# Lecture Notes in Artificial Intelligence 2777

Edited by J. G. Carbonell and J. Siekmann

)3

Subseries of Lecture Not

D0862852

**Springer**
*Berlin*
*Heidelberg*
*New York*
*Hong Kong*
*London*
*Milan*
*Paris*
*Tokyo*

Bernhard Schölkopf   Manfred K. Warmuth (Eds.)

# Learning Theory and Kernel Machines

16th Annual Conference on Learning Theory
and 7th Kernel Workshop, COLT/Kernel 2003
Washington, DC, USA, August 24-27, 2003
Proceedings

 Springer

Series Editors

Jaime G. Carbonell, Carnegie Mellon University, Pittsburgh, PA, USA
Jörg Siekmann, University of Saarland, Saarbrücken, Germany

Volume Editors

Bernhard Schölkopf
Max Planck Institute for Biological Cybernetics
Empirical Inference Department
Spemannstr. 38, 72076 Tübingen, Germany
E-mail: bs@tuebingen.mpg.de

Manfred K. Warmuth
University of California
Department of Computer Science
227 Baskin Engineering, Santa Cruz, CA 95064,USA
E-mail: manfred@cse.ucsc.edu

Cataloging-in-Publication Data applied for

A catalog record for this book is available from the Library of Congress.

Bibliographic information published by Die Deutsche Bibliothek
Die Deutsche Bibliothek lists this publication in the Deutsche Nationalbibliografie;
detailed bibliographic data is available in the Internet at <http://dnb.ddb.de>.

CR Subject Classification (1998): I.2.6, I.2.3, I.2, F.4.1, F.2, F.1.1

ISSN 0302-9743
ISBN 3-540-40720-0 Springer-Verlag Berlin Heidelberg New York

Springer-Verlag Berlin Heidelberg New York
a member of BertelsmannSpringer Science+Business Media GmbH

http://www.springer.de

© Springer-Verlag Berlin Heidelberg 2003
Printed in Germany

Typesetting: Camera-ready by author, data conversion by Olgun Computergrafik
Printed on acid-free paper      SPIN: 10931424      06/3142      5 4 3 2 1 0

# Preface

This volume contains papers presented at the joint 16th Annual Conference on Learning Theory (COLT) and the 7th Annual Workshop on Kernel Machines, held in Washington, DC, USA, during August 24–27, 2003. COLT, which recently merged with EuroCOLT, has traditionally been a meeting place for learning theorists. We hope that COLT will benefit from the collocation with the annual workshop on kernel machines, formerly held as a NIPS postconference workshop.

The technical program contained 47 papers selected from 92 submissions. All 47 papers were presented as posters; 22 of the papers were additionally presented as talks. There were also two target areas with invited contributions. In *computational game theory*, a tutorial entitled "Learning Topics in Game-Theoretic Decision Making" was given by Michael Littman, and an invited paper on "A General Class of No-Regret Learning Algorithms and Game-Theoretic Equilibria" was contributed by Amy Greenwald. In *natural language processing*, a tutorial on "Machine Learning Methods in Natural Language Processing" was presented by Michael Collins, followed by two invited talks, "Learning from Uncertain Data" by Mehryar Mohri and "Learning and Parsing Stochastic Unification-Based Grammars" by Mark Johnson.

In addition to the accepted papers and invited presentations, we solicited short open problems that were reviewed and included in the proceedings. We hope that reviewed open problems might become a new tradition for COLT. Our goal was to select simple signature problems whose solutions are likely to inspire further research. For some of the problems the authors offered monetary rewards. Yoav Freund acted as the open problem area chair. The open problems were presented as posters at the conference.

The Mark Fulk award is presented annually for the best paper contributed by a student. This year's award was won by Ulrike von Luxburg for the paper "Distance-Based Classification with Lipschitz Functions" (co-authored with Olivier Bousquet). Owing to generous support from the Journal of Machine Learning, we were able to award two second prizes for the best student paper. They went to Gilles Stoltz, "Internal Regret in On-line Portfolio Selection" (co-authored with Gabor Lugosi), and Petra Philips, "Random Subclass Bounds" (co-authored with Shahar Mendelson).

We thank all the people and organizations who helped make this conference successful. We are especially grateful to the program committee for their efforts in evaluating and selecting the papers in this volume:

| | |
|---|---|
| Kristin Bennett | Rensselaer Polytechnic Institute |
| Avrim Blum | Carnegie Mellon University |
| Nicolò Cesa-Bianchi | University of Milan |
| Nello Cristianini | University of California at Davis |
| Yoav Freund | Banter Inc. |
| Michael Kearns | University of Pennsylvania |
| Efim Kinber | Sacred Heart University, Fairfield, CT |
| Vladimir Koltchinskii | The University of New Mexico |
| Yishay Mansour | Tel Aviv University |
| Rob Schapire | Princeton University |

The program committee solicited the help of the following reviewers. We obtained at least two independent reviews for each paper in addition to the reviews and discussions carried out by the program committee:

| | | |
|---|---|---|
| Naoki Abe | Rusins Freivalds | Wolfgang Merkle |
| Dana Angluin | Nir Friedman | Jochen Nessel |
| Peter Auer | Bill Gasarch | Kamal Nigam |
| Peter Bartlett | Claudio Gentile | Noam Nisan |
| Satinder Baveja | Sally Goldman | Bill Noble |
| Jonathan Baxter | Geoff Gordon | Luis Ortiz |
| Amos Beimel | Thore Graepel | Dmitry Panchenko |
| Shai Ben-David | Peter Grunwald | Relu Patrascu |
| Yoshua Bengio | Patrick Haffner | John Platt |
| Gilles Blanchard | Lisa Hellerstein | Gunnar Rätsch |
| Stephane Boucheron | Jeff Jackson | Vijay Raghavan |
| Olivier Bousquet | Thorsten Joachims | Dana Ron |
| Nader Bshouty | Adam Kalai | Roman Rosipal |
| Chris Burges | Jaz Kandola | Dale Schuurmans |
| Colin Campbell | Balazs Kegl | Rocco Servedio |
| Rafael Carrasco | Jyrki Kivinen | John Shawe-Taylor |
| John Case | John Lafferty | Yoram Singer |
| Moses Charikar | Gert Lanckriet | Bob Sloan |
| Alex Conconi | John Langford | Frank Stephan |
| Sanjoy Dasgupta | Christina Leslie | Christino Tamon |
| Tijl DeBie | Chi-jen Lin | Koji Tsuda |
| Nigel Duffy | Philip Long | Alexandre Tsybakov |
| Pierre Dupont | Fernando Lozano | Nicolas Vayatis |
| Ran El-Yaniv | Gabor Lugosi | Jean-Philippe Vert |
| Andre Ellisseef | Ulrike von Luxburg | Volodya Vovk |
| Eyal Even-Dar | Olvi Mangasarian | Grace Wahba |
| Theodoros Evgeniou | Shie Mannor | Osamu Watanabe |
| Amos Fiat | David McAllester | Rolf Wiehagen |
| Karim Filali | Ron Meir | Tong Zhang |
| Peter Flach | Shahar Mendelson | Sandra Zilles |

Special thanks go to our local conference chairs: to Carl Smith, whose health problems would not let him finish the job (Carl, get better soon!), and to John Case, who thankfully agreed to take over this job. Together with the invaluable help of Cecilia Kullman, John saved us when things were gradually getting into a state of emergency. We would also like to thank Richard van de Stadt, Karin Bierig, and Sabrina Nielebock for help with the paper submissions and with the preparation of the proceedings, and Stephen Kwek for maintaining the conference Web site. Finally, we thank the National ICT Australia (www.nicta.com.au), the University of Maryland Institute for Advanced Computer Studies, and the Max Planck Institute for Biological Cybernetics for their generous sponsorship and administrative help.

June 2003                          Bernhard Schölkopf (Max Planck Instititute Tübingen)
                             Manfred K. Warmuth (University of California at Santa Cruz)
                                                                      Program Chairs

# Sponsors

MAX-PLANCK-INSTITUT FÜR
BIOLOGISCHE KYBERNETIK

# Table of Contents

## Poster Session 1

## Statistical Learning Theory

## Online Learning

## Other Approaches

## Poster Session 2

## Target Area: Natural Language Processing

### Invited Talks

## Inductive Inference Learning

# Open Problems

# Tutorial: Learning Topics
# in Game-Theoretic Decision Making

Michael L. Littman

Rutgers University

The tutorial will cover some topics of recent interest in AI and economics concerning design making in a computational game-theory framework. It will highlight areas in which computational learning theory has played a role and could play a greater role in the future. Covered areas include recent representational and algorithmic advances, stochastic games and reinforcement learning, no regret algorithms, and the role of various equilibrium concepts.

B. Schölkopf and M.K. Warmuth (Eds.): COLT/Kernel 2003, LNAI 2777, p. 1, 2003.
© Springer-Verlag Berlin Heidelberg 2003

# A General Class of No-Regret Learning Algorithms and Game-Theoretic Equilibria

Amy Greenwald[1] and Amir Jafari[2]

[1] Department of Computer Science
Brown University, Box 1910
Providence, RI 02906
amy@brown.edu
http://www.cs.brown.edu/~amy
[2] Department of Mathematics
Brown University, Box 1917
Providence, RI 02906
amir@math.brown.edu
http://www.math.brown.edu/~amir

**Abstract.** A general class of no-regret learning algorithms, called $\Phi$-no-regret learning algorithms is defined, which spans the spectrum from no-internal-regret learning to no-external-regret learning, and beyond. $\Phi$ describes the set of strategies to which the play of a learning algorithm is compared: a learning algorithm satisfies $\Phi$-no-regret iff no regret is experienced for playing as the algorithm prescribes, rather than playing according to any of the transformations of the algorithm's play prescribed by elements of $\Phi$. Analogously, a class of game-theoretic equilibria, called $\Phi$-equilibria, is defined, and it is shown that the empirical distribution of play of $\Phi$-no-regret algorithms converges to the set of $\Phi$-equilibria. Perhaps surprisingly, the strongest form of no-regret algorithms in this class are no-internal-regret algorithms. Thus, the tightest game-theoretic solution concept to which $\Phi$-no-regret algorithms (provably) converge is correlated equilibrium. In particular, Nash equilibrium is not a necessary outcome of learning via any $\Phi$-no-regret learning algorithms.

## 1 Introduction

Consider an agent that repeatedly faces some decision problem. The agent is presented with a choice of actions, each with a different outcome, or set of outcomes. After each choice is made, and the corresponding outcome is observed, the agent achieves a reward. In this setting, one reasonable objective for an agent is to maximize its average rewards. If each outcome is deterministic, and if the action set is finite, the agent need only undertake a linear search for an action that yields the maximal reward, and choose that action forever after. But if there is a set of outcomes associated with each choice of action, i.e., if the outcome is nondeterministic, even if the action set is finite, a more complex strategy, or *learning algorithm*, is called for, if indeed the agent seeks to maximize rewards.

B. Schölkopf and M.K. Warmuth (Eds.): COLT/Kernel 2003, LNAI 2777, pp. 2–12, 2003.

*No-regret* learning algorithms are geared toward maximizing rewards in nondeterministic settings. The efficacy of a no-regret algorithm is determined by comparing the performance of the algorithm with the performance of a set of alternative strategies. For example, one might compare the performance of a learning algorithm with the set of strategies that always choose the same action $a$, for all actions $a$. Learning algorithms that outperform this strategy set are said to exhibit no-external-regret [11]. As another example, consider the set of strategies that choose action $a'$ rather than action $a$, whenever a given learning algorithm chooses $a$, for all possible actions $a$ and $a'$. Learning algorithms that outperform all strategies in this set are said to satisfy no-internal-regret [6].

This paper studies the outcome of no-regret learning among a set of agents, or players, playing a repeated game. In a game, each player is presented with a choice of actions, and the outcome of the game is jointly determined by all players' choices. Each outcome assigns a reward to each player. In general, players choose their actions nondeterministically; thus, the outcome of a game can be viewed as nondeterministic, as in the single agent decision problem. Interestingly, in two-player, zero-sum games, if each player plays using a no-external-regret learning algorithm, then the empirical distribution of play converges to the set of minimax equilibria (see, for example, Freund and Schapire [8]). Also of interest, in multi-player games, if each agent plays using a no-internal-regret learning algorithm, then the empirical distribution of play converges to the set of correlated equilibria (see, for example, Hart and Mas-Colell [12]).

In this article, we define a general class of no-regret learning algorithms, called $\Phi$-no-regret learning algorithms, which spans the spectrum from no-internal-regret learning to no-external-regret learning, and beyond. $\Phi$ describes the set of strategies to which the play of a learning algorithms is compared: a learning algorithm satisfies $\Phi$-no-regret iff no regret is experienced for playing as the algorithm prescribes, rather than playing according to any of the transformations of the algorithm's play prescribed by elements of $\Phi$. Analogously, we define a class of game-theoretic equilibria, called $\Phi$-equilibria, and we show that the empirical distribution of play of $\Phi$-no-regret algorithms converges to the set of $\Phi$-equilibria. Perhaps surprisingly, no-internal-regret algorithms are the strongest form of no-regret algorithms in this class. Thus, the tightest game-theoretic solution concept to which $\Phi$-no-regret algorithms (provably) converge is correlated equilibrium. In particular, Nash equilibrium is not a necessary outcome of learning via any $\Phi$-no-regret learning algorithms.

This article is organized as follows. In the next section, we present Blackwell's approachability theory, which provides the technology for the proofs that appear throughout this work. In Section 3, we define $\Phi$-no-regret learning, and we show that no-external-regret and no-internal-regret are special cases of $\Phi$-no-regret. We also directly establish the existence of an algorithm that exhibits $\Phi$-no-regret, for an arbitrary choice of $\Phi$. In Section 4, we define $\Phi$-equilibrium, and we prove that $\Phi$-no-regret learning converges to the set of $\Phi$-equilibria. The content of this article is largely based on Jafari's Master's thesis [14].

## 2  Approachability

Consider an agent with a set of actions $A$ ($a \in A$) playing a game against a set of opponents with joint action set $A'$ ($a' \in A'$). Associated with each possible outcome is some vector given by the vector-valued function $\rho : A \times A' \to V$. The sets $A$ and $A'$ are $\sigma$-algebras, and $V$ is a vector space with an inner product $\cdot$ and a distance metric $d$ defined by the inner product.

Given a game with the vector-valued function $\rho$, a (deterministic) *learning algorithm* $\mathcal{A}$ is a sequence of functions $q_t = q_t(\rho) : (A \times A')^{t-1} \to \Delta(A)$, for $t = 1, 2, \ldots$, where $\Delta(A)$ is the set of all probability measures on $A$ and $(A \times A')^0$ is defined as a single point: i.e., $q_1 \in \Delta(A)$. Note that a deterministic learning algorithm $\mathcal{A}$ generates nondeterministic actions. A nondeterministic learning algorithm $\mathcal{A}$ assumes values in $\mathcal{P}(\Delta(A))$, the set of all subsets of $\Delta(A)$.

Many examples of learning algorithms appear throughout the literature. A history-independent learning algorithm returns some constant element of $\Delta(A)$. The best-reply learning algorithm [4] returns an element of $\Delta(A)$, at time $t$, that maximizes the agent's rewards w.r.t. only $a'_{t-1}$. Fictitious play [3, 15] returns returns an element of $\Delta(A)$, at time $t$, that maximizes the agent's rewards w.r.t. the empirical distribution of play through time $t - 1$.

Following Blackwell [2], we define the notion of approachability as follows.

**Definition 1.** *Given a game with vector-valued function $\rho$, a subset $G \subseteq V$ is said to be $\rho$-approachable iff there exists learning algorithm $\mathcal{A} = q_1, q_2, \ldots$ s.t. for any sequence of opponents' actions $a'_1, a'_2, \ldots$, for all $\epsilon > 0$, there exists $t_0$ s.t. for all $t \geq t_0$, $d(G, \bar{\rho}_t) = \inf_{g \in G} d(g, \bar{\rho}_t) < \epsilon$, almost surely, where $\bar{\rho}_t$ denotes the average value of $\rho$ through time $t$: i.e., $\bar{\rho}_t = \frac{1}{t} (\rho(a_1, a'_1) + \ldots + \rho(a_t, a'_t))$.*

*Technically, for any sequence of opponents' actions $a'_1, a'_2, \ldots$, for all $\epsilon, \delta > 0$, there exists $t_0$ s.t. for all $t \geq t_0$, $P^t ((a_1, \ldots, a_t) | d(G, \bar{\rho}_t) > \delta) < \epsilon$, where $P^t$ is the product measure on $A^t$ induced by $q_1, \ldots, q_t$ as follows:*

$$P^t = q_1 \times q_2(a_1, a'_1) \times \ldots \times q_t((a_1, a'_1), \ldots, (a_{t-1}, a'_{t-1}))$$

In other words, a subset $G \subseteq V$ is $\rho$-approachable iff there exists a learning algorithm for an agent that generates nondeterministic actions for the agent which ensure that the distance from the set $G$ to the average value of $\rho$ through time $t$ tends to zero as $t$ tends to infinity, almost surely, for any sequence of opponents' actions $a'_1, a'_2, \ldots$.

Throughout the remainder of this paper, we restrict attention to $V = \mathbb{R}^S$ and $G = \mathbb{R}^S_- = \{(x_s)_{s \in S} | x_s \leq 0\}$, for various choices of some finite set $S$. Ultimately, we interpret the vector-valued function in games as *regrets* (rather than rewards). Thus, we seek learning algorithms that approach the negative orthant: i.e., learning algorithms that achieve no-regret.

Blackwell's seminal approachability theorem [2] gives a sufficient condition on learning algorithms which ensures that $\mathbb{R}^S_- \subseteq \mathbb{R}^S$ (or, more generally, any convex subset $G \subseteq V$) is approachable. We present Blackwell's condition, as well as a generalization of the approachability theorem due to Jafari [14].

**Definition 2.** *Let $\Lambda : \mathbb{R}^S \to \mathbb{R}^S$ be a function that is zero on $\mathbb{R}_-^S$. Given a game with vector-valued function $\rho$, a learning algorithm $\mathcal{A} = q_1, q_2, \ldots$ is $\Lambda$-compatible iff for any sequence of opponents' actions $a_1', a_2', \ldots$, there exists some constant $c \in \mathbb{R}$ and there exists $t_0 \in \mathbb{N}$ s.t. for all $t \geq t_0$,*

$$\Lambda(\bar{\rho}_t) \cdot \rho(q_{t+1}, a') \leq \frac{c}{t+1} \tag{1}$$

*for all $a' \in A'$. Here $\rho(q, a') = \int_A \rho(a, a') dq(a)$ is the expected value of $\rho$.*

This definition of $\Lambda$-compatibility is inspired by Hart and Mas-Colell [13], who introduce the notion of $\Lambda$-compatibility for $c = 0$. Blackwell's condition can be stated in terms of $\Lambda$-compatibility for a particular choice of $\Lambda$, namely $\Lambda_0$, which is defined as follows: $\Lambda_0((x_s)_{s \in S}) = (x_s^+)_{s \in S}$, where $x_s^+ = \max\{x_s, 0\}$.

**Theorem 1 (Blackwell, 1956).** *Given a game with vector-valued function $\rho$, if $A$ and $A'$ finite, then the set $\mathbb{R}_-^S$ is $\rho$-approachable by learning algorithm $\mathcal{A}$ if $\mathcal{A}$ is $\Lambda_0$-compatible, with $c = 0$: i.e., for any sequence of opponents' actions $a_1', a_2', \ldots$, there exists $t_0 \in \mathbb{N}$ s.t. for all $t \geq t_0$, $\bar{\rho}_t^+ \cdot \rho(q_{t+1}, a') \leq 0$. Conversely, if no such learning algorithm exists, then the set $\mathbb{R}_-^S$ is not $\rho$-approachable.*

The following generalization of Blackwell's theorem, due to Jafari [14], states that $\Lambda_0$-compatibility implies $\rho$-approachability, even for $c \neq 0$.

**Theorem 2 (Jafari, 2003).** *Given a game with vector-valued function $\rho$, if $\rho(A \times A')$ is bounded, then the set $\mathbb{R}_-^S$ is $\rho$-approachable by learning algorithm $\mathcal{A}$ if $\mathcal{A}$ is $\Lambda_0$-compatible: i.e., for any sequence of opponents' actions $a_1', a_2', \ldots$, there exists some constant $c \in \mathbb{R}$ and there exists $t_0 \in \mathbb{N}$ s.t. for all $t \geq t_0$, $\bar{\rho}_t^+ \cdot \rho(q_{t+1}, a') \leq \frac{c}{t+1}$. Conversely, if no such learning algorithm exists, then the set $\mathbb{R}_-^S$ is not $\rho$-approachable.*

## 3   No-Regret Learning

Let $\Phi$ be a finite subset of stochastic matrices: i.e., linear maps $\phi : \Delta(A) \to \Delta(A)$ s.t. for all $0 \leq \alpha \leq 1$, for all $q_1, q_2 \in \Delta(A)$,

$$\phi(\alpha q_1 + (1 - \alpha)q_2) = \alpha\phi(q_1) + (1 - \alpha)\phi(q_2) \tag{2}$$

Thus, each $\phi \in \Phi$ converts one nondeterministic action for an agent into another. Given $\Phi$, and given one distinguished agent's reward function $r : A \times A' \to \mathbb{R}$, we define regret vector $\rho_\Phi : A \times A' \to \mathbb{R}^\Phi$ as follows:

$$\rho_\Phi(a, a') = (r(\phi(\delta_a), a') - r(a, a'))_{\phi \in \Phi} \tag{3}$$

Here $\delta_a$ is the Dirac $\delta$ function: i.e., all mass is concentrated at $a$. In words, $\rho_\Phi(a, a')$ is a vector indexed by $\phi \in \Phi$ for which each entry describes the regret the agent feels for choosing action $a$ rather than action $\phi(\delta_a)$, given action $a'$. Using this framework, we define $\Phi$-no-regret learning.

**Definition 3.** *A $\Phi$-no-regret learning algorithm is one that $\rho_\Phi$-approaches $\mathbb{R}^\Phi_-$.*

Given a game, if an agent with reward function $r$ learns to play in such a way that $\rho_\Phi$ approaches the negative orthant, then the agent's learning algorithm is said to exhibit no-regret. There are two well-studied examples of the $\Phi$-no-regret property: *no-external-regret* and *no-internal-regret*.

Given an agent with finite action set $A$, let $\Phi_{\text{EXT}} = \{\phi_a | a \in A\}$ be the set of constant maps: i.e., $\phi_a(q) = \delta_a$. Thus, $\phi_a(q)$ is a probability density concentrated at $a$—it ascribes zero probability to any action $b \neq a$. Intuitively, a learning algorithm satisfies $\Phi_{\text{EXT}}$-no-regret iff it precludes the agent from experiencing regret relative to any fixed strategy. $\Phi_{\text{EXT}}$-no-regret corresponds to no-external-regret, also known as Hannan, or universal, consistency [11].

Our next choice of $\Phi$, once again for $A$ finite, gives rise to the definition of no-internal-regret [6]. Let $\Phi_{\text{INT}} = \{\phi_{a,b} | a \neq b \in A\}$, where

$$\phi_{a,b}(q)(c) = \begin{cases} q(c) & \text{if } c \neq a, b \\ 0 & \text{if } c = a \\ q(a) + q(b) & \text{if } c = b \end{cases} \tag{4}$$

For $a \neq b$, $\phi_{a,b}$ maps nondeterministic action $q$ into another that ascribes zero probability to $a$, but instead adds $a$'s probability mass according to $q$ to the probability $q$ ascribes to $b$. Thus, an algorithm satisfies $\Phi_{\text{INT}}$-no-regret if the agent does not feel regret when it plays $a$ instead of $b$, for all pairs of distinct actions $a \neq b$. Following Foster and Vohra [6], we call this property no-internal-regret, but it is sometimes called conditional universal consistency [9].

Perhaps surprisingly, no-internal-regret is the strongest form of $\Phi$-no-regret, as Proposition 1 demonstrates. To prove this claim, we rely on two lemmas.

**Lemma 1.** *If learning algorithm $\mathcal{A}$ satisfies $\Phi$-no-regret, then $\mathcal{A}$ also satisfies $\Phi'$-no-regret, for all finite subsets $\Phi'$ contained in the convex hull of $\Phi$.*

*Proof.* If $\Phi'$ is contained in the convex hull of $\Phi$, then $\rho_{\Phi'} = M\rho_\Phi$, for some matrix $M$ with non-negative entries and rows that sum to 1. (Note that $M$ need not be stochastic since $M$ need not be square.) If learning algorithm $\mathcal{A}$ satisfies $\Phi$-no-regret (i.e., if $\mathbb{R}^\Phi_-$ is $\rho_\Phi$-approachable), then $d(\mathbb{R}^\Phi_-, \overline{\rho}_{\Phi,t}) \to 0$, as $t \to \infty$, almost surely. But then, by the continuity of $M$, $d(M\mathbb{R}^\Phi_-, M\overline{\rho}_{\Phi,t}) = d(M\mathbb{R}^\Phi_-, \overline{\rho}_{\Phi',t}) \to 0$, as $t \to \infty$, almost surely. In other words, $M\mathbb{R}^\Phi_-$ is $\rho_{\Phi'}$-approachable. Now since all entries in $M$ are non-negative, it follows that $M\mathbb{R}^\Phi_- \subseteq \mathbb{R}^{\Phi'}_-$. Therefore, $\mathbb{R}^{\Phi'}_-$ is $\rho_{\Phi'}$-approachable: i.e., $\mathcal{A}$ satisfies $\Phi'$-no-regret.

**Lemma 2.** *If learning algorithm $\mathcal{A}$ satisfies $\Phi$-no-regret, then $\mathcal{A}$ also satisfies $\alpha_1\phi_1 + \ldots + \alpha_k\phi_k + \alpha_{k+1}I$-no-regret, where $\phi_i \in \Phi$, $\alpha_i \geq 0$, for $1 \leq i \leq k$, $\alpha_{k+1} \in \mathbb{R}$, $\sum_{i=1}^{k+1} \alpha_i = 1$, and $I$ is the identity map.*

*Proof.* Let $\phi = \alpha_1\phi_1 + \ldots + \alpha_k\phi_k + \alpha_{k+1}I$. By the following calculation, $\rho_\phi = \alpha_1\rho_{\phi_1} + \ldots + \alpha_k\rho_{\phi_k} + \alpha_{k+1}\rho_I$.

$$\rho_\phi(a, a') = r(\phi(\delta_a), a') - r(a, a')$$
$$= r((\alpha_1 \phi_1 + \ldots + \alpha_k \phi_k + \alpha_{k+1} I)(\delta_a), a') - r(a, a')$$
$$= \alpha_1 r(\phi_1(\delta_a), a') + \ldots + \alpha_k r(\phi_k(\delta_a), a') + \alpha_{k+1} r(I(\delta_a), a') - r(a, a')$$
$$= \alpha_1 r(\phi_1(\delta_a), a') + \ldots + \alpha_k r(\phi_k(\delta_a), a') + \alpha_{k+1} r(I(\delta_a), a') - \sum_{i=1}^{k+1} \alpha_i r(a, a')$$
$$= \alpha_1 \rho_{\phi_1}(a, a') + \ldots + \alpha_k \rho_{\phi_k}(a, a') + \alpha_{k+1} \rho_I(a, a')$$
$$= (\alpha_1 \rho_{\phi_1} + \ldots + \alpha_k \rho_{\phi_k} + \alpha_{k+1} \rho_I)(a, a')$$

But, in fact, $\rho_\phi = \alpha_1 \rho_{\phi_1} + \ldots + \alpha_k \rho_{\phi_k}$, since $\rho_I(a, a') = r(I(\delta_a), a') - r(a, a') = r(a, a') - r(a, a') = 0$.

By assumption, $\mathcal{A}$ satisfies $\Phi$-no-regret: i.e., $\mathbb{R}^\Phi_-$ is $\rho_\Phi$-approachable. In other words, for all $\phi_i \in \Phi$, $d(\mathbb{R}^\Phi_-, \overline{\rho}_{\phi_i, t}) \to 0$, as $t \to \infty$, almost surely. But then, $d(\mathbb{R}^\Phi_-, \overline{\rho}_{\phi, t}) = d(\mathbb{R}^\Phi_-, \overline{(\alpha_1 \rho_{\phi_1} + \ldots + \alpha_k \rho_{\phi_k})}_t) \to 0$, as $t \to \infty$, almost surely, since $\alpha_i \geq 0$, for $1 \leq i \leq k$. Therefore, $\mathbb{R}^\phi_-$ is $\rho_\phi$-approachable: i.e., $\mathcal{A}$ also satisfies $\alpha_1 \phi_1 + \ldots + \alpha_k \phi_k + \alpha_{k+1} I$-no-regret.

**Proposition 1.** *If learning algorithm $\mathcal{A}$ satisfies no-internal-regret, then $\mathcal{A}$ also satisfies $\Phi$-no-regret for all finite subsets $\Phi$ of the set of stochastic matrices.*

*Proof.* An elementary matrix is one with exactly one 1 per row, and 0's elsewhere. By Lemma 1, if an algorithm is $\Phi$-no-regret for the set $\Phi$ of elementary matrices, then the algorithm satisfies $\Phi'$-no-regret for all finite subsets $\Phi'$ of the set of stochastic matrices, since the set of stochastic matrices is the convex hull of the set of elementary matrices. Thus, it suffices to show that an algorithm that satisfies no-internal-regret is $\Phi$-no-regret for the set $\Phi$ of elementary matrices.

But by Lemma 2, it further suffices to show that any elementary matrix $M$ can be expressed as follows: $M = \alpha_1 \phi_1 + \ldots + \alpha_k \phi_k - \alpha_{k+1} I$, where $\phi_i \in \Phi_{\text{INT}}$ and $\alpha_i \geq 0$, for $1 \leq i \leq k$, $\alpha_{k+1} \in \mathbb{R}$, $\sum_{i=1}^{k+1} \alpha_i = 1$, and $I$ is the identity map.

Let $A = \{1, \ldots, m\}$. Let $M(n_1, \ldots, n_m)$ denote the elementary matrix with 0's everywhere except 1's at entries $(i, n_i)$ for $1 \leq i \leq m$. Now the linear map $\phi_{i,j}$ defined in Equation 4 is represented by the elementary matrix with 1's on the diagonal except in row $i$, where the 1 appears in column $j$. Thus, $\phi_{1n_1} + \ldots + \phi_{mn_m}$ corresponds to the matrix with 0's everywhere, except 1's at entries $(i, n_i)$ for $1 \leq i \leq m$, and $m - 1$'s on the diagonal. It follows that

$$M(n_1, \ldots, n_m) = \phi_{1n_1} + \ldots + \phi_{mn_m} - (m-1)I \tag{5}$$

Indeed, $\Phi$-no-regret learning algorithms exists. In particular, no-external-regret algorithms pervade the literature. The earliest date back to Blackwell [2] and Hannan [11]; but, more recently, Foster and Vohra [5] Freund and Schapire [7], Fudenberg and Levine [10], Hart and Mas-Colell [13], and others have studied such algorithms. To our knowledge, only Foster and Vohra [6] have proposed an algorithm that satisfies no-internal-regret.

The next theorem directly establishes the existence of $\Phi$-no-regret algorithms. The method of proof is related to that of Foster and Vohra [6].

**Theorem 3.** *Given a game $\rho : A \times A' \to \mathbb{R}$. If $\rho(A \times A')$ is bounded, then there exists a learning algorithm that satisfies $\Phi$-no-regret, for all finite subsets $\Phi$ of the set of continuous, linear maps on $\Delta(A)$.*

*Proof.* It suffices to show that for all $x \in \mathbb{R}^\Phi \setminus \mathbb{R}^\Phi_-$, there exists $q = q(x) \in \Delta(A)$ s.t. $x^+ \cdot \rho_\Phi(q, a') \leq 0$, for all $a' \in A$. Letting $x = \overline{\rho}_t$, for $t = 1, 2, \ldots$, the result follows from Blackwell's approachability theorem. In fact, we show equality:

$$
\begin{aligned}
0 &= x^+ \cdot \rho_\Phi(q, a') \\
&= \sum_{\phi \in \Phi} x_\phi^+ (r(\phi(q), a') - r(q, a')) \\
&= \sum_{\phi \in \Phi} x_\phi^+ (r(\phi(q), a') - \sum_{\phi \in \Phi} x_\phi^+ r(q, a')) \\
&= r\left( \left( \sum_{\phi \in \Phi} x_\phi^+ \phi \right)(q), a' \right) - r\left( \left( \sum_{\phi \in \Phi} x_\phi^+ \right) q, a' \right)
\end{aligned}
$$

Now it suffices to show the following:

$$
\left( \sum_{\phi \in \Phi} x_\phi^+ \phi \right)(q) = \left( \sum_{\phi \in \Phi} x_\phi^+ \right) q \tag{6}
$$

Define $M : \Delta(A) \to \Delta(A)$ as follows:

$$
M = \frac{\sum_{\phi \in \Phi} x_\phi^+ \phi}{\sum_{\phi \in \Phi} x_\phi^+} \tag{7}
$$

The function $M$ maps a compact space, namely $\Delta(A)$, into itself. Moreover, it is continuous, since all $\phi \in \Phi$ are continuous, by assumption. Therefore, by Brouwer's fixed point theorem, $M$ has a fixed point.

Technically speaking, this theorem does not establish the existence of an "algorithm," as stated, because the proof of Brouwer's fixed point theorem is not constructive. Moreover, the solution to Equation 6 need not be unique. Thus, at best, this theorem establishes the existence of a *nondeterministic*, $\Phi$-no-regret "algorithm." But if $A$ is finite, then the function $M$ defined in Equation 7 is a stochastic matrix, and a solution to Equation 6 arises from the fact that any stochastic matrix has a positive fixed point. In this case, the least squares method of solving systems of equations yields a deterministic, $\Phi$-no-regret algorithm.

## 4  $\Phi$-Equilibrium

In this section, we define the notion of $\Phi$-equilibrium, and we prove that learning algorithms that satisfy $\Phi$-no-regret converge to $\Phi$-equilibria. In particular, $\Phi_{\mathrm{EXT}}$-no-regret algorithms (i.e., no-external-regret algorithms) converge to (generalized) minimax equilibria; and $\Phi_{\mathrm{INT}}$-no-regret algorithms (i.e., no-internal-regret algorithms) converge to correlated equilibria.

Consider an $n$-player game where each player $i$ chooses an action from the set $A_i$, and rewards are determined by the function $r : A_1 \times \ldots \times A_n \to \mathbb{R}^n$. Let $\Phi_i$ be a finite subset of stochastic matrices: i.e., linear maps $\phi_i : \Delta(A_i) \to \Delta(A_i)$. A linear map $\phi_i$ extends to a linear map $\phi_i : \Delta(A_1 \times \ldots \times A_n) \to \Delta(A_1 \times \ldots \times A_n)$ as follows:

$$\phi_i(q)(b_i, a_{-i}) \equiv \phi_i((q(a_i, a_{-i}))_{a_i \in A_i})(b_i)$$

$$= \phi_i \left( \sum_{a_i \in A_i} q(a_i, a_{-i}) \delta_{a_i} \right)(b_i)$$

$$= \sum_{a_i \in A_i} q(a_i, a_{-i}) \phi_i(\delta_{a_i})(b_i) \qquad (8)$$

An element $q \in \Delta(A_1 \times \ldots \times A_n)$ is called independent iff it can be written as the product $q = q_1 \times \ldots \times q_n$ of $n$ independent elements $q_i \in \Delta(A_i)$. For independent $q \in \Delta(A_1 \times \ldots \times A_n)$,

$$\phi_i(q)(a_1, \ldots, a_{i-1}, b_i, a_{i+1}, \ldots, a_n)$$

$$= \sum_{a_i \in A_i} (q_1 \times \ldots \times q_i \times \ldots \times q_n)(a_1, \ldots, a_i, \ldots, a_n) \phi_i(\delta_{a_i})(b_i)$$

$$= \sum_{a_i \in A_i} q_1(a_1) \ldots q_i(a_i) \ldots q_n(a_n) \phi_i(\delta_{a_i})(b_i)$$

$$= q_1(a_1) \ldots q_{i-1}(a_{i-1}) q_{i+1}(a_{i+1}) \ldots q_n(a_n) \sum_{a_i \in A_i} q_i(a_i) \phi_i(\delta_{a_i})(b_i)$$

$$= q_1(a_1) \ldots q_{i-1}(a_{i-1}) q_{i+1}(a_{i+1}) \ldots q_n(a_n) \phi_i \left( \sum_{a_i \in A_i} q_i(a_i) \delta_{a_i} \right)(b_i)$$

$$= q_1(a_1) \ldots q_{i-1}(a_{i-1}) q_{i+1}(a_{i+1}) \ldots q_n(a_n) \phi_i(q_i)(b_i)$$

The stated definition of the extended map $\phi_i$ applies to all $q \in \Delta(A_1 \times \ldots \times A_n)$, with the property that $\phi(q) = q_1 \times \ldots \times \phi_i(q_i) \times \ldots \times q_n$, for independent $q$. Note also that this definition yields an extension that is indeed a probability measure, since

$$\sum_{b_i, a_{-i}} \phi_i(q)(b_i, u_{-i}) - \sum_{b_i, a_{-i}} \left( \sum_{a_i \in A_i} q(a_i, a_{-i}) \phi_i(\delta_{a_t})(b_i) \right)$$

$$= \sum_{a_i, a_{-i}} q(a_i, a_{-i}) \sum_{b_i} \phi_i(\delta_{a_i})(b_i)$$

$$= 1$$

**Definition 4.** *Given a game (i.e., given reward function $r$), and given vector $\Phi = (\Phi_i)_{1 \leq i \leq n}$, an element $q \in \Delta(A_1 \times \ldots \times A_n)$ is called a $\Phi$-equilibrium iff $r_i(q) \geq r_i(\phi_i(q))$, for all players $i$ and for all $\phi_i \in \Phi_i$.*

Generalized minimax and correlated equilibrium are both special cases of $\Phi$-equilibrium. We define generalized minimax equilibria as $\Phi$-equilibria, with $\Phi_i = \Phi_{\text{EXT}}$ for all players $i$. Correlated equilibria are $\Phi$-equilibria, where $\Phi_i = \Phi_{\text{INT}}$ for all players $i$. Next we discuss two convexity properties of the set of $\Phi$-equilibria, and the relationship between $\Phi$-equilibria and Nash equilibria.

**Lemma 3.** *Given a game (i.e., given reward function $r$), and given vector $\Phi = (\Phi_i)_{1 \leq i \leq n}$, the set of $\Phi$-equilibria is convex.*

*Proof.* If $q$ and $q'$ are both $\Phi$-equilibria, then $r_i(q) \geq r_i(\phi_i q)$ and $r_i(q') \geq r_i(\phi_i q')$, for all players $i$ and for all $\phi_i \in \Phi_i$. Since $r_i$ and $\phi_i$ are linear on $\Delta(A_1 \times \ldots \times A_n)$, it follows that

$$
\begin{aligned}
&r_i(\alpha q + (1-\alpha)q') \\
&= \alpha r_i(q) + (1-\alpha)r_i(q') \\
&\geq \alpha r_i(\phi_i q) + (1-\alpha)r_i(\phi_i q') \\
&= r_i(\alpha \phi_i q + (1-\alpha)\phi_i q') \\
&= r_i(\phi_i(\alpha q + (1-\alpha)q'))
\end{aligned}
$$

**Lemma 4.** *Given a game (i.e., given reward function $r$), and given vector $\Phi = (\Phi_i)_{1 \leq i \leq n}$, if $q \in \Delta(A_1 \times \ldots \times A_n)$ is a $\Phi$-equilibrium, then it is also a $\Phi'$-equilibrium, where $\Phi' = (\Phi'_i)_{1 \leq i \leq n}$ and $\Phi'_i$ is the convex hull of $\Phi_i$, for $1 \leq i \leq n$.*

*Proof.* Since $q$ is a $\Phi$-equilibrium, $r_i(q) \geq r_i(\phi_i(q))$, for all players $i$ and for all $\phi_i \in \Phi_i$. In particular, $r_i(q) \geq r_i(\phi_{i_1}(q))$ and $r_i(q) \geq r_i(\phi_{i_2}(q))$. Since $r_i$, $\phi_{i_1}$, and $\phi_{i_2}$ are linear on $\Delta(A_1 \times \ldots \times A_n)$, it follows that

$$
\begin{aligned}
&r_i(q) \\
&= \alpha r_i(q) + (1-\alpha)r_i(q) \\
&\geq \alpha r_i(\phi_{i_1}(q)) + (1-\alpha)r_i(\phi_{i_2}(q)) \\
&= r_i(\alpha \phi_{i_1}(q)) + (1-\alpha)\phi_{i_2}(q)) \\
&= r_i((\alpha \phi_{i_1} + (1-\alpha)\phi_{i_2})(q))
\end{aligned}
$$

A Nash equilibrium $q \in \Delta(A_1 \times \ldots \times A_n)$ is an independent $\Phi$-equilibrium: if $r_i(q) \geq r_i(\phi_i(q)) = r(q_1, \ldots, q_{i-1}, \phi_i(q_i), q_{i+1}, \ldots, q_n)$, for all players $i$ and for all $\phi_i \in \Phi_i$, then $r(q) \geq r(q_1, \ldots, q_{i-1}, q'_i, q_{i+1}, \ldots, q_n)$, for all players $i$ and for all $q'_i \in \Delta(A_i)$. In other words, the set of $\Phi$-equilibria contains the set of Nash equilibria. Moreover, since the set of $\Phi$-equilibria is convex, this set also contains the convex hull of the set of Nash equilibria. But the convex hull of the set of Nash equilibria need not contain even the smallest set of $\Phi$-equilibria: in particular, the convex hull of the set of Nash equilibria need not contain the set of correlated equilibria [1].

**Theorem 4.** *Given a game described by reward function $r$, if all players $i$ play via some $\Phi_i$-no-regret learning algorithm, then the joint empirical distribution of play converges to the set of $\Phi$-equilibrium, almost surely.*

*Proof.* Define the empirical distribution $z_t$ of play through time $t$ as follows:

$$z_t(a_i, a_{-i}) = \frac{1}{t} \sum_{\tau=1}^{t} \mathbf{1}_{a_{i,\tau}=a_i} \mathbf{1}_{a_{-i,\tau}=a_{-i}} \tag{9}$$

for all actions $a_i \in A_i$ and $a_{-i} \in A_{-i} \equiv \prod_{j \neq i} A_j$. (The notation $\mathbf{1}_{a_{i,\tau}=a_i}$ denotes the indicator function, which equals 1 whenever $a_{i,\tau} = a_i$, and 0 otherwise.) It suffices to show that for all players $i$ and for all $\phi_i \in \Phi_i$, $r_i(\phi_i(z_t)) - r_i(z_t) \to 0$, as $t \to \infty$, almost surely.

First, for arbitrary player $i$ and for arbitrary $\phi_i \in \Phi_i$,

$$
\begin{aligned}
r_i(\phi_i(z_t)) &= \sum_{b_i, a_{-i}} \phi_i(z_t)(b_i, a_{-i}) r_i(b_i, a_{-i}) \\
&= \sum_{b_i, a_{-i}} \sum_{a_i \in A_i} z_t(a_i, a_{-i}) \phi_i(\delta_{a_i})(b_i) r_i(b_i, a_{-i}) \\
&= \sum_{a_i, a_{-i}} z_t(a_i, a_{-i}) r_i(\phi_i(\delta_{a_i}), a_{-i}) \\
&= \frac{1}{t} \sum_{\tau=1}^{t} r_i(\phi_i(\delta_{a_{i,\tau}}), a_{-i,\tau})
\end{aligned}
$$

In the first step, we expand the definition of the expectation $r_i(q, a_{-i})$; and in the third step we collapse this definition. The second step relies on the extended definition of $\phi_i : \Delta(A_1 \times \ldots \times A_n) \to \Delta(A_1 \times \ldots \times A_n)$—see Equation 8. The last step follows from the definition of the empirical distribution $z_t$.

Second, for arbitrary player $i$,

$$r_i(z_t) = \frac{1}{t} \sum_{\tau=1}^{t} r_i(a_{i,\tau}, a_{-i,\tau})$$

Now, by assumption all players $i$ play according to some $\Phi_i$-no-regret learning algorithm: i.e., for all players $i$, for all $\phi_i \in \Phi_i$, for all $\epsilon > 0$, there exists $t_0$ s.t. for all $t \geq t_0$,

$$
\begin{aligned}
& r_i(\phi_i(z_t)) - r_i(z_t) \\
&= \frac{1}{t} \sum_{\tau=1}^{t} r_i(\phi_i(\delta_{a_{i,\tau}}), a_{-i,\tau}) - \frac{1}{t} \sum_{\tau=1}^{t} r_i(a_{i,\tau}, a_{-i,\tau}) \\
&< \epsilon
\end{aligned}
$$

almost surely. Therefore, for all players $i$, $r_i(z_t)$ approaches $r_i(\phi_i(z_t))$, almost surely, for all $\phi_i \in \Phi_i$. In other words, the joint empirical distribution of play converges to the set of $\Phi$-equilibrium, almost surely.

# 5  Conclusion

In this article, we defined a general class of no-regret learning algorithms, called $\Phi$-no-regret learning algorithms, which spans the spectrum from no-internal-regret learning to no-external-regret Analogously, we defined a general class of game-theoretic equilibria, called $\Phi$-equilibria, and we showed that the empirical distribution of play of $\Phi$-no-regret algorithms converges to the set of $\Phi$-equilibria. But the set $\Phi$ was restricted: it contained only linear maps. In future work, we plan to generalize this framework to include nonlinear, as well as, linear maps. Perhaps by doing so, we can obtain convergence results to tighter solution concepts than correlated equilibrium.

# References

1. R. Aumann. Subjectivity and correlation in randomized strategies. *Journal of Mathematical Economics*, 1:67–96, 1974.
2. D. Blackwell. An analog of the minimax theorem for vector payoffs. *Pacific Journal of Mathematics*, 6:1–8, 1956.
3. G. Brown. Iterative solutions of games by fictitious play. In T. Koopmans, editor, *Activity Analysis of Production and Allocation*. Wiley, New York, 1951.
4. A. Cournot. *Recherches sur les Principes Mathematics de la Theorie de la Richesse.* Hachette, 1838.
5. D. Foster and R. Vohra. A randomization rule for selecting forecasts. *Operations Research*, 41(4):704–709, 1993.
6. D. Foster and R. Vohra. Regret in the on-line decision problem. *Games and Economic Behavior*, 21:40–55, 1997.
7. Y. Freund and R. Schapire. A decision-theoretic generalization of on-line learning and an application to boosting. In *Computational Learning Theory: Proceedings of the Second European Conference*, pages 23–37. Springer-Verlag, 1995.
8. Y. Freund and R. Schapire. Game theory, on-line prediction, and boosting. In *Proceedings of the 9th Annual Conference on Computational Learning Theory*, pages 325–332. ACM Press, May 1996.
9. D. Fudenberg and D. K. Levine. Conditional universal consistency. *Games and Economic Behavior*, Forthcoming.
10. D. Fudenberg and D.K. Levine. Universal consistency and cautious fictitious play. *Journal of Economic Dyanmics and Control*, 19:1065–1090, 1995.
11. J. Hannan. Approximation to Bayes risk in repeated plays. In M. Dresher, A.W. Tucker, and P. Wolfe, editors, *Contributions to the Theory of Games*, volume 3, pages 97–139. Princeton University Press, 1957.
12. S. Hart and A. Mas Colell. A simple adaptive procedure leading to correlated equilibrium. *Econometrica*, 68:1127–1150, 2000.
13. S. Hart and A. Mas Colell. A general class of adaptive strategies. *Economic Theory*, 98:26–54, 2001.
14. A. Jafari. *On the Notion of Regret in Infinitely Repeated Games*. Master's Thesis, Brown University, Providence, May 2003.
15. J. Robinson. An iterative method of solving a game. *Annals of Mathematics*, 54:298–301, 1951.

# Preference Elicitation and Query Learning

Avrim Blum[1], Jeffrey C. Jackson[2], Tuomas Sandholm[1], and Martin Zinkevich[1]

[1] Carnegie Mellon University, Pittsburgh PA 15213, USA
maz@cs.cmu.edu
http://www.cs.cmu.edu/~avrim,sandholm,maz/
[2] Duquesne University, Pittsburgh PA 15282, USA
jackson@mathcs.duq.edu
http://www.mathcs.duq.edu/~jackson/

**Abstract.** In this paper we initiate an exploration of relationships between "preference elicitation", a learning-style problem that arises in combinatorial auctions, and the problem of learning via queries studied in computational learning theory. Preference elicitation is the process of asking questions about the preferences of bidders so as to best divide some set of goods. As a learning problem, it can be thought of as a setting in which there are multiple target concepts that can each be queried separately, but where the goal is not so much to learn each concept as it is to produce an "optimal example". In this work, we prove a number of similarities and differences between preference elicitation and query learning, giving both separation results and proving some connections between these problems.

## 1 Introduction

In a combinatorial auction, an entity (the "auctioneer") has a set $S$ of $n$ items that he would like to partition among a set of $k$ bidders. What makes an auction *combinatorial* is that the valuations of the bidders (how much they would be willing to pay for different subsets of items) may not necessarily be linear functions over the items. For instance, if item $a$ is a left shoe and item $b$ is a right shoe, then a bidder might be willing to pay a reasonable amount for the bundle $\{a, b\}$ but very little for just $\{a\}$ or just $\{b\}$. In the other direction, if $a$ and $b$ are each *pairs* of shoes, then a bidder might value $\{a, b\}$ less than the sum of his valuations on $\{a\}$ and $\{b\}$ (especially if he just needs one pair of shoes right now). A standard goal for the auctioneer in such a setting is to determine the allocation of goods that maximizes *social welfare*: this is the sum, over all bidders, of the value that each bidder places on the set of items that he receives. This goal is perhaps most natural if one thinks of the auctioneer as not having a financial interest of its own but simply as an agent acting to help divide up a given set of items in a way that maximizes overall happiness. For example, the case of $k = 2$ can be thought of as a situation in which one of the bidders represents a buyer (with various preferences over bundles of items) and the other bidder represents a marketplace (with various discounts and package-deals), and

B. Schölkopf and M.K. Warmuth (Eds.): COLT/Kernel 2003, LNAI 2777, pp. 13–25, 2003.
© Springer-Verlag Berlin Heidelberg 2003

the auctioneer is acting as an agent to help the buyer decide what subset of items to purchase from the marketplace[1].

There are a number of issues that arise in the combinatorial auction setting. For example, there is much work on designing protocols (mechanisms) so that bidders will be truthful in reporting their valuations and not want to "game" the system (e.g., [1–3]). But another issue is that even if we can get bidders to be truthful, their valuation functions can be quite complicated. Because of this, bidding in a traditional manner can require an exponential amount of communication. This has led researchers to study the notion of preference elicitation, in which the auctioneer asks questions of the bidders in order to learn (elicit) enough information about their preferences so as to be able to decide on the best (or approximately best) allocation of the items. Because the issues of truthfulness can be handled even in this setting of incremental preference elicitation via known mechanisms [4], much of this previous work—as well as this paper—focuses solely on the elicitation question of how to extract the necessary information needed for allocation.

## 1.1  Preference Elicitation and Query Learning

We can think of preference elicitation in the context of query learning by thinking of the $n$ items as features, thinking of a subset of items (a "bundle") as an example $x \in \{0,1\}^n$ indicating which items are in the subset, and thinking of the bidder's valuation function as a target function. The standard assumption of "free disposal" (bidders can throw away items for free), means we can assume that these valuation functions are *monotone*, though they typically will not be boolean-valued. Furthermore, one of the natural types of queries studied in preference elicitation, the *value query* (where the auctioneer asks the bidder how much he values some bundle), corresponds exactly with the learning-theoretic notion of a membership query.

On the other hand, a key difference between preference elicitation and query learning is in the goals. In learning, the objective is to exactly or approximately recover the target function. In preference elicitation, however, the goal is more one of finding the "best example". For instance, if there are just two bidders with preference functions $f$ and $g$, then the goal is to find a partition $(S', S'')$ of the $n$ items to maximize $f(S') + g(S'')$. Thinking in terms of functions over $\{0,1\}^n$, the goal is to find $x \in \{0,1\}^n$ to maximize $f(x) + g(\bar{x})$.

Notice that one of the immediate differences between preference elicitation and query learning is that preference elicitation makes sense even if the target functions do not have short descriptions, or even short approximations. We will see some interesting examples later, but as a simple case, if we learn that bidder $A$ will pay \$100 for the entire set of $n$ items but no more than \$50 for any subset of size $n - 1$ (she is a collector and wants the whole set), and $B$ will pay a

---

[1] To think of this as a combinatorial auction, it is easiest to imagine that the auctioneer has pre-purchased *all* the items, and then is deciding which the buyer should keep and which should be returned for a refund.

maximum of \$50 even for the whole lot, then we know we might as well give all items to $A$, and we do not need to know exactly how much each bidder would have paid for different subsets. On the other hand, it is quite possible for allocation of items to be *computationally* hard, even if the preferences of all the bidders are known. For example, even if each bidder's preferences can be expressed as a simple conjunction (these are called "single-minded" bidders), then if there are many bidders, allocation is equivalent to the NP-hard set-packing problem. For somewhat more complicated preference functions, such as read-once formulas, allocation can be NP-hard even for two bidders [5].

Another difference concerns the types of queries that are most natural in each setting. While value/membership queries are common to both, equivalence queries are quite *un*natural in the context of preference elicitation. On the other hand, the *demand query*, a powerful type of query for preference elicitation introduced by Nisan [6], does not seem to have been studied in query learning[2].

In this paper, we discuss similarities and differences between the three objectives of exact learning, approximate learning, and preference elicitation. We then give a number of upper and lower bounds for preference elicitation of natural preference (concept) classes. We focus primarily on the case of $k = 2$ bidders, because even this case is quite interesting, both practically (since it models a buyer and a marketplace as mentioned above) and technically. We show that monotone DNF formulas (long known to be hard to learn exactly from membership queries alone but easy to learn approximately) are *hard* for preference elicitation, even with demand queries. However, the hardness we show is $2^{\Omega(\sqrt{n})}$-hard rather than $2^{\Omega(n)}$-hard. On the other hand, $\log(n)$-DNF are *easy* for preference-elicitation, even if the functions have more than polynomially many terms. We also give a number of general statements about when the ability to succeed for one of these goals implies being able to succeed in the others. We then end with a number of open problems.

## 1.2  Related Work on Combinatorial Auctions

Combinatorial auctions are economically efficient mechanisms for selling $n$ items to multiple bidders, and are attractive when the bidders' valuations on bundles exhibit *complementarity* (a bundle of items is worth more than the sum of its parts) and/or *substitutability* (a bundle is worth less than the sum of its parts). Determining the winners in such auctions, given the bids, is a complex optimization problem that has received considerable attention (e.g., [7–9, 2, 10, 11]). Equally important, however, is the problem of communication. There are $2^n - 1$ bundles, and each agent may need to bid on all of them to fully express its preferences. Appropriate bidding languages [8, 12, 9, 2, 13, 14] can address the communication overhead in some cases where the bidder's utility function is compressible. However, they still require the agents to completely determine

---

[2] In this query, the auctioneer proposes a set of item prices and then asks the bidder what set of items he would choose to buy at those prices. These will be discussed further in Section 2.

and transmit their valuation functions and as such do not solve all the issues. So in practice, when the number of items for sale is even moderate, the bidders cannot bid on all bundles. Instead, they may bid on bundles which they will not win, and they may fail to bid on bundles they would have won. The former problem leads to wasted effort, and the latter problem leads to reduced economic efficiency of the resulting allocation of items to bidders.

Selective *incremental preference elicitation* by the auctioneer was recently proposed to address these problems, and several papers have studied different types of elicitors [4, 15, 16, 6, 17]. On the negative side, if valuations are arbitrary monotone functions, then the worst-case communication complexity to find an (even approximately) optimal allocation is exponential in the number of items, no matter what query types are used [6]. However, experimentally, only a small decreasing fraction of the bidders' preferences can be elicited before the provably optimal allocation is found [16].

Vickrey-Clark-Groves [18–20] schemes provide a method for charging bidders so that each is motivated to tell the truth about its valuations. Briefly, in this scheme the elicitor first finds the optimal allocation $OPT$. Then, for each bidder $i$, it finds the optimal allocation $OPT_i$ without bidder $i$. Bidder $i$ is charged a fee based on the difference between the utility of the other agents in $OPT$ and $OPT_i$. One then proves that in such a scheme, each bidder is motivated to be truthful. This means that if one can elicit the optimal allocation exactly assuming that agents tell the truth, one can determine the Vickrey payments that make truth-telling a good strategy for the bidders. Because of this, for the remainder of the paper we assume that the bidders are truthful.

Driven by the same concerns as preference elicitation in combinatorial auctions, there has been significant recent work on ascending combinatorial auctions (e.g., [21–26]). These are multistage mechanisms. At each stage the auctioneer announces prices (on items or in some cases on bundles of items), and each bidder states which bundle of items he would prefer (that is, which bundle would maximize his valuation minus the price he would have to pay for the bundle) at those prices. The auctioneer increases the prices between stages, and the auction usually ends when the optimal allocation is found. Ascending auctions can be viewed as a special case of preference elicitation where the queries are demand queries ("If these were the prices, what bundle would you buy from the auction?") and the query policy is constrained to increasing the prices in the queries over time. Recently it was shown that if *per-item* prices suffice to support an optimal allocation (i.e., a *Walrasian equilibrium* exists), then the optimal allocation can be found with a polynomial number of queries (where each query and answer is of polynomial size) [6].

Recently, some of us [5], noticing the connection to query learning, showed how the AHK algorithm [27] could be adapted to elicit preferences expressable as read-once-formulas over gates that are especially natural in the context of combinatorial auctions. This work goes on to discuss the computational problem of determining the best allocation once the formulas are elicited. On the negative side, it shows that even for two bidders with read-once-formula preferences, allocation can be NP-hard, but on the other hand, if one of the two bidders has a linear value function, then allocation can be done in polynomial time.

## 2    Notation and Definitions

Because subset notation is most natural from the point of view of preference elicitation, we will use both subset notation and bit-vector notation in this paper. That is, we will think of the instance space $X$ both as elements of $\{0,1\}^n$ and as the power set of some set $S$ of $n$ *items*. We will also interchangeably call a subset of $S$ a "bundle" or an "example". When discussing preference elicitation, we assume there are $k$ bidders with monotone real-valued preference functions over the instance space. The objective of preference elicitation is to determine a $k$-way partition $(S_1, \ldots, S_k)$ of $S$ to maximize $f_1(S_1) + f_2(S_2) + \ldots + f_k(S_k)$, where $f_1, \ldots, f_k$ are the $k$ real-valued preference functions. Typically we will assume $k = 2$.

Let $C$ be a class of monotone functions. We will be interested in the learnability of various $C$ in the exact learning, approximate learning, and preference elicitation models given the ability to make various types of queries. By "approximate learning" we mean learning with respect to the uniform distribution on inputs — i.e., finding a hypothesis function that agrees with the target over almost all of the instance space. While learning algorithms are typically considered efficient if they run in time polynomial in the number of items $n$ and in the length of the representation of the target (and possibly other parameters), we will at times explicitly require run time bounds independent of description length in order to demonstrate a fundamental advantage of preference elicitation for problems involving complex targets. The hardness observations for learning problems when this restriction is in place are therefore not hardness results in the standard learning-theoretic sense.

*Query types:* A *membership query* or *value query* is a request $x \in \{0,1\}^n$ to an oracle for a target $f$. The oracle responds with the value $f(x)$ corresponding to $x$. We can think of these queries as asking the following question of a bidder: "How much are you willing to pay for this bundle of items?"

A *demand query* is a request $w \in (\mathbf{R}^+)^n$ ($\mathbf{R}^+$ here represents non-negative real values) to an oracle for a target $f$. The oracle responds with an example $x \in \{0,1\}^n$ that maximizes $f(x) - w \cdot x$. We can think of these queries as asking the following question of a bidder: "If these are the costs of items, what would you choose to buy?"

We can illustrate the power of demand queries with the following observation due to Nisan. If one of the bidders has a linear valuation function, and the other is arbitrary, then preference elicitation can be done with $n + 1$ queries: $n$ value queries and one demand query. Specifically, we simply ask the linear bidder $n$ value queries to determine his value on each item, and then send the other bidder these values as prices and ask him what he would like to buy. Thus it is interesting that our main lower bounds hold for demand queries as well.

*Natural function/representation classes:* One of the most natural representation classes of monotone functions in machine learning is that of monotone DNF formulas. In preference elicitation, the analog of this representation is called the "XOR bidding language"[3]. A preference in this representation is a set of bundles (terms) $T = \{T_1, T_2, \ldots, T_m\}$ along with values $v_i$ for each bundle $T_i$. The value of this preference for all $S' \subseteq S$ is:

$$f_{T,v}(S') = \max_{T_i \subseteq S'} v_i.$$

In other words, the value of a set of items $S'$ is the maximum value of any of the "desired bundles" in $T$ that are contained in $S'$. We will call this the *DNF representation* of preferences, or "DNF preferences" for short. Our hardness results for this class will all go through for the boolean case (all $v_i$ are equal to 1), but our positive results will hold for general $v_i$.

## 3 DNF Preferences

Angluin [28] shows that monotone DNF formulas are hard to exactly learn from membership queries alone, but are easy to learn approximately. Angluin's example showing hardness of exact learning can be thought of as follows: imagine the $n$ items are really $n/2$ pairs of shoes. The buyer would be happy with any bundle containing at least one pair of shoes (any such bundle is worth \$1). But then we add one final term to the DNF: a bundle of size $n/2$ containing exactly one shoe from each pair, where for each pair we flip a coin to decide whether to include the left or right shoe. Since the learning algorithm already knows the answer will be positive to any query containing a pair of shoes, the only interesting queries are those that contain no such pair, and therefore it has to match the last term *exactly* to provide any information. Thus even for a randomized algorithm, an expected $2^{n/2-1}$ queries are needed for exact learning of monotone DNF.

We now consider the preference elicitation problem when one or more preferences are represented as monotone DNF expressions, beginning with a few simple observations.

**Observation 1** *If $f$ is a known DNF preference function with $m$ terms, and $g$ is an arbitrary unknown monotone preference function, then preference elicitation can be performed using $m$ value queries.*

*Proof.* Because $g$ is monotone, the optimal allocation will be of the form $(T_i, S - T_i)$ for some term $T_i$ in $f$. So, we simply need to query $g$ once for each set $S - T_i$ and then pick the best of these $m$ partitions. □

---

[3] This terminology is to indicate that the bidder wants only one of his listed bundles and will not pay more for a set of items that contains multiple bundles inside it. This usage is very different from the standard definition of XOR as a sum modulo 2. Therefore, to avoid confusion, we will not use the XOR terminology here.

**Observation 2** *If $f$ and $g$ are boolean DNF preferences each containing exactly one term that is not size 2 (the hard case in Angluin's construction) then preference elicitation can be performed using polynomially (in $n$) many value queries.*

*Proof.* We begin by finding all terms in $f$ of size 2 by asking $n^2$ queries. Suppose two of these terms $T_1$ and $T_2$ are disjoint. In that case, we query $g$ on $S - T_1$ and $S - T_2$. If one answer is "yes" then we are done. If both answers are "no" then this means all of $g$'s terms intersect both $T_1$ and $T_2$. In particular, $g$ can have only a constant number of terms, and therefore *exactly* learning $g$ is easy, after which we can then apply Observation 1 (swapping $f$ and $g$). On the other hand, if $f$ does not have two disjoint terms of size 2, then the only way $f$ can have more than 3 such terms is if they all share some common item $x_i$. It is thus now easy to learn the large term in $f$: if $f(S - \{x_i\})$ is positive, we can "walk downward" from that example to find it, else we can walk downward from the example in which all the *other* items in the small terms have been removed. Once $f$ has been learned, we can again apply Observation 1.     □

We now show that even though Angluin's specific example is no longer hard in the preference elicitation model, monotone DNF formulas remain hard for preference elicitation using value queries, even when the preference functions are quite small. We then extend this result to demand queries as well.

**Theorem 1.** *Preference elicitation of monotone DNF formulas requires $2^{\Omega(\sqrt{n})}$ value queries. This holds even if each bidder's preference function has only $O(\sqrt{n})$ terms.*

*Proof.* We construct a hard example as follows. There will be $n = m^2$ items, arranged in an $m$-by-$m$ matrix. Let us label the items $x_{ij}$ for $1 \le i, j \le m$. We will call the two preference functions $f_R$ and $f_C$. Both will be boolean functions. Bidder $f_R$ is happy with any row: that is, $f_R = x_{11}x_{12}\cdots x_{1m} \vee x_{21}x_{22}\cdots x_{2m} \vee \ldots \vee x_{m1}x_{m2}\cdots x_{mm}$. Bidder $f_C$ is happy with any column: that is, $f_C = x_{11}x_{21}\cdots x_{m1} \vee x_{21}x_{22}\cdots x_{m2} \vee \ldots \vee x_{1m}x_{2m}\cdots x_{mm}$. Thus, at this point, it is impossible to make both bidders happy. However, we now add one additional term to each preference function. We flip a coin for each of the $n$ items in $S$, labeling the item as heads or tails. Let $H$ be the set of all items labeled heads, and $T$ be the set of all items labeled tails. We now add the conjunction of all items in $H$ as one additional term to $f_R$, and the conjunction of all items in $T$ as one additional term to $f_C$. Thus now it *is* possible to make both bidders happy, and the optimal allocation will be to give the items in $H$ to the "row bidder" and the items in $T$ to the "column bidder".

We now argue that no query algorithm can find this allocation in less than $\frac{1}{2}2^{\sqrt{n}} - 2$ queries in expectation. Let us enforce that the last two questions of the query protocol are the values of the actual allocation. That is, if the elicitor assigns the items in $H$ to the row agent and $T$ to the column agent, it must ask the row agent the value of $H$ and the column agent the value of $T$. This constraint only increases the length of the protocol by at most 2 questions.

Let us assume that the elicitor knows in advance the structure of the problem, the row sets and the column sets, and the only information the elicitor does not know are the sets $H$ and $T$. In this case, we can assume without loss of generality that the elicitor never asks the row bidder about any bundle containing a row (because he already knows the answer will be "yes") and similarly never asks the column bidder about any bundle containing a column.

We now argue as follows. If the elicitor asks a query of the row bidder, the query must be missing at least one item in each row, and if the elicitor ask a query of the column bidder, it must be missing at least one item in each column. However, notice that in the first case, the answer will be positive only if all missing items are in $T$, and in the second case, the answer will be positive only if all missing items are in $H$. Therefore, for any given such query, the probability that the answer will be positive taken over the random coin flips is at most $2^{-\sqrt{n}}$. Thus, for any elicitation strategy, the probability the elicitor gets a positive response in the first $k$ queries is at most $k2^{-\sqrt{n}}$ and therefore the expected number of queries is at least $\frac{1}{2}2^{\sqrt{n}}$. $\qquad\square$

We now show that preference elicitation remains hard for DNF preferences even if we allow demand queries.

**Theorem 2.** *Even if both demand queries and value queries are allowed, preference elicitation of monotone DNF formulas requires $2^{\Omega(\sqrt{n})}$ queries. This holds even if each bidder's preference function has only $O(\sqrt{n})$ terms.*

*Proof.* We use the same example as in the proof of Theorem 1. As in that proof, we can insist that the last question be a demand query where the agent responds with the set $H$ or $T$ respectively. Let us without loss of generality consider a sequence of demand queries to the "row bidder". What we need to calculate now is the probability, for any given cost vector $w$, that the set $H$ happens to be the cheapest term in his DNF formula. The intuition is that this is highly unlikely because $H$ is so much larger than the other terms.

Specifically, for a given query cost vector $w$, let $w_i$ be the total cost of the $i$th row. Thus, the cheapest row has cost $\min(w_1, \ldots, w_m)$ and the *expected* cost of $H$ is $\frac{1}{2}(w_1 + \ldots + w_m)$. One simple observation that helps in the analysis is that if we define $h_i$ as the cost of the items in $H$ that are in the $i$th row, then $\Pr(h_i \geq w_i/2) \geq 1/2$. That is because if any particular subset of the $i$th row has cost less than $w_i/2$, its complement in the $i$th row must have cost greater than $w_i/2$. Furthermore, these events are independent over the different rows.

So, we can reduce the problem to the following: we have $m$ independent events each of probability at least $1/2$. If at least two of these events occur, the elicitor gets no information ($H$ is not the cheapest bundle because it is not cheaper than the cheapest row). Thus, the probability the elicitor *does* get some information is at most $(m+1)2^{-m}$ and the expected number of queries is at least $\frac{1}{2(m+1)}2^m$. $\qquad\square$

**Open Problem 1** *Can preferences expressible as polynomial-size DNF formulas be elicited in $2^{O(\sqrt{n})}$ value queries or demand queries?*

### 3.1   log(n)-DNF Preferences

In the previous problem, even though there were only $O(\sqrt{n})$ terms in each preference function, the terms themselves were fairly large. What if all of the terms are small, of size no more than $\log n$? Observe that there are $\binom{n}{\log n}$ possible terms of size $\log n$, so some members of this class cannot be represented in $\text{poly}(n)$ bits.

**Theorem 3.** *If $f$ and $g$ are DNF-preferences where no term is of size more than $\log_2 n$, then preference elicitation can be performed in a number of value queries polynomial in $n$.*

*Proof.* We begin by giving a randomized construction and then show a derandomization.

For convenience let us put an empty term $T_0$ of value 0 into both $f$ and $g$. With this convention we can assume the optimal allocation satisfies some term $T' \in f$ and some term $T'' \in g$.

We now simply notice that since $T'$ and $T''$ are both of size at most $\log_2 n$, a random partition $(S', S'')$ has probability at least $1/n^2$ of satisfying $S' \supseteq T'$ and $S'' \supseteq T''$. So, we simply need to try $O(n^2 \log \frac{1}{\delta})$ random partitions and take the best one, and with probability at least $1 - \delta$ we will have found the optimal allocation.

We can now derandomize this algorithm using the $(n, k)$-universal sets of Naor and Naor [29]. A set of assignments to $n$ boolean variables is $(n, k)$-universal if for every subset of $k$ variables, the induced assignments to those variables covers all $2^k$ possible settings. Naor and Naor [29] give efficient explicit constructions of such sets using only $2^{O(k)} \log n$ assignments. In our case, we can use the case of $k = 2\log_2 n$, so the construction is polynomial time and size. Each of these assignments corresponds to a partition of the items, and we simply ask $f$ and $g$ for their valuations on each one and take the best.     □

## 4   General Relationships

In this section we describe some general relationships between query learning and preference elicitation. We begin with an example in which preference elicitation is easy but exact learning is hard, even though the function has a small description. We then show that in certain circumstances, however, the ability to elicit does imply the ability to learn with queries.

### 4.1   Almost-Threshold Preferences

We now define a class of preference functions that we call *almost-threshold*. This class will be used to show that, even if all of the functions in a class have representations of size polynomial in $n$, we can still separate exact learning and preference elicitation with respect to membership queries.

An "almost threshold" preference function is defined by specifying a single set $S'$. This set in turn defines a preference function that is 1 for any set of size greater than or equal to $|S'|$, except for $S'$ itself, and is 0 otherwise. Formally, for any $S' \neq \emptyset$, define:

$$h_{S'}(S'') = \begin{cases} 1 \text{ if } S'' \neq S' \text{ and } |S''| \geq |S'| \\ 0 \text{ otherwise} \end{cases}$$

The class $H_{AT}$ of almost-threshold preference functions is then $H_{AT} = \{h_{S'}\}$.

**Observation 3** *It requires at least $\binom{n}{\lceil n/2 \rceil - 1}$ membership queries to exactly learn the class $H_{AT}$.*

**Theorem 4.** *If $f, g \in H_{AT}$ then the optimal allocation can be elicited in $4 + \log_2 n$ membership queries.*

*Proof.* Assume $|S| > 2$ and suppose $f = h_{S'}$. The first step is to determine $|S'|$. We can do this in $\log_2 n + 1$ queries using binary search. We next use two more queries to find two sets $T, T'$ of size $|S'|$ such that $f(T) = f(T') = 1$. This can be done by just picking three arbitrary sets of size $|S'|$ and querying the first two: if either has value 0 then the third has value 1. Then, we test if $g(S \backslash T) = 1$. If it is, then $T, S \backslash T$ is an optimal allocation. Otherwise, $T', S \backslash T'$, regardless of its value, is an optimal allocation.    $\square$

## 4.2    Positive Results

We now show that in certain circumstances, however, the ability to elicit does imply the ability to learn with queries. In particular, we will show that in certain cases, the ability to perform preference elicitation will provide us with a Superset Query oracle, which together with membership queries can allow us to to learn concept classes not learnable by membership queries alone.

**Definition 1.** *A **superset query oracle** for a concept class $H$ takes in a function $f \in H$ as input. If $f$ is a superset of the target $f^*$, that is, $\{x : f(x) = 1\} \supseteq \{x : f^*(x) = 1\}$, then the query returns "true". Otherwise the query produces a counterexample: an $x$ such that $f(x) = 0$ but $f^*(x) = 1$.*

Notice that Angluin's algorithm [28] for learning Monotone DNF can use superset queries instead of equivalence queries, because the hypothesis is always a subset of the target function. Furthermore, any subclass of Monotone DNF that is closed under removal of terms can be learned from superset queries and membership queries by the same algorithm.

What makes this interesting is the following relationship between preference elicitation and superset queries. First, for any boolean function $f$, let us define its "dual"

$$\hat{f}(S') = 1 - f(S \backslash S').$$

Or, in other words, $\hat{f}(x) = \bar{f}(\bar{x})$. Given a hypothesis space $H$, define $\hat{H} = \{\hat{f} : f \in H\}$. For example, the dual of $\log(n)$-DNF preferences is $\log(n)$-CNF preferences. The set of monotone functions is closed under dual.

**Theorem 5.** *If, given $f \in H$ and $g \in \hat{H}$, one can elicit the optimal allocation $S, S'$ using $M$ value queries, then one can perform a superset query on $H$ using $M + 2$ membership queries.*

*Proof.* Suppose that $f^*$ is the target concept and one wants to perform a superset query with $g \in H$. First, compute $\hat{g} \in \hat{H}$. Then, perform preference elicitation on $f^*, \hat{g}$. If this procedure returns an allocation satisfying both parties, this means we have an $x$ such that $f^*(x) = 1$ and $\hat{g}(\bar{x}) = 1$. But, $\hat{g}(\bar{x}) = \bar{g}(x)$ so this means that $x$ is a counterexample to the superset query. On the other hand if the elicitation procedure fails to do so, then this means no such $x$ exists so the superset query can return "true". □

**Corollary 1.** *If $H$ is a subclass of monotone DNF that is closed under removal of terms, and if one can perform preference elicitation for $(H, \hat{H})$, then $H$ is learnable from membership queries alone.*

## 5   Conclusions and Open Problems

In machine learning, one's objective is nearly always to learn or approximately learn some target function. In this paper, we relate this to the notion of preference elicitation, in which the goal instead is to find the optimal partitioning of some set of items (to find an example $x$ maximizing $f(x) + g(\bar{x})$.)

We now describe several open problems left by this work. We begin with a problem stated above in Section 3.

**Open Problem 1** *Can preferences expressible as polynomial-size DNF formulas be elicited in $2^{O(\sqrt{n})}$ value queries or demand queries?*

A somewhat fuzzier question related to our results on $\log(n)$-DNF is the following. Our algorithm in this case was non-adaptive: the questions asked did not depend on answers to previous questions. It seems natural that for some classes adaptivity should help. In fact, it not hard to generate artificial examples in which this is the case. However, we know of no natural example having this property.

**Open Problem 2** *Are there natural classes of functions for which exact learning is information-theoretically hard, preference elicitation via a non-adaptive algorithm is hard (i.e., one in which the questions can all be determined in advance) but elicitation by an adaptive algorithm is easy.*

One of the oldest techniques for preference elicitation is an ascending auction. An ascending auction can be considered to be a sequence of increasing demand queries, where if one asks a query $w'$ after a query $w$, then it must be the case that for all $i$, $w'_i \geq w_i$. One interesting open question is:

**Open Problem 3** *Does there exist a preference elicitation problem that is hard (or impossible) to elicit using an ascending auction but easy to elicit using demand queries?*

## Acknowledgements

This material is based upon work supported under NSF grants CCR-0105488, ITR CCR-0122581, CCR-0209064, ITR IIS-0081246, and ITR IIS-0121678. Any opinion, findings, conclusions or recommendations expressed in this publication are those of the authors and do not necessarily reflect the views of the National Science Foundation.

## References

1. Sandholm, T.: eMediator: A next generation electronic commerce server. Computational Intelligence **18** (2002) 656–676 Special issue on Agent Technology for Electronic Commerce. Early versions appeared in the Conference on Autonomous Agents (AGENTS-00), pp. 73–96, 2000; AAAI-99 Workshop on AI in Electronic Commerce, Orlando, FL, pp. 46–55, July 1999; and as a Washington University, St. Louis, Dept. of Computer Science technical report WU-CS-99-02, Jan. 1999.
2. Nisan, N.: Bidding and allocation in combinatorial auctions. In: Proceedings of the ACM Conference on Electronic Commerce (ACM-EC), Minneapolis, MN (2000) 1–12
3. Lehmann, D., O'Callaghan, L.I., Shoham, Y.: Truth revelation in rapid, approximately efficient combinatorial auctions. Journal of the ACM (2003) To appear. Early version appeared in ACMEC-99.
4. Conen, W., Sandholm, T.: Preference elicitation in combinatorial auctions: Extended abstract. In: Proceedings of the ACM Conference on Electronic Commerce (ACM-EC), Tampa, FL (2001) 256–259 A more detailed description of the algorithmic aspects appeared in the IJCAI-2001 Workshop on Economic Agents, Models, and Mechanisms, pp. 71–80.
5. Zinkevich, M., Blum, A., Sandholm, T.: On polynomial-time preference elicitation with value queries. In: Proceedings of the ACM Conference on Electronic Commerce (ACM-EC), San Diego, CA (2003)
6. Nisan, N., Segal, I.: The communication complexity of efficient allocation problems (2002) Draft. Second version March 5th.
7. Rothkopf, M.H., Pekeč, A., Harstad, R.M.: Computationally manageable combinatorial auctions. Management Science **44** (1998) 1131–1147
8. Sandholm, T.: Algorithm for optimal winner determination in combinatorial auctions. Artificial Intelligence **135** (2002) 1–54 First appeared as an invited talk at the First International Conference on Information and Computation Economies, Charleston, SC, Oct. 25–28, 1998. Extended version appeared as Washington Univ., Dept. of Computer Science, tech report WUCS-99-01, January 28th, 1999. Conference version appeared at the International Joint Conference on Artificial Intelligence (IJCAI), pp. 542–547, Stockholm, Sweden, 1999.
9. Fujishima, Y., Leyton-Brown, K., Shoham, Y.: Taming the computational complexity of combinatorial auctions: Optimal and approximate approaches. In: Proceedings of the Sixteenth International Joint Conference on Artificial Intelligence (IJCAI), Stockholm, Sweden (1999) 548–553
10. Andersson, A., Tenhunen, M., Ygge, F.: Integer programming for combinatorial auction winner determination. In: Proceedings of the Fourth International Conference on Multi-Agent Systems (ICMAS), Boston, MA (2000) 39–46

11. Sandholm, T., Suri, S., Gilpin, A., Levine, D.: CABOB: A fast optimal algorithm for combinatorial auctions. In: Proceedings of the Seventeenth International Joint Conference on Artificial Intelligence (IJCAI), Seattle, WA (2001) 1102–1108

12. Sandholm, T.: eMediator: A next generation electronic commerce server. In: Proceedings of the Fourth International Conference on Autonomous Agents (AGENTS), Barcelona, Spain (2000) 73–96 Early version appeared in the AAAI-99 Workshop on AI in Electronic Commerce, Orlando, FL, pp. 46–55, July 1999, and as a Washington University, St. Louis, Dept. of Computer Science technical report WU-CS-99-02, Jan. 1999.

13. Hoos, H., Boutilier, C.: Bidding languages for combinatorial auctions. In: Proceedings of the Seventeenth International Joint Conference on Artificial Intelligence (IJCAI), Seattle, WA (2001) 1211–1217

14. Sandholm, T., Suri, S.: Side constraints and non-price attributes in markets. In: IJCAI-2001 Workshop on Distributed Constraint Reasoning, Seattle, WA (2001) 55–61

15. Conen, W., Sandholm, T.: Differential-revelation VCG mechanisms for combinatorial auctions. In: AAMAS-02 workshop on Agent-Mediated Electronic Commerce (AMEC), Bologna, Italy (2002)

16. Hudson, B., Sandholm, T.: Effectiveness of preference elicitation in combinatorial auctions. In: AAMAS-02 workshop on Agent-Mediated Electronic Commerce (AMEC), Bologna, Italy (2002) Extended version: Carnegie Mellon University, Computer Science Department, CMU-CS-02-124, March. Also: Stanford Institute for Theoretical Economics workshop (SITE-02).

17. Smith, T., Sandholm, T., Simmons, R.: Constructing and clearing combinatorial exchanges using preference elicitation. In: AAAI-02 workshop on Preferences in AI and CP: Symbolic Approaches. (2002) 87–93

18. Vickrey, W.: Counterspeculation, auctions, and competitive sealed tenders. Journal of Finance **16** (1961) 8–37

19. Clarke, E.H.: Multipart pricing of public goods. Public Choice **11** (1971) 17–33

20. Groves, T.: Incentives in teams. Econometrica **41** (1973) 617–631

21. Parkes, D.C.: Optimal auction design for agents with hard valuation problems. In: Agent-Mediated Electronic Commerce Workshop at the International Joint Conference on Artificial Intelligence, Stockholm, Sweden (1999)

22. Parkes, D.C.: iBundle: An efficient ascending price bundle auction. In: Proceedings of the ACM Conference on Electronic Commerce (ACM-EC), Denver, CO (1999) 148–157

23. Ausubel, L.M., Milgrom, P.: Ascending auctions with package bidding. Technical report (2001) Draft June 7th.

24. Wurman, P.R., Wellman, M.P.: AkBA: A progressive, anonymous-price combinatorial auction. In: Proceedings of the ACM Conference on Electronic Commerce (ACM-EC), Minneapolis, MN (2000) 21–29

25. Bikhchandani, S., de Vries, S., Schummer, J., Vohra, R.V.: Linear programming and Vickrey auctions (2001) Draft.

26. Bikhchandani, S., Ostroy, J.: The package assignment model. UCLA Working Paper Series, mimeo (2001)

27. Angluin, D., Hellerstein, L., Karpinski, M.: Learning read-once formulas with queries. In: Journal of the ACM. Volume 40. (1993) 185–210

28. Angluin, D.: Queries and concept learning. Machine Learning **2** (1988) 319–342

29. Naor, J., Naor, M.: Small-bias probability spaces: Efficient constructions and applications. In: Proc. 22nd Annual ACM Symposium on Theory of Computing, Baltimore (1990) 213–223

# Efficient Algorithms
# for Online Decision Problems

Adam Kalai and Santosh Vempala

Massachusetts Institute of Technology, 77 Mass. Ave.
Cambridge, MA 02139, USA
{akalai,vempala}@math.mit.edu

**Abstract.** In an online decision problem, one makes a sequence of decisions without knowledge of the future. Tools from learning such as Weighted Majority and its many variants [4, 13, 18] demonstrate that online algorithms can perform nearly as well as the best single decision chosen in hindsight, even when there are exponentially many possible decisions. However, the naive application of these algorithms is *inefficient* for such large problems. For some problems with nice structure, specialized efficient solutions have been developed [3, 6, 10, 16, 17].
We show that a very simple idea, used in Hannan's seminal 1957 paper [9], gives *efficient* solutions to all of these problems. Essentially, in each period, one chooses the decision that worked best in the past. To guarantee low regret, it is necessary to add randomness. Surprisingly, this simple approach gives additive $\epsilon$ regret per period, efficiently. We present a simple general analysis and several extensions, including a $(1+\epsilon)$-competitive algorithm as well as a lazy one that rarely switches between decisions.

## 1 Introduction

In an online decision problem, one has to make a sequence of decisions without knowledge of the future. Exponential weighting schemes for these problems have been discovered and rediscovered in may areas [7]. Even in learning, there are too many results to mention (for a survey, see [1]).

We show that Hannan's original idea[1] of doing what worked best against the past (with perturbed totals) gives efficient and simple algorithms for online decision problems. We extend his algorithm to get multiplicative $(1+\epsilon)$ guarantees as well as algorithms that do few updates. Fortunately, the same algorithm and analysis apply to many such problems, including some open problems. Let us begin with examples.

**Experts problem.** There are $n$ experts, each of which incurs a cost between 0 and 1 each period. Each period, we have to pick a single expert, and then we incur the same cost as that expert. After we pick the expert, the costs of all experts are revealed. The goal is to have a total cost not much larger than the minimum total cost of any expert.

---

[1] We are grateful to Sergiu Hart for the pointer to Hannan's algorithm; we regret that we were unaware of it in an earlier version of this paper [11].

B. Schölkopf and M.K. Warmuth (Eds.): COLT/Kernel 2003, LNAI 2777, pp. 26–40, 2003.
© Springer-Verlag Berlin Heidelberg 2003

– Follow the perturbed leading expert: On each period $t = 1, 2, \ldots$,
1. For each expert $e$, pick $p_t[e] \geq 0$ randomly from the exponential distribution $d\mu(x) = \epsilon e^{-\epsilon x}$.
2. Choose the expert with smallest $c[e] - p_t[e]$, where $c[e]$ is the total cost of expert $e$ so far.

As we discuss later, one can show that on any period,

$$E[\text{cost}] \leq (1 + \epsilon)(\text{min cost in hindsight}) + \frac{O(\log n)}{\epsilon}.$$

The above algorithm and guarantees are similar to the randomized version of Weighted Majority. We present this application just as motivation, for those familiar with Weighted Majority[2].

**Online shortest path.** [16] One has a directed graph with $n$ nodes and $m$ edges, and a fixed pair of nodes $(s, t)$. Each period, one has to pick a path from $s$ to $t$, and then the times on all the edges are revealed. The per-period cost is the sum of the times on the edges of the chosen path.

The standard solution to this type of problem would be to view each *path* as an expert, and use an algorithm such as Weighted Majority. The difficulty is that there may be exponentially many paths, and so this is inefficient. Fortunately, by following the perturbed leader, we can now take advantage of the structure of the problem and only add randomness to the edges individually rather than considering each path seperately:

– Follow the perturbed leading path: On each period $t = 1, 2, \ldots$,
1. For each edge $e$, pick $p_t[e] \in \mathbb{R}$ randomly from an exponential distribution. (See Section 2.4 for the exact parameters.)
2. Use the shortest path in the graph with weight $s[e] + p_t[e]$ on edge $e$, where $s[e]$ is the total time on edge $e$ so far.

As a corollary of Theorem 2,

$$E[\text{time}] \leq (1 + \epsilon)(\text{best time in hindsight}) + \frac{O(mn \log n)}{\epsilon}.$$

As is standard, "best time in hindsight" refers to the minimum total time spent, if one had to use the same path each period, and we are assuming all edge times are between 0 and 1. This is similar to the bounds of Takimoto and Warmuth [16], and their specialized algorithm is also efficient. For the next problem, no efficient near optimal algorithm was previously known.

**Tree update problem.** This problem is a classic online problem [15] introduced by Sleator and Tarjan with Splay Trees, around the same time as they introduced

---

[2] The natural idea of following the leader without randomness fails on the following example. Imagine just two experts whose cost sequence is $(0, \frac{1}{2})$, $(1, 0)$, $(0, 1)$, $(1, 0)$, $(0, 1), \ldots$. The leader, i.e. best expert so far, always happens to be the one that costs 1 next. So, following the leader will cost about $t$, while staying with either expert by itself will cost about $t/2$ (worse example with $n > 2$).

the list update problem [14]. In the tree update problem, one maintains a binary search tree over $n$ items in the face of an unknown sequence of accesses to these items. For each access, i.e. lookup, the cost is the number of comparisons necessary to find the item, which is equal to its depth in the tree.

One could use "follow the perturbed leader" mentioned above for this problem as well. This would maintain frequency counts for each item in the tree, and then before each access it would find the best tree given these frequencies plus perturbations (which can be computed in $\Theta(n^2)$ using dynamic programming). But doing so much computation and so many tree rotations, just to prepare for a lookup seems a little bit ridiculous. Instead, we give a way to achieve the same effect with little computation and few updates to the tree:

- Follow the lazy tree($N$):
  1. For $1 \leq i \leq n$, let $s_i := 0$ and choose $v_i$ randomly from $\{1, 2, \ldots, N\}$
  2. Start with the best tree as if there were $v_i$ accesses to node $i$.
  3. After each access, set $a$ to be the accessed item, and:
     (a) $s_a := s_a + 1$
     (b) If $s_a \geq v_a$ then
         i. $v_a := v_a + N$
         ii. Change trees to the best tree as if there were $v_i$ accesses to node $i$.

Over $T$ accesses, for $N = \sqrt{T/n}$, one gets the following *static* bounds[3] as a corollary of Theorem 1,

$$E[\text{cost of lazy trees}] \leq (\text{cost of best tree}) + 2n\sqrt{nT}$$

Because any algorithm must pay at least 1 per acccess, the above additive regret bound is even stronger than a multiplicative $(1+\epsilon)$-competitive bound, i.e. $T \leq (\text{cost of best tree})$. In contrast, Splay Trees have a guarantee of $3\log_2 3 \times$ (cost of best tree) plus an additive term, but they have other desirable properties. Standard tricks can be used if $T$ is not known in advance.

The key point here is that step (ii) is executed with probability at most $1/N$, so one expects to update only $\sqrt{nT}$ times over $T$ accesses. Thus the computational costs and movement costs, which he have thus far ignored, are small. This algorithm has what Blum et. al. call *strong static optimality* [3]. They also presented a follow the perturbed leader type of algorithm for the easier list update problem. Theirs was the original motivation for our work, and they were also unaware of the similarity to Hannan's algorithm.

## 1.1   Generalization

What is important about the above problems is that in each problem there are a small number of summary features, e.g. the total time on each edge and the total number of accesses to each item. The cost of any decision, e.g. path or tree,

---
[3] We do not give dynamic guarantees and our results do not apply to the dynamic optimality conjecture.

is *additive* in terms of these summary feature. That is, the cost of a decision over two sequences is the cost when we add the two sets of summary features. The computational savings comes from adding randomness only to each summary feature, because there are typically a small number of summary features compared to the exponentially (or even infinitely many) possible decisions.

We give (expected) $(1+\epsilon)$-competitive bounds for any such additive problem. We also give guarantees on having (expected) $\epsilon$ fraction of periods where any calculation or changes of decision are necessary. It is remarkable that Hannan in 1957 [9], in addition to inventing the problem, came up with an algorithm that has efficiency properties better than those of many modern algorithms. While he wasn't concerned with efficiency and only studied additive regret, the algorithm we call "follow the perturbed leader" for additive regret is essentially his algorithm. Perhaps the reason his particular algorithm hasn't often been revisited is because his analysis is quite complex. In fact, we don't understand it, and we present simple proofs of all our results. However, his is inspirational paper may be worth mining for other good ideas.

We discuss various extensions, such as to the case when you can only approximate the leader and to the case when the set of decisions is a convex set, where you can average decisions. We discuss several applications, including online shortest path, the tree update problem, online decision tree pruning, online linear programming, and adaptive Huffman coding. For the tree update problem and adaptive Huffman coding, no efficient $(1 + \epsilon)$-optimal algorithms were known. We hope the technique will be useful for other natural problems.

The focus of an earlier version of this paper [11] was the general problem of online linear optimization, which we describe later. Independently, Zinkevich has introduced an elegant deterministic algorithm for the more general online convex optimization problem [19]. His algorithm is well-suited for convex problems but not for the discrete problems which we focus on here.

## 2    Algorithms

In this section we define the model for online decision problems and describe Hannan's basic algorithm which leads to a bound on the (additive) regret. Then we describe an extension that changes decisions rarely, and another extension which has a (multiplicative) competitive bound.

### 2.1    The Model

A decision maker must make a series of decisions from a possibly infinite set $\mathcal{D}$. After each decision is made, a *state* is revealed. We assume that each state can be represented by a nonnegative vector $s \in \mathbb{R}^n_+$ from some set of feasible states $S \subset \mathbb{R}^n_+$. In the online path example, this would be the vector with a component for each edge indicating the time on that edge. In the online tree problem, it would simply be the vector $e_i$ (the vector of all 0s with a 1 in the $i$th position) for an access to item number $i$. Moreover we assume there is a non-negative cost for each decision and state, represented by a function $c : \mathcal{D} \times S \rightarrow \mathbb{R}_+$. We assume this function is *additive* and extend it to $\mathcal{D} \times \mathbb{R}^n$. By additive, we mean that the cost for a single decision $d$ on a sequence of states $s_1, s_2, \ldots, s_t$ can be computed by

$$c(d, s_1) + c(d, s_2) + \ldots + c(d, s_t) = c(d, s_1 + s_2 + \ldots + s_t).$$

Here the sum $s_1 + \ldots + s_t$ are the summary features of the problem. It follows that each decision $d$ can be equated to a point in $d \in \mathbb{R}^n$, where the $i$th coordinate is $c(d, e_i)$. For example, for a path, this would be a $\{0, 1\}$ vector with a 1 in every position corresponding to an edge in the path. For a tree, this would be the vector where the $i$th component is the depth of $i$ in the tree. For notational ease, we make no distinction between a decision and its corresponding vector, so that $\mathcal{D} \subset \mathbb{R}^n$. Thus the cost of a decision on the sequence $s_1, s_2, \ldots, s_t$ can be written as

$$c(d, s_1) + c(d, s_2) + \ldots + c(d, s_t) = d \cdot (s_1 + s_2 + \ldots + s_t).$$

For further succinctness, we use the notational shortcut

$$s_{1:t} = s_1 + s_2 + \ldots + s_t.$$

In order to avoid searching over all decisions, we need to assume that there is some oracle $M$ that can tell us, for any summary vector $s \in \mathbb{R}^n$, what the best decision would have been.

$$M(s) = \arg\min_{d \in \mathcal{D}} c(d, s) = \arg\min_{d \in \mathcal{D}} d \cdot s$$

In the path problem, this could be implemented by the shortest path algorithm applied to the total times on each edge. In the tree problem, this could be implemented by a dynamic programming algorithm that takes as input the total number of times each item was accessed. For a state sequence $s_1, s_2, \ldots, s_t$, the minimum achievable *offline* static cost is $M(s_{1:t}) \cdot s_{1:t}$.

Finally, we need to bound the costs and other vectors. Suppose,

$$c(d, s) \in [0, R], \text{ for all } d \in \mathcal{D}, s \in S$$
$$|s|_1 \leq A, \text{ for all } s \in S$$
$$|d - d'|_1 \leq D, \text{ for all } d, d' \in \mathcal{D}$$

Here $|x|_1 = |x_1| + |x_2| + \ldots + |x_n|$ is the $L_1$ norm of $x \in \mathbb{R}^n$. The parameter $D$, the $L_1$ diameter of the set of decisions, is a geometric parameter that we use to bound the performance. In the above bounds, we actually only need to consider "reasonable" decisions, i.e. decisions that are the possible output of the oracle $M(s)$ for some $s \in \mathbb{R}^n$. For example, one need not consider paths that visit a node more than once. Also, $R$ need only be an upper bound on the difference between the cost of two decisions on a single period.

The $L_1$ norm may seem arbitrary, but it is quite natural for many discrete applications as we will presently see. In [11], we also discuss the $L_2$ norm.

## 2.2   Follow the Perturbed Leader

In this section, we describe Hannan's algorithm in the context of an additive online decision problem. Recall that $s_{1:t} = s_1 + s_2 + \ldots + s_t$.

- **FPL($\epsilon$)**: On each period $t$,
  1. Choose $p_t$ uniformly at random from the cube $\left[0, \frac{1}{\epsilon}\right]^n$.
  2. Use $M(s_{1:t-1} + p_t)$.

We will now bound the performance of FPL on any particular sequence of states.

**Theorem 1.** *Let $s_1, s_2, \ldots \in \mathbb{R}^n$ be any state sequence. For any $T > 0$, the expected cost of FPL($\epsilon$) on the first $T$ periods is bounded by,*

$$E[\text{cost of FPL}(\epsilon)] \leq M(s_{1:T}) \cdot s_{1:T} + \epsilon RAT + \frac{D}{\epsilon},$$

*where $D, R$ and $A$ are defined in Section 2.1.*

We defer all proofs to the appendix. The idea is to first analyze a version of the algorithm where we use $M(s_{1:t})$ on period $t$ (instead of $M(s_{1:t-1})$). Of course, this is only a hypothetical algorithm since we don't know $s_t$ in advance. But, as we show, this "be the leader" algorithm has no regret. The point of adding randomness is that it makes following the leader not that different than being the leader. The more randomness we add, the closer they are (and the smaller the $\epsilon RAT$ term). However, there is a cost to adding randomness. Namely, a large amount of randomness may make a worse choice seem better. This accounts for the $D/\epsilon$ term. The analysis is relatively straightforward.

If $T$ is known in advance, $\epsilon = \sqrt{D/(RAT)}$ minimizes the above bound giving $2\sqrt{DRAT}$ regret,

$$E[\text{cost of FPL}(\sqrt{D/RAT})] \leq M(s_{1:t}) \cdot s_{1:t} + 2\sqrt{DRAT}$$

Without advance knowledge of $T$, using a standard $\epsilon$-halving technique, where every so often you restart with a smaller $\epsilon$, you can achieve slightly worse bounds. Hannan gives a more elegent solution, where he slowly increased the size of the perturbation:

- **Hannan($\delta$)**: On each period $t$,
  1. Choose $p_t$ uniformly at random from the cube $\left[0, \frac{\sqrt{t}}{\delta}\right]^n$.
  2. Use $M(s_{1:t-1} + p_t)$.

In the appendix, we will show the following (similar to what Hannan showed) but our proof is significantly simpler:

$$E[\text{cost of Hannan}(\delta = \sqrt{D/2AR})] \leq M(s_{1:T}) \cdot s_{1:T} + 2\sqrt{2DRAT}$$

Thus one loses only a factor of $\sqrt{2}$ for not knowing $T$, setting $\delta = \sqrt{D/(2AR)}$,

## 2.3   Follow the Lazy Leader

Here, we introduce an algorithm called Follow the Lazy Leader or FLL, with the following properties:

- FLL is equivalent to FPL, in terms of expected cost.
- FLL rarely calls the oracle $M$.
- FLL rarely changes decision from one period to the next.

If calling the oracle is a computationally expensive operation or if there is a cost to switching between different decisions, then this is a desirable property. For example, to find the best binary search tree in hindsight on $n$ items takes time $O(n^2)$, and it would be ridiculous to do this between every access to the tree.

The trick is to take advantage of the fact that we can correlate our perturbations from one period to the next – this will not change the expected totals. We will choose the perturbations so that $s_{1:t-1} + p_t = s_{1:t} + p_{t+1}$, or in terms of FLL, $g_{t-1} = g_t$, as often as possible.

- **FLL($\epsilon$):**
    1. Once, at the beginning, choose $p \in \left[0, \frac{1}{\epsilon}\right]^n$ uniformly, determining a grid $G = \{p + \frac{1}{\epsilon}z | z \in \mathbb{Z}^n\}$.
    2. On period $t$, use $M(g_{t-1})$, where $g_{t-1}$ is the unique point in $G \cap (s_{1:t-1} + [0, \frac{1}{\epsilon})^n)$. (Clearly if $g_t = g_{t-1}$, then there is no need to re-evaluate $M(g_t) = M(g_{t-1})$.)

It is not difficult to see that the point $g_{t-1}$ is uniformly distributed over $s_{1:t-1} + [0, \frac{1}{\epsilon})^n$, like FPL. Thus FPL($\epsilon$) and FLL($\epsilon$) behave identically on any single period, for any fixed sequence of states. Furthermore, since often $g_{t-1} = g_t$, rarely does a decision need to be changed or even computed. To be more precise,

**Lemma 1.** *For any fixed sequence of states $s_1, s_2, \ldots$, FPL($\epsilon$) and FLL($\epsilon$) behave identically on each period $t$, i.e. the distribution over $g_{t-1}$ for FLL($\epsilon$) is identical to the distribution over $s_{1:t-1} + p_t$ for FPL($\epsilon$). Also, for FLL($\epsilon$), $\Pr[g_{t-1} \neq g_t] \leq \epsilon |s_t|_1 \leq \epsilon A$.*

The main *disadvantage* of the FLL algorithm is that it is predictable – its choices in different rounds are very related. This means that an adaptive adversary can force the algorithm to have large regret. This is true of any algorithm that uses very little randomness.

## 2.4   Competitive Versions of FLL and FPL

In this section, we give algorithms that are nearly optimal in a multiplicative sense.

- **FPL*($\epsilon$):** On each period $t$,
    1. Choose $p_t$ at random according to the density $d\mu(x) \propto e^{-\epsilon|x|_1}$. (This can be done by, for each coordinate, choosing $r \geq 0$ according to the standard exponential density $e^{-r}$ and setting the $i$th coordinate of $p_t$ to $\pm(r/\epsilon)$.)
    2. Use $M(s_{1:t-1} + p_t)$.

- **FLL\*($\epsilon$):**
  1. Choose $p_1$ at random according to the density $d\mu(x) \propto e^{-\epsilon|x|_1}$.
  2. On each period $t$, use $M(s_{1:t-1} + p_t)$.
  3. Update
     (a) With probability $\min\left(1, \frac{d\mu(p_t - s_t)}{d\mu(p_t)}\right)$, set $p_{t+1} = p_t - s_t$ (so that $s_{1:t} + p_{t+1} = s_{1:t-1} + p_t$).
     (b) Otherwise, set $p_{t+1} := -p_t$.

**Lemma 2.** *On any period $t$, FPL\*($\epsilon$) and FLL\*($\epsilon$) behave identically. In other words, the distribution over $s_{t-1} + p_t$ for both is the same. Also, for FLL\*($\epsilon$), $\Pr[s_{1:t-1} + p_t \neq s_{1:t} + p_{t+1}] \leq \epsilon|s_t|_1 \leq \epsilon A$.*

Again, the above shows that the oracle need be called very rarely – only when $s_{1:t-1} + p_t$ changes. The main theorem here is:

**Theorem 2.** *For any state sequence $s_1, s_2, \ldots, s_t$ and any $0 \leq \epsilon \leq 1/A$, the cost of FPL\*($\epsilon$) is bounded by,*

$$E[\text{cost of FPL\*}(\epsilon)] \leq (1 + \epsilon 2A)M(s_{1:T}) \cdot s_{1:T} + \frac{D(1 + \log n)}{\epsilon}$$

Using $\epsilon' = \epsilon/2A$, one can get $(1 + \epsilon)$ guarantees with an $O(AD\log(n)/\epsilon)$ additive term. A small technical difficulty arises in that for these multiplicative algorithms, $s_{1:t-1} + p_t$ may have negative components, especially for small $t$. For some problems, like the online path problem, this can cause difficulty because there may be negative cycles in the graph. (Coincidentally, Takimoto and Warmuth make the assumption that the graph has no cycles whatsoever [16].) A less-restrictive approach to solving this problem in general is to add large fixed pretend costs at the beginning, i.e. $s_0 = (M, M, \ldots, M)$. For a sufficiently large $M$, with high probability all of the components of $s_{0:t-1} + p_t$ will be non-negative. Furthermore, one can show that these costs do not have too large an effect.

## 2.5   Follow the Expected Leader and Online Linear Optimization

A simple extension is possible for convex sets, which we call Follow the Expected Leader (FEL):

- **FEL($\epsilon, m$):** On each period $t$,
  1. Choose $p_t^1, p_t^2, \ldots, p_t^m$ independently and uniformly at random from the cube $[0, \frac{1}{\epsilon}]^n$.
  2. Use $\frac{1}{m}\sum_{i=1}^m M(s_{1:t-1} + p_t^i)$.

For this algorithm, we are assuming that the set of possible decisions is convex so that we may take the average of several decisions. In this case, the expected guarantees can be converted into high-probability guarantees. Formulated another way, FEL applies to the following problem.

**Online linear optimization:** *Given a feasible convex set $\mathcal{D} \subset \mathbb{R}^n$, and a sequence of objective vectors $s_1, s_2, \ldots \in \mathbb{R}^n$, choose a sequence of points $d_1, d_2, \ldots \in \mathcal{D}$ that minimizes $\sum_{t=1}^T d_t \cdot s_t$. When choosing $d_t$, only $s_1, s_2, \ldots s_{t-1}$ are known.*

Since linear optimization is a general framework, this models many on-line problems. The parameters $D$ and $A$ now take on special geometric significance as $D$ is the diameter of the feasible set and $A$ is a bound on the objective vectors. Other extensions for this problem are to allow for negative objective vectors and costs, in the additive regret case.

In [11], we discussed this problem in greater detail. Independently, Zinkevich has introduced a deterministic algorithm for an online convex optimization problem [19], which is more general than the problem described in this section. His nice algorithm is well-suited for convex problems like the one mentioned in this section but not for the discrete problems which we focused on earlier.

## 3   Applications

We have already discussed the online shortest paths and binary search tree applications. For these problems, it is just a matter of calculating the parameters. For example, in the tree problem, $R = n$, $A = 1$, and $D = n^2$ will suffice as upper bounds. In the online path problem, $A = m$ and $D = 2n$ will suffice, assuming times are in $[0, 1]$, and of course we only need to consider paths of length at most $n$.

The Adaptive Huffman coding problem [12] is not normally considered as an online algorithm. But it fits naturally into the framework. There, one wants to choose a prefix tree for each symbol in a message, "on the fly" without knowledge of the sequence of symbols in advance. The cost is the length of the encoding of the symbol, i.e. again its depth in the tree. Adaptive Huffman coding is exactly the follow-the-leader algorithm applied to this problem. For such a problem, however, it is natural to be concerned about sequences of alternating 0s and 1s. Adaptive Huffman coding does not give $(1 + \epsilon)$ guarantees. If the encoder and decoder have a shared random (or pseudorandom) sequence, then they can apply FPL or FLL as well. The details are similar to the tree update problem.

Efficient $(1 + \epsilon)$ algorithms have been designed for online pruning of decision trees, decision graphs, and their variants [10, 17]. Not surprisingly, FPL* and FLL* will apply.

### 3.1   Predicting from Expert Advice

We would like to apply our algorithm to the predicting from expert advice problem [4], where one has to choose a particular expert each period. Here, it would seem that $D = 1$ and $A = n$. This is unfortunate because we need $A = 1$ to get the standard bounds. For the multiplicative case, we can fix this problem by observing that the worst case for our algorithm (and in fact most algorithms) is when each period only one expert incurs cost[4]. Thus we may as well imagine that $A = 1$, and we get the standard $(1 + \epsilon) \times (\text{best expert}) + O(\log n/\epsilon)$ bounds of Weighted Majority.

---

[4] Imagine comparing two scenarios, one with one period $s_1 = (a, b)$ and the second with two periods $s_1 = (a, 0)$ and $s_2 = (0, b)$. It is not difficult to see that our cost in the second scenario is larger, because we have more weight on the second expert after the first period. Nevertheless, the cost of the best expert in both scenarios is the same.

In fact, one can give a very simple direct analysis of FPL* for the experts problem in less than a page (which we cannot afford). In summary, one first observes that if the leader never changes, then following the leader gives no regret. Second, one observes that the total additive regret is at most the number of times the leader has changed. Third, one checks that by adding randomness with an exponential distribution, the probability that the leader changes during any period is very small, in particular at most $\epsilon$ times the expected cost of the algorithm during that period. Finally, one checks that adding randomness of that magnitude doesn't hurt too much.

## 4    Conclusions and Open Problems

For many problems, exponential weighting schemes such as the weighted majority provide inefficient online algorithms that perform almost as well as the offline analogs. Hannan's original idea leads to an efficient algorithm, with similar guarantees, provided that the offline problem can be solved efficiently.

This separation of the adaptive problem into its online and offline components seems helpful. In many cases, the guarantees of this approach may be slightly worse than custom-designed algorithms for problems (the additive term may be slightly larger). However, we believe that this separation at least highlights where the difficulty of a problem enters. For example, an online shortest-path algorithm [16] must be sophisticated enough at least to solve the offline shortest path problem.

Furthermore, the simplicity of the "follow the leader" approach sheds some light on the static online framework. The worst-case framework makes it problematic to simply follow the leader, which is a natural, justifiable approach that works in other models. Adding randomness simply makes the analysis work, and is necessary only in the worst case kind of sequence where the leader changes often. (Such a sequence may be plausible in some scenarios, such as compressing the sequence 0101....)

As one can see, there are several ways to extend the algorithm. One natural variation is tracking (following the best decision that may change a few times). Another variation would be a bandit version, but it may be challenging to come up with a good model of revealed information.

A problem with our approach is that one needs to solve the optimization problem exactly in order for our theorems to work. For some problems, only an approximate solution is possible. If, for any $\epsilon$, there is an efficient algorithm for finding a $1 + \epsilon$ optimal solution, i.e. one of cost at most $1 + \epsilon$ times the cost of the best static offline solution, then the given approach can still be made to work. However, an interesting problem is to extend it to the case where only worse approximations are known.

In [11], we point out that some approximation algorithms have a pointwise guarantee which allows our analysis to work. Such problems include the max-cut algorithm of [8] and others. We find the online max-cut problem particularly natural: edges are added, one at a time, to a multigraph. At each time period, we must choose a cut, and receive a score of 1 if the added edge crosses the cut and 0 otherwise.

Finally, while Hannan's algorithm and our variants are quite general, there are of course many problems for which they cannot be used. It would be great to generalize FPL to nonlinear problems such as portfolio prediction [5]. For this kind of problem, it is not sufficient to maintain additive summary statistics.

## Acknowledgements

We would like to thank Avrim Blum, Danny Sleator, and the anonymous referees for their helpful comments.

## References

1. A. Blum. On-line algorithms in machine learning. Technical Report CMU-CS-97-163, Carnegie Mellon University, 1997
2. Avrim Blum and Carl Burch. On-line learning and the metrical task system problem. *Machine Learning*, 39(1):35–58, April 2000.
3. Avrim Blum, Shuchi Chawla, and Adam Kalai. Static Optimality and Dynamic Search Optimality in Lists and Trees. In *Proceedings of the Thirteenth Annual ACM-SIAM Symposium on Discrete Algorithms (SODA '02), 2002.*
4. N. Cesa-Bianchi, Y. Freund, D. Haussler, D. Helmbold, R. Schapire, and M. Warmuth. How to use expert advice. *Journal of the ACM*, 44(3):427-485, 1997.
5. Thomas Cover. Universal Portfolios. In *Math. Finance* 1, 1-29, 1991.
6. Y. Freund, R. Schapire, Y. Singer, and M. Warmuth. Using and combining predictors that specialize. In *Proceedings of the Twenty-Ninth Annual ACM Symposium on the Theory of Computing*, pp. 334–343, 1997.
7. D. Foster and R. Vohra. Regret in the on-line decision problem. *Games and Economic Behavior*, vol.29, pp.1084-1090, 1999.
8. M. Goemans and D. Williamson, "Improved Approximation Algorithms for Maximum Cut and Satisfiability Problems Using Semidefinite Programming", J. ACM, 42, 1115–1145, 1995.
9. J. Hannan. Approximation to Bayes risk in repeated plays. In M. Dresher, A. Tucker, and P. Wolfe, editors, *Contributions to the Theory of Games, volume 3*, pages 97-139. Princeton University Press, 1957.
10. D. Helmbold and R. Schapire. Predicting nearly as well as the best pruning of a decision tree. *Machine Learning*, 27(1):51-68, 1997.
11. A. Kalai and S. Vempala. Geometric algorithms for online optimization. MIT Technical report MIT-LCS-TR-861, 2002.
12. D. Knuth. Dynamic Huffman Coding. *J. Algorithms*, 2:163-180, 1985.
13. N. Littlestone and M. K. Warmuth. The weighted majority algorithm. *Information and Computation*, 108:212–261, 1994.
14. Daniel Sleator and Robert Tarjan. Amortized efficiency of list update and paging rules. *Communications of the ACM*, 28:202-208, 1985.
15. Daniel Sleator and Robert Tarjan. Self-Adjusting Binary Search Trees. *Journal of the ACM* 32:652-686, 1985.
16. E. Takimoto and M. Warmuth. Path Kernels and Multiplicative Updates. In *Proceedings of the Thirteenth Annual Conference on Computational Learning Theory*, pp. 74-89, 2002.

17. E. Takimoto and M. Warmuth. Predicting Nearly as Well as the Best Pruning of a Planar Decision Graph. *Theoretical Computer Science*, 288(2): 217-235, 2002.
18. V. Vovk. Aggregating strategies. In *Proc. 3rd Ann. Workshop on Computational Learning Theory*, pp. 371–383, 1990.
19. M. Zinkevich. Online Convex Programming and Generalized Infinitesimal Gradient Ascent. CMU Technical Report CMU-CS-03-110, 2003.

# A   Analysis

The motivation for following the perturbed leader can be seen in the simple two-expert example given earlier. In that example, we would have no regret had we stayed with the same expert the whole time, and low regret so long as we didn't switch often. Now, imagine adding a pretend day 0, on which each expert had a random cost, chosen from some large range $[0, 1/\epsilon]$. As long as the two numbers are sufficiently far apart, follow the leader will stick with one expert the whole time. If these two numbers happen to be within 1 of each other, follow the leader will again alternate. This is the intuition behind the $(1 + \epsilon)$ term. However, there is a penalty for adding randomness. The more randomness one adds, the more periods it will take to compensate for a false bias if one of the paths is actually better than the other, which leads to the additive term.

In the above motivation, we assumed that the randomness was chosen once in advance. By linearity of expectation, the expectation does not change if randomness is chosen anew each period. Furthermore, choosing new randomness protects against an adaptive adversary that can see one's previous decisions (but not one's random coins).

Here we present the proofs of the guarantees of the various algorithms.

## A.1   FPL

First, we see by induction on $T$ that using $M(s_{1:t})$ on day $t$ gives 0 regret,

$$\sum_{t=1}^{T} M(s_{1:t}) \cdot s_t \leq M(s_{1:T}) \cdot s_{1:T}. \tag{1}$$

For $T = 1$, it is trivial. For the induction step from $T - 1$ to $T$, notice that

$$M(s_{1:T-1}) \cdot s_{1:T-1} \leq M(s_{1:T}) \cdot s_{1:T-1},$$

by definition of $M$. Combining this with $s_{1:T} = s_T + s_{1:T-1}$ completes the induction step.

Equation (1) shows that if one used $M(s_{1:t})$ on period $t$, one would have no regret. Essentially, this means that the hypothetical "be the leader" algorithm would have no regret.

Next we prove Theorem 1 of Section 2.2. We first show that perturbations don't hurt too much. Conceptually, it is easiest to bound this cost when $p_t = p_{t-1}$, because this is as if there was a pretend 0th period on which these perturbations actually happened. In general, we get:

**Lemma 3.** *For and state sequence* $s_1, s_2, \ldots,$ *any* $T > 0$, *and any vectors* $p_0 = 0$, $p_1, p_2, \ldots, p_t \in \mathbb{R}^n$,

$$\sum_{t=1}^{T} M(s_{1:t} + p_t) \cdot s_t \leq M(s_{1:T}) \cdot s_{1:T} + D \sum_{t=1}^{T} |p_t - p_{t-1}|_\infty$$

*Proof.* Pretend the cost vector $s_t$ on period $t$ was actually $s_t + p_t - p_{t-1}$. Then the cumulative $s_{1:t}$ would actually be $s_{1:t} + p_t$, by telescoping. Making these substitutions in (1) gives,

$$\sum_{t=1}^{T} M(s_{1:t} + p_t) \cdot (s_t + p_t - p_{t-1}) \leq M(s_{1:T} + p_T) \cdot (s_{1:T} + p_T)$$

$$\leq M(s_{1:T}) \cdot (s_{1:T} + p_T)$$

By un-telescoping, we can rewrite this as,

$$\sum_{t=1}^{T} M(s_{1:t} + p_t) \cdot s_t \leq M(s_{1:T}) \cdot s_{1:T} + \sum_{t=1}^{T} (M(s_{1:T}) - M(s_{1:t} + p_t)) \cdot (p_t - p_{t-1})$$

Recall that $D \geq |d - d'|_1$ for any decision vectors $d, d'$. Also note that $u \cdot v \leq |u|_1 |v|_\infty$.

*Proof (Proof of Theorem 1).* In terms of expected performance, it wouldn't matter whether we chose a new $p_t$ each day or whether $p_t = p_1$ for all $t > 1$. Applying Lemma 3 to the latter scenario gives,

$$E\left[ \sum_{t=1}^{T} M(s_t + p_1) \cdot s_t \right] \leq M(s_{1:T}) \cdot s_{1:T} + D|p_1|_\infty \leq M(s_{1:T}) \cdot s_{1:T} + \frac{D}{\epsilon} \quad (2)$$

Thus, it just remains to show that the expected difference between using $M(s_{1:t-1} + p_t)$ instead of $M(s_{1:t} + p_t)$ on each period $t$ is at most $\epsilon AR$.

**Key idea:** we notice that the *distributions* over $s_{1:t-1} + p_t$ and $s_{1:t} + p_t$ are similar. In particular, they are both distributions over cubes. If the cubes were identical, i.e. $s_{1:t-1} = s_{1:t}$, then $E[M(s_{1:t-1} + p_t) \cdot s_t] = E[M(s_{1:t} + p_t) \cdot s_t]$. If they overlap on a fraction $f$ of their volume, then we could say,

$$E[M(s_{1:t-1} + p_t) \cdot s_t] \leq E[M(s_{1:t} + p_t) \cdot s_t] + (1 - f)R$$

This is because on the fraction that they overlap, the expectation is identical, and on the fraction that they do not overlap, one can only be $R$ larger, by the definition of $R$. By Lemma 4 following this proof, $1 - f \leq \epsilon |s_t|_1 \leq \epsilon A$.

**Lemma 4.** *For any* $v \in \mathbb{R}^n$, *the cubes* $\left[0, \frac{1}{\epsilon}\right]^n$ *and* $v + \left[0, \frac{1}{\epsilon}\right]^n$ *overlap in at least a* $(1 - \epsilon |v|_1)$ *fraction.*

*Proof.* Take a random point $x \in \left[0, \frac{1}{\epsilon}\right]^n$. If $x \notin v + \left[0, \frac{1}{\epsilon}\right]^n$, then for some $i$, $x_i \notin v_i + [0, \frac{1}{\epsilon}]$, which happens with probability at most $\epsilon |v_i|$ for any particular $i$. By the union bound, we're done.

## A.2   Hannan

The following theorem was used at the end of Section 2.2:

**Theorem 3.** *For any state sequence* $s_1, s_2, \ldots$, *after any number of periods* $T > 0$,

$$E[cost\ of\ Hannan(\delta)] \le M(s_{1:T}) \cdot s_{1:T} + 2\delta RA\sqrt{T} + \frac{D\sqrt{T}}{\delta}$$

*Proof.* WLOG we may choose $p_t = (\sqrt{t})p_1$, because all the $p_t$ are identically distributed, and we are only bounding the expectation. Applying Lemma 3 to this scenario gives,

$$E\left[\sum_{t=1}^{T} M(s_{1:t} + \sqrt{t}p_1) \cdot s_t\right] \le M(s_{1:T}) \cdot s_{1:T} + D|p_1|_\infty \sum_{t=1}^{T}(\sqrt{j} - \sqrt{j-1})$$

The last term is at most $D(1/\delta)\sqrt{T}$.

Now, $M(s_{1:t-1} + p_t)$ and $M(s_{1:t} + p_t)$ are distributions over cubes of side $\sqrt{t}/\delta$. By Lemma 4, they overlap in a fraction that is at least $1 - |s_t|_1\delta/\sqrt{t} \ge 1 - A\delta/\sqrt{t}$. On this fraction, their expectation is identical so,

$$E[(M(s_{1:t-1} + p_t) - M(s_{1:t} + p_t)) \cdot s_t] \le \frac{\delta RA}{\sqrt{t}}$$

Thus we have shown,

$$E\left[\sum_{t=1}^{T} M(s_{1:t-1} + p_t) \cdot s_t\right] \le M(s_{1:T}) \cdot s_{1:T} + \frac{D\sqrt{T}}{\delta} + \sum_{t=1}^{T} \frac{\delta RA}{\sqrt{t}}.$$

Finally, straightforward induction shows $\sum_{t=1}^{T} \frac{1}{\sqrt{t}} \le 2\sqrt{T}$.

## A.3   FLL

*Proof (Proof of Lemma 1).* FLL($\epsilon$) chooses a uniformly random grid of spacing $1/\epsilon$. There will be exactly one grid point inside $s_{t-1} + [0, \frac{1}{\epsilon})^n$, and by symmetry, it is uniformly distributed over that set. Thus we see that the grid point $g_{t-1}$ will be distributed exactly like FPL($\epsilon$), uniform over $s_{1:t-1} + \left[0, \frac{1}{\epsilon}\right]^n$.

Now, $g_{t-1} \neq g_t$ iff the grid point in $s_{1:t-1} + \left[0, \frac{1}{\epsilon}\right]^n$, which we know is uniform over this set, is not in $s_{1:t} + \left[0, \frac{1}{\epsilon}\right]^n$. By Lemma 4, we know this is at most $\epsilon|s_t|_1$.

## A.4   FPL* and FLL*

*Proof (Proof of Theorem 2).* WLOG, we may assume $p_t = p_1$ for all $t > 1$, because this does not change the expectation. As before, by Lemma 1,

$$E\left[\sum_{t=1}^{T} M(s_{1:t} + p_1) \cdot s_t\right] \le M(s_{1:T}) \cdot s_{1:T} + D|p_1|_\infty$$

In expectation, the magnitude of each coordinate of $p_1$ is $1/\epsilon$, as it is a number from the exponential distribution scaled by a $1/\epsilon$ factor. To bound the expected maximum, note that the expectation of a nonnegative random variable $X$ is $E[X] = \int_0^\infty \Pr[X \geq x]dx$. Consider $x_1, x_2, \ldots, x_n$, each drawn independently from the exponential distribution $e^{-x}$. The expected maximum is

$$\int_0^\infty \Pr[\max(x_1, x_2, \ldots, x_n) \geq x]dx \leq \left(\int_{\log n}^\infty ne^{-x}dx\right) + \log n = 1 + \log n$$

Furthermore, we claim that

$$E[M(s_{1:t-1} + p_1) \cdot s_t] \leq e^{\epsilon A} E[M(s_{1:t} + p_1) \cdot s_t] \tag{3}$$

To see this, notice that the *distributions* over $s_{1:t-1} + p_1$ and $s_{1:t} + p_1$ are similar. In particular,

$$E[M(s_{1:t-1} + p_1) \cdot s_t] = \int_{x \in \mathbb{R}^n} M(s_{1:t-1} + x) \cdot s_t d\mu(x)$$

$$= \int_{y \in \mathbb{R}^n} M(s_{1:t} + y) \cdot s_t d\mu(y + s_t)$$

$$= \int_{y \in \mathbb{R}^n} M(s_{1:t} + y) \cdot s_t e^{-\epsilon(|y+s_t|_1 - |y|_1)} d\mu(y)$$

Finally, $-\epsilon(|y + s_t|_1 - |y|_1) \leq \epsilon|s_t|_1 \leq \epsilon A$ by the triangle inequality. This establishes (3). For $\epsilon \leq 1/A$, $e^{\epsilon A} \leq 1 + 2\epsilon A$.

*Proof (Proof of Lemma 2).* We first argue by induction on $t$ that the distribution over $p_t$ for FLL*($\epsilon$) has the same density $d\mu(x) \propto e^{-\epsilon|x|_1}$. (In fact, this holds for any center-symmetric $d\mu$.) For $t = 1$ this is trivial. For $t + 1$, the density at $x$ is

$$d\mu(x + s_t) \min\{1, \frac{d\mu(x)}{d\mu(x + s_t)}\} + d\mu(-x)(1 - \min\{1, \frac{d\mu(-x - s_t)}{d\mu(-x)}\}) \tag{4}$$

This is because we can reach $p_{t+1} = x$ by either being at $p_t = x + s_t$ or $p_t = -x$. Observing that $d\mu(-x) = d\mu(x)$,

$$d\mu(x + s_t) \min\{1, \frac{d\mu(x)}{d\mu(x + s_t)}\} = \min\{d\mu(x + s_t), d\mu(x)\}$$

$$= d\mu(-x) \min\{1, \frac{d\mu(-x - s_t)}{d\mu(-x)}\}$$

Thus, (4) is equal to $d\mu(x)$.

Finally, the probability of switching is at most

$$1 - \frac{d\mu(p_t + s_t)}{d\mu(p_t)} = 1 - e^{-\epsilon(|p_t + s_t|_1 - |p_t|_1)}$$

$$\leq 1 - e^{-\epsilon|s_t|_1}$$

$$\leq \epsilon|s_t|_1$$

# Positive Definite Rational Kernels

Corinna Cortes, Patrick Haffner, and Mehryar Mohri

AT&T Labs – Research
180 Park Avenue, Florham Park, NJ 07932, USA
{corinna,haffner,mohri}@research.att.com

**Abstract.** Kernel methods are widely used in statistical learning techniques. We recently introduced a general kernel framework based on weighted transducers or rational relations, *rational kernels*, to extend kernel methods to the analysis of variable-length sequences or more generally weighted automata. These kernels are efficient to compute and have been successfully used in applications such as spoken-dialog classification. Not all rational kernels are *positive definite and symmetric* (PDS) however, a sufficient property for guaranteeing the convergence of discriminant classification algorithms such as Support Vector Machines. We present several theoretical results related to PDS rational kernels. We show in particular that under some conditions these kernels are closed under sum, product, or Kleene-closure and give a general method for constructing a PDS rational kernel from an arbitrary transducer defined on some non-idempotent semirings. We also show that some commonly used string kernels or similarity measures such as the edit-distance, the convolution kernels of Haussler, and some string kernels used in the context of computational biology are specific instances of rational kernels. Our results include the proof that the edit-distance over a non-trivial alphabet is not *negative definite*, which, to the best of our knowledge, was never stated or proved before.

## 1 Motivation

Many classification algorithms were originally designed for fixed-length vectors. Recent applications in text and speech processing and computational biology require however the analysis of variable-length sequences and even more generally weighted automata. Indeed, the output of a large-vocabulary speech recognizer for a particular input speech utterance, or that of a complex information extraction system combining several information sources for a specific input query, is typically a weighted automaton compactly representing a large set of alternative sequences. The weights assigned by the system to each sequence are used to rank different alternatives according to the models the system is based on. The error rate of such complex systems is still too high in many tasks to rely only on their one-best output, thus it is preferable instead to use the full output weighted automata which contain the correct result in most cases.

Kernel methods [13] are widely used in statistical learning techniques such as Support Vector Machines (SVMs) [2, 4, 14] due to their computational efficiency in high-dimensional feature spaces. Recently, a general kernel framework

B. Schölkopf and M.K. Warmuth (Eds.): COLT/Kernel 2003, LNAI 2777, pp. 41–56, 2003.

**Table 1.** *Semiring examples.* $\oplus_{\log}$ *is defined by:* $x \oplus_{\log} y = -\log(e^{-x} + e^{-y})$.

| SEMIRING | SET | $\oplus$ | $\otimes$ | $\bar{0}$ | $\bar{1}$ |
|---|---|---|---|---|---|
| Boolean | $\{0,1\}$ | $\vee$ | $\wedge$ | 0 | 1 |
| Probability | $\mathbb{R}_+$ | $+$ | $\times$ | 0 | 1 |
| Log | $\mathbb{R} \cup \{-\infty, +\infty\}$ | $\oplus_{\log}$ | $+$ | $+\infty$ | 0 |
| Tropical | $\mathbb{R} \cup \{-\infty, +\infty\}$ | $\min$ | $+$ | $+\infty$ | 0 |

based on weighted transducers or rational relations, *rational kernels*, was introduced to extend kernel methods to the analysis of variable-length sequences or more generally weighted automata [3]. It was shown that there are general and efficient algorithms for computing rational kernels. Rational kernels have been successfully used for applications such as spoken-dialog classification.

Not all rational kernels are *positive definite and symmetric* (PDS), or equivalently verify the Mercer condition [1], a condition that guarantees the convergence of discriminant classification algorithms such as SVMs. This motivates the study undertaken in this paper. We present several theoretical results related to PDS rational kernels. In particular, we show that under some conditions these kernels are closed under sum, product, or Kleene-closure and give a general method for constructing a PDS rational kernel from an arbitrary transducer defined on some non-idempotent semirings. We also study the relationship between rational kernels and some commonly used string kernels or similarity measures such as the edit-distance, the convolution kernels of Haussler [6], and some string kernels used in the context of computational biology [8]. We show that these kernels are all specific instances of rational kernels. In each case, we explicitly describe the corresponding weighted transducer. These transducers are often simple and efficient for computing kernels. Their diagram often provides more insight into the definition of kernels and can guide the design of new kernels. Our results also include the proof of the fact that the edit-distance over a non-trivial alphabet is not *negative definite*, which, to the best of our knowledge, was never stated or proved before.

## 2   Preliminaries

In this section, we present the algebraic definitions and notation necessary to introduce rational kernels.

**Definition 1 ([7]).** *A system* $(\mathbb{K}, \oplus, \otimes, \bar{0}, \bar{1})$ *is a* semiring *if:* $(\mathbb{K}, \oplus, \bar{0})$ *is a commutative monoid with identity element* $\bar{0}$; $(\mathbb{K}, \otimes, \bar{1})$ *is a monoid with identity element* $\bar{1}$; $\otimes$ *distributes over* $\oplus$; *and* $\bar{0}$ *is an annihilator for* $\otimes$: *for all* $a \in \mathbb{K}, a \otimes \bar{0} = \bar{0} \otimes a = \bar{0}$.

Thus, a semiring is a ring that may lack negation. Table 1 lists some familiar semirings.

**Definition 2.** *A weighted finite-state transducer* $T$ *over a semiring* $\mathbb{K}$ *is an 8-tuple* $T = (\Sigma, \Delta, Q, I, F, E, \lambda, \rho)$ *where:* $\Sigma$ *is the finite input alphabet of the* *transducer; $\Delta$ is the finite output alphabet; $Q$ is a finite set of states; $I \subseteq Q$ the set of initial states; $F \subseteq Q$ the set of final states; $E \subseteq Q \times (\Sigma \cup \{\epsilon\}) \times (\Delta \cup \{\epsilon\}) \times \mathbb{K} \times Q$ a finite set of transitions; $\lambda : I \to \mathbb{K}$ the initial weight function; and $\rho : F \to \mathbb{K}$ the final weight function mapping $F$ to $\mathbb{K}$.*

*Weighted automata* can be formally defined in a similar way by simply omitting the input or output labels.

Given a transition $e \in E$, we denote by $p[e]$ its origin or previous state and $n[e]$ its destination state or next state, and $w[e]$ its weight. A *path* $\pi = e_1 \cdots e_k$ is an element of $E^*$ with consecutive transitions: $n[e_{i-1}] = p[e_i]$, $i = 2, \ldots, k$. We extend $n$ and $p$ to paths by setting: $n[\pi] = n[e_k]$ and $p[\pi] = p[e_1]$. The weight function $w$ can also be extended to paths by defining the weight of a path as the $\otimes$-product of the weights of its constituent transitions: $w[\pi] = w[e_1] \otimes \cdots \otimes w[e_k]$. We denote by $P(q, q')$ the set of paths from $q$ to $q'$ and by $P(q, x, y, q')$ the set of paths from $q$ to $q'$ with input label $x \in \Sigma^*$ and output label $y$. These definitions can be extended to subsets $R, R' \subseteq Q$, by: $P(R, x, y, R') = \cup_{q \in R, q' \in R'} P(q, x, y, q')$. A transducer $T$ is *regulated* if the output weight associated by $T$ to any pair of input-output string $(x, y)$ by:

$$[\![T]\!](x, y) = \bigoplus_{\pi \in P(I, x, y, F)} \lambda(p[\pi]) \otimes w[\pi] \otimes \rho[n[\pi]] \tag{1}$$

is well-defined and in $\mathbb{K}$. $[\![T]\!](x, y) = \bar{0}$ when $P(I, x, y, F) = \emptyset$. If for all $q \in Q$ $\bigoplus_{\pi \in P(q, \epsilon, \epsilon, q)} w[\pi] \in \mathbb{K}$, then $T$ is regulated. In particular, when $T$ does not have any $\epsilon$-cycle, it is regulated. In the following, we will assume that all the transducers considered are regulated. Regulated weighted transducers are closed under $\oplus$, $\otimes$ and Kleene-closure. For any transducer $T$, we denote by $T^{-1}$ its *inverse*, that is the transducer obtained from $T$ by transposing the input and output labels of each transition. The *composition* of two weighted transducers $T_1$ and $T_2$ is a weighted transducer denoted by $T_1 \circ T_2$ when the sum:

$$[\![T_1 \circ T_2]\!](x, y) = \bigoplus_{z \in \Sigma^*} [\![T_1]\!](x, z) \otimes [\![T_2]\!](z, y) \tag{2}$$

is well-defined and in $\mathbb{K}$ for all $x \in \Sigma^*$ and $y \in \Delta^*$ [7].

## 3 Rational Kernels – Definition

**Definition 3.** *A kernel $K$ is said to be* rational *if there exist a weighted transducer $T = (\Sigma, \Delta, Q, I, F, E, \lambda, \rho)$ over the semiring $\mathbb{K}$ and a function $\psi : \mathbb{K} \to \mathbb{R}$ such that for all $x \in \Sigma^*$ and $y \in \Delta^*$:*

$$K(x, y) = \psi([\![T]\!](x, y)) \tag{3}$$

This definition and many of the results presented in this paper can be generalized by replacing the free monoids $\Sigma^*$ and $\Delta^*$ with arbitrary monoids $M_1$ and $M_2$.

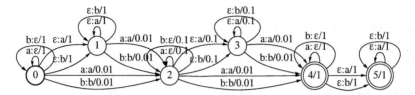

**Fig. 1.** Gappy bigram rational kernel with decay factor $\lambda = .1$. Bold face circles represent initial states and double circles indicate final states.

Also, note that we are not making any particular assumption about the function $\psi$ in this definition. In general, it is an arbitrary function mapping $\mathbb{K}$ to $\mathbb{R}$.

Figure 1 shows an example of a transducer over the probability semiring corresponding to the gappy $n$-gram kernel with decay factor $\lambda$ as defined by [10]. Such gappy $n$-gram kernels are rational kernels [3].

Rational kernels can be naturally extended to kernels over weighted automata. Let $A$ be a weighted automaton defined over the semiring $\mathbb{K}$ and the alphabet $\Sigma$ and $B$ a weighted automaton defined over the semiring $\mathbb{K}$ and the alphabet $\Delta$, $K(A, B)$ is defined by:

$$K(A, B) = \psi \left( \bigoplus_{(x,y) \in \Sigma^* \times \Delta^*} [\![A]\!](x) \otimes [\![T]\!](x, y) \otimes [\![B]\!](y) \right) \qquad (4)$$

for all weighted automata $A$ and $B$ such that the $\oplus$-sum:

$$\bigoplus_{(x,y) \in \Sigma^* \times \Delta^*} [\![A]\!](x) \otimes [\![T]\!](x, y) \otimes [\![B]\!](y)$$

is well-defined and in $\mathbb{K}$. This sum is always defined and in $\mathbb{K}$ when $A$ and $B$ are acyclic weighted automata since the sum then runs over a finite set. It is defined for all weighted automata in all *closed semirings* [7] such as the tropical semiring. In the probability semiring, the sum is well-defined for all $A$, $B$, and $T$ representing probability distributions. When $K(A, B)$ is defined, Equation 4 can be equivalently written as:

$$K(A, B) = \psi \left( \bigoplus_{(x,y) \in \Sigma^* \times \Delta^*} [\![A \circ T \circ B]\!](x, y) \right) \qquad (5)$$

A general algorithm for computing rational kernels efficiently was given in [3]. It is based on the composition of weighted transducers and a general shortest-distance algorithm in a semiring $\mathbb{K}$.

In learning techniques such as those based on SVMs, we are particularly interested in kernels that are *positive definite symmetric* (PDS), or, equivalently, kernels verifying Mercer's condition, which guarantee the existence of a Hilbert space and a dot product associated to the kernel considered. Thus, in what follows, we will focus on theoretical results related to the construction of rational kernels that are PDS. Due to the symmetry condition, the input and output alphabets $\Sigma$ and $\Delta$ will coincide in the rest of the paper.

# 4 Theoretical Results on Positive Definite Rational Kernels

This section reviews a number of results related to PDS kernels and extends them to *PDS rational kernels*, that is the class of rational kernels that have the Mercer property [1]. These results can be used to combine PDS rational kernels to design new PDS rational kernels or to determine if a rational kernel is PDS.

**Definition 4.** *Let $X$ be a non-empty set. A function $K : X \times X \to \mathbb{R}$ is said to be a PDS kernel if it is symmetric ($K(x,y) = K(y,x)$ for all $x, y \in X$) and*

$$\sum_{i,j=1}^{n} c_i c_j K(x_i, x_j) \geq 0 \tag{6}$$

*for all $n \geq 1$, $\{x_1, \ldots, x_n\} \subseteq X$ and $\{c_1, \ldots, c_n\} \subseteq \mathbb{R}$.*

It is clear from classical results of linear algebra that $K$ is a PDS kernel iff the matrix $K(x_i, x_j)_{i,j \leq n}$ for all $n \geq 1$ and all $\{x_1, \ldots, x_n\} \subseteq X$ is symmetric and all its eigenvalues are non-negative.

PDS kernels can be used to construct other families of kernels that also meet these conditions [13]. *Polynomial kernels* of degree $p$ are formed from the expression $(K + a)^p$, and *Gaussian kernels* can be formed as $\exp(-d^2/\sigma^2)$ with $d^2(x,y) = K(x,x) + K(y,y) - 2K(x,y)$. The following sections will provide other ways of constructing PDS rational kernels.

## 4.1 General Closure Properties of PDS Kernels

The following theorem summarizes general closure properties of PDS kernels [1].

**Theorem 1.** *Let $X$ and $Y$ be two non-empty sets.*

1. *Closure under sum: Let $K_1, K_2 : X \times X \to \mathbb{R}$ be PDS kernels, then $K_1 + K_2 : X \times X \to \mathbb{R}$ is a PDS kernel.*
2. *Closure under product: Let $K_1, K_2 : X \times X \to \mathbb{R}$ be PDS kernels, then $K_1 \cdot K_2 : X \times X \to \mathbb{R}$ is a PDS kernel.*
3. *Closure under tensor product: Let $K_1 : X \times X \to \mathbb{R}$ and $K_2 : Y \times Y \to \mathbb{R}$ be PDS kernels, then their tensor product $K_1 \odot K_2 : (X \times Y) \times (X \times Y) \to \mathbb{R}$, where $K_1 \odot K_2((x_1, y_1), (x_2, y_2)) = K_1(x_1, x_2) \cdot K_2(y_1, y_2)$ is a PDS kernel.*
4. *Closure under pointwise limit: Let $K_n : X \times X \to \mathbb{R}$ be a PDS kernel for all $n \in \mathbb{N}$ and assume that $\lim_{n \to \infty} K_n(x,y)$ exists for all $x, y \in X$, then $K$ defined by $K(x,y) = \lim_{n \to \infty} K_n(x,y)$ is a PDS kernel.*

5. Closure under composition with a power series: Let $K : X \times X \to \mathbb{R}$ be a PDS kernel such that $|K(x,y)| < \rho$ for all $(x,y) \in X \times X$. Then if the radius of convergence of the power series $S = \sum_{n=0}^{\infty} a_n x^n$ is $\rho$ and $a_n \geq 0$ for all $n \geq 0$, the composed kernel $S \circ K$ is a PDS kernel. In particular, if $K : X \times X \to \mathbb{R}$ is a PDS kernel, then so is $\exp(K)$.

Clearly, these closure properties all apply to PDS rational kernels as well. In the next section, we present other closure properties more specific to the class of PDS rational kernels.

## 4.2   Closure Properties of PDS Rational Kernels

By definition, weighted transducers are closed under rational operations. The rational operations (sum, product, and closure operations) are defined as follows for all transducers $T_1$ and $T_2$ and $(x,y) \in \Sigma^* \times \Sigma^*$:

$$[\![T_1 \oplus T_2]\!](x,y) = [\![T_1]\!](x,y) \oplus [\![T_2]\!](x,y) \tag{7}$$

$$[\![T_1 \otimes T_2]\!](x,y) = \bigoplus_{x=x_1 x_2, y=y_1 y_2} [\![T_1]\!](x_1,y_1) \otimes [\![T_2]\!](x_2,y_2)$$

$$[\![T^*]\!](x,y) = \bigoplus_{n=0}^{\infty} T^n(x,y)$$

In this section, we assume that a fixed function $\psi$ is used in the definition of all the rational kernels mentioned. We denote by $K_T$ the rational kernel corresponding to the transducer $T$ and defined for all $x, y \in \Sigma^*$ by $K_T(x,y) = \psi([\![T]\!](x,y))$.

**Theorem 2.** Let $\Sigma$ be a non-empty alphabet. The following closure properties hold for PDS rational kernels.

1. Closure under $\oplus$-sum: Assume that $\psi : (\mathbb{K}, \oplus, \overline{0}) \to (\mathbb{R}, +, 0)$ is a monoid morphism. Let $K_{T_1}, K_{T_2} : \Sigma^* \times \Sigma^* \to \mathbb{R}$ be PDS rational kernels, then $K_{T_1 \oplus T_2} : \Sigma^* \times \Sigma^* \to \mathbb{R}$ is a PDS rational kernel and $K_{T_1 \oplus T_2} = K_{T_1} + K_{T_2}$.
2. Closure under $\otimes$-product: Assume that $\psi : (\mathbb{K}, \oplus, \otimes, \overline{0}, \overline{1}) \to (\mathbb{R}, +, \times, 0, 1)$ is a semiring morphism. Let $K_{T_1}, K_{T_2} : \Sigma^* \times \Sigma^* \to \mathbb{R}$ be PDS rational kernels, then $K_{T_1 \otimes T_2} : \Sigma^* \times \Sigma^* \to \mathbb{R}$ is a PDS rational kernel.
3. Closure under Kleene-closure: Assume that $\psi : (\mathbb{K}, \oplus, \otimes, \overline{0}, \overline{1}) \to (\mathbb{R}, +, \times, 0, 1)$ is a continuous semiring morphism. Let $K_T : \Sigma^* \times \Sigma^* \to \mathbb{R}$ be a PDS rational kernel, then $K_{T^*} : \Sigma^* \times \Sigma^* \to \mathbb{R}$ is a PDS rational kernel.

*Proof.* The closure under $\oplus$-sum follows directly Theorem 1 and the fact that for all $x, y \in \Sigma^*$:

$$\psi([\![T_1]\!](x,y) \oplus [\![T_2]\!](x,y)) = \psi([\![T_1]\!](x,y)) + \psi([\![T_2]\!](x,y))$$

when $\psi : (\mathbb{K}, \oplus, \overline{0}) \to (\mathbb{R}, +, 0)$ is a monoid morphism. For the closure under $\otimes$-product, when $\psi$ is a semiring morphism, for all $x, y \in \Sigma^*$:

$$\psi(\llbracket T_1 \otimes T_2 \rrbracket (x, y)) = \sum_{x_1 x_2 = x, y_1 y_2 = y} \psi(\llbracket T_1 \rrbracket (x_1, y_1)) \cdot \psi(\llbracket T_2 \rrbracket (x_2, y_2)) \qquad (8)$$

$$= \sum_{x_1 x_2 = x, y_1 y_2 = y} K_{T_1} \odot K_{T_2}((x_1, x_2), (y_1, y_2))$$

By Theorem 1, since $K_{T_1}$ and $K_{T_2}$ are PDS kernels, their tensor product $K_{T_1} \odot K_{T_2}$ is a PDS kernel and there exists a Hilbert space $H \subseteq \mathbb{R}^{\Sigma^*}$ and a mapping $u \to \phi_u$ such that $K_{T_1} \odot K_{T_2}(u, v) = \langle \phi_u, \phi_v \rangle$ [1]. Thus

$$\psi(\llbracket T_1 \otimes T_2 \rrbracket (x, y)) = \sum_{x_1 x_2 = x, y_1 y_2 = y} \langle \phi_{(x_1, x_2)}, \phi_{(y_1, y_2)} \rangle \qquad (9)$$

$$= \left\langle \sum_{x_1 x_2 = x} \phi_{(x_1, x_2)}, \sum_{y_1 y_2 = y} \phi_{(y_1, y_2)} \right\rangle$$

Since a dot product is positive definite, this equality implies that $K_{T_1 \otimes T_2}$ is a PDS kernel. The closure under Kleene-closure is a direct consequence of the closure under $\oplus$-sum and $\otimes$-product of PDS rational kernels and the closure under pointwise limit of PDS kernels (Theorem 1). $\qquad\square$

Theorem 2 provides a general method for constructing complex PDS rational kernels from simpler ones. PDS rational kernels defined to model specific prior knowledge sources can be combined to create a more general PDS kernel. In contrast to Theorem 2, PDS rational kernels are not closed under composition. This is clear since the ordinary matrix multiplication does not preserve positive definiteness in general[1]. The next section studies a general construction of PDS rational kernels using composition.

## 4.3   A General Construction of PDS Rational Kernels

In this section, we assume that $\psi : (\mathbb{K}, \oplus, \otimes, \overline{0}, \overline{1}) \to (\mathbb{R}, +, \times, 0, 1)$ is a continuous semiring morphism[2]. We show that there exists a general way of constructing a PDS rational kernel from any transducer $T$. The construction is based on composing $T$ with its inverse $T^{-1}$. The composition of two weighted transducers $T_1$ and $T_2$ is a weighted transducer denoted by $T_1 \circ T_2$ and defined by:

$$\llbracket T_1 \circ T_2 \rrbracket (x, y) = \bigoplus_{z \in \Sigma^*} \llbracket T_1 \rrbracket (x, z) \otimes \llbracket T_2 \rrbracket (z, y) \qquad (10)$$

---

[1] It is not difficult to prove however that the composition of two PDS transducers $T_1$ and $T_2$ is a PDS transducer when $T_1 \circ T_2 = T_2 \circ T_1$.

[2] In some cases such a morphism may not exist. Its existence implies among other properties that $\mathbb{K}$ is commutative and that $\mathbb{K}$ is non-idempotent. Indeed, if $\mathbb{K}$ is idempotent, for any $x \in \mathbb{K}$, $\psi(x) = \psi(x \oplus x) = \psi(x) + \psi(x) = 2\psi(x)$, which implies that $\psi(x) = 0$ for all $x$.

**Proposition 1.** *Let $T = (\Sigma, \Delta, Q, I, F, E, \lambda, \rho)$ be a weighted transducer defined over $(\mathbb{K}, \oplus, \otimes, \bar{0}, \bar{1})$. Assume that the weighted transducer $T \circ T^{-1}$ is regulated, then $T \circ T^{-1}$ defines a PDS rational kernel over $\Sigma^* \times \Sigma^*$.*

*Proof.* Denote by $S$ the composed transducer $T \circ T^{-1}$. Let $K$ be the rational kernel defined by $S$. By definition of composition

$$K(x,y) = \psi([\![S]\!](x,y)) = \psi\left(\bigoplus_{z \in \Delta^*} [\![T]\!](x,z) \otimes [\![T]\!](y,z)\right) \quad (11)$$

for all $x, y \in \Sigma^*$. Since $\psi$ is a continuous semiring morphism, for all $x, y \in \Sigma^*$

$$K(x,y) = \psi([\![S]\!](x,y)) = \sum_{z \in \Delta^*} \psi([\![T]\!](x,z)) \cdot \psi([\![T]\!](y,z)) \quad (12)$$

For all $n \in \mathbb{N}$ and $x, y \in \Sigma^*$, define $K_n(x,y)$ by:

$$K_n(x,y) = \sum_{|z| \leq n} \psi([\![T]\!](x,z)) \cdot \psi([\![T]\!](y,z)) \quad (13)$$

where the sum runs over all strings $z \in \Delta^*$ of length less than or equal to $n$. Clearly, $K_n$ defines a symmetric kernel. For any $l \geq 1$ and any $x_1, \ldots, x_l \in \Sigma^*$, define the matrix $M_n$ by: $M_n = (K_n(x_i, x_j))_{i \leq l, j \leq l}$. Let $z_1, z_2, \ldots, z_m$ be an arbitrary ordering of the strings of length less than or equal to $n$. Define the matrix $A$ by:

$$A = (\psi([\![T]\!](x_i, z_j)))_{i \leq l, j \leq m} \quad (14)$$

By definition of $K_n$, $M_n = AA^t$. Thus, the eigenvalues of $M_n$ are all non-negative, which implies that $K_n$ is a PDS kernel. Since $K$ is a pointwise limit of $K_n$, $K(x,y) = \lim_{n \to \infty} K_n(x,y)$, by Theorem 1, $K$ is a PDS kernel. This ends the proof of the proposition. □

The next propositions provide results related to the converse of Proposition 1.

**Proposition 2.** *Let $S = (\Sigma, \Sigma, Q, I, F, E, \lambda, \rho)$ be an acyclic weighted transducer over $(\mathbb{K}, \oplus, \otimes, \bar{0}, \bar{1})$ defining a PDS rational kernel over $\Sigma^* \times \Sigma^*$, then there exists a weighted transducer $T$ such that $S = T \circ T^{-1}$.*

*Proof.* The proof is based on the classical result of linear algebra that any positive definite (finite) matrix $M$ can be written as $M = AA^t$ for some matrix $A$. The full proof of the proposition is reserved to a longer version of the paper. □

Assume that the same continuous semiring morphism $\psi$ is used in the definition of all the rational kernels.

**Proposition 3.** *Let $\Theta$ be the subset of weighted transducers over $(\mathbb{K}, \oplus, \otimes, \bar{0}, \bar{1})$ defining a PDS rational kernel such that for any $S \in \Theta$ there exists a weighted transducer $T$ such that $S = T \circ T^{-1}$. Then $\Theta$ is closed under $\oplus$-sum, $\otimes$-product, and Kleene-closure.*

*Proof.* The proof is based on various technical arguments related to the composition of weighted transducers and is left to a longer version of the paper.    □

Proposition 1 leads to a natural question: under the same assumptions, are all weighted transducers $S$ defining a PDS rational kernel of the form $S = T \circ T^{-1}$? We conjecture that this is the case and that this property provides a characterization of the weighted transducers defining PDS rational kernels under the assumptions made in Proposition 1. Indeed, we have not (yet) found a counter-example contradicting this statement and have proved a number of results in support of it, including the two propositions above.

## 4.4   Negative Definite Kernels

As mentioned before, given a set $X$ and a distance or dis-similarity measure $d : X \times X \to \mathbb{R}_+$, a common method used to define a kernel $K$ is the following. For all $x, y \in X$,

$$K(x, y) = \exp(-td^2(x, y)) \tag{15}$$

where $t > 0$ is some constant typically used for normalization. Gaussian kernels are defined in this way. However, such kernels $K$ are not necessarily positive definite, e.g., for $X = \mathbb{R}$, $d(x, y) = |x - y|^p$, $p > 1$ and $t = 1$, $K$ is not positive definite. The positive definiteness of $K$ depends on $t$ and the properties of the function $d$. The classical results presented in this section exactly address such questions [1]. They include a characterization of PDS kernels based on *negative definite kernels* which may be viewed as distances with some specific properties[3].

   The results we are presenting are general, but we are particularly interested in the case where $d$ can be represented by a rational kernel. We will use these results later when dealing with the case of the edit-distance.

**Definition 5.** *Let $X$ be a non-empty set. A function $K : X \times X \to \mathbb{R}$ is said to be a negative definite symmetric kernel (NDS kernel) if it is symmetric ($K(x, y) = K(y, x)$ for all $x, y \in X$) and*

$$\sum_{i,j=1}^{n} c_i c_j K(x_i, x_j) \leq 0 \tag{16}$$

*for all $n \geq 1$, $\{x_1, \ldots, x_n\} \subseteq X$ and $\{c_1, \ldots, c_n\} \subseteq \mathbb{R}$ with $\sum_{i=1}^{n} c_i = 0$.*

   Clearly, if $K$ is a PDS kernel then $-K$ is a NDS kernel, however the converse does not hold in general. Negative definite kernels often correspond to distances, e.g., $K(x, y) = (x - y)^\alpha$, with $0 < \alpha \leq 2$ is a negative definite kernel.

   The next theorem summarizes general closure properties of NDS kernels [1].

**Theorem 3.** *Let $X$ be a non-empty set.*

---

[3] Many of the results described by [1] are also included in [12] with the terminology of *conditionally positive definite* instead of *negative definite kernels*. We adopt the original terminology used by [1].

1. *Closure under sum: Let $K_1, K_2 : X \times X \to \mathbb{R}$ be NDS kernels, then $K_1 + K_2 : X \times X \to \mathbb{R}$ is a NDS kernel.*
2. *Closure under log and exponentiation: Let $K : X \times X \to \mathbb{R}$ be a NDS kernel with $K \geq 0$, and $\alpha$ a real number with $0 < \alpha < 1$, then $\log(1 + K), K^{\alpha} : X \times X \to \mathbb{R}$ are NDS kernels.*
3. *Closure under pointwise limit: Let $K_n : X \times X \to \mathbb{R}$ be a NDS kernel for all $n \in \mathbb{N}$, then $K$ defined by $K(x, y) = \lim_{n \to \infty} K_n(x, y)$ is a NDS kernel.*

The following theorem clarifies the relation between NDS and PDS kernels and provides in particular a way of constructing PDS kernels from NDS ones [1].

**Theorem 4.** *Let $X$ be a non-empty set, $x_o \in X$, and let $K : X \times X \to \mathbb{R}$ be a symmetric kernel.*

1. *$K$ is negative definite iff $\exp(-tK)$ is positive definite for all $t > 0$.*
2. *Let $K'$ be the function defined by:*

$$K'(x, y) = K(x, x_0) + K(y, x_0) - K(x, y) - K(x_0, x_0) \qquad (17)$$

*Then $K$ is negative definite iff $K'$ is positive definite.*

The theorem gives two ways of constructing a positive definite kernel using a negative definite kernel. The first construction is similar to the way Gaussian kernels are defined. The second construction has been put forward by [12].

## 5   Relationship with Some Commonly Used Kernels or Similarity Measures

This section studies the relationships between several families of kernels or similarities measures and rational kernels.

### 5.1   Edit-Distance

A common similarity measure in many applications is that of the *edit-distance* [9]. We denote by $d_e(x, y)$ the edit-distance between two strings $x$ and $y$ over the alphabet $\Sigma$ with cost 1 assigned to all edit operations.

**Proposition 4.** *Let $\Sigma$ be a non-empty finite alphabet and let $d_e$ be the edit-distance over $\Sigma$, then $d_e$ is a symmetric rational kernel. Furthermore, (1): $d_e$ is not a PDS kernel, and (2): $d_e$ is a NDS kernel iff $|\Sigma| = 1$.*

*Proof.* The edit-distance between two strings, or weighted automata, can be represented by a simple weighted transducer over the tropical semiring [11]. Since the edit-distance is symmetric, this shows that $d_e$ is a symmetric rational kernel. Figure 2(a) shows the corresponding transducer when the alphabet is $\Sigma = \{a, b\}$. The cost of the alignment between two sequences can also be computed by a weighted transducer over the probability semiring [11], see Figure 2(b).

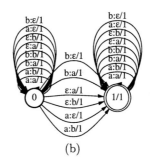

(a)                                           (b)

**Fig. 2.** (a) Weighted transducer over the tropical semiring representing the edit-distance over the alphabet $\Sigma = \{a, b\}$. (b) Weighted transducer over the probability semiring computing the cost of alignments over the alphabet $\Sigma = \{a, b\}$.

Let $a \in \Sigma$, then the matrix $(d_e(x_i, x_j))_{1 \leq i,j \leq 2}$ with $x_1 = \epsilon$ and $x_2 = a$ has a negative eigenvalue $(-1)$, thus $d_e$ is not a PDS kernel.

When $|\Sigma| = 1$, the edit-distance simply measures the absolute value of the difference of length between two strings. A string $x \in \Sigma^*$ can then be viewed as a vector of the Hilbert space $\mathbb{R}^\infty$. Denote by $\| \cdot \|$ the corresponding norm. For all $x, y \in \Sigma^*$:

$$d_e(x, y) = \|x - y\|$$

The square distance $\| \cdot \|^2$ is negative definite, thus by Theorem 3, $d_e = (\| \cdot \|^2)^{1/2}$ is also negative definite.

Assume now that $|\Sigma| > 1$. We show that $\exp(-d_e)$ is not PDS. By theorem 4, this implies that $d_e$ is not negative definite. Let $x_1, \cdots, x_{2^n}$ be any ordering of the strings of length $n$ over the alphabet $\{a, b\}$. Define the matrix $M_n$ by:

$$M_n = (\exp(-d_e(x_i, x_j)))_{1 \leq i,j, \leq 2^n} \qquad (18)$$

Figure 3(a) shows the smallest eigenvalue $\alpha_n$ of $M_n$ as a function of $n$. Clearly, there are values of $n$ for which $\alpha_n < 0$, thus the edit-distance is not negative definite. Table 3(b) provides a simple example with five strings of length 3 over the alphabet $\Sigma = \{a, b, c, d\}$ showing directly that the edit-distance is not negative definite. Indeed, it is easy to verify that: $\sum_{i=1}^{5} \sum_{j=1}^{5} c_i c_j K(x_i, x_j) = \frac{2}{3} > 0$. □

To our knowledge, this is the first statement and proof of the fact that $d_e$ is not NDS for $|\Sigma| > 1$. This result has a direct consequence on the design of kernels in computational biology, often based on the edit-distance or other related similarity measures. When $|\Sigma| > 1$, Proposition 4 shows that $d_e$ is not NDS. Thus, there exists $t > 0$ for which $\exp(-t d_e)$ is not PDS. Similarly, $d_e^2$ is not NDS since otherwise by Theorem 3, $d_e = (d_e^2)^{1/2}$ would be NDS.

### 5.2   Haussler's Convolution Kernels for Strings

D. Haussler describes a class of kernels for strings built by applying iteratively *convolution kernels* [6]. We show that these convolution kernels for strings are

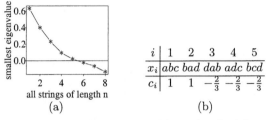

**Fig. 3.** (a) Smallest eigenvalue of the matrix $M_n = (\exp(-d_e(x_i, x_j)))_{1 \leq i,j, \leq 2^n}$ as a function of $n$. (b) Example demonstrating that the edit-distance is not negative definite.

specific instances of rational kernels. To define these kernels, Haussler introduces for $0 \leq \gamma < 1$ the $\gamma$-infinite iteration of a mapping $H : \Sigma^* \times \Sigma^* \to \mathbb{R}$ by:

$$H_\gamma^* = (1 - \gamma) \sum_{n=1}^{\infty} \gamma^{n-1} H^{(n)} \tag{19}$$

where $H^{(n)} = H \star H^{(n-1)}$ is the result of the convolution of $H$ with itself $n - 1$ times. Note that $H_\gamma^* = 0$ for $\gamma = 0$.

**Lemma 1.** *For $0 < \gamma < 1$, the $\gamma$-infinite iteration of a rational transduction $H : \Sigma^* \times \Sigma^* \to \mathbb{R}$ can be defined in the following way with respect to the Kleene †-operator:*

$$H_\gamma^* = \frac{1 - \gamma}{\gamma} (\gamma H)^\dagger \tag{20}$$

*Proof.* Haussler's convolution simply corresponds to the Cauchy product or concatenation in the case of rational transductions. Thus, for $0 < \gamma < 1$, by definition of the †-operator:

$$(\gamma H)^\dagger = \sum_{n=1}^{\infty} (\gamma H)^n = \sum_{n=1}^{\infty} \gamma^n H^n = \frac{\gamma}{1 - \gamma} \sum_{n=1}^{\infty} (1 - \gamma) \gamma^{n-1} H^n = \frac{\gamma}{1 - \gamma} H_\gamma^* \qquad \square$$

Given a probability distribution $p$ over all symbols of $\Sigma$, Haussler's convolution kernels for strings are defined by:

$$K_H(x, y) = \gamma K_2 \star (K_1 \star K_2)_\gamma^* + (1 - \gamma) K_2$$

where $K_1$ is the specific polynomial PDS rational transduction over the probability semiring defined by: $K_1(x, y) = \sum_{a \in \Sigma} p(x|a) p(y|a) p(a)$ and models substitutions, and $K_2$ another specific PDS rational transduction over the probability semiring modeling insertions.

**Proposition 5.** *For any $0 \leq \gamma < 1$, Haussler's convolution kernels $K_H$ coincide with the following special cases of rational kernels:*

$$K_H = (1 - \gamma)[K_2 (\gamma K_1 K_2)^*] \tag{21}$$

**Fig. 4.** Haussler's convolution kernels $K_H$ for strings: specific instances of rational kernels. $K_1$, $(K_2)$, corresponds to a specific weighted transducer over the probability semiring and modeling substitutions (resp. insertions).

*Proof.* As mentioned above, Haussler's convolution simply corresponds to concatenation in this context. When $\gamma = 0$, by definition, $K_H$ is reduced to $K_2$ which is a rational transducer and the proposition's formula above is satisfied. Assume now that $\gamma \neq 0$. By lemma 1, $K_H$ can be re-written as:

$$K_H = \gamma K_2(K_1 K_2)^\star_\gamma + (1-\gamma)K_2 = \gamma K_2 \frac{1-\gamma}{\gamma}(\gamma K_1 K_2)^\dagger + (1-\gamma)K_2 \quad (22)$$

$$= (1-\gamma)[K_2(\gamma K_1 K_2)^\dagger + K_2] = (1-\gamma)[K_2(\gamma K_1 K_2)^*]$$

Since rational transductions are closed under rational operations, $K_H$ also defines a rational transduction. Since $K_1$ and $K_2$ are PDS kernels, by theorem 2, $K_H$ defines a PDS kernel.                                                                     □

The transducer of Figure 4 illustrates the convolution kernels for strings proposed by Haussler. They correspond to special cases of rational kernels whose mechanism is clarified by the figure: the kernel corresponds to a substitution with weight $(1-\gamma)$ modeled by $K_2$ followed by any number of sequences of insertions modeled by $K_1$ and substitutions modeled by $K_2$ with weight $\gamma$. Clearly, there are many other ways of defining kernels based on weighted transducers with more complex definitions and perhaps more data-driven definitions.

### 5.3   Other Kernels Used in Computational Biology

In this section we show the relationship between rational kernels and another class of kernels used in computational biology.

A family of kernels, *mismatch string kernels*, was introduced by [8] for protein classification using SVMs. Let $\Sigma$ be a finite alphabet, typically that of amino acids for protein sequences. For any two sequences $z_1, z_2 \in \Sigma^*$ of same length ($|z_1| = |z_2|$), we denote by $d(z_1, z_2)$ the total number of mismatching symbols between these sequences. For all $m \in \mathbb{N}$, we define the bounded distance $d_m$ between two sequences of same length by:

$$d_m(z_1, z_2) = \begin{cases} 1 & \text{if } (d(z_1, z_2) \leq m) \\ 0 & \text{otherwise} \end{cases} \quad (23)$$

and for all $k \in \mathbb{N}$, we denote by $F_k(x)$ the set of all factors of $x$ of length $k$:

$$F_k(x) = \{z : x \in \Sigma^* z \Sigma^*, |z| = k\}$$

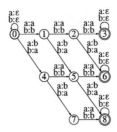

**Fig. 5.** Mismatch kernel $K_{(k,m)} = T_{k,m} \circ T_{k,m}^{-1}$ [8] with $k = 3$ and $m = 2$ and with $\Sigma = \{a, b\}$. The transducer $T_{3,2}$ defined over the probability semiring is shown. All transition weights and final weights are equal to one. Note that states 3, 6, and 8 of the transducer are equivalent and thus can be merged and similarly that states 2 and 5 can then be merged as well.

For any $k, m \in \mathbb{N}$ with $m \leq k$, a $(k, m)$-mismatch kernel $K_{(k,m)} : \Sigma^* \times \Sigma^* \to \mathbb{R}$ is the kernel defined over protein sequences $x, y \in \Sigma^*$ by:

$$K_{(k,m)}(x, y) = \sum_{z_1 \in F_k(x),\, z_2 \in F_k(y),\, z \in \Sigma^k} d_m(z_1, z)\, d_m(z, z_2) \tag{24}$$

**Proposition 6.** *For any* $k, m \in \mathbb{N}$ *with* $m \leq k$, *the* $(k, m)$-*mismatch kernel* $K_{(k,m)} : \Sigma^* \times \Sigma^* \to \mathbb{R}$ *is a PDS rational kernel.*

*Proof.* Let $M$, $S$, and $D$ be the weighted transducers over the probability semiring defined by:

$$M = \sum_{a \in \Sigma}(a, a) \qquad S = \sum_{a \neq b}(a, b) \qquad D = \sum_{a \in \Sigma}(a, \epsilon) \tag{25}$$

$M$ associates weight 1 to each pair of identical symbols of the alphabet $\Sigma$, $S$ associates 1 to each pair of distinct or mismatching symbols, and $D$ associates 1 to all pairs with second element $\epsilon$.

For $i, k \in \mathbb{N}$ with $0 \leq i \leq k$, Define the *shuffle* of $S^i$ and $M^{k-i}$, denoted by $S^i \sqcup\!\sqcup M^{k-i}$, as the the sum over all products made of factors $S$ and $M$ with exactly $i$ factors $S$ and $k - i$ factors $M$. As a finite sum of products of $S$ and $M$, $S^i \sqcup\!\sqcup M^{k-i}$ is rational. Since weighted transducers are closed under rational operations the following defines a weighted transducer $T$ over the probability semiring for any $k, m \in \mathbb{N}$ with $m \leq k$: $T_{k,m} = D^* R D^*$ with $R = \sum_{i=0}^{m} S^i \sqcup\!\sqcup M^{k-i}$. Consider two sequences $z_1, z_2$ such that $|z_1| = |z_2| = k$. By definition of $M$ and $S$ and the shuffle product, for any $i$, with $0 \leq i \leq m$,

$$[\![S^i \sqcup\!\sqcup M^{k-i}]\!](z_1, z_2) = \begin{cases} 1 & \text{if } (d(z_1, z_2) = i) \\ 0 & \text{otherwise} \end{cases} \tag{26}$$

Thus,
$$[\![R]\!](z_1, z_2) = \sum_{i=0}^{m} S^i \sqcup\!\sqcup M^{k-i}(z_1, z_2) = \begin{cases} 1 & \text{if } (d(z_1, z_2) \leq m) \\ 0 & \text{otherwise} \end{cases}$$
$$= d_m(z_1, z_2)$$

By definition of the product of weighted transducers, for any $x \in \Sigma^*$ and $z \in \Sigma^k$,

$$T_{k,m}(x, z) = \sum_{x=uvw, z=u'v'w'} [\![D^*]\!](u, u') \, [\![R]\!](v, v') \, [\![D^*]\!](w, w') \qquad (27)$$

$$= \sum_{v \in F_k(x), z=v'} [\![R]\!](v, v') = \sum_{v \in F_k(x)} d_m(v, z)$$

It is clear from the definition of $T_{k,m}$ that $T_{k,m}(x, z) = 0$ for all $x, z \in \Sigma^*$ with $|z| > k$. Thus, by definition of the composition of weighted transducer, for all $x, y \in \Sigma^*$

$$[\![T_{k,m} \circ T_{k,m}{}^{-1}]\!](x, y) = \sum_{z_1 \in F_k(x), z_2 \in F_k(y), z \in \Sigma^*} d_m(z_1, z) \, d_m(z, z_2) \qquad (28)$$

$$= \sum_{z_1 \in F_k(x), z_2 \in F_k(y), z \in \Sigma^k} d_m(z_1, z) \, d_m(z, z_2) = K_{(k,m)}(x, y)$$

By proposition 1, this proves that $K_{(k,m)}$ is a PDS rational kernel. $\qquad \square$

Figure 5 shows $T_{3,2}$, a simple weighted transducer over the probability semiring that can be used to compute the mismatch kernel $K_{(3,2)} = T_{3,2} \circ T_{3,2}{}^{-1}$. Such transducers provide a compact representation of the kernel and are very efficient to use with the composition algorithm already described in [3]. The transitions of these transducers can be defined implicitly and expanded on-demand as needed for the particular input strings or weighted automata. This substantially reduces the space needed for their representation, e.g., a single transition with labels $x : y$, $x \neq y$ can be used to represent all transitions with similar labels $((a : b), a, b \in \Sigma$, with $a \neq b)$. Similarly, composition can also be performed on-the-fly. Furthermore, the transducer of Figure 5 can be made more compact since it admits several states that are equivalent.

## 6    Conclusion

In general, the transducer representation provides a very compact representation benefiting from existing and well-studied optimizations and leads to an efficient computation of rational kernels. It further avoids the design of special-purpose algorithms for the computation of the kernels covered by the framework of rational kernels. We gave the proof of several new and general properties related to PDS rational kernels. These results can be used to design a PDS rational kernel from simpler ones or from an arbitrary weighted transducer over an appropriate semiring, or from negative definite kernels. Rational kernels provide a unified framework for the design of computationally efficient kernels for strings or weighted automata. The framework includes in particular pair-HMM string kernels [5, 15], Haussler's convolution kernels for strings and other classes of string kernels introduced for computational biology.

# References

1. Christian Berg, Jens Peter Reus Christensen, and Paul Ressel. *Harmonic Analysis on Semigroups*. Springer-Verlag: Berlin-New York, 1984.
2. B. E. Boser, I. Guyon, and V. N. Vapnik. A training algorithm for optimal margin classifiers. In *Proceedings of the Fifth Annual Workshop of Computational Learning Theory*, volume 5, pages 144–152, Pittsburg, 1992. ACM.
3. Corinna Cortes, Patrick Haffner, and Mehryar Mohri. Rational Kernels. In *NIPS 2002*, Vancouver, Canada, March 2003. MIT Press.
4. Corinna Cortes and Vladimir N. Vapnik. Support-Vector Networks. *Machine Learning*, 20(3):273–297, 1995.
5. R. Durbin, S.R. Eddy, A. Krogh, and G.J. Mitchison. *Biological Sequence Analysis: Probabilistic Models of Proteins and Nucleic Acids*. Cambridge University Press, Cambridge UK, 1998.
6. David Haussler. Convolution Kernels on Discrete Structures. Technical Report UCSC-CRL-99-10, University of California at Santa Cruz, 1999.
7. Werner Kuich and Arto Salomaa. *Semirings, Automata, Languages*. Number 5 in EATCS Monographs on Theoretical Computer Science. Springer-Verlag, 1986.
8. Christina Leslie, Eleazar Eskin, Jason Weston, and William Stafford Noble. Mismatch String Kernels for SVM Protein Classification. In *NIPS 2002*, Vancouver, Canada, March 2003. MIT Press.
9. Vladimir I. Levenshtein. Binary codes capable of correcting deletions, insertions, and reversals. *Soviet Physics - Doklady*, 10:707–710, 1966.
10. Huma Lodhi, John Shawe-Taylor, Nello Cristianini, and Chris Watkins. Text classification using string kernels. In Todd K. Leen, Thomas G. Dietterich, and Volker Tresp, editors, *NIPS 2000*, pages 563–569. MIT Press, 2001.
11. Mehryar Mohri. Edit-Distance of Weighted Automata: General Definitions and Algorithms. *International Journal of Foundations of Computer Science*, 2003.
12. Bernhard Schölkopf. The Kernel Trick for Distances. In Todd K. Leen, Thomas G. Dietterich, and Volker Tresp, editors, *NIPS 2001*, pages 301–307. MIT Press, 2001.
13. Bernhard Schölkopf and Alex Smola. *Learning with Kernels*. MIT Press: Cambridge, MA, 2002.
14. Vladimir N. Vapnik. *Statistical Learning Theory*. John Wiley & Sons, 1998.
15. Chris Watkins. Dynamic alignment kernels. Technical Report CSD-TR-98-11, Royal Holloway, University of London, 1999.

# Bhattacharyya and Expected Likelihood Kernels

Tony Jebara and Risi Kondor

Columbia University, New York, NY 10027, USA
{jebara,risi}@cs.columbia.edu

**Abstract.** We introduce a new class of kernels between distributions. These induce a kernel on the input space between data points by associating to each datum a generative model fit to the data point individually. The kernel is then computed by integrating the product of the two generative models corresponding to two data points. This kernel permits discriminative estimation via, for instance, support vector machines, while exploiting the properties, assumptions, and invariances inherent in the choice of generative model. It satisfies Mercer's condition and can be computed in closed form for a large class of models, including exponential family models, mixtures, hidden Markov models and Bayesian networks. For other models the kernel can be approximated by sampling methods. Experiments are shown for multinomial models in text classification and for hidden Markov models for protein sequence classification.

## 1 Introduction

A variety of efforts in machine learning have explored the fusion of discriminative and generative estimation to exploit their complementary advantages. Some approaches use discriminative learning algorithms and paradigms for generative models. For instance, a generative model may be estimated conditionally [5, 3, 21] or discriminatively [11, 23] to improve its performance for classification. Other approaches explore the use of generative models within standard discriminative classifiers such as support vector machines (SVMs). These generative models help induce appropriate feature space mappings or kernels. For example, the Fisher kernel method forms a generative model of the aggregated data set to compute a kernel on the resulting statistical manifold [10]. Alternatively, information diffusion gives kernels by solving heat equations on a statistical manifold over a given generative model's parameter space [16]. Nevertheless, kernels are frequently engineered independently of generative modeling to obtain desired properties [20, 9]. For instance, string kernels and sequential data kernels [18, 17, 6, 7, 26, 25] do not specifically address the generative hidden Markov model (HMM) literature. However, there may potentially be much to gain by building upon generative modeling, HMM-variants and statistical tools to facilitate the kernel design process.

In this paper, we propose another point of contact between generative models and kernels. We describe a general class of kernels that are computed by estimating a generative probability model for each given datum (or multiple data

B. Schölkopf and M.K. Warmuth (Eds.): COLT/Kernel 2003, LNAI 2777, pp. 57–71, 2003.

points) in the input space via maximum likelihood or another criterion. The kernel's output value for a pair of data points is then obtained by integrating the product of their corresponding probability models taken to a power. This measure of affinity is a generalized form of the Bhattacharyya similarity measure. The kernel readily accommodates many popular distributions allowing us to consider a variety of input spaces (sequences, discrete structures, etc.) while inheriting properties and invariances of the probabilistic modeling. For instance, the kernel applies to exponential family distributions, mixtures and HMMs.

Previous efforts involved generative modeling with statistical manifolds using the Kullback-Leibler (KL) divergence to set up affinity measures between probabilistic models [10, 16]. The KL-divergence is asymmetric and typically is approximated by a local metric (i.e. in the neighborhood of a single maximum likelihood estimate for the whole data set) to generate, for instance, the Fisher kernel [10]. One disadvantage of such a local approximation is that exponential family distributions only generate linear Fisher kernels (see Section 3). Recent work in information diffusion kernels [16] proposes an alternative way of dealing with the statistical manifold by partial differential methods and heat equations as opposed to a local maximum likelihood estimate for the whole dataset. The authors explicate the cases of the multinomial on the sphere and the Gaussian variance on a hyperbolic space which are both solvable and yield interesting nonlinear kernels. However, the latter work has yet to be extended to the wide class of exponential family or mixture model distributions due to the difficulty in finding closed form solutions to the heat equation for arbitrary geometries. In contrast, the measure we choose gives a symmetric kernel from the outset which handles a wide variety of generative models in closed form and can even be computed via sampling methods for arbitrary distributions.

This paper is organized as follows. We first present the general form of our kernel as a product of two distributions each induced from data and note certain properties. We then show how the kernel can be computed in closed form for any distribution in the exponential family, thereby covering a wide range of classical generative models. We derive the particular formulas for the Gaussian, the Bernoulli and the multinomial distribution. We then discuss how to extend the kernel to any mixture model as well as structured mixture models such as HMMs. For generative models that are not straightforward, we show how we can readily use sampling methods to compute the kernel. We then present other implications of the kernel in terms of the regularization and the reproducing kernel Hilbert space. Preliminary experiments are shown for the SCOP protein sequence dataset and the WebKB text dataset. We conclude with discussions.

## 2      A Kernel on Distributions

Given a positive (semi-) definite kernel $K : \mathcal{X} \times \mathcal{X} \mapsto \mathbb{R}$ on the input space $\mathcal{X}$, and examples $x_1, x_2, \ldots, x_m \in \mathcal{X}$ with labels $y_1, y_2, \ldots y_m \in \mathcal{Y}$, kernel based learning algorithms return hypotheses of the form $h(x) = \sum_i \alpha_i K(x_i, x) + b$. Instead of defining a kernel directly between examples $x, x' \in \mathcal{X}$, in this paper we define a class of kernels $K_\rho : \mathcal{P} \times \mathcal{P} \mapsto \mathbb{R}$ on the space of normalized probability distributions over some probability space $\Omega$. Specifically, we define the general **Probability Product Kernel** between distributions $p$ and $p'$ as

$$K_\rho(p, p') = \int_\Omega p(x)^\rho \, p'(x)^\rho \, dx. \tag{1}$$

Examples can be of the form of a single data point $\chi = \{x \in \Omega\}$ or a set of data points $\chi = \{x_1, x_2, \ldots, x_n : x_i \in \Omega\}$. We assume that for each $\chi$ there is an underlying distribution generating data points, and that $\chi$ is a set of independent, identically distributed set of samples from that distribution. We then induce a kernel between $\chi$ and $\chi'$ by forming estimates $p$ and $p'$ of their underlying distributions and computing the probability product kernel between these estimates:

$$\overline{K}_\rho(\chi, \chi') = K_\rho(p, p') = \int_\Omega p(x)^\rho \, p'(x)^\rho \, dx.$$

For any $p_1, p_2, \ldots, p_n \in \mathcal{P}$ and $\alpha_1, \alpha_2, \ldots, \alpha_n \in \mathbb{R}$,

$$\sum_i \sum_j \alpha_i \alpha_j K_\rho(p_i, p_i) = \int_\Omega \left( \sum_i \alpha_i p_i(x)^\rho \right)^2 dx \geq 0 \,, \tag{2}$$

hence $K$ is trivially positive definite on $\mathcal{P}$. This implies that for any deterministic estimation procedure $\Phi : \chi \mapsto p$, $\overline{K}$ is positive definite on $\mathcal{X}$ and hence a suitable kernel for use in learning algorithms in its own right. Additionally, $\overline{K}$ is invariant (symmetric) with respect to permutations of the individual data points comprising $\chi$ and $\chi'$. In the following, we shall omit the bar sign over the induced kernel and may omit the subscript $\rho$ when that does not risk causing confusion.

The space of distributions $\mathcal{P}$ can trivially be embedded in the Hilbert space of functions $L_1(\Omega)$, and the estimation mapping $\Phi : \mathcal{X} \mapsto \mathcal{P}$ can be regarded as the feature map. By appropriate choice of $\Phi$ and $\rho$, a powerful family of kernels can be constructed, combining the advantages of parametric and non-parametric statistical methods. Essentially, the Probability Product Kernel acts as a measure of the degree of similarity or affinity[1] between the two distributions.

For $\rho = 1/2$,

$$K(\chi, \chi') = \int \sqrt{p(x)} \sqrt{p'(x)} \, dx \tag{3}$$

which we shall call the **Bhattacharyya Kernel**, because in the statistics literature it is known as Bhattacharyya's measure of affinity between distributions [4, 1], related to the better known Hellinger's distance

$$H(p, p') = \frac{1}{2} \int \left( \sqrt{p(x)} - \sqrt{p'(x)} \right)^2 dx$$

---

[1] The proposed kernels (probability product, Bhattacharyya and expected likelihood) are not the only possible measures of similarity between distributions. A more customary measure is the Kullback-Leibler divergence $D(p_1 \| p_2) = \int_\Omega p_1(x) \log p_1(x) \, dx - \int_\Omega p_1(x) \log p_2(x) \, dx$ yet it not positive definite, not symmetric, and often not as straightforward to use as a kernel.

by $H = \sqrt{2-2K}$. Note that the Hellinger distance can be seen as a principled symmetric approximation of the Kullback Leibler (KL) divergence and in fact is a bound on KL as shown in [24] where relationships between many information theoretic divergences are characterized. Unlike some divergences, Hellinger naturally implies a symmetric (Bhattacharyya) affinity. Kernels of this form were introduced in [15] and have the special property $K(x, x') = 1$. For $\rho = 1$, we note another interesting configuration where the kernel behaves as the expectation of one distribution under the other:

$$K(x, x') = \int p(x)\, p'(x)\, dx = \mathrm{E}_p[p'(x)] = \mathrm{E}_{p'}[p(x)], \qquad (4)$$

which we shall refer to as the **Expected Likelihood Kernel**. This kernel is particularly easy to evaluate by sampling methods, as we discuss in Section 6.

## 2.1  Frequentist and Bayesian Methods of Estimation

Various strategies may be used to estimate $p(x)$ from the sample $x$. Given a parametric family $\{p(x|\theta)\}_\theta$, the simplest approach is to choose $p(x) = p(x|\hat{\theta})$ corresponding to the maximum likelihood estimator $\hat{\theta} = \arg\max \log p(x|\theta)$, but other point estimators can plugged into $\hat{\theta}$. The Bayesian approach postulates a prior $p(\theta)$ on the parameters and invokes Bayes' rule

$$p(\theta|x) = \frac{p(x|\theta)\, p(\theta)}{\int p(x|\theta)\, p(\theta)\, d\theta}\ .$$

One could use the Maximum a Posteriori estimate $p(x|\hat{\theta}_{\mathrm{MAP}})$, where $\hat{\theta}_{\mathrm{MAP}} = \arg\max p(\theta|x)$, or the true posterior

$$p(x|x) = \int p(x|\theta)\, p(\theta|x)\, d\theta. \qquad (5)$$

In practice, the samples $x_i$ are often very small, or consist of just a single datum, and in this case the Bayesian approach may provide regularization to avoid over-fitting. Both MAP and maximum likelihood estimators can be seen as approximations to the full posterior. Another type of regularization to consider is a form of shrinkage which draws estimates from all training points closer together:

$$\theta = \arg\max\left[\log p(x|\theta) + \lambda \sum_i \log(x_i|\theta)\right].$$

In the following we shall investigate particular estimation methods for which the kernel can be computed in closed form.

**Table 1.** Definition of $\mathcal{A}$ and $\mathcal{K}$ in natural form for some exponential families.

| Family | $\mathcal{A}(X)$ | $\mathcal{K}(\theta)$ | Parameter |
|---|---|---|---|
| Gaussian (mean) | $-\frac{1}{2}X^TX - \frac{D}{2}\log(2\pi)$ | $\frac{1}{2}\theta^T\theta$ | $\theta \in \mathbb{R}^D$ |
| Gaussian (variance) | $-\frac{1}{2}\log(2\pi)$ | $-\frac{1}{2}\log(\theta)$ | $\theta \in \mathbb{R}_+$ |
| Multinomial | $\log(\Gamma(\eta+1)) - \log(\nu)$ | $\eta\log(1 + \sum_{d=1}^{D}\exp(\theta_d))$ | $\theta \in \mathbb{R}^D$ |
| Exponential | $0$ | $-\log(-\theta)$ | $\theta \in \mathbb{R}_-$ |
| Gamma | $-\exp(X) - X$ | $\log\Gamma(\theta)$ | $\theta \in \mathbb{R}_+$ |
| Poisson | $\log(X!)$ | $\exp(\theta)$ | $\theta \in \mathbb{R}$ |

## 3   Exponential Families

A family of distributions is said to form an exponential family [2] if it can be written in the form

$$p(x|\theta) = \exp(\mathcal{A}(x) + \theta^T T(x) - \mathcal{K}(\theta))$$

where the measure is denoted $\mathcal{A}$, the cumulant generating function is denoted $\mathcal{K}$, the so-called sufficient statistics are computed via $T$ and the $\theta$ is the natural parameter of the distribution. Often, $T(x)$ is just $x$.

Many familiar distributions, such as the Normal, Bernoulli, Multinomial, Poisson and Gamma distributions can be written in this form (Table 1). Note that $\mathcal{A}$ and $\mathcal{K}$ are related through the Laplace transform

$$\mathcal{K}(\theta) = \log \int \exp(\mathcal{A}(x) + \theta^T T(x))\, dx$$

since $p(x|\theta)$ is normalized. Furthermore, it is straightforward to show that $\mathcal{K}$ is convex. The maximum likelihood estimate for $\theta$ under this distribution is given by equating the gradient (which we will denote as $\mathcal{G}(\theta)$) of the cumulant generating function to the (empirical) expected value of the sufficient statistic:

$$\mathcal{G}(\theta) \;=\; \frac{\partial\mathcal{K}(\theta)}{\partial\theta} \;=\; \frac{1}{n}\sum_{i=1}^{n}T(x_i)$$

For exponential families, the Bhattacharyya kernel ($\rho = 1/2$) is:

$$K(x, x') = K(p, p') = \int p(x|\theta)^{1/2}p(x|\theta')^{1/2}dx$$
$$= \exp\left(\mathcal{K}\left(\tfrac{1}{2}\theta + \tfrac{1}{2}\theta'\right) - \tfrac{1}{2}\mathcal{K}(\theta) - \tfrac{1}{2}\mathcal{K}(\theta')\right).$$

We can expand the above in terms of the actual data $x$ and $x'$ by using (for instance) their corresponding maximum likelihood settings for $\theta$ and $\theta'$.

It is interesting to note that the above kernel is in general nonlinear for e-family models (and possibly infinite dimensional in feature space) and we expect the choice of generative distribution to greatly influence the resulting kernel formula we obtain (the Fisher kernel for e-family models which is typically linear[2] in $T(x)$ unlike our kernel). For particular families, more explicit formulae also exist for general $\rho$. In the following, we examine some of these cases.

## 3.1  Gaussian Models

The $D$ dimensional Gaussian distribution $p(x) \sim \mathcal{N}(\mu, \Sigma)$ is of the form

$$p(x) = (2\pi)^{-D/2} \, |\Sigma|^{-1/2} \, \exp\left(-\tfrac{1}{2}(x-\mu)^T \Sigma^{-1}(x-\mu)\right)$$

where $\Sigma$ is a positive definite matrix and $|\Sigma|$ denotes its determinant. For a pair of Gaussians $p \sim \mathcal{N}(\mu, \Sigma)$ and $p' \sim \mathcal{N}(\mu', \Sigma')$, completing the square in the exponent gives the general probability product kernel:

$$\begin{aligned}
K_\rho(x, x') = K_\rho(p, p') &= \int_{\mathbb{R}^D} p(x)^\rho p'(x)^\rho dx \\
&= (2\pi)^{(1-2\rho)D/2} \, |\Sigma^\dagger|^{1/2} |\Sigma|^{-\rho/2} \, |\Sigma'|^{-\rho/2} \\
&\quad \exp\left(-\frac{\rho}{2}\mu^T \Sigma^{-1}\mu - \frac{\rho}{2}\mu'^T \Sigma'^{-1}\mu' + \frac{1}{2}\mu^{\dagger T} \Sigma^\dagger \mu^\dagger\right)
\end{aligned}$$

where $\Sigma^\dagger = \left(\rho\Sigma^{-1} + \rho\Sigma'^{-1}\right)^{-1}$ and $\mu^\dagger = \rho\Sigma^{-1}\mu + \rho\Sigma'^{-1}\mu'$. If the covariance is isotropic and fixed: $\Sigma = \sigma^2 I$, this simplifies to:

$$K_\rho(p, p') = 2^{D/2} \, (2\pi\sigma^2)^{(1-2\rho)D/2} \, \exp\left((\rho-1)\frac{\mu^T\mu + \mu'^T\mu'}{2\sigma^2} - \frac{(\mu'-\mu)^T(\mu'-\mu)}{4\sigma^2}\right),$$

which, for $\rho=1$ (the expected likelihood kernel) simply gives the following Gaussian (whose variance is effectively double the original $\Sigma = \sigma^2 I$):

$$K(p, p') = \frac{1}{(4\pi\sigma^2)^{D/2}} \, e^{-\|\mu'-\mu\|^2/(4\sigma^2)}$$

Writing the above explicitly in terms of the maximum likelihood setting $\mu = \bar{x} = \frac{1}{n}\sum_{i=1}^n x_i$ and $\mu' = \bar{x}' = \frac{1}{n'}\sum_{i=1}^{n'} x_i'$, yields the traditional radial basis function (RBF) kernel:

$$K(x, x') = \frac{1}{(4\pi\sigma^2)^{D/2}} \, \exp\left(-\|\bar{x}-\bar{x}'\|^2/(4\sigma^2)\right)$$

Similarly for $\rho=1/2$ (the Bhattacharyya kernel), we also obtain the RBF kernel.

---

[2] Recall the Fisher kernel computed at the dataset's maximum likelihood estimate $\theta^*$ has the following form: $K(x, x') = U_x I_{\theta^*}^{-1} U_{x'}$ where $U_x = \nabla_\theta \log P(x|\theta)|_{\theta^*}$ is the general formula. For the exponential family, this reduces to $U_x = T(x) - \mathcal{G}(\theta^*)$ which is linear in $T(x)$.

## 3.2  Bernoulli and Naive Bayes Models

The Bernoulli distribution $p(x) = \gamma^x (1-\gamma)^{1-x}$ with parameter $\gamma \in [0,1]$, and its $D$ dimensional variant, sometimes referred to as Naive Bayes,

$$p(x) = \prod_{d=1}^{D} \gamma_d^{x_d} (1-\gamma_d)^{1-x_d}$$

with $\gamma \in [0,1]^D$, are used to model binary $x \in \{0,1\}$ or multidimensional binary $x \in \{0,1\}^D$ observations, respectively. The Bhattacharyya kernel between a pair of such distributions

$$K_\rho(x, x') = K_\rho(p, p') = \sum_{x \in \{0,1\}^D} \prod_{d=1}^{D} (\gamma_d \gamma_d')^{\rho x_d} ((1-\gamma_d)(1-\gamma_d'))^{\rho(1-x_d)}$$

factorizes trivially (for any setting of $\rho$) as:

$$K_\rho(p, p') = \prod_{d=1}^{D} \left[ (\gamma_d \gamma_d')^\rho + (1-\gamma_d)^\rho (1-\gamma_d')^\rho \right].$$

## 3.3  Multinomial Models

For discrete count data, when $x = (x_1, x_2, \ldots, x_D)$ is a vector of non-negative integer counts summing to $X$, we can use the multinomial model

$$p(x) = \frac{X!}{x_1! x_2! \ldots x_D!} \alpha_1^{x_1} \alpha_2^{x_2} \ldots \alpha_D^{x_D}$$

with parameter vector $\alpha = (\alpha_1, \alpha_2, \ldots, \alpha_D)$ subject to $\sum_{d=1}^{D} \alpha_d = 1$. The maximum likelihood estimate given observations $x^{(1)}, x^{(2)}, \ldots, x^{(n)}$ is

$$\hat{\alpha}_d = \frac{\sum_{i=1}^{n} x_d^{(i)}}{\sum_{i=1}^{n} \sum_{d=1}^{D} x_d^{(i)}}.$$

For the case $\rho = 1/2$, fixing $X$, the Bhattacharyya kernel $K(x, x') = K(p, p')$ for counts can be computed explicitly using the multinomial theorem, giving:

$$K(p, p') = \sum_{\substack{x = (x_1, x_2, \ldots, x_D) \\ \sum_i x_i = X}} \frac{X!}{x_1! x_2! \ldots x_D!} \prod_{d=1}^{D} (\alpha_d \alpha_d')^{x_d/2} = \left[ \sum_{d=1}^{D} (\alpha_d \alpha_d')^{1/2} \right]^X \quad (6)$$

which is equivalent to the homogeneous polynomial kernel of order $X/2$ between $(\alpha_1, \alpha_2, \ldots, \alpha_D)$ and $(\alpha_1', \alpha_2', \ldots, \alpha_D')$. If we do not wish to hold $X$ constant, we may sum over all its possible values

$$K(p, p') = \sum_{X=0}^{\infty} \left[ \sum_{d=1}^{D} (\alpha_d \alpha_d')^{1/2} \right]^X = \left( 1 - \sum_{d=1}^{D} (\alpha_d \alpha_d')^{1/2} \right)^{-1}$$

or weight each power differently (i.e. a power series expansion). For the general case of $\rho \neq 1/2$, a general formula for discrete multinomial events is available (if $\rho \neq 1/2$ there is no general closed form formula for counts except for $X = 1$ where, as opposed to counts, we really have single mutually exclusive events). This discrete events scenario if arguably more relevant and yields the form:

$$K(p, p') = \sum_{d=1}^{D} (\alpha_d \alpha'_d)^\rho.$$

## 4   Mixture Models

For extensions to a mixture model setting, it is clear that the Bhattacharyya kernel with $\rho = 1/2$ becomes less attractive than the expected likelihood kernel since the square root of a mixture probability is unwieldly[3]. However, with $\rho = 1$, we can easily evaluate any mixture model via the subkernel evaluations over the cross-product of all the hidden states as follows. Consider the case of mixture models $p = \sum_m p(m)p(x|m)$ and $p' = \sum_n p'(n)p'(x|n)$ (with slight abuse of notation). Here, the first mixture is over $M$ configurations while the second is over $N$ configurations. The expected likelihood kernel trivially reduces to a sum of $M \times N$ elementary expected likelihood subkernels $K_{i,j}(x, x')$ for each setting of the hidden variables:

$$K(x, x') = \sum_m \sum_n p(m)p'(n) \int p(x|m)p'(x|n)\, dx = \sum_{m,n} p(m)p'(n) K_{m,n}(x, x').$$

A generalization of the above is possible for $\rho = 2, 3, \ldots$ provided that the higher order kernel $K(p_1, p_2, \ldots, p_{2\rho}) = \int p_1(x)p_2(x) \ldots p_{2\rho}(x)\, dx$ is easy to compute. The above mixture models can be readily applied to our previous solutions for the Gaussian, the multinomial (if we have a single event, i.e. $X = 1$ as opposed to counts) and the Bernoulli since these were computed explicitly for $\rho = 1$. No such solution is readily available for $\rho = 1/2$, and general mixture models of other exponential family forms need to be derived specifically for $\rho = 1$. One heuristic is to simply impute the $\rho = 1/2$ value for the subkernel exponential family evaluations while maintaining $\rho = 1$ for handling the mixture model.

## 5   Hidden Markov Models and Bayesian Networks

Perhaps more interestingly, the above mixture modeling and latent variable framework extends naturally to HMMs and general latent Bayesian networks without considering the brute force cross product of their hidden variables. This is done by taking advantage of conditional independencies in the graphical models. We thus consider new forms of sequence-based or network-based kernels.

---

[3] Approximations may be possible for the setting $\rho = 1/2$ via Jensen's inequality.

Recall, for instance, the general form of an HMM for a sequence of observations $X = (x_1, \ldots, x_T)$ (as discrete or continuous vectors):

$$p(X) = \sum_{S=s_1,\ldots,s_T} p(s_1)\, p(x_1|s_1) \prod_{t=2}^{T} p(s_t|s_{t-1})\, p(x_t|s_t) \, .$$

The expected likelihood kernel is merely the co-emission probability of two different HMMs [19, 14]. We compute a kernel between two sequences $x$ and $x'$ by fitting an HMM to each and summing (or integrating) the product over all possible input sequences $X$. Given an HMM $p(X|\theta)$ with discrete states $s_t$ of cardinality $M$ and an HMM $p(X|\theta')$ with discrete states $u_t$ of cardinality $N$, a brute force evaluation would explore $M^T \times N^T$ configurations of their joint hidden variables and compute a subkernel for each. This is because both HMMs need to be marginalized over their hidden variables $S = (s_1, \ldots, s_T)$ and $U = (u_1, \ldots, u_T)$. However, due to the Markov structure, we need not consider all possible configurations of each HMM as shown below[4]:

$$K(x, x') = \sum_{X=(x_1,\ldots,x_T)} p(X)\, p'(X)$$

$$= \sum_{S} \sum_{U} \prod_{t=1}^{T} p(s_t|s_{t-1}) p'(u_t|u_{t-1}) \sum_{x_t} p(x_t|s_t) p'(x_t|u_t)$$

$$= \sum_{S} \sum_{U} \prod_{t=1}^{T} p(s_t|s_{t-1}) p'(u_t|u_{t-1}) \psi(s_t, u_t) \, .$$

The above indicates only subkernels $K_{s_t,u_t} = \sum_{x_t} p(x_t|s_t) p'(x_t|u_t)$ need to be computed for each of the $T$ $x_t$ variables independently under each setting of their parent variables $s_t$ and $u_t$. Thus, we evaluate $T \times M \times N$ subkernels. These effectively form positive clique functions $\psi(s_t, u_t) = K_{s_t,u_t}$ over the common parents of each $x_t$ variable in the network. It is then straightforward to sum over hidden states of the resulting graphical model via a junction tree algorithm (see Figure 1). The two graphs are coupled via common children in $X$ and cliques over their joint parents emerge as we propagate messages [13].

The above efficient approach extends to general Bayesian networks. These are directed acyclic graphs whose probability distribution factorizes as $P(X) = \prod_i P(x_i|\pi_i)$ where $\pi_i$ is the set of random variables that are parents of the variable $x_i$ in the graph. Some of the variables may be latent while others are in the input or sample space. Ultimately, we only need to compute subkernels over the configurations of the common parents for each subvariable of $X$ in our network. These form positive clique functions that couple the common parents:

$$\psi(\pi_i, \pi_i') = K_{\pi_i, \pi_i'} = \int p(x_i|\pi_i) p'(x_i|\pi_i') dx.$$

---

[4] For brevity in the product over $t$ we assume $p(s_1|s_0) = p(s_1)$ and $p(u_1|u_0) = p(u_1)$.

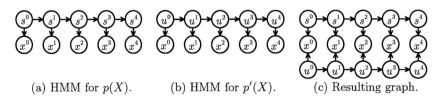

(a) HMM for $p(X)$.      (b) HMM for $p'(X)$.      (c) Resulting graph.

**Fig. 1.** The resulting graphical model from two hidden Markov models as the kernel couples common parents for each node creating undirected edges between them.

The two Bayesian networks need not be the same as long as, when marginalized over their hidden variables, they are distributions over the sample space $X$. Computations grow tractably with the enlarged clique sizes of the joint parents. Furthermore, if the original networks do not have loops, the resulting fused network from the expected likelihood kernel will not give rise to loops itself.

## 6   Sampling Approximation

To accommodate the complete class of generative models (i.e. beyond mixture models and other latent models) when we can no longer find closed form formulas for the probability product kernel for any setting of $\rho$, the expected likelihood kernel can be approximated by sampling methods. This hinges on our ability to generate samples and evaluate their likelihood with a given generative model yet these operations are often assumed to be readily available.

For $\rho=1$ (the expected likelihood kernel) the approximation (c.f. eq. 4)

$$K(x, x') = K(p, p') \approx \frac{\beta}{N} \sum_{\substack{x_i \sim p(x) \\ i=1,...,N}} p'(x_i) + \frac{(1-\beta)}{N'} \sum_{\substack{x'_i \sim p'(x) \\ i=1,...,N'}} p(x'_i)$$

(where $x_1, x_2, \ldots, x_N$ and $x'_1, x'_2, \ldots, x'_{N'}$ are iid samples from $p$ and $p'$ respectively and $\beta \in [0, 1]$ is a parameter of our choosing) is guaranteed to converge to the true value of the kernel by the law of large numbers.

Often unusual distributions occur in the context of generative models. Hence, at least for the expected likelihood kernel, when the analytic approach to calculating $K(x, x')$ fails, we will often find that we can easily and efficiently generate samples and compute the kernel using this approximation. In the case of infinite samples, the above is an exact evaluation of the kernel. However, in practice we can use a finite number of samples yet still consistently obtain a rapidly converging, reliable numerical estimate for the kernel. Furthermore, in the cases where sampling from the distribution is difficult, we may use importance sampling and related methods to compute the kernel.

# 7   Reproducing Kernel Hilbert Spaces

The mapping $\Phi : \mathcal{X} \mapsto \mathcal{P}$ described in Section 2 is not the only Hilbert space representation of $K$ satisfying $K(x, x') = \langle \Phi(x), \Phi(x') \rangle$. The so-called Reproducing Kernel Hilbert Space (RKHS) representation associates with each $x$ the function $\Phi_{\text{RKHS}}(x) = f_x = K(x, \cdot)$. Defining the inner product as $\langle \Phi_{\text{RKHS}}(x),$ $\Phi_{\text{RKHS}}(x') \rangle = K(x, x')$ lends the resulting Hilbert space $\mathcal{H}$ the special property that for any $f \in \mathcal{H}$, $\langle f, f_x \rangle = f(x)$, in particular, $\langle f_x, f_{x'} \rangle = f_x(x') = f_{x'}(x) = K(x, x')$.

Note that by construction of the kernel, $\mathcal{H}$ only contains functions symmetric in $\{x_1, x_2, \dots, x_n\}$, i.e. invariant under permutations of the components of $x$. The above inner product can be related to the standard product between functions by $\langle f, f' \rangle = \int_x (Pf)(x) (Pf')(x) \, dx$ for some regularization operator $P : \mathcal{H} \mapsto \mathcal{H}$ [8].

Kernel based learning algorithms generally return hypotheses of the form $h(x) = \langle h, \Phi(x) \rangle + b = h(x) + b$ where $h \in \mathcal{H}$ and $b \in \mathbb{R}$ together minimize the regularized risk $R_{\text{reg}}(h, b) = \frac{1}{m} \sum_i^m L(y_i, h(x_i)) + \frac{1}{2} \langle h, h \rangle$, where $(x_i)_{i=1}^m$ is the training data, $(y_i)_{i=1}^m$ are the training labels and $L$ is a loss function. Hence, understanding $P$ is the key to understanding the way our kernel implements capacity control, i.e. avoids over-fitting.

For our kernel defined by way of a kernel between distributions, if $\mathcal{P}$ is parameterized by $\theta \in \Theta$, we can introduce an analogous RKHS construction with respect to $\Theta$ by setting $f_\theta(\theta') = K(p_\theta, p_{\theta'})$ and $\langle f_\theta, f_{\theta'} \rangle = K(p_\theta, p_{\theta'})$ leading to $\langle f, f_\theta \rangle = f(\theta)$. A family of distributions indexed by $\theta \in \mathbb{R}^d$ is called a location family if $p_\theta(x) = p'_\theta(x - \theta' + \theta)$. An example of a location family is the family of unit variance Normal distributions on $\mathbb{R}^D$. When our parametric model for computing Bhattacharyya or expected likelihood kernels is chosen from a location family, the kernel will be translation invariant in the sense that

$$K(p_\theta, p_{\theta'}) = \int p_\theta(x) \, p_{\theta'}(x) \, dx = k(\theta' - \theta),$$

where, for simplicity, we have set $\rho = 1$, although the generalization to other values is obvious. We then have

$$k(\theta' - \theta) = \int p_0(x) \, p_0(x - \theta' + \theta) \, dx$$

and by the convolution theorem, the Fourier transform of $k$ will be $\hat{k}(\omega) = [\hat{p}_0(\omega)]^2$. On the other hand, by the RKHS property, $\hat{f}_\theta(\omega) = e^{i\omega\theta} [\hat{p}_0(\omega)]^2$. Hence, we can recover our kernel in the form

$$K(p_\theta, p_{\theta'}) = k(\theta' - \theta) = \int_\Theta (Pf_\theta)(\vartheta) \, (Pf_{\theta'})(\vartheta) \, d\vartheta = \int_{\hat{\Theta}} (\hat{P}\hat{f}_\theta)(\omega) \, \overline{(\hat{P}\hat{f}_{\theta'})(\omega)} \, d\omega$$

by setting $\hat{P} : \hat{f}(\omega) \mapsto \hat{f}(\omega) / |\hat{p}_0(\omega)|$.

The analogous result for "ordinary" stationary kernels has been well known for some time [22]. The significance of the above is that it explains the regularization properties implied by $K(x, x')$ in terms of the base distribution $p_0$ for our

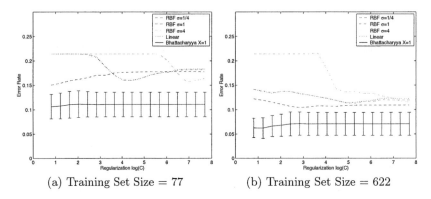

(a) Training Set Size = 77          (b) Training Set Size = 622

**Fig. 2.** SVM error rates (and standard deviation) for the Bhattacharyya kernel for multinomial models as well as error rates for traditional kernels on the WebKB dataset. Various levels of regularization are explored and various training set sizes are examined. Results are shown for 20-fold cross-validation.

choice of models $\mathcal{P}$. For "smooth" distributions, $|\hat{p}_0(\omega)|$ drops off sharply with increasing $|\omega|$. For instance, for the unit Normal distribution, $\hat{p}_0(\omega) \sim e^{-\omega^2/2}$. The above expression for the regularization operator implies that our learning algorithm will correspondingly heavily penalize high frequency Fourier modes in $\hbar$, favoring hypotheses that appear "smooth" in the parameter space $\Theta$.

## 8   Text Experiments

In one experiment we attempted to classify HTML documents for the freely available WebKB dataset using only the text component of each web page and discarding hyperlink information. Text was represented via a bag-of-words description which only tracks the frequency of appearance of words in each document without maintaining information on word orderings. The counts for each document are computed and normalized to sum to unity which corresponds to the maximum likelihood estimate of the document under a multinomial distribution over counts. This effectively gives the multinomial parameter vector $\alpha = (\alpha_1, \alpha_2, \ldots, \alpha_D)$ subject to $\sum_{d=1}^{D} \alpha_d = 1$ for each document.

SVMs were used to discriminate between two categories in the WebKB dataset: faculty web pages and student web pages. We compare the Bhattacharyya kernel for multinomials 6 (with the setting $X = 1$) against the (linear) dot product kernel and the Gaussian RBF kernel. The dataset contains a total of 1641 student web pages and 1124 faculty web pages. The data for each class is further split into 4 universities and 1 miscellaneous category and we performed the usual training and testing split as described by [16, 12] where testing is performed on a held out university. We averaged the results over 20-fold cross-validation and show the error rates for the various kernels in Figure 2.

The figure shows error rates for different sizes of the training set ranging over 77 and 622 training points. Each figure plots the average error rate of each kernel

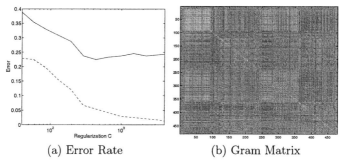

|(a) Error Rate|(b) Gram Matrix|

**Fig. 3.** SVM error rates for the expected likelihood kernel for HMMs. In (a) error under various levels of regularization is shown (dashed line is training error, solid is test error). In (b) the corresponding Gram matrix is shown.

as a function of the SVM regularization parameter $C$. In addition, we show the standard deviation of the error rate for the Bhattacharyya kernel. Even though we only used a single arbitrary setting of $X = 1$ for the Bhattacharyya kernel, we note that it performs better than the linear kernel as well as the RBF at multiple settings of its $\sigma$ parameter (where we attempted $\sigma = \{1/4, 1, 4\}$). Exploring other settings of $X$ (or summing over all settings of $X$ as previously discussed) as well as exploring various settings of $\lambda$ to perform shrinkage-like regularization might further improve our results. Nevertheless, in this preliminary application the Bhattacharyya kernel is promising and the kernel provides a more appropriate affinity measure for count data which reduces error (although similar squashing functions on word frequencies have already been explored in text retrieval).

## 9    Sequence Experiments

In another preliminary experiment, we computed the expected likelihood kernel on HMMs for the SCOP protein sequence dataset [10, 17, 19]. These sequences are variable length discrete emissions from an alphabet of roughly 20 symbols. For simplicity, we only considered a single sub-task in the SCOP experiments, namely distinguishing proteins into negative and positive classes for SCOP sub-families 2.1.1.4 and 2.1. We followed the same train and test split suggested for the SCOP 1.37 PDB-90 database experiments but reduced the size of the training set and testing set to keep computations simple. Therefore, we only used a total of 120 positive and 120 negative training examples and evaluated the resulting SVM on the appropriately held out 120 positive and 120 negative testing examples. The HMMs were trained on each sequence in the dataset. Thus, we have a total of 480 distinct HMM parameters with a fixed topology of 2 hidden states. Subsequently, we computed the Gram matrix over the whole dataset using the approach in Section 5.

Figure 3 shows the error rate under varying levels of regularization for the expected likelihood kernel. In addition, we show the Gram matrix which was verified to be positive definite by a singular value decomposition. One open issue is the potential of the individual HMMs to overfit under maximum likelihood due to the shortness of the sequences and the large alphabet size for protein sequences (this is less problematic with, e.g. gene sequences, which are longer yet have smaller 4-element alphabets). Further experiments and comparisons will be investigated in future work.

## 10   Discussion

We have introduced a new and simple kernel between probability distributions, the Probability Product Kernel, which eschews some of the complexities that kernels based on the Kullback-Leibler divergence often contend with. In special cases, our kernel reduces to Bhattacharyya's measure of similarity or the expected likelihood kernel. Furthermore, as a kernel between distributions the proposed computations are available in closed form for many common distributions and can be efficiently approximated in other cases.

To use the probability product kernel for learning from examples, we proposed the following general procedure. First, select a class of parametric generative models suitable for the data at hand. Then for each data point, estimate the parameters of the generative model using an appropriate frequentist or Bayesian procedure. Finally, for each pair of datapoints, define the kernel between them as the value of the probability product kernel between the corresponding distributions. The resulting kernel between datapoints can then be plugged into the kernel based learning algorithm of choice (SVM, Gaussian Process, Kernel ICA, etc.) for classification, regression or data analysis.

The proposed kernel marries discriminative learning frameworks with flexible generative modeling and can exploit advantages of both parametric an nonparametric approaches. We discussed the form our kernel takes for several members of the exponential family, mixture models, HMMs and Bayesian networks. For the special case of location families we also developed the regularization theory corresponding to our new kernel and discussed the link between the form of the distribution used as generative model and the regularization operator on parameter space. Experiments on text data and sequence data indicate that the approach is feasible and may be promising in practice.

## Acknowledgments

Thanks to A. Jagota and R. Lyngsoe for profile HMM comparison code, C. Leslie and R. Kuang for SCOP data and the referees for important corrections.

## References

1. F Aherne, N. Thacker, and P. Rockett. The Bhattacharyya metric as an absolute similarity measure for frequency coded data. *Kybernetika*, 32(4):1–7, 1997.
2. O. Barndorff-Nielsen. *Information and Exponential Families in Statistical Theory*. John Wiley & Sons, 1978.

3. Y. Bengio and P. Frasconi. Input-output HMM's for sequence processing. *IEEE Transactions on Neural Networks*, 7(5):1231–1249, September 1996.
4. A. Bhattacharyya. On a measure of divergence between two statistical populations defined by their probability distributions. *Bull. Calcutta Math Soc.*, 1943.
5. C. Bishop. *Neural Networks for Pattern Recognition*. Oxford Press, 1996.
6. M. Collins and N. Duffy. Convolution kernels for natural language. In *Neural Information Processing Systems 14*, 2002.
7. C. Cortes, P. Haffner, and M. Mohri. Rational kernels. In *Neural Information Processing Systems 15*, 2002.
8. F. Girosi, M. Jones, and T. Poggio. Regularization theory and neural network architectures. *Neural Computation*, 7:219–269, 1995.
9. D. Haussler. Convolution kernels on discrete structures. Technical Report UCSC-CRL-99-10, University of California at Santa Cruz, 1999.
10. T. Jaakkola and D. Haussler. Exploiting generative models in discriminative classifiers. In *Neural Information Processing Systems 11*, 1998.
11. T. Jaakkola, M. Meila, and T. Jebara. Maximum entropy discrimination. In *Neural Information Processing Systems 12*, 1999.
12. T. Joachims, N. Cristianini, and J. Shawe-Taylor. Composite kernels for hypertext categorisation. In *International Conference on Machine Learning*, 2001.
13. M. Jordan. *Learning in Graphical Models*. Kluwer Academic, 1997.
14. T. Kin, K. Tsuda, and K. Asai. Marginalized kernels for rna sequence data analysis. In *Proc. Genome Informatics*, 2002.
15. R. Kondor and T. Jebara. A kernel between sets of vectors. Machine Learning: Tenth International Conference, ICML 2003, February 2003.
16. J. Lafferty and G. Lebanon. Information diffusion kernels. In *Neural Information Processing Systems*, 2002.
17. C. Leslie, E. Eskin, J. Weston, and W.S. Noble. Mismatch string kernels for svm protein classification. In *Neural Information Processing Systems*, 2002.
18. H. Lodhi, C. Saunders, J. Shawe-Taylor, N. Cristianini, and C. Watkins. Text classification using string kernels. *Journal of Machine Learning Research*, 2:419–444, February 2002.
19. R.B. Lyngso, C.N.S. Pedersen, and H. Nielsen. Metrics and similarity measures for hidden markov models. In *Proceedings of the 7th International Conference on Intelligent Systems for Molecular Biology (ISMB)*, 1999.
20. C. Ong, A. Smola, and R. Williamson. Superkernels. In *Neural Information Processing Systems*, 2002.
21. C. Rathinavelu and L. Deng. Speech trajectory discrimination using the minimum classification error learning. In *IEEE Trans. on Speech and Audio Processing*, 1997.
22. A. J. Smola and B. Schölkopf. From regularization operators to support vector machines. In *Neural Information Processing Systems*, pages 343–349, 1998.
23. N. Tishby, W. Bialek, and F. Pereira. The information bottleneck method: Extracting relevant information from concurrent data. Technical report, NEC Research Institute, 1998.
24. F. Topsoe. Some inequalities for information divergence and related measures of discrimination. *J. of Inequalities in Pure and Applied Mathematics*, 2(1), 1999.
25. S.V.N. Vishawanathan and A.J. Smola. Fast kernels for string and tree matching. In *Neural Information Processing Systems 15*, 2002.
26. C. Watkins. *Advances in kernel methods*, chapter Dynamic Alignment Kernels. MIT Press, 2000.

# Maximal Margin Classification for Metric Spaces

Matthias Hein and Olivier Bousquet

Max Planck Institute for Biological Cybernetics
Spemannstr. 38
72076 Tuebingen, Germany
{matthias.hein,olvier.bousquet}@tuebingen.mpg.de

**Abstract.** In this article we construct a maximal margin classification algorithm for arbitrary metric spaces. At first we show that the Support Vector Machine (SVM) is a maximal margin algorithm for the class of metric spaces where the negative squared distance is conditionally positive definite (CPD). This means that the metric space can be isometrically embedded into a Hilbert space, where one performs linear maximal margin separation. We will show that the solution only depends on the metric, but not on the kernel. Following the framework we develop for the SVM, we construct an algorithm for maximal margin classification in arbitrary metric spaces. The main difference compared with SVM is that we no longer embed isometrically into a Hilbert space, but a Banach space. We further give an estimate of the capacity of the function class involved in this algorithm via Rademacher averages. We recover an algorithm of Graepel *et al.* [6].

## 1 Introduction

It often occurs that real-world data does not have a natural vector space structure. It is rather common, however that a natural (semi)-metric exists on this data that measures pairwise dissimilarities. For the task of classification in a (semi)-metric space $(\mathcal{X}, d)$, where $\mathcal{X}$ is a set and $d$ a (semi)-metric on $\mathcal{X}$, in the absence of other information or prior knowledge, we can only use the metric. Therefore all algorithms for classification on metric spaces assume that the metric is somehow adapted to the classification task. This means heuristically that the inner class distances should be low compared with the distance between the two classes. If the metric fulfills these conditions, then it reveals valuable information for the classification problem. Therefore any kind of transformation of $\mathcal{X}$ that distorts this distance structure (the only information we have on the data) should be avoided.

On the other hand the idea of maximal margin separation of two sets, which is equivalent to finding the distance between the convex hulls of the two sets, is a very appealing geometric concept. Obviously we cannot do this for all (semi)-metric spaces, because in general no linear structure is available. Therefore we employ isometric embeddings into linear spaces which, on the one hand, preserve the distance structure of the input space, which can be seen as our prior

B. Schölkopf and M.K. Warmuth (Eds.): COLT/Kernel 2003, LNAI 2777, pp. 72–86, 2003.

knowledge on the data, and on the other hand, provide us with the linearity to do maximal margin separation.

In the first section we start by reviewing the formulation of the SVM. Then we turn around the normal viewpoint on SVM, and show that the SVM is actually a maximal-margin algorithm for (semi)-metric spaces. This means that one can start with a (semi)-metric space, where the negative squared metric is CPD, then embed this (semi)-metric space isometrically into a Hilbert space, and then use the linear structure of the Hilbert space to do maximal margin separation. We emphasize this point by showing that any CPD kernel, which includes any positive definite (PD) kernel, can be expressed as a sum of the squared (semi)-metric and some function, and only the (semi)-metric enters the solution of the SVM. We also show that the optimization problem and the solution can be written in terms of the (semi)-metric of the input space only.

Unfortunately only the class of metric spaces where the negative square of the distance is CPD can be used in the SVM. We thus provide a generalization of the maximum margin principle to arbitrary metric spaces. The main idea is that any (semi)-metric space can be embedded isometrically into a Banach space. Since a Banach space is linear and the concept of maximal margin separation between convex sets can be extended to Banach spaces [2, 12], it is then possible to write down a maximal margin classification algorithm, which can be applied to arbitrary (semi)-metric spaces. However the solution of this algorithm differs from the SVM solution if applied to the same metric space.

Next, we compare semi-metric spaces to metric spaces with respect to classification. It turns out that a semi-metric space can be seen as a space where certain invariances are realized. Therefore using a semi-metric means that one implicitly uses prior knowledge about invariances of the data. If the data does not share this invariance property, the use of semi-metrics may lead to a bad classifier.

In the end we compare both algorithms in terms of their generalization ability and other properties. In particular, we show that the capacity of the class of functions generated by the proposed embedding is directly related to the metric entropy of the input space.

## 2   SVM as a Maximal Margin Algorithm for Metric Spaces

### 2.1   The RKHS and the Formulation of the SVM

In this section we construct the Reproducing Kernel Hilbert Space (RKHS) and state the problem of the SVM; see [11] for an overview on kernel methods. We first need the definition of the two classes of kernels that are used in the SVM:

**Definition 1.** *A real valued function $k$ on $\mathcal{X} \times \mathcal{X}$ is positive definite (resp. conditionally positive definite) if and only if $k$ is symmetric and*

$$\sum_{i,j}^{n} c_i c_j k(x_i, x_j) \geq 0, \tag{1}$$

*for all $n \in \mathbb{N}$, $x_i \in \mathcal{X}, i = 1, ..., n$, and for all $c_i \in \mathbb{R}, i = 1, ..., n$, (resp. for all $c_i \in \mathbb{R}, i = 1, ..., n$, with $\sum_i^n c_i = 0$).*

Notice that a PD kernel is always CPD.

A PD kernel allows the construction of a RKHS $\mathcal{H}$ in the following way:

1. Define a feature map $\Phi : \mathcal{X} \to \mathbb{R}^{\mathcal{X}}$, $x \to \Phi_x = k(x, .)$
2. Turn it into a vector space by considering all finite linear combinations of $\Phi_{x_i}$: $f = \sum_{i=1}^n \alpha_i \Phi_{x_i}$
3. Turn it into a pre-Hilbert space $\tilde{\mathcal{H}}$ by introducing the dot product:
   $< \Phi_x, \Phi_y > = k(x, y)$
4. Turn it into a Hilbert space $\mathcal{H}$ by completing $\tilde{\mathcal{H}}$

With these definitions, we can describe the SVM algorithm as follows. The input space $\mathcal{X}$ is mapped into a Hilbert space $\mathcal{H}$ via the feature map $\Phi$, and a maximal margin hyperplane is searched for in this space. Hyperplanes correspond to linear continuous functionals on the Hilbert space. The margin of such a hyperplane is defined as twice the distance from the hyperplane to the closest data point. The margin of the optimal hyperplane is equal to the distance between the convex hulls of the two classes [2, 12]. Due to Riesz theorem, each continuous linear functional can be considered as a vector of the Hilbert space (the normal vector of the corresponding hyperplane).

Given a training set $\{(x_i, y_i)\}_{i=1..n}, x_i \in \mathcal{X}, y_i \in \{-1, +1\}$, the optimization problem corresponding to the maximum margin hyperplane can be written as

$$\min_{\alpha} \left\| \sum_{i:y_i=+1} \alpha_i \Phi_{x_i} - \sum_{i:y_i=-1} \alpha_i \Phi_{x_i} \right\|_{\mathcal{H}}^2$$

$$\text{s.th} : \sum_{i:y_i=+1} \alpha_i = \sum_{i:y_i=-1} \alpha_i = 1, \quad \alpha_i \geq 0,$$

which is equivalent to

$$\min_{\alpha} \left\| \sum_i y_i \alpha_i \Phi_{x_i} \right\|_{\mathcal{H}}^2 = \sum_{i,j} y_i y_j \alpha_i \alpha_j k(x_i, x_j)$$

$$\text{s.th} : \sum_i y_i \alpha_i = 0, \quad \sum_i \alpha_i = 2, \quad \alpha_i \geq 0,$$

where the normal vector to the hyperplane is given by

$$w = \sum_{i=1}^n \alpha_i y_i \Phi_{x_i} .$$

## 2.2   The Input Space as a (Semi)-metric Space

Let us first put the standard point of view on SVM like this:

$$\mathcal{X} \xrightarrow{\text{kernel } k} \mathcal{H} \longrightarrow \text{maximal margin separation} \qquad (2)$$

In this section we show by using results which date back to Schoenberg that there exists an equivalent point of view, which allows us to generalize later on to arbitrary metric spaces. It can be summarized with the following scheme:

$$(\mathcal{X}, d) \xrightarrow{\ isometric\ } \mathcal{H} \longrightarrow \text{maximal margin separation} \qquad (3)$$

Recall that a semi-metric is a non-negative symmetric function, $d : \mathcal{X} \times \mathcal{X} \to \mathbb{R}$, which satisfies the triangle inequality and $d(x, x) = 0$ (it is a metric if $d(x, y) = 0 \Rightarrow x = y$).

First we note that through the previous construction of the RKHS, we can induce a semi-metric on $\mathcal{X}$ by the following definition:

$$d^2(x, y) := \|\Phi_x - \Phi_y\|_{\mathcal{H}}^2 = k(x, x) + k(y, y) - 2\,k(x, y). \qquad (4)$$

Note that $d$ will be a metric if $\Phi_x$ is injective (and a semi-metric otherwise). A simple example of a kernel whose feature map is not injective is $k(x, y) = \langle x, y \rangle^2$. We will consider the difference between a metric and semi-metric with respect to classification in a later section.

The next proposition can be found in a different form in Berg et al. (see Proposition 3.2 of [3]). We have rewritten it in order to stress the relevant parts for the SVM.

**Proposition 1.** *Let $\mathcal{X}$ be the input space and $k : \mathcal{X} \times \mathcal{X} \to \mathbb{R}$ a CPD kernel. Then the function $d$, defined as*

$$d(x, y) = \sqrt{k(x, x) + k(y, y) - 2\,k(x, y)}, \qquad (5)$$

*is a semi-metric on $\mathcal{X}$ such that $-d^2$ is CPD. All CPD kernels $k : \mathcal{X} \times \mathcal{X} \to \mathbb{R}$ are generated by a (semi)-metric $d$ (with $-d^2$ CPD) in the sense that there exists a function $g : \mathcal{X} \to \mathbb{R}$ such that*

$$k(x, y) = -\frac{1}{2} d^2(x, y) + g(x) + g(y), \qquad (6)$$

*and any kernel of this form induces the semi-metric $d$ via Equation (5).*

This proposition states that semi-metrics $d$, where $-d^2$ is CPD, are up to a function $f$ equivalent to the whole class of CPD kernels. Next, one can show that the obtained metric space can be isometrically embedded into a Hilbert space (see also Proposition 3.2 of [3]).

**Proposition 2.** *Let $(\mathcal{X}, d)$ be the semi-metric space defined in Proposition 1.*

*(i) It can be isometrically embedded into a Hilbert space $\mathcal{H}$;*
*(ii) if $k$ is bounded, $\mathcal{H}$ can be continuously embedded into $(C_b(\mathcal{X}), \|\cdot\|_\infty)$.*

Moreover, the class of semi-metric spaces defined in Proposition 1 consists of all metric spaces that can be embedded isometrically into a Hilbert space, which is a result of Schoenberg [9]. Schoenberg proved this theorem already in 1938 and introduced the notion of PD and CPD functions. We are getting back to the roots of the kernel industry.

**Theorem 1.** *A necessary and sufficient condition for a (semi)-metric space $(\mathcal{X}, d)$ to be isometrically embeddable into a Hilbert space is that $\tilde{k}(x, y) = -\frac{1}{2}d(x, y)^2$ is CPD.*

We now try to show the relevance of these results for the SVM. This theorem together with Proposition 1 gives the full equivalence of the standard (2) and our (3) point of view on SVM. This can be summarized as follows: defining a CPD kernel on the input space $\mathcal{X}$ is equivalent to defining a unique (semi)-metric $d$ on the input space $\mathcal{X}$ via (5); and in the other direction any (semi)-metric $d$ on $\mathcal{X}$, where $-d^2$ is CPD, defines a non-unique PD kernel via (6) and (7), such that $(\mathcal{X}, d)$ can be embedded isometrically into the corresponding RKHS.

We will also use these results to show in the next section that the SVM classifier only depends on the metric, so that all the kernels of the form (6) are equivalent from the SVM point of view.

In the rest of this section we give the proofs of the propositions.

*Proof (Proposition 1).* If $k$ is CPD but not PD, we consider for an arbitrary $x_0 \in \mathcal{X}$,

$$\tilde{k}(x, y) := k(x, y) - k(x, x_0) - k(x_0, y) + k(x_0, x_0). \tag{7}$$

This kernel is PD if and only if $k$ is CPD (see [3]) and $\tilde{k}(x, x) + \tilde{k}(y, y) - 2\tilde{k}(x, y) = k(x, x) + k(y, y) - 2k(x, y)$, so that $\tilde{k}$ defines the same semi-metric $d$ as $k$ (via Equation (5)). Note that $k(x, y) = \hat{k}(x, y) + g(x) + g(y)$ is CPD, if $\hat{k}$ is CPD:

$$\sum_{i,j} c_i c_j k(x_i, x_j) = \sum_{i,j} c_i c_j \hat{k}(x_i, x_j) + 2 \sum_j c_j \sum_i c_i g(x_i)$$

$$= \sum_{i,j} c_i c_j \hat{k}(x_i, x_j) \geq 0,$$

where the second term vanishes because $\sum_i c_i = 0$.

Thus from (5) we get that $-d^2$ is CPD with $f(x) = -\frac{1}{2}k(x, x)$. On the other hand, if we start with a semi-metric $d$, where $-\frac{1}{2}d^2(x, y)$ is CPD, then $k$ defined by (6) is CPD and $k$ induces $d$ as a semi-metric via (5). Now if two CPD kernels $k$ and $\hat{k}$ induce the same (semi)-metric, then they fulfill $k(x, y) = \hat{k}(x, y) + \frac{1}{2}[(k(x, x) - \hat{k}(x, x)) + (k(y, y) - \hat{k}(y, y))]$. Thus they differ by a function $g : \mathcal{X} \to \mathbb{R}$ with $g(.) = \frac{1}{2}(k(., .) - \hat{k}(., .))$. $\qquad\square$

*Proof (Proposition 2).* We have shown in the proof of Proposition 1 that each CPD kernel $k$ defines a PD kernel $\tilde{k}$ via (7), which induces the same (semi)-metric. With the PD kernel $\tilde{k}$ we define a reproducing kernel Hilbert space $\mathcal{H}$ as above, with associated feature map $\Phi$ ($\Phi_x = \tilde{k}(x, \cdot)$). It trivially defines an isometry.

We note that the kernel is always continuous with respect to the (semi)-metric it induces:

$$|k(x, y) - k(x', y')| = |<k_x, k_y - k_{y'}> + <k_x - k_{x'}, k_{y'}>|$$

$$\leq \|k_x\| \|k_y - k_{y'}\| + \|k_x - k_{x'}\| \|k_{y'}\|$$

$$= \sqrt{k(x, x)}\sqrt{d(y, y')} + \sqrt{k(y', y')}\sqrt{d(x, x')}.$$

Furthermore, if the kernel is bounded, then for any $f \in \mathcal{H}$,

$$|f(x)| = |\langle f, k(x, \cdot)\rangle| \leq \|f\|_{\mathcal{H}} \sqrt{k(x, x)}$$

so that $f$ is bounded, and similarly

$$|f(x) - f(y)| \leq \|f\| \, \|k(x, \cdot) - k(y, \cdot)\| = \|f\| \, d(x, y),$$

hence $f$ is continuous.                                                    □

## 2.3   Formulation of the SVM in Terms of the (Semi)-metric

It was already recognized by Schölkopf [10] that the SVM relies only on distances in the RKHS. This can be seen directly from the optimization problem (2), where we minimize the euclidean distance of the convex hulls in $\mathcal{H}$, which is translation invariant. Schölkopf showed that this implies one can use the bigger class of CPD kernels in SVM. One can show this by directly plugging in the expression of the PD kernel in terms of a CPD kernel from (7) into the optimization problem. All terms except the CPD kernel $k(x, y)$ part cancel out because of the constraints.

We have shown in the last section that a (semi)-metric lies at the core of every CPD kernel, and that there exists a whole class of CPD kernels which induce the same (semi)-metric on $\mathcal{X}$. Applying the results of the last section we go one step further and show that the SVM is a maximal-margin algorithm for a certain class of (semi)-metric spaces.

**Theorem 2.** *The SVM method can be applied to the class of (semi)-metric spaces $(\mathcal{X}, d)$, where $-d^2$ is CPD. The (semi)-metric space $(\mathcal{X}, d)$ is embedded isometrically via the corresponding positive definite kernel into a Hilbert space. Using the linear structure of the Hilbert space, the two sets of points, corresponding to the two classes, are linearly separated so that the margin between the two sets is maximized. The distance between the convex hulls of the two classes is twice the margin. The solution of the SVM does not depend on the specific isometric embedding $\Phi$, nor on the corresponding choice of the kernel. The optimization problem and the solution can be completely expressed in terms of the (semi)-metric $d$ of the input space,*

$$\min_{\alpha} \left\| \sum_i y_i \alpha_i \Phi_{x_i} \right\|_{\mathcal{H}}^2 = -\frac{1}{2} \sum_{i,j} y_i y_j \alpha_i \alpha_j d^2(x_i, x_j)$$

$$s.th : \sum_i y_i \alpha_i = 0, \quad \sum_i \alpha_i = 2, \quad \alpha_i \geq 0.$$

*The solution can be written as*

$$f(x) = -\frac{1}{2} \sum_i y_i \alpha_i d^2(x_i, x) + c.$$

*Proof.* By combining the Proposition 1 and the theorem of Schoenberg, we showed the equivalence of the standard view on SVM and the view of an isometric embedding of the (semi)-metric space $(\mathcal{X}, d)$ into a Hilbert space $\mathcal{H}$. Therefore the SVM is restricted to metric spaces $(\mathcal{X}, d)$, where $-d^2$ is CPD. The statement about the equivalence of maximal-margin separation and the distance between the convex hulls of the two classes can be found in [2, 12]. Now the expression of the optimization problem of the SVM in terms of the (semi)-metric follows from (6);

$$\left\| \sum_i y_i \alpha_i \Phi_{x_i} \right\|_{\mathcal{H}}^2 = \sum_{i,j} y_i y_j \alpha_i \alpha_j k(x_i, x_j)$$

$$= \sum_{i,j} y_i y_j \alpha_i \alpha_j [-\frac{1}{2} d^2(x_i, x_j) + g(x_i) + g(x_j)]$$

$$= -\frac{1}{2} \sum_{i,j} y_i y_j \alpha_i \alpha_j d^2(x_i, x_j),$$

where $f$ drops out due to the constraint $\sum_i y_i \alpha_i = 0$.

The solution expressed in terms of a CPD kernel $k$ can also be expressed in terms of the (semi)-metric by using (6):

$$f(x) = \sum_i y_i \alpha_i k(x_i, x) + b = \sum_i y_i \alpha_i [-\frac{1}{2} d(x_i, x)^2 + g(x_i) + g(x)]$$

$$= -\frac{1}{2} \sum_i y_i \alpha_i d^2(x_i, x) + c,$$

where again $\sum_i y_i \alpha_i g(x)$ drops out and $c = b + \sum_i y_i \alpha_i g(x_i)$, but $c$ can also be directly calculated with the average value of $b = y_j + \frac{1}{2} \sum_i y_i \alpha_i d^2(x_i, x_j)$, where $j$ runs over all indices with $\alpha_j > 0$. Since neither the specific isometric embedding $\Phi$ nor a corresponding kernel $k$ enter the optimization problem or the solution, the SVM only depends on the (semi)-metric.  $\square$

The kernel is sometimes seen as a similarity measure. The last theorem, however, shows that this property of the kernel does not enter the algorithm. On the contrary the (semi)-metric as a dissimilarity measure of the input space only enters the algorithm. Nevertheless it seems to be easier to construct a CPD kernel than a function $d(x, y)$, where $d$ is a (semi)-metric and $-d^2$ is CPD, but one should remain aware that only the induced (semi)-metric has an influence on the solution, and therefore compare two different kernels through their induced (semi)-metrics.

One can use the high ambiguity in the kernel to chose from the whole class of kernels which induce the same (semi)-metric (6) that which is computationally the cheapest, because the solution does not change as is obvious from the last theorem. As a final note we would like to add that the whole argumentation on the isometric embedding of the (semi)-metric space into a Hilbert space also applies to the soft-margin-formulation of the SVM. The reformulation in terms of reduced convex hulls is a little bit tricky, and we refer to [2, 12] for this issue.

# 3   Maximal Margin Algorithm for Arbitrary (Semi)-metric Spaces

The maximal margin algorithm where the space one embeds the data isometrically is a Hilbert space, which is equivalent to the SVM, is limited to a subclass of all metric spaces. In this section we will treat arbitrary metric spaces trying to follow the same steps described at the end of the last section. We first define an isometric embedding of an arbitrary metric space into a Banach space. We then use the fact that in Banach spaces the problem of a maximal margin hyperplane is equivalent to finding the distance between the convex hulls. With this property we are able to formulate the problem and discuss the algorithm. The scheme we use can be stated as follows

$$(\mathcal{X}, d) \xrightarrow{\ isometric\ } (\bar{D}, \|.\|_\infty) \subset (C_b(\mathcal{X}), \|.\|_\infty) \longrightarrow \text{maximal margin separation}$$

where $\bar{D}$ is a Banach space of (continuous and bounded) functions defined on $\mathcal{X}$ (see definitions below).

## 3.1   Isometric Embedding of a General Metric Space into a Banach Space

In this section we construct a pair of dual Banach spaces. The metric space $\mathcal{X}$ will be isometrically embedded into the first one, and the second one will be used to define continuous linear functionals (i.e. hyperplanes).

Let $(\mathcal{X}, d)$ be a compact[1] metric space and denote by $C_b(\mathcal{X})$ the Banach space of continuous and bounded functions on $\mathcal{X}$ endowed with the supremum norm. The topological dual of $C_b(\mathcal{X})$ is the space of Baire measures $\mathcal{M}(\mathcal{X})$ with the measure norm $\|\mu\| = \int_\mathcal{X} d\mu_+ - \int_\mathcal{X} d\mu_-$ (where $\mu_+$ and $\mu_-$ are respectively the positive and negative parts of $\mu$).

Consider an arbitrary $x_0 \in \mathcal{X}$ and define the following maps

$$\begin{aligned} \Phi : \mathcal{X} &\to \mathbb{R}^\mathcal{X} & \text{and} \quad \Psi : \mathcal{X} &\to \mathbb{R}^\mathcal{X} \\ x &\mapsto \Phi_x := d(x, \cdot) - d(x_0, \cdot) & x &\mapsto \Psi_x := d(\cdot, x) - d(x_0, x) \,. \end{aligned}$$

Let $D = \mathrm{span}\{\Phi_x : x \in \mathcal{X}\}$ and $E = \mathrm{span}\{\Psi_x : x \in \mathcal{X}\}$ be the linear spans of the images of the maps $\Phi$ and $\Psi$.

We will show that $\Phi$ defines an isometric embedding of the metric space $\mathcal{X}$ into the closure $\bar{D}$ of $D$ (with respect to the infinity norm). Moreover, $\bar{D}$ is a Banach space whose dual is isometrically isomorphic to (hence can be identified with) the completion $\bar{E}$ of $E$ with respect to the norm

$$\|e\|_E = \inf \left\{ \sum_{i \in I} |\beta_i| \; : \; e = \sum_{i \in I} \beta_i \psi_{x_i}, \; x_i \in \mathcal{X}, \; |I| < \infty \right\} .$$

The following results formalize the above statements.

---

[1] Compactness is needed for the analysis but the algorithm we present in the next section works without this assumption since it performs an approximation on a finite set.

**Lemma 1.** $\Phi$ *is an isometry from* $(\mathcal{X}, d)$ *into the Banach space* $(\bar{D}, \|\cdot\|_\infty) \subset (C_b(\mathcal{X}), \|\cdot\|_\infty)$.

*Proof.* We have $\|\Phi_x\|_\infty \leq d(x, x_0) < \infty$ and $|\Phi_x(y) - \Phi_x(y')| \leq |d(x,y) - d(x,y')| + |d(x_0, y) - d(x_0, y')| \leq 2d(y, y')$, so that $\Phi_x \in C_b(\mathcal{X})$. In addition $\|\Phi_x - \Phi_y\|_\infty = \|d(x, \cdot) - d(y, \cdot)\|_\infty \leq d(x, y)$ and the supremum is attained at $x$ and $y$. Hence, $\Phi$ is an isometry from $(\mathcal{X}, d)$ into $(D, \|\cdot\|_\infty)$ which is a subspace of $C_b(\mathcal{X})$. Defining $\bar{D}$ as the closure of $D$ in $C_b(\mathcal{X})$ which is a Banach space yields that $\bar{D}$ is complete. $\qquad\square$

Note that, as an isometry, $\Phi$ is continuous, and $x_0$ is mapped to the origin of $D$.

**Lemma 2.** $\|\cdot\|_E$ *is a norm on* $E$.

*Proof.* It is easy to see that $\|\cdot\|_E$ satisfies the properties of a semi-norm. To prove that it is a norm, consider $e \in E$ such that $\|e\|_E = 0$. Then there exist sequences $(I_n), (\beta_{i,n})$ and $x_{i,n}$ such that $e = \sum_{i \in I_n} \beta_{i,n} \Psi_{x_{i,n}}$ and $\sum_{i \in I_n} |\beta_{i,n}| \to 0$. As a consequence, for any $x \in \mathcal{X}$, $|e(x)| = |\sum_{i \in I_n} \beta_{i,n} \Psi_{x_{i,n}}(x)| \leq d(x, x_0) \sum_{i \in I_n} |\beta_{i,n}|$, so that taking the limit $n \to \infty$ we obtain $e(x)$. This proves $e \equiv 0$ and concludes the proof. $\qquad\square$

As a normed space, $E$ can be completed with respect to the norm $\|\cdot\|_E$ into a Banach space $\bar{E}$ with extended norm $\|\cdot\|_{\bar{E}}$. Let $\bar{D}'$ be the topological dual of $\bar{D}$ with dual norm $\|\cdot\|_{\bar{D}'}$.

**Theorem 3.** $(\bar{E}, \|\cdot\|_{\bar{E}})$ *is isometrically isomorphic to* $(\bar{D}', \|\cdot\|_{\bar{D}'})$.

*Proof.* Let $\bar{D}^\perp = \{d' \in \bar{D}' : \langle d', d \rangle = 0, \forall d \in D\}$ and consider the space $\mathcal{M}(\mathcal{X})/\bar{D}^\perp$ of equivalence classes of measures that are identical on the subspace $\bar{D}$ and endow this space with the quotient norm $\|\tilde{\mu}\| = \inf\{\|\mu\| : \mu \in \tilde{\mu}\}$. Then by theorem 4.9 of [8] $(\bar{D}', \|\cdot\|_{\bar{D}'})$ is isometrically isomorphic to $(\mathcal{M}(\mathcal{X})/\bar{D}^\perp, \|\cdot\|)$.

Recall that the span of measures with finite support is dense in $\mathcal{M}(\mathcal{X})$, so the same is true for the quotient space $\mathcal{M}(\mathcal{X})/\bar{D}^\perp$. The linear map $\sigma : E \to \mathrm{span}\{\delta_x : x \in \mathcal{X}\}/\bar{D}^\perp$ defined as $\sigma(\Psi_x) = \delta_x|_D$ induces an isometric isomorphism between $E$ and $\mathrm{span}\{\delta_x : x \in \mathcal{X}\}/\bar{D}^\perp$, which can be extended to the closure of these spaces. $\qquad\square$

### 3.2 Duality of Maximal Margin Hyperplanes and Distance of Convex Hulls in Banach Spaces

We have stated in the beginning that the two problems of finding the distance between two disjoint convex hulls and finding a maximal margin hyperplane are equivalent for Banach spaces. This can be seen by the following theorem (see [12] for a proof), where we define $co(T) = \{\sum_{i \in I} \alpha_i x_i | \sum_{i \in I} \alpha_i = 1, x_i \in T, \alpha_i \in \mathbb{R}^+, |I| < \infty\}$.

**Theorem 4.** *Let* $T_1$ *and* $T_2$ *be two finite sets of points in a Banach space* $B$ *then if* $co(T_1) \cap co(T_2) = \emptyset$

$$d(co(T_1), co(T_2)) = \inf_{y \in co(T_1), z \in co(T_2)} \|y - z\| = \sup_{x' \in B'} \frac{\inf_{y \in T_1, z \in T_2} <x', y - z>}{\|x'\|}.$$

We now rewrite the right term by using the definition of the infimum:

$$\inf_{x' \in B', c, d} \frac{\|x'\|}{c - d}$$

$$\text{subject to:} \quad x'(y) \geq c, \quad \forall y \in T_1, \quad x'(z) \leq d, \quad \forall z \in T_2.$$

Now subtract $-\frac{c+d}{2}$ from both inequalities, and define the following new quantities: $b = \frac{c+d}{d-c}$, $w' = \frac{2}{c-d}x'$, $T = T_1 \cup T_2$. Then one gets the standard form:

$$\min_{w' \in B', b} \|w'\| \tag{8}$$

$$\text{subject to:} \quad y_i(w'(x_i) + b) \geq 1 \quad \forall x_i \in T = T_1 \cup T_2.$$

## 3.3   The Algorithm

We now plug our isometric embedding into the equation (8) to get the optimization problem for maximal margin classification in arbitrary (semi)-metric spaces:

$$\min_{w' \in \bar{D}', b \in \mathbb{R}} \|w'\|$$

$$\text{subject to:} \quad y_j(w'(\Phi_{x_j}) + b) \geq 1 \quad \forall x_j \in T.$$

We are using the isometric isomorphism between $\bar{D}'$ and $\bar{E}$ to state it equivalently in $\bar{E}$. By density of $E$ in $\bar{E}$ and by continuity of the norm and of the duality-product, the minimum on $\bar{E}$ can be replaced by an infimum on $E$:

$$\inf_{e \in E, b} \|e\| = \inf_{m \in \mathbb{N}, \, x_1, \ldots, x_m \in \mathcal{X}^m, \, b} \sum_{i=1}^{m} |\beta_i|$$

$$\text{s.t. } y_j\left(\sum_{i=1}^{m} \beta_i \psi_{x_i}(\Phi_{x_j}) + b\right) = y_j\left(\sum_{i=1}^{m} \beta_i(d(x_j, x_i) - d(x_0, x_i)) + b\right) \geq 1 \, \forall x_j \in T.$$

Notice that the infimum may not be attained in $E$. Unlike in the SVM case there seems to be no guarantee such as a representer theorem that the solution can be expressed in terms of points in the training set only.

In order to make the problem computationally tractable, we have to restrict the problem to a finite dimensional subspace of $E$. A simple way to do this is to consider only the subspace of $E$ generated by a finite subset $Z \in \mathcal{X}, |Z| = m$. We are free to choose the point $x_0$, so we choose it as $x_0 = z_1, z_1 \in Z$. Since the problem stated in Theorem 4 is translation invariant, this choice has no influence on the solution. This leads to the following optimization problem:

$$\min_{\beta_i, b} \sum_{i=1}^{m} |\beta_i|$$

$$\text{subject to:} \quad y_j\left(\sum_{i=1}^{m} \beta_i(d(x_j, z_i) - d(z_1, z_i)) + b\right) \geq 1, \quad \forall x_j \in T.$$

In general, a convenient choice for $Z$ is $Z = T$. In a transduction setting one can use for $Z$ the union of labelled and unlabelled data.

As $\sum_{i=1}^{m} \beta_i d(z_1, z_i)$ does not depend on $j$, due to translation invariance, we can put it in the constant $b$ and solve the equivalent problem:

$$\min_{\beta_i, c} \sum_{i=1}^{m} |\beta_i|$$

$$\text{subject to:} \quad y_j \left( \sum_{i=1}^{m} \beta_i \, d(x_j, z_i) + c \right) \geq 1, \quad \forall x_j \in T.$$

The corresponding decision function is given by

$$f(x) = \text{sgn} \left( \sum_{i=1}^{m} \beta_i \, d(x, z_i) + c \right).$$

The above optimization problem can be transformed into a linear programming problem, and is easily solvable with standard methods. Note that if we take $Z = T$ we recover the algorithm proposed by Graepel et al. [6]. We also note that it is easily possible to obtain a soft-margin version of this algorithm. In this case there still exists the equivalent problem of finding the distance between the reduced convex hulls [2, 12]. This algorithm was compared to other distance based classifiers by Pekalska et al. in [7] and showed good performance.

Using Theorem 4, we can also formulate the problem (in dual form) as follows

$$\min_{\alpha_i \in \mathbb{R}} \sup_{x \in \mathcal{X}} \left| \sum_{i=1}^{n} y_i \alpha_i d(x, x_i) \right|$$

$$\text{subject to:} \quad \sum_{i=1}^{n} y_i \alpha_i = 0, \ \sum_{i=1}^{n} \alpha_i = 2, \alpha_i \geq 0.$$

Unfortunately, there is no simple relationship between primal $(\beta_i)$ and dual $(\alpha_i)$ variables which allows to compute the decision function from the $\alpha_i$. However, it is interesting to notice that the approximation of the primal problem which consists in looking for a solution generated by a finite subset $Z$ corresponds, in dual form, to restricting the supremum to $Z$ only. This means for finite metric spaces the problem can be solved without approximation.

## 4    Semi-metric Spaces Compared to Metric Spaces for Classification

In the last two sections we made no distinction between semi-metric and metric spaces. In fact there is a connection between both of them which we want to clarify in this section.

**Theorem 5.** *Let $(\mathcal{X}, d)$ be a (semi)-metric space and $\sim$ be the equivalence relation defined by $x \sim y \Leftrightarrow d(x, y) = 0$. Then $(\mathcal{X}/\sim, d)$ is a metric space, and if $-d^2(x, y)$ is a CPD Kernel and $k$ a PD Kernel on $\mathcal{X}$ which induces $d$ on $\mathcal{X}$, then $-d^2$ is also a CPD Kernel and $k$ a PD kernel on $(\mathcal{X}/\sim, d)$.*

*Proof.* The property $d(x, y) = 0$ defines an equivalence relation on $\mathcal{X}$, $x \sim y \iff d(x, y) = 0$. Symmetry follows from the symmetry of $d$, and transitivity $x \sim y, y \sim z \Rightarrow x \sim z$ follows from the triangle inequality $d(x, z) \leq d(x, y) + d(y, z) = 0$. Then $d(x, y)$ is a metric on the quotient space $\mathcal{X}/\sim$ because all points with zero distance are identified, so

$$d(x, y) = 0 \iff x = y,$$

and obviously symmetry and the triangle inequality are not affected by this operation. $d$ is well-defined because if $x \sim z$ then $|d(x, .) - d(z, .)| \leq d(x, z) = 0$.

The fact that $-d^2$ is CPD on $\mathcal{X}/\sim$ follows from the fact that all possible representations of equivalence classes are points in $\mathcal{X}$ and $-d^2$ is CPD on $\mathcal{X}$. It is also well defined because if $x \sim z$ then

$$|d^2(x, .) - d^2(z, .)| \leq d(x, z)|(d(x, .) + d(z, .)| = 0.$$

The argumentation that $k$ is also PD on $\mathcal{X}/\sim$ is the same as above. It is well defined because if $x \sim x'$ then $\|\Phi_x - \Phi_{x'}\| = 0$, so that actually $k(x, \cdot) = k(x', \cdot)$ (since for all $y \in \mathcal{X}$, $|k(x, y) - k(x', y)| \leq \|\Phi_x - \Phi_{x'}\| \|\Phi_y\|$). $\square$

The equivalence relation defined in Theorem 5 can be seen as defining a kind of global invariance on $\mathcal{X}$. For example in the SVM setting when we have the kernel $k(x, y) = \langle x, y \rangle^2$, the equivalence relation identifies all points which are the same up to a reflection. This can be understood as one realization of an action of the discrete group $D = \{-e, +e\}$ on $\mathbb{R}^n$, so this kernel can be understood as a kernel on $\mathbb{R}^n/D$.

Assume now that there are no invariances in the data and two different points $x \neq y$ with different labels are such that $d(x, y) = 0$. Then they cannot be separated by any hyperplane. This means that using semi-metrics implicitly assumes invariances in the data, which may not hold.

## 5    Generalization Bounds Using Rademacher Averages

In this section we calculate the Rademacher averages corresponding to the function classes of the two algorithms presented. The Rademacher average is a measure of capacity of a function class with respect to classification, and can be used to derive upper bounds on the error of misclassification (see e.g. Theorems 7 and 11 from [1]).

Let $P$ be a probability distribution on $\mathcal{X} \times \{\pm 1\}$ and consider a training sample $T = \{(X_i, Y_i)_{i=1}^n\}$ drawn according to $P^n$. Let $\widehat{R}_n$ be the empirical Rademacher average of the function class $\mathcal{F}$, defined as

$$\widehat{R}_n(\mathcal{F}) = E_\sigma \sup_{f \in \mathcal{F}} |\frac{1}{n} \sum_{i=1}^n \sigma_i f(x_i)|,$$

where $\sigma$ are Rademacher variables and $E_\sigma$ denotes the expectation conditional to the sample (i.e. with respect to the $\sigma_i$ only). The function classes we are interested in are those of continuous linear functionals on Hilbert or Banach spaces. More precisely, we consider the following two classes. For a given PD kernel $k$, let $\tilde{k}$ be defined as $\tilde{k}(x, \cdot) = k(x, \cdot) - k(x_0, \cdot)$ [2] and $\mathcal{H}$ be the associated RKHS for $\tilde{k}$. We define $\mathcal{F}_1 = \{g : g \in \mathcal{H}, \|g\| \le B\}$. Also, with the notations of the previous section, we define $\mathcal{F}_2 = \{e \in \bar{E}, \|e\| \le B\}$.

**Theorem 6.** *With the above notation, we have*

$$\widehat{R}_n(\mathcal{F}_1) \le \frac{B}{n}\sqrt{\sum_{i=1}^{n} d(x_i, x_0)^2}\,.$$

*where $d(x_i, x_0) = \|k(x_i, \cdot) - k(x_0, \cdot)\|_\mathcal{H}$ is the distance induced by the kernel on $\mathcal{X}$. Also, there exists a universal constant $C$ such that*

$$\widehat{R}_n(\mathcal{F}_2) \le \frac{CB}{\sqrt{n}} \int_0^\infty \sqrt{\log N(\frac{\varepsilon}{2}, \mathcal{X}, d)}\, d\varepsilon.$$

*Proof.* We first compute the Rademacher average for $\mathcal{F}_2$:

$$\widehat{R}_n(\mathcal{F}_2) = E_\sigma \sup_{e \in \bar{E}, \|e\| \le B} \left| \frac{1}{n}\sum_{i=1}^{n} \sigma_i \langle e, \Phi_{x_i} \rangle \right| = E_\sigma \sup_{e \in \bar{E}, \|e\| \le B} \left| \left\langle e, \frac{1}{n}\sum_{i=1}^{n} \sigma_i \Phi_{x_i} \right\rangle \right|$$

$$= \frac{B}{n} E_\sigma \left\| \sum_{i=1}^{n} \sigma_i \Phi_{x_i} \right\|_\infty = \frac{B}{n} E_\sigma \sup_{x \in \mathcal{X}} \left| \sum_{i=1}^{n} \sigma_i \Phi_{x_i}(x) \right| \tag{9}$$

We will use Dudley's upper bound on the empirical Rademacher average [5] which gives that there exists an absolute constant $C$ for which the following holds: for any integer $n$, any sample $\{x_i\}_{i=1}^n$ and every class $\mathcal{F}_2$,

$$\widehat{R}_n(\mathcal{F}_2) \le \frac{C}{\sqrt{n}} \int_0^\infty \sqrt{\log N(\varepsilon, \mathcal{F}_2, L_2(\mu_n))}\, d\varepsilon, \tag{10}$$

where $\mu_n$ is the empirical measure supported on the sample and $N(\varepsilon, \mathcal{F}_2, L_2(\mu_n))$ are the covering numbers of the function class $\mathcal{F}_2$ with respect to $L_2(\mu_n)$.

In order to apply this result of Dudley, we notice that the elements of $\mathcal{X}$ can be considered as functions defined on $\mathcal{X}$. Indeed, for each $x \in \mathcal{X}$, one can define the function $f_y : x \mapsto \Phi_x(y)$. We denote by $\mathcal{G}$ the class of all such functions, i.e. $\mathcal{G} = \{f_y : y \in \mathcal{X}\}$. Then using (9), we get

$$\widehat{R}_n(\mathcal{F}_2) = B\, E_\sigma \sup_{x \in \mathcal{X}} \left| \frac{1}{n}\sum_{i=1}^{n} \sigma_i \Phi_{x_i}(x) \right| = B\, \widehat{R}_n(\mathcal{G}). \tag{11}$$

---

[2] where $k(x_0, \cdot)$ corresponds to the origin in $\mathcal{H}$ and is introduced to make the comparison with the space $\bar{E}$ easier.

We now try to upper bound the empirical $L_2$-norm of $\mathcal{G}$:

$$\|f_{y_1} - f_{y_2}\|_{L_2(\mu_n)} \leq \|f_{y_1} - f_{y_2}\|_{L_\infty(\mu_n)} = \max_{x_i \in T} |\Phi_{x_i}(y_1) - \Phi_{x_i}(y_2)|$$

$$= \max_{x_i \in T} |d(x_i, y_1) - d(x_i, y_2) + d(x_0, y_2) - d(x_0, y_1)|$$

$$\leq 2d(y_1, y_2). \tag{12}$$

Combining (10) and (12) we get

$$\widehat{R}_n(\mathcal{G}) \leq \frac{C}{\sqrt{n}} \int_0^\infty \sqrt{\log N(\frac{\varepsilon}{2}, \mathcal{X}, d)} d\varepsilon$$

This gives the first result. Similarly, we have

$$\widehat{R}_n(\mathcal{F}_1) = \frac{B}{n} E_\sigma \left\| \sum_{i=1}^n \sigma_i(k(x_i, .) - k(x_0, .)) \right\|_{\mathcal{H}} \leq \frac{B}{n} \sqrt{\sum_{i=1}^n d(x_i, x_0)^2},$$

where the second step follows from Jensen's inequality (applied to the concave function $\sqrt{\cdot}$). □

Notice that a trivial bound on $\widehat{R}_n(\mathcal{F}_2)$ can be found from (9) and

$$\left| \sum_{i=1}^n \sigma_i(d(x_i, x) - d(x_0, x)) \right| \leq \sum_{i=1}^n d(x_i, x_0),$$

which gives the upper bound

$$\widehat{R}_n(\mathcal{F}_2) \leq \frac{B}{n} \sum_{i=1}^n d(x_i, x_0),$$

which is also an upper bound on $\widehat{R}_n(\mathcal{F}_1)$. However, this upper bound is loose since if all the data is at approximately the same distance from $x_0$ (e.g. on a sphere), then this quantity does not decrease with $n$.

## 6   Conclusion and Perspectives

In this article we have built a general framework for the generation of maximal margin algorithms for metric spaces. We first use an isometric embedding of the metric space into a Banach space followed by a maximal margin separation. It turned out that the SVM uses the same principle, but is restricted to the special class of metric spaces that allow an isometric embedding into a Hilbert space. In the following diagram the structure of both algorithms is shown:

$$RKHS \xrightarrow{continuous} C(\mathcal{X})$$

$$(\mathcal{X}, d) \xrightarrow{isometric} \nearrow$$
$$\searrow$$

$$(\bar{D}, \|.\|_\infty) \xrightarrow{isometric} (C_b(\mathcal{X}), \|.\|_\infty)$$

The structural difference between the two algorithms is the space into which they embed. Since there exist several isometric embeddings of metric spaces into normed linear spaces, this raises two questions. First what is their difference in terms of mathematical structure, and second what are the consequences for a learning algorithm, especially its generalization ability?

Further on in the SVM case we shifted the problem of choosing a kernel on $\mathcal{X}$ to the problem of choosing a metric on $\mathcal{X}$. Maybe one can construct a measure on the space of metrics for a given space $\mathcal{X}$, which can be calculated on the data, that captures the heuristic notion of "small inner class distance and big distance between the classes".

## Acknowledgements

We would like to thank Ulrike von Luxburg, Bernhard Schölkopf and Arthur Gretton for helpful discussions and comments during the preparation of this article.

## References

1. P. L. Bartlett, S. Mendelson, *Rademacher and Gaussian Complexities: Risk Bounds and Structural Results*, JLMR, **3**, 463-482, (2002).
2. K. P. Bennett,E. J. Bredensteiner, *Duality and Geometry in SVM classifiers*, Proceedings of the Seventeenth International Conference on Machine Learning, 57-64, (2000).
3. C. Berg, J.P.R. Cristensen, P. Ressel, *Harmonic Analysis on Semigroups*, Springer Verlag, New York, (1984).
4. F. Cucker, S. Smale, *On the Mathematical Foundations of Learning*, Bull. Amer. Math. Soc., **39**, 1-49, (2002).
5. R. M. Dudley, *Universal Donsker Classes and Metric Entropy*, Ann. Prob.,**15**,1306-1326, (1987).
6. T. Graepel, R. Herbrich, B. Schölkopf, A. Smola, P. Bartlett, K.R. Müller, K. Obermayer and R. Williamson, *Classification on proximity data with LP-machines*, International Conference on Artificial Neural Networks, 304-309, (1999).
7. E. Pekalska, P. Paclik, R.P.W. Duin, *A Generalized Kernel Approach to Dissimilarity-based Classification*, Journal of Machine Learning Research, **2**, 175-211, (2001).
8. W. Rudin, *Functional Analysis*, McGraw Hill, (1991).
9. I. J. Schoenberg, *Metric Spaces and Positive Definite Functions*, TAMS, **44**, 522-536, (1938).
10. B. Schölkopf, *The Kernel Trick for Distances*, Neural Information Processing Systems (NIPS), **13**, (2000).
11. B. Schölkopf, A. J. Smola *Learning with Kernels*, MIT Press, MA, Cambridge, (2002).
12. D. Zhou, B. Xiao, H. Zhou, R. Dai, *Global Geometry of SVM Classifiers*, Technical Report 30-5-02, AI Lab, Institute of Automation, Chinese Academy of Sciences, (2002).

# Maximum Margin Algorithms
# with Boolean Kernels

Roni Khardon[1,*] and Rocco A. Servedio[2,**]

[1] Department of Computer Science, Tufts University
Medford, MA 02155, USA
roni@cs.tufts.edu
[2] Department of Computer Science, Columbia University
New York, NY 10027, USA
rocco@cs.columbia.edu

**Abstract.** Recent work has introduced Boolean kernels with which one can learn over a feature space containing all conjunctions of length up to $k$ (for any $1 \leq k \leq n$) over the original $n$ Boolean features in the input space. This motivates the question of whether maximum margin algorithms such as support vector machines can learn Disjunctive Normal Form expressions in the PAC learning model using this kernel. We study this question, as well as a variant in which structural risk minimization (SRM) is performed where the class hierarchy is taken over the length of conjunctions.

We show that such maximum margin algorithms do not PAC learn $t(n)$-term DNF for any $t(n) = \omega(1)$, even when used with such a SRM scheme. We also consider PAC learning under the uniform distribution and show that if the kernel uses conjunctions of length $\tilde{\omega}(\sqrt{n})$ then the maximum margin hypothesis will fail on the uniform distribution as well. Our results concretely illustrate that margin based algorithms may overfit when learning simple target functions with natural kernels.

## 1 Introduction

### 1.1 Background

Maximum margin algorithms, notably Support Vector Machines (SVM) [3], have received considerable attention in recent years (see e.g. [21] for an introduction). In their basic form, SVM learn linear threshold hypotheses and combine two powerful ideas. The first idea is to learn using the linear separator which achieves the *maximum margin* on the training data rather than an arbitrary consistent hypothesis. The second idea is to use an implicit feature expansion by a *kernel function*. The kernel $K : X \times X \to \mathbb{R}$, where $X$ is the original space of examples, computes the inner product in the expanded feature space. Given a kernel $K$

* This work has been partly supported by NSF Grant IIS-0099446.
** Much of this work was done while supported by an National Science Foundation Mathematical Sciences Postdoctoral Research Fellowship.

B. Schölkopf and M.K. Warmuth (Eds.): COLT/Kernel 2003, LNAI 2777, pp. 87–101, 2003.

which corresponds to some expanded feature space, the SVM hypothesis $h$ is (an implicit representation of) the maximum margin linear threshold hypothesis over this expanded feature space rather than the original feature space. SVM theory implies that if the kernel $K$ is efficiently computable then it is possible to efficiently construct this maximum margin hypothesis $h$ and that $h$ itself is efficiently computable. Several on-line algorithms have also been proposed which iteratively construct large margin hypotheses in the feature space, see e.g. [6].

Another major focus of research in learning theory is the question of whether various classes of Boolean functions can be learned by computationally efficient algorithms. The canonical open question in this area is whether there exist efficient algorithms in Valiant's PAC learning model [23] for learning Boolean formulas in Disjunctive Normal Form, or DNF. This question has been open since the introduction of the PAC model nearly twenty years ago, and has been intensively studied by many researchers (see e.g. [1, 2, 4, 7, 8, 10, 12, 14, 15, 18, 22, 24, 25]).

## 1.2  Can SVMs Learn DNF?

In this paper we analyze the performance of maximum margin algorithms when used with Boolean kernels to learn DNF formulas. Several authors [11, 17, 26, 13] have recently proposed a family of kernel functions $K_k : \{0,1\}^n \times \{0,1\}^n \to \mathbb{N}$, where $1 \leq k \leq n$, such that $K_k(x,y)$ computes the number of (monotone or unrestricted) conjunctions of length (exactly or up to) $k$ which are true in both $x$ and $y$. This is equivalent to expanding the original feature space of $n$ Boolean features to include all such conjunctions[1]. Since linear threshold elements can represent disjunctions, one can naturally view any DNF formula as a linear threshold function over this expanded feature space. It is thus natural to ask whether the $K_k$ kernel maximum margin learning algorithms are good algorithms for learning DNF.

Additional motivation for studying DNF learnability with the $K_k$ kernels comes from recent progress on the DNF learning problem. The fastest known algorithm for PAC learning DNF is due to Klivans and Servedio [12]; it works by explicitly expanding each example into a feature space of monotone conjunctions and explicitly learning a consistent linear threshold function over this expanded feature space. Since the $K_k$ kernel enables us to do such expansions implicitly in a computationally efficient way, it is natural to investigate whether the $K_k$-kernel maximum margin algorithm yields a computationally efficient algorithm for PAC learning DNF.

We note that it is easily seen that standard convergence bounds on large margin classifiers do not imply that the $K_k$ kernel maximum margin algorithm

---

[1] This Boolean kernel is similar to the well known polynomial kernel in that all monomials of length up to $k$ are represented. The main difference is that the polynomial kernel assigns weights to monomials which depend on certain binomial coefficients; thus the weights of different monomials can differ by an exponential factor. In the Boolean kernel all monomials have the same weight.

is an efficient algorithm for PAC learning DNF. Indeed, the bound given by, e.g., Theorem 4.18 of [21] only implies nontrivial generalization error for the $K_k$ kernel algorithm if a sample of size $n^{\Omega(k)}$ is used, and with such a large sample the computational advantage of using the $K_k$ kernel is lost. However, such upper bounds do not imply that the $K_k$ kernel maximum margin algorithm must have poor generalization error if run with a smaller sample. The situation is analogous to that of [19] where the generalization error of the Perceptron and Winnow algorithms were studied. For both Perceptron and Winnow the standard bounds gave only an exponential upper bound on the number of examples required to learn various classes, but a detailed algorithm-specific analysis gave positive PAC learning results for Perceptron and negative PAC results for Winnow for the problems considered. Analogously, in this paper we perform detailed algorithm-specific analyses for the $K_k$ kernel maximum margin algorithms.

### 1.3 Previous Work

Khardon *et al.* constructed a simple Boolean function and an example sequence and showed that this sequence causes the $K_n$ kernel perceptron algorithm (i.e. the Perceptron algorithm run over a feature space of all $2^n$ monotone conjunctions) to make exponentially many mistakes [11]. The current paper differs in several ways from this earlier work: we study the maximum margin algorithm rather than Perceptron, we consider PAC learning from a random sample rather than online learning, and we analyze the $K_k$ kernels for all $1 \leq k \leq n$.

### 1.4 Our Results

Throughout this paper we study the kernels corresponding to all monotone monomials of length up to $k$, which we denote by $K_k$. In addition to maximum margin algorithms we also consider a natural scheme of structural risk minimization (SRM) that can be used with this family of Boolean kernels. In SRM, given a hierarchy of classes $C_1 \subseteq C_2 \subseteq \ldots$, one learns with each class separately and uses a cost function combining the complexity of the class with its observed accuracy to choose the final hypothesis. The cost function typically balances various criteria such as the observed error and the (bound on) generalization error. A natural scheme here is to use SRM over the classes formed by $K_k$ with $k = 1, \ldots, n$ [2].

We prove several negative results which establish strong limitations on the ability of maximum margin algorithms to PAC learn DNF formulas (or other simple Boolean classes) using the monomial kernels. Our first result says essentially that for any $t(n) = \omega(1)$, for all $k = 1, \ldots, n$ the $K_k$ kernel maximum margin algorithm cannot PAC learn $t(n)$-term DNF. More precisely, we prove

**Result 1:** Let $t(n) = \omega(1)$ and let $\epsilon = \frac{1}{4 \cdot 2^{t(n)}}$. There is a $O(t(n))$-term monotone DNF over $t(n)$ relevant variables, and a distribution $\mathcal{D}$ over $\{0,1\}^n$ such that

---

[2] This is standard practice in experimental work with the polynomial kernel, where typically small values of $k$ are tried (e.g. 1 to 5) and the best is chosen.

for all $k \in \{1, \ldots, n\}$ the $K_k$ maximum margin hypothesis has error larger than $\epsilon$ (with overwhelmingly high probability over the choice of a polynomial size random sample from $\mathcal{D}$).

Note that this result implies that the $K_k$ maximum margin algorithms fail even when combined with SRM *regardless of the cost function*. This is simply because the maximum margin hypothesis has error $> \epsilon$ for all $k$, and hence the final SRM hypothesis must also have error $> \epsilon$.

While our accuracy bound in the above result is small (it is $o(1)$ since $t(n) = \omega(1)$), a simple variant of the construction used for Result 1 also proves:

**Result 2:** Let $f(x) = x_1$ be the target function. There is a distribution $\mathcal{D}$ over $\{0,1\}^n$ such that for any $k = \omega(1)$ the $K_k$ maximum margin hypothesis has error at least $\frac{1}{2} - 2^{-n^{\Omega(1)}}$ (with overwhelmingly high probability over the choice of a polynomial size random sample from $\mathcal{D}$).

Thus any attempt to learn using monomials of non-constant size can provably lead to overfitting. Note that for any $k = \Theta(1)$, standard bounds on maximum margin algorithms show that the $K_k$ kernel algorithm can learn $f(x) = x_1$ from a polynomial size sample.

Given these strong negative results for PAC learning under arbitrary distributions, we next consider the problem of PAC learning monotone DNF under the uniform distribution. This is one of the few frameworks in which some positive results have been obtained for learning DNF from random examples only (see e.g. [5, 20]). In this scenario a simple variant of the construction for Result 1 shows that learning must fail if $k$ is too small:

**Result 3:** Let $t(n) = \omega(1)$ and $\epsilon = \frac{1}{4 \cdot 2^{t(n)}}$. There is a $O(t(n))$-term monotone DNF over $t(n)$ relevant variables such that for all $k < t(n)$ the $K_k$ maximum margin hypothesis has error at least $\epsilon$ (with probability 1 over the choice of a random sample from the uniform distribution).

On the other hand, we also show that the $K_k$ algorithm fails under the uniform distribution for large $k$:

**Result 4:** Let $f(x) = x_1$ be the target function. For any $k = \tilde{\omega}(\sqrt{n})$, the $K_k$ maximum margin hypothesis will have error $\frac{1}{2} - 2^{-\Omega(n)}$ with probability at least 0.028 over the choice of a polynomial size random sample from the uniform distribution.

Note that there is a substantial gap between the "low" values of $k$ (for which learning is guaranteed to fail) and the "high" values of $k$ (for which we show that learning fails with constant probability). We feel that it is of significant interest to characterize the performance of the $K_k$ maximum margin algorithm under the uniform distribution for these intermediate values of $k$; a discussion of this point is given in Section 5.

Finally, we note here that some of our results can be adapted to give similar negative results for the standard polynomial kernel.

## 2   Preliminaries

We consider learning Boolean functions over the Boolean cube $\{0,1\}^n$ so that $f : \{0,1\}^n \to \{0,1\}$. It is convenient to consider instead the range $\{-1,1\}$ with 0 mapped to $-1$ and 1 mapped to 1. This is easily achieved by the transformation $f'(x) = 1 - 2f(x)$ and since we deal with linear function representations this can be done without affecting the results. For the rest of the paper we assume this representation.

Our arguments will refer to $L_1$ and $L_2$ norms of vectors. We use the notation $|x| = \sum |x_l|$ and $\|x\| = \sqrt{\sum x_l^2}$.

**Definition 1.** *Let $h : \mathbb{R}^N \to \{-1,1\}$ be a linear threshold function $h(x) = sign(W \cdot x - \theta)$ for some $W \in \mathbb{R}^N, \theta \in \mathbb{R}$. The margin of $h$ on $\langle z, b \rangle \in \mathbb{R}^N \times \{-1,1\}$ is*

$$m_h(z,b) = \frac{b(W \cdot z - \theta)}{\|W\|}.$$

Note that $|m_h(z,b)|$ is the Euclidean distance from $z$ to the hyperplane $W \cdot x = \theta$.

**Definition 2.** *Let $S = \{\langle x^i, b_i \rangle\}_{i=1,\dots,m}$ be a set of labeled examples where each $x^i \in \mathbb{R}^N$ and each $b_i \in \{-1,1\}$. Let $h(x) = sign(W \cdot x - \theta)$ be a linear threshold function. The margin of $h$ on $S$ is*

$$m_h(S) = \min_{\langle x,b \rangle \in S} m_h(x,b).$$

*The maximum margin classifier for $S$ is the linear threshold function $h(x) = sign(W \cdot x - \theta)$ such that*

$$m_h(S) = \max_{W' \in \mathbb{R}^N, \theta' \in \mathbb{R}} \min_{\langle x,b \rangle \in S} \frac{b(W' \cdot x - \theta')}{\|W'\|}. \tag{1}$$

*The quantity (1) is called the margin of $S$ and is denoted $m_S$.*

Note that $m_S > 0$ iff $S$ is consistent with some linear threshold function. If $m_S > 0$ then the maximum margin classifier for $S$ is unique [21].

Let $\phi$ be a transformation which maps $\{0,1\}^n$ to $\mathbb{R}^N$ and let $K : \{0,1\}^n \times \{0,1\}^n \to \mathbb{R}$ be the corresponding kernel function $K(x,y) = \phi(x) \cdot \phi(y)$. Given a set of labeled examples $S = \{\langle x^i, b_i \rangle\}_{i=1,\dots,m}$ where each $x^i$ belongs to $\{0,1\}^n$ we write $\phi(S)$ to denote the set of transformed examples $\{\langle \phi(x^i), b_i \rangle\}_{i=1,\dots,m}$.

We refer to the following learning algorithm as the $K$-*maximum margin learner*:

- The algorithm first draws a sample $S = \{\langle x^i, f(x^i) \rangle\}_{i=1,\dots,m}$ of $m = \mathrm{poly}(n)$ labeled examples from some fixed probability distribution $\mathcal{D}$ over $\{0,1\}^n$; here $f : \{0,1\}^n \to \{-1,1\}$ is the unknown function to be learned.
- The algorithm's hypothesis is $h : \{0,1\}^n \to \{-1,1\}, h(x) = sign(W \cdot \phi(x) - \theta)$ where $sign(W \cdot x - \theta)$ is the maximum margin classifier for $\phi(S)$. Without loss of generality we assume that $W$ is normalized, that is $\|W\| = 1$. We also assume that $S$ contains both positive and negative examples since otherwise the maximum margin classifier is not defined.

SVM theory tells us that if $K(x, y)$ can be computed in poly$(n)$ time then the $K$-maximum margin learning algorithm runs in poly$(n, m)$ time and the output hypothesis $h(x)$ can be evaluated in poly$(n, m)$ time [21].

Our goal is to analyze the PAC learning ability of various kernel maximum margin learning algorithms. Recall (see e.g. [9]) that a PAC learning algorithm for a class $\mathcal{C}$ of functions over $\{0, 1\}^n$ is an algorithm which runs in time polynomial in $n$ and $\frac{1}{\delta}, \frac{1}{\epsilon}$ where $\delta$ is a confidence parameter and $\epsilon$ is an accuracy parameter. We assume here, as is the case throughout the paper, that each function in $\mathcal{C}$ has a description of size poly$(n)$. Given access to random labelled examples $\langle x, f(x) \rangle$ for any $f \in \mathcal{C}$ and any distribution $\mathcal{D}$ over $\{0, 1\}^n$, with probability at least $1 - \delta$ a PAC learning algorithm must output an efficiently computable hypothesis $h$ such that $\Pr_{x \in \mathcal{D}}[h(x) \neq f(x)] \leq \epsilon$. If an algorithm only satisfies this criterion for a particular distribution such as the uniform distribution on $\{0, 1\}^n$, we say that it is a uniform distribution PAC learning algorithm.

Let $\rho_k(n) = \sum_{i=1}^{i=k} \binom{n}{i}$. Note that the number of nonempty monotone conjunctions (i.e. monomials) of size at most $k$ on $n$ variables is $\rho_k(n)$. For $x \in \{0, 1\}^n$ we write $\phi_k(x)$ to denote the $\rho_k(n)$-dimensional vector $(x_T)_{T \subseteq \{1,\ldots,n\}, 1 \leq |T| \leq k}$ where $x_T = \prod_{i \in T} x_i$, i.e. the components of $\phi_k(x)$ are all monotone conjunctions of the desired size. We note that for an example $x \in \{0, 1\}^n$, the $L_1$ norm of the expanded example $\phi_k(x)$ is $|\phi_k(x)| = \rho_k(|x|)$.

For $x, y \in \{0, 1\}^n$ we write $x \cdot y$ to denote $\sum_{i=1}^n x_i y_i$, i.e. the number of bits which are 1 in both $x$ and $y$.

**Definition 3.** *We write $K_k(x, y)$ to denote $\phi_k(x) \cdot \phi_k(y)$. We refer to $K_k$ as the $k$-monomials kernel.*

The following theorem shows that the $k$-monomial kernels are easy to compute:

**Theorem 1 ([11]).** *For all $1 \leq k \leq n$ we have $K_k(x, y) = \sum_{i=1}^k \binom{x \cdot y}{i}$.*

We will frequently use the following observation which is a direct consequence of the Cauchy-Schwarz inequality:

**Observation 1** *If $U \in \mathbb{R}^{N_1}$ with $\|U\| = L$ and $I \subseteq \{1, \ldots, N_1\}$, $|I| = N_2$, then $\sum_{i \in I} |U_i| \leq L \cdot \sqrt{N_2}$.*

As a consequence of Observation 1 we have that if $\rho_k(n) = N_1$ is the number of features in the expanded feature space and $|\phi_k(x)| = \rho_k(|x|) = N_2$, then $U \cdot \phi_k(x) \leq L \cdot \sqrt{N_2}$.

## 3    Distribution-Free Non-learnability

We give a DNF and a distribution which are such that the $k$-monomials kernel fails to learn, for all $1 \leq k \leq n$. The DNF we consider is a read once monotone DNF over $t(n)$ variables where $t(n) = \omega(1)$ and $t(n) = O(\log n)$. In fact our results hold for any $t(n) = \omega(1)$ but for concreteness we use $t(n) = \log n$ as a running example. We have

$$f(x) = (x_1 \cdots x_{4\ell^2}) \vee (x_{4\ell^2+1} \cdots x_{8\ell^2}) \vee \cdots \vee (x_{4\ell^3-4\ell^2+1} \cdots x_{4\ell^3}) \qquad (2)$$

where $4\ell^3 = t(n) = \log n$ so that the number of terms $\ell = \Theta(t(n)^{1/3}) = \Theta((\log n)^{1/3})$. For the rest of this section $f(x)$ will refer to the function defined in Equation (2) and $\ell$ to its size parameter.

A *polynomial threshold function* is defined by a multivariate polynomial $p(x_1, \ldots, x_n)$ with real coefficients. The output of the polynomial threshold function is 1 if $p(x_1, \ldots, x_n) \geq 0$ and $-1$ otherwise. The degree of the function is simply the degree of the polynomial $p$. Note that any hypothesis output by the $K_k$ kernel maximum margin algorithm must be a polynomial threshold function of degree at most $k$. Minsky and Papert [16] (see also [12]) gave the following lower bound on polynomial threshold function degree for DNF:

**Theorem 2.** *Any polynomial threshold function for $f(x)$ in Equation (2) must have degree at least $\ell$.*

The distribution $\mathcal{D}$ on $\{0,1\}^n$ we consider is the following:

- With probability $\frac{1}{2}$ the distribution outputs $0^n$.
- With probability $\frac{1}{2}$ the distribution outputs a string $x \in \{0,1\}^n$ drawn from the following product distribution $\mathcal{D}'$: the first $t(n)$ bits are drawn uniformly, and the last $n - t(n)$ bits are drawn from the product distribution which assigns 1 to each bit with probability $\frac{1}{n^{1/3}}$.

For small values of $k$ the result is representation based and does not depend on the sample drawn:

**Lemma 1.** *If the maximum margin algorithm uses the kernel $K_k$ for $k < \ell$ when learning $f(x)$ under $\mathcal{D}$ then its hypothesis has error greater than $\epsilon = \frac{1}{4 \cdot 2^{t(n)}} = \frac{1}{4n}$.*

*Proof.* If hypothesis $h$ has error at most $\epsilon = \frac{1}{4 \cdot 2^{t(n)}}$ under $\mathcal{D}$ then clearly it must have error at most $\frac{1}{2 \cdot 2^{t(n)}}$ under $\mathcal{D}'$. Since we are using the kernel $K_k$, the hypothesis $h$ is some polynomial threshold function of degree at most $k$ which has error $\tau \leq \frac{1}{2 \cdot 2^{t(n)}}$ under $\mathcal{D}'$. So there must be some setting of the last $n - t(n)$ variables which causes $h$ to have error at most $\tau$ under the uniform distribution on the first $t(n)$ bits. Under this setting of variables the hypothesis is a degree-$k$ polynomial threshold function on the first $t(n)$ variables. By Minsky and Papert's theorem, this polynomial threshold function cannot compute the target function exactly, so it must be wrong on at least one setting of the first $t(n)$ variables. But under the uniform distribution, every setting of those variables has probability at least $\frac{1}{2^{t(n)}}$. This contradicts $\tau \leq \frac{1}{2 \cdot 2^{t(n)}}$. $\qquad \square$

For larger values of $k$ (in fact for all $k = \omega(1)$) we show that the maximum margin hypothesis will with high probability overfit the sample. The following definition captures typical properties of a sample from distribution $\mathcal{D}$:

**Definition 4.** *A sample $S$ is a $\mathcal{D}$-typical sample if*

- *The sample includes the example $0^n$.*
- *Any nonzero example $x$ in the sample has $0.99n^{2/3} \leq |x| \leq 1.01n^{2/3}$.*
- *Every pair of positive and negative examples $x^i$, $x^j$ in $S$ satisfies $x^i \cdot x^j \leq 1.01n^{1/3}$.*

We are interested in cases where a polynomial size sample is used by the algorithm. The following two lemmas hold by standard Chernoff bound arguments:

**Lemma 2.** *For $m = poly(n)$, with probability $1 - 2^{-n^{\Omega(1)}}$ a random i.i.d. sample of $m$ draws from $\mathcal{D}$ is a $\mathcal{D}$-typical sample.*

**Definition 5.** *Let $S$ be a sample. The set $Z(S)$ includes all positive examples $z$ such that every example $x$ in $S$ satisfies $x \cdot z \leq 1.01n^{1/3}$.*

**Lemma 3.** *Let $S$ be a $\mathcal{D}$-typical sample of size $m = poly(n)$ examples. Then $\Pr_{\mathcal{D}}[z \in Z(S)|f(z) = 1] = 1 - 2^{-n^{\Omega(1)}}$.*

We now show that for a $\mathcal{D}$-typical sample one can achieve a very large margin:

**Lemma 4.** *Let $S$ be a $\mathcal{D}$-typical sample. Then the maximum margin $m_S$ satisfies*

$$m_S \geq M_{h'} \equiv \frac{1}{2} \cdot \frac{\rho_k(.99n^{2/3}) - m\rho_k(1.01n^{1/3})}{\sqrt{m\rho_k(1.01n^{2/3})}}$$

*Proof.* We exhibit an explicit linear threshold function $h'$ which has margin at least $M_{h'}$ on the data set. Let $h'(x) = \text{sign}(W' \cdot \phi(x) - \theta')$ be defined as follows:

- $W'_T = 1$ if $T$ is active in some positive example;
- $W'_T = 0$ if $T$ is not active in any positive example.
- $\theta'$ is the value that gives the maximum margin on $\phi_k(S)$ for this $W'$, i.e. $\theta'$ is the average of the smallest value of $W' \cdot \phi_k(x^{i,+})$ and the largest value of $W' \cdot \phi_k(x^{j,-})$.

Since each positive example $x^+$ in $S$ has at least $.99n^{2/3}$ ones, we have $W' \cdot \phi(x^+) \geq \rho_k(.99n^{2/3})$. Since each positive example has at most $1.01n^{2/3}$ ones, each positive example in the sample contributes at most $\rho_k(1.01n^{2/3})$ ones to $W'$, so $\|W'\| \leq \sqrt{m\rho_k(1.01n^{2/3})}$. Finally, since each negative example $x^-$ in the sample and each positive example $x^+$ in the sample share at most $1.01n^{1/3}$ ones, for any $x^-$ in the sample $W' \cdot \phi(x^-) \leq m\rho_k(1.01n^{1/3})$. Putting these conditions together, we get that the margin of $h'$ on the sample is at least

$$\frac{1}{2} \cdot \frac{\rho_k(.99n^{2/3}) - m\rho_k(1.01n^{1/3})}{\sqrt{m\rho_k(1.01n^{2/3})}}$$

as desired.                                                                $\square$

**Lemma 5.** *If $S$ is a $\mathcal{D}$-typical sample, then the threshold $\theta$ in the maximum margin classifier for $S$ is at least $M_{h'}$.*

*Proof.* Let $h(x) = \text{sign}(W \cdot \phi(x) - \theta)$ be the maximum margin hypothesis. Since $\|W\| = 1$ we have

$$\theta = \frac{\theta}{\|W\|} = m_h(\phi_k(0^n), -1) \geq m_{h'}(S) \geq M_{h'}$$

where the second equality holds because $W \cdot \phi(0^n) = 0$ and the last inequality is by Lemma 4. □

**Lemma 6.** *If the maximum margin algorithm uses the kernel $K_k$ for $k = \omega(1)$ when learning $f(x)$ under $\mathcal{D}$ then with probability $1 - 2^{-n^{\Omega(1)}}$ its hypothesis has error greater than $\epsilon = \frac{1}{4 \cdot 2^{t(n)}} = \frac{1}{4n}$.*

*Proof.* Let $S$ be the sample used for learning and let $h(x) = \text{sign}(W \cdot \phi_k(x) - \theta)$ be the maximum margin hypothesis. It is well known (see e.g. Proposition 6.5 of [21]) that the maximum margin weight vector $W$ is a linear combination of the support vectors, i.e. of certain examples $\phi_k(x)$ in the sample $\phi_k(S)$. Hence the only coordinates $W_T$ of $W$ that can be nonzero are those corresponding to features (conjunctions) $T$ such that $x_T = 1$ for some example $x$ in $S$.

By Lemma 2 we have that with probability $1 - 2^{-n^{\Omega(1)}}$ the sample $S$ is $\mathcal{D}$-typical. Consider any $z \in Z(S)$. It follows from the above observations on $W$ that $W \cdot \phi_k(z)$ is a sum of at most $m\rho_k(1.01n^{1/3})$ nonzero numbers, and moreover the sum of the squares of these numbers is at most 1. Thus by Observation 1 we have that $W \cdot \phi_k(z) \leq \sqrt{m\rho_k(1.01n^{1/3})}$. The positive example $z$ is erroneously classified as negative by $h$ if $\theta > W \cdot \phi_k(z)$; by Lemma 5 this inequality holds if

$$\frac{1}{2} \cdot \frac{\rho_k(.99n^{2/3}) - m\rho_k(1.01n^{1/3})}{\sqrt{m\rho_k(1.01n^{2/3})}} > \sqrt{m\rho_k(1.01n^{1/3})},$$

i.e. if

$$\rho_k(.99n^{2/3}) > 2m\sqrt{\rho_k(1.01n^{1/3})\rho_k(1.01n^{2/3})} + m\rho_k(1.01n^{1/3}). \tag{3}$$

One can show that this equation holds for any $k = \omega(1)$; the proof is omitted for lack of space and will be given in the full version of the paper.

Finally, observe that positive examples have probability at least $\frac{1}{2^{t(n)}} = \frac{1}{n}$. The above argument shows that any $z \in Z(S)$ is misclassified, and Lemma 3 guarantees that the relative weight of $Z(S)$ in positive examples is $1 - 2^{-n^{\Omega(1)}}$. Thus the overall error rate of $h$ under $\mathcal{D}$ is at least $\frac{1}{4 \cdot 2^{t(n)}} = \frac{1}{4n}$ as claimed. □

Together, Lemma 1 and Lemma 6 imply Result 1:

**Theorem 3.** *For any value of $k$, if the maximum margin algorithm uses the kernel $K_k$ when learning $f(x)$ under $\mathcal{D}$ then with probability $1 - 2^{-n^{\Omega(1)}}$ its hypothesis has error greater than $\epsilon = \frac{1}{4 \cdot 2^{t(n)}} = \frac{1}{4n}$.*

With a small modification we can also obtain Result 2. In particular, since we do not need to deal with small $k$ we can use a simple function $f = x_1$ and modify $\mathcal{D}$ slightly so that the probability that $f(x) = 1$ is 0.5. Now the argument of Lemma 6 yields

**Theorem 4.** *For $k = \omega(1)$, if the maximum margin algorithm uses the kernel $K_k$ when learning $f(x) = x_1$ under $\mathcal{D}$ then with probability $1 - 2^{-n^{\Omega(1)}}$ its hypothesis has error at least $\epsilon = \frac{1}{2} - 2^{-n^{\Omega(1)}}$.*

## 4   Uniform Distribution

While Theorem 3 tells us that the $K_k$-maximum margin learner is not a PAC learning algorithm for monotone DNF in the distribution-free PAC model, it does not rule out the possibility that the $K_k$-maximum margin learner might succeed for particular probability distributions such as the uniform distribution on $\{0,1\}^n$. In this section we investigate the uniform distribution.

In Section 3 we took advantage of the fact that $0^n$ occurred with high weight under the distribution $\mathcal{D}$. This let us give a lower bound (of 0) on the value of $W \cdot \phi_k(x)$ for some negative example in the sample, and we then could argue that the value of $\theta$ in the maximum margin classifier must be at least as large as $m_S$. For the uniform distribution, though, this lower bound no longer holds, so we must use a more subtle analysis.

Before turning to the main result, it is easy to observe that the proof of Lemma 1 goes through for the uniform distribution as well (we actually gain a factor of 2). This therefore proves Result 3: if the algorithm uses too low a degree $k$ then its hypothesis cannot possibly be a sufficiently accurate approximation of the target. In contrast, the next result will show that if a rather large $k$ is used then the algorithm is likely to overfit.

For the next result, we consider the target function $f(x) = x_1$. Let $S = S^+ \cup S^-$ be a data set drawn from the uniform distribution $\mathcal{U}$ and labelled according to the function $f(x)$ where $S^+ = \{\langle x^{i,+}, 1\rangle\}_{i=1,\dots,m_+}$ are the positive examples and $S^- = \{\langle x^{j,-}, -1\rangle\}_{j=1,\dots,m_-}$ are the negative examples. Let $u_i$ denote $|x^{i,+}|$ the weight of the $i$-th positive example, and let the positive examples be ordered so that $u_1 \leq u_2 \leq \cdots \leq u_{m^+}$. Similarly let $v_j$ denote $|x^{j,-}|$ the weight of the $j$-th negative example with $v_1 \leq v_2 \leq \cdots \leq v_{m^-}$.

**Definition 6.** *A sample $S$ is a $\mathcal{U}$-typical sample if*

- *Every example $x \in S$ satisfies $0.49n \leq |x| \leq 0.51n$.*
- *Every pair of positive and negative examples $x^{i,+}, x^{j,-}$ in $S$ satisfy $x^{i,+} \cdot x^{j,-} \leq 0.26n$.*

A straightforward application of Chernoff bounds yields the next two lemmas:

**Lemma 7.** *For $m = poly(n)$, with probability $1 - 2^{-\Omega(n)}$ a random i.i.d. sample of $m$ draws from $\mathcal{U}$ is a $\mathcal{U}$-typical sample.*

**Definition 7.** *Let $S$ be a sample. The set $Z(S)$ includes all positive examples $z$ such that every example $x$ in $S$ satisfies $x \cdot z \leq 0.26n$.*

**Lemma 8.** *Let $S$ be a $\mathcal{U}$-typical sample of size $m = poly(n)$ examples. Then $\Pr_{\mathcal{U}}[z \in Z(S)|f(z) = 1] = 1 - 2^{-\Omega(n)}$.*

The following lemma is analogous to Lemma 4:

**Lemma 9.** *Let $S$ be a $\mathcal{U}$-typical sample of size $m$. Then the maximum margin $m_S$ satisfies*

$$m_S \geq \frac{1}{2}\left(\frac{1}{\sqrt{m}}\sqrt{\rho_k(u_1)} - \sqrt{m\rho_k(.26n)}\right).$$

*Proof.* We exhibit an explicit linear threshold function $h'$ which has this margin. Let $h'(x) = \text{sign}(W' \cdot \phi_k(x) - \theta')$ be defined as follows:

- For each positive example $x^{i,+}$ in $S$, pick a set of $\rho_k(u_1)$ features (monomials) which take value 1 on $x^{i,+}$. This can be done since each positive example $x^{i,+}$ has at least $u_1$ bits which are 1. For each feature $T$ in each of these sets, assign $W'_T = 1$.
- For all remaining features $T$ set $W'_T = 0$.
- Set $\theta'$ to be the value that gives the maximum margin on $\phi_k(S)$ for this $W'$, i.e. $\theta'$ is the average of the smallest value of $W' \cdot \phi_k(x^{i,+})$ and the largest value of $W' \cdot \phi_k(x^{j,-})$.

Note that since each positive example contributes at most $\rho_k(u_1)$ nonzero coefficients to $W'$, the number of 1's in $W'$ is at most $m\rho_k(u_1)$, and hence $\|W'\| \leq \sqrt{m\rho_k(u_1)}$. By construction we also have that each positive example $x^{i,+}$ satisfies $W' \cdot \phi_k(x^{i,+}) \geq \rho_k(u_1)$.

Since $S$ is a $\mathcal{U}$-typical sample, each negative example $x^{j,-}$ in $S$ shares at most $.26n$ ones with any positive example in $S$. Hence the value of $W' \cdot \phi_k(x^{j,-})$ is a sum of at most $m\rho_k(.26n)$ numbers whose squares sum to at most $m\rho_k(u_1)$. By Observation 1 we have that $W' \cdot \phi_k(x^{j,-}) \leq \sqrt{m\rho_k(.26n)}\sqrt{m\rho_k(u_1)}$.

The lemma follows by combining the above bounds on $\|W'\|$, $W' \cdot \phi_k(x^{i,+})$ and $W' \cdot \phi_k(x^{j,-})$. □

It turns out that the relative sizes of $u_1$ and $v_1$ (the weights of the lightest positive and negative examples in $S$) play an important role.

**Definition 8.** *A sample $S$ of size $m$ is* positive-skewed *if $u_1 \geq v_1 + B$, i.e. the lightest positive example in $S$ weighs at least $B$ more than the lightest negative example, where $B = \frac{1}{66}\sqrt{\frac{n}{\log m}}$.*

The following lemma shows that a random sample is positive skewed with constant probability (the proof is omitted for lack of space and is given in the full version of the paper):

**Lemma 10.** *Let $S$ be a sample of size $m = \text{poly}(n)$ drawn from the uniform distribution. Then $S$ is positive-skewed with probability at least 0.029.*

Now we can give a lower bound on the threshold $\theta$ for the maximum margin classifier.

**Lemma 11.** *Let $S$ be a labeled sample of size $m$ which is $\mathcal{U}$-typical and positive skewed, and let $h(x) = \text{sign}(W \cdot \phi_k(x) - \theta)$ be the maximum margin hypothesis for $S$. Then*

$$\theta \geq \frac{1}{2} \left( \frac{1}{\sqrt{m}} \sqrt{\rho_k(u_1)} - \sqrt{m\rho_k(.26n)} \right) - \sqrt{\rho_k(u_1 - B)}.$$

*Proof.* Since $S$ is positive-skewed we know that $W \cdot \phi_k(x^{1,-})$ is a sum of at most $\rho_k(u_1 - B)$ weights $W_T$, and since $W$ is normalized the sum of the squares of these weights is at most 1. By Observation 1 we thus have $W \cdot \phi_k(x^{1,-}) \geq -\sqrt{\rho_k(u_1 - B)}$. Since $\theta \geq W \cdot \phi_k(x^{1,-}) + m_S$, together with Lemma 9 this proves the lemma. $\qquad\square$

Putting all of the pieces together, we have:

**Theorem 5.** *If the maximum margin algorithm uses the kernel $K_k$ for $k = \omega(\sqrt{n} \log^{\frac{3}{2}} n)$ when learning $f(x) = x_1$ under the uniform distribution then with probability at least 0.028 its hypothesis has error $\epsilon = \frac{1}{2} - 2^{-\Omega(n)}$.*

*Proof.* By Lemmas 7 and 10, the sample $S$ used for learning is both $\mathcal{U}$-typical and positive skewed with probability at least $0.029 - 1/2^{-\Omega(n)} > 0.028$. Consider any $z \in Z(S)$. Using the reasoning from Lemma 6, $W \cdot \phi(z)$ is a sum of at most $m\rho_k(.26n)$ numbers whose squares sum to at most 1, so $W \cdot \phi(z) \leq \sqrt{m\rho_k(.26n)}$. The example $z$ is erroneously classified as negative by $h$ if

$$\frac{1}{2} \left( \frac{1}{\sqrt{m}} \sqrt{\rho_k(u_1)} - \sqrt{m\rho_k(.26n)} \right) - \sqrt{\rho_k(u_1 - B)} > \sqrt{m\rho_k(.26n)}.$$

so it suffices to show that

$$\sqrt{\rho_k(u_1)} > 3m \left( \sqrt{\rho_k(.26n)} + \sqrt{\rho_k(u_1 - B)} \right). \tag{4}$$

In Appendix A we show that this holds for all $k = \omega(\sqrt{n} \log^{\frac{3}{2}} n)$ as required.

The above argument shows that any $z \in Z(S)$ is misclassified, and Lemma 8 guarantees that the relative weight of $Z(S)$ in positive examples is $1 - 2^{-\Omega(n)}$. Since $\Pr_{x \in \mathcal{U}}[f(x) = 1]$ is $1/2$, we have that with probability at least 0.028 the hypothesis $h$ has error rate at least $\epsilon = \frac{1}{2} - 2^{-\Omega(n)}$, and we are done. $\qquad\square$

## 5    Conclusions and Future Work

Boolean kernels offer an interesting new algorithmic approach to one of the major open problems in computational learning theory, namely learnability of DNF expressions. We have studied the performance of a maximum margin algorithm with the Boolean kernels, giving negative results for several settings of the problem. Our results indicate that the maximum margin algorithm can overfit even when learning simple target functions and using natural and expressive kernels for such functions, and even when combined with structural risk minimization.

We hope that these negative results will be used as a tool to explore alternate approaches which may succeed; we now discuss these briefly.

One direction for future work is to modify the basic learning algorithm. Many interesting variants of the basic maximum margin algorithm have been used in recent years, such as soft margin criteria, kernel regularization, etc.. It may be possible to prove positive results for some DNF learning problems using these approaches. A starting point would be to test their performance on the counterexamples (functions and distributions) which we have constructed.

A more immediate goal is to close the gap between small and large $k$ in our results for the uniform distribution. It is well known [24] that when learning polynomial size DNF under uniform, conjunctions of length $\omega(\log n)$ can be ignored with little effect. Hence the most interesting setting of $k$ for the uniform distribution learning problem is $k = \Theta(\log n)$. Learning under uniform with a $k = \Theta(\log n)$ kernel is qualitatively quite different from learning with the large values of $k$ which we were able to analyze. For example, for $k = \Theta(\log n)$ if a sufficiently large polynomial size sample is taken, then with very high probability all features (monomials of size at most $k$) are active in the sample.

As a first concrete problem in this scenario, one might consider the question of whether a $k = \Theta(\log n)$ kernel maximum margin algorithm can efficiently PAC learn the target function $f(x) = x_1$ under uniform. For this problem it is easy to show that that the naive hypothesis $h'$ constructed in our proofs achieves both a large margin and high accuracy. Moreover, it is possible to show that with high probability the maximum margin hypothesis has a margin which is within a multiplicative factor of $(1 + o(1))$ of the margin achieved by $h'$. Though these preliminary results do not answer the above question they suggest that the answer may be positive. A positive answer, in our view, would be strong motivation to analyze the general case.

# References

1. A. Blum, M. Furst, J. Jackson, M. Kearns, Y. Mansour, and S. Rudich. Weakly learning DNF and characterizing statistical query learning using Fourier analysis. In *Proceedings of the Twenty-Sixth Annual Symposium on Theory of Computing*, pages 253–262, 1994.
2. A. Blum and S. Rudich. Fast learning of $k$-term DNF formulas with queries. *Journal of Computer and System Sciences*, 51(3):367–373, 1995.
3. B. Boser, I. Guyon, and V. Vapnik. A training algorithm for optimal margin classifiers. In *Proceedings of the Fifth Annual Workshop on Computational Learning Theory*, pages 144–152, 1992.
4. N. Bshouty. A subexponential exact learning algorithm for DNF using equivalence queries. *Information Processing Letters*, 59:37–39, 1996.
5. N. Bshouty and C. Tamon. On the Fourier spectrum of monotone functions. *Journal of the ACM*, 43(4):747–770, 1996.
6. C. Gentile. A new approximate maximal margin classification algorithm. *Journal of Machine Learning Research*, 2:213–242, 2001.
7. T. Hancock and Y. Mansour. Learning monotone $k$-$\mu$ DNF formulas on product distributions. In *Proceedings of the Fourth Annual Conference on Computational Learning Theory*, pages 179–193, 1991.

8. J. Jackson. An efficient membership-query algorithm for learning DNF with respect to the uniform distribution. *Journal of Computer and System Sciences*, 55:414–440, 1997.

9. M. Kearns and U. Vazirani. *An introduction to computational learning theory*. MIT Press, Cambridge, MA, 1994.

10. R. Khardon. On using the Fourier transform to learn disjoint DNF. *Information Processing Letters*, 49:219–222, 1994.

11. R. Khardon, D. Roth, and R. Servedio. Efficiency versus convergence of boolean kernels for on-line learning algorithms. In T. G. Dietterich, S. Becker, and Z. Ghahramani, editors, *Advances in Neural Information Processing Systems 14*, Cambridge, MA, 2002. MIT Press.

12. A. Klivans and R. Servedio. Learning DNF in time $2^{\tilde{o}(n^{1/3})}$. In *Proceedings of the Thirty-Third Annual Symposium on Theory of Computing*, pages 258–265, 2001.

13. A. Kowalczyk, A. J. Smola, and R. C. Williamson. Kernel machines and boolean functions. In T. G. Dietterich, S. Becker, and Z. Ghahramani, editors, *Advances in Neural Information Processing Systems 14*, Cambridge, MA, 2002. MIT Press.

14. L. Kucera, A. Marchetti-Spaccamela, and M. Protassi. On learning monotone DNF formulae under uniform distributions. *Information and Computation*, 110:84–95, 1994.

15. E. Kushilevitz and D. Roth. On learning visual concepts and DNF formulae. In *Proceedings of the Sixth Annual Conference on Computational Learning Theory*, pages 317–326, 1993.

16. M. Minsky and S. Papert. *Perceptrons: an introduction to computational geometry*. MIT Press, Cambridge, MA, 1968.

17. K. Sadohara. Learning of boolean functions using support vector machines. In *Proc. of the 12th International Conference on Algorithmic Learning Theory*, pages 106–118. Springer, 2001. LNAI 2225.

18. Y. Sakai and A. Maruoka. Learning monotone log-term DNF formulas under the uniform distribution. *Theory of Computing Systems*, 33:17–33, 2000.

19. R. Servedio. On PAC learning using winnow, perceptron, and a perceptron-like algorithm. In *Proceedings of the Twelfth Annual Conference on Computational Learning Theory*, pages 296–307, 1999.

20. R. Servedio. On learning monotone DNF under product distributions. In *Proceedings of the Fourteenth Annual Conference on Computational Learning Theory*, pages 473–489, 2001.

21. J. Shawe-Taylor and N. Cristianini. *An introduction to support vector machines*. Cambridge University Press, 2000.

22. J. Tarui and T. Tsukiji. Learning DNF by approximating inclusion-exclusion formulae. In *Proceedings of the Fourteenth Conference on Computational Complexity*, pages 215–220, 1999.

23. L. Valiant. A theory of the learnable. *Communications of the ACM*, 27(11):1134–1142, 1984.

24. K. Verbeurgt. Learning DNF under the uniform distribution in quasi-polynomial time. In *Proceedings of the Third Annual Workshop on Computational Learning Theory*, pages 314–326, 1990.

25. K. Verbeurgt. Learning sub-classes of monotone DNF on the uniform distribution. In *Proceedings of the Ninth Conference on Algorithmic Learning Theory*, pages 385–399, 1998.

26. C. Watkins. Kernels from matching operations. Technical Report CSD-TR-98-07, Computer Science Department, Royal Holloway, University of London, 1999.

## A   Proof of Equation (4)

We must show that $\sqrt{\rho_k(u_1)} > 3m\left(\sqrt{\rho_k(.26n)} + \sqrt{\rho_k(u_1 - B)}\right)$. Since we are assuming that the sample $S$ is $\mathcal{U}$-typical, we have $u_1 \geq .49n$ so $u_1 - B > 0.26n$. It thus suffices to show that $\rho_k(u_1) > 36m^2\rho_k(u_1 - B)$.

**Case 1: $k \leq \frac{1}{2}(u_1 - B)$.** Since $\rho_k(\ell) = \sum_{i=1}^{k}\binom{\ell}{i}$, for $k \leq \ell/2$ we have $\rho_k(\ell) \leq k\binom{\ell}{k}$. Also for all $k$, $\rho_k(\ell) \geq \binom{\ell}{k}$ so it suffices to show that

$$\binom{u_1}{k} > 36m^2k\binom{u_1 - B}{k}.$$

This inequality is true if

$$\left(\frac{u_1}{u_1 - B}\right)^k > 36m^2k.$$

Recall that $B = \frac{1}{66}\sqrt{\frac{n}{\log m}}$. Now using the fact that

$$\frac{u_1}{u_1 - B} = 1 + \frac{B}{u_1 - B} > 1 + \frac{B}{n} = 1 + \frac{1}{66\sqrt{n\log m}}$$

it suffices to show that

$$\left(1 + \frac{1}{66\sqrt{n\log m}}\right)^k > 36m^2k.$$

Using the fact that $1 + x \geq e^{x/2}$ for $0 < x < 1$, we can see that this inequality holds if $k > 132\sqrt{n\log(m)}\ln(36m^2n)$. Since $m = \text{poly}(n)$, this is the case for $k = \omega(\sqrt{n}\log^{\frac{3}{2}}n)$.

**Case 2: $\frac{1}{2}(u_1 - B) < k$.** Since $\rho_k(u_1 - B) \leq 2^{u_1 - B}$, it suffices to show that

$$\sum_{i=1}^{\frac{u_1}{2} - \frac{B}{2}}\binom{u_1}{i} > 36m^2 \cdot 2^{u_1 - B}.$$

Since $\sqrt{u_1} > B/2$ it suffices to show that

$$\sum_{i=1}^{\frac{u_1}{2} - \sqrt{u_1}}\binom{u_1}{i} > 36m^2 \cdot 2^{u_1 - B}.$$

Standard binomial coefficient properties imply that the left side above is $\Theta(2^{u_1})$. Since $m = \text{poly}(n)$ and $B = \frac{1}{66}\sqrt{\frac{n}{\log m}}$ this is greater than the right side.

# Knowledge-Based Nonlinear Kernel Classifiers

Glenn M. Fung, Olvi L. Mangasarian*, and Jude W. Shavlik

Computer Sciences Department, University of Wisconsin
Madison, WI 53706
{gfung,olvi,shavlik}@cs.wisc.edu

**Abstract.** Prior knowledge in the form of multiple polyhedral sets, each belonging to one of two categories, is introduced into a reformulation of a nonlinear kernel support vector machine (SVM) classifier. The resulting formulation leads to a linear program that can be solved efficiently. This extends, in a rather unobvious fashion, previous work [3] that incorporated similar prior knowledge into a *linear* SVM classifier. Numerical tests on standard-type test problems, such as exclusive-or prior knowledge sets and a checkerboard with 16 points and prior knowledge instead of the usual 1000 points, show the effectiveness of the proposed approach in generating sharp nonlinear classifiers based mostly or totally on prior knowledge.

**Keywords:** prior knowledge, support vector machines, linear programming

## 1 Introduction

Support vector machines (SVMs) have played a major role in classification problems [15, 2, 10]. However unlike other classification tools such as knowledge-based neural networks [13, 14, 4], little work [11, 3] has gone into incorporating prior knowledge into support vector machines. In this work we extend the previous work [3] of incorporating multiple polyhedral sets as prior knowledge for a linear classifier to nonlinear kernel-based classifiers. This extension is not an obvious one, since it depends critically on the theory of *linear* inequalities and cannot be incorporated directly into a nonlinear kernel classifier. However, if the "kernel trick" is employed *after* one uses a theorem of the alternative for linear inequalities [9, Chapter 2], then incorporation of polyhedral knowledge sets into a nonlinear kernel classifier can be achieved. We show this in Section 2 of the paper. In Section 3 we derive a linear programming formulation that generates a nonlinear kernel SVM classifier that is based on conventional data as well as two groups of polyhedral sets, each group of which belongs to one of two classes. We note that conventional datasets are not essential to our formulation and can be surrogated by samples taken from the knowledge sets. In Section 4 we test our formulation on standard-type test problems. The first test problem is the exclusive-or (XOR) problem consisting of four points in 2-dimensional input space plus four

---

* Also Department of Mathematics, University of California at San Diego, La Jolla, CA 92093.

B. Schölkopf and M.K. Warmuth (Eds.): COLT/Kernel 2003, LNAI 2777, pp. 102–113, 2003.

polyhedral knowledge sets, all of which get classified perfectly by a Gaussian kernel knowledge-based classifier. The second test problem is the checkerboard problem consisting of 16 two-colored squares. Typically this problem is classified based on 1000 points. Here, by using only 16 points plus prior knowledge, our knowledge-based nonlinear kernel classifier, generates a sharp classifier that is as good as that obtained by using 1000 points. Section 5 concludes the paper.

We now describe our notation. All vectors will be column vectors unless transposed to a row vector by a prime $'$. The scalar (inner) product of two vectors $x$ and $y$ in the $n$-dimensional real space $R^n$ will be denoted by $x'y$. For $x \in R^n$, $\|x\|_p$ denotes the $p$-norm, $p = 1, 2, \infty$. The notation $A \in R^{m \times n}$ will signify a real $m \times n$ matrix. For such a matrix, $A'$ will denote the transpose of $A$ and $A_i$ will denote the $i$-th row of $A$. A vector of ones in a real space of arbitrary dimension will be denoted by $e$. Thus for $e \in R^m$ and $y \in R^m$ the notation $e'y$ will denote the sum of the components of $y$. A vector of zeros in a real space of arbitrary dimension will be denoted by 0. The identity matrix of arbitrary dimension will be denoted by $I$. A *separating plane*, with respect to two given point sets $\mathcal{A}$ and $\mathcal{B}$ in $R^n$, is a plane that attempts to separate $R^n$ into two halfspaces such that each open halfspace contains points mostly of $\mathcal{A}$ or $\mathcal{B}$. A *bounding plane* to the set $\mathcal{A}$ is a plane that places $\mathcal{A}$ in one of the two closed halfspaces that the plane generates. The abbreviation "s.t." stands for "such that". For $A \in R^{m \times n}$ and $B \in R^{n \times k}$, a *kernel* $K(A, B)$ maps $R^{m \times n} \times R^{n \times k}$ into $R^{m \times k}$. In particular, if $x$ and $y$ are column vectors in $R^n$ then, $K(x', y)$ is a real number, $K(x', A')$ is a row vector in $R^m$ and $K(A, A')$ is an $m \times m$ matrix. We shall make no assumptions on our kernels other than symmetry, that is $K(x', y)' = K(y', x)$, and in particular we shall not assume or make use of Mercer's positive definiteness condition [15, 12]. The base of the natural logarithm will be denoted by $\varepsilon$. A frequently used kernel in nonlinear classification is the Gaussian kernel [15, 2, 10] whose $ij$th element, $i = 1 \ldots, m$, $j = 1 \ldots, k$, is given by: $(K(A, B))_{ij} = \varepsilon^{-\mu \|A_i' - B_{.j}\|^2}$, where $A \in R^{m \times n}$, $B \in R^{n \times k}$ and $\mu$ is a positive constant.

## 2  Prior Knowledge in a Nonlinear Kernel Classifier

We begin with a brief description of support vector machines (SVMs). SVMs are used principally for classification [10, 15, 12]. The simplest classifier is a *linear separating surface*, a plane in $R^n$:

$$x'w = \gamma, \tag{1}$$

where $w \in R^n$ determines the orientation of the plane (1), in fact it is the normal to the plane, and $\gamma$ determines the location of the plane relative to the origin. The separating plane (1) lies midway between two parallel *bounding planes*:

$$\begin{aligned} x'w &= \gamma + 1, \\ x'w &= \gamma - 1, \end{aligned} \tag{2}$$

each of which attempts to place each class of points in one of the two halfspaces:

$$\begin{aligned} &\{x \mid x'w \geq \gamma + 1\}, \\ &\{x \mid x'w \leq \gamma - 1\}. \end{aligned} \tag{3}$$

In addition, these bounding planes are pushed apart as far as possible. To obtain a more complex classifier, one resorts to a nonlinear separating surface in $R^n$ instead of the linear separating surface (1) defined as follows [10]:

$$K(x', A')Du = \gamma, \tag{4}$$

where $K$ is an arbitrary nonlinear kernel as defined in the Introduction, and $(u, \gamma)$ are determined by solving the linear program (19). Here, $A \in R^{m \times n}$ represents a set of $m$ points in $R^n$ each of which belonging to class $A^+$ or $A^-$ depending on whether the corresponding element of a given $m \times m$ diagonal matrix $D$ is $+1$ or $-1$, and $u \in R^m$ is a dual variable. The linear separating surface (1) becomes a special case of the nonlinear surface (4) if we use the linear kernel $K(A, A') = AA'$ and set $w = A'Du$ [10, 8].

We turn now to the incorporation of prior knowledge in the form of a polyhedral set into a nonlinear kernel classifier. But first, we show that a routine incorporation of such knowledge leads to a nonlinear system of nonconvex inequalities that are not very useful.

Suppose that the polyhedral $\{x \mid Bx \le b\}$ where $B \in R^{\ell \times n}$ and $b \in R^\ell$, must lie in the halfspace $\{x \mid x'w \ge \gamma + 1\}$ for some given $w \in R^n$ and $\gamma \in R$. We thus have the implication:

$$Bx \le b \implies x'w \ge \gamma + 1. \tag{5}$$

By letting $w$ take on its dual representation $w = A'Du$ [10, 8], the implication (5) becomes:

$$Bx \le b \implies x'A'Du \ge \gamma + 1. \tag{6}$$

If we now "kernelize" this implication by letting $x'A' \longrightarrow K(x', A')$, where $K$ is some nonlinear kernel as defined in the Introduction, we then have the implication, for a given $A$, $D$, $u$ and $\gamma$, that:

$$Bx \le b \implies K(x', A')Du \ge \gamma + 1. \tag{7}$$

This is equivalent to the following nonlinear, and generally nonconvex, system of inequalities *not* having a solution $x$ for a given $A$, $D$, $u$ and $\gamma$:

$$Bx \le b, \; K(x', A')Du < \gamma + 1. \tag{8}$$

Unfortunately, the nonlinearity and nonconvexity of the system (8) precludes the use of any theorem of the alternative for either linear or convex inequalities [9]. We thus have to backtrack to the implication (6) and rewrite it equivalently as the following system of homogeneous linear inequalities not having a solution $(x, \zeta) \in R^{n+1}$ for a given fixed $u$ and $\gamma$:

$$\begin{aligned} Bx \qquad\quad -b\zeta &\le 0, \\ u'DAx -(\gamma+1)\zeta &< 0, \\ -\zeta &< 0. \end{aligned} \tag{9}$$

Here, the positive variable $\zeta$ is introduced in order to make the inequalities (9) homogeneous in $(x, \zeta)$, thus enabling us to use a desired theorem of the alternative [9] for such linear inequalities. It follows by Motzkin's Theorem of the Alternative [9], that (9) is equivalent to the following system of linear inequalities having a solution in $(v, \eta, \tau) \in R^{\ell+1+1}$ for a given fixed $u$ and $\gamma$:

$$
\begin{aligned}
B'v + (A'Du)\eta & = 0, \\
-b'v - (\gamma+1)\eta \quad -\tau & = 0, \\
v & \geq 0, \\
0 \neq (\eta, \tau) & \geq 0.
\end{aligned}
\tag{10}
$$

Here, the last constraint signifies that at most one of the two nonnegative variables $\eta$ and $\tau$ can be zero. Hence, if $\eta = 0$, then $\tau > 0$. It follows then from (10) that there exists a $v$ such that: $B'v = 0$, $-b'v > 0$, $v \geq 0$, which contradicts the natural assumption that the knowledge set $\{x \mid Bx \leq b\}$ is nonempty. Otherwise, we have the contradiction:

$$
0 = v'Bx \leq b'v < 0.
\tag{11}
$$

Hence $\eta > 0$ and $\tau \geq 0$. Dividing the inequalities of (10) by $\eta$ and redefining $v$ as $\frac{v}{\eta}$, we have from (10) that the following system of linear equalities has a solution $v$ for a given $u$ and $\gamma$:

$$
\begin{aligned}
B'v + A'Du & = 0, \\
b'v + \gamma + 1 & \leq 0, \\
v & \geq 0.
\end{aligned}
\tag{12}
$$

Under the rather natural assumption that $A$ has linearly independent columns, this in turn is equivalent to following system of linear equalities having a solution $v$ for a given $u$ and $\gamma$:

$$
\begin{aligned}
AB'v + AA'Du & = 0, \\
b'v \quad + \gamma + 1 & \leq 0, \\
v & \geq 0.
\end{aligned}
\tag{13}
$$

Note that the linear independence is needed only for (13) to imply (12). Replacing the the linear kernels $AB'$ and $AA'$ by the general nonlinear kernels $K(A, B')$ and $K(A, A')$, we obtain that the following system of linear equalities has a solution $v$ for a given $u$ and $\gamma$:

$$
\begin{aligned}
K(A, B')v + K(A, A')Du & = 0, \\
b'v \quad + \gamma + 1 & \leq 0, \\
v & \geq 0.
\end{aligned}
\tag{14}
$$

This is the set of constraints that we shall impose on our nonlinear classification formulation as a surrogate for the implication (7). Since the derivation of the conditions were not directly obtained from (7), it is useful to state precisely what the conditions (14) are equivalent to. By using a similar reasoning that employs theorems of the alternative as we did above, we can derive the following equivalence result which we state without giving its explicit proof. The proof is very similar to the arguments used above.

**Proposition 21 Knowledge Set Classification** *Let*

$$\{y \mid K(B, A')y \leq b\} \neq \emptyset. \tag{15}$$

*Then the system (14) having a solution $v$, for a given $u$ and $\gamma$, is equivalent to the implication:*

$$K(B, A')y \leq b \implies u'DK(A, A')y \geq \gamma + 1. \tag{16}$$

We note that the implication is not precisely the implication (7) that we started with, but can be thought of as a kernelized version of it. To see this we state a corollary to the above proposition which shows what the implication means for a linear kernel $AA'$.

**Corollary 22 Linear Knowledge Set Classification** *Let*

$$\{y \mid Bx \leq b, \ x = A'y\} \neq \emptyset. \tag{17}$$

*For a linear kernel $K(A, A') = AA'$, the system (14) having a solution $v$, for a given $u$ and $\gamma$, is equivalent to the implication:*

$$Bx \leq b, \ x = A'y \implies w'x \geq \gamma + 1, \ w = A'Du, \ x = A'y. \tag{18}$$

We immediately note that the implication (18) is equivalent to the desired implication (5) for linear knowledge sets, under the rather unrestrictive assumption that $A$ has linearly independent columns. That the columns of $A$ are linearly independent is equivalent to assuming that in the input space, features are not linearly dependent on each other. If they were, then linearly dependent features could be easily removed from the problem.

We turn now to a linear programming formulation of a nonlinear kernel classifier that incorporates prior knowledge in the form of multiple polyhedral sets.

# 3    Knowledge-Based Linear Programming Formulation of Nonlinear Kernel Classifiers

A standard [10, 1] linear programming formulation of a nonlinear kernel classifier is given by:

$$\min_{u, \gamma, r, y} \quad \nu e'y + e'r$$
$$\text{s.t. } D(K(A, A')Du - e\gamma) + y \geq e, \tag{19}$$
$$-r \leq u \leq r,$$
$$y \geq 0.$$

The $(u, \gamma)$ taken from a solution $(u, \gamma, r, y)$ of (19) generates the nonlinear separating surface (4). Suppose now that we are given the following *knowledge sets*:

$$p \text{ sets belonging to } A+ : \{x \mid B^i x \leq b^i\}, \ i = 1, \ldots, p,$$
$$q \text{ sets belonging to } A- : \{x \mid C^i x \leq c^i\}, \ i = 1, \ldots, q. \tag{20}$$

It follows from the implication (7) for $B = B^i$ and $b = b^i$ for $i = 1, \ldots, p$ and its consequence, the existence of a solution to (14), and a similar implication for the sets $\{x \mid C^i x \leq c^i\}$, $i = 1, \ldots, q$, that the following holds:

There exist $s^i$, $i = 1, \ldots, p$, $t^j$, $j = 1, \ldots, q$, such that:

$$K(A, B^{i'})s^i + K(A, A')Du = 0, \ b^{i'}s^i + \gamma + 1 \leq 0, \ s^i \geq 0, \ i = 1, \ldots, p, \quad (21)$$
$$K(A, C^{j'})t^j - K(A, A')Du = 0, \ c^{j'}t^j - \gamma + 1 \leq 0, \ t^j \geq 0, \ j = 1, \ldots, q.$$

We now incorporate the knowledge sets (20) into the nonlinear kernel classifier linear program (19) by adding conditions (21) as constraints to (19) as follows:

$$\min_{u, \gamma, r, (y, s^i, t^j) \geq 0} \quad \nu e'y + e'r$$
$$\text{s.t.} \quad D(K(A, A')Du - e\gamma) + y \geq e,$$
$$-r \leq u \leq r,$$
$$K(A, B^{i'})s^i + K(A, A')Du = 0, \quad (22)$$
$$b^{i'}s^i + \gamma + 1 \leq 0, \ i = 1, \ldots, p,$$
$$K(A, C^{j'})t^j - K(A, A')Du = 0,$$
$$c^{j'}t^j - \gamma + 1 \leq 0, \ j = 1, \ldots, q.$$

This linear programming formulation incorporates the knowledge sets (20) into the appropriate halfspaces in the higher dimensional feature space. However since there is no guarantee that we are able to place each knowledge set in the appropriate halfspace, we need to introduce error variables $z_1^i, \zeta_1^i, i = 1, \ldots, p, z_2^j, \zeta_2^j, j = 1, \ldots, q$, just like the error variable $y$ of the SVM formulation (19), and attempt to drive these error variables to zero by modifying our last formulation above as follows:

$$\min_{u, \gamma, r, z_1^i, z_2^j, (y, s^i, t^j, \zeta_1^i, \zeta_2^j) \geq 0} \quad \nu e'y + e'r + \mu \left( \sum_{i=1}^{p} (e'z_1^i + \zeta_1^i) \ + \sum_{j=1}^{q} (e'z_2^j + \zeta_2^j) \right)$$
$$\text{s.t.} \quad D(K(A, A')Du - e\gamma) + y \geq e,$$
$$-r \leq u \leq r,$$
$$-z_1^i \leq K(A, B^{i'})s^i + K(A, A')Du \leq z_1^i,$$
$$b^{i'}s^i + \gamma + 1 \leq \zeta_1^i, \ i = 1, \ldots, p,$$
$$-z_2^j \leq K(A, C^{j'})t^j - K(A, A')Du \leq z_2^j,$$
$$c^{j'}t^j - \gamma + 1 \leq \zeta_2^j, \ j = 1, \ldots, q.$$
$$(23)$$

This is our final knowledge-based linear programming formulation which incorporates the knowledge sets (20) into the linear classifier with weight $\mu$, while the (empirical) error term $e'y$ is given weight $\nu$. As usual, the value of these two parameters, $\nu, \mu$, are chosen by means of a tuning set extracted from the training set.

**Remark 31 Data-Based and Knowledge-Based Classifiers.** *If we set* $\mu = 0$*, then the linear program (23) degenerates to (19), the linear program associated with an ordinary data-based nonlinear kernel SVM. We can also make the linear program (23), which generates a nonlinear classifier, to be* **only knowledge-based** *and not dependent on any specific training data* **if** *we replace the matrix A appearing everywhere in (23) by a random sample of points taken from the knowledge sets (20) together with the associated diagonal matrix D. This might be a useful paradigm for situations where training datasets are not easily available, but expert knowledge, such as doctors' experience in diagnosing certain diseases, is readily available. In fact, using this idea of making A and D random samples drawn from the knowledge sets (20), the linear programming formulation (23)* **as is** *can be made* **totally** *dependent on prior knowledge only.*

We turn now to our numerical experiments.

## 4   Numerical Experience

The focus of this paper is rather theoretical. However, in order to illustrate the power of the proposed formulation, we tested our algorithm on two synthetic examples for which most or all the data is constituted of knowledge sets. Experiments involving real world knowledge sets will be utilized in future work.

### Exclusive-Or (XOR) Knowledge Sets

This example generalizes the well known XOR example which consists of the four vertices of a rectangle in 2-dimensions, with the pair of vertices on the end of one diagonal belonging to one class (crosses) while the other pair belongs to another class (stars). Figure 1 depicts two such pairs of vertices symmetrically placed around the origin. It also depicts two pairs of knowledge sets with each pair belonging to one class (two triangles and two parallelograms respectively).

The given points in this XOR example can be considered in two different ways. We note that in line with Remark 31, this classifier can be considered either partially or totally dependent on prior knowledge, depending on whether the four data points are given independently of the knowledge sets or as points contained in them. Our knowledge-based linear programming classifier (23) with a Gaussian kernel yielded the depicted nonlinear separating surface that classified all given points and sets correctly.

Another realization of the XOR example is depicted in Figure 2. Here the data points are not positioned symmetrically with respect to the origin and only one of them is contained in a knowledge set. The resulting nonlinear separating surface for this XOR example is constrained by one of the knowledge sets, in fact it is tangent to one of the diamond-shaped knowledge sets.

### Checkerboard

Our second example is the classical checkerboard dataset [5, 6, 8, 7] which consists of 1000 points taken from a 16-square checkerboard. The following experiment

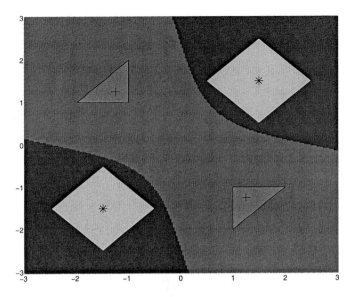

**Fig. 1.** Totally or partially knowledge-based XOR classification problem. The nonlinear classifier obtained by using a Gaussian kernel in our linear programming formulation (23), completely separates the two pairs of prior knowledge sets as well the two pairs of points. The points can be treated as samples taken from the knowledge sets or given independently of them.

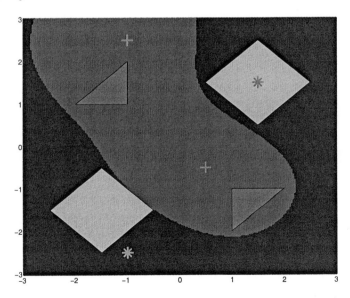

**Fig. 2.** Another XOR classification problem where only one of the points is contained in a knowledge set. The nonlinear classifier obtained by using a Gaussian kernel in our linear programming formulation (23), completely separates the two pairs of prior knowledge sets as well the two pairs of points. Note the strong influence of the knowledge sets on the separating surface which is tangent to one of the knowledge sets.

on this dataset shows the strong influence of knowledge sets on the separating surface.

We first took a subset of 16 points only, each one is the "center" of one of the 16 squares. Since we are using a nonlinear Gaussian kernel to model the separating surface, this particular choice of the training set is very appropriate for the checkerboard dataset. However, due to the nature of the Gaussian function it is hard for it to learn the "sharpness" of the checkerboard by using only a 16-point Gaussian kernel basis. We thus obtain a fairly poor Gaussian-based representation of the checkerboard depicted in Figure 3 with correctness of only 89.66% on a testing set of uniformly randomly generated 39,601 points labeled according to the true checkerboard pattern.

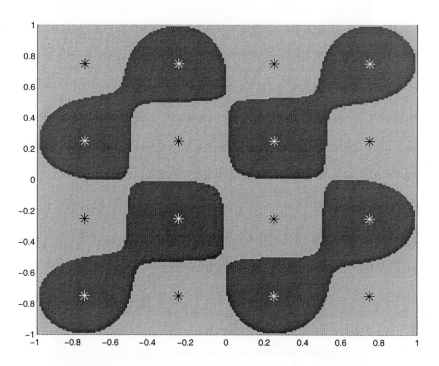

**Fig. 3.** A poor nonlinear classifier based on 16 points taken from each of the 16 squares of a checkerboard. The nonlinear classifier was obtained by using a Gaussian kernel in a conventional linear programming formulation (19).

On the other hand, if we use these same 16 points in the linear program (23) as a distinct dataset in conjunction with prior knowledge in the form of 8 linear inequalities characterizing *only two* subsquares fully contained in the leftmost two squares of the bottom row of squares, we obtain the very sharply defined checkerboard depicted in Figure 4, with a correctness of 98.5% on a 39, 601-point testing set. We note that, it does not matter which two subsquares are taken

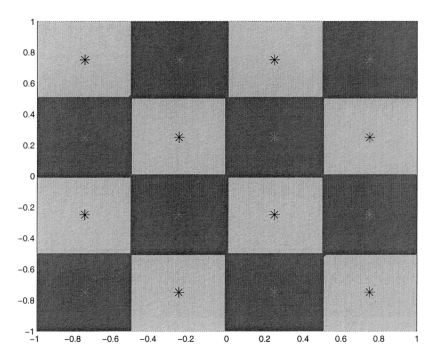

**Fig. 4.** Knowledge-based checkerboard classification problem. The nonlinear classifier was obtained by using a Gaussian kernel in our linear programming formulation (23) with the 16 depicted points as a given dataset together with prior knowledge consisting of 8 linear inequalities characterizing *only two* subsquares contained in the leftmost two squares of the bottom row of squares. The sharply defined checkerboard has a correctness of 98.5% on a 39, 601-point testing set.

as prior knowledge, as long as there is one from each class. Also the size of the subsquare is not critical either. Figure 4 was obtained with subsquares with sides equal to 0.75 times the the original sides and centered around the given data points. Squares down to size 0.25 of the original squares, gave similar results. We emphasize here that the prior knowledge given to the linear program (23) here is truly a partial knowledge set in the sense that it gives the linear program information on only 2 of 16 squares.

It is interesting to note that by using prior knowledge from *only two* squares, our linear programming formulation (23) is capable of transforming a complex boundary between the union of eight squares in each class, into a *single* nonlinear classifier equation given by (4).

## 5    Conclusion

We have presented a knowledge-based formulation of a nonlinear kernel SVM classifier. The classifier is obtained using a linear programming formulation with any nonlinear symmetric kernel with no positive definiteness (Mercer) condition assumed. The formulation works equally well with or without conventional datasets. We note that unlike the linear kernel case with prior knowledge [3], where the absence of conventional datasets was handled by deleting some constraints from a linear programming formulation, here arbitrary representative points from the knowledge sets are utilized to play the role of such datasets, that is $A$ and $D$ in (23). The issues associated with sampling the knowledge sets, in situations where there are no conventional data points, constitute an interesting topic for future research.

Future application to medical problems, computer vision, microarray gene classification, and efficacy of drug treatment, all of which have prior knowledge available, are planned.

## Acknowledgments

Research described in this UW Data Mining Institute Report 03-02, March 2003, was supported by NSF Grant CCR-138308, by NLM Grant 1 R01 LM07050-01, and by Microsoft.

## References

1. P. S. Bradley and O. L. Mangasarian. Feature selection via concave minimization and support vector machines. In J. Shavlik, editor, *Machine Learning Proceedings of the Fifteenth International Conference(ICML '98)*, pages 82–90, San Francisco, California, 1998. Morgan Kaufmann. ftp://ftp.cs.wisc.edu/math-prog/tech-reports/98-03.ps.
2. V. Cherkassky and F. Mulier. *Learning from Data - Concepts, Theory and Methods*. John Wiley & Sons, New York, 1998.
3. G. Fung, O. L. Mangasarian, and J. Shavlik. Knowledge-based support vector machine classifiers. Technical Report 01-09, Data Mining Institute, Computer Sciences Department, University of Wisconsin, Madison, Wisconsin, November 2001. ftp://ftp.cs.wisc.edu/pub/dmi/tech-reports/01-09.ps, NIPS 2002 Proceedings, to appear.
4. F. Girosi and N. Chan. Prior knowledge and the creation of "virtual" examples for RBF networks. In *Neural networks for signal processing, Proceedings of the 1995 IEEE-SP Workshop*, pages 201–210, New York, 1995. IEEE Signal Processing Society.
5. T. K. Ho and E. M. Kleinberg. Building projectable classifiers of arbitrary complexity. In *Proceedings of the 13th International Conference on Pattern Recognition*, pages 880–885, Vienna, Austria, 1996. http://cm.bell-labs.com/who/tkh/pubs.html. Checker dataset at: ftp://ftp.cs.wisc.edu/math-prog/cpo-dataset/machine-learn/checker.
6. T. K. Ho and E. M. Kleinberg. Checkerboard dataset, 1996. http://www.cs.wisc.edu/math-prog/mpml.html.
7. Y.-J. Lee and O. L. Mangasarian. RSVM: Reduced support vector machines. Technical Report 00-07, Data Mining Institute, Computer Sciences Department, University of Wisconsin, Madison, Wisconsin, July 2000. Proceedings of the First SIAM International Conference on Data Mining, Chicago, April 5-7, 2001, CD-ROM Proceedings. ftp://ftp.cs.wisc.edu/pub/dmi/tech-reports/00-07.ps.

8. Y.-J. Lee and O. L. Mangasarian. SSVM: A smooth support vector machine. *Computational Optimization and Applications*, 20:5–22, 2001. Data Mining Institute, University of Wisconsin, Technical Report 99-03. ftp://ftp.cs.wisc.edu/pub/dmi/tech-reports/99-03.ps.
9. O. L. Mangasarian. *Nonlinear Programming*. SIAM, Philadelphia, PA, 1994.
10. O. L. Mangasarian. Generalized support vector machines. In A. Smola, P. Bartlett, B. Schölkopf, and D. Schuurmans, editors, *Advances in Large Margin Classifiers*, pages 135–146, Cambridge, MA, 2000. MIT Press. ftp://ftp.cs.wisc.edu/math-prog/tech-reports/98-14.ps.
11. B. Schölkopf, P. Simard, A. Smola, and V. Vapnik. Prior knowledge in support vector kernels. In M. Jordan, M. Kearns, and S. Solla, editors, *Advances in Neural Information Processing Systems 10*, pages 640 – 646, Cambridge, MA, 1998. MIT Press.
12. A. Smola and B. Schölkopf. *Learning with Kernels*. MIT Press, Cambridge, MA, 2002.
13. G. G. Towell and J. W. Shavlik. Knowledge-based artificial neural networks. *Artificial Intelligence*, 70:119–165, 1994.
14. G. G. Towell, J. W. Shavlik, and M. Noordewier. Refinement of approximate domain theories by knowledge-based artificial neural networks. In *Proceedings of the Eighth National Conference on Artificial Intelligence (AAAI-90)*, pages 861–866, 1990.
15. V. N. Vapnik. *The Nature of Statistical Learning Theory*. Springer, New York, second edition, 2000.

# Fast Kernels for Inexact String Matching

Christina Leslie and Rui Kuang

Columbia University, New York NY 10027, USA
{rkuang,cleslie}@cs.columbia.edu

**Abstract.** We introduce several new families of string kernels designed in particular for use with support vector machines (SVMs) for classification of protein sequence data. These kernels – restricted gappy kernels, substitution kernels, and wildcard kernels – are based on feature spaces indexed by $k$-length subsequences from the string alphabet $\Sigma$ (or the alphabet augmented by a wildcard character), and hence they are related to the recently presented $(k, m)$-mismatch kernel and string kernels used in text classification. However, for all kernels we define here, the kernel value $K(x, y)$ can be computed in $O(c_K(|x| + |y|))$ time, where the constant $c_K$ depends on the parameters of the kernel but is independent of the size $|\Sigma|$ of the alphabet. Thus the computation of these kernels is linear in the length of the sequences, like the mismatch kernel, but we improve upon the parameter-dependent constant $c_K = k^{m+1}|\Sigma|^m$ of the mismatch kernel. We compute the kernels efficiently using a recursive function based on a trie data structure and relate our new kernels to the recently described transducer formalism. Finally, we report protein classification experiments on a benchmark SCOP dataset, where we show that our new faster kernels achieve SVM classification performance comparable to the mismatch kernel and the Fisher kernel derived from profile hidden Markov models.

**Keywords:** Kernel methods, string kernels, computational biology.

## 1   Introduction

Recently, there has been considerable interest in the development of string kernels for use with support vector machine classifiers and other kernel methods in applications like text categorization, speech recognition, and protein sequence classification. Previous work includes convolution kernels defined by Haussler [5], dynamic alignment kernels based on pair hidden Markov models by Watkins [15], and the gappy $n$-gram kernel developed for text classification by Lodhi *et al.* [11]. A practical disadvantage of these string kernels is their computational expense. Most of the kernels rely on dynamic programming algorithms for which the computation of each kernel value $K(x, y)$ is quadratic in the length of the input sequences $x$ and $y$, that is, $O(|x||y|)$ with constant factor that depends on the parameters of the kernel. The recently presented $k$-spectrum (gap-free $k$-gram) kernel gave a linear time $(O(k(|x|+|y|))$ implementation of a kernel based on a trie data structure for use in SVM protein classification. Vishwanathan *et al.* [13] extended this work to compute the weighted sum of $k$-spectrum kernels for different $k$ by using suffix trees and suffix links, allowing elimination of

B. Schölkopf and M.K. Warmuth (Eds.): COLT/Kernel 2003, LNAI 2777, pp. 114–128, 2003.
© Springer-Verlag Berlin Heidelberg 2003

the constant factor in the spectrum kernel for a compute time of $O(|x| + |y|)$. Finally, the $(k, m)$-mismatch kernel [9] achieved improved performance on the protein classification task by incorporating the biologically important notion of character mismatches. Using a mismatch tree data structure, the complexity of the kernel calculation was shown to be $O(c_K(|x| + |y|))$, with $c_K = k^{m+1}|\Sigma|^m$ for $k$-grams with up to $m$ mismatches from alphabet $\Sigma$.

In this paper, we introduce several new families of string kernels designed for use with SVMs for classification of protein sequence data. These kernels – restricted gappy kernels, substitution kernels, and wildcard kernels – are based on feature spaces indexed by $k$-length subsequences from the string alphabet $\Sigma$ (or the alphabet augmented by a wildcard character), and hence they are closely related to the $(k, m)$-mismatch kernel and string kernels used in text classification. However, for all kernels we define here, the kernel value $K(x, y)$ can be computed in $O(c_K(|x| + |y|))$ time, where the constant $c_K$ depends on the parameters of the kernel but is independent of the size $|\Sigma|$ of the alphabet. Thus the computation of these kernels is linear in the length of the sequences, like the mismatch kernel, but we improve upon the parameter-dependent constant. Therefore, we provide a number of different models for incorporating a notion of inexact matching while maintaining fast computation. We describe how to compute these kernels efficiently using a recursive function based on a trie data structure. We also relate our new kernels to the recently described transducer formalism [2] and give transducers corresponding to some of our kernels.

Finally, we report protein classification experiments on a benchmark SCOP dataset, where we show that our new faster kernels achieve SVM classification performance comparable to the mismatch kernel and the Fisher kernel derived from profile hidden Markov models.

## 2    Definitions of Feature Maps and String Kernels

Below, we review the definition of mismatch kernels [9] and introduce three new families: restricted gappy kernels, substitution kernels, and wildcard kernels.

In each case, the kernel is defined via an explicit feature map map from the space of all finite sequences from an alphabet $\Sigma$ to a vector space indexed by the set of $k$-length subsequences from $\Sigma$ or, in the case of wildcard kernels, $\Sigma$ augmented by a wildcard character. For protein sequences, $\Sigma$ is the alphabet of $|\Sigma| = 20$ amino acids. We refer to a $k$-length contiguous subsequence occurring in an input sequence as an instance $k$-mer (also called a $k$-gram in the literature). The mismatch kernel feature map obtains inexact matching of instance $k$-mers from the input sequence to $k$-mer features by allowing a restricted number of mismatches; the new kernels achieve inexact matching by allowing a restricted number of gaps, by enforcing a probabilistic threshold on character substitutions, or by permitting a restricted number of matches to wildcard characters.

### 2.1    Spectrum and Mismatch Kernels

In previous work, we defined the $(k, m)$-mismatch kernel via a feature map $\Phi_{(k,m)}^{\text{Mismatch}}$ to the $|\Sigma|^k$-dimensional vector space indexed by the set of $k$-mers from $\Sigma$. For a fixed $k$-mer $\alpha = a_1 a_2 \ldots a_k$, with each $a_i$ a character in $\Sigma$, the $(k, m)$-neighborhood generated by $\alpha$ is the set of all $k$-length sequences $\beta$ from $\Sigma$ that differ from $\alpha$ by at most $m$ mismatches. We denote this set by $N_{(k,m)}(\alpha)$. For a $k$-mer $\alpha$, the feature map is defined as

$$\Phi_{(k,m)}^{\mathrm{Mismatch}}(\alpha) = (\phi_\beta(\alpha))_{\beta \in \Sigma^k}$$

where $\phi_\beta(\alpha) = 1$ if $\beta$ belongs to $N_{(k,m)}(\alpha)$, and $\phi_\beta(\alpha) = 0$ otherwise. For a sequence $x$ of any length, we extend the map additively by summing the feature vectors for all the $k$-mers in $x$:

$$\Phi_{(k,m)}^{\mathrm{Mismatch}}(x) = \sum_{k\text{-mers } \alpha \text{ in } x} \Phi_{(k,m)}^{\mathrm{Mismatch}}(\alpha)$$

Each instance of a $k$-mer contributes to all coordinates in its mismatch neighborhood, and the $\beta$-coordinate of $\Phi_{(k,m)}^{\mathrm{Mismatch}}(x)$ is just a count of all instances of the $k$-mer $\beta$ occurring with up to $m$ mismatches in $x$. The $(k, m)$-mismatch kernel $K_{(k,m)}$ is then given by the inner product of feature vectors:

$$K_{(k,m)}^{\mathrm{Mismatch}}(x, y) = \langle \Phi_{(k,m)}^{\mathrm{Mismatch}}(x), \Phi_{(k,m)}^{\mathrm{Mismatch}}(y) \rangle.$$

For $m = 0$, we obtain the $k$-spectrum [8] or $k$-gram kernel [11].

## 2.2    Restricted Gappy Kernels

For the $(g, k)$-gappy string kernel, we use the same $|\Sigma|^k$-dimensional feature space, indexed by the set of $k$-mers from $\Sigma$, but we define our feature map based on gappy matches of $g$-mers to $k$-mer features. For a fixed $g$-mer $\alpha = a_1 a_2 \ldots a_g$ (each $a_i \in \Sigma$), let $G_{(g,k)}(\alpha)$ be the set of all the $k$-length subsequences occurring in $\alpha$ (with up to $g - k$ gaps). Then we define the gappy feature map on $\alpha$ as

$$\Phi_{(g,k)}^{\mathrm{Gap}}(\alpha) = (\phi_\beta(\alpha))_{\beta \in \Sigma^k}$$

where $\phi_\beta(\alpha) = 1$ if $\beta$ belongs to $G_{(g,k)}(\alpha)$, and $\phi_\beta(\alpha) = 0$ otherwise. In other words, each instance $g$-mer contributes to the set of $k$-mer features that occur (in at least one way) as subsequences with up to $g - k$ gaps in the $g$-mer. Now we extend the feature map to arbitrary finite sequences $x$ by summing the feature vectors for all the $g$-mers in $x$:

$$\Phi_{(g,k)}^{\mathrm{Gap}}(x) = \sum_{g\text{-mers } \alpha \in x} \Phi_{g,k}^{\mathrm{Gap}}(\alpha)$$

The kernel $K_{(g,k)}^{\mathrm{Gap}}(x, y)$ is defined as before by taking the inner product of feature vectors for $x$ and $y$.

Alternatively, given an instance $g$-mer, we may wish to count the number of occurrences of each $k$-length subsequence and weight each occurrence by the number of gaps. Following [11], we can define for $g$-mer $\alpha$ and $k$-mer feature $\beta = b_1 b_2 \dots b_k$ the weighting

$$\phi_\beta^\lambda(\alpha) = \frac{1}{\lambda^k} \sum_{\substack{1 \le i_1 < i_2 < \dots < i_k \le g \\ a_{i_j} = b_j \text{ for } j=1\dots k}} \lambda^{i_k - i_1 + 1}$$

where the multiplicative factor satisfies $0 < \lambda \le 1$. We can then obtain a weighted version of the gappy kernel $K_{(g,k,\lambda)}^{\text{Weighted Gap}}$ from the feature map:

$$\Phi_{(g,k,\lambda)}^{\text{Weighted Gap}}(x) = \sum_{g\text{-mers } \alpha \in x} (\phi_\beta^\lambda(\alpha))_{\beta \in \Sigma^k}$$

This feature map is related to the gappy $k$-gram kernel defined in [11] but enforces the following restriction: here, only those $k$-character subsequences that occur with at most $g - k$ gaps, rather than all gappy occurrences, contribute to the corresponding $k$-mer feature. When restricted to input sequences of length $g$, our feature map coincides with that of the usual gappy $k$-gram kernel. Note, however, that for our kernel, a gappy $k$-mer instance (occurring with at most $g - k$ gaps) is counted in all (overlapping) $g$-mers that contain it, whereas in [11], a gappy $k$-mer instance is only counted once. If we wish to approximate the gappy $k$-gram kernel, we can define a small variation of our restricted gappy kernel where one only counts a gappy $k$-mer instance if its first character occurs in the first position of a $g$-mer window. That is, the modified feature map is defined on each $g$-mer $\alpha$ by coordinate functions

$$\widetilde{\phi}_\beta^\lambda(\alpha) = \frac{1}{\lambda^k} \sum_{\substack{1 = i_1 < i_2 < \dots < i_k \le g \\ a_{i_j} = b_j \text{ for } j=1\dots k}} \lambda^{i_k - i_1 + 1},$$

$0 < \lambda \le 1$, and is extended to longer sequences by adding feature vectors for $g$-mers. This modified feature map now gives a "truncation" of the usual gappy $k$-gram kernel.

In Section 3, we show that our restricted gappy kernel has $O(c(g,k)(|x|+|y|))$ computation time, where constant $c(g,k)$ depends on size of $g$ and $k$, while the original gappy $k$-gram kernel has complexity $O(k(|x||y|))$. Note in particular that we do not compute the standard gappy $k$-gram kernel on every pair of $g$-grams from $x$ and $y$, which would necessarily be quadratic in sequence length since there are $O(|x||y|)$ such pairs. We will see that for reasonable choices of $g$ and $k$, we obtain much faster computation time, while in experimental results reported in Section 5, we still obtain good classification performance.

## 2.3   Substitution Kernels

The substitution kernel is similar to the mismatch kernel, except that we replace the combinatorial definition of a mismatch neighborhood with a similarity neighborhood based on a probabilistic model of character substitutions. In computational biology, it is standard to compute pairwise alignment scores for protein sequences using a substitution matrix [6, 12, 1] that gives pairwise scores $s(a, b)$ derived from estimated evolutionary substitution probabilities. In one scoring system [12], the scores $s(a, b)$ are based on estimates of conditional substitution probabilities $P(a|b) = p(a, b)/q(b)$, where $p(a, b)$ is the probability that $a$ and $b$ co-occur in an alignment of closely related proteins, $q(a)$ is the background frequency of amino acid $a$, and $P(a|b)$ represents the probability of a mutation into $a$ during fixed evolutionary time interval given that the ancestor amino acid was $b$. We define the mutation neighborhood $M_{(k,\sigma)}(\alpha)$ of a $k$-mer $\alpha = a_1 a_2 \ldots a_k$ as follows:

$$M_{(k,\sigma)}(\alpha) = \{\beta = b_1 b_2 \ldots b_k \in \Sigma^k : -\sum_i^k \log P(a_i|b_i) < \sigma\}$$

Mathematically, we can define $\sigma = \sigma(N)$ such that $\max_{\alpha \in \Sigma^k} |M_{(k,\sigma)}(\alpha)| < N$, so we have theoretical control over the maximum size of the mutation neighborhoods. In practice, choosing $\sigma$ to allow an appropriate amount of mutation while restricting neighborhood size may require experimentation and cross-validation.

Now we define the substitution feature map analogously to the mismatch feature map:

$$\Phi_{(k,\sigma)}^{\text{Sub}}(x) = \sum_{k\text{-mers } \alpha \text{ in } x} (\phi_\beta(\alpha))_{\beta \in \Sigma^k}$$

where $\phi_\beta(\alpha) = 1$ if $\beta$ belongs to the mutation neighborhood $M_{(k,\sigma)}(\alpha)$, and $\phi_\beta(\alpha) = 0$ otherwise.

### 2.4   Wildcard Kernels

Finally, we can augment the alphabet $\Sigma$ with a wildcard character denoted by $*$, and we map to a feature space indexed by the set $\mathcal{W}$ of $k$-length subsequences from $\Sigma \cup \{*\}$ having at most $m$ occurrences of the character $*$. The feature space has dimension $\sum_{i=0}^m \binom{k}{i} |\Sigma|^{k-i}$.

A $k$-mer $\alpha$ matches a subsequence $\beta$ in $\mathcal{W}$ if all non-wildcard entries of $\beta$ are equal to the corresponding entries of $\alpha$ (wildcards match all characters). The wildcard feature map is given by

$$\Phi_{(k,m,\lambda)}^{\text{Wildcard}}(x) = \sum_{k\text{-mers } \alpha \text{ in } x} (\phi_\beta(\alpha))_{\beta \in \mathcal{W}}$$

where $\phi_\beta(\alpha) = \lambda^j$ if $\alpha$ matches pattern $\beta$ containing $j$ wildcard characters, $\phi_\beta(\alpha) = 0$ if $\alpha$ does not match $\beta$, and $0 < \lambda \le 1$.

Other variations of the wildcard idea, including specialized weightings and use of groupings of related characters, are described in [3].

## 3   Efficient Computation

All the kernels we define above can be efficiently computed using a trie data structure, similar to the mismatch tree approach previously presented [9]. We will describe the computation of the gappy kernel in most detail, since the other kernels are easier adaptations of the mismatch kernel computation. For simplicity, we explain how to compute a single kernel value $K(x, y)$ for a pair of input sequences; computation of the full kernel matrix in one traversal of the data structure is a straightforward extension.

## 3.1   $(g, k)$-Gappy Kernel Computation

For the $(g, k)$-gappy kernel, we represent our feature space as a rooted tree of depth $k$ where each internal node has $|\Sigma|$ branches and each branch is labeled with a symbol from $\Sigma$. In this depth $k$ trie, each leaf node represents a fixed $k$-mer in feature space by concatenating the branch symbols along the path from root to leaf and each internal node represents the prefix for those for the set of $k$-mer features in the subtree below it.

Using a depth-first traversal of this tree, we maintain at each node that we visit a set of pointers to all $g$-mer instances in the input sequences that contain a subsequence (with gaps) that matches the current prefix pattern; we also store, for each $g$-mer instance, an index pointing to the last position we have seen so far in the $g$-mer. At the root, we store pointers to all $g$-mer instances, and for each instance, the stored index is 0, indicating that we have not yet seen any characters in the $g$-mer. As we pass from a parent node to a child node along a branch labeled with symbol $a$, we process each of parent's instances by scanning ahead to find the next occurrence of symbol $a$ in each $g$-mer. If such a character exists, we pass the $g$-mer to the child node along with its updated index; otherwise, we drop the instance and do not pass it to the child. Thus at each node of depth $d$, we have effectively performed a greedy gapped alignment of $g$-mers from the input sequences to the current $d$-length prefix, allowing insertion of up to $g - k$ gaps into the prefix sequence to obtain each alignment. When we encounter a node with an empty list of pointers (no valid occurrences of the current prefix), we do not need to search below it in the tree; in fact, unless there is a valid $g$-mer instance from each of $x$ and $y$, we do not have to process the subtree. When we reach a leaf node, we sum the contributions of all instances occurring in each source sequence to obtain feature values for $x$ and $y$ corresponding to the current $k$-mer, and we update the kernel by adding the product of these feature values. Since we are performing a depth-first traversal, we can accomplish the algorithm with a recursive function and do not have to store the full trie in memory. Figure 1 shows expansion down a path during the recursive traversal.

The computation at the leaf node depends on which version of the gappy kernel one uses. For the unweighted feature map, we obtain the feature values of $x$ and $y$ corresponding to the current $k$-mer by counting the $g$-mer instances at the leaf coming from $x$ and from $y$, respectively; the product of these counts gives the contribution to the kernel for this $k$-mer feature. For the $\lambda$-weighted gappy feature map, we need a count of all alignments of each valid $g$-mer instance against the $k$-mer feature allowing up to $g - k$ gaps. This can be computed with a simple dynamic programming routine (similar to the Needleman-Wunsch

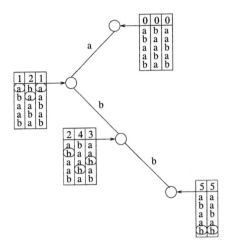

**Fig. 1. Trie traversal for gappy kernel.** Expansion along a path from root to leaf during traveral of the trie for the $(5,3)$-gappy kernel, showing only the instance 5-mers for a single sequence $x = abaabab$. Each node stores its valid 5-mer instances and the index to the last match for each instance. Instances at the leaf node contribute to the kernel for 3-mer feature $abb$.

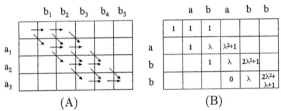

**Fig. 2. Dynamic programming at the leaf node.** The trellis in (A) shows the restricted paths for aligning a $g$-mer against a $k$-mer, with insertion of up to $g-k$ gaps in the $k$-mer, for $g = 5$ and $k = 3$. The basic recursion for summing path weights is $S(i,j) = m(a_i, b_j)S(i-1, j-1) + g(i)S(i, j-1)$, where $m(a,b) = 1$ if $a$ and $b$ match, 0 if they are different, and the gap penalty $g(i) = 1$ for $i = 0, k$ and $g(i) = \lambda$ for other rows. Trellis (B) shows the example of aligning $ababb$ against 3-mer $abb$.

algorithm), where we sum over a restricted set of paths, as shown in Figure 2. The complexity is $O(k(g-k))$, since we fill a restricted trellis of $(k+1)(g-k+1)$ squares. Note that when we align a subsequence $b_{i_1}b_{i_2}\ldots b_{i_k}$ against a $k$-mer $a_1 a_2 \ldots a_k$, we only penalize interior gaps corresponding to non-consecutive indices in $1 \le i_1 < i_2 \ldots < i_k \le g$. Therefore, the multiplicative gap cost is 1 in the zeroth and last rows of the trellis and $\lambda$ in the other rows.

Each $g$-mer instance in the input data can contribute to $\binom{g}{k} = O(g^{g-k})$ $k$-mer features (assuming that $g-k$ is smaller than $k$). Therefore, we visit at most $O(g^{g-k}(|x|+|y|))$ leaf nodes in the traversal. Since we iterate through at most $g$ positions of each $g$-mer instance as we pass from root to leaf, the traversal time is

$O(g^{g-k+1}(|x|+|y|))$. The total processing time at leaf nodes is $O(g^{g-k}(|x|+|y|))$ for the unweighted gappy kernel and $O(k(g-k)g^{g-k}(|x|+|y|))$ for the weighted gappy kernel. Therefore, in both cases, we have total complexity of the form $O(c(g,k)(|x|+|y|))$, with $c(g,k) = O((g-k)g^{g-k+1})$ for the more expensive kernel.

Note that with the definition of the gappy feature maps given above, a gappy $k$-character subsequence occuring with $c \leq g-k$ gaps is counted in each of the $g-(k+c)+1$ $g$-length windows that contain it. To obtain feature maps that count a gappy $k$-character subsequence only once, we can make minor variations to the algorithm by requiring that the first character of a gappy $k$-mer occurs in the first position of the $g$-length window in order to contribute to the corresponding $k$-mer feature.

### 3.2 $(k, \sigma)$-Substitution Kernel Computation

For the substitution kernel, computation is very similar to the mismatch kernel algorithm. We use a depth $k$ trie to represent the feature space. We store, at each depth $d$ node that we visit, a set of pointers to all $k$-mer instances $\alpha$ in the input data whose $d$-length prefixes have current mutation score $-\sum_{i=1}^{d} \log P(a_i|b_i) < \sigma$ of the current prefix pattern $b_1 b_2 \ldots b_d$, and we store the current mutation score for each $k$-mer instance. As we pass from a parent node at depth $d$ to a child node at depth $d+1$ along a branch labeled with symbol $b$, we process each $k$-mer $\alpha$ by adding $-\log P(a_{d+1}|b)$ to the mutation score and pass it to the child if and only if the score is still less than $\sigma$. As before, we update the kernel at the leaf node by computing the contribution of the corresponding $k$-mer feature.

The number of leaf nodes visited is in the traversal is $O(N_\sigma(|x|+|y|))$, where $N_\sigma = \max_{\alpha \in \Sigma^k} |M_{(k,\sigma)}|$. We can choose $\sigma$ sufficiently small to get any desired bound on $N_\sigma$. Total complexity for the kernel value computation is $O(kN_\sigma(|x|+|y|))$.

### 3.3 $(k, m)$-Wildcard Kernel Computation

Computation of the wildcard kernel is again very similar to the mismatch kernel algorithm. We use a depth $k$ trie with branches labeled by characters in $\Sigma \cup \{*\}$, and we prune (do not traverse) subtrees corresponding to prefix patterns with greater than $m$ wildcard characters. At each node of depth $d$, we maintain pointers to all $k$-mers instances in the input sequences whose $d$-length prefixes match the current $d$-length prefix pattern (with wildcards) represented by the path down from the root.

Each $k$-mer instance in the data matches at most $\sum_{i=0}^{m} \binom{k}{i} = O(k^m)$ $k$-length patterns having up to $m$ wildcards. Thus the number of leaf nodes visited is in the traversal is $O(k^m(|x|+|y|))$, and total complexity for the kernel value computation is $O(k^{m+1}(|x|+|y|))$.

## 3.4   Comparison with Mismatch Kernel Complexity

For the $(k, m)$ mismatch kernel, the size of the mismatch neighborhood of an instance $k$-mer is $O(k^m |\Sigma|^m)$, so total kernel value computation is $O(k^{m+1} |\Sigma|^m (|x| + |y|))$. All the other kernels presented here have running time $O(c_K(|x| + |y|))$, where constant $c_K$ depends on the parameters of the kernel but not on the size of the alphabet $\Sigma$. Therefore, we have improved constant term for larger alphabets (such as the alphabet of 20 amino acids). In Section 5, we show that these new, faster kernels have performance comparable to the mismatch kernel in protein classification experiments.

## 4   Transducer Representation

Cortes *et al.* [2] recently showed that many known string kernels can be associated with and constructed from weighted finite state transducers with input alphabet $\Sigma$. We briefly outline their transducer formalism and give transducers for some of our newly defined kernels. For simplicity, we only describe transducers over the probability semiring $\mathbb{R}_+ = [0, \infty)$, with regular addition and multiplication.

Following the development in [2], a weighted finite state transducer over $\mathbb{R}_+$ is defined by a finite input alphabet $\Sigma$, a finite output alphabet $\Delta$, a finite set of states $Q$, a set of input states $I \subset Q$, a set of output states $F \subset Q$, a finite set of transitions $E \subset Q \times (\Sigma \cup \{\epsilon\}) \times (\Delta \cup \{\epsilon\}) \times \mathbb{R}_+ \times Q$, an initial weight function $\lambda : I \to \mathbb{R}_+$, and a final weight function $\rho : F \to \mathbb{R}_+$. Here, the symbol $\epsilon$ represents the empty string. The transducer can be represented by a weighted directed graph with nodes indexed by $Q$ and each transition $e \in E$ corresponding to a directed edge from its origin state $p[e]$ to its destination state $n[e]$ and labeled by the input symbol $i[e]$ it accepts, the output symbol $o[e]$ it emits, and the weight $w[e]$ it assigns. We write the label as $i[e] : o[e]/w[e]$ (abbreviated as $i[e] : o[e]$ if the weight is 1).

For a path $\pi = e_1 e_2 \ldots e_k$ of consecutive transitions (directed path in graph), the weight for the path is $w[\pi] = w[e_1] w[e_2] \ldots w[e_k]$, and we denote $p[\pi] = p[e_1]$ and $n[\pi] = n[e_k]$. We write $\Sigma^* = \cup_{k \geq 0} \Sigma^k$ for the set of all strings over $\Sigma$. For an input string $x \in \Sigma^*$ and output string $z \in \Delta^*$, we denote by $P(I, x, z, F)$ the set of paths from initial states $I$ to final states $F$ that accept string $x$ and emit string $z$. A transducer $T$ is called regulated if for any pair of input and output strings $(x, z)$, the output weight $[[T]](x, z)$ that $T$ assigns to the pair is well-defined. The output weight is given by:

$$[[T]](x, z) = \sum_{\pi \in P(I, x, z, F)} \lambda(p[\pi]) w[\pi] \rho(n[\pi])$$

A key observation from [2] is that there is a general method for defining a string kernel from a weighted transducer $T$. Let $\Psi : \mathbb{R}_+ \to \mathbb{R}$ be a semiring morphism (for us, it will simply be inclusion), and denote by $T^{-1}$ the transducer obtained from $T$ by transposing the input and output labels of each transition.

Then if the composed transducer $S = T \circ T^{-1}$ is regulated, one obtains a rational string kernel for alphabet $\Sigma$ via

$$K(x, y) = \Psi([[S]](x, y)) = \sum_z \Psi([[T]](x, z))\Psi([[T]](y, z))$$

where the sum is over all strings $z \in \Delta^*$ (where $\Delta$ is the output alphabet for $T$) or equivalently, over all output strings that can be emitted by $T$. Therefore, we can think of $T$ as defining a feature map indexed by all possible output strings $z \in \Delta^*$ for $T$.

Using this construction, Cortes *et al.* showed that the $k$-gram counter transducer $T_k$ corresponds to the $k$-gram or $k$-spectrum kernel, and the gappy $k$-gram counter transducer $T_{k,\lambda}$ gives the unrestricted gappy $k$-gram kernel from [11]. Figure 3 shows diagrams of the 3-gram transducer $T_3$ and gappy 3-gram transducer $T_{3,\lambda}$. Our $(g, k, \lambda)$-gappy kernel $K^{\text{Weighted Gap}}_{(g,k,\lambda)}$ can be obtained from the composed transducer $T = T_{k,\lambda} \circ T_g$ using the $T \circ T^{-1}$ construction. (In all our examples, we use $\lambda(s) = 1$ for every initial state $s$ and $\rho(t) = 1$ for every final state $t$.)

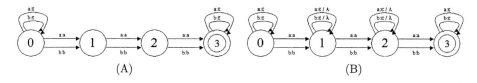

**Fig. 3. The $k$-gram and gappy $k$-gram transducers.** The diagrams show the 3-gram transducer (A) and the gappy 3-gram transducer (B) for a two-letter alphabet.

For the $(k, m)$-wildcard kernel, we set the output alphabet to be $\Delta = \Sigma \cup \{*\}$ and define a transducer with $m + 1$ final states, as indicated in the figure. The $m + 1$ final states correspond to destinations of paths that emit $k$-grams with 0, 1, ..., $m$ wildcard characters, respectively. The $(3, 1)$-wildcard transducer is shown in Figure 4.

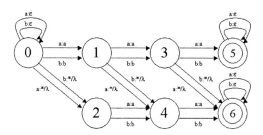

**Fig. 4. The $(k, m)$-wildcard transducer.** The diagram shows the $(3, 1)$-wildcard transducer for a two-letter alphabet.

The $(k, \sigma)$-substitution kernel does not appear to fall exactly into this framework, though if we threshold individual substitution probabilities independently rather than threshold the product probability over all positions in the $k$-mer, we can define a transducer that generates a similar kernel. Starting with the $k$-gram transducer, we add additional transitions (between "consecutive" states of the $k$-gram) of the form $a : b$ for those pairs of symbols with $-\log P(a|b) < \sigma_o$. Now there will be a (unique) path in the transducer that accepts $k$-mer $\alpha = a_1 a_2 \ldots a_k$ and emits $\beta = b_1 b_2 \ldots b_k$ if and only if every substitution satisfies $-\log P(a_i|b_i) < \sigma_o$.

## 5   Experiments

We tested all the new string kernels with SVM classifiers on a benchmark SCOP dataset from Jaakkola *et al.* [7], which is designed for the remote protein homology detection problem, in order to compare to results with the mismatch kernel reported in [9]. In these experiments, remote homology is simulated by holding out all members of a target SCOP family from a given superfamily as a test set, while examples chosen from the remaining families in the same superfamily form the positive training set. The negative test and training examples are chosen from disjoint sets of folds outside the target family's fold, so that negative test and negative training sets are unrelated to each other and to the positive examples. More details of the experimental set-up can be found in [7].

We compare the SVM classification performance of the three new string kernels with both the mismatch kernel and the Fisher kernel of Jaakkola *et al.* [7]. In the Fisher kernel method, the feature vectors are derived from profile HMMs trained on the positive training examples. The feature vector for sequence $x$ is the gradient of the log likelihood function $\log P(x|\theta)$ defined by the model and evaluated at the maximum likelihood estimate for model parameters: $\Phi(x) = \nabla_\theta \log P(x|\theta)|_{\theta=\theta_0}$. The Fisher kernel was the best performing method on this dataset prior to the mismatch-SVM approach, whose performance is as good as Fisher-SVM and better than all other standard methods tried [9].

We note that there is another successful feature representation for protein classification, the SVM-pairwise method presented in [10]. Here one uses an empirical kernel map based on pairwise Smith-Waterman [14] alignment scores

$$\Phi(x) = (d(x_1, x), \ldots, d(x_m, x))$$

where $x_i$, $i = 1 \ldots m$, are the training sequences and $d(x_i, x)$ is the E-value for the alignment score between $x$ and $x_i$. In the longer version of [9], we will show that the mismatch kernel used with an SVM classifier is competitive with SVM-pairwise on the smaller SCOP benchmark presented in [10]. For this reason, and because the SVM-pairwise feature map is expensive to compute on the larger SCOP dataset from [7] (each feature vector is $O(|x|^2 m)$, where $m$ is the number of training sequences), we compare the new kernels only to the mismatch kernel and the Fisher kernel.

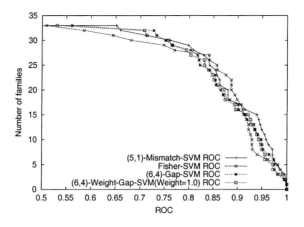

**Fig. 5. Comparison of of Mismatch-SVM, Fisher-SVM and Gappy-SVM.**
The graph plots the total number of families for which a given method exceeds an
ROC score threshold. The $(6, 4)$-Gap-SVM uses the unweighted gappy string kernel, in
which an instance $g$-mer contributes a value of 1 to a $k$-mer feature if the $k$-mer occurs
in it as a subsequence. The $(6, 4)$-Weight-Gap-SVM uses the weighted version of the
gappy string kernel, which counts the total number alignments of a $k$-mer against a
$g$-mer with multiplicative gap penalty of $\lambda$.

All methods are evaluated using the receiver operating characteristic (ROC)
score, which is the area under the graph of the rate of true positives as a function
of the rate of false positives as the threshold for the classifier varies [4]. Perfect
ranking of all positives above all negatives gives an ROC score of 1, while a
random classifier has an expected score close to 0.5.

## 5.1   Restricted Gappy Kernels

We tested the $(g, k)$-gappy kernel with parameter choices $(g, k) = (6, 4)$, $(7, 4)$,
$(8, 5)$, $(8, 6)$, and $(9, 6)$. Among them $(g, k) = (6, 4)$ yielded the best results,
though other choices of parameters had quite similar performance (data not
shown). We also tested the alternative weighted gappy kernel, where the contribution of an instance $g$-mer to a $k$-mer feature is a weighted sum of all the
possible matches of the $k$-mer to subsequences in the $g$-mer with multiplicative
gap penalty $\lambda$ $(0 < \lambda \leq 1)$. We used gap penalty $\lambda = 1.0$ and $\lambda = 0.5$ with the
$(6, 4)$ weighted gappy kernel. We found that $\lambda = 0.5$ weighting slightly weakened performance (results not shown). In Figure 5, we see that unweighted and
weighted $(\lambda = 1.0)$ gappy kernels have comparable results to $(5, 1)$-mismatch
kernel and Fisher kernel.

## 5.2   Substitution Kernels

We tested the substitution kernels with $(k, \sigma) = (4, 6.0)$. Here, $\sigma = 6.0$ was
chosen so that the members of a mutation neighborhood of a particular 4-mer

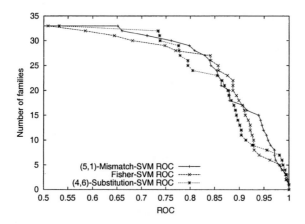

**Fig. 6. Comparison of mismatch-SVM, Fisher-SVM and substitution-SVM.**
The graph plots the total number of families for which a given method exceeds an ROC
score threshold.

would typically have only one position with a substitution, and such substitutions
would have fairly high probability. Therefore, the mutation neighborhoods were
much smaller than, for example, $(4, 1)$-mismatch neighborhoods. The results are
shown in Figure 6. Again, the substitution kernel has comparable performance
with mismatch-SVM and Fisher-SVM, though results are perhaps slightly weaker
for more difficult test families.

## 5.3   Wildcard Kernels

In order to compare with the $(5, 1)$-mismatch kernel, we tested wildcard kernels
with parameters $(k, m, \lambda) = (5, 1, 1.0)$ and $(k, m, \lambda) = (5, 1, 0.5)$. Results are
shown in Figure 7. The wildcard kernel with $\lambda = 1.0$ seems to perform as well
or almost as well as the $(5, 1)$-mismatch kernel and Fisher kernel, while enforcing a penalty on wildcard characters of $\lambda = 0.5$ seems to weaken performance
somewhat.

## 6   Discussion

We have presented a number of different kernels that capture a notion of inexact
matching – through use of gaps, probabilistic substitutions, and wildcards –
but maintain fast computation time. Using a recursive function based on a trie
data structure, we show that for all our new kernels, the time to compute a
kernel value $K(x, y)$ is $O(c_K(|x| + |y|))$, where the constant $c_K$ depends on the
parameters of the kernel but not on the size of the alphabet $\Sigma$. Thus we improve
on the constant factor involved in the mismatch kernel computation, in which
$|\Sigma|$ as well as $k$ and $m$ control the size of the mismatch neighborhood and hence
the constant $c_K$.

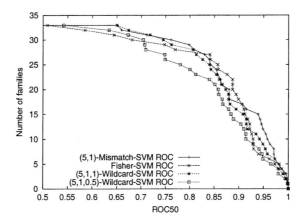

**Fig. 7. Comparison of mismatch-SVM, Fisher-SVM and wildcard-SVM.** The graph plots the total number of families for which a given method exceeds an ROC score threshold.

We also show how many of our kernels can be obtained through the recently presented transducer formalism of rational $T \circ T^{-1}$ kernels and give the transducer $T$ for several examples. This connection gives an intuitive understanding of the kernel definitions and could inspire new string kernels.

Finally, we present results on a benchmark SCOP dataset for the remote protein homology detection problem and show that many of the new, faster kernels achieve performance comparable to the mismatch kernel. Therefore, these new kernels seem promising for applications in computational biology and other domains involving learning from sequence data.

## Acknowledgments

We would like to thank Eleazar Eskin, Risi Kondor and William Stafford Noble for helpful discussions and Corinna Cortes, Patrick Haffner and Mehryar Mohri for explaining their transducer formalism to us. CL is supported by an Award in Informatics from the PhRMA Foundation and by NIH grant LM07276-02.

## References

1. S. F. Altschul, W. Gish, W. Miller, E. W. Myers, and D. J. Lipman. A basic local alignment search tool. *Journal of Molecular Biology*, 215:403–410, 1990.
2. C. Cortes, P. Haffner, and M. Mohri. Rational kernels. *Neural Information Processing Systems*, 2002.
3. E. Eskin, W. S. Noble, Y. Singer, and S. Snir. A unified approach for sequence prediction using sparse sequence models. Technical report, Hebrew University, 2003.

4. M. Gribskov and N. L. Robinson. Use of receiver operating characteristic (ROC) analysis to evaluate sequence matching. *Computers and Chemistry*, 20(1):25–33, 1996.

5. D. Haussler. Convolution kernels on discrete structure. Technical report, UC Santa Cruz, 1999.

6. S. Henikoff and J. G. Henikoff. Amino acid substitution matrices from protein blocks. *PNAS*, 89:10915–10919, 1992.

7. T. Jaakkola, M. Diekhans, and D. Haussler. Using the Fisher kernel method to detect remote protein homologies. In *Proceedings of the Seventh International Conference on Intelligent Systems for Molecular Biology*, pages 149–158. AAAI Press, 1999.

8. C. Leslie, E. Eskin, and W. S. Noble. The spectrum kernel: A string kernel for SVM protein classification. *Proceedings of the Pacific Biocomputing Symposium*, 2002.

9. C. Leslie, E. Eskin, J. Weston, and W. S. Noble. Mismatch string kernels for SVM protein classification. *Neural Information Processing Systems 15*, 2002.

10. C. Liao and W. S. Noble. Combining pairwise sequence similarity and support vector machines for remote protein homology detection. *Proceedings of the Sixth Annual International Conference on Research in Computational Molecular Biology*, 2002. To appear.

11. Huma Lodhi, Craig Saunders, John Shawe-Taylor, Nello Cristianini, and Chris Watkins. Text classification using string kernels. *Journal of Machine Learning Research*, 2:419–444, 2002.

12. R. M. Schwartz and M. O. Dayhoff. Matrices for detecing distant relationships. In *Atlas of Protein Sequence and Structure*, pages 353–358, Silver Spring, MD, 1978. National Biomedical Research Foundation.

13. S. V. N. Vishwanathan and A. Smola. Fast kernels for string and tree matching. *Neural Information Processing Systems 15*, 2002.

14. M. S. Waterman, J. Joyce, and M. Eggert. *Computer alignment of sequences*, chapter Phylogenetic Analysis of DNA Sequences. Oxford, 1991.

15. C. Watkins. Dynamic alignment kernels. Technical report, UL Royal Holloway, 1999.

# On Graph Kernels:
# Hardness Results and Efficient Alternatives

Thomas Gärtner[1,2,3], Peter Flach[3], and Stefan Wrobel[1,2]

[1] Fraunhofer Institut Autonome Intelligente Systeme, Germany
{Thomas.Gaertner,Stefan.Wrobel}@ais.fraunhofer.de
[2] Department of Computer Science III, University of Bonn, Germany
[3] Department of Computer Science, University of Bristol, UK
Peter.Flach@bristol.ac.uk

**Abstract.** As most 'real-world' data is structured, research in kernel methods has begun investigating kernels for various kinds of structured data. One of the most widely used tools for modeling structured data are graphs. An interesting and important challenge is thus to investigate kernels on instances that are represented by graphs. So far, only very specific graphs such as trees and strings have been considered.

This paper investigates kernels on labeled directed graphs with general structure. It is shown that computing a strictly positive definite graph kernel is at least as hard as solving the graph isomorphism problem. It is also shown that computing an inner product in a feature space indexed by all possible graphs, where each feature counts the number of subgraphs isomorphic to that graph, is *NP*-hard. On the other hand, inner products in an alternative feature space, based on walks in the graph, can be computed in polynomial time. Such kernels are defined in this paper.

## 1 Introduction

Support vector machines [1] are among the most successful recent developments within the machine learning community. Along with some other learning algorithms they form the class of kernel methods [15]. The computational attractiveness of kernel methods is due to the fact that they can be applied in high dimensional feature spaces without suffering from the high cost of explicitly computing the feature map. This is possible by using a positive definite kernel $k$ on any set $\mathcal{X}$. For such $k : \mathcal{X} \times \mathcal{X} \to \mathbb{R}$ it is known that a map $\phi : \mathcal{X} \to \mathcal{H}$ into a Hilbert space $\mathcal{H}$ exists, such that $k(x, x') = \langle \phi(x), \phi(x') \rangle$ for all $x, x' \in \mathcal{X}$.

Kernel methods have so far successfully been applied to various tasks in attribute-value learning. Much 'real-world' data, however, is structured – there is no natural representation of the instances of the learning problem as a tuple of constants. In computer science graphs are a widely used tool for modeling structured data. They can be used, for example, as a representation for molecules.

Unfortunately, due to the powerful expressiveness of graphs, defining appropriate kernel functions for graphs has proven difficult. In order to control the

B. Schölkopf and M.K. Warmuth (Eds.): COLT/Kernel 2003, LNAI 2777, pp. 129–143, 2003.

complexity of such kernels, one line of existing research has concentrated on special kinds of graphs, in particular, trees [2] or strings [17, 14] which results in efficient kernels, but loses most of the power of general graphs. More recently, [4, 9] have investigated efficient kernels for general graphs based on particular kinds of walks, which captures more, but still far from all of the structure of the graph. An interesting open problem is thus whether approaches such as the latter can be further generalized, and if so, if it is possible to define kernels that take the entire structure of graphs into account.

In this paper, we give answers to both of these questions. Firstly, we prove that computing any kernel function that is capable of fully recognizing the structure of graphs (using subgraph-isomorphism) is *NP*-hard, making it extremely unlikely that efficient kernels can be found. Secondly, we show that nonetheless there is room for improvement by presenting a generalized family of kernels based on walks which includes the kernels proposed in [4, 9] as special cases while still being polynomially computable.

The outline of the paper is as follows: Section 1.1 first gives an intuitive overview over the important results of this paper. Section 2 gives then a brief overview of graph theoretic concepts. Section 3 defines what might be the ideal graph kernel but also shows that such kernels cannot be computed in polynomial time. Section 4 and 5 introduce alternative graph kernels. Section 6 shows how these kernels can be extended and computed efficiently. Finally, section 7 discusses related work and section 8 concludes with future work.

## 1.1   Motivation and Approach

Consider a graph kernel that has one feature $\Phi_H$ for each possible graph $H$, each feature $\Phi_H(G)$ measuring how many subgraphs of $G$ have the same structure as graph $H$. Using the inner product in this feature space, graphs satisfying certain properties can be identified. In particular, one could decide whether a graph has a Hamiltonian path, i.e., a sequence of adjacent vertices and edges that contains every vertex and edge exactly once. Now this problem is known to be *NP*-hard, i.e., it is strongly believed that this problem can not be solved in polynomial time. Thus we need to consider alternative graph kernels.

We investigate mainly two alternative approaches. One is to define a similarity of two graphs based on the length of all walks between each pair of vertices in the graph. The other is to measure the number of times given label sequences occur in this graph. The inner product in this feature space can be computed directly, by first building the product graph and then computing the limit of a matrix power series of the adjacency matrix. In both cases the computation is possible in polynomial time.

To illustrate these kernels, consider a simple graph with four vertices labeled 'c', 'a', 'r', and 't', respectively. We also have four edges in this graph: one from the vertex labeled 'c' to the vertex labeled 'a', one from 'a' to 'r', one from 'r' to 't', and one from 'a' to 't'. The non-zero features in the label pair feature space are $\phi_{c,c} = \phi_{a,a} = \phi_{r,r} = \phi_{t,t} = \lambda_0$, $\phi_{c,a} = \phi_{a,r} = \phi_{r,t} = \lambda_1$, $\phi_{a,t} = \lambda_1 + \lambda_2$, $\phi_{c,r} = \lambda_2$, and $\phi_{c,t} = \lambda_2$. The non-zero features in the label sequence feature space are

$\phi_c = \phi_a = \phi_r = \phi_t = \sqrt{\lambda_0}$, $\phi_{ca} = \phi_{ar} = \phi_{at} = \phi_{rt} = \sqrt{\lambda_1}$, $\phi_{car} = \phi_{cat} = \lambda_2$, and $\phi_{cart} = \sqrt{\lambda_3}$. The $\lambda_i$ are user defined weights and the square-roots appear only to make the computation of the kernel more elegant. In particular, we show how closed forms of the inner products in this feature space can be computed for exponential and geometric choises of $\lambda_i$.

## 2   Graphs

This section gives a brief overview of graphs. For a more in-depth discussion of these and related concepts the reader is referred to [3, 13].

### 2.1   Basic Terminology and Notation

Generally, a *graph* $G$ is described by a finite set of *vertices* $\mathcal{V}$, a finite set of *edges* $\mathcal{E}$, and a function $\Psi$. For *hypergraphs* this function maps each edge to a set of vertices $\Psi : \mathcal{E} \to \{X \subseteq \mathcal{V}\}$. For *undirected* graphs the codomain of the function is restricted to sets of vertices with two elements only $\Psi : \mathcal{E} \to \{X \subseteq \mathcal{V} : |X| = 2\}$. For *directed* graphs the function maps each edge to the tuple consisting of its initial and terminal node $\Psi : \mathcal{E} \to \{(u, v) \in \mathcal{V} \times \mathcal{V}\}$. Edges $e$ in a directed graph for which $\Psi(e) = (v, v)$ are called $s$. Two edges $e, e'$ are *parallel* if $\Psi(e) = \Psi(e')$. We will sometimes assume some enumeration of the vertices in a graph, i.e., $\mathcal{V} = \{\nu_i\}_{i=1}^n$ where $n = |\mathcal{V}|$.

For *labeled* graphs there is additionally a set of labels $\mathcal{L}$ along with a function *label* assigning a label to each edge and/or vertex. In *edge-labeled* graphs, labels are assigned to edges only; in *vertex-labeled* graphs, labels are assigned to vertices only; and in *fully-labeled* graphs, labels are assigned to edges and vertices. It is useful to have some enumeration of all possible labels at hand, i.e., $\mathcal{L} = \{\ell_r\}_{r \in \mathbb{N}}$ [1].

In this paper we are mainly concerned with labeled directed graphs without parallel edges. In this case we can – for simplicity of notation – identify an edge with its image under the map $\Psi$. In what follows 'graph' will always refer to labeled directed graphs without parallel edges. Each graph will be described by a two-tuple $G = (\mathcal{V}, \mathcal{E})$ such that $\mathcal{E} \subseteq \mathcal{V} \times \mathcal{V}$. To refer to the vertex and edge set of a specific graph we will use the notation $\mathcal{V}(G), \mathcal{E}(G)$. Wherever we distinguish two graphs by their subscript $(G_i)$ or some other symbol $(G', G^*)$ the same notation will be used to distinguish their vertex and edge sets.

A generalization of the concepts and functions described in this paper to graphs with parallel edges is straightforward, however, directly considering them in this paper would obscure notation. Graphs with undirected edges can – for all purposes of this paper – be identified with a directed graph that has two edges for each edge in the undirected graph. Graphs without labels can be seen as a special case of labeled graphs where the same label is assigned to each edge and/or vertex. Hypergraphs are not considered in this paper.

---

[1] While $\ell_1$ will be used to always denote the same label, $l_1$ is a variable that can take different values, e.g., $\ell_1, \ell_2, \ldots$ .. The same holds for vertex $\nu_1$ and variable $v_1$.

Last but not least we need to define some special graphs. A *walk*[2] $w$ is a sequence of vertices $w = v_1, v_2, \ldots v_{n+1}$; $v_i \in \mathcal{V}$ such that $(v_i, v_{i+1}) \in \mathcal{E}$. The *length* of the walk is equal to the number of edges in this sequence, i.e., $n$ in the above case. A *path* is a walk in which $v_i \neq v_j \Leftrightarrow i \neq j$. A *cycle* is a path with $(v_{n+1}, v_1) \in \mathcal{E}$.

A graph $G = (\mathcal{V}, \mathcal{E})$ is called *connected* if there is a walk between any two vertices in the following graph: $(\mathcal{V}, \mathcal{E} \cup \{(u, v) : (v, u) \in \mathcal{E}\})$. For a graph $G = (\mathcal{V}(G), \mathcal{E}(G))$, we denote by $G[\mathcal{V}^*]$ the subgraph *induced* by the set of vertices $\mathcal{V}^* \subseteq \mathcal{V}(G)$, that is $G[\mathcal{V}^*] = (\mathcal{V}^*, \{(u, v) \in \mathcal{E}(G) : u, v \in \mathcal{V}^*\})$. A *subgraph* of $G$ is a graph $H = (\mathcal{V}(H), \mathcal{E}(H))$ with $\mathcal{V}(H) \subseteq \mathcal{V}(G)$ and $\mathcal{E}(H) \subseteq \mathcal{E}(G[\mathcal{V}(H)])$. A subgraph $H$ of $G$ is *proper* if $\mathcal{V}(H) \subset \mathcal{V}(G)$; it is *spanning* if $\mathcal{V}(H) = \mathcal{V}(G)$. If a path or a cycle is a subgraph of a graph $G$, it is often called a walk or cycle in $G$. A spanning path in $G$ is called a *Hamiltonian path*; a spanning cycle in $G$ is called a *Hamiltonian cycle*.

## 2.2    Matrix Notation and Some Functions

For the description of our graph kernels it turns out to be useful to have a matrix representation for (labeled directed) graphs. Let $[A]_{ij}$ denote the element in the $i$-th row and $j$-th column of matrix $A$. For two $m \times n$ matrices $A, B$ (given by $[A]_{ij}, [B]_{ij} \in \mathbb{R}$) the inner product is defined as $\langle A, B \rangle = \sum_{i,j} [A]_{ij} [B]_{ij}$. Furthermore, $\mathbf{I}$ denotes the identity matrix; $\mathbf{0}, \mathbf{1}$ denote matrices with all elements equal to $0, 1$, respectively.

A graph $G$ can uniquely be described by its label and adjacency matrices. The label matrix $L$ is defined by $[L]_{ri} = 1 \Leftrightarrow \ell_r = label(\nu_i)$, $[L]_{ri} = 0 \Leftrightarrow \ell_r \neq label(\nu_i)$. The adjacency matrix $E$ is defined by $[E]_{ij} = 1 \Leftrightarrow (\nu_i, \nu_j) \in \mathcal{E}$, $[E]_{ij} = 0 \Leftrightarrow (\nu_i, \nu_j) \notin \mathcal{E}$. We also need to define some functions describing the neighborhood of a vertex $v$ in a graph $G$: $\delta^+(v) = \{(v, u) \in \mathcal{E}\}$ and $\delta^-(v) = \{(u, v) \in \mathcal{E}\}$. Here, $|\delta^+(v)|$ is called the *outdegree* of a vertex and $|\delta^-(v)|$ the *indegree*. Furthermore, the maximal indegree and outdegree are denoted by $\Delta^-(G) = max\{|\delta^-(v)|, v \in \mathcal{V}\}$ and $\Delta^+(G) = max\{|\delta^+(v)|, v \in \mathcal{V}\}$, respectively. It is clear that the maximal indegree equals the maximal column sum of the adjacency matrix and that the maximal outdegree equals the maximal row sum of the adjacency matrix. For $a \geq min\{\Delta^+(G), \Delta^-(G)\}$, $a^n$ is an upper bound on each component of the matrix $E^n$. This will be useful to determine the convergence properties of some graph kernels.

## 2.3    Interpretation of Matrix Powers

First consider the diagonal matrix $LL^\top$. The $i$-th element of the diagonal of this matrix, i.e. $[LL^\top]_{ii}$, corresponds to the number of times label $\ell_i$ is assigned to a vertex in the graph. Now consider the matrix $E$. The component $[E]_{ij}$ describes whether there is an edge between vertex $\nu_i$ and $\nu_j$. Now we combine the label

---

[2] What we call 'walk' is sometimes called an 'edge progression'.

and adjacency matrix as $LEL^\mathsf{T}$. Each component $[LEL^\mathsf{T}]_{ij}$ corresponds to the number of edges between vertices labeled $\ell_i$ and vertices labeled $\ell_j$.

Replacing the adjacency matrix $E$ by its $n$-th power ($n \in \mathbb{N}, n \geq 0$), the interpretation is quite similar. Each component $[E^n]_{ij}$ of this matrix gives the number of walks of length $n$ from vertex $\nu_i$ to $\nu_j$. Multiplying this with the label matrix, we obtain the matrix $LE^nL^\mathsf{T}$. Each component $[LE^nL^\mathsf{T}]_{ij}$ now corresponds to the number of walks of length $n$ between vertices labeled $\ell_i$ and vertices labeled $\ell_j$.

## 2.4   Product Graphs

Product graphs [8] are a very interesting tool in discrete mathematics. The four most important graph products are the Cartesian, the strong, the direct, and the lexicographic product. While the most fundamental one is the Cartesian graph product, in our context the direct graph product is the most important ones.

Usually, graph products are defined on unlabeled graphs. However, in many real-world machine learning problems it could be important to be able to deal with labeled graphs. We extend the definition of graph products to labeled graphs and give the relevant definition in the appropriate places in this paper.

# 3   Complete Graph Kernels

In this section, all vertices and edges are assumed to have the same label. If there is no polynomial time algorithm for this special case then there is obviously no polynomial time algorithm for the general case.

When considering the set of all graphs $\mathcal{G}$, many graphs in this set differ only in the enumeration of vertices, and thus edges, and not in their structure: these graphs are *isomorphic*. Since usually in learning, the names given to vertices in different graphs have no meaning, we want kernels not to distinguish between isomorphic graphs. Formally, two graphs $G, H$ are isomorphic if there is a bijection $\psi : \mathcal{V}(G) \to \mathcal{V}(H)$ such that for all $(u, v) \in \mathcal{E}(G) \Leftrightarrow (\psi(u), \psi(v)) \in \mathcal{E}(H)$. We denote that $G, H$ are isomorphic by $G \simeq H$. In the remainder of this paper we define all kernels and maps on the quotient set of the set of all graphs with respect to isomorphism, i.e., the set of equivalence classes. To keep the notation simple, we will continue to refer to this set as $\mathcal{G}$, and also refer to each equivalence class simply by one of its representative graphs.

While it is easy to see that graph isomorphism is in *NP* it is – in spite of a lot of research devoted to this question – still not known whether graph isomorphism is in *P* or if it is *NP*-complete. It is believed that graph isomorphism lies between *P* and *NP*-complete [11].

The first class of graph kernels we are going to consider is those kernels that allow to distinguish between all (non-isomorphic) graphs in feature space. If a kernel does not allow us to distinguish between two graphs then there is no way any learning machine based on this kernel function can separate these two graphs. Investigating the complexity of graph kernels that distinguish between all graphs is thus an interesting problem.

**Definition 1.** *Let $\mathcal{G}$ denote the set of all graphs and let $\Phi : \mathcal{G} \to \mathcal{H}$ be a map from this set into a Hilbert space $\mathcal{H}$. Furthermore, let $k : \mathcal{G} \times \mathcal{G} \to \mathbb{R}$ be such that $\langle \Phi(G), \Phi(G') \rangle = k(G, G')$. If $\Phi$ is injective, $k$ is called a* complete *graph kernel.*

**Proposition 1.** *Computing any complete graph kernel is at least as hard as deciding whether two graphs are isomorphic.*

*Proof.* Let all functions be as in definition 1. As $\Phi$ is injective, $k(G, G) - 2k(G, G')$ $+ k(G', G') = \langle \Phi(G) - \Phi(G'), \Phi(G) - \Phi(G') \rangle = 0$ if and only if $G \simeq G'$.    □

It is well known that there are polynomial time algorithms to decide isomorphism for several restricted graph classes [11], for example, planar graphs. However, considering kernels on restricted graph classes is beyond the scope of this paper. The remaining question for us is whether the above complexity result is tight, i.e., if there is a complete graph kernel that is (exactly) as hard as deciding graph isomorphism. This is obvious considering the kernel $k(G, G') = 1 \Leftrightarrow G \simeq G'$ and $k(G, G') = 0 \Leftrightarrow G \not\simeq G'$. Now the following corollary is interesting.

**Corollary 1.** *Computing any strictly positive definite graph kernel is at least as hard as deciding whether two graphs are isomorphic.*

*Proof.* This follows directly from proposition 1 and strictly positive definite graph kernels being complete.    □

We will now look at another interesting class of graph kernels. Intuitively, it is useful to base the similarity of two graphs on their common subgraphs.

**Definition 2.** *Let $\mathcal{G}$ denote the set of all graphs and let $\lambda$ be a sequence $\lambda_1, \lambda_2, \ldots$ of weights ($\lambda_n \in \mathbb{R}; \lambda_n > 0$ for all $n \in \mathbb{N}$). The* subgraph feature space *is defined by the map $\Phi : \mathcal{G} \to \mathcal{H}$ into the Hilbert space $\mathcal{H}$ with one feature $\Phi_H$ for each connected graph $H \in \mathcal{G}$, such that for every graph $G \in \mathcal{G}$*

$$\Phi_H(G) = \lambda_{|\mathcal{E}(H)|} |\{G' \text{ is subgraph of } G : G' \simeq H\}|$$

Clearly, the inner product in the above feature space is a complete graph kernel and thus computing the inner product is at least as hard as solving the graph isomorphism problem. However, we are able to show an even stronger result.

**Proposition 2.** *Computing the inner product in the subgraph feature space is NP-hard.*

*Proof.* Let $P_n \in \mathcal{G}$ be the path graph with $n$ edges and let $\mathbf{e}_H$ be a vector in the subgraph feature space such that the feature corresponding to graph $H$ equals 1 and all other features equal 0. Let $G$ be any graph with $m$ vertices. As $\{\Phi(P_n)\}_{n \in \mathbb{N}}$ is linearly independent, there are $\alpha_1, \ldots, \alpha_m$ such that $\alpha_1 \Phi(P_1) + \ldots + \alpha_m \Phi(P_m) = \mathbf{e}_{P_m}$. These $\alpha_1, \ldots, \alpha_m$ can be found in polynomial time, as in each image of a path $P_n$ under the map $\Phi$ only $n$ features are different from 0. Then, $\alpha_1 \langle \Phi(P_1), \Phi(G) \rangle + \ldots + \alpha_m \langle \Phi(P_m), \Phi(G) \rangle > 0$ if and only if $G$ has a Hamiltonian path. However, it is well known that the decision problem whether a graph has a Hamiltonian path is *NP*-complete.    □

A first approach to defining graph kernels for which there is a polynomial time algorithm might be to restrict the feature space of $\Phi$ to features $\Phi_H$ where $H$ is a member of a restricted class of graphs. However, even if $H$ is restricted to paths the above proof still applies. Closely related to the Hamiltonian path problem is the problem of finding the longest path in a graph. This problem is known to be *NP*-complete even on (most) restricted graph classes [16]. Thus even restricting the domain of $\Phi$ is not likely to improve the computational complexity.

The results shown in this section indicate that it is intractable to compute complete graph kernels and inner products in feature spaces made up by graphs isomorphic to subgraphs. Our approach to define polynomial time computable graph kernels is to have the feature space be made up by graphs homomorphic to subgraphs. In the remainder of this paper we will thus concentrate on walks instead of paths in graphs.

## 4   Kernels Based on Label Pairs

In this section we consider vertex-labeled graphs only. In some applications there is reason to suppose that only the distance between (all) pairs of vertices of some label has an impact on the classification of the graph. In such applications we suggest the following feature space.

**Definition 3.** *Let $W_n(G)$ denote the set of all possible walks with $n$ edges in $G$ and let $\lambda$ be a sequence $\lambda_0, \lambda_1, \ldots$ of weights ($\lambda_n \in \mathbb{R}; \lambda_n \geq 0$ for all $n \in \mathbb{N}$). For a given walk $w \in W_n(G)$ let $l_1(w)$ denote the label of the first vertex of the walk and $l_{n+1}(w)$ denote the label of the last vertex of the walk.*

*The label pair feature space is defined by one feature $\phi_{\ell_i, \ell_j}$ for each pair of labels $\ell_i, \ell_j$:*

$$\phi_{\ell_i, \ell_j}(G) = \sum_{n=0}^{\infty} \lambda_n \left|\{w \in W_n(G) : l_1(w) = \ell_i \wedge l_{n+1}(w) = \ell_j\}\right|$$

Let all functions and variables be defined as in definition 3. The key to efficient computation of the kernel corresponding to the above feature map is the following equation:

$$\langle \phi(G), \phi(G') \rangle = \left\langle L \left( \sum_{i=0}^{\infty} \lambda_i E^i \right) L^\top, L' \left( \sum_{j=0}^{\infty} \lambda_j E'^j \right) L'^\top \right\rangle$$

As we are only interested in cases in which $||\phi(G)||$ is finite, we generally assume that $\sum_i \lambda_i a^i$ for $a = \min\{\Delta^+(G), \Delta^-(G)\}$ converges. To compute this graph kernel, it is then necessary to compute the above matrix power series. See section 6.1 for more details.

Although the map $\phi_{\ell_i, \ell_j}$ is injective if the function *label* is injective, the dimensionality of the label pair feature space is low, if the number of different labels is low. In particular the dimensionality of the label pair feature space equals the number of different labels squared (that is $|\mathcal{L}|^2$). In domains in which only few labels occur, this might be a feature space of too low dimension.

One obvious way to achieve a higher dimensional – and thus more expressive – feature space is to use a more expressive label set including, for example, some information about the neighborhood of the vertices. Still, this manual enrichment of the feature space is not in all cases desired. For that reason, in the next section we describe a kernel function that operates in a more expressive feature space. The key idea of the kernel is to have each dimension of the feature space correspond to one particular label sequence. Thus even with very few – and even with a single – labels, the feature space will already be of infinite dimension.

## 5    Kernels Based on Contiguous Label Sequences

In this section we consider graphs with labels on vertices and/or edges. In the presence of few labels, the kernel described in the previous section suffers from too little expressivity. The kernel described in this section overcomes this by defining one feature for every possible label sequence and then counting how many walks in a graph match this label sequence. In order not to have to distinguish all three cases of edge-labeled, vertex-labeled, and fully-labeled graphs explicitly, we extend the domain of the function *label* to include all vertices and edges. In edge-labeled graphs we define $label(v) = \#$ for all vertices $v$ and in vertex-labeled graphs we define $label(u, v) = \#$ for all edges $(u, v)$.

We begin by defining the feature space of contiguous (or unbroken) label sequences and the *direct graph product*, central to the further developments in this section.

**Definition 4.** *Let $\mathcal{S}_n$ denote the set of all possible label sequences of walks with $n$ edges and let $\lambda$ be a sequence $\lambda_0, \lambda_1, \ldots$ of weights ($\lambda_i \in \mathbb{R}; \lambda_i \geq 0$ for all $i \in \mathbb{N}$). Furthermore, let $\mathcal{W}_n(G)$ denote the set of all possible walks with $n$ edges in graph $G$. For a given walk $w \in \mathcal{W}_n(G)$ let $l_i(w)$ denote the $i$-th label of the walk.*

*The sequence feature space is defined by one feature for each possible label sequence. In particular, for any given length $n$ and label sequence $s = s_1, \ldots, s_{2n+1}$; $s \in \mathcal{S}_n$, the corresponding feature value for every graph $G$ is:*

$$\phi_s(G) = \sqrt{\lambda_n} \, |\{w \in \mathcal{W}_n(G), \forall \, i : \, s_i = l_i(w)\}|$$

**Definition 5.** *We denote the direct product of two graphs $G_1 = (\mathcal{V}_1, \mathcal{E}_1), G_2 = (\mathcal{V}_2, \mathcal{E}_2)$ by $G_1 \times G_2$. The vertex and edge set of the direct product are respectively defined as:*

$$\mathcal{V}(G_1 \times G_2) = \{(v_1, v_2) \in \mathcal{V}_1 \times \mathcal{V}_2 : (label(v_1) = label(v_2))\}$$

$$\mathcal{E}(G_1 \times G_2) = \{((u_1, u_2), (v_1, v_2)) \in \mathcal{V}^2(G_1 \times G_2) :$$
$$(u_1, v_1) \in \mathcal{E}_1 \wedge (u_2, v_2) \in \mathcal{E}_2 \wedge (label(u_1, v_1) = label(u_2, v_2))\}$$

*A vertex (edge) in graph $G_1 \times G_2$ has the same label as the corresponding vertices (edges) in $G_1$ and $G_2$.*

Before giving the definition of direct product graph kernels we will now describe and interpret some properties of the product graph. The following proposition relates the number of times a label sequence occurs in the product graph to the number of times it occurs in each factor.

**Proposition 3.** *Let all variables and functions be defined as in definition 4 and 5. Furthermore, let $G, G'$ be two graphs. Then*

$$|\{w \in W_n(G \times G'), \forall i : s_i = l_i(w)\}|$$
$$= |\{w \in W_n(G), \forall i : s_i = l_i(w)\}| \cdot |\{w \in W_n(G'), \forall i : s_i = l_i(w)\}|$$

*Proof.* It is sufficient to show a bijection between every walk in the product graph and one walk in both graphs such that their label sequences match.

Consider first a walk in the product graph $w^* \in W_n(G \times G')$:

$$w^* = (v_1, v_1'), (v_2, v_2'), \dots, (v_n, v_n')$$

with $(v_i, v_i') \in V(G \times G')$. Now let $w = v_1, v_2, \dots, v_n$ and $w' = v_1', v_2', \dots, v_n'$. Clearly $w \in W_n(G)$, $w' \in W_n(G')$, and

$$\forall i : l_i(w^*) = l_i(w) = l_i(w')$$

The opposite holds as well: For every two walks $w \in W_n(G)$, $w' \in W_n(G')$ with matching label sequences, there is a walk $w^* \in W_n(G \times G')$ with a label sequence that matches the label sequences of $w$ and $w'$. □

Having introduced product graphs and having shown how these can be interpreted, we are now able to define the direct product kernel.

**Definition 6.** *Let $G_1, G_2$ be two graphs, let $E_\times$ denote the adjacency matrix of their direct product $E_\times = E(G_1 \times G_2)$, and let $V_\times$ denote the vertex set of the direct product $V_\times = V(G_1 \times G_2)$. With a sequence of weights $\lambda = \lambda_0, \lambda_1, \dots$ ($\lambda_i \in \mathbb{R}; \lambda_i \geq 0$ for all $i \in \mathbb{N}$) the direct product kernel is defined as*

$$k_\times(G_1, G_2) = \sum_{i,j=1}^{|V_\times|} \left[ \sum_{n=0}^{\infty} \lambda_n E_\times^n \right]_{ij}$$

*if the limit exists.*

**Proposition 4.** *Let $\phi$ be as in definition 4 and $k_\times$ as in definition 6. For any two graphs $G, G'$, $k_\times(G, G') = \langle \phi(G), \phi(G') \rangle$*

*Proof.* This follows directly from proposition 3. □

To compute this graph kernel, it is then necessary to compute the above matrix power series. See section 6.1 for more details.

# 6    Extensions and Computation

This section shows how the limits of matrix power series can efficiently be computed, how the concepts presented above can be extended to graphs with transition probabilities, and how a kernel based on non-contiguous label sequences can be computed.

## 6.1    Computation of Matrix Power Series

In this section we show how matrix power series of the type $\lim_{n \to \infty} \sum_{i=0}^{n} \lambda_i E^i$ can efficiently be computed for some choices of $\lambda$.

*Exponential Series* Similar to the exponential of a scalar value ($e^b = 1 + b/1! + b^2/2! + b^3/3! + \ldots$) the exponential of the square matrix $E$ is defined as

$$e^{\beta E} = \lim_{n \to \infty} \sum_{i=0}^{n} \frac{(\beta E)^i}{i!}$$

where we use $\frac{\beta^0}{0!} = 1$ and $E^0 = \mathbf{I}$. Feasible exponentiation of matrices in general requires diagonalising the matrix. If the matrix $E$ can be diagonalized such that $E = T^{-1}DT$ we can easily calculate arbitrary powers of the matrix as $E^n = (T^{-1}DT)^n = T^{-1}D^nT$ and for a diagonal matrix we can calculate the power component-wise $[D^n]_{i,i} = [D_{i,i}]^n$. Thus $e^{\beta E} = T^{-1}e^{\beta D}T$ where $e^{\beta D}$ is calculated component-wise. Once the matrix is diagonalized, computing the exponential matrix can be done in linear time. Matrix diagonalization is a matrix eigenvalue problem and such methods have roughly cubic time complexity.

*Geometric Series* The geometric series $\sum_i \gamma^i$ is known to converge if and only if $|\gamma| < 1$. In this case the limit is given by $\lim_{n \to \infty} \sum_{i=0}^{n} \gamma^i = \frac{1}{1-\gamma}$. Similarly, we define the geometric series of a matrix as

$$\lim_{n \to \infty} \sum_{i=0}^{n} \gamma^i E^i$$

if $\gamma < 1/a$, where $a \geq \min\{\Delta^+(G), \Delta^-(G)\}$ as above. Feasible computation of the limit of a geometric series is possible by inverting the matrix $\mathbf{I} - \gamma E$. To see this, let $(\mathbf{I} - \gamma E)x = 0$, thus $\gamma E x = x$ and $(\gamma E)^i x = x$. Now, note that $(\gamma E)^i \to 0$ as $i \to \infty$. Therefore $x = 0$ and $\mathbf{I} - \gamma E$ is regular. Then $(\mathbf{I} - \gamma E)(\mathbf{I} + \gamma E + \gamma^2 E^2 + \cdots) = \mathbf{I}$ and $(\mathbf{I} - \gamma E)^{-1} = (\mathbf{I} + \gamma E + \gamma^2 E^2 + \cdots)$ is obvious. Matrix inversion is roughly of cubic time complexity.

## 6.2    Transition Graphs

In some cases graphs are employed to model discrete random processes such as Markov chains [7]. In these cases a *transition probability* is assigned to each edge.

We only consider the case that the transition probability does not change over time. Such graphs will be called *transition graphs*. In transition graphs vertices are often called *states*. We denote the probability of going from vertex $u$ to $v$ by $p_{(u,v)}$. More precisely this denotes the probability of the process being in state $v$ at time $t + 1$ given that it was in state $u$ at time $t$. Usually, transitions are without loss, i.e., $\forall u \in \mathcal{V} : \sum_{(u,v) \in \mathcal{E}} p_{(u,v)} = 1$. In some cases, there is a probability $p_{\text{stop}}$ that the process stops at any time.

In order to deal with graphs modeling random processes, we replace the adjacency matrix $E$ of a graph by the transition matrix $R$ with $[R]_{ij} = p_{(\nu_i,\nu_j)}(1 - p_{\text{stop}})$ if $(\nu_i, \nu_j) \in \mathcal{E}$ and $[R]_{ij} = 0$ otherwise. Without loss of generality we assume $p_{(\nu_i,\nu_j)} > 0 \Leftrightarrow (\nu_i, \nu_j) \in \mathcal{E}$. Before we can apply the kernel introduced in the previous section to transition graphs we have to redefine the functions $\Delta^+(G), \Delta^-(G)$ to be the maximal row and column sum of the matrix $R$ of a graph $G$, respectively. Clearly $\Delta^+(G), \Delta^-(G) \leq 1$.

If we use the transition matrix $R$ instead of the adjacency matrix, we get to a similar interpretation. $[R^n]_{ij}$ determines then the probability of getting from vertex $\nu_i$ to vertex $\nu_j$ in $n$ steps. The interpretation of $[LR^nL^\top]_{ij}$ is a bit more complicated. If we divide by the number of times label $\ell_i$ occurs, however, interpretation becomes easy again. Thus consider $[LR^nL^\top]_{ij}/[LL^\top]_{ii}$. This is the probability that having started at any vertex labeled $\ell_i$ and taking $n$ steps, we arrive at any vertex labeled $\ell_j$. The division by $[LL^\top]_{ii}$ can be justified by assuming a uniform distribution for starting at a particular vertex with label $\ell_i$.

A graph with some transition matrix $R$ and stopping probability $p_{\text{stop}} = 0$ can be interpreted as a *Markov chain*. A vertex $v$ with a transition probability $p_{(v,v)} = 1$ in a Markov chain is called *absorbing*. An absorbing Markov chain is a Markov chain with a vertex $v$ such that $v$ is absorbing and there is a walk from any vertex $u$ to the absorbing vertex $v$. It is known [7] that in absorbing Markov chains the limit of $R^n$ for $n \to \infty$ is $\mathbf{0}$. If we define $N = \mathbf{I} + R + R^2 + \cdots$ then $[N]_{ij}$ is the expected number of times the chain is in vertex $\nu_j$ given that it starts in vertex $\nu_i$. $N$ can be computed as the inverse of the matrix $\mathbf{I} - R$.

In the case of graphs with transition probabilities on the edges, the edges in the product graph have probability $p_{(u_{12},v_{12})} = p_{(u_1,v_1)}p_{(u_2,v_2)}$ where $u_{12} = (u_1, u_2) \in \mathcal{V}(G_1 \times G_2)$ and $v_{12} = (v_1, v_2) \in \mathcal{V}(G_1 \times G_2)$. Let $p_1, p_2$ denote the stopping probability in graphs $G_1, G_2$ respectively. The stopping probability $p_{12}$ in the product graph is then given by $p_{12} = 1 - (1 - p_1)(1 - p_2)$. A similar interpretation to proposition 3 can be given for graphs with transition probabilities by replacing the cardinality of the sets of walks with the sum over the probabilities of the walks.

## 6.3   Non-contiguous Label Sequences

The (implicit) representation of a graph by a set of walks through the graph suggests a strong relation to string kernels investigated in literature [14]. There, the similarity of two strings is based on the number of common substrings. In contrast to the direct product kernel suggested in section 5, however, the substrings need not be contiguous.

In this section we will describe a graph kernel such that the similarity of two graphs is based on common non-contiguous label sequences. We will consider only edge-labeled graphs in this section. A similar technique can be used for fully-labeled graphs, however, its presentation becomes more lengthy.

Before defining the desired feature space we need to introduce the wildcard symbol '?' and the function $match(l, l') \Leftrightarrow (l = l') \vee (l =?) \vee (l' =?)$. In the following 'label' will refer to an element of the set $\mathcal{L} \cup \{?\}$.

**Definition 7.** *Let $\mathcal{S}_{n,m}$ denote the set of all possible label sequences of length $n$ containing $m \geq 0$ wildcards. Let $\lambda$ be a sequence $\lambda_0, \lambda_1, \ldots$ of weights $(\lambda_n \in \mathbb{R}; \lambda_n \geq 0$ for all $n \in \mathbb{N})$ and let $0 \leq \alpha \leq 1$ be a parameter for penalizing gaps. Furthermore, let $\mathcal{W}_n(G)$ denote the set of all possible walks with $n$ edges in graph $G$ and let $\mathcal{W}(G) = \bigcup_{i=0}^{n} \mathcal{W}_n(G)$. For a given walk $w \in \mathcal{W}(G)$ let $l_i(w)$ denote the label of the $i$-th edge in this walk.*

*The sequence feature space is defined by one feature for each possible label sequence. In particular, for any given $n, m$ and label sequence $s = s_1, \ldots, s_n \in \mathcal{S}_{n,m}$, the corresponding feature value is*

$$\phi_s(G) = \sqrt{\lambda_n \alpha^m} \, |\{w \in \mathcal{W}(G), \forall i : match(s_i, l_i(w))\}|$$

We proceed directly with the definition of the non-contiguous sequence kernel.

**Definition 8.** *Let $G_1, G_2$ be two graphs, let $G_\times = G_1 \times G_2$ be their direct product, and let $G_o$ be their direct product when ignoring the labels in $G_1$ and $G_2$. With a sequence of weights $\lambda = \lambda_0, \lambda_1, \ldots$ $(\lambda_i \in \mathbb{R}; \lambda_i \geq 0$ for all $i \in \mathbb{N})$ and a factor $0 \leq \alpha \leq 1$ penalizing gaps, the non-contiguous sequence kernel is defined as*

$$k_*(G_1, G_2) = \sum_{i,j=1}^{|V_\times|} \left[ \sum_{n=0}^{\infty} \lambda_n \left( (1-\alpha)E_\times + \alpha E_o \right)^n \right]_{ij}$$

*if the limit exists.*

This kernel is very similar to the direct product kernel. The only difference is that instead of the adjacency matrix of the direct product graph, the matrix $(1 - \alpha)E_\times + \alpha E_o$ is used. The relationship can be seen by adding – parallel to each edge – a new edge labeled $\#$ with weight $\sqrt{\alpha}$ in both factor graphs.

Note, that the above defined feature space contains features for 'trivial label sequences', i.e., label sequences that consist only of wildcard symbols. This can be corrected by using the kernel $k_*(G_1, G_2) - \sum_n \lambda_n \alpha^n E_o^n$ instead.

## 7   Discussion and Related Work

This section briefly describes the work most relevant to this paper. For an extensive overview of kernels on structured data, the reader is referred to [5].

Graph kernels are an important means to extend the applicability of kernel methods to structured data. Diffusion kernels on graphs [12] allow for the computation of a kernel if the instance space has a graph structure. This is different from the setting in this paper where we consider that every instance has a graph structure.

A preliminary version of the label pair graph kernel has been presented in [4]. The feature space of this kernel is based on the distance of all labeled vertices in graphs. The dimensionality of the feature space is the number of different labels squared. In applications, where this is not sufficiently discriminative, inner products in a feature space where each feature counts the number of times a path with a given label sequence is homomorphic to a subgraph can be used. Such kernels can be extended to cover graphs with a transition probability associated to each edge.

A kernel function on transition graphs has previously been described in [9][3]. In the feature space considered there, each feature corresponds to the probability with which a label sequence is generated by a random walk on the direct product graph. There transition graphs with a uniform distribution over all edges leaving the same vertex are considered and convergence is guaranteed by assuming a non-zero halting probability. In section 6 we showed how our graph kernels can be extended to cover general transition graphs. The kernel proposed in [9] is a special case of this extended kernel.

Tree kernels have been described in [2] and compute the similarity of two trees based on their common subtrees. However, the trees considered there are restricted to labeled trees where the label of each vertex determines the number of children of that vertex. Furthermore, a fixed order of the children of each vertex is assumed. In this case [2] devises an algorithm for computing the kernel with quadratic time complexity. The graph kernels suggested in the paper at hand can clearly also be applied to trees but do not require any restriction on the set of trees. They are thus a more flexible alternative.

String kernels that base the similarity of two strings on the common non-contiguous substrings are strongly related to the non-contiguous graph kernel with geometric weights. Such string kernels have been investigated deeply in literature, see for example [17, 14]. However, using a similar idea on graphs – as done with the non-contiguous graph kernel – is new.

The main differences between string kernels and graph kernels for strings are which features are used and how the label sequences are matched. String kernels use a label sequence without wildcards and count how often this sequence or a sequence created by inserting wildcard symbols occurs. Graph kernels for strings use a label sequence with wildcards and count how often this sequence occurs. Consider, for example, the two strings 'art' and 'ant'. For string kernels the common substrings are 'a', 't', and 'at' – 'at' occurs with a gap of length 1 in both strings. For direct product graph kernels the common sequences are only 'a' and 't'. For non-contiguous graph kernels the common sequences are 'a', 't', 'a?', '?t', 'a??', '??t', and 'a?t'. The most interesting difference between string kernels

---

[3] An extended version of this paper appeared recently [10].

and non-contiguous graph kernels is the feature 'at' and 'a?t', respectively. Now consider the string 'at'. The sequence 'a?t' does not occur in 'at', while the substring 'at' obviously occurs in 'at'.

## 8   Conclusions and Future Work

In this paper we showed that computing a complete graph kernel is at least as hard as deciding whether two graphs are isomorphic, and that the problem of computing a graph kernel based on common (isomorphic) subgraphs is *NP*-hard. Therefore, we presented alternative graph kernels that are conceptually based on the label sequences of all possible walks in the kernel. Efficient computation of these kernels is made possible by the use of product graphs and by choosing the weights such that a closed form of the resulting matrix power series exists.

The advantage of the label pair graph kernel is that the feature space can be computed explicitly and thus linear optimization methods for support vector machines can be applied. Therefore, learning with this kernel can be very efficient. The advantage of the direct product kernel and the non-contiguous graph kernel is the expressivity of their feature spaces. Both definitions are based on the concept of graph products.

We have shown that the direct graph product can be employed to count the number of contiguous label sequences occurring in two graphs and that it can be to extended to count the number of non-contiguous label sequences occurring in two graphs.

We believe that such graph kernels can successfully be applied in many real-world applications. Such applications will be investigated in future work. One step towards real world applications is an experiment in a relational reinforcement learning setting, described in [6]. There we applied Gaussian processes with graph kernels as the covariance function. Experiments were performed in blocks worlds with up to ten blocks with three different goals. In this setting our algorithm proofed competitive or superior to all previous implementations of relational reinforcement learning algorithms, although it did not use any sophisticated instance selection strategies.

Real world experiments will apply graph kernels to different molecule classification tasks from bioinformatics and computational chemistry.

## Acknowledgments

Research supported in part by the EU Framework V project (IST-1999-11495) *Data Mining and Decision Support for Business Competitiveness: Solomon Virtual Enterprise* and by the DFG project (WR 40/2-1) *Hybride Methoden und Systemarchitekturen für heterogene Informationsräume*. The authors thank Tamás Horváth and Jan Ramon for valuable discussions.

# References

1. B. E. Boser, I. M. Guyon, and V. N. Vapnik. A training algorithm for optimal margin classifiers. In D. Haussler, editor, *Proceedings of the 5th Annual ACM Workshop on Computational Learning Theory*, pages 144–152, Pittsburgh, PA, July 1992. ACM Press.

2. M. Collins and N. Duffy. Convolution kernels for natural language. In T. G. Dietterich, S. Becker, and Z. Ghahramani, editors, *Advances in Neural Information Processing Systems*, volume 14, Cambridge, MA, 2002. MIT Press.

3. R. Diestel. *Graph Theory*. Springer-Verlag, 2000.

4. T. Gärtner. Exponential and geometric kernels for graphs. In *NIPS Workshop on Unreal Data: Principles of Modeling Nonvectorial Data*, 2002.

5. T. Gärtner. Kernel-based multi-relational data mining. *SIGKDD Explorations*, 2003. to appear.

6. T. Gärtner, K. Driessens, and J. Ramon. Graph kernels and gaussian processes for relational reinforcement learning. In *Proceedings of the 13th International Conference on Inductive Logic Programming*, 2003. submitted.

7. R. Gray. *Probability, Random Processes, and Ergodic Properties*. Springer-Verlag, 1987.

8. W. Imrich and S. Klavžar. *Product Graphs: Structure and Recognition*. John Wiley, 2000.

9. H. Kashima and A. Inokuchi. Kernels for graph classification. In *ICDM Workshop on Active Mining*, 2002.

10. H. Kashima, K. Tsuda, and A. Inokuchi. Marginalized kernels between labeled graphs. In *Proceedings of the 20th International Conference on Machine Learning*, 2003. to appear.

11. J. Köbler, U. Schöning, and J. Torán. *The Graph Isomorphism Problem: Its Structural Complexity*. Progress in Theoretical Computer Science. Birkhäuser, 1993.

12. R. I. Kondor and J. Lafferty. Diffusion kernels on graphs and other discrete input spaces. In C. Sammut and A. Hoffmann, editors, *Proceedings of the 19th International Conference on Machine Learning*, pages 315–322. Morgan Kaufmann, 2002.

13. B. Korte and J. Vygen. *Combinatorial Optimization: Theory and Algorithms*. Springer-Verlag, 2002.

14. H. Lodhi, C. Saunders, J. Shawe-Taylor, N. Cristianini, and C. Watkins. Text classification using string kernels. *Journal of Machine Learning Research*, 2:419–444, 2002.

15. B. Schölkopf and A. J. Smola. *Learning with Kernels*. The MIT Press, 2002.

16. S. Skiena. *The Algorithm Design Manual*. Springer-Verlag, 1997.

17. C. Watkins. Kernels from matching operations. Technical report, Department of Computer Science, Royal Holloway, University of London, 1999.

# Kernels and Regularization on Graphs

Alexander J. Smola[1] and Risi Kondor[2]

[1] Machine Learning Group, RSISE
Australian National University
Canberra, ACT 0200, Australia
Alex.Smola@anu.edu.au
[2] Department of Computer Science
Columbia University
1214 Amsterdam Avenue, M.C. 0401
New York, NY 10027, USA
risi@cs.columbia.edu

**Abstract.** We introduce a family of kernels on graphs based on the notion of regularization operators. This generalizes in a natural way the notion of regularization and Greens functions, as commonly used for real valued functions, to graphs. It turns out that diffusion kernels can be found as a special case of our reasoning. We show that the class of positive, monotonically decreasing functions on the unit interval leads to kernels and corresponding regularization operators.

## 1 Introduction

There has recently been a surge of interest in learning algorithms that operate on input spaces $X$ other than $\mathbb{R}^n$, specifically, discrete input spaces, such as strings, graphs, trees, automata etc.. Since kernel-based algorithms, such as Support Vector Machines, Gaussian Processes, Kernel PCA, etc. capture the structure of $X$ via the kernel $K : X \times X \mapsto \mathbb{R}$, as long as we can define an appropriate kernel on our discrete input space, these algorithms can be imported wholesale, together with their error analysis, theoretical guarantees and empirical success.

One of the most general representations of discrete metric spaces are graphs. Even if all we know about our input space are local pairwise similarities between points $x_i, x_j \in X$, distances (e.g shortest path length) on the graph induced by these similarities can give a useful, more global, sense of similarity between objects. In their work on Diffusion Kernels, Kondor and Lafferty [2002] gave a specific construction for a kernel capturing this structure. Belkin and Niyogi [2002] proposed an essentially equivalent construction in the context of approximating data lying on surfaces in a high dimensional embedding space, and in the context of leveraging information from unlabeled data.

In this paper we put these earlier results into the more principled framework of Regularization Theory. We propose a family of regularization operators (equivalently, kernels) on graphs that include Diffusion Kernels as a special case, and show that this family encompasses all possible regularization operators invariant under permutations of the vertices in a particular sense.

B. Schölkopf and M.K. Warmuth (Eds.): COLT/Kernel 2003, LNAI 2777, pp. 144–158, 2003.
© Springer-Verlag Berlin Heidelberg 2003

*Outline of the Paper:* Section 2 introduces the concept of the graph Laplacian and relates it to the Laplace operator on real valued functions. Next we define an extended class of regularization operators and show why they have to be essentially a function of the Laplacian. An analogy to real valued Greens functions is established in Section 3.3, and efficient methods for computing such functions are presented in Section 4. We conclude with a discussion.

## 2    Laplace Operators

An undirected unweighted graph $G$ consists of a set of vertices $V$ numbered 1 to $n$, and a set of edges $E$ (i.e., pairs $(i,j)$ where $i,j \in V$ and $(i,j) \in E \Leftrightarrow (j,i) \in E$). We will sometimes write $i \sim j$ to denote that $i$ and $j$ are neighbors, i.e. $(i,j) \in E$. The adjacency matrix of $G$ is an $n \times n$ real matrix $W$, with $W_{ij} = 1$ if $i \sim j$, and 0 otherwise (by construction, $W$ is symmetric and its diagonal entries are zero). These definitions and most of the following theory can trivially be extended to weighted graphs by allowing $W_{ij} \in [0, \infty)$.

Let $D$ be an $n \times n$ diagonal matrix with $D_{ii} = \sum_j W_{ij}$. The **Laplacian** of $G$ is defined as $L := D - W$ and the **Normalized Laplacian** is $\tilde{L} := D^{-\frac{1}{2}} L D^{-\frac{1}{2}} = I - D^{-\frac{1}{2}} W D^{-\frac{1}{2}}$. The following two theorems are well known results from spectral graph theory [Chung-Graham, 1997]:

**Theorem 1 (Spectrum of $\tilde{L}$).** $\tilde{L}$ *is a symmetric, positive semidefinite matrix, and its eigenvalues* $\lambda_1, \lambda_2, \ldots, \lambda_n$ *satisfy* $0 \leq \lambda_i \leq 2$. *Furthermore, the number of eigenvalues equal to zero equals to the number of disjoint components in* $G$.

The bound on the spectrum follows directly from Gerschgorin's Theorem.

**Theorem 2 ($L$ and $\tilde{L}$ for Regular Graphs).** *Now let $G$ be a **regular** graph of degree $d$, that is, a graph in which every vertex has exactly $d$ neighbors. Then* $L = dI - W$ *and* $\tilde{L} = I - \frac{1}{d}W = \frac{1}{d}L$. *Finally, $W, L, \tilde{L}$ share the same eigenvectors* $\{\mathbf{v}_i\}$, *where* $\mathbf{v}_i = \lambda_i^{-1}W\mathbf{v}_i = (d - \lambda_i)^{-1}L\mathbf{v}_i = (1 - d^{-1}\lambda_i)^{-1}\tilde{L}\mathbf{v}_i$ *for all $i$.*

$L$ and $\tilde{L}$ can be regarded as linear operators on functions $f : V \mapsto \mathbb{R}$, or, equivalently, on vectors $f = (f_1, f_2, \ldots, f_n)^\top$. We could equally well have defined $L$ by

$$\langle f, Lf \rangle = f^\top Lf = -\frac{1}{2}\sum_{i \sim j}(f_i - f_j)^2 \text{ for all } f \in \mathbb{R}^n, \tag{1}$$

which readily generalizes to graphs with a countably infinite number of vertices.

The Laplacian derives its name from its analogy with the familiar Laplacian operator $\Delta = \frac{\partial^2}{\partial x_1^2} + \frac{\partial^2}{\partial x_2^2} + \ldots + \frac{\partial^2}{\partial x_m^2}$ on continuous spaces. Regarding (1) as inducing a semi-norm $\| f \|_L = \langle f, Lf \rangle$ on $\mathbb{R}^n$, the analogous expression for $\Delta$ defined on a compact space $\Omega$ is

$$\| f \|_\Delta = \langle f, \Delta f \rangle = \int_\Omega f(\Delta f)\, d\omega = \int_\Omega (\nabla f) \cdot (\nabla f)\, d\omega. \tag{2}$$

Both (1) and (2) quantify how much $f$ and $f$ vary locally, or how "smooth" they are over their respective domains.

More explicitly, when $\Omega = \mathbb{R}^m$, up to a constant, $-L$ is exactly the finite difference discretization of $\Delta$ on a regular lattice:

$$\Delta f(x) = \sum_{i=1}^{m} \frac{\partial^2}{\partial x_i^2} f \approx \sum_{i=1}^{m} \frac{\frac{\partial}{\partial x_i} f(x + \frac{1}{2} e_i) - \frac{\partial}{\partial x_i} f(x - \frac{1}{2} e_i)}{\delta}$$

$$\approx \sum_{i=1}^{m} \frac{f(x + e_i) + f(x - e_i) - 2f(x)}{\delta^2} =$$

$$\frac{1}{\delta^2} \sum_{i=1}^{m} \left( f_{x_1,\dots,x_i+1,\dots,x_m} + f_{x_1,\dots,x_i-1,\dots,x_m} - 2 f_{x_1,\dots,x_m} \right) = -\frac{1}{\delta^2} [Lf]_{x_1,\dots,x_m},$$

where $e_1, e_2, \dots, e_m$ is an orthogonal basis for $\mathbb{R}^m$ normalized to $\| e_i \| = \delta$, the vertices of the lattice are at $x = x_1 e_1 + \dots + x_m e_m$ with integer valued coordinates $x_i \in \mathbb{N}$, and $f_{x_1,x_2,\dots,x_m} = f(x)$.

Moreover, both the continuous and the discrete Laplacians are canonical operators on their respective domains, in the sense that they are invariant under certain natural transformations of the underlying space, and in this they are essentially unique.

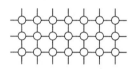

Regular grid in two dimensions

The Laplace operator $\Delta$ is the unique self-adjoint linear second order differential operator invariant under transformations of the coordinate system under the action of the special orthogonal group $SO_m$, i.e. invariant under rotations. This well known result can be seen by using Schur's lemma and the fact that $SO_m$ is irreducible on $\mathbb{R}^m$.

We now show a similar result for $L$. Here the permutation group plays a similar role to $SO_m$. We need some additional definitions: denote by $S_n$ the group of permutations on $\{1, 2, \dots, n\}$ with $\pi \in S_n$ being a specific permutation taking $i \in \{1, 2, \dots n\}$ to $\pi(i)$. The so-called defining representation of $S_n$ consists of $n \times n$ matrices $\Pi_\pi$, such that $[\Pi_\pi]_{i,\pi(i)=1}$ and all other entries of $\Pi_\pi$ are zero.

**Theorem 3 (Permutation Invariant Linear Functions on Graphs).** *Let $L$ be an $n \times n$ symmetric real matrix, linearly related to the $n \times n$ adjacency matrix $W$, i.e. $L = \mathcal{T}[W]$ for some linear operator $L$ in a way invariant to permutations of vertices in the sense that*

$$\Pi_\pi^\top \mathcal{T}[W] \Pi_\pi = \mathcal{T}\left[ \Pi_\pi^\top W \Pi_\pi \right] \tag{3}$$

*for any $\pi \in S_n$. Then $L$ is related to $W$ by a linear combination of the following three operations: identity; row/column sums; overall sum; row/column sum restricted to the diagonal of $L$; overall sum restricted to the diagonal of $W$.*

**Proof** Let

$$L_{i_1 i_2} = \mathcal{T}[W]_{i_1 i_2} := \sum_{i_3=1}^{n} \sum_{i_4=1}^{n} T_{i_1 i_2 i_3 i_4} W_{i_3 i_4} \tag{4}$$

with $T \in \mathbb{R}^{n^4}$. Eq. (3) then implies $T_{\pi(i_1)\pi(i_2)\pi(i_3)\pi(i_4)} = T_{i_1 i_2 i_3 i_4}$ for any $\pi \in S_n$.

The indices of $T$ can be partitioned by the equality relation on their values, e.g. $(2, 5, 2, 7)$ is of the partition type $[\,1\,3\,|\,2\,|\,4\,]$, since $i_1 = i_3$, but $i_2 \neq i_1$, $i_4 \neq i_1$ and $i_2 \neq i_4$. The key observation is that under the action of the permutation group, elements of $T$ with a given index partition structure are taken to elements with the same index partition structure, e.g. if $i_1 = i_3$ then $\pi(i_1) = \pi(i_3)$ and if $i_1 \neq i_3$, then $\pi(i_1) \neq \pi(i_3)$. Furthermore, an element with a given index index partition structure can be mapped to any other element of $T$ with the same index partition structure by a suitable choice of $\pi$.

Hence, a necessary and sufficient condition for (4) is that all elements of $T$ of a given index partition structure be equal. Therefore, $T$ must be a linear combination of the following tensors (i.e. multilinear forms):

$$A_{i_1 i_2 i_3 i_4} = 1$$

$$B^{[1,2]}_{i_1 i_2 i_3 i_4} = \delta_{i_1 i_2} \qquad B^{[1,3]}_{i_1 i_2 i_3 i_4} = \delta_{i_1 i_3} \qquad B^{[1,4]}_{i_1 i_2 i_3 i_4} = \delta_{i_1 i_4}$$

$$B^{[2,3]}_{i_1 i_2 i_3 i_4} = \delta_{i_2 i_3} \qquad B^{[2,4]}_{i_1 i_2 i_3 i_4} = \delta_{i_2 i_4} \qquad B^{[3,4]}_{i_1 i_2 i_3 i_4} = \delta_{i_3 i_4}$$

$$C^{[1,2,3]}_{i_1 i_2 i_3 i_4} = \delta_{i_1 i_2} \delta_{i_2 i_3} \qquad C^{[2,3,4]}_{i_1 i_2 i_3 i_4} = \delta_{i_2 i_3} \delta_{i_3 i_4}$$

$$C^{[3,4,1]}_{i_1 i_2 i_3 i_4} = \delta_{i_3 i_4} \delta_{i_4 i_1} \qquad C^{[4,1,2]}_{i_1 i_2 i_3 i_4} = \delta_{i_4 i_1} \delta_{i_1 i_2}$$

$$D^{[1,2][3,4]}_{i_1 i_2 i_3 i_4} = \delta_{i_1 i_2} \delta_{i_3 i_4} \qquad D^{[1,3][2,4]}_{i_1 i_2 i_3 i_4} = \delta_{i_1 i_3} \delta_{i_2 i_4} \qquad D^{[1,4][2,3]}_{i_1 i_2 i_3 i_4} = \delta_{i_1 i_4} \delta_{i_2 i_3}$$

$$E^{[1,2,3,4]}_{i_1 i_2 i_3 i_4} = \delta_{i_1 i_2} \delta_{i_1 i_3} \delta_{i_1 i_4} \,.$$

The tensor $A$ puts the overall sum in each element of $L$, while $B^{[1,2]}$ returns the the same restricted to the diagonal of $L$.

Since $W$ has vanishing diagonal, $B^{[3,4]}$, $C^{[2,3,4]}$, $C^{[3,4,1]}$, $D^{[1,2][3,4]}$ and $E^{[1,2,3,4]}$ produce zero. Without loss of generality we can therefore ignore them.

By symmetry of $W$, the pairs $(B^{[1,3]}, B^{[1,4]})$, $(B^{[2,3]}, B^{[2,4]})$, $(C^{[1,2,3]}, C^{[4,1,2]})$ have the same effect on $W$, hence we can set the coefficient of the second member of each to zero. Furthermore, to enforce symmetry on $L$, the coefficient of $B^{[1,3]}$ and $B^{[2,3]}$ must be the same (without loss of generality 1) and this will give the row/column sum matrix $(\sum_k W_{ik}) + (\sum_k W_{kl})$.

Similarly, $C^{[1,2,3]}$ and $C^{[4,1,2]}$ must have the same coefficient and this will give the row/column sum restricted to the diagonal: $\delta_{ij} [(\sum_k W_{ik}) + (\sum_k W_{kl})]$.

Finally, by symmetry of $W$, $D^{[1,3][2,4]}$ and $D^{[1,4][2,3]}$ are both equivalent to the identity map. ∎

The various row/column sum and overall sum operations are uninteresting from a graph theory point of view, since they do not heed to the topology of the graph. Imposing the conditions that each row and column in $L$ must sum to zero, we recover the graph Laplacian. Hence, up to a constant factor and trivial additive components, the graph Laplacian (or the normalized graph Laplacian if we wish to rescale by the number of edges per vertex) is the only "invariant" differential operator for given $W$ (or its normalized counterpart $\tilde{W}$). Unless stated otherwise, all results below hold for both $L$ and $\tilde{L}$ (albeit with a different spectrum) and we will, in the following, focus on $\tilde{L}$ due to the fact that its spectrum is contained in $[0, 2]$.

## 3  Regularization

The fact that $L$ induces a semi-norm on $\boldsymbol{f}$ which penalizes the changes between adjacent vertices, as described in (1), indicates that it may serve as a tool to design regularization operators.

### 3.1  Regularization via the Laplace Operator

We begin with a brief overview of translation invariant regularization operators on continuous spaces and show how they can be interpreted as powers of $\Delta$. This will allow us to repeat the development almost verbatim with $\tilde{L}$ (or $L$) instead.

Some of the most successful regularization functionals on $\mathbb{R}^n$, leading to kernels such as the Gaussian RBF, can be written as [Smola et al., 1998]

$$\langle f, Pf \rangle := \int |\tilde{f}(\omega)|^2 \, r(\|\omega\|^2) \, d\omega = \langle f, r(\Delta)f \rangle . \tag{5}$$

Here $f \in L_2(\mathbb{R}^n)$, $\tilde{f}(\omega)$ denotes the Fourier transform of $f$, $r(\|\omega\|^2)$ is a function penalizing frequency components $|\tilde{f}(\omega)|$ of $f$, typically increasing in $\|\omega\|^2$, and finally, $r(\Delta)$ is the extension of $r$ to operators simply by applying $r$ to the spectrum of $\Delta$ [Dunford and Schwartz, 1958]

$$\langle f, r(\Delta)f' \rangle = \sum_i \langle f, \psi_i \rangle \, r(\lambda_i) \, \langle \psi_i, f' \rangle$$

where $\{(\psi_i, \lambda_i)\}$ is the eigensystem of $\Delta$. The last equality in (5) holds because applications of $\Delta$ become multiplications by $\|\omega\|^2$ in Fourier space. Kernels are obtained by solving the self-consistency condition [Smola et al., 1998]

$$\langle k(x, \cdot), Pk(x', \cdot) \rangle = k(x, x') . \tag{6}$$

One can show that $k(x, x') = \kappa(x - x')$, where $\kappa$ is equal to the inverse Fourier transform of $r^{-1}(\|\omega\|^2)$. Several $r$ functions have been known to yield good results. The two most popular are given below:

|  | $r(\|\omega\|^2)$ | $k(x, x')$ | $r(\Delta)$ |
|---|---|---|---|
| Gaussian RBF | $\exp\left(\dfrac{\sigma^2}{2}\|\omega\|^2\right)$ | $\exp\left(-\dfrac{1}{2\sigma^2}\|x - x'\|^2\right)$ | $\displaystyle\sum_{i=0}^{\infty} \dfrac{\sigma^{2i}}{i!} \Delta^i$ |
| Laplacian RBF | $1 + \sigma^2\|\omega\|^2$ | $\exp\left(-\dfrac{1}{\sigma}\|x - x'\|\right)$ | $1 + \sigma^2\Delta$ |

In summary, regularization according to (5) is carried out by penalizing $\tilde{f}(\omega)$ by a function of the Laplace operator. For many results in regularization theory one requires $r(\|\omega\|^2) \to \infty$ for $\|\omega\|^2 \to \infty$.

### 3.2  Regularization via the Graph Laplacian

In complete analogy to (5), we define a class of regularization functionals on graphs as

$$\langle \boldsymbol{f}, P\boldsymbol{f} \rangle := \langle \boldsymbol{f}, r(\tilde{L})\boldsymbol{f} \rangle . \tag{7}$$

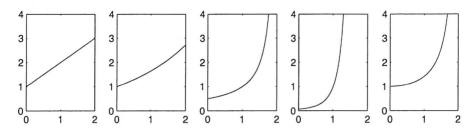

**Fig. 1.** Regularization function $r(\lambda)$. From left to right: regularized Laplacian ($\sigma^2 = 1$), diffusion process ($\sigma^2 = 1$), one-step random walk ($a = 2$), 4-step random walk ($a = 2$), inverse cosine.

Here $r(\tilde{L})$ is understood as applying the scalar valued function $r(\lambda)$ to the eigenvalues of $\tilde{L}$, that is,

$$r(\tilde{L}) := \sum_{i=1}^{m} r(\lambda_i)\, \boldsymbol{v}_i \boldsymbol{v}_i^{\top}, \tag{8}$$

where $\{(\lambda_i, \boldsymbol{v}_i)\}$ constitute the eigensystem of $\tilde{L}$. The normalized graph Laplacian $\tilde{L}$ is preferable to $L$, since $\tilde{L}$'s spectrum is contained in $[0, 2]$. The obvious goal is to gain insight into what functions are appropriate choices for $r$.

- From (1) we infer that $\boldsymbol{v}_i$ with large $\lambda_i$ correspond to rather uneven functions on the graph $G$. Consequently, they should be penalized more strongly than $\boldsymbol{v}_i$ with small $\lambda_i$. Hence $r(\lambda)$ should be monotonically increasing in $\lambda$.
- Requiring that $r(\tilde{L}) \succeq 0$ imposes the constraint $r(\lambda) \geq 0$ for all $\lambda \in [0, 2]$.
- Finally, we can limit ourselves to $r(\lambda)$ expressible as power series, since the latter are dense in the space of $C_0$ functions on bounded domains.

In Section 3.5 we will present additional motivation for the choice of $r(\lambda)$ in the context of spectral graph theory and segmentation. As we shall see, the following functions are of particular interest:

$$r(\lambda) = 1 + \sigma^2\lambda \qquad \text{(Regularized Laplacian)} \tag{9}$$
$$r(\lambda) = \exp\left(\sigma^2/2\lambda\right) \qquad \text{(Diffusion Process)} \tag{10}$$
$$r(\lambda) = (aI - \lambda)^{-1} \text{ with } a \geq 2 \qquad \text{(One-Step Random Walk)} \tag{11}$$
$$r(\lambda) = (aI - \lambda)^{-p} \text{ with } a \geq 2 \qquad \text{($p$-Step Random Walk)} \tag{12}$$
$$r(\lambda) = (\cos \lambda\pi/4)^{-1} \qquad \text{(Inverse Cosine)} \tag{13}$$

Figure 1 shows the regularization behavior for the functions (9)-(13).

## 3.3 Kernels

The introduction of a regularization matrix $P = r(\tilde{L})$ allows us to define a Hilbert space $\mathcal{H}$ on $\mathbb{R}^m$ via $\langle f, f \rangle_{\mathcal{H}} := \langle \boldsymbol{f}, P\boldsymbol{f} \rangle$. We now show that $\mathcal{H}$ is a reproducing kernel Hilbert space.

**Theorem 4.** *Denote by $P \in \mathbb{R}^{m \times m}$ a (positive semidefinite) regularization matrix and denote by $\mathcal{H}$ the image of $\mathbb{R}^m$ under $P$. Then $\mathcal{H}$ with dot product $\langle f, f \rangle_{\mathcal{H}} := \langle f, Pf \rangle$ is a Reproducing Kernel Hilbert Space and its kernel is $k(i,j) = \left[P^{-1}\right]_{ij}$, where $P^{-1}$ denotes the pseudo-inverse if $P$ is not invertible.*

**Proof** Since $P$ is a positive semidefinite matrix, we clearly have a Hilbert space on $P\mathbb{R}^m$. To show the reproducing property we need to prove that

$$f(i) = \langle f, k(i, \cdot) \rangle_{\mathcal{H}}. \tag{14}$$

Note that $k(i,j)$ can take on at most $m^2$ different values (since $i, j \in [1 : m]$). In matrix notation (14) means that for all $f \in \mathcal{H}$

$$f(i) = \boldsymbol{f}^{\top} P K_{i,:} \text{ for all } i \quad \Longleftrightarrow \quad \boldsymbol{f}^{\top} = \boldsymbol{f}^{\top} P K. \tag{15}$$

The latter holds if $K = P^{-1}$ and $\boldsymbol{f} \in P\mathbb{R}^m$, which proves the claim. $\blacksquare$

In other words, $K$ is the Greens function of $P$, just as in the continuous case. The notion of Greens functions on graphs was only recently introduced by Chung-Graham and Yau [2000] for $L$. The above theorem extended this idea to arbitrary regularization operators $\hat{r}(\tilde{L})$.

**Corollary 1.** *Denote by $P = r(\tilde{L})$ a regularization matrix, then the corresponding kernel is given by $K = r^{-1}(\tilde{L})$, where we take the pseudo-inverse wherever necessary. More specifically, if $\{(\boldsymbol{v}_i, \lambda_i)\}$ constitute the eigensystem of $\tilde{L}$, we have*

$$K = \sum_{i=1}^{m} r^{-1}(\lambda_i) \, \boldsymbol{v}_i \boldsymbol{v}_i^{\top} \text{ where we define } 0^{-1} \equiv 0. \tag{16}$$

## 3.4   Examples of Kernels

By virtue of Corollary 1 we only need to take (9)-(13) and plug the definition of $r(\lambda)$ into (16) to obtain formulae for computing $K$. This yields the following kernel matrices:

$$K = (I + \sigma^2 \tilde{L})^{-1} \qquad \text{(Regularized Laplacian)} \tag{17}$$

$$K = \exp(-\sigma^2/2\tilde{L}) \qquad \text{(Diffusion Process)} \tag{18}$$

$$K = (aI - \tilde{L})^p \text{ with } a \geq 2 \qquad \text{(p-Step Random Walk)} \tag{19}$$

$$K = \cos \tilde{L}\pi/4 \qquad \text{(Inverse Cosine)} \tag{20}$$

Equation (18) corresponds to the diffusion kernel proposed by Kondor and Lafferty [2002], for which $K(x, x')$ can be visualized as the quantity of some substance that would accumulate at vertex $x'$ after a given amount of time if we injected the substance at vertex $x$ and let it diffuse through the graph along the edges. Note that this involves matrix exponentiation defined via the limit $K = \exp(B) = \lim_{n \to \infty}(I + B/n)^n$ as opposed to component-wise exponentiation $K_{i,j} = \exp(B_{i,j})$.

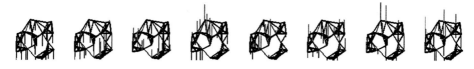

**Fig. 2.** The first 8 eigenvectors of the normalized graph Laplacian corresponding to the graph drawn above. Each line attached to a vertex is proportional to the value of the corresponding eigenvector at the vertex. Positive values (red) point up and negative values (blue) point down. Note that the assignment of values becomes less and less uniform with increasing eigenvalue (i.e. from left to right).

For (17) it is typically more efficient to deal with the inverse of $K$, as it avoids the costly inversion of the sparse matrix $\tilde{L}$. Such situations arise, e.g., in Gaussian Process estimation, where $K$ is the covariance matrix of a stochastic process [Williams, 1999].

Regarding (19), recall that $(aI - \tilde{L})^p = ((a-1)I + \tilde{W})^p$ is up to scaling terms equivalent to a $p$-step random walk on the graph with random restarts (see Section A for details). In this sense it is similar to the diffusion kernel. However, the fact that $K$ involves only a finite number of products of matrices makes it much more attractive for practical purposes. In particular, entries in $K_{ij}$ can be computed cheaply using the fact that $\tilde{L}$ is a sparse matrix.

A nearest neighbor graph.

Finally, the inverse cosine kernel treats lower complexity functions almost equally, with a significant reduction in the upper end of the spectrum. Figure 2 shows the leading eigenvectors of the graph drawn above and Figure 3 provide examples of some of the kernels discussed above.

### 3.5   Clustering and Spectral Graph Theory

We could also have derived $r(\tilde{L})$ directly from spectral graph theory: the eigenvectors of the graph Laplacian correspond to functions partitioning the graph into clusters, see e.g., [Chung-Graham, 1997, Shi and Malik, 1997] and the references therein. In general, small eigenvalues have associated eigenvectors which vary little between adjacent vertices. Finding the smallest eigenvectors of $\tilde{L}$ can be seen as a real-valued relaxation of the min-cut problem[1].

For instance, the smallest eigenvalue of $\tilde{L}$ is 0, its corresponding eigenvector is $D^{\frac{1}{2}}1_n$ with $1_n := (1,\dots,1) \in \mathbb{R}^n$. The second smallest eigenvalue/eigenvector pair, also often referred to as the **Fiedler**-vector, can be used to split the graph

---

[1] Only recently, algorithms based on the celebrated semidefinite relaxation of the mincut problem by Goemans and Williamson [1995] have seen wider use [Torr, 2003] in segmentation and clustering by use of spectral bundle methods.

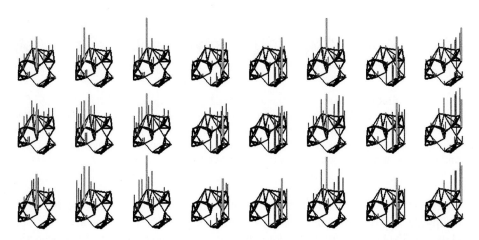

**Fig. 3.** Top: regularized graph Laplacian; Middle: diffusion kernel with $\sigma = 5$, Bottom: 4-step random walk kernel. Each figure displays $K_{ij}$ for fixed $i$. The value $K_{ij}$ at vertex $i$ is denoted by a bold line. Note that only adjacent vertices to $i$ bear significant value.

into two distinct parts [Weiss, 1999, Shi and Malik, 1997], and further eigenvectors with larger eigenvalues have been used for more finely-grained partitions of the graph. See Figure 2 for an example.

Such a decomposition into functions of increasing complexity has very desirable properties: if we want to perform estimation on the graph, we will wish to bias the estimate towards functions which vary little over large homogeneous portions[2]. Consequently, we have the following interpretation of $\langle f, f \rangle_{\mathcal{H}}$. Assume that $f = \sum_i \beta_i v_i$, where $\{(v_i, \lambda_i)\}$ is the eigensystem of $\tilde{L}$. Then we can rewrite $\langle f, f \rangle_{\mathcal{H}}$ to yield

$$\langle f, r(\tilde{L})f \rangle = \left\langle \sum_i \beta_i v_i, \sum_j r(\lambda_j) v_j v_j^\top \sum_l \beta_l v_l \right\rangle = \sum_i \beta_i^2 r(\lambda_i). \quad (21)$$

This means that the components of $f$ which vary a lot over coherent clusters in the graph are penalized more strongly, whereas the portions of $f$, which are essentially constant over clusters, are preferred. This is exactly what we want.

### 3.6   Approximate Computation

Often it is not necessary to know all values of the kernel (e.g., if we only observe instances from a subset of all positions on the graph). There it would be wasteful to compute the full matrix $r(L)^{-1}$ explicitly, since such operations typically scale with $O(n^3)$. Furthermore, for large $n$ it is not desirable to compute $K$ via (16), that is, by computing the eigensystem of $\tilde{L}$ and assembling $K$ directly.

---

[2] If we cannot assume a connection between the structure of the graph and the values of the function to be estimated on it, the entire concept of designing kernels on graphs obviously becomes meaningless.

Instead, we would like to take advantage of the fact that $\tilde{L}$ is sparse, and consequently any operation $\tilde{L}\alpha$ has cost at most linear in the number of nonzero elements of $\tilde{L}$, hence the cost is bounded by $O(|E|+n)$. Moreover, if $d$ is the largest degree of the graph, then computing $L^p e_i$ costs at most $|E| \sum_{i=1}^{p-1} (\min(d+1, n))^i$ operations: at each step the number of non-zeros in the rhs decreases by at most a factor of $d+1$. This means that as long as we can approximate $K = r^{-1}(\tilde{L})$ by a low order polynomial, say $\rho(\tilde{L}) := \sum_{i=0}^{N} \beta_i \tilde{L}^i$, significant savings are possible.

Note that we need not necessarily require a uniformly good approximation and put the main emphasis on the approximation for small $\lambda$. However, we need to ensure that $\rho(\tilde{L})$ is positive semidefinite.

*Diffusion Kernel:* The fact that the series $r^{-1}(x) = \exp(-\beta x) = \sum_{m=0}^{\infty} (-\beta)^m \frac{x^m}{m!}$ has alternating signs shows that the approximation error at $r^{-1}(x)$ is bounded by $\frac{(2\beta)^{N+1}}{(N+1)!}$, if we use $N$ terms in the expansion (from Theorem 1 we know that $\|\tilde{L}\| \leq 2$). For instance, for $\beta = 1$, 10 terms are sufficient to obtain an error of the order of $10^{-4}$.

*Variational Approximation:* In general, if we want to approximate $r^{-1}(\lambda)$ on $[0, 2]$, we need to solve the $L_\infty([0, 2])$ approximation problem

$$\operatorname*{minimize}_{\beta,\epsilon} \; \epsilon \; \text{ subject to } \left| \sum_{i=0}^{N} \beta_i \lambda^i - r^{-1}(\lambda) \right| \leq \epsilon \quad \forall \lambda \in [0, 2] \qquad (22)$$

Clearly, (22) is equivalent to minimizing $\sup_{\tilde{L}} \|\rho(\tilde{L}) - r^{-1}(\tilde{L})\|$, since the matrix norm is determined by the largest eigenvalues, and we can find $\tilde{L}$ such that the discrepancy between $\rho(\lambda)$ and $r^{-1}(\lambda)$ is attained. Variational problems of this form have been studied in the literature, and their solution may provide much better approximations to $r^{-1}(\lambda)$ than a truncated power series expansion.

## 4     Products of Graphs

As we have already pointed out, it is very expensive to compute $K$ for arbitrary $\hat{r}$ and $\tilde{L}$. For special types of graphs and regularization, however, significant computational savings can be made.

### 4.1     Factor Graphs

The work of this section is a direct extension of results by Ellis [2002] and Chung-Graham and Yau [2000], who study factor graphs to compute inverses of the graph Laplacian.

**Definition 1 (Factor Graphs).** *Denote by $(V, E)$ and $(V', E')$ the vertices $V$ and edges $E$ of two graphs, then the factor graph $(V_f, E_f) := (V, E) \otimes (V', E')$ is defined as the graph where $(i, i') \in V_f$ if $i \in V$ and $i' \in V'$; and $((i, i'), (j, j')) \in E_f$ if and only if either $(i, j) \in E$ and $i' = j'$ or $(i', j') \in E'$ and $i = j$.*

For instance, the factor graph of two rings is a torus. The nice property of factor graphs is that we can compute the eigenvalues of the Laplacian on products very easily (see e.g., Chung-Graham and Yau [2000]):

**Theorem 5 (Eigenvalues of Factor Graphs).** *The eigenvalues and eigenvectors of the normalized Laplacian for the factor graph between a regular graph of degree $d$ with eigenvalues $\{\lambda_j\}$ and a regular graph of degree $d'$ with eigenvalues $\{\lambda_l'\}$ are of the form:*

$$\lambda_{j,l}^{\text{fact}} = \frac{d}{d+d'}\lambda_j + \frac{d'}{d+d'}\lambda_l' \tag{23}$$

*and the eigenvectors satisfy $e_{(i,i')}^{j,l} = e_i^j e_{i'}^{\prime l}$, where $e^j$ is an eigenvector of $\tilde{L}$ and $e^{\prime l}$ is an eigenvector of $\tilde{L}'$.*

This allows us to apply Corollary 1 to obtain an expansion of $K$ as

$$K = (r(L))^{-1} = \sum_{j,l} r^{-1}(\lambda_{jl})\, e^{j,l}\left(e^{j,l}\right)^{\top}. \tag{24}$$

While providing an explicit recipe for the computation of $K_{ij}$ without the need to compute the full matrix $K$, this still requires $O(n^2)$ operations per entry, which may be more costly than what we want (here $n$ is the number of vertices of the factor graph).

Two methods for computing (24) become evident at this point: if $r$ has a special structure, we may exploit this to decompose $K$ into the products and sums of terms depending on one of the two graphs alone and pre-compute these expressions beforehand. Secondly, if one of the two terms in the expansion can be computed for a rather general class of values of $r(x)$, we can pre-compute this expansion and only carry out the remainder corresponding to (24) explicitly.

## 4.2   Product Decomposition of $r(x)$

Central to our reasoning is the observation that for certain $r(x)$, the term $\frac{1}{r(a+b)}$ can be expressed in terms of a product and sum of terms depending on $a$ and $b$ only. We assume that

$$\frac{1}{r(a+b)} = \sum_{m=1}^{M} \rho_n(a)\tilde{\rho}_n(b). \tag{25}$$

In the following we will show that in such situations the kernels on factor graphs can be computed as an analogous combination of products and sums of kernel functions on the terms constituting the ingredients of the factor graph. Before we do so, we briefly check that many $r(x)$ indeed satisfy this property.

$$\exp(-\beta(a+b)) = \exp(-\beta a)\exp(-\beta b) \tag{26}$$

$$(A - (a+b)) = \left(\frac{A}{2} - a\right) + \left(\frac{A}{2} - b\right) \tag{27}$$

$$(A - (a+b))^p = \sum_{n=0}^{p} \binom{p}{n}\left(\frac{A}{2} - a\right)^n \left(\frac{A}{2} - b\right)^{p-n} \tag{28}$$

$$\cos\frac{(a+b)\pi}{4} = \cos\frac{a\pi}{4}\cos\frac{b\pi}{4} - \sin\frac{a\pi}{4}\sin\frac{b\pi}{4} \tag{29}$$

In a nutshell, we will exploit the fact that for products of graphs the eigenvalues of the joint graph Laplacian can be written as the sum of the eigenvalues of the Laplacians of the constituent graphs. This way we can perform computations on $\rho_n$ and $\tilde{\rho}_n$ separately without the need to take the other part of the the product of graphs into account. Define

$$k_m(i, j) := \sum_l \rho_l \left( \frac{d\lambda_l}{d + d'} \right) e_i^l e_j^l \text{ and } \tilde{k}_m(i', j') := \sum_l \tilde{\rho}_l \left( \frac{d\lambda_l}{d + d'} \right) \tilde{e}_{i'}^l \tilde{e}_{j'}^l. \quad (30)$$

Then we have the following composition theorem:

**Theorem 6.** *Denote by $(V, E)$ and $(V', E')$ connected regular graphs of degrees $d$ with $m$ vertices (and $d'$, $m'$ respectively) and normalized graph Laplacians $\tilde{L}, \tilde{L}'$. Furthermore denote by $r(x)$ a rational function with matrix-valued extension $\hat{r}(X)$. In this case the kernel $K$ corresponding to the regularization operator $\hat{r}(L)$ on the product graph of $(V, E)$ and $(V', E')$ is given by*

$$k((i, i'), (j, j')) = \sum_{m=1}^M k_m(i, j) \tilde{k}_m(i', j') \quad (31)$$

**Proof** Plug the expansion of $\frac{1}{r(a+b)}$ as given by (25) into (24) and collect terms.
∎

From (26) we immediately obtain the corollary (see Kondor and Lafferty [2002]) that for diffusion processes on factor graphs the kernel on the factor graph is given by the product of kernels on the constituents, that is $k((i, i'), (j, j')) = k(i, j)k'(i', j')$.

The kernels $k_m$ and $\tilde{k}_m$ can be computed either by using an analytic solution of the underlying factors of the graph or alternatively they can be computed numerically. If the total number of kernels $k_n$ is small in comparison to the number of possible coordinates this is still computationally beneficial.

### 4.3   Composition Theorems

If no expansion as in (31) can be found, we may still be able to compute kernels by extending a reasoning from [Ellis, 2002]. More specifically, the following composition theorem allows us to accelerate the computation in many cases, whenever we can parameterize $(\hat{r}(L + \alpha I))^{-1}$ in an efficient way. For this purpose we introduce two auxiliary functions

$$K_\alpha(i, j) := \left( \hat{r} \left( \frac{d}{d + d'} L + \frac{\alpha d'}{d + d'} I \right) \right)^{-1} = \sum_l \left( r \left( \frac{d\lambda_l + \alpha d'}{d + d'} \right) \right)^{-1} e_l(i) e_l(j)$$

$$G'_\alpha(i, j) := (L' + \alpha I)^{-1} = \sum_l \frac{1}{\lambda_l + \alpha} e_l(i) e_l(j). \quad (32)$$

In some cases $K_\alpha(i, j)$ may be computed in closed form, thus obviating the need to perform expensive matrix inversion, e.g., in the case where the underlying graph is a chain [Ellis, 2002] and $K_\alpha = G_\alpha$.

**Theorem 7.** *Under the assumptions of Theorem 6 we have*

$$K((j,j'),(l,l')) = \frac{1}{2\pi i} \int_C K_\alpha(j,l) G'_{-\alpha}(j',l') d\alpha = \sum_v K_{\lambda_v}(j,l) e^v_{j'} e^v_{l'} \qquad (33)$$

*where $C \subset \mathbb{C}$ is a contour of the $\mathbb{C}$ containing the poles of $(V',E')$ including 0.*

For practical purposes, the third term of (33) is more amenable to computation. **Proof** From (24) we have

$$K((j,j'),(l,l')) = \sum_{u,v} \left( r \left( \frac{d\lambda_u + d'\lambda_v}{d + d'} \right) \right)^{-1} e^u_j e^u_l e^v_{j'} e^v_{l'} \qquad (34)$$

$$= \frac{1}{2\pi i} \int_C \sum_u \left( r \left( \frac{d\lambda_u + d'\alpha}{d + d'} \right) \right)^{-1} e^u_j e^u_l \sum_v \frac{1}{\lambda_v - \alpha} e^v_{j'} e^v_{l'} d\alpha$$

Here the second equality follows from the fact that the contour integral over a pole $p$ yields $\int_C \frac{f(\alpha)}{p-\alpha} d\alpha = 2\pi i f(p)$, and the claim is verified by checking the definitions of $K_\alpha$ and $G'_\alpha$. The last equality can be seen from (34) by splitting up the summation over $u$ and $v$. ∎

## 5    Conclusions

We have shown that the canonical family of kernels on graphs are of the form of power series in the graph Laplacian. Equivalently, such kernels can be characterized by a real valued function of the eigenvalues of the Laplacian. Special cases include diffusion kernels, the regularized Laplacian kernel and $p$-step random walk kernels. We have developed the regularization theory of learning on graphs using such kernels and explored methods for efficiently computing and approximating the kernel matrix.

## Acknowledgments

This work was supported by a grant of the ARC. The authors thank Eleazar Eskin, Patrick Haffner, Andrew Ng, Bob Williamson and S.V.N. Vishwanathan for helpful comments and suggestions.

## A    Link Analysis

Rather surprisingly, our approach to regularizing functions on graphs bears resemblance to algorithms for scoring web pages such as PageRank [Page et al., 1998], HITS [Kleinberg, 1999], and randomized HITS [Zheng et al., 2001]. More specifically, the random walks on graphs used in all three algorithms and the stationary distributions arising from them are closely connected with the eigensystem of $L$ and $\tilde{L}$ respectively.

We begin with an analysis of PageRank. Given a set of web pages and links between them we construct a directed graph in such a way that pages correspond to vertices and edges correspond to links, resulting in the (nonsymmetric) matrix $W$. Next we consider the random walk arising from following each of the links with equal probability in addition to a random restart at an arbitrary vertex with probability $\epsilon$. This means that the probability distribution over states follows the discrete time evolution equation

$$p(t+1) = \left[\epsilon I + (1 - \epsilon)WD^{-1}\right] p(t) \tag{35}$$

where $D$ is a diagonal matrix with $D_{ii} = \sum_j W_{ij}$ and $p$ is the vector of probabilities of being on a certain page. The PageRank is then determined from the stationary distribution of $p$. Clearly the largest eigenvalue/eigenvector pair of $\left[\epsilon I + (1 - \epsilon)WD^{-1}\right]$ will determine the stationary distribution $p(\infty)$, and the contribution of the other eigenvectors decays geometrically (one may conjecture that in practice only few iterations are needed).

Now consider the same formalism in the context of a 1-step random walk (11): here one computes $aI - \tilde{L} = (a - 1)I + D^{-\frac{1}{2}}WD^{-\frac{1}{2}}$. Rescaling by $\frac{1}{a}$ and setting $\epsilon = \frac{1-a}{a}$ yields a matrix with the same spectrum as the linear difference equation (35). Furthermore, for all eigenvectors $v_i$ of $\epsilon I + (1 - \epsilon)WD^{-1}$ we can find eigenvectors of $aI - \tilde{L}$ of the form $D^{-\frac{1}{2}}v_i$.

The main difference, however, is that while graphs arising from web pages are directed (following the direction of the link), which leads to asymmetric $W$, the graphs we studied in this paper are all undirected, leading to symmetric $W$ and $L, \tilde{L}$. We can now view the assignment of a certain PageRank to a page, as achieved via the stationary distribution of the random walk, as a means of finding a "simple" function on the graph of web pages.

In HITS [Kleinberg, 1999] one uses the concept of hubs and authorities to obtain a ranking between web pages. Given the graph $G$, as represented by $W$, one seeks to find the largest eigenvalue of the matrix $M := \begin{bmatrix} 0 & W \\ W^\top & 0 \end{bmatrix}$, which can be shown to be equivalent to finding singular value decomposition of $W$ [Zheng et al., 2001] (the latter is also used if we wish to perform latent semantic indexing on the matrix $W$). More specifically, with $\{v_i, \lambda_i\}$ being the eigensystem of $WW^\top$ (we assume that the eigenvalues are sorted in increasing order), one uses $v_{mj}^2$ as the weight of page $j$.

This setting was modified by Zheng et al. [2001] to accommodate for a larger subspace (Subspace HITS), which renders the system more robust with respect to small perturbations. More specifically, they use $\sum_{i=1}^{m} g(\lambda_i)v_{ij}^2$ for some monotonically increasing function $g(\lambda)$ to assess the relevance of page $j$. The latter, however, is identical to the diagonal entry of $g(W)$. Note the similarity to 7, where we used an essentially rescaled version of $W$ to determine the complexity of the functions under consideration. More specifically, if for regular graphs of order $d$ we set $g(\lambda) = \frac{1}{\tau(1-\lambda/d)}$ we can see that the HITS rank assigned to pages $j$ is simply the "length" of the corresponding page in "feature space" as given by $K_{ii}$. In other words, pages with a high HITS rank correspond to unit vectors which are considered simple with respect to the regularizer induced by the underlying graph.

# Bibliography

M. Belkin and P. Niyogi. Laplacian eigenmaps for dimensionality reduction and data representation. Technical Report TR-2002-01, The University of Chichago, January 2002.

F. Chung-Graham. *Spectral Graph Theory*. Number 92 in CBMS Regional Conference Series in Mathematics. AMS, 1997.

F. Chung-Graham and S. T. Yau. Discrete green's functions. *Journal of Combinatorial Theory*, 91:191–214, 2000.

N. Dunford and J. Schwartz. *Linear operators*. Pure and applied mathematics, v. 7. Interscience Publishers, New York, 1958.

R. Ellis. Discrete green's functions for products of regular graphs. Technical report, University of California at San Diego, 2002. Preliminary Report.

M.X. Goemans and D.P. Williamson. Improved approximation algorithms for maximum cut and satisfiability problems using semidefinite programming. *Journal of the ACM*, 42(6):1115–1145, 1995.

J. Kleinberg. Authoritative sources in a hyperlinked environment. *Journal of the ACM*, 46(5):604–632, November 1999.

R. S. Kondor and J. Lafferty. Diffusion kernels on graphs and other discrete structures. In *Proceedings of the ICML*, 2002.

L. Page, S. Brin, R. Motwani, and T. Winograd. The pagerank citation ranking: Bringing order to the web. Technical report, Stanford Digital Library Technologies Project, Stanford University, Stanford, CA, USA, November 1998.

J. Shi and J. Malik. Normalized cuts and image segmentation. *IEEE Conf. Computer Vision and Pattern Recognition*, June 1997.

A. Smola, B. Schölkopf, and K.-R. Müller. The connection between regularization operators and support vector kernels. *Neural Networks*, 11:637–649, 1998.

P.H.S. Torr. Solving Markov random fields using semidefinite programming. In *Artificial Intelligence and Statistics AISTATS*, 2003.

Y. Weiss. Segmentation using eigenvectors: A unifying view. In *International Conference on Computer Vision ICCV*, pages 975–982, 1999.

C. K. I. Williams. Prediction with Gaussian processes: From linear regression to linear prediction and beyond. In Micheal Jordan, editor, *Learning and Inference in Graphical Models*, pages 599–621. MIT Press, 1999.

A. Zheng, A. Ng, and M. Jordan. Stable eigenvector algorithms for link analysis. In W. Croft, D. Harper, D. Kraft, and J. Zobel, editors, *Proceedings of the 24th Annual International ACM SIGIR Conference on Research and Development in Information Retrieval*, pages 258–266, New York, 2001. ACM Press.

# Data-Dependent Bounds for Multi-category Classification Based on Convex Losses

Ilya Desyatnikov and Ron Meir

Department of Electrical Engineering
Technion, Haifa 32000, Israel
(ilyad,rmeir)@(tx,ee).technion.ac.il

**Abstract.** Algorithms for solving multi-category classification problems using output coding have become very popular in recent years. Following initial attempts with discrete coding matrices, recent work has attempted to alleviate some of their shortcomings by considering real-valued 'coding' matrices. We consider an approach to multi-category classification, based on minimizing a convex upper bound on the $0-1$ loss. We show that this approach is closely related to output coding, and derive data-dependent bounds on the performance. These bounds can be optimized in order to obtain effective coding matrices, which guarantee small generalization error. Moreover, our results apply directly to kernel based approaches.

## 1 Introduction

The problem of multi-category classification plays an important role in both the theory and the practice of Machine Learning, and has been the focus of attention of much recent work. A particularly interesting line of research resulted from the work of Dietterich and Bakiri [6] based on error-correcting output codes. This work led to many extensions focusing on various approaches to selecting the so-called coding matrices, usually focusing on discrete codes (some examples, among many, are [18,9,1,19]). The computational problems inherent in using discrete output codes led Crammer and Singer [4] to suggest a relaxation to continuous codes, which resulted in an efficiently solvable convex optimization problem. In this work we consider a framework which bears strong affinities to both the continuous code approach of [4] and to the multi-category support vector machine classifier introduced in [13]. The approach is based on a non-linear mapping to a feature space, similarly to support vector machines, followed by a winner-take-all classifier operating in this space. Instead of working with the $0-1$ classification loss, we consider convex upper bounds on the $0-1$ loss, which enable us to derive rather tight data-based generalization error bounds. These bounds can be used to effectively select a good coding matrix. The approach is sufficiently flexible to allow the incorporation of various types of constraints, such as inter-row and iter-column correlations.

The remainder of the paper is organized as follows. We begin in Section 2 by formally defining the problem and quoting some relevant results. Section 3 then

B. Schölkopf and M.K. Warmuth (Eds.): COLT/Kernel 2003, LNAI 2777, pp. 159–172, 2003.

introduces two continuous convex functions which upper bound the $0-1$ loss, and shows that minimizing these functions makes good statistical sense. We then move on in Section 4 to the derivation of data-dependent bounds, concluding and discussing open problem in Section 5.

## 2    Problem Formulation and Preliminary Results

We consider the problem of learning a multi-category classification problem. We are given a sequence of data pairs, $S = \{(\mathbf{x}_1, y_1), \ldots, (\mathbf{x}_1, y_1)\}$, where $\mathbf{x}_i \in \mathcal{X}$ and $y_i \in \mathcal{Y} = \{1, 2, \ldots, k\}$. A multi-class classifier $F$ maps an input $\mathbf{x} \in \mathcal{X}$ to a label $y \in \mathcal{Y}$.

We consider multi-category classification based on using $k$ soft binary classifiers $f_1(\mathbf{x}), \ldots, f_k(\mathbf{x})$. The label corresponding to an input $\mathbf{x}$ will be defined as

$$F(\mathbf{x}) = \underset{1 \leq r \leq k}{\operatorname{argmax}} f_r(\mathbf{x}). \tag{1}$$

Ideally one would like to construct a learning algorithm which achieves the minimum of the expected $0-1$ loss, where

$$\ell_{0-1}(F(\mathbf{x}), y) = \mathbf{I}(y \neq F(\mathbf{x})),$$

and where $\mathbf{I}(\mathcal{E})$ is the indicator function of the event $\mathcal{E}$. Minimizing the $0-1$ loss is in general intractable, and we are led to consider smooth cost functions, which upper bound the $0-1$ loss, and whose minimization leads to good performance with respect to the $0-1$ loss. Let $\mathbf{f}(\mathbf{x}) = (f_1(\mathbf{x}), \ldots, f_k(\mathbf{x}))$, and introduce a loss function $\phi(\mathbf{f}(\mathbf{x}), y)$ which dominates the $0-1$ loss, namely for every $\mathbf{x}$ and $y$

$$\ell_{0-1}(F(\mathbf{x}), y) \leq \phi(\mathbf{f}(\mathbf{x}), y),$$

where $F$ and $\mathbf{f}$ are related through (1). We use the notation $(\phi \circ \mathbf{f})(\mathbf{x}, y) = \phi(\mathbf{f}(\mathbf{x}), y)$ to denote function composition.

Consider a class of real-valued functions $\mathcal{F}$, and a set of $n$ random variables $X_1^n = \{X_1, \ldots, X_n\}$ drawn independently at random from some distribution $P$. The *empirical* Rademacher complexity of the class is defined as

$$\hat{R}_n(\mathcal{F}) = \mathbf{E}_\sigma \sup_{f \in \mathcal{F}} \frac{1}{n} \sum_{i=1}^n \sigma_i f(X_i) \tag{2}$$

where the i.i.d. random variables $\{\sigma_i\}_{i=1}^n$ assume the values $\pm 1$ with equal probabilities and $\sigma = \{\sigma_1, \ldots, \sigma_n\}$. Note that the current definition differs slightly from the standard definition of Rademacher complexity (e.g. [20]), which uses an absolute value inside the supremum. The two definitions coincide when the class $\mathcal{F}$ is closed under negation, namely $f \in \mathcal{F}$ implies $-f \in \mathcal{F}$. The current definition is never larger than the standard Rademacher complexity, is easier to work with, and has the added benefit that it equals zero for a class consisting of a single constant function (see [15] for other properties). The Rademacher complexity $R_n(\mathcal{F})$ is given by $R_n(\mathcal{F}) = \mathbf{E}_{X_1^n} \hat{R}_n(\mathcal{F})$.

We begin by recalling a uniform convergence result from [11,2]. In fact we present a slight refinement of Theorem 8 in [2] which is based on the observation that the proof of that result only requires the weakened version of the Rademacher complexity (2). This allows one to slightly improve the constants and simplify the claim. Note that [15] contains an extension of this result to unbounded functions.

Let $\{\mathcal{F}_1,\ldots,\mathcal{F}_k\}$ be classes of real-valued functions, and consider the class of vector-valued functions

$$\mathcal{F} = \left\{ \mathbf{f} : \mathbf{f}(\mathbf{x}) = (f_1(\mathbf{x}), f_2(\mathbf{x}),\ldots, f_k(\mathbf{x})), \ f_j \in \mathcal{F}_j, \ \sum_{j=1}^k f_j(\mathbf{x}) = 0 \right\}. \quad (3)$$

The condition $\sum_{j=1}^k f_j(\mathbf{x}) = 0$ is a technical condition which will be used in the sequel. The class $\phi \circ \mathcal{F}$ is given by $\{g : g(\mathbf{x}, y) = \phi(\mathbf{f}(\mathbf{x}), y), \ \mathbf{f} \in \mathcal{F}\}$.

**Theorem 1.** (Modified from Theorem 8 in [2]) *Let $\{\mathcal{F}_r\}_{r=1}^k$ be classes of real-valued functions, and let $\mathcal{F}$ be defined as in (3). Consider a loss function $\phi(\mathbf{f}(\mathbf{x}), y)$ which uniformly dominates the $0 - 1$ loss $\ell_{0-1}(F(\mathbf{x}), y)$, and such that $\phi(\mathbf{f}(\mathbf{x}), y) \leq B$ for all $\mathbf{x}$ and $y$. Let $\{(X_i, Y_i)\}_{i=1}^n$ be independently selected according to a probability measure $P$, and set $\hat{\mathbf{E}}_n \phi(\mathbf{f}(X), Y)$ to be the empirical mean of $\phi(\mathbf{f}(X), Y)$, namely $(1/n) \sum_{i=1}^n \phi(\mathbf{f}(X_i), Y_i)$. Then for any integer $n$ and $0 < \delta < 1$, with probability at least $1 - \delta$ over samples of length $n$, every $\mathbf{f} \in \mathcal{F}$ satisfies*

$$\mathbf{P}\{F(X) \neq Y\} \leq \hat{\mathbf{E}}_n \phi(\mathbf{f}(X), Y) + 2R_n(\phi \circ \mathcal{F}) + B\sqrt{\frac{2\log(1/\delta)}{n}}.$$

## 3   Convex Upper Bounds on the $0 - 1$ Loss

We consider two convex loss functions which upper bound the $0 - 1$ loss. The first loss function was suggested in [13], while the second is an extension of the logistic loss function used in two-class Boosting [7].

For any $y \in \mathcal{Y} = \{1, 2, \ldots, k\}$ define vector valued variables $\mathbf{y} \in (-1, +1)^k$ and $\boldsymbol{\xi}(y) \in \{0, 1\}^k$ by

$$(\boldsymbol{\xi}(y))_i = 1 - \delta_{y,i}$$
$$(\mathbf{y})_i = \delta_{y,i} - (1/(k-1))(1 - \delta_{y,i}).$$

For example, if $y = 1$ we have $\mathbf{y} = (1, -1/(k-1), \cdots, -1/(k-1))$ and $\boldsymbol{\xi}(y) = (0, 1, \ldots, 1)$.

Next, following [13] introduce the *hinge* loss function $\phi_{\mathrm{H}}$ through

$$(\phi_{\mathrm{H}} \circ \mathbf{f})(\mathbf{x}, y) = (2(k-1)/k)(\langle \boldsymbol{\xi}(y), (\mathbf{f}(\mathbf{x}) - \mathbf{y}) \rangle)_+$$
$$= (2(k-1)/k) \sum_{r \neq y} (f_r(\mathbf{x}) + 1/(k-1))_+ , \quad (4)$$

where $\langle \cdots, \cdot \rangle$ denotes a scalar product and $(x)_+ = \max(x, 0)$. Note that for $k = 2$, the standard SVM loss function is recovered [13]. We begin by relating $\phi_H$ to the $0 - 1$ loss.

**Lemma 1.** *Let* $\mathbf{f}(\mathbf{x}) = (f_1(\mathbf{x}), \ldots, f_k(\mathbf{x}))$ *where* $\sum_{r=1}^{k} f_r(\mathbf{x}) = 0$, *and set* $F(\mathbf{x}) = \operatorname{argmax}_{1 \le r \le k} f_r(\mathbf{x})$. *Then, for any* $\mathbf{x}$ *and* $y$,

$$\ell_{0-1}(F(\mathbf{x}), y) \le \phi_H(\mathbf{f}(\mathbf{x}), y).$$

*Proof.* Observe that if $F(\mathbf{x}) = y$, the $0 - 1$ loss is zero so the bound trivially holds since $\phi_H(\mathbf{f}(\mathbf{x}), y) \ge 0$. We therefore assume that $F(\mathbf{x}) \ne y$. Without loss of generality assume that $y = 1$, implying that there exists a value of $r \in \{2, \ldots, k\}$ such that $F(\mathbf{x}) = r$, say $r = 2$. Since we consider fixed values of $\mathbf{x}$ and $y$, we simplify the notation by replacing $f_r(\mathbf{x})$ by $f_r$. We then consider the cost function

$$\phi_H(\mathbf{f}) = \frac{2(k-1)}{k} \sum_{r=2}^{k} (f_r + 1/(k-1))_+ .$$

We need to show that $\phi_H(\mathbf{f}) \ge 1$. Set $\mathbf{f}^* = (f_1^*, \ldots, f_k^*)$, where

$$f_r^* = \begin{cases} \frac{k-2}{2(k-1)} & \text{if } r = 1 \text{ or } r = 2 \\ -\frac{1}{(k-1)} & \text{otherwise .} \end{cases}$$

It is easy to see that $\sum_{r=1}^{k} f_r = 0$ and $\phi_H(\mathbf{f}^*) = 1$. Assume that $\mathbf{f} = (f_1, f_2, \cdots, f_k)$ minimizes $\phi_H(\mathbf{f})$. We will show that $\mathbf{f} = \mathbf{f}^*$.

First, we show that for any $r \ge 3$, $f_r = f_r^* = -b$, where we set $b = 1/(k-1)$. The proof proceeds by contradiction. We consider two cases.

**Case 1:** Assume there exists a value of $r \ge 3$, such that $f_r = c < -b$. Then we construct $\mathbf{f}'$ as follows. If $f_2 > -b$

$$\begin{aligned} f_1' &= f_1 + (c+b)/2 & f_2' &= f_2 + (c+b)/2 \\ f_r' &= f_r - (c+b) = -b & f_s' &= f_s \quad (s \notin \{1, 2, r\}). \end{aligned}$$

We then find that

$$\begin{aligned} \phi_H(\mathbf{f}') &= \frac{2(k-1)}{k} \left[ (f_2 + b + (c+b)/2)_+ + \sum_{l \ne 1,2,r}^{k} (f_l + b)_+ \right] \\ &< \frac{2(k-1)}{k} \sum_{l=2}^{k} (f_l + b)_+ \\ &= \phi_H(\mathbf{f}). \end{aligned}$$

If $f_2 \le -b$ then there exists $s \ge 3$, so that $f_s > -b$ (because the sum is 0). In this case set $\mathbf{f}'$ as follows.

$$f_r' = f_r - (c+b) = -b \quad ; \quad f_s' = f_s + (c+b) \quad ; \quad f_l' = f_l \quad (l \notin \{r, s\})$$

we then have

$$\phi_{\mathrm{H}}(\mathbf{f}') = \frac{2(k-1)}{k}\left[(f_s + b + (c+b))_+ + \sum_{l \neq 1, r, s}^{k} (f_l + b)_+\right]$$

$$< \frac{2(k-1)}{k}\sum_{l=2}^{k}(f_l + b)_+$$

$$= \phi_{\mathrm{H}}(\mathbf{f}).$$

In both cases we obtain $\phi_{\mathrm{H}}(\mathbf{f}') < \phi_{\mathrm{H}}(\mathbf{f})$ contradicting the assumption that $\mathbf{f}$ minimizes $\phi_{\mathrm{H}}(\mathbf{f})$. This implies that for all $r \geq 3$, $f_r \geq -b$.

**Case 2.** Assume there exists a value of $r \geq 3$, such that $f_r = c > -b$. We construct $\mathbf{f}'$ as follows.

$$f_1' = f_1 + (c+b)/2 \qquad f_2' = f_2 + (c+b)/2$$
$$f_r' = f_r - (c+b) = -b \qquad f_l' = f_l \quad (l \notin \{1, 2, r\})$$

We then conclude that

$$\phi_{\mathrm{H}}(\mathbf{f}') = \frac{2(k-1)}{k}\left[(f_2 + b + (c+b)/2)_+ + (f_r' + b) + \sum_{l \neq 1, 2, r}^{k} (f_l + b)_+\right]$$

$$< \frac{2(k-1)}{k}\left[(f_2 + b)_+ + (c+b)_+ + \sum_{l \neq 1, 2, r}^{k} (f_l + b)_+\right]$$

$$< \frac{2(k-1)}{k}\left[(f_2 + b)_+ + (f_r + b)_+ + \sum_{l \neq 1, 2, r}^{k} (f_l + b)_+\right]$$

$$= \phi_{\mathrm{H}}(\mathbf{f}).$$

And once again we get a contradiction. The conclusion from the cases considered so far is that for all $r \geq 3$, $f_r = f_r^* = -b$.

It remains to show that $f_1 = f_1^*$ and $f_2 = f_2^*$. Since $\sum_{r=1}^{k} f_r = 0$, it follows that $f_1 + f_2 = (k-2)b = 2f_1^* = 2f_2^* > 0$. Note that $f_1 > f_2$ is impossible, since we assumed that a classification error occurred. Assume that $f_2 > f_1$. We then have

$$\phi_{\mathrm{H}}(\mathbf{f}^*) = \frac{2(k-1)}{k}\left[(f_2^* + b)_+ + \sum_{l=3}^{k}(f_l^* + b)_+\right]$$

$$= \frac{2(k-1)}{k}\left[((f_1 + f_2)/2 + b)_+ + \sum_{l=3}^{k}(f_l + b)_+\right]$$

$$< \frac{2(k-1)}{k}\left[(f_2 + b)_+ + \sum_{l=3}^{k}(f_l + b)_+\right]$$

$$= \phi_{\mathrm{H}}(\mathbf{f})$$

which contradicts the assumption on the optimality of $\mathbf{f}$. In conclusion we get $\mathbf{f} = \mathbf{f}^*$, which completes the proof. $\qquad\square$

The hinge loss $\phi_{\mathrm{H}}$ described above has the following nice feature. Assuming that the class of functions $\mathcal{F}$ is 'rich enough', the minimizer of the expected value of $\phi_{\mathrm{H}}$, $\mathbf{E}\phi_{\mathrm{H}}(\mathbf{f}(X), Y)$, coincides with the optimal Bayes classifier [13]. It is well known that for the two-category case, the hinge loss $\phi$ considered above is not unique in this respect (see, for example, [22]). In fact, most of the results in this paper hold for general functions $\phi$ which dominate the $0-1$ loss. As a specific example we introduce an additional loss function, and show that minimizing it leads, in the limit, to the Bayes classifier. This loss function, denotes $\phi_{\mathrm{L}}$, extends the logistic loss for binary classification, and is given by

$$\phi_{\mathrm{L}}(\mathbf{f}(\mathbf{x}), y) = (2(k-1)/k) \sum_{r \neq y} \log_2 \left(1 + \exp\{f_r(\mathbf{x}) + 1/(k-1)\}\right). \tag{5}$$

It is easy to see that this function upper bounds the hinge loss defined in (4), and therefore provides an upper bound on the $0-1$ loss. We show that minimizing the expected value of this function leads to the Bayes classifier.

**Lemma 2.** *Let $F^*(\mathbf{x}) = \operatorname{argmax} f_r^*(\mathbf{x})$, where $\mathbf{f} = (f_1^*, \ldots, f_k^*)$ minimizes $\mathbf{E}\phi_L(\mathbf{f}(X), Y)$. Then $F^*$ is the Bayes classifier.*

*Proof.* Set $\eta_i(\mathbf{x}) = P(Y = i|\mathbf{x})$. It is well known that the optimal Bayes classifier is obtained by setting $F_{\mathrm{B}}(\mathbf{x}) = \operatorname{argmax}_{1 \leq i < k} \eta_i(\mathbf{x})$. We then have

$$(k/2(k-1))\phi_{\mathrm{L}}(\mathbf{f}(\mathbf{x})) \triangleq (k/2(k-1))\mathbf{E}_Y \phi_{\mathrm{L}}(\mathbf{f}(\mathbf{x}), Y) \tag{6}$$

$$= (k/2(k-1)) \sum_{i=1}^{k} \eta_i(\mathbf{x})\phi_{\mathrm{L}}(\mathbf{f}(\mathbf{x}), i)$$

$$= \sum_{r=1}^{k} \log_2 \left(1 + e^{f_r(\mathbf{x}) + \frac{1}{k-1}}\right)$$

$$- \sum_{r=1}^{k} \eta_r(\mathbf{x}) \log_2 \left(1 + e^{f_r(\mathbf{x}) + \frac{1}{k-1}}\right)$$

Since $\mathbf{x}$ is fixed, we slightly abuse notation and eliminate the $\mathbf{x}$ dependence in the proof. Let $\mathbf{f}^* = (f_1^*, \ldots, f_k^*)$ minimize $\phi_{\mathrm{L}}(\mathbf{f})$. In order to show that $F^* = \operatorname{argmax}_r f_r^*$ is the Bayes classifier, we need to show that $\operatorname{argmax}_r f_r^* = \operatorname{argmax}_r \eta_r$. Let us assume the contrary, namely that $\operatorname{argmax}_r f_r^* \neq \operatorname{argmax}_r \eta_r$.

In this case we define a new classifier $\mathbf{f}'$ as follows. We take $(f_1^*, f_2^*, \cdots, f_k^*)$ and rearrange the order of the vector elements so that they are ordered similarly to $\eta_r$ [1]. Due to our assumption $\mathbf{f}' \neq \mathbf{f}^*$. Next, observe that for two real-valued sequences $\{a_i\}$ and $\{b_i\}$,

$$\sum_i a_i b_i \leq \sum_i a_i b_i'$$

---

[1] Two sequences $\{a_i\}$ and $\{b_i\}$ are similarly ordered if $(a_i - a_j)(b_i - b_j) \geq 0$ for all $i$ and $j$.

where $\{b_i'\}$ is a permutation of $\{b_i\}$ which ensures that $\{b_i'\}$ and $\{a_i\}$ are similarly ordered (e.g., Theorem 10.368 in [8]). In view of (6) and the monotonicity of the logarithm, we find that $\phi_L(\mathbf{f}') < \phi_L(\mathbf{f}^*)$, in contradiction to the assumption. $\square$

## 4    Data-Dependent Bounds

Until now we have imposed no restrictions on the structure of the functions $\{f_r\}$. At this point we make the assumption that $f_r$ is obtained by first mapping the input $\mathbf{x}$ using an $\ell$-dimensional mapping $\mathbf{h}(\mathbf{x}) = (h_1(\mathbf{x}), \ldots, h_\ell(\mathbf{x}))$, $h_j(\mathbf{x}) \in \mathcal{H}$, followed by a $k$-dimensional linear map, namely

$$f_r(\mathbf{x}) = \langle \mathbf{m}_r, \mathbf{h}(\mathbf{x}) \rangle.$$

One can envisage two situations here. If $\ell$ is finite, consider the $k \times \ell$ matrix $M$, the $r'$th row of which is given by $\mathbf{m}_r$. In this case, observe that the transition from the $k$ classifiers $\{f_r\}$ to the multi-category classifier $F$, as described in (1) is identical to a form of the *decoding step* of the error correcting procedures introduced in [6]. One can then view the functions $\{h_j(\mathbf{x})\}_{j=1}^\ell$ as the soft binary classifiers associated with the columns of the coding matrix $M$. In this context, one of the interesting unsolved issues is the construction of effective procedures for selecting good coding matrices. For example, [4] have recently suggested procedures for constructing such coding matrices based on convex optimization using a margin based cost function. In this work we start by deriving data-dependent generalization error bounds, which depend explicitly on the properties of the coding matrix $M$. One may choose optimal coding matrices $M$ by optimizing these bounds. It is interesting to observe that the mapping studied here may be considered as a two-layer neural network with a winner-take-all function operating in the output layer. This observation has also been made recently in [5].

A second interpretation of the approach presented, pursued in [13], is that of kernel methods. Consider a positive semi-definite Mercer kernel $k(\mathbf{x}, \mathbf{x}')$ with associated eigenfunctions $\psi_j(\mathbf{x})$ and non-negative eigenvalues $\lambda_j$ with respect to a measure $P$, where the latter are arranged in descending order of magnitude $\lambda_1 \geq \lambda_2 \geq \cdots$. We select the functions $h_j$ so that $h_j(\mathbf{x}) = \sqrt{\lambda_j} \psi_j(\mathbf{x})$. It is well known (e.g. [21]) that in this case

$$k(\mathbf{x}, \mathbf{x}') = \sum_j h_j(\mathbf{x}) h_j(\mathbf{x}') = \langle \mathbf{h}(\mathbf{x}), \mathbf{h}(\mathbf{x}') \rangle.$$

As we show below, the bounds obtained do not depend explicitly on $\ell$, but rather on $\|\mathbf{h}(\mathbf{x})\|^2 = k(\mathbf{x}, \mathbf{x})$, allowing our bounds to be applied to the multi-category support vector machines introduced in [13].

Let $\tilde{\mathbf{m}} = \{\mathbf{m}_1, \ldots, \mathbf{m}_k\}$ and set $\mathbf{a} = (a_1, \ldots, a_s)$ for some real numbers $\{a_1, \ldots, a_s\}$. Assume a domain $\mathcal{M}(\mathbf{a})$ is defined by the following set of $s$ constraints

$$\mathcal{M}(\mathbf{a}) = \{\tilde{\mathbf{m}} : g_1(\tilde{\mathbf{m}}) \leq a_1, \cdots, g_s(\tilde{\mathbf{m}}) \leq a_s\}, \tag{7}$$

where $\{g_1, g_2, \ldots, g_s\}$ are non-negative constraint functions. We consider the associated set of functions

$$\mathcal{F}(\mathbf{a}) = \{\mathbf{f} : \ \mathbf{f}(\mathbf{x}) = (\langle \mathbf{m}_1, \mathbf{h}(\mathbf{x}) \rangle, \cdots, \langle \mathbf{m}_k, \mathbf{h}(\mathbf{x}) \rangle), \ \tilde{\mathbf{m}} \in \mathcal{M}(\mathbf{a})\} .$$

Introduce the class of functions

$$\mathcal{G}(\mathbf{a}) = \left\{ g : g(\mathbf{x}) = \sum_{r=1}^{k} \langle \mathbf{m}_r, \mathbf{h}(\mathbf{x}) \rangle, \ \tilde{\mathbf{m}} \in \mathcal{M}(\mathbf{a}) \right\} . \tag{8}$$

For each constraint $g_j(\tilde{\mathbf{m}})$ define a conjugate function

$$g_j^*(\mathbf{z}) = \sup_{\tilde{\mathbf{m}} \in \mathcal{M}(\mathbf{a})} \left\{ \sum_{r=1}^{k} \langle \mathbf{m}_r, \mathbf{z} \rangle - g_j(\tilde{\mathbf{m}}) \right\} , \quad (j = 1, 2, \ldots, s).$$

An immediate consequence of this definition (the so-called Fenchel inequality in Convex Analysis [17]) is that for all $\{\mathbf{m}_1, \ldots, \mathbf{m}_k\}$ and $\mathbf{z}$

$$\sum_{r=1}^{k} \langle \mathbf{m}_r, \mathbf{z} \rangle \leq g_j(\tilde{\mathbf{m}}) + g_j^*(\tilde{\mathbf{z}}) , \quad (j = 1, 2, \ldots, s).$$

Combining these inequalities we have that

$$\sum_{r=1}^{k} \langle \mathbf{m}_r, \mathbf{z} \rangle \leq \min_{1 \leq j \leq s} \{ g_j(\tilde{\mathbf{m}}) + g_j^*(\tilde{\mathbf{z}}) \} . \tag{9}$$

Setting $\mathbf{z} = (\lambda/n) \sum_{i=1}^{n} \sigma_i \mathbf{h}(\mathbf{x}_i)$ in (9), and using $g_j(\tilde{\mathbf{m}}) \leq a_j$, we conclude from the definition of the Rademacher complexity that for any positive $\lambda$

$$\hat{R}_n(\mathcal{G}(\mathbf{a})) = \mathbf{E}_\sigma \sup_{\tilde{\mathbf{m}} \in \mathcal{M}(\mathbf{a})} \left\{ \frac{1}{n} \sum_{i=1}^{n} \sigma_i \sum_{r=1}^{k} \langle \mathbf{m}_r, \mathbf{h}(\mathbf{x}_i) \rangle \right\}$$

$$\leq \frac{1}{\lambda} \mathbf{E}_\sigma \min_{1 \leq j \leq s} \left\{ a_j + g_j^* \left( (\lambda/n) \sum_{i=1}^{n} \sigma_i \mathbf{h}(\mathbf{x}_i) \right) \right\}$$

$$\leq \frac{1}{\lambda} \min_{1 \leq j \leq s} \left\{ a_j + \mathbf{E}_\sigma g_j^* \left( (\lambda/n) \sum_{i=1}^{n} \sigma_i \mathbf{h}(\mathbf{x}_i) \right) \right\} . \tag{10}$$

Since (10) holds for each $\lambda$ we obtain the best bound by minimizing over $\lambda$.

The bound on $\hat{R}_n(\phi \circ \mathcal{F}(\mathbf{a}))$ required for the utilization of Theorem 1 contains an explicit dependence on the parameters $\{a_1, \ldots, a_s\}$ defining the constraint set $\mathcal{M}(\mathbf{a})$. Introduce the notation

$$\varUpsilon(\mathbf{a}) = R_n(\phi \circ \mathcal{F}(\mathbf{a})),$$

where the notation makes the functional dependence of $\varUpsilon$ on $\mathbf{a}$ (rather than on $\phi \circ \mathcal{F}(\mathbf{a})$) explicit. Observe that by definition $\varUpsilon(\mathbf{a})$ is monotonically increasing in each of its arguments $a_i$.

The next Theorem provides a fully data-dependent bound, which can in turn be used for model selection. The derivation is a generalization of Theorems 3 and 4 in [16] and extends the proof in [15] to the case of multiple constraints. We use the notation $F_{\tilde{\mathbf{m}}}$ and $\mathbf{f}_{\tilde{\mathbf{m}}}$ to denote the dependence of the classifiers on $\tilde{\mathbf{m}}$. We begin with a simple lemma.

**Lemma 3.** *Let $\{i_1, i_2, \ldots, i_s\}$ be an s-tuple of positive integers. Then, for any s and $i_j \in \mathbb{Z}^+$ (the set of positive integers),*

$$\sum_{j=1}^{s}(i_j - 1) + 1 \leq \prod_{j=1}^{s} i_j.$$

*Proof.* We proceed by induction on $s$. For $s = 1$ the claim holds trivially. Assume it holds for $s$, and proceed to $s + 1$. We have

$$\sum_{j=1}^{s+1}(i_j - 1) + 1 = \sum_{j=1}^{s}(i_j - 1) + (i_{s+1} - 1) + 1$$

$$\leq \prod_{j=1}^{s} i_j + i_{s+1} - 1$$

$$\leq \prod_{j=1}^{s+1} i_j,$$

where the last inequality follows from the observation that $in + 1 - n - i = (n-1)(i-1) \geq 0$ for $i \geq 1, n \geq 1$. $\square$

**Theorem 2.** *Let $S = \{(X_i, Y_i)\}_{i=1}^{n}$, $X_i \in \mathcal{X}$, $Y_i \in \mathcal{Y} = \{1, \ldots, k\}$ be a sample of n points generated independently at random from a distribution P. Assume that $F_{\tilde{\mathbf{m}}}(\mathbf{x}) = \operatorname{argmax}_{1 \leq r \leq k} \langle \mathbf{m}_r, \mathbf{h}(\mathbf{x}) \rangle$ and that $\phi$ dominates the $0-1$ loss and is uniformly bounded by B. Let $g_{0,j} > 0$, $j = 1, 2, \ldots, s$, be a set of positive numbers, and set $\tilde{g}_j(\tilde{\mathbf{m}}) = 2 \max(g_j(\tilde{\mathbf{m}}), g_{0,j})$ where the constraint functions $g_j(\tilde{\mathbf{m}})$ were introduced in (7). Then with probability at least $1 - \delta$, for all $\mathbf{f}_{\tilde{\mathbf{m}}}$,*

$$\mathbf{P}\{F_{\tilde{\mathbf{m}}}(X) \neq Y\} \leq \frac{1}{n}\sum_{i=1}^{n}\phi(\mathbf{f}_{\tilde{\mathbf{m}}}(X_i), Y_i) + 2\Upsilon(\tilde{g}_1(\tilde{\mathbf{m}}), \ldots, \tilde{g}_s(\tilde{\mathbf{m}}))$$

$$+ B\sqrt{\frac{2\sum_{j=1}^{s}\log 2^{1/s}\log_2(\tilde{g}_j(\tilde{\mathbf{m}})/g_{0,j})}{n}} + B\sqrt{\frac{2\log(1/\delta)}{n}}.$$

*Proof.* Consider the $s$-dimensional grid defined by the coordinates $(i_1, \ldots, i_s)$, $i_j \in \mathbb{Z}^+$, and introduce a mapping $\zeta$ from $(\mathbb{Z}^+)^s$ to $\mathbb{Z}^+$ by requiring

$$i \leq \prod_{j=1}^{s} i_j \quad ; \quad i = \zeta(i_1, \ldots, i_s). \tag{11}$$

This can be done, for example, by setting $\zeta(i_1, \ldots, i_s)$ to be the Manhattan distance of the grid point $(i_1, \ldots, i_s)$ from the origin, given by $1 + \sum_{j=1}^{s}(i_j - 1)$. Equally (Manhattan) distant points are arbitrarily assigned an index $i$ consistent with (11) so that a unique mapping is achieved. Lemma 3 establishes (11) in this case.

Let $\{p_i\}$ be a set of positive numbers such that $\sum_i p_i = 1$, where for concreteness we set $p_i = 1/i(i+1)$, $i = 1, 2, \ldots$. For each $1 \le j \le s$ let $a_{i_j}^j = g_{0,j}2^{i_j}$, $i_j = 1, 2, \ldots$.

For each $(i_1, \ldots, i_s)$ and $i = \zeta(i_1, \ldots, i_s)$ set $\mathbf{a}_i = (a_{i_1}^1, \ldots, a_{i_s}^s)$, and denote by $\mathcal{M}(\mathbf{a}_i)$ the domain

$$\mathcal{M}(\mathbf{a}_i) = \left\{ \tilde{\mathbf{m}} : g_1(\tilde{\mathbf{m}}) \le a_{i_1}^1, \cdots, g_s(\tilde{\mathbf{m}}) \le a_{i_s}^s \right\}.$$

From Theorem 1 and the multiple testing lemma (essentially a slightly refined union bound; e.g. Lemma (4.14) in [10]) we have that for all $\tilde{\mathbf{m}} \in \mathcal{M}(\mathbf{a}_i)$, with probability at least $1 - \delta$

$$\mathbf{P}\{F_{\tilde{\mathbf{m}}}(X) \ne Y\} \le \hat{\mathbf{E}}_n \phi(\mathbf{f}(X), Y) + 2\Upsilon(\mathbf{a}_i) + B\sqrt{\frac{2\log(1/p_i\delta)}{n}}. \qquad (12)$$

For each $\tilde{\mathbf{m}}$ and $j$ let $i_j(\tilde{\mathbf{m}})$ be the smallest index for which $a_{i_j(\tilde{\mathbf{m}})}^j \ge g_j(\tilde{\mathbf{m}})$. By the construction and the definition of $\tilde{g}_j(\tilde{\mathbf{m}})$, it follows that for each $j$, $i_j(\tilde{\mathbf{m}}) \le \log_2(\tilde{g}_j(\tilde{\mathbf{m}})/g_{0,j})$, and $a_{i_j(\tilde{\mathbf{m}})}^j \le \tilde{g}_j(\tilde{\mathbf{m}})$. Let $i(\tilde{\mathbf{m}}) = \zeta(i_1(\tilde{\mathbf{m}}), \ldots, i_s(\tilde{\mathbf{m}})) \le \prod_{j=1}^{s} i_j(\tilde{\mathbf{m}})$. This implies that

$$\log(1/p_{i(\tilde{\mathbf{m}})}) \le 2\log(i(\tilde{\mathbf{m}}) + 1)$$

$$\le 2\log\left[\prod_j \log_2(\tilde{g}_j(\tilde{\mathbf{m}})/g_{0,j}) + 1\right]$$

$$\le 2\sum_{j=1}^{s} \log 2^{1/s} \log_2(\tilde{g}_j(\tilde{\mathbf{m}})/g_{0,j}).$$

Combining these results with (12), and using the monotonicity of $\Upsilon(\mathbf{a})$ in each of its arguments completes the proof. $\qquad \square$

*Remark 1.* Note that $\{g_{0,j}\}$ in Theorem 2 set the scale of each constraint. If $g_j(\tilde{\mathbf{m}}) \le g_{0,j}$ for all $j$, we obtain a data *independent* bound, depending solely on $g_{0,j}$ rather than $g_j(\tilde{\mathbf{m}})$.

*Remark 2.* The bound in Theorem 2 can be made 'more' data-dependent by using the empirical Rademacher complexity instead of the expected Rademacher complexity used to define $\Upsilon(\mathbf{a})$. This can be done using a simple consequence of a concentration inequality from [3]. In particular, one finds that with probability at least $1 - \delta$

$$R_n(\phi \circ \mathcal{F}(\mathbf{a})) \le \hat{R}_n(\phi \circ \mathcal{F}(\mathbf{a})) + \sqrt{\frac{B\hat{R}_n(\phi \circ \mathcal{F}(\mathbf{a}))\log(1/\delta)}{n}} + \frac{B\log(1/\delta)}{n},$$

which can be used in order to replace the expected Rademacher complexity in Theorem 2 by its empirical version, keeping in mind that $\delta$ needs to be appropriately scaled.

*Remark 3.* The results of Theorem 2 seem to apply only for a fixed (data-independent) choice of $\mathbf{h}$. However, assume that $\mathcal{H} = \{\bar{h}_1, \bar{h}_2, \dots, \}$ is a countable class of functions. In this case, any function of the form $\langle \mathbf{m}_r, \mathbf{h}(\mathbf{x}) \rangle$ can be written as $\langle \bar{\mathbf{m}}_r, \bar{\mathbf{h}}(\mathbf{x}) \rangle$ (where the inner product now is in an infinite-dimensional space) for some $\bar{\mathbf{m}}_r$. Since $\mathbf{m}_r$ can be chosen after seeing the data, there is in principle (but not in practice) no loss of generality using Theorem 2 with $\langle \bar{\mathbf{m}}_r, \bar{\mathbf{h}}(\mathbf{x}) \rangle$ to find optimal bounds.

In order to estimate $\hat{R}_n(\phi_{\mathrm{H}} \circ \mathcal{F}(\mathbf{a}))$ we quote the following Lemma from [15] (this is a slight refinement of Theorem 4.12 in [12]).

**Lemma 4 (Lemma 5 from [15].** *] Let $\{g_i(\theta)\}$ and $\{h_i(\theta)\}$ be sets of functions defined for all $\theta$ in some domain $\Theta$. If for all $i$, $\theta$, $\theta'$, $|g_i(\theta) - g_i(\theta')| \leq |h_i(\theta) - h_i(\theta')|$, then*

$$\mathbf{E}_\sigma \sup_{\theta \in \Theta} \left\{ \sum_{i=1}^n \sigma_i g_i(\theta) \right\} \leq \mathbf{E}_\sigma \sup_{\theta \in \Theta} \left\{ \sum_{i=1}^n \sigma_i h_i(\theta) \right\}.$$

Let $\mathcal{F}(\mathbf{a})$ consist of all vector-valued functions $(f_1, \dots, f_k)$ where $f_r(\mathbf{x}) = \langle \mathbf{m}_r, \mathbf{h}(\mathbf{x}) \rangle$ and $\sum_{r=1}^k \mathbf{m}_r = \mathbf{0}$ and where $\tilde{\mathbf{m}} \in \mathcal{M}(\mathbf{a})$. Denote by $\mathcal{M}'(\mathbf{a})$ the intersection of $\mathcal{M}(\mathbf{a})$ with the set defined by $\sum_{r=1}^k \mathbf{m}_r = 0$. It is easy to see that for any real numbers $a, b$ and $c$,

$$|(a + c)_+ - (b + c)_+| \leq |a - b|. \tag{13}$$

Denote the set of indices for which $y_i = r$ by $I_r$, and let $n_r$, $1 \leq r \leq k$, denote the number of training points for which $y_i = r$. We then have

$$\hat{R}_n(\phi_{\mathrm{H}} \circ \mathcal{F}(\mathbf{a})) = \frac{1}{n} \mathbf{E}_\sigma \sup_{\tilde{\mathbf{m}} \in \mathcal{M}'(\mathbf{a})} \sum_{i=1}^n \sigma_i \sum_{r \neq y_i} \left( \langle \mathbf{m}_r, \mathbf{h}(\mathbf{x}_i) \rangle + \frac{1}{k-1} \right)_+$$

$$\overset{(a)}{\leq} \frac{1}{n} \mathbf{E}_\sigma \sup_{\tilde{\mathbf{m}} \in \mathcal{M}'(\mathbf{a})} \sum_{i=1}^n \sigma_i \sum_{r \neq y_i} \langle \mathbf{m}_r, \mathbf{h}(\mathbf{x}_i) \rangle$$

$$\overset{(b)}{=} \frac{1}{n} \mathbf{E}_\sigma \sup_{\tilde{\mathbf{m}} \in \mathcal{M}'(\mathbf{a})} \sum_{i=1}^n \sigma_i \langle \mathbf{m}_{y_i}, \mathbf{h}(\mathbf{x}_i) \rangle$$

$$= \frac{1}{n} \mathbf{E}_\sigma \sup_{\tilde{\mathbf{m}} \in \mathcal{M}'(\mathbf{a})} \left\{ \sum_{i \in I_1} \sigma_i \langle \mathbf{m}_1, \mathbf{h}(\mathbf{x}_i) \rangle + \cdots + \sum_{i \in I_k} \sigma_i \langle \mathbf{m}_k, \mathbf{h}(\mathbf{x}_i) \rangle \right\}$$

$$\leq \frac{1}{n} \mathbf{E}_\sigma \sup_{\tilde{\mathbf{m}} \in \mathcal{M}'(\mathbf{a})} \left\{ \sum_{i \in I_1} \sigma_i \langle \mathbf{m}_1, \mathbf{h}(\mathbf{x}_i) \rangle \right\} + \cdots$$

$$+ \frac{1}{n} \mathbf{E}_\sigma \sup_{\tilde{\mathbf{m}} \in \mathcal{M}'(\mathbf{a})} \left\{ \sum_{i \in I_k} \sigma_i \langle \mathbf{m}_k, \mathbf{h}(\mathbf{x}_i) \rangle \right\}$$

Here $(a)$ used (13) and Lemma 4 while $(b)$ is based on the condition $\sum_r \mathbf{m}_r = \mathbf{0}$ and on a symmetry argument. Each one of the terms on the r.h.s. of the final inequality can be bounded using the techniques used to establish (10). In particular, define

$$g_{j,r}^*(\mathbf{z}) = \sup_{\tilde{\mathbf{m}} \in \mathcal{M}(\mathbf{a})} \{\langle \mathbf{m}_r, \mathbf{z} \rangle - g_j(\tilde{\mathbf{m}})\}.$$

Analogously to (10), we then find that for each $r \in \{1, 2, \ldots, k\}$ and $\lambda > 0$

$$\mathbf{E}_\sigma \sup_{\tilde{\mathbf{m}} \in \mathcal{M}(\mathbf{a})} \frac{1}{n_r} \sum_{i \in I_r} \sigma_i \langle \mathbf{m}_r, \mathbf{h}(\mathbf{x}_i) \rangle \leq \frac{1}{\lambda} \min_{1 \leq j \leq s} \left\{ a_j + \mathbf{E}_\sigma g_{j,r}^* \left( \frac{\lambda}{n_r} \sum_{i \in I_r} \sigma_i \mathbf{h}(\mathbf{x}_i) \right) \right\}.$$
(14)

This result can be used in Theorem 2 in order to establish bounds which depend explicitly on the constraint functions $\{g_1, \ldots, g_s\}$.

A simple upper bound can be obtained using the following argument. Consider the restriction $\tilde{\mathbf{m}} \in \mathcal{M}(\mathbf{a})$ in (7). For each $r \in \{1, 2, \ldots k\}$ this defines a domain over which $\mathbf{m}_r$ is allowed to vary. Define the set $B(\mathbf{a})$ to contain the largest region allowed for each of the components $\mathbf{m}_r$ of $\tilde{\mathbf{m}}$. Note that

$$\mathbf{E}_\sigma \sup_{\tilde{\mathbf{m}} \in \mathcal{M}'(\mathbf{a})} \left\{ \sum_{i \in I_r} \sigma_i \langle \mathbf{m}_r, \mathbf{h}(\mathbf{x}_i) \rangle \right\} \leq \mathbf{E}_\sigma \sup_{\mathbf{m}_r \in B(\mathbf{a})} \left\{ \sum_{i \in I_r} \sigma_i \langle \mathbf{m}_r, \mathbf{h}(\mathbf{x}_i) \rangle \right\},$$

where the domain on the r.h.s. involves only $\mathbf{m}_r$. We thus conclude that

$$\hat{R}_n(\phi_{\mathrm{H}} \circ \mathcal{F}(\mathbf{a})) \leq \frac{n_1}{n} \hat{R}_{n_1}(B(\mathbf{a})) + \cdots + \frac{n_k}{n} \hat{R}_{n_k}(B(\mathbf{a})),$$

where each of the terms $\hat{R}_{n_r}(B(\mathbf{a}))$ can be estimated using the results in [15]. However, such a bound essentially neglects the detailed structure of the region $\mathcal{M}(\mathbf{a})$ defined through the constraints in (7).

We defer the full elaboration of the more precise bounds resulting from (14) and the provision of examples to the full version of the paper. Note that a similar result can be established for the logistic loss $\phi_{\mathrm{L}}$.

## 5   Discussion

We have considered a general formulation of multi-category classification based on minimizing a convex upper bound on the $0 - 1$ loss. The presented formulation is related to both the output coding approach of [6] and to the multi-category support vector machine approach of [13]. We have derived general data-dependent bounds which enable one to select good coding matrices in the output coding framework, while allowing for the flexibility of attaining the Bayes risk in the support vector machine framework. The framework is sufficiently flexible so that many types of constraints can be incorporated, and any prior knowledge available may be incorporated into the problem.

There are many directions for extending this work. First, it would be interesting to extend the results to other loss functions which weight the different classes asymmetrically, as suggested in [13]. Second, while some very preliminary simulations indicate that the bounds correlate well with the true generalization error and lead to very effective model selection algorithms, this issue needs to be fully corroborated, followed by a comparison of the resulting algorithms to standard approaches that use fixed coding matrices such as all-pairs. A particularly interesting issue is the astute selection of constraint functions $g_j(\tilde{\mathbf{m}})$. This selection may strongly influence the quality of the bounds, and should be made based on prior information. In fact, it would be interesting to see whether it is possible to learn the correct functions from the data. Finally, we have considered generalization bounds based on a fixed selection of basis functions $\mathbf{h}$, as in standard support vector machines (but see Remark 3). We plan to extend these results to incorporate adaptive selection of $\mathbf{h}$, as is done, for example in Boosting. The methods developed in [14] should be very useful in this context. On a technical level, we have assumed that the convex loss functions bounding the $0-1$ loss are bounded. This assumption can be alleviated using the techniques presented in [15].

## Acknowledgments

We are grateful to Tong Zhang for allowing us to use some of the ideas from [15] prior to publication. Helpful discussions with Coby Crammer, Ran El-Yaniv and Yoram Singer are gratefully acknowledged. The research of R.M. is partially supported by the fund for promotion of research at the Technion and by the Ollendorff foundation of the Electrical Engineering department at the Technion.

## References

1. E.L. Allwein, R.E. Schapire, and Y. Singer. Reducing multiclass to binary: a unifying approach for margin classifiers. *Journal of Machine Learning Research*, 1:113–141, 2000.
2. P.L. Bartlett and S. Mendelson. Rademacher and Gaussian complexities: Risk bounds and structural results. *Journal of Machine Learning Research*, 3:463–482, 2002.
3. S. Boucheron, G. Lugosi, and P. Massart. Concentration inequalities using the entropy method. *The Annals of Probability*, 2, 2003. To appear.
4. K. Crammer and Y. Singer. On the learnability and design of output codes for multiclass problems. *Machine Learning*, 47(2), 2002.
5. K. Crammer and Y. Singer. Improved output coding for classification using continuous relaxation. In *Advances in Neural Information Processing Systems*, volume 15, 2003.
6. T.G. Dietterich and G. Bakiri. Solving multiclass learning problems via error-correcting output codes. *Journal of Aritifical Intelligence Research*, 2:263–286, 1995.

7. J. Friedman, T. Hastie, and R. Tibshirani. Additive logistic regression: a statistical view of boosting. *The Annals of Statistics*, 38(2):337–374, 2000.
8. G. Hardy, J.E. Littlewood, and G. Polya. *Inequalities*. Cambridge University Press, second edition, 1952.
9. T. Hastie and R. Tibshirani. Classification by pairwise clustering. *The Annals of Statistics*, 16(1):451–471, 1998.
10. R. Herbrich. *Learning Kernel Classifiers: Theory and Algorithms*. MIT Press, Boston, 2002.
11. V. Koltchinksii and D. Panchenko. Empirical margin distributions and bounding the generalization error of combined classifiers. *The Annals of Statistics*, 30(1), 2002.
12. M. Ledoux and M. Talgrand. *Probability in Banach Spaces: Isoperimetry and Processes*. Springer Press, New York, 1991.
13. Y. Lee, Y. LIin, and G. Wahba. Multicategory Support Vector Machines, theory and applications to the classification of microarray data and satellite radiance data. Technical Report 1064, University of Wisconsin, Department of Statistics, 2002.
14. S. Mannor, R. Meir, and T. Zhang. The consistency of greedy algorithms for classification. In *Proceedings of the fifteenth Annual conference on Computational learning theory*, volume 2375 of *LNAI*, pages 319–333, Sydney, 2002. Springer.
15. R. Meir and T. Zhang. Generalization bounds for Bayesian mixture algorithms. Submitted for publication.
16. R. Meir and T. Zhang. Data-dependent bounds for Bayesian mixture methods. In *Advances in Neural Information Processing Systems 15*, 2003. To eppear.
17. R.T. Rockafellar. *Convex Analysis*. Princeton University Press, Princeton, N.J., 1970.
18. R. Schapire. Using outpout codes to boost multiclass learning problems. In *Proceeding of the Fourteenth International Conference on Machine Learning*, pages 313–321, 1997.
19. R.E. Schapire and Y. Singer. Improved boosting algorithms using confidence-rated predictions. *Machine Learning*, 37(3):297–336, 1999.
20. A.W. van der Vaart and J.A. Wellner. *Weak Convergence and EmpiricalProcesses*. Springer Verlag, New York, 1996.
21. V. N. Vapnik. *Statistical Learning Theory*. Wiley Interscience, New York, 1998.
22. T. Zhang. Statistical behavior and consistency of classification methods based on convex risk minimization. *The Annals of Statistics*, 2003. To appear.

# Comparing Clusterings
# by the Variation of Information

Marina Meilă

University of Washington
Box 354322
Seattle WA 98195-4322
mmp@stat.washington.edu

**Abstract.** This paper proposes an information theoretic criterion for comparing two partitions, or *clusterings*, of the same data set. The criterion, called variation of information (VI), measures the amount of information lost and gained in changing from clustering $\mathcal{C}$ to clustering $\mathcal{C}'$. The criterion makes no assumptions about how the clusterings were generated and applies to both soft and hard clusterings. The basic properties of VI are presented and discussed from the point of view of comparing clusterings. In particular, the VI is positive, symmetric and obeys the triangle inequality. Thus, surprisingly enough, it is a true metric on the space of clusterings.

**Keywords:** Clustering; Comparing partitions; Measures of agreement; Information theory; Mutual information

## 1 Introduction

This paper proposes a simple information theoretic criterion for comparing two clusterings. The concepts of entropy and information have proved themselves as useful vehicles for formalizing intuitive notions related to uncertainty. By approaching the relationship between two clusterings from the point of view of the information exchange – loss and gain – between them, we are exploiting once again this quality of information theoretic concepts. As it will be shown, the choice is also fortunate from other points of view. In particular, the variation of information is provably a metric on the space of clusterings.

To address the ill-posedness of the search for a "best" criterion, the paper presents a variety of properties of the variation of information and discusses their meaning from the point of view of comparing clusterings. We will check whether the properties of the new criterion are "reasonable" and "desirable" in a generic setting. The reader with a particular application in mind has in these properties a precise description of the criterion's behavior.

The paper starts by presenting previously used comparison criteria (section 2). The variation of information is introduced in section 3 and its properties are presented in section 4. In section 5 the variation of information is compared with other metrics and criteria of similarity between clusterings.

B. Schölkopf and M.K. Warmuth (Eds.): COLT/Kernel 2003, LNAI 2777, pp. 173–187, 2003.

## 2    Related Work

A clustering $\mathcal{C}$ is a partition of a set of points, or *data set* $D$ into sets $C_1, C_2, \ldots$ $C_K$ called *clusters* such that $C_k \cap C_l = \emptyset$ and $\bigcup_{k=1}^K C_k = D$. Let the number of data points in $D$ and in cluster $C_k$ be $n$ and $n_k$ respectively. We have, of course, that $n = \sum_{k=1}^K n_k$. We also assume that $n_k > 0$; in other words, that $K$ represents the number of non-empty clusters. Let a second clustering of the same data set $D$ be $\mathcal{C}' = \{C_1', C_2', \ldots C_{K'}'\}$, with cluster sizes $n_{k'}'$. Note that the two clusterings may have different numbers of clusters.

Virtually all criteria for comparing clustering can be described using the so-called *confusion matrix*, or *association matrix* or *contingency table* of the pair $\mathcal{C}, \mathcal{C}'$. The contingency table is a $K \times K'$ matrix, whose $kk'$-th element is the number of points in the intersection of clusters $C_k$ of $\mathcal{C}$ and $C_{k'}'$ of $\mathcal{C}'$.

$$n_{kk'} = |C_k \cap C_{k'}'|$$

### 2.1    Comparing Clusterings by Counting Pairs

An important class of criteria for comparing clusterings, is based on counting the pairs of points on which two clusterings agree/disagree. A pair of points from $D$ can fall under one of four cases described below.

$N_{11}$ the number of point pairs that are in the same cluster under both $\mathcal{C}$ and $\mathcal{C}'$
$N_{00}$ number of point pairs in different clusters under both $\mathcal{C}$ and $\mathcal{C}'$
$N_{10}$ number of point pairs in the same cluster under $\mathcal{C}$ but not under $\mathcal{C}'$
$N_{01}$ number of point pairs in the same cluster under $\mathcal{C}'$ but not under $\mathcal{C}$

The four counts always satisfy $N_{11} + N_{00} + N_{10} + N_{01} = n(n-1)/2$. They can be obtained from the contingency table $[n_{kk'}]$. See [3] for details.

Wallace [12] proposed the two asymmetric criteria $\mathcal{W}_I, \mathcal{W}_{II}$ below.

$$\mathcal{W}_I(\mathcal{C}, \mathcal{C}') = \frac{N_{11}}{\sum_k n_k(n_k - 1)/2} \qquad \mathcal{W}_{II}(\mathcal{C}, \mathcal{C}') = \frac{N_{11}}{\sum_{k'} n_{k'}'(n_{k'}' - 1)/2} \qquad (1)$$

They represent the probability that a pair of points which are in the same cluster under $\mathcal{C}$ (respectively $\mathcal{C}'$) are also in the same cluster under the other clustering.

Fowlkes and Mallows [3] introduced a criterion which is symmetric, and is the geometric mean of $\mathcal{W}_I, \mathcal{W}_{II}$.

$$\mathcal{F}(\mathcal{C}, \mathcal{C}') = \sqrt{\mathcal{W}_I(\mathcal{C}, \mathcal{C}')\mathcal{W}_{II}(\mathcal{C}, \mathcal{C}')} \qquad (2)$$

The Fowlkes-Mallows index $\mathcal{F}$ has a base-line that is the expected value of the criterion under a null hypothesis corresponding to "independent" clusterings [3]. The index is used by subtracting the base-line and normalizing by the range, so that the expected value of the normalized index is 0 while the maximum (attained for identical clusterings) is 1. The adjusted Rand index is a similar transformation introduced by [4] of Rand's [10] criterion

$$\mathcal{R}(\mathcal{C}, \mathcal{C}') = \frac{N_{11} + N_{00}}{n(n-1)/2} \qquad (3)$$

A problem with adjusted indices is that the baseline is an expectation under a null hypothesis. The null hypothesis is that a) the two clusterings are sampled independently, and b) the clusterings are sampled from the set of all partition pairs with fixed $n_k$, $n'_{k'}$ points in each cluster [3,4]. In practice, the second assumption is normally violated. Many algorithms take a number of clusters $K$ as input, but the numbers of points in each cluster are a result of the execution of the algorithm. In most exploratory data analysis situations, it is unnatural to assume that anyone can know exactly how many points are in each cluster. The problems listed above have been known in the statistical community for a long time; see for example [12].

On the other hand, the range of values of the unadjusted $\mathcal{F}$ and $\mathcal{R}$ varies sharply for values of $K, K'$ smaller than $n/3$ making comparisons across different values of $K, K'$ unreliable [3].

There are other criteria in the literature, to which the above discussion applies, such as the Jacard [1] index

$$\mathcal{J}(\mathcal{C}, \mathcal{C}') = \frac{N_{11}}{N_{11} + N_{01} + N_{10}} \tag{4}$$

an improved version of the Rand index, and the Mirkin [9] metric

$$\mathcal{M}(\mathcal{C}, \mathcal{C}') = \sum_k n_k^2 + \sum_{k'} n_{k'}'^2 - 2 \sum_k \sum_{k'} n_{kk'}^2 \tag{5}$$

The latter is obviously 0 for identical clusterings and positive otherwise. In fact, this metric corresponds to the Hamming distance between certain binary vector representations of each partition [9]. This metric can also be rewritten as

$$\mathcal{M}(\mathcal{C}, \mathcal{C}') = 2(N_{01} + N_{10}) = n(n-1)[1 - \mathcal{R}(\mathcal{C}, \mathcal{C}')] \tag{6}$$

Thus the Mirkin metric is another adjusted form of the Rand index.

## 2.2  Comparing Clusterings by Set Matching

A second category of criteria is based on set cardinality alone. Meilă and Heckerman [8] computed the criterion $\mathcal{H}$: First, each cluster of $\mathcal{C}$ is given a "best match" in $\mathcal{C}'$. This is done by scanning the elements $n_{kk'}$ of the contingency table in decreasing order. The largest of them, call it $n_{ab}$, entails a match between $C_a$ and $C'_b$, the second largest not in row $a$ or column $b$ entails the second match, and so on until $\min(K, K')$ matches are made. Denote by $match(k)$ the index of the cluster $C'_{k'}$ in $\mathcal{C}'$ that matches cluster $C_k$. Then

$$\mathcal{H}(\mathcal{C}, \mathcal{C}') = \frac{1}{n} \sum_{k'=match(k)} n_{kk'} \tag{7}$$

The index is symmetric and takes value 1 for identical clusterings. Larsen et al., [5] use

$$\mathcal{L}(\mathcal{C}, \mathcal{C}') = \frac{1}{K} \sum_k \max_{k'} \frac{2n_{kk'}}{n_k + n'_k} \tag{8}$$

This is an asymmetric criterion that is 1 when the clusterings are identical. A criterion that is a metric was introduced by van Dongen [11]

$$\mathcal{D}(\mathcal{C}, \mathcal{C}') = 2n - \sum_k \max_{k'} n_{kk'} - \sum_{k'} \max_k n_{kk'} \tag{9}$$

All three above criteria suffer from the "problem of matching" that we discuss now. One way or another, $\mathcal{L}, \mathcal{H}, \mathcal{D}$ all first find a "best match" for each cluster, then add up the contributions of the matches found. In doing so, the criteria completely ignore what happens to the "unmatched" part of each cluster. For example, suppose $\mathcal{C}$ is a clustering with $K$ equal size clusters. The clustering $\mathcal{C}''$ is obtained from $\mathcal{C}$ by moving a fraction $f$ of the points in each $C_k$ to the cluster $C_{k+1(modK)}$. The clustering $\mathcal{C}'$ is obtained from $\mathcal{C}$ by reassigning a fraction $f$ of the points in each $C_k$ evenly between the other clusters. If $f < 0.5$ then $\mathcal{L}(\mathcal{C}, \mathcal{C}') = \mathcal{L}(\mathcal{C}, \mathcal{C}'')$, $\mathcal{H}(\mathcal{C}, \mathcal{C}') = \mathcal{H}(\mathcal{C}, \mathcal{C}'')$, $\mathcal{D}(\mathcal{C}, \mathcal{C}') = \mathcal{D}(\mathcal{C}, \mathcal{C}'')$. This contradicts the intuition that $\mathcal{C}'$ is a less disrupted version of $\mathcal{C}$ than $\mathcal{C}''$.

## 3    The Variation of Information

Now we introduce the variation of information, the criterion we propose for comparing two clusterings.

We start by establishing how much information is there in each of the clusterings, and how much information one clustering gives about the other. For more details about the information theoretical concepts presented here, the reader is invited to consult [2].

Imagine the following game: if we were to pick a point of $D$, how much uncertainty is there about which cluster is it going to be in? Assuming that each point has an equal probability of being picked, it is easy to see that the probability of the outcome being in cluster $C_k$ equals

$$P(k) = \frac{n_k}{n} \tag{10}$$

Thus we have defined a discrete random variable taking $K$ values, that is uniquely associated to the clustering $\mathcal{C}$. The uncertainty in our game is equal to the *entropy* of this random variable

$$H(\mathcal{C}) = -\sum_{k=1}^{K} P(k) \log P(k) \tag{11}$$

We call $H(\mathcal{C})$ the *entropy associated with clustering* $\mathcal{C}$. Entropy is always non-negative. It takes value 0 only when there is no uncertainty, namely when there is only one cluster. Note that the uncertainty does not depend on the number of points in $D$ but on the relative proportions of the clusters.

We now define the *mutual information* between two clusterings, i.e the information that one clustering has about the other. Denote by $P(k)$, $k = 1, \ldots K$ and $P'(k')$, $k' = 1, \ldots K'$ the random variables associated with the clusterings

$C$, $C'$. Let $P(k, k')$ represent the probability that a point belongs to $C_k$ in clustering $C$ and to $C'_{k'}$ in $C'$, namely the joint distribution of the random variables associated with the two clusterings.

$$P(k, k') = \frac{|C_k \cap C'_{k'}|}{n} \tag{12}$$

We define $I(C, C')$ the mutual information between the clusterings $C$, $C'$ to be equal to the mutual information between the associated random variables

$$I(C, C') = \sum_{k=1}^{K} \sum_{k'=1}^{K'} P(k, k') \log \frac{P(k, k')}{P(k)P'(k')} \tag{13}$$

Intuitively, we can think of $I(C, C')$ in the following way: We are given a random point in $D$. The uncertainty about its cluster in $C'$ is measured by $H(C')$. Suppose now that we are told which cluster the point belongs to in $C$. How much does this knowledge reduce the uncertainty about $C'$? This reduction in uncertainty, averaged over all points, is equal to $I(C, C')$.

The mutual information between two random variables is always non-negative and symmetric.

$$I(C, C') = I(C', C) \geq 0 \tag{14}$$

Also, the mutual information can never exceed the total uncertainty in a clustering, so

$$I(C, C') \leq \min(H(C), H(C')) \tag{15}$$

Equality in the above formula occurs when one clustering completely determines the other. For example, if $C'$ is obtained from $C$ by merging two or more clusters, then

$$I(C, C') = H(C') < H(C)$$

When the two clusterings are equal, and only then, we have

$$I(C, C') = H(C') = H(C)$$

We propose to use as a comparison criterion for two clusterings $C$, $C'$ the quantity

$$VI(C, C') = H(C) + H(C') - 2I(C, C') \tag{16}$$

At a closer examination, this is the sum of two positive terms

$$VI(C, C') = [H(C) - I(C, C')] + [H(C') - I(C, C')] \tag{17}$$

By analogy with the total variation of a function, we call it *variation of information* between the two clusterings. The two terms represent the conditional entropies $H(C|C')$, $H(C'|C)$. The first term measures the amount of information about $C$ that we loose, while the second measures the amount of information about $C'$ that we have to gain, when going from clustering $C$ to clustering $C'$.

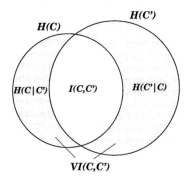

**Fig. 1.** The variation of information (represented by the sum of the shaded areas) and related quantities.

From the above considerations it follows that an equivalent expression for the variation of information (VI) is

$$VI(\mathcal{C},\mathcal{C}') \;=\; H(\mathcal{C}|\mathcal{C}') + H(\mathcal{C}'|\mathcal{C}) \tag{18}$$

Noting that

$$I(\mathcal{C},\mathcal{C}') \;=\; H(\mathcal{C}) + H(\mathcal{C}') - H(\mathcal{C},\mathcal{C}')$$

where $H(\mathcal{C},\mathcal{C}')$ is the entropy of $P(k,k)$, or the *joint entropy* of the two clusterings [2], we obtain a third equivalent expression for the variation of information

$$VI(\mathcal{C},\mathcal{C}') \;=\; 2H(\mathcal{C},\mathcal{C}') - H(\mathcal{C}) - H(\mathcal{C}') \tag{19}$$

## 4    Properties of the Variation of Information

We now list some basic properties of the variation of information with the goal of better understanding the structure it engenders on the set of all clusterings. These properties will also help us decide whether this comparison criterion is appropriate for the clustering problem at hand. Here we will not be focusing on a specific application, but rather we will try to establish whether the properties are "reasonable" and in agreement with the general intuition of what "more different" and "less different" should mean for two clusterings of a set.

Most of the properties below have elementary proofs that are left as an exercise to the reader. The proofs for properties 1, 8 are given in the long version of the paper [7].

**Property 1 The VI is a metric.** *(1)* $VI(\mathcal{C},\mathcal{C}')$ *is always non-negative and* $VI(\mathcal{C},\mathcal{C}') \;=\; 0$ *if and only if* $\mathcal{C} = \mathcal{C}'$. *(2)* $VI(\mathcal{C},\mathcal{C}') \;=\; VI(\mathcal{C}',\mathcal{C})$ *(3) (Triangle inequality) For any 3 clusterings* $\mathcal{C}_1, \mathcal{C}_2, \mathcal{C}_3$ *of* $D$

$$VI(\mathcal{C}_1,\mathcal{C}_2) + VI(\mathcal{C}_2,\mathcal{C}_3) \;\geq\; VI(\mathcal{C}_1,\mathcal{C}_3) \tag{20}$$

The space of all clusterings being finite, the VI metric is necessarily bounded. A comparison criterion that is a metric has several important advantages. The properties of a metric – mainly the symmetry and the triangle inequality – make the criterion more understandable. Human intuition is more at ease with a metric than with an arbitrary function of two variables.

Second, the triangle inequality tells us that if two elements of a metric space (i.e clusterings) are close to a third they cannot be too far apart from each other. This property is extremely useful in designing efficient data structures and algorithms. With a metric, one can move from simply comparing two clusterings to analyzing the structure of large sets of clusterings. For example, one can design algorithms a la K-means [6] that cluster a set of clusterings, one can construct ball trees of clusterings for efficient retrieval, or one can estimate the speed at which a search algorithm (e.g simulated annealing type algorithms) moves away from its initial point.

**Upper bounds.** The following properties give some intuition of scale in this metric space.

**Property 2 $n$-invariance.** *The value of $VI(\mathcal{C}, \mathcal{C}')$ depends only on the relative sizes of the clusters. It does not directly depend on the number of points in the data set.*

**Property 3** *The following bound is attained for all $n$.*

$$VI(\mathcal{C}, \mathcal{C}') \leq \log n \tag{21}$$

For example, $\mathcal{C} = \{\{1\}, \{2\}, \{3\}, \ldots \{n\}\}$ and $\mathcal{C}' = \{D\}$ always achieve $VI(\mathcal{C}, \mathcal{C}') = \log n$.

We have said before that the VI distance does not depend on $n$. The bound in the above inequality however depends on $n$. This does not show a contradiction, but merely the fact that with more data points more clusterings are possible. For example, if two data sets $D_1, D_2$ have respectively $n_1, n_2$ points, with $n_1 < n_2$ then no clustering of $D_1$ will have more than $n_1$ clusters, while for the set $D_2$ there can be clusterings with $K > n_1$ clusters.

If the number of clusters is bounded by a constant $K^*$ we can derive a bound that is dependent on $K^*$ only.

**Property 4** *If $\mathcal{C}$ and $\mathcal{C}'$ have at most $K^*$ clusters each, with $K^* \leq \sqrt{n}$, then $VI(\mathcal{C}, \mathcal{C}') \leq 2 \log K^*$.*

For any fixed $K^*$ the bound is approached arbitrarily closely in the limit of large $n$ and is attained in every case where $n$ is an exact multiple of $(K^*)^2$. This shows that for large enough $n$, clusterings of different data sets, with different numbers of data points, but with bounded numbers of clusters are really on the same scale in the metric VI.

The above consequence is extremely important if the goal is to compare clustering algorithms instead of clusterings of one data set only. The previous three properties imply that, everything else being equal, distances obtained from

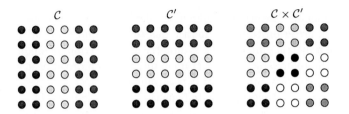

**Fig. 2.** Two maximally separated clusterings $\mathcal{C}$ and $\mathcal{C}'$, having each $K = 3$ clusters, and their join $\mathcal{C} \times \mathcal{C}'$, having 9 clusters.

data sets of different sizes are comparable. For example, if one ran a clustering algorithm with the same parameters and the same $K^*$ on 3 data sets produced by the same generative process, then one could compare the clusterings obtained by the algorithm with the gold standard for each of the 3 data sets and average the resulting 3 distances to obtain the average "error" of the algorithm. Other less restrictive comparisons are also possible and are being often used in practice, but their results should be regarded with caution. To summarize, if it makes sense to consider the clustering problems on two data sets as equivalent, then it also makes sense to compare, add, subtract VI distances across the two clustering spaces independently of the sizes of the underlying data sets.

**The local neighborhood.** A consequence of having a metric is that we can define $\epsilon$-radius balls around any clustering. The following properties give the distances at which the nearest neighbors of a clustering $\mathcal{C}$ will lie. They also give an intuition of what kind of clusterings lie "immediately near" a given one, or, in other words, what changes to a clustering are small according to the VI distance?

**Property 5 Splitting a cluster.** *Assume $\mathcal{C}'$ is obtained from $\mathcal{C}$ by splitting $C_k$ into clusters $C'_{k_1}, \ldots C'_{k_m}$. The cluster probabilities in $\mathcal{C}'$ are*

$$P'(k') = \begin{cases} P(k') & \text{if } C'_{k'} \in \mathcal{C} \\ P(k'|k)P(k) & \text{if } C'_{k'} \subseteq C_k \in \mathcal{C} \end{cases} \qquad (22)$$

*In the above $P(k'|k)$ for $k' \in \{k_1, \ldots k_m\}$ is*

$$P(k_l|k) = \frac{|C'_{k_l}|}{|C_k|} \qquad (23)$$

*and its entropy, representing the uncertainty associated with splitting $C_k$, is*

$$H_{|k} = -\sum_l P(k_l|k) \log P(k_l|k)$$

*Then,*

$$VI(\mathcal{C}, \mathcal{C}') = P(k)H_{|k} \qquad (24)$$

The same value is obtained when performing the reverse operation, i.e when a set of clusters is merged into a single one. Equation (24) shows that the distance achieved by splitting a cluster is proportional to the relative size of the cluster times the entropy of the split. Hence, splitting (or merging) smaller clusters has less impact on the VI then splitting or merging larger ones. Note also that the variation of information at splitting or merging a cluster is independent of anything outside the cluster involved. This is a desirable property; things that are equal in two clusterings should not be affecting the distance between them.

The next two properties are direct consequences of Property 5.

**Property 6 Splitting a cluster into equal parts.** *If $C'$ is obtained from $C$ by splitting $C_k$ into $q$ equal size clusters, then $VI(C,C') = P(k) \log q$.*

**Property 7 Splitting off one point.** *If $C'$ is obtained from $C$ by splitting one point off $C_k$ and making it into a new cluster, then*

$$VI(C,C') = \frac{1}{n}[n_k \log n_k - (n_k - 1) \log(n_k - 1)] \qquad (25)$$

Since splitting off one point represents the lowest entropy split for a given cluster, it follows that splitting one point off the smallest non-singleton cluster results in the nearest $C'$ with $K' > K$ to a given $C$. This suggests that the nearest neighbors of a clustering $C$ in the VI metric are clusterings obtained by splitting or merging small clusters in $C$. In the following we prove that this is indeed so.

First some definitions. We shall say that a clustering $C'$ *refines* another clustering $C$ if for each cluster $C'_{k'} \in C'$ there is a (unique) cluster $C_k \in C$ so that $C'_{k'} \subseteq C_k$. In other words, a refinement $C'$ is obtained by splitting some clusters of the original $C$. If $C'$ refines $C$ it is easy to see that $K' \geq K$, with equality only if $C' = C$.

We define the *join* of clusterings $C$ and $C'$ by

$$C \times C' = \{C_k \cap C'_{k'} \mid C_k \in C, \ C'_{k'} \in C', \ C_k \cap C'_{k'} \neq \emptyset\}$$

Hence, the join of two clusterings is the clustering formed from all the nonempty intersections of clusters from $C$ with clusters from $C'$. The join $C \times C'$ contains all the information in $C$ and $C'$, i.e knowing a point's cluster in the join uniquely determines its cluster in $C$ and $C'$. Note that if $C'$ is a refinement of $C$, then $C \times C' = C'$.

**Property 8 Collinearity of the join.** *The triangle inequality holds with equality for two clusterings and their join.*

$$VI(C,C') = VI(C, C \times C') + VI(C', C \times C') \qquad (26)$$

Thus, the join of two clusterings is "collinear" with and "in between" the clusterings in this metric space. Finally, this leads us to the following property, which implies that the nearest neighbor of any clustering $C$ is either a refinement of $C$ or a clustering whose refinement is $C$.

**Property 9** *For any two clusterings we have*

$$VI(\mathcal{C}, \mathcal{C}') \ \geq \ VI(\mathcal{C}, \mathcal{C} \times \mathcal{C}') \tag{27}$$

*with equality only if* $\mathcal{C}' = \mathcal{C} \times \mathcal{C}'$.

From the above, we conclude that the nearest neighbor of $\mathcal{C}$, with $K' < K$ is obtained by merging the two smallest clusters in $\mathcal{C}$. We now have, due to Properties 7 and 9, a lower bound on the distance between a clustering $\mathcal{C}$ and any other clustering of the same data set. The lower bound depends on $\mathcal{C}$. Taking its minimum for all clusterings, which is attained when two singleton clusters are merged (or conversely, a cluster consisting of two points is split) we obtain $VI(\mathcal{C}, \mathcal{C}') \geq 2/n$ for $\mathcal{C} \neq \mathcal{C}'$.

The last property implies that the smallest distance between two clusterings decreases when the total number of points increases. In other words, the space of clusterings has not only a larger diameter for larger $n$ but it also has finer granularity. This is natural, since a larger $n$ allows clusterings not possible with smaller $n$'s. If we multiply $n$ by an integer, obtaining $n' = \alpha n$ and a new data set $D'$ that has $\alpha$ points for each point of $D$, then it is easy to see that all the clusterings of $D$ are possible in $D'$ and that their respective distances in $D$ are preserved by the metric in $D'$. In addition, $D'$ will have clusterings not possible in $D$, that will be interspersed between the clusterings from $D$.

**Linearity.** Looking at property 5 (splitting a cluster) from a different angle we can derive another interesting property of the variation of information.

**Property 10 Linearity of composition.** *Let* $\mathcal{C} = \{C_1, \ldots C_K\}$ *be a clustering and* $\mathcal{C}'$, $\mathcal{C}''$ *be two refinements of* $\mathcal{C}$. *Denote by* $\mathcal{C}'_k$ ($\mathcal{C}''_k$) *the partitioning induced by* $\mathcal{C}'$ *(respectively* $\mathcal{C}''$*) on* $C_k$. *Let* $P(k)$ *represent the proportion of data points that belong to cluster* $C_k$. *Then*

$$VI(\mathcal{C}', \mathcal{C}'') \ = \ \sum_{k=1}^{K} P(k) VI(\mathcal{C}'_k, \mathcal{C}''_k) \tag{28}$$

This property is illustrated in figure 3 for $K = 2$. The property can be interpreted in a way reminiscent of hierarchical clusterings. If two hierarchical clusterings have exactly two levels and they coincide on the higher level but differ on the lower level, then the VI distance between the two clusterings (regarded as flat clusterings) is a weighted sum of the VI distances between the second level partitions of each of the common first level clusters.

Property 10 can be seen in another way yet. If two clustered data sets are merged, they induce a clustering on their union. If there are two ways of clustering each of the data sets, the VI distance between any two induced clusterings is a linear combination of the VI distances at the level of the component data sets.

Finally, a property pertaining to the computation time of the variation of information.

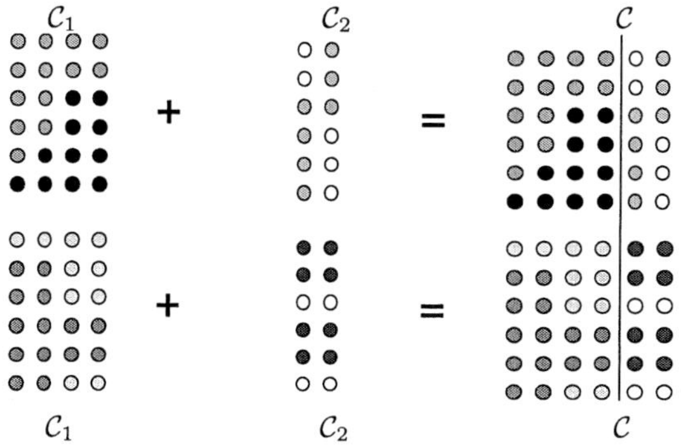

**Fig. 3.** Illustration of linearity. If $C = C_1 \cup C_2$ and $C' = C'_1 \cup C'_2$ then $VI(C, C') = \frac{n_1}{n_1+n_2} VI(C_1, C'_1) + \frac{n_2}{n_1+n_2} VI(C_2, C'_2)$.

**Property 11** $VI(C, C')$ can be computed in $\mathcal{O}(n + KK')$ time.

This is not surprising, since $VI(C, C')$, just like the previously presented criteria, is completely determined by the contingency table $[n_{kk'}]$. The first term in the above formula corresponds to the computation of the contingency table, while the second represents the computation of the VI from it.

## 5  Discussion

### 5.1  Scaled Distances between Clusterings

Here we consider some of the other indices and metrics for comparing clusterings, and examine whether they can be made invariant with $n$ (of the criteria discussed in section 2 only the $\mathcal{H}$ and $\mathcal{L}$ criteria are). We give invariance with $n$ particular attention because, in any situation where comparisons are not restricted to a single data set, the value of a criterion that is not $n$-invariant would be useless without being accompanied by the corresponding $n$.

The Rand, Fowlkes-Mallows, Jacard, and Wallace indices are asymptotically $n$-invariant in the limit of large $n$. For finite values of $n$ the dependence on $n$ is weak. It is also non-linear, and we don't see a natural way of making these criteria exactly $n$-invariant.

A more interesting case is represented by the two metrics: the Mirkin metric $\mathcal{M}$, which is related to the Rand index and thus to counting pairs, and the van Dongen metric $\mathcal{D}$ based on set matching. These metrics depend strongly on $n$ but they can be scaled to become $n$-invariant. We denote the $n$-invariant versions of $\mathcal{D}$, $\mathcal{M}$ by $\mathcal{D}_{inv}$, $\mathcal{M}_{inv}$.

$$\mathcal{D}_{inv}(C, C') = \frac{\mathcal{D}(C, C')}{2n}$$

$$\mathcal{M}_{inv}(C, C') = \frac{\mathcal{M}(C, C')}{n^2}$$

Since the Mirkin distance is related to the Rand index, by inspecting (6) we see that the Rand index is asymptotically equivalent to an $n$-invariant metric.

It is instructive to compare the behavior of the three invariant metrics $VI$, $\mathcal{M}_{inv}$, $\mathcal{D}_{inv}$ for two clusterings with $K$ clusters that are maximally separated under the VI distance. Such a situation is depicted in figure 2. The two clusterings have $n_k = n'_k = n/K$ and $n_{kk'} = n/K^2$ for all $k, k' = 1, \ldots K$. It is assumed that $n$ is a multiple of $K^2$ for simplicity. It can be shown that this pair of clusterings is also maximizing the $\mathcal{D}_{inv}$ and $\mathcal{M}_{inv}$ metrics under the constraint that $K = K'$.

We compute now the values of $VI, \mathcal{D}_{inv}$ and $\mathcal{M}_{inv}$ for this particular pair, as a function of $K$.

$$VI^{max} = 2\log K$$
$$\mathcal{D}^{max}_{inv} = 1 - \frac{1}{K}$$
$$\mathcal{M}^{max}_{inv} = \frac{2}{K} - \frac{1}{K^2} \tag{29}$$

It follows that while the VI distance grows logarithmically with $K$, the other two metrics have values bounded between 0 and 1 for any value of $K$. The $\mathcal{D}_{inv}$ metric grows with $K$ toward the upper bound of 1, while the $\mathcal{M}_{inv}$ metric decreases toward 0 approximately as $1/K$.

## 5.2   Linearity and Locality

Now we compare the scaled metrics with the VI distance from the point of view of linearity. The following proposition can be easily proved.

**Property 12 Linearity of composition for $\mathcal{D}_{inv}$, $\mathcal{M}_{inv}$.** *Let $\mathcal{C} = \{C_1, \ldots C_K\}$ be a clustering and $\mathcal{C}', \mathcal{C}''$ be two refinements of $\mathcal{C}$. Denote by $\mathcal{C}'_k$ ($\mathcal{C}''_k$) the partitioning induced by $\mathcal{C}'$ (respectively $\mathcal{C}''$) on $C_k$. Let $n_k$ represent the number of data points that belong to cluster $C_k$. Then*

$$\mathcal{D}_{inv}(\mathcal{C}', \mathcal{C}'') = \sum_{k=1}^{K} \frac{n_k}{n} \mathcal{D}_{inv}(\mathcal{C}'_k, \mathcal{C}''_k)$$
$$\mathcal{M}_{inv}(\mathcal{C}', \mathcal{C}'') = \sum_{k=1}^{K} \frac{n_k^2}{n^2} \mathcal{M}_{inv}(\mathcal{C}'_k, \mathcal{C}''_k)$$

Hence, the $\mathcal{D}_{inv}$ metric behaves like the VI metric in that the resulting distance is a convex combination of the distances between the subclusterings. The $\mathcal{M}_{inv}$ metric is linear too, but the coefficients depend quadratically on $n_k/n$ so that the resulting distance is smaller than the convex combinations of distances between subclusterings. This is in agreement with equation (29) showing that the Mirkin metric has to decrease rapidly with the number of clusters. Note also that the unscaled versions of $\mathcal{D}$, $\mathcal{M}$ are additive, hence also linear.

Linearity for a metric entails the following property, called *locality*: If $\mathcal{C}'$ is obtained from $\mathcal{C}$ by splitting one cluster, then the distance between $\mathcal{C}$ and $\mathcal{C}'$ depends only on the cluster undergoing the split. Metrics that are linear are also *local*. For example, for the Mirkin metric in the case of splitting cluster $C_k$ into $C_k^1, C_k^2$, locality is expressed as

$$\mathcal{M}_{inv}(\mathcal{C}, \mathcal{C}') = \frac{n_k^2}{n^2} \mathcal{M}_{inv}(\{C_k\}, \{C_k^1, C_k^2\})$$

The r.h.s of the above formula depends only on quantities related to $C_k$ and its split. It is invariant to the configuration of the other clusters in the partition. Locality for the VI distance is reflected by property 7.

The VI distance as well as the $\mathcal{D}$ and $\mathcal{M}$ metrics and their $n$-invariant versions are local. It can be easily shown that the Rand and the Meilă-Heckerman $\mathcal{H}$ indices are also local. The Larsen, Fowlkes-Mallos and Jacard indices are not local. See [7] for details.

Whether a criterion for comparing clusterings should be local or not depends ultimately on the specific requirements of the application. A priori, however, a local criterion is more intuitive and easier to understand.

## 5.3   Concluding Remarks

This paper has presented a new criterion for comparing two clusterings of a data set, that is derived from information theoretic principles.

The criterion is more discriminative than the previously introduced criteria that are based on set matching. In contrast with the comparison criteria based on counting pairs, the variation of information is not directly concerned with relationships between pairs of points, or with triples like [4]. One could say that the variation of information is based on the relationship between a point and its cluster in each of the two clusterings that are compared. This is neither a direct advantage, nor a disadvantage w.r.t the criteria based on pair counts. If pairwise relationships between data points are fundamental to the current application, then a criterion based on pair counts should be used. Model based clustering and centroid based clustering (e.g the K-means algorithm of [6]) focus not on pairwise relationships but on the relationship between a point and its cluster or centroid. Therefore, the VI distance is a priori better suited with applications of model based clustering than indices based on counting pairs.

The vast literature on the subject suggests that criteria like $\mathcal{R}, \mathcal{F}, \mathcal{K}, \mathcal{J}$ need to be shifted and rescaled in order allow their values to be compared. However, the existing rescaling methods make strong assumptions about the way the clusterings were generated, that are commonly violated in practice. By contrast, the variation of information makes no assumptions about how the clusterings were generated and requires no rescaling to compare values of $VI(\mathcal{C}, \mathcal{C}')$ for arbitrary pairs of clusterings of a data set.

Moreover, the variation of information does not directly depend on the number of data points in the set. This gives a much stronger ground for comparisons across data sets, something we need to do if we want to compare clustering algorithms against each other.

As $K$ grows, the VI distance between two clusterings can grow as large as $2 \log K$. This sets the VI distance apart from all other indices and metrics discussed here. The scaled metrics $\mathcal{M}_{inv}$, $\mathcal{D}_{inv}$ as well as the indices $\mathcal{R}$, $\mathcal{F}$, $\mathcal{J}$, $\mathcal{W}$, $\mathcal{H}$ are bounded between 0 and 1. Hence they carry the implicit assumption that clusterings can only get negligibly more diverse if at all as the number of clusters increases. Whether a bounded or unbounded criterion for comparing clusterings is better depends on the clustering application at hand. This paper's aim in this respect is to underscore the possible choices.

In the practice of comparing clusterings, one deals more often with clusterings that are close to each other than with clusterings that are maximally apart. For example, one often needs to compare partitions obtained by several clustering algorithms to a gold standard. It is reasonable to expect that the clusterings so obtained are somewhat similar to each other. The results on locality and the local neighborhood help one understand the behavior of VI in this context. Note for example that the fact that the maximum VI distance grows like $\log K$ does not affect the local properties of the variation of information.

It has been shown here that VI is a metric. This is extremely fortunate as it allows one to see past simple pairwise comparisons between clusterings into the global structure of the space of clusterings. A metric also entails the existence of local neighborhoods, and this in turn allows us to apply to clusterings a vast array of already existing algorithmic techniques. One could for example cluster a set of clusterings obtained by different algorithms. This has already been suggested as a tool for results summarization but so far no existent metric has been used for this problem.

Last but not least, the variation of information fares well compared to other criteria in that it is easy to understand. For those readers who are familiar with information theory, VI is a natural extension of basic concepts. For the other readers, this paper has given a thorough description of the behavior of VI. The very fact that this paper contains more proved results than any of [1,3,4,5,10,11,12] and that most results were easy to obtain is an argument for the "understandabilty" and "predictablity" of this metric. In addition to understanding the VI per se, the properties of variation of information presented represent a tool that helps us think about the space of clusterings in a precise way and brings it nearer our intuition.

Just as one cannot define a "best" clustering method out of context, one cannot define a criterion for comparing clusterings that fits every problem optimally. This paper has strived to present a comprehensible picture of the properties of the VI criterion, in order to allow a potential user to make informed decisions.

# References

1. Asa Ben-Hur, Andre Elisseeff, and Isabelle Guyon. A stability based method for discovering structure in clustered data. In *Pacific Symposium on Biocomputing*, pages 6–17, 2002.
2. Thomas M. Cover and Joy A. Thomas. *Elements of Information Theory*. Wiley, 1991.
3. E. B. Fowlkes and C. L. Mallows. A method for comparing two hierarchical clusterings. *Journal of the American Statistical Association*, 78(383):553–569, 1983.
4. Lawrence Hubert and Phipps Arabie. Comparing partitions. *Journal of Classification*, 2:193–218, 1985.
5. B. Larsen and C. Aone. Fast and effective text mining using linear time document clustering. In *Proceedings of the conference on Knowledge Discovery and Data Mining*, pages 16–22, 1999.
6. S. P. Lloyd. Least squares quantization in PCM. *IEEE Transactions on Information Theory*, 28:129–137, 1982.
7. Marina Meilă. Comparing clusterings. Technical Report 419, University of Washington, 2002. www.stat.washington.edu/reports.
8. Marina Meilă and David Heckerman. An experimental comparison of model-based clustering methods. *Machine Learning*, 42(1/2):9–29, 2001.
9. Boris Mirkin. *Mathematical classification and clustering*. Kluwer Academic Press, 1996.
10. W. M. Rand. Objective criteria for the evaluation of clustering methods. *Journal of the American Statistical Association*, 66:846–850, 1971.
11. Stijn van Dongen. Performance criteria for graph clustering and Markov cluster experiments. Technical Report INS-R0012, Centrum voor Wiskunde en Informatica, 2000.
12. David L. Wallace. Comment. *Journal of the American Statistical Association*, 78(383):569–576, 1983.

# Multiplicative Updates for Large Margin Classifiers

Fei Sha[1], Lawrence K. Saul[1], and Daniel D. Lee[2]

[1] Department of Computer and Information Science
[2] Department of Electrical and Systems Engineering
University of Pennsylvania
200 South 33rd Street, Philadelphia, PA 19104
{feisha,lsaul,ddlee}@seas.upenn.edu

**Abstract.** Various problems in nonnegative quadratic programming arise in the training of large margin classifiers. We derive multiplicative updates for these problems that converge monotonically to the desired solutions for hard and soft margin classifiers. The updates differ strikingly in form from other multiplicative updates used in machine learning. In this paper, we provide complete proofs of convergence for these updates and extend previous work to incorporate sum and box constraints in addition to nonnegativity.

## 1 Introduction

Many problems in machine learning involve optimizations with nonnegativity constraints. Examples include classification by support vector machines [22], density estimation in Bayesian networks [1], and dimensionality reduction by nonnegative matrix factorization [13]. The optimizations for these problems cannot be solved in closed form; thus, iterative learning rules are required that converge in the limit to actual solutions.

The simplest such learning rule is gradient descent. Minimizing an objective function $F(\mathbf{v})$ by gradient descent involves the additive update:

$$v_i \leftarrow v_i - \eta(\partial F/\partial v_i) \ , \tag{1}$$

where $\eta > 0$ is a positive learning rate, and all the elements of the parameter vector $v = (v_1, v_2, \dots, v_N)$ are updated in parallel. Gradient descent is not particularly well suited to constrained optimizations, however, because the additive update in (1) can lead to violations of the constraints.

For optimizations with nonnegativity constraints, an equally simple but more appropriate learning rule involves the so-called Exponentiated Gradient (EG) [12]:

$$v_i \leftarrow v_i e^{-\eta(\partial F/\partial v_i)} \ . \tag{2}$$

Equation (2) is an example of a multiplicative update. Because the elements of the exponentiated gradient are always positive, this update naturally enforces the nonnegativity constraints on $v_i$. By taking the logarithm of both sides of (2), we can view the EG update as an additive update[1] in the log domain:

$$\log v_i \leftarrow \log v_i - \eta(\partial F/\partial v_i) \ . \tag{3}$$

---

[1] This update differs slightly from gradient descent in the variable $u_i = \log v_i$, which would involve the partial derivative $\partial F/\partial u_i = v_i(\partial F/\partial v_i)$ as opposed to what appears in (3).

B. Schölkopf and M.K. Warmuth (Eds.): COLT/Kernel 2003, LNAI 2777, pp. 188–202, 2003.

Multiplicative updates such as EG typically lead to faster convergence than additive updates [12] if the solution $\mathbf{v}^*$ of the optimization problem is sparse, containing a large number of zero elements. Note, moreover, that sparse solutions are more likely to arise in problems with nonnegativity constraints because in these problems minima can emerge at $v_i^* = 0$ without the the precise vanishing of the partial derivative $(\partial F/\partial v_i)|_{\mathbf{v}^*}$ (as would be required in an unconstrained optimization).

The EG update in (2) – like gradient descent in (1) – depends on the explicit introduction of a learning rate $\eta > 0$. The size of the learning rate must be chosen to avoid divergent oscillations (if $\eta$ is too large) and unacceptably slow convergence (if $\eta$ is too small). The necessity of choosing a learning rate can be viewed as a consequence of the generality of these learning rules; they do not assume or exploit any structure in the objective function $F(\mathbf{v})$ beyond the fact that it is differentiable.

Not surprisingly, many objective functions in machine learning have structure that can be exploited in their optimizations – and in particular, by multiplicative updates. Such updates need not involve learning rates, and they may also involve intuitions rather different from the connection between EG and gradient descent in (2–3). For example, the Expectation-Maximization (EM) algorithm [2] for hidden Markov models and the generalized iterative scaling (GIS) algorithm [8] for logistic regression can be viewed as multiplicative updates, but unlike the EG update, they can not be cast as simple variants of gradient descent in the log domain.

In this paper, we derive multiplicative updates for the various problems in nonnegative quadratic programming that arise in the training of large margin classifiers [18, 19, 22]. Our multiplicative updates have the property that they lead to monotonic improvement in the loss function for these classifiers. Interestingly, their form is strikingly different from those of other multiplicative updates used in machine learning, including EG, EM, and GIS. A previous, shorter paper [21] presented our updates for nonnegative quadratic programming in their simplest form. This paper has a stronger theoretical component, not only providing complete proofs of convergence, but also deriving extensions that incorporate sum and box constraints in addition to nonnegativity. It also includes the results of experiments on a larger and more difficult data set. The techniques behind this work should be of general interest to researchers in machine learning faced with problems in constrained optimization.

## 2   Nonnegative Quadratic Programming

We begin by studying the problem of nonnegative quadratic programming in its simplest form. Consider the minimization of the objective function

$$F(\mathbf{v}) = \frac{1}{2}\mathbf{v}^T\mathbf{A}\mathbf{v} + \mathbf{b}^T\mathbf{v} \ , \tag{4}$$

subject to the constraints that $v_i \geq 0$ for all $i$. We assume that the matrix $\mathbf{A}$ is symmetric and semipositive definite, so that the objective function $F(\mathbf{v})$ is bounded below, and its optimization is convex. Due to the nonnegativity constraints, however, there does not exist an analytical solution for the global minimum (or minima), and an iterative solution is needed.

## 2.1 Multiplicative Updates

Our multiplicative updates are expressed in terms of the positive and negative components of the matrix $\mathbf{A}$ in (4). Let $\mathbf{A}^+$ and $\mathbf{A}^-$ denote the *nonnegative* matrices:

$$A_{ij}^+ = \begin{cases} A_{ij} & \text{if } A_{ij} > 0, \\ 0 & \text{otherwise,} \end{cases} \quad \text{and } A_{ij}^- = \begin{cases} |A_{ij}| & \text{if } A_{ij} < 0, \\ 0 & \text{otherwise.} \end{cases} \quad (5)$$

It follows that $\mathbf{A} = \mathbf{A}^+ - \mathbf{A}^-$. In terms of these nonnegative matrices, the objective function can be decomposed as the combination of three terms, which we write as

$$F(\mathbf{v}) = F_a(\mathbf{v}) + F_b(\mathbf{v}) - F_c(\mathbf{v}) \quad (6)$$

for reasons that will become clear shortly. We use the first and third terms in (6) to "split" the quadratic piece of $F(\mathbf{v})$, and the second term to capture the linear piece:

$$F_a(\mathbf{v}) = \frac{1}{2}\mathbf{v}^T \mathbf{A}^+ \mathbf{v} \ , \quad (7)$$

$$F_b(\mathbf{v}) = \mathbf{b}^T \mathbf{v} \ , \quad (8)$$

$$F_c(\mathbf{v}) = \frac{1}{2}\mathbf{v}^T \mathbf{A}^- \mathbf{v} \ . \quad (9)$$

The gradient of $F(\mathbf{v})$ can be similarly decomposed in terms of contributions from these three pieces. We have chosen our notation in (4) and (8) so that $b_i = \partial F_b/\partial v_i$; for the quadratic terms in the objective function, we define the corresponding derivatives:

$$a_i = \frac{\partial F_a}{\partial v_i} = (\mathbf{A}^+\mathbf{v})_i \ , \quad (10)$$

$$c_i = \frac{\partial F_c}{\partial v_i} = (\mathbf{A}^-\mathbf{v})_i \ . \quad (11)$$

Note that these partial derivatives are themselves nonnegative[2]: that is, $a_i \geq 0$ and $c_i \geq 0$. In terms of these derivatives, our updates take the form:

$$v_i \longleftarrow v_i \left[ \frac{-b_i + \sqrt{b_i^2 + 4a_ic_i}}{2a_i} \right] \ . \quad (12)$$

These updates are meant to be applied in parallel to all the elements of $\mathbf{v}$. They are remarkably simple to implement, as they neither involve a learning rate nor other heuristic

---

[2] Some of our proofs in the appendices rely additionally on the *positivity* of $a_i = (\mathbf{A}^+\mathbf{v})_i$ and $c_i = (\mathbf{A}^-\mathbf{v})_i$ whenever $\mathbf{v}$ has no zero elements. If $\mathbf{A}^+$ and $\mathbf{A}^-$ are defined as in (5), then these terms will be strictly positive as long as the matrix $\mathbf{A}$ has at least one positive and negative element in each row. If $\mathbf{A}$ does not satisfy this condition, then $\mathbf{A}^+$ and $\mathbf{A}^-$ can be redefined (for example, by adding a small positive number to each element) so that the proofs remain valid. In this case, the multiplicative updates are not changed in form, merely the definitions of $\mathbf{A}^+$ and $\mathbf{A}^-$. Alternatively, in certain of these degenerate cases, the proofs can be modified while keeping the original decomposition in (5).

criteria that must be tuned to ensure convergence. As we show later, moreover, these updates are guaranteed to decrease the value of $F(\mathbf{v})$ at each iteration.

The reader will recognize the factor multiplying $v_i$ on the right hand side of (12) as the quadratic formula for the positive root of the polynomial $a_i z^2 + b_i z - c_i$. This factor is guaranteed to be nonnegative, as we observed earlier that $a_i \geq 0$ and $c_i \geq 0$. The updates thus naturally enforce the nonnegativity constraints on $v_i$. The updates are notable for their absence of a learning rate, but even beyond this, their basic form is strikingly different than the EG update in (2). How does this seemingly mysterious combination of partial derivatives [17] serve to minimize the objective function $F(\mathbf{v})$?

An intuition for these multiplicative updates can be gained by examining their fixed points. One fixed point for (12) occurs at $v_i^* = 0$; the other occurs when the positive root of the polynomial $a_i z^2 + b_i z - c_i = 0$ is located at $z = 1$, since in this case the multiplicative factor in (12) is equal to unity. The latter condition, together with the definitions in (6–11), implies that $(\partial F / \partial v_i)|_{\mathbf{v}^*} = a_i + b_i - c_i = 0$. Thus the two criteria for fixed points are either (i) $v_i^* = 0$, or (ii) $(\partial F / \partial v_i)|_{\mathbf{v}^*} = 0$. These are ultimately the same criteria as the EG update in (2).

Further intuition is gained by considering the effects of the multiplicative update away from its fixed points. Although the partial derivative $\partial F / \partial v_i$ does not appear explicitly in (12), there is a close link between the sign of this derivative and the effect of the update on $v_i$. In particular, using the fact that $\partial F / \partial v_i = a_i + b_i - c_i$, it is easy to show that the update decreases $v_i$ if $\partial F / \partial v_i > 0$ and increases $v_i$ if $\partial F / \partial v_i < 0$. Thus, the multiplicative update in (12) moves each element $v_i$ in the same direction as the EG update in (2), though not in general by the same amount.

The above intuitions are useful, but insufficient to establish that the updates converge to global minima of $F(\mathbf{v})$. In Appendix A, we prove the following theorem:

**Theorem 1.** *The function $F(\mathbf{v})$ in (4) decreases monotonically to the value of its global minimum under the multiplicative updates in (12).*

The proof of this theorem relies on the construction of an auxiliary function which provides an upper bound on $F(\mathbf{v})$. While many algorithms in machine learning [2, 5, 8, 9, 14, 17] are derived from auxiliary functions, the proof in this paper introduces a particular inequality for nonnegative matrices that we have not seen in previous work.

## 2.2  Sum Constraint

The multiplicative updates in (12) can be extended to incorporate additional constraints beyond nonnegativity. One such constraint is a linear equality of the form:

$$\sum_i \beta_i v_i = \beta , \tag{13}$$

with constant coefficients $\beta_i$ and constant sum $\beta$. We will refer to such a constraint as a sum constraint. In what follows, we assume that the feasible region resulting from the sum and nonnegativity constraints is not empty.

The sum constraint in (13) is enforced by introducing a Lagrange multiplier $\lambda$ at each iteration of the multiplicative updates. In particular, to incorporate the sum constraint, we consider the "extended" objective function:

$$F(\mathbf{v}, \lambda) = \frac{1}{2}\mathbf{v}^T\mathbf{A}\mathbf{v} + \mathbf{b}^T\mathbf{v} + \lambda\left(\sum_i \beta_i v_i - \beta\right) . \tag{14}$$

Suppose that $\lambda$ is fixed to some value; then its overall effect in (14) is to alter the coefficients of the term that is linear in $v_i$ by an amount $\lambda\beta_i$. As shorthand notation to capture this effect in the multiplicative update, we let

$$r_i(\lambda) = \frac{-(b_i + \lambda\beta_i) + \sqrt{(b_i + \lambda\beta_i)^2 + 4a_ic_i}}{2a_i} \tag{15}$$

denote the positive root of the polynomial $a_iz^2 + (b_i + \lambda\beta_i)z - c_i$, where as in the previous section, $a_i = (\mathbf{A}^+\mathbf{v})_i$ and $c_i = (\mathbf{A}^-\mathbf{v})_i$. Then, a multiplicative update that decreases $F(\mathbf{v}, \lambda)$ for fixed $\lambda$ is given by:

$$v_i \longleftarrow v_i r_i(\lambda) . \tag{16}$$

At each iteration, the unknown $\lambda$ should be chosen so that the updated values of $v_i$ satisfy the sum constraint in (13). In terms of the existing values of $v_i$, this is done by choosing $\lambda$ to satisfy:

$$\sum_i \beta_i v_i r_i(\lambda) = \beta . \tag{17}$$

If $\lambda$ is chosen at each iteration[3] to enforce the constraint, such that $F(\mathbf{v}) = F(\mathbf{v}, \lambda)$, then the multiplicative updates in (16) will serve to minimize $F(\mathbf{v})$ while preserving both the sum and nonnegativity constraints on $v_i$. The proof of convergence in Appendix A generalizes in a straightforward way to this case. Though impossible to solve (17) for $\lambda$ in closed form, a simple iterative procedure exists to compute a solution. In particular, in Appendix B, we prove the following:

**Theorem 2.** *Equation (17) has a unique solution, $\lambda^*$, that can be computed by iterating:*

$$\lambda \leftarrow \frac{1}{R}\left(\sum_i \beta_i v_i r_i(\lambda) - \beta\right) + \lambda , \tag{18}$$

*where $R$ is any positive constant satisfying $|\sum_i \beta_i v_i \frac{dr_i}{d\lambda}| < R$ for all $\lambda$.*

## 2.3   Box Constraints

The multiplicative updates in (12) can also be extended to incorporate constraints of the form $v_i \leq \kappa$ for all $i$, where $\kappa$ is a constant. These are referred to as box constraints, since they bound $v_i$ from both above and below. A more general constraint is that each $v_i$ has a different upper bound $\kappa_i$. By linearly rescaling the variables $v_i$, however, this problem can be transformed into the previous one. Interestingly, though box constraints are nonlinear, their handling is fairly trivial and indeed much simpler than enforcing the linear sum constraint in the previous section. The simplest way to enforce the box constraints is to clip the output of the updates in (12), such as:

$$v_i \longleftarrow \min\left\{\kappa, v_i\left[\frac{-b_i + \sqrt{b_i^2 + 4a_ic_i}}{2a_i}\right]\right\} . \tag{19}$$

---

[3] The required value of $\lambda$ changes from one iteration to the next (though eventually it stabilizes).

This clipped update is also guaranteed to decrease the objective function $F(\mathbf{v})$ in (4) if it results in a change of $v_i$. It is not straightforward, however, to combine this clipped update with the sum constraint in the previous section. Thus, for problems in which both sum and box constraints are active, we have developed an additional approach.

Recall that the multiplicative update in (12) increases $v_i$ if $\partial F/\partial v_i < 0$ and decreases $v_i$ if $\partial F/\partial v_i > 0$. Since increasing $v_i$ is equivalent to decreasing $(\kappa - v_i)$, we devise a multiplicative update that "operates" on $v_i$ if $\partial F/\partial v_i \geq 0$ and on $(\kappa - v_i)$ if $\partial F/\partial v_i < 0$. In particular, at each iteration, we define the new variables:

$$\hat{v}_i = \begin{cases} v_i & \text{if } \frac{\partial F}{\partial v_i} \geq 0, \\ \kappa - v_i & \text{otherwise.} \end{cases} \tag{20}$$

Note that since $v_i$ and $\hat{v}_i$ are linearly related, minimizing $F(\mathbf{v})$ is equivalent to minimizing the quadratic form $\hat{F}(\hat{\mathbf{v}})$ obtained by the change of variables in (20). Let

$$\hat{F}(\hat{\mathbf{v}}) = \frac{1}{2}\hat{\mathbf{v}}^{\mathrm{T}}\hat{\mathbf{A}}\hat{\mathbf{v}} + \hat{\mathbf{b}}^{\mathrm{T}}\hat{\mathbf{v}} \ , \tag{21}$$

where the coefficients $\hat{A}_{ij}$ and $\hat{b}_i$ are chosen such that $\hat{F}(\hat{\mathbf{v}}) - F(\mathbf{v})$ is a constant that does not depend on $\mathbf{v}$. To compute these coefficients, we let $s_i = \mathrm{sgn}(\partial F/\partial v_i)$ denote the sign of $\partial F/\partial v_i$, with $\mathrm{sgn}(0)$ equal to 1. Then $v_i$ can be expressed in terms of $\hat{v}_i$ as:

$$v_i = \hat{v}_i s_i + \kappa(1 - s_i)/2 \ . \tag{22}$$

The coefficients $\hat{A}_{ij}$ and $\hat{b}_i$ are obtained by substituting (22) into (4) and extracting the coefficients of the terms $\hat{v}_i\hat{v}_j$ and $\hat{v}_i$, respectively. This gives:

$$\hat{A}_{ij} = s_i s_j A_{ij} \ , \tag{23}$$

$$\hat{b}_i = b_i s_i + (\kappa/2)\sum_j s_i(1 - s_j)A_{ij} \ . \tag{24}$$

By constructing $\hat{F}(\hat{\mathbf{v}})$ in this way, we ensure that all the elements of its gradient are nonnegative: $\partial \hat{F}/\partial \hat{v}_i \geq 0$. Thus, if we define matrices $\hat{A}^{\pm}$ from $\hat{A}$ using the same construction as in (5), and if we define $\hat{a}_i = (\hat{A}^+\hat{\mathbf{v}})_i$ and $\hat{c}_i = (\hat{A}^-\hat{\mathbf{v}})_i$, then the multiplicative update

$$\hat{v}_i \longleftarrow \hat{v}_i \left[ \frac{-\hat{b}_i + \sqrt{\hat{b}_i^2 + 4\hat{a}_i\hat{c}_i}}{2\hat{a}_i} \right] \tag{25}$$

will decrease $\hat{F}(\hat{\mathbf{v}})$ by driving all the variables $\hat{v}_i$ toward zero. Note that by decreasing $\hat{F}(\hat{\mathbf{v}})$, the update also decreases $F(\mathbf{v})$ since the two differ only by a constant. Moreover, by enforcing the nonnegativity constraint on $\hat{v}_i$, the update enforces the box constraint on $v_i$: in particular, either $v_i$ decreases toward zero or increases toward $\kappa$. To distinguish this scheme from the clipped multiplicative update in (19), we will refer to (25) as the "flipped" multiplicative update, noting that the effect of the change of variables in (20) is simply to reverse the direction of the multiplicative update.

Sum and box constraints can be jointly enforced by combining the ideas in this section and the previous one. In this case, at each iteration the change of variables in (20) is first used to obtain a quadratic form $\hat{F}(\hat{\mathbf{v}})$ with $\partial \hat{F}/\partial \hat{v}_i \geq 0$ for all $i$. Next, the sum constraint in (13) is rewritten in terms of the variables $\hat{v}_i$. Finally, the multiplicative update in (16) is applied to the variables $\hat{v}_i$.

## 3 Large Margin Classifiers

The problems in nonnegative quadratic programming studied in Section 2 arise in the training of large margin classifiers. These classifiers – though decades old – have generated renewed interest due to their underlying role in support vector machines (SVMs). SVMs use kernel methods to map inputs into a higher, potentially infinite, dimensional feature space. The maximum margin hyperplane in this feature space is then computed as the decision boundary between classes. SVMs have been applied successfully to many problems in machine learning and statistical pattern recognition [7, 18, 19, 22].

Computing the maximum margin hyperplane in SVMs gives rise to a quadratic programming problem with nonnegativity constraints. There is a large literature on iterative algorithms for nonnegative quadratic programming in general and for SVMs as a special case [3, 7, 18, 19]. In this section, we will begin by briefly reviewing the constrained optimizations that arise in SVMs, then show how the multiplicative updates from Section 2 are applied to these problems. Finally, we will compare the updates to other algorithms for training SVMs.

### 3.1 Costs and Constraints

Let $\{(\mathbf{x}_i, y_i)\}_{i=1}^N$ denote a training set of labeled examples with binary labels $y_i = \pm 1$, and let $K(\mathbf{x}_i, \mathbf{x}_j)$ denote the kernel used to compute dot products between inputs in the feature space. We consider first the realizable setting where the examples are linearly separable in the feature space generated by the choice of kernel. The decision rule of the maximum margin classifier is given by the signed function:

$$y = \text{sgn}\left(K(\mathbf{w}^*, \mathbf{x}) + b^*\right) ,\qquad (26)$$

where $\mathbf{w}^*$ is the normal vector to the maximum margin hyperplane and $|b^*|$ is its distance from the origin. The vector $\mathbf{w}^*$ can be written as a weighted sum over examples,

$$\mathbf{w}^* = \sum_i \alpha_i^* y_i \mathbf{x}_i ,\qquad (27)$$

where the coefficients $\alpha_i^*$ are non-zero only for the so-called support vectors that lie closest to the hyperplane. By convention, the scale of $\mathbf{w}^*$ is set by requiring

$$y_i[K(\mathbf{w}^*, \mathbf{x_i}) + b^*] \geq 1 \qquad (28)$$

for all examples in the training set, with equality holding only for support vectors.

A special case of the above occurs when we simply set $b^* = 0$, constraining the separating hyperplane to pass through the origin. In this case, the weight vector $\mathbf{w}^*$ for the maximum margin classifier (assuming the examples remain linearly separable) is obtained by minimizing the loss function:

$$L(\alpha) = \frac{1}{2} \sum_{ij} \alpha_i \alpha_j y_i y_j K(\mathbf{x}_i, \mathbf{x}_j) - \sum_i \alpha_i ,\qquad (29)$$

subject to the nonnegativity constraints $\alpha_i \geq 0$. The coefficients $\alpha_i^*$ of the weight vector are determined by the minimum of this loss function, and the solution satisfies $y_i K(\mathbf{w}^*, \mathbf{x}_i) \geq 1$ for all examples in the training set.

The optimization is only slightly changed when we no longer constrain the separating hyperplane to pass through the origin. In this case, the coefficients $\alpha_i^*$ in (27) are again obtained by minimizing (29), but subject to the sum constraint

$$\sum_i y_i \alpha_i = 0 \ , \tag{30}$$

in addition to the nonnegativity constraints $\alpha_i \geq 0$. The threshold $b^*$ does not appear in (29), but it can be computed from the optimal weight vector using (28). The classifier with $b^* \neq 0$ resulting from the additional sum constraint is guaranteed to have an equal or larger margin than the one whose separating hyperplane is constrained to pass through the origin.

In the realizable setting, there is no need to relax or soften the constraints in (28), and the resulting classifiers are known as hard margin classifiers. For examples that are not linearly separable, one must relax these constraints while attempting to minimize the required degree of slack. The resulting classifiers are known as soft margin classifiers. If a one-norm is used to penalize slack, then the problem for computing the optimal classifier is hardly changed from the realizable setting. In this case, the weight vector $\mathbf{w}^*$ is again obtained by minimizing (29), but now subject to the box constraints

$$0 \leq \alpha_i \leq \kappa \tag{31}$$

in addition to the sum constraint in (30) and the nonnegativity constraints $\alpha_i \geq 0$. The constant $\kappa$ is a free parameter that measures the penalty per unit slack in the margin constraints (28). The determination of the bias $b^*$ is somewhat more complicated for soft margin classifiers; further details can be found in standard treatments [19].

## 3.2  Multiplicative Margin Maximization ($\mathbf{M}^3$ )

The optimizations required for large margin classifiers are special cases of the problems in nonnegative quadratic programming considered in Section 2. In particular, the loss function in (29) is a special case of (4) with $A_{ij} = y_i y_j K(\mathbf{x}_i, \mathbf{x}_j)$ and $b_i = -1$. The simplest SVM occurs in the realizable setting where the separating hyperplane is constrained to pass through the origin. This SVM can be trained by the update rule:

$$\alpha_i \longleftarrow \alpha_i \left[ \frac{1 + \sqrt{1 + 4(\mathbf{A}^+\alpha)_i (\mathbf{A}^-\alpha)_i}}{2(\mathbf{A}^+\alpha)_i} \right] \ , \tag{32}$$

where $\mathbf{A}^\pm$ are defined as in (5). For hard margin classifiers whose separating hyperplanes do not pass through the origin, the sum constraint in (30) corresponds to the constraint in Section 2.2; for soft margin classifiers, the box constraints in (31) corresponds to the constraints in Section 2.3. The multiplicative updates in these sections are easily specialized to SVMs, and we refer to this general framework for training large margin classifiers as Multiplicative Margin Maximization ($M^3$ ).

We have applied $M^3$ algorithms for SVMs to three well-known data sets. The first two are the sonar [11] and breast cancer [15] data sets from the UCI Machine Learning Repository. These are small data sets containing 208 and 683 examples, respectively. The third data set is the collection of USPS handwritten digits [20]; this is a larger data set, containing 7291 examples for training. All these data sets have been benchmarked using SVMs. Using $M^3$ algorithms, we obtained large margin classifiers with similar error rates on training and test sets. This is not too surprising since the same maximum margin hyperplane was being computed for all the benchmarks. Arguably, then, the interesting comparisons are not in terms of error rates, but in terms of other criteria. These are discussed next.

### 3.3   Comparison to Other Approaches

A large number of algorithms have been investigated for nonnegative quadratic programming in SVMs. We have not attempted an exhaustive comparison, but instead have focused on similarly motivated approaches (such as EG) and on competing approaches that represent the state-of-the-art for large applications.

EG updates have been used to train SVMs [6]. These updates share many of the advantages of $M^3$ updates: natural handling of nonnegativity constraints, ease of implementation, and simple parallelization. A drawback of EG updates is the need to choose a learning rate and the lack of theoretical guidance for choosing it; this issue does not arise in $M^3$ updates, which additionally provide a guarantee of monotonic convergence. Note that both EG and $M^3$ updates are complicated by the sum constraint in (30). It is worth pointing out, however, that for many problems, the bias term in large margin classifiers (though well motivated) does not have a significant effect on generalization.

EG and $M^3$ updates for training SVMs are both applied in parallel to all the coefficients $\alpha_i$ that appear in the loss function (29). Subset methods constitute a fundamentally different approach to nonnegative quadratic programming. These methods split the variables at each iteration into two sets: a *fixed* set in which the variables are held constant, and a *working* set in which the variables are optimized by an internal subroutine. At the end of each iteration, a heuristic is used to transfer variables between the two sets and improve the objective function.

Two subset methods have been widely used for training SVMs. The first is the method of sequential minimal optimization (SMO) [16], which updates only two coefficients of the weight vector per iteration. In this case, there exists an analytical solution for the updates, so that one avoids the expense of an iterative optimization within each iteration of the main loop. SMO enforces the sum and box constraints for soft margin classifiers. If the sum constraint is lifted, then it is possible to update the coefficients of the weight vector sequentially, one at a time, with an adaptive learning rate that ensures monotonic convergence. This approach is known as the Kernel Adatron [4, 10].

SMO and Kernel Adatron are among the most viable methods for training SVMs on large data sets. Figures 1 and 2 compare the amount of CPU time for these approaches and two types of $M^3$ updates (flipped and clipped) on the USPS data set of handwritten digits. SVMs were trained to distinguish the digit "2" from the rest of the digits. A Gaussian kernel $K(\mathbf{x}_i, \mathbf{x}_j) = e^{-||\mathbf{x}_i - \mathbf{x}_j||^2 / 2\sigma^2}$ was used, with $\sigma = 6.0$, and digit images were smoothed prior to training and testing. The slack penalty was $\kappa = 10$. Parameters

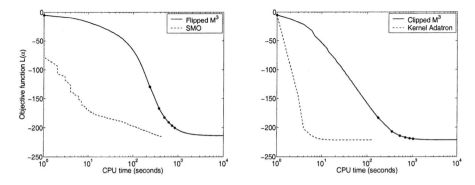

**Fig. 1.** Plots of the objective $L(\alpha)$ in (29) versus training time on USPS handwritten digits. Left: SMO and the flipped $M^3$ update in (25). Right: Kernel Adatron and the clipped $M^3$ update in (19). The circles mark batches of one hundred $M^3$ updates.

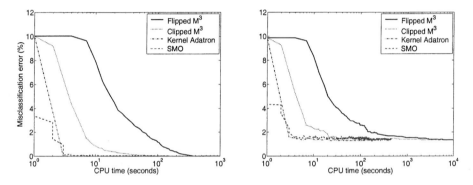

**Fig. 2.** Left: Percentage of misclassification against training time of the flipped $M^3$ algorithm and SMO on USPS training data. Right: Percentage of misclassification against training time of the clipped $M^3$ algorithm and Kernel Adatron algorithm on the testing data.

ensuring rapid convergence of SMO [16] and Kernel Adatron [4, 10] were set as in previous implementations. Note that SMO and the flipped $M^3$ updates in (25) enforce both sum and box constraints, while the Kernel Adatron and the clipped $M^3$ updates in (19) enforce only box constraints. On this data set, the figures show that the $M^3$ updates take one to two orders of magnitude longer to converge to solutions of similar quality, as measured either by the minimum value of the objective function, $L(\alpha)$, or by the error rates on the training and test sets.

From these results, it appears that the main utility of the $M^3$ updates lies in their application to small data sets [21], where computation time is not a primary concern. The simple, parallel form of $M^3$ updates makes them easy to implement in higher-level languages, such as MATLAB. The parallel form, however, also has its drawbacks. Parallel $M^3$ updates require more computation per iteration than subset methods, involving the whole Gram matrix for each update. Also, on large data sets with redundant inputs, subset methods such as SMO and Kernel Adatron appear to have the same advantages over $M^3$ updates as on-line learning algorithms have over batch algorithms. A final draw-back of $M^3$ updates, in their simplest form, is that they cannot set a variable directly to zero. Despite these issues, however, we believe $M^3$ updates provide an attractive starting point for experimenting with large margin classifiers.

## 4   Conclusion

In this paper, we have derived multiplicative updates for nonnegative quadratic pro-gramming by exploiting hidden structure in the objective function. Several interesting questions remain. For example, the decomposition of $\mathbf{A} = \mathbf{A}^+ - \mathbf{A}^-$ could be achieved in many ways; the particular scheme in (5) is probably not optimal. The optimal de-composition and resulting performance of the algorithm are likely to depend on specific properties of the data set. Of potential interest is the algorithm's behavior on data sets (such as text documents[4]) with sparse inputs and unbalanced numbers of positive and negative examples. The updates could also be used as part of a subset method, instead of being applied completely in parallel. This might be one way to accelerate the $M^3$ updates for SVMs, by removing the need to multiply by the entire Gram matrix at each itera-tion. Finally, we are interested in nonnegative quadratic programming problems that arise on graphs – in particular, problems with connections to inference and learning in probabilistic graphical models.

## References

1. E. Bauer, D. Koller, and Y. Singer. Update rules for parameter estimation in Bayesian networks. In *Proceedings of the 13th Annual Conference on Uncertainty in AI*, 1997.
2. L. Baum. An inequality and associated maximization technique in statistical estimation of probabilistic functions of Markov processes. *Inequalities*, 3:1–8, 1972.
3. C. J. C. Burges. A tutorial on support vector machines for pattern recognition. *Knowledge Discovery and Data Mining*, 2(2):121–167, 1998.
4. C. Campbell and N. Cristianini. Simple learning algorithms for training support vector machines. Technical report, University of Bristol., 1998.
5. M. Collins, R. Schapire, and Y. Singer. Logistic regression, adaBoost, and Bregman distances. In *Proceedings of the Thirteenth Annual Conference on Computational Learning Theory*, 2000.
6. N. Cristianini, C. Campbell, and J. Shawe-Taylor. Multiplicative updatings for support vector machines. In *Proceedings of ESANN'99*, pages 189–194, 1999.
7. N. Cristianini and J. Shawe-Taylor. *An Introduction to Support Vector Machines*. Cambridge University Press, Cambridge, UK, 2000.
8. J. N. Darroch and D. Ratcliff. Generalized iterative scaling for log-linear models. *Annals of Mathematical Statistics*, 43:1470–1480, 1972.
9. A. P. Dempster, N. M. Laird, and D. B. Rubin. Maximum likelihood from incomplete data via the EM algorithm. *Journal of the Royal Statistical Society B*, 39:1–37, 1977.
10. T. Friess, N. Cristianini, and C. Campbell. The Kernel Adatron algorithm: a fast and simple learning procedure for support vector machines. In *Proc. 15th International Conference on Machine Learning*, 1998.

---

[4] We are grateful to the anonymous reviewers for suggesting this line of research.

11. R. P. Gorman and T. J. Sejnowski. Analysis of hidden units in a layered network trained to classify sonar targets. *Neural Networks*, 1(1):75–89, 1988.

12. J. Kivinen and M. Warmuth. Exponentiated gradient versus gradient descent for linear predictors. *Information and Computation*, 132(1):1–63, 1997.

13. D. D. Lee and H. S. Seung. Learning the parts of objects with nonnegative matrix factorization. *Nature*, 401:788–791, 1999.

14. D. D. Lee and H. S. Seung. Algorithms for non-negative matrix factorization. In T. K. Leen, T. G. Dietterich, and V. Tresp, editors, *Advances in Neural and Information Processing Systems*, volume 13, Cambridge, MA, 2001. MIT Press.

15. O. L. Mangasarian and W. H. Wolberg. Cancer diagnosis via linear programming. *SIAM News*, 23(5):1–18, 1990.

16. J. Platt. Fast training of support vector machines using sequential minimal optimization. In B. Schölkopf, C. J. C. Burges, and A. J. Smola, editors, *Advances in Kernel Methods – Support Vector Learning*, pages 185–208, Cambridge, MA, 1999. MIT Press.

17. L. K. Saul and D. D. Lee. Multiplicative updates for classification by mixture models. In T. G. Dietterich, S. Becker, and Z. Ghahramani, editors, *Advances in Neural and Information Processing Systems*, volume 14, Cambridge, MA, 2002. MIT Press.

18. B. Schölkopf, C. J. C. Burges, and A. J. Smola. *Advances in Kernel Methods – Support Vector Learning*. MIT Press, Cambridge, MA, 1999.

19. B. Schölkopf and A. J. Smola. *Learning with Kernels*. MIT Press, Cambridge, MA, 2002.

20. B. Schölkopf, K Sung, C. Burges, F. Girosi, P. Niyogi, T. Poggio, and V. Vapnik. Comparing support vector machines with Gaussian kernels to radial basis function classiers. *IEEE Trans. on Signal Processing*, 45(11), 1997.

21. F. Sha, L. K. Saul, and D. D. Lee. Multiplicative updates for nonnegative quadratic programming in support vector machines. In S. Becker, S. Thrun, and K. Obermayer, editors, *Advances in Neural and Information Processing Systems*, volume 15, Cambridge, MA, 2003. MIT Press.

22. V. Vapnik. *Statistical Learning Theory*. Wiley, N.Y., 1998.

# A    Proof of Theorem 1

The proof of monotonic convergence is based on the derivation of an auxiliary function. Similar proofs have been used for many models in statistical learning [5, 8, 9, 14, 17].

## A.1    Monotonic Convergence

An auxiliary function $G(\tilde{\mathbf{v}}, \mathbf{v})$ has the two crucial properties that $F(\tilde{\mathbf{v}}) \leq G(\tilde{\mathbf{v}}, \mathbf{v})$ and $F(\mathbf{v}) = G(\mathbf{v}, \mathbf{v})$ for all nonnegative $\tilde{\mathbf{v}}, \mathbf{v}$. From such an auxiliary function, we can derive the update rule $\mathbf{v}' = \arg\min_{\tilde{\mathbf{v}}} G(\tilde{\mathbf{v}}, \mathbf{v})$ which never increases (and generally decreases) the objective function $F(\mathbf{v})$:

$$F(\mathbf{v}') \leq G(\mathbf{v}', \mathbf{v}) \leq G(\mathbf{v}, \mathbf{v}) = F(\mathbf{v}) \ . \tag{33}$$

By iterating this procedure, we obtain a series of estimates that improve the objective function. For nonnegative quadratic programming, we derive an auxiliary function $G(\tilde{\mathbf{v}}, \mathbf{v})$ by decomposing $F(\mathbf{v})$ in (4) into three terms and then bounding each term separately:

$$F(\mathbf{v}) = \frac{1}{2} \sum_{ij} A_{ij}^+ v_i v_j - \frac{1}{2} \sum_{ij} A_{ij}^- v_i v_j + \sum_i b_i v_i \ , \tag{34}$$

$$G(\tilde{\mathbf{v}}, \mathbf{v}) = \frac{1}{2} \sum_i \frac{(\mathbf{A}^+ \mathbf{v})_i}{v_i} \tilde{v}_i^2 - \frac{1}{2} \sum_{ij} A_{ij}^- v_i v_j \left(1 + \log \frac{\tilde{v}_i \tilde{v}_j}{v_i v_j}\right) + \sum_i b_i \tilde{v}_i \ . \tag{35}$$

In the following, we show that $F(\tilde{\mathbf{v}}) \leq G(\tilde{\mathbf{v}}, \mathbf{v})$. We begin by focusing on the first term on the right hand side of (34–35) and establishing that:

$$\frac{1}{2} \sum_{ij} A_{ij}^+ \tilde{v}_i \tilde{v}_j \ \leq \ \frac{1}{2} \sum_i \frac{(\mathbf{A}^+ \mathbf{v})_i}{v_i} \tilde{v}_i^2 \ . \tag{36}$$

To this end, let $\delta_{ij}$ denote the Kronecker delta function, and let $\mathbf{K}$ be the diagonal matrix with elements

$$K_{ij} \ = \ \delta_{ij} \frac{(\mathbf{A}^+ \mathbf{v})_i}{v_i} \ . \tag{37}$$

Equation (36) is equivalent to the statement that the matrix $(\mathbf{K} - \mathbf{A}^+)$ is semipositive definite. To show this, we consider the matrix $\mathbf{M}$ whose elements

$$M_{ij} \ = \ v_i (K_{ij} - A_{ij}^+) v_j \tag{38}$$

are obtained by rescaling componentwise the elements of $(\mathbf{K} - \mathbf{A}^+)$. Thus, $(\mathbf{K} - \mathbf{A}^+)$ is semipositive definite if $\mathbf{M}$ is semipositive definite. We note that for all vectors $\mathbf{u}$:

$$\mathbf{u}^T \mathbf{M} \mathbf{u} = \sum_{ij} u_i M_{ij} u_j \tag{39}$$

$$= \sum_{ij} u_i u_j v_j \delta_{ij} (\mathbf{A}^+ \mathbf{v})_i - \sum_{ij} v_i v_j u_i u_j A_{ij}^+ \tag{40}$$

$$= \sum_{ij} v_i v_j A_{ij}^+ u_i^2 - \sum_{ij} v_i v_j u_i u_j A_{ij}^+ \tag{41}$$

$$= \sum_{ij} v_i v_j A_{ij}^+ \left[\frac{1}{2} u_i^2 + \frac{1}{2} u_j^2 - u_i u_j\right] \tag{42}$$

$$= \frac{1}{2} \sum_{ij} A_{ij}^+ v_i v_j (u_i - u_j)^2 \tag{43}$$

$$\geq 0 \ . \tag{44}$$

Thus, $(\mathbf{K} - \mathbf{A}^+)$ is semipositive definite, proving the bound in (36). To bound the second term on the right hand side of (34), we use the inequality: $z \geq 1 + \log z$. The second term on the right hand side of (35) is obtained by substituting $z = \tilde{v}_i \tilde{v}_j / (v_i v_j)$ into this inequality:

$$\tilde{v}_i \tilde{v}_j \geq v_i v_j \left(1 + \log \frac{\tilde{v}_i \tilde{v}_j}{v_i v_j}\right) \ . \tag{45}$$

Combining (36) and (45), and noting that the third terms on the right hand sides of (34–35) are the same, we have shown that:

$$F(\tilde{\mathbf{v}}) \leq G(\tilde{\mathbf{v}}, \mathbf{v}) \ . \tag{46}$$

It is easy to verify that $F(\mathbf{v}) = G(\mathbf{v}, \mathbf{v})$. Therefore, $G(\tilde{\mathbf{v}}, \mathbf{v})$ is an auxiliary function, and we can use it to improve $F(\mathbf{v})$. Note that $G(\tilde{\mathbf{v}}, \mathbf{v})$ diverges as $\tilde{v}_i \to 0$; thus, except in degenerate cases, its minimum occurs at positively valued $\tilde{v}_i$. The minimization of $G(\tilde{\mathbf{v}}, \mathbf{v})$ is performed by setting its derivative with respect to $\tilde{v}_i$ to zero, leading to the multiplicative updates in (12). Minimizing $G(\tilde{\mathbf{v}}, \mathbf{v})$ with box constraints on $\tilde{v}_i$ leads to the clipped multiplicative updates in (19).

### A.2    Convergence to Global Minimum

The equality in (46) is satisfied if and only if $\tilde{\mathbf{v}} = \mathbf{v}$, implying that the update rule has reached a fixed point. The existence of an auxiliary function guarantees monotonic convergence to a fixed point, though not (in general) convergence to a global minimum. The optimization in nonnegative quadratic programming, however, is convex. Using this, one can prove the second statement of Theorem 1, namely that under the multiplicative updates, the objective function $F(\mathbf{v})$ converges to the value of its global minimum.

Let $\mathbf{v}^*$ be a fixed point that emerges from iteratively applying the update in (12) to an initial vector $\mathbf{v}$ with no zero elements. By examining the sign of the gradient at $\mathbf{v}^*$, we can show that $F(\mathbf{v}^*)$ represents a global minimum. In particular, if $v_i^* \neq 0$, then as shown in Section 2.1, it follows that $(\partial F/\partial v_i)|_{\mathbf{v}^*} = 0$. Alternatively, if $v_i^* = 0$, we can show that $(\partial F/\partial v_i)|_{\mathbf{v}^*} \geq 0$. Together, these are precisely the conditions of the Kuhn-Tucker Theorem, establishing that $F(\mathbf{v})$ attains its global minimum value at $\mathbf{v}^*$.

To prove the latter statement, we suppose that $v_i^* = 0$ occurs at a "reachable" fixed point and show that $(\partial F/\partial v_i)|_{\mathbf{v}^*} < 0$ leads to a contradiction. If the partial derivative is negative at $v_i^* = 0$, then by continuity there exists an $\epsilon > 0$ such that $(\partial F/\partial v_i)|_{\mathbf{v}'} < 0$ for all $\mathbf{v}'$ such that $|\mathbf{v}' - \mathbf{v}^*| < \epsilon$. As observed in Section 2.1, the multiplicative update increases $v_i$ if $\partial F/\partial v_i < 0$; thus in this region, the update will push $v_i$ to larger and larger values until it escapes from the $\epsilon$-region. This leaves only one scenario in which $v_i^* = 0$ could emerge as a reachable fixed point – namely, if an update from outside the $\epsilon$-region sets $v_i$ directly to zero. Examining the update rule, we see that this cannot happen if the terms $a_i = (\mathbf{A}^+\mathbf{v})_i$ and $c_i = (\mathbf{A}^-\mathbf{v})_i$ are strictly positive when $\mathbf{v}$ does not contain any zero elements. This is easily guaranteed by construction of the matrices $A_{ij}^+$ and $A_{ij}^-$; see the footnote in Section 2.1. Thus, we have a contradiction.

## B    Proof of Theorem 2

First, we show that (17) has a unique solution. Computing the derivative of the left hand side with respect to $\lambda$ gives:

$$\sum_i \beta_i v_i r_i'(\lambda) = \sum_i \frac{\beta_i^2 v_i}{2 a_i} \left[ -1 + \frac{b_i + \lambda \beta_i}{\sqrt{(b_i + \lambda \beta_i)^2 + 4 a_i c_i}} \right] . \tag{47}$$

Every term in this sum is strictly negative if $a_i > 0$ and $c_i > 0$, which can be assumed without loss of generality. (See the footnote in Section 2.1.) Thus, the sum as a whole is always negative, implying that the left hand side of (17) decreases monotonically with $\lambda$.

The existence of a solution to (17) is implied by the assumption of a non-empty feasible region, while the monotonicity of the left hand side establishes uniqueness.

To prove convergence of (18), let $\lambda^t$ denote the value after $t$ iterations of the update rule, and let $\lambda^*$ denote its fixed point. The proof is typical of fixed point theorems in that we will show each update moves $\lambda^{t+1}$ closer to $\lambda^*$ than $\lambda^t$. To begin, note that:

$$\left|\lambda^{t+1} - \lambda^*\right| = \left|\lambda^t - \lambda^* + \frac{1}{R}\left(\sum_i \beta_i v_i[r_i(\lambda^t) - r_i(\lambda^*)]\right)\right| . \qquad (48)$$

Consider the final term on the right hand side of (48). By Taylor's Theorem, there exists a value $\bar{\lambda}$ between $\lambda^t$ and $\lambda^*$ such that:

$$\sum_i \beta_i v_i[r_i(\lambda^t) - r_i(\lambda^*)] = \sum_i \beta_i v_i(\lambda^t - \lambda^*)r_i'(\bar{\lambda}) . \qquad (49)$$

Substituting (49) into the right hand side of (48) and collecting terms, we obtain a mapping of the form:

$$\left|\lambda^{t+1} - \lambda^*\right| = \left|\lambda^t - \lambda^*\right|\left|1 + \frac{1}{R}\sum_i \beta_i v_i r_i'(\bar{\lambda})\right| . \qquad (50)$$

We now exploit the fact that the left hand side of (17) decreases monotonically with $\lambda$, and that its derivative is negative and bounded below. In particular, by setting

$$R = \sum_i \frac{\beta_i^2 v_i}{a_i} \qquad (51)$$

and appealing to the form of the derivative in (47), it is easily shown that the factor multiplying $|\lambda^t - \lambda^*|$ in (50) is less than unity. It follows that (48) is a contraction mapping, with $|\lambda^{t+1} - \lambda^*| < |\lambda^t - \lambda^*|$. In practice, we have found the iterative procedure in (18) to work well for solving (17), though more sophisticated root-finding methods are certainly possible.

# Simplified PAC-Bayesian Margin Bounds

David McAllester

Toyota Technological Institute at Chicago
mcallester@tti-c.org

**Abstract.** The theoretical understanding of support vector machines is largely based on margin bounds for linear classifiers with unit-norm weight vectors and unit-norm feature vectors. Unit-norm margin bounds have been proved previously using fat-shattering arguments and Rademacher complexity. Recently Langford and Shawe-Taylor proved a dimension-independent unit-norm margin bound using a relatively simple PAC-Bayesian argument. Unfortunately, the Langford-Shawe-Taylor bound is stated in a variational form making direct comparison to fat-shattering bounds difficult. This paper provides an explicit solution to the variational problem implicit in the Langford-Shawe-Taylor bound and shows that the PAC-Bayesian margin bounds are significantly tighter. Because a PAC-Bayesian bound is derived from a particular prior distribution over hypotheses, a PAC-Bayesian margin bound also seems to provide insight into the nature of the learning bias underlying the bound.

## 1   Introduction

Margin bounds play a central role in learning theory. Margin bounds for convex combination weight vectors (unit $\ell_1$ norm weight vectors) provide a theoretical foundation for boosting algorithms [15, 9, 8]. Margin bounds for unit-norm weight vectors provide a theoretical foundation for support vector machines [3, 17, 2]. This paper concerns the unit-norm margin bounds underlying support vector machines. Earlier unit-norm margin bounds were proved using fat shattering dimension. This paper, building on results by Langford and Shawe-Taylor [11], gives a PAC-Bayesian unit-norm margin bound that is tighter than known unit-norm margin bounds derived from fat shattering arguments.

Consider a fixed distribution $D$ on pairs $\langle x, y \rangle$ with $x \in R^d$ satisfying $||x|| = 1$ and $y \in \{-1, 1\}$. We are interested in finding a weight vector $w$ with $||w|| = 1$ such that the sign of $w \cdot x$ predicts $y$. For $\gamma > 0$ the error rate of $w$ on distribution $D$ relative to safety margin $\gamma$, denoted $\ell_\gamma(w, D)$ is defined as follows.

$$\ell_\gamma(w, D) = \mathrm{P}_{\langle x, y \rangle \sim D}\left[(w \cdot x)y \leq \gamma\right]$$

Let $S$ be a sample of $m$ pairs drawn IID from the distribution $D$. The sample $S$ can be viewed as an empirical distribution on pairs. We are interested in

B. Schölkopf and M.K. Warmuth (Eds.): COLT/Kernel 2003, LNAI 2777, pp. 203–215, 2003.
© Springer-Verlag Berlin Heidelberg 2003

bounding $\ell_0(w, D)$ in terms of $\ell_\gamma(w, S)$ and the margin $\gamma$. Bartlett and Shawe-Taylor use fat shattering arguments [2] to show that with probability at least $1 - \delta$ over the choice of the sample $S$ we have the following simultaneously for all weight vectors $w$ with $||w|| = 1$ and margins $\gamma > 0$.

$$\ell_0(w, D) \leq \ell_\gamma(w, S) + 27.18\sqrt{\frac{\log^2 m + 84}{m\gamma^2}} + O\left(\sqrt{\frac{\ln \frac{1}{\delta}}{m}}\right) \tag{1}$$

Note that the bound is independent of the dimension $d$ (the number of features and corresponding weights). Intuitively the quantity $1/\gamma^2$ acts like the complexity of the weight vector. Bound (1) has been recently improved using Rademacher complexity — Theorem 21 of [4] implies the following where $k$ is $m\gamma^2$.

$$\ell_0(w, D) \leq \ell_\gamma(w, S) + 8\sqrt{\frac{\ln \frac{4}{\delta}}{k}} + \frac{4}{\sqrt{k}} + \sqrt{\frac{\ln \frac{4}{\delta}}{m}} \tag{2}$$

Bound (2) has the nice scaling property that the bound remains meaningful in a limit where $k$ is held constant while $m$ goes to infinity. Further improvements on (2) are possible within the Rademacher complexity framework [1].

Initial attempts to use PAC-Bayesian arguments to derive unit-norm margin bounds resulted in bounds that depended on $d$ [6]. Here, building on the work of Langford and Shawe-Taylor [11], we use a PAC-Bayesian argument to show that with probability at least $1 - \delta$ over the choice of the sample $S$ we have the following simultaneously for all $w$ with $||w|| = 1$ and where $\ln^+ (x)$ abbreviates $\max(0, lnx)$.

$$\ell_0(w, D) \leq \ell_\gamma(w, S) + 2\sqrt{\frac{2\left(\ell_\gamma(w, S) + \frac{4}{k}\right)\ln \frac{k}{4}}{k}} + \frac{8\left(1 + \ln \frac{k}{4}\right)}{k}$$

$$+ O\left(\sqrt{\frac{\ln m + \ln \frac{1}{\delta}}{m}}\right) \tag{3}$$

Like (2), bound (3) is meaningful in a limit where $k$ is held constant while $m$ goes to infinity. Bound (3) also interpolates the realizable and unrealizable case — in the case where the training error $\ell_\gamma(w, S)$ is zero the bound is $O((\ln k)/k)$. Note however, that even for $\ell_\gamma(w. S) = 1/2$ we have that (3) is an improvement on (1) and (2) for modest values of $k$.

Bound (3) is derived from a bound given by Langford and Shawe-Taylor [11]. The Langford and Shawe-Taylor bound is tighter than (3) but is given in an implicit form which makes explicit comparison with earlier bounds difficult. Langford and Shawe-Taylor also use PAC-Bayesian analysis to define more refined notions of margin leading to new learning algorithms. The contribution of this paper is to solve the variational problems implicit in the Langford and Shawe-Taylor bound and show clearly how the PAC-Bayesian bounds compare with earlier bounds. PAC-Bayesian bounds seem competitive with the best known bounds derivable by shattering and Rademacher methods.

The derivation of a margin bound from the PAC-Bayesian theorem presents the bias of the learning algorithm in the familiar form of a prior distribution on hypotheses. In particular, the derivation of (3) is based on an isotropic Gaussian prior over the weight vectors. PAC-Bayesian arguments have also been used to give what appears to be the tightest known bounds for Gaussian process classifiers [16] and useful bounds for convex weight vector linear threshold classifiers [9]. In these cases as well, PAC-Bayesian derivations present the bias of the algorithm in the familiar form of a prior distribution.

## 2   The PAC-Bayesian Theorem

A first version of the PAC-Bayesian theorem appeared in [12]. The improved statement of the theorem given here is due to Langford and the simplified proof in the appendix is due to Seeger [10, 16]. Let $D$ be a distribution on a set $Z$, let $P$ be a distribution on a set $H$, and let $\ell$ be a "loss function" from $H \times Z$ to $[0, 1]$. For any distribution $W$ on $Z$ and $h \in H$ let $\ell(h, W)$ be $E_{z \sim W}[\ell(h, z)]$. Let $S$ be an IID sample of $m$ elements of $Z$ drawn according to the distribution $D$. We are interested in using the sample $S$ to select $h \in H$ so as to minimize the loss $\ell(h, D)$. We will treat the sample as a distribution in the standard way so that $\ell(h, S)$ is the (training) loss of $h$ on the sample $S$ and $\ell(h, D)$ is the (generalization) loss of $h$ on $D$. A common case is where the set $Z$ is of the form $X \times \{0, 1\}$, $H$ is a set of functions from $X$ to $\{0, 1\}$, and $\ell(h, \langle x, y \rangle)$ is 1 if $h(x) \neq y$ and 0 otherwise. In this case $\ell(h, S)$ is the training error rate of rule $h$ on the sample $S$ and $\ell(h, D)$ is $P_{\langle x, y \rangle \sim D}[h(x) \neq y]$. We will be interested in Gibbs classifiers, i.e., classifiers which select $h$ stochastically [5]. For any distribution $Q$ on $H$ and distribution $W$ on $Z$ let $\ell(Q, W)$ denote $E_{h \sim Q, z \sim W}[\ell(h, z)]$. $\ell(Q, S)$ is the training loss of the Gibbs rule defined by $Q$ and $\ell(Q, D)$ is the generalization loss of this rule. For two distributions $Q$ and $P$ on the same set $H$ the Kullback-Leibler divergence $KL(Q||P)$ is defined to be $E_{h \sim Q}[\ln(dQ(h)/dP(h))]$. For $p, q \in [0, 1]$ let $KL(p||q)$ denote the Kullback-Leibler divergence from a Bernoulli variable with bias $p$ to a Bernoulli variable with bias $q$. We have $KL(p||q) = p\ln(p/q) + (1-p)\ln((1-p)/(1-q))$. Let $\forall^\delta S\ \Phi(S, \delta)$ mean that with probability at least $1 - \delta$ over the choice of $S$ we have that $\Phi(S, \delta)$ holds. The two-sided PAC-Bayesian theorem is the following where $P$ is a fixed "prior" distribution on $H$ and $Q$ ranges over arbitrary "posterior" distributions on $H$.

$$\forall^\delta S\ \forall Q\ KL(\ell(Q, S)||\ell(Q, D)) \leq \frac{KL(Q||P) + \ln \frac{2m}{\delta}}{m - 1} \tag{4}$$

Note that $\ell(Q, D)$ is the error rate of a Gibbs classifier that first selects a rule stochastically according to the distribution $Q$ and then uses the prediction of that rule. Intuitively, the theorem states that if $KL(Q||P)$ is small then $\ell(Q, D)$ is near $\ell(Q, S)$. Formula (4) bounds the difference between the empirical loss $\ell(Q, S)$ of the Gibbs classifier and its true (generalization) loss $\ell(Q, D)$.

A one-sided version can be stated as follows where $2/\delta$ in the two-sided version becomes $1/\delta$ in the one-sided version.

$$\forall^\delta S \; \forall Q \; \ell(Q, D) \leq \sup\left\{\epsilon : KL(\ell(Q, S)||\epsilon) \leq \frac{KL(Q||P) + \ln\frac{m}{\delta}}{m - 1}\right\} \quad (5)$$

For $q > p$ we have that $KL(p||q) \geq (q - p)^2/(2q)$. This inequality implies that if $KL(p||q) \leq x$ then $q \leq p + \sqrt{2px} + 2x$. So (5) implies the following somewhat weaker but perhaps clearer statement.

$$\ell(Q, D) \leq \ell(Q, S) + \sqrt{\frac{2\ell(Q, S)\left(KL(Q||P) + \ln\frac{m}{\delta}\right)}{m - 1}} + \frac{2\left(KL(Q||P) + \ln\frac{m}{\delta}\right)}{m - 1} \quad (6)$$

Note if the empirical loss $\ell(Q, S)$ is small compared to $KL(Q||P)/m$ then the last term dominates (the realizable case). If $\ell(Q, S)$ is large compared to $KL(Q||P)/m$ then the first term dominates. Because the arithmetic mean bounds the geometric mean, we have that in general the bound is $O(\ell(Q, S) + KL(Q||P)/m)$. Proofs of these theorems are given in an appendix.

# 3   Gibbs Linear Threshold Classifiers

In this section we use the PAC-Bayesian theorem to prove a margin bound for a Gibbs classifier which stochastically selects a linear threshold function. The next section uses similar methods to prove a margin bound for a single (deterministic) linear threshold classifier. In both this section and the next we take $Z$ to be the set of pairs $\langle x, y \rangle$ with $x \in R^d$ satisfying $||x|| = 1$ and $y \in \{-1, 1\}$. Both these sections take $H$ to be weight vectors in $R^d$ and take the prior $P$ on $H$ to be a unit-variance isotropic (the same in all directions) multivariate Gaussian on $R^d$. For each $\gamma \geq 0$ we define a loss function $\ell_\gamma$ as follows.

$$\ell_\gamma(w, \langle x, y \rangle) = \begin{cases} 1 \text{ if } y(w \cdot x) \leq \gamma \\ 0 \text{ otherwise} \end{cases}$$

For $w \in R^d$ with $||w|| = 1$ and $\mu > 0$ define the "posterior" $Q(w, \mu)$ by the following density function $q$ where $p$ is the density function of the "prior" $P$ and $Z$ is a normalizing constant.

$$q(w') = \frac{1}{Z}\begin{cases} p(w') \text{ if } w' \cdot w \geq \mu \\ 0 \qquad \text{otherwise} \end{cases}$$

Note that $w'$ is drawn from a unit-variance multivariate Gaussian and $w$ is a fixed vector with $||w|| = 1$. Since $Q(w, \mu)$ is just the prior renormalized on a subset of the space we have the following where $\Phi(\mu)$ is the probability that a unit-variance Gaussian real-value random variable exceeds $\mu$.

$$KL(Q(w,\mu)||P) = \ln \frac{1}{Z} = \ln \frac{1}{P(w' \cdot w \geq \mu)} = \ln \frac{1}{\Phi(\mu)}$$

Now for $\gamma > 0$, any hypothesis distribution $Q$, and any data distribution $W$, define $\ell_\gamma(Q, W)$ as follows.

$$\ell_\gamma(Q, W) = \mathrm{E}_{w \sim Q, \langle x, y \rangle \sim W} [\ell_\gamma(w, \langle x, y \rangle)]$$

We will often write $\ell_\gamma(w, W)$ where $w \in R^d$ as a notation for $\ell_\gamma(Q, W)$ where $Q$ places all of its weight on $w$. These quantities are error rates relative to a "safety margin" of $\gamma$. The fundamental idea behind the PAC-Bayesian approach to margin bounds is that a small error rate relative to a large safety margin ensures the existence of a posterior distribution (a Gibbs classifier) with a small training error and a small KL-divergence from the prior. We first consider the training error. Langford and Shawe-Taylor prove the following.

**Lemma 1 (Langford&Shawe-Taylor).** *For $w \in R^d$ with $||w|| = 1$, and for $\mu \geq 0$, we have the following for all $\gamma \geq 0$.*

$$\ell_0(Q(w,\mu), S) \leq \ell_\gamma(w, S) + \Phi(\gamma\mu)$$

*Proof.* For $x \in R^d$ with $||x|| = 1$ we let $x_{||}$ be $(w \cdot x)w$ ($x_{||}$ is the component of $x$ parallel to $w$), and let $x_\perp$ be $x - x_{||}$ ($x_\perp$ is the component of $x$ perpendicular to $w$). Let $\langle x, y \rangle$ be a tuple in $S$. We say that $\langle x, y \rangle$ is $\gamma$-safe (for $w$) if $y(w \cdot x) \geq \gamma$. Note that the Gaussian prior on weight vectors has the property that, for any two orthogonal directions, the components of a random vector in those two directions are independent and normally distributed. Fix a $\gamma$-safe point $\langle x, y \rangle$ and consider the orthogonal components $w' \cdot x_\perp$ and $w' \cdot x_{||}$ as we select random weight vectors $w'$. If $w' \cdot w \geq \mu$, and $\langle x, y \rangle$ is $\gamma$-safe for $w$ then $y(w' \cdot x_{||}) \geq \gamma\mu$. More specifically we have the following.

$$
\begin{aligned}
\mathrm{P}_{w' \sim Q(w,\mu)} [y(w' \cdot x) \leq 0] &= \mathrm{P}_{w' \sim Q(w,\mu)} \left[ -y(w' \cdot x_\perp) \geq y(w' \cdot x_{||}) \right] \\
&= \mathrm{P}_{w' \sim Q(w,\mu)} \left[ -y(w' \cdot x_\perp) \geq y(x \cdot w)(w' \cdot w)) \right] \\
&\leq \mathrm{P}_{w' \sim Q(w,\mu)} \left[ -y(w' \cdot x_\perp) \geq \gamma\mu \right] \\
&= \Phi \left( \frac{\gamma\mu}{||x_\perp||} \right) \\
&\leq \Phi(\gamma\mu)
\end{aligned}
$$

This yields the following.

$$
\begin{aligned}
\ell_0(Q(w,\mu), S) &= \mathrm{E}_{\langle x, y \rangle \sim S} \left[ \mathrm{P}_{w' \sim Q(w,\mu)} [y(w' \cdot x) \leq 0] \right] \\
&\leq \ell_\gamma(w, S) + \mathrm{E}_{\langle x, y \rangle \sim S} \left[ \mathrm{P}_{w' \sim Q(w,\mu)} [y(w' \cdot x) \leq 0] \mid y(x \cdot w) \geq \gamma \right] \\
&\leq \ell_\gamma(w, S) + \Phi(\gamma\mu) \qquad\qquad \square
\end{aligned}
$$

Formula (5) (for the loss function $\ell_0$) and Lemma 1 together yield the following.

**Theorem 1 (Langford&Shawe-Taylor).** *With probability at least $1-\delta$ over the choice of the sample we have that the following holds simultaneously for all $w \in R^d$ with $||w|| = 1$, $\mu \geq 0$ and $\gamma \geq 0$.*

$$\ell_0(Q(w,\mu), D) \leq \sup\left\{\epsilon: KL\left(\ell_\gamma(w,\ S) + \Phi\left(\gamma\mu\right)\ ||\ \epsilon\right) \leq \frac{\ln\frac{1}{\Phi(\mu)} + \ln\frac{m}{\delta}}{m-1}\right\}$$

The main contribution of this paper is to give a particular value for $\mu$ and then "solve" for the upper bound on $\ell_0(Q(w,\ \mu))$ implicit in Theorem 1. In particular we define $\mu(\gamma)$ as follows.

$$\mu(\gamma) = \frac{\sqrt{2\ln(m\gamma^2)}}{\gamma}$$

For this choice of $\mu$ we have the following.

**Theorem 2.** *With probability at least $1-\delta$ over the choice of the sample $S$ we have that the following holds simultaneously for all $w \in R^d$ with $||w|| = 1$ and $\gamma > 0$.*

$$\ell_0(Q(w,\mu(\gamma)), D) \leq \sup\left\{\epsilon: \begin{array}{c} KL\left(\ell_\gamma(w,\ S) + \frac{1}{m\gamma^2}\ ||\ \epsilon\right) \\ \leq \frac{\frac{\ln^+\left(m\gamma^2\right)}{\gamma^2} + \frac{3}{2}\ln m + \ln\frac{1}{\delta} + 3}{m-1} \end{array}\right\}$$

Theorem 2 follows from the following of two lemmas.

**Lemma 2.** *For $\gamma > 0$ we have the following.*

$$\ln\frac{1}{\Phi(\mu(\gamma))} \leq \frac{\ln^+(m\gamma^2)}{\gamma^2} + \frac{1}{2}\ln m + 3$$

*Proof.* First, if $\mu(\gamma) \leq 3/2$ we have the following.

$$\ln\frac{1}{\Phi(\mu(\gamma))} \leq \ln\frac{1}{\Phi(3/2)} \leq 3 \qquad (7)$$

In this case $\ln(m\gamma^2)$ might be negative, but the lemma still follows. Now suppose $\mu(\gamma) \geq 3/2$. For $\mu \geq 0$ we have the following well known lower bound on $\Phi(\mu)$ (see [14]).

$$\Phi(\mu) \geq \left(1 - \frac{1}{\mu^2}\right)\frac{1}{\sqrt{2\pi}}\frac{1}{\mu}\exp\left(-\frac{\mu^2}{2}\right) \qquad (8)$$

For $\mu(\gamma) \geq 3/2$ formula 8 yields the following.

$$\Phi(\mu(\gamma)) \geq \frac{5}{9} \frac{1}{\sqrt{2\pi}} \frac{1}{\mu(\gamma)} \exp\left(-\mu^2(\gamma)/2\right)$$

This yields the following.

$$\ln \frac{1}{\Phi(\mu(\gamma))} \leq 2 + \ln\mu(\gamma) + \frac{\ln(m\gamma^2)}{\gamma^2} \tag{9}$$

We have that $\mu(\gamma)$ goes to zero as $\gamma$ goes to infinity and goes to negative infinity as $\gamma$ goes to zero. Furthermore, a simple calculation shows that the derivative is zero at only a single point given by $\gamma = \sqrt{e/m}$ and at this point $\mu(\gamma)$ is positive. These facts imply that this point is a maximum of $\mu(\gamma)$ and we get the following which implies the lemma.

$$\mu(\gamma) \leq \sqrt{\frac{2m}{e}} \tag{10}$$

$\square$

**Lemma 3.** *For $\gamma > 0$ we have the following.*

$$\Phi(\gamma\mu(\gamma)) \leq \frac{1}{m\gamma^2}$$

*Proof.* For $\gamma \leq 1/\sqrt{m}$ we have $1/(m\gamma^2) \geq 1$ and the lemma follows from $\Phi(x) \leq 1$. For $\gamma \geq 1/\sqrt{m}$ we have $\mu(\gamma) \geq 0$ and the lemma follows from the fact that for $z \geq 0$ we have $\Phi(z) \leq \exp(-z^2/2)$. $\square$

Theorem 2 now follows from Theorem 1 and Lemmas 2 and 3. Using $KL(p\|q) \leq \frac{1}{2}q(q-p)^2$ for $p \leq q$ we get the following corollary of Theorem 2.

**Corollary 1.** *With probability at least $1 - \delta$ over the choice of the sample $S$ we have that the following holds simultaneously for all $w \in R^d$ with $\|w\| = 1$ and $\gamma > 0$.*

$$\ell_0(Q(w, \mu(\gamma)), D) \leq \hat{\ell} + \sqrt{2\hat{\ell}\Delta} + 2\Delta$$
$$where$$
$$\hat{\ell} = \ell_\gamma(w, S) + \frac{1}{m\gamma^2}$$

$$\Delta = \frac{\frac{\ln^+(m\gamma^2)}{\gamma^2} + \frac{3}{2}\ln m + \ln\frac{1}{\delta} + 3}{m - 1}$$

The body of Corollary 1 can be rewritten as follows.

$$\ell_0(Q(w, \mu(\gamma)), D) \leq \ell_\gamma(w, S) + \sqrt{\frac{2\left(\ell_\gamma(w, S) + \frac{1}{k}\right)\ln^+(k)}{k}} + \frac{1 + 2\ln^+(k)}{k}$$

$$+ O\left(\sqrt{\frac{\ln m + \ln\frac{1}{\delta}}{m}}\right) \tag{11}$$

Note that (11) is vacuously true for $k \leq 1$. For $k \geq 1$ the constants in the big O expression are modest and independent of $k$ (i.e., independent of $\gamma$). For large sample size the big O term vanishes and either the error is very near zero or the bound is dominated by the terms involving $k$. This bound has a nice limiting behavior in a "thermodynamic limit" where $\ell_\gamma(w, S)$ and $k$ are held constant while $m \to \infty$. This thermodynamic limit corresponds to a realistic regime where $m$ is large but $\ell_\gamma(w, S)$ and $1/k$ are still significantly greater than zero. For the realizable case, i.e., when $\ell_\gamma(w, S) = 0$, we get the following.

$$\ell_0(Q(w, \mu(\gamma)), D) \leq \frac{1 + \sqrt{2\ln^+(k)} + 2\ln^+(k)}{k} + O\left(\sqrt{\frac{\ln m + \ln\frac{1}{\delta}}{m}}\right) \tag{12}$$

## 4   Deterministic Linear Classifiers

Theorem 2 gives a margin bound for the loss of a Gibbs classifier — a classifier that stochastically selects the classification rule at classification time. There are two ways of converting Theorem 2 into a margin guarantee on a deterministic linear classification rule. First we observe that the deterministic classification rule defined by the weight vector $w$ corresponds to the majority vote over the distribution $Q(w, \mu)$. More formally we have that $P_{w' \sim Q(w,\mu)}\left[w' \cdot x \geq 0\right] \geq 1/2$ if and only if $x \cdot w \geq 0$. For any Gibbs classifier, the error rate of the majority vote classifier can be at most twice the error rate of the Gibbs classifier. This is because each error of the majority vote classifier requires that at least half (under the voting measure) of the individual classifiers are making an error and so the error rate of the Gibbs classifier must be at least half the error rate of the majority vote classifier. This general factor of two bound on the error rate of the majority classifier together with (11) yields the following.

$$\ell_0(w, D) \leq 2\ell_\gamma(w, S) + 2\sqrt{\frac{2\left(\ell_\gamma(w, S) + \frac{1}{k}\right)\ln^+(k)}{k}} + \frac{2\left(1 + 2\ln^+(k)\right)}{k}$$

$$+ O\left(\sqrt{\frac{\ln m + \ln\frac{1}{\delta}}{m}}\right) \tag{13}$$

Again it is interesting to consider the thermodynamic limit where $\ell_\gamma(w, S)$ and $k$ are held constant as $m \to \infty$. Note that (3) is tighter than (13) in the regime where $1/k$ is small compared to $\ell_\gamma(w, S)$. We now prove (3). We start with the following generalization of Lemma 1.

**Lemma 4 (Langford&Shawe-Taylor).** *Let $W$ be any distribution on pairs $\langle x, y \rangle$ with $x \in R^d$ satisfying $||x|| = 1$ and $y \in \{-1, 1\}$. Let $w$ be any vector in $R^d$ satisfying $||w|| = 1$. For $\mu \geq 0$ and $\gamma \geq 0$ and any real value $\beta$ we have the following.*

$$\mathop{\mathrm{P}}_{\langle x, y \rangle \sim W, w' \sim Q(w, \mu)} \left[ y(w' \cdot x) \leq \beta \right] \leq \mathop{\mathrm{P}}_{\langle x, y \rangle \sim W} \left[ y(w \cdot x) \leq \beta + \gamma \right] + \Phi(\gamma\mu) \quad (14)$$

$$\mathop{\mathrm{P}}_{\langle x, y \rangle \sim W, w' \sim Q(w, \mu)} \left[ y(w' \cdot x) > \beta \right] \leq \mathop{\mathrm{P}}_{\langle x, y \rangle \sim W} \left[ y(w \cdot x) > \beta - \gamma \right] + \Phi(\gamma\mu) \quad (15)$$

Formula (14) is a generalization of Lemma 1 and the proof of (14) is a straightforward generalization of the proof of Lemma 1. The proof of (15) is similar. Lemma 4 yields the following corollary.

**Corollary 2 (Langford&Shawe-Taylor).**

$$\ell_{\gamma/2}(Q(w, \mu), S) \leq \ell_\gamma(w, S) + \Phi(\gamma\mu/2) \quad (16)$$

$$\ell_0(w, D) \leq \ell_{\gamma/2}(Q(w, \mu), D) + \Phi(\gamma\mu/2) \quad (17)$$

*Proof.* Formula (16) is an instance of (14) with $\beta = \gamma/2$ and $\gamma$ replaced by $\gamma/2$. To prove (17) we construct the following instance of (15) again with $\beta = \gamma/2$ and $\gamma$ replaced by $\gamma/2$.

$$1 - \ell_{\gamma/2}(Q(w, \mu), D) \leq 1 - \ell_0(w, D) + \Phi(\gamma\mu/2)$$

$\square$

To get a bound on $\ell_0(w, D)$ it now suffices to bound $\ell_{\gamma/2}(Q(w, \mu), D)$ in terms of $\ell_{\gamma/2}(Q(w, \mu), S)$. An application of (5) to the loss function $\ell_\gamma$ yields the following.

$$\forall \gamma \forall^\delta S \ \forall Q \ \ell_\gamma(Q, D) \leq \sup \left\{ \epsilon : KL(\ell_\gamma(Q, S) || \epsilon) \leq \frac{KL(Q||P) + \ln \frac{m}{\delta}}{m - 1} \right\} \quad (18)$$

We now consider discrete values of $\gamma$ satisfying the statements that $k = m\gamma^2 = i/m$ for $i \in \{1, 2, \ldots, m^2\}$. By a union bound over the $m^2$ different possible values of $\gamma$ we get that with probability at least $1 - \delta$ over the choice of the sample the following holds for all $Q$ and for all $\gamma$ satisfying $k \in \{1/m, 2/m, \ldots, m^2/m\}$.

$$\ell_{\gamma/2}(Q, D) \leq \sup \left\{ \epsilon : KL(\ell_{\gamma/2}(Q, S) || \epsilon) \leq \frac{KL(Q||P) + \ln \frac{m^3}{\delta}}{m - 1} \right\} \quad (19)$$

Formulas (16), (17), and (19) together yield the following variant of a theorem in [11].

**Theorem 3 (Langford and Shawe-Taylor).** *With probability at least* $1 - \delta$ *over the choice of the sample we have the following simultaneously for all* $\mu \geq 0$ *and* $\gamma \in \{1/m, 2/m \ldots, m/m\}$.

$$\ell_0(w, D) \leq \sup \left\{ \epsilon : \, KL \left( \ell_\gamma(w, S) + \Phi(\gamma\mu/2) \| \epsilon - \Phi(\gamma\mu/2) \right) \leq \frac{\ln \frac{1}{\Phi(\mu)} + \ln \frac{m^3}{\delta}}{m - 1} \right\}$$

Again, the main contribution of this paper is to construct more explicit forms of the bounds implicit in Theorems 1 and 3. Using $\mu(\gamma/2)$ in Theorem 3 together with Lemmas 2 and 3 yields the following.

$$\ell_0(w, D) \leq \sup \left\{ \epsilon : \begin{array}{c} KL \left( \ell_\gamma(w, S) + \frac{4}{m\gamma^2} \| \epsilon - \frac{4}{m\gamma^2} \right) \\[2mm] \leq \frac{\frac{4 \ln^+ \left( m\gamma^2/4 \right)}{\gamma^2} + \frac{7}{2} \ln m + \ln \frac{1}{\delta} + 3}{m - 1} \end{array} \right\} \tag{20}$$

By the arguments deriving (11) from Theorem 2 we then have the following for the allowed discrete values of $k$.

$$\ell_0(w, D) \leq \ell_\gamma(w, S) + 2\sqrt{\frac{2 \left( \ell_\gamma(w, S) + \frac{4}{k} \right) \ln^+ \left( \frac{k}{4} \right)}{k}} + \frac{8 \left( 1 + \ln^+ \left( \frac{k}{4} \right) \right)}{k}$$

$$+ O \left( \sqrt{\frac{\ln m + \ln \frac{1}{\delta}}{m}} \right) \tag{21}$$

To derive (3) for arbitrary $\gamma$ we first note that (3) is vacuously true for $k \leq 8$. For $k \geq 8$ we have $\gamma \geq 4/\sqrt{m}$. Let $\alpha$ be the largest value with $\alpha \leq \gamma$ such that $m\alpha^2$ has the form $i/m$ for $i \in \{1, \ldots, m^2\}$. Let $k'$ be $m\alpha$. Note that we have $k' \geq 8$. We now get that (21) holds for $\alpha$ and $k'$ replacing $\gamma$ and $k$ respectively. Note that $\ell_\alpha(w, S) \leq \ell_\gamma(w, S)$ and $k' \geq k - 1/m$. This give the following for arbitrary $\gamma$ satisfying $k \geq 8$.

$$\ell_0(w, D) \leq \ell_\gamma(w, S) + 2\sqrt{\frac{2 \left( \ell_\gamma(w, S) + \frac{4}{k-1/m} \right) \ln^+ \left( \frac{k}{4} \right)}{k - 1/m}} + \frac{8 \left( 1 + \ln^+ \left( \frac{k}{4} \right) \right)}{k - 1/m}$$

$$+ O \left( \sqrt{\frac{\ln m + \ln \frac{1}{\delta}}{m}} \right) \tag{22}$$

The difference between $k$ and $k - 1/m$ can then be absorbed into the final term and we get (3).

# References

1. Peter Bartlett. Personal communication. 2003.
2. Peter Bartlett and John Shawe-Taylor. Generalization performance of support vector machines and other pattern classifiers. In Bernhard Schölkopf, Christopher J. C. Burges, and Alexander J. Smola, editors, *Advances in Kernel Methods - Support Vector Learning*. MIT Press, 1998.
3. Peter L. Bartlett. The sample complexity of pattern classification with neural networks: the size of the weights is more important than the the size of the network. *IEEE Transactions on Information Theory*, March 1998.
4. P.L. Bartlett and S. Mendelson. Rademacher and gaussian complexities: risk bounds and structural results. *Journal of Machine Learning Research*, 3:463–482, 2002.
5. Olivier Catoni. Gibbs estimators. to appear in Probability Theory and Related Fields.
6. Ralph Herbrich and Thore Graepel. A PAC-Bayesian margin bound for linear clasifiers: Why svms work. In *Advances in Neural Information Processing Systems (NIPS)*, 2001.
7. W. Hoeffding. Probability inequalities for sums of bounded random variables. *Journal of the American Statistical Association*, 58:13–30, 1963.
8. V. Koltchinskii and D. Panchenko. Empirical margin distributions and bounding the generalization error of combined classifiers. *Annals of Statistics*, 30, 2002.
9. John Langford, Matthias Seeger, and Nimrod Megiddo. An improved predictive accuracy bound for averaging classifiers. In *ICML2001*, 2001.
10. John Langford and Matthias Seger. Bounds for averaging classifiers. CMU Technical Report CMU-CS-01-102, 2002.
11. John Langford and John Shawe-Taylor. PAC-Bayes and margins. In *Neural Information Processing Systems (NIPS)*, 2002.
12. David McAllester. PAC-Bayesian stochastic model selection. *Machine Learning*, 5:5–21, 2003. A short version appeared as "PAC-Bayesian Model Averaging" in COLT99.
13. David McAllester and Luis Ortiz. Concentration inequalities for the missing mass and for histogram rule error. In *Neural Information Processing systems (NIPS)*, 2002.
14. Harold Ruben. A new asymptotic expansion for the normal probability integral and mill's ratio. *Journal of the Royal Statistical Society. Series B (Methodological)*, 24(1):177–179, 1962.
15. Robert Schapire, Yoav Freund, Peter Bartlett, and Wee Sun Lee. Boosting the margin: A new explanation for the effectiveness of voting methods. In *Machine Learning: Proceedings of the Fourteenth International Conference*, 1997.
16. Matthias Seeger. PAC-Bayesian generalization bounds for gaussian processes. *Journal of Machine Learning Research*, 3:233–269, 2002.
17. John Shawe-Taylor, Peter Bartlett, Robert Williamson, and Martin Anthony. A framework for structural risk minimization. *IEEE Transactions on Information Theory*, 44(5):1926–1940, 1998.

# A    Appendix: Proofs of PAC-Bayesian Theorems

McAllester's original form of the theorem used a square root rather than an inverse KL divergence. The inverse KL divergence form is due to John Langford. The simple proof based on Jensen's inequality is due to Matthias Seeger. We prove the one-sided version (5). A lower bound version of (5) follows by applying (5) to the loss function $1 - \ell$ and the two-sided version (4) follows by a union bound from the upper and lower bound versions. To prove (5) we first prove the following lemma.

**Lemma 5.** *Let $X$ be a real valued random variable satisfying*

$$P(X \leq x) \leq e^{-mf(x)}$$

*where $f(x)$ is non-negative. For any such $X$ we have the following.*

$$\mathrm{E}\left[e^{(m-1)f(X)}\right] \leq m$$

*Proof.* If $P(X \leq x) \leq e^{-mf(x)}$ then $P(e^{(m-1)f(X)} \geq \nu) \leq \min(1, \ \nu^{-m/(m-1)})$. We can then use the general fact that for $W$ non-negative we have $\mathrm{E}[W] = \int_0^\infty P(W \geq \nu)d\nu$. This gives the following.

$$\mathrm{E}\left[e^{(m-1)f(X)}\right] \leq 1 + \int_1^\infty \nu^{-m/(m-1)}d\nu$$

$$= 1 - (m-1)\left[\nu^{-1/(m-1)}\right]_1^\infty$$

$$= m \qquad \qquad \square$$

Now let $KL^+(p||q)$ be zero if $p \geq q$ and $KL(p||q)$ if $p \leq q$. Hoeffding [7] proved essentially the following[1].

**Lemma 6 (Hoeffding).** *If $X_1, \ldots, X_m$ are IID random variables restricted to the interval $[0, 1]$, and $\hat{X}$ is the empirical average $(X_1 + \cdots + X_m)/m$, then for $\epsilon \in [0, 1]$ we have the following.*

$$P(\hat{X} \leq \epsilon) \leq e^{-mKL^+(\epsilon||\mathrm{E}[X_i])}$$

---

[1] It is interesting to note that Lemma 6 generalizes to an arbitrary real-valued random variable $X$. Let $P_\beta$ be the Gibbs distribution on $X$ at inverse temperature $\beta$, let $\mathrm{E}_\beta[f(X)]$ be the expectation of $f(X)$ under $P_\beta$, and let $Z_\beta$ be the partition function at inverse temperature $\beta$.

$$P_\beta(X = x) = \frac{1}{Z_\beta}e^{-\beta x}P(X = x)$$

$$\mathrm{E}_\beta[f(X)] = \frac{1}{Z_\beta}\mathrm{E}\left[f(X)e^{-\beta X}\right]$$

$$Z_\beta = \mathrm{E}\left[e^{-\beta X}\right]$$

Let $DP(x)$ be $P(X \leq x)$ if $x \leq \mathrm{E}[X]$ and $P(X \geq x)$ if $x \geq \mathrm{E}[X]$. In general we have $DP(x) \leq \exp(-KL(P_\beta||P))$ where $\beta$ satisfies $\mathrm{E}_\beta[X] = x$. This is, in general, the tightest bound provable by Chernoff's exponential moment method [13].

**Lemma 7.**
$$\forall^\delta S \; E_{h\sim P}\left[e^{(m-1)KL^+(\ell(h,S)||\ell(h,D))}\right] \le \frac{m}{\delta}$$

*Proof.* Lemma 5 and Lemma 6 together imply the following for any fixed $h \in H$.

$$E_{S\sim D^m}\left[e^{(m-1)KL^+(\ell(h,S)||\ell(h,D))}\right] \le m$$

This implies the following.

$$E_{S\sim D^m}\left[E_{h\sim H}\left[e^{(m-1)KL^+(\ell(h,S)||\ell(h,D))}\right]\right] \le m$$

The lemma now follows from Markov's inequality. □

We now prove the following shift of measure lemma.

**Lemma 8.**
$$E_{x\sim Q}\left[f(x)\right] \le KL(Q||P) + \ln E_{x\sim P}\left[e^{f(x)}\right]$$

*Proof.*

$$
\begin{aligned}
E_{x\sim Q}\left[f(x)\right] &= E_{x\sim Q}\left[\ln e^{f(x)}\right] \\
&= E_{x\sim Q}\left[\ln \frac{dP(x)}{dQ(x)}e^{f(x)} + \ln \frac{dQ(x)}{dP(x)}\right] \\
&= KL(Q||P) + E_{x\sim Q}\left[\ln \frac{dP(x)}{dQ(x)}e^{f(x)}\right] \\
&\le KL(Q||P) + \ln E_{x\sim Q}\left[\frac{dP(x)}{dQ(x)}e^{f(x)}\right] \\
&= KL(Q||P) + \ln E_{x\sim P}\left[e^{f(x)}\right]
\end{aligned}
$$

□

Formula (5) can now be proved by assuming the body of Lemma 8 (which holds with probability at least $1 - \delta$) and then observing the following where the last step follows from Jensen's inequality and strong convexity properties of KL-divergence.

$$E_{h\sim Q}\left[(m-1)KL^+(\ell(h,S)||\ell(h,D))\right] \le KL(Q||P)$$
$$+ \ln E_{h\sim P}\left[e^{(m-1)KL^+(\ell(h,S)||\ell(h,D))}\right]$$

$$\le KL(Q||P) + \ln \frac{m}{\delta}$$

$$(m-1)KL^+(\ell(Q,S)||\ell(Q,D)) \le KL(Q||P) + \ln \frac{m}{\delta}$$

# Sparse Kernel Partial Least Squares Regression

Michinari Momma[1] and Kristin P. Bennett[2]

[1] Department of Decision Sciences and Engineering Systems,
Rensselaer Polytechnic Institute, Troy NY 12180, USA
mommam@rpi.edu
[2] Department of Mathematical Sciences,
Rensselaer Polytechnic Institute, Troy NY 12180, USA
bennek@rpi.edu
http://www.rpi.edu/~bennek

**Abstract.** Partial Least Squares Regression (PLS) and its kernel version (KPLS) have become competitive regression approaches. KPLS performs as well as or better than support vector regression (SVR) for moderately-sized problems with the advantages of simple implementation, less training cost, and easier tuning of parameters. Unlike SVR, KPLS requires manipulation of the full kernel matrix and the resulting regression function requires the full training data. In this paper we rigorously derive a sparse KPLS algorithm. The underlying KPLS algorithm is modified to maintain sparsity in all steps of the algorithm. The resulting $\nu$-KPLS algorithm explicitly models centering and bias rather than using kernel centering. An $\epsilon$-insensitive loss function is used to produce sparse solutions in the dual space. The final regression function for the $\nu$-KPLS algorithm only requires a relatively small set of support vectors.

## 1   Introduction

Partial Least Squares (PLS) has proven to be a popular and effective approach to problems in chemometrics such as predicting the bioactivity of molecules in order to facilitate discovery of novel pharmaceuticals [11, 4, 2]. On such data, PLS is very resistant to overfitting, fast provided the data fit in memory, easy to implement, and relatively simple to tune. Chemometric problems frequently have training data with few points and very high dimensionality. On this type of problem, simple linear least squares regression fails, but linear PLS excels. This property makes PLS an ideal candidate for a kernel approach. Rosipal and Trejo first extended PLS to nonlinear regression using kernel functions [6].

As demonstrated in [6, 2], kernel partial least squares (KPLS) is a very effective general-purpose regression approach competitive with other support vector regression (SVR) approaches [9]. KPLS is robust and generalizes well. Another advantage of KPLS is ease of tuning of the parameters. All kernel methods depend on the choice of kernel so we discuss only the algorithm parameters. KPLS has only one integer parameter: the number of latent variables. Alternative SV regression methods have one or two continuous parameters that indicate the tradeoff between training error and capacity and define the loss function in $\epsilon$-insensitive approaches. The KPLS algorithm requires no large convex op-

B. Schölkopf and M.K. Warmuth (Eds.): COLT/Kernel 2003, LNAI 2777, pp. 216–230, 2003.

timization routines or equation solvers. The algorithm is simple and easy to implement. Readers should consult [2] for a tutorial on PLS and KPLS.

But $\epsilon$-insensitive SVR retains one great advantage over KPLS – sparsity. Any kernel method creates a kernel function of the form $f(\mathbf{x}) = \sum_{i=1}^{m} \alpha_i K(\mathbf{x}, \mathbf{x}_i)$ where $\mathbf{x}_1, \ldots, \mathbf{x}_m$ are the $m$ training points. We say that the function is sparse in the dual space if most of the kernel coefficients $\alpha_i$ are zero. Unfortunately the solution produced by KPLS is fully dense — $\alpha_i \neq 0$ for every point! This contrasts with $\epsilon$-insensitive SVR which constructs functions with only relatively few points with $\alpha_i \neq 0$ depending on the choice of $\epsilon$. These are exactly the support vectors that give the approach its name.

To achieve sparsity in KPLS is a multi-step process. KPLS constructs low-dimensional approximations of the data called latent variables which are closely related to the principal components in principal component analysis (PCA). Then these components are used in a least squares regression model. The primary difference between PLS and PCA is that the latent variables take into account the response variable. KPLS starts by centering the data to generate directions with maximum covariance and to eliminate the need for a bias term in the regression function. Then an optimization problem is solved to compute the first component. The latent variables are used to predict the response. Then the data are "deflated" to take into account the portion of the data explained by the latent variables. Centering the data, optimizing the latent variables, and deflation are all steps that result in fully dense solutions and algorithms in KPLS.

This paper revises the mathematical models underlying KPLS and derives the resulting algorithm in order to produce sparse kernel regression functions. Section 2 reviews KPLS and discusses the barriers to sparsity. Section 3 shows how to modify linear PLS to preserve sparsity and to explicitly model centering and bias thus eliminating the need for the dense kernel centering operation. In Section 4, we alter the latent variable optimization problem to use the $\epsilon$-insensitive loss and incorporate centering. As in SVR, the resulting dual optimal solution is sparse. In Section 5, we derive the final kernel version of the proposed algorithm and examine its properties. Computational results for the $\nu$-KPLS algorithm in Section 6 demonstrate $\nu$-KPLS performs as well as the dense KPLS while using fewer support vectors. We end with a discussion of the open issues in sparse KPLS and possible generalizations of the approach to other methods.

Assume we are given a training data set of size $m$ with a single response, $((\mathbf{x}_1, \mathbf{y}_1), \ldots, (\mathbf{x}_m, \mathbf{y}_m))$ $\mathbf{x}_i \in R^{n \times 1}$, $\mathbf{y}_i \in R$. Note that PLS and KPLS are applicable to multiple regression problems with $\mathbf{y}_i \in R^c$, $c > 1$. The data matrix is $\mathbf{X} = [\mathbf{x}_1, \ldots, \mathbf{x}_m]'$ and the response vector is $\mathbf{y} = [\mathbf{y}_1, \ldots, \mathbf{y}_m]'$. We assume the reader is familiar with the basics of kernel methods. $\mathbf{K}$ denotes the kernel or Gram matrix in feature space with $\mathbf{K}_{ij} = K(\mathbf{x}_i, \mathbf{x}_j)$ for a given kernel function $K$. $\|\mathbf{y}\|$ denotes the 2-norm of $\mathbf{y}$. The dot product of two column vectors $\mathbf{u}$ and $\mathbf{v}$ is denoted by $\mathbf{u}'\mathbf{v}$. The outer product of $\mathbf{u}$ and $\mathbf{v}$ is denoted by $\mathbf{u}\mathbf{v}'$. The reader should be careful to distinguish the use of dot products from that of outer products. Iteration indices are expressed as superscripts. Subscripts indicate components of a matrix or vector. diag$(\mathbf{y})$ denotes the diagonal matrix with $\mathbf{y}$ as its diagonal.

## 2   Partial Least Squares and Dense Matrix Manipulation

PLS and KPLS regression consist of four main steps. First, the data are centered. Second, latent variables based on linear projections of the data are constructed. Then the data are deflated to account for the parts of the data explained by a low-rank approximation of the data based on this projection. The first three major steps are repeated until the desired number of latent variables, $L$, is reached. Then the final regression function is constructed by minimizing the least squares error between the projected data and the response $\mathbf{y}$. Regularization is achieved by using only a small number of latent variables. The number of latent variables is the only algorithm parameter. In this process, PLS and KPLS construct low-rank approximations of $\mathbf{X}$ and $\mathbf{y}$. More specifically, PLS and KPLS construct $\mathbf{X} \approx \mathbf{T}\mathbf{P}'$ and $\mathbf{y} \approx \mathbf{T}\mathbf{C}'$ where $\mathbf{T} \in R^{m \times L}$, $\mathbf{P} \in R^{n \times L}$ and $\mathbf{C} \in R^{1 \times L}$. These low-rank approximations of the data and the response are used to solve an approximation of the least squares problem. Because the same first matrix is used for both $\mathbf{X}$ and $\mathbf{y}$, the final least squares problem is simplified. The low-rank approximations are constructed by selecting a series of orthogonal basis vectors such that reconstruction error is minimized much like in principal component analysis. Understanding PLS based on only the code is very challenging. See [2] for a tutorial and derivation of PLS and KPLS.

The original KPLS algorithm simplified to one response variable [6, 2] is given in Algorithm 1. In later parts of the paper, we will discuss details of the origins of the steps of this algorithm and how they must be modified to allow sparsity. For now let us simply examine the algorithm and consider the challenges that must be overcome in order to create a sparse version of KPLS.

**Algorithm 1 (KPLS)** *Input: kernel matrix* $\mathbf{K}$, *response variables* $\mathbf{y}$, *the number of latent variables* $L$.

1. *Center data and compute mean of response variable:* $\mu = \frac{1}{m}\mathbf{K}\mathbf{e}$, $\mathbf{K}^1 = (\mathbf{K} - \mathbf{e}\mu')(\mathbf{I} - \frac{1}{m}\mathbf{e}\mathbf{e}')$, $\tilde{\mathbf{y}} = \frac{1}{m}\mathbf{e}'\mathbf{y}$

2. $\mathbf{u}^1 = \mathbf{y} - \tilde{\mathbf{y}}$

3. *For* $i = 1$ *to* $L$

4.     *Compute latent variables:* $\mathbf{t}^i = \mathbf{K}^i\mathbf{u}^i$, $\mathbf{t}^i \leftarrow \mathbf{t}^i/\|\mathbf{t}^i\|$

5.     *Deflate:* $\mathbf{K}^{i+1} = (\mathbf{I} - \mathbf{t}^i\mathbf{t}^{i\prime})\mathbf{K}^i(\mathbf{I} - \mathbf{t}^i\mathbf{t}^{i\prime})$

6.     *Compute regression coefficients:* $\mathbf{c}^i = \mathbf{t}^{i\prime}\mathbf{u}^i$

7.     *Compute residual:* $\mathbf{u}^{i+1} = \mathbf{u}^i - \mathbf{t}^i\mathbf{c}^{i\prime}$

8. *end*

9. *Compute final regression coefficients:* $\tilde{\mathbf{g}} = \mathbf{U}\left(\mathbf{T}'\mathbf{K}^{1\prime}\mathbf{U}\right)^{-1}\mathbf{T}'\mathbf{y}$ *where the* $m^{th}$ *columns of* $\mathbf{U}$ *and* $\mathbf{T}$ *are* $\mathbf{u}^i$ *and* $\mathbf{t}^i$ *respectively.*

10. *Predict test data* $\mathbf{x}$. *First, center kernel.* *If* $\mathbf{v} = [K(\mathbf{x}, \mathbf{x}_1) - \mu_1, ..., K(\mathbf{x}, \mathbf{x}_m) - \mu_m]$, $\bar{\mathbf{v}} = \frac{1}{m}\sum_{i=1}^{m}\mathbf{v}_i$ *then the centered kernel is* $\hat{K}(\mathbf{x}, \mathbf{x}_i) = \mathbf{v}_i - \bar{\mathbf{v}}$. *Second, compute final* $f(\mathbf{x}) = \sum_{i=1}^{m}\hat{K}(\mathbf{x}, \mathbf{x}_i)\tilde{g}_i + \tilde{\mathbf{y}}$.

Several steps of KPLS require fully dense manipulation of the kernel matrix. Step 1 centers the kernel. Centering the kernel requires that the full training kernel be constructed and then modified. Step 4 computes the latent variables $\mathbf{t}^i$. Each $\mathbf{t}^i$ is a function of the full kernel matrix. Since the vectors $\mathbf{u}^i$, the error residuals, are fully dense, the resulting $\mathbf{t}^i$ is also fully dense. Thus deflation, Step 5, also requires manipulation of the full kernel matrix.

The final KPLS regression function is fully dense since the vector $\widetilde{\mathbf{g}}$ computed in Step 9 is dense. Any sparse KPLS algorithm must compute a sparse coefficient vector $\widetilde{\mathbf{g}}$. Note that the final KPLS regression function is based on the centered kernel. To compute this centered kernel, one must store all of the training data. Explicit centering of the kernel must be eliminated.

## 3   The New PLS

To construct sparse kernel functions, every step of KPLS must be altered to ensure that solutions are sparse and that sparsity is preserved. To understand what KPLS does, we move back to the primal linear PLS algorithm. Then we will make the necessary changes in the primal space and then derive the kernel algorithm. The linear PLS algorithm for one response variable is:

**Algorithm 2 (Original Linear PLS)** *Input: $\mathbf{X}$, $\mathbf{y}$, and $L$.*

1.  *Center data and compute mean of response: $\boldsymbol{\mu} = \frac{1}{m}\mathbf{X}'\mathbf{e}$, $\mathbf{X}^1 = \mathbf{X} - \mathbf{e}\boldsymbol{\mu}'$, $\tilde{\mathbf{y}} = \frac{1}{m}\mathbf{e}'\mathbf{y}$.*
2.  $\mathbf{u}^1 = \mathbf{y} - \tilde{\mathbf{y}}$
3.  *For $i = 1$ to $L$*
4.  *Compute optimal projection: $\mathbf{w}^i = \mathbf{X}^{i\prime}\mathbf{u}^i$*
5.  *Compute latent variables: $\mathbf{t}^i = \mathbf{X}^i\mathbf{w}^i$, $\mathbf{t}^i \leftarrow \mathbf{t}^i/\|\mathbf{t}^i\|$*
6.  *Deflate: $\mathbf{p}^i = \mathbf{X}^{i\prime}\mathbf{t}^i$, $\mathbf{X}^{i+1} = \mathbf{X}^i - \mathbf{t}^i\mathbf{p}^{i\prime}$*
7.  *Compute regression function:     $\mathbf{c}^i = \mathbf{u}^{i\prime}\mathbf{t}^i$*
8.  *Compute residual: $\mathbf{u}^{i+1} = \mathbf{u}^i - \mathbf{t}^i\mathbf{c}^i$*
9.  *end*
10. *Compute regression coefficients: $\mathbf{g} = \mathbf{W}\left(\mathbf{P}'\mathbf{W}\right)^{-1}\mathbf{C}'$ where $\mathbf{W}$, $\mathbf{P}$, and $\mathbf{C}$ has as their columns $\mathbf{t}^i$, $\mathbf{p}^i$, and $\mathbf{c}^i$ respectively.*
11. *Thus final prediction function is: $f(\mathbf{x}) = (\mathbf{x} - \boldsymbol{\mu})'\mathbf{g} + \tilde{\mathbf{y}}$.*

For comparison we now give the proposed linear $\nu$-PLS algorithm and then discuss how the $\nu$-PLS algorithm was derived.

**Algorithm 3 ($\nu$-PLS)** *input: data $\mathbf{X}$, response $\mathbf{y}$, and number of latent variables $L$.*

1.  *initialize $\mathbf{u}^1 = \mathbf{y}$, $\mathbf{T} = [\ ]$*
2.  *for $i = 1$ to $L$*
3.  *Compute dual optimal shifted projection: $\widehat{\boldsymbol{\alpha}}^i$ and $\widehat{\boldsymbol{\beta}}^i$ given in Section 4.*

4.    *Construct primal projection:* $\mathbf{w}^i = \mathbf{X}^{i\prime}\widehat{\boldsymbol{\alpha}}^i$, $\mathbf{w}^i = \mathbf{w}^i/\|\mathbf{w}^i\|$.

5.    *Compute* $\mathbf{s}^i$ *and shift data:* $\mathbf{s}^i = \mathbf{X}^{i\prime}\widehat{\boldsymbol{\beta}}^i$, $\widetilde{\mathbf{X}}^i = \mathbf{X}^i - \mathbf{e}\mathbf{s}^{i\prime}$.

6.    *Compute latent variable:* $\mathbf{t}^i = \widetilde{\mathbf{X}}^i\mathbf{w}^i$, $\tau_i = \|\mathbf{t}^i\|$, $\mathbf{t}^i \leftarrow \mathbf{t}^i/\tau_i$, $\mathbf{T} = [\mathbf{T} \ \ \mathbf{t}^i]$.

7.    *Deflate:* $\mathbf{X}^{i+1} = \widetilde{\mathbf{X}}^i(\mathbf{I} - \mathbf{w}^i\mathbf{w}^{i\prime})$

8.    *Compute regression function:* $\mathbf{C}, \gamma_y = \mathrm{argmin}_{\mathbf{C},\gamma_y}\|\mathbf{u}^1 - \mathbf{T}\mathbf{C}' - \gamma_y\mathbf{e}\|^2$

9.    *Compute residual:* $\mathbf{u}^{i+1} = \mathbf{u}^1 - \mathbf{T}\mathbf{C}' - \gamma_y\mathbf{e}$

10.   *end*

11.   *Compute regression coefficients:* $\mathbf{g} = \mathbf{W}\mathrm{diag}(\boldsymbol{\tau})^{-1}\mathbf{C}'$.

12.   *Prediction functions:* $f(\mathbf{x}) = (\mathbf{x}' - \sum_{i=1}^{L}\mathbf{s}^{i\prime})\mathbf{g} + \gamma_y = \mathbf{x}'\mathbf{g} + \gamma$ *with*

$$\gamma = -\mathbf{e}'\mathbf{S}'\mathbf{g} + \gamma_y \ \text{ where } \ \mathbf{S} = [\mathbf{s}^1, \ldots, \mathbf{s}^L].$$

Recall that centering the data and computation of $\mathbf{w}^i$ made the original KPLS algorithm fully dense. We tackle the issues of centering the data in this section and leave details on sparsifying the computation of $\mathbf{w}^i$ (Step 3) to the next section. First, we must eliminate centering of the kernel matrix, Step 1 of Algorithm 2. Centering in PLS eliminates the need to consider bias in the model. The original PLS fits linear models of the form, $f(\mathbf{x}_i) = \mathbf{x}_i'\mathbf{w}$ where $\mathbf{w} \in R^n$. By fitting linear models with a threshold $\gamma \in R$: $f(\mathbf{x}_i) = \mathbf{x}_i'\mathbf{w} - \gamma$, we can eliminate Steps 1 and 2. But the ramifications of this change on the other steps of the algorithms are quite profound.

Steps 4-7 of PLS compute an optimal projection of the data and then use this projection as the basis of a low-rank approximation of the input data and response. More specifically, these steps first construct the linear projection of the data as represented by the projection vector $\mathbf{w}^i$. The distance from the origin to the projection of each data point $\mathbf{x}_j$ onto $\mathbf{w}^i$ is known as the scalar latent variable $t_j^i$. The latent variables at each iteration, $\mathbf{t}^i$, are part of a factorization of $\mathbf{X}$, $\mathbf{X} \approx \mathbf{T}\mathbf{P}'$. In a process much like an ensemble algorithm, the derived features $\mathbf{t}^i$ are constructed such that the residual responses, $\mathbf{u}^i$, are "well explained" by a weak model. The next section describes in detail how the $\mathbf{w}^i$ are selected. The latent variables are used to construct a linear least squares regression model such that $\mathbf{C} = \mathrm{argmin}_{\mathbf{C}}\|\mathbf{T}\mathbf{C}' - \mathbf{y}\|^2$. By construction, the latent variables $\mathbf{T}$ are orthonormal. Thus, $\mathbf{C}$ can be computed component-wise in Step 7 as the latent variables are constructed. At the end, $\mathbf{T}$ and $\mathbf{C}$ form a low-rank factorization of the response: $\mathbf{y} \approx \mathbf{T}\mathbf{C}'$.

Since the input data are not centered, $\nu$-PLS allows for shifts in the data and allows for bias in the regression function. Let $\mathbf{e}_m$ and $\mathbf{e}_L$ be vectors of ones of dimension $m$ and $L$ respectively. We define a shifted low-rank approximation by introducing $\mathbf{S} \in R^{n \times L}$ such that at the end of the algorithm $\mathbf{X} \approx \mathbf{T}\mathbf{P}' + \mathbf{e}_m\mathbf{e}_L'\mathbf{S}'$ with the accuracy depending on the size of $L$. Similarly, define $\gamma_y \in R$ as the bias term in the model for approximating the response, $\mathbf{y} \approx \mathbf{T}\mathbf{C}' + \mathbf{e}_m\gamma_y$. $\mathbf{S}$ has as its columns the constant shift in input space, $\mathbf{s}^i$, required for each latent variable $\mathbf{t}^i$. Since $\mathbf{t}^i = \widetilde{\mathbf{X}}^i\mathbf{w}^i/\tau_i$, where we define $\widetilde{\mathbf{X}}^i = \mathbf{X}^i - \mathbf{e}\mathbf{s}^{i\prime}$, Step 4 in PLS must be replaced by some operation that appropriately constructs the best projection of the data $\mathbf{w}^i = \mathbf{X}^{i'}\widehat{\boldsymbol{\alpha}}^i$ and shift of the data $\mathbf{s}^i = \mathbf{X}^{i'}\widehat{\boldsymbol{\beta}}^i$. Note that in the original PLS algorithm, $\widehat{\boldsymbol{\alpha}}^i = \mathbf{u}^i/m$ and $\widehat{\boldsymbol{\beta}}^i = \mathbf{e}_m/m$. So $\mathbf{s}^i = 0$ since the data have been centered. In Section 4, we show that $\widehat{\boldsymbol{\alpha}}^i$ and $\widehat{\boldsymbol{\beta}}^i$ are the dual optimal solutions of a problem that constructs an optimal low-rank representation based on $\mathbf{w}^i$ and $\mathbf{s}^i$ of the input data. Both $\widehat{\boldsymbol{\alpha}}^i$ and $\widehat{\boldsymbol{\beta}}^i$ are sparse with identical support vectors. For now assume that such an $\widehat{\boldsymbol{\alpha}}^i$ and $\widehat{\boldsymbol{\beta}}^i$ can be constructed.

Step 5 of original PLS computes the latent variable for the centered data. In $\nu$-PLS we first shift the data by $\mathbf{s}^i$ and then compute the latent variables. The $\mathbf{s}^i$ are sparse (in the dual sense) approximations of the mean of $\mathbf{X}^i$. Thus Steps 5 and 6 in Algorithm 3 shift the data and compute the $i^{th}$ latent variable.

Step 6 of PLS deflates the data by removing the current low-rank approximation. PLS multiplies the data by the dense vector $\mathbf{t}^i$ to compute $\mathbf{p}^i$ and then deflates using $\mathbf{t}^i\mathbf{p}^{i'}$. This operation destroys sparsity in the dual space. In PLS, the best approximation of $\mathbf{X}^i$ for a fixed $\mathbf{t}^i$ is the $\mathbf{p}^{i'}$ calculated in Step 6 that solves the following problem with $\|\mathbf{A}\|_F^2$ defined as $\sum_{i,j} \mathbf{A}_{ij}^2$: $\min_{\mathbf{p}} \|\mathbf{X}^i - \mathbf{t}^i\mathbf{p}^{i'}\|_F^2$.

Deflation in $\nu$-PLS preserves sparsity by changing the low-rank approximation to be based on $\mathbf{w}^i$ instead of $\mathbf{t}^i$. The vector $\mathbf{t}^i = \mathbf{X}^i\mathbf{w}^i$ is the optimal solution of $\min_{\mathbf{t}} \|\mathbf{X}^i - \mathbf{es}^{i'} - \mathbf{tw}^{i'}\|^2$. Thus deflation becomes $\mathbf{X}^{i+1} = \widetilde{\mathbf{X}}^i - \mathbf{t}^i\mathbf{w}^{i'} = \widetilde{\mathbf{X}}^i(\mathbf{I} - \mathbf{w}^i\mathbf{w}^{i'})$. For numerical robustness, we rescale $\mathbf{t}^i$ to have unit length by dividing by $\tau_i$. Thus $\mathbf{p}^i = \tau^i\mathbf{w}^i$, or $\mathbf{P} = \mathbf{W}\mathrm{diag}(\boldsymbol{\tau})$ so that the factorization is well defined. These $\mathbf{p}^i$ need not be stored explicitly.

Both the linear PLS and $\nu$-PLS have the property that the projection vectors $\mathbf{w}^i$ are orthogonal, i.e. $\mathbf{w}^{i'}\mathbf{w}^j = 0$ for $i \neq j$. The original PLS also has the property that the $\mathbf{t}^i$ are orthogonal. Unfortunately, the orthogonality of $\mathbf{t}^i$ is not preserved in $\nu$-PLS. Thus additional changes are required in the subsequent steps of $\nu$-PLS. Although in practice we observe that very few of the latent variables have significant correlation with each other, sparse deflation that preserves orthogonality of $\mathbf{t}^i$ would be preferred both for computation and generalization.

In PLS, the residual, $\mathbf{u}^i$, is reduced by the current prediction of the response in Steps 7 and 8. PLS does not solve this problem in the original space, but rather in the space of the latent variables $\mathbf{t}^i$. These steps must be altered to take into account the new biased model and the fact that the $\mathbf{t}^i$ are no longer orthonormal. Let the matrix $\mathbf{T}$ have as its columns all the latent variables, $\mathbf{t}^i$, constructed so far. In PLS, the best current least squares model for the current set of latent variables is selected by solving the optimization problem: $\min_{\mathbf{C}} \|\mathbf{u}^1 - \mathbf{TC}'\|$ where $\mathbf{u}^1 = \mathbf{y}$. This implies $\mathbf{C}' = (\mathbf{T}'\mathbf{T})^{-1}\mathbf{T}'\mathbf{u}^1$. Because $\mathbf{T}$ is orthonormal, this reduces to Steps 7 and 8 in PLS. In $\nu$-PLS, we introduce the bias term $\gamma_y$ to yield: $\min_{\mathbf{C},\gamma_y} \|\mathbf{u}^1 - \mathbf{TC}' - \gamma_y\mathbf{e}\|^2$. If we use the usual trick of defining $\widehat{\mathbf{T}} = [\mathbf{T}\ \mathbf{e}]$ then $\begin{bmatrix} \mathbf{C}' \\ \gamma_y \end{bmatrix} = (\widehat{\mathbf{T}}'\widehat{\mathbf{T}})^{-1}\widehat{\mathbf{T}}\mathbf{u}^1$. Typically $\mathbf{C}$ and $\gamma_y$ can be calculated very efficiently since $\widehat{\mathbf{T}}$ only has $i \leq L$ rows and $L$ is small.

These steps are repeated until the desired number of latent variables is reached. The final step is to compute the coefficients of the regression functions. The original PLS algorithm by this point has constructed low-rank approximations of the data $\mathbf{X} \approx \mathbf{TP}'$ and the response $\mathbf{y} \approx \mathbf{TC}'$. In Step 10, PLS uses these approximations instead of the original variables to construct the final least squares model. The original PLS recomputes the latent variables by multiplying $\mathbf{TP}'$ by $\mathbf{W}$ and then fits the least squares model. Thus in original PLS the final least squares regression problem is: construct $\mathbf{v}$ such that

$$\min_{\mathbf{v}} ||\mathbf{TC}' - (\mathbf{TP}')\mathbf{Wv}||^2 \;=\; \min_{\mathbf{v}} ||\mathbf{T}(\mathbf{C}' - \mathbf{P}'\mathbf{Wv})||^2 \tag{1}$$

Since $\mathbf{T}$ is orthogonal and $\mathbf{P}'\mathbf{W}$ is an invertible matrix, $\mathbf{v} = (\mathbf{P}'\mathbf{W})^{-1}\mathbf{C}'$. The final regression coefficients must be used in the original space so they become $\mathbf{g} = \mathbf{Wv} = \mathbf{W}(\mathbf{P}'\mathbf{W})^{-1}\mathbf{C}'$.

$\nu$-PLS constructs shifted low-rank approximations of the data $\mathbf{X} \approx \mathbf{TP}' + \mathbf{e}_m\mathbf{e}'_L\mathbf{S}'$ and the response $\mathbf{y} \approx \mathbf{TC}' + \gamma_y\mathbf{e}_m$. Using these approximations and a model with bias $\psi$, Problem 1 becomes the following for $\nu$-PLS:

$$\min_{\mathbf{v},\psi} ||(\mathbf{TC}' + \gamma_y\mathbf{e}_m) - (\mathbf{TP}' + \mathbf{e}_m\mathbf{e}'_L\mathbf{S}')\mathbf{Wv} - \psi\mathbf{e}_m||^2 \tag{2}$$

The optimal solution is $\mathbf{v} = (\mathbf{P}'\mathbf{W})^{-1}\mathbf{C}'$ and $\psi = \gamma_y - \mathbf{e}'_L\mathbf{S}'\mathbf{Wv}$ since the objective function equals its lower bound 0. Thus $\mathbf{g} = \mathbf{W}(\mathbf{P}'\mathbf{W})^{-1}\mathbf{C}' = \mathbf{W}\mathrm{diag}(\tau)^{-1}\mathbf{C}'$ since $\mathbf{P} = \mathbf{W}\mathrm{diag}(\tau)$ and $\mathbf{W}$ is orthonormal. Thus our prediction for a point $\mathbf{x}$ is $\hat{\mathbf{y}} = (\mathbf{x} - \mathbf{Se})'\mathbf{g} + \gamma_y = \mathbf{x}'\mathbf{g} + \gamma$, where $\gamma = -\mathbf{e}'\mathbf{S}'\mathbf{g} + \gamma_y$.

## 4  Computing Projection

In this section we discuss the issue of how to compute Step 3 of $\nu$-PLS and the kernel version Algorithm 4 given in the next section. The goal of Step 3 is to compute a shift and projection of the data that are sparse in the dual sense and work well for regression. $\nu$-PLS computes the projection $\mathbf{w}^i = \mathbf{X}^{i'}\hat{\alpha}^i$ and shift $\mathbf{s}^i = \mathbf{X}^{i'}\hat{\beta}^i$ vectors. If the $\hat{\alpha}^i$ and $\hat{\beta}^i$ are sparse at each iteration of $\nu$-PLS then the final regression function will not include any additional support vectors.

The original PLS picks the projection by maximizing the covariance between $\mathbf{X}^i\mathbf{w}$ and $\mathbf{u}^i$, i.e. $\max_{\mathbf{w}} \; cov(\mathbf{X}^i\mathbf{w}, \mathbf{u}^i) \;\; s.t. \;\; ||\mathbf{w}||^2 = 1$. Recall that the original PLS assumes that the data are centered and the response is normalized. Thus as shown in [2], this is equivalent to solving $\min_{\mathbf{w}} \sum_{i=1}^{L} ||\mathbf{x}_i - u_i\mathbf{w}||^2$ with $\mathbf{x}'_i = \mathbf{X}^j_i$ and $u_i = \mathbf{u}^j_i$, and $||\mathbf{w}||^2 = 1$. This optimal solution can be computed in closed form $\mathbf{w}^i = \mathbf{X}^{i'}\mathbf{u}^i/\mathbf{u}^{i'}\mathbf{X}^i\mathbf{X}^{i'}\mathbf{u}^i$ – a dense solution in the dual space.

We now redefine this problem to remove the assumptions that the data are centered and that the optimal solution is sparse in the dual space. To center the data we can simply introduce the shift vector $\mathbf{s}$. The revised problem becomes

$$\min_{\mathbf{w},\mathbf{s}} \sum_{i=1}^{L} ||\mathbf{x}_i - \mathbf{s} - u_i\mathbf{w}||^2. \tag{3}$$

If Problem 3 is applied to centered data, then $\mathbf{s} = 0$ and $\mathbf{w}$ is optimal for the original PLS problem.

To introduce dual sparsity, we use the $\epsilon$-insensitive loss function in the objective of Problem 3. A similar loss function has been used in support vector regression to produce sparse kernel regression functions that generalize well [9]. Since it is difficult to specify a fixed value of $\epsilon$, we make $\epsilon$ a variable of the problem and instead specify the desired degree of sparsity $\nu \in [0,1]$ as a parameter of the problem. Since the resulting approach is closely related to $\nu$-support-vector regression, which explicitly shrinks the regression tube [8], the algorithm is called $\nu$-PLS. The primal form of the $\nu$-PLS optimization problem is:

$$\min_{\mathbf{w,s},\xi,\epsilon} \frac{1}{\nu m} \sum_i \xi_i + \epsilon$$
$$\text{s.t.} \quad \frac{1}{2}||\mathbf{x}_i - \mathbf{s} - u_i\mathbf{w}||^2 - \xi_i \leq \epsilon, \qquad \xi_i \geq 0, \quad i = 1, \ldots, m \tag{4}$$

The dual optimization problem is constructed by adding a Lagrangian multiplier $\alpha_i$ for each of the data constraints and $v_i$ for each nonnegativity constraint. The dual problem maximizes the Lagrangian function:

$$L(\mathbf{w,s},\xi,\epsilon,\boldsymbol{\alpha},\mathbf{v}) = \frac{1}{\nu m}\sum_i \xi_i + \epsilon + \sum_i \alpha_i(\frac{1}{2}||\mathbf{x}_i - \mathbf{s} - u_i\mathbf{w}||^2 - \xi_i - \epsilon) - \sum_i v_i\xi_i \tag{5}$$

subject to the constraints that the multipliers are nonnegative, $\boldsymbol{\alpha}, \mathbf{v} \geq 0$, and that the Lagrangian derivatives with respect to the primal variables are zero:

$$\nabla_{\mathbf{w}} L(\mathbf{w,s},\xi,\epsilon,\boldsymbol{\alpha},\mathbf{v}) = -\sum_i \alpha_i u_i(\mathbf{x}_i - \mathbf{s} - u_i\mathbf{w}) = 0$$
$$\nabla_{\mathbf{s}} L(\mathbf{w,s},\xi,\epsilon,\boldsymbol{\alpha},\mathbf{v}) = -\sum_i \alpha_i(\mathbf{x}_i - \mathbf{s} - u_i\mathbf{w}) = 0$$
$$\nabla_{\epsilon} L(\mathbf{w,s},\xi,\epsilon,\boldsymbol{\alpha},\mathbf{v}) = 1 - \sum_i \alpha_i = 0$$
$$\nabla_{\xi} L(\mathbf{w,s},\xi,\epsilon,\boldsymbol{\alpha},\mathbf{v}) = \frac{1}{\nu m}\mathbf{e} - \boldsymbol{\alpha} - \mathbf{v} = 0$$

The primal variables can be simplified and then eliminated from the problem. If we define $\delta_\alpha = \sum_i u_i^2\alpha_i - (\sum_i u_i\alpha_i)^2$, then we get

$$\mathbf{w} = \left(\sum_i u_i\alpha_i\mathbf{x}_i - (\sum_j u_j\alpha_j)\sum_i \alpha_i\mathbf{x}_i\right)/\delta_\alpha$$
$$\mathbf{s} = \sum_i \alpha_i\mathbf{x}_i - (\sum_j u_j\alpha_j)\left[\sum_i u_i\alpha_i\mathbf{x}_i - (\sum_q u_q\alpha_q)\sum_i \alpha_i\mathbf{x}_i\right]/\delta_\alpha.$$

After substitution for $\mathbf{w}$ and $\mathbf{s}$ the final dual objective function becomes

$$\min_{\boldsymbol{\alpha}} \sum_i \alpha_i\mathbf{x}_i'\mathbf{x}_i$$
$$- \frac{[(\sum_q \alpha_q u_q^2)\sum_{ij}\alpha_i\alpha_j\mathbf{x}_i'\mathbf{x}_j + \sum_{ij}\alpha_i\alpha_j u_i u_j\mathbf{x}_i'\mathbf{x}_j - 2(\sum_q \alpha_q u_q)\sum_{ij}\alpha_i\alpha_j u_i\mathbf{x}_i'\mathbf{x}_j]}{\sum_i u_i^2\alpha_i - (\sum_i u_i\alpha_i)^2}$$
$$\text{s.t.} \quad \sum_i \alpha_i = 1, \quad \frac{1}{\nu m} \geq \alpha_i \geq 0, \quad i = 1, \ldots, m \tag{6}$$

This problem has a convex nonlinear objective with simple linear constraints. The data only appear in inner products so the formulation can be used in feature space by simply substituting kernel functions for the inner products. At the jth iteration, the optimal primal variables are $\mathbf{w}^j = \mathbf{X}^{j\prime}\widehat{\boldsymbol{\alpha}}^j$ and $\mathbf{s}^j = \mathbf{X}^{j\prime}\widehat{\boldsymbol{\beta}}^j$ with

$$\widehat{\boldsymbol{\alpha}}^j = \frac{\text{diag}(\mathbf{u}^j)\boldsymbol{\alpha} - (\mathbf{u}^{j\prime}\boldsymbol{\alpha})\boldsymbol{\alpha}}{\delta_\alpha} \qquad \widehat{\boldsymbol{\beta}}^j = \boldsymbol{\alpha} - (\mathbf{u}^{j\prime}\boldsymbol{\alpha})\widehat{\boldsymbol{\alpha}}^j \tag{7}$$

where $\boldsymbol{\alpha}$ solves Problem 6 with $u_i = \mathbf{u}_i^j$ and $\mathbf{x}_i' = \mathbf{X}_i^j$. Clearly $\hat{\beta}_i \neq 0$ implies $\hat{\alpha}_i \neq 0$, so $\mathbf{s}$ does not require any support vectors other than those required for $\mathbf{w}$. From the dual constraints in Problem 6, the number of support vectors is bounded below by $\nu m$. By complementarity, the number of points with reconstruction error $||\mathbf{x}_i - \mathbf{s} - u_i \mathbf{w}||^2$ strictly greater than $\epsilon$, or equivalently $\alpha_i = \frac{1}{\nu m}$, will be at most $\nu$ fraction of the data.

The price of sparsity is additional computational cost in Step 3. For the fully dense case, $\nu = 1$, the only feasible solution is $\alpha_i = \frac{1}{m}$. For $\nu < 1$, Problem 6 can be solved using any of the many general purpose methods for nonlinear programming with linear equality constraints. For this paper, we simply used the FMINCON function in the MATLAB Optimization Toolbox. Problem 6 is closely related to quadratic SVR, thus it is likely that special purpose algorithms similar to the SMO algorithm [5] can be defined that exploit the structure of the problem and that do not require manipulation of the full kernel matrix. Of course for $\nu < 1$ the computational cost will always be more expensive than the closed form solution for the original PLS and KPLS algorithms since the algorithm must effectively search for appropriate support vectors.

## 5    The New Kernel PLS

In this section we derive the kernel version of the $\nu$-PLS algorithm. If all references to the matrix $\mathbf{X}$ are in the form of inner products $\mathbf{XX}'$ then these inner products can be replaced by the equivalent Kernel or Gram matrix $\mathbf{K}$ with $\mathbf{K}_{i,j} = K(\mathbf{x}_i, \mathbf{x}_j)$ for some appropriate kernel function [9]. This effectively maps the data (usually nonlinearly) to a feature space and the linear PLS constructs a linear function in feature space that corresponds to a nonlinear regression function in the original space. We assume the reader is familiar with this now-standard practice for kernel methods and the reader should consult [9] for more details. The kernel $\nu$-KPLS algorithm is as follows:

**Algorithm 4 ($\nu$-KPLS)** *Input: kernel matrix* $\mathbf{K}$, *response variable* $\mathbf{y}$, *and number of latent variables* $L$.

1. *Initialize* $\mathbf{u}^1 = \mathbf{y}$, $\mathbf{K}^1 = \mathbf{K}$, $\mathbf{T} = [\ ]$
2. *for* $i = 1$ *to* $L$
3.     *Compute dual optimal shifted projection:* $\widehat{\boldsymbol{\alpha}}^i$ *and* $\widehat{\boldsymbol{\beta}}^i$ *given in Section 4.*
4.     *Compute latent variables:* $\mathbf{t}^i = \left(\mathbf{I} - \mathbf{e}\widehat{\boldsymbol{\beta}}^{i\prime}\right) \mathbf{K}^i \widehat{\boldsymbol{\alpha}}^i$, $\tau_i = ||\mathbf{t}^i||$, $\mathbf{t}^i = \mathbf{t}^i/\tau_i$,
    $\mathbf{T} = [\mathbf{T}\ \ \mathbf{t}^i]$.
5.     *Deflate:* $r^i = \sqrt{\widehat{\boldsymbol{\alpha}}^{i\prime}\mathbf{K}^i\widehat{\boldsymbol{\alpha}}^i}$,

$$\mathbf{K}^{i+1} = \left(\mathbf{I} - \mathbf{e}\widehat{\boldsymbol{\beta}}^{i\prime}\right) \mathbf{K}^i \left(\mathbf{I} - \widehat{\boldsymbol{\beta}}^i \mathbf{e}'\right) - \left(\frac{\tau_i}{r_i}\right)^2 \mathbf{t}^i \mathbf{t}^{i\prime}.$$

6.     *Compute regression function:* $\begin{bmatrix} \mathbf{C}' \\ \gamma_y \end{bmatrix} = ([\mathbf{T}\ \ \mathbf{e}]'[\mathbf{T}\ \ \mathbf{e}])^{-1}[\mathbf{T}\ \ \mathbf{e}]'\mathbf{u}^1.$

7.    *Compute residual:* $\mathbf{u}^{i+1} = \mathbf{u}^i - \mathbf{T}\mathbf{C}' - \gamma_y \mathbf{e}$

8.  *end*

9.  *Compute* $\mathbf{A}$ *and* $\mathbf{B}$ *such that* $\mathbf{w}^i = \mathbf{X}^{1\prime}\mathbf{a}^i$ *and* $\mathbf{s}^i = \mathbf{X}^{1\prime}\mathbf{b}^i$

10. *Compute regression coefficients and bias:*

$$\widetilde{\mathbf{g}} = \mathbf{A}\,\mathrm{diag}(\boldsymbol{\tau})^{-1}\mathbf{C}', \qquad \gamma = -\mathbf{e}'\mathbf{B}'\mathbf{K}^1\mathbf{A}\,\mathrm{diag}(\boldsymbol{\tau})^{-1}\mathbf{C}' + \gamma_y$$

11. *Prediction function is:* $f(\mathbf{x}) = \sum_i K(\mathbf{x}, \mathbf{x}_i)\widetilde{g}_i + \gamma.$

## 5.1   Kernel Algorithm Derivation

The primal variables $\mathbf{X}^i$, $\mathbf{w}^i$, $\mathbf{s}^i$ in Algorithm 3 must be expressed in terms of dual variables $\widehat{\boldsymbol{\alpha}}^i$ and $\widehat{\boldsymbol{\beta}}^i$ computed by solving Problem 6 and computing Equation (7). In order to avoid direct reference to $\mathbf{w}^i$ and $\mathbf{s}^i$ and to express all reference to the data as inner products, Steps 4-6 of Algorithm 3 are condensed into one operation much as in the original KPLS. By using relations $\widetilde{\mathbf{X}}^i = \mathbf{X}^i - \mathbf{e}\mathbf{s}^{i\prime}$, $\mathbf{s}^i = \mathbf{X}^{i\prime}\widehat{\boldsymbol{\beta}}^i$, and $\mathbf{w}^i = \mathbf{X}^{i\prime}\widehat{\boldsymbol{\alpha}}^i$, $\mathbf{t}^i$ becomes $\widetilde{\mathbf{X}}^i\mathbf{w}^i/\tau_i = \left(\mathbf{X}^i - \mathbf{e}\widehat{\boldsymbol{\beta}}^{i\prime}\mathbf{X}^i\right)\mathbf{X}^{i\prime}\widehat{\boldsymbol{\alpha}}^i/\tau_i,$ or equivalently $\mathbf{t}^i = \left(\mathbf{I} - \mathbf{e}\widehat{\boldsymbol{\beta}}^{i\prime}\right)\mathbf{K}^i\widehat{\boldsymbol{\alpha}}^i/\tau_i$ after nonlinear transformation, where $\tau_i$ is the normalization factor which is defined to be $\left\|\left(\mathbf{I} - \mathbf{e}\widehat{\boldsymbol{\beta}}^{i\prime}\right)\mathbf{K}^i\right\|.$

Deflation of the data matrix in Step 5 of Algorithm 4 is replaced by deflation of the kernel matrix $\mathbf{K}^i$. In the primal, we have $\mathbf{X}^{i+1} = \widetilde{\mathbf{X}}^i\left(\mathbf{I} - \mathbf{w}^i\mathbf{w}^{i\prime}/r_i^2\right),$ where $r^i$ is the norm of $\mathbf{w}^i$, $r^i = \|\mathbf{w}^i\| = \sqrt{\widehat{\boldsymbol{\alpha}}^{i\prime}\mathbf{X}^i\mathbf{X}^{i\prime}\widehat{\boldsymbol{\alpha}}^i}$. The deflation becomes:

$$\mathbf{X}^{i+1}\mathbf{X}^{i+1\prime} = \widetilde{\mathbf{X}}^i\left(\mathbf{I} - \mathbf{w}^i\mathbf{w}^{i\prime}/r_i^2\right)\widetilde{\mathbf{X}}^{i\prime} = \widetilde{\mathbf{X}}^i\widetilde{\mathbf{X}}^{i\prime} - \left(\frac{\tau_i}{r_i}\right)^2\mathbf{t}^i\mathbf{t}^{i\prime}$$

$$= \left(\mathbf{I} - \mathbf{e}\widehat{\boldsymbol{\beta}}^{i\prime}\right)\mathbf{X}^i\mathbf{X}^{i\prime}\left(\mathbf{I} - \widehat{\boldsymbol{\beta}}^i\mathbf{e}'\right) - \left(\frac{\tau_i}{r_i}\right)^2\mathbf{t}^i\mathbf{t}^{i\prime}.$$

Therefore, we deflate the kernel matrix in the following way:

$$\mathbf{K}^{i+1} = \left(\mathbf{I} - \mathbf{e}\widehat{\boldsymbol{\beta}}^{i\prime}\right)\mathbf{K}^i\left(\mathbf{I} - \widehat{\boldsymbol{\beta}}^i\mathbf{e}'\right) - \left(\frac{\tau_i}{r_i}\right)^2\mathbf{t}^i\mathbf{t}^{i\prime}. \tag{8}$$

Due to the deflation of the kernel matrix, the calculations required to predict new data points, Steps 9 and 10, are much more challenging. Step 9 translates operations performed on the deflated matrix to operations on the original kernel matrix and these are used to predict new points in Step 10. The derivations of Steps 9 and 10 are given in the next section. Section 5.3 gives theorems proving properties of the algorithm needed to support the derivations of Steps 9 and 10.

## 5.2   Prediction of New Data

Now, we derive the formula for predicting a new point by rewriting the primal variables in terms of inner products of the data followed by the nonlinear feature mapping. In the primal of linear $\nu$-PLS, we have $\hat{y} = (\mathbf{x} - \mathbf{Se})'\mathbf{g} + \gamma_y$ where $\mathbf{g} = \mathbf{W}\text{diag}(\tau)^{-1}\mathbf{C}'$. At each iteration, $\nu$-PLS constructs $\mathbf{W}$ and $\mathbf{S}$ using the deflated kernel matrix. $\mathbf{W}$ and $\mathbf{S}$ must be expressed in terms of the original matrix $\mathbf{X}^1$ in order to avoid computing deflation each time we predict test data. We define matrices $\mathbf{A}$ and $\mathbf{B}$ such that $\mathbf{W} = \mathbf{X}^{1'}\mathbf{A}$ and $\mathbf{S} = \mathbf{X}^{1'}\mathbf{B}$. Theorems 1 and 2 in the next section give formulas for $\mathbf{A}$ and $\mathbf{B}$. Once $\mathbf{A}$ and $\mathbf{B}$ are calculated, the regression coefficient and bias become $\mathbf{g} = \mathbf{W}\text{diag}(\tau)^{-1}\mathbf{C}' = \mathbf{X}^{1'}\mathbf{A}\text{diag}(\tau)^{-1}\mathbf{C}'$ and $\mathbf{e}'\mathbf{S}'\mathbf{g} = \mathbf{e}'\mathbf{B}'\mathbf{X}^1\mathbf{X}^{1'}\mathbf{A}$. Prediction for test data is:

$$
\begin{aligned}
f(\mathbf{x}) &= (\mathbf{x} - \mathbf{Se})'\mathbf{g} + \gamma_y \\
&= (\mathbf{x} - \mathbf{X}^{1'}\mathbf{Be})'\mathbf{W}\text{diag}(\tau)^{-1}\mathbf{C}' + \gamma_y \\
&= (\mathbf{x} - \mathbf{X}^{1'}\mathbf{Be})'\mathbf{X}^{1'}\mathbf{A}\text{diag}(\tau)^{-1}\mathbf{C}' + \gamma_y \\
&= \mathbf{x}'\mathbf{X}^{1'}\mathbf{A}\text{diag}(\tau)^{-1}\mathbf{C}' - \mathbf{e}'\mathbf{B}'\mathbf{X}^1\mathbf{X}^{1'}\mathbf{A}\text{diag}(\tau)^{-1}\mathbf{C}' + \gamma_y \\
&= \mathbf{x}'\mathbf{X}^{1'}\tilde{\mathbf{g}} + \gamma,
\end{aligned} \tag{9}
$$

where $\tilde{\mathbf{g}} = \mathbf{A}\text{diag}(\tau)^{-1}\mathbf{C}'$ and $\gamma = -\mathbf{e}'\mathbf{B}'\mathbf{X}^1\mathbf{X}^{1'}\mathbf{A}\text{diag}(\tau)^{-1}\mathbf{C}' + \gamma_y$. Therefore, the final kernel function for a given kernel $K$ is $f(\mathbf{x}) = \sum_{i=1}^m K(\mathbf{x}, \mathbf{x}_i)\tilde{g}_i + \gamma$ where $\gamma$ is obtained by $\gamma = -\mathbf{e}'\mathbf{B}'\mathbf{K}^1\mathbf{A}\text{diag}(\tau)^{-1}\mathbf{C}' + \gamma_y$.

## 5.3　Properties of the Algorithm

In this section we provide the theorems to support the above derivation and to illuminate properties of $\nu$-PLS and $\nu$-KPLS. The first two theorems were used above to simplify calculation of the final prediction function.

**Theorem 1 (Representation of deflated matrices).** *The relationship between the original and deflated matrices for $\nu$-PLS is:*

$$
\begin{aligned}
\mathbf{X}^i &= \mathbf{X}^1 - \mathbf{e}\sum_{j=1}^{i-1}\mathbf{s}^{j'} - \sum_{j=1}^{i-1}\left(\frac{\tau_j}{r_j^2}\right)\mathbf{t}^j\mathbf{w}^{j'} \\
&= \mathbf{X}^1 - \mathbf{e}\sum_{j=1}^{i-1}\hat{\beta}^{j'}\mathbf{X}^j - \sum_{j=1}^{i-1}\left(\frac{\tau_j}{r_j^2}\right)\mathbf{t}^j\hat{\alpha}^{j'}\mathbf{X}^j.
\end{aligned} \tag{10}
$$

*Proof.* For $i = 1$ and $i = 2$, the equality holds. Assume it holds for $i = k$.

$$
\begin{aligned}
\mathbf{X}^{k+1} &= \tilde{\mathbf{X}}^k\left(\mathbf{I} - \mathbf{w}^k\mathbf{w}^{k'}/r_k^2\right) \\
&= \mathbf{X}^k - \mathbf{e}\mathbf{s}^{k'} - \left(\frac{\tau_k}{r_k^2}\right)\mathbf{t}^k\mathbf{w}^{k'} \quad \text{by assumption} \\
&= \mathbf{X}^1 - \mathbf{e}\sum_{l=1}^k\mathbf{s}^{l'} - \sum_{l=1}^k\left(\frac{\tau_l}{r_l^2}\right)\mathbf{t}^l\mathbf{w}^{l'}.
\end{aligned} \tag{11}
$$

The second part of the equality follows by using $\mathbf{s}^i = \mathbf{X}^{i'}\hat{\beta}^i$ and $\mathbf{w}^i = \mathbf{X}^{i'}\hat{\alpha}^i$. □

**Theorem 2 (Representation of W and S).** *In Algorithms 3 and 4, the primal variables* $\mathbf{w}^i$ *and* $\mathbf{s}^i$ *can be written in terms of the original matrix:*

$$\mathbf{w}^i = \mathbf{X}^{i\prime}\widehat{\boldsymbol{\alpha}}^i = \mathbf{X}^{1\prime}\mathbf{a}^i \quad \text{and} \quad \mathbf{s}^i = \mathbf{X}^{i\prime}\widehat{\boldsymbol{\beta}}^i = \mathbf{X}^{1\prime}\mathbf{b}^i, \tag{12}$$

*where* $\mathbf{a}^i$ *and* $\mathbf{b}^i$ *are given by*

$$\mathbf{a}^i = \left(\mathbf{I} - \sum_{j=1}^{i-1} \mathbf{b}^j \mathbf{e}' - \sum_{j=1}^{i-1} \left(\frac{T_j}{r_j^2}\right) \mathbf{a}^j \mathbf{t}^{j\prime}\right)\widehat{\boldsymbol{\alpha}}^i,$$

$$\mathbf{b}^i = \left(\mathbf{I} - \sum_{j=1}^{i-1} \mathbf{b}^j \mathbf{e}' - \sum_{j=1}^{i-1} \left(\frac{T_j}{r_j^2}\right) \mathbf{a}^j \mathbf{t}^{j\prime}\right)\widehat{\boldsymbol{\beta}}^i. \tag{13}$$

*In matrix notation,* **W** *and* **S** *are expressed in terms of* **A** *and* **B** *such that* $\mathbf{W} = \mathbf{X}^1\mathbf{A}$ *and* $\mathbf{S} = \mathbf{X}^1\mathbf{B}$.

*Proof.* Clearly Equations (12) hold for the first iteration. Assume they hold up to the $k^{th}$ iteration. Then equations (10) can be written by using $\mathbf{a}^i$ and $\mathbf{b}^i$:

$$\mathbf{X}^{k+1} = \left(\mathbf{I} - \sum_{i=1}^{k} \mathbf{e}\mathbf{b}^{i\prime} - \sum_{i=1}^{k} \left(\frac{T_i}{r_i^2}\right) \mathbf{t}^i \mathbf{a}^{i\prime}\right)\mathbf{X}^1. \tag{14}$$

Since $\mathbf{X}^{k+1\prime}\widehat{\boldsymbol{\alpha}}^{k+1} = \mathbf{X}^{1\prime}\widehat{\mathbf{a}}^{k+1}$ and $\mathbf{X}^{k+1\prime}\widehat{\boldsymbol{\beta}}^{k+1} = \mathbf{X}^{1\prime}\widehat{\mathbf{b}}^{k+1}$, equation (13) holds for $i = k + 1$. □

By Equations (12) we can see that the sparsity of the final kernel function is identical to the sparsity of the $\widehat{\boldsymbol{\alpha}}^k$ and $\widehat{\boldsymbol{\beta}}^k$ taken over all of the latent variables.

**Corollary 1 (Sparsity of A and B).** *If*

$$SV_{\boldsymbol{\alpha},\boldsymbol{\beta}} = \left\{i \mid \widehat{\boldsymbol{\alpha}}^i \neq 0 \text{ or } \widehat{\boldsymbol{\beta}}^i \neq 0, \ i = 1, \ldots, k\right\}$$

*and* $SV_{\mathbf{a},\mathbf{b}} = \left\{i \mid \widehat{\mathbf{a}}^i \neq 0 \text{ or } \widehat{\mathbf{b}}^i \neq 0, \ i = 1, \ldots, k\right\}$, *then* $SV_{\boldsymbol{\alpha},\boldsymbol{\beta}} = SV_{\mathbf{a},\mathbf{b}}$

$\nu$-KPLS produces orthogonal projections of the data in feature space.

**Theorem 3 (Orthogonality of Projections).** *In* $\nu$-*PLS, the primal projection vectors are orthogonal, i.e.* $\mathbf{w}^{i\prime}\mathbf{w}^j = 0$ *for* $i \neq j$ *and* $\|\mathbf{w}^i\| \neq 0$.

*Proof.*

i). for $i = j + 1$, $\mathbf{w}^{j+1\prime}\mathbf{w}^j = \widehat{\boldsymbol{\alpha}}^{j+1\prime}\mathbf{X}^{j+1\prime}\mathbf{w}^j = \widehat{\boldsymbol{\alpha}}^{j+1\prime}\mathbf{X}^j \left(\mathbf{I} - \mathbf{w}^j\mathbf{w}^{j\prime}/r_j^2\right)\mathbf{w}^j = 0$.

ii). for $i = j + k$, where $k \geq 2$, assume $\mathbf{w}^{l\prime}\mathbf{w}^j = 0$ holds for $k - 1 \geq l \geq j + 1$.

$$\begin{aligned}
\mathbf{w}^{j+k\prime}\mathbf{w}^j &= \widehat{\boldsymbol{\alpha}}^{j+k\prime}\mathbf{X}^{j+k\prime}\mathbf{w}^j \\
&= \widehat{\boldsymbol{\alpha}}^{j+k\prime}\widetilde{\mathbf{X}}^{j+k-1} \left(\mathbf{I} - \mathbf{w}^{j+k-1}\mathbf{w}^{j+k-1\prime}/r_{j+k-1}^2\right)\mathbf{w}^j \\
&= \widehat{\boldsymbol{\alpha}}^{j+k\prime}\widetilde{\mathbf{X}}^{j+k-1}\mathbf{w}^j \\
&= \widehat{\boldsymbol{\alpha}}^{j+k\prime} \left(\mathbf{I} - \mathbf{e}\widehat{\boldsymbol{\beta}}^{j+k-1\prime}\right)\mathbf{X}^{j+k-1}\mathbf{w}^j
\end{aligned}$$

By iterating the above step, we can reduce the index to obtain

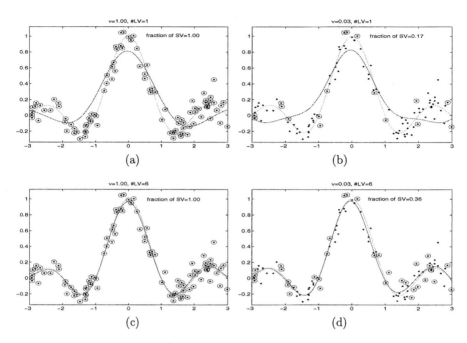

**Fig. 1.** Sinc Function. a) original KPLS with 1 LV. b) $\nu$-KPLS with $\nu = 0.03$ and 1 LV. c) original KPLS with 6 LVs. d) $\nu$-KPLS with $\nu = 0.03$ and 6 LVs.

$$\mathbf{w}^{j+k'}\mathbf{w}^j = \widehat{\alpha}^{j+k'}\mathbf{Z}\left(\mathbf{I} - \mathbf{w}^j\mathbf{w}^{j'}/r_j^2\right)\mathbf{w}^j = 0, \quad \text{where} \quad \mathbf{Z} = \prod_{l=j}^{j+k-1}\left(\mathbf{I} - \mathbf{e}\widehat{\beta}^{l'}\right)\mathbf{X}^j$$

Therefore, combining i) and ii), we prove the $\mathbf{w}^i$ are orthogonal. $\square$

## 6   Computational Results

We provide computational results for generated and real-world data.

**Results on Generated Data:** First, we illustrate the behavior of $\nu$-KPLS on randomly generated data with known solution. Figure 1 gives results for the sinc function with noise: $y_i = \sin(\pi x_i)/(\pi x_i) + n_i$ where $n_i$ is drawn from standard normal. The 100 training points were drawn randomly from: $x_i \in [-3, 3]$. We used the RBF kernel with $\sigma = 1$, i.e. $K(\mathbf{x}_i, \mathbf{x}_j) = \exp(-\|\frac{\mathbf{x}_i - \mathbf{x}_j}{\sigma}\|^2) = \exp(-\|\mathbf{x}_i - \mathbf{x}_j\|^2)$. In Figure 1, the dashed curves represent the prediction obtained by $\nu$-KPLS. Dotted curves are the target sinc functions. Dots represent the training data. The circled dots are support vectors.

$\nu$-KPLS works much like regression ensemble methods. It iteratively constructs a series of latent variables using a "weak learner" based on the residuals and then takes a linear combination of these as the regression function. Figure 1 (a) and (b) show the results for the first latent variable constructed by KPLS

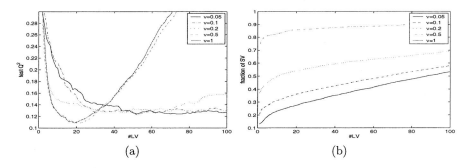

**Fig. 2.** Boston Housing Results. (a) Error curve and (b) fraction of support vectors with respect to number of latent variables.

and by $\nu$-KPLS with $\nu = 0.03$ respectively. $\nu$-KPLS approximates the first latent vector with very few support vectors. Since $\nu$ is only the lower bound on the fraction of support vectors and the following iterations typically require additional support vectors, the value of $\nu$ is set very small. Figure 1 (c) and (d) show the behavior for 6 latent variables for original KPLS and $\nu$-KPLS respectively. $\nu$-KPLS represented a prediction function very similar to that of KPLS using only 36% of the possible support vectors versus 100% for KPLS.

**Results on Real-World Data:** The behavior of $\nu$-KPLS is further illustrated using the well-known Boston Housing Data [3]. The $Q^2$-statistic was used to evaluate the models. $Q^2$ is the mean square error normalized by the variance, $Q^2 = \frac{\sum_{i=1}^{m}(\hat{y}_i - y_i)^2}{\sum_{i=1}^{m}(\bar{y} - y_i)^2}$. All the statistics obtained were averaged over 10-fold cross validation. All the experiments were done using the same partitions of the dataset. The RBF kernel was used with $\sigma = 4$. The dataset was preprocessed to make the attributes all have mean 0 and standard deviation 1. Figure 2 (a) and (b) shows the error curve and fraction of support vectors with respect to the number of latent variables (LV) for the external test set. Each curve is associated with different choice of the sparsity parameter $\nu$=0.05, 0.1, 0.2, and 0.5. For comparison, the result by the regular KPLS is also shown ($\nu = 1$). As $\nu$ increases less LVs are needed to make good prediction. Since $\nu$ is only the lower bound on the number of support vectors for each iteration, taking a large $\nu$ may produce a very dense solution. Since our goal is to obtain a model with as much sparsity as possible without losing the generalization ability of the regular KPLS, small values of $\nu$ produce the desired results. $\nu$-KPLS requires more iterations and each iteration is more expensive than KPLS, but it is possible to obtain sparse solutions with the same quality as the regular KPLS. If efficient approximations to Problem (6) are used, then the computational costs of $\nu$-KPLS are dramatically decreased with similar or even better generalization. We leave presentation of this work to future papers.

# 7   Conclusions and Future Work

We have proposed a sparse KPLS method, $\nu$-KPLS. Centering and computing the low-rank factorizations of the data proved to be the key stumbling blocks to sparsity. By adopting the $\epsilon$-insensitive loss, the optimal centering and projection vectors are sparse in the dual sense. This sparsity was maintained by modifying deflation. $\nu$-PLS can produce sparse kernel functions that generalized similarly to those for dense KPLS. Many open research questions remain. *Can $\nu$-KPLS be computationally competitive with SVR?* $\nu$-PLS's computational costs are dominated by the optimization problem in Step 3 of Algorithm 4. The efficiency of $\nu$-KPLS can be dramatically improved by approximately solving Problem 6 in Step 3. Explicit deflation of the kernel matrix in Step 5 of $\nu$-KPLS can be removed by revising the kernel function at each iteration. *Can the method be altered to preserve sparsity and force orthogonality of the latent variables?* This may improve both efficiency and generalization. *Can the sparsity techniques developed for $\nu$-KPLS be adapted to closely related approaches such as kernel principal component, canonical correlation, factor and Fisher discriminant analysis [7, 10, 1]? From learning theory or statistical perspectives, why does $\nu$-KPLS generalize well?*

# Acknowledgements

This work was supported by NSF grant IIS-9979860.

# References

1. F. Bach and M. Jordan. Kernel independent component analysis. *Journal of Machine Learning Research*, 3:1–48, 2002.
2. K. Bennett and M. Embrechts. An optimization perspective on kernel partial least squares. In *Proc. of NATO Adv. Study Inst. on Learning Theory and Prac.*, 2003.
3. C. L. Blake and C. J. Merz. UCI repository of machine learning databases, 1998. http://www.ics.uci.edu/~mlearn/MLRepository.html.
4. A. Höskuldsson. PLS Regression Methods. *Journ. of Chemometrics*, 2:211–228, 1988.
5. J. Platt. Fast training of svm using sequential minimal optimization. In *Adv, in Kernel Methods - Support Vector Learning*. MIT Press, 1999.
6. R. Rosipal and L. Trejo. Kernel partial least squares regression in reproducing kernel Hilbert space. *Journal of Machine Learning Research*, 2:97–123, 2001.
7. B. Schölkopf, A. Smola, and K.-R. Müller. Kernel principal component analysis. In *Adv. in Kernel Methods - Support Vector Learning*. MIT Press, 1999.
8. B. Schölkopf, A. Smola, and R. Williamson. Shrinking the tube: A new support regression algorithm. In *Adv. in Neural Info. Proc. Systems 11*. MIT Press, 1999.
9. V. Vapnik. *The Nature of Statistical Learning Theory*. Springer, New York, 1996.
10. A. Vinokourov, J. Shawe-Taylor, and N. Cristianini. Finding language-independent semantic representation of text using kernel canonical correlation analysis. Neuro-COLT Technical Report NC-TR-02-119, 2002.
11. H. Wold. Estimation of principal components and related models by iterative least squares,. In *Multivariate Analysis*, New York, 1966. Academic Press.

# Sparse Probability Regression
# by Label Partitioning

Shantanu Chakrabartty[1], Gert Cauwenberghs[1], and Jayadeva[2]

[1] Center for Language and Speech Processing
Johns Hopkins University, Baltimore, MD 21218, USA
{shantanu,gert}@jhu.edu
[2] Department of Electrical Engineering,
Indian Institute of Technology,
Hauz Khas, New Delhi - 110058, INDIA
jayadeva@ee.iitd.ernet.in

**Abstract.** A large-margin learning machine for sparse probability regression is presented. Unlike support vector machines and other forms of kernel machines, nonlinear features are obtained by transforming labels into higher-dimensional label space rather than transforming data vectors into feature space. Linear multi-class logistic regression with partitioned classes of labels yields a nonlinear classifier in the original labels. With a linear kernel in data space, storage and run-time requirements are reduced from the number of support vectors to the number of partitioned labels. Using the partitioning property of KL-divergence in label space, an iterative alignment procedure produces sparse training coefficients. Experiments show that label partitioning is effective in modeling nonlinear decision boundaries with same, and in some cases superior, generalization performance to Support Vector Machines with significantly reduced memory and run-time requirements.

## 1 Introduction

Support Vector Machines [1, 2] derive their approximation power by mapping the training data vectors into a higher dimensional feature space, where a linear maximal margin separating hyper-plane can be found to efficiently discriminate between respective classes. Computation in this higher dimensional feature space is made feasible with the aid of reproducing Hilbert space kernels, which are equivalent to computing inner-products in these higher dimensions. Even though SVMs have demonstrated state-of-art classification performance, some challenges remain:

1. The efficiency of real-time classification for SVMs depends on the degree of sparsity as measured by the number of support vectors required for a given task. In most practical scenarios there exists significant overlap between class distributions which results in large numbers of support vectors for classification. For a given Bayes error rate, the number of error support vectors scales directly with the number of training points, and significantly outgrows the number of margin support vectors for very large datasets.

B. Schölkopf and M.K. Warmuth (Eds.): COLT/Kernel 2003, LNAI 2777, pp. 231–242, 2003.

2. The complexity of SVM training scales with the square of the number of support vectors, and becomes prohibitively slow for huge datasets with significant class overlaps.
3. The choice of kernel is heuristic, and is governed by prior knowledge about the problem which usually is not available.

The first two problems can be attributed to the need to represent error vectors as support vectors in the dual formulation, assuming a non-linear kernel. It has been shown [3] that the same classification boundary can be obtained by optimizing a primal reformulation of the SVM cost function, leading to a reduction of the number of effective support vectors, although sparsity is not guaranteed and depends on the kernel used. Reduced Set Methods [4] project the decision surface onto a sparser kernel representation formed by a number of basis functions that are chosen based on an unconstrained non-convex optimization procedure. Relevance Vector Machines (RVM) [5] offer an alternative to obtaining sparse kernel expansions in a Bayesian setting, and have demonstrated same or better generalization performance with fewer 'relevance' vectors, although practical implementation has been limited to relatively small datasets.

We introduce the *Partitioned Label Machine* (PLM) to improve on sparsity of representation and generalization performance in large-margin kernel classification and probability regression. PLMs map the labels, rather than the data vectors, into a higher dimensional space. Through partitioning of the labels, the resulting partitioned classes can be linearly classified. Linear multi-class probability regression can then be used to map decision boundaries and combine hypotheses to form nonlinear classification decisions. The linear form gives rise to a sparse representation in the primal formulation, with an expansion that scales not with the number of training data, but with the number of label partitions. We show that label partitioning implies a nonlinear map similar to that implied in data space by a Mercer kernel in the SVM dual formulation. The PLM method is very general and easily extends from two-class to multi-class problems.

Committee machines [6], voting machines and mixture of experts [7–9] are based on similar lines of combining simple decision surfaces by voting/mixing. Linear weighting of simple hypotheses cannot result in a more complex hypothesis, and we show how PLMs model nonlinear decision surfaces even though the underlying classification functions are linear. SVMs are not combined by linear mixing; rather, partitioned subclasses combine nonlinearly through the competitive and self-normalizing functional form of multinomial logistic regression, applied once to all partitioned classes. Since the classification machine outputs class probabilities, partitioning of the labels can be accomplished in an iterative scheme similar to expectation maximization.

Section 2 describes the probability model used for PLM and provides its justification based on generalization performance. Section 3 formulates the problem in terms of KL-divergence and logistic kernel regression, and compares properties of label partitioning with those of Mercer kernels. Section 4 summarizes the experiments performed on PLMs and section 5 provides concluding remarks.

## 2    Model Selection

Partitioned Label Machines (PLMs) map an input feature vector $\mathbf{x} \in R^d$ onto one of the respective $S$ label classes based on a compound selection criterion derived from partitioning of the label classes. The class decisions are based on choosing the class $i \in 1..S$ with the highest probability measure $P_i(\mathbf{x})$:

$$P_i(\mathbf{x}) = \Pr(i|\mathbf{x}) = \sum_j^K P_{ij}(\mathbf{x}) \tag{1}$$

obtained by pooling probability mass $P_{ij}(\mathbf{x})$ over $K$ corresponding partitioned sub-classes $j$:

$$P_{ij}(\mathbf{x}) = \Pr(i,j|\mathbf{x}) = \frac{\exp(\mathbf{w}_{ij}.\mathbf{x} + b_{ij})}{\sum_p^S \sum_q^K \exp(\mathbf{w}_{pq}.\mathbf{x} + b_{pq})}. \tag{2}$$

A special case of interest is that of binary classification with decision function

$$y = \theta(P_1(\mathbf{x}) - 0.5) = \theta(\sum_j^K P_{1j}(\mathbf{x}) - 0.5) \tag{3}$$

where $\theta(\cdot)$ is the Heaviside function mapping onto two respective classes $\{1,0\}$ and the function $P_{1j}(\mathbf{x}) \in \mathcal{H}_s$ is given by

$$P_{1j}(\mathbf{x}) = \frac{\exp(\mathbf{w}_{1i}.\mathbf{x} + b_{1i})}{\sum_q \exp(\mathbf{w}_{0q}.\mathbf{x} + b_{0q}) + \sum_q \exp(\mathbf{w}_{1q}.\mathbf{x} + b_{1q})}. \tag{4}$$

The $\mathcal{P}$-dimension [10] $dim_{\mathcal{P}}$ of the class of functions $\mathcal{H}_s$ is bounded above by $d + 1$. This can be easily verified by observing that $P_{1j}(\mathbf{x})$ forms a soft-max of $K$ linear decision surfaces. Using results directly from [11] the scale sensitive dimension $fat_{\mathcal{H}}$ of the class of $\mathcal{H}$ of functions $P_1(\mathbf{x})$ in (3) is given by

$$fat_{\mathcal{H}}(\beta) \leq \frac{cK^2 d}{\beta^2} \log(1/\beta) \tag{5}$$

for some universal constant $c$ and margin $\beta$. This shows that the upper-bound on complexity of decision space $H$ is polynomial in the number of sub-classes $K$, suggesting poor generalization for large values of $K$. However, appropriately maximizing the margin $\beta$ allows to control the complexity of the hypothesis class and hence the generalization ability. Equation (5) also suggests to adjust the margin $\beta$ with with the number of partitions $K$ as to maintain a fixed upper-bound on the complexity of $\mathcal{H}$.

## 3    Label Partitioning and Re-estimation

For training the learning machine, we assume access to a training sequence $\mathbf{x}[n] \in R^d$ with labels (class memberships) $y[n] \in R^S$, where $n$ denotes the data index, $d$ the dimension of the input vectors, and $S$ the number of classes. Continuous (soft) labels could be assigned rather than binary indicator labels, to signify uncertainty in the training data over the classes. Like probabilities, label assignments are normalized: $\sum_{i=1}^{S} y_i[n] = 1, y_i[n] \geq 0$ where $S$ is the total number of classes.

Training could be formulated as minimization of the regularized empirical KL-divergence between the probabilities estimated by the learning machine $P_i[n] = \Pr(i|\mathbf{x}[n])$, and the label vectors $y_i[n]$:

$$H(\mathbf{W}) = \frac{1}{2} \sum_{i}^{S} \sum_{j}^{K} |\mathbf{w}_{ij}|^2 + C \sum_{n=1}^{N} \sum_{i=1}^{S} y_i[n] \log \frac{y_i[n]}{P_i[n]} \tag{6}$$

where $C \geq 0$ is a regularization constant, and $\mathbf{W} = \bigcup_{ij}(\mathbf{w}_{ij}, b_{ij})$ denotes the set of hyperplane parameters of the model.

The cost function (6) is non-convex for the probability model given by (2). To arrive at a convex optimization problem, we derive an auxiliary function upper-bounding the decrease in cost function $\delta H(\mathbf{W}, \mathbf{W}^*) = H(\mathbf{W}^*) - H(\mathbf{W})$, where $\mathbf{W}$ and $\mathbf{W}^*$ denote the current and the previous estimates of parameters. $\delta H(\mathbf{W}, \mathbf{W}^*)$ can be written as

$$\delta H(\mathbf{W}, \mathbf{W}^*) = \delta\Omega(\mathbf{W}, \mathbf{W}^*) + C\delta F(\mathbf{W}, \mathbf{W}^*) \tag{7}$$

with

$$\delta\Omega(\mathbf{W}, \mathbf{W}^*) = \frac{1}{2} \sum_{i}^{S} \sum_{j}^{K} [|\mathbf{w}_{ij}^*|^2 - |\mathbf{w}_{ij}|^2] \tag{8}$$

and

$$\delta F(\mathbf{W}, \mathbf{W}^*) = -\sum_{n}^{N} \sum_{i}^{S} \frac{y_i[n] \sum_j P_{ij}^*[n]}{\sum_j P_{ij}^*[n]} \log \frac{\sum_j P_{ij}^*[n]}{\sum_j P_{ij}[n]} \tag{9}$$

where

$$P_{ij}^*[n] = \frac{\exp(\mathbf{w}_{ij}^* . \mathbf{x}[n] + b_{ij}^*)}{\sum_s^S \sum_k^K \exp(\mathbf{w}_{sk}^* . \mathbf{x}[n] + b_{sk}^*)} \tag{10}$$

$$P_{ij}[n] = \frac{\exp(\mathbf{w}_{ij} . \mathbf{x}[n] + b_{ij})}{\sum_s^S \sum_k^K \exp(\mathbf{w}_{sk} . \mathbf{x}[n] + b_{sk})}. \tag{11}$$

We use the celebrated log-sum inequality to bound (9):

**Lemma:** For a sequence of non-negative numbers $\{a_i\}_{i=1}^n$ and $\{b_i\}_{i=1}^n$, and for $a = \sum_{i=1}^n a_i$ and $b = \sum_{i=1}^n b_i$, the following inequality holds

$$\sum_{i}^{n} a_i \log \frac{a_i}{b_i} \geq a \log \frac{a}{b} \tag{12}$$

with equality iff $a_i/b_i = a/b$ for all $i$. The proof of lemma (12) is simple and is obtained by application of Jensen's inequality to the convex function $t \log(t)$.

Applying (12) to (9) the following expectation-maximization (EM) auxiliary function is obtained

$$A(\mathbf{W}, \mathbf{W}^*) = \frac{1}{2} \sum_{i,j} |\mathbf{w}_{ij}|^2 + C \sum_n^N \sum_{i,j} y_{ij}^*[n] \log \frac{P_{ij}^*[n]}{P_{ij}[n]} \tag{13}$$

where

$$y_{ij}^*[n] = y_i[n] \frac{P_{ij}^*[n]}{P_i^*[n]} \tag{14}$$

with $P_i^*[n] = \sum_l P_{il}^*[n]$. It it easy to verify that $A(\mathbf{W}, \mathbf{W}^*) \geq 0$. Minimizing the auxiliary function (13) is therefore equivalent to decreasing an upper bound on the cost function (6), and by subsequent iteration of computing the new labels based on previous estimates the procedure converges at least to a local minimum. The upper-bound $A(\mathbf{W}, \mathbf{W}^*)$ bears resemblance to conditional EM bounds in [12] within a regularization framework. One can directly see from the condition for equality in the above log-sum inequality that the solution converges to the global minimum if the following condition is satisfied:

$$\frac{P_{ij}[n]}{P_i[n]} = \frac{y_{ij}[n]}{y_i[n]}. \tag{15}$$

This condition, unfortunately cannot be strictly ensured by the probability measures $P_i(\mathbf{x})$ and therefore has to be satisfied to close approximation. The initialization sub-labels $y_{ij}$ should therefore be chosen such that they can be easily classified using a large margin classifier which can be obtained by using disjoint partitioning or clustering methods like Gaussian mixture modeling.

The principle of mapping the a low-dimension label vector into higher dimensional space yields advantages similar to the 'kernel trick', in this case however one can work in the higher dimensional space directly using a linear kernel. Partitioning the classes into sub-classes yields easily separable classes which can then efficiently combined using multi-class probabilistic regression techniques, reviewed next.

## 3.1   Logistic Probability Regression

Optimization of the lower-bound in (13) amounts to regressing probabilities over $S \times K$ (partitioned) classes. Estimation of probabilities $P_{ij}[n]$, for partitions $j$ of class $i$, from training data $\mathbf{x}[n]$ and partitioned labels $y_{ij}^*[n]$, is obtained using a regularized form of logistic probability regression. The model (2) assumes a multinomial logistic form

$$P_{ij}[n] = \exp(f_{ij}(\mathbf{x}[n])) / \sum_s^S \sum_k^K \exp(f_{sk}(\mathbf{x}[n])). \tag{16}$$

**Primal Formulation:** In the primal formulation, the discriminant functions $f_{ij}(\mathbf{x})$ are expressed in the primal variables defining the coordinates of the hyperplane in feature space. In particular, for a *linear* kernel,

$$f_{ij}(\mathbf{x}) = \mathbf{w}_{ij}.\mathbf{x} + b_{ij}. \tag{17}$$

The objective function of logistic regression expresses regularized divergence (13) of the logistic model (16) in the form [13, 14]

$$H_1 = \sum_{i,j} \frac{1}{2}|\mathbf{w}_{ij}|^2 + C \sum_n [\sum_{i,j} y_{ij}^*[n] f_{ij}(\mathbf{x}[n]) + \log(\sum_{s,k} e^{f_{sk}(\mathbf{x}[n])})] . \tag{18}$$

Use of a linear kernel enables use of primal gradient related methods that directly optimizes (13). The advantage of the primal formulation with linear kernel is that the number of variables is fixed by the vector dimension $d$, and not by the number of training vectors $N$. In PLM, this implies that the number of terms in the expansion is proportional to the number of partitions, determined by the complexity of the task rather than the size of the data. Partitioning of the labels allows to use a linear kernel and yet model a nonlinear decision surface. Still, it may be advantageous to use a nonlinear Mercer kernel, or to resort to the dual representation otherwise and gain in terms of computational efficiency.

**Dual Formulation:** Dual formulation of (18) yields a regularized kernel-based form of logistic regression [15, 14]. As with SVMs, dot products in the expression for $f_{ij}(\mathbf{x})$ in (16) convert into kernel expansions over the training data $\mathbf{x}[m]$ by transforming the data to feature space [4]

$$f_{ij}(\mathbf{x}) = \sum_m \lambda_{ij}^m K(\mathbf{x}[m], \mathbf{x}) + b_{ij}. \tag{19}$$

The parameters $\lambda_{ij}^m$ in (19) are determined by minimizing a dual formulation of the objective function (18) obtained through the Legendre transformation, which for logistic regression takes the form of an entropy-based objective function [15]

$$H_2 = \sum_{i,j} [\frac{1}{2} \sum_l^N \sum_m^N \lambda_{ij}^l Q_{lm} \lambda_{ij}^m + C \sum_m^N (y_{ij}^*[m] - \lambda_{ij}^m/C) \log(y_{ij}^*[m] - \lambda_{ij}^m/C)] \tag{20}$$

with $Q_{lm} = K(\mathbf{x}[l], \mathbf{x}[m])$, to be minimized in the dual parameters subject to constraints

$$\sum_m \lambda_{ij}^m = 0 \tag{21}$$

$$\sum_{i,j} \lambda_{ij}^m = 0 \tag{22}$$

$$C(y_{ij}^*[m] - 1) \leq \lambda_{ij}^m \leq C y_{ij}^*[m], \qquad \forall \, i, j. \tag{23}$$

Newton-Raphson based techniques can be used to solve the dual optimization problem (20) but exhibit slow convergence on account of the non-differentiability of the Shannon entropy factor in (20). $GiniSVM$ [16] offers an approximate dual procedure based on a Gini quadratic form of entropy [17] to solve (20) efficiently. Like in soft-margin SVM classification, $GiniSVM$ recasts the optimization problem into a quadratic programming (QP) problem, and produces a sparse kernel expansion.

In the following we assume the use of a linear kernel, and the distinction between primal and dual formulations becomes immaterial other than computational issues in the implementation.

## 3.2   Training Algorithm

The training algorithm can be summarized as follows:

1. Given the number of classes $S$, choose the number of sub-classes. This is determined by the constraints imposed by memory and computational resources for a specific application. Let the number of sub-classes be $K$. Therefore the total memory required scales with $K \times S$.
2. For each of the classes, partition the data vectors into disjoint $K$ sub-classes using vector quantization or any clustering technique. This step is crucial to ensure that the equality (15) holds approximately.
3. Train probability regression with a linear kernel for $K$ classes, to obtain $K \times S$ partition vectors $\mathbf{w}_{ij}$ and corresponding estimates $P_{ij}[n]$.
4. Re-estimate the new labels $y_{ij}^*[n]$ using (14) and retrain.

In most cases two or three EM iterations are enough to obtain a good solution. It is also demonstrated in Section 4 that this re-estimation procedure prevents over-fitting which may occur when more sub-classes $K$ are chosen than required for discrimination.

## 3.3   Correspondence between Label-Partitioning and Mercer Kernels

The similarity between using the partition method and using non-linear kernels can be observed through cost function (20) re-written as

$$H_2 = \frac{1}{2} \sum_{l}^{N} \sum_{m}^{N} Q_{lm}(\sum_{i,j} \lambda_{ij}^l \lambda_{ij}^m) + C \sum_{m}^{N} \sum_{i,j} (y_{ij}^*[m] - \frac{\lambda_{ij}^m}{C}) \log(y_{ij}^*[m] - \frac{\lambda_{ij}^m}{C}). \quad (24)$$

The term $\sum_{i,j}^{M} \lambda_{ij}^l \lambda_{ij}^m$ could be interpreted as an inner product in a higher-dimensional 'label' space $\phi(\lambda^m).\phi(\lambda^l)$. This implies that even if the data kernel $Q_{lm}$ is not powerful enough to model the desired non-linear decision boundaries, the kernel formed by inner-product of the coefficient label 'vectors' obtained by training augments the modeling power of PLM. Figure 1 compares the data kernel matrix $Q_{lm}$ for a linear kernel with the PLM label 'kernel' matrix formed

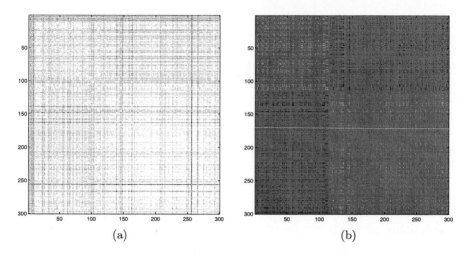

(a)                                  (b)

**Fig. 1.** Kernel maps formed over UCI Pima-Indians database. (a) Linear Mercer kernel $Q_{lm}$. (b) Label "kernel" formed by inner-product of the coefficient vectors $\sum_{i,j} \lambda_{ij}^l \lambda_{ij}^m$ after training.

by the trained label coefficients $\sum_{i,j} \lambda_{ij}^l \lambda_{ij}^m$, using 300 training points from the UCI Pima-Indian dataset.

Unfortunately, unlike standard kernel machines the decision surface cannot be directly expressed in original label space. This necessitates explicit use of inner products of coefficients in partitioned label space, which is accomplished by means of the partition method of Section 3.

## 4   Experiments and Results

The first set of experiments were performed with synthetic data generated using a mixture of Gaussians. The aim of the first set of experiments was to validate/observe the following:

1. PLM forms a decision surface similar to a full SVM solution but with much smaller number of partition labels than support vectors.
2. The large-margin decision surface does not change appreciably if larger number of sub-classes $K$ are chosen than required. This illustrates that PLM does not over-fit in the scenario when more partition vectors are used than actually required. This is important because one cannot determine *a priori* the number of sub-classes necessary for good generalization.
3. The PLM formulation directly extends to the multi-class case, since the underlying probability model is multi-class (multinomial logistic).

Figures 2 illustrates the strong similarity in decision surface between PLM and conventional SVM classification, but with significantly fewer partition vectors $\mathbf{w}_{ij}$ than support vectors $\mathbf{x}[m]$. Figure 3 depicts an example where the SVM

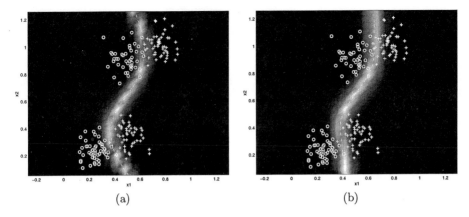

**Fig. 2.** (a) 2-class decision surface obtained by SVM with a third order polynomial kernel. Support vectors in this case comprise 58% of the training data. (b) Decision surface obtained by PLM with linear kernel, and $K = 2$ partitions per class. Label partition vectors comprise 4% of the training data.

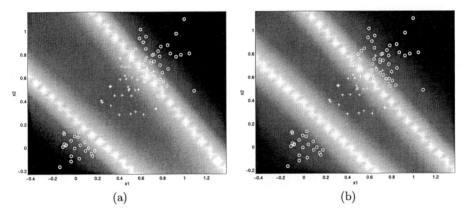

**Fig. 3.** (a) 2-Class decision surface formed by third order polynomial SVM with 20% support vectors. (b) 3-Partition PLM decision surface with 4% partitioned label vectors. Note that the solution obtained by SVM in this case is not a true large-margin solution in the original data-space, while PLM adjusts the margin locally by differentiating between clusters.

formulation does not produce large margin in data-space, because the true 'margin' of separation varies between pairs of clusters. Label partitioning allows to differentiate between clusters of data, and adapt the margin locally.

Figures 4 and 5 show the effect of choosing more partition vectors than actually required. One can observe in Figure 5 the effect of EM re-estimation on the large margin partitioned hyperplane, smoothing out artifacts of over-partitioning in Figure 4. Figure 6 shows probability contours obtained by applying the PLM method to the multi-class case.

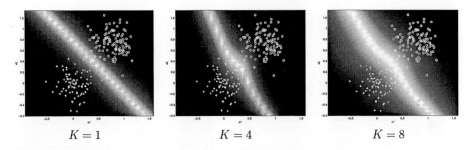

$$K = 1 \qquad\qquad K = 4 \qquad\qquad K = 8$$

**Fig. 4.** Decision surface obtained by increasing the total number of partitions before EM re-estimation.

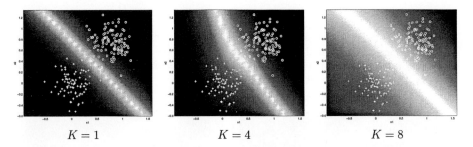

$$K = 1 \qquad\qquad K = 4 \qquad\qquad K = 8$$

**Fig. 5.** Decision surface obtained after EM re-estimation of partitions in Figure 4.

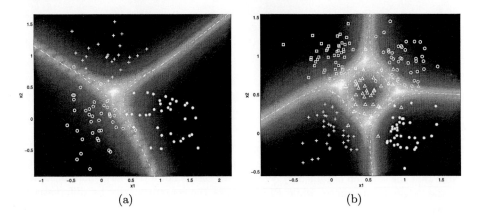

$$\text{(a)} \qquad\qquad\qquad \text{(b)}$$

**Fig. 6.** (a) Probability contours formed by using PLM for a 3-class problem with 9 partitions. (b) Probability contours formed by PLM for a 5-class problem with 10 partitions.

The second set of experiments compares the performance of SVM with PLM on databases chosen from the UCI repository. For each of the selected datasets, a 10-fold cross-validation technique was used and the test errors were averaged over all the subsets. The size of the training set used $N$, the test error rates (Err) and the obtained number of support/partition vectors (#sv/#pv) are given in

**Table 1.** Results on UCI data

| Database | $N$ | SVM (Err) | PLM (Err) | SVM (#sv) | PLM (#pv) |
|---|---|---|---|---|---|
| Ionosphere | 300 | 8.1% | 7.2% | 76 | 4 |
| Pima Diabetes | 650 | 21.6% | 21.0% | 284 | 4 |
| Wisc Breast Cancer | 600 | 3.0% | 3.7% | 81 | 6 |
| Sonar | 160 | 7.6% | 5.7% | 122 | 12 |

Table 1, which shows that PLM exhibits same or better generalization performance compared to binary soft-margin SVM, with improved sparsity in the representation.

## 5    Conclusions

We presented the *Partitioned Label Machine* (PLM) as a technique to obtain sparse classification and probability regression within the framework of large margin kernel methods and support vector machines. Advantages include:

1. PLM directly finds a decision surface subject to memory constraints imposed on the problem, expressed in number of label partitions.
2. The method is *non-parametric*, because there is no choice of kernel unlike support vector machines, and the only flexibility involves choosing the regularization constant $C$, and the number of sub-classes $K$.
3. PLMs provide comparable generalization performance in comparison with SVMs, but with much fewer partition labels than support vectors. Generalization performance of PLM is superior when the data is non-uniformly distributed, with variable margin in data space.
4. Because the algorithm is linear in each of the sub-classes, the training algorithm is fast, as only a single inner-product computation has to be performed to calculate the margin of any data vector.
5. The run-time classification is significantly reduced and only depends on the number of sub-classes $K$, which in turn can be fixed by memory constraints pre-specified during training.
6. The technique is very general and extends directly to multi-class problems.

## Acknowledgment

This work was supported by the Catalyst Foundation, New York (*http://www.catalyst-foundation.org*), and National Science Foundation IIS-0209289.

## References

1. Vapnik, V. *The Nature of Statistical Learning Theory,* New York: Springer-Verlag, 1995.
2. Schölkopf, B., Burges, C. and Smola, A., Eds., *Advances in Kernel Methods-Support Vector Learning,* MIT Press, Cambridge, 1998.

3. Osuna, E, and Girosi, F. "Reducing the Run-time Complexity in Support Vector Machines", *Advances in Kernel Methods-Support Vector Learning*, MIT Press, 1998.

4. Burges, C.J.C "Simplified Support Vector Decision Rules", *Proc. 13$^{th}$ Intl. Conf. on Machine Learning,* San Mateo, CA: Morgan Kaufmann, pp. 71-77, 1996.

5. Tipping, R. "Sparse Bayesian Learning and the Relevance Vector Machine", *Journal of Machine Learning Research,* vol. **1**, pp. 211-244, 2001.

6. Tresp, V. "A Bayesian Committee Machine", *Neural Computation,* vol. **12**, pp. 2719-2741, 2000.

7. Jacobs, R.A., Jordan, M.I., Nowlan, S.J and Hinton, G.E. "Adaptive Mixtures of Local Experts", *Neural Computation,* vol. **3** (1), pp. 79-87, 1991.

8. Collobert, R., Bengio, Y. and Bengio, S. "Scaling Large Learning Problems with Hard Parallel Mixtures", *IEEE Int. Conf. of Pattern Recognition: SVM workshop. (ICPR'2002),* Niagara Falls, 2002.

9. Kwok, J.T. "Support Vector Mixtures for Classification and Regression Problems", *Proc. of the International Conference on Pattern Recognition (ICPR),* pp. 255-258, Brisbane, Queensland, Australia, 1998.

10. Pollard, D. *Convergence of Stochastic Processes* New York: Springer-Verlag, 1984.

11. Bartlett, P "The Sample Complexity of Pattern Classification with Neural Networks: The Size of the Weights is More Important than the Size of the Network", *IEEE Transactions on Information Theory,* vol. **44** (2), March 1998.

12. Jebara, T. *Discriminative, Generative and Imitative Learning*, PhD Thesis, Media Laboratory, MIT, December 2001.

13. Wahba, G. *Support Vector Machine, Reproducing Kernel Hilbert Spaces and Randomized GACV*, Technical Report 984, Department of Statistics, University of Wisconsin, Madison WI.

14. Zhu, J and Hastie, T., "Kernel Logistic Regression and Import Vector Machine", *Adv. IEEE Neural Information Processing Systems (NIPS'2001),* Cambridge, MA: MIT Press, 2002.

15. Jaakkola, T. and Haussler, D. "Probabilistic kernel regression models", *Proc. Seventh International Workshop on Artificial Intelligence and Statistics,* 1999.

16. Chakrabartty, S. and Cauwenberghs, G. "Forward Decoding Kernel Machines: A hybrid HMM/SVM Approach to Sequence Recognition", *IEEE Int. Conf. of Pattern Recognition: SVM workshop. (ICPR'2002),* Niagara Falls, 2002.

17. Breiman, L. Friedman, J. H. et al. *Classification and Regression Trees*, Wadsworth and Brooks, Pacific Grove, CA, 1984.

# Learning with Rigorous Support Vector Machines

Jinbo Bi[1] and Vladimir N. Vapnik[2]

[1] Department of Mathematical Sciences,
Rensselaer Polytechnic Institute, Troy NY 12180, USA
`bij2@rpi.edu`
[2] NEC Labs America, Inc. Princeton NJ 08540, USA
`vlad@nec-labs.com`

**Abstract.** We examine the so-called rigorous support vector machine (RSVM) approach proposed by Vapnik (1998). The formulation of RSVM is derived by explicitly implementing the structural risk minimization principle with a parameter $H$ used to directly control the VC dimension of the set of separating hyperplanes. By optimizing the dual problem, RSVM finds the optimal separating hyperplane from a set of functions with VC dimension approximate to $H^2 + 1$. RSVM produces classifiers equivalent to those obtained by classic SVMs for appropriate parameter choices, but the use of the parameter $H$ facilitates model selection, thus minimizing VC bounds on the generalization risk more effectively. In our empirical studies, good models are achieved for an appropriate $H^2 \in [5\%\ell, 30\%\ell]$ where $\ell$ is the size of training data.

## 1   Introduction

Support vector machines (SVMs) have proven to be a powerful and robust methodology for learning from empirical data. They originated from the concept in Vapnik-Chervonenkis (VC) theory which provides bounds on the generalization risk of a function $f$. Consider the learning problem of finding a function $f$, from a set of functions $\mathcal{F}$, which minimizes the expected risk functional $R[f] = \int L(y, f(\mathbf{x})) \, dP(\mathbf{x}, y)$ provided data $(\mathbf{x}, y)$ follows the distribution $P(\mathbf{x}, y)$. The loss functional $L(y, f(\mathbf{x}))$ measures the distance between the observation $y$ and the prediction $f(\mathbf{x})$. However, $R[f]$ can not be directly calculated due to the unknown distribution $P$. Given $\ell$ training points $(\mathbf{x}_1, y_1), \cdots, (\mathbf{x}_\ell, y_\ell)$ i.i.d. drawn from $P$, the empirical risk is computed as $R_{emp}[f] = \frac{1}{\ell} \sum_{i=1}^{\ell} L(y_i, f(\mathbf{x}_i))$ to approximate $R[f]$. A typical form of VC bounds is stated as [13]: with probability $1 - \eta$, $R[f]$ is bounded from above by

$$R_{emp}[f] + \frac{h}{\ell} \cdot \mathcal{E} \left( 1 + \sqrt{1 + \frac{4R_{emp}[f]}{\mathcal{E}h/\ell}} \right), \tag{1}$$

where $\mathcal{E} = 1 - \ln\left(\frac{h}{2\ell}\right) - \frac{1}{h}\ln\left(\frac{\eta}{4}\right)$, $\ell$ is the size of training data, and $h$ is the VC dimension of $\mathcal{F}$. The second term of the bound (1) that controls the VC

B. Schölkopf and M.K. Warmuth (Eds.): COLT/Kernel 2003, LNAI 2777, pp. 243–257, 2003.

confidence is basically a monotonically increasing function in terms of $h$ for a fixed $\ell$, and the ratio $\frac{h}{\ell}$ is the dominating factor in this term.

This paper focuses on binary classification problems. SVMs construct classifiers that generalize well by minimizing the VC bound. The classic SVM formulation (C-SVM) was derived based on a simplified version of the VC bound. In contrast, the SVM formulation examined in this paper is derived by explicitly implementing the structural risk minimization (SRM) principle without simplification. This approach can more effectively minimize the VC bound due to the easier tuning of the model parameter, so we name it "rigorous" SVM (RSVM). Instead of using a parameter $C$ as in C-SVMs, RSVM uses a parameter $H$ to provide an effective estimate of VC dimension $h$.

We follow Vapnik ([13], Chapter 10) in deriving the RSVM formulations in Section 2. Then we investigate basic characteristics of the RSVM approach (Section 3), compare RSVM to other SVM methods (Section 4), and solve RSVM by discussing strategies for choosing $H$ and developing a decomposition algorithm (Section 5). Computational results are included in Section 6.

The following notation is used through this paper. Vectors are denoted by bold lower case letters such as $\mathbf{x}$, and presumed to be column vectors unless otherwise stated. The $\mathbf{x}'$ is the transpose of $\mathbf{x}$. Matrices are denoted by bold capital letters such as $\mathbf{Q}$. The $||\cdot||$ denotes the $\ell_2$ norm of a vector. The inner product between two vectors such as $\mathbf{w}$ and $\mathbf{x}$ is denoted as $(\mathbf{w} \cdot \mathbf{x})$.

## 2     Review of RSVM Formulations

We briefly review the derivation of the RSVM approach in this section. Readers can consult [13] for a complete description. SVMs construct classifiers based on separating hyperplanes. A separating hyperplane $\{\mathbf{x} : (\mathbf{w} \cdot \mathbf{x}) + b = 0\}$ is in a canonical form if it satisfies $y_i((\mathbf{w} \cdot \mathbf{x}_i) + b) \geq 1$, $i = 1, \ldots, \ell$ [12]. The margin of separation is defined as the Euclidean distance between the separating hyperplane and either of the planes determined by $(\mathbf{w} \cdot \mathbf{x}) + b = 1$ and $(\mathbf{w} \cdot \mathbf{x}) + b = -1$. For a hyperplane of canonical form, the margin equals $1/||\mathbf{w}||$. For any such separating hyperplane characterized uniquely by a pair $(\mathbf{w}, b)$, a classifier can be constructed based on it as $g_{\mathbf{w},b}(\mathbf{x}) = \mathrm{sgn}((\mathbf{w} \cdot \mathbf{x}) + b)$.

Consider the set of classifiers $\mathcal{F} = \{g_{\mathbf{w},b} : ||\mathbf{w}|| \leq \frac{1}{\Delta}\}$ where $\Delta$ determines that any separating hyperplane $(\mathbf{w}, b)$ in this set separates training points $\mathbf{x}$ with a margin at least $\Delta$. If input vectors $\mathbf{x}$ belong to a ball $B_R$ of radius $R$, this set of classifiers defined on $B_R$ has its VC dimension $h$ bounded from above by $\frac{R^2}{\Delta^2} + 1$ [13] assuming that the dimension of $\mathbf{x}$ is larger than the ratio $\frac{R^2}{\Delta^2}$. This is often the case encountered in practice, especially for a kernel method. For instance, employing a RBF kernel corresponds to constructing hyperplanes in a feature space of infinite dimension. In real-world applications, a separating hyperplane does not always exist. To allow for errors, we use slack variables $\xi_i = \max\{0, 1 - y_i((\mathbf{w} \cdot \mathbf{x}_i) + b)\}$ [4], and the empirical risk is approximated by the $\ell_1$ error metric $\frac{1}{\ell} \sum_{i=1}^{\ell} \xi_i$.

In C-SVMs, $R^2||\mathbf{w}||^2$ is regarded as a rough estimate of the VC dimension of $\mathcal{F}$ provided $\frac{1}{\Delta}$ can be attained at a $||\mathbf{w}||$. C-SVMs minimize the objective function $C\sum_{i=1}^{\ell}\xi_i + \frac{1}{2}||\mathbf{w}||^2$ on purpose to minimize the VC bound (1) with $R_{emp}[f]$ evaluated by $\frac{1}{\ell}\sum_{i=1}^{\ell}\xi_i$ and VC dimension $h$ approximated by $R^2||\mathbf{w}||^2$. Comparing the objective function with the bound (1) yields that in order to achieve the goal, $C$ should be chosen so that $1/C \approx \left(2R^2\mathcal{E}\left(1+\sqrt{1+\frac{4R_{emp}}{\mathcal{E}\hat{h}/\ell}}\right)\right)$ where $R_{emp}$ and $\hat{h}$ are the smallest possible empirical risk and VC dimension respectively. Obviously, it is difficult to estimate this $C$ due to no access to the $R_{emp}$ and $\hat{h}$ beforehand. In practice, $C$ is usually selected from a set of candidates according to cross-validation performance. The obtained $C$ could be far from the desirable value if the candidate set is not well-selected.

Based on the bound (1), $R_{emp}[f]$ and $h$ are the only two factors that a learning machine can control in order to minimize the bound. We thus do not directly minimize the bound as done in C-SVMs. Instead we regulate the two factors by fixing one and minimizing the other. RSVM restricts the set of functions $\mathcal{F}$ to one with VC dimension close to a pre-specified value, and minimizes the empirical risk by finding an optimal function from this set $\mathcal{F}$.

In RSVM formulations, the upper bound $R^2||\mathbf{w}||^2 + 1$ is used as an estimate of the VC dimension. If data is uniformly distributed right on the surface of the ball $B_R$, the VC dimension of $\mathcal{F}$ is exactly equal to $R^2||\mathbf{w}||^2 + 1$ according to the derivation of the bound [13]. However, data following such a distribution is not commonplace in real life. To make the estimation effective, we approximate the distribution by performing the transformation for each training point $\mathbf{x}_i$ as:

$$(\mathbf{x}_i - \bar{\mathbf{x}})/||\mathbf{x}_i - \bar{\mathbf{x}}|| \tag{2}$$

where $\bar{\mathbf{x}} = \frac{1}{\ell}\sum_{i=1}^{\ell}\mathbf{x}_i$ is the mean. The transformed points live on the surface of the unit ball ($R = 1$) centered at the origin. In C-SVMs, the VC dimension is commonly estimated using the same bound with the radius $R$ of the smallest ball containing input data, which amounts to having most data points inside a unit ball after proper rescaling. The upper bound is closer to the true VC dimension when data points are on the surface of the ball than inside the ball. Hence with the transformation (2), $||\mathbf{w}||^2 + 1$ becomes a more accurate estimate of the VC dimension $h$. Then the VC dimension of $\mathcal{F}$ can be effectively controlled by restricting $||\mathbf{w}|| \leq H$ with a given $H$. RSVM Primal is formulated in variables $\mathbf{w}$, $b$ and $\boldsymbol{\xi}$ as [13]:

$$\min \quad E(\mathbf{w}, b, \boldsymbol{\xi}) = \sum_{i=1}^{\ell}\xi_i \tag{3}$$
$$\text{s.t.} \quad y_i\left((\mathbf{w}\cdot\mathbf{x}_i) + b\right) \geq 1 - \xi_i, \; \xi_i \geq 0, \; i = 1,\cdots,\ell, \tag{4}$$
$$(\mathbf{w}\cdot\mathbf{w}) \leq H^2. \tag{5}$$

Let $\gamma$ be the Lagrange multiplier corresponding to the constraint (5), and $\alpha_i$, $s_i$ be the Lagrange multiplier to the constraints $y_i((\mathbf{w}\cdot\mathbf{x}_i) + b) \geq 1 - \xi_i$ and $\xi_i \geq 0$ respectively. The index $i$ is understood to run over $1,\cdots,\ell$ unless otherwise noted. We can write the Lagrangian as

$$L = \sum \xi_i - \sum \alpha_i \left( y_i \left( (\mathbf{w} \cdot \mathbf{x}) + b \right) - 1 + \xi_i \right) - \gamma \left( H^2 - (\mathbf{w} \cdot \mathbf{w}) \right) - \sum s_i \xi_i, \quad (6)$$

and compute its derivatives with respect to the primal variables $\mathbf{w}$, $b$ and $\boldsymbol{\xi}$. At optimality, these derivatives equal to 0. We thus have the optimality conditions:

$$\gamma \mathbf{w} = \sum \alpha_i y_i \mathbf{x}_i, \quad (7)$$

$$\sum \alpha_i y_i = 0, \quad (8)$$

$$0 \leq \alpha_i \leq 1, \quad \gamma \geq 0. \quad (9)$$

We derive the dual formulation based on the discussion of two cases: $\gamma = 0$ and $\gamma > 0$. By complementarity, either $\gamma = 0$ or $(\mathbf{w} \cdot \mathbf{w}) - H^2 = 0$ at optimality. Without loss of generality, we assume they are not both equal to 0 at optimality. 1. If $\gamma = 0$ or $(\mathbf{w} \cdot \mathbf{w}) < H^2$ at optimality, by the KKT conditions, the optimal solution to RSVM Primal is also optimal for the relaxation problem by removing the constraint (5) from RSVM Primal. The relaxation problem degenerates to a linear program, so the dual problem becomes a linear program as follows:

$$\begin{aligned} \min_{\boldsymbol{\alpha}} \quad & \sum_{i=1}^{\ell} \alpha_i \\ \text{s.t.} \quad & \sum_{i=1}^{\ell} \alpha_i y_i \mathbf{x}_i = 0, \\ & \sum_{i=1}^{\ell} \alpha_i y_i = 0, \quad 0 \leq \alpha_i \leq 1. \end{aligned} \quad (10)$$

2. If $\gamma > 0$ or $(\mathbf{w} \cdot \mathbf{w}) = H^2$ at optimality, by Eq.(7), we have $\mathbf{w} = \frac{1}{\gamma} \sum_i \alpha_i y_i \mathbf{x}_i$. Substituting $\mathbf{w}$ into the Lagrangian, simplifying and adding in the dual constraints (8) and (9) yield the following optimization problem:

$$\begin{aligned} \max_{\boldsymbol{\alpha}, \gamma} \quad W(\boldsymbol{\alpha}, \gamma) = & \sum_{i=1}^{\ell} \alpha_i - \frac{1}{2\gamma} \sum_{i,j=1}^{\ell} \alpha_i \alpha_j y_i y_j (\mathbf{x}_i \cdot \mathbf{x}_j) - \frac{\gamma H^2}{2} \\ \text{s.t.} \quad & \sum_{i=1}^{\ell} \alpha_i y_i = 0, \\ & 0 \leq \alpha_i \leq 1, \quad \gamma > 0. \end{aligned} \quad (11)$$

The optimal $\gamma$ can be obtained by optimizing the unconstrained problem $\max_\gamma W(\alpha, \gamma)$. Set the derivative of $W$ with respect to $\gamma$ equal to 0. Solving the resulting equation produces two roots. The positive root $\frac{1}{H} \sqrt{\sum_{i,j=1}^{\ell} \alpha_i \alpha_j y_i y_j (\mathbf{x}_i \cdot \mathbf{x}_j)}$ is the optimal $\gamma$ for Problem (11). Substituting this optimal $\gamma$ into $W(\boldsymbol{\alpha}, \gamma)$ and adding a minus sign to $W$ yield the dual problem [13]:

$$\begin{aligned} \min_{\boldsymbol{\alpha}} \quad W(\boldsymbol{\alpha}) = & H \sqrt{\sum_{i,j=1}^{\ell} \alpha_i \alpha_j y_i y_j (\mathbf{x}_i \cdot \mathbf{x}_j)} - \sum_{i=1}^{\ell} \alpha_i \\ \text{s.t.} \quad & \sum_{i=1}^{\ell} \alpha_i y_i = 0, \\ & 0 \leq \alpha_i \leq 1. \end{aligned} \quad (12)$$

To perform capacity control, we should choose $H$ such that $(\mathbf{w} \cdot \mathbf{w}) = H^2$ at optimality, which means the constraint (5) is *active*. Otherwise, RSVM corresponds to just the training error minimization without capacity control. Therefore the second case, $\gamma > 0$, is of our concern. We refer to Problem (12) as RSVM Dual and assume the optimal $\gamma$ is positive through later sections. A question naturally arises as how Dual (12) behaves in case $\gamma = 0$. Denote the optimal solution to Dual (12) by $\hat{\alpha}$. Define $S(\hat{\alpha}) = \sum_{i,j=1}^{\ell} \hat{\alpha}_i \hat{\alpha}_j y_i y_j k(\mathbf{x}_i, \mathbf{x}_j)$, and $S(\alpha) \geq 0$ for any $\alpha$ due to the positive semi-definiteness of $k$. As shown in the expression of the optimal $\gamma$, once $S(\hat{\alpha}) > 0$, the optimal $\gamma > 0$. Hence in the case of $\gamma = 0$, $S(\hat{\alpha})$ has to be 0. Many solvers for nonlinear programs use the KKT conditions to construct termination criteria. To evaluate the KKT conditions of Dual (12), the derivative of $W(\alpha)$ with respect to each $\alpha_i$ needs to be computed:

$$\nabla_i W = \frac{H y_i \left( \sum_j \alpha_j y_j k(\mathbf{x}_i, \mathbf{x}_j) \right)}{\sqrt{S(\alpha)}} - 1. \tag{13}$$

Realize that the derivative is not well-defined if $S(\alpha) = 0$. Hence no solution can be obtained for Dual (12) if $H$ is so large that $\gamma = 0$.

## 3  Characteristics of RSVM

In this section we discuss some characteristics of RSVM that are fundamental to its construction and optimization. Given a series of candidates for the parameter $H$, such that $0 < H_1 < H_2 < \cdots < H_t < \cdots$, we show that solving RSVM Primal (3) with respect to this series of values for $H$ and choosing the best solution $(\mathbf{w}, b)$ actually yields a direct implementation of the induction principle of SRM. The following proposition characterizes this result. The C-SVM was also formulated following the SRM principle but not an explicit implementation.

**Proposition 1.** *Let* $0 < H_1 < H_2 < \cdots < H_t < \cdots$. *It follows the induction principle of SRM to solve RSVM (3) respectively with* $H_1, H_2, \cdots, H_t, \cdots$ *and choose the solution* $(\mathbf{w}, b)$ *that achieves the minimal value of the bound (1).*

*Proof.* Let $\mathcal{F}$ be the set consisting of all hyperplanes. We only need to prove that the series of subsets of $\mathcal{F}$, from each of which RSVM finds a solution, are nested with respect to $H_1, H_2, \cdots, H_t, \cdots$. In other words, they satisfy $\mathcal{F}_1 \subset \mathcal{F}_2 \subset \cdots \subset \mathcal{F}_t \subset \cdots$. Consider the two consecutive sets $\mathcal{F}_{t-1}$ and $\mathcal{F}_t$. It is clear that the set $\mathcal{F}_{t-1} = \{g_{\mathbf{w},b}(\mathbf{x}) : (\mathbf{w} \cdot \mathbf{w}) \leq H_{t-1}^2\}$ is a subset of $\mathcal{F}_t = \{g_{\mathbf{w},b}(\mathbf{x}) : (\mathbf{w} \cdot \mathbf{w}) \leq H_t^2\}$ for $H_{t-1} < H_t$. Recall that $g_{\mathbf{w},b}(\mathbf{x}) = \mathrm{sgn}\,((\mathbf{w} \cdot \mathbf{x}) + b)$. Then we verify that each element in the series has the structure:

1. $\mathcal{F}^t$ has a finite VC dimension $h_t \leq H_t^2 + 1$.

2. $\mathcal{F}_t$ contains the functions of the form $g_{\mathbf{w},b}(\mathbf{x})$, for which the loss function is an indicator function.

Similar to C-SVMs, RSVM constructs optimal hyperplanes by optimizing in the dual space. In general, solving the dual does not necessarily produce the optimal value of the primal unless there is no duality gap. In other words, the strong duality should be met, which requires that $W(\boldsymbol{\alpha}, \gamma) = E(\mathbf{w}, b, \boldsymbol{\xi})$ at the respective primal and dual optimal solutions. Equivalently, this imposes $W(\boldsymbol{\alpha}) = -E(\mathbf{w}, b, \boldsymbol{\xi})$ at the optimal RSVM Primal and Dual solutions.

**Theorem 1.** *There is no duality gap between Primal (3) and Dual (12).*

*Proof.* We use the following theorem [2]:
If (i) the problem $\min\{f(\mathbf{x}) : \mathbf{c}(\mathbf{x}) \leq 0, \mathbf{x} \in \mathbb{R}^n\}$ has a finite optimal value, (ii) the functions $f$ and $\mathbf{c}$ are convex, and (iii) an interior point $\mathbf{x}$ exists, i.e., $\mathbf{c}(\mathbf{x}) < 0$, then there is no duality gap.
It is obvious that RSVM Primal satisfies the first two conditions. If $H > 0$, a feasible $\mathbf{w}$ exists for $(\mathbf{w} \cdot \mathbf{w}) < H^2$. With this $\mathbf{w}$, an interior point $(\mathbf{w}, b, \boldsymbol{\xi})$ can be constructed by choosing $\boldsymbol{\xi}$ large enough to satisfy $y_i((\mathbf{w} \cdot \mathbf{x}_i) + b) > 1 - \xi_i, \xi_i > 0, i = 1, \cdots, \ell$.

RSVM Primal is a quadratically-constrained quadratic program that is a convex program. For a convex program, a local minimizer is also a global minimizer. If the solution is not unique, the set of global solutions is convex. Although the objective of RSVM Dual is not surely convex, RSVM Dual is in principle a convex program since it can be recast as a second-order cone program (SOCP) by substituting $t$ for the square root term in the objective and adding a constraint to restrict the square root term no more than $t$. SOCPs are non-linear convex programs [7]. Therefore same as C-SVMs, RSVM does not get trapped at any local minimizer. We leave investigation of SOCPs in RSVM to future research.

Examining uniqueness of the solution can provide insights into the algorithm as shown for C-SVMs [5]. Since the goal is to construct a separating hyperplane characterized by $(\mathbf{w}, b)$, and the geometric interpretation of SVMs mainly rests on the primal variables, we provide Theorem 2 only addressing the conditions for the primal $\hat{\mathbf{w}}$ to be unique. In general, the optimal $\hat{\mathbf{w}}$ of RSVM is not necessarily unique, which is different from C-SVMs where even if the optimal solutions $(\mathbf{w}, b, \boldsymbol{\xi})$ may not be unique, they share the same optimal $\mathbf{w}$ [5]. Arguments about the offset $\hat{b}$ can be drawn similarly to those in [5], and will not be discussed here.

**Theorem 2.** *If the constraint $(\mathbf{w} \cdot \mathbf{w}) \leq H^2$ is active at any optimal solution to RSVM Primal, then the optimal $\mathbf{w}$ is unique.*

*Proof.* Realize that the optimal solution set of RSVM Primal is a convex set. Let $\hat{\mathbf{w}}$ be an optimal solution of RSVM, and $(\hat{\mathbf{w}} \cdot \hat{\mathbf{w}}) = H^2$. Assume that RSVM has another solution $\bar{\mathbf{w}}$ also satisfying $(\bar{\mathbf{w}} \cdot \bar{\mathbf{w}}) = H^2$. Then the middle point on the line segment connecting $\hat{\mathbf{w}}$ and $\bar{\mathbf{w}}$ is also optimal, but it cannot satisfy $(\mathbf{w} \cdot \mathbf{w}) = H^2$, contradicting the assumption.

Since RSVM Dual (12) is derived assuming $\gamma > 0$, solving it always produces a primal solution with $(\mathbf{w} \cdot \mathbf{w}) = H^2$. From the primal perspective, however, alternative solutions may exist satisfying $(\mathbf{w} \cdot \mathbf{w}) < H^2$, so Theorem 2 will not hold. Notice that such a solution is also optimal to the relaxation problem

$$\min \quad \sum_{i=1}^{\ell} \xi_i$$
$$\text{s.t. } y_i((\mathbf{w} \cdot \mathbf{x}_i) + b) \geq 1 - \xi_i, \ i = 1, \cdots, \ell, \tag{14}$$
$$\xi_i \geq 0, \ i = 1, \cdots, \ell.$$

If the relaxation problem (14) has a unique solution $\bar{\mathbf{w}}$ and let $\bar{H} = ||\bar{\mathbf{w}}||$, there exist only two cases: 1. if $H < \bar{H}$, the constraint (5) must be active at any RSVM optimal solution, and thus Theorem 2 holds; 2. if $H \geq \bar{H}$, Primal (3) has only one solution $\bar{\mathbf{w}}$. In both cases, the optimal $\mathbf{w}$ of Primal (3) is unique. We hence conclude with Theorem 3.

**Theorem 3.** *If the relaxation problem (14) has a unique solution, then for any $H > 0$, RSVM (3) has a unique optimal $\mathbf{w}$.*

One of the principal characteristics of SVMs is the use of kernels [12]. It is clear that RSVM can construct nonlinear classifiers by substituting the kernel $k(\mathbf{x}_i, \mathbf{x}_j)$ for the inner product $(\mathbf{x}_i \cdot \mathbf{x}_j)$ in Dual (12). By using a kernel $k$, we map the original data $\mathbf{x}$ to $\Phi(\mathbf{x})$ in a feature space so that $k(\mathbf{x}_i, \mathbf{x}_j) = (\Phi(\mathbf{x}_i) \cdot \Phi(\mathbf{x}_j))$. From the perspective of primal, solving Dual (12) with inner products replaced by kernel entries corresponds to constructing a linear function $f(\mathbf{x}) = (\mathbf{w} \cdot \Phi(\mathbf{x})) + b$ in feature space. Similarly, by optimality conditions, $\mathbf{w} = \frac{1}{\gamma} \sum \alpha_i y_i \Phi(\mathbf{x}_i)$, and the function $f(\mathbf{x}) = \frac{1}{\gamma} \sum \alpha_i y_i k(\mathbf{x}_i, \mathbf{x})$ with $\gamma = \frac{1}{H} \sqrt{\sum_{i,j=1}^{\ell} \alpha_i \alpha_j y_i y_j k(\mathbf{x}_i, \mathbf{x}_j)}$. Notice that the transformation (2) now has to be taken in the feature space, i.e., $(\Phi(\mathbf{x}_i) - \bar{\Phi})/||\Phi(\mathbf{x}_i) - \bar{\Phi}||$ where $\bar{\Phi}$ denotes the mean of all $\Phi(\mathbf{x}_i)$s. We verify that this transformation can be implicitly performed by defining a kernel associated with $k$ as $\tilde{k}(\mathbf{x}_i, \mathbf{x}_j) = \frac{\hat{k}(\mathbf{x}_i, \mathbf{x}_j)}{\sqrt{\hat{k}(\mathbf{x}_i, \mathbf{x}_i)\hat{k}(\mathbf{x}_j, \mathbf{x}_j)}}$ (normalizing) where $\hat{k}(\mathbf{x}_i, \mathbf{x}_j) = k(\mathbf{x}_i, \mathbf{x}_j) - \frac{1}{\ell} \sum_{q=1}^{\ell} k(\mathbf{x}_i, \mathbf{x}_q) - \frac{1}{\ell} \sum_{p=1}^{\ell} k(\mathbf{x}_p, \mathbf{x}_j) + \frac{1}{\ell^2} \sum_{p,q=1}^{\ell} k(\mathbf{x}_p, \mathbf{x}_q)$ (centering).

## 4    Comparison with Other SVMs

We compare RSVM to other SVM formulations in this section to identify their relationships. These approaches include the C-SVM with a parameter $C$ [4, 13], the geometric Reduced convex Hull approach (RHSVM) with a parameter $D$ [1, 3], and the $\nu$-SVM classification with a parameter $\nu$ [11]. The comparison reveals the equivalence of these approaches for properly-selected parameter choices. We emphasize the equivalence of the normal vector $\mathbf{w}$ constructed by these approaches. Two $\mathbf{w}$ vectors are said to be "equivalent" if they are precisely the same or only scale differently.

Let $(\hat{\boldsymbol{\alpha}}, \hat{\mathbf{w}})$ be optimal to the RSVM Dual and Primal. Denote the corresponding solutions of the C-SVM, RHSVM, and $\nu$-SVM respectively by $(\boldsymbol{\alpha}^C, \mathbf{w}^C)$, $(\boldsymbol{\alpha}^D, \mathbf{w}^D)$ and $(\boldsymbol{\alpha}^\nu, \mathbf{w}^\nu)$. We obtain the following three propositions.

**Proposition 2.** *If $C = \frac{1}{\hat{\gamma}} = \frac{\sqrt{S(\hat{\boldsymbol{\alpha}})}}{H}$, then $\boldsymbol{\alpha}^C = \frac{\hat{\boldsymbol{\alpha}}}{\hat{\gamma}}$ is a solution to C-SVM.*

*Proof.* Consider Problem (11). Note that this problem is equivalent to RSVM Dual (12). We rewrite the objective function $W(\boldsymbol{\alpha}, \gamma) =$

$$\gamma \left( \sum_{i=1}^{\ell} \alpha_i - \frac{1}{2} \sum_{i,j=1}^{\ell} \alpha_i \alpha_j y_i y_j k(\mathbf{x}_i, \mathbf{x}_j) - \frac{H^2}{2} \right)$$

where $\boldsymbol{\alpha}$ has been rescaled by dividing by $\gamma$. Since $H$ is a pre-specified constant in the above parentheses, for any fixed $\gamma \geq 0$, solving Problem (11) is equivalent to solving the following problem

$$
\min_{\boldsymbol{\alpha}} \frac{1}{2} \sum_{i,j=1}^{\ell} \alpha_i \alpha_j y_i y_j k(\mathbf{x}_i, \mathbf{x}_j) - \sum_{i=1}^{\ell} \alpha_i \tag{15}
$$

$$
\text{s.t.} \quad \sum_{i=1}^{\ell} \alpha_i y_i = 0,
$$
$$
0 \leq \alpha_i \leq \tfrac{1}{\gamma}, \quad i = 1, \cdots, \ell.
$$

Multiplying the solution to Problem (15) by $\gamma$ produces a solution to Problem (11). Realize that Problem (15) is exactly the dual C-SVM formulation with the parameter $C = \frac{1}{\gamma}$. Set $C = \frac{1}{\hat{\gamma}}$ where $\hat{\gamma} = \frac{\sqrt{S(\hat{\boldsymbol{\alpha}})}}{H}$ is optimal to Problem (11). With this $C$, C-SVM has a solution $\boldsymbol{\alpha}^C = \frac{\hat{\boldsymbol{\alpha}}}{\hat{\gamma}}$.

**Proposition 3.** *If* $D = \frac{2}{\sum \hat{\alpha}_i}$, *then* $\boldsymbol{\alpha}^D = \frac{2\hat{\boldsymbol{\alpha}}}{\sum \hat{\alpha}_i}$ *is a solution to RHSVM.*

*Proof.* Consider RSVM Dual (12). The equality constraint can be rewritten as $\sum_{y_i=1} \alpha_i = \sum_{y_i=-1} \alpha_i = \delta$ for $\delta = \frac{1}{2} \sum_{i=1}^{\ell} \alpha_i$. Now define $\boldsymbol{\beta} = \frac{\hat{\boldsymbol{\alpha}}}{\hat{\delta}}$ where $\hat{\delta} = \frac{1}{2} \sum \hat{\alpha}_i$, and then $\sum \beta_i = 2$. It can be shown by contradiction that $\boldsymbol{\beta}$ is an optimal solution to the following problem

$$
\min_{\boldsymbol{\alpha}} \quad \frac{1}{2} \sum_{i,j=1}^{\ell} \alpha_i \alpha_j y_i y_j k(\mathbf{x}_i, \mathbf{x}_j) \tag{16}
$$

$$
\text{s.t.} \ \sum_{y_i=1} \alpha_i = 1, \ \sum_{y_i=-1} \alpha_i = 1,
$$
$$
0 \leq \alpha_i \leq \tfrac{1}{\hat{\delta}}, \quad i = 1, \cdots, \ell.
$$

Realize that Problem (16) is exactly the dual RHSVM formulation [1] with the parameter $D = \frac{1}{\hat{\delta}}$. Then $D = \frac{2}{\sum \hat{\alpha}_i}$, and $\boldsymbol{\alpha}^D = \boldsymbol{\beta} = \frac{\hat{\boldsymbol{\alpha}}}{\hat{\delta}} = \frac{2\hat{\boldsymbol{\alpha}}}{\sum \hat{\alpha}_i}$.

**Proposition 4.** *If* $\nu = \frac{\sum \hat{\alpha}_i}{\ell}$, *then* $\boldsymbol{\alpha}^\nu = \frac{\hat{\boldsymbol{\alpha}}}{\ell}$ *is a solution to $\nu$-SVM.*

*Proof.* Consider Problem (15) with parameter $\gamma$ equal to the $\hat{\gamma}$. Multiply the $\boldsymbol{\alpha}$ in (15) by $\frac{\hat{\gamma}}{\ell}$. Set $\nu = \frac{\hat{\gamma}}{\ell} \sum \alpha_i^C = \frac{\sum \hat{\alpha}_i}{\ell}$. Solving the dual $\nu$-SVM formulation [11]:

$$
\min_{\boldsymbol{\alpha}} \frac{1}{2} \sum_{i,j=1}^{\ell} \alpha_i \alpha_j y_i y_j k(\mathbf{x}_i, \mathbf{x}_j) \tag{17}
$$

$$
\text{s.t.} \quad \sum_{i=1}^{\ell} \alpha_i y_i = 0,
$$
$$
0 \leq \alpha_i \leq \tfrac{1}{\ell}, \quad i = 1, \cdots, \ell,
$$
$$
\sum_{i=1}^{\ell} \alpha_i = \nu.
$$

yields a solution $\boldsymbol{\alpha}^\nu = \frac{\hat{\gamma}}{\ell} \boldsymbol{\alpha}^C = \frac{\hat{\boldsymbol{\alpha}}}{\ell}$.

We summarize the above results in Table 1 along with comparison of primal $\hat{\mathbf{w}}$. Solving the four formulations with their parameters chosen according to Table

**Table 1.** Relations of the RSVM, C-SVM, RHSVM, and $\nu$-SVM. The $S(\hat{\alpha}) = \sum_{i,j=1}^{\ell} \hat{\alpha}_i \hat{\alpha}_j y_i y_j k(\mathbf{x}_i, \mathbf{x}_j)$. For appropriate parameter choices as defined in the table, the optimal separating hyperplanes produced by the four methods are parallel.

| | PARAMETER | DUAL | PRIMAL |
|---|---|---|---|
| RSVM | $H$ | $\hat{\alpha}$ | $\hat{\mathbf{w}}$ |
| C-SVM | $\dfrac{H}{\sqrt{S(\hat{\alpha})}}$ | $\hat{\alpha}\dfrac{H}{\sqrt{S(\hat{\alpha})}}$ | $\mathbf{w}^C = \hat{\mathbf{w}}$ |
| RHSVM | $\dfrac{2}{\sum \hat{\alpha}_i}$ | $\hat{\alpha}\dfrac{2}{\sum \hat{\alpha}_i}$ | $\mathbf{w}^D = \hat{\mathbf{w}}\dfrac{2\sqrt{S(\hat{\alpha})}}{H\sum \hat{\alpha}_i}$ |
| $\nu$-SVM | $\dfrac{\sum \hat{\alpha}_i}{\ell}$ | $\hat{\alpha}\dfrac{1}{\ell}$ | $\mathbf{w}^\nu = \hat{\mathbf{w}}\dfrac{\sqrt{S(\hat{\alpha})}}{H\ell}$ |

1 yields equivalent solutions, namely, the same orientation of the optimal separating hyperplanes. In RSVM, the VC dimension is pre-specified approximate to $H^2 + 1$ prior training. In C-SVM, instead of pre-specified, the VC dimension can be evaluated via $(\mathbf{w}^C \cdot \mathbf{w}^C)$ only after a solution $\mathbf{w}^C$ has been obtained. For the other two approaches, it is not straightforward to estimate VC dimension based on their solutions or parameter values.

## 5    Choosing $H$ and the Decomposition Scheme

According to duality analysis, the parameter $H$ should be selected within an upper limit $\hat{H}$ or otherwise Dual (12) will not produce a solution. We focus on finding an upper bound $\hat{H}$ on valid choices of $H$. A choice of $H$ is valid for RSVM if there exists an optimal RSVM solution satisfying $(\mathbf{w} \cdot \mathbf{w}) = H^2$.

To proceed with our discussion, we first define separability. A set of data $(\mathbf{x}_i, y_i), i = 1, \cdots, \ell$, is linearly separable (or strictly separable) if there exists a hyperplane $\{\mathbf{x} : f(\mathbf{x}) = 0\}$, such that $y_i f(\mathbf{x}_i) \geq 0$ (or $y_i f(\mathbf{x}_i) > 0$); otherwise, it is linearly inseparable. Note that linear separability can be extended to hyperplanes in feature space, and thus it is not linear in input space. In terms of RSVM (3), if the minimal objective value is 0 for a choice of $H$, meaning $\xi_i = 0$ for all $i$, the data are strictly separable, whereas for inseparable data, the objective $E$ will never achieve 0 for any choice of $H$. Without loss of generality, we discuss the strictly separable case and the inseparable case.

1. For the strictly separable case, a valid $H$ exists so that $E(\hat{\mathbf{w}}, \hat{b}, \hat{\xi}) = 0$. By strong duality, the dual $W(\hat{\alpha}) = H\sqrt{S(\hat{\alpha})} - \sum \hat{\alpha}_i = 0$, so $H = \dfrac{\sum \hat{\alpha}_i}{\sqrt{S(\hat{\alpha})}}$, which is well-defined since $S(\hat{\alpha}) > 0$ for a valid $H$. Rescaling $\hat{\alpha}$ by $\hat{\delta} = \frac{1}{2}\sum_{i=1}^{\ell} \hat{\alpha}_i$ does not change the fraction, and $H = \dfrac{2}{\sqrt{S(\beta)}}$ where $\beta = \dfrac{\hat{\alpha}}{\hat{\delta}}$. As shown in Proposition 3, $\beta$ is optimal for RHSVM dual problem (16). Notice that the largest valid $H$ can be evaluated by computing the smallest possible $S(\beta)$. We thus relax Problem (16) by removing the upper bound on $\alpha$, $\alpha_i \leq \frac{1}{\delta}$, to produce the smallest $S(\hat{\beta})$. Now $\hat{\beta}$ is a solution to the RHSVM dual for the linearly separable case [1] where RHSVM finds the closest points in the convex hulls of each class of data,

and $\sqrt{S(\hat{\beta})}$ is the distance between the two closest points. So $\frac{1}{2}\sqrt{S(\hat{\beta})}$ is the maximum margin of the problem. We therefore have the following proposition.

**Proposition 5.** *For linearly separable problems, $H > \frac{1}{\Delta}$ is not valid for RSVM (3) where $\Delta$ is the maximum hard margin.*

2. For the inseparable case, we can solve the relaxation problem (14) to have a solution $\bar{\mathbf{w}}$. Then $\|\bar{\mathbf{w}}\|$ is a potential upper bound on valid choices of $H$. In a more general case, if a kernel is employed, the point $\mathbf{x}_i$ in Problem (14) has to be replaced by its image $\Phi(\mathbf{x}_i)$ which is often not explicitly expressed, so it is impossible to directly solve Problem (14). We instead solve the problem with the substitution of $\mathbf{w} = \sum \beta_i y_i \Phi(\mathbf{x}_i)$, and the problem becomes

$$\min_{\beta, b, \xi} \quad E(\beta, b, \xi) = \sum_{i=1}^{\ell} \xi_i$$
$$\text{s.t.} \quad y_i \left( \sum_{j=1}^{\ell} \beta_j y_j k(\mathbf{x}_i, \mathbf{x}_j) + b \right) \geq 1 - \xi_i, \tag{18}$$
$$\xi_i \geq 0, \quad i = 1, \cdots, \ell.$$

This is a linear program in terms of $\beta$ not $\mathbf{w}$. Let $\mathcal{B}$ be the entire set of optimal solutions to Problem (18). Denote the $\mathbf{w}$ constructed based on any solution in $\mathcal{B}$ by $\mathbf{w}_\beta$. If the supremum of $\|\mathbf{w}_\beta\|$ ($= \sqrt{S(\beta)}$) on $\mathcal{B}$ is finite, then it is an upper bound on valid $H$. We show this result in the following proposition.

**Proposition 6.** *If $\hat{H} = \sup\limits_{\beta \in \mathcal{B}} \|\mathbf{w}_\beta\| < \infty$, $H > \hat{H}$ is not valid for RSVM (3).*

*Proof.* Assume $H > \hat{H}$ is valid. We show that by contradiction, there exists another solution $\hat{\beta}$ that is optimal to Problem (18) but not included in $\mathcal{B}$.

If $H$ is valid, then $\gamma > 0$. The optimal $\hat{\mathbf{w}}$ to the Primal (3) with $\mathbf{x}_i$ replaced by $\Phi(\mathbf{x}_i)$ can be expressed as $\hat{\mathbf{w}} = \sum \hat{\beta}_i y_i \Phi(\mathbf{x}_i)$ where $\hat{\beta} = \frac{\hat{\alpha}}{\gamma}$ and $\hat{\alpha}$ is optimal for Dual (12). Let the respective optimal objective values of Problem (3) and (18) be $\hat{E}$ and $\bar{E}$. Since the feasible region of Primal (3) is a subset of the feasible region of Problem (18), $\hat{E} \geq \bar{E}$. However, any $\mathbf{w}_\beta$ is feasible to Primal (3) for $H > \hat{H}$, and thus optimal for Primal (3), so $\hat{E} = \bar{E}$. Then $\hat{\beta}$ is also an optimal solution to Problem (18) but not included in $\mathcal{B}$ since $\|\hat{\mathbf{w}}\| = H > \hat{H}$.

We devise our strategies for choosing $H$ based the above two propositions. Since $H^2$ is used to provide an estimate of the VC dimension and VC dimension is typically a positive integer no greater than $\ell$, we consider just positive integers in $[0, \ell] \cap [0, \hat{H}^2]$ where $\hat{H}$ is calculated depending on the linear separability. Actually $\hat{H}$ can be obtained with small computational cost by solving either a hard margin C-SVM (separable) or a linear program (18) (inseparable). Moreover, previous research [13, 10] suggested that $\frac{h}{\ell} \in [0.05, 0.25]$ might be a good choice for the capacity control. We recommend selecting integers first from a small range, such as $[0.05\ell, 0.25\ell] \cap [0, \hat{H}^2]$, as candidates for $H^2$. If it does not produce desirable performance, the range can be augmented to include choices in $[0, \ell] \cap [0, \hat{H}^2]$.

We next explore the possibility of large-scale RSVM learning by developing a decomposition scheme for RSVM based on the one proposed for C-SVMs [6, 8]. A decomposition algorithm consists of two steps. First, select the working set $B$ of $q$ variables. Second, decompose the problem and optimize $W(\alpha)$ on $B$. The algorithm repeats the two steps until the termination criteria are met. We show that the decomposition algorithm can be carried over on RSVM with small extra cost of computation as compared with the algorithm for C-SVMs.

For notational convenience, we switch to the matrix vector product notation here. Define the matrix $\mathbf{Q}$ as $\mathbf{Q}_{ij} = y_i y_j k(\mathbf{x}_i, \mathbf{x}_j)$. Then $W(\alpha) = H\sqrt{S(\alpha)} - \mathbf{e}'\alpha$ where $S(\alpha) = \alpha'\mathbf{Q}\alpha$ and $\mathbf{e}$ is a vector of ones of appropriate dimension. Let variables $\alpha$ be separated into a working set $B$ and the remaining set $N$. We properly arrange $\alpha$, $\mathbf{y}$ and $\mathbf{Q}$ with respect to $B$ and $N$ so that

$$\alpha = \begin{pmatrix} \alpha_B \\ \alpha_N \end{pmatrix}, \quad \mathbf{y} = \begin{pmatrix} \mathbf{y}_B \\ \mathbf{y}_N \end{pmatrix}, \quad \mathbf{Q} = \begin{pmatrix} \mathbf{Q}_{BB} & \mathbf{Q}_{BN} \\ \mathbf{Q}_{NB} & \mathbf{Q}_{NN} \end{pmatrix}.$$

Decompose $S(\alpha)$ to the sum of three terms $S_{BB} = \alpha'_B \mathbf{Q}_{BB}\alpha_B$, $S_{BN} = 2(\mathbf{Q}_{BN}\alpha_N)'\alpha_B$, and $S_{NN} = \alpha'_N \mathbf{Q}_{NN}\alpha_N$, and rewrite $\mathbf{e}'\alpha = \mathbf{e}'\alpha_B + \mathbf{e}'\alpha_N$. Since the $\alpha_N$ are fixed, $\mathbf{p}_{BN} = \mathbf{Q}_{BN}\alpha_N$, $S_{NN}$ and $\mathbf{e}'\alpha_N$ are constant. The $\mathbf{e}'\alpha_N$ can be omitted from $W(\alpha)$ without changing the solution. Dual (12) can be reformulated as the following subproblem in variables $\alpha_B$:

$$\min_{\alpha_B} H\sqrt{\alpha'_B \mathbf{Q}_{BB}\alpha_B + 2\mathbf{p}'_{BN}\alpha_B + S_{NN}} - \mathbf{e}'\alpha_B$$
$$\text{s.t.} \qquad \mathbf{y}'_B\alpha_B = -\mathbf{y}'_N\alpha_N, \tag{19}$$
$$0 \le \alpha_B \le \mathbf{e}.$$

Note that $S_{NN}$ can not be omitted as in C-SVMs since it stays inside the square root. Typically the working set $B$ consists of merely a few variables, and $N$ contains the majority of variables. Computing $\mathbf{p}_{BN}$ and $S_{NN}$ consumes significant time. If the kernel matrix is large and not stored in memory, computing $\mathbf{Q}_{NN}$ and $\mathbf{Q}_{BN}$ collapses the efficiency of the decomposition. Let $(\mathbf{Q}\alpha)_B$ be the vector consisting of the first $q$ components (in the working set $B$) of $\mathbf{Q}\alpha$. Then $(\mathbf{Q}\alpha)_B = \mathbf{Q}_{BB}\alpha_B + \mathbf{Q}_{BN}\alpha_N$. The key to our scheme is the use of the two equations:

$$\mathbf{p}_{BN} = (\mathbf{Q}\alpha)_B - \mathbf{Q}_{BB}\alpha_B, \tag{20}$$
$$S_{NN} = S(\alpha) - S_{BB} - S_{BN}, \tag{21}$$

in computing $\mathbf{p}_{BN}$ and $S_{NN}$ instead of a direct evaluation. We keep track of the value of $S(\alpha)$ after solving each subproblem. Compared with the algorithm for C-SVMs, the update of $S(\alpha)$ and the evaluation of $S_{NN}$ introduce the extra computation which, however, takes only a few arithmetic operations. See our implementation[1] for more details of the algorithm.

---

[1] A preliminary solver for RSVM written in C++ is available at
*http://www.cs.rpi.edu/~bij2/rsvm.html.*

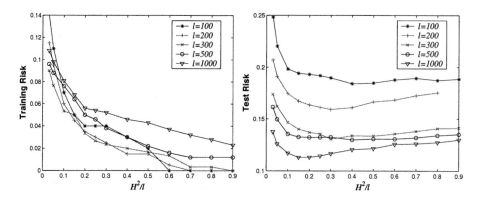

**Fig. 1.** Curves of the error rates versus the ratio $H^2/\ell$ for various choices of $\ell$: *left*, the training risk; *right*, the test risk.

## 6    Experimental Studies

The goals of our experiments were to demonstrate the performance of RSVM, discover knowledge for choosing proper $H$, and compare RSVM to other SVM approaches. We conducted our experiments on the MNIST hand-written digit database (60,000 digits, 784 variables), the Wisconsin Breast Cancer (569 observations, 30 variables) and Adult-4 (4781 examples, 123 variables) benchmark datasets[2]. For the digit dataset, we want to distinguish odd numbers from even numbers. The proportion of positive examples to negative examples is roughly even in the digit data, but the proportions in the Adult-4 and Breast Cancer data are 1188/3593 and 212/357, respectively. We randomly took 200 examples from Breast Cancer and 1000 examples from Adult-4, respectively, for training such that the ratios of positive to negative examples of training data are the same as of the entire data. The remaining examples were used for test.

The data were preprocessed in the following way: examples were centered to have mean **0** by subtracting the mean of the training examples; then each variable (totally $28 \times 28 = 784$ variables) was scaled to have standard deviation 1; after that, each example was normalized to have $\ell_2$-norm equal 1. Note that the test data should be blinded to the learning algorithm. Hence the test data were preprocessed using the mean of training data and the standard deviation of each variable computed based on training data. We simply used the inner product (a linear kernel) in all our experiments.

We first performed a series of experiments on the digit dataset. The first $\ell$ digits of the database were adopted as the training dataset, and $\ell$ was respectively equal to 100, 200, 300, 500, 1000. The last 10,000 digits comprised the test set for all the experiments. Figure 1 presents the performance of RSVM obtained

---

[2] MNIST data was downloaded from *http://yann.lecun.com/exdb/mnist/*. The Breast Cancer and Adult-4 datasets were obtained respectively from UC-Irvine data repository and *http://www.research.microsoft.com/~jplatt* [9].

**Table 2.** Results obtained using the training sets of $\ell = 200$ (left) and $\ell = 1000$ (right) digits. The N_SV stands for the number of support vectors. $R_{trn}$ and $R_{tst}$ are the percentages of errors on the training and test datasets, respectively. Numbers in the column of the parameter $D$ should be multiplied by $10^{-2}$.

| $H^2/\ell$ | N_SV | $R_{trn}$ | $R_{tst}$ | $C$ | $D$ | $\nu$ | N_SV | $R_{trn}$ | $R_{tst}$ | $C$ | $D$ | $\nu$ |
|---|---|---|---|---|---|---|---|---|---|---|---|---|
| 0.03 | 184 | 11.5 | 20.7 | 0.075 | 1.097 | 0.912 | 599 | 10.8 | 13.8 | 0.124 | 0.345 | 0.579 |
| 0.05 | 167 | 9.5 | 19.1 | 0.129 | 1.258 | 0.795 | 518 | 9.8 | 12.6 | 0.247 | 0.414 | 0.482 |
| 0.1 | 140 | 6.0 | 17.4 | 0.298 | 1.623 | 0.616 | 431 | 8.1 | 11.7 | 0.636 | 0.534 | 0.374 |
| 0.15 | 127 | 4.5 | 16.7 | 0.476 | 1.890 | 0.529 | 394 | 6.8 | 11.3 | 1.021 | 0.600 | 0.333 |
| 0.2 | 119 | 3.5 | 16.3 | 0.712 | 2.215 | 0.452 | 378 | 5.6 | 11.3 | 1.407 | 0.650 | 0.308 |
| 0.25 | 114 | 3.0 | 16.0 | 0.982 | 2.528 | 0.396 | 363 | 5.4 | 11.5 | 1.906 | 0.711 | 0.281 |
| 0.3 | 105 | 2.5 | 16.0 | 1.21 | 2.732 | 0.366 | 351 | 5.2 | 11.7 | 2.378 | 0.756 | 0.265 |
| 0.4 | 100 | 1.5 | 16.1 | 1.71 | 3.153 | 0.317 | 333 | 4.6 | 12.1 | 3.323 | 0.830 | 0.241 |
| 0.5 | 100 | 1.5 | 16.6 | 2.25 | 3.567 | 0.280 | 325 | 4.3 | 12.2 | 4.255 | 0.890 | 0.225 |
| 0.6 | 95 | 0.5 | 16.8 | 2.90 | 4.079 | 0.245 | 322 | 3.7 | 12.6 | 5.190 | 0.942 | 0.212 |
| 0.7 | 96 | 0 | 17.2 | 3.64 | 4.649 | 0.215 | 320 | 3.2 | 12.6 | 6.208 | 0.996 | 0.200 |
| 0.8 | 94 | 0 | 17.5 | 4.50 | 5.326 | 0.188 | 318 | 2.8 | 12.7 | 7.233 | 1.046 | 0.191 |

on distinct sizes of training data with a large spread of choices of $H^2$. The training risk monotonically decreases as $H^2$ increases for all the choices of $\ell$. The corresponding test risk curve, however, has the minimum point as shown in Figure 1(right). Although the optimal ratios $H^2/\ell$ are different for various sizes of training data, they are roughly located around $[0.05, 0.30]$ except when $\ell = 100$, it is a little off. In this case, we may want to explore the full range of valid $H$, $[0, \min\{\hat{H}^2, \ell\}]$, where $\hat{H}^2 = 90$ obtained by solving the hard-margin C-SVM for $\ell = 100$. Table 2 provides in detail the results obtained by RSVM for $\ell = 200$ and $\ell = 1000$. We applied the heuristic of choosing the ratio $H^2/\ell$ in $[0.05, 0.30]$ into the subsequent experiments on the Adult-4 and Breast Cancer data. Results are summarized in Table 3 which shows that this heuristic is useful since good models are achieved with $H^2/\ell$ chosen in this much smaller range.

As shown in Table 2, the ratio $H^2/\ell$ was chosen from 0.03 to 0.8 in the experiments on digits. The corresponding value of $C$ for C-SVM spreads within a small range, for instance, from 0.124 to 7.233 for $\ell = 1000$. As in Table 3, the ratio was chosen in a smaller range for experiments with Adult-4. But the value of $C$ jumped from small numbers to very big numbers. Hence it is hard to pre-determine the proper range for C-SVM and to evaluate what happens in training when using a $C$ far beyond the acceptable range. In addition, the proper range of $C$ (not only the best $C$) is problem-dependent by cross referencing the results for $\ell = 200$ and $\ell = 1000$ in Table 2 and results in Table 3. Hence it is not straightforward to distinguish if $C$ takes a proper value so that $H^2$ is valid.

Because of the geometric motivation for RHSVM, the parameter $D$ scales with the size of training data. From Table 2, RHSVM used rather small values of $D$ in our experiments, especially for a large training set and a small $h$ (or small $H^2$). Since $D$ is the upper bound on each $\alpha$, too small $D$ may cause computation unstable. As $\nu$ is the lower bound on the fraction of support vectors as well as

**Table 3.** Results obtained on Adult-4 (left, $\ell = 1000$) and Breast Cancer (right, $\ell = 200$) datasets. FP/FN$_r$ and FP/FN$_t$ represent false positive versus false negative rates respectively for training and test.

| $H^2/\ell$ | $R_{trn}$ | FP/FN$_r$ | $R_{tst}$ | FP/FN$_t$ | $C$ | $R_{trn}$ | FP/FN$_r$ | $R_{tst}$ | FP/FN$_t$ | $C$ |
|---|---|---|---|---|---|---|---|---|---|---|
| 0.03 | 15.1 | 8.1/17.3 | 16.7 | 11.4/18.5 | 3.2e-1 | 2.5 | 0/4.0 | 2.4 | 0.7/3.4 | 2.1e-2 |
| 0.05 | 13.7 | 10.8/14.6 | 16.8 | 14.5/17.6 | 6.4e-1 | 2.5 | 0/4.0 | 2.4 | 0.7/3.4 | 3.7e-1 |
| 0.1 | 13.9 | 4.4/17.0 | 18.0 | 10.9/20.4 | 1.0e+5 | 1.5 | 1.3/1.6 | 2.2 | 0.7/3.0 | 1.3e+0 |
| 0.15 | 15.4 | 6.0/18.5 | 19.3 | 12.8/21.4 | 1.2e+5 | 1.5 | 1.3/1.6 | 2.4 | 0.7/3.4 | 2.6e+0 |
| 0.2 | 13.8 | 6.0/16.4 | 19.8 | 22.0/19.1 | 1.5e+5 | 1.0 | 2.7/0 | 2.4 | 0.7/3.4 | 3.8e+0 |
| 0.25 | 13.4 | 4.0/16.5 | 19.5 | 12.7/21.7 | 1.6e+5 | 1.0 | 2.7/0 | 3.8 | 2.1/4.7 | 4.8e+0 |
| 0.3 | 12.5 | 2.4/15.8 | 18.5 | 9.5/21.1 | 1.7e+5 | 1.0 | 2.7/0 | 3.5 | 2.1/4.3 | 5.5e+0 |

the upper bound on the fraction of error examples, the range of $\nu$ is conceptually $[0\%, 100\%]$. Hence it does not bear the problem of potentially lying in a wrong range. But results from our experiments suggest that $\nu$ should be tuned carefully at the lower end because small variation (from 0.2 to 0.191) on $\nu$ may cause a large change on $h$ (from 700 to 800), especially on large datasets. All parameters in these methods change monotonically when increasing $H$, so these methods can effectively trade off between the training risk and the VC dimension. They can perform similarly provided there is a cogent way to tune their parameters.

## 7   Conclusion

We have described the RSVM approach and examined how to tune its parameter $H$ and how to train it in large-scale. We compared RSVM with other SVM approaches, and the comparison revealed the relationships between each other of these methods. This work made efforts to address the derivation of SVM algorithms from the fundamentals. C-SVMs minimize the VC bound in a straightforward way with a constant $C$ used to approximate a varying term in bound (1). The RSVM approach uses a parameter $H$ to directly estimate the VC dimension of the hypothesis space. The bound (1) can be effectively minimized by minimizing the training risk with a given $H$, and finding the $H$ which results in the minimum value of the bound. To date, no appropriate parameter range has been proposed for C-SVMs generally effective for problems of all kinds. On the contrary, a proper range for $H$ can be easily determined by solving simple optimization problems as discussed in Section 5. Furthermore, we can shrink the parameter range even more by examining integer values in the range $[0.05\ell, 0.30\ell] \cap [0, \hat{H}]$ first. Based on our empirical observation, the resulting models based on this range were not far from the best model.

One important open problem is to develop fast and efficient solvers for the RSVM dual problem. We may convert RSVM dual to a SOCP since SOCPs can be solved with the same complexity as the C-SVM dual quadratic program. Our preliminary investigation shows that large-scale RSVM learning is possible by means of a decomposition scheme. A SMO-like algorithm [9], (a decomposition scheme with $q = 2$,) may provide a more efficient implementation for RSVM.

# Acknowledgements

The material is mainly based on research supported by NEC Labs America, Inc. Many thanks to the reviewers for their valuable comments.

# References

1. K. P. Bennett and E. J. Bredensteiner. Duality and geometry in SVM classifiers. In *Proc. 17th International Conf. on Machine Learning*, pages 57–64, San Francisco, CA, 2000. Morgan Kaufmann.
2. D. P. Bertsekas. *Nonlinear Programming*. Athena Scientific, Belmont, MA, 1999.
3. J. Bi and K. P. Bennett. Duality, geometry, and support vector regression. In *Advances in Neural Information Processing Systems, Volumn 14*, Cambridge, MA., 2001. MIT Press.
4. B. E. Boser, I. M. Guyon, and V. N. Vapnik. A training algorithm for optimal margin classifiers. In D. Haussler, editor, *Proceedings of the 5th Annual ACM Workshop on Computational Learning Theory*, pages 144–152, Pittsburgh, PA, July 1992. ACM Press.
5. C. J. C. Burges and D. J. Crisp. Uniqueness theorems for kernel methods. *Technical Report MSR-TR-2002-11*, 2002.
6. T. Joachims. Making large-scale support vector machine learning practical. In B. Schölkopf, C. J. C. Burges, and A. J. Smola, editors, *Advances in Kernel Methods - Support Vector Learning*, pages 169–184. MIT Press, 1999.
7. M. Lobo, L. Vandenberghe, S. Boyd, and H. Lebret. Applications of second-order cone programming. *Linear Algebra and its Applications*, 284:193–228, 1998.
8. E. Osuna, R. Freund, and F. Girosi. Improved training algorithm for support vector machines. In *Proceedings of IEEE Neural Networks for Signal Processing VII Workshop*, pages 276–285, Piscataway, NY, 1997. IEEE Press.
9. J. Platt. Sequential minimal optimization: A fast algorithm for training support vector machines. In B. Schölkopf, C. J. C. Burges, and A. J. Smola, editors, *Advances in Kernel Methods - Support Vector Learning*, pages 185–208. MIT Press, 1999.
10. B. Schölkopf, C.J.C. Burges, and V. N. Vapnik. Extracting support data for a given task. In U. M. Fayyad and R. Uthurusamy, editors, *Proceedings of First International Conference on Knowledge Discovery & Data Mining*, Menlo Park, 1995. AAAI Press.
11. B. Schölkopf, A. J. Smola, R. C. Williamson, and P. L. Bartlett. New support vector algorithms. *Neural Computation*, 12:1207–1245, 2000.
12. B. Schölkopf and A. J. Smola. *Learning with Kernels: Support Vector Machines, Regularization, Optimization and Beyond*. MIT Press, Cambridge, MA., 2002.
13. V. N. Vapnik. *Statistical Learning Theory*. Wiley, New York, 1998.

# Robust Regression by Boosting the Median*

Balázs Kégl

Department of Computer Science and Operations Research
University of Montreal,
CP 6128 succ. Centre-Ville,
Montréal, Canada H3C 3J7
kegl@iro.umontreal.ca

**Abstract.** Most boosting regression algorithms use the weighted average of base regressors as their final regressor. In this paper we analyze the choice of the weighted median. We propose a general boosting algorithm based on this approach. We prove boosting-type convergence of the algorithm and give clear conditions for the convergence of the robust training error. The algorithm recovers ADABOOST and ADABOOST$_\varrho$ as special cases. For boosting confidence-rated predictions, it leads to a new approach that outputs a different decision and interprets robustness in a different manner than the approach based on the weighted average. In the general, non-binary case we suggest practical strategies based on the analysis of the algorithm and experiments.

## 1 Introduction

Most boosting algorithms designed for regression use the weighted *average* of the base regressors as their final regressor (e.g., [5, 8, 14]). Although these algorithms have several theoretical and practical advantages, in general they are not natural extensions of ADABOOST in the sense that they do not recover ADABOOST as a special case. The main focus of this paper is the analysis of MEDBOOST, a generalization of ADABOOST that uses the weighted median as the final regressor.

Although average-type boosting received more attention in the regression domain, the idea of using the weighted median as the final regressor is not new. Freund [6] briefly mentions it and proves a special case of the main theorem of this paper. The ADABOOST.R algorithm of Freund and Schapire [7] returns the weighted median but the response space is restricted to [0, 1] and the parameter updating steps are rather complicated. Drucker [4] also uses the weighted median of the base regressors as the final regressor but the parameter updates are heuristic and the convergence of the method is not analyzed. Bertoni et al. [2] consider an algorithm similar to MEDBOOST with response space [0, 1], and prove a convergence theorem in that special case that is weaker than our result by a factor of two. Avnimelech and Intrator [1] construct triplets of weak learners and show that the median of the three regressors has a smaller error than

---

* This research was supported in part by the Natural Sciences and Engineering Research Council (NSERC) of Canada.

B. Schölkopf and M.K. Warmuth (Eds.): COLT/Kernel 2003, LNAI 2777, pp. 258–272, 2003.

the individual regressors. The idea of using the weighted median has recently appeared in the context of bagging under the name of "bragging" [3].

The main result of this paper is the proof of algorithmic convergence of MEDBOOST. The theorem also gives clear conditions for the convergence of the robust training error. The algorithm synthesizes several versions of boosting for binary classification. In particular, it recovers ADABOOST and the marginal boosting algorithm ADABOOST$_\varrho$ of Rätsch and Warmuth [10] as special cases. For boosting confidence-rated predictions it leads to a strategy different from Schapire and Singer's approach [13]. In particular, MEDBOOST outputs a different decision and interprets robustness in a different manner than the approach based on the weighted average.

In the general, non-binary case we suggest practical strategies based on the analysis of the algorithm. We show that the algorithm provides a clear criteria for growing regression trees for base regressors. The analysis of the algorithm also suggests strategies for controlling the capacity of the base regressors and the final regressor. We also propose an approach to use window base regressors that can abstain. Learning curves obtained from experiments with this latter model show that MEDBOOST in regression behaves very similarly to ADABOOST in classification.

The rest of the paper is organized as follows. In Section 2 we describe the algorithm and state the result on the algorithmic convergence. In Section 3 we show the relation between MEDBOOST and other boosting algorithms in the special case of binary classification. In Section 4 we analyse MEDBOOST in the general, non-binary case. Finally we present some experimental results in Section 5 and draw conclusions in Section 6.

## 2    The MedBoost Algorithm and the Convergence Result

The algorithm (Figure 1) basically follows the lines of ADABOOST. The main difference is that it returns the *weighted median* of the base regressors rather than their *weighted average*, which is consistent with ADABOOST in the binary classification as shown in Section 3.1. Other differences come from the subtleties associated with the general case.

For the formal description, let the training data be $D_n = ((\mathbf{x}_1, y_1), \ldots, (\mathbf{x}_n, y_n))$ where data points $(\mathbf{x}_i, y_i)$ are from the set $\mathbb{R}^d \times \mathbb{R}$. The algorithm maintains a weight distribution $\mathbf{w}^{(t)} = (w_1^{(t)}, \ldots, w_n^{(t)})$ over the data points. The weights are initialized uniformly in line 1, and are updated in each iteration in line 12. We suppose that we are given a *base learner* algorithm $\text{BASE}(D_n, \mathbf{w})$ that, in each iteration $t$, returns a base regressor $h^{(t)}$ coming from a subset of $\mathcal{H} = \{h : \mathbb{R}^d \mapsto \mathbb{R}\}$. In general, the base learner should attempt to minimize the average weighted cost $\sum_{i=1}^{n} w_i C_\epsilon(h^{(t)}(\mathbf{x}_i), y_i)$ on the training data[1], where

---

[1] If the base learner cannot handle weighted data, we can, as usual, resample using the weight distribution.

---

$\text{MEDBOOST}(D_n, C_\epsilon(y', y), \text{BASE}(D_n, \mathbf{w}), \gamma, T)$

1   $\mathbf{w} \leftarrow (1/n, \ldots, 1/n)$
2   **for** $t \leftarrow 1$ **to** $T$
3      $h^{(t)} \leftarrow \text{BASE}(D_n, \mathbf{w})$     $\triangleright$ *try to minimize* $\sum_{i=1}^{n} w_i C_\epsilon(h^{(t)}(\mathbf{x}_i), y_i)$
4      **for** $i \leftarrow 1$ **to** $n$
5        $\theta_i \leftarrow 1 - 2C_\epsilon(h^{(t)}(\mathbf{x}_i), y_i)$     $\triangleright$ *base awards*
6      $\alpha^{(t)} \leftarrow \arg\min_\alpha e^{\gamma\alpha} \sum_{i=1}^{n} w_i^{(t)} e^{-\alpha\theta_i}$
7      **if** $\alpha^{(t)} = \infty$     $\triangleright$ $\theta_i \geq \gamma$ *for all* $i = 1, \ldots, n$
8        **return** $f^{(t)}(\cdot) = \text{med}_\alpha(\mathbf{h}(\cdot))$
9      **if** $\alpha^{(t)} < 0$     $\triangleright$ *equivalent to* $\sum_{i=1}^{n} w_i^{(t)} \theta_i < \gamma$
10       **return** $f^{(t-1)}(\cdot) = \text{med}_\alpha(\mathbf{h}(\cdot))$
11      **for** $i \leftarrow 1$ **to** $n$
12       $w_i^{(t+1)} \leftarrow w_i^{(t)} \dfrac{\exp(-\alpha^{(t)}\theta_i)}{\sum_{j=1}^{n} w_j^{(t)} \exp(-\alpha^{(t)}\theta_j)} = w_i^{(t)} \dfrac{\exp(-\alpha^{(t)}\theta_i)}{Z^{(t)}}$
13 **return** $f^{(T)}(\cdot) = \text{med}_\alpha(\mathbf{h}(\cdot))$

---

**Fig. 1.** The pseudocode of the MEDBOOST algorithm. $D_n$ is the training data, $C_\epsilon(y', y) \geq I_{\{|y - y'| > \epsilon\}}$ is the cost function, $\text{BASE}(D_n, \mathbf{w})$ is the base regression algorithm that attempts to minimize the weighted cost $\sum_{i=1}^{n} w_i C_\epsilon(h^{(t)}(\mathbf{x}_i), y_i)$, $\gamma$ is the robustness parameter, and $T$ is the number of iterations.

$C_\epsilon(y, y')$ is an *ε-tube loss function* satisfying

$$C_\epsilon(y, y') \geq I_{\{|y - y'| > \epsilon\}}, \tag{1}$$

where the indicator function $I_{\{A\}}$ is 1 if its argument $A$ is true and 0 otherwise. The most often we will consider two cost functions that satisfy this condition, the $(0-1)$ cost function

$$C_\epsilon^{(0-1)}(y, y') = I_{\{|y - y'| > \epsilon\}}, \tag{2}$$

and the $L_1$ cost function

$$C_\epsilon^{(1)}(y, y') = \frac{1}{\epsilon}|y - y'|. \tag{3}$$

To emphasize the relation to binary classification and to simplify the notation in Figure 1 and in Theorem 1 below, we define the *base awards* $\theta_i^{(t)}$ for each training point $(\mathbf{x}_i, y_i)$, $i = 1, \ldots, n$, and base regressor $h^{(t)}$, $t = 1, \ldots, T$, as

$$\theta_i^{(t)} = 1 - 2C_\epsilon(h^{(t)}(\mathbf{x}_i), y_i). \tag{4}$$

Note that by condition (1) on the cost function, the base awards are upper bounded by

$$\theta_i^{(t)} \leq \begin{cases} 1 & \text{if } |h^{(t)}(\mathbf{x}_i) - y_i| \leq \epsilon, \\ -1 & \text{otherwise.} \end{cases} \tag{5}$$

After computing the base awards in line 5, the algorithm sets the weight $\alpha^{(t)}$ of the base regressor $h^{(t)}$ to the value that minimizes $E^{(t)}(\alpha) = e^{\gamma\alpha}\sum_{i=1}^{n} w_i^{(t)}e^{-\alpha\theta_i}$. If all base awards are larger than $\gamma$, then $\alpha^{(t)} = \infty$ and $E^{(t)}(\alpha^{(t)}) = 0$, so the algorithm returns the actual regressor (line 8). Intuitively, this means that the capacity of the set of base regressors is too large. If $\alpha^{(t)} < 0$, or equivalently[2], if $\sum_{i=1}^{n} w_i^{(t)}\theta_i < \gamma$, the algorithm returns the weighted median of the base regressors up to the last iteration (line 10). Intuitively, this means that the capacity of the set of base regressors is too small, so we cannot find a new base regressor that would decrease the training error. In general, $\alpha^{(t)}$ can be found easily by line-search because of the convexity of $E^{(t)}(\alpha)$. In several special cases, $\alpha^{(t)}$ can be computed analytically. Note that in practice, $\text{BASE}(D_n, \mathbf{w})$ does not have to actually minimize the weighted cost[3] $\sum_{i=1}^{n} w_i C_\epsilon(h^{(t)}(\mathbf{x}_i), y_i)$. The algorithm can continue with any base regressor for which $\alpha^{(t)} > 0$.

In lines 8, 10, or 13, the algorithm returns the weighted median of the base regressors. For the analysis of the algorithm, we formally define the final regressor in a more general manner. Let $f_{\gamma+}^{(T)}(\mathbf{x})$ and $f_{\gamma-}^{(T)}(\mathbf{x})$ be the *weighted* $\left(\frac{1+\gamma}{2}\right)$- and $\left(\frac{1-\gamma}{2}\right)$-*quantiles*, respectively, of the base regressors $h^{(1)}(\mathbf{x}), \ldots, h^{(T)}(\mathbf{x})$ with respective weights $\alpha^{(1)}, \ldots, \alpha^{(T)}$. Formally, for $0 \leq \gamma < 1$, let

$$f_{\gamma+}^{(T)}(\mathbf{x}) = \min_j \left\{ h^{(j)}(\mathbf{x}) : \frac{\sum_{t=1}^{T} \alpha^{(t)} I_{\{h^{(j)}(\mathbf{x}) < h^{(t)}(\mathbf{x})\}}}{\sum_{t=1}^{T} \alpha^{(t)}} < \frac{1-\gamma}{2} \right\}, \tag{6}$$

$$f_{\gamma-}^{(T)}(\mathbf{x}) = \max_j \left\{ h^{(j)}(\mathbf{x}) : \frac{\sum_{t=1}^{T} \alpha^{(t)} I_{\{h^{(j)}(\mathbf{x}) > h^{(t)}(\mathbf{x})\}}}{\sum_{t=1}^{T} \alpha^{(t)}} < \frac{1-\gamma}{2} \right\}. \tag{7}$$

Then the *weighted median* is defined as

$$f^{(T)}(\cdot) = \text{med}_\alpha(\mathbf{h}(\cdot)) = f_{0+}^{(T)}(\cdot). \tag{8}$$

For the analysis of the robust error, we define the $\gamma$-*robust prediction* $\widehat{y}_i(\gamma)$ as the furthest of the two quantiles $f_{\gamma+}^{(T)}(\mathbf{x}_i)$ and $f_{\gamma-}^{(T)}(\mathbf{x}_i)$ from the real response $y_i$. Formally, for $i = 1, \ldots, n$, we let

$$\widehat{y}_i(\gamma) = \begin{cases} f_{\gamma+}^{(T)}(\mathbf{x}_i) & \text{if } \left| f_{\gamma+}^{(T)}(\mathbf{x}_i) - y_i \right| \geq \left| f_{\gamma-}^{(T)}(\mathbf{x}_i) - y_i \right|, \\ f_{\gamma-}^{(T)}(\mathbf{x}_i) & \text{otherwise}. \end{cases} \tag{9}$$

With this notation, the *prediction* at $\mathbf{x}_i$ is $\widehat{y}_i = \widehat{y}_i(0) = f^{(T)}(\mathbf{x}_i)$.

The main result of the paper analyzes the relative frequency of training points on which the $\gamma$-robust prediction $\widehat{y}_i(\gamma)$ is not $\epsilon$-*precise*, that is, $\widehat{y}_i(\gamma)$ has a larger $L_1$ error than $\epsilon$. Formally, let the $\gamma$-*robust training error* of $f^{(T)}$ defined[4] as

---

[2] Since $E^{(t)}(\alpha)$ is convex and $E^{(t)}(0) = 1$, $\alpha^{(t)} < 0$ is equivalent to $E^{(t)'}(0) = \gamma - \sum_{i=1}^{n} w_i^{(t)}\theta_i > 0$.

[3] Equivalent to minimizing $E^{(t)'}(0)$, which is consistent to Mason et al.'s gradient descent approach in the function space [9].

[4] For the sake of simplicity, in the notation we suppress the fact that $L^{(\gamma)}$ depends on the whole sequence of base regressors and weights, not only on the final regressor $f^{(T)}$.

$$L^{(\gamma)}(f^{(T)}) = \frac{1}{n} \sum_{i=1}^{n} I_{\{|\hat{y}_i(\gamma) - y_i| > \epsilon\}}. \tag{10}$$

If $\gamma = 0$, $L^{(0)}(f^{(T)})$ gives the relative frequency of training points on which the regressor $f^{(T)}$ has a larger $L_1$ error than $\epsilon$. If we have equality in (1), this is exactly the average cost of the regressor $f^{(T)}$ on the training data. A small value for $L^{(0)}(f^{(T)})$ indicates that the regressor predicts most of the training points with $\epsilon$-precision, whereas a small value for $L^{(\gamma)}(f^{(T)})$ suggests that the prediction is not only precise but also robust in the sense that a small perturbation of the base regressors and their weights will not increase $L^{(0)}(f^{(T)})$.

The following theorem upper bounds the $\gamma$-robust training error $L^{(\gamma)}$ of the regressor $f^{(T)}$ output by MEDBOOST.

**Theorem 1.** *Let $L^{(\gamma)}(f^{(T)})$ defined as in (10) and suppose that condition (1) holds for the cost function $C_\epsilon(\cdot, \cdot)$. Define the base awards $\theta_i^{(t)}$ as in (4), let $w_i^{(t)}$ be the weight of training point $\mathbf{x}_i$ after the $t$th iteration (updated in line 12 in Figure 1), and let $\alpha^{(t)}$ be the weight of the base regressor $h^{(t)}(\cdot)$ (computed in line 6 in Figure 1). Then*

$$L^{(\gamma)}(f^{(T)}) \leq \prod_{t=1}^{T} E^{(t)}(\alpha^{(t)}) = \prod_{t=1}^{T} e^{\gamma \alpha^{(t)}} \sum_{i=1}^{n} w_i^{(t)} e^{-\alpha^{(t)} \theta_i^{(t)}}. \tag{11}$$

The proof (see Appendix) is based on the observation that if the median of the base regressors goes further than $\epsilon$ from the real response $y_i$ at training point $\mathbf{x}_i$, then most of the base regressors must also be far from $y_i$, giving small base awards to this point. Then the proof follows the proof of Theorem 5 in [12] by exponentially bounding the step function. Note that the theorem implicitly appears in [6] for $\gamma = 0$ and for the $(0-1)$ cost function (2). A weaker result[5] with an explicit proof in the case of $y, h^{(t)}(\mathbf{x}) \in [0,1]$ can be found in [2].

Note also that since $E^{(t)}(\alpha)$ is convex and $E^{(t)}(0) = 1$, a positive $\alpha^{(t)}$ means that $\min_\alpha E^{(t)}(\alpha) = E^{(t)}(\alpha^{(t)}) < 1$, so the condition in line 9 in Figure 1 guarantees that the the upper bound of (11) decreases in each step.

## 3   Binary Classification as a Special Case

In this section we show that, in a certain sense, MEDBOOST is a natural extension of the original ADABOOST algorithm. We then derive marginal boosting [10], a recently developed variant of ADABOOST, as a special case of MEDBOOST. Finally, we show that, as another special case, MEDBOOST provides an approach for boosting confidence-rated predictions that is different from the algorithm proposed by Schapire and Singer [13].

---

[5] $\epsilon$ is replaced by $2\epsilon$ in (9).

## 3.1   AdaBoost

In the problem of binary classification, the response variable $y$ comes from the set $\{-1, 1\}$. In the original ADABOOST algorithm, it is assumed that the base learners generate binary functions from a function set $\mathcal{H}_b$ that contains base decisions from the set $\{h : \mathbb{R}^d \mapsto \{-1, 1\}\}$. ADABOOST returns the weighted average $g_A^{(T)}(\mathbf{x}) = \frac{\sum_{t=1}^T \alpha^{(t)} h^{(t)}(\mathbf{x})}{\sum_{t=1}^T \alpha^{(t)}}$ of the base decision functions, which is then converted to a decision by the simple rule

$$f_A^{(T)}(\mathbf{x}) = \begin{cases} 1 & \text{if } g_A^{(T)}(\mathbf{x}) \geq 0, \\ -1 & \text{otherwise.} \end{cases} \tag{12}$$

The weighted median $f^{(T)}(\cdot) = \text{med}_\alpha(\mathbf{h}(\cdot))$ returned by MEDBOOST is identical to $f_A^{(T)}$ in this simple case. Training errors of base decisions are counted in a natural way by using the cost function $C_1^{(0-1)}$. With this cost function, the base awards are familiarly defined as

$$\theta_i^{(t)} = \begin{cases} 1 & \text{if } h^{(t)}(\mathbf{x}_i) = y_i, \\ -1 & \text{otherwise.} \end{cases}$$

The base decisions $h^{(t)}$ are found by minimizing the weighted error $\epsilon^{(t)} = \sum_{h^{(t)}(\mathbf{x}_i) \neq y_i} w_i^{(t)}$ (line 3 in Figure 1), and the optimal weights of the base decisions can be computed explicitly (line 6 in Figure 1) as $\alpha^{(t)} = \frac{1}{2} \log \left( \frac{1 - \epsilon^{(t)}}{\epsilon^{(t)}} \right)$. Another convenient property of ADABOOST is that the stopping condition in line 9 reduces to $\epsilon^{(t)} > \frac{1}{2}$ which is never satisfied if $\mathcal{H}_b$ is closed under multiplication by $-1$. With these settings, $L^{(0)}(f^{(T)})$ becomes the training error of $f^{(T)}$, and Theorem 1 reduces to Theorem 9 in [7], that is, $L^{(0)}(f^{(T)}) \leq \prod_{t=1}^T 2\sqrt{\epsilon^{(t)}(1 - \epsilon^{(t)})}$. One observation that partly explains the good generalization ability of ADABOOST is that it tends to minimize not only the training error but also the $\gamma$-robust training error. In their groundbreaking paper, Schapire et al. [12] define the $\gamma$-robust training error of the real valued function $g_A^{(T)}$ as

$$L_A^{(\gamma)}(g_A^{(T)}) = \frac{1}{n} \sum_{i=1}^n I_{\left\{ g_A^{(T)}(\mathbf{x}_i) y_i \leq \gamma \right\}}. \tag{13}$$

One of the main tools in this analysis is Theorem 5 [12] which shows that

$$L_A^{(\gamma)}(g_A^{(T)}) \leq \prod_{t=1}^T 2\sqrt{\epsilon^{(t)}{}^{1-\gamma}(1 - \epsilon^{(t)})^{1+\gamma}}. \tag{14}$$

The following lemma shows that in this special case, the two definitions of the $\gamma$-robust training errors coincide, so (14) is a special case of Theorem 1.

**Lemma 1.** *Let* $(h^{(1)}, \ldots, h^{(n)}) \in \mathcal{H}_b^t$ *be a sequence of binary decisions, let* $(\alpha^{(1)}, \ldots, \alpha^{(n)})$ *be a sequence of positive, real numbers, let* $g_A^{(T)}(\mathbf{x}) = \frac{\sum_{t=1}^T \alpha^{(t)} h^{(t)}(\mathbf{x})}{\sum_{t=1}^T \alpha^{(t)}}$, *and define* $f^{(T)}(\mathbf{x})$ *as in (8). Then* $L_A^{(\gamma)}(g_A^{(T)}) = L^{(\gamma)}(f^{(T)})$, *where* $L_A^{(\gamma)}(g_A^{(T)})$ *and* $L^{(\gamma)}(f^{(T)})$ *are defined by (13) and (10), respectively.*

*Proof.* First observe that in this special case of binary base decisions, $|\widehat{y}_i(\gamma) - y_i| > 1$ is equivalent to $\widehat{y}_i(\gamma)y_i = -1$. Because of the one-sided error,

$$\widehat{y}_i(\gamma) = \begin{cases} f_{\gamma+}^{(T)}(\mathbf{x}_i) & \text{if } y_i = -1, \\ f_{\gamma-}^{(T)}(\mathbf{x}_i) & \text{if } y_i = 1, \end{cases}$$

where $f_{\gamma+}^{(T)}$ and $f_{\gamma-}^{(T)}$ are the weighted $(\frac{1+\gamma}{2})$- and $(\frac{1-\gamma}{2})$-quantiles, respectively, defined in (6-7). Without the loss of generality, suppose that $y_i = 1$. Then $\widehat{y}_i(\gamma)y_i = -1$ is equivalent to $f_{\gamma-}^{(T)}(\mathbf{x}_i) = -1$. Hence, by definition (7), we have

$$\frac{1-\gamma}{2} \leq \frac{\sum_{t=1}^T I_{\{1 > h^{(t)}(\mathbf{x}_i)\}} \alpha^{(t)}}{\sum_{t=1}^T \alpha^{(t)}} = \frac{\sum_{t=1}^T I_{\{h^{(t)}(\mathbf{x}_i) = -1\}} \alpha^{(t)}}{\sum_{t=1}^T \alpha^{(t)}} = \frac{\sum_{t=1}^T \frac{1 - h^{(t)}(\mathbf{x}_i)}{2} \alpha^{(t)}}{\sum_{t=1}^T \alpha^{(t)}},$$

which is equivalent to $g_A^{(T)}(\mathbf{x}_i) \leq \gamma$. □

### 3.2   AdaBoost$_\varrho$

Although Schapire et al. [12] analyzed the $\gamma$-robust training error in the general case of $\gamma > 0$, the idea to modify ADABOOST such that the right hand side of (11) is explicitly minimized has been proposed only later by Rätsch and Warmuth [10]. The algorithm was further analyzed in a recent paper by the same authors [11]. In this case, the optimal weights of the base decisions can still be computed explicitly (line 6 in Figure 1) as $\alpha^{(t)} = \frac{1}{2} \log \left( \frac{1 - \epsilon^{(t)}}{\epsilon^{(t)}} \times \frac{1-\gamma}{1+\gamma} \right)$. The stopping condition in line 9 becomes $\epsilon^{(t)} > \frac{1}{2} - \gamma$, so, in principle, it can become true even if $\mathcal{H}_b$ is closed under multiplication by $-1$. For the above choice of $\alpha^{(t)}$, Theorem 1 is identical to Lemma 2 in [10]. In particular,

$$L^{(\gamma)}(f^{(T)}) \leq \prod_{t=1}^T 2 \sqrt{\epsilon^{(t)1-\gamma}(1 - \epsilon^{(t)})^{1+\gamma}} \sqrt{\frac{1}{(1-\gamma)^{1-\gamma}(1+\gamma)^{1+\gamma}}}.$$

### 3.3   Confidence-Rated AdaBoost

Another general direction in which ADABOOST can be extended is to relax the requirement that base-decisions must be binary. In Schapire and Singer's approach [13], weak hypotheses $h^{(t)}$ range over $\mathbb{R}$. As in ADABOOST, the algorithm returns the weighted sum of the base decisions which is then converted to a decision by (12). An upper bound on the training error is proven for this general case, and the base decisions and their weights (in lines 3 and 6 in Figure 1) are found by minimizing this bound. The upper bound is formally identical to the right hand side of (11) with $\gamma = 0$, but with the setting of base awards to

$$\theta_i^{(t)} = h^{(t)}(\mathbf{x}_i)y_i. \tag{15}$$

Interestingly, this algorithm is not a special case of MEDBOOST, and the differences give some interesting insights. The first, rather technical difference is that the choice of $\theta_i^{(t)}$ (15) does not satisfy (4) if the range of $h^{(t)}$ is the whole real line. In MEDBOOST, Theorem 1 suggests to set $\epsilon = 1$ in (10) so that $L^{(0)}(f^{(T)})$ is the training error of the decision generated from $f^{(T)}$ by (12). If the range of the base decisions is restricted to $[-1, 1]^6$, then the choice of the cost function $C_1^{(1)}$ generates base awards that are identical to (15) up to a factor of two. Note that the general settings of MEDBOOST allow other cost functions, such as $C_1^{(2)}(y, y') = (y - y')^2$, which might make the optimization easier in practice.

The second, more fundamental difference between the two approaches is the decision they return and the way they measure the robustness of the decision. Unlike in the case of binary base decisions (Lemma 1), in this case $L_A^{(\gamma)}(g_A^{(T)})$ is not equal to $L^{(\gamma)}(f^{(T)})$. The following lemma shows that for given robustness of $f^{(T)}(\mathbf{x})$, $g_A^{(T)}(\mathbf{x})$ can vary in a relatively large interval, depending on the actual base predictors and their weights.

**Lemma 2.** *For every margin $0 < \gamma < 1$ and $0 < \delta \leq \frac{1-\gamma}{2}$, it is possible to construct a set of base predictors and weights such that*

1. $f_{\gamma-}^{(T)}(\mathbf{x}) \geq 0$ *and* $g_A^{(T)}(\mathbf{x}) < -\frac{1-\gamma}{2} + \delta$,
2. $f_{\gamma-}^{(T)}(\mathbf{x}) < 0$ *and* $g_A^{(T)}(\mathbf{x}) \geq \frac{1+\gamma}{2} - \delta$

*Proof.* For the first statement, consider $h^{(1)}(\mathbf{x}) = 0$ with weight $c^{(1)} = \frac{1+\gamma}{2}$, and $h^{(2)}(\mathbf{x}) = -1$ with weight $c^{(2)} = \frac{1-\gamma}{2}$. For the second statement, let $h^{(1)}(\mathbf{x}) = 1$ with weight $c^{(1)} = \frac{1+\gamma}{2}$, and $h^{(2)}(\mathbf{x}) = -\frac{2\delta}{1-\gamma}$ with weight $c^{(2)} = \frac{1-\gamma}{2}$.  □

The lemma shows that it is even possible that the two methods predict different labels on a given point even though the base predictors and their weights are identical. Lemma 2 and the robustness definitions (10) and (13) suggest that average-type boosting gives high confidence to a set of base-decisions if their *weighted average is far from 0* (even if they are highly dispersed around this mean), while MEDBOOST prefers sets of base-decisions such that *most of their weight is on the good side* (even if they are close to the decision threshold 0).

---

[6] This is not a real restriction: allowing one-sided cost functions and looking at only the lower quantiles for $y = 1$ and upper quantiles for $y = -1$ is the same as truncating the range of base functions into $[-1, 1]$.

## 3.4   Base Decisions That Abstain

Schapire and Singer [13] considers a special case of confidence-rated boosting when base decisions are binary but they are allowed to abstain, so they come from the subset $\mathcal{H}_t$ of the set $\{h : \mathbb{R}^d \mapsto \{-1, 0, 1\}\}$. The problem is interesting because it seems to be the most complicated case when the optimal weights can be computed analytically. We also use a similar model in the experiments (Section 4) that illustrate the algorithm in the general case.

If the final regressor $f^{(T)}$ is converted to a decision differently from (12), this special case of Schapire and Singer's approach is also a special case of MEDBOOST. In general, the asymmetry of (12) causes problems only in degenerate cases. If the median of the base decisions from $\mathcal{H}_t$ is returned, then there are non-degenerate cases when $f^{(T)} = 0$. In this case (12) would always assign label 1 to the given point which seems unreasonable. To solve this problem, let

$$g^{(T)}(\mathbf{x}) = \begin{cases} 1 & \text{if } \sum_{t=1}^{T} I_{\{h^{(t)}(\mathbf{x})=1\}} \geq \sum_{t=1}^{T} I_{\{h^{(t)}(\mathbf{x})=-1\}}, \\ -1 & \text{otherwise.} \end{cases} \quad (16)$$

be the binary decision assigned to the output of MEDBOOST. With this modification, and by using the cost function $C_1^{(0-0.5-1)}(y, y') = \frac{1}{2} I_{\{|y-y'|>\frac{1}{2}\}} + \frac{1}{2} I_{\{|y-y'|>1\}}$, MEDBOOST is identical to the algorithm in [13]. The base awards are defined as

$$\theta_i^{(t)} = h^{(t)}(\mathbf{x}_i) y_i = \begin{cases} 1 & \text{if } h^{(t)}(\mathbf{x}_i) = y_i, \\ 0 & \text{if } h^{(t)}(\mathbf{x}_i) = 0, \\ -1 & \text{otherwise.} \end{cases} \quad (17)$$

Base decisions $h^{(t)}$ are found by minimizing $\left(\epsilon_0^{(t)} + 2\sqrt{\epsilon_+^{(t)} \epsilon_-^{(t)}}\right)$, where $\epsilon_-^{(t)} = \sum_{i=1}^{n} w_i^{(t)} I_{\{h^{(t)}(\mathbf{x}_i)y_i=-1\}}$ is the weighted error in the $t$th iteration, $\epsilon_0^{(t)} = \sum_{i=1}^{n} w_i^{(t)} I_{\{h^{(t)}(\mathbf{x}_i)=0\}}$ is the weighted abstention rate, and $\epsilon_+^{(t)} = 1 - \epsilon_-^{(t)} - \epsilon_0^{(t)}$ is the weighted correct rate. The optimal weights of the base decisions (line 6 in Figure 1) are

$$\alpha^{(t)} = \frac{1}{2} \log \left( \frac{\epsilon_+^{(t)}}{\epsilon_-^{(t)}} \right). \quad (18)$$

The stopping condition in line 9 reduces to $\epsilon_-^{(t)} > \epsilon_+^{(t)}$. For the $\gamma$-robust training error Theorem 1 gives[7]

$$L^{(\gamma)}(g^{(T)}) \leq \prod_{t=1}^{T} \left(\epsilon_0^{(t)} + 2\sqrt{\epsilon_+^{(t)} \epsilon_-^{(t)}}\right) \sqrt{\frac{\epsilon_+^{(t)}}{\epsilon_-^{(t)}}}^{\gamma}.$$

---

[7] Note that these settings minimize the upper bound for $L^{(0)}(f^{(T)})$. One could also minimize $L^{(\gamma)}(f^{(T)})$ as in ADABOOST$_\varrho$ to obtain a regularized version. The minimization can be done analytically, but the formulas are quite complicated so we omit them.

In the case of MEDBOOST, another possibility would be to let the final decision also to abstain by not using (16) to convert $f^{(T)}$ to a binary decision. In this case, we can make abstaining more costly by setting $\gamma$ to a small but non-zero value. Another option is to choose $C_1^{(1)}(y, y')$ as the cost function. In this case, the base awards become

$$\theta_i^{(t)} = \begin{cases} 1 & \text{if } h^{(t)}(\mathbf{x}_i) = y_i, \\ -1 & \text{if } h^{(t)}(\mathbf{x}_i) = 0, \\ -3 & \text{otherwise,} \end{cases}$$

so abstentions are also penalized. The optimization becomes more complicated but the optimal parameters can still be found analytically.

## 4 The General Case

In theory, the general fashion of the algorithm and the theorem allows the use of different cost functions, sets of base regressors, and base learning algorithms. In practice, however, base regressors of which the capacity cannot be controlled (e.g., linear regressors, regression stumps) seem to be impractical. To see why, consider the case of the $(0-1)$ cost function (2) and $\gamma = 0$. In this case, Theorem 1 can be translated into the following PAC-type statement on weak/strong learning [6]: "if each weak regressor is $\epsilon$-precise on more than 50% of the weighted points than the final regressor is $\epsilon$-precise on all points". In the first extreme case, when we cannot even find a base regressor that is $\epsilon$-precise on more than 50% of the (unweighted) points, the algorithm terminates in the first iteration in line 9 in Figure 1. In the second extreme case, when all points are within $\epsilon$ from the base regressor $h^{(t)}$, the algorithm would simply return $h^{(t)}$ in line 8 in Figure 1. This means that the capacity of the set of the base regressors must be carefully chosen such that the weighted errors $\epsilon^{(t)} = \sum_{i=1}^{n} I_{\{|h^{(t)}(\mathbf{x}_i) - y_i| > \epsilon\}} w_i^{(t)}$ are less than half but, to avoid overfitting, not too close to zero.

**Regression Trees.** A possible and practically feasible choice is to use regression trees as base regressors. The minimization of the weighted cost (line 3 in Figure 1) provides a clear criteria for splitting and pruning. The complexity can also be easily controlled by allowing a limited number of splits. According to the stopping criterion in line 9 in Figure 1, the growth of the tree must be continued until $\alpha^{(t)}$ becomes positive, which is equivalent to $\epsilon^{(t)} < 1/2$ if the $(0-1)$ cost function (2) is used. The algorithm stops either after $T$ iterations, or when the tree returned by the base regressor is judged to be too complex. The complexity of the final regressor can also be controlled by using "strong" trees (with $\epsilon^{(t)} \ll 1/2$) as base regressors with a nonzero $\gamma$.

**Regressors That Abstain.** Another general solution to the capacity control problem is to use base regressors that can abstain. Formally, we define the cost function

$$C_\epsilon^{(0-A-1)}(y,y') = \begin{cases} \frac{1}{2} & \text{if } h^{(t)} \text{ abstains on } \mathbf{x}_i, \\ C_\epsilon^{(0-1)}(y,y') & \text{otherwise,} \end{cases}$$

so the base awards become

$$\theta_i^{(t)} = \begin{cases} 1 & \text{if } |h^{(t)}(\mathbf{x}_i) - y_i| \le \epsilon, \\ 0 & \text{if } h^{(t)} \text{ abstains on } \mathbf{x}_i, \\ -1 & \text{otherwise.} \end{cases}$$

In the experiments in Section 5 we use window base functions that are constant inside a ball of radius $r$ centered around data points, and abstain outside the ball. The minimization in line 3 in Figure 1 is straightforward since there are only finite number of base functions with different average costs. $E^{(t)}(\alpha)$ in line 6 can be minimized analytically as in (18). The case of $\alpha^{(t)} = \infty$ must be handled with care if we want to minimize not only the error rate but also the abstain rate. The problem can be solved formally by setting $\gamma$ to a small but non-zero value.

**Validation.** To be able to assess the regressor and to validate the parameters of the algorithm, suppose that the observation $X$ and its response $Y$ form a pair $(X, Y)$ of random variables taking values in $\mathbb{R}^d \times \mathbb{R}$. We define the $\epsilon$-tube error of a function $f : \mathbb{R}^d \to \mathbb{R}$ as $L_\epsilon(f) = \Pr(Y > f(X) + \epsilon) + \Pr(Y < f(X) - \epsilon)$. Suppose that the $\epsilon$-mode function of the conditional distribution, defined as $\mu_\epsilon^* = \arg\min_f L_\epsilon(f)$, exists and that it is unique. Let $L_\epsilon^* = L_\epsilon(\mu_\epsilon^*)$ be the $\epsilon$-tube Bayes error of the distribution of $(X, Y)$. Using an $\epsilon$-tube cost function in MEDBOOST, $L^{(0)}(f^{(T)})$ is the empirical $\epsilon$-tube error of $f^{(T)}$, so, we can interpret the objective of MEDBOOST as that of minimizing the empirical $\epsilon$-tube error. For a given $\epsilon$, this also gives a clear criteria for validation as that of minimizing the $\epsilon$-tube test error.

Validating $\epsilon$ seems to be a much tougher problem. First note that because of the terminating condition in line 9 in Figure 1 we need base regressors with an empirical weighted $\epsilon$-tube error smaller than $1/2$, so if $\epsilon$ is such that $L_\epsilon^* > 1/2$ then overfitting seems unavoidable (note that this situation cannot happen in the special case of binary classification). The practical behavior of the algorithm in this case is that it either returns an overfitting regressor (if the set of base regressors have a large enough capacity), or it stops in the first iteration in line 9. In both cases, the problem of a too small $\epsilon$ can be detected. If $\epsilon$ is such that $L_\epsilon^* < 1/2$, then the algorithm is well-behaving. If $L_\epsilon^* = 0$, similarly to the case of binary classification, we expect that the algorithm works particularly well (see Section 5.1). At this point, we can give no general criteria for choosing the best $\epsilon$, and it seems that $\epsilon$ is a design parameter rather than a parameter to validate. On the other hand, if the goal is to minimize a certain cost function (e.g, quadratic or absolute error), then all the parameters can be validated based on the test cost. In the second set of experiments (Section 5.2) we know $\mu_\epsilon^*$ and we know that it is the same for all $\epsilon$ so we can validate $\epsilon$ based on the $L_1$ error between $\mu_\epsilon^*$ and $f^{(T)}$. In practice, when $\mu_\epsilon^*$ is unknown, this is clearly unfeasible.

**Table 1.** MEDBOOST versus linear regression.

| Noise distribution | Noise PDF in $[-0.2.0.2]$ | Noise STD | Best $\epsilon$ | $L_1$ distance from $\mu_\epsilon^*$ | |
|---|---|---|---|---|---|
| | | | | MEDBOOST | LINEAR |
| Uniform | 2.5 | 0.1155 | 0.19 | 0.0133 (0.0078) | 0.0204 (0.0108) |
| Inverted triangle | $25\|\delta\|$ | 0.1414 | 0.2 | 0.0101 (0.0069) | 0.0250 (0.0132) |
| Quadratic | $1.25(1 - \|5\delta\|)^{-1/2}$ | 0.1461 | 0.2 | 0.0066 (0.0053) | 0.0261 (0.0136) |
| Extreme | $\pm 0.2$ w. prob. $0.5 - 0.5$ | 0.2 | 0.21 | 0.0147 (0.0153) | 0.0358 (0.0191) |

## 5   Experiments

The experiments in this section were designed to illustrate the method in the general case. We concentrated on the similarities and differences between classification and regression rather than the practicalities of the method. Clearly, more experiments will be required to evaluate the algorithm from a practical viewpoint.

### 5.1   Linear Base Regressors

The objective of these experiments is to show that if $L_\epsilon^* \approx 0$ and the base regressors are adequate in terms of the data generating distribution, then MEDBOOST works very well. To this end, we used a data generating model where $X$ is uniform in $[0,1]$ and $Y = 1 + X + \delta$ where $\delta$ is a random noise generated by different symmetric distributions in the interval $[-0.2, 0.2]$. We used linear base regressors that minimize the weighted quadratic error in each iteration. To generate the base awards, we used the cost function $C_\epsilon^{(0-1)}$. We set $\gamma = 0$ and $T = 100$ although the algorithm usually stopped before reaching this limit. The final regressor was compared to the linear regressor that minimized the quadratic error. Both the comparison and the validation of $\epsilon$ was based on the $L_1$ error between the regressor and $\mu_\epsilon^*$ which is $x + 1$ if $\epsilon$ is large enough. Table 1 shows the average $L_1$ errors and their standard deviations over 10000 experiments with $n = 40$ points generated in each. The results show that MEDBOOST beats the individual linear regressor in all experiments, and the margin grows with the variance of the noise distribution. Since the base learner minimizes the quadratic error, $h^{(1)}$ is the linear regressor, so we can say that additional base regressors improve the best linear regressor.

### 5.2   Window Base Regressors That Abstain

In these experiments we tested MEDBOOST with window base regressors that abstain (Section 4) on a toy problem. The same data model was used as in Section 5.1 but this time the noise $\delta$ was Gaussian with zero mean and standard deviation of 0.1. In each experiment, 200 training and 10000 test points were used. We tested several combinations of $\epsilon$ and $r$. The typical learning curves in Figure 2 indicate that the algorithm behaves similarly to the binary classification

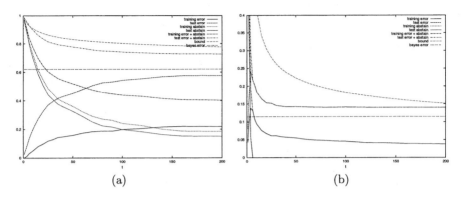

**Fig. 2.** Learning curves of MEDBOOST with window base regressors that abstain. (a) $\epsilon = 0.05$, $r = 0.02$. (b) $\epsilon = 0.16$, $r = 0.2$.

**Table 2.** Validation of the parameters of MEDBOOST.

| $\epsilon$ | best $r$ in $L_1$ sense | $L_1$ dist. from $\mu_\epsilon^*$ | best $r$ by test er. | test er. | $L_\epsilon^*$ | test er. $-L_\epsilon^*$ |
|---|---|---|---|---|---|---|
| 0.1 | 0.12 | 0.032 | 0.12 | 0.359 | 0.3274 | 0.032 |
| 0.13 | 0.16 | 0.033 | 0.16 | 0.227 | 0.1936 | 0.033 |
| 0.16 | 0.2 | 0.032 | 0.2 | 0.14 | 0.1096 | 0.03 |

case. First, there is no overfitting in the overtraining sense: the test error plus the rate of data points where $f^{(t)}$ abstains decreases monotonically. The second similarity is that the test error decreases even after the training error crosses $L_\epsilon^*$ which may be explained by the observation that MEDBOOST minimizes the $\gamma$-robust training error. Interestingly, when $L_\epsilon^* > 1/2$ (Figure 2(a)), the actual test error goes below $L_\epsilon^*$, and even the test error plus the rate of data points where $f^{(t)}$ abstains approaches $L_\epsilon^*$ quite well. Intuitively, this means that the algorithm "gives up" on hard points by abstaining rather than overfitting by trying to predict them.

We also compared the two validation strategies based on test error and $L_1$ distance from $\mu_\epsilon^*$. For a given $\epsilon$, we found that the test error and $L_1$ distance were always minimized at the same radius $r$. As expected, the $L_1$ distance tends to be small for $\epsilon$'s for which $L_\epsilon^* < 1/2$. When validating $\epsilon$, we found that the minimum $L_1$ distance is quite stable in a relatively large range of $\epsilon$ (Table 2).

## 6  Conclusion

In this paper we have presented and analyzed MEDBOOST, a boosting algorithm for regression that uses the weighted median of base regressors as final regressor. We have proven boosting-type convergence of the algorithm and have given clear conditions for the convergence of the robust training error. We have shown that ADABOOST is recovered as a special case of MEDBOOST. For boosting confidence-rated predictions we have proposed a new approach based on

MEDBOOST. In the general, non-binary case we have suggested practical strategies and presented two feasible choices for the set of base regressors. Experiments
with one of these models have shown that MEDBOOST in regression behaves similarly to ADABOOST in classification.

## Appendix

### Proof of Theorem 1

First, observe that by the definition (9) of the robust prediction $\widehat{y}_i(\gamma)$, it follows
from $|\widehat{y}_i(\gamma) - y_i| > \epsilon$ that $\max\left(\left|f_{\gamma+}^{(T)}(\mathbf{x}_i) - y_i\right|, \left|f_{\gamma-}^{(T)}(\mathbf{x}_i) - y_i\right|\right) > \epsilon$. Then we
have three cases.

1. $\left|f_{\gamma+}^{(T)}(\mathbf{x}_i) - y_i\right| > \left|f_{\gamma-}^{(T)}(\mathbf{x}_i) - y_i\right|$.

   Since $\left|f_{\gamma+}^{(T)}(\mathbf{x}_i) - y_i\right| > \epsilon$ and $f_{\gamma+}^{(T)}(\mathbf{x}_i) \geq f_{\gamma-}^{(T)}(\mathbf{x}_i)$, we also have that
   $f_{\gamma+}^{(T)}(\mathbf{x}_i) - y_i > \epsilon$. This together with the definition (6) of $f_{\gamma+}^{(T)}$ implies that
   $\frac{\sum_{t=1}^{T} \alpha^{(t)} I_{\left\{h^{(t)}(\mathbf{x}_i) - y_i > \epsilon\right\}}}{\sum_{t=1}^{T} \alpha^{(t)}} \geq \frac{1-\gamma}{2}$, thus $\frac{\sum_{t=1}^{T} \alpha^{(t)} I_{\left\{\left|h^{(t)}(\mathbf{x}_i) - y_i\right| > \epsilon\right\}}}{\sum_{t=1}^{T} \alpha^{(t)}} \geq \frac{1-\gamma}{2}$. Since
   $\frac{1-\theta_i^{(t)}}{2} \geq I_{\left\{\left|h^{(t)}(\mathbf{x}_i) - y_i\right| > \epsilon\right\}}$ by (5), we have $\frac{\sum_{t=1}^{T} \alpha^{(t)} \frac{1-\theta_i^{(t)}}{2}}{\sum_{t=1}^{T} \alpha^{(t)}} \geq \frac{1-\gamma}{2}$, and so

$$\gamma \sum_{t=1}^{T} \alpha^{(t)} \geq \sum_{t=1}^{T} \alpha^{(t)} \theta_i^{(t)}. \tag{19}$$

2. $\left|f_{\gamma+}^{(T)}(\mathbf{x}_i) - y_i\right| < \left|f_{\gamma-}^{(T)}(\mathbf{x}_i) - y_i\right|$.

   (19) follows similarly as in Case 1 from the definition (7) of $f_{\gamma-}^{(T)}$ and the
   fact that in this case $y_i - f_{\gamma-}^{(T)}(\mathbf{x}_i) > \epsilon$.

3. $\left|f_{\gamma+}^{(T)}(\mathbf{x}_i) - y_i\right| = \left|f_{\gamma-}^{(T)}(\mathbf{x}_i) - y_i\right|$.

   If $f_{\gamma+}^{(T)}(\mathbf{x}_i) \geq y_i$ then (19) follows as in Case 1, otherwise (19) follows as in
   Case 2.

We have shown that $|\widehat{y}_i(\gamma) - y_i| > \epsilon$ implies (19), hence

$$
\begin{aligned}
L^{(\gamma)}(f^{(T)}) &= \frac{1}{n} \sum_{i=1}^{n} I_{\{|\widehat{y}_i(\gamma) - y_i| > \epsilon\}} \leq \frac{1}{n} \sum_{i=1}^{n} I_{\left\{\gamma \sum_{t=1}^{T} \alpha^{(t)} - \sum_{t=1}^{T} \alpha^{(t)} \theta_i^{(t)} \geq 0\right\}} \\
&\leq \frac{1}{n} \sum_{i=1}^{n} \exp\left(\gamma \sum_{t=1}^{T} \alpha^{(t)} - \sum_{t=1}^{T} \alpha^{(t)} \theta_i^{(t)}\right) \quad (\text{since } e^x \geq I_{\{x \geq 0\}}) \quad (20) \\
&= \exp\left(\gamma \sum_{t=1}^{T} \alpha^{(t)}\right) \frac{1}{n} \sum_{i=1}^{n} \exp\left(-\sum_{t=1}^{T} \alpha^{(t)} \theta_i^{(t)}\right) \\
&= \exp\left(\gamma \sum_{t=1}^{T} \alpha^{(t)}\right) \prod_{t=1}^{T} Z^{(t)} \sum_{i=1}^{n} w_i^{(T+1)} \quad (\text{by line 12 in Figure 1})
\end{aligned}
$$

$$= \exp\left(\gamma \sum_{t=1}^{T} \alpha^{(t)}\right) \prod_{t=1}^{T} Z^{(t)}$$

$$= \prod_{t=1}^{T} e^{\gamma \alpha^{(t)}} Z^{(t)} = \prod_{t=1}^{T} e^{\gamma \alpha^{(t)}} \sum_{i=1}^{n} w_i^{(t)} e^{-\alpha^{(t)} \theta_i^{(t)}},$$

where $Z^{(t)} = \sum_{i=1}^{n} w_i^{(t)} e^{-\alpha^{(t)} \theta_i^{(t)}}$ is the normalizing factor used in line 12 in Figure 1. Note that from (20), the proof is identical to the proof of Theorem 5 in [12]. □

# References

1. R. Avnimelech and N. Intrator. Boosting regression estimators. *Neural Computation*, 11:491–513, 1999.
2. A. Bertoni, P. Campadelli, and M. Parodi. A boosting algorithm for regression. In *Proceedings of the Int. Conf. on Artificial Neural Networks*, pages 343–348, 1997.
3. P. Bühlmann. Bagging, subagging and bragging for improving some prediction algorithms. In M.G. Akritas and D.N. Politis, editors, *Recent Advances and Trends in Nonparametric Statistics (to appear)*. 2003.
4. H. Drucker. Improving regressors using boosting techniques. In *Proceedings of the 14th International Conference on Machine Learning*, pages 107–115, 1997.
5. N. Duffy and D. P. Helmbold. Leveraging for regression. In *Proceedings of the 13th Conference on Computational Learning Theory*, pages 208–219, 2000.
6. Y. Freund. Boosting a weak learning algorithm by majority. *Information and Computation*, 121(2):256–285, 1995.
7. Y. Freund and R. E. Schapire. A decision-theoretic generalization of on-line learning and an application to boosting. *Journal of Computer and System Sciences*, 55(1):119–139, 1997.
8. J. Friedman. Greedy function approximation: a gradient boosting machine. Technical report, Dept. of Statistics, Stanford University, 1999.
9. L. Mason, P. Bartlett, J. Baxter, and M. Frean. Boosting algorithms as gradient descent. In *NIPS'99*, volume 12, pages 512–518. The MIT Press, 2000.
10. G. Rätsch and M. K. Warmuth. Marginal boosting. In *Proceedings of the 15th Conference on Computational Learning Theory*, 2002.
11. G. Rätsch and M. K. Warmuth. Efficient margin maximizing with boosting. *Journal of Machine Learning Research (submitted)*, 2003.
12. R. E. Schapire, Y. Freund, P. Bartlett, and W. S. Lee. Boosting the margin: a new explanation for the effectiveness of voting methods. *Annals of Statistics*, 26(5):1651–1686, 1998.
13. R. E. Schapire and Y. Singer. Improved boosting algorithms using confidence-rated predictions. *Machine Learning*, 37(3):297–336, 1999.
14. R. S. Zemel and T. Pitassi. A gradient-based boosting algorithm for regression problems. In *NIPS'00*, volume 13, pages 696–702, 2001.

# Boosting with Diverse Base Classifiers

Sanjoy Dasgupta[1] and Philip M. Long[2]

[1] Department of Computer Science
University of California at San Diego
dasgupta@cs.ucsd.edu
[2] Genome Institute of Singapore
gislongp@nus.edu.sg

**Abstract.** We establish a new bound on the generalization error rate of the Boost-by-Majority algorithm. The bound holds when the algorithm is applied to a collection of base classifiers that contains a "diverse" subset of "good" classifiers, in a precisely defined sense. We describe cross-validation experiments that suggest that Boost-by-Majority can be the basis of a practically useful learning method, often improving on the generalization of AdaBoost on large datasets.

## 1 Introduction

Boosting [46, 14, 16] is an approach to training class prediction rules in which an algorithm is applied repeatedly on a variety of datasets constructed from the original dataset; an effort is made for each dataset to emphasize examples that were often classified incorrectly by rules output by previous invocations of the algorithm. After a number of rounds of this process, the class prediction rules returned (the "base classifiers") are often combined into a single rule by some kind of voting; for example, each base classifier can be assigned a weight, and the final classifier classifies an object as 1 if the total weight of the base classifiers that classify it as 1 is more than the total weight of the classifiers outputting a 0 prediction. For a wide variety of applied problems, the best algorithms known use boosting.

One interesting aspect of the behavior of boosting is that it appears to run counter to Occam's Razor, a principle that has played an important role in guiding the design of machine learning algorithms. Occam's Razor says that, all else being equal, an algorithm should prefer class prediction rules that are in some sense simple. Algorithms designed following this principle are viewed as balancing a classifier's fit to the data against its complexity.

Boosting seemed to contradict Occam's Razor because the generalization enjoyed by boosting algorithms was seen to improve as the number of rounds of boosting increased, even after the algorithm obtained zero training error [43, 10]. This improvement was seen despite the fact that the final classifier output by the boosting algorithm was getting more complex, without any accompanying decrease in training error.

Schapire, et al [47] provided an theoretical explanation of this phenomenon. This took the form of a bound on the generalization error of the boosted classifier in terms of the "margin." The margin by which a voting classifier correctly

B. Schölkopf and M.K. Warmuth (Eds.): COLT/Kernel 2003, LNAI 2777, pp. 273–287, 2003.

classifies an instance is the difference between the fraction of the weight voting correctly and the fraction voting incorrectly. Their bound can be paraphrased as saying that it is highly likely that if most examples in the training data are classified correctly with a large margin, then generalization will be good. They also demonstrated experimentally that AdaBoost, the main boosting algorithm, tends to improve the margin of the voting classifier during training. It has since been proved that some related algorithms maximize the margin [44, 45]. Improved bounds have also been obtained [24]. This analysis has had a substantial impact on the subsequent design and analysis of boosting algorithms.

Some experimental results suggested that it might be worth supplementing the margin analysis with alternative explanations of the generalization ability of boosting algorithms [10, 19, 36, 29, 30]. In the paper presenting the margin analysis, Schapire, et al also posed the problem of searching for alternative modes of analysis.

In this paper, we show theoretically that boosting is able to take advantage of situations in which the set of base classifiers is diverse, i.e. when there are many base classifiers that perform moderately well individually, but complement one another as sources of evidence of the correct classification of random objects. (The importance of diversity in the pool of base classifiers has been discussed in a number of papers, including [1, 34, 41, 3].)

To formalize this, we use the standard assumption that the training data, and any subsequent test data, is generated independently at random according to an underlying probability distribution $\mathbb{P}$ over instance-classification pairs. We further assume that the set $H$ of $n$ base classifiers used by the boosting algorithm contains a set $H^*$ of $k$ classifiers that are correct with probability at least $\frac{1}{2}+\gamma_*$. Finally, we assume that the random variables indicating whether the base classifiers in $H^*$ are correct or not are mutually independent with respect to $\mathbb{P}$. We do not make any assumptions regarding the base classifiers in $H - H^*$; our analysis allows for them to depend on one another, and the classifiers in $H^*$, in a manner that is maximally confusing to the learning algorithm.

Note that the Hoeffding bound implies that a vote over the base classifiers in $H^*$ is incorrect with probability at most $e^{-2\gamma_*^2 k}$. This is what can be achieved if $H^*$ is known. We show that, with probability $1 - \delta$, if $\gamma_*$ is a constant, given $m$ examples, the Boost-by-Majority algorithm [14] achieves accuracy

$$e^{-\Omega(k)} + O\left(\frac{k^{3/2} \log \frac{nk}{\delta}}{m}\right). \tag{1}$$

One can apply existing theory to show that an algorithm, essentially proposed in [4], that chooses a voting classifier to maximize the number of examples correctly classified with a margin $\gamma_*$, which we call a MAM algorithm, achieves

$$e^{-\Omega(k)} + O\left(\frac{(\log^2 m)(\log n) \log \frac{1}{\delta}}{m}\right). \tag{2}$$

The Boost-by-Majority algorithm runs in polynomial time – in fact, for reasonable collections of base classifiers, it can be very fast. We do not address how to carry out the optimization for the MAM algorithm; it is not obvious to us how to do it efficiently.

Note that since one can always choose a smaller $H^*$, loosely speaking, the above bounds can be minimized over $k$. The second term will dominate unless $k$ is polylogarithmic in $m$, so (1) and (2) are incomparable.

Note that any statistically consistent algorithm will approach accuracy at least as good as $e^{-2\gamma_*^2 k}$ with high probability as $m$ approaches infinity. A number of algorithms related to boosting have been shown to be consistent [9, 22, 31–33, 11, 51].

In one of these papers, Lugosi and Vayatis [31] informally discussed the behavior of an algorithm related to AdaBoost in the setting of this paper. They pointed out that, as the number of examples approaches infinity, the accuracy of this algorithm approaches $e^{-2\gamma_*^2 k}$ with high probability. They did not work out a detailed bound on the error probability for a finite number $m$ of examples; the most direct extension of their line of reasoning[1] leads to a bound, for constant $\gamma_*$, of

$$e^{-\Omega(k)} + e^{O(k)} \tilde{O}\left(\sqrt{\frac{1}{m}}\right).$$

One issue that arose during the course of performing our analysis surprised us. Our analysis leading to (1) concerns the version of Boost-by-Majority that performs Boosting-by-Filtering [14]. That is, in each round of boosting, the algorithm generates a dataset by randomly choosing a subset of the original dataset, where the probability of choosing an example depends on how many of the previously chosen base classifiers correctly classified the example. We started out trying to analyze algorithms, like AdaBoost, that evaluate base classifiers based on the total weight of the examples that are classified correctly, where the weight of an example is determined by the number of previously chosen base classifiers that got it correct. We planned to view this weighted sum as an estimate of the expected error with respect to a modified distribution over the whole domain. However, we were unable to prove (1) in this way. The trouble seemed to come at this error estimation step.

In fact, this appears to be an instance of a phenomenon that has already been discussed in the literature (see [27]). The problem of evaluating the accuracy of a base classifier in one of the later rounds of boosting can be described as estimating the expection of a random variable according to a distribution $\mathbb{Q}$, given a random sample drawn according to $\mathbb{P}$, where the function $V$ such that $V(x) = \mathbb{Q}(x)/\mathbb{P}(x)$ is known. Estimating the expectation of $f$ as is done in the view of AdaBoost adopted in this paper, by drawing $x_1, ..., x_m$ according to $\mathbb{P}$, and then taking $\frac{1}{m}\sum_{i=1}^m Q(x_i)f(x_i)$ as the estimate, is called *importance sampling*, whereas performing this estimation as is done in Boosting-by-Filtering is called variously the *acceptance method*, the *rejection method*, and the *acceptance-rejection method*. When $\mathbb{Q}$ is quite different from $\mathbb{P}$ over much of the domain, as often happens in boosting, the estimates obtained through importance sampling

---

[1] In their notation, setting $\lambda = N$.

are well known to suffer from high variance – the theoretical potential for this high variance is what prevented us from proving (1) for algorithms like AdaBoost that work this way.

Inspired by this observation, we experimentally evaluated a simple algorithm, similar to Boost-by-Majority, that we call BBM\*. For most of the larger benchmark datasets we tried them on, BBM\* generalized better than AdaBoost, providing preliminary evidence of the practical utility of boosting by filtering.

## 2 Preliminaries

### 2.1 The Main Model

Let $\mathcal{X}$ be a countable domain. A *class prediction rule* maps domain elements in $\mathcal{X}$ to classifications in $\{-1, 1\}$.

An algorithm is given access to a set $H$ of $n$ base class prediction rules. An unknown probability distribution $\mathbb{P}$ over $\mathcal{X} \times \{-1, 1\}$ is used to generate $m$ examples $(x_1, y_1), ..., (x_m, y_m)$, which are passed to the algorithm, which uses them, together with the base classifiers $H$, to output a class prediction rule $h$.

We will analyze the Boost-by-Majority Algorithm[2] [14], which uses parameters $\alpha$ and $T$:

- Divide the $m$ examples into $T$ bins: put the first $\left\lfloor \frac{m}{2\sqrt{T((T-1)-0)}} \right\rfloor$ in bin 0, the next $\left\lfloor \frac{m}{2\sqrt{T((T-1)-1)}} \right\rfloor$ in bin 1, ..., the next $\left\lfloor \frac{m}{2\sqrt{T((T-1)-(T-2))}} \right\rfloor$ in bin $T - 2$, and the remaining examples in bin $T - 1$. Denote the indices of the examples in bin $t$ by $S_t$.
- For rounds $t = 0, ..., T - 1$
  - for each $i \in S_t$
    * let $r_{t,i}$ be the the number of previous base classifiers $h_0, ..., h_{t-1}$ that are correct on $(x_i, y_i)$, and
    * $w_{t,i} = \binom{T-t-1}{\lfloor \frac{T}{2} \rfloor - r_{t,i}} (\frac{1}{2} + \alpha)^{\lfloor \frac{T}{2} \rfloor - r_{t,i}} (\frac{1}{2} - \alpha)^{\lceil \frac{T}{2} \rceil - t - 1 + r_{t,i}}$,
  - let $w_{t,\max} = \max_r \binom{T-t-1}{\lfloor \frac{T}{2} \rfloor - r} (\frac{1}{2} + \alpha)^{\lfloor \frac{T}{2} \rfloor - r} (\frac{1}{2} - \alpha)^{\lceil \frac{T}{2} \rceil - t - 1 + r}$ be the largest possible value that any $w_{t,i}$ could take,
  - apply the rejection method as follows, where $a_{t,i}$ is interpreted as indicating whether example $i$ was accepted: for each $i \in S_t$,
    * choose $u_{t,i}$ uniformly from $[0, 1]$,
    * let $a_{t,i} = \begin{cases} 1 \text{ if } u_{t,i} \le \frac{w_{t,i}}{w_{t,\max}} \\ 0 \text{ otherwise.} \end{cases}$
  - choose a base classifier $h_t$ from $H$ to maximize the number of examples in the filtered dataset that are classified correctly: $\{i \in S_t : a_{t,i} = 1 \text{ and } h(x_i) = y_i\}$.
- Output the classifier obtained by taking a majority vote over $h_0, ..., h_{T-1}$.

---

[2] We have simplified the algorithm somewhat for the purposes of our analysis, but as the spirit of the algorithm is maintained, we refer to the modified algorithm also as Boost-by-Majority.

## 2.2    Correctness Functions

For a class prediction rule $h$, its associated *correctness function* is an indicator function $r_h$ that tells, for a given pair $(x, y)$, whether it is the case that $h(x) = y$; $r_h$ evaluates to 1 in that case, and 0 otherwise. When $h$ is defined over a domain with an associated probability distribution, we will naturally refer to $r_h$ as its correctness random variable.

## 2.3    Main Result

**Theorem 1.** *Fix a constant $\gamma_* > 0$. Suppose the set $H$ of base classifiers has a subset $H^*$ of $k$ base classifiers*

- *whose associated correctness random variables are mutually independent with respect to the underlying distribution $\mathbb{P}$, and*
- *each of which is correct with probability at least $1/2 + \gamma_*$ (again, with respect to $\mathbb{P}$).*

*Then if the Boost-by-Majority Algorithm is run with $T = k$ and $\alpha = \frac{\gamma_*}{8}$, there are constants $c_1, c_2 \geq 1$ such that, for any underlying probability distribution $\mathbb{P}$, with probability at least $1 - \delta$, the output $h$ of the Boost-by-Majority Algorithm applied to $m$ random examples chosen independently according to $\mathbb{P}$ satisfies*

$$\mathbb{P}(h(x) \neq y) \leq e^{-c_1 k} + \frac{c_2 k^{3/2} \log \frac{nk}{\delta}}{m}.$$

# 3    Some Lemmas

In this section, we establish some useful lemmas.

Since the rescaling factor for each example in each round of the Boost-by-Majority Algorithm is determined by the number of previously chosen base classifiers that classified the example correctly, we have the following.

**Lemma 1.** *Suppose the Boost-by-Majority algorithm is run on a dataset generated independently at random according to an underlying distribution $\mathbb{P}$. Then, for each round $t$, after conditioning on the examples seen before round $t$, the examples accepted by the algorithm in round $t$ are mutually independent, and are distributed according to a probability distribution $\mathbb{P}_t$ over the whole of $\mathcal{X} \times \{-1, 1\}$ defined as follows.*

- $R_t(x, y) = |\{s < t : h_s(x) = y\}|$,
- $W_t(x, y) = \binom{T-t-1}{\lfloor \frac{T}{2} \rfloor - R_t(x,y)} (\frac{1}{2} + \alpha)^{\lfloor \frac{T}{2} \rfloor - R_t(x,y)} (\frac{1}{2} - \alpha)^{\lceil \frac{T}{2} \rceil - t - 1 + R_t(x,y)}$
- $\mathbb{P}_t(x, y) = W_t(x, y) \mathbb{P}(x, y) / Z_t$, *where $Z_t$ is chosen so that $\mathbb{P}_t$ is a probability distribution.*

The following lemma will be used to show that Boost-by-Majority is often able to find accurate classifiers in rounds in which the distribution $\mathbb{P}_t$ is not too different from $\mathbb{P}$. It uses one known probabilistic method trick [42, 20, 47, 4].

**Lemma 2.** *Suppose* $\mathbb{P}$ *satifies the requirements of Theorem 1: there is a subset* $H^*$ *of* $k$ *elements of* $H$ *whose correctness random variables are mutually independent with respect to* $\mathbb{P}$, *and each of which are correct with probability at least* $\frac{1}{2} + \gamma_*$, *where* $\gamma_* > 0$. *For any probability distribution* $\mathbb{Q}$ *such that for all* $(x, y) \in X \times \{-1, 1\}$,

$$\mathbb{Q}(x, y) \leq \frac{\gamma_*}{3} e^{\gamma_*^2 k/2} \mathbb{P}(x, y),$$

*there is a* $g \in H^*$ *such that*

$$\mathbb{Q}(g(x) = y) \geq \frac{1}{2} + \frac{\gamma_*}{4}.$$

*Proof.* Let $g_1, ..., g_k$ (the "good" ones) be the elements of $H^*$. For each $i \in \{1, ..., k\}$, denote $r_{g_i}$, the correctness random variable for $g_i$, simply by $r_i$. The mutual independence of the $r_i$'s with respect to $\mathbb{P}$, together with the Hoeffding bound, implies

$$\mathbb{P}\left(\frac{1}{k} \sum_{i=1}^{k} r_i < \frac{1}{2} + \frac{\gamma_*}{2}\right) \leq e^{-\gamma_*^2 k/2}. \tag{3}$$

Let us refer to the set of pairs $(x, y) \in X \times \{-1, 1\}$ on which $\frac{1}{k} \sum_{i=1}^{k} r_i \geq \frac{1}{2} + \frac{\gamma_*}{2}$ as the good *examples*, and call them $U$. The complement are the bad examples $B$.

First, we claim that for *any* probability distribution $\mathbb{R}$ for which $\mathbb{R}(B) = 0$, there is an $i \in \{1, ..., k\}$ such that $\mathbb{R}(r_i = 1) \geq \frac{1}{2} + \frac{\gamma_*}{2}$. For all examples in $U$, $\frac{1}{k} \sum_{i=1}^{k} r_i \geq \frac{1}{2} + \frac{\gamma_*}{2}$ so $\mathbf{E}_{(x,y) \sim \mathbb{R}}(\frac{1}{k} \sum_{i=1}^{k} r_i) \geq \frac{1}{2} + \frac{\gamma_*}{2}$ which implies $\frac{1}{k} \sum_{i=1}^{k} \mathbb{R}(r_i = 1) \geq \frac{1}{2} + \frac{\gamma_*}{2}$. So there is an $i$ such that $\mathbb{R}(r_i = 1) \geq \frac{1}{2} + \frac{\gamma_*}{2}$.

The above claim implies that there is an $i$ such that $\mathbb{Q}(g_i(x) = y|U) \geq \frac{1}{2} + \frac{\gamma_*}{2}$. Fix such an $i$. Then

$$\mathbb{Q}(g_i(x) = y) \geq \mathbb{Q}(g_i(x) = y|U)\mathbb{Q}(U)$$

$$\geq \left(\frac{1}{2} + \gamma_*/2\right)\mathbb{Q}(U)$$

$$= \left(\frac{1}{2} + \gamma_*/2\right)(1 - \mathbb{Q}(B))$$

$$\geq \left(\frac{1}{2} + \gamma_*/2\right)\left(1 - \frac{\gamma_*}{3} e^{\gamma_*^2 k/2} \mathbb{P}(B)\right)$$

$$\geq \left(\frac{1}{2} + \gamma_*/2\right)\left(1 - \frac{\gamma_*}{3}\right) \quad \text{(by (3))}$$

$$\geq \frac{1}{2} + \gamma_*/4,$$

completing the proof. ☐

For the most part, Freund's original analysis [14] can take us the rest of the way to prove Theorem 1. For completeness, we provide the details of how.

**Lemma 3.** *Suppose the Boost-by-Majority is run with parameters $\alpha$ and $T$, and generates classifiers $h_0, ..., h_{T-1}$ for which*

$$\mathbb{P}_0(h_0(x) = y) = \frac{1}{2} + \gamma_0, ..., \mathbb{P}_{T-1}(h_{T-1}(x) = y) = \frac{1}{2} + \gamma_{T-1}.$$

*Then, for a random element of $\mathbb{P}$, a majority vote over the predictions of the base classifiers $h_0, ..., h_{T-1}$ is incorrect with probability at most*

$$e^{-2\alpha^2 T} + \sum_{t=0}^{T-1} (\alpha - \gamma_t) Z_t.$$

*Proof.* Define $B(t, R)$ recursively as follows:

$$B(T, R) = \begin{cases} 1 \text{ if } R \le T/2 \\ 0 \text{ otherwise} \end{cases}$$

$$B(t, R) = \left(\frac{1}{2} - \alpha\right) B(t+1, R) + \left(\frac{1}{2} + \alpha\right) B(t+1, R+1).$$

The following is equivalent:

$$B(t, R) = \sum_{i=0}^{\lfloor T/2 \rfloor - R} \binom{T-t}{i} \left(\frac{1}{2} + \alpha\right)^i \left(\frac{1}{2} - \alpha\right)^{T-t-i}.$$

Define the potential $\Phi_t$ to be

$$\Phi_t = \sum_{(x,y) \in \mathcal{X} \times \{-1,1\}} \mathbb{P}(x, y) B(t, R_t(x, y)).$$

The Hoeffding bound implies

$$\Phi_0 \le e^{-2\alpha^2 T}. \tag{4}$$

Freund [14, Lemma 3.7] proved that

$$\Phi_{t+1} = \Phi_t + (\alpha - \gamma_t) Z_t. \tag{5}$$

Finally, the probability with respect to $\mathbb{P} = \mathbb{P}_0$ that a majority vote over $h_0, ..., h_{T-1}$ is wrong can be rewritten as $\mathbb{P}_0(R_T(x, y) \le T/2)$, which is $\Phi_T$. Putting this together with (4) and (5) completes the proof. □

**Lemma 4 (Lemma 3.9 of [14]).** *For all iterations $t \le T - 2$, $w_{t,\max} < \frac{2}{\sqrt{T-1-t}}$.*

## 4   Proof of Theorem 1

Recall that $T = k$ and $\alpha = \gamma_*/8$. Since the theorem is vacuously true if $4k < m$, we can assume without loss of generality that $m \ge 4k$, which means that the rejection method is applied to at least $\left\lceil \frac{m}{4\sqrt{T((T-1)-t)}} \right\rceil \geq \frac{m}{8\sqrt{T((T-1)-t)}}$ examples in each round $t \leq T - 2$.

Let

$$\epsilon = \max \left\{ 4096 \frac{T^{3/2} \left( \log \frac{nT}{2\delta} \right)}{\gamma_*^2 m}, \frac{3T}{\gamma_*} e^{-\gamma_*^2 T/2} \right\}. \tag{6}$$

Solving for $m$, we get

$$m \geq 4096 \frac{T^{3/2} \left( \log \frac{nT}{2\delta} \right)}{\gamma_*^2 \epsilon}. \tag{7}$$

**Lemma 5.** *If $T = k$, for any $t$ such that $Z_t > \epsilon/T$, with probability at least $1 - \delta/T$, $\gamma_t \geq \gamma_*/8 (= \alpha)$.*

*Proof.* We will give the details assuming $t \leq T - 2$. The case $t = T - 1$ can be proved similarly.

Let $m_t$ be the number of examples accepted in round $t$. Since the probability that an example is accepted is $Z_t/w_{t,\max}$, the standard Chernoff bound implies the probability that $m_t < \frac{Z_t m}{16 w_{t,\max} \sqrt{T((T-1)-t)}}$ is at most

$$\exp\left( -\frac{Z_t m}{64 w_{t,\max} \sqrt{T((T-1)-t)}} \right).$$

Since, by assumption, $Z_t > \epsilon/T$, and, by Lemma 4, $w_{t,\max} < \frac{2}{\sqrt{T-1-t}}$, (7) implies that this probability is at most $\delta/(2T)$.

The definition of $\epsilon$, (6), implies that

$$Z_t > \epsilon/T \geq \frac{3}{\gamma_*} e^{-\gamma_*^2 k/2}.$$

This implies that for all $(x, y)$,

$$\mathbb{P}_t(x, y)/\mathbb{P}(x, y) \leq 1/Z_t \leq \frac{\gamma_*}{3} e^{\gamma_*^2 k/2}.$$

Applying Lemma 2, there is a base classifier $h_t^* \in H$ such that

$$\mathbb{P}_t(h_t^*(x) = y) \geq \frac{1}{2} + \frac{\gamma_*}{4}.$$

For each $t$, let $\hat{\mathbb{P}}_t$ be the empirical distribution over the examples $(x_i, y_i)$ in the filtered dataset of round $t$, i.e. the examples such that $a_{t,i} = 1$. Then

$$\Pr(\gamma_t < \alpha)$$
$$= \Pr\left( \gamma_t < \frac{\gamma_*}{8} \right)$$
$$\leq \Pr\left( \hat{\mathbb{P}}_t(h_t^*(x) = y) - \mathbb{P}_t(h_t^*(x) = y) > \frac{\gamma_*}{16} \right.$$
$$\left. \text{or } \mathbb{P}_t(h_t(x) = y) - \hat{\mathbb{P}}_t(h_t(x) = y) > \frac{\gamma_*}{16} \right)$$
$$\leq \Pr\left( \text{There is an } h \in H, \, |\hat{\mathbb{P}}_t(h(x) = y) - \mathbb{P}_t(h(x) = y)| > \frac{\gamma_*}{16} \right).$$

Applying Hoeffding bounds,

$$\Pr(\gamma_t \leq \alpha) \leq 2n \exp\left(-\frac{\gamma_*^2 m_t}{128}\right).$$

If $m_t \geq \dfrac{Z_t m}{16 w_{t,\max}\sqrt{T((T-1)-t)}}$, then since $Z_t > \epsilon/T$ and $w_{t,\max} \leq 2/\sqrt{((T-1)-t)}$, we have $m_t \geq \frac{\epsilon m}{32 T^{3/2}}$, and the definition of $m$ then implies $\Pr(\gamma_t \leq \alpha) \leq \frac{\delta}{2T}$, completing the proof. □

Let us return to proving Theorem 1. Lemma 5 implies that with probability at least $1 - \delta$, for every $t$ for which $Z_t > \epsilon/T$, $\gamma_t \geq \alpha$. Thus, applying Lemma 3, with probability at least $1 - \delta$

$$\Pr(\text{MAJORITY}(h_0, ..., h_{T-1}) \text{ incorrect})$$

$$\leq e^{-\frac{\gamma_*^2 k}{8}} + \sum_{t=0}^{T-1}(\alpha - \gamma_t)Z_t$$

$$= e^{-\frac{\gamma_*^2 k}{8}} + \left(\sum_{t: Z_t \leq \epsilon/T}(\alpha - \gamma_t)Z_t\right) + \left(\sum_{t: Z_t > \epsilon/T}(\alpha - \gamma_t)Z_t\right)$$

$$\leq e^{-\frac{\gamma_*^2 k}{8}} + \epsilon + 0,$$

completing the proof. □

## 5    A Margin-Based Bound

Recall that $H$ is formally a set of $\{-1, 1\}$-valued functions. Let $co(H)$ be the set of all convex combinations of functions in $H$. In this section, we analyze the algorithm that chooses $f$ from $co(H)$ to maximize the number of examples $(x_i, y_i)$ for which $y_i f(x_i) \geq \gamma_*$, and outputs the classifier $h_f$ defined by $h_f(x) = \text{sign}(f(x))$. In other words, this algorithm chooses weights with which each of the classifiers in $H$ vote in order to maximize the number of training examples that are classified correctly with a margin of $\gamma_*$. Since it maximizes agreements with a margin, let us call such an algorithm a MAM algorithm.

Our analysis of this algorithm begins with the following lemma, which is an immediate consequence of Theorems 13.9, 12.8 and 14.20 of [4] (see also [2, 5]).

**Lemma 6.** *Fix a constant $\gamma_* > 0$. There are positive constants $c_3$ and $c_4$ such that, for any underlying distribution $\mathbb{P}$, if $(x_1, y_1), ..., (x_m, y_m)$ are drawn independently at random according to $\mathbb{P}$, then*

$$\Pr\left(\exists f \in co(H),\ \mathbb{P}_{(x,y)}(h_f(x) \neq y) > 2\frac{|\{i : y_i f(x_i) < \gamma_*\}|}{m} + \beta\right)$$

$$\leq \exp(c_3(\log^2 m)\log n - c_4 \beta m).$$

We will make use of the following standard Chernoff bounds.

**Lemma 7 (see [40]).** *Let $\hat{p}$ be the fraction of successes in $m$ independent Bernoulli trials with success probability $p$. Then*

- *if $0 < \beta \leq 1$, $\Pr(\hat{p} > (1+\beta)p) \leq e^{-\beta^2 pm/3}$,*
- *if $\beta > 1$, $\Pr(\hat{p} > (1+\beta)p) \leq e^{-(1+\beta)\ln(1+\beta)pm/4}$.*

We then easily obtain the following.

**Theorem 2.** *Fix a constant $\gamma_* > 0$. There are positive constants $c_5$ and $c_6$ such that, for $H$, $\mathbb{P}$ and $\gamma_*$ satisfying the requirements of Theorem 1, with probability $1 - \delta$, the output $h$ of an MAM algorithm applied to $m$ random examples chosen independently according to $\mathbb{P}$ satisfies*

$$\mathbb{P}(h(x) \neq y) \leq e^{-c_5 k} + \frac{c_6 (\log^2 m)(\log n) \log \frac{1}{\delta}}{m}.$$

*Proof.* First, we claim that it is likely that there is a voting classifier that correctly classifies all but a fraction $2e^{-\gamma_*^2 k/2} + \frac{8 \ln \frac{2}{\delta}}{m}$ of the training examples correctly with a margin $\gamma_*$. (Let $B$ be the event that this does not happen.) If $f(\cdot) = \frac{1}{k} \sum_{h \in H_*} h(\cdot)$, then the Hoeffding bound implies $\mathbb{P}(yf(x) < \gamma_*) \leq e^{-\gamma_*^2 k/2}$. Applying Lemma 7 then establishes that $\Pr(B) \leq 1 - \delta/2$ (use the $\beta = 1$ bound if $m \geq 3e^{\gamma_*^2 k/2} \ln \frac{2}{\delta}$, and $\beta > 1$ bound otherwise).

Applying Lemma 6 completes the proof. □

## 6    Experiments

The fact that we were only able to prove Theorem 1 using Boost-by-Majority made us wonder whether an algorithm like Boost-by-Majority might perform well in practice. In this section, we describe some preliminary experiments aimed at addressing this question.

Our experiments compare the performance of AdaBoost with an algorithm we call BBM*, which is like Boost-by-Majority, but with a few changes. Both algorithms were applied in conjunction with decision stumps, and the decision stump for each attribute was chosen to minimize the empirical error.

The differences between BBM* and Boost-by-Majority are as follows:

- When run for $T$ rounds, instead of partitioning the training data into $T$ disjoint parts to be used in the various rounds, BBM* uses all of the examples in each round. The rejection method is applied to choose a subset of the examples in each round in a manner analogous to Boost-by-Majority.
- If the number of examples accepted in a given round is less than 5, then, in BBM*, the round is skipped: no base classifier is added to the list of voters in that round. (This is similar to the practice Freund [14] analyzed: when the number of accepted examples is too small, add a base classifier that predicts randomly. The cutoff of 5 was chosen arbitrarily and not optimized, and the same value of 5 was used on all of the datasets.)

- If more than one attribute has a decision stump that minimizes training error on the filtered dataset in a given round, then an attribute is chosen uniformly at random from the list of minimizers.
- The parameter $\alpha$ is chosen using 5-fold cross-validation on the training data. The values $\{0.002, 0.005, 0.01, 0.02, 0.05\}$ are tried, and the value minimizing the cross-validation error is used. In case of a tie, the geometric mean of the values attaining the minimum is used.

In our experiments, both BBM* and AdaBoost were applied in conjunction with decision stumps, and both were run for 100 rounds. We evaluated the algorithms using the protocol of Dudoit, et al [13], in which the data is randomly split 100 times into a training set with 2/3 of the examples, and a test set with 1/3 of the examples. Both algorithms were evaluated on the same 100 training-test splits, and the average test-set error was tabulated. We applied both algorithms to a list of datasets from the UC Irvine repository previously used for evaluating AdaBoost [15], together with one microarray dataset called ER (see [49, 30] for a description).

Our results are summarized in Table 1.

Table 1. Summary of our experimental comparison between the BBM* algorithm and AdaBoost when both are applied for 100 rounds in conjunction with decision stumps. On each dataset, the percentage of test examples misclassified by each of the algorithms, together with the number of attributes and number of examples in the dataset, are shown.

| Dataset | BBM* | AdaBoost | # attrs. | # examples |
|---|---|---|---|---|
| ER | 20.0 | 18.1 | 7129 | 49 |
| promoters | 10.8 | 9.9 | 57 | 106 |
| hepatitis | 18.2 | 19.2 | 19 | 155 |
| ionosphere | 11.4 | 10.3 | 34 | 351 |
| house | 4.2 | 4.0 | 16 | 435 |
| breast | 3.4 | 4.5 | 9 | 699 |
| pima | 25.7 | 24.7 | 8 | 768 |
| hypothyroid | 0.86 | 1.01 | 25 | 3163 |
| sick-euthyroid | 2.5 | 3.1 | 25 | 3163 |
| kr-vs-kp | 3.0 | 4.3 | 36 | 3196 |

BBM* appears to significantly improve on the performance of AdaBoost on most of the larger datasets.

The code for these experiments is a modification of the code from [30]. The site

http://giscompute.gis.nus.edu.sg/~plong/bbm_star

has the new code.

# 7   Conclusion

We have provided a theoretical analysis of boosting that shows how a boosting algorithm can take advantage of a collection of base classifiers that contains a large, diverse collection of fairly good classifiers. Inspired by this analysis, we have investigated the practical utility of an algorithm like Freund's Boost-by-Majority algorithm, and found that, on some large datasets, it appears to perform better than AdaBoost. We have also showed that a better bound can be obtained by an algorithm that maximizes the number of examples classified correctly with a certain margin, but we have not shown how to efficiently perform this optimization.

It is trivial to generalize our results to the case in which the correctness random variables of the good base classifiers $H^*$ are *negatively associated*, say in the sense studied in Dubhashi and Ranjan's [12] paper. An analysis in which a limited amount of positive association among the errors of classifiers in $H^*$ was allowed would be interesting.

All that we use about our assumption is that it implies that there is a convex combination $f$ of the classifiers in $H$ such that $\mathbb{P}(yf(x) \leq \gamma_*) \leq e^{-\gamma_*^2 k/2}$. Thus, more general theorems concerning this form of assumption are implicit in our analyses. This implies that our results can also be strengthened to apply when the *average* (instead of the maximum) error rate of the classifiers in $H^*$ is at most $1/2 - \gamma_*$.

Directly applying (1.5) from [25] (see also [24]) leads to a bound, for the MAM algorithm, of

$$
c \left( e^{-\gamma_*^2 k/2} + \frac{(1/\gamma_*)^{\frac{\log_2 n}{1+\log_2 n}}}{m^{-\frac{1+\frac{\log_2 n}{2}}{1+\log_2 n}}} + \frac{\ln \frac{1}{\delta}}{m} \right).
$$

If $\gamma_*$ is a constant and $n$ is moderately large, the dependence on $m$ is roughly as $1/\sqrt{m}$. However, it seems likely that some the techniques used in [24] can be applied to improve Theorem 2, at least by a factor of $\log m$.

It would be good to prove a bound like Theorem 2 for a provably fast algorithm. One promising avenue is to try to use boosting to do the optimization, possibly approximately, for an algorithm like MAM.

In our analysis, the parameters of the Boost-by-Majority algorithm were set as a function of $k$ and $\gamma^*$. It would be nice to be able to prove a similar theorem for an algorithm that did not need to do this. A modification of the smooth boosting algorithm studied by Gavinsky [21, 23, 18] to use boosting-by-filtering seems a good place to start. (Similarly, the MAM algorithm used knowledge of $\gamma_*$.)

Another question is whether the bounds of this paper, or better bounds, can be obtained by an algorithm that minimizes a convex function of the voting weights that is an upper bound on the number of misclassifications, as some boosting algorithms can be seen to do (see [8, 35, 17]). Recently, significant progress has been made on the analysis of such algorithms (see [31, 50, 6,

7]). Recent strong bounds obtained for Support Vector Machines [26, 37] using the PAC-Bayes methodology [39, 38] also raise hope for that technique to be profitably applied here. Either of these would result in guarantees with the flavor of the margin analysis, as well as for the framework of this paper, for the same, efficient, algorithm.

It also appears possible that improved analysis could be obtained with an algorithm like Boost-by-Majority. For example, can improved bounds be obtained for an algorithm like BBM* that, in each round, applies the rejection method on *all* the examples?

Finally, we view BBM* as a crude first step in investigation of the practical utility of the rejection method in the context of boosting. It appears possible that sophisticated hybrids of the rejection method and importance sampling, as have been developed for other applications (see [28]), might lead to significant improvements in practical performance for boosting algorithms. Another tantalizing possibility is that recent refinements to importance sampling that reduce the variance while remaining unbiased (see [48]) might have a role to play in boosting, both in theory and in practice.

## Acknowledgements

We are grateful to Peter Bartlett, Gábor Lugosi, David McAllester, Partha Niyogi and Adai Ramasamy for helpful discussions and email messages, including in some cases pointers to the literature and in some cases helpful comments on previous versions of this paper. We would also like to thank anonymous referees for stimulating comments.

## References

1. K. M. Ali and M. J. Pazzani. Error reduction through learning multiple descriptions. *Machine Learning*, 24:173–202, 1996.
2. N. Alon, S. Ben-David, N. Cesa-Bianchi, and D. Haussler. Scale-sensitive dimensions, uniform convergence, and learnability. *Journal of the Association for Computing Machinery*, 44(4):616–631, 1997.
3. Y. Amit and G. Blanchard. Multiple randomized classifiers: MRCL, 2001. Manuscript.
4. M. Anthony and P. L. Bartlett. *Neural Network Learning: Theoretical Foundations*. Cambridge University Press, 1999.
5. P. L. Bartlett. The sample complexity of pattern classification with neural networks: the size of the weights is more important than the size of the network. *IEEE Transactions on Information Theory*, 44(2):525–536, 1998.
6. P. L. Bartlett, M. I. Jordan, and J. D. McAuliffe. Convexity, classification, and risk bounds. Technical Report 638, Department of Statistics, U.C. Berkeley, 2003.
7. G. Blanchard, G. Lugosi, and N. Vayatis. On the rate of convergence of regularized boosting methods, 2003. Manuscript.
8. L. Breiman. Prediction games and arcing algorithms. *Neural Computation*, 11(7), 1999.

9. L. Breiman. Some infinity theory for predictor ensembles. Technical Report 577, Statistics Department, UC Berkeley, 2000.

10. Leo Breiman. Arcing classifiers. *The Annals of Statistics*, 1998.

11. P. Bülmann and B. Yu. Boosting with the l2 loss: regression and classification. *Journal of the American Statistical Association*, to appear.

12. D. Dubhashi and D. Ranjan. Balls and bins: A study in negative dependence. *Random Structures & Algorithms*, 13(2):99–124, Sept 1998.

13. S. Dudoit, J. Fridlyand, and T. P. Speed. Comparison of discrimination methods for the classification of tumors using gene expression data. *Journal of the American Statistical Association*, 97(457):77–87, 2002.

14. Y. Freund. Boosting a weak learning algorithm by majority. *Information and Computation*, 121(2):256–285, 1995.

15. Y. Freund and R. Schapire. Experiments with a new boosting algorithm. *Proceedings of the Thirteenth International Conference on Machine Learning*, 1996.

16. Y. Freund and R. E. Schapire. A decision-theoretic generalization of on-line learning and an application to boosting. *Proceedings of the Second European Conference on Computational Learning Theory*, pages 23–37, 1995.

17. J. Friedman, T. Hastie, and R. Tibshirani. Additive logistic regression: A statistical view of boosting. *The Annals of Statistics*, 38(2):337–407, 2000.

18. D. Gavinsky. Optimally-smooth adaptive boosting and application to agnostic learning. *Proceedings of the 13th International Workshop on Algorithmic Learning Theory*, 2002.

19. A.J. Grove and D. Schuurmans. Boosting in the limit: Maximizing the margin of learned ensembles. In *Proceedings of the Fifteenth National Conference on Artifical Intelligence*, 1998.

20. A. Hajnal, W. Maass, P. Pudlák, M. Szegedy, and G. Turán. Threshold circuits of bounded depth. *Journal of Computer and System Sciences*, 46:129–154, 1993.

21. Russell Impagliazzo. Hard-core distributions for somewhat hard problems. In *IEEE Symposium on Foundations of Computer Science*, pages 538–545, 1995.

22. W. Jiang. Process consistency for AdaBoost. *Annals of Statistics*, to appear.

23. Adam Klivans and Rocco A. Servedio. Boosting and hard-core sets. In *IEEE Symposium on Foundations of Computer Science*, pages 624–633, 1999.

24. V. Koltchinskii and D. Panchenko. Empirical margin distributions and bounding the generalization error of combined classifiers. *Annals of Statistics*, 30(1), 2002.

25. V. Koltchinskii and D. Panchenko. Complexities of convex combinations and bounding the generalization error in classification, 2003. Manuscript.

26. J. Langford and J. Shawe-Taylor. PAC-bayes and margins. *NIPS, 2002*.

27. J. S. Liu. *Monte Carlo Strategies in Scientific Computing*. Springer, 2001.

28. J. S. Liu and R. Chen. Sequential Monte Carlo methods for dynamic systems. *Journal of the American Statistical Association*, 93(443):1032–1044, 1998.

29. P. M. Long. Minimum majority classification and boosting. *Proceedings of the The Eighteenth National Conference on Artificial Intelligence*, 2002.

30. P. M. Long and V. B. Vega. Boosting and microarray data. *Machine Learning*, to appear.

31. G. Lugosi and N. Vayatis. On the bayes-risk consistency of regularized boosting methods. *Annals of Statistics*, 2004. Preliminary version in COLT'02.

32. S. Mannor, R. Meir, and S. Mendelson. The consistency of boosting algorithms. Manuscript, 2001.

33. S. Mannor, R. Meir, and T. Zhang. The consistency of greedy algorithms for classification. *Proc. Fifteenth Annual Conference on Computational Learning Theory*, 2002.

34. Dragos D. Margineantu and Thomas G. Dietterich. Pruning adaptive boosting. In *Proc. 14th International Conference on Machine Learning*, pages 211–218. Morgan Kaufmann, 1997.

35. L. Mason, J. Baxter, P. L. Bartlett, and M. Frean. Boosting algorithms as gradient descent. In *Advances in Neural Information Processing Systems 12*, pages 512–518. MIT Press, 2000.

36. Llew Mason, Peter L. Bartlett, and Jonathan Baxter. Improved generalization through explicit optimization of margins. *Machine Learning*, 38(3):243–255, 2000.

37. D. McAllester. Simplified PAC-Bayesian margin bounds. *Proceedings of the 2003 Conference on Computational Learning Theory*, 2003.

38. David A. McAllester. PAC-Bayesian model averaging. In *Proc. 12th Annu. Conf. on Comput. Learning Theory*, pages 164–170. ACM Press, New York, NY, 1999.

39. David A. McAllester. Some PAC-Bayesian theorems. *Machine Learning*, 37(3):355–363, 1999.

40. R. Motwani and P. Raghavan. *Randomized Algorithms*. Cambridge University Press, 1995.

41. P. Niyogi, J.-B. Pierrot, and O. Siohan. On decorrelating classifiers and combining them, 2001. Manuscript, see `people.cs.uchicago.edu/~niyogi/decorrelation.ps`.

42. G. Pisier. Remarques sur un resultat non publi'e de B. Maurey. *Sem. d'Analyse Fonctionelle*, 1(12):1980–81, 1981.

43. J. Quinlan. Bagging, boosting and c4.5. In *Proceedings of the Thirteenth National Conference on Artifiicial Intelligence*, pages 725–730. AAAI/MIT Press, 1996.

44. G. Rätsch and M. K. Warmuth. Marginal boosting. *Proceedings of the Annual Conference on Computational Learning Theory*, 2002.

45. S. Rosset, J. Zhu, and T. Hastie. Boosting as a regularized path to a maximum margin classifier. *NIPS*, 2002.

46. R. Schapire. The strength of weak learnability. *Machine Learning*, 5:197–227, 1990.

47. Robert E. Schapire, Yoav Freund, Peter Bartlett, and Wee Sun Lee. Boosting the margin: A new explanation for the effectiveness of voting methods. *The Annals of Statistics*, 26(5):1651–1686, 1998.

48. F. Southey, D. Schuurmans, and A. Ghodsi. Regularized greedy importance sampling. *NIPS'02*.

49. M. West, et al. Predicting the clinical status of human breast cancer by using gene expression profiles. *Proc. Natl. Acad. Sci. USA*, 98(20):11462–11467, 2001.

50. T. Zhang. Statistical behavior and consistency of classification methods based on convex risk minimization. *Annals of Statistics*, to appear.

51. T. Zhang and B. Yu. Boosting with early stopping: convergence and consistency. Technical Report 635, Statistics Department, UC Berkeley, 2003.

# Reducing Kernel Matrix Diagonal Dominance Using Semi-definite Programming

Jaz Kandola[1], Thore Graepel[2], and John Shawe-Taylor[1]

[1] Dept. Computer Science
Royal Holloway, University of London UK
{jaz,john}@cs.rhul.ac.uk
[2] Microsoft Research
Cambridge UK
thoreg@microsoft.com

**Abstract.** Kernel-based learning methods revolve around the notion of a *kernel* or Gram matrix between data points. These square, symmetric, positive semi-definite matrices can informally be regarded as encoding pairwise similarity between all of the objects in a data-set. In this paper we propose an algorithm for manipulating the diagonal entries of a kernel matrix using semi-definite programming. Kernel matrix diagonal dominance reduction attempts to deal with the problem of learning with almost orthogonal features, a phenomenon commonplace in kernel matrices derived from string kernels or Gaussian kernels with small width parameter. We show how this task can be formulated as a semi-definite programming optimization problem that can be solved with readily available optimizers. Theoretically we provide an analysis using Rademacher based bounds to provide an alternative motivation for the 1-norm SVM motivated from kernel diagonal reduction. We assess the performance of the algorithm on standard data sets with encouraging results in terms of approximation and prediction.

## 1 Introduction

Kernel-based methods (for an overview see [1] [2] [3]) are increasingly being used for data modelling and prediction because of their conceptual simplicity and outstanding performance on many tasks. Kernel-based learning algorithms can often be formulated as convex optimization problems and—as a consequence—do not suffer from problems of convergence to local minima and dependence on parameter initialization. The convexity is a result of the fact that the objective function involves only inner products in a feature space corresponding to the kernel used. Hence, kernel algorithms can be viewed as selecting linear functions in feature space which often leads to convex optimisation problems. The kernel function must satisfy two mathematical requirements in order to correspond to an inner product in some feature space: it must be symmetric and positive semi-definite. Given such a kernel function kernel methods revolve around the notion of a *kernel matrix* or Gram matrix whose entries characterise the pairwise similarity between objects in the training sample. As observed by [4] the

B. Schölkopf and M.K. Warmuth (Eds.): COLT/Kernel 2003, LNAI 2777, pp. 288–302, 2003.

construction of appropriate positive semi-definite kernels is not a simple task, and this is why (with a few notable exceptions) kernel methods have mostly been confined to Euclidean input spaces. Recent work by [5] has shown how the kernel matrix can be *learned* using a semi-definite programming approach in a transductive setting. Semi-definite programming is a branch of convex optimization that deals with the optimization of convex functions over the convex cone of positive semi-definite matrices [6]. Hence, semi-definite programming is an attractive framework for kernel methods since the crucial positive semi-definite constraint on the kernel matrix is implicit in the formulation of an SDP.

The main contribution of this paper is in the exploitation of SDP for the *manipulation* of kernel matrices. In *kernel matrix diagonal dominance reduction* we aim at individually reducing the diagonal entries of the kernel matrix in an attempt to deal with the problem of learning with almost orthogonal features commonplace in kernel matrices on structured objects such as strings.

This paper is structured as follows. In Section 2 we review some basic concepts about kernel methods and detail the conditions a kernel function must satisfy. In Section 3 we introduce semi-definite programming and review its relation to linear and quadratic programming, both of which are commonly used in machine learning. Section 4 formulates a semi-definite program to deal with the problem of learning with almost orthogonal features which gives rise to what are referred to as diagonally dominant kernel matrices. Experimental results are presented in Section 5 and the paper is summarized in Section 6 where we also provide some ideas for future work.

## Notation

We denote vectors by bold lower-case letters, e.g., $\mathbf{x}$. Matrices are denoted by bold upper-case letters, e.g., $\mathbf{A}$. We denote sets other than the standard sets $\mathbb{R}$ and $\mathbb{N}$ by calligraphic upper-case letters, e.g., $\mathcal{X}$. The mapping $\phi$ maps to the feature space $\mathcal{F}$. We assume $m$ examples and a feature space dimensionality of $N$. The kernel function is $k : \mathcal{X} \times \mathcal{X} \to \mathbb{R}$.

## 2    Overview of Kernel Methods

Kernels methods for pattern analysis work by embedding data into a vector space where patterns can be more easily detected. This is achieved in a computationally efficient way by implicitly computing the inner products between the images of the data items in such a space, rather than invoking their coordinates. Several pattern recognition algorithms exist that only require the knowledge of inner products between data, and it is often the case that the inner product between feature vectors is much easier to compute than their explicit representation in coordinates. The function that returns the inner product between images of two data items in some embedding space is called the kernel function.

Of course, the quality of the pattern analysis will depend on the quality of the embedding provided by the kernel chosen. Ideally, we would like the embedding to be such that objects that are similar with respect to the task given are close in feature space. The kernel function thus requires us to put in knowledge of the domain. Once such a kernel is available, it can be used for tasks such as classification, clustering, and ranking. Formally, we will call any function that calculates the inner product between inputs mapped to feature space a *kernel function*. For any mapping $\phi : \mathcal{X} \rightarrow \mathcal{F}$, from the input space $\mathcal{X}$ to the feature space $\mathcal{F}$, we will denote the kernel by $k(x_i, x_j) = \langle \phi(x_i), \phi(x_j) \rangle$. The mapping $\phi$ transforms an example $x \in \mathcal{X}$ into an $N$-dimensional feature vector.

$$\phi(x) = (\phi_1(x), \ldots, \phi_N(x))'$$

Mapping the data explicitly to feature space generally has very high computational cost. However, a kernel function provides a way to handle this problem. A kernel function is a symmetric, positive-definite function, that is the $m \times m$ matrix with entries of the form $K_{ij} = k(x_i, x_j)$ (known as the kernel matrix) is always a symmetric, positive semi-definite matrix.

Given a sample $x := (x_1, x_2, \ldots, x_m)$, the information available to kernel-based algorithms is contained entirely in the matrix of kernel evaluations

$$\mathbf{K} = (k(x_i, x_j))_{i,j=1}^{m} \tag{1}$$

referred to as the Gram or Kernel matrix. Kernels can be used without actually knowing the feature space $\mathcal{F}$ being implicitly defined, as long as one can guarantee that such a space exists, that is, that the kernel can actually be regarded as an inner product in *some* space. This is done by exploiting properties that characterize kernel functions. One can characterize valid kernel functions in many ways, the simplest one probably being the following:

**Proposition 1. Saitoh** *[7] A function $k(x, \tilde{x})$ is a valid kernel if and only if for any finite set of data $\{x_1, x_2, \ldots, x_m\}$, for any $(a_1, .., a_m)' \in \mathbb{R}^m$ we have $\sum_{i,j=1}^{m} a_i a_j k(x_i, x_j) \geq 0$.*

Note that this proposition is a characterisation very similar to Mercer's theorem but taking recourse to instantiations of the kernel matrix resulting from a kernel rather than the integral operator corresponding to the kernel. While it might in fact be difficult to determine if the condition is true for every finite subset of $\mathcal{X}$, the proposition does emphasize the importance of the positive semi-definiteness of the kernel matrix.

## 3    Semi-definite Programming

Semi-definite optimization can be described as the problem of optimizing a linear function of a symmetric matrix subject to linear equality constraints and the condition that the matrix be positive semi-definite [8]. The well-known linear programming problem can be generalized to a semi-definite optimization by replacing the vector of variables with a symmetric matrix, and replacing the

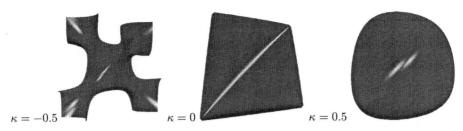

$\kappa = -0.5$          $\kappa = 0$          $\kappa = 0.5$

**Fig. 1.** Visualisation of positive semi-definite constraints. Points $(x, y, z)'$ on the surface of the depicted body correspond to the solutions of the determinant Equation $\det|((1, x, y)', (x, 1, z)', (y, z, 1)')| = \kappa$. $\kappa = 0$, (c) $\kappa = 0.5$. Points inside the body correspond to positive definite matrices, points on the surface to positive semi-definite, and point outside the body to indefinite matrices.

non-negativity constraints with positive semi-definite constraints. This generalization inherits several properties: it is convex, has a rich duality theory and allows theoretically efficient solution algorithms based on iterating interior point methods to either follow a central path or decrease a potential function. An important difference to linear programming is that the feasible region is no longer a polyhedron and hence the simplex method cannot be used directly. However, as observed by [6] most interior point methods for linear programs have been generalized to semi-definite programs. Also the simplex method has been generalized to semi-definite programs. As in linear programming these algorithms have polynomial worst-case complexity.

Let $C \in \mathbb{S}_m$ be in the set $\mathbb{S}_m$ of $m \times m$ symmetric matrices and define the inner product $\langle \cdot, \cdot \rangle : \mathbb{S}_m \times \mathbb{S}_m \to \mathbb{R}$ between matrices $A, B \in \mathbb{S}_m$ by $\langle A, B \rangle :=$ trace$(AB)$. Then semi-definite programs with unknown $X$ can be cast into the form [6]

$$\text{minimise}_{\mathbf{X}} \ \langle \mathbf{C}, \mathbf{X} \rangle$$
$$\text{subject to } \mathcal{A}\mathbf{X} = \mathbf{b} \quad \text{and} \quad \mathbf{X} \succeq 0. \tag{2}$$

The condition $\mathbf{X} \succeq 0$ constrains the solution to lie in the cone $\mathbb{S}_m^+$ of positive semi-definite matrices. This constraint turns out to be very powerful, because it effectively corresponds to infinitely many linear constraints, $\forall v \in \mathbb{R}^m : v'Xv \geq 0$. The type of convex region that can be described by positive semi-definite constraints is illustrated in Figure 1. Also we may have a linear equality constraint $\mathcal{A}\mathbf{X} = \mathbf{b}$ with $\mathcal{A} : \mathbb{S}_m \to \mathbb{R}^l$ being a linear operator from the set $\mathbb{S}_m$ of symmetric $m \times m$ matrices to $\mathbb{R}^l$.

In order to appreciate the generality of SDPs note that we have

$$\mathbf{X}_1 \succeq 0, \ldots, \mathbf{X}_k \succeq 0 \quad \Leftrightarrow \quad \text{diag}(\mathbf{X}_1, \ldots \mathbf{X}_k) \succeq 0, \tag{3}$$

for diagonal block matrices, and the Schur complement

$$\begin{pmatrix} \mathbf{A} & \mathbf{B} \\ \mathbf{B}' & \mathbf{C} \end{pmatrix} \succeq 0 \quad \Leftrightarrow \quad \mathbf{C} - \mathbf{B}'\mathbf{A}^{-1}\mathbf{B} \succeq 0, \tag{4}$$

for $\mathbf{A} \in \mathbb{S}_k^+$, $\mathbf{C} \in \mathbb{S}_l$, and $\mathbf{B}$ a $k \times l$ matrix.

From (3) it is easy to see that a linear program, $\text{minimise}_{\mathbf{x} \geq 0} \langle \mathbf{c}, \mathbf{x} \rangle$, s.t. $\mathbf{Ax} = \mathbf{b}$, can be cast as a semi-definite program interpreting each single component $x_i$ of $\mathbf{x}$ as a positive semi-definite matrix in (3). Similarly, a quadratically constrained convex quadratic program (QCQP), $\text{minimise}_{\mathbf{x} \geq 0} \mathbf{x}'\mathbf{Q}_0\mathbf{x} - \mathbf{q}_0'\mathbf{x} - c_0$, s.t. $\forall i \, \mathbf{x}'\mathbf{Q}_i\mathbf{x} - \mathbf{q}_i'\mathbf{x} - c_i \leq \mathbf{0}$ can be formulated as a semi-definite program. Using (4) a convex quadratic constraint $\mathbf{x}'\mathbf{Q}_i\mathbf{x} - \mathbf{q}_i'\mathbf{x} - c_i \leq \mathbf{0}$ is equivalent to the linear matrix constraint

$$\begin{pmatrix} \mathbf{I} & \mathbf{C}_i\mathbf{x} \\ \mathbf{x}'\mathbf{C}_i' & \mathbf{q}_i'\mathbf{x} + c_i \end{pmatrix} \succeq \mathbf{0} \quad \Leftrightarrow \quad \mathbf{x}'\mathbf{Q}_i\mathbf{x} - \mathbf{q}_i'\mathbf{x} - c_i \leq \mathbf{0},$$

where $\mathbf{Q}_i =: \mathbf{C}_i'\mathbf{C}_i$. Thus solving the semi-definite program

$$\text{minimise}_{t,\mathbf{x}} \quad t$$

$$\text{subject to} \quad \begin{pmatrix} \mathbf{I} & \mathbf{C}_0\mathbf{x} \\ \mathbf{x}'\mathbf{C}_0' & \mathbf{q}_0'\mathbf{x} + c_0 + t \end{pmatrix} \succeq \mathbf{0} \quad \text{and} \quad \forall i \begin{pmatrix} \mathbf{I} & \mathbf{C}_i\mathbf{x} \\ \mathbf{x}'\mathbf{C}_i' & \mathbf{q}_i'\mathbf{x} + c_i + t \end{pmatrix} \succeq \mathbf{0}$$

is equivalent to solving the QCQP. It should be noted, however, that these formulations are often not efficient in practice, where the particular structure of the problem should be considered. The two special cases discussed are of particular interest in machine learning: They show that the linear and quadratic programs that have become so popular in the context of support vector machines and kernel machines in general [1], can be cast into the more general framework of semi-definite programming (SDP), an insight that might pave the way for yet more sophisticated learning algorithms based on convex programming.

Although semi-definite programs are much more general than linear programs [6] observe that they are not much harder to solve. It is now generally accepted that interior-point methods for linear programs are competitive with the simplex method and even faster for problems with more than 100,000 variables or constraints. As a very rough rule of thumb, interior-point methods solve semi-definite problems in about 5-50 iterations where each iteration can be considered as basically being a least-square problem of the same size as the original problem. From a theoretical perspective, a worst-case analysis of interior point methods for semi-definite programming shows that the effort required to solve a semi-definite program to a given accuracy grows no faster than a polynomial of the problem size.

## 4   Kernel Diagonal Reduction

As observed by [1] an important feature of kernel methods is that the input domain $\mathcal{X}$ does not have to be a vector space. Both, [9] and [10] have considered kernel construction over discrete objects such as strings. As observed by [11] the feature map $\phi$ might incorporate rather complex features of the inputs such as all (even non-contiguous) sub-strings of a given string. As a consequence, it has been observed in practice that the resulting kernel matrices are often diagonally dominant [11], that is,

$$k(x_i, x_i) \gg \|k(x_i, x_j)\| \text{ for } x_i \neq x_j, \ i, j \in \{1, \cdots, m\}. \tag{5}$$

This reflects the fact that under very generic kernels such as string kernels the feature vectors in $\mathcal{F}$ may be almost orthogonal. Having orthogonal features means that when a kernel matrix is constructed every point is most similar to itself (corresponding to a large norm $k(x_i, x_i) = \|\phi(x_i)\|^2$) and very dissimilar to every other point $\tilde{x} \neq x$ (corresponding to a small inner product $k(x_i, x_j) = \langle x_i, x_j \rangle$). This may lead to severe over-fitting, because the high effective dimensionality of $\mathcal{F}$ leads to a high complexity of the function class used for learning. The most naive approach to this problem simply subtracts a constant from the diagonal such that the resulting matrix remains positive semi-definite. Another approach suggested by [11] attempts to reduce the *dynamic range* of the kernel matrix. In this approach a scaling function, e.g., the logarithm or a sigmoidal function is applied element wise to the entries of the kernel matrix. From the resulting matrix a positive semi-definite kernel matrix is constructed, e.g., by squaring. We suggest a more refined approach based on a semi-definite programming formulation of the problem.

## 4.1   Diagonal-Reduction by Semi-definite Programming

We consider the problem of diagonal dominance reduction as a semi-definite program,

$$\text{maximise}_{\mathbf{d}} \ \mathbf{1}'_m \mathbf{d} \tag{6}$$
$$\text{subject to } \mathbf{K} - \text{diag}(\mathbf{d}) \succeq \mathbf{0}.$$

The objective is to find the vector $\mathbf{d}$ with maximum 1-norm, $\|\mathbf{d}\|_1$ such that the expression $\mathbf{K} - \text{diag}(\mathbf{d})$ remains positive semi-definite. It turns out that this simple semi-definite program does not only capture the essence of diagonal dominance reduction in a computationally efficient way. The program (6) also bears an interesting relation to the so-called Max-Cut problem and its semi-definite relaxations [12]. In order to see this, we consider the dual (see [6] for SDP duality) of the SDP (6),

$$\text{maximise}_{\mathbf{Y}} \ \langle \mathbf{K}, \mathbf{Y} \rangle \tag{7}$$
$$\text{subject to } \text{diag}(\mathbf{Y}) = \mathbf{1}_m$$
$$\mathbf{Y} \succeq \mathbf{0}.$$

Numerical results for this approach are presented in Section 5 using diagonally dominant kernel matrices constructed based on real data-sets.

This semi-definite program is well-known as a relaxation of the NP-hard combinatorial optimisation problem Max-Cut, which is concerned with finding the maximum-weight cut of a graph with weighted edges. Consider a complete undirected graph $\mathcal{G} = (\mathcal{N}, \mathcal{E})$ consisting of a node set $\mathcal{N}$ and an edge set $\mathcal{E}$, and a real-valued matrix $\mathbf{W} \in \mathbb{S}_m$ of weights. For a subset $\mathcal{K}$ of nodes let $\delta(\mathcal{K}) := \{ij \in \mathcal{E} : i \in \mathcal{K}, j \notin \mathcal{K}\}$ denote the set of edges cut and let their weight be given by $w(\delta(\mathcal{K})) := \sum_{ij \in \delta(\mathcal{K})} w_{ij}$. The Max-Cut problem is to find $\mathcal{K}$ such that $w(\delta(\mathcal{K}))$ is maximised. In [8] (following work by [12]) non-convex quadratic programming formulations of the Max-Cut problem are considered, which can be further relaxed to semi-definite programs. Formally, if $y \in \mathbb{R}^m$ with each $y_i = \pm 1$ is used to represent the cut $\delta(K)$, where $y_i = 1$ iff $i \in \mathcal{K}$. It follows that $y_i y_j = -1$ if $ij \in \delta(\mathcal{K})$ and $y_i y_j = 1$ otherwise. Let $\mathbf{K} \in \mathbb{S}_m$ with entries $k_{ij} := -w_{ij}/4$ for $i \neq j$ and $k_{ii} = \sum_j w_{ij}/4 \,\forall\, i$. Then the weight of the cut determined by $y$ can be written as,

$$w(\delta(\mathcal{K})) = \frac{1}{2} \sum_{i<j} w_{ij}(1 - y_i y_j) = \frac{1}{4} \sum_i \sum_j w_{ij}(1 - y_i y_j) = y'\mathbf{K}y \quad (8)$$

As observed by [8] since every $(+1, -1)$ vector corresponds to a cut, the Max-Cut problem can be written as the integer quadratic programming problem,

$$\text{maximize}_y \ y'\mathbf{K}y \quad (9)$$
$$\text{subject to} \ y_i \in \{+1, -1\}, i \in \mathcal{N}, \quad (10)$$

or, equivalently, as the non-convex quadratically constrained quadratic problem

$$\text{maximize}_y \ y^T\mathbf{K}y \quad (11)$$
$$\text{subject to} \ y_i^2 = 1, i \in \mathcal{N}.$$

The following theorem provides a way of encoding the constraint in terms of a linear matrix inequality:

**Theorem 1.** *[13] Let $\mathbf{Y}$ be an $m \times m$ symmetric matrix and $\mathbf{Y} \in \{\pm 1\}^{m \times m}$. Then $\mathbf{Y} \succeq 0$ if and only if $\mathbf{Y} = yy'$ for some $y \in \{\pm 1\}^m$.*

By noting that $y'\mathbf{K}y$ is equivalent to $\langle \mathbf{K}, yy' \rangle$ and removing the rank one constraint on $\mathbf{Y}$, (11) can be relaxed to the SDP (7) which is the dual of the diagonal reduction SDP (6).

If we define the duality gap $\eta$ as the difference between the primal and the dual objectives we obtain

$$\eta := -\mathbf{1}'_m\mathbf{d} + \langle \mathbf{K}, \mathbf{Y} \rangle = \langle \mathbf{K} - \text{diag}(\mathbf{d}), \mathbf{Y} \rangle. \quad (12)$$

Assuming that both the primal and the dual are strictly feasible we have $\eta = 0$ at the optimal solution, i.e., we have

$$\langle \mathbf{K} - \text{diag}(\mathbf{d}^*), \mathbf{Y}^* \rangle = 0. \quad (13)$$

The diagonally reduced kernel matrix $\mathbf{K} - \text{diag}(\mathbf{d})$ is orthogonal in the sense of the Frobenius inner product to the solution matrix $\mathbf{Y}$ of the corresponding Max-Cut problem.

## 4.2   A Bound-Based Motivation for Diagonal Reduction

Work by [14] has given rise to a bound on the generalisation ability of the Support
Vector Machine. More recently the use of Rademacher based bounds has led to
a bound of the form

$$O\left(\frac{\sqrt{\sum_{i=1}^{m}\|\phi(x_i)\|^2}}{\sqrt{m}\gamma}\right). \tag{14}$$

We will therefore motivate the diagonal reduction criterion by considering how
it will affect the expression (14). Before considering how to reduce a weighted
diagonal recall the method introduced in [15] for increasing the diagonal weight
in order to implement a soft margin SVM. A slight extension of the method
constructs a space of delta functions derived from the input space $\mathcal{X}$,

$$L(\mathcal{X}) = \left\{\sum_{i=1}^{S} \alpha_i \delta_{y_i}(\mathcal{X}) \ : s \in \mathbb{N}, y \in \mathcal{X}, 1 \le i \le S\right\}$$

The modified construction now embeds the input space $\mathcal{X}$ into the space $(\mathcal{X} \times L(\mathcal{X}))$ through the mapping

$$\tau_{\mathbf{d}} \to (z, d(z)\delta_z(x)) .$$

Note that a natural inner product is defined on the space $L(\mathcal{X})$ by

$$\left\langle \sum_{i=1}^{S} \alpha_i \delta_{y_i}(x), \sum_{j=1}^{S} \beta_j \delta_{z_i}(x) \right\rangle = \sum_{i,j:y_i=z_j} \alpha_i \beta_j . \tag{15}$$

This then extends the kernel defined inner product on $\mathcal{X}$ to $(\mathcal{X} \times L(X))$ to give

$$\langle \tau(y), \tau(z) \rangle = \begin{cases} \langle \phi(y), \phi(z) \rangle = k(y, z), & \text{if } y \ne z \\ \langle \phi(y), \phi(z) + d(z)^2 \rangle = k(z, z) + d(z)^2, & \text{if } y = z \end{cases} . \tag{16}$$

Hence, if we perform diagonal reduction we can recover the original space using
the construction to add back the amount originally removed. This leads to the
same bound value for the expression

$$\sum_{i=1}^{m} \|\phi(x_i)\|^2 . \tag{17}$$

However, we now have the freedom to add less to the diagonal while still achieving the same margin, since for those points that were not support vectors the
margin satisfies

$$y_i \sum_{j=1}^{m} \alpha_j y_j k(x_j, x_i) > 1 ,$$

so that reducing the value of the entry $k(x_i, x_i)$ will not affect the SVM solution.
Hence, we can obtain the same margin while reducing the numerator of the bound

giving an overall improvement. The above observations lead to the following optimisation criterion for maximising the expected reduction in the size of the bound,

$$\text{maximise}_{\mathbf{d}} \ \|\mathbf{d}\|^2$$
$$\text{subject to: } \mathbf{K} - \text{diag}(d_1^2, \cdots, d_n^2) \succeq 0 \,.$$

Here we have explicitly restricted the input space to the training set. The condition ensures that the resulting kernel matrix after diagonal removal is still a valid kernel. Hence, we seek a feature mapping from the space $\hat{\phi}(x)$ such that the original mapping $\phi(x)$ can be expressed up to isomorphism as

$$\phi(x) = \tau_d \hat{\phi}(x) \,, \tag{18}$$

with $\sum_{i=1}^m \|\hat{\phi}(x)\|^2$ minimal. There is an apparent difficulty that when constructing a soft SVM we do not have the freedom to add different elements to the diagonal. Note that the numerator of the bound (15) for the mapping $\phi$ can be expressed as

$$\left\| \sum \hat{\phi}(x) \right\|^2 + \|\mathbf{d}\|^2 \,. \tag{19}$$

We can consider constraining this to have a fixed value and maximise the margin by fixing a functional margin of 1 and minimising the norm of the weight vectors in the original feature space $\mathcal{F}$ and the augmented feature space $\hat{\mathcal{F}}$. What we would like to solve is the following optimisation problem

$$\text{minimise}_{\mathbf{d},\mathbf{w},\mathbf{w}'} \ D\|\mathbf{d}\|^2 + \frac{1}{2}\|\mathbf{w}\|^2 + \frac{1}{2}\|\mathbf{w}'\|^2$$
$$\text{subject to: } y_i \left( \langle \mathbf{w}, \hat{\phi}(\mathbf{x}_i) \rangle + \langle \mathbf{w}', \phi_{\mathbf{d}}(\mathbf{x}_i) \rangle \right) \geq 1 \,,$$

since this corresponds to minimising the bound (15). It can be shown (the proof is described in Appendix 1) that solving this problem is equivalent to solving the 1-norm SVM in the feature space $\hat{\mathcal{F}}$ with $C$ parameter $C = \sqrt{2D}$. Hence, the bound can be minimised by the following strategy. First perform diagonal reduction and then solve a 1-norm SVM in the resulting feature space for some value of $D$. This is equivalent to adding a flexible amount $d_i$ to each input to minimise the bound (15). Numerical evaluations for this kernel matrix diagonal dominance reduction algorithm are presented in section 5.

## 5     Experiments

### 5.1     Kernel Matrix Diagonal Dominance Reduction

Two artificial problems, dealing with string classification and microarray cancer detection, originally proposed by [11] were used in this work. A string kernel was created from two classes of strings that were generated with equal probability by two different Markov models. Both classes of strings consisted of letters from the same alphabet of 20 letters, and strings from both classes were fixed to be of length 20. Strings from the negative class were generated by a model where transitions from any letter to any other letter were equally likely. Strings from the positive class were generated by a model where transitions from one letter to itself had probability 0.43, and all other transitions have a probability of 0.03. The task is to predict which class a given string belongs to. The second problem considered is a microarray classification problem using a dataset with extra noisy features (again considered by [11]). The task here is to distinguish between cancerous and normal tissue in a colon cancer problem given the expression of genes measured by microarray technology. As noted in [11], this dataset does *not* give rise to kernel matrices with large diagonals, hence the original dataset was augmented with extra noisy features to simulate the problem of diagonally dominant kernel matrices. In order to solve the kernel diagonal reduction problem, we used a general purpose semi-definite programming solver[1] and subsequently trained a 1-norm SVM. A 5-fold cross validation procedure was used to set the value of the SVM capacity control parameter $C$. The results for this method for the microarray dataset and string kernel matrices are reported in the tables below:

**Table 1.** Support Vector Classifier error: (Left: microarray dataset) and (Right: string dataset). The value in brackets is the result obtained using the dynamic range technique found in [11].

| Matrix | SVC Error | Matrix | SVC Error |
|--------|-----------|--------|-----------|
| $K$ | 0.50 | $K$ | 0.38 |
| $K_{AS}$ | 0.11 (0.25) | $K_{AS}$ | 0.16 (0.28) |

From Figures 2 and 4 it can be seen that the semi-definite program clearly does reduce the diagonal of the original diagonally dominant matrix. Looking at the generalisation error experimental results confirms the observation that the learning algorithm is now able to exploit the latent structure in the reduced kernel matrix. Whilst the dynamic range approach from [11] also gives a reduction in generalisation error the SDP based approach on these two datasets reduced the error still further. An interesting avenue of future work would be to test the validity of the SDP approach on larger possibly commercial datasets. The effect of the SDP reduction can also be seen when we look at the eigenspectra of the original kernel matrix compared to the reduced matrix where we see a faster decay in eigenvalues for the SDP matrix. This observation is in accordance with our expectations where a kernel matrix with a fast decaying eigenspectrum is likely to generalise well.

The second set of experiments use the Breast cancer dataset obtained from the UCI repository. A 50-50 split of the data into training and test sets was made. Using a Gaussian kernel with varying width parameters a support vector

---

[1] A matlab toolbox for solving optimisation problems over symmetric cones (SeDuMi) can be downloaded from http://fewcal.kub.nl/sturm/software/sedumi.html

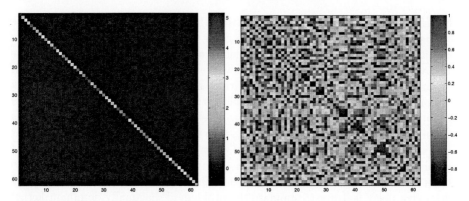

**Fig. 2.** Visualisation of a diagonally dominant kernel matrix (left) derived from the Colon dataset and its reduced form after manipulation via semi-definite programming (right). Note that the gray value coding is different in the two images.

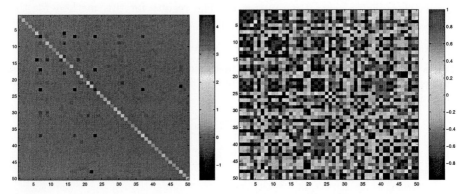

**Fig. 3.** Visualisation of a diagonally dominant kernel matrix derived from the string microarray dataset (left) and its reduced form after manipulation via semi-definite programming (right). Note that the gray value coding is different in the two images.

classifier was run on both the original diagonally dominant kernel matrix and the SDP reduced kernel matrix. The results are summarised in Figure 5. The generalisation performance of the diagonally reduced matrices is better than that of the original matrix showing that reducing the orthogonality of the features is beneficial. The biggest gain in performance appears to be when the original matrix is the most dominant, that is when the $\sigma$ parameter of the Gaussian is set to 0.01.

## 6    Conclusions and Outlook

In this paper we have proposed an algorithm for manipulating the entries of a kernel matrix using semi-definite programming. This approach was considered to be attractive since it ensures the resulting matrix remains a valid kernel matrix.

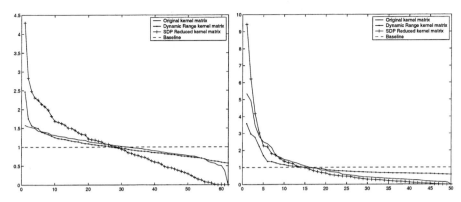

**Fig. 4.** The eigenspectra of the three kernel matrices considered in these experiments for the microarray and the colon cancer datasets.

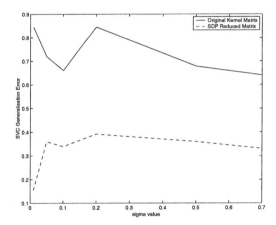

**Fig. 5.** Generalisation performance of a support vector classifier trained using both a diagonally dominant kernel matrix and a reduced matrix.

The task we considered was kernel matrix diagonal dominance reduction which attempts to deal with the problem of learning with almost orthogonal features, a phenomenon commonplace in kernel matrices derived from string kernels or Gaussian kernels with small width parameter. We formulated this problem as a semi-definite programming optimization problem that can be solved with readily available optimizers. We assessed the performance of the algorithms on standard data sets with encouraging results in terms of approximation and prediction. A further extension of this approach has been considered in [16] in which the diagonal reduction technique was combined with spectral clustering methods. A Bayesian interpretation of the algorithms described in this paper is also under consideration.

## Appendix 1

In this section we expand the Rademacher based bound motivation for performing diagonal reduction by formulating an optimisation problem similar to that of an SVM, however an additional weight vector $\mathbf{w}'$ is introduced, to deal with the augmented feature space described above, where each component is multiplied by a weight $d_i$ given to each training vector. In the following $e_i$ has replaced the $d_i^2$ that appeared in the main paper to avoid confusion. The resulting optimisation problem can be written as:

$$\text{minimise}_{\mathbf{e},\mathbf{w},\mathbf{w}'} \, D \sum_{i=1}^{m} e_i + \frac{1}{2}||\mathbf{w}||^2 + \frac{1}{2}||\mathbf{w}'||^2, \tag{20}$$

subject to

$$y_i \left( \langle \mathbf{w}, \hat{\boldsymbol{\phi}}_{\mathbf{e}}(x_i) \rangle + \langle \mathbf{w}', \boldsymbol{\phi}_{\mathbf{e}}(x_i) \rangle \right), \, e_i \geq 0 \geq 1, \, i = 1, \ldots, m,$$

where $\phi(x_i) = \sqrt{e_i}\delta_i(\cdot)$ and we use $k_e(x, z) = \langle \boldsymbol{\phi}_{\mathbf{e}}(x), \boldsymbol{\phi}_{\mathbf{e}}(z) \rangle$.

This optimisation problem can be thought of as maximising the standard SVM margin whilst allowing the algorithm to add components to the diagonal of the kernel matrix in order to improve the value of (20). The tradeoff between the margin and this quantity is controlled by a fixed regularisation constant $D$. Making use of Lagrange multipliers we have the following Lagrangian:

$$L(\boldsymbol{\alpha}, \mathbf{e}, \mathbf{w}, \mathbf{w}') = D \sum_{i=1}^{m} e_i + \frac{1}{2}||\mathbf{w}||^2 + \frac{1}{2}||\mathbf{w}'||^2 \tag{21}$$

$$- \sum_{i=1}^{m} \alpha_i \left[ y_i \left( \langle \mathbf{w}, \hat{\boldsymbol{\phi}}_{\mathbf{e}}(x_i) \rangle + \langle \mathbf{w}', \boldsymbol{\phi}_{\mathbf{e}}(x_i) \rangle \right) - 1 \right] - \sum_{i=1}^{m} \xi_i e_i$$

with the constraints $\alpha_i \geq 0$, $\xi_i \geq 0$  $i = 1, \ldots, m$.
Differentiating w.r.t. $\mathbf{w}$ and $\mathbf{w}'$ we obtain:

$$\frac{\partial L}{\partial \mathbf{w}} = \mathbf{w} - \sum_{i=1}^{m} \alpha_i y_i \hat{\boldsymbol{\phi}}_{\mathbf{e}}(x_i) = 0 \tag{22}$$

$$\mathbf{w} = \sum_{i=1}^{m} \alpha_i y_i \hat{\boldsymbol{\phi}}_{\mathbf{e}}(x_i) \tag{23}$$

$$\frac{\partial L}{\partial \mathbf{w}'} = \mathbf{w}' - \sum_{i=1}^{m} \alpha_i y_i \boldsymbol{\phi}_{\mathbf{e}}(x_i) = 0 \tag{24}$$

$$\mathbf{w}' = \sum_{i=1}^{m} \alpha_i y_i \boldsymbol{\phi}_{\mathbf{e}}(x_i) \tag{25}$$

$$\frac{\partial L}{\partial e_i} = D - \frac{\alpha_i y_i}{2\sqrt{e_i}} \langle \mathbf{w}', \delta_i(\cdot) \rangle - \xi_i = 0 \tag{26}$$

$$D - \frac{\alpha_i y_i}{2\sqrt{e_i}} \sum_j \alpha_j y_j \langle \phi_e(x_j), \delta_i(\cdot) \rangle - \xi_i = 0 \tag{27}$$

$$D - \frac{\alpha_i^2}{2} - \xi_i = 0 \tag{28}$$

Hence $\alpha_i \leq \sqrt{2D}$. Making the substitution for $\mathbf{w}$ and $\mathbf{w}'$ in Equation (21) gives the dual optimisation problem,

$$\text{maximise}_{\alpha,e} D \sum_{i=1}^{m} e_i + \frac{1}{2} \sum_{i,j=1}^{m} \alpha_i \alpha_j y_i y_j k(x_i, x_j) + \frac{1}{2} \sum_{i,j=1}^{m} \alpha_i \alpha_j y_i y_j \hat{k}(x_i, x_j) -$$

$$\sum_{i=1}^{m} \alpha_i \left[ y_i \left( \sum_{j=1}^{m} \alpha_j y_j k(x_i, x_j) + \sum_{j=1}^{m} \alpha_j y_j \hat{k}(x_i, x_j) \right) - 1 \right] - \sum_{i=1}^{m} \xi_i e_i,$$

given that $\sum_{i,j=1}^{m} \alpha_i \alpha_j y_i y_j k_d(x_i, x_j) = \sum_{i=1}^{m} \alpha_i^2 e_i$, we can write the above as

$$\text{maximise}_{\alpha} - \frac{1}{2} \sum_{i,j=1}^{m} \alpha_i \alpha_j y_i y_j k(x_i, x_j) + \sum_{i=1}^{m} \alpha_i, \text{ subject to } \alpha_i \geq 0. \tag{29}$$

which is equivalent to the 1-norm SVM when setting the $C$ parameter to $\sqrt{2D}$.

## Acknowledgements

The authors would like to thank Jason Weston for supplying the microarray and string kernel matrices and for helpful discussions on kernel matrix diagonal dominance. We also thank Anna Fukshansky, Craig Saunders, Bernhard Schölkopf, Ralf Herbrich, Hugo Zaragoza and Alex Smola for their valuable comments on this work. This work was supported by the EPSRC.

## References

1. N. Cristianini and J. Shawe-Taylor, An Introduction to Support Vector Machines, Cambridge University Press, 2000.
2. B. Schölkopf and A. Smola. Learning With Kernels – Support Vector Machines, Regularization, Optimization and Beyond, MIT Press, 2002.
3. R. Herbrich. Learning Kernel Classifiers. MIT Press. 2002.
4. R.I. Kondor and J. Lafferty. Diffusion Kernels on Graphs and Other Discrete Structures. Proceedings of Intenational Conference on Machine Learning (ICML 2002), 2002.
5. G. Lanckriet and N. Cristianini and P. Bartlett and L. El-Ghoui and M.I. Jordan. Learning the Kernel Matrix using Semi-Definite Programming. International Conference on Machine Learning (ICML 2002). 2002.
6. L. Vanderberghe and S. Boyd. Semidefinite programming. SIAM Review. A Publication of the Society for Industrial and Applied Mathematics, pp49-95. 1996.

7. S. Saitoh. Theory of Reproducing Kernels and its Applications, Longman Scientific & Technical 1988.

8. M.J. Todd. Semidefinite Programming, Technical report: Cornell University 2000.

9. D. Haussler. Convolutional Kernels on Discrete Structures. Technical Report: Computer Science Department, University of California at Santa Cruz. 1999

10. C. Watkins. Dynamic Alignment Kernels. Advances in Large Margin Classifiers. MIT Press. 2000

11. B. Schölkopf and J. Weston and E. Eskin and C. Les lie and W. Noble. A Kernel Approach for Learning from almost Orthogonal Patterns. Proceedings of European Conference on Machine Learning (ECML 2002) 2002.

12. M.X. Goemans and D.P. Williamson. Improved approximation algorithms for maximum cut and satisfiability problems using semidefinite programming. JACM 1115-1145. 1995.

13. H. Wolkowicz and M.F. Anjoz. Semi-definite Programming for Discrete Optimisation and Matrix Completion Problems. Technical Report: University of Waterloo 2000.

14. J. Shawe-Taylor and P. L. Bartlett and R. C. Williamson and M. Anthony. Structural Risk Minimization over Data-Dependent Hierarchies. IEEE Transactions on Information Theory 1998.

15. J. Shawe-Taylor and N. Cristianini. Margin Distribution Bounds on Generalization. Proceedings of the European Conference on Computational Learning Theory, EuroCOLT1999.

16. J. Kandola and J. Shawe-Taylor. Spectral Clustering using Diagonally Reduced Gram Matrices. Submitted to Neural Information Processing Systems 16, 2003.

# Optimal Rates of Aggregation

Alexandre B. Tsybakov

Laboratoire de Probabilités et Modèles Aléatoires, Université Paris 6, 4 pl. Jussieu,
75252 Paris Cedex 05, France
tsybakov@ccr.jussieu.fr

**Abstract.** We study the problem of aggregation of $M$ arbitrary estimators of a regression function with respect to the mean squared risk. Three main types of aggregation are considered: model selection, convex and linear aggregation. We define the notion of optimal rate of aggregation in an abstract context and prove lower bounds valid for any method of aggregation. We then construct procedures that attain these bounds, thus establishing optimal rates of linear, convex and model selection type aggregation.

## 1   Introduction

Consider the regression model

$$Y_i = f(X_i) + \xi_i, \quad i = 1, \dots, n, \tag{1}$$

where $X_1, \dots, X_n$ are i.i.d. random vectors with values in a Borel subset $\mathcal{X}$ of $\mathbf{R}^d$, $\xi_i$ are i.i.d. zero-mean random variables in $\mathbf{R}$ such that $(\xi_1, \dots, \xi_n)$ is independent of $(X_1, \dots, X_n)$ and $f : \mathcal{X} \to \mathbf{R}$ is an unknown regression function. The problem is to estimate the function $f$ from the data $D_n = ((X_1, Y_1), \dots, (X_n, Y_n))$.

Denote $P_f$ and $P^X$ the probability distributions of $D_n$ and of $X_1$ respectively. For an estimator $\hat{f}_n$ of $f$ based on the sample $D_n$, define the $L_2$-risk

$$R(\hat{f}_n, f) = E_f \|\hat{f}_n - f\|^2$$

where $E_f$ denotes the expectation w.r.t. the measure $P_f$ and, for a Borel function $g : \mathcal{X} \to \mathbf{R}$,

$$\|g\| = \left( \int_{\mathcal{X}} g^2(x) P^X(dx) \right)^{1/2}.$$

Suppose that we have $M \geq 2$ arbitrary estimators $f_{n,1}, \dots f_{n,M}$ of the function $f$ based on the sample $D_n$. The aim of aggregation is to construct a new estimate of $f$ (called *aggregate*) that mimics in a certain sense the behavior of the best among the estimators $f_{n,j}$. We will consider the following three well-known aggregation problems (cf. Nemirovski (2000)).

**Problem (L).** (*Linear aggregation.*) Find an aggregate estimator $\tilde{f}_n$ which is at least as good as the best linear combination of $f_{n,1}, \dots, f_{n,M}$, up to a small remainder term, i.e.

$$R(\tilde{f}_n, f) \leq \inf_{\lambda \in \mathbf{R}^M} R(f_\lambda^*, f) + \Delta_{n,M}^{\mathbf{L}}$$

B. Schölkopf and M.K. Warmuth (Eds.): COLT/Kernel 2003, LNAI 2777, pp. 303–313, 2003.
© Springer-Verlag Berlin Heidelberg 2003

for every $f$ belonging to a large class of functions $\mathcal{F}$, where

$$f_\lambda^* = \sum_{j=1}^M \lambda_j f_{n,j}, \quad \lambda = (\lambda_1, \ldots, \lambda_M),$$

and $\Delta_{n,M}^{\mathbf{L}}$ is a remainder term that does not depend on $f$.

**Problem (C).** (*Convex aggregation.*) Find an aggregate estimator $\tilde{f}_n$ which is at least as good as the best convex combination of $f_{n,1}, \ldots, f_{n,M}$, up to a small remainder term, i.e.

$$R(\tilde{f}_n, f) \le \inf_{\lambda \in \Lambda^M} R(f_\lambda^*, f) + \Delta_{n,M}^{\mathbf{C}}$$

for every $f$ belonging to a large class of functions $\mathcal{F}$, where

$$\Lambda^M = \left\{ \lambda \in \mathbf{R}^M : \lambda_j \ge 0, \sum_{j=1}^M \lambda_j \le 1 \right\}$$

and $\Delta_{n,M}^{\mathbf{C}}$ is a remainder term that does not depend on $f$.

**Problem (MS).** (*Model selection aggregation.*) Find an aggregate estimator $\tilde{f}_n$ which is at least as good as the best among $f_{n,1}, \ldots, f_{n,M}$, up to a small remainder term, i.e.

$$R(\tilde{f}_n, f) \le \min_{1 \le j \le M} R(f_{n,j}, f) + \Delta_{n,M}^{\mathbf{MS}}$$

for every $f$ belonging to a large class of functions $\mathcal{F}$, where $\Delta_{n,M}^{\mathbf{MS}}$ is a remainder term that does not depend on $f$.

Clearly,

$$\min_{1 \le j \le M} R(f_{n,j}, f) \ge \inf_{\lambda \in \Lambda^M} R(f_\lambda^*, f) \ge \inf_{\lambda \in \mathbf{R}^M} R(f_\lambda^*, f). \tag{2}$$

The smallest possible remainder terms $\Delta_{n,M}^{\mathbf{L}}$, $\Delta_{n,M}^{\mathbf{C}}$ and $\Delta_{n,M}^{\mathbf{MS}}$ characterize the price to pay for aggregation. We will see that they satisfy a relation that is in a sense inverse to (2): the largest price $\Delta_{n,M}$ is to be paid for linear aggregation and the smallest one for model selection aggregation. Convex aggregation has an intermediate price.

Aggregation of arbitrary estimators for regression with random design (1) under the $L_2$-risk has been studied by several authors, mostly in the case of model selection (Yang (2000), Catoni (2001), Wegkamp (2000), Györfi, Kohler, Krzyżak and Walk (2002), Birgé (2002)) and convex aggregation (Nemirovski (2000), Juditsky and Nemirovski (2000), Yang (2001)). Linear aggregation for the Gaussian white noise model is discussed by Nemirovski (2000). Aggregation procedures are typically based on sample splitting. The initial sample $D_n$ is divided into two independent subsamples $D_m^1$ and $D_l^2$ of sizes $m$ and $l$ respectively where $m \gg l$ and $m + l = n$. The first subsample $D_m^1$ is used to construct estimators $f_{n,1}, \dots, f_{n,M}$ and the second subsample $D_l^2$ is used to aggregate them, i.e. to construct $\tilde{f}_n$ (thus, $\tilde{f}_n$ is measurable w.r.t. the whole sample $D_n$). In this paper we will not consider sample splitting schemes but rather deal with an idealized framework (following Nemirovski (2000), Juditsky and Nemirovski (2000)) where the first subsample is fixed and thus instead of the estimators $f_{n,1}, \dots, f_{n,M}$ we have fixed functions $f_1, \dots, f_M$. The problem is to find linear, convex and model selection aggregates of $f_1, \dots, f_M$ based on the sample $D_n$ that would converge with the fastest possible rate (i.e. with the smallest possible remainder terms $\Delta_{n,M}$) in a minimax sense. A partial solution of this problem for the case of convex aggregation has been given by Juditsky and Nemirovski (2000) and Yang (2001). Here we solve the problem for all the three types of aggregation, in particular, improving these results concerning convex aggregation. The main goal of this paper is to find optimal rates of aggregation in the sense of a general definition given below.

## 2    Main Definition and Lower Bounds

We start with the following definition that covers more general framework than the one considered in the paper.

**Definition 1.** *Let $H$ be a given abstract index set and let $\mathcal{F}$, $\mathcal{F}'$ be a given classes of Borel functions on $\mathcal{X}$.*

*A sequence of positive numbers $\psi_n$ is called **optimal rate of aggregation** for $(H, \mathcal{F}, \mathcal{F}')$ if*

- *for any family of Borel functions $\{f_\lambda, \lambda \in H\}$ indexed by $H$ and contained in $\mathcal{F}'$ there exists an estimator $\tilde{f}_n$ of $f$ (aggregate) such that*

$$\sup_{f \in \mathcal{F}} \left[ R(\tilde{f}_n, f) - \inf_{\lambda \in H} \|f_\lambda - f\|^2 \right] \leq C\psi_n, \qquad (3)$$

*for some constant $C < \infty$ and any integer $n$,*
*and*
- *there exists a family of Borel functions $\{f_\lambda, \lambda \in H\}$ indexed by $H$ and contained in $\mathcal{F}'$ such that for all estimators $T_n$ of $f$ we have*

$$\sup_{f \in \mathcal{F}} \left[ R(T_n, f) - \inf_{\lambda \in H} \|f_\lambda - f\|^2 \right] \geq c\psi_n, \qquad (4)$$

*for some constant $c > 0$ and any integer $n$.*

In this paper we are interested in the following index sets:

$$H = \begin{cases} \{1, \dots, M\} & \text{for Problem (MS)}, \\ \Lambda^M & \text{for Problem (C)}, \\ \mathbf{R}^M & \text{for Problem (L)}, \end{cases}$$

and we consider $\mathcal{F} = \mathcal{F}_0$ defined by

$$\mathcal{F}_0 = \{f : \|f\|_\infty \leq L\}, \tag{5}$$

where $\|\cdot\|_\infty$ denotes the $L_\infty$ norm associated with the measure $P^X$ and $L < \infty$ is an unknown constant. We take also $\mathcal{F}' = \mathcal{F}_0$ for Problems (MS) and (C), and $\mathcal{F}' = L_2(\mathcal{X}, P^X)$ for Problem (L).

Optimal rates of aggregation for $(\{1, \ldots, M\}, \mathcal{F}_0, \mathcal{F}_0)$, for $(\Lambda^M, \mathcal{F}_0, \mathcal{F}_0)$ and for $(\mathbf{R}^M, \mathcal{F}_0, L_2(\mathcal{X}, P^X))$ will be called for brevity optimal rates of model selection, convex and linear aggregation respectively.

In the rest of the paper the notation $f_\lambda$ for a vector $\lambda = (\lambda_1, \ldots, \lambda_M) \in \mathbf{R}^M$ is understood in the following sense:

$$f_\lambda = \sum_{j=1}^{M} \lambda_j f_j.$$

In this section we prove lower bounds of the type (4) for model selection, convex and linear aggregation. The proofs will be based on the following lemma on minimax lower bounds which can be obtained, for example, by combining Theorems 2.2 and 2.5 in Tsybakov (2003).

**Lemma 1.** *Let $\mathcal{C}$ be a finite set of functions on $\mathcal{X}$ such that $N = \mathrm{card}(\mathcal{C}) \geq 2$,*

$$\|f - g\|^2 \geq 4\psi_n > 0, \quad \forall \, f, g \in \mathcal{C}, \quad f \neq g,$$

*and the Kullback divergences $K(P_f, P_g)$ between the measures $P_f$ and $P_g$ satisfy*

$$K(P_f, P_g) \leq (1/16) \log N, \quad \forall \, f, g \in \mathcal{C}.$$

*Then*

$$\inf_{T_n} \sup_{f \in \mathcal{C}} R(T_n, f) \geq c_1 \psi_n,$$

*where $\inf_{T_n}$ denotes the infimum over all estimators and $c_1 > 0$ is a constant.*

Throughout the paper we denote by $c_i$ finite positive constants. Introduce the following assumptions.

**(A1)** The errors $\xi_i$ are i.i.d. Gaussian $\mathcal{N}(0, \sigma^2)$ random variables, $0 < \sigma < \infty$.

**(A2)** There exists a cube $S \subset \mathcal{X}$ such that $P^X$ admits a bounded density $\mu(\cdot)$ on $S$ w.r.t. the Lebesgue measure and $\mu(x) \geq \mu_0 > 0$ for all $x \in S$.

**(A3)** There exists a constant $c_0$ such that $\log M \leq c_0 n$.

**(A4)** There exists a constant $c_0$ such that $M \leq c_0 n$.

**Theorem 1.** *Under assumptions (A1)–(A3) we have*

$$\sup_{f_1, \ldots, f_M \in \mathcal{F}_0} \inf_{T_n} \sup_{f \in \mathcal{F}_0} \left[ R(T_n, f) - \min_{1 \leq j \leq M} \|f_j - f\|^2 \right] \geq c\psi_n^{\mathbf{MS}}(M)$$

*for some constant $c > 0$ and any integer $n$, where $\inf_{T_n}$ denotes the infimum over all estimators and*

$$\psi_n^{\mathbf{MS}}(M) = \frac{\log M}{n}.$$

*Proof.* Let $\{\varphi_j\}_{j=1}^M$ be an orthogonal system of functions in $L_2(S, dx)$ for the cube $S$ given in assumption (A2) and satisfying $\|\varphi_j\|_\infty \leq A < \infty$ for $j = 1, \ldots, M$. Such functions can be constructed, for example, by taking $\varphi_j(x) = A_1 \cos(a j x_1 + b)$ for $x \in S$ and for suitably chosen constants $A_1$, $a$ and $b$, where $x_1$ is the first coordinate of $x$. Define the functions

$$f_j(x) = \gamma \sqrt{\frac{\log M}{n}} \varphi_j(x) I(x \in S), \quad j = 1, \ldots, M,$$

where $I(\cdot)$ denotes the indicator function and $\gamma$ is a positive constant to be chosen. In view of assumption (A3), $\{f_1, \ldots, f_M\} \subset \mathcal{F}_0$ if $\gamma$ is small enough. Thus, it suffices to prove the lower bound of the theorem for $f \in \{f_1, \ldots, f_M\}$. But for such $f$ we have $\min_{1 \leq j \leq M} \|f_j - f\|^2 = 0$, and to finish the proof of the theorem it is sufficient to bound from below by $c\psi_n^{\mathrm{MS}}(M)$ the quantity $\sup_{f \in \{f_1, \ldots, f_M\}} R(T_n, f)$ uniformly over all estimators $T_n$. This is done by applying Lemma 1. Using assumption (A2) and orthogonality of the system $\{f_j\}_{j=1}^M$ on $S$ we get, for $j \neq k$,

$$\|f_j - f_k\|^2 \asymp \int_S (f_j(x) - f_k(x))^2 dx = \int_S f_j^2(x) dx + \int_S f_k^2(x) dx \asymp \frac{\gamma^2 \log M}{n}. \quad (6)$$

Since $\xi_j$'s are $\mathcal{N}(0, \sigma^2)$ random variables, the Kullback divergence $K(P_{f_j}, P_{f_k})$ between $P_{f_j}$ and $P_{f_k}$ satisfies

$$K(P_{f_j}, P_{f_k}) = \frac{n}{2\sigma^2} \|f_j - f_k\|^2, \quad j = 1, \ldots, M. \quad (7)$$

In view of (6) and (7), one can choose $\gamma$ small enough to have $K(P_{f_j}, P_{f_k}) \leq (1/16) \log M$, $j, k = 1, \ldots, M$. To finish the proof it remains to use this inequality, (6) and Lemma 1.

**Theorem 2.** *Under assumptions (A1)–(A3) we have*

$$\sup_{f_1, \ldots, f_M \in \mathcal{F}_0} \inf_{T_n} \sup_{f \in \mathcal{F}_0} \left[ R(T_n, f) - \min_{\lambda \in \Lambda^M} \|f_\lambda - f\|^2 \right] \geq c\psi_n^{\mathbf{C}}(M)$$

*for some constant $c > 0$ and any integer $n$, where $\inf_{T_n}$ denotes the infimum over all estimators and*

$$\psi_n^{\mathbf{C}}(M) = \begin{cases} M/n & \text{if } M \leq \sqrt{n}, \\[2mm] \sqrt{\frac{1}{n} \log\left(\frac{M}{\sqrt{n}} + 1\right)} & \text{if } M > \sqrt{n}. \end{cases}$$

*Proof.* Consider first the case where $M > \sqrt{n}$. Let the functions $\{\varphi_j\}_{j=1}^M$ be as in the proof of Theorem 1. Set

$$f_j(x) = \gamma \varphi_j(x) I(x \in S), \quad j = 1, \ldots, M, \quad (8)$$

for some constant $\gamma$ to be chosen later. Define an integer

$$m = \left\lceil c_2 \left[ n / \log \left( \frac{M}{\sqrt{n}} + 1 \right) \right]^{1/2} \right\rceil \tag{9}$$

for a constant $c_2 > 0$ chosen in such a way that $M \geq 6m$. Denote by $\mathcal{C}$ the finite set of such convex combinations of $f_1, \ldots, f_M$ that $m$ of the coefficients $\lambda_j$ are equal to $1/m$ and the remaining $M - m$ coefficients are zero. For every pair of functions $g_1, g_2 \in \mathcal{C}$ we have

$$\|g_1 - g_2\|^2 \leq c_3 \gamma^2 / m. \tag{10}$$

Clearly, $\mathcal{C} \subset \mathcal{F}_0$ for $\gamma$ small enough and $\min_{\lambda \in \Lambda^M} \|f_\lambda - f\|^2 = 0$ for any $f \in \mathcal{C}$. Therefore, to prove the theorem for $M > \sqrt{n}$ it is sufficient to bound from below by $c \sqrt{\frac{1}{n} \log \left( \frac{M}{\sqrt{n}} + 1 \right)}$ the supremum $\sup_{f \in \mathcal{C}} R(T_n, f)$ uniformly over all estimators $T_n$. In fact, we will show that the required lower bound holds already for the quantity $\sup_{f \in \mathcal{N}} R(T_n, f)$ where $\mathcal{N}$ is a subset of $\mathcal{C}$ of cardinality $\text{card}(\mathcal{N})$ satisfying

$$\log(\text{card}(\mathcal{N})) \geq c_4 m \log \left( \frac{M}{m} + 1 \right) \tag{11}$$

and such that for every two functions $g_1, g_2 \in \mathcal{N}$ we have

$$\|g_1 - g_2\|^2 \geq c_5 \gamma^2 / m.$$

The existence of such a subset $\mathcal{N}$ of $\mathcal{C}$ follows, for example, from Lemma 4 of Birgé and Massart (2001). Now, using (7) – (11) and the definition of $m$ we get that, for any $g_1, g_2 \in \mathcal{N}$,

$$K(P_{g_1}, P_{g_2}) \leq c_6 \gamma^2 n / m \leq c_7 \gamma^2 \log(\text{card}(\mathcal{N})).$$

Finally, we choose $\gamma$ small enough to have $c_7 \gamma^2 < 1/16$ and we apply Lemma 1 to get the result.

Consider now the case $M \leq \sqrt{n}$. Define the functions $f_j$ by (8) and introduce a finite set of functions

$$\mathcal{C}_1 = \left\{ f = \frac{1}{\sqrt{n}} \sum_{j=1}^{M} \omega_j f_j : \omega \in \Omega \right\} \tag{12}$$

where $\Omega$ is the set of all vectors $\omega$ of length $M$ with binary coordinates $\omega_j \in \{0, 1\}$. Since $M \leq \sqrt{n}$ we have $\mathcal{C}_1 \subset \mathcal{F}_0$ for $\gamma$ small enough and $\mathcal{C}_1 \subset \{f_\lambda : \lambda \in \Lambda^M\}$. Therefore, similarly to the previous proofs, it is sufficient to bound from below $\inf_{T_n} \sup_{f \in \mathcal{C}_1} R(T_n, f)$. Using assumption (A2) we get that, for any $g_1, g_2 \in \mathcal{C}_1$,

$$\|g_1 - g_2\|^2 \leq c_8 \gamma^2 M / n. \tag{13}$$

If $M < 8$ we have $\psi_n^{\mathbf{C}}(M) \asymp 1/n$, and the lower bound of the theorem can be easily deduced from testing between two hypotheses: $f_1 \equiv 0$ and $f_2(x) =$

$n^{-1/2}I(x \in S)$. For $M \geq 8$ it follows from the Varshamov-Gilbert bound (see e.g. Tsybakov (2003), Ch.2) that there exists a subset $\mathcal{N}_1$ of $\mathcal{C}_1$ such that $\operatorname{card}(\mathcal{N}_1) \geq 2^{M/8}$ and

$$\|g_1 - g_2\|^2 \geq c_9 \gamma^2 M/n. \tag{14}$$

for any $g_1, g_2 \in \mathcal{N}_1$. Using (7) and (13) we get, for any $g_1, g_2 \in \mathcal{N}_1$,

$$K(P_{g_1}, P_{g_2}) \leq c_{10} \gamma^2 M \leq c_{11} \gamma^2 \log(\operatorname{card}(\mathcal{N}_1)),$$

and by choosing $\gamma$ small enough, we can finish the proof in the same way as in the case $M > \sqrt{n}$.

Note that Theorem 2 generalizes the lower bounds for convex aggregation given by Juditsky and Nemirovski (2000) and Yang (2001). Juditsky and Nemirovski (2000) considered the case of very large $M$ (satisfying $M \geq n/\log n$) and they proved the lower bound with the rate $\sqrt{n^{-1} \log M}$ which coincides in order with $\psi_n^C(M)$ in this zone. Yang (2001) obtained the lower bounds for convex aggregation with polynomial $M$, i.e. $M \asymp n^\tau$ for $0 < \tau < \infty$. His bounds also follow as a special case from Theorem 2.

**Theorem 3.** *Under assumptions (A1), (A2), (A4) we have*

$$\sup_{f_1,\ldots,f_M \in \mathcal{F}_0} \inf_{T_n} \sup_{f \in \mathcal{F}_0} \left[ R(T_n, f) - \min_{\lambda \in \mathbf{R}^M} \|f_\lambda - f\|^2 \right] \geq c\psi_n^{\mathbf{L}}(M)$$

*for some constant $c > 0$ and any integer $n$, where $\inf_{T_n}$ denotes the infimum over all estimators and*

$$\psi_n^{\mathbf{L}}(M) = \frac{M}{n}.$$

*Proof.* Assume w.l.o.g. that there exist disjoint subsets $S_1, \ldots, S_M$ of $S$ such that the Lebesgue measure of $S_j$ is $1/M$. Define the functions $f_j(x) = \gamma I(x \in S_j)$, $j = 1, \ldots, M$, for a constant $\gamma > 0$, and the set

$$\mathcal{C}_2 = \left\{ f = \sqrt{\frac{M}{n}} \sum_{j=1}^M \omega_j f_j : \omega \in \Omega \right\}$$

with $\Omega$ as in (12). Assumption (A4) guarantees that $\mathcal{C}_2 \subset \mathcal{F}_0$ for $\gamma$ small enough. Since the functions $f_j$ are mutually orthogonal and $\int f_j^2(x) dx = \gamma^2/M$, the rest of the proof is identical to the part of the proof of Theorem 2 after (13) (with $\mathcal{C}_1$ replaced by $\mathcal{C}_2$), and it is therefore omitted.

## 3  Attainability of the Lower Bounds

In this section we show that the lower bounds of Theorems 1–3 give optimal rates of aggregation. We start with the problem of linear aggregation (Problem (L)) in which case we construct an aggregate attaining in order the lower bound of Theorem 3.

Denote by $\mathcal{L}$ the linear span of $f_1, \ldots, f_M$. Let $\varphi_1, \ldots, \varphi_{M'}$ with $M' \leq M$ be an orthonormal basis of $\mathcal{L}$ in $L_2(\mathcal{X}, P^X)$. Consider a linear aggregate

$$\tilde{f}_n^{\mathbf{L}}(x) = \sum_{j=1}^{M'} \hat{\lambda}_j \varphi_j(x), \quad x \in \mathcal{X, } \tag{15}$$

where

$$\hat{\lambda}_j = \frac{1}{n} \sum_{i=1}^{n} Y_i \varphi_j(X_i).$$

**Theorem 4.** *Let* $\mathbf{E}(\xi_i) = 0$, $\mathbf{E}(\xi_i^2) \leq \sigma^2 < \infty$. *Then*

$$R(\tilde{f}_n^{\mathbf{L}}, f) - \min_{\lambda \in \mathbf{R}^M} \|f_\lambda - f\|^2 \leq \frac{(\sigma^2 + L^2) M}{n}$$

*for any integers* $M \geq 2$, $n \geq 1$ *and any* $f, f_1, \ldots, f_M \in \mathcal{F}_0$, *where* $L$ *is the constant in (5).*

*Proof.* We have $\min_{\lambda \in \mathbf{R}^M} \|f_\lambda - f\|^2 = \|f_\lambda^* - f\|^2$ where $f_\lambda^* = \sum_{j=1}^{M'} \lambda_j^* \varphi_j$, $\lambda_j^* = (f, \varphi_j)$, and $(\cdot, \cdot)$ is the scalar product in $L_2(\mathcal{X}, P^X)$. Now,

$$\|\tilde{f}_n^{\mathbf{L}} - f\|^2 = \sum_{j=1}^{M'} (\hat{\lambda}_j - \lambda_j^*)^2 + \|f_\lambda^* - f\|^2,$$

and to finish the proof it suffices to note that $\mathbf{E}(\hat{\lambda}_j) = \lambda_j^*$, $\mathbf{E}\left[(\hat{\lambda}_j - \lambda_j^*)^2\right] = \mathrm{Var}(\hat{\lambda}_j) \leq (\sigma^2 + L^2)/n$.

Theorems 3 and 4 imply the following result.

**Corollary 1.** *Under assumptions (A1), (A2), (A4) the sequence* $\psi_n^{\mathbf{L}}(M)$ *is optimal rate of linear aggregation.*

Consider now the problem of convex aggregation (Problem (C)). If $M \leq \sqrt{n}$ the lower bound of Theorem 2 is identical to the linear aggregation case, so we can use the linear aggregate $\tilde{f}_n^{\mathbf{L}}$ defined in (15) that attains this bound in view of Theorem 4. For $M > \sqrt{n}$ we use a different procedure. To define this procedure, consider first the Kullback divergence based model selection aggregate (Catoni (2001), Yang (2000)). This aggregate, for the problem of model selection with $N$ Borel functions $g_1, \ldots, g_N$ on $\mathcal{X}$, is defined by

$$\tilde{g}_{n,N}(x) = \frac{1}{n+1} \sum_{k=0}^{n} p_{k,N}(x)$$

where

$$p_{k,0}(x) = \frac{1}{N} \sum_{j=1}^{N} g_j(x)$$

and, for $k = 1, \ldots, N$,

$$p_{k,N}(x) = \frac{\sum_{j=1}^{N} g_j(x) \prod_{i=1}^{k} \exp(-(Y_i - g_j(X_i))^2/2\sigma^2)}{\sum_{j=1}^{N} \prod_{i=1}^{k} \exp(-(Y_i - g_j(X_i))^2/2\sigma^2)} .$$

As shown by Catoni (2001), for any integers $M \geq 2$, $n \geq 1$ and any functions $f, g_1, \ldots, g_M \in \mathcal{F}_0$,

$$R(\tilde{g}_{n,N}, f) \leq \min_{1 \leq j \leq N} \|g_j - f\|^2 + C_0 \frac{\log N}{n} \qquad (16)$$

where $C_0 < \infty$ is a constant that depends only on $L$ and $\sigma^2$.

Now, define $m$ by (9) and denote by $\mathcal{C}'$ the set of all linear combinations of $f_1, \ldots, f_M$ such that at most $m$ coefficients of these combinations are equal to $1/m$ and the remaining coefficients are zero. We have

$$\mathrm{card}(\mathcal{C}') = \sum_{j=1}^{m} \binom{M}{j} \leq \left(\frac{eM}{m}\right)^m \qquad (17)$$

(cf., e.g., Devroye, Györfi and Lugosi (1996, p.218)). Let $N = \mathrm{card}(\mathcal{C}')$, let $g_1, \ldots, g_N$ be the elements of $\mathcal{C}'$, and denote by $\tilde{f}_{n,m}^{\mathrm{MS}}$ the corresponding model selection aggregate $\tilde{g}_{n,N}$. Then (16) takes the form

$$R(\tilde{f}_{n,m}^{\mathrm{MS}}, f) \leq \min_{g \in \mathcal{C}'} \|g - f\|^2 + C_0 \frac{\log(\mathrm{card}(\mathcal{C}'))}{n} , \qquad (18)$$

which holds for every $f \in \mathcal{F}_0$.

Finally, define a compound method of convex aggregation by

$$\tilde{f}_n^{\mathbf{C}} = \begin{cases} \tilde{f}_n^{\mathbf{L}} & \text{if } M \leq \sqrt{n}, \\ \tilde{f}_{n,m}^{\mathbf{MS}} & \text{if } M > \sqrt{n}. \end{cases}$$

This definition emphasizes an intermediate character of convex aggregation: it switches from linear to model selection aggregates. If $M > \sqrt{n}$ we are in a "sparse case": convex aggregation oracle concentrates only on a relatively small number of functions $f_j$, and optimal rate is attained on a model selection type procedure. On the contrary, for $M \leq \sqrt{n}$ convex aggregation oracle does not concentrate on the boundary of the set $\Lambda^M$, and therefore it essentially behaves as a linear oracle giving solution to unrestricted minimization problem.

**Theorem 5.** *Under assumption (A1) we have*

$$R(\tilde{f}_n^{\mathbf{C}}, f) - \min_{\lambda \in \Lambda^M} \|f_\lambda - f\|^2 \leq C\psi_n^{\mathbf{C}}(M)$$

*for some constant $C < \infty$, any integers $M \geq 2$, $n \geq 1$ and any $f, f_1, \ldots, f_M \in \mathcal{F}_0$.*

*Proof.* In view of Theorem 4, it suffices to consider the case $M > \sqrt{n}$. Let $\lambda^0 = (\lambda_1^0, \ldots, \lambda_M^0)$ be the weights of a convex aggregation oracle, i.e. a vector $\lambda^0$ satisfying $\|f_{\lambda^0} - f\| = \min_{\lambda \in \Lambda^M} \|f_\lambda - f\|$. Applying the argument of Nemirovski (2000, p.192–193) to the vector $\lambda^0$ instead of $\lambda(z)$ and putting there $K = m$ we find

$$\sum_{i=1}^{J} p_i \|h_i - f\|^2 \le \min_{\lambda \in \Lambda^M} \|f_\lambda - f\|^2 + \frac{L^2}{m}$$

where $J = \operatorname{card}(\mathcal{C}')$, $(p_1, \ldots, p_J)$ is a probability vector (i.e. $p_1 + \cdots + p_J = 1$, $p_j \ge 0$) that depends on $\lambda^0$ and the functions $h_i$ are the elements of the set $\mathcal{C}'$. This immediately implies that

$$\min_{g \in \mathcal{C}'} \|g - f\|^2 \le \min_{\lambda \in \Lambda^M} \|f_\lambda - f\|^2 + \frac{L^2}{m} . \tag{19}$$

Combining (17)–(19) we obtain

$$R(\tilde{f}_{n,m}^{\mathbf{MS}}, f) \le \min_{\lambda \in \Lambda^M} \|f_\lambda - f\|^2 + \frac{L^2}{m} + c_{12}\frac{m}{n}\left[\log\left(\frac{M}{m}\right) + 1\right]$$

$$\le \min_{\lambda \in \Lambda^M} \|f_\lambda - f\|^2 + C\sqrt{\frac{1}{n}\log\left(\frac{M}{\sqrt{n}} + 1\right)}$$

for a constant $C < \infty$.

Theorems 2 and 5 imply the following result.

**Corollary 2.** *Under assumptions (A1)–(A3) the sequence $\psi_n^{\mathbf{C}}(M)$ is optimal rate of convex aggregation.*

Finally, for the Problem (MS), the attainability of the lower bound of Theorem 1 follows immediately from (16) with $N = M$ and $g_j = f_j$. Thus, we have the following corollary.

**Corollary 3.** *Under assumptions (A1)–(A3) the sequence $\psi_n^{\mathbf{MS}}(M)$ is optimal rate of model selection aggregation.*

# References

1. Birgé, L.: Model selection for Gaussian regression with random design. Prépublication n. 783, Laboratoire de Probabilités et Modèles Aléatoires, Universités Paris 6 - Paris 7 (2002).
2. Birgé, L., Massart, P.: Gaussian model selection. J. Eur. Math. Soc. **3** (2001) 203–268.
3. Catoni, O.: *Statistical Learning Theory and Stochastic Optimization.* Ecole d'Eté de Probabilités de Saint-Flour 2001, Lecture Notes in Mathematics, Springer, N.Y. (to appear).
4. Devroye, L., Györfi, L., Lugosi, G.: *A Probabilistic Theory of Pattern Recognition.* Springer, N.Y. (1996).

5. Györfi, L., Kohler, M., Krzyżak, A., Walk, H.: *A Distribution-Free Theory of Non-parametric Regression*. Springer, N.Y.(2002).
6. Juditsky, A., Nemirovski, A.: Functional aggregation for nonparametric estimation. Annals of Statistics **28** (2000) 681–712.
7. Nemirovski, A.: *Topics in Non-parametric Statistics*. Ecole d'Eté de Probabilités de Saint-Flour XXVIII - 1998, Lecture Notes in Mathematics, v. 1738, Springer, N.Y. (2000).
8. Tsybakov, A.: *Introduction à l'estimation non-paramétrique*. (2003) Springer (to appear).
9. Wegkamp, M.: Model selection in nonparametric regression. Annals of Statistics **31** (2003) (to appear).
10. Yang, Y.: Combining different procedures for adaptive regression. J.of Multivariate Analysis **74** (2000) 135–161.
11. Yang, Y.: Aggregating regression procedures for a better performance (2001). Manuscript.

# Distance-Based Classification
# with Lipschitz Functions

Ulrike von Luxburg and Olivier Bousquet

Max Planck Institute for Biological Cybernetics, Tübingen, Germany
{ule,olivier.bousquet}@tuebingen.mpg.de

**Abstract.** The goal of this article is to develop a framework for large
margin classification in metric spaces. We want to find a generalization
of linear decision functions for metric spaces and define a corresponding
notion of margin such that the decision function separates the training
points with a large margin. It will turn out that using Lipschitz functions as decision functions, the inverse of the Lipschitz constant can be
interpreted as the size of a margin. In order to construct a clean mathematical setup we isometrically embed the given metric space into a
Banach space and the space of Lipschitz functions into its dual space.
Our approach leads to a general large margin algorithm for classification
in metric spaces. To analyze this algorithm, we first prove a representer
theorem. It states that there exists a solution which can be expressed
as linear combination of distances to sets of training points. Then we
analyze the Rademacher complexity of some Lipschitz function classes.
The generality of the Lipschitz approach can be seen from the fact that
several well-known algorithms are special cases of the Lipschitz algorithm, among them the support vector machine, the linear programming
machine, and the 1-nearest neighbor classifier.

## 1   Introduction

Support vector machines construct linear decision boundaries in Hilbert spaces
such that the training points are separated with a large margin. The goal of this
article is to extend this approach from Hilbert spaces to metric spaces: we want
to find a generalization of linear decision functions for metric spaces and define
a corresponding notion of margin such that the decision function separates the
training points with a large margin.

SVMs can be seen from two different points of view. In the regularization
interpretation, for a given positive definite kernel $k$, the SVM chooses a decision
function of the form $f(x) = \sum_i \alpha_i k(x_i, x) + b$ which has a low empirical error
$R_{\text{emp}}$ and is as smooth as possible. According to the large margin point of view,
SVMs construct a linear decision boundary in a Hilbert space $\mathcal{H}$ such that the
training points are separated with a large margin and the sum of the margin
errors is small. Both viewpoints can be connected by embedding the sample
space $X$ into the reproducing kernel Hilbert space $\mathcal{H}$ via the so called "feature
map" and the function space $\mathcal{F}$ into the dual $\mathcal{H}'$. Then the regularizer $\|f\|^2$

B. Schölkopf and M.K. Warmuth (Eds.): COLT/Kernel 2003, LNAI 2777, pp. 314–328, 2003.

corresponds to the inverse margin $\|\omega\|_{\mathcal{H}'}^2$ and the empirical error to the margin error (cf. sections 4.3 and 7 of [6]) . The benefits of these two dual viewpoints are that the regularization framework gives some intuition about the geometrical meaning of the norm $\|\cdot\|_{\mathcal{H}}$, and the large margin framework leads to statistical learning theory bounds on the generalization error of the classifier.

Now consider the situation where the sample space is a metric space $(X, d)$. From the regularization point of view, a convenient class of functions on a metric space is the class of Lipschitz functions, as functions with a small Lipschitz constant have low variation. Thus it seems desirable to separate the different classes by a decision function which has a small Lipschitz constant. In this article we want to construct the dual point of view to this approach. To this end, we embed the metric space $(X, d)$ in a Banach space $\mathcal{B}$ and the space of Lipschitz functions into its dual space $\mathcal{B}'$. Remarkably, both embeddings can be realized as isometries simultaneously. By this construction, each $x \in X$ will correspond to some $m_x \in \mathcal{B}$ and each Lipschitz function $f$ on $X$ to some functional $T_f \in \mathcal{B}'$ such that $f(x) = T_f m_x$ and the Lipschitz constant $L(f)$ is equal to the operator norm $\|T_f\|$. Then we can construct a geometrical margin in $\mathcal{B}$ which allows to apply the usual large margin generalization bounds from statistical learning theory. The size of the margin will be given by the inverse of the operator norm of the decision functional. The basic algorithm implementing this approach is

$$\text{minimize } R_{\text{emp}}(f) + \lambda L(f)$$

in regularization language and

$$\text{minimize } L(f) + C \sum_i \xi_i \text{ subject to } y_i f(x_i) \geq 1 - \xi_i, \ \xi_i \geq 0$$

in large margin language. In both cases, $L(f)$ denotes the Lipschitz constant of the function $f$, and the minimum is taken over a subset of Lipschitz functions on $X$. To apply this algorithm in practice, the choice of this subset will be important. We will see that by choosing different subsets we can recover the SVM (in cases where the metric on $X$ is induced by a kernel), the linear programming machine (cf. [4]), and even the 1-nearest neighbor classifier. In particular this shows that all these algorithms are large margin algorithms. So the Lipschitz framework can help to analyze a wide range of algorithms which do not seem to be connected at the first glance. Furthermore, the Banach space in which we will embed $X$ is in some sense the largest possible Banach space in which $X$ can be embedded isometrically. This means that the Lipschitz algorithm on this space can be seen as a prototype for large margin algorithms on metric spaces. All other large margin algorithms are special cases of this general one.

This paper is organized as follows: in section 2 we provide the necessary functional analytic background for the Lipschitz algorithm, which is then derived in section 3. We investigate representer theorems for this algorithm in section 4. It will turn out that the algorithm always has a solution which can be expressed as a vector lattice combination of the functions $d(x_i, \cdot)$ where $x_i$ are the training points. In plain words this means that we always find solutions which are linear combinations of distances to *sets* of training points. In section 5 we analyze the Lipschitz algorithm in terms of its Rademacher complexities. In particular, this gives valuable information about how fast the algorithm converges for different choices of subsets of Lipschitz functions.

## 2   Preliminaries: Lipschitz Function Spaces

In this section we introduce several Lipschitz function spaces and their properties. For a more detailed treatment we refer to [10].

A metric space $(X, d)$ is a set $X$ together with a metric $d$ (i.e., $d$ is non-negative, symmetric, fulfills $d(x, y) = 0 \Leftrightarrow x = y$ and the triangle inequality $d(x, y) + d(y, z) \leq d(x, z)$). A function $f : X \to \mathbb{R}$ on a metric space $(X, d)$ is called a Lipschitz function if there exists a constant $L$ such that $|f(x) - f(y)| \leq L d(x, y)$ for all $x, y \in X$. The smallest constant $L$ such that this inequality holds is called the Lipschitz constant of $f$, denoted by $L(f)$. For Lipschitz functions $f, g$ and scalars $a \in \mathbb{R}$ the Lipschitz constant has the properties $L(f + g) \leq L(f) + L(g)$, $L(af) \leq |a| L(f)$ and $L(\min(f, g)) \leq \max\{L(f), L(g)\}$, where $\min(f, g)$ denotes the pointwise minimum of the functions $f$ and $g$. For a metric space $(X, d)$ consider the set

$$\text{Lip}(X) := \{f : X \to \mathbb{R}; \ f \text{ is a bounded Lipschitz function}\}.$$

It forms a vector space, and the Lipschitz constant $L(f)$ is a seminorm on this space. To define a convenient norm on this space we restrict ourselves to *bounded* metric spaces, i.e., spaces which have a finite diameter $\text{diam}(X) := \sup_{x, y \in X} d(x, y)$. For the learning framework this is not a big drawback as the training and test data can always be assumed to come from a bounded region of the underlying space. For a bounded metric space $X$ we choose the norm

$$\|f\|_L := \max\left\{L(f), \frac{\|f\|_\infty}{\text{diam}(X)}\right\}$$

as our default norm on the space $\text{Lip}(X)$. It is easy to see that this indeed is a norm. One reason why it fits nicely in the learning setting is the following. Functions that are used as classifiers are supposed to take positive and negative values on the respective classes and thus satisfy $\|f\|_\infty = \sup_x |f(x)| \leq \sup_{x,y} |f(x) - f(y)| \leq \text{diam}(X) L(f)$, that is $\|f\|_L = L(f)$. Hence, the norm of a classification function is determined by the quantity we use as regularizer later on. Some technical reasons for the choice of $\|\cdot\|_L$ will become clear later.

Another important space of Lipschitz functions is constructed as follows. Let $(X_0, d)$ be a metric space with a distinguished "base point" $e$ which is fixed in advance. Then,

$$\text{Lip}_0(X_0) := \{f \in \text{Lip}(X_0); \ f(e) = 0\}.$$

On this set, the Lipschitz constant $L(\cdot)$ is a norm. However, its disadvantage in the learning framework is the condition $f(e) = 0$ which is an inconvenient a priori restriction on our classifier. To overcome this restriction, for a given bounded metric space $(X, d)$ we define a corresponding extended space $X_0 := X \cup \{e\}$ for a new base element $e$ with the metric

$$d_{X_0}(x, y) = \begin{cases} d(x, y) & \text{for } x, y \in X \\ \text{diam}(X) & \text{for } x \in X, y = e. \end{cases} \qquad (1)$$

Note that $\text{diam}(X_0) = \text{diam}(X)$. Then we define the map

$$\psi : \text{Lip}(X) \to \text{Lip}_0(X_0), \quad \psi(f)(x) = \begin{cases} f(x) & \text{if } x \in X \\ 0 & \text{if } x = e \end{cases} \qquad (2)$$

Obviously, $\psi$ is bijective, and it is even an isometry: for $f_0 := \psi(f)$ we have

$$L(f_0) = \sup_{x,y \in X_0} \frac{|f_0(x) - f_0(y)|}{d_{X_0}(x, y)} = \max \{ \sup_{x,y \in X} \frac{|f(x) - f(y)|}{d(x, y)}, \sup_{x \in X} \frac{|f(x) - f(e)|}{d_{X_0}(x, e)} \} =$$

$$= \max \{ L(f), \frac{\|f\|_\infty}{\text{diam}(X)} \} = \|f\|_L$$

The space $(\text{Lip}_0(X_0), L(\cdot))$ has some very useful duality properties. Let $(X_0, d)$ be a metric space with distinguished base element $e$. A *molecule* of $X_0$ is a function $m : X_0 \to \mathbb{R}$ such that its support (i.e., the set where $m$ has non-zero values) is a finite set and $\sum_{x \in X_0} m(x) = 0$. For $x, y \in X_0$ we define the *basic molecules* $m_{xy} := \mathbb{1}_x - \mathbb{1}_y$. It is easy to see that every molecule $m$ can be written as a (non unique) finite linear combination of basic molecules. Thus we can define

$$\|m\|_{AE} := \inf \left\{ \sum_i |a_i| d(x_i, y_i); \ m = \sum_i a_i m_{x_i y_i} \right\}$$

which is a norm on the space of molecules. We call the completion of the space of molecules with respect to $\| \cdot \|_{AE}$ the *Arens-Eells space* $AE(X_0)$. Denoting its dual space (i.e., the space of all continuous linear forms on $AE(X_0)$) by $AE(X_0)'$ the following theorem holds (cf. [10]).

**Theorem 1.** $AE(X_0)'$ *is isometrically isomorphic to* $\text{Lip}_0(X_0)$.

This means that we can regard a Lipschitz function $f$ on $X_0$ as a linear functional $T_f$ on the space of molecules, and the Lipschitz constant $L(f)$ coincides with the operator norm of the corresponding functional $T_f$. For a molecule $m$ and a Lipschitz function $f$ this duality can be expressed as

$$\langle f, m \rangle = \sum_{x \in X_0} m(x) f(x). \qquad (3)$$

It can be proved that $\|m_{xy}\|_{AE} = d(x, y)$ holds for all basic molecules $m_{xy}$. Hence, it is possible to embed $X_0$ isometrically in $AE(X_0)$ via

$$\Gamma : X_0 \to AE(X_0), \ x \mapsto m_{xe} \qquad (4)$$

In this context note that the Arens-Eells space is a free Banach space over $X_0$. This means that we can express every map $g : X_0 \to V$ in some vector space $V$ as a linear functional $T_g$ on $AE(X_0)$ via $T_g m_{xe} := g(x)$. In particular, we can realize every isometric embedding $g$ of $X$ in some vector space $V$ by composing $\Gamma$ with the linear functional $T_g$. In this sense, $AE(X_0)$ is the biggest Banach space in which $X$ can be embedded isometrically.

The norm $\| \cdot \|_{AE}$ has a nice geometrical interpretation in terms of the mass transportation problem: some product is manufactured in varying amounts at several factories and has to be distributed to several shops. The (discrete) transportation problem is to find an optimal way to transport the product from the factories to the shops. The costs of such a transport are defined as $\sum a_{ij} d(f_i, s_j)$ where $a_{ij}$ denotes the amount of the product transported from factory $f_i$ to shop $s_j$ and $d(f_i, s_j)$ the distance between them. To connect the Arens-Eells space to this problem we identify the locations of the factories and shops with a molecule $m$. The points $x$ with $m(x) > 0$ represent the factories, the ones with $m(x) < 0$ the shops. It can be proved that $\|m\|_{AE}$ equals the minimal transportation costs for molecule $m$. A special case is when the given molecule has the form $m_0 = \sum m_{x_i y_j}$. In this case, the transportation problem reduces to the bipartite minimal matching problem: given $2m$ points $(x_1, \ldots, x_m, y_1, \ldots, y_m)$ in a metric space, we want to match each of the $x$-points to one of the $y$-points such that the sum of the distances between the matched pairs is minimal (cf. [8]).

In section 4 we will also need the notion of a vector lattice. A vector lattice is a vector space $V$ with an ordering $\preceq$ which respects the vector space structure (i.e., for $x, y, z \in V, a > 0 : x \preceq y \implies x+z \preceq y+z$ and $ax \preceq ay$) and such that for any two elements $f, g \in V$ there exists a greatest lower bound $\inf(f, g)$. In particular, the space of Lipschitz functions with the ordering $f \preceq g \iff \forall x \; f(x) \leq g(x)$ forms a vector lattice.

## 3   The Lipschitz Classifier

Let $(X, d)$ be a metric space and $(x_i, y_i)_{i=1,\ldots,n} \subset X \times \{\pm 1\}$ some training data. In order to be able to define hyperplanes, we want to embed $(X, d)$ into a vector space, but without loosing or changing the underlying metric structure. Our first step is to embed $X$ by the identity mapping into the extended space $X_0$ as described in (1), which in turn is embedded into $AE(X_0)$ via (4). We denote the resulting composite embedding by

$$\Phi : X \to AE(X_0), \; x \mapsto m_x := m_{xe}$$

Secondly, we identify $\mathrm{Lip}(X)$ with $\mathrm{Lip}_0(X_0)$ according to (2) and then $\mathrm{Lip}_0(X_0)$ with $AE(X_0)'$ according to Theorem 1. Together this defines the map

$$\Psi : \mathrm{Lip}(X) \to AE(X_0)', \; f \mapsto T_f$$

**Proposition 2.** *The mappings $\Phi$ and $\Psi$ have the following properties:*

1. $\Phi$ is an isometric embedding of $X$ into $AE(X_0)$: to every point $x \in X$ corresponds a molecule $m_x \in AE(X_0)$ such that $d(x,y) = \|m_x - m_y\|_{AE}$ for all $x, y \in X$.
2. $\mathrm{Lip}(X)$ is isometrically isomorphic to $AE(X_0)'$: to every Lipschitz function $f$ on $X$ corresponds an operator $T_f$ on $AE(X_0)$ such that $\|f\|_L = \|T_f\|$ and vice versa.
3. It makes no difference whether we evaluate operators on the image of $X$ in $AE(X_0)$ or apply Lipschitz functions on $X$ directly: $T_f m_x = f(x)$.
4. Scaling a linear operator is the same as scaling the corresponding Lipschitz function: for $a \in \mathbb{R}$ we have $aT_f = T_{af}$.

*Proof.* All these properties are direct consequences of the construction and equation (3).                                                                    ☺

The message of this proposition is that it makes no difference whether we classify our training data on the space $X$ with the decision function $\mathrm{sgn}\, f(x)$ or on $AE(X_0)$ with the hyperplane $\mathrm{sgn}(T_f m_x)$. The advantage of the latter is that there we can construct the margin of the classifier in a straightforward way: for a functional $T_f \in AE(X_0)'$ let $H_f := \{m \in AE(X_0); T_f m = 0\}$ be the hyperplane induced by $T_f$. We normalize the representation of the hyperplane such that $\min_{i=1,\ldots,n} |T_f m_{x_i}| = 1$. Note that normalizing $T_f$ is the same as normalizing $f$ itself according to part 4 of Proposition 2. We define the margin of $H_f$, which we also call the margin of $f$, as

$$\rho := \inf_{\substack{i=1,\ldots,n \\ m_h \in H_f}} \|m_{x_i} - m_h\|_{AE}.$$

Now for each training point $m_{x_i}$ and each point $m_h$ on the hyperplane,

$$1 \le |T_f m_{x_i}| = |T_f m_{x_i} - T_f m_h| = |T_f(m_{x_i} - m_h)| \le \|T_f\|\|m_{x_i} - m_h\|_{AE}$$

and thus $\rho \ge 1/\|T_f\| = 1/\|f\|_L$ because of part 2 of Proposition 2. If the training data are nontrivial (i.e., they contain points from both classes), then the decision function $f$ has to take positive and negative values. Hence, $\|f\|_L = L(f)$ holds as we already explained in the last section. So we have proved the following theorem:

**Theorem 3 (Margin of the Lipschitz classifier).** *Let $(X, d)$ be a metric space, $(x_i, y_i)_{i=1,\ldots,n} \subset X \times \{\pm 1\}$ some training data containing points of both classes, and $f \in \mathrm{Lip}(X)$ such that $y_i f(x_i) \ge 1$ $(i = 1, \ldots, n)$ and $\min_{i=1,\ldots,n} |f(x_i)| = 1$. Then the margin $\rho$ of the decision function $\mathrm{sgn}\, f(x)$ satisfies $\rho \ge 1/L(f)$.*

One nice aspect about the above construction is that the margin also has a geometrical meaning in the input space $X$ itself: it is the minimal distance between the "separation surface" $S := \{s \in X; f(s) = 0\}$ and the training points. To see this, observe that for normalized $f$ and $s \in S$ we have $1 \le |f(x_i) - f(s)| \le L d(x_i, s)$, and thus $d(x_i, s) \ge 1/L(f)$. Note also that the relation between margins and Lipschitz constants in the context of normed vector spaces has already been observed in [7].

As a consequence of Theorem 3, a large margin algorithm on a metric space has to construct decision functions with small Lipschitz constant. This leads to the following optimization problem:

$$\text{minimize}_{f \in Lip(X)} \, L(f) \text{ subject to } y_i f(x_i) \geq 1, \, i = 1, \ldots, n \qquad (*)$$

We call a solution of this problem a (hard margin) Lipschitz classifier. Analogously to SVMs (e.g., [6]) we define the soft margin version of this algorithm

$$\text{minimize}_{f \in Lip(X)} \, L(f) + C \sum_{i=1}^{n} \xi_i \text{ subject to } y_i f(x_i) \geq 1 - \xi_i, \, \xi_i \geq 0 \qquad (**)$$

To implement this algorithm in practice we will have to choose reasonable subsets of Lipschitz functions. Consider the following special cases: if the metric on $X$ is induced by a kernel $k$ and we choose a classifier of the form $f(x) = \sum_i \alpha_i k(x_i, x) + b$, then the solution of the Lipschitz classifier coincides with the solution of the SVM. The reason is that the norm of a linear functional coincides with its Lipschitz constant. In the case where we choose the subset of all linear combinations of distance functions of the form $f(x) = \sum_{i=1}^{n} a_i d(x_i, x) + b$ the Lipschitz algorithm is the same as the linear programming machine (cf. [4]). The reason for this is that the Lipschitz constant of a function $f(x) = \sum_{i=1}^{n} a_i d(x_i, x) + b$ is upper bounded by $\sum |a_i|$. Furthermore, if we do not restrict the function space at all, then we will see in the next section that the 1-nearest neighbor classifier is a solution of the algorithm. These examples show that the Lipschitz algorithm is a very general approach. By choosing different subsets of Lipschitz functions we recover several well known algorithms. As the Lipschitz algorithm is a large margin algorithm according to Theorem 3, the same thus holds for the recovered algorithms. For instance the linear programming machine, originally designed with little theoretical justification, can now be understood as a large margin algorithm.

## 4   Representer Theorems

A crucial theorem in the context of SVMs and other kernel algorithms is the representer theorem (cf. [6]). It states that, even though the space of possible solutions of these algorithms forms an infinite dimensional space, there always exists a solution in the finite dimensional subspace spanned by the training points. It is because of this theorem that SVMs overcome the curse of dimensionality and yield computationally tractable solutions. In this section we prove a similar theorem for the Lipschitz classifier $(*)$. To simplify the discussion, denote $\mathcal{D} := \{d(x, \cdot); \, x \in X\} \cup \{\mathbb{1}\}$ and $\mathcal{D}_{\text{train}} := \{d(x_i, \cdot); \, x_i \text{ training point }\} \cup \{\mathbb{1}\}$ where $\mathbb{1}$ is the constant-1 function.

**Theorem 4 (Representer theorem I).** *Problem $(*)$ has a solution in the vector lattice spanned by $\mathcal{D}_{\text{train}}$.*

This is remarkable as the space $\mathrm{Lip}(X)$ of possible solutions of $(*)$ contains the whole vector lattice spanned by $\mathcal{D}$. The theorem thus states that even though the Lipschitz algorithm searches for solutions in the whole lattice spanned by $\mathcal{D}$ it always manages to come up with a solution in the sublattice spanned by $\mathcal{D}_{\mathrm{train}}$. Another way to state this theorem is the following:

**Theorem 5 (Representer theorem II).** *Problem $(*)$ always has a solution which is a linear combination of distances to sets of training points.*

To prove these theorems we first need a simple proposition. We denote the set of all training points with positive label by $X^+$, the set of the training points with negative label by $X^-$, and for two subsets $A, B \subset X$ we define $d(A, B) := \inf_{a \in A, b \in B} d(a, b)$.

**Proposition 6.** *The Lipschitz constant $L^*$ of a solution of $(*)$ satisfies*
$$L^* \geq \tfrac{2}{d(X^+, X^-)}.$$

*Proof.* For a solution $f$ of $(*)$ we have

$$L(f) = \sup_{x,y \in X} \frac{|f(x) - f(y)|}{d(x, y)} \geq \max_{i,j=1,\dots,n} \frac{|f(x_i) - f(x_j)|}{d(x_i, x_j)}$$

$$\geq \max_{i,j=1,\dots,n} \frac{|y_i - y_j|}{d(x_i, x_j)} = \frac{2}{\min_{x_i \in X^+, x_j \in X^-} d(x_i, x_j)} = \frac{2}{d(X^+, X^-)}. \qquad ☺$$

**Proposition 7.** *Let $L^* = \tfrac{2}{d(X^+, X^-)}$. The following functions solve $(*)$:*

$$f_l(x) := \max_i(y_i - L^* d(x, x_i))$$

$$f_u(x) := \min_i(y_i + L^* d(x, x_i))$$

$$f_0(x) := \frac{d(x, X^-) - d(x, X^+)}{d(X^+, X^-)}$$

*Proof.* It is easy to see that $f_l, f_u$, and $f_0$ fulfill the constraint $y_i f(x_i) \geq 1$. Using the properties of Lipschitz constants stated in section 2 and the fact that the function $d(x, \cdot)$ has Lipschitz constant 1 we see that all three functions have Lipschitz constants $\leq L^*$. Thus they are solutions of $(*)$ by Proposition 6. ☺

The functions $f_l, f_u$, and $f_0$ lie in the vector lattice spanned by $\mathcal{D}_{\mathrm{train}}$. This proves Theorem 4. As $f_0$ is a linear combination of distances to sets of training points we also have proved Theorem 5.

A further remarkable fact of Proposition 7 is that the function $f_0$ realizes the 1-nearest neighbor classifier. This means that according to section 3 this classifier actually is a large margin classifier.

So far we have proved that $(*)$ always has a solution which can be stated as a linear combination of distances to sets of training points. But maybe we even get a theorem stating that we always find a solution which is a linear combination of distance functions to single training points? Unfortunately, in the metric space setting such a theorem is not true in general. This can be seen by the following counterexample:

*Example 8.* Assume four training points $x_1, x_2, x_3, x_4$ with (singular!) distance matrix $[0\ 2\ 1\ 1;\ 2\ 0\ 1\ 1;\ 1\ 1\ 0\ 2;\ 1\ 1\ 2\ 0\,]$ (in matlab notation) and label vector $y = (1, 1, -1, -1)$. Then the system $f(x) = \sum_{i=1}^{4} a_i d(x_i, x) + b,\ y_i f(x_i) \geq 1$ of linear inequalities has no solution. Hence, in this example, (*) has no solution which is a linear combination of distances to single training points. But it still has a solution as linear combination of distances to sets of training points according to Theorem 5.

This means that, in order to construct solutions for (*), we are in the interesting situation that it is not enough to consider distances to single training points – we have to deal with distances to sets of training points.

## 5 Rademacher Complexities

In this section we compute capacities of $\|\cdot\|_L$-balls of Lipschitz functions. The measures of capacity we consider are the Rademacher complexity $R_n$ and the related maximum discrepancy $\tilde{R}_n$. Both can be used effectively to bound the generalization error of a classifier (cf. [1]). For an arbitrary class $\mathcal{F}$ of functions, they are defined as

$$R_n(\mathcal{F}) := E(\frac{1}{n} \sup_{f \in \mathcal{F}} | \sum_{i=1}^{n} \sigma_i f(X_i)|) \geq \frac{1}{2} E(\frac{1}{n} \sup_{f \in \mathcal{F}} | \sum_{i=1}^{n} f(X_i) - f(Y_i)|) =: \tilde{R}_n(\mathcal{F})$$

where $\sigma_i$ are iid Rademacher random variables (i.e., $Prob(\sigma_i = +1) = Prob(\sigma_i = -1) = 1/2$), $X_i$ and $Y_i$ are iid sample points according to the (unknown) sample distribution, and the expectation is taken with respect to all occurring random variables. We will describe two different ways to compute these complexities for sets of Lipschitz functions. One way is a classical approach using entropy numbers and leads to an upper bound on $R_n$. For this approach we always assume that the metric space $(X, d)$ is precompact (i.e., it can be covered by finitely many balls of radius $\varepsilon$ for every $\varepsilon > 0$). The other way is more elegant: because of the definition of $\|\cdot\|_L$ and the resulting isometries, the maximum discrepancy of a $\|\cdot\|_L$-unit ball of $\text{Lip}(X)$ is the same as of the corresponding unit ball in $AE(X_0)'$. Hence it will be possible to express $\tilde{R}_n$ as the norm of an element of the Arens-Eells space. This norm can then be computed via bipartite minimal matching. In the following, $B$ always denotes the unit ball of the considered function space.

### 5.1 The Duality Approach

The main insight to compute the maximum discrepancy by the duality approach is the following observation:

$$\sup_{\|f\|_L \leq 1} | \sum_{i=1}^{n} f(x_i) - f(y_i)| = \sup_{\|T_f\| \leq 1} | \sum_{i=1}^{n} T_f m_{x_i} - T_f m_{y_i}| =$$

$$= \sup_{\|T_f\| \leq 1} |\langle T_f, \sum_{i=1}^{n} m_{x_i} - m_{y_i}\rangle| = \| \sum_{i=1}^{n} m_{x_i y_i} \|_{AE}$$

Applying this to the definition of the maximum discrepancy immediately yields

$$\tilde{R}_n(B) = \frac{1}{n} E \| \sum_{i=1}^{n} m_{X_i Y_i} \|_{AE} \tag{5}$$

As we already explained in section 2, the norm $\| \sum_{i=1}^{n} m_{X_i Y_i} \|_{AE}$ can be interpreted as the costs of a minimal bipartite matching between $\{X_1, \ldots, X_n\}$ and $\{Y_1, \ldots, Y_n\}$. To compute the right hand side of (5) we need to know the expected value of random instances of the bipartite minimal matching problem where we assume that the points $X_i$ and $Y_i$ are drawn iid from the sample distribution. In particular we want to know how this value scales with the number $n$ of points as this indicates how fast we can learn. This question has been solved for some special cases of random bipartite matching. Let the random variable $C_n$ describe the minimal bipartite matching costs for a matching between the points $X_1, \ldots, X_n$ and $Y_1, \ldots, Y_n$ drawn iid according to some distribution $P$. In [11] it was has been proved that for an arbitrary distribution on the unit square of $\mathbb{R}^d$ with $d \geq 3$ we have $\lim C_n / n^{d-1/d} = c > 0$ a.s. for some constant $c$. The upper bound $EC_n \leq c\sqrt{n \log n}$ for arbitrary distributions on the unit square in $\mathbb{R}^2$ was presented in [9]. These results, together with equation (5), lead to the following maximum discrepancies:

**Theorem 9 (Maximum discrepancy of unit ball of Lip$([0,1]^d)$).** *Let $X = [0,1]^d \subset \mathbb{R}^d$ with the Euclidean metric. Then the maximum discrepancy of the $\| \cdot \|_L$-unit ball $B$ of $\mathrm{Lip}(X)$ is given by*

$$\tilde{R}_n(B) \begin{cases} = c_1 \frac{1}{\sqrt[d]{n}} & \text{if } d \geq 3 \\ \leq c_2 \frac{\sqrt{\log n}}{\sqrt{n}} & \text{if } d = 2 \end{cases}$$

*for some constants $c_1, c_2$ which are independent of $n$.*

Note that this gives exact results rather than upper bounds in cases where we have exact results on the bipartite matching costs. This is for example the case for cubes in $\mathbb{R}^d, d \geq 3$ as Yukich's theorem gives an exact limit result, or for $\mathbb{R}^2$ with the uniform distribution.

## 5.2   Covering Number Approach

To derive the Rademacher complexity in more general settings than Euclidean spaces we use an adapted version of the classical entropy bound of Dudley. The proof of this theorem can be found in the appendix.

**Theorem 10 (Generalized entropy bound).** *Let $\mathcal{F}$ be a class of functions and $X_1, \ldots, X_n$ iid sample points with empirical distribution $\mu_n$. Then, for every $\varepsilon > 0$,*

$$R_n(\mathcal{F}) \leq 2\varepsilon + \frac{4\sqrt{2}}{\sqrt{n}} \int_{\varepsilon/4}^{\infty} \sqrt{\log N(\mathcal{F}, u, \| \cdot \|_{L_2(\mu_n)})} \, du$$

To apply this theorem we need to know covering numbers of spaces of Lipschitz functions. This can be found for example in [5], pp.353–357.

**Theorem 11 (Covering numbers for Lipschitz function balls).** *For a totally bounded metric space $(X, d)$ and the unit ball $B$ of $(\mathrm{Lip}(X), \|\cdot\|_L)$,*

$$2^{N(X, 4\varepsilon, d)} \leq N(B, \varepsilon, \|\cdot\|_\infty) \leq \left( 2 \left\lceil \frac{2 \operatorname{diam}(X)}{\varepsilon} \right\rceil + 1 \right)^{N(X, \frac{\varepsilon}{4}, d)}.$$

*If, in addition, $X$ is connected and centered (i.e., for all subsets $A \in X$ with $\operatorname{diam}(A) \leq 2r$ there exists a point $x \in X$ such that $d(x, a) \leq r$ for all $a \in A$),*

$$2^{N(X, 2\varepsilon, d)} \leq N(B, \varepsilon, \|\cdot\|_\infty) \leq \left( 2 \left\lceil \frac{2 \operatorname{diam}(X)}{\varepsilon} \right\rceil + 1 \right) \cdot 2^{N(X, \frac{\varepsilon}{2}, d)}.$$

Combining Theorems 10 and 11 and using $N(\mathcal{F}, u, \|\cdot\|_{L_2(\mu_n)}) \leq N(\mathcal{F}, u, \|\cdot\|_\infty)$ now gives a bound on the Rademacher complexity of balls of $\mathrm{Lip}(X)$:

**Theorem 12 (Rademacher complexity of unit ball of $\mathrm{Lip}(X)$).** *Let $(X, d)$ be a totally bounded metric space with diameter $\operatorname{diam}(X)$ and $B$ the ball of Lipschitz functions with $\|f\|_L \leq 1$. Then, for every $\varepsilon > 0$,*

$$R_n(B) \leq 2\varepsilon + \frac{4\sqrt{2}}{\sqrt{n}} \int_{\varepsilon/4}^{4 \operatorname{diam}(X)} \sqrt{N\left(X, \frac{u}{4}, d\right) \log\left( 2 \left\lceil \frac{2 \operatorname{diam}(X)}{u} \right\rceil + 1 \right)} \, du$$

*If, in addition, $X$ is connected and centered, we have*

$$R_n(B) \leq 2\varepsilon + \frac{4\sqrt{2}}{\sqrt{n}} \int_{\varepsilon/4}^{2 \operatorname{diam}(X)} \sqrt{N\left(X, \frac{u}{2}, d\right) \log 2 + \log(2 \left\lceil \frac{2 \operatorname{diam}(X)}{u} \right\rceil + 1)} \, du$$

In our framework this is a nice result as the bound on the complexity of balls of $\mathrm{Lip}(X)$ only uses the metric properties of the underlying space $X$.

*Example 13.* Let $X = [0, 1]^d \subset \mathbb{R}^d, d \geq 3$, with the Euclidean metric $\|\cdot\|_2$. This is a connected and centered space. We choose $\varepsilon = 1/\sqrt[d]{n}$ and use that the covering numbers of $X$ have the form $N(X, \varepsilon, \|\cdot\|_2) = c/\varepsilon^d$. After evaluating the second integral of Theorem 12 we find that $R_n(B)$ scales as $1/\sqrt[d]{n}$.

*Example 14.* Let $X = [0, 1]^2 \subset \mathbb{R}^2$ with the Euclidean metric. Applying Theorem 12 similar to Example 13 yields a bound on $R_n(B)$ that scales as $\log n/\sqrt{n}$.

In case of example 13 the scaling behavior of the upper bound on $R_n(B)$ obtained by the covering number approach coincides with the exact result for $\tilde{R}_n(B)$ derived in Theorem 9. In case of example 14 the covering number result $\log n/\sqrt{n}$ is slightly worse than the result $\sqrt{\log(n)}/\sqrt{n}$ obtained in Theorem 9.

## 5.3  Complexity of Lipschitz RBF Classifiers

In this section we want to derive a bound for the Rademacher complexity of radial basis function classifiers of the form

$$\mathcal{F}_{rbf} := \{f : X \to \mathbb{R}|\ f(x) = \sum_{k=1}^{l} a_k g_k(d(p_k, x)),\ g_k \in \mathcal{G}\} \tag{6}$$

where $p_k \in X$, $a_k \in \mathbb{R}$, and $\mathcal{G} \subset Lip(X)$ is a (small) set of $\|\cdot\|_\infty$-bounded Lipschitz functions on $\mathbb{R}$ whose Lipschitz constants are bounded from below by a constant $c > 0$. As an example, consider $\mathcal{G} = \{g : \mathbb{R} \to \mathbb{R}|\ g(x) = exp(-x^2/\sigma^2), \sigma \geq 1\}$. The special case $\mathcal{G} = \{id\}$ corresponds to the function class which is used by the linear programming machine. It can easily be seen that the Lipschitz constant of an RBF function satisfies $L(\sum_k a_k g_k(d(p_k, \cdot))) \leq \sum_k |a_k| L(g_k)$. We define a norm on $\mathcal{F}_{rbf}$ by

$$\|f\|_{rbf} := \inf \left\{ \sum_k |a_k| L(g_k);\ f = \sum_k a_k g_k(d(p_k, \cdot)) \right\}$$

and derive the Rademacher complexity of a unit ball $B$ of $(\mathcal{F}_{rbf}, \|\cdot\|_{rbf})$. Substituting $a_k$ by $c_k/L(g_k)$ in the expansion of $f$ we get

$$\sup_{f \in B} |\sum_{i=1}^{n} \sigma_i f(x_i)| = \sup_{\sum |a_k| L(g_k) \leq 1, p_k \in X, g_k \in \mathcal{G}} |\sum_{i=1}^{n} \sigma_i \sum_{k=1}^{l} a_k g_k(d(p_k, x_i))|$$

$$= \sup_{\sum |c_k| \leq 1, p_k \in X, g_k \in \mathcal{G}} |\sum_{i=1}^{n} \sigma_i \sum_{k=1}^{l} \frac{c_k}{L(g_k)} g_k(d(p_k, x_i))|$$

$$= \sup_{\sum |c_k| \leq 1, p_k \in X, g_k \in \mathcal{G}} |\sum_{k=1}^{l} c_k \sum_{i=1}^{n} \sigma_i \frac{1}{L(g_k)} g_k(d(p_k, x_i))|$$

$$= \sup_{p \in X, g \in \mathcal{G}} |\sum_{i=1}^{n} \sigma_i \frac{1}{L(g)} g(d(p, x_i))| \tag{7}$$

For the last step observe that the supremum in the linear expansion in the second last line is obtained when one of the $c_k$ is 1 and all the others are 0. To proceed we introduce the notations $h_{p,g}(x) := g(d(p, x_i))/L(g)$, $\mathcal{H} := \{h_{p,g};\ p \in X, g \in \mathcal{G}\}$, and $\mathcal{G}_1 := \{g/L(g);\ g \in \mathcal{G}\}$. We rewrite the right hand side of equation (7) as

$$\sup_{p \in X, g \in \mathcal{G}} |\sum_{i=1}^{n} \sigma_i \frac{1}{L(g)} g(d(p, x_i))| = \sup_{h_{p,g} \in \mathcal{H}} |\sum_{i=1}^{n} \sigma_i h_{p,g}(x_i)|$$

and thus obtain $R_n(B) = R_n(\mathcal{H})$. To calculate the latter we need the following:

**Lemma 15.** $N(\mathcal{H}, 2\varepsilon, \|\cdot\|_\infty) \leq N(X, \varepsilon, d) N(\mathcal{G}_1, \varepsilon, \|\cdot\|_\infty)$.

*Proof.* First we observe that for $h_{p_1,g_1}, h_{p_2,g_2} \in \mathcal{H}$

$$\|h_{p_1,g_1} - h_{p_2,g_2}\|_\infty = \sup_{x \in X} \left| \frac{g_1(d(p_1, x))}{L(g_1)} - \frac{g_2(d(p_2, x))}{L(g_2)} \right|$$

$$\leq \sup_{x \in X} \left( \left| \frac{g_1(d(p_1, x))}{L(g_1)} - \frac{g_1(d(p_2, x))}{L(g_1)} \right| + \left| \frac{g_1(d(p_2, x))}{L(g_1)} - \frac{g_2(d(p_2, x))}{L(g_2)} \right| \right)$$

$$\leq \sup_{x \in X} |d(p_1, x) - d(p_2, x)| + \left\| \frac{g_1}{L(g_1)} - \frac{g_2}{L(g_2)} \right\|_\infty$$

$$\leq d(p_1, p_2) + \left\| \frac{g_1}{L(g_1)} - \frac{g_2}{L(g_2)} \right\|_\infty =: d_\mathcal{H}(h_{p_1,g_1}, h_{p_2,g_2}) \tag{8}$$

For the step from the second to the third line we used the Lipschitz property of $g_1$. Finally, it is easy to see that $N(\mathcal{H}, 2\varepsilon, d_\mathcal{H}) \leq N(X, \varepsilon, d)N(\mathcal{G}_1, \varepsilon, \|\cdot\|_\infty)$.  ☺

Plugging lemma 15 in Theorem 10 yields the following Rademacher complexity:

**Theorem 16 (Rademacher complexity of unit ball of $\mathcal{F}_{rbf}$).** *Let $B$ the unit ball of $(\mathcal{F}_{rbf}, \|\cdot\|_{rbf})$, $\mathcal{G}_1$ the rescaled functions of $\mathcal{G}$ as defined above, and $w := \max\{\mathrm{diam}(X, d), \mathrm{diam}(\mathcal{G}_1, \|\cdot\|_\infty)\}$. Then, for every $\varepsilon > 0$,*

$$R_n(B) \leq 2\varepsilon + \frac{4\sqrt{2}}{\sqrt{n}} \int_{\varepsilon/4}^w \sqrt{\log N\left(X, \frac{u}{2}, d\right) + \log N\left(\mathcal{G}_1, \frac{u}{2}, \|\cdot\|_\infty\right)} \; du$$

This theorem is a huge improvement compared to Theorem 12 as instead of the covering numbers we now have log-covering numbers in the integral. As an example consider the linear programming machine on $X = [0, 1]^d$. Because of $\mathcal{G} = \{id\}$, the second term in the square root vanishes, and the integral over the log-covering numbers of $X$ can be bounded by a constant independent of $\varepsilon$. As result we obtain that in this case $R_n(B)$ scales as $1/\sqrt{n}$.

## 6   Conclusion

We derived a general approach to large margin classification on metric spaces. Our theoretical analysis led to a general algorithm that works directly on the given metric space and uses Lipschitz functions as decision functions. It specializes to well-known algorithms, as the support vector machine or the linear programming machine. Especially for the latter, our analysis gave new insights into its learning theoretic properties.

## Acknowledgements

We would like to thank Matthias Hein and Bernhard Schölkopf for helpful discussions.

# Appendix: Proof of Theorem 10

The idea of the proof of Theorem 10 is the following. Instead of bounding the Rademacher complexity on the whole set of functions $\mathcal{F}$, we first consider a maximal $\varepsilon$-separating subset $\mathcal{F}_\varepsilon$ of $\mathcal{F}$. This is a maximal subset such that all its points have distance at least $\varepsilon$ to each other. To this special set we will apply the classical entropy bound of Dudley [3]:

**Theorem 17 (Classical entropy bound).** *For every class $\mathcal{F}$ of functions there exists a constant $C$ such that*

$$R_n(\mathcal{F}) \leq \frac{C}{\sqrt{n}} \int_0^\infty \sqrt{\log N(u, \mathcal{F}, L_2(\mu_n))} \, du$$

*where $\mu_n$ is the empirical distribution of the sample.*

As a second step we then bound the error we make by computing the Rademacher complexity of $\mathcal{F}_\varepsilon$ instead of $\mathcal{F}$. This will lead to the additional offset of $2\varepsilon$ in Theorem 10. The following lemma can be found as Lemma 3.10 in [2].

**Lemma 18 ($\varepsilon$-separations of an empirical process).** *Let $\{Z_t; t \in T\}$ be a separable stochastic process satisfying for $\lambda > 0$ the increment condition*

$$\forall s, t \in T : E\left(e^{\lambda(Z_t - Z_s)}\right) \leq e^{\lambda^2 c^2 d^2(s,t)/2}.$$

*Let $\varepsilon \geq 0$ and $\delta > 0$. If $\varepsilon > 0$, let $T_\varepsilon$ denote a maximal $\varepsilon$-separated subset of $T$ and let $T_\varepsilon = T$ otherwise. Then for all $t_0$,*

$$E\left(\sup_{t \in T_\varepsilon, d(t,t_0) \leq \delta} Z_t - Z_{t_0}\right) \leq 4\sqrt{2}c \int_{\varepsilon/4}^{\delta/2} \sqrt{\log N(T, u, d)} \, du$$

To apply this lemma to the Rademacher complexity of a function class $\mathcal{F}$, we choose the index set $T = \mathcal{F}$, the fixed index $t_0 = f_0$ for some $f_0 \in \mathcal{F}$, the empirical process $Z_f = \frac{1}{n} \sum \sigma_i f(X_i)$, and $\delta = \infty$. Note that the Rademacher complexity satisfies the increment condition of Lemma 18 with respect to the $L_2(\mu_n)$–distance with constant $c = \sqrt{n}$. Using $E(Z_{t_0}) = E(\frac{1}{n} \sum \sigma_i f_0(X_i)) = 0$ and the symmetry of the distribution of $Z_f$ we thus get the next lemma:

**Lemma 19 (Entropy bound for $\varepsilon$-separations).** *Let $(X_i)_{i=1,\ldots,n}$ iid training points with empirical distribution $\mu_n$, $\mathcal{F}$ an arbitrary class of functions, and $\mathcal{F}_\varepsilon$ a maximal $\varepsilon$-separating subset of $\mathcal{F}$ with respect to $L_2(\mu_n)$- norm. Then*

$$E\left(\sup_{f \in \mathcal{F}_\varepsilon} \frac{1}{n} \Big| \sum_i \sigma_i f(X_i) \Big| \, \Big| X_1, \ldots, X_n\right) \leq \frac{4\sqrt{2}}{\sqrt{n}} \int_{\varepsilon/4}^\infty \sqrt{\log N(T, u, L_2(\mu_n))} \, du$$

With this lemma we achieved that the integral over the covering numbers starts at $\varepsilon/4$ instead of 0 as it is the case in Theorem 17. The price we pay is that the supremum on the left hand side is taken over the smaller set $\mathcal{F}_\varepsilon$ instead of the whole class $\mathcal{F}$. Our next step is to bound the mistake we make by this procedure.

**Lemma 20.** *Let $\mathcal{F}$ be a class of functions and $\mathcal{F}_\varepsilon$ a maximal $\varepsilon$-separating subset of $\mathcal{F}$ with respect to $\|\cdot\|_{L_2(\mu_n)}$. Then $|R_n(\mathcal{F}) - R_n(\mathcal{F}_\varepsilon)| \leq 2\varepsilon$.*

*Proof.* We want to bound the expression

$$|R_n(\mathcal{F}) - R_n(\mathcal{F}_\varepsilon)| = E\frac{1}{n}\left|\sup_{f\in\mathcal{F}}|\sum\sigma_i f(X_i)| - \sup_{f\in\mathcal{F}_\varepsilon}|\sum\sigma_i f(X_i)|\right|.$$

First look at the expression inside the expectation, assume that the $\sigma_i$ and $X_i$ are fixed and that $\sup_{f\in\mathcal{F}}|\sum\sigma_i f(x_i)| = |\sum\sigma_i f^*(x_i)|$ for some function $f^*$ (if $f^*$ doesn't exist we additionally have to use a limit argument). Let $f_\varepsilon \in \mathcal{F}_\varepsilon$ such that $\|f^* - f_\varepsilon\|_{L_2(\mu_n)} \leq 2\varepsilon$. Then,

$$\frac{1}{n}\left|\sup_{f\in\mathcal{F}}|\sum\sigma_i f(x_i)| - \sup_{f\in\mathcal{F}_\varepsilon}|\sum\sigma_i f(x_i)|\right| \leq \frac{1}{n}\left||\sum\sigma_i f^*(x_i)| - |\sum\sigma_i f_\varepsilon(x_i)|\right|$$

$$\leq \frac{1}{n}\left|\sum\sigma_i(f^*(x_i) - f_\varepsilon(x_i))\right| \leq \|f^* - f_\varepsilon\|_{L_1(\mu_n)} \leq \|f^* - f_\varepsilon\|_{L_2(\mu_n)} \leq 2\varepsilon$$

As this holds conditioned on every fixed values of $\sigma_i$ and $X_i$ we get the same for the expectation. This proves the lemma.     ☺

To prove Theorem 10 we now combine lemmas 19 and 20.     ☺

# References

1. P. Bartlett and S. Mendelson. Rademacher and Gaussian complexities: Risk bounds and structural results. *JMLR*, 3:463–482, 2002.
2. O. Bousquet. Concentration inequalities and empirical processes theory applied to the analysis of learning algorithms. PhD Thesis, 2002.
3. R. M. Dudley. Universal Donsker classes and metric entropy. *Ann. Probab.*, 15(4):1306–1326, 1987.
4. T. Graepel, R. Herbrich, B. Schölkopf, A. Smola, P. Bartlett, K. Müller, K. Obermayer, and R. Williamson. Classification of proximity data with LP machines. In *Proceedings of the Ninth International Conference on Artificial Neural Networks*, pages 304–309, 1999.
5. A. N. Kolmogorov and V. M. Tihomirov. $\varepsilon$-entropy and $\varepsilon$-capacity of sets in functional space. *Amer. Math. Soc. Transl. (2)*, 17:277–364, 1961.
6. B. Schölkopf and A. Smola. *Learning with Kernels. Support Vector Machines, Regularization, Optimization and Beyond*. MIT press, 2002.
7. B. Schölkopf, A.J. Smola, R.C. Williamson, and P.L. Bartlett. New support vector algorithms. *Neural Computation*, 12(5):1207–1245, 2000.
8. J. Michael Steele. *Probability theory and combinatorial optimization*, volume 69 of *CBMS-NSF Regional Conference Series in Applied Mathematics*. Society for Industrial and Applied Mathematics (SIAM), Philadelphia, PA, 1997.
9. M. Talagrand. The Ajtai-Komlos-Tusnady matching theorem for general measures. In *Progress in Probability*, volume 30, 1991.
10. N. Weaver. *Lipschitz algebras*. World Scientific, 1999.
11. J. Yukich. Asymptotics for transportation costs in high dimensions. *J. Theor. Probab.*, 8(1):97–118, 1995.

# Random Subclass Bounds

Shahar Mendelson and Petra Philips

RSISE, The Australian National University, Canberra, ACT 0200, Australia
{shahar.mendelson,petra.philips}@anu.edu.au

**Abstract.** It has been recently shown that sharp generalization bounds can be obtained when the function class from which the algorithm chooses its hypotheses is "small" in the sense that the Rademacher averages of this function class are small [8, 9]. Seemingly based on different arguments, generalization bounds were obtained in the compression scheme [7], luckiness [13], and algorithmic luckiness [6] frameworks in which the "size" of the function class is not specified a priori.
We show that the bounds obtained in all these frameworks follow from the same general principle, namely that coordinate projections of this function subclass evaluated on random samples are "small" with high probability.

**Keywords:** statistical learning theory, generalization bounds, data-dependent complexity

## 1   Introduction

The generalization performance of learning machines is quantified through generalization bounds, which express the probability that the function produced by a learning algorithm has a small error. The classical approach to obtain these bounds is to study the deviation of empirical means from the actual mean *uniformly* over the whole set of hypothesis functions. The quantity investigated is therefore the probability that, for *any* hypothesis, this deviation is larger than a given threshold,

$$Pr\left\{\sup_{f\in F}\left|\mathbb{E}_\mu f - \frac{1}{n}\sum_{i=1}^{n}f(X_i)\right| \geq t\right\},\tag{1}$$

where $\mu$ is an unknown probability measure on $\Omega$, $X_1, ..., X_n$ are independent random variables distributed according to $\mu$, $\mathbb{E}_\mu$ is the expectation with respect to $\mu$, and $F$ is the loss class associated with the learning problem.

Since $F$ is a class of loss functions we can and will assume that it is a class of real-valued functions defined on a measurable space $\Omega$ which take values in $[-1, 1]$.

Classes of functions which, independently of the underlying measure $\mu$, satisfy the uniform law of large numbers are called *uniform Glivenko-Cantelli classes*. For these classes, learning is guaranteed for large enough training samples. Historically, uniform Glivenko-Cantelli classes were characterized by a finite combinatorial dimension (e.g. a finite VC dimension in the Boolean case). In [10, 8] it

B. Schölkopf and M.K. Warmuth (Eds.): COLT/Kernel 2003, LNAI 2777, pp. 329–343, 2003.
© Springer-Verlag Berlin Heidelberg 2003

has been shown that parameters which also characterize the uniform Glivenko-Cantelli property are the *uniform Rademacher averages of the class*, defined as

$$R_n(F) := \sup_{\{x_1,\ldots,x_n\} \subset \Omega^n} \mathbb{E}_\varepsilon \sup_{f \in F} \Big| \sum_{i=1}^n \varepsilon_i f(x_i) \Big|,$$

where $(\varepsilon_i)_{i=1}^n$ are independent, symmetric, $\{-1, 1\}$-valued random variables, also known as Rademacher random variables. The necessary and sufficient condition for a class $F$ to be a uniform Glivenko-Cantelli class is that $R_n(F) = o(n)$. Sharp generalization bounds for (1) which are independent of the underlying measure $\mu$ can be obtained in terms of the Rademacher averages. Therefore, they seem to be a reasonable notion of "size" for a function class $F$ in the context of learning via the uniform law of large numbers.

Seemingly based on different arguments, generalization bounds were obtained in the compression scheme [7], luckiness [13], and algorithmic luckiness [6] frameworks in which the "size" of the function class is not specified a priori. Their common starting point is that, ultimately, one wants to control the generalization ability *only* for the hypothesis functions which are reachable by the specific learning algorithm when presented with the actual training sample.

Therefore, it suffices to obtain estimates for

$$Pr\Big\{ \sup_{f \in F'} \Big| \mathbb{E}_\mu f - \frac{1}{n} \sum_{i=1}^n f(X_i) \Big| \geq t \Big\}, \tag{2}$$

where $F' \subset F$ and $\hat{f} \in F'$, where $\hat{f}$ is the loss of the function produced by the algorithm from the sample $(X_1, \ldots, X_n)$. Although one can hope that $F'$ has a smaller "size" than $F$, it is not possible to use the classical uniform generalization bounds because $F'$ depends on the random training sample and could change with the sample. In all the frameworks mentioned, it is possible to avoid the detour via the worst-case quantity in equation (1) and to derive bounds by using additional prior knowledge about the learning algorithm or the training sample. Let us consider a few such examples.

In the compression framework, it is a property of the learning algorithm which restricts the number of reachable hypothesis functions and therefore the number of possible errors. This property states that the hypothesis produced by the algorithm from the training sample can be reproduced by presenting only a small ("compressed") subset of the training sample. For example, the maximal margin hyperplane produced by support vector machines can be reproduced using only the support vectors of the training sample. The size of the compressed sample, called *compression size*, is the quantity which governs the generalization rate.

In the luckiness framework, prior knowledge about the connection between the sample and the functions in $F$ is quantified through a luckiness function. A "fortunate" property of this luckiness function ($\omega$-smallness) ensures good tail estimates for (2). One example for a luckiness function is the size of the margin for linear classifiers.

The algorithmic luckiness framework generalizes both the compression scheme and the luckiness framework. Prior knowledge on the link between the functions learned by the algorithm and the sample are formulated through an algorithmic luckiness function whose property of "$\omega$-smallness" enables one to bound the generalization error.

In this paper we will show that all these bounds follow from the same general principle, directly generalizing the original proof of the uniform Glivenko-Cantelli property. This principle states that there are three main ingredients sufficient to ensure learnability and tight generalization bounds: a symmetrization procedure, a sharp concentration inequality, and a small "size" for the set of random coordinate projections. The difference between the new version and the original proof of the GC theorem is that symmetrization is performed with respect to a random subclass of functions instead of the whole class. In this way, the probability in equation (2) can be related to the probability of having large Rademacher sums – and thus a large "size" – for the projections of this random subclass of functions evaluated on a random sample. Sharp generalization bounds can be obtained when the "size" of the set of coordinate projections of the random subclass is "small" in the sense that the Rademacher sums associated with this set are small. We will show that in the compression scheme, luckiness, and algorithmic luckiness frameworks, the additional exploited properties are only different ways of ensuring that the "size" of the set of coordinate projections of specific symmetric subsets are "small" in the above sense.

Results on generalization bounds for data-dependent hypothesis classes which use a symmetrization argument similar to ours were presented previously in [4, 2]. We will show in section 3.2 that they are special cases of the framework presented in this paper, where the notion of "size" which they employ is simply that of cardinality.

**Notation.** In the following, $F$ is a class of real-valued functions defined on a measurable space $\Omega$ which take values in $[-1, 1]$ and $\mu$ is a probability measure on $\Omega$. $\Omega^n$ denotes the product space $\Omega \times \cdots \times \Omega$. Let $X_1, ..., X_n$ be independent random variables distributed according to $\mu$ and let $(Y_1, ..., Y_n)$ be an independent copy of $(X_1, ..., X_n)$. $\mu_n$ denotes the random empirical probability measure supported on $\{X_1, ..., X_n\}$, that is, $\mu_n := n^{-1} \sum_{i=1}^{n} \delta_{X_i}$. $Pr_\mu$ and $\mathbb{E}_\mu$ denote the probability and the expectation with respect to $\mu$ and, $Pr_X$ and $\mathbb{E}_X$ denote the probability and the expectation with respect to the random vector $X = (X_1, ..., X_n)$ (and therefore with respect to $\mu^n$), and, in general, for any random variable $Z$, $Pr_Z$ and $\mathbb{E}_Z$ denote the probability and the expectation with respect to the distribution of $Z$. $\text{var}(f)$ is the variance of the random variable $f(X)$.

Set $\ell_p^n$ to be $\mathbb{R}^n$ with the norm $\|x\|_p := \left( \sum_{i=1}^{n} |x_i|^p \right)^{1/p}$ and put $B_p^n$ to be the unit ball of $\ell_p^n$. $\ell_\infty^n$ is $\mathbb{R}^n$ endowed with the norm $\|x\|_\infty := \sup_{1 \le i \le n} |x_i|$. Let $L_\infty(\Omega)$ be the set of bounded functions on $\Omega$ with respect to the norm $\|f\|_\infty := \sup_{\omega \in \Omega} |f(\omega)|$, and denote its unit ball by $B(L_\infty(\Omega))$. For a probability measure $\mu$ on a measurable space $\Omega$ and $1 \le p < \infty$, let $L_p(\mu)$ be the space of measurable functions on $\Omega$ with a finite norm $\|f\|_{L_p(\mu)} := \left( \int |f|^p d\mu \right)^{1/p}$.

Let $(Y, d)$ be a metric space. If $F \subset Y$ then for every $\varepsilon > 0$, $N(\varepsilon, F, d)$ is the minimal number of open balls (with respect to the metric $d$) needed to cover $F$. A corresponding set $\{y_1, ..., y_m\} \subset Y$ of minimal cardinality chosen such that for every $f \in F$ there is some $y_i$ with $d(f, y_i) < \varepsilon$ is called an $\varepsilon$-cover of $F$. For $1 \le p < \infty$, denote by $N(\varepsilon, F, L_p(\mu_n))$ the covering number of $F$ at scale $\varepsilon$ with respect to the $L_p(\mu_n)$ norm. Similarly, one can define the packing number at scale $\varepsilon$, which is the maximal cardinality of a set $\{y_1, ..., y_k\} \subset F$ such that for every $i \ne j$, $d(y_i, y_j) \ge \varepsilon$. Denote the $\varepsilon$-packing numbers by $D(\varepsilon, F, d)$ and note that for every $\varepsilon > 0$, $N(\varepsilon, F, d) \le D(\varepsilon, F, d) \le N(\varepsilon/2, F, d)$. If $S$ is a set, we denote its complement by $S^c$, and for every two sets $A$, $B$, $A + B = \{a + b : a \in A, b \in B\}$.

Finally, throughout this article all absolute constants are denoted by $c$, $C$ or $K$. Their values may change from line to line, or even within the same line.

## 2    Random Subclass Bounds

For every integer $n$, let $F_n$ denote a set-valued function which assigns to each $x \in \Omega^n$ a subset of $F$. The quantity we want to bound in the sequel is the probability

$$Pr_X \left\{ \sup_{f \in F_n(\sigma_n)} \left| \mathbb{E}_\mu f - \frac{1}{n} \sum_{i=1}^n f(X_i) \right| \ge t \right\}, \tag{3}$$

where $\sigma_n = (X_1, ..., X_n)$ is a random sample.

In the context of classical Statistical Learning Theory, $F_n(\sigma_n) = F$, which means one provides a worst-case bound on the generalization error which holds uniformly over the entire hypothesis class. As a matter of fact, the goal is $F_n(\sigma_n)$ to be the singleton containing the loss of the function produced by a specific learning algorithm from $\sigma_n$. For example, for support vector machines this function could be the loss of a maximum margin hyperplane. Another example, which is useful in the case of noisy data, is the set of all the losses of hyperplanes having a margin which differs by at most $\epsilon$ from the margin of the maximal margin hyperplane.

### 2.1    Symmetrization

The main result we present in this section, Theorem 3, is a random symmetrization claim which will enable us to bound the quantity in equation (3) in terms of Rademacher sums associated with sets of coordinate projections. Using the same line of thought as in the original proof of the Glivenko-Cantelli case, we employ a symmetrization procedure in two steps: a symmetrization by a ghost sample which relates the deviation of the mean from the empirical mean by the deviation of the empirical means evaluated on two different samples; and a symmetrization by signs which relates the latter deviation to the probability of having "large" Rademacher sums.

Variations on the first symmetrization step were stated and proved in [4, 6, 11]. The second symmetrization step requires an additional property of the random subclass, namely, that it is invariant under permutations of the sample. Therefore, let $F_n^{\text{sym}}$ be a set-valued map from $\Omega^n$ to subsets of $F$, such that for every $\sigma_n \in \Omega^n$ and every permutation $\pi(\sigma_n)$ of $\sigma_n$, $F_n^{\text{sym}}(\sigma_n) = F_n^{\text{sym}}(\pi(\sigma_n))$. In this case we say that $F_n^{\text{sym}}$ is *symmetric*.

**Lemma 1 (Symmetrization by a Ghost Sample)** *For   any   probability measure $\mu$ and every $t > 0$,*

$$\left(1 - \frac{4n}{t^2} \sup_{f \in F} \text{var}(f)\right) Pr_X \left\{ \exists f \in F_n(\sigma_n), \left| \sum_{i=1}^{n} (f(X_i) - \mathbb{E}_\mu f) \right| \geq t \right\}$$

$$\leq Pr_{X \times Y} \left\{ \exists f \in F_n(\sigma_n), \left| \sum_{i=1}^{n} (f(X_i) - f(Y_i)) \right| \geq \frac{t}{2} \right\},$$

*where $\sigma_n = (X_1, ..., X_n)$ and $(Y_1, ..., Y_n)$ is an independent copy of $\sigma_n$.*

*Proof.* A complete proof can be found in [11].

**Lemma 2 (Symmetrization by Random Signs)** *Let $F_{2n}^{sym}$ be a symmetric map. Then, for any probability measure $\mu$ and every $t > 0$,*

$$Pr_{X \times Y} \left\{ \exists f \in F_{2n}^{sym}(\sigma_n, \tau_n), \left| \frac{1}{n} \sum_{i=1}^{n} (f(X_i) - f(Y_i)) \right| \geq t \right\}$$

$$\leq 2 Pr_{X \times Y} Pr_\varepsilon \left\{ \exists f \in F_{2n}^{sym}(\sigma_n, \tau_n), \left| \sum_{i=1}^{n} \varepsilon_i f(X_i) \right| \geq \frac{nt}{2} \right\},$$

*where $\sigma_n = (X_1, ..., X_n)$, $\tau_n = (Y_1, ..., Y_n)$, and $(\varepsilon_i)_{i=1}^n$ are independent Rademacher variables.*

*Proof.* By the symmetry of $F_{2n}^{\text{sym}}$ it follows that for every $\{\varepsilon_1, ..., \varepsilon_n\} \in \{-1, 1\}^n$,

$$Pr_{X \times Y} \left\{ \exists f \in F_{2n}^{\text{sym}}(\sigma_n, \tau_n), \left| \frac{1}{n} \sum_{i=1}^{n} (f(X_i) - f(Y_i)) \right| \geq t \right\}$$

$$= Pr_{X \times Y} \left\{ \exists f \in F_{2n}^{\text{sym}}(\sigma_n, \tau_n), \left| \frac{1}{n} \sum_{i=1}^{n} \varepsilon_i (f(X_i) - f(Y_i)) \right| \geq t \right\}.$$

Taking the expectation with respect to the random signs (that is, with respect to the Rademacher random variables), the proof follows from the triangle inequality and the fact that $(X_1, ..., X_n)$ has the same distribution as $(Y_1, ..., Y_n)$.

In order to relate the two symmetrization results, we use the following assumption on the functions $F_n$ and $F_n^{\text{sym}}$:

**Assumption 1** *There exists a constant $\delta > 0$ such that for every $t > 0$,*

$$Pr_{X \times Y}\left\{\exists f \in F_n(\sigma_n), \left|\frac{1}{n}\sum_{i=1}^{n}(f(X_i) - f(Y_i))\right| \geq t\right\} \leq$$

$$Pr_{X \times Y}\left\{\exists f \in F_{2n}^{sym}(\sigma_n, \tau_n), \left|\frac{1}{n}\sum_{i=1}^{n}(f(X_i) - f(Y_i))\right| \geq t\right\} + \delta, \quad (4)$$

*where $\sigma_n = (X_1, ..., X_n)$ and $\tau_n = (Y_1, ..., Y_n)$.*

This assumption holds trivially with a constant $\delta = 0$ if for every double-sample $(\sigma_n, \tau_n)$, $F_n(\sigma_n) \subseteq F_{2n}^{sym}(\sigma_n, \tau_n)$. An extreme case occurs when both set-valued maps are the constant function, $F_n(\sigma_n) = F_n^{sym}(\sigma_n) = F$.

Given $F_n$, one can always define a mapping $F_{2n}^{sym}$ to satisfy Assumption 1 as the symmetric extension of $F_n$, that is, for every double-sample $(\sigma_n, \tau_n)$, $F_{2n}^{sym}(\sigma_n, \tau_n)$ is defined to be the union of all subsets corresponding to the first half of permutations of the double-sample $(\sigma_n, \tau_n)$,

$$F_{2n}^{sym}(\sigma_n, \tau_n) := \bigcup_{\pi \in S_{2n}} F_n\left(\pi(\sigma_n, \tau_n)|_{i=1}^{n}\right). \quad (5)$$

In general, the assumption quantifies that by replacing the original random subset of hypotheses with another symmetric random subset dependent on the double-sample – and which is therefore invariant under permutations of this double-sample – the probability of having large deviations of empirical means evaluated on the sample and ghost sample increases by at most $\delta$. This allows us to replace the original subset $F_n(\sigma_n)$ even with a potentially "smaller" symmetric subset $F_{2n}^{sym}(\sigma_n, \tau_n)$ as long as the change in probabilities can be controlled. This is exactly the idea in the luckiness and algorithmic luckiness frameworks, where the $\omega$-condition ensures both a small symmetric set and that this probability doesn't increase "too much".

By combining Lemma 1, Assumption 1 and Lemma 2, the symmetrization theorem follows directly:

**Theorem 3** *If Assumption 1 holds then for every $t > 0$,*

$$\left(1 - \frac{4}{nt^2}\sup_{f \in F}\text{var}(f)\right) \cdot Pr_X\left\{\exists f \in F_n(\sigma_n), \left|\mathbb{E}_\mu f - \frac{1}{n}\sum_{i=1}^{n}f(X_i)\right| \geq t\right\}$$

$$\leq 2Pr_{X \times Y}Pr_\varepsilon\left\{\exists f \in F_{2n}^{sym}(\sigma_n, \tau_n), \left|\sum_{i=1}^{n}\varepsilon_i f(X_i)\right| \geq \frac{nt}{4}\right\} + 2\delta, \quad (6)$$

*where $\sigma_n = (X_1, ..., X_n)$ and $\tau_n = (Y_1, ..., Y_n)$.*

As the examples we present in section 3 show, most of the standard methods used in Learning Theory fall within the general framework of Theorem 3. The advantage of Theorem 3 is that it reduces the analysis of (3) to a geometric problem, namely, estimating the Rademacher sums associated with the coordinate projection onto $\sigma_n = (X_1, ..., X_n)$ of the random class $F_{2n}^{\mathrm{sym}}(\sigma_n, \tau_n)$,

$$F_{2n}^{\mathrm{sym}}(\sigma_n, \tau_n)/\sigma_n := \left\{ \left( f(X_1), ..., f(X_n) \right) : f \in F_{2n}^{\mathrm{sym}}(\sigma_n, \tau_n) \right\}.$$

For a fixed $(\sigma_n, \tau_n)$ and by employing concentration inequalities for the random variable

$$Z = \sup_{f \in F_{2n}^{\mathrm{sym}}(\sigma_n, \tau_n)} \left| \sum_{i=1}^{n} \varepsilon_i f(X_i) \right| = \sup_{v \in F_{2n}^{\mathrm{sym}}(\sigma_n, \tau_n)/\sigma_n} \left| \sum_{i=1}^{n} \varepsilon_i v_i \right|$$

around its conditional mean $\mathbb{E}_\varepsilon (Z | X_1, ..., X_n, Y_1, ..., Y_n)$, the probability of having large Rademacher sums can be related to the probability of having large Rademacher averages associated with $F_{2n}^{\mathrm{sym}}(\sigma_n, \tau_n)/\sigma_n$.

## 2.2   Concentration Result

In this section we state one particular concentration result which will be used in the next section. Note that for every set $V \subset B_\infty^n$ and by setting $h(\varepsilon_1, ..., \varepsilon_n) := \sup_{v \in V} \left| \sum_{i=1}^{n} \varepsilon_i v_i \right|$, it follows by the triangle inequality that $\forall i \in \{1, ..., n\}$,

$$\sup_{\{\varepsilon_1, ..., \varepsilon_n, \tilde{\varepsilon}_i\}} \left| h(\varepsilon_1, ..., \varepsilon_n) - h(\varepsilon_1, ..., \varepsilon_{i-1}, \tilde{\varepsilon}_i, \varepsilon_{i+1}, ..., \varepsilon_n) \right| \leq 2.$$

Thus, by McDiarmid's inequality [12], for every $t > 0$,

$$Pr_\varepsilon \left\{ \sup_{v \in V} \left| \sum_{i=1}^{n} \varepsilon_i v_i \right| - \mathbb{E}_\varepsilon \sup_{v \in V} \left| \sum_{i=1}^{n} \varepsilon_i v_i \right| > t \right\} \leq e^{-\frac{t^2}{2n}}. \tag{7}$$

**Corollary 4** *If Assumption 1 holds, then for every $t > 0$*

$$\left( 1 - \frac{4}{nt^2} \sup_{f \in F} \mathrm{var}(f) \right) \cdot Pr_X \left\{ \exists f \in F_n(\sigma_n), \left| \mathbb{E}_\mu f - \frac{1}{n} \sum_{i=1}^{n} f(X_i) \right| \geq t \right\}$$

$$\leq 2 \left( Pr_{X \times Y} \{A_t^c\} + e^{-\frac{nt^2}{128}} \right) + 2\delta,$$

*with $V = F_{2n}^{\mathrm{sym}}(\sigma_n, \tau_n)/\sigma_n$ and $A_t = \{(\sigma_n, \tau_n) : \mathbb{E}_\varepsilon \sup_{v \in V} \left| \sum_{i=1}^{n} \varepsilon_i v_i \right| \leq nt/8 \}$.*

*Proof.* Since equation (7) implies that

$$Pr_{X \times Y} Pr_\varepsilon \left\{ \exists f \in F_{2n}^{\mathrm{sym}}(\sigma_n, \tau_n), \left| \sum_{i=1}^{n} \varepsilon_i f(X_i) \right| > \frac{nt}{4} \right\} \leq Pr_{X \times Y}(A_t^c) + e^{-\frac{nt^2}{128}},$$

the proof follows directly by Theorem 3.

As we see from this corollary, Assumption 1 is sufficient to guarantee a generalization bound with tails of order $e^{-cnt^2}$ for a learning algorithm drawing its hypotheses from the random set $F_n(\sigma_n)$, as soon as the Rademacher averages of the projection of $F_{2n}^{\mathrm{sym}}(\sigma_n, \tau_n)$ onto $\sigma_n$ are "small" with high probability.

## 3    Examples

In the previous section we have proved that, in order to obtain tail estimates of the order of $e^{-cnt^2}$ over random subsets $F_n(\sigma_n)$, it is sufficient to find symmetric random subsets $F_{2n}^{\mathrm{sym}}(\sigma_n, \tau_n)$ which satisfy Assumption 1 and for which the probability

$$Pr_{X \times Y}\left\{\mathbb{E}_\varepsilon\left(\sup_{f \in F_{2n}^{\mathrm{sym}}(\sigma_n, \tau_n)} \Big|\sum_{i=1}^n \varepsilon_i f(X_i)\Big| \Big| X_1, ..., X_n, Y_1, ..., Y_n\right) > \frac{nt}{8}\right\},$$

is small.

In this section we will show that many apparently different approaches fall within this framework. In all these examples we will prove that, given the specific maps $F_n$ and $F_{2n}^{\mathrm{sym}}$, for every fixed double-sample $(\sigma_n, \tau_n)$,

$$\mathbb{E}_\varepsilon \sup_{f \in F_{2n}^{\mathrm{sym}}(\sigma_n, \tau_n)} \Big|\sum_{i=1}^n \varepsilon_i f(x_i)\Big|,$$

are sufficiently small (of the order $o(n)$), and thus, one can apply Corollary 4.

### 3.1    Uniform Glivenko-Cantelli Classes

If $F$ is a uniform GC class, one can recover the optimal deviation estimates by selecting the constant functions

$$F_n(\sigma_n) = F_n^{\mathrm{sym}}(\sigma_n) = F.$$

Assumption 1 is therefore satisfied with $\delta = 0$ and

$$F_{2n}^{\mathrm{sym}}(\sigma_n, \tau_n)/\sigma_n = \{(f(X_1), ..., f(X_n)) : f \in F\}$$

for every double-sample $(\sigma_n, \tau_n)$. The fact that these coordinate projections are "small" follows from the characterization of uniform GC classes. A class of uniformly bounded functions is a uniform GC class if and only if $R_n(F) :=$ $\sup_{\{x_1,...,x_n\} \subset \Omega^n} \mathbb{E}_\varepsilon \sup_{f \in F} \big|\sum_{i=1}^n \varepsilon_i f(x_i)\big| = o(n)$ [8], which ensures that the bound obtained from Theorem 3 is nonempty.

In particular, for every $t > 0$ let $n_0$ be such that for every $n \geq n_0$, $R_n(F) \leq nt/8$. Since $F \subset B(L_\infty(\Omega))$ then $\sup_{f \in F} \mathrm{var}(f) \leq 1$, and thus, for $n \geq 8/t^2$, $1 - 4\sup_{f \in F}\mathrm{var}(f)/nt^2 \geq 1/2$. Therefore, by Corollary 4, it follows that for every integer $n > \max\{8/t^2, n_0\}$ and for any probability measure $\mu$,

$$Pr_X\left\{\sup_{f \in F}\Big|\mathbb{E}_\mu f - \frac{1}{n}\sum_{i=1}^n f(X_i)\Big| \geq t\right\} \leq 8e^{-\frac{nt^2}{128}}.$$

In cases where one has a priori estimates on the size of the class (e.g. the shattering dimension or the uniform entropy), one can recover the optimal GC deviation results. For example, if $VC(F) = d$, then $R_n(F) \leq C\sqrt{dn}$ where $C$ is an absolute constant [10]. Similar estimates can be recovered for classes with a polynomial shattering dimension by applying the bounds on $R_n(F)$ from [8].

In [9, 10, 1] it was proved that one can obtain sharper generalization bounds for so-called Bernstein classes of functions which are star-shaped. As was shown in [11], the bound from [9, 10] can be obtained using Theorem 3. Indeed, as in [9, 10] (under mild assumptions on the class $F$)

$$Pr_X\left\{\exists f \in F, \ \frac{1}{n}\sum_{i=1}^n f(X_i) \le t, \ \mathbb{E}_\mu f \ge 2t\right\}$$

$$\le 2Pr_X\left\{\sup_{f \in F, \ \mathbb{E}_\mu f^2 \le t}\left|\mathbb{E}_\mu f - \frac{1}{n}\sum_{i=1}^n f(X_i)\right| \ge t\right\},$$

then by setting $F_n(\sigma_n) = F_{2n}^{\mathrm{sym}}(\sigma_n, \tau_n) := \{f \in F, \ \mathbb{E}_\mu f^2 \le t\}$ and replacing (7) with a sharper concentration result based on Talagrand's convex-distance inequality [11], tail estimates which are of the order of $e^{-cnt}$ (instead of $e^{-cnt^2}$) follow from Theorem 3. Note that this recovers the PAC-bounds in the zero-error case when $\frac{1}{n}\sum_{i=1}^n \hat{f}(X_i) = 0$ and $F$ consists of nonnegative functions [13].

## 3.2 Data-Dependent Class Bounds

In [4, 2] data-dependent class bounds were formulated for sample-dependent hypothesis classes and binary losses, using a similar symmetrization argument to the one presented in section 2.1. $F_{2n}^{\mathrm{sym}}(\sigma_n, \tau_n)$ is defined to be the union of all subsets corresponding to the first half of permutations of the double-sample $(\sigma_n, \tau_n)$,

$$F_{2n}^{\mathrm{sym}}(\sigma_n, \tau_n) := \bigcup_{\pi \in S_{2n}} F_n\big(\pi(\sigma_n, \tau_n)|_{i=1}^n\big).$$

Thus, by construction, $F_{2n}^{\mathrm{sym}}(\sigma_n, \tau_n)$ is symmetric and $F_n(\sigma_n) \subseteq F_{2n}^{\mathrm{sym}}(\sigma_n, \tau_n)$, satisfying Assumption 1 with $\delta = 0$.

In [4], the cardinality of $F_{2n}^{\mathrm{sym}}(\sigma_n, \tau_n)$ is bounded by assumption by a function which is sample-independent and only depends on the sample size $n$, i.e.

$$|F_{2n}^{\mathrm{sym}}(\sigma_n, \tau_n)| \le d(n).$$

We will show that a small $d(n)$ is just a way of guaranteeing that the projection $F_{2n}^{\mathrm{sym}}(\sigma_n, \tau_n)/\sigma_n$ has small Rademacher averages, and therefore, by Corollary 4, one can obtain learnability and generalization bounds in terms of $d(n)$.

Since the class $F$ consists of functions bounded by 1, $V := F_{2n}^{\mathrm{sym}}(\sigma_n, \tau_n)/\sigma_n \subset B_\infty^n \subset \sqrt{n}B_2^n$. For every $V \subset \ell_2^n$, the Rademacher process indexed by $V$ is subgaussian and therefore, by a chaining argument [14], there is an absolute constant $C$ such that

$$\mathbb{E}_\varepsilon \sup_{v \in V}\left|\sum_{i=1}^n \varepsilon_i v_i\right| \le C\int_0^{\sqrt{n}}\sqrt{\log(N(\varepsilon, V, \ell_2^n))}d\varepsilon \le C\sqrt{n}\sqrt{\log(|V|)}.$$

Hence, for any sample $(\sigma_n, \tau_n)$,

$$\mathbb{E}_\varepsilon \sup_{v \in F_{2n}^{\mathrm{sym}}(\sigma_n, \tau_n)/\sigma_n} \left| \sum_{i=1}^n \varepsilon_i v_i \right| \le C \sqrt{\log \left| F_{2n}^{\mathrm{sym}}(\sigma_n, \tau_n)/\sigma_n \right|} \sqrt{n}, \tag{8}$$

and since $|F_{2n}^{\mathrm{sym}}(\sigma_n, \tau_n)/\sigma_n| \le d(n)$ it follows that

$$\mathbb{E}_\varepsilon \sup_{v \in F_{2n}^{\mathrm{sym}}(\sigma_n, \tau_n)/\sigma_n} \left| \sum_{i=1}^n \varepsilon_i v_i \right| \le C \sqrt{n \log(d(n))}.$$

In [2] the "smallness" of $F_{2n}^{\mathrm{sym}}(\sigma_n, \tau_n)$ is ensured by the assumption that the quantity

$$S_{2n/n}(F) := \sup_{(\sigma_n, \tau_n)} \left| \{ (f(X_1), ..., f(X_n), f(Y_1), ..., f(Y_n)) : f \in F_{2n}^{\mathrm{sym}}(\sigma_n, \tau_n) \} \right|$$

is small. Obviously, $|F_{2n}^{\mathrm{sym}}(\sigma_n, \tau_n)/\sigma_n| \le S_{2n/n}(F)$, implying once again, using (8), that

$$\mathbb{E}_\varepsilon \sup_{v \in F_{2n}^{\mathrm{sym}}(\sigma_n, \tau_n)/\sigma_n} \left| \sum_{i=1}^n \varepsilon_i v_i \right| \le C \sqrt{n \log(S_{2n/n})},$$

where $C$ is an absolute constant.

## 3.3    Compression Schemes

In [7, 3] generalization bounds are formulated for a particular class of learning algorithms called compression schemes, which can reconstruct the hypothesis produced from a given training sample using only a small "compressed" subset of it. We denote by $\mathcal{C}(\zeta)$ the size of the smallest compressed sample by which the compression scheme algorithm $\mathcal{A}$, when presented with the training sample $\zeta$, can reconstruct its hypothesis. A sample compression scheme of size at most $\mathcal{K}$ is one for which $\mathcal{C}(\zeta) \le \mathcal{K}$ for every sample $\zeta$.

Let $\mathcal{A}(\sigma_n)$ be the loss of the function produced by the algorithm from a training sample $\sigma_n$. We set $F_n(\sigma_n) := \{\mathcal{A}(\sigma_n)\}$ and let $F_{2n}^{\mathrm{sym}}(\sigma_n, \tau_n)$ be the set of all losses of functions learned by the algorithm from the first half of all permutations of a double sample $(\sigma_n, \tau_n)$,

$$F_{2n}^{\mathrm{sym}}(\sigma_n, \tau_n) := \left\{ \mathcal{A}(\pi(\sigma_n, \tau_n)|_{i=1}^n) : \pi \in S_{2n} \right\}.$$

As before, Assumption 1 is satisfied with $\delta = 0$.

We will show that a small compression size $\mathcal{K}$ guarantees that $F_{2n}^{\mathrm{sym}}(\sigma_n, \tau_n)/\sigma_n$ has small Rademacher averages, and thus, Corollary 4 implies learnability and recovers the results of [7, 3]. Indeed, the number of functions in $F_{2n}^{\mathrm{sym}}(\sigma_n, \tau_n)$ is upper bounded by the maximal number of functions which can be reproduced from a training sample of size at most $\mathcal{K}$. For binary losses taking values only in $\{-1, 1\}$, the number of functions which can be reproduced from a sample of size $i$ is less than $2^i$, and so $|F_{2n}^{\text{sym}}(\sigma_n, \tau_n)| \leq \sum_{i=0}^{\mathcal{K}} 2^i = 2^{\mathcal{K}+1} - 1$. From equation (8),

$$\mathbb{E}_\varepsilon \sup_{v \in F_{2n}^{\text{sym}}(\sigma_n, \tau_n)/\sigma_n} \left| \sum_{i=1}^n \varepsilon_i v_i \right| \leq C\sqrt{\mathcal{K}n},$$

where $C$ is an absolute constant.

## 3.4   Luckiness and Algorithmic Luckiness

In the luckiness framework introduced in [13], bounds on the generalization error of functions are formulated a-posteriori, after having seen a sample $\sigma_n$. The bounds are given in terms of an upper bound on some empirical, computable quantity dependent on the sample.

In the algorithmic luckiness framework [6], the generalization error bound is similarly formulated a-posteriori. It differs from the luckiness framework because it gives bounds on the generalization error only of the function learned by the learning algorithm from the sample at hand. Again, the bound is given in terms of a computable quantity dependent on the sample and on the algorithm.

In both frameworks, an (algorithmic) luckiness function and an $\omega$-function are introduced in order to define the functions $F_n$ and $F_{2n}^{\text{sym}}$. The functions $L$ and $\omega$ satisfy a joint smallness condition which, as we will show, ensures that Assumption 1 holds, and that the "size" of the projection $F_{2n}^{\text{sym}}(\sigma_n, \tau_n)/\sigma_n$ is sufficiently small. Whereas in the previous examples the notion of "size" was a trivial one, that of cardinality, in the luckiness frameworks it is slightly more refined. The notion of size employed in the luckiness frameworks is that of covering numbers, and we prove that, again, it implies that the Rademacher averages of a random coordinate projection are small. We will present the proof of the result only in the algorithmic luckiness case. A similar proof for the luckiness can be found in [11].

In the following, let $n$ be a fixed sample size, $d$ is a given fixed integer, and set $\delta \in (0, 1]$. Recall that $F$ is a loss function class. Denote by $\mathcal{A}$ a fixed learning algorithm, by $\mathcal{A}(\zeta)$ the loss of the function produced by the algorithm from the sample $\zeta$, and set $\mathcal{A}(F) = \{f = \mathcal{A}(\zeta) : \zeta \in \Omega^n\}$.

Three concepts are used in the algorithmic luckiness framework: The first is the algorithmic luckiness function which is a function $L : \mathcal{A}(F) \longrightarrow \mathbb{R}$. Using the algorithmic luckiness function one can construct sample dependent subsets of $F$, called *lucky sets* in the following manner: for every sample $\zeta$ of size $2n$, the *lucky set* $G(\zeta)$ is defined as the subset of losses of functions learned by the algorithm on the first half of the sample, when permuting the whole sample, as long as the function the algorithm produced on the first half of the permuted sample is "luckier" than on the original one. Formally, define the lucky set as

$$G(\zeta) := \left\{ \mathcal{A}(\pi(\zeta)|_{i=1}^n) : L(\mathcal{A}(\pi(\zeta)|_{i=1}^n)) \geq L(\mathcal{A}(\zeta|_{i=1}^n)), \ \pi \in S_{2n} \right\}. \quad (9)$$

If $G_{\mathcal{A}}(\zeta)$ is the subset of losses corresponding to functions learned by $\mathcal{A}$ on the first half of all the permutations of the double-sample $\zeta$, then $G(\zeta) \subset G_{\mathcal{A}}(\zeta)$, and clearly, $|G_{\mathcal{A}}(\zeta)| \leq (2n)! < \infty$. Therefore, we can order the functions in $G_{\mathcal{A}}(\zeta)$ in decreasing order according to their luckiness. Define the ordered set

$$G_{\mathcal{A}}(\zeta) := \underbrace{\left[f_1, f_2, f_3, \ldots, f_{k-1}, f_k, f_{k+1}, \ldots, f_m\right]}_{G(\zeta)}, \qquad (10)$$

and for the sake of simplicity, assume that for every $i < j$, $L(f_i) > L(f_j)$. Only a small modification is required in the general case, where some functions might have the same luckiness.

Set $f_k = \mathcal{A}(\zeta|_{i=1}^n)$ and let $G_{\mathcal{A}}^\ell(\zeta)$ be the subset consisting of the first $\ell$ functions in $G_{\mathcal{A}}(\zeta)$, i.e. $G_{\mathcal{A}}^\ell(\zeta) = \{f_1, f_2, f_3, \ldots, f_\ell\}$. For the given integer $d$ and the double-sample $(\sigma_n, \tau_n)$ put $k^*$ to be the largest integer such that

$$D\left(\tfrac{1}{n}, G_{\mathcal{A}}^{k^*}((\sigma_n, \tau_n)), L_1(\mu_{2n})\right) \leq 2^d \text{ and } D\left(\tfrac{1}{n}, G_{\mathcal{A}}^{k^*+1}((\sigma_n, \tau_n)), L_1(\mu_{2n})\right) > 2^d.$$

Then, by setting

$$F_{2n}^{\mathrm{sym}}(\sigma_n, \tau_n) := G_{\mathcal{A}}^{k^*}((\sigma_n, \tau_n)) \qquad (12)$$

it follows that $F_{2n}^{\mathrm{sym}}$ is symmetric, since the learning algorithm is permutation invariant.

The second ingredient, the $\omega$-function, $\omega : \mathbb{R} \times \mathbb{N} \times (0, 1] \longrightarrow \mathbb{N}$ is used to define $F_n(\sigma_n)$. Indeed, define

$$F_n(\sigma_n) := \begin{cases} \{\mathcal{A}(\sigma_n)\} & \text{if } \omega\big(L(\mathcal{A}(\sigma_n)), n, \delta\big) \leq 2^d \\ \emptyset & \text{otherwise,} \end{cases} \qquad (13)$$

and note that $|F_n(\sigma_n)| \leq 1$.

The third ingredient is the $\omega$-smallness condition, which is a joint property of the algorithmic luckiness and $\omega$ functions. It states that for every integer $n$, every $\delta \in (0, 1]$, and every probability measure $\mu$,

$$Pr_{X \times Y}\left\{D\left(\tfrac{1}{n}, G((\sigma_n, \tau_n)), L_1(\mu_{2n})\right) \geq \omega\big(L(\mathcal{A}(\sigma_n)), n, \delta\big)\right\} < \delta. \qquad (14)$$

The following result shows that the $\omega$-smallness of $L$ ensures that Assumption 1 holds, and that, with high probability, $F_{2n}^{\mathrm{sym}}(\sigma_n, \tau_n)/\sigma_n$ is sufficiently small.

**Lemma 5** *Let $\mathcal{A}$ be a learning algorithm, fix an integer $d$ and some $\delta \in (0, 1]$, and let $F_n$ and $F_{2n}^{\mathrm{sym}}$ be as in (13) and (12). If an algorithmic luckiness function $L$ and an $\omega$-function satisfy the $\omega$-smallness condition (14), then for every $t > 0$*

$$Pr_{X \times Y}\left\{\exists f \in F_n(\sigma_n) : \left|\frac{1}{n}\sum_{i=1}^n (f(X_i) - f(Y_i))\right| \geq t\right\}$$

$$\leq Pr_{X \times Y}\left\{\exists f \in F_{2n}^{\mathrm{sym}}(\sigma_n, \tau_n) : \left|\frac{1}{n}\sum_{i=1}^n (f(X_i) - f(Y_i))\right| \geq t\right\} + \delta.$$

*Proof.* For every double sample $\zeta = (\sigma_n, \tau_n)$, let $\mu_{2n}$ be the empirical measure supported on $(\sigma_n, \tau_n)$ and define two random sets in the following manner. Let $A_\zeta := \{A(\sigma_n)\}$ if $D(\frac{1}{n}, G((\sigma_n, \tau_n)), L_1(\mu_{2n})) < \omega(L(A(\sigma_n)), n, \delta)$ and the empty set otherwise, and put $B_\zeta := \{A(\sigma_n)\}$ if $D(\frac{1}{n}, G((\sigma_n, \tau_n)), L_1(\mu_{2n})) \leq 2^d$ and the empty set otherwise. Note that for every $\zeta$, $F_n(\sigma_n) \cap A_\zeta \subset B_\zeta \subset F_{2n}^{\text{sym}}(\sigma_n, \tau_n)$. Moreover, if $F_n(\sigma_n) \cap (A_\zeta)^c \neq \emptyset$, then $F_n(\sigma_n) = \{A(\sigma_n)\}$ and $A_\zeta = \emptyset$. Thus, by the $\omega$-smallness condition,

$$Pr_{X \times Y}\Big\{ F_n(\sigma_n) \cap (A_\zeta)^c \neq \emptyset \Big\} \leq Pr_{X \times Y}\Big\{ A_\zeta = \emptyset \Big\} < \delta.$$

The claim of the lemma follows now directly from the union bound for the disjoint sets $F_n(\sigma_n) \cap A_\zeta$ and $F_n(\sigma_n) \cap (A_\zeta)^c$.

Now, we are ready to formulate the generalization bound for the algorithmic luckiness framework which recovers the main result of [6]. The main part of the proof is to show that the definition of $F_{2n}^{\text{sym}}(\sigma_n, \tau_n)$ ensures that the covering numbers and therefore the Rademacher averages of $F_{2n}^{\text{sym}}(\sigma_n, \tau_n)$ are small.

**Theorem 6** *Let $A$ be a learning algorithm which takes values in $B(L_\infty(\Omega))$, and let $L$ and $\omega$ be functions satisfying the $\omega$-smallness condition (14). Then, for every probability measure $\mu$, every $d \in \mathbb{N}$ and every $\delta \in (0, 1]$, there is a set of probability at least $1 - 12\delta$ such that if $\omega(L(A(\sigma_n)), n, \delta) \leq 2^d$, then*

$$\Big| \mathbb{E}_\mu(A(\sigma_n)) - \mathbb{E}_{\mu_n}(A(\sigma_n)) \Big| \leq C\sqrt{\frac{d}{n} \log \frac{1}{\delta}},$$

*where $C$ is an absolute constant.*

*Proof.* Let $F_n$ and $F_{2n}^{\text{sym}}$ be defined as above, and observe that

$$D(\tfrac{1}{n}, F_{2n}^{\text{sym}}(\sigma_n, \tau_n), L_1(\mu_{2n})) \leq 2^d \qquad (15)$$

for every $(\sigma_n, \tau_n)$. Let $V := F_{2n}^{\text{sym}}(\sigma_n, \tau_n)/\sigma_n \subset \ell_2^n$, put $\mu_{2n}$ to be the empirical measure supported on $\zeta = (\sigma_n, \tau_n)$, and set $\nu_n$ to be the empirical measure supported on $\sigma_n$. Note that for every $f, g$, $\mathbb{E}_{\mu_{2n}}|f - g| \geq \mathbb{E}_{\nu_n}|f - g|/2$. Thus, every $1/n$-cover of $F_{2n}^{\text{sym}}(\sigma_n, \tau_n)$ in $L_1(\mu_{2n})$ is a $2/n$-cover of the same set in $L_1(\nu_n)$. In particular, if $A$ is a maximal $1/n$-packing of $F_{2n}^{\text{sym}}(\sigma_n, \tau_n)$ in $L_1(\mu_{2n})$, it is a $2/n$ cover of that set in $L_1(\nu_n)$. It is easy to verify that $B(L_1(\nu_n)) = nB_1^n$, and in particular, $V \subset A + \frac{2}{n} \cdot nB_1^n = A + 2B_1^n$, and by the triangle inequality,

$$\mathbb{E}_\varepsilon \sup_{v \in V} \Big| \sum_{i=1}^n \varepsilon_i v_i \Big| \leq \mathbb{E}_\varepsilon \sup_{a \in A} \Big| \sum_{i=1}^n \varepsilon_i a_i \Big| + 2\mathbb{E}_\varepsilon \sup_{b \in B_1^n} \Big| \sum_{i=1}^n \varepsilon_i b_i \Big|.$$

By equation (8) and because $|A| \leq 2^d$ by (15), the first term can be bounded by $\mathbb{E}_\varepsilon \sup_{a \in A} \Big| \sum_{i=1}^n \varepsilon_i a_i \Big| \leq C\sqrt{\log |A|}\sqrt{n} \leq C\sqrt{nd}$. For the second term, one can apply the triangle inequality to show that $\mathbb{E}_\varepsilon \sup_{b\in B_1^n}\left|\sum_{i=1}^n \varepsilon_i b_i\right| \le 1$. Therefore,

$$\mathbb{E}_\varepsilon \sup_{f\in F_{2n}^{\mathrm{sym}}(\sigma_n,\tau_n)}\left|\sum_{i=1}^n \varepsilon_i f(x_i)\right| \le C\sqrt{nd}.$$

To complete the proof, apply Corollary 4 for $t = C\sqrt{\frac{d}{n}\log(1/\delta)}$.

**Sparsity Luckiness.** An application of the algorithmic luckiness approach is a data dependent version of compression schemes, known as the sparsity luckiness [6, 5]. Using our framework, it is possible to recover the data-dependent compression bounds in terms of the data-dependent compression size $\mathcal{C}(\zeta)$, where $C(\zeta)$ denotes the size of the smallest compressed sub-sample by which the compression scheme algorithm $\mathcal{A}$ can reconstruct the hypothesis when presented with the training sample $\zeta$.

We define the sparsity luckiness function to be $L(\mathcal{A}(\zeta)) = -\mathcal{C}(\zeta)$. Then, by (9), for every sample $\sigma_n$, the sparsity lucky set for a double sample $(\sigma_n,\tau_n)$ consists of at most the functions corresponding to all different compressed sub-samples of size smaller or equal to $\mathcal{C}(\sigma_n)$,

$$G((\sigma_n,\tau_n)) = \left\{\mathcal{A}(\pi(\sigma_n,\tau_n)|_{i=1}^n) : \mathcal{C}(\pi(\sigma_n,\tau_n)|_{i=1}^n) \le \mathcal{C}(\sigma_n), \ \pi\in S_{2n}\right\}.$$

Since the number of different subsamples of $(\sigma_n,\tau_n)$ of size at most $\mathcal{C}(\sigma_n)$ is $\sum_{i=0}^{\mathcal{C}(\sigma_n)}\binom{2n}{i}$, it follows that

$$|G((\sigma_n,\tau_n))| \le \sum_{i=0}^{\mathcal{C}(\sigma_n)}\binom{2n}{i}.$$

We define $F_{2n}^{\mathrm{sym}}$ to be

$$F_{2n}^{\mathrm{sym}}(\sigma_n,\tau_n) := G_{\mathcal{A}}^{k^*}((\sigma_n,\tau_n)),$$

where $k^*$ is defined as the largest integer such that $k^* \le \log_2\left(\sum_{i=0}^{\mathcal{C}(\sigma_n)}\binom{2n}{i}\right)$, and $G_{\mathcal{A}}^{k^*}((\sigma_n,\tau_n))$ is the subset consisting of the first $k^*$ functions in $G_{\mathcal{A}}(\sigma_n,\tau_n)$ defined as in (10). Then, if $n \ge \mathcal{C}(\sigma_n)$

$$|F_{2n}^{\mathrm{sym}}(\sigma_n,\tau_n)| \le \left(\frac{2en}{\mathcal{C}(\sigma_n)}\right)^{\mathcal{C}(\sigma_n)}$$

and thus by (8)

$$\mathbb{E}_\varepsilon \sup_{f\in F_{2n}^{\mathrm{sym}}(\sigma_n,\tau_n)}\left|\sum_{i=1}^n \varepsilon_i f(x_i)\right| \le C\sqrt{n\mathcal{C}(\sigma_n)\log\left(\frac{2en}{\mathcal{C}(\sigma_n)}\right)},$$

where $C$ is an absolute constant.

# References

1. P.L. Bartlett, O. Bousquet, S. Mendelson: Local Rademacher Complexities, preprint.
2. A.H. Cannon, J.M. Ettinger, D.R. Hush, J.C. Scovel: Machine learning with data dependent hypothesis classes, JMLR 2, 335-358, 2002.
3. S. Floyd, M. Warmuth: Sample compression, learnability, and the Vapnik-Chervonenkis dimension, Machine Learning 21(3), 269-304, 1995.
4. Y. Gat: A bound concerning the generalization ability of a certain class of learning algorithms, Tech. Rep. No. 548, Univ. of California, Berkeley, March 1999.
5. T. Graepel, R. Herbrich, J. Shawe-Taylor: Generalisation Error Bounds for Sparse Linear Classifiers, Proc. 13th Annu. Conf. on Comput. Learning Theory, 2000.
6. R. Herbrich, R.C. Williamson: Algorithmic luckiness, JMLR 3, 175-212, 2002.
7. N. Littlestone, M. Warmuth: Relating Data Compression and Learnability, unpublished manuscript, Univ. of California Santa Cruz, 1986.
8. S. Mendelson: Rademacher averages and phase transitions in Glivenko-Cantelli class, IEEE Trans. on Inform. Th., 48(1), 251-263, 2002.
9. S. Mendelson, Improving the sample complexity using global data, IEEE Trans. on Inform. Th. 48(7), 1977-1991, 2002.
10. S. Mendelson: A few notes on Statistical Learning Theory, in *Proc. of the Machine Learning Summer School, Canberra 2002, S. Mendelson and A. Smola (Eds.)*, Lect. Notes in Comp. Sc. 2600, Springer 2003.
11. S. Mendelson, P. Philips: On the importance of small coordinate projections, JMLR, to appear.
12. McDiarmid, C: On the method of bounded differences, in *Surveys in Combinatorics*, London Math. Soc. Lect. Note Series 141, 1989, pp 148–188.
13. J. Shawe-Taylor, P.L. Bartlett, R.C. Williamson, M. Anthony: Structural risk minimization over data-dependent hierarchies, IEEE Trans. on Inform. Th., 44(5), 1926-1940, 1998.
14. M. Talagrand: Majorizing measures: The generic chaining, Ann Probab. 24, 1996, 1049-1103.

# PAC-MDL Bounds

Avrim Blum[1,*] and John Langford[2]

[1] Computer Science Department, Carnegie Mellon University avrim@cs.cmu.edu
[2] IBM, Watson Research Center jcl@cs.cmu.edu

**Abstract.** We point out that a number of standard sample complexity bounds (VC-dimension, PAC-Bayes, and others) are all related to the number of bits required to communicate the labels given the unlabeled data for a natural communication game. Motivated by this observation, we give a general sample complexity bound based on this game that allows us to unify these different bounds in one common framework.

> *One Bound to rule them all, One Bound to find them,*
> *One Bound to bring them all and in the darkness bind them.*
> *–J.R.R. Tolkien (roughly)[1]*

## 1 Introduction

One of the most basic results about learning in the PAC model is the "Occam's razor" theorem [1] that states that if we can explain the labels of a set of $m$ training examples by a hypothesis that can be described using only $k \ll m$ bits, then we can be confident that this hypothesis generalizes well to future data. One way to view this statement is to consider a setting in which two players Alice and Bob are each given the $m$ examples, but only Alice is given the $m$ labels, and Alice must communicate these labels to Bob. In this case, the result tells us that compression implies learning *for the description language of hypotheses* (that is, Alice communicates the $m$ labels by sending a hypothesis $h$ to Bob, and Bob then reconstitutes the labels by evaluating $h$ on each example).

What if we allow more general procedures for label transmission? In particular, a label transmission procedure is simply an agreement on how a string of bits $\sigma$, together with a list of $m$ unlabeled examples, should produce a list of $m$ labels. Instead of being a function from $X$ to $Y$ (which is then run $m$ times by the receiver), in general, a compressed string could represent any function from $X^m$ to $Y^m$.

We start by pointing out that a number of standard sample complexity bounds can be viewed as stating that "compression implies learning" for different description languages in the above game. Motivated by this observation,

---

* This work is supported in part by NSF grants CCR-0105488 and NSF-ITR CCR-0122581.

[1] This quote is intended to describe the motivation for this line of work rather than our current state — our hope here is to have made some progress in this direction.

B. Schölkopf and M.K. Warmuth (Eds.): COLT/Kernel 2003, LNAI 2777, pp. 344–357, 2003.
© Springer-Verlag Berlin Heidelberg 2003

we give a general bound showing that for any description language, if Alice can communicate the labels of the training data in a small number of bits, then Alice can be confident in her ability to predict well on new data (see Section 2 for a formal description). We then show how this statement allows us to derive these other bounds as special cases. In particular, besides the Occam's razor bound, the standard bounds we consider include:

1. The PAC-Bayes bound [7], which states for any "prior" $P(c)$ and any "posterior" $Q(c)$, a bound on the true error rate of a stochastic classifier as a function of the KL divergence between $P$ and $Q$.
2. The VC bound [8] (of which there are many variants), which states that any classifier chosen from a class of VC dimension $d$ (or a fixed covering number, or a VC entropy) has a true error bound related to $d$.
3. The Compression bound [6][3], which states that any classifier learned using only a small subset of the training examples has a true error bound related to performance on unused examples[2].

## 1.1   Viewing Sample Complexity Bounds as Label Compression

Consider the case of VC-dimension. Suppose Alice and Bob agree on a hypothesis class $H$ of VC-dimension $d$, and Alice is able to find a hypothesis in $H$ that is consistent with the training data. This means that in the above communication game, Alice can send the labels to Bob using only $O(d \log m)$ bits. That is because $H$ makes only $O(m^d)$ different partitions of the data and, since Bob has the unlabeled sample, Alice can just send the index of the appropriate one in some canonical ordering[3]. For Structural Risk-Minimization, in which a set of nested hypothesis classes are used, Alice first uses $O(\log d)$ bits to send the hypothesis class, a low-order additive term. Thus, the statement that we can have confidence in consistent hypotheses from a class of low VC-dimension can be thought of as an instantiation of the statement that label compression implies learning, for this particular transmission language. In fact, not surprisingly, the proof for this generalized form of Occam's razor involves a similar random-partitioning trick as used in the standard proof of VC-dimension bounds. The bound also works for lossy compression, so we can recover the VC guarantees in the unrealizable case as well.

As another example, consider PAC-Bayes bounds (the realizable case for simplicity). In this case, instead of agreeing on a hypothesis *class*, Alice and Bob agree in advance on a "prior" $P(c)$ over hypotheses. Notice, now, that given any list of $m$ unlabeled examples $x^m = (x_1, \ldots, x_m)$, this prior on hypotheses induces

---

[2] Unlike the other bounds considered we can not, quite, reproduce the Compression bound with our results.

[3] One might be concerned that the *computational* task of finding the index of this partition could be quite expensive. But since this is just for the purpose of a sample-complexity bound that depends on the number of bits transmitted, Alice does not need to actually produce this index so long as she knows an upper bound on its length.

a prior over labelings $P(y^m) = \sum_{c:c(x_1)=y_1,c(x_2)=y_2,...,c(x_m)=y_m} P(c)$. This means that any particular labeling $y^m$ can be described in roughly $\log(1/P(y^m))$ bits. Thus, if the data is such that the "version space" of consistent classifiers has high total probability mass under $P$ (i.e., $P(y^m)$ is large), then this labeling can be transmitted in a small number of bits.

## 1.2   Stating a PAC-MDL Bound

Our goal, then, is to state a kind of Occam's razor bound, which we call a PAC-MDL bound, that holds for this general communication game. One technical "detail" we need to address in order to give such a bound is a method for interpreting an arbitrary compression procedure as a way of predicting on new examples. In particular, even though the string $\sigma$ is a function from $X^m$ to $Y^m$, it is not necessarily in itself a good prediction rule on new data. For example, in the "VC-dimension language" considered above, Alice might send to Bob a string indicating that she is using the 57th linear separator in some canonical ordering — but on some new data set, the 57th linear separator might look totally different depending on how this canonical ordering is defined and perform very badly.

To address this issue without introducing a lot of excess baggage, we define the bound in a transductive setting. In particular, we assume that Alice is given both a set of labeled training data and a set of unlabeled test data. Bob has the all the data without labels, given in some canonical order (e.g., lexicographic) so that he does not know which are training examples and which are test examples. Alice is required to send a string that uncompresses to a labeling on the entire data set. The conclusion is that if this string is small and uncompresses to a labeling with low error on the training set, then Alice can be confident in the labels it yields on the test set.

Working in the transductive setting somewhat complicates arguments like those above for viewing standard bounds in the context of label compression. The VC-dimension case does not change by much: if there are $m$ training examples and $n$ test examples, then Alice sends $O(d \log(m + n))$ bits to transmit the labeling given by some function in the class. However, for the PAC-Bayes language, the different consistent hypotheses may well not agree over the test data. We could just send the shortest string corresponding to a labeling that agrees with the training data, but we use a somewhat different argument in order to get the best bounds.

In Sections 3.1 and 5 we show how these transductive bounds can be used to imply standard *inductive* sample-complexity bounds. The high-level idea of the argument is the same as one that appears in standard VC-dimension arguments. In particular, to take the contrapositive, if there were a significant probability of having a hypothesis with low empirical error but high true error, then there must also be a significant probability of having a hypothesis with low empirical error on the training set and high error on a similarly-sized test set, violating the transductive bounds.

## 2    The Setup

We consider the following compression game between two players Alice and Bob. Alice has available a training set $S_{\text{train}}$ consisting of $m$ labeled examples drawn independently from $D$. Alice also has a test set $S_{\text{test}}$ of $n$ unlabeled examples drawn independently from $D$. Bob has available just the unlabeled versions of the test set and the training set, sorted together in some canonical order (e.g., lexicographic) so that he does not know which are training and which are test examples. Pictorially, the available information is:

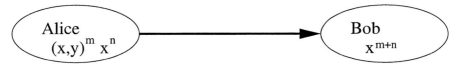

Alice's goal is to communicate labels to Bob using as few bits as possible. Alice encodes with a function $A : (X \times Y)^m \times X^n \to \{0,1\}^*$ and Bob decodes with a function $B : X^{m+n} \times \{0,1\}^* \to Y^{m+n}$. We assume the string $\sigma$ sent is self-terminating, i.e., is given in a prefix-free code. Given any compression/decompression procedure $(A, B)$, we can view the transmitted string $\sigma$ as representing a function $\sigma : X^{m+n} \to Y^{m+n}$. Formally, we define the labeling given by $\sigma$ to be the labeling produced by running $\sigma$ on the $m + n$ examples in sorted order (the order in which Bob has the examples). Thus, we can view the encoded information as something more general than just a hypothesis from $X$ to $Y$.

For a compression algorithm $A$, labeled training set $S_{\text{train}}$ and unlabeled test set $S_{\text{test}}$, the output $\sigma = A(S_{\text{train}}, S_{\text{test}})$ has a specific number of bits $|\sigma|$ sent to Bob in order to label the training and test sets. Let $y(x)$ be the correct labeling of some example $x$ and $y_\sigma(x)$ be the labeling that Bob computes. We can then define $\hat{e}(\sigma, S_{\text{test}}) = \frac{1}{n} \sum_{x \in S_{\text{test}}} I(y_\sigma(x) \neq y(x))$ to be the rate of errors on the test set of the labeling induced by $\sigma$. Similarly, $\hat{e}(\sigma, S_{\text{train}})$ is the rate of errors on the training set.

## 3    Realizable Case

We begin by considering the realizable case: that is, the setting in which the string $\sigma$ provides a lossless compression of the labels on the training set. We then use our bounds to derive the realizable case of a number of standard sample complexity bounds.

**Theorem 1** *(Realizable PAC-MDL bound) For all description languages (i.e., methods of describing the labels via strings $\sigma$), for all $\delta > 0$:*

$$\mathbf{Pr}_{S \sim D^m, S' \sim D^n} \left( \forall \sigma : \ \hat{e}(\sigma, S) > 0 \ or \ \hat{e}(\sigma, S') \leq \frac{|\sigma| \ln 2 + \ln \frac{1}{\delta}}{n \ln \left(1 + \frac{m}{n}\right)} \right) > 1 - \delta$$

In other words, it is unlikely there will exist a short string $\sigma$ that uncompresses perfectly on the training data and yet has high error on the test set. This statement has a bound which is linear in the description complexity, $|\sigma|$. The exact bound is controlled by the size of the sample set $m$, test set $n$, and the required confidence, $\delta$.

*Proof.* Rather than give a proof from first principles, we simplify our more general Theorem 6 (Section 4) for the realizable case of $\hat{e}(\sigma, S) = 0$, using a prior $P(\sigma) = 2^{-|\sigma|}$. Since the training error is 0 in this setting, Theorem 6 simplifies as:

With probability at least $1 - \delta$, all $\sigma$ with $\hat{e}(\sigma, S) = 0$ satisfy:

$$\frac{\binom{n}{n\hat{e}(\sigma, S')}}{\binom{m+n}{n\hat{e}(\sigma, S')}} \geq 2^{-|\sigma|}\delta$$

$$\Rightarrow \frac{n(n-1)...(n - n\hat{e}(\sigma, S') + 1)}{(m+n)(m+n-1)...(m+n - n\hat{e}(\sigma, S') + 1)} \geq 2^{-|\sigma|}\delta$$

Using the crude approximation: $\frac{n(n-1)...(n-t+1)}{(m+n)(m+n-1)...(m+n-t+1)} \leq \left(\frac{n}{m+n}\right)^t$ we get:

$$\left(\frac{n}{m+n}\right)^{n\hat{e}(\sigma, S')} \geq 2^{-|\sigma|}\delta$$

Taking the ln of both sides, we get:

$$n\hat{e}(\sigma, S') \ln\left(1 + \frac{m}{n}\right) \leq \ln 2^{|\sigma|} + \ln\frac{1}{\delta}$$

$$\Rightarrow \hat{e}(\sigma, S') \leq \frac{\ln 2^{|\sigma|} + \ln\frac{1}{\delta}}{n \ln\left(1 + \frac{m}{n}\right)} \leq \frac{|\sigma| \ln 2 + \ln\frac{1}{\delta}}{n \ln\left(1 + \frac{m}{n}\right)}$$

$\square$

## 3.1 Comparison to Standard Bounds: Qualitative Results

In the transductive setting discussed above, we have a training set and test set and desire a bound on the number of mistakes on the test set based on observable quantities (like the error rate on the training set and the number of bits needed to communicate the labels). In the inductive setting, which most standard bounds are concerned with, we simply have a training set and desire a bound on the future error rate of a resulting prediction procedure. In this section we show how the PAC-MDL bound can be used to derive standard bounds at the qualitative level. By "qualitative" we mean that we are not concerned with exact constants and we will only focus on the realizable case. Later, we discuss the agnostic case and quantitative comparisons.

Let us begin by considering two special cases of Theorem 1: the limit as $n \to \infty$, and the case of $n = m$.

**Corollary 2** *For all description languages over strings* $\sigma$,

$$\lim_{n \to \infty} \mathbf{Pr}_{S \sim D^m, S' \sim D^n} \left( \forall \sigma \; \hat{e}(\sigma, S) > 0 \text{ or } \hat{e}(\sigma, S') \leq \frac{|\sigma| \ln 2 + \ln \frac{1}{\delta}}{m} \right) > 1 - \delta$$

*Proof.* Apply the asymptotically tight approximation, $n \ln \left(1 + \frac{m}{n}\right) = n\frac{m}{n} = m$ to Theorem 1.    □

**Corollary 3** *For all description languages over strings* $\sigma$,

$$\mathbf{Pr}_{S \sim D^m, S' \sim D^m} \left( \forall \sigma \; \hat{e}(\sigma, S) > 0 \text{ or } \hat{e}(\sigma, S') \leq \frac{|\sigma| + \log_2 \frac{1}{\delta}}{m} \right) > 1 - \delta$$

*Proof.* Just plug in $n = m$ into Theorem 1.    □

One first observation is that Corollary 2 immediately implies the standard Occam's Razor bound, because in that case $|\sigma|$ is just the size in bits of the hypothesis, and as $n \to \infty$, $\hat{e}(\sigma, S')$ approaches the true error with probability 1.

## 3.2 VC-Bounds

For the case of VC-dimension, the number of bits sent *does* depend on the number of test examples, so we instead use Corollary 3, together with the fact that any hypothesis violating the VC bound (having zero empirical error but high true error) likely has a high error rate on a randomly chosen test set. Notice that this argument is also used in the standard proof of VC-bounds.

**Theorem 4** *Let $H$ be a hypothesis class of VC-dimension $d$. Then,*

$$\mathbf{Pr}_{S \sim D^m} \left( \exists c \in H : \hat{e}(c, S) = 0 \text{ and } e(c) > \frac{1}{m} \left( d \log_2(2m) + \log_2 \frac{4}{\delta} \right) \right) \leq \delta.$$

*Proof.* Suppose this were false. That is, suppose there were a chance greater than $\delta$ that a hypothesis in $H$ existed with zero empirical error but true error greater than the above bound. Then, since the mean and median of the binomial are within 1, this implies that

$$\mathbf{Pr}_{S \sim D^m, S' \sim D^m} \left( \exists c \in H : \hat{e}(c, S) = 0 \text{ and } \hat{e}(c, S') > \frac{1}{m} \left( d \log_2(2m) + \log_2 \frac{2}{\delta} \right) \right)$$

$$> \delta/2.$$

But, now we appeal to Sauer's lemma which states that the number of ways to label any $m$ examples using hypotheses in a class of VC-dimension $d$ is at most $m^d$. Thus, for the setting of Corollary 3 where we have $2m$ examples, the labeling given by any $c \in H$ can be transmitted in only a number of bits $|\sigma| = d \log(2m)$ by sending its index in some canonical ordering. But then this violates Corollary 3 using "$\delta$" of $\delta/2$.    □

## 3.3   PAC-Bayes Bounds

We can also reconstruct PAC-Bayes bounds (again, focusing on the realizable case for simplicity). PAC-Bayes bounds state that for any "prior" $P(c)$ over hypotheses, if the learning algorithm finds a set of consistent hypotheses $U$ with large probability mass, then we can be confident that the stochastic prediction strategy that randomizes over concepts in $U$ has low true error. To view this in our setting, we consider a communication protocol in which Alice and Bob agree on the prior $P$, and also agree on a common random string. This common random string is then used to repeatedly sample from the prior $P$, and the message $\sigma$ that Alice sends to Bob is just the index of the first consistent hypothesis produced by this sampling. Notice that (as with the Occam bounds) the string $\sigma$ does not depend on the test data and so we are able to use Corollary 2. In the statement below, let $P(U) = \sum_{c \in U} P(c)$.

**Theorem 5** *Let $P(c)$ be any distribution over classifiers. Then,*

$$\mathbf{Pr}_{S \sim D^m} \left( \exists U : \hat{e}(U, S) = 0 \text{ and } e(U) > \frac{1}{m} \left( \ln \frac{m}{P(U)} + \ln \ln \frac{2}{\delta} + \ln \frac{2}{\delta} + 1 \right) \right) \leq \delta,$$

*where $e(U)$ is the expected true error of a random hypothesis drawn from $U$ (according to $P|_U$), and likewise $\hat{e}(U, S)$ is the expected empirical error of a random hypothesis from $U$ on set $S$.*

The argument used here is (essentially) a derandomization of the bits-back argument used by Hinton and van Camp [4]. A similar argument also appears in the Slepian-Wolf theorem [2] of information theory.

*Proof.* Suppose this were false. That is, there was a chance greater than $\delta$ that a bad set $U$ existed (one satisfying the conditions of the theorem). For any such set $U$, let $U' = \{c \in U : e(c) \geq e(U) - 1/m\}$. Since the error rate of any classifier is at most 1, we know $P(U') \geq P(U)/m$. Now, for any fixed such $U'$, if we repeatedly sample from $P$, the expected number of samples until we first pick a classifier in $U'$ is at most $\frac{m}{P(U)}$. Furthermore, the chance that we do not pick such a classifer in $\frac{m}{P(U)} \ln \frac{2}{\delta}$ samples is at most $\delta/2$. This means that over the sample $S$ and the common random oracle between Alice and Bob, there is a greater than $\delta/2$ chance that a consistent classifier $c \in U'$ exists whose description length $|\sigma_c|$ satisfies

$$|\sigma_c| \leq \log_2 \left( \frac{m}{P(U)} \ln \frac{2}{\delta} \right).$$

Now, by definition of $U'$, we have

$$e(c) \geq e(U) - 1/m$$
$$> \frac{1}{m} \left( \ln \frac{m}{P(U)} + \ln \ln \frac{2}{\delta} + \ln \frac{2}{\delta} \right)$$
$$\geq \frac{1}{m} \left( |\sigma_c| \ln 2 + \ln \frac{2}{\delta} \right).$$

Putting this all together, there is a probability greater than $\delta/2$ over the sample and common random oracle that such a classifier exists, violating Corollary 2 for "$\delta$" of $\delta/2$.                                                                □

# 4   The Agnostic Case

To discuss the agnostic case, it will be convenient to make the following definitions. First, imagine we have a bucket with $m$ red balls and $n$ blue balls, and we draw $a + b$ of them without replacement. Let us define Bucket$(m, n, a, b)$ to be the probability that we get at least $b$ blue balls. That is,

$$\text{Bucket}(m, n, a, b) = \sum_{t=b}^{a+b} \frac{\binom{n}{t}\binom{m}{a+b-t}}{\binom{n+m}{a+b}}.$$

Notice that Bucket is a decreasing function of $b$. Now, for a given value of $\delta$, let $b_{\max}\left(n, \frac{a}{m}, \delta\right)$ be the largest value of $b$ such that Bucket$(m, n, a, b) \geq \delta$. In other words, for any $b > b_{\max}\left(n, \frac{a}{m}, \delta\right)$, if we pick $a + b$ balls out of the $m + n$, the chance we get more than $b$ blue balls is less than $\delta$. We now give our main result.

**Theorem 6** *(PAC-MDL bound) Let $P(\sigma)$ be any probability distribution over strings $\sigma$ (a "prior"). With probability at least $1 - \delta$ over the draw of the train and test sets $S, S' \sim D^{m+n}$:*

$$\forall \sigma \quad n\hat{e}(\sigma, S') \leq b_{\max}\left(n, \hat{e}(\sigma, S), P(\sigma)\delta\right).$$

Intuitively, this theorem statement can be thought of as "with high probability, the test set error rate is not too much larger than the the training error rate."

*Proof.* Assume for the moment that we have a fixed vector of labeled examples, $(x, y)^{m+n}$ so that we can use an argument similar to the "double sample trick" in VC bounds. Let $S, S' \sim \pi(m, n)$ denote a binary partition drawn uniformly from the set of $\binom{m+n}{n}$ possible binary partitions into sets of size $m, n$. For any particular string, $\sigma$, there is a total number of errors $e_\sigma$ on the labeled data. What we wish to disallow is the possibility that most of these errors are in the test set. We know that:

$$\mathbf{Pr}_{S,S' \sim \pi(m,n)}(t \text{ test set errors and } e_\sigma - t \text{ train set errors}) = \frac{\binom{n}{t}\binom{m}{e_\sigma - t}}{\binom{m+n}{e_\sigma}}$$

In order to construct a confidence interval we must choose some set of "bad events" to exclude. In our case, this set of bad events consists of all test errors $t \geq \min\{b : \text{Bucket}(m, n, e_\sigma - b, b) < P(\sigma)\delta\}$. Notice that there is at most a $P(\sigma)\delta$ probability that the number of test errors is such that:

$$\text{Bucket}(m, n, m\hat{e}(\sigma, S), n\hat{e}(\sigma, S')) < P(\sigma)\delta.$$

Therefore, we have:

$$\forall (x,y)^{m+n} \forall \sigma \; \mathbf{Pr}_{S,S' \sim \pi(m,n)} (\text{Bucket}(m,n,m\hat{e}(\sigma,S), n\hat{e}(\sigma,S')) < P(\sigma)\delta)$$
$$\leq P(\sigma)\delta$$

(note that this is the step which requires that Bob not know which samples are in the train set and which are in the test set) The union bound implies:

$$\forall (x,y)^{m+n} \; \mathbf{Pr}_{S,S' \sim \pi(m,n)} (\exists \sigma : \text{Bucket}(m,n,m\hat{e}(\sigma,S), n\hat{e}(\sigma,S')) < P(\sigma)\delta) \leq \delta$$

Taking the expectation over draws, $(x,y)^{m+n} \sim D^{m+n}$, we get:

$$E_{(x,y)^{m+n} \sim D^{m+n}} \mathbf{Pr}_{S,S' \sim \pi(m,n)} (\exists \sigma \; \text{Bucket}(m,n,m\hat{e}(\sigma,S), n\hat{e}(\sigma,S')) < P(\sigma)\delta)$$
$$\leq \delta$$

$$\Rightarrow \mathbf{Pr}_{(x,y)^{m+n} \sim D^{m+n}} (\exists \sigma \; \text{Bucket}(m,n,m\hat{e}(\sigma,S), n\hat{e}(\sigma,S')) < P(\sigma)\delta) \leq \delta$$

Negating this statement, we get:

$$\Rightarrow \mathbf{Pr}_{(x,y)^{m+n} \sim D^{m+n}} (\forall \sigma \; \text{Bucket}(m,n,m\hat{e}(\sigma,S), n\hat{e}(\sigma,S')) \geq P(\sigma)\delta) > 1 - \delta$$

To construct a bound we must take a worst case over unknown quantities. In this case, the unknown quantity is the number of test errors, or equivalently the total number of errors. Taking the worst case over the number of test errors, we get the theorem. □

## 4.1   Lower Bound

Here, we show that there exists no other bound which is a significant improvement on the PAC-MDL bound for the communication game we consider.

**Theorem 7** (PAC-MDL lower bound) *For all "priors" over descriptions, $P(\sigma)$ there exists transductive classifiers $\sigma$ and distributions $D$ so that with probability*
$$\frac{\delta}{(n+1)(m+1)} - \frac{\delta^2}{(n+1)^2(m+1)^2}$$

$$\exists \sigma : \; n\hat{e}(\sigma,S') > b_{\max}(n, \hat{e}(\sigma,S), P(\sigma)\delta).$$

*Furthermore, if any $\sigma$ satisfies the clause, it is the $\sigma$ with smallest train error.*

Intuitively, this theorem says "the probabability that one of the transductive classifiers has a large test error rate is within a $(n+1)(m+1)$ fraction of $\delta$".

*Proof.* Let $D$ be the distribution which is uniform on any domain $X$ and always chooses $Y = 0$.

Pick any fixed train error rate $e_{\text{train}}$. For each possible string, $\sigma$, pick $e_\sigma$ according to:

$$e_\sigma = e_{\text{train}} + b_{\max}(n, \hat{e}(\sigma,S), P(\sigma)\delta).$$

Define $F_e$ to be the set of all functions from $X^{m+n}$ to $Y^{m+n}$ such that for every input we have exactly $e$ 1's in the output. We now define $\sigma$ to be a random element in $F_{e_\sigma}$. This choice implies that every description decodes to $e_\sigma$ total errors. Since errors in the test set and errors in the train set have a constant total, any string with a too-large number of test errors has a number of train errors less than $e_{\text{train}}$.

We have:

$$\forall \sigma \ \mathbf{Pr}_{S,S' \sim D^{m+n}}(\hat{e}(\sigma, S') > b_{\max}(n, \hat{e}(\sigma, S), P(\sigma)\delta))$$

$$\geq \text{Bucket}(m, n, e_{\text{train}} - 1, e_\sigma - e_{\text{train}} + 1)$$

Noting that $\begin{pmatrix} n \\ k+1 \end{pmatrix} > \dfrac{1}{n}\begin{pmatrix} n \\ k \end{pmatrix}$ and $\begin{pmatrix} n \\ k-1 \end{pmatrix} > \dfrac{1}{n}\begin{pmatrix} n \\ k \end{pmatrix}$ We get:

$$\forall \sigma \ \mathbf{Pr}_{S,S' \sim D^{m+n}}(\hat{e}(\sigma, S') > b_{\max}(n, \hat{e}(\sigma, S), P(\sigma)\delta)) \geq \frac{P(\sigma)\delta}{(n+1)(m+1)}$$

Negating, we get:

$$\forall \sigma \ \mathbf{Pr}_{S,S' \sim D^{m+n}}(\hat{e}(\sigma, S') \leq b_{\max}(n, \hat{e}(\sigma, S), P(\sigma)\delta)) \leq 1 - \frac{P(\sigma)\delta}{(n+1)(m+1)}$$

Using independence from the construction of the $\sigma$, we get:

$$\mathbf{Pr}_{S,S' \sim D^{m+n}}(\forall \sigma \ \hat{e}(\sigma, S') \leq b_{\max}(n, \hat{e}(\sigma, S), P(\sigma)\delta)) \leq \prod_\sigma (1 - \frac{P(\sigma)\delta}{(n+1)(m+1)})$$

Approximating the product, we get:

$$\mathbf{Pr}_{S,S' \sim D^{m+n}}(\forall \sigma \ \hat{e}(\sigma, S') \leq b_{\max}(n, \hat{e}(\sigma, S), P(\sigma)\delta))$$

$$\leq 1 - (\frac{\delta}{(n+1)(m+1)} - \frac{\delta^2}{(n+1)^2(m+1)^2})$$

And negating again, we get:

$$\mathbf{Pr}_{S,S' \sim D^{m+n}}(\exists \sigma \ \hat{e}(\sigma, S') > b_{\max}(n, \hat{e}(\sigma, S), P(\sigma)\delta))$$

$$\geq \frac{\delta}{(n+1)(m+1)} - \frac{\delta^2}{(n+1)^2(m+1)^2}$$

$\square$

## 5   Comparison to Standard Bounds: Quantitative Results

The goal of this section is making a quantitatively tight comparison of the PAC-MDL bound to various other bounds in the inductive setting where other bounds are typically stated. For a fair quantitative comparison, we state bounds in their tightest forms, and for this we work directly with the Binomial tail and its inverse.

**Definition 8** *(Binomial Tail Distribution)*

$$Bin\left(\frac{k}{m}, p\right) \equiv \mathbf{Pr}_{X_1, \dots X_m \sim p^m}\left(\sum_{i=1}^{m} X_i \leq k\right) = \sum_{j=1}^{k} \binom{m}{j} p^j (1-p)^{m-j}$$

= *the probability a given classifier of true error $p$ has empirical error at most $\frac{k}{m}$ on a sample of size $m$.*

Since we are interested in calculating a bound on the true error rate given a confidence, $\delta$, and an empirical error, $\hat{e}_S(c)$, it is handy to define the inversion of a Binomial tail.

**Definition 9** *(Binomial Tail Inversion)*

$$\overline{Bin}\left(\frac{k}{m}, \delta\right) \equiv \max_{p}\left\{p: Bin\left(\frac{k}{m}, p\right) = \delta\right\}$$

= *the largest true error rate such that the probability of having empirical error $\leq \frac{k}{m}$ is at least $\delta$.*

We next state each of the bounds in their tightest form and show how each bound is related to the description complexity of the labels given the unlabeled data.

## 5.1   The Occam's Razor bound

The Occam's Razor Bound applies to any measure $P$ over a set of classifiers, $c$

**Theorem 10** *[1] (Occam's Razor Bound) For all "priors" $p(c)$ over the classifiers, $c$, for all $\delta \in (0, 1]$:*

$$\forall p(c) \ \mathbf{Pr}_{S \sim D^m}\left(\exists c: \ e(c) \geq \overline{Bin}\left(\hat{e}_S(c), \delta p(c)\right)\right) \leq \delta$$

The prior $p(c)$ can be interpreted as a language for describing classifiers, $c$. Given any prior $p(c)$, we can construct a language $L(c)$ which uses code words of length approximately $2^{-|L(c)|} = p(c)$.

The appropriate method for constructing the Occam's Razor bound from the PAC-MDL bound uses the limit as $n \to \infty$, similar to Corollary 2 (although really using Theorem 6 in order to cover the agnostic case).

Using the PAC-MDL bound, we can construct an inductive bound on the true error rate given any "prior" on classifiers, $p(c)$. How does this compare with the bound constructed with the Occam's Razor bound directly?

For the agnostic case, we can do a numerical calculation with $m_{\text{train}} = 100$ training examples, a confidence of $\delta p(c) = 0.001$, a near-infinite (size 10000) test set, and a varying training error. Then, the two true error bounds yield the following graph:

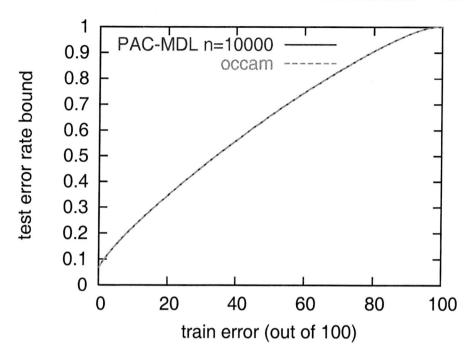

Quantitatively, the Occam's Razor bound is essentially a specialization of the PAC-MDL bound where the description language is given by the prior on the classifiers.

## 5.2   The Compression Bound

The compression bound works from the observation that examples which do not affect the output hypothesis are "sort of" test examples. In particular, if we knew in advance which examples are unnecessary, then the "unnecessary" examples would be independent of the chosen hypothesis and a test set bound would apply. We don't know in advance, so it is necessary to worsen the results by some factor.

Let $|A(S)|$ be the number of examples used by the learning algorithm and $\bar{A}(S)$ be the set of examples not used by the learning algorithm.

**Theorem 11** *(Compression Bound)* *[6][3]*

$$\mathbf{Pr}_{S \sim D^m}\left( e(c) \geq \overline{Bin}\left( \hat{e}_{\bar{A}(S)}(c), \frac{\delta}{\binom{m}{|A(S)|}(m+1)} \right) \right) \leq \delta$$

(Note: we have improved the compression bound here to work in the agnostic setting)

The language here is quite simple. First, specify the size of the compression set using $\log(m+1)$ bits, then specify the compression set using $\log \binom{m}{|A(S)|}$ bits, and then specify the labels using $|A(S)|$ bits. Given the labels of the compression set, the decoding end can run the learning algorithm and produce labels for all of the examples.

The compression bound is similar (but not identical) to the PAC-MDL bound with a specific language: the language which states the labels of the critical subset of $|A(S)|$ labels. Given the critical subset, it is possible to learn the hypothesis, and given the hypothesis, a labeling of all the data exists.

The number of bits required to specify the critical subset of labels is $\log_2(m+n+1)$ (to specify the size of the subset) plus $\log_2 \binom{m+n}{|A(S)|}$ (to specify the particular subset) plus $|A(S)|$ (to specify the labels of the subset). We compare these two bounds (with $\delta = 0.05$ on a training set of size 100) and find the following graph:

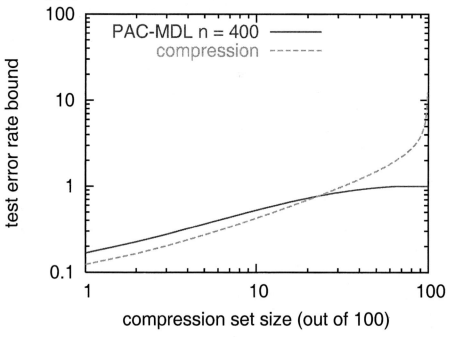

The PAC-MDL bound does somewhat worse because we are forced to choose from a larger set, of size $m + n$ rather than $n$.

## 6    Discussion

There are a few things we have accomplished here.

1. Bound unification. All of the major bounds can be thought of as (approximate or exact) applications of the PAC-MDL bound.

2. Generalization. We have a better understanding of the transductive setting since the PAC-MDL bound is naturally transductive. This allows us to bound the error rate on a given test set in many situations where it might be much more difficult to state an inductive bound.
3. Simplification. Proving bounds becomes an exercise in showing that we have some language for labels.

The qualitative and quantitative comparisons with the inductive bounds were made in the inductive setting where a "home court advantage" exists for naturally inductive bounds. If instead, we compare in a transductive setting, with a specific train and test set, the advantage shifts towards the naturally transductive PAC-MDL bound.

Information theory has a few implications for the PAC-MDL bound. If we let $H(Y|X)$ be the conditional entropy of the label given the unlabeled data, we know that asymptotically $H(Y|X)$ bits per label are required transfer the labels. Thus, for the realizable case, we can (asymptotically) find a code where $|\sigma|/(m+n) = H(Y|X)$.

It is worth noting that there are a few effects which are *not* captured by the PAC-MDL bound. Results which depend upon the distribution of observed empirical errors, such as shell bounds, are not captured. It may be possible to create an PAC-MDL bound which handles this as well, but that is an item for future work.

# References

1. A. Blumer, A. Ehrenfeucht, D. Haussler, M. Warmuth. "Occam's Razor." Information Processing Letters 24: 377-380, 1987.
2. Thomas Cover and Joy Thomas, "Elements of Information Theory" Wiley, New York 1991.
3. Sally Floyd and Manfred Warmuth, "Sample Compression, Learnability, and the Vapnik-Chervonenkis Dimension", Machine Learning, Vol.21 (3), pp. 269–304.
4. G. E. Hinton and D. van Camp, "Keeping neural networks simple by minimizing the description length of the weights", COLT 1993.
5. John Langford "Quantitatively Tight Sample Complexity Bounds", Carnegie Mellon Thesis, 2002.
6. Nick Littlestone and Manfred Warmuth, "Relating Data Compression and Learnability", Unpublished manuscript. June 10, 1986.
7. David McAllester, "PAC-Bayesian Model Averaging" COLT 1999.
8. V. N. Vapnik and A. Y. Chervonenkis. "On the uniform convergence of relative frequencies of events to their probabilities." Theory of Probab. and its Applications, 16(2):264-280, 1971.
9. Vladimir N. Vapnik, "Statistical Learning Theory", Wiley, December 1999.

# Universal Well-Calibrated Algorithm for On-Line Classification

Vladimir Vovk

Computer Learning Research Center
Department of Computer Science
Royal Holloway, University of London
Egham, Surrey TW20 0EX, UK
vovk@cs.rhul.ac.uk

**Abstract.** We study the problem of on-line classification in which the prediction algorithm is given a "confidence level" $1 - \delta$ and is required to output as its prediction a range of labels (intuitively, those labels deemed compatible with the available data at the level $\delta$) rather than just one label; as usual, the examples are assumed to be generated independently from the same probability distribution $P$. The prediction algorithm is said to be "well-calibrated" for $P$ and $\delta$ if the long-run relative frequency of errors does not exceed $\delta$ almost surely w.r. to $P$. For well-calibrated algorithms we take the number of "uncertain" predictions (i.e., those containing more than one label) as the principal measure of predictive performance. The main result of this paper is the construction of a prediction algorithm which, for any (unknown) $P$ and any $\delta$: (a) makes errors independently and with probability $\delta$ at every trial (in particular, is well-calibrated for $P$ and $\delta$); (b) makes in the long run no more uncertain predictions than any other prediction algorithm that is well-calibrated for $P$ and $\delta$; (c) processes example $n$ in time $O(\log n)$.

## 1 Introduction

Typical machine learning algorithms output a point prediction for the label of an unknown object. This paper continues study of an algorithm, called Transductive Confidence Machine (TCM) and introduced in [11, 6], that complements its predictions with some measures of confidence. There are different ways of presenting TCM's output; in this paper (as in the related [9, 8]) we use TCM as a "region predictor", in the sense that for any confidence level $1 - \delta$ it outputs a predictive region rather than a point prediction.

Any TCM is well-calibrated when used in the on-line mode: for any confidence level $1 - \delta$ the long-run relative frequency of erroneous predictions does not exceed $\delta$. What makes this feature of TCM especially appealing is that it is far from being just an asymptotic phenomenon: a slight modification of TCM called randomized TCM (rTCM; randomization is needed to break ties and deal efficiently with borderline cases) makes errors independently at different trials and with probability $\delta$ at each trial; the property of being well-calibrated then immediately follows by the Borel strong law of large numbers. For proofs and further information, see [9].

B. Schölkopf and M.K. Warmuth (Eds.): COLT/Kernel 2003, LNAI 2777, pp. 358–372, 2003.

The justification of the study of TCM given in [9] was its good performance on real-world and standard benchmark data sets. For example, Figure 1 shows that for the standard confidence levels 99% and 95% most examples in the well-known USPS data set (randomly permuted) can be predicted categorically (by a simple 1-Nearest Neighbor TCM): the predictive region contains only one label.

This paper presents theoretical results about TCM's performance; we show that there exists a *universal* rTCM, which, for any confidence level $1 - \delta$ and without knowing the true distribution $P$ generating the examples:

- produces, asymptotically, no more uncertain predictions than any other prediction algorithm that is well-calibrated for $P$ and $\delta$;
- produces, asymptotically, at least as many empty predictions as any other prediction algorithm that is well-calibrated for $P$ and $\delta$ and whose percentage of uncertain predictions is optimal (in the sense of the previous item).

The importance of the first item is obvious: we want to minimize the number of uncertain predictions. This criterion ceases to work, however, when the number of uncertain predictions stabilizes, as in Figure 1 (bottom). In such cases the number of empty predictions becomes important: empty predictions (automatically leading to an error) provide a warning that the object is untypical (looks very different from the previous objects), and one would like to be warned as often as possible, taking into account that the relative frequency of errors (including empty predictions) is guaranteed not to exceed $\delta$ in the long run.

This paper's result elaborates on [8], where it was shown that an optimal TCM exists when the distribution $P$ generating the examples is known. Here we consider only randomized TCM, so we drop the adjective "randomized".

The two areas of mainstream machine learning that are most closely connected with this paper are PAC learning theory and Bayesian learning theory. Whereas we often use the rich arsenal of mathematical tools developed in these fields, they do not provide the same kind of guarantees (a prespecified probability of error, with errors at different trials independent) under unknown $P$; for more details, see [9] and references therein. Several papers (such as [5, 4]) extend the standard PAC framework by allowing the prediction algorithm to abstain from making a prediction at some trials. Our results show that for any confidence level $1 - \delta$ there exists a prediction algorithm that: (a) makes a wrong prediction with relative frequency at most $\delta$; (b) has an optimal frequency of abstentions among the prediction algorithms that satisfy property (a) (for details, see Remark 2 below). Paper [4] is especially close to the approach of this paper, defining a very natural TCM in the situation where a hypothesis class is given (the "empirical log ratio" of [4], taken with appropriate sign, can be used as "individual strangeness measure", as defined in §3).

## 2   Main Result

In our learning protocol, Reality outputs pairs $(x_1, y_1), (x_2, y_2), \ldots$ called *examples*. Each example $(x_i, y_i)$ consists of an *object* $x_i$ and its *label* $y_i$; the objects

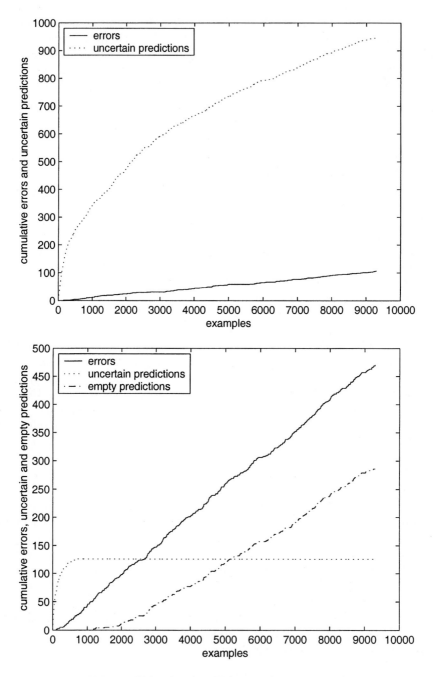

**Fig. 1.** TCM at 99% (top) and 95% (bottom) on the USPS data set

are chosen from a measurable space $\mathbf{X}$ called the *object space* and the labels are elements of a measurable space $\mathbf{Y}$ called the *label space*. In this paper we assume that $\mathbf{Y}$ is finite (and endowed with the $\sigma$-algebra of all subsets). The protocol includes variables $\text{Err}_n$ (the total number of errors made up to and including trial $n$) and $\text{err}_n$ (the binary variable showing whether an error is made at trial $n$); it also includes analogous variables $\text{Unc}_n$, $\text{unc}_n$, $\text{Emp}_n$, $\text{emp}_n$ for uncertain and empty predictions:

$\text{Err}_0 := 0$; $\text{Unc}_0 := 0$; $\text{Emp}_0 := 0$;
FOR $n = 1, 2, \ldots$:
    Reality outputs $x_n \in \mathbf{X}$;
    Predictor outputs $\Gamma_n \subseteq \mathbf{Y}$;
    Reality outputs $y_n \in \mathbf{Y}$;
$$\text{err}_n := \begin{cases} 1 \text{ if } y_n \notin \Gamma_n \\ 0 \text{ otherwise} \end{cases}; \quad \text{Err}_n := \text{Err}_{n-1} + \text{err}_n;$$
$$\text{unc}_n := \begin{cases} 1 \text{ if } |\Gamma_n| > 1 \\ 0 \text{ otherwise} \end{cases}; \quad \text{Unc}_n := \text{Unc}_{n-1} + \text{unc}_n;$$
$$\text{emp}_n := \begin{cases} 1 \text{ if } |\Gamma_n| = 0 \\ 0 \text{ otherwise} \end{cases}; \quad \text{Emp}_n := \text{Emp}_{n-1} + \text{emp}_n$$
END FOR.

We will use the notation $\mathbf{Z} := \mathbf{X} \times \mathbf{Y}$ for the *example space*; $\Gamma_n$ will be called the *predictive region* (or just *prediction*).

We will assume that each example $z_n = (x_n, y_n)$, $n = 1, 2, \ldots$, is output according to a probability distribution $P$ in $\mathbf{Z}$ and the examples are independent of each other (so the sequence $z_1 z_2 \ldots$ is output by the power distribution $P^\infty$). This is Reality's randomized strategy.

A *region predictor* is a measurable function

$$\Gamma_\gamma(x_1, \tau_1, y_1, \ldots, x_{n-1}, \tau_{n-1}, y_{n-1}, x_n, \tau_n),$$

where $\gamma \in (0, 1)$, $n = 1, 2, \ldots$, the $(x_i, y_i) \in \mathbf{Z}$, $i = 1, \ldots, n - 1$, are examples, $x_n \in \mathbf{X}$ is an object, and $\tau_i \in [0, 1]$ ($i = 1, \ldots, n$), which satisfies

$$\Gamma_{\gamma_1}(x_1, \tau_1, y_1, \ldots, x_{n-1}, \tau_{n-1}, y_{n-1}, x_n, \tau_n)$$
$$\subseteq \Gamma_{\gamma_2}(x_1, \tau_1, y_1, \ldots, x_{n-1}, \tau_{n-1}, y_{n-1}, x_n, \tau_n)$$

whenever $\gamma_1 \leq \gamma_2$. Since we are interested in prediction with confidence, the region predictor is given an extra input $\gamma = 1 - \delta \in (0, 1)$, which we call the *confidence level* (typically it is close to 1, standard values being 99% and 95%); the complementary value $\delta$ is called the *significance level*. We will always assume that $\tau_n$ are independent random variables uniformly distributed in $[0, 1]$; this makes a region predictor a family (indexed by $\gamma \in (0, 1)$) of Predictor's randomized strategies.

We will often use the notation $\text{err}_n$, $\text{unc}_n$, etc., in the case where Predictor and Reality are using given randomized strategies: for example, $\text{err}_n(P^\infty, \Gamma_{1-\delta})$ is the random variable equal to 1 if Predictor is right at trial $n$ and 0 otherwise.

It is always assumed that the random numbers $\tau_n$ used by $\Gamma$ and the random examples $z_n$ chosen by Reality are independent.

We say that a region predictor $\Gamma$ is (conservatively) *well-calibrated* for a probability distribution $P$ in $\mathbf{Z}$ and a significance level $\delta \in (0,1)$ if

$$\limsup_{n\to\infty} \frac{\mathrm{Err}_n(P^\infty, \Gamma_{1-\delta})}{n} \le \delta \quad \text{a.s.}$$

We say (following [8]) that $\Gamma$ is *optimal* for $P$ and $\delta$ if, for any region predictor $\Gamma^\dagger$ which is well-calibrated for $P$ and $\delta$,

$$\limsup_{n\to\infty} \frac{\mathrm{Unc}_n(P^\infty, \Gamma_{1-\delta})}{n} \le \liminf_{n\to\infty} \frac{\mathrm{Unc}_n(P^\infty, \Gamma^\dagger_{1-\delta})}{n} \quad \text{a.s.} \tag{1}$$

(the symbol "a.s." in such a context always assumes that the random numbers used by $\Gamma$ and $\Gamma^\dagger$ are independent). Of course, the definition of optimality is natural only for well-calibrated $\Gamma$.

A region predictor $\Gamma$ is *universal well-calibrated* if:

- it is well-calibrated for any $P$ and $\delta$;
- it is optimal for any $P$ and $\delta$;
- for any $P$, any $\delta$, and any region predictor $\Gamma^\dagger$ which is well-calibrated and optimal for $P$ and $\delta$,

$$\liminf_{n\to\infty} \frac{\mathrm{Emp}_n(P^\infty, \Gamma_{1-\delta})}{n} \ge \limsup_{n\to\infty} \frac{\mathrm{Emp}_n(P^\infty, \Gamma^\dagger_{1-\delta})}{n} \quad \text{a.s.}$$

Recall that a measurable space $\mathbf{X}$ is *Borel* if it is isomorphic to a measurable subset of the interval $[0,1]$. The class of Borel spaces is very rich; for example, all Polish spaces (such as finite-dimensional Euclidean spaces $\mathbb{R}^n$, $\mathbb{R}^\infty$, functional spaces $C$ and $D$) are Borel.

**Theorem 1.** *Suppose the object space $\mathbf{X}$ is Borel. There exists a universal well-calibrated region predictor.*

This is the main result of the paper; in §3 we construct a universal well-calibrated region predictor (processing example $n$ in time $O(\log n)$) and in §4 outline the idea of the proof that it indeed satisfies the required properties.

*Remark 1.* In this paper we are interested in the theoretical properties of region predictors for a fixed confidence level. This does not mean, however, that fixing a confidence level in advance is the right thing to do in practice; at the very least, two or more conventional levels should be used. For example, we could say that the prediction is "highly certain" if $|\Gamma_{0.99}| \le 1$ and "certain" if $|\Gamma_{0.95}| \le 1$; similarly, we could say that the new object (whose label is being predicted) is "highly untypical" if $|\Gamma_{0.99}| = 0$ and "untypical" if $|\Gamma_{0.95}| = 0$. To avoid the dependence on arbitrarily chosen conventional levels, the range of possible predictive regions $\Gamma_{1-\delta}$, $\delta \in (0,1)$, can be summarized by reporting the *confidence*

$$\sup\{\gamma : |\Gamma_\gamma| \le 1\},$$

the *credibility*

$$\inf\{\delta : |\Gamma_{1-\delta}| = 0\},$$

and the *prediction* $\Gamma_\gamma$, where $\gamma$ is the confidence ($\Gamma_\gamma$ is certain for TCM and usually contains exactly one label). Reporting the prediction, confidence, and credibility, as in [11, 6], is analogous to reporting the observed level of significance ([2], p. 66) in statistics.

*Remark 2.* The protocol of [5, 4] is in fact a restriction of our protocol, in which Predictor is only allowed to output a one-element set or the whole of $\mathbf{Y}$; the latter is interpreted as abstention. (And in the situation where $\mathrm{Err}_n$ and $\mathrm{Unc}_n$ are of primary interest, as in this paper, the difference between these two protocols is not very significant.) The universal well-calibrated region predictor can be adapted to the restricted protocol by replacing an uncertain prediction with $\mathbf{Y}$ and replacing an empty prediction with a randomly chosen label. In this way we obtain a prediction algorithm in the restricted protocol which is well-calibrated and has an optimal frequency of abstentions, in the sense of (1), among the well-calibrated algorithms.

## 3   Construction of a Universal Well-Calibrated Region Predictor

### 3.1   Preliminaries

If $\tau$ is a number in $[0, 1]$, we split it into two numbers $\tau', \tau'' \in [0, 1]$ as follows: if the binary expansion of $\tau$ is $0.a_1 a_2 \ldots$ (redefine the binary expansion of 1 to be $0.11 \ldots$), set $\tau' := 0.a_1 a_3 a_5 \ldots$ and $\tau'' := 0.a_2 a_4 a_6 \ldots$. If $\tau$ is distributed uniformly in $[0, 1]$, then both $\tau'$ and $\tau''$ are, and they are independent of each other.

We will often apply our procedures (e.g., the "individual strangeness measure" in §3.2, the Nearest Neighbors rule in §3.3) not to the original objects $x \in \mathbf{X}$ but to *extended objects* $(x, \sigma) \in \tilde{\mathbf{X}} := \mathbf{X} \times [0, 1]$, where $x$ is complemented by a random number $\sigma$ (to be extracted from one of the $\tau_n$). In other words, along with examples $(x, y)$ we will also consider *extended examples* $(x, \sigma, y) \in \tilde{\mathbf{Z}} := \mathbf{X} \times [0, 1] \times \mathbf{Y}$.

Let us set $\mathbf{X} := [0, 1]$; we can do this without loss of generality since $\mathbf{X}$ is Borel. This makes the extended object space $\tilde{\mathbf{X}} = [0, 1]^2$ a linearly ordered set with the lexicographic order: $(x_1, \sigma_1) < (x_2, \sigma_2)$ means that either $x_1 = x_2$ and $\sigma_1 < \sigma_2$ or $x_1 < x_2$. We say that $(x_1, \sigma_1)$ is *nearer* to $(x_3, \sigma_3)$ than $(x_2, \sigma_2)$ is if

$$|x_1 - x_3, \sigma_1 - \sigma_3| < |x_2 - x_3, \sigma_2 - \sigma_3|, \tag{2}$$

where

$$|x, \sigma| := \begin{cases} (x, \sigma) & \text{if } (x, \sigma) \geq (0, 0) \\ (-x, -\sigma) & \text{otherwise.} \end{cases}$$

Our construction will be based on the Nearest Neighbors algorithm, which is known to be strongly universally consistent in the traditional theory of pattern recognition (see, e.g., [3], Chapter 11); the random components $\sigma$ are needed for tie-breaking. As usual, to give a precise meaning to the expression "the $k$th nearest neighbor" in a sequence of extended objects to another extended object $v$, we use the convention that extended objects with smaller indices in the sequence are considered to be nearer to $v$ (this particular convention is not essential, since adding the random components $\sigma$ ensures that ties will occur with probability zero).

## 3.2    Transductive Confidence Machines

TCM is a way of transition from what we call an "individual strangeness measure" to a region predictor. A family of measurable functions $\{A_n : n = 1, 2, \ldots\}$, where $A_n : \check{\mathbf{Z}}^n \to \mathbb{R}^n$ for all $n$, is called an *individual strangeness measure* if, for any $n = 1, 2, \ldots$, each $\alpha_i$ in

$$A_n : (w_1, \ldots, w_n) \mapsto (\alpha_1, \ldots, \alpha_n) \tag{3}$$

is determined by $w_i$ and the multiset $\wr w_1, \ldots, w_n \wr$.

The *TCM associated with an individual strangeness measure* $A_n$ is the following region predictor $\Gamma_{1-\delta}(x_1, \tau_1, y_1, \ldots, x_{n-1}, \tau_{n-1}, y_{n-1}, x_n, \tau_n)$: at any trial $n$ and for any label $y \in \mathbf{Y}$, define

$$(\alpha_1, \ldots, \alpha_n) := A_n((x_1, \tau_1', y_1), \ldots, (x_{n-1}, \tau_{n-1}', y_{n-1}), (x_n, \tau_n', y)),$$

and include $y$ in $\Gamma_{1-\delta}$ if and only if

$$\tau_n'' < \frac{\#\{i = 1, \ldots, n : \alpha_i \geq \alpha_n\} - n\delta}{\#\{i = 1, \ldots, n : \alpha_i = \alpha_n\}} \tag{4}$$

(in particular, include $y$ in $\Gamma_{1-\delta}$ if $\#\{i = 1, \ldots, n : \alpha_i > \alpha_n\}/n > \delta$ and do not include $y$ in $\Gamma_{1-\delta}$ if $\#\{i = 1, \ldots, n : \alpha_i \geq \alpha_n\}/n \leq \delta$).

A *TCM* is the TCM associated with some individual strangeness measure. It was shown in [9] that

**Proposition 1.** *Every TCM is well-calibrated for every $P$ and $\delta$.*

## 3.3    Universal TCM

Fix a monotonically non-decreasing sequence of integer numbers $K_n$, $n = 1, 2, \ldots$, such that

$$K_n \to \infty, \ K_n = o(n/\ln n) \tag{5}$$

as $n \to \infty$. The *Nearest Neighbors TCM* is defined as follows. Let $w_1, \ldots, w_n$ be a sequence of extended examples $w_i = (x_i, \sigma_i, y_i)$. To define the corresponding $\alpha$s (see (3)), we first define Nearest Neighbors approximations $P_n^{\neq}(y \mid x_i, \sigma_i)$ to the true (but unknown) conditional probabilities $P(y \mid x_i)$: for every extended example $(x_i, \sigma_i, y_i)$ in the sequence,

$$P_n^{\neq}(y \mid x_i, \sigma_i) := N^{\neq}(x_i, \sigma_i, y)/K_n, \tag{6}$$

where $N^{\neq}(x_i, \sigma_i, y)$ is the number of $j = 1, \ldots, n$ such that $y_j = y$ and $(x_j, \sigma_j)$ is one of the $K_n$ nearest neighbors of $(x_i, \sigma_i)$ in the sequence $((x_1, \sigma_1), \ldots, (x_{i-1}, \sigma_{i-1}), (x_{i+1}, \sigma_{i+1}), \ldots, (x_n, \sigma_n))$. (The upper index $\neq$ reminds us of the fact that $(x_i, \sigma_i)$ is not counted as one of its own nearest neighbors in this definition.) If $K_n \geq n$ or $K_n \leq 0$, this definition does not work, so set, e.g., $P_n^{\neq}(y \mid x_i, \sigma_i) := 1/|\mathbf{Y}|$ for all $y$ and $i$ (this particular convention is not essential since, by (5), $0 < K_n < n$ from some $n$ on).

Define the "empirical predictability function" $f_n^{\neq}$ by

$$f_n^{\neq}(x_i, \sigma_i) := \max_{y \in \mathbf{Y}} P_n^{\neq}(y \mid x_i, \sigma_i).$$

For each $(x_i, \sigma_i)$ fix some

$$\hat{y}_n(x_i, \sigma_i) \in \arg\max_y P_n^{\neq}(y \mid x_i, \sigma_i)$$

(e.g., take the first element of $\arg\max_y P_n^{\neq}(y \mid x_i, \sigma_i)$ in a fixed ordering of $\mathbf{Y}$) and define the mapping (3) (where $w_i = (x_i, \sigma_i, y_i)$, $i = 1, \ldots, n$) setting

$$\alpha_i := \begin{cases} -f_n^{\neq}(x_i, \sigma_i) & \text{if } y_i = \hat{y}_n(x_i, \sigma_i) \\ f_n^{\neq}(x_i, \sigma_i) & \text{otherwise.} \end{cases} \tag{7}$$

This completes the definition of the Nearest Neighbors TCM, which will later be shown to be universal.

**Proposition 2.** *If* $\mathbf{X} = [0, 1]$ *and* $K_n \to \infty$ *sufficiently slowly, the Nearest Neighbors TCM can be implemented so that computations at trial $n$ are performed in time* $O(\log n)$.

Proposition 2 assumes a computational model that allows operations (such as comparison) with real numbers. If $\mathbf{X}$ is an arbitrary Borel space, for this proposition to be applicable $\mathbf{X}$ should be imbedded in $[0, 1]$ first; e.g., if $\mathbf{X} \subseteq [0, 1]^n$, an $x = (x_1, \ldots, x_n) \in \mathbf{X}$ can be represented as

$$(x_{1,1}, x_{2,1}, \ldots, x_{n,1}, x_{1,2}, x_{2,2}, \ldots, x_{n,2}, \ldots) \in [0, 1],$$

where $0.x_{i,1}x_{i,2}\ldots$ is the binary expansion of $x_i$.

## 4   Fine Details of Region Prediction

In this section we make first steps towards the proof of Theorem 1. Let $P$ be the true distribution in $\mathbf{Z}$ generating the examples. We denote by $P_{\mathbf{X}}$ the marginal distribution of $P$ in $\mathbf{X}$ (i.e., $P_{\mathbf{X}}(E) := P(E \times \mathbf{Y})$) and by $P_{\mathbf{Y}|\mathbf{X}}(y \mid x)$ the conditional probability that, for a random example $(X, Y)$ chosen from $P$, $Y = y$ provided $X = x$ (we fix arbitrarily a regular version of this conditional probability). We will often omit lower indices $\mathbf{X}$ and $\mathbf{Y}|\mathbf{X}$ and $P$ itself from our notation.

The *predictability* of an object $x \in \mathbf{X}$ is

$$f(x) := \max_{y \in \mathbf{Y}} P(y \mid x).$$

and the *predictability distribution function* is the function $F : [0,1] \to [0,1]$ defined by

$$F(\beta) := P\{x : f(x) \le \beta\}.$$

An example of such a function $F$ is given in Figure 2 (left), where the graph of $F$ is the thick line.

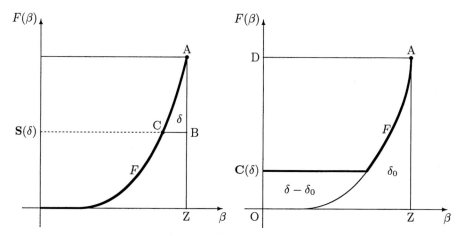

**Fig. 2.** The predictability distribution function $F$ and the success curve $\mathbf{S}(\delta)$ (left); the complementary success curve $\mathbf{C}(\delta)$ (right)

The *success curve* $\mathbf{S}$ of $P$ is defined by the equality

$$\mathbf{S}_P(\delta) = \inf\left\{B \in [0,1] : \int_0^1 (F(\beta) - B)^+ d\beta \le \delta\right\},$$

where $t^+$ stands for $\max(t, 0)$; the function $\mathbf{S}$ is also of the type $[0,1] \to [0,1]$. Geometrically, $\mathbf{S}_P(\delta)$ is defined from the graph of $F$ as follows (see Figure 2, left; we usually drop the lower index $p$): move the point B from A to Z until the area of the curvilinear triangle ABC becomes $\delta$ or B reaches Z; the ordinate of B is then $\mathbf{S}(\delta)$.

The *complementary success curve* $\mathbf{C}$ of $P$ is defined by

$$\mathbf{C}_P(\delta) = \sup\left\{B \in [0,1] : B + \int_0^1 (F(\beta) - B)^+ d\beta \le \delta\right\}.$$

Similarly to the case of $\mathbf{S}(\delta)$, $\mathbf{C}(\delta)$ is defined as the value such that the area of the part of the box AZOD below the thick line in Figure 2 (right) is $\delta$ ($\mathbf{C}(\delta) = 0$ if such a value does not exist).

Define the *critical significance level* $\delta_0$ as

$$\delta_0 := \int_0^1 F(\beta) d\beta.$$

It is clear that

$$\delta \leq \delta_0 \implies \int_0^1 (F(\beta) - \mathbf{S}(\delta))^+ d\beta = \delta \;\&\; \mathbf{C}(\delta) = 0$$

$$\delta \geq \delta_0 \implies \mathbf{S}(\delta) = 0 \;\&\; \mathbf{C}(\delta) + \int_0^1 (F(\beta) - \mathbf{C}(\delta))^+ d\beta = \delta.$$

The following result is proven in [8].

**Proposition 3.** *Let $P$ be a probability distribution in $\mathbf{Z}$ with success curve $\mathbf{S}$ and $\delta > 0$ be a significance level. If a region predictor $\Gamma$ is well-calibrated for $P$ and $\delta$, then*

$$\liminf_{n \to \infty} \frac{\mathrm{Unc}_n(P^\infty, \Gamma_{1-\delta})}{n} \geq \mathbf{S}(\delta) \quad a.s.$$

In this paper we complement Proposition 3 with

**Proposition 4.** *Let $P$ be a probability distribution in $\mathbf{Z}$ with success curve $\mathbf{S}$ and complementary success curve $\mathbf{C}$ and $\delta > 0$ be a significance level. If a region predictor $\Gamma$ is well-calibrated for $P$ and $\delta$ and satisfies*

$$\limsup_{n \to \infty} \frac{\mathrm{Unc}_n(P^\infty, \Gamma_{1-\delta})}{n} \leq \mathbf{S}(\delta) \quad a.s., \tag{8}$$

*then*

$$\limsup_{n \to \infty} \frac{\mathrm{Emp}_n(P^\infty, \Gamma_{1-\delta})}{n} \leq \mathbf{C}(\delta) \quad a.s.$$

Theorem 1 immediately follows from Propositions 1, 3, 4 and the following proposition.

**Proposition 5.** *Suppose $\mathbf{X}$ is Borel. The Nearest Neighbors TCM constructed in §3.3 satisfies, for any $P$ and any significance level $\delta$,*

$$\limsup_{n \to \infty} \frac{\mathrm{Unc}_n(P^\infty, \Gamma_{1-\delta})}{n} \leq \mathbf{S}_P(\delta) \quad a.s. \tag{9}$$

*and*

$$\liminf_{n \to \infty} \frac{\mathrm{Emp}_n(P^\infty, \Gamma_{1-\delta})}{n} \geq \mathbf{C}_P(\delta) \quad a.s. \tag{10}$$

Proof sketches of Propositions 2 and 4 are given in the appendix; the proof of Proposition 5 is too long for this paper and can be found in its fuller version [10].

## Acknowledgments

I am grateful to anonymous referees whose comments and suggestions helped to improve the quality of presentation. This work was partially supported by EPSRC (grant GR/R46670/01), BBSRC (grant 111/BIO14428), and EU (grant IST-1999-10226).

# References

1. Thomas H. Cormen, Charles E. Leiserson, Ronald L. Rivest, and Clifford Stein. *Introduction to Algorithms*. MIT Press, Cambridge, MA, second edition, 2001.
2. David R. Cox and David V. Hinkley. *Theoretical Statistics*. Chapman and Hall, London, 1974.
3. Luc Devroye, László Györfi, and Gábor Lugosi. *A Probabilistic Theory of Pattern Recognition*. Springer, New York, 1996.
4. Yoav Freund, Yishay Mansour, and Robert E. Schapire. Generalization bounds for averaged classifiers. July 2002. To appear in *Annals of Statistics*.
5. Ronald L. Rivest and R. Sloan. Learning complicated concepts reliably and usefully. In *Proceedings of the First Annual Conference on Computational Learning Theory*, pages 69–79, San Mateo, CA, 1988. Morgan Kaufmann.
6. Craig Saunders, Alex Gammerman, and Vladimir Vovk. Transduction with confidence and credibility. In *Proceedings of the Sixteenth International Joint Conference on Artificial Intelligence*, pages 722–726, 1999.
7. Albert N. Shiryaev. *Probability*. Springer, New York, second edition, 1996.
8. Vladimir Vovk. Asymptotic optimality of Transductive Confidence Machine. In *Proceedings of the Thirteenth International Conference on Algorithmic Learning Theory*, volume 2533 of *Lecture Notes in Artificial Intelligence*, pages 336–350, 2002.
9. Vladimir Vovk. On-line Confidence Machines are well-calibrated. In *Proceedings of the Forty Third Annual Symposium on Foundations of Computer Science*, pages 187–196. IEEE Computer Society, 2002.
10. Vladimir Vovk. Universal well-calibrated algorithm for on-line classification, On-line Compression Modelling project, `http://vovk.net/kp`, Working Paper #3, November 2002.
11. Vladimir Vovk, Alex Gammerman, and Craig Saunders. Machine-learning applications of algorithmic randomness. In *Proceedings of the Sixteenth International Conference on Machine Learning*, pages 444–453, San Francisco, CA, 1999. Morgan Kaufmann.

# Appendix: Proofs

## A.1    Proof Sketch of Proposition 2

For simplicity we will assume that all extended objects $(x_i, \tau_i') \in [0,1]^2$ are different (in any case, this is true with probability one, since $\tau_i'$ are independent random numbers uniformly distributed in $[0,1]$). Our computational model has an operation of splitting $\tau \in [0,1]$ into $\tau'$ and $\tau''$ (or is allowed to generate both $\tau_n'$ and $\tau_n''$ at every trial $n$).

We will use two main data structures in our implementation of the Nearest Neighbors TCM:

- a red-black binary *search tree* (see, e.g., [1], Chapters 13–15; the only two operations on red-black trees we need in this paper are the query SEARCH and the modifying operation INSERT);

- a growing *array* of nonnegative integer numbers indexed by numbers $k \in \{-K_n, -K_n + 1, \ldots, K_n\}$ (where $n$ is the ordinal number of the example being processed).

Immediately after processing the $n$th extended example $(x_n, \tau_n, y_n)$ the contents of these data structures are as follows:

- The search tree contains $n$ vertices, corresponding to the extended examples $(x_i, \tau_i, y_i)$ seen so far. The key of vertex $i$ is the extended object $(x_i, \tau_i') \in [0,1]^2$; the linear order on the keys is the lexicographic order. The other information contained in vertex $i$ is the random number $\tau_i''$, the label $y_i$, the set $\{P_n^{\neq}(y \,|\, x_i, \tau_i') : y \in \mathbf{Y}\}$ of conditional probability estimates (6), the pointer to the following vertex (i.e., the vertex that has the smallest key greater than $(x_i, \tau_i')$; if there is no greater key, the pointer is NIL), and the pointer to the previous vertex (i.e., the vertex that has the greatest key smaller than $(x_i, \tau_i')$; if $(x_i, \tau_i')$ is the smallest key, the pointer is NIL).
- The array contains the numbers

$$N(k) := \# \{i = 1, \ldots, n : \alpha_i = k/K_n\}.$$

Notice that the information contained in vertex $i$ of the search tree is sufficient to find $\hat{y}_n(x_i, \tau_i')$ and $\alpha_i$ in time $O(1)$.

We will say that an extended object $(x_j, \tau_j')$ is in the *vicinity* of an extended object $(x_i, \tau_i')$ if there are less than $K_n$ extended objects $(x_k, \tau_k')$ (strictly) between $(x_i, \tau_i')$ and $(x_j, \tau_j')$.

When a new object $x_n$ becomes known, the algorithm does the following:

- Generates $\tau_n'$ and $\tau_n''$.
- Locates the successor and predecessor of $(x_n, \tau_n')$ in the search tree (using the query SEARCH and the pointers to the following and previous vertices); this requires time $O(\log n)$.
- Computes the conditional probabilities $\{P_n^{\neq}(y \,|\, x_n, \tau_n') : y \in \mathbf{Y}\}$; this also gives $\hat{y}_n(x_n, \tau_n')$. The required time is $O(K_n) = O(\log n)$.
- For each $y \in \mathbf{Y}$ looks at what happens if the $n$th example is $(x_n, \tau_n, y_n) = (x_n, \tau_n, y)$: computes $\alpha_n$ and updates (if necessary) $\alpha_i$ for $(x_i, \tau_i')$ in the vicinity of $(x_n, \tau_n')$; using the array and $\tau_n''$, finds if $y \in \Gamma_n$. This requires time $O(K_n^2) = O(\log n)$.
- Outputs the predictive region $\Gamma_n$ (time $O(1)$).

When the label $y_n$ arrives, the algorithm:

- Inserts the new vertex $(x_n, \tau_n', \tau_n'', y_n, \{P_n^{\neq}(y \,|\, x_n, \tau_n') : y \in \mathbf{Y}\})$ in the search tree, repairs the pointers to the following and previous elements for $(x_n, \tau_n')$'s left and right neighbors, initializes the pointers to the following and previous elements for $(x_n, \tau_n')$ itself, and rebalances the tree (time $O(\log n)$).
- Updates (if necessary) the conditional probabilities

$$\{P_{n-1}^{\neq}(y \,|\, x_i, \tau_i') : y \in \mathbf{Y}\} \mapsto \{P_n^{\neq}(y \,|\, x_i, \tau_i') : y \in \mathbf{Y}\}$$

for the $2K_n$ existing vertices $(x_i, \tau_i')$ in the vicinity of $(x_n, \tau_n')$; this requires time $O(K_n^2) = O(\log n)$. The conditional probabilities for other $(x_i, \tau_i')$, $i = 1, \ldots, n - 1$, do not change.

- Updates the array, changing $N(K_n \alpha_i)$ for the $(x_i, \tau_i') \neq (x_n, \tau_n')$ in the vicinity of $(x_n, \tau_n')$ and for both old and new values of $\alpha_i$ and changing $N(K_n \alpha_n)$ (time $O(K_n) = O(\log n)$).

In conclusion we discuss how to do the updates required when $K_n$ increases. An *epoch* is defined to be a maximal sequence of $ns$ with the same $K_n$. Since the changes that need to be done when a new epoch starts are substantial, they will be spread over the whole preceding epoch. An epoch is *odd* if the corresponding $K_n$ is odd and *even* if $K_n$ is even. At every step in an epoch we prepare the ground for the next epoch. By the end of epoch $n = A + 1, A + 2, \ldots, B$ we need to change $B$ sets $\{P_n^{\neq}(y \,|\, x_i, \tau_i') : y \in \mathbf{Y}\}$ in $B - A$ steps (the duration of the epoch). Therefore, each vertex of the search tree should contain not only $\{P_n^{\neq}(y \,|\, x_i, \tau_i')\}$ for the current epoch but also $\{P_n^{\neq}(y \,|\, x_i, \tau_i')\}$ for the next epoch (two structures for holding $\{P_n^{\neq}(y \,|\, x_i, \tau_i')\}$ will suffice, one for even epochs and one for odd epochs). If $K_n$ grows slowly enough (say, as $\log n$), $B/A = O(1)$. At each step, $O(1)$ sets $\{P_n^{\neq}(y \,|\, x_i, \tau_i')\}$ for the next epoch are added. This will take time $O(K_n) = O(\log n)$. As soon as a set $\{P_n^{\neq}(y \,|\, x_i, \tau_i')\}$ for the next epoch is added at some trial, both sets (for the current and next epoch) will have to be updated for each new example. In a similar way the array for the next epoch is gradually built up.

## A.2    Proof Sketch of Proposition 4

The proof of Proposition 4 is similar to (but more complicated than) the proof of Theorems 1 and 1r in [8]; this proof sketch can be made rigorous using the Neyman-Pearson lemma, as in [8].

We will use the notations $g'_{\text{left}}$ and $g'_{\text{right}}$ for the left and right derivatives, respectively, of a function $g$. The following lemma parallels Lemma 2 in [8], which deals with $\mathbf{S}(\delta)$.

**Lemma 1.** *The complementary success curve* $\mathbf{C} : [0, 1] \to [0, 1]$ *always satisfies these properties:*

1. *There is a point* $\delta_0 \in [0, 1]$ *(viz. the critical significance level) such that* $\mathbf{C}(\delta) = 0$ *for* $\delta \leq \delta_0$ *and* $\mathbf{C}(\delta)$ *is concave for* $\delta \geq \delta_0$.
2. $\mathbf{C}'_{\text{right}}(\delta_0) < \infty$ *and* $\mathbf{C}'_{\text{left}}(1) \geq 1$; *therefore, for* $\delta \in (\delta_0, 1)$, $1 \leq \mathbf{C}'_{\text{right}}(\delta) \leq \mathbf{C}'_{\text{left}}(\delta) < \infty$ *and the function* $\mathbf{C}(\delta)$ *is increasing.*
3. $\mathbf{C}(\delta)$ *is continuous at* $\delta = \delta_0$; *therefore, it is continuous everywhere in* $[0, 1]$.

*If a function* $\mathbf{C} : [0, 1] \to [0, 1]$ *satisfies these properties, there exist a measurable space* $\mathbf{X}$, *a finite set* $\mathbf{Y}$, *and a probability distribution* $P$ *in* $\mathbf{X} \times \mathbf{Y}$ *for which* $\mathbf{C}$ *is the complementary success curve.*

**Proof sketch** The statement of the lemma follows from the fact that the complementary success curve $\mathbf{S}$ can be obtained from the predictability distribution function $F$ using these steps (labeling the horizontal and vertical axes as $x$ and $y$ respectively):

1. Invert $F$: $F_1 := F^{-1}$.
2. Integrate $F_1$: $F_2(x) := \int_0^x F_1(t)dt$.
3. Increase $F_2$: $F_3(x) := F_2(x) + \delta_0$, where $\delta_0 := \int_0^1 F(x)dx$.
4. Invert $F_3$: $F_4 := F_3^{-1}$.

It can be shown that $\mathbf{C} = F_4$, if we define $g^{-1}(y) := \sup\{x : g(x) \le y\}$ for non-decreasing $g$ (so that $g^{-1}$ is continuous on the right). ∎

Complement the protocol of §2 in which Reality plays $P^\infty$ and Predictor plays $\Gamma_{1-\delta}$ with the following variables:

$$\overline{\text{err}}_n := (P \times \mathbf{U})\{(x, y, \tau) : y \notin \Gamma_{1-\delta}(x_1, \tau_1, y_1, \ldots, x_{n-1}, \tau_{n-1}, y_{n-1}, x, \tau)\},$$
$$\overline{\text{unc}}_n := (P_{\mathbf{X}} \times \mathbf{U})\{(x, \tau) : |\Gamma_{1-\delta}(x_1, \tau_1, y_1, \ldots, x_{n-1}, \tau_{n-1}, y_{n-1}, x, \tau)| > 1\},$$
$$\overline{\text{emp}}_n := (P_{\mathbf{X}} \times \mathbf{U})\{(x, \tau) : |\Gamma_{1-\delta}(x_1, \tau_1, y_1, \ldots, x_{n-1}, \tau_{n-1}, y_{n-1}, x, \tau)| = 0\},$$

$\mathbf{U}$ standing for the uniform distribution in $[0, 1]$, and

$$\overline{\text{Err}}_n := \sum_{i=1}^n \overline{\text{err}}_i, \quad \overline{\text{Unc}}_n := \sum_{i=1}^n \overline{\text{unc}}_i, \quad \overline{\text{Emp}}_n := \sum_{i=1}^n \overline{\text{emp}}_i.$$

By the martingale strong law of large numbers, to prove the proposition it suffices to consider only these "predictable" versions of $\text{Err}_n$, $\text{Unc}_n$, and $\text{Emp}_n$: indeed, since $\text{Err}_n - \overline{\text{Err}}_n$, $\text{Unc}_n - \overline{\text{Unc}}_n$, and $\text{Emp}_n - \overline{\text{Emp}}_n$ are martingales (with increments bounded by 1 in absolute value) with respect to the filtration $\mathcal{F}_n$, $n = 0, 1, \ldots$, where each $\mathcal{F}_n$ is generated by $(x_1, \tau_1, y_1), \ldots, (x_n, \tau_n, y_n)$, we have

$$\lim_{n \to \infty} \frac{\text{Err}_n - \overline{\text{Err}}_n}{n} = 0 \quad \text{a.s.},$$

$$\lim_{n \to \infty} \frac{\text{Unc}_n - \overline{\text{Unc}}_n}{n} = 0 \quad \text{a.s.},$$

and

$$\lim_{n \to \infty} \frac{\text{Emp}_n - \overline{\text{Emp}}_n}{n} = 0 \quad \text{a.s.}$$

(see, e.g., [7], Theorem VII.5.4).

Without loss of generality we can assume that Predictor's move $\Gamma_n$ at trial $n$ is $\{\hat{y}(x_n)\}$ (where $x \mapsto \hat{y}(x) \in \arg\max_y P(y \,|\, x)$ is a fixed "choice function") or the empty set $\emptyset$ or the whole label space $\mathbf{Y}$. Furthermore, we can assume that

$$\overline{\text{unc}}_n = \mathbf{S}(\overline{\text{err}}_n), \quad \overline{\text{emp}}_n = \mathbf{C}(\overline{\text{err}}_n),$$

at every trial, since the optimal way (which is essentially the only optimal way) to spend the allowance of $\overline{\text{err}}_n$ is to be certain on objects $x$ with the largest (uppermost in Figure 2) representations $F(f(x))$ and, if part of the allowance is still left when certainty is attained for all objects (i.e., if $\overline{\mathrm{err}}_n > \delta_0$), be empty on objects $x$ with the smallest (lowermost in Figure 2) representations $F(f(x))$. (A formal argument for the statement about $\mathbf{S}$ is given in [8].)

From the argument of [8] (Proof of Theorems 1 and 1r) it is clear that to achieve (8) the region predictor must satisfy

$$\delta < \delta_0 \implies \limsup_{n \to \infty} \frac{1}{n} \sum_{i=1}^{n} (\overline{\mathrm{err}}_i - \delta_0)^+ = 0$$

$$\delta \geq \delta_0 \implies \limsup_{n \to \infty} \frac{1}{n} \sum_{i=1}^{n} (\delta_0 - \overline{\mathrm{err}}_i)^+ = 0.$$

Using the fact that the complementary success curve $\mathbf{C}$ is concave, increasing, and (uniformly) continuous for $\delta \geq \delta_0$ (see Lemma 1), we obtain: if $\delta < \delta_0$,

$$\frac{\overline{\mathrm{Emp}_n}}{n} = \frac{1}{n} \sum_{i=1}^{n} \overline{\mathrm{emp}}_i = \frac{1}{n} \sum_{i=1}^{n} \mathbf{C}(\overline{\mathrm{err}}_i)$$

$$\leq \frac{1}{n} \mathbf{C}'_{\mathrm{right}}(\delta_0) \sum_{i=1}^{n} (\overline{\mathrm{err}}_i - \delta_0)^+ \to 0 \quad (n \to \infty);$$

if $\delta \geq \delta_0$,

$$\frac{\overline{\mathrm{Emp}_n}}{n} = \frac{1}{n} \sum_{i=1}^{n} \mathbf{C}(\overline{\mathrm{err}}_i) = \frac{1}{n} \sum_{i=1}^{n} \mathbf{C}(\overline{\mathrm{err}}_i \vee \delta_0)$$

$$\leq \mathbf{C}\left( \frac{1}{n} \sum_{i=1}^{n} (\overline{\mathrm{err}}_i \vee \delta_0) \right) = \mathbf{C}\left( \frac{1}{n} \sum_{i=1}^{n} \overline{\mathrm{err}}_i + \frac{1}{n} \sum_{i=1}^{n} (\delta_0 - \overline{\mathrm{err}}_i)^+ \right)$$

$$\leq \mathbf{C}\left( \frac{1}{n} \sum_{i=1}^{n} \overline{\mathrm{err}}_i \right) + o(1) \leq \mathbf{C}(\delta) + \epsilon,$$

the last inequality holding almost surely for an arbitrary $\epsilon > 0$ from some $n$ on and $\delta$ being the significance level used.

# Learning Probabilistic Linear-Threshold Classifiers via Selective Sampling

Nicolò Cesa-Bianchi[1], Alex Conconi[1], and Claudio Gentile[2]

[1] Dept. of Information Technologies
Università degli Studi di Milano, Crema, Italy
{cesa-bianchi,conconi}@dti.unimi.it
[2] Dipartimento di Informatica e Comunicazione
Università dell'Insubria, Varese, Italy
gentile@dsi.unimi.it

**Abstract.** In this paper we investigate selective sampling, a learning model where the learner observes a sequence of i.i.d. unlabeled instances each time deciding whether to query the label of the current instance. We assume that labels are binary and stochastically related to instances via a linear probabilistic function whose coefficients are arbitrary and unknown. We then introduce a new selective sampling rule and show that its expected regret (with respect to the classifier knowing the underlying linear function and observing the label realization after each prediction) grows not much faster than the number of sampled labels. Furthermore, under additional assumptions on the true margin distribution, we prove that the number of sampled labels grows only logarithmically in the number of observed instances. Experiments carried out on a text categorization problem show that: (1) our selective sampling algorithm performs better than the Perceptron algorithm even when the latter is given the true label after each classification; (2) when allowed to observe the true label after each classification, the performance of our algorithm remains the same. Finally, we note that by expressing our selective sampling rule in dual variables we can learn nonlinear probabilistic functions via the kernel machinery.

## 1 Introduction

In many real-world learning applications obtaining labels is an expensive process and several learning models have been proposed in the past to address this issue. In the membership query model, introduced in [1] and extensively investigated under adversarial and statistical assumptions, the learner can query the label of an arbitrary instance in the domain. In the label-efficient model of [10] the learner decides which labels to query from an adversarially chosen sequence of instances. A different setup is the active learning model (see, e.g., [4, 15]), where the learner is allowed to interactively choose which labels to obtain from an i.i.d. training set of unlabeled instances. In this paper we are interested in a sequential variant of active learning, called selective sampling in [2]. In the selective sampling model the learner observes a sequence of i.i.d. unlabeled instances and

B. Schölkopf and M.K. Warmuth (Eds.): COLT/Kernel 2003, LNAI 2777, pp. 373–387, 2003.
© Springer-Verlag Berlin Heidelberg 2003

decides whether to query the label of the current instance. Note that, in contrast with active learning where the learner has access to the entire training set, here the learner must base each query only on previously observed instances and labels. A very comprehensive study of selective sampling is carried out in [8] where it is shown that, under certain conditions, the query-by-committee (QBC) algorithm learns using a number of labels which is *exponentially smaller* than the number of observed instances. In particolar, QBC is shown to use exponentially fewer labels than instances when learning linear-threshold classifiers (LTC) under the hypothesis that: instances are drawn from a quasi-uniform distribution and labels are generated by a target LTC also drawn from a quasi-uniform distribution over the set of all LTCs. In this work, we obtain an exponential rate of labels over instances with a different algorithm and under slightly different conditions. We assume that labels are stochastically related to instances via a linear probabilistic function whose linear coefficients are arbitrary and unknown. To learn these coefficients we use a least-squares estimate which is incrementally built over the set of instances for which we obtained the label[1]. Each time a new instance is observed, the algorithm decides to ask for a label if the magnitude of the *estimated* margin on the current instance falls below a certain threshold. This threshold is dynamically adjusted according to a large deviation analysis based on the number of observed instances and labels. Under additional conditions on the instance distribution, we show that the number of labels grows logarithmically in the number of observed instances, thus achieving the desired exponential rate. More discussion on the relationships between our results and those proven in [8] is deferred to the full paper.

The main motivation driving our research was the design of an algorithm with good empirical behavior. In the last part of the paper, we describe some experiments on text categorization with Reuters Corpus Volume 1. These experiments show that our algorithm makes, in a certain sense, optimal use of the label information. In particular, the performance curve of our selective sampling classifier does not improve when feeding more labels than those asked by the algorithm. Moreover, the performance curve flattens approximately when the frequency of queried labels flattens. This may be interpreted as the ability of the selective sampler to ask labels in proportion to the information that can be gained at each stage of the learning process, irrespective to (and without much affecting) the actual rate of mistakes that are being made.

The paper is organized as follows. In Section 2 we recall basic preliminaries, introduce the notational conventions used throughout the paper, and define our selective sampling model. In Section 3 we introduce our selective sampling algorithm and provide a theoretical analysis of its performance. In Section 4 we present the results of experiments run on text data. In Section 5 we summarize our work and describe our future directions of research.

---

[1] This least-squares estimate is a sparse variant of the ridge regression estimator [12], similar in spirit to those studied (in different settings) in [3, 5, 7, 17].

## 2    Learning Model, Preliminaries and Notation

We assume instances $X_1, X_2, \ldots$ are drawn independently from a fixed and unknown distribution on the surface of the unit Euclidean sphere in $\mathbb{R}^d$, so that $\|X_t\| = 1$ for all $t \geq 1$. The label of each instance $X_t$ is given by a $\{-1, 1\}$-valued random variable $Y_t$. We assume there exists a fixed and unknown vector $u \in \mathbb{R}^d$, with Euclidean norm $\|u\| = 1$, such that $\mathbb{E}[Y_t \mid X_t = x_t] = u^\top x_t$ for all $t \geq 1$. Hence $X_t = x_t$ is labelled 1 with probability $(1 + u^\top x_t)/2 \in [0, 1]$. We call the pair $(X, Y)$ an example. All probabilities and expectations will be understood with respect to the joint distribution of the i.i.d. process $\{(X_1, Y_1), (X_2, Y_2), \ldots\}$.

In this model, we want to perform almost as well as the algorithm that knows $u$ and labels $X_t$ with 1 if and only if $u^\top X_t \geq 0$. We consider linear-threshold algorithms that predict the value of $Y_t$ through $\mathrm{SGN}(W^\top X_t)$, where $W \in \mathbb{R}^d$ is a dynamically updated weight vector which might be intended as the current estimate for $u$.

We use $\Delta_t$ to denote the margin $u^\top X_t$ and $\widehat{\Delta}_t$ to denote the margin $W^\top X_t$ whenever $W$ is understood from the context. We will sometimes abuse the notation and write $\Delta_t$ to denote both the random variable $u^\top X_t$ and its realization $u^\top x_t$. No confusion will arise. We define the *regret* of the linear-threshold algorithm at time $t$ on the given instance $X_t$ as $\mathbb{P}(Y_t \widehat{\Delta}_t < 0) - \mathbb{P}(Y_t \Delta_t < 0)$ Our goal is to bound the cumulative regret

$$\sum_{t=1}^{n} \left( \mathbb{P}(Y_t \widehat{\Delta}_t < 0) - \mathbb{P}(Y_t \Delta_t < 0) \right)$$

over a sequence of $n$ examples $(X_1, Y_1), \ldots, (X_n, Y_n)$ drawn i.i.d. as specified above.

In the selective sampling model, at each time step $t$ the learner observes the instance $x_t$ (a realization of $X_t$), outputs a binary prediction, and possibly issues a query to access the label $y_t$ (a realization of $Y_t$). Note that while each prediction of the learner (which we henceforth call *selective sampler*) must only depend on the previously observed instances and on the previously queried labels, the cumulative regret is computed on all time steps; that is, taking also into account those times $t$ when the algorithm did not issue a query.

Let $\{\phi\}$ denote the Bernoulli random variable which is 1 if and only if predicate $\phi$ is true. Observe that $\{Y_t \widehat{\Delta}_t < 0\} \leq \{Y_t \Delta_t < 0\} + \{\widehat{\Delta}_t \Delta_t \leq 0\}$. Hence the cumulative regret satisfies

$$\sum_{t=1}^{n} \left( \mathbb{P}(Y_t \widehat{\Delta}_t < 0) - \mathbb{P}(Y_t \Delta_t < 0) \right) \leq \sum_{t=1}^{n} \mathbb{P}(\widehat{\Delta}_t \Delta_t \leq 0) . \tag{1}$$

We will prove bounds on the right-hand side of (1) that are inversely proportional to the square of the smallest margin $\Delta = \min_{1 \leq t \leq n} |\Delta_t|$.

**Parameters:** integer $R$.

**Initialization:** weight vector $\boldsymbol{W} = (0,\dots,0)$; query counter $N = 0$.

At each time $t = 1, 2, \dots$ do the following:

1. observe instance $\boldsymbol{X}_t$
2. predict the label $Y_t \in \{-1, 1\}$ with SGN($\widehat{\Delta}$), where $\widehat{\Delta} = \boldsymbol{W}^\top \boldsymbol{X}_t$
3. if $N < R$, then query the label of $\boldsymbol{X}_t$
4. if $N \geq R$ and $\widehat{\Delta} \leq (4 \ln t)/N$, then query the label of $\boldsymbol{X}_{t+1}$
5. if $Y_t$ is available, then increment $N$ and update $\boldsymbol{W}$ using $(\boldsymbol{X}_t, Y_t)$.

**Fig. 1.** The selective sampling procedure.

## 3   Definition and Analysis of the Algorithm

Our selective sampler (see Figure 1) stores each instance whose label has been queried. During the first $R$ steps, where $R$ depens only on the eigenstructure of the process generating the data, the sampler queries all labels. When this transient regime is over, the sampler queries a label at time $t > R$ based on the margin $\widehat{\Delta}_t$ of the current instance $\boldsymbol{X}_t$, as we explain below. Let $S$ be the matrix whose columns are the instances stored before observing instance $\boldsymbol{X}_t$, and let $\boldsymbol{Y}$ be the vector of labels that have been queried for these stored instances. The margin $\widehat{\Delta}_t = \boldsymbol{W}^\top \boldsymbol{X}_t$ is computed using

$$\boldsymbol{W} = \left(I + S S^\top\right)^{-1} S \boldsymbol{Y} , \tag{2}$$

where $I$ is the $d \times d$ identity matrix[2]. Let $N_t$ be the number of data elements whose labels have been observed up to and including time $t$, so that $N_R = R$ (in what follows, we write $\widehat{\Delta}_{N_{t-1}, t}$ instead of $\widehat{\Delta}_t$ to stress the dependence of $\widehat{\Delta}_t$ on the number of queried labels/stored instances). If the margin is small, that is $\widehat{\Delta}^2_{N_{t-1}, t} \leq (4 \ln t)/N_{t-1}$, then the label of the *next* instance $\boldsymbol{X}_{t+1}$ is queried.

In the following, we show that $\widehat{\Delta}_{N_{t-1}, t}$ is a (biased) estimate of the true margin $\Delta_t$. To guarantee that, at time $t$, the regret increases as $1/t$ (so to achieve the desired logarithmic cumulative regret), we sample often enough to make sure that the size of $\widehat{\Delta}_t$'s confidence interval, at a confidence value of $1/t$, is smaller than $\Delta_t$ (note that we must do that without knowing the exact value of $\Delta_t$). The main scaling factor in the sample size turns out to be related to the expected value of $1/\Delta_t^2$, which is the same for all $t$ due to the i.i.d. assumption. Once we collect evidence that the number $N_{t-1}$ of queried labels is smaller than our current estimate of $1/\Delta_t^2$, that is when $\widehat{\Delta}^2_{N_{t-1}, t} \leq (4 \ln t)/N_{t-1}$, then we query a new label. Note that this technique is designed just to detect the need of an additional label, which we assume is queried from the next random instance. A more refined technique (see Section 4) would query instead the label of the *current* instance, following the obvious intuition that we should make

---

[2] Adding $I$ to matrix $S S^\top$ ensures the invertibility of $I + S S^\top$ but, as we will see later, it makes the margin estimator $\widehat{\Delta}_t$ additively biased.

"more progress" towards $u$. Unfortunately, we have not been able to analyze the performance of this latter method.

The next theorem is our main theoretical result.

**Theorem 1.** *Let $u \in \mathbb{R}^d$ be such that $\|u\| = 1$ and let $(X_1, Y_1), \dots, (X_n, Y_n)$ be an i.i.d. sample such that $\|X_t\| = 1$ with probability 1 and $Y_t \in \{-1, 1\}$, where $\mathbb{E}[Y_t \mid X_t] = u^\top X_t = \Delta_t$, $t = 1, \dots, n$. Let $\lambda$ be the minimal eigenvalue of the process covariance matrix $\{\mathbb{E}[X_i X_j]\}_{i,j=1}^d$, where $(X_1, \dots, X_d) = X_1$. Assume $\lambda > 0$ and set $R = \lceil \max\{96\, d,\, 912 \ln n\}/\lambda^2 \rceil$. Then the cumulative regret of our selective sampling algorithm is at most*

$$R + \mathbb{E}\,L + 4 \ln n + 6 = \mathbb{E}\,L + O\left(\frac{d + \ln n}{\lambda^2}\right),$$

*where $L$ is the number of queried labels after the first $R$ time steps (thus $R + L$ is the total number of queried labels). In turn, $L$ satisfies*

$$\mathbb{E}\,L \le \mathbb{E}\left[\frac{16 \ln n}{\lambda\, \Delta^2}\right] + 4\,, \qquad \text{where} \quad \Delta = \min_{1 \le t \le n} |\Delta_t|\,.$$

*Remark 1.* This theorem says that the expected regret of our algorithm grows only logarithmically above the expected number of requested labels, $R + \mathbb{E}\,L$. In turn, $L$ depends on the minimum margin $\Delta$. A more explicit bound on the expectation of $L$ is one in which $\Delta$ is replaced by the process margin $\Delta_1 = u^\top X_1$. In order to obtain such a bound, it is sufficient to require that the distribution of instances is such that the distribution of the inverse squared margin $1/\Delta_1^2$ has a tail decreasing as fast as a gaussian, that is,

$$\ln \mathbb{E}\left[e^{\alpha/\Delta_1^2}\right] \le \alpha\,\mathbb{E}\left[1/\Delta_1^2\right] + (\alpha\sigma)^2,$$

for all $\alpha > 0$ and for some $\sigma > 0$. In such a case, it is not hard to show the following bound:

$$\mathbb{E}\,L \le \mathbb{E}\left[\frac{16 \ln n}{\lambda\, \Delta_1^2}\right] + \frac{32}{\lambda}\sigma(\ln n)^{3/2}\,.$$

*Remark 2.* As other least-squares estimators, our algorithm can be turned into an equivalent dual form. This is needed when we want to use the feature expansion facility provided by kernel functions (see, e.g., [6,16] and references therein) to efficiently handle nonlinear probabilistic models of the data. Moreover, the estimator (2) can be computed incrementally as new instances are stored, by exploiting known adjustment formulas for partitioned matrices such as those mentioned in [5].

We now introduce our main technical tools. The proof of the first lemma, along with a few ancillary definitions, is given in the appendix.

**Lemma 1.** *For each $i \ge 1$ let $T_i + 1$ be the time at which we store an instance for the $i$-th time and let $Z_{T_i} = (X_{T_i}, Y_{T_i})$ be the example whose margin caused instance $X_{T_i+1}$ to be stored. Then $Z_{T_1+1}, Z_{T_2+1}, \dots$ are independent random variables distributed as $Z_1$.*

Lemma 1 is used, together with the next result, to control the bias of $\widehat{\Delta}_t$. The next lemma, which can be easily derived as a consequence of Theorem 8 in [14], establishes a concentration property about the eigenvalues of an empirical correlation matrix whose items are generated by an i.i.d. process.

**Lemma 2.** *Let $\boldsymbol{X} = (X_1, \ldots, X_d) \in \mathbb{R}^d$ be a random vector such that $\|\boldsymbol{X}\| = 1$ with probability 1, and $\lambda$ be the* smallest *eigenvalue of the covariance matrix $\{\mathbb{E}[X_i X_j]\}_{i,j=1}^d$ (note that $\lambda \geq 0$). Let $\boldsymbol{X}_1, \ldots, \boldsymbol{X}_s$ be i.i.d. random vectors distributed as $\boldsymbol{X}$, $S$ be the $d \times s$ matrix whose columns are $\boldsymbol{X}_1, \ldots, \boldsymbol{X}_s$, $A = S S^{\mathsf{T}}$ be the associated empirical correlation matrix, and $\hat{\lambda}_s$ be the* smallest *eigenvalue of $A$ (note that $\hat{\lambda}_s \geq 0$). Then:*

$$\mathbb{P}\left(\frac{\hat{\lambda}_s}{s} < \lambda/2\right) \leq 2(s+1)\, e^{-s\, \lambda^2/304} \, , \tag{3}$$

*provided $s \geq 96d/\lambda^2$. Note that if $s \geq (912 \ln n)/\lambda^2$, for some $n > s$, then the right-hand side of (3) is less than $2(n+1)/n^3$.*

Further, we recall that if $A$ is a $d \times d$ positive definite matrix, the *spectral norm* of $A$, denoted by $\|A\|$, coincides with the spectral radius of $A$, i.e., with the largest eigenvalue of $A$. If $\boldsymbol{x} \in \mathbb{R}^d$ then the (Cauchy-Schwartz) inequality $\|A\boldsymbol{x}\| \leq \|A\|\,\|\boldsymbol{x}\|$ holds. Moreover, $\|A^{-1}\| = 1/\|A\|$. See, e.g., [13, Ch. 5].

A final notational remark. In the analysis below we denote by $\widehat{\Delta}_{s,t}$ the random variable obtained by restricting to those sample realizations such that $N_{t-1}$ takes on value $s$. In other words, any predicate $\phi = \phi(\widehat{\Delta}_{s,t})$ involving $\widehat{\Delta}_{s,t}$ should actually be intended as a shorthand for the joint predicate $\phi(\widehat{\Delta}_{N_{t-1},t})$ and "$N_{t-1} = s$".

Armed with these tools, we are ready to prove Theorem 1.

**Proof of Theorem 1.** We say that $t$ is a *marking step* if the instance observed at time $t$ triggered a query on the label of the next instance. We split the regret into a contribution due to marking steps and a contribution due to nonmarking steps keeping the initial $R$ time steps apart,

$$\sum_{t=1}^n \left(\mathbb{P}(Y_t\, \widehat{\Delta}_{N_{t-1},t} < 0) - \mathbb{P}(Y_t\, \Delta_t < 0)\right)$$

$$\leq \sum_{t=1}^n \mathbb{P}\left(\widehat{\Delta}_{N_{t-1},t} \Delta_t \leq 0\right) \qquad \text{(by inequality (1))}$$

$$\leq R + \sum_{t=R+1}^n \mathbb{P}\left(\widehat{\Delta}_{N_{t-1},t} \Delta_t \leq 0\right)$$

$$\leq R + \sum_{t=R+1}^n \mathbb{P}\left(\widehat{\Delta}_{N_{t-1},t} \Delta_t \leq 0,\ \widehat{\Delta}_{N_{t-1},t}^2 \leq (4 \ln t)/N_{t-1}\right) \tag{4}$$

$$+ \sum_{t=R+1}^n \mathbb{P}\left(\widehat{\Delta}_{N_{t-1},t} \Delta_t \leq 0,\ \widehat{\Delta}_{N_{t-1},t}^2 > (4 \ln t)/N_{t-1}\right) . \tag{5}$$

Since instances in marking steps have a small margin, we cannot say much concerning the probability of making a mistake on those steps. Therefore, we bound (4) as follows

$$R + \sum_{t=R+1}^{n} \mathbb{P}\left(\widehat{\Delta}_{N_{t-1},t}\Delta_t \leq 0, \, \widehat{\Delta}^2_{N_{t-1},t} \leq (4\ln t)/N_{t-1}\right)$$

$$\leq R + \sum_{t=R+1}^{n} \mathbb{P}\left(\widehat{\Delta}^2_{N_{t-1},t} \leq (4\ln t)/N_{t-1}\right)$$

$$= R + \mathbb{E}\left[\sum_{t=R+1}^{n} \left\{\widehat{\Delta}^2_{N_{t-1},t} \leq (4\ln t)/N_{t-1}\right\}\right] = R + \mathbb{E}\, L \ .$$

Clearly, $N_R = R$. We now focus on time steps $t \geq R+1$. On those time steps a label is queried if and only if $N_{t-1} \leq (4\ln t)/\widehat{\Delta}^2_{N_{t-1},t}$, and, if a query is issued, then $N_t = N_{t-1} + 1$. Moreover, for any integer $M \geq 1$, if the sampler queried at least $R + M$ labels, then there exists some time step $s \geq R + M$ where $N_s \geq R + M$. Let then $M$ be any integer satisfying $M \geq (16\ln n)/\Delta^2$. Recalling that the total number of queries is $R + L$, we have

$$L \leq M + \sum_{t=R+1}^{n} \left\{N_{t-1} \leq \frac{4\ln t}{\widehat{\Delta}^2_{N_{t-1},t}}, \, N_{t-1} \geq M\right\}$$

$$\leq M + \sum_{t=1}^{n} \sum_{s=\max\{M,R\}}^{t-1} \left\{s \leq \frac{4\ln t}{\widehat{\Delta}^2_{s,t}}\right\} \qquad \text{(recall that } N_R = R)$$

$$\leq M + \sum_{t=1}^{n} \sum_{s=\max\{M,R\}}^{t-1} \left(\left\{s \leq \frac{16\ln t}{\Delta_t^2}\right\} + \left\{|\widehat{\Delta}_{s,t}| \leq |\Delta_t|/2\right\}\right)$$

$$= M + \sum_{t=1}^{n} \sum_{s=\max\{M,R\}}^{t-1} \left\{|\widehat{\Delta}_{s,t}| \leq |\Delta_t|/2\right\} \qquad \text{(since } s \geq M \geq (16\ln n)/\Delta_t^2)$$

$$\leq M + \sum_{t=1}^{n} \sum_{s=\max\{M,R\}}^{t-1} \left\{|\widehat{\Delta}_{s,t} - \Delta_t| \geq |\Delta_t|/2\right\}$$

$$\leq M + \sum_{t=1}^{n} \sum_{s=\max\{M,R\}}^{t-1} \left\{|\widehat{\Delta}_{s,t} + B_{s,t} - \Delta_t| \geq |\Delta_t|/2 - |B_{s,t}|\right\}$$

$$\leq M + \sum_{t=1}^{n} \sum_{s=\max\{M,R\}}^{t-1} \left(\left\{|\widehat{\Delta}_{s,t} + B_{s,t} - \Delta_t| \geq |\Delta_t|/4\right\}\right.$$

$$\left. + \{|B_{s,t}| \geq |\Delta_t|/4\}\right), \tag{6}$$

where the $B_{s,t}$ are arbitrary real numbers whose values will be related to the bias of our estimator $\widehat{\Delta}_{s,t}$, as specified next.

Let $X'_1, \ldots, X'_s$ be the $s$ stored instances in $\widehat{\Delta}_{s,t}$ and let $Y'_1, \ldots, Y'_s$ be their labels. Recalling (2), we compute the conditional expectation of $\widehat{\Delta}_{s,t}$ as follows.

$$
\mathbb{E}\left[\widehat{\Delta}_{s,t} \mid X'_1 = x'_1, \ldots, X'_s = x'_s, X_t = x_t\right]
$$
$$
= \mathbb{E}\left[Y^\top \mid X'_1 = x'_1, \ldots, X'_s = x'_s, X_t = x_t\right] S^\top \left(I + S S^\top\right)^{-1} x_t
$$
$$
= u^\top S S^\top \left(I + S S^\top\right)^{-1} x_t = \Delta_t - u^\top \left(I + S S^\top\right)^{-1} x_t
$$
$$
= \Delta_t - B_{s,t} , \tag{7}
$$

where the bias $B_{s,t}$ satisfies

$$
B_{s,t} = u^\top \left(I + S S^\top\right)^{-1} x_t \le \|u\| \left\|\left(I + S S^\top\right)^{-1}\right\| \|x_t\|
$$
$$
= \left\|\left(I + S S^\top\right)^{-1}\right\| = \frac{1}{1 + \hat{\lambda}_s} \tag{8}
$$

where $\hat{\lambda}_s$ denotes the smallest eigenvalue of the empirical correlation matrix $S S^\top$. Let us now turn to the (conditional) variance of $\widehat{\Delta}_{s,t}$. We have

$$
\widehat{\Delta}_{s,t} = \sum_{i=1}^{s} Y'_i v_i \qquad \text{where} \quad v = S^\top \left(I + S S^\top\right)^{-1} x_t
$$

and, using the simple properties of matrix norms mentioned earlier, $\|v\|^2$ satisfies

$$
\|v\|^2 = x_t^\top \left(I + S S^\top\right)^{-1} S S^\top \left(I + S S^\top\right)^{-1} x_t
$$
$$
\le \|x_t\| \left\|\left(I + S S^\top\right)^{-1} S S^\top \left(I + S S^\top\right)^{-1}\right\| \|x_t\|
$$
$$
= \left\|\left(I + S S^\top\right)^{-1} S S^\top \left(I + S S^\top\right)^{-1}\right\|
$$
$$
= \hat{\lambda}/(1 + \hat{\lambda})^2 \qquad \text{(for some eigenvalue $\hat{\lambda}$ of $S S^\top$)}
$$
$$
\le \max_{x \ge 0} \ x/(1 + x)^2 = 1/4. \tag{9}
$$

We now continue by upper bounding the double sum in (6). Recalling (8), we can write

$$
\{|B_{s,t}| \ge |\Delta_t|/4\} \le \left\{ \frac{1}{1 + \hat{\lambda}_s} \ge |\Delta_t|/4 \right\}
$$
$$
\le \left\{ \frac{1}{1 + \lambda s/2} \ge |\Delta_t|/4 \right\} + \left\{ \frac{\hat{\lambda}_s}{s} < \lambda/2 \right\}. \tag{10}
$$

We observe that if $s > \frac{2}{\lambda}\left(\frac{4}{|\Delta_t|} - 1\right)$ then the first term in (10) vanishes. Hence choosing $M \ge 8/(\lambda \Delta)$ in (6), where $\Delta = \min_{t=1,\ldots,n} |\Delta_t|$, implies

$$
L \le M + \sum_{t=1}^{n} \sum_{s=\max\{M,R\}}^{t-1} \left( \left\{|\widehat{\Delta}_{s,t} + B_{s,t} - \Delta_t| \ge |\Delta_t|/4\right\} + \left\{ \frac{\hat{\lambda}_s}{s} < \lambda/2 \right\} \right).
$$

Therefore

$$L \le M + \sum_{t=1}^{n}\sum_{s=M}^{t-1}\left\{|\widehat{\Delta}_{s,t}+B_{s,t}-\Delta_t| \ge |\Delta_t|/4\right\} + \sum_{t=1}^{n}\sum_{s=R}^{t-1}\left\{\frac{\hat{\lambda}_s}{s} < \lambda/2\right\}.$$

We want to apply expectations to both sides of the last inequality. Lemma 1 states that the stored variables $(X'_1, Y'_1), \ldots, (X'_s, Y'_s)$ are a set of independent random variables distributed as $X_1$. Hence, we drop the primes and simply write $(X_1, Y_1), \ldots, (X_s, Y_s)$. We have

$$\mathbb{P}(Y_1, \ldots, Y_s \mid X_1, \ldots, X_s) = \frac{\mathbb{P}(X_1, Y_1, \ldots, X_s, Y_s)}{\mathbb{P}(X_1, \ldots, X_s)}$$

$$= \frac{\mathbb{P}(X_1, Y_1) \ldots \mathbb{P}(X_s, Y_s)}{\mathbb{P}(X_1) \ldots \mathbb{P}(X_s)}$$

$$= \mathbb{P}(Y_1 \mid X_1) \ldots \mathbb{P}(Y_s \mid X_s).$$

Hence the $Y_i$ are independent when conditioned on the stored examples and we can apply Chernoff-Hoeffding [11] bounds. Conditioning further on $X_t$, and recalling (7) and (9), we thus obtain (w.p.1)

$$\mathbb{P}\left(|\widehat{\Delta}_{s,t}+B_{s,t}-\Delta_t| \ge |\Delta_t|/4 \mid X_1, \ldots, X_s, X_t\right) \le 2\,e^{-s\,\Delta_t^2/2}.$$

Similarly, if $R \ge \max\left\{\frac{96d}{\lambda^2}, \frac{912\ln n}{\lambda^2}\right\}$ we can apply Lemma 2 and get

$$\mathbb{P}\left(\frac{\hat{\lambda}_s}{s} < \lambda/2\right) \le 2(s+1)\,e^{-s\,\lambda^2/304} \le \frac{2(n+1)}{n^3}.$$

Thus we can write

$$\mathbb{E}\,L \le \mathbb{E}\,M + \mathbb{E}\left[\sum_{t=1}^{n}\sum_{s=M}^{t-1}\mathbb{E}\left[\left\{|\widehat{\Delta}_{s,t}+B_{s,t}-\Delta_t| \ge |\Delta_t|/4\right\} \mid X_1, \ldots, X_s, X_t\right]\right]$$

$$+ \mathbb{E}\left[\sum_{t=1}^{n}\sum_{s=R}^{t-1}\left\{\frac{\hat{\lambda}_s}{s} > \lambda/2\right\}\right]$$

$$\le \mathbb{E}\,M + \mathbb{E}\left[\sum_{t=1}^{n}\sum_{s=M}^{t-1}2\,e^{-s\,\Delta_t^2/2}\right] + \sum_{t=1}^{n}\sum_{s=R}^{t-1}\mathbb{P}\left(\frac{\hat{\lambda}_s}{s} < \lambda/2\right)$$

$$\le \mathbb{E}\,M + \sum_{t=1}^{n}\frac{2}{n^7} + \sum_{t=1}^{n}\frac{2(n-1)(n+1)}{n^3} \quad \text{(recall that } M \ge (16\ln n)/\Delta^2)$$

$$\le \mathbb{E}\,M + 4.$$

We now bound the remaining term (5) by adapting a technique from [9]. Let

$$\beta_{s,t} = \sqrt{\frac{\ln t}{\Delta_t^2 s}}, \qquad \widehat{\beta}_{N_{t-1},t} = \sqrt{\frac{\ln t}{\widehat{\Delta}_{N_{t-1},t}^2 \, N_{t-1}}}, \qquad \widehat{\varepsilon}_{N_{t-1},t} = \frac{\widehat{\beta}_{N_{t-1},t}}{1 - \widehat{\beta}_{N_{t-1},t}}$$

for $s = R, \ldots, t-1$. We have

$$\left\{ \widehat{\Delta}_{N_{t-1},t} \Delta_t \leq 0, \; \widehat{\Delta}^2_{N_{t-1},t} > (4\ln t)/N_{t-1} \right\}$$

$$\leq \left\{ |\widehat{\Delta}_{N_{t-1},t} - \Delta_t| \geq |\Delta_t|, \; N_{t-1} > \frac{4\ln t}{\widehat{\Delta}^2_{N_{t-1},t}} \right\}$$

$$\leq \left\{ |\widehat{\Delta}_{N_{t-1},t} - \Delta_t| \geq \beta_{N_{t-1},t}|\Delta_t| \right\} + \left\{ \beta_{N_{t-1},t} \geq \widehat{\varepsilon}_{N_{t-1},t} \right\}$$

$$+ \left\{ \widehat{\varepsilon}_{N_{t-1},t} > 1, \; N_{t-1} > \frac{4\ln t}{\widehat{\Delta}^2_{N_{t-1},t}} \right\}$$

$$= \left\{ |\widehat{\Delta}_{N_{t-1},t} - \Delta_t| \geq \beta_{N_{t-1},t}|\Delta_t| \right\} + \left\{ |\widehat{\Delta}_{N_{t-1},t}| \geq (1 + \beta_{N_{t-1},t})|\Delta_t| \right\}$$

$$+ \left\{ \widehat{\varepsilon}_{N_{t-1},t} > 1, \; N_{t-1} > \frac{4\ln t}{\widehat{\Delta}^2_{N_{t-1},t}} \right\} \qquad \text{(by the very definition of } \widehat{\varepsilon}_{N_{t-1},t})$$

$$\leq 2 \left\{ |\widehat{\Delta}_{N_{t-1},t} - \Delta_t| \geq \beta_{N_{t-1},t}|\Delta_t| \right\} + \left\{ \widehat{\varepsilon}_{N_{t-1},t} > 1, \; N_{t-1} > \frac{4\ln t}{\widehat{\Delta}^2_{N_{t-1},t}} \right\}$$

$$\leq 2 \sum_{s=R}^{t-1} \left\{ |\widehat{\Delta}_{s,t} - \Delta_t| \geq \beta_{s,t}|\Delta_t| \right\} + \left\{ \widehat{\varepsilon}_{N_{t-1},t} > 1, \; N_{t-1} > \frac{4\ln t}{\widehat{\Delta}^2_{N_{t-1},t}} \right\}$$

$$\leq 2 \sum_{s=R}^{t-1} \left( \left\{ |\widehat{\Delta}_{s,t} + B_{s,t} - \Delta_t| \geq \beta_{s,t}|\Delta_t|/2 \right\} + \left\{ |B_{s,t}| \geq \beta_{s,t}|\Delta_t|/2 \right\} \right)$$

$$+ \left\{ \widehat{\varepsilon}_{N_{t-1},t} > 1, \; N_{t-1} > \frac{4\ln t}{\widehat{\Delta}^2_{N_{t-1},t}} \right\}$$

$$= 2 \sum_{s=R}^{t-1} \left( \left\{ |\widehat{\Delta}_{s,t} + B_{s,t} - \Delta_t| \geq \beta_{s,t}|\Delta_t|/2 \right\} + \left\{ |B_{s,t}| \geq \beta_{s,t}|\Delta_t|/2 \right\} \right), \qquad (11)$$

since $\left\{ \widehat{\varepsilon}_{N_{t-1},t} > 1, \; N_{t-1} > \frac{4\ln t}{\widehat{\Delta}^2_{N_{t-1},t}} \right\} = 0$. Now, as for (10), we can argue that

$$\{|B_{s,t}| \geq \beta_{s,t}|\Delta_t|/2\} \leq \left\{ \frac{1}{1 + \lambda s/2} \geq \beta_{s,t}|\Delta_t|/2 \right\} + \left\{ \frac{\widehat{\lambda}_s}{s} < \lambda/2 \right\}.$$

Recalling the definition of $\beta_{s,t}$, it is not hard to show that $s \geq 16/(\lambda^2 \ln t)$ makes the first term on the right-hand side equal to zero. Hence choosing $R \geq 16/\lambda^2$ in (11) implies

$$\left\{ \widehat{\Delta}_{N_{t-1},t} \Delta_t \leq 0, \; \widehat{\Delta}^2_{N_{t-1},t} > (4\ln t)/N_{t-1} \right\}$$

$$\leq 2 \sum_{s=R}^{t-1} \left( \left\{ |\widehat{\Delta}_{s,t} + B_{s,t} - \Delta_t| \geq \beta_{s,t}|\Delta_t|/2 \right\} + \left\{ \frac{\widehat{\lambda}_s}{s} < \lambda/2 \right\} \right)$$

We sum over $t = R + 1, \ldots, n$ and take expectations. As before, we apply both Chernoff-Hoeffding bounds and Lemma 2 (we assumed $R \geq \max\{\frac{96d}{\lambda^2}, \frac{912 \ln n}{\lambda^2}\}$). This results in the following chain of inequalities:

$$\sum_{t=R+1}^{n} \mathbb{P}\left(\widehat{\Delta}_{N_{t-1},t}\Delta_t \leq 0, \; \widehat{\Delta}^2_{N_{t-1},t} > (4 \ln t)/N_{t-1}\right)$$

$$\leq 2 \sum_{t=R+1}^{n} \sum_{s=R}^{t-1} \mathbb{E}\left[2 e^{-2s\beta^2_{s,t}\Delta^2_t}\right] + 2 \sum_{t=R+1}^{n} \sum_{s=R}^{t-1} \mathbb{P}\left(\frac{\hat{\lambda}_s}{s} < \lambda/2\right)$$

$$\leq \sum_{t=R+1}^{n} \frac{4}{t} + \sum_{t=R+1}^{n} \frac{2(n-1)(n+1)}{n^3} \leq 6 + 4 \ln n \; .$$

Piecing together, collecting the conditions on $M$ and $R$ we spread throughout and overapproximating gives the desired bound. □

## 4   Experimental Results

The selective sampling algorithm of Section 3 uses the margin on the current instance to decide whether further sampling is needed. If the margin falls below the current threshold value, then the algorithm asks for the label of the *next* instance. Intuitively, requesting the label of the same instance that realized the small margin should give us a better estimate, and this intuition is empirically confirmed. In fact, the only reason why we ask for the label of the next instance is technical: to analyze the algorithm, we need the time instants at which instances are stored to be stopping times (as specified in the appendix). To carry out the experiments described in this section, we have thus used the smarter variant requesting the labels of the same instances whose margin fell below the current threshold value.

We tested our algorithm on a dataset consisting of the first 100,000 newswire stories from the Reuters Corpus Volume 1. Documents were mapped to real vectors using the bag-of-words representation. More precisely, after tokenization we lemmatized the tokens using a general-purpose finite-state morphological English analyzer and then removed stopwords (we also replaced all digits with a single special character). Document vectors were built by removing all words which did not occur at least three times in the corpus and using the TF-IDF encoding in the form $(1 + \ln \text{TF}) \ln(N/\text{DF})$, where TF is the word frequency in the document, DF is the number of documents containing the word, and $N$ is the total number of documents (if TF$= 0$ the TF-IDF coefficient was also set to 0). To simulate a truly on-line classification task, the DF coefficient was computed incrementally, that is, it was based on the actual documents observed so far according to the original Reuters numbering (to seed the statistics, we used the first three documents that were not subsequently fed to the algorithm). Finally, all document vectors were normalized to length 1.

We associated a binary classification task with each one of the 102 Reuters topics. For each topic, a positive example is any document labelled with that

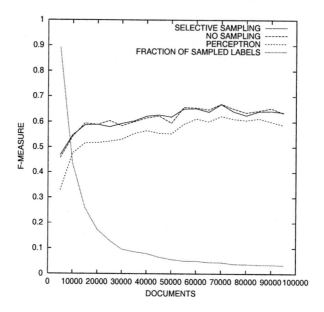

**Fig. 2.** Plot of the instantaneous $F$-measure, averaged over all 102 topics, as the sequence of documents is fed to the classification algorithms. The performance of the selective sampling algorithm is compared to that of its variant which observes all labels and stores only mistaken instances ("NO SAMPLING"), and to that of the standard Perceptron algorithm (also receiving all labels). We also plotted the fraction of sampled labels. The selective sampling algorithm seems to be fairly unaffected by the fact that it observes less and less labels.

topic and a negative example is any document not labelled with that topic. We measured the classification performance using the $F$-measure $2RP/(R+P)$, where $P$ is precision (fraction of correctly classified documents among all documents that were classified positive for the given topic) and $R$ is recall (fraction of correctly classified documents among all documents that are labelled with the given topic).

Figure 2 shows that, on average, the empirical performance of our selective sampling algorithm is essentially unaffected by observing progressively fewer labels (performance of the standard Perceptron algorithm is included as a sanity check). This surprising behavior — we point out again that the selective sampling rule may make a mistake irrespective of whether the label was sampled or not — could be interpreted as the ability of the selective sampling algorithm to match the rate of sampled labels with the achievable learning rate (in other words, as the performance curve flattens, fewer labels are sampled).

Figure 3 shows the performance on each individual topic over the last 5,000 documents in the sequence (this is different from the usual test set performance, as in our case learning was never stopped). Note that performance decreases, on average, according to the frequency of positive examples (which is decreasing from left to right in the plot). On the other hand, the overall fraction of sampled

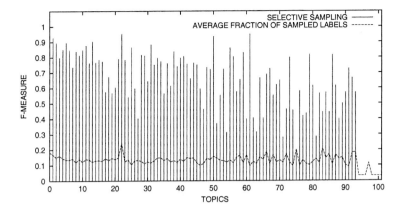

**Fig. 3.** Plot of the final $F$-measure over each of the 102 binary classification tasks sorted according to decreasing frequency of positive examples. The performance of our algorithm (as measured by the $F$-measure) tends to decrease as the fraction of positive examples decreases. On the other hand, the fraction of observed labels tends to remain constant. On the very infrequent topics (right-most side of the plot) the selective sampling algorithm exhibits a degenerate behavior.

labels stays about the same (13%) throughout the different topics, but for the last few ones where learning did not take place at all due to the scarcity of positive examples (right-most side of the plot).

## 5    Conclusions and Ongoing Research

We have introduced a new selective sampling algorithm for probabilistic linear threshold classifiers. The algorithm maintains a least-squares estimate of the true (unknown) margin on the data and compares such an estimate with a dinamically adjusted threshold whose value is suggested by a large deviation analysis. We have proven a bound on the cumulative expected regret which grows only logarithmically above the expected number of requested labels. In turn, under suitable assumptions on the margin distribution (see Remark 1), the expected number of labels grows only logarithmically with the horizon $n$. We have reported on experiments with a "smarter" (or just "more reasonable") variant of the selective sampling algorithm which asks for the label of the instance that caused the small margin. We have shown that on textual data this algorithm seems to be unaffected by observing progressively fewer labels.

Our analysis in Section 3 works under a fair amount of side assumptions. For instance, the algorithm needs prior knowledge of both the horizon $n$ and the smallest eigenvalue $\lambda$. This information is needed to keep the bias of the algorithm suitably small. We are currently investigating the extent to which this assumption could be removed without paying the price of a larger regret. By the same token, we are trying to prove bounds in terms of the margin of the process with no side conditions on the margin distribution.

Analyzing the algorithm we used in the experiments does not seem to be easy, since a direct concentration analysis appears to be inapplicable. We are currently exploring different avenues.

Finally, we are performing more extensive experiments applying our algorithms to other datasets, to see whether the surprising behavior reported in Section 4 recurs.

## Acknowledgements

This research was partially supported by the European Commission under the KerMIT Project No. IST-2001-25431. Warm thanks to Jean-Michel Renders of Xerox Research Centre Europe for the customized preprocessing of the Reuters Corpus. We would also like to thank the Colt reviewers for helpful comments.

## References

1. Angluin, D. (1988). Queries and concept learning. *Machine Learning*, 2(4):319–342.
2. Atlas, L., Cohn, R., and Ladner, R. (1990). Training connectionist networks with queries and selective sampling. In *NIPS 2*. MIT Press.
3. Azoury, K., and Warmuth, M.K. (2001). Relative loss bounds for on-line density estimation with the exponential family of distributions, *Machine Learning*, 43:211–246.
4. Campbell, C., Cristianini, N., and Smola, A. (2000). Query learning with large margin classifiers. In Proc. *17th ICML*, pages 111–118. Morgan Kaufmann.
5. Cesa-Bianchi, N., Conconi, A., and Gentile, C. (2002). A second-order Perceptron algorithm. In *Proc. COLT'02*, pages 121–137. LNAI 2375, Springer.
6. Cristianini, N. & Shawe-Taylor, J. (2001). *An Introduction to Support Vector Machines*. Cambridge University Press.
7. Forster, J., and Warmuth, M. K. (2001). Relative Loss Bounds for Temporal-Difference Learning. *Machine Learning*, to appear.
8. Freund, Y., Seung, S., Shamir, E., and Tishby, N. (1997). Selective sampling using the query by committee algorithm. *Machine Learning*, 28(2/3):133–168.
9. Gavaldà, R., and Watanabe, O. (2001). Sequential sampling algorithms: Unified analysis and lower bounds. In *Proc. SAGA'01*, pages 173–187. Springer.
10. Helmbold, D.P., and Panizza, S. (1997). Some label efficient learning results. In *Proc. 10th COLT*, pages 218–230. ACM Press.
11. Hoeffding, W. (1963). Probability inequalities for sums of bounded random variables. *Journal of the American Statistical Association*, 58:13–30.
12. Hoerl, A., and Kennard, R. (1970). Ridge regression: biased estimation for nonorthogonal problems. *Technometrics*, 12:55–67.
13. Horn, R.A., & Johnson, C.R. (1985). *Matrix Analysis*. Cambridge University Press.
14. Shawe-Taylor, J., Williams, C., Cristianini, N., Kandola, J. (2003). On the eigenspectrum of the Gram matrix and the generalization error of kernel PCA. Unpublished. Preliminary version: Shawe-Taylor, J., Cristianini, N., Kandola, J., On the concentration of spectral properties, NIPS 14, MIT Press, 2002.
15. Tong, S., and Koller, D. (2000). Support vector machine active learning with applications to text classification. In *Proc. 17th ICML*. Morgan Kaufmann.
16. Vapnik, V. (1998). *Statistical learning theory*. New York: J. Wiley & Sons.
17. Vovk, V. (2001). Competitive on-line statistics. *International Statistical Review*, 69:213–248.

## A    Appendix

This appendix contains the proof of Lemma 1. Before proving it, we need a few definitions and a technical lemma.

An integer-valued random variable $T$ is a stopping time w.r.t. a random process $Z_1, Z_2, \ldots$ if, for each $k \geq 1$, $\{T = k\}$ belongs to the $\sigma$-algebra $\sigma(Z_1, \ldots, Z_k)$ generated by the random variables $Z_1, \ldots, Z_k$. A stopping time $T$ is finite if $\mathbb{P}(T = \infty) = 0$. The next result proves an elementary property of stopping times.

**Lemma 3.** *If $T$ is a finite stopping time w.r.t. the i.i.d. random variables $Z_1$, $Z_2, \ldots$, then $Z_{T+1}$ is independent of $Z_1, \ldots, Z_T$ and distributed as $Z_1$.*

**Proof.** Choose any $A \in \sigma(Z_1, \ldots, Z_T)$ and choose any subset $B$ of the range of $Z_{T+1}$ such that $\{Z_{T+1} \in B\}$ is measurable. We have

$$\mathbb{P}(A \cap \{Z_{T+1} \in B\}) = \sum_{j=1}^{\infty} \mathbb{P}(A \cap \{T = j\} \cap \{Z_{j+1} \in B\})$$

$$= \sum_{j=1}^{\infty} \mathbb{P}(A \cap \{T = j\}) \, \mathbb{P}(Z_{j+1} \in B)$$

$$\text{(since } A \cap \{T = j\} \text{ is } \sigma(Z_1, \ldots, Z_j)\text{-measurable)}$$

$$= \sum_{j=1}^{\infty} \mathbb{P}(A \cap \{T = j\}) \, \mathbb{P}(Z_1 \in B) = \mathbb{P}(A) \, \mathbb{P}(Z_1 \in B). \quad (12)$$

Hence, taking $A = \Omega$, we get $\mathbb{P}(Z_{T+1} \in B) = \mathbb{P}(Z_1 \in B)$, showing that $Z_{T+1}$ is distributed as $Z_1$. Consequently, from (12) we get that $\mathbb{P}(A \cap \{Z_{T+1} \in B\}) = \mathbb{P}(A)\mathbb{P}(Z_{T+1} \in B)$, as desired.    □

**Proof of Lemma 1.** The random variables $T_1, T_2, \ldots$ are finite stopping times with respect to the i.i.d. process $Z_1, Z_2, \ldots$ according to which the examples are generated. Indeed, $\{T_i = k\}$ is completely determined by the values taken by $Z_1, \ldots, Z_k$. Furthermore, $\mathbb{P}(T_i = \infty) = 0$ as, for each $i \geq 1$ and for $t$ large enough, $\widehat{\Delta}^2_{N_{t-1}, t} \leq (4 \ln t)/N_{t-1}$, where $N_{t-1} = i - 1$, will hold.

Pick any $i \geq 1$. By Lemma 3, $Z_{T_i+1}$ is independent of $Z_1, \ldots, Z_{T_i}$ and distributed as $Z_1$. Since $Z_{T_1+1}, \ldots, Z_{T_{i-1}+1}$ are $\sigma(Z_1, \ldots, Z_{T_i})$-measurable (this is guaranteed by the fact that $T_{i-1} < T_i$ always holds), we get that $Z_{T_i+1}$ is also independent of $Z_{T_1+1}, \ldots, Z_{T_{i-1}+1}$. As $i$ was chosen arbitrarily, we get that $Z_{T_1+1}, Z_{T_2+1}, \ldots$ are independent random variables distributed as $Z_1$.    □

# Learning Algorithms for Enclosing Points in Bregmanian Spheres

Koby Crammer and Yoram Singer

School of Computer Science & Engineering
The Hebrew University, Jerusalem 91904, Israel
{kobics,singer}@cs.huji.ac.il

**Abstract.** We discuss the problem of finding a generalized sphere that encloses points originating from a single source. The points contained in such a sphere are within a maximal divergence from a center point. The divergences we study are known as the Bregman divergences which include as a special case both the Euclidean distance and the relative entropy. We cast the learning task as an optimization problem and show that it results in a simple dual form which has interesting algebraic properties. We then discuss a general algorithmic framework to solve the optimization problem. Our training algorithm employs an auxiliary function that bounds the dual's objective function and can be used with a broad class of Bregman functions. As a specific application of the algorithm we give a detailed derivation for the relative entropy. We analyze the generalization ability of the algorithm by adopting margin-style proof techniques. We also describe and analyze two schemes of online algorithms for the case when the radius of the sphere is set in advance.

## 1 Introduction

To motivate the topic of this paper let us discuss briefly the following application. The task of speaker verification is concerned with determining whether a speech segment is uttered by a pre-specified speaker or by an imposter. This problem is inherently different than classification problems since in general the verification system is provided at the training stage with examples only from the speaker whose voice we wish to verify in the test phase. Although a verification system might receive supervised data from different speakers, casting the problem as a multiclass problem might be problematic since the number of classes is not fixed and an imposter is not necessarily one of the speakers in the training set. Therefore, a common approach in speaker verification systems is to build a different model for each speaker where each model is trained based on examples from a single source (speaker).

In the problem setting we discuss, we indeed observe examples from a single source and our goal is to find a body of a small volume such most of the examples lie inside the learned body. Since we observe examples from a single source we term this problem the *uniclass*[1] problem. To illustrate the problem,

---

[1] In a similar setting [18], this problem was called the *one-class* problem. We believe however that the term uniclass is more appropriate.

B. Schölkopf and M.K. Warmuth (Eds.): COLT/Kernel 2003, LNAI 2777, pp. 388–402, 2003.

let us assume that the examples are points in an Euclidean space. A natural and simple candidate for enclosing points from a single source is a ball. The learning problem therefore reduces to the problem of finding the center and the radius of a ball enclosing the points. Clearly, a finite sample can always be enclosed in a sphere of a large radius. However, such a sphere is very likely to include points not belonging to the source. Therefore, we give some leeway to the learning algorithm so that a few of the points may not lie inside the ball. This view cast a natural tradeoff between the radius of the enclosing sphere and the portion of points outside this ball.

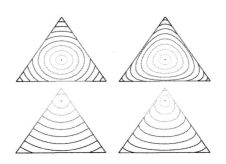

**Fig. 1.** The level sets induced by the Euclidean distance (left column) and the relative entropy (right column). The points are in the three dimensional simplex and are projected onto the plane. Each line represents equidistant points from a center where the center is at [0.3 0.3 0.3] in the top figures and at [0.8 0.2 0.2] in the bottom figures.

In quite a few applications, the examples do not reside in an Euclidean space. For instance, in text retrieval applications documents are often represented by word frequencies and information theoretic measures are more natural than the Euclidean distance as the means for assessing divergences between documents. We therefore employ a rather general notion of divergence, called *Bregman divergences* [3]. A Bregman divergence is defined via a strictly convex function $F : X \to \mathbb{R}$ defined on a closed, convex set $X \subseteq \mathbb{R}^n$. A Bregman function $F$ needs to specify a set of constraints. We omit the discussion of the constraints and refer the reader to [4]. All the functions we discuss in this paper fulfill these constraints and are hence Bregman functions. In this paper we occasionally require that $X$ is also bounded and therefore compact. Assume that $F$ is continuously differentiable at all points of $X_{\text{int}}$, the interior of $X$, which we assume is nonempty. The Bregman divergence associated with $F$ is defined for $\mathbf{x} \in X$ and $\mathbf{w} \in X_{\text{int}}$ to be

$$B_F\left(\mathbf{x}\|\mathbf{w}\right) \overset{\text{def}}{=} F(\mathbf{x}) - [F(\mathbf{w}) + \nabla F(\mathbf{w}) \cdot (\mathbf{x} - \mathbf{w})] \ .$$

Thus, $B_F$ measures the difference between $F$ and its first-order Taylor expansion about $\mathbf{w}$, evaluated at $\mathbf{x}$. Bregman distances generalize some commonly studied distance measures. The divergences we employ are defined via a single scalar convex function $f$ such that $F(\mathbf{x}) = \sum_{l=1}^{n} f(x_l)$, where $x_l$ is the $l$th coordinate of $\mathbf{x}$. In this paper we exemplify our algorithms and their analyses with two commonly used divergences. The first, when $X \subset \mathbb{R}^n$ is derived by setting $f(x) = (1/2)\, x^2$ and thus $B_F$ becomes the squared Euclidean distance between $\mathbf{x}$ and $\mathbf{w}$, $B_F\left(\mathbf{x}\|\mathbf{w}\right) = (1/2)\, \|\mathbf{x} - \mathbf{w}\|^2$. The second divergence we consider is derived by setting $f(x) = x \log(x) - x$. In this case $B_F$ is the (unnormalized) relative entropy,

$B_{\text{RE}}(\mathbf{x}\|\mathbf{w}) = \sum_{l=1}^{n} \left( x_l \log \left( \frac{x_l}{w_l} \right) - x_l + w_l \right)$. While the above divergence can be defined over a convex subset of $\mathbb{R}_+^n$, in this paper we restrict the domain in the case of the relative entropy to be a compact subset of the $n$th dimensional simplex, $\Delta_n = \{\mathbf{x} \mid x_l \geq 0; \sum_l x_l = 1\}$. For this specific choice of domain, the relative entropy reduces to $B_{\text{RE}}(\mathbf{x}\|\mathbf{w}) = \sum_{l=1}^{n} x_l \log(x_l/w_l)$ which is often referred to as the Kullback-Leibler divergence. An illustration of the Bregmanian spheres for the Euclidean norm and the relative entropy is given in Fig. 1. The two divergences exhibit different characteristics: the level sets of the Euclidean distance intersect the boundary of the simplex, the relative entropy bends close to the boundary and all the level sets remain strictly within the simplex.

The problem we consider in this paper is the construction of a simple sub-set that encloses a large portion of a set of instances. Concretely, we are given a set of examples $S = \{\mathbf{x}_i\}_{i=1}^{m}$ where $\mathbf{x}_i \in X$. Our goal is to find $\mathbf{w} \in X$ such that many of the examples attain a Bregman divergence from $\mathbf{w}$ that is smaller than $R$ ($R \geq 0$). Informally, we seek $\mathbf{w} \in X$ and a small scalar $R$ such that most of $\mathbf{x}_i \in S$ are in a Bregmanian ball of radius $R$, $B_F(\mathbf{x}_i\|\mathbf{w}) \leq R$. Clearly, the smaller $R$ is, the less likely we are to succeed in our task. Therefore, there is a natural tradeoff between the size of $R$ and the number of points in $S$ that are within a divergence $R$ from $\mathbf{w}$. We thus associate a loss with each example $\mathbf{x}_i$ that falls outside the Bregmanian ball of radius $R$ This loss is equal to excess Bregman divergence of a point $\mathbf{x}_i$ from $\mathbf{w}$ over the maximal radius $R$, that is, $B_F(\mathbf{x}_i\|\mathbf{w}) - R$. We cast the tradeoff between the need to find a Bregmanian ball with a small radius and the need to attain a small excess loss on each point as the following optimization problem,

$$\min_{\mathbf{w},R,\xi} R + \frac{1}{\nu m} \sum_{i=1}^{m} \xi_i \quad \text{s.t} \quad B_F(\mathbf{x}_i\|\mathbf{w}) \leq R + \xi_i \; ; \; \xi_i \geq 0 \quad i = 1,\ldots,m \; . \quad (1)$$

Here $\nu \in [0,1]$ is a parameter that governs the tradeoff between the value of $R$ and the total amount of discrepancies from the Bregmanian sphere. We also need to require that $R$ is non-negative and $\mathbf{w}$ to be in $X$. However, these constraints are automatically fulfilled at the optimal solution. We would also like to note that although a Bregman divergence is not necessarily convex in its second argument $\mathbf{w}$, the dual problem of Eq. (1) is concave and attains a unique optimal solution.

The optimization problem defined in Eq. (1) was originally cast for the squared distance by Schölkopf [14] and Tax and Duin [18]. Later on, Schölkopf et al. [15] introduced and analyzed a closely related problem in which the goal is to separate most of the examples from the origin using a single hyperplane. We adopt the notation used in [15]. However, our setting is more general since we allow the use of any Bregman divergence that satisfies the conditions above.

The uniclass problem has many potential applications such as simple clustering, outliers detection (e.g. intrusion detection), novelty detection, and density estimation. Due to the lack of space we refer the reader to the work of Tax [17], Tax and Duin [18] and Schölkopf et al. [15] and the references therein. Finally, we would like to emphasize that although the use of the Bregman divergences in the context of uniclass problems is novel, Bregman divergences have been trendy and useful tools in other learning settings such as online learning [1, 10, 9], boosting [6], and principal component analysis [5]. We now turn to the dual form of the optimization problem described in Eq. (1) and its properties.

## 2   The Optimization Problem

The Lagrangian of Eq. (1) is equal to,

$$\mathcal{L} = R + \frac{1}{\nu m} \sum_{i=1}^{m} \xi_i + \sum_{i=1}^{m} \alpha_i \left[ B_F(\mathbf{x}_i \| \mathbf{w}) - R - \xi_i \right] - \gamma_i \xi_i$$

$$= R \left( 1 - \sum_{i=1}^{m} \alpha_i \right) + \sum_{i=1}^{m} \xi_i \left( \frac{1}{\nu m} - \alpha_i - \gamma_i \right) + \sum_{i=1}^{m} \alpha_i B_F(\mathbf{x}_i \| \mathbf{w}) . \quad (2)$$

We first compute the derivatives of the Lagrangian with respect to its primal variables $R$ and $\xi_i$ and equate them to 0,

$$\frac{\partial}{\partial R} \mathcal{L} = 1 - \sum_{i=1}^{m} \alpha_i = 0 \quad \Rightarrow \quad \sum_{i=1}^{m} \alpha_i = 1 \quad (3)$$

$$\frac{\partial}{\partial \xi_i} \mathcal{L} = \frac{1}{\nu m} - \alpha_i - \gamma_i = 0 \quad \Rightarrow \quad \alpha_i \le \frac{1}{\nu m} \quad (4)$$

Next we compute the derivate of $B_F(\mathbf{x} \| \mathbf{w})$ with respect to $\mathbf{w}$,

$$\nabla_{\mathbf{w}} B_F(\mathbf{x} \| \mathbf{w}) = \nabla_{\mathbf{w}} \left[ F(\mathbf{x}) - F(\mathbf{w}) - \nabla F(\mathbf{w}) \cdot (\mathbf{x} - \mathbf{w}) \right]$$
$$= -\nabla F(\mathbf{w}) - \triangle F(\mathbf{w})(\mathbf{x} - \mathbf{w}) + \nabla F(\mathbf{w}) = -\triangle F(\mathbf{w})(\mathbf{x} - \mathbf{w}) , (5)$$

where $\triangle F(\mathbf{w})$ is the matrix of the second order derivatives of $F$ with respect to $\mathbf{w}$ and we write all vectors as column vectors. Using Eq. (5) we calculate the derivative of the Lagrangian with respect to $\mathbf{w}$, $\nabla_{\mathbf{w}} \mathcal{L} = \sum_{i=1}^{m} \alpha_i \nabla_{\mathbf{w}} B_F(\mathbf{x}_i \| \mathbf{w}) = -\sum_{i=1}^{m} \alpha_i \triangle F(\mathbf{w}) \cdot (\mathbf{x}_i - \mathbf{w})$. Setting $\nabla_{\mathbf{w}} \mathcal{L} = 0$ we get,

$$-\sum_{i=1}^{m} \alpha_i \triangle F(\mathbf{w}) \cdot (\mathbf{x}_i - \mathbf{w}) = 0 \quad \Rightarrow \quad \triangle F(\mathbf{w}) \left[ \sum_{i=1}^{m} \alpha_i \mathbf{x}_i - \mathbf{w} \sum_{i=1}^{m} \alpha_i \right] = 0 . (6)$$

Since $F(\mathbf{w})$ is strictly convex, then $\triangle F(\mathbf{w})$ is positive definite and thus its inverse exists[2]. Multiplying both sides of Eq. (6) and using the fact that $\sum_i \alpha_i = 1$ (Eq. (3)) we now get,

$$\mathbf{w} = \sum_{i=1}^{m} \alpha_i \mathbf{x}_i . \quad (7)$$

---

[2] Since we assume that $F(\mathbf{x}) = \sum_{l=1}^{n} f(x_l)$, we thus have that $\triangle F(\mathbf{w})$ is a diagonal matrix, with positive elements on the diagonal.

Substituting Eqs. (3), (4) and (7) in the Lagrangian given by Eq. (2) we get the following dual objective function,

$$Q(\alpha) = \sum_{i=1}^{m} \alpha_i B_F(\mathbf{x}_i\| \sum_{j=1}^{m} \alpha_j \mathbf{x}_j) = \sum_{i=1}^{m} \alpha_i F(\mathbf{x}_i) - F\left(\sum_{j=1}^{m} \alpha_j \mathbf{x}_j\right) \sum_{i=1}^{m} \alpha_i$$

$$-\nabla F\left(\sum_{j=1}^{m} \alpha_j \mathbf{x}_j\right)\left(\sum_{i=1}^{m} \alpha_i \mathbf{x}_i - \sum_{j=1}^{m} \alpha_j \mathbf{x}_j \sum_{i=1}^{m} \alpha_i\right) . \quad (8)$$

Using again Eq. (3) we finally get, $Q(\alpha) = \sum_{i=1}^{m} \alpha_i F(\mathbf{x}_i) - F\left(\sum_{i=1}^{m} \alpha_i \mathbf{x}_i\right)$. In summary, we get the following dual problem for Eq. (1)

$$\begin{aligned} \max_\alpha \ & Q(\alpha) = \sum_{i=1}^{m} \alpha_i F(\mathbf{x}_i) - F\left(\sum_{i=1}^{m} \alpha_i \mathbf{x}_i\right) \\ \text{s.t.} \ & \sum_{i=1}^{m} \alpha_i = 1 \ ; \ 0 \le \alpha_i \le \frac{1}{\nu m} \quad i = 1,\ldots,m \end{aligned} \quad (9)$$

We would like to underscore a few properties of the above constrained optimization problem before turning to an algorithm for finding the optimal solution. First, the objective function, $Q(\alpha)$, is strictly concave and also non-negative due to the convexity of $F$. This function is the difference between the convex combination of $F$ evaluated at each sample point (the line in Fig. 2) and $F$ applied to the convex combination of the sample (the curve in in Fig. 2). Second, if $\nu = 1$ than there is a unique assignment that satisfies the two constraints, namely $\alpha_j = 1/m$ for all $j = 1,\ldots,m$. Using similar arguments to Schölkopf et al. [15], it is rather simple to prove that $\nu$ is a lower bound on the fraction of examples for which whose Lagrange multiplier $\alpha_i$ is greater than zero, and also that $\nu$ is an upper bound on the fraction of examples which are outliers (examples for which $\xi_i > 0$).

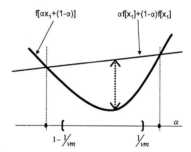

**Fig. 2.** Illustration of the dual's objective function for the uniclass problem.

## 3    A Parallel-Update Algorithm

In this section we describe and analyze an algorithm that finds the optimal set of $\alpha$'s by solving the dual optimization problem given in Eq. (9). Our algorithm can be used in conjunction with a rather general class of Bregman divergences. We would like to note in passing that although there exists a wide range of algorithms for finding the optimal solution of a concave function under linear constraints (see for instance [8, 4]), these algorithms are rather general and do not take advantage of the particular form of the optimization problem on hand.

In contrast, we describe in this section a specialized algorithm that is simple to implement and to analyze. Our algorithm employs an auxiliary function that bounds the objective function from below and is reminiscent of a recent learning algorithm for SVMs by Sha et. al [16] and also bears resemblance to fixed-point algorithms such as the NMF algorithm [11] and the EM algorithm [7].

Before diving into the specifics of the algorithm we first provide a high level overview of its operation. Let $Q(\alpha)$ be the objective function of Eq. (9). We employ an auxiliary function $R(\cdot, \cdot)$ which for any $\alpha^* > 0$ satisfies two properties:

$$Q(\alpha) = R(\alpha, \alpha) \qquad (10)$$
$$Q(\alpha) \geq R(\alpha, \alpha^*) \ .$$

**Input:**

– A set of examples $\{\mathbf{x}_i\}_{i=1}^m$ , $x_{i,l} > 0$
– A Bregman function $F(\mathbf{x})$

**Initialize:** Set $\alpha_i^1 = \frac{1}{m}$

**Loop:** For $t = 1, 2, ..., T$

– Set $\mathbf{w}_t = \sum_i \alpha_i^t \mathbf{x}_i$
– Update

$$\alpha^{t+1} \leftarrow \texttt{NewWeights}(\mathbf{w}_t, \{\mathbf{x}_i\}_i^m, \alpha^t)$$

**Compute sphere's parameters:**

– Set $\mathbf{w} = \sum_i \alpha_i^T \mathbf{x}_i$
– Choose $i$ such that $\alpha_i^T \in (0, \frac{1}{\nu m})$
– Define $R = B_F(\mathbf{x}_i \| \mathbf{w})$

**Output :**   Center $\mathbf{w}$ ; Radius $R$

**Fig. 3.** The parallel - update algorithm for the uniclass problem.

The algorithm is initialized with any $\alpha^1$ that satisfies Eq. (9). It then works in rounds. On round $t$ it sets $\alpha^{t+1}$ to be the maximizer of $R(\alpha, \alpha^t)$. As we show in the sequel, the above two properties of $R$ imply that the value of $Q(\alpha^t)$ is a non-decreasing function with a single fixed-point at the optimal solution. The analysis we provide below further motivates the following construction of $R$.

The function $R$ that we use for Eq. (9) is,

$$R\left(\alpha, \alpha^t\right) = \sum_{l=1}^n \sum_i \alpha_i f\left(x_{i,l}\right) - \sum_{l=1}^n \frac{1}{\sum_j \alpha_j^t x_{j,l}} \sum_i \alpha_i^t x_{i,l} f\left(\frac{\alpha_i}{\alpha_i^t} \sum_j \alpha_j^t x_{j,l}\right) \ , (11)$$

where $f$ is the per-coordinate Bregman function. For simplicity, we assume that $x_{i,l} > 0$ though there are less restrictive terms for which Eq. (11) is well defined. Let us assume for now that $R$ satisfies Eq. (10). Replacing $Q(\alpha)$ with $R\left(\alpha, \alpha^t\right)$ we get the following optimization problem,

$$\alpha^{t+1} = \arg\max_\alpha R\left(\alpha, \alpha^t\right) \ \text{s.t.} \ \sum_{i=1}^m \alpha_i = 1 \ ; \ 0 \leq \alpha_i \leq \frac{1}{\nu m} \quad i = 1, \ldots, m \ .(12)$$

The above constrained optimization problem constitutes the core of the algorithm. To solve Eq. (12) we first write its appropriate Lagrangian and get,

$$\mathcal{L}(\alpha) = R\left(\alpha, \alpha^t\right) - \gamma\left(\sum_{i=1}^m \alpha_i - 1\right) + \sum_{i=1}^m \mu_i \alpha_i - \sum_{i=1}^m \eta_i\left(\alpha_i - 1/(\nu m)\right) \ , \text{where}$$

$\mu_i, \eta_i \geq 0$ $(1 \leq i \leq m)$ and $\gamma$ are the Lagrange multipliers. Taking the derivative of $\mathcal{L}$ with respect to $\alpha_i$ we get,

$$\frac{\partial}{\partial \alpha_i} \mathcal{L} = -\sum_{l=1}^{n} x_{i,l} f'\left(\frac{\alpha_i}{\alpha_i^t} \sum_j \alpha_j^t x_{j,l}\right) + \sum_{l=1}^{n} f(x_{i,l}) - \gamma + \mu_i - \eta_i \ . \quad (13)$$

Rearranging and adding terms which do not depend on $i$ in Eq. (13) we get,

$$\sum_{l=1}^{n} x_{i,l} f'\left(\frac{\alpha_i}{\alpha_i^t} \sum_j \alpha_j^t x_{j,l}\right) - \sum_{l=1}^{n} f(x_{i,l}) + \gamma - \mu_i + \eta_i$$

$$= -B_F\left(\mathbf{x}_i \| \sum_j \alpha_j^t \mathbf{x}_j\right) + \mathbf{x}_i \cdot \left[\nabla F\left(\frac{\alpha_i}{\alpha_i^t} \sum_j \alpha_j^t \mathbf{x}_j\right) - \nabla F\left(\sum_j \alpha_j^t \mathbf{x}_j\right)\right]$$

$$+\gamma' - \mu_i + \eta_i \ ,$$

where $\gamma' = \gamma + \sum_{l=1}^{n}\left[-f\left(\sum_j \alpha_j^t x_{j,l}\right) + f'\left(\sum_j \alpha_j^t x_{j,l}\right)\sum_j \alpha_j^t x_{j,l}\right]$. For clarity, we denote by $\mathbf{w}_t = \sum_j \alpha_j^t \mathbf{x}_j$. Setting the derivative of the Lagrangian, in the manipulated form above, to zero we get,

$$\mathbf{x}_i \cdot \left[\nabla F\left(\frac{\alpha_i}{\alpha_i^t} \mathbf{w}_t\right) - \nabla F(\mathbf{w}_t)\right] = B_F(\mathbf{x}_i \| \mathbf{w}_t) - \gamma' + \mu_i - \eta_i \ . \quad (14)$$

Eq. (14) is the heart of a single weight-update iteration: given $\alpha^t$ we set $\mathbf{w}_t = \sum_j \alpha_j^t \mathbf{x}_j$; we then solve Eq. (14) for $\alpha$ by fixing $\mathbf{w}_t$ and $\alpha^t$. The Lagrange multipliers are still present and are set so that the constraints of Eq. (9) are satisfied along with their corresponding Karush-Kuhn-Tucker (KKT) conditions. Before proceeding to the description of the full algorithm. We would like to note that the solution of Eq. (14) takes a multiplicative form, $\alpha_i^{t+1} = \alpha_i^t g(\mathbf{w}_t, \mathbf{x}_i, \gamma', \mu_i, \eta_i)$.

Pseudo-code for the algorithm is given in Fig. 3. The algorithm starts with an initialization of $\alpha_i$ that satisfies the constraints by setting $\alpha_i^1 = 1/m$. It then alternates between setting $\mathbf{w}_t$ from the current $\alpha^t$ and finding a new set $\alpha^{t+1}$ from the newly calculated $\mathbf{w}_t$. The radius of the resulting Bregmanian sphere is the computed by choosing any point $\mathbf{x}_i$ that lies on the sphere itself and computing its distance to the center of the sphere $\mathbf{w}$. Such a point can be easily identified since KKT conditions imply that its Lagrange multiplier should be inside $(0, 1/(\nu m))$.

**Analysis:** We now turn our attention to the convergence properties of the above algorithm and its correctness. The following lemma serves as a basic technical tool in our analysis. The lemma is a generalization of Eq. (29) in [11].

**Lemma 1.** *Let $f(x)$ be a convex function. Let $\{a_i\}_{i=1}^{m}$ and $\{z_i\}_{i=1}^{m}$ be two sets of variables such that $a_i > 0$ for all $i$ and $\sum_i a_i = 1$. Then, the following bound holds, $f(\sum_i z_i) \leq \sum_i a_i f(z_i/a_i)$ .*

*Proof.* The convexity of $f$ implies , $f\left(\sum_i z_i\right) = f\left(\sum_i a_i \frac{z_i}{a_i}\right) \le \sum_i a_i f(z_i/a_i)$ . $\qquad \square$

We now state the main conditions of the function $R$.

**Lemma 2.** *Assume that $x_{i,l} > 0$ and $\alpha_i^t > 0$ for all $i$ and $l$, then $Q$ (defined in Eq. (9)) and $R$ (defined in Eq. (11)) satisfy,* (1) $R(\alpha, \alpha) = Q(\alpha)$ *and* (2) $R(\alpha, \alpha^t) \le Q(\alpha)$.

We omit the proof due to lack of space and proceed to the main result of this section. In the following theorem we show that the process of solving Eq. (12) repeatedly never decrease the value of the objective function, and furthermore, the only fixed point of the algorithm is the solution of Eq. (9).

**Theorem 1.** *Let $\alpha^t$, $t = 1, 2, \ldots$ be the solutions obtained by the algorithm for Eq. (12). Then, $Q(\alpha^t) \le Q(\alpha^{t+1})$ for all $t \ge 1$. Furthermore, $\alpha^t = \alpha^{t+1}$ iff $\alpha^t$ is the optimal solution of Eq. (9).*

*Proof.* To prove the first property we apply Lemma 2. The first part of Lemma 2 implies that $Q(\alpha^t) = R(\alpha^t, \alpha^t)$. Since $\alpha^t$ satisfies the constraints of Eq. (12) and $\alpha^{t+1}$ is the maximizer of Eq. (12) we have that $R(\alpha^t, \alpha^t) \le R(\alpha^{t+1}, \alpha^t)$. Using the second part of Lemma 2 we have, $R(\alpha^{t+1}, \alpha^t) \le Q(\alpha^{t+1})$. Summing up we get, $Q(\alpha^t) = R(\alpha^t, \alpha^t) \le R(\alpha^{t+1}, \alpha^t) \le Q(\alpha^{t+1})$, which proves property (1).

For the second property, let us start with Eq. (12). We have showed that Eq. (13), when set to zero, defines a set of constraints that serve as the conditions needed for solving Eq. (12). A fixed point of Eq. (13) is obtained when $\alpha^t = \alpha^{t+1}$. Put another way, $\alpha^t$ is a fixed point of Eq. (13) if and only if it is a solution for the following set of equations (for $i = 1, \ldots, m$),

$$\sum_{l=1}^n x_{i,l} f'\left(\sum_j \alpha_j^t x_{j,l}\right) - \sum_{l=1}^n f(x_{i,l}) + \gamma - \mu_i + \eta_i = 0 . \qquad (15)$$

Similarly, solving Eq. (9) by writing the appropriate Lagrangian and comparing its derivative with respect to $\alpha_i$ to zero yields the same set of equations as Eq. (15). Since the fixed points of Eq. (12) and the optimal solution of Eq. (9) yield the same set of equations, which cast necessary and sufficient conditions for optimality, we obtain that a fixed point of Eq. (12) is the optimal solution for Eq. (9). $\qquad \square$

## 4   A Closed-Form Update for the Relative Entropy

In the previous section we described a general iterative algorithm for solving the constrained optimization problem for the Bregmanian uniclass problem. We have left unspecified though the algorithmic details of finding $\alpha^{t+1}$ that minimizes $R(\alpha, \alpha^t)$. In this section we demonstrate the applicability of our approach by describing an efficient algorithm for the relative entropy as the Bregman divergence. Similar updates can be devised for the squared norm. We focus though on the relative entropy which has not been explored in the context of uniclass problems.

To cast the relative entropy as a Bregman divergence we set $f(x) = x \log(x) - x$ as the convex Bregman function of a single component. This implies that $f'(x) = \log(x)$. We restrict ourselves to the more common case where $\mathbf{x}$ defines a discrete distribution, i.e, each instance $\mathbf{x}_i$ conforms with $x_{i,l} \geq 0$ and $\sum_l x_{i,l} = 1$. In this case Eq. (14) reduces to,

$$\sum_{l=1}^{n} x_{i,l} \left[ \log(\frac{\alpha_i}{\alpha_i^t} \sum_j \alpha_j^t x_{j,l}) - \log(\sum_j \alpha_j^t x_{j,l}) \right] = B_F(\mathbf{x}_i \| \mathbf{w}_t) - \gamma' + \mu_i - \eta_i$$

Since $\log\left( \frac{\alpha_i}{\alpha_i^t} \sum_j \alpha_j^t x_{j,l} \right) = \log\left( \sum_j \alpha_j^t x_{j,l} \right) + \log\left( \frac{\alpha_i}{\alpha_i^t} \right)$ and $\sum_l x_{i,l} = 1$ we get that the update rule is of the form, $\alpha_i^{t+1} = \alpha_i^t \exp\left[ B_F(\mathbf{x}_i \| \mathbf{w}_t) - \gamma' + \mu_i - \eta_i \right]$. Note that if $\alpha_i^t > 0$ then $\alpha_i^{t+1} > 0$ as well. Thus, KKT conditions imply that $\mu_i = 0$. Next note that the requirement that $\sum_i \alpha_i^{t+1} = 1$ implies that $\gamma'$, which does not depend on $i$, is a normalization constraint and we can rewrite the update rule as,

$$\alpha_i^{t+1} = \frac{1}{Z_t} \exp\left[ B_F(\mathbf{x}_i \| \mathbf{w}_t) + \log(\alpha_i^t) - \eta_i \right] , \qquad (16)$$

where $Z_t = \sum_i \exp\left[ B_F(\mathbf{x}_i \| \mathbf{w}_t) + \log(\alpha_i^t) - \eta_i \right]$. We are not done yet: Eq. (16) is not sufficient to devise an iterative update that computes $\alpha^{t+1}$ since each Lagrange multiplier $\eta_i$ is not bound to a specific value. The following lemma provides a monotonicity property that in turn serves as a tool for setting $\eta_i$.

**Lemma 3.** *Let $\eta_i$ and $\alpha_i^{t+1}$ are chosen so as to satisfy both Eq. (16) and the KKT conditions for Eq. (12). Then, $B_F(\mathbf{x}_i \| \mathbf{w}_t) + \log(\alpha_i^t) \geq B_F(\mathbf{x}_j \| \mathbf{w}_t) + \log(\alpha_j^t)$ implies that $\eta_i \geq \eta_j$.*

*Proof.* The KKT condition of Eq. (12) imply that the Lagrange multipliers (for all $k$) $\eta_k$ and $\alpha_k^{t+1}$ must satisfy $\eta_k(\alpha_k^{t+1} - 1/(\nu m)) = 0$ while $\eta_k \geq 0$. Assume for contradiction that $B_F(\mathbf{x}_i \| \mathbf{w}_t) + \log(\alpha_i^t) \geq B_F(\mathbf{x}_j \| \mathbf{w}_t) + \log(\alpha_j^t)$, but $\eta_i < \eta_j$. From Eq. (16) we get that,

$$\log\left( \alpha_i^{t+1} \right) - \log\left( \alpha_j^{t+1} \right)$$
$$= \left[ B_F(\mathbf{x}_i \| \mathbf{w}_t) + \log(\alpha_i^t) \right] - \left[ B_F(\mathbf{x}_j \| \mathbf{w}_t) + \log(\alpha_j^t) \right] - \eta_i + \eta_j .$$

The above equation is strictly greater than zero since $B_F(\mathbf{x}_i \| \mathbf{w}_t) + \log(\alpha_i^t) \geq B_F(\mathbf{x}_j \| \mathbf{w}_t) + \log(\alpha_j^t)$ and we assumed $\eta_j > \eta_i$ and therefore, $\alpha_i^{t+1} > \alpha_j^{t+1}$. However, using the assumption that $\eta_j > \eta_i \geq 0$ in conjunction with the KKT condition $\eta_j(\alpha_j^{t+1} - 1/(\nu m)) = 0$, we must have $\alpha_j^{t+1} = 1/(\nu m)$. Alas, $\alpha_i^{t+1}$ must be within the box constraints, that is, $0 \leq \alpha_i^{t+1} \leq 1/(\nu m)$ and thus $\alpha_i^{t+1} \leq 1/(\nu m) = \alpha_j^{t+1}$ which leads to a contradiction. $\qquad \square$

The above lemma sheds more light on the form of solution for Eq. (16). We get that the values of the Lagrange multiplies are ordered in according to the (known) sums of the relative entropy between each point and $\mathbf{w}_t$ and the logarithm of the current estimate for $\alpha^t$. Combining this property with the box constraints yields the following lemma.

**Lemma 4.** *Assume that $\eta_i$ and $\alpha_i^{t+1}$ satisfy Eq. (16) and the KKT conditions of Eq. (12). Denote by $v_i = B_F(\mathbf{x}_i\|\mathbf{w}_t) + \log(\alpha_i^t)$. Then, there exists a constant $\psi$ such that, $\alpha_i^{t+1} = \exp(u_i)/Z_t$ where $u_i = \min\{\psi, v_i\}$.*

*Proof.* Assume w.l.o.g. that the indices are sorted according to $v_i$, i.e., $v_1 \geq v_2 \geq \cdots \geq v_m$. Using Lemma 3 together with KKT conditions we get $\eta_1 \geq \eta_2 \cdots \geq \eta_m \geq 0$. Denote by $k$ the maximal index for which $\eta_i$ is strictly greater than zero, that is, $\eta_1 \geq \eta_2 \cdots \geq \eta_k > 0$ and $\eta_{k+1} = \ldots = \eta_m = 0$. From the KKT conditions we have that whenever $\eta_i > 0$ (meaning $v_i \geq v_k$), $\alpha_i^{t+1}$ is on boundary of constraints and is equal to $1/(\nu m)$. An analogous argument implies that for $i$ such that $\eta_i = 0$ (and thus $v_i \leq v_{k+1}$), $\alpha_i^{t+1}$ is inside the simplex of constraints and is equal to $\exp\left[B_F(\mathbf{x}_i\|\mathbf{w}_t) + \log(\alpha_i^t)\right]/Z_t = \exp(v_i)/Z_t$. Summing up, there exists a threshold, $\psi \in [v_{k+1}, v_k)$, such that for $v_i > \psi$, $\alpha_i^{t+1} = \exp(\psi)/Z_t$ and for $v_i \leq \psi$ $\alpha_i^{t+1} = \exp(v_i)/Z_t$. Finally, $\psi$ is set such that $1/(\nu m) = \exp(\psi)/Z_t$. $\square$

As noted in Lemma 4, the exact value of $\psi$ is the solution of $1/(\nu m) = \exp(\psi)/Z_t$. As in the lemma, let us assume that $v_i = B_F(\mathbf{x}_i\|\mathbf{w}) + \log(\alpha_i^t)$ are sorted in descending order and for boundary conditions we define $v_0 = \infty$. An immediate consequence of the lemma is that we can write $\alpha_i^{t+1}$ as $\alpha_i^{t+1} = \exp(\min\{v_i, \psi\})/[\sum_j \exp(\min\{v_j, \psi\})]$. Let $k$ be the index such that $v_k > \psi \geq v_{k+1}$. Then from the above we get that,

$$\frac{1}{\nu m} = \alpha_k^{t+1} = \frac{e^\psi}{k e^\psi + \sum_{j=k+1}^m e^{v_j}} \ . \tag{17}$$

Put another way, had we set $\psi$ wrongly to be $v_k$ we would have gotten that,

$$\frac{1}{\nu m} < \frac{e^{v_k}}{k e^{v_k} + \sum_{j=k+1}^m e^{v_j}} \ . \tag{18}$$

Analogously, since $\psi \geq v_{k+1}$ we must have,

$$\frac{1}{\nu m} \geq \frac{e^{v_{k+1}}}{(k+1) e^{v_{k+1}} + \sum_{j=k+2}^m e^{v_j}} \ . \tag{19}$$

Eq. (18) and Eq. (19) do not depend on the exact value of $\psi$. Therefore, in order to find the interval $[v_{k+1}, v_k)$ in which $\psi$ resides, it suffices to find the index $k$ for which Eq. (18) and Eq. (19) are both satisfied.

A direct calculation of Eq. (18) takes $\mathcal{O}(m)$ time for each $r$ and thus the total search would take $\mathcal{O}(m^2)$ time. However, we can reduce the search time to be linear in $m$ by defining the following auxiliary variables, $\Phi(r) = \frac{e^{v_r}}{Z(r)}$ and $Z(r) = r e^{v_r} + \sum_{j=r+1}^m e^{v_j}$. We can rewrite $Z(r)$ recursively as, $Z(r+1) = Z(r) + r(e^{v_{r+1}} - e^{v_r})$. To find the value of $\psi$, we first perform a linear search to find the index $r$ for which $\Phi(r) > 1/(\nu m)$ and $\Phi(r+1) \leq 1/(\nu m)$, which, from Eq. (18) and Eq. (19), implies that $\psi \in [v_{r+1}, v_r)$ . To find the exact value of $\psi$ we use Eq. (17) and get, $\psi = \log[(\sum_{j=r+1}^{m} e^{v_j})/(\nu m - r)]$. (Note that the above equation implies that $r \leq \nu m$.) The search process is linear in $m$ and with the sorting of $v_i$ we get that finding $\psi$ and $\alpha_i^{t+1}$ afterwards takes $\mathcal{O}(m \log(m))$ time.

## 5    Generalization

We now analyze the generalization of the uniclass algorithm for Eq. (1) in terms of the empirical discrepancies from the sphere enclosing the points in the sample. Informally, the theorem below states that the true probability of observing a point outside the enclosing sphere, depends on the empirical distribution of the points in a divergence $r$ from the origin where $r \in [R - \theta, R]$. This probability is also inversely proportional to $\theta$. Similar bounds have been derived for the generalization of margin classifiers. Indeed, our proof is closely related to the proofs in [2, 13, 12]. The proof exploits the fact that the solution to the batch problem is a convex combination of the points in the sample (Eq. (7)). The proof is omitted due to lack of space.

**Theorem 2.** *Let $\mathcal{D}$ be a distribution over a compact domain $X \subset \mathbb{R}^n$, and let $S$ be a sample of $m$ examples chosen independently according to $\mathcal{D}$. Let $B_F$ be a Bregman divergence with $f'$ continuous over $X$. Define*

$$\mathcal{H} = \left\{ h : X \to \mathbb{R} \mid h(\mathbf{x}) = R - B_F\left(\mathbf{x} \| \mathbf{w}\right) \; ; \; \mathbf{w} = \sum_{i=1}^{m} \alpha_i \mathbf{x}_i \, , \, \alpha_i \geq 0, \sum_i \alpha_i = 1 \right\}$$

*and assume that $0 < R \leq \theta_0$. Then with probability at least $1 - \delta$ over the random choice of the training set $S$, every function $h \in \mathcal{H}$ satisfies the following bound for all $0 < \theta \leq \theta_0$,*

$$P_{\mathcal{D}}\left[h(\mathbf{x}) \leq 0\right] \leq P_S\left[h(\mathbf{x}) \leq \theta\right] + \mathcal{O}\left(\frac{n \log(m)}{\theta \sqrt{m}} \left(\log(m) + \log\left(\frac{\theta_0}{\delta}\right)\right)\right) \quad .$$

## 6    Online Algorithms

In this section we describe online algorithms for the uniclass problems and analyze their mistake bounds. In online settings we receive examples one at a time. We therefore need to employ a somewhat different assumptions in order to analyze the algorithms. We cast the learning goal as the task of constructing a Bregmanian sphere whose radius is competitive with the radius of the smallest sphere that encloses all of the sample points. Formally, we observe a sequence of points $\mathbf{x}_1, \mathbf{x}_2, \ldots, \mathbf{x}_t, \ldots (\mathbf{x}_s \in X)$ and assume that there exists a radius $r$ and a center $\mathbf{u}$ such that $\forall t : B_F(\mathbf{x}_t \| \mathbf{u}) \leq r$. The goal of the learning algorithm is to construct a sphere that encloses all of the points with a small radius. The algorithms we present in this section assume that the radius of the sphere we need to construct, denoted $R = (1 + \delta)r$, is given.

We also assume that $R$ is strictly greater than $r$, $(\delta > 0)$. We start with an initial value for the center of the sphere and modify the center on any input point that lies outside the current sphere. We prove bounds on the number of center modifications, that is, the number of times a newly observed point resides outside the Bregmanian sphere of radius $R$. Our analysis implies that after a *finite* number of examples, we find a center such that all future points lie inside a ball of radius $R$. In Fig. 4 we give the skeleton for all of our online algorithms. Upon a mistake, i.e., when a new example $\mathbf{x}_t$ is found to be outside the current ball, we set the new center $\mathbf{w}_{t+1}$ to be a convex combination of the current center $\mathbf{w}_t$ and the new example $\mathbf{x}_t$. We describe below two schemes to set the interpolation parameter, denoted $\alpha_t \in [0, 1]$. The first is very simple as it employs a fixed value for $\alpha_t$ where we only require that $\alpha_t$ is be bounded above by a number which depends only on $\delta$. The second scheme chooses on each round $t$ a different value for $\alpha_t$ that depends on $\mathbf{x}_t$, $\mathbf{w}_t$, and $R$. While the mistake bound for the second scheme is potentially better, finding $\alpha_t$ requires solving a single dimension optimization problem over the interval $[0, 1]$. In our analyses we use of the following equality that was derived by Kivinen and Warmuth [10]:

$$B_F(\mathbf{x}\|\mathbf{u}) = B_F(\mathbf{x}\|\mathbf{w}) + B_F(\mathbf{w}\|\mathbf{u}) + (\nabla F(\mathbf{w}) - \nabla F(\mathbf{u})) \cdot (\mathbf{x} - \mathbf{w}) \quad , \quad (20)$$

for any $\mathbf{x}, \mathbf{w}, \mathbf{u} \in X$. This equality generalizes the Euclidean cosine rule to Bregman divergences.

Let us first describe and analyze the version that chooses different value for $\alpha_t$ on each round. In this version we set $\alpha_t$ as the minimizer of the following (convex) problem,

$$\alpha_t = \min_\alpha \quad \mathcal{Q}(\alpha) = B_F(\alpha\mathbf{x}_t + (1 - \alpha)\mathbf{w}_t\|\mathbf{w}_t) - \alpha B_F(\mathbf{x}_t\|\mathbf{w}_t) + \alpha R \quad (21)$$

$$\text{s.t.} \quad \alpha \in [0, 1] \ .$$

The rationale for this choice of $\alpha_t$ is as follows. On one hand, if $B_F(\mathbf{x}_t\|\mathbf{u}) \leq R$ then the optimal value for $\alpha_t$ is zero. If, on the other hand, $B_F(\mathbf{x}_t\|\mathbf{u}) > R$ then the optimal value for $\alpha$ is set aggressively in order to enclose $\mathbf{x}_t$ in a sphere centered at $\mathbf{w}_{t+1}$. The next theorem shows that the cumulative sum of $\alpha_t$ is bounded. This result enables us to prove the corresponding mistake bound.

**Theorem 3.** *Let $\mathbf{x}_1, \ldots, \mathbf{x}_T$ be a input sequence of points in $X$ fed to the online uniclass algorithm of Fig. 4 where $\alpha_t$ is chosen according to Eq. (21). Assume that there exists a center $\mathbf{u} \in X$ and a radius $r$ such that $B_F(\mathbf{x}_t\|\mathbf{u}) \leq r$ for all $t \in \{1, \ldots, T\}$. Then, for any $R = (1+\delta)r$ with $\delta > 0$ the following bound holds, $\sum_{t=1}^T \alpha_t \leq \frac{1}{\delta}$.*

---

**Input:** Divergence $B_F$  ;  Radius $R > 0$
**Initialize:** Set $\mathbf{w}_1 = \mathbf{x}_0$
**Loop:** For $t = 1, 2, \ldots, T$

- Get a new instance $\mathbf{x}_t \in \mathbb{R}^n$
- If $B_F(\mathbf{x}_t\|\mathbf{w}_t) \geq R$ update:
  1. Choose $\alpha_t \in [0, 1]$
  2. Set $\mathbf{w}_{t+1} = \alpha_t\mathbf{x}_t + (1 - \alpha_t)\mathbf{w}_t$
  Else: $\mathbf{w}_{t+1} = \mathbf{w}_t$

**Return:** sphere's center – $\mathbf{w}_{T+1}$

---

**Fig. 4.** The uniclass online algorithm.

*Proof.* Denote by, $\Delta^t = B_F(\mathbf{w}_{t+1}\|\mathbf{u}) - B_F(\mathbf{w}_t\|\mathbf{u})$. To prove the theorem we bound $\sum_{t=1}^{T} \Delta^t$ from below and above. First note that the sum is telescopic with $\mathbf{w}_1 = \mathbf{x}_0$ and thus,

$$\sum_{t=1}^{T} \Delta^t = B_F(\mathbf{w}_{T+1}\|\mathbf{u}) - B_F(\mathbf{w}_1\|\mathbf{u}) \geq -B_F(\mathbf{w}_1\|\mathbf{u}) = -B_F(\mathbf{x}_0\|\mathbf{u}) \geq -r . \quad (22)$$

To bound the sum from above we bound each term of $\Delta^t$ independently. Let us assume that $B_F(\mathbf{x}_t\|\mathbf{w}_t) > R$ (otherwise $\Delta^t = 0$). In this case $\mathbf{w}_{t+1} = \alpha_t \mathbf{x}_t + (1 - \alpha_t)\mathbf{w}_t$. We rewrite $\Delta^t$ as

$$\begin{aligned}
\Delta^t &= F(\mathbf{w}_{t+1}) - F(\mathbf{u}) - \nabla F(\mathbf{u}) \cdot (\mathbf{w}_{t+1} - \mathbf{u}) \\
&\quad - [F(\mathbf{w}_t) - F(\mathbf{u}) - \nabla F(\mathbf{u}) \cdot (\mathbf{w}_{t+1} - \mathbf{u})] \\
&= F(\mathbf{w}_{t+1}) - F(\mathbf{w}_t) - \nabla F(\mathbf{u}) \cdot (\mathbf{w}_{t+1} - \mathbf{w}_t) . \quad (23)
\end{aligned}$$

Substituting $\mathbf{w}_{t+1} = \alpha_t \mathbf{x}_t + (1 - \alpha_t)\mathbf{w}_t$, we get,

$$\begin{aligned}
\Delta^t &= F(\mathbf{w}_{t+1}) - F(\mathbf{w}_t) - \nabla F(\mathbf{u}) \cdot (\alpha_t \mathbf{x}_t + (1 - \alpha_t)\mathbf{w}_t - \mathbf{w}_t) \\
&= F(\mathbf{w}_{t+1}) - F(\mathbf{w}_t) - \alpha_t \nabla F(\mathbf{u}) \cdot (\mathbf{x}_t - \mathbf{w}_t) . \quad (24)
\end{aligned}$$

Using the "generalized cosine equality" of Eq. (20) we get, $(\nabla F(\mathbf{w}_t) - \nabla F(\mathbf{u})) \cdot (\mathbf{x}_t - \mathbf{w}_t) = B_F(\mathbf{x}_t\|\mathbf{u}) - B_F(\mathbf{x}_t\|\mathbf{w}_t) - B_F(\mathbf{w}_t\|\mathbf{u})$. Substituting in Eq. (24),

$$\begin{aligned}
\Delta^t &= F(\mathbf{w}_{t+1}) - F(\mathbf{w}_t) \\
&\quad + \alpha_t \left[ -\nabla F(\mathbf{w}_t) \cdot (\mathbf{x}_t - \mathbf{w}_t) + B_F(\mathbf{x}_t\|\mathbf{u}) - B_F(\mathbf{x}_t\|\mathbf{w}_t) - B_F(\mathbf{w}_t\|\mathbf{u}) \right] \\
&= F(\mathbf{w}_{t+1}) - F(\mathbf{w}_t) - \alpha_t \nabla F(\mathbf{w}_t) \cdot (\mathbf{x}_t - \mathbf{w}_t) \\
&\quad + \alpha_t B_F(\mathbf{x}_t\|\mathbf{u}) - \alpha_t B_F(\mathbf{x}_t\|\mathbf{w}_t) - \alpha_t B_F(\mathbf{w}_t\|\mathbf{u}) \quad (25)
\end{aligned}$$

We use the definition of $B_F$ to further develop Eq. (25),

$$\begin{aligned}
\Delta^t &= B_F(\mathbf{w}_{t+1}\|\mathbf{w}_t) + \alpha_t B_F(\mathbf{x}_t\|\mathbf{u}) - \alpha_t B_F(\mathbf{x}_t\|\mathbf{w}_t) - \alpha_t B_F(\mathbf{w}_t\|\mathbf{u}) \\
&= B_F(\alpha_t \mathbf{x}_t + (1 - \alpha_t)\mathbf{w}_t\|\mathbf{w}_t) - \alpha_t B_F(\mathbf{x}_t\|\mathbf{w}_t) + \alpha_t R \\
&\quad - \alpha_t R + \alpha_t B_F(\mathbf{x}_t\|\mathbf{u}) - \alpha_t B_F(\mathbf{w}_t\|\mathbf{u}) \\
&= \mathcal{Q}(\alpha_t) - \alpha_t R + \alpha_t B_F(\mathbf{x}_t\|\mathbf{u}) - \alpha_t B_F(\mathbf{w}_t\|\mathbf{u}) , \quad (26)
\end{aligned}$$

where we used the definition of $\mathcal{Q}(\alpha)$ to obtain the last equality. It is straightforward to verify that $\mathcal{Q}(0) = 0$ and thus $\mathcal{Q}(\alpha_t) \leq 0$ since $\alpha_t$ is the minimizer of $\mathcal{Q}(\alpha)$. Since we assumed that $B_F(\mathbf{x}_t\|\mathbf{u}) \leq r$ we can upper bound $\Delta^t$,

$$\Delta^t \leq -\alpha_t R + \alpha_t r = -\alpha_t ((1 + \delta)r - r) = -\alpha_t \delta r . \quad (27)$$

Combining the lower bound on $\Delta^t$ with Eq. (27) we get, $\sum_t \alpha_t \delta r \leq \sum_{t=1}^{T} \Delta^t \leq r \Rightarrow \sum_t \alpha_t \leq \frac{1}{\delta}$ , which concludes the proof. $\square$

Note that the above theorem does not equip us with a mistake bound. A priori, one would hope that it is possible to derive a bound on the number of times a new point would no reside inside the learned ball. However, the situation seems a bit more delicate and we could not derive such a bound. We give below a somewhat weaker bound. In a nutshell, the theorem states that the number of rounds on which the divergence $B_F(\mathbf{x}_t \| \mathbf{w}_t)$ exceeds $\tilde{R} > R$ is bounded.

**Theorem 4.** *Assume that the first eigenvalue of the Hessian of $F(\mathbf{x})$ is bounded by $\lambda$ for any $\mathbf{x} \in X$ and that $\|\mathbf{x}_t\|_2 \leq B$ for $1 \leq t \leq T$. Then, for the same conditions of Thm. 3 and for any $\tilde{R} = (1 + \tilde{\delta})r$ such that $\tilde{\delta} > \delta$, the number of rounds for which $B_F(\mathbf{x}_t \| \mathbf{w}_t) \geq \tilde{R}$ is bounded above by, $\frac{4\lambda B^2}{r\delta(\tilde{\delta}-\delta)}$ .*

*Proof.* Due to the lack of space we only give a sketch of the proof. We want to bound the number of rounds for which $B_F(\mathbf{x}_t \| \mathbf{w}_t) \geq \tilde{R}$. To do so we find a lower bound on $\alpha_t$ for all such rounds. To derive the bound we use the second order Taylor expansion of $Q$ and write $Q'(\alpha_t) = Q'(0) + \alpha_t Q''(\xi)$ where $\xi \in [0, \alpha_t]$. Since $\alpha_t$ is the minimizer of $Q$ we know that $Q'(\alpha_t) = 0$. Combining this property with tedious calculus yields that,

$$\alpha_t(\mathbf{x}_t - \mathbf{w}_t)^T H \left[ (\mathbf{w}_t + \xi(\mathbf{x}_t - \mathbf{w}_t)) \right] (\mathbf{x}_t - \mathbf{w}_t) = B_F(\mathbf{x}_t \| \mathbf{w}_t) - R \ , \quad (28)$$

where $H$ is the Hessian of $F$. Using the assumption that $B_F(\mathbf{x}_t \| \mathbf{w}_t) \geq \tilde{R}$ we can bound the the right hand side of Eq. (28) with $r(\tilde{\delta} - \delta)$. Using the Hessian's eigenvalue bound, the left hand side of Eq. (28) is lower bounded by, $4\lambda B^2$. Therefore, we lower bound $\alpha_t$ on each round for which $B_F(\mathbf{x}_t \| \mathbf{w}_t) \geq \tilde{R}$ by, $\alpha_t \geq \frac{r(\tilde{\delta}-\delta)}{4\lambda B^2}$ . Since we know from Thm. 3 that $\sum_t \alpha_t \leq 1/\delta$ we get that the number of rounds with $B_F(\mathbf{x}_t \| \mathbf{w}_t) \geq \tilde{R}$ cannot exceed the desired bound.    □

Finally, to conclude the section on online algorithms we would like to mention in passing the formal results obtained for the fixed-$\alpha$ update. Using similar proof techniques it is possible to prove the following mistake bound.

**Theorem 5.** *Let $\mathbf{x}_1, \ldots, \mathbf{x}_T$ be a input sequence of points in $X$ fed to the online uniclass algorithm of Fig. 4 used with a fixed-rate update ($\forall t : \alpha_t = \alpha$). Then, under the same conditions of Thm. 4, there exist $\alpha$ such that the number of rounds for which $B_F(\mathbf{x}_t \| \mathbf{w}_t) \geq \tilde{R}$ is bounded from above by, $4(1 + \delta)/\delta^2$.*

## 7    Discussion

We introduced and analyzed a general algorithmic framework for uniclass problems that can be used with a broad family of Bregman divergences. We provided a new parallel-update algorithm for solving the optimization problem and demonstrated its usage by with the relative entropy. We also introduced and analyzed an apparatus for online learning of Bregmanian sphere. There are numerous directions in which this work can be extended and further investigated. A particularly interesting extension builds on the relation of Bregman divergences to the exponential family of distributions. One of the more challenging questions that arises from this view is whether the uniclass framework can to be generalized and applied to complex distribution models which arise in speech recognition, information retrieval, and biological sequence analysis.

**Acknowledgments.** We would like to thank Yair Censor for his comments and advice throughout the research and to Ran Bachrach for his valuable comments. Thanks also to Guy Lebanon for his help in producing the figures and to Leo Kontorovich for comments and suggestions. This work was partially funded by EU project KerMIT No. IST-2000-25341.

# References

1. K. Azoury and M. Warmuth. Relative loss bounds for on-line density estimation with the exponential family of distributions. *Machine Learning*, 43:211–246, 2001.
2. P.L. Bartlett. The sample complexity of pattern classification with neural networks: the size of the weights is more important than the size of the network. *IEEE Transactions on Information Theory*, 44(2):525–536, March 1998.
3. L. M. Bregman. The relaxation method of finding the common point of convex sets and its application to the solution of problems in convex programming. *USSR Computational Mathematics and Mathematical Physics*, 7:200–217, 1967.
4. Y. Censor and S.A. Zenios. *Parallel optimization: Theory, Algorithms and Applications*. Oxford University Press, 1997.
5. M. Collins, S. Dasgupta, and R. Schapire. A generalization of principal component analysis to the exponential family. In *Adv. in NIPS 13*, 2001.
6. M. Collins, R.E. Schapire, and Y. Singer. Logistic regression, adaboost and bregman distances. *Machine Learning*, 47(2/3):253–285, 2002.
7. A.P. Dempster, N.M. Laird, and D.B. Rubin. Maximum likelihood from incomplete data via the EM algorithm. *J. of the Royal Stat. Soc., Ser. B*, 39:1–38, 1977.
8. R. Fletcher. *Practical Methods of Optimization*. John Wiley, second edition, 1987.
9. C. Gentile and M. Warmuth. Linear hinge loss and average margin. In *Advances in Neural Information Processing Systems 10*, 1998.
10. J. Kivinen and M. K. Warmuth. Relative loss bounds for multidimensional regression problems. *Journal of Machine Learning*, 45(3):301–329, July 2001.
11. D.D. Lee and H.S. Seung. Algorithms for non-negative matrix factorization. In *Advances in Neural Information Processing Systems 13*, pages 556–562, 2000.
12. R. E. Schapire and Y. Singer. Improved boosting algorithms using confidence-rated predictions. *Machine Learning*, 37(3):1–40, 1999.
13. R.E. Schapire, Y. Freund, P. Bartlett, and W.S. Lee. Boosting the margin: A new explanation for the effectiveness of voting methods. *The Annals of Statistics*, 26(5):1651–1686, October 1998.
14. B. Schölkopf, C. Burges, and V.N. Vapnik. Extracting support data for a given task. In U.M. Fayyad and R. Uthurusamy, editors, *First International Conference on Knowledge Discovery & Data Mining (KDD)*. AAAI Press, 1995.
15. B. Schölkopf, J. Platt, J. Shawe-Taylor, A. J. Smola, and R. C. Williamson. Estimating the support of a high-dimensional distribution. *Neural Computation*, 13(7):1443–1472, 2001.
16. F. Sha, L.K. Saul, and D.D. Lee. Multiplicative updates for nonnegative quadratic programming in support vector machines. In S. Becker, S. Thrun, and K. Obermayer, editors, *Advances in Neural Information Processing Systems 15*, 2002.
17. D.M.J. Tax. *One-class classification; Concept-learning in the absence of counterexamples*. PhD thesis, Delft University of Technology, 2001.
18. D.M.J. Tax and R.P.W. Duin. Data domain description using support vectors. In M. Verleysen, editor, *Proceedings of the European Symposium on Artificial Neural Networks*, pages 251–256, April 1999.

# Internal Regret in On-Line Portfolio Selection[*]

Gilles Stoltz[1] and Gábor Lugosi[2]

[1] Laboratoire de Mathématiques, Université Paris-Sud,
91405 Orsay Cedex, France
gilles.stoltz@math.u-psud.fr
[2] Department of Economics, Pompeu Fabra University,
08005 Barcelona, Spain
lugosi@upf.es

**Abstract.** This paper extends the game-theoretic notion of internal regret to the case of on-line potfolio selection problems. New sequential investment strategies are designed to minimize the cumulative internal regret for all possible market behaviors. Some of the introduced strategies, apart from achieving a small internal regret, achieve an accumulated wealth almost as large as that of the best constantly rebalanced portfolio. It is argued that the low-internal-regret property is related to stability and experiments on real stock exchange data demonstrate that the new strategies achieve usually better returns compared to some known algorithms.

## 1  Introduction

The problem of sequential portfolio allocation is well-known to be closely related to the on-line prediction of individual sequences under expert advice, see, for example, Cover [6], Cover and Ordentlich [7], Helmbold, Schapire, Singer, and Warmuth [14], Ordentlich and Cover [15], Blum and Kalai [2], Cesa-Bianchi and Lugosi [4]. In the on-line prediction problem the goal is to minimize the predictor's cumulative loss with respect to the best cumulative loss in a pool of "experts". In a certain equivalent game-theoretic formulation of the problem, this is the same as minimizing the predictor's *external regret*, see Foster and Vohra [9]. External regret measures the difference between the predictor's cumulative loss and that of the best expert. However, another notion of regret, called *internal regret* in [9] has also been in the focus of attention mostly in the theory of playing repeated games, see Foster and Vohra [8, 9], Fudenberg and Levine [10, 11], Hart and Mas Colell [12, 13], Cesa-Bianchi and Lugosi [5]. Roughly speaking, a predictor has a small internal regret if for each pair of experts $(i, j)$, the predictor does not regret of not having followed expert $i$ each time it followed expert $j$. It is easy to see that requiring a small internal regret is a more difficult

---

[*] The work of the first author was supported by PAI Picasso grant 02543RM and by the French CNRS research network AS66 (SVM and kernel algorithms). The work of the second author was supported by DGI grant BMF2000-0807.

B. Schölkopf and M.K. Warmuth (Eds.): COLT/Kernel 2003, LNAI 2777, pp. 403–417, 2003.
© Springer-Verlag Berlin Heidelberg 2003

problem since a small internal regret in the prediction problem implies small external regret as well. A brief summary of the basic properties is given below.

The goal in the sequential investment problem is to distribute one's capital in each trading period among a certain number of stocks such that the total achieved wealth is almost as large as the wealth of the largest in a certain class of investment strategies. This problem is easily seen to be the generalization of an external regret minialization problem in the "expert" setting under the logarithmic loss function. The main purpose of this paper is to extend the notion of internal regret to the sequential investment problem, understand its relationship to the external regret, and design investment strategies minimizing this new notion of regret. The definition of internal regret given here has a natural interpretation and the investment strategies designed to minimize it have several desirable properties both in theory and in the experimental study described below.

The paper is organized as follows. In Section 2 we briefly summarize the sequential prediction problem based on expert advice and describe the notions of internal and external regrets. In Section 3 the sequential portfolio selection problem is described, and basic properties of Cover's universal portfolio and the EG investment strategy are discussed. In Section 4 we introduce the notion of the internal regret for sequential portfolio selection, and describe some basic properties. In Section 5 we introduce new investment strategies aiming at the minimization of the internal regret. In Section 6 the notion of internal regret is generalized for an uncountable class of investment strategies and an algorithm inspired by Cover's universal portfolio is proposed which minimizes the new notion of internal regret.

## 2   Sequential Prediction

In the (randomized) sequential prediction problem the predictor, at each time instance $t = 1, 2, \ldots$, chooses a probability distribution $\mathbf{P}_t = (P_{1,t}, \ldots, P_{N,t})$ over the set $\{1, 2, \ldots, N\}$ of experts. After the choice is made, expert $i$ suffers loss $\ell_{i,t}$, and the predictor suffers loss

$$\ell_t(\mathbf{P}_t) = \sum_{i=1}^{N} P_{i,t}\ell_{i,t} \ .$$

This loss may be interpreded as the expected loss if the predictor chooses an expert randomly, according to the distribution $\mathbf{P}_t$, and predicts according to the selected expert's advice. The *external regret* of the predictor, after $n$ rounds of play, is

$$\sum_{t=1}^{n} \ell_t(\mathbf{P}_t) - \min_{i=1,\ldots,N} \sum_{t=1}^{n} \ell_{i,t} = \max_{i=1,\ldots,N} \sum_{j=1}^{N} \sum_{t=1}^{n} P_{j,t}(\ell_{j,t} - \ell_{i,t}) \ .$$

It is well known (see, e.g., [3]) that if the losses $\ell_{i,t}$ are all bounded between zero and $B > 0$, then the exponentially weighted average predictor defined, for $t = 1, 2, \ldots$, by

$$P_{i,t+1} = \frac{\exp(-\eta \sum_{s=1}^{t} \ell_{i,s})}{\sum_{j=1}^{N} \exp(-\eta \sum_{s=1}^{t} \ell_{j,s})}$$

with $\eta = B^{-1}\sqrt{8\ln N/n}$ has an external regret bounded by

$$B\sqrt{(n/2)\ln N} \; . \tag{2.1}$$

Also, a whole family of predictors with similar performance guarantees may be defined, see [5].

The *internal regret* of a sequential predictor $\mathbf{P}_t$ is defined by

$$\max_{i,j\in\{1,\dots,N\}} \sum_{t=1}^{n} r_{(i,j),t}$$

where $r_{(i,j),t} = P_{i,t}(\ell_{i,t} - \ell_{j,t})$. Thus, $r_{(i,j),t}$ expresses the predictor's regret of having put the probability mass $P_{i,t}$ on the $i$-th expert instead of on the $j$-th one, and

$$R_{(i,j),n} = \sum_{t=1}^{n} r_{(i,j),t} = \sum_{t=1}^{n} P_{i,t}(\ell_{i,t} - \ell_{j,t})$$

is the corresponding cumulative regret. Now clearly, the external regret of the predictor $\mathbf{P}_t$ equals

$$\max_{i=1,\dots,N} \sum_{j=1}^{N} R_{(i,j),n} \le N \max_{i,j\in\{1,\dots,N\}} R_{(i,j),n}$$

which shows that any algorithm with a small (i.e., sublinear in $n$) internal regret also has a small external regret. On the other hand, it is easy to see that a small external regret does not imply small internal regret. In fact, as it is shown in the next example, even the exponential weighted average algorithm defined above may have a linearly growing internal regret.

*Example 1. (Weighted average predictor has a large internal regret.)* Consider the following example with three experts, $A$, $B$, and $C$. Let $n$ be a large multiple of 3 and assume that time is divided in three equally long regimes, characterized by a constant loss for each expert. In the first regime $\ell_{A,t}, \ell_{B,t}, \ell_{C,t}$ equal 0, 1, and 5, respectively. In the second these values are 1, 0, 5, while in the third 1, 0, −1. We claim that the regret $R_{(B,C),n}$ of $B$ versus $C$ grows linearly with $n$, that is,

$$\liminf_{n\to\infty} \frac{1}{n} \sum_{t=1}^{n} P_{B,t} \left( \ell_{B,t} - \ell_{C,t} \right) = \gamma > 0 \; ,$$

where $P_{B,t} = e^{-\eta L_{B,t}} / \left( e^{-\eta L_{A,t}} + e^{-\eta L_{B,t}} + e^{-\eta L_{C,t}} \right)$ denotes the weight assigned by the exponential weighted averge predictor to expert $B$, where $L_{i,t} = \sum_{s=1}^{t} \ell(i,t)$ denotes the cumulative loss of expert $i$ and $\eta$ is chosen as defined above, that is, $\eta = (1/6)\sqrt{(8\ln 3)/n} = K/\sqrt{n}$ with $K = \sqrt{8\ln 3}/6$. The intuition behind this example is that at the end of the second regime the predictor quickly switches from $A$ to $B$, and the weight of expert $C$ can never recover because of its disastrous behavior in the first two regimes. But since expert $C$ behaves much better than $B$ in the third regime, the weighted average predictor will regret of not having followed the advice of $C$ each time it followed $B$.

More precisely, we show that during the first two regimes, the number of times when $P_{B,t}$ is more than $\epsilon$ is of the order of $\sqrt{n}$ and that, in the third regime, $P_{B,t}$ is always more than a fixed constant $(1/3$, say$)$. In the first regime, a sufficient condition for $P_{B,t} \leqslant \epsilon$ is that $e^{-\eta L_{B,t}} \leqslant \epsilon$. This occurs whenever $t \geqslant t_0 = K(-\ln \epsilon)\sqrt{n}$. For the second regime, we lower bound the time instant $t_1$ when $P_{B,t}$ gets larger than $\epsilon$. To this end, note that $P_{B,t} \geqslant \epsilon$ implies

$$(1-\epsilon)e^{-\eta L_{B,t}} \geqslant \epsilon \left(e^{-\eta L_{A,t}} + e^{-\eta L_{C,t}}\right) \geqslant \epsilon e^{-\eta L_{A,t}} ,$$

which leads to $t_1 \geqslant \frac{2n}{3} + K\left(\ln \frac{\epsilon}{1-\epsilon}\right)\sqrt{n}$. Finally, in the third regime, we have at each time instant $L_{B,t} \leqslant L_{A,t}$ and $L_{B,t} \leqslant L_{C,t}$, so that $P_{B,t} \geqslant 1/3$. Putting these three steps together, we obtain the following lower bound for the internal regret of $B$ versus $C$:

$$\sum_{t=1}^{n} P_{B,t}\left(\ell_{B,t} - \ell_{C,t}\right) \geqslant \frac{n}{9} - 5\left(\frac{2n}{3}\epsilon + K\left(\ln \frac{1-\epsilon}{\epsilon^2}\right)\sqrt{n}\right) ,$$

which is of the order $n$ if $\epsilon$ is sufficiently small.

The example above shows that special algorithms need to be designed to guarantee a small internal regret. Indeed, such predictors exist, as was shown by Foster and Vohra [8], see also Fudenberg and Levine [10, 11], and Hart and Mas Colell [12, 13]. Here we briefly describe a predictor described in Cesa-Bianchi and Lugosi [5], based on Hart and Mas Colell [13]. To this end, recall that defining the *exponential potential function* $\Phi : \mathbb{R}^M \to [0, \infty)$ by

$$\Phi(\mathbf{u}) = \sum_{i=1}^{M} \exp\left(\eta u_i\right) ,$$

where $M = N(N-1)$ and writing $\mathbf{r}_t$ for the $M$-vector with components $r_{(i,j),t}$ and $\mathbf{R}_t = \sum_{s=1}^{t} \mathbf{r}_s$, any predictor predictor satisfying the so-called "Blackwell condition"

$$\nabla\Phi(\mathbf{R}_{t-1}) \cdot \mathbf{r}_t \leqslant 0 \qquad (2.2)$$

for all $t \geqslant 1$, satisfies

$$\max_{1 \leqslant i,j \leqslant N} R_{(i,j),t} \leqslant \frac{\ln N(N-1)}{\eta} + \frac{\eta}{2} t B^2$$

where $B = \max_{1 \leqslant i,j \leqslant N, 1 \leqslant s \leqslant t} r_{(i,j),s}^2$, so that choosing $\eta$ optimally, one obtains an internal regret of the order of $B\sqrt{n \ln N}$ (Cesa-Bianchi and Lugosi [5]). To design a predictor satifying the Blackwell condition, recall that

$$\nabla \Phi(\mathbf{R}_{t-1}) \cdot \mathbf{r}_t = \sum_{i=1}^{N} \ell_{i,t} \left( \sum_{j=1}^{N} \nabla_{(i,j)} \Phi(\mathbf{R}_{t-1}) P_{i,t} - \sum_{j=1}^{N} \nabla_{(j,i)} \Phi(\mathbf{R}_{t-1}) P_{j,t} \right)$$

(see [5] for the details). To make sure that this quantity is nonpositive, it suffices to require that

$$\sum_{j=1}^{N} \nabla_{(i,j)} \Phi(\mathbf{R}_{t-1}) P_{i,t} - \sum_{j=1}^{N} \nabla_{(j,i)} \Phi(\mathbf{R}_{t-1}) P_{j,t} = 0$$

for all $j$. The existence of such a vector $\mathbf{P}_t$ may be seen by noting that $\mathbf{P}_t$ is an element of the kernel of the $N \times N$ matrix $A$ whose entries are $A_{i,j} = \nabla_{(j,i)} \Phi(\mathbf{R}_{t-1})$ if $i \neq j$ and $A_{i,i} = -\sum_{j \neq i,\ 1 \leqslant j \leqslant N} \nabla_{(i,j)} \Phi(\mathbf{R}_{t-1})$. As the rows of $A$ sum to zero, its kernel is nonempty, but we also need $\mathbf{P}_t$ to have nonnegative entries. To this end, consider the matrix $S = A/\alpha + I_N$, where $I_N$ is the $N \times N$ identity matrix and $\alpha$ denotes an upper bound on the absolute value of the elements of $A$. Then $S$ is a row stochastic matrix, since $\nabla_{(j,i)} \Phi(\mathbf{R}_{t-1}) \geqslant 0$. Now, it is well-known that $S$ admits a probability distribution $\mathbf{P}_t$ as a fixed point. However, a fixed point of $S$ is also an element of the kernel of $A$. Foster and Vohra [9], suggest a Gaussian elimination method over $A$ for the practical computation of $\mathbf{P}_t$.

We remark here that instead of the exponential potential defined above, other potential functions may also be used with success. For example, polynomial potentials of the form $\Phi(\mathbf{u}) = \sum_{i=1}^{N} (u_i)_+^p$ lead to the bound $\max_{1 \leqslant i,j \leqslant N} R_{(i,j),t} \leqslant B\sqrt{2(p-1)tN^{4/p}}$, see [5].

## 3    Sequential Portfolio Selection

In this section we describe the problem of sequential portfolio selection, recall some previous results, and take a new look at the EG strategy of Helmbold, Schapire, Singer, and Warmuth [14].

A *market vector* $\mathbf{x} = (x_1, \ldots, x_N)$ for $N$ assets is a vector of nonnegative numbers representing price relatives for a given trading period. In other words, the quantity $x_i \geq 0$ denotes the ratio of closing to opening price of the $i$-th asset for that period. Hence, an initial wealth invested in the $N$ assets according to fractions $Q_1, \ldots, Q_N$ multiplies by a factor of $\sum_{i=1}^{N} x_i Q_i$ at the end of period. The market behavior during $n$ trading periods is represented by a sequence $\mathbf{x}_1^n = (\mathbf{x}_1, \ldots, \mathbf{x}_n)$ of market vectors. $x_{t,j}$, the $j$-th component of $\mathbf{x}_t$, denotes the the factor by which the wealth invested in asset $j$ increases in the $t$-th period. We denote the probability simplex in $\mathbb{R}^N$ by $\mathcal{X}$.

An *investment strategy* $Q$ for $n$ trading periods is a sequence $\mathbf{Q}_1, \ldots, \mathbf{Q}_n$ of vector-valued functions $\mathbf{Q}_t : \mathbb{R}_+^{t-1} \to \mathcal{X}$, where the $i$-th component $Q_{t,i}(\mathbf{x}_1^{t-1})$ of the vector $\mathbf{Q}_t(\mathbf{x}_1^{t-1})$ denotes the fraction of the current wealth invested in the $i$-th asset at the beginning of the $t$-th period based on the past market behavior $\mathbf{x}_1^{t-1}$. We use

$$S_n(Q, \mathbf{x}_1^n) = \prod_{t=1}^{n} \left( \sum_{i=1}^{N} x_{t,i} Q_{t,i}(\mathbf{x}_1^{t-1}) \right)$$

to denote the wealth factor of strategy $Q$ after $n$ trading periods.

The simplest examples of investment strategies are the so called *buy-and-hold* strategies. A buy-and-hold strategy simply distributes its initial wealth among the $N$ assets according to some distribution $\mathbf{Q}_1 \in \mathcal{X}$ before the first trading period, and does not trade anymore. The wealth factor of such a strategy, after $n$ periods, is simply

$$S_n(Q, \mathbf{x}_1^n) = \sum_{j=1}^{N} Q_{1,j} \prod_{t=1}^{n} x_{t,j} \ .$$

Clearly, this wealth factor is at most as large as the gain $\max_{j=1,\dots,N} \prod_{t=1}^{n} x_{t,j}$ of the best stock over the investment period, and achieves this maximal wealth if $\mathbf{Q}_1$ concentrates on the best stock.

Another simple and important class of investment strategies is the class of *constantly rebalanced portfolios*. Such a strategy $B$ is parametrized by a probability vector $\mathbf{B} = (B_1, \dots, B_N) \in \mathcal{X}$, and simply $\mathbf{Q}_t(\mathbf{x}_1^{t-1}) = \mathbf{B}$ regardless of $t$ and the past market behavior $\mathbf{x}_1^{t-1}$. Thus, an investor following such a strategy rebalances, at every trading period, his current wealth according to the distribution $\mathbf{B}$ by investing a proportion $B_1$ of his wealth in the first stock, a proportion $B_2$ in the second stock, etc. The wealth factor achieved after $n$ trading periods is

$$S_n(\mathbf{B}, \mathbf{x}_1^n) = \prod_{t=1}^{n} \left( \sum_{i=1}^{N} x_{t,i} B_i \right) \ .$$

Now given a class $\mathcal{Q}$ of investment strategies, we define the *worst-case logarithmic wealth ratio* of strategy $P$ by

$$W_n(P, \mathcal{Q}) = \sup_{\mathbf{x}_1^n} \sup_{Q \in \mathcal{Q}} \ln \frac{S_n(Q, \mathbf{x}_1^n)}{S_n(P, \mathbf{x}_1^n)} \ .$$

The worst-case logarithmic wealth ratio is the analog of the external regret in the sequential portfolio selection problem. $W_n(P, \mathcal{Q}) = o(n)$ means that the investment strategy $P$ achieves the same exponent of growth as the best reference strategy in the class $\mathcal{Q}$ for all possible market behaviors.

For example, it is immediate to see that if $\mathcal{Q}$ is the class of all buy-and-hold strategies, then if $P$ is chosen to be the buy-and-hold strategy based on the uniform distribution $\mathbf{Q}_1$, then $W_n(P, \mathcal{Q}) \le \ln N$.

The class of constantly rebalanced portfolios is a significanlty richer class and achieving a small worst-case logarithmic wealth ratio is a greater challenge. Cover's *universal portfolio* [6] was the first example to achieve this goal. The universal portfolio strategy $P$ is defined by

$$P_{t,j}(\mathbf{x}_1^{t-1}) = \frac{\int_{\mathcal{X}} B_j S_{t-1}(\mathbf{B}, \mathbf{x}_1^{t-1}) \phi(\mathbf{B}) d\mathbf{B}}{\int_{\mathcal{X}} S_{t-1}(\mathbf{B}, \mathbf{x}_1^{t-1}) \phi(\mathbf{B}) d\mathbf{B}} \ , j = 1, \dots, N; t = 1, \dots, n$$

where $\phi$ is a density function on $\mathcal{X}$. In the simplest case $\phi$ is the uniform density over $\mathcal{X}$. In that case, the worst-case logarithmic wealth ratio of $P$ with respect to the class $\mathcal{Q}$ of all universal portfolios satisfies $W_n(P, \mathcal{Q}) \leq (N-1)\ln(n+1)$ . If the universal portfolio is defined using the Dirichlet$(1/2, \cdots, 1/2)$ density $\phi$, then the bound improves to

$$W_n(P, \mathcal{Q}) \leq \frac{N-1}{2}\ln n + \ln \frac{\Gamma(1/2)^N}{\Gamma(N/2)} + \frac{N-1}{2}\ln 2 + o(1) ,$$

see Cover and Ordentlich [7]. The worst-case performance of the universal portfolio is basically unimprovable (see [15]) but it has some practical disadvantages, including computational difficulties for not very small values of $N$. Helmbold, Schapire, Singer, and Warmuth [14] suggest their EG strategy to overcome these difficulties. The EG strategy is defined by

$$P_{i,t+1} = \frac{P_{i,t}\exp\left(\eta x_{i,t}/\mathbf{P}_t \cdot \mathbf{x}_t\right)}{\sum_{j=1}^{N} P_{j,t}\exp\left(\eta x_{j,t}/\mathbf{P}_t \cdot \mathbf{x}_t\right)} . \tag{3.1}$$

Helmbold, Schapire, Singer, and Warmuth [14] prove that if the market values $x_{i,t}$ all fall between the positive constants $m$ and $M$, then the worst-case logarithmic wealth ratio of the EG investment strategy is bounded by

$$\frac{\ln N}{\eta} + \frac{n\eta}{8}\frac{M^2}{m^2} = \frac{M}{m}\sqrt{\frac{n}{2}\ln N} ,$$

where the equality holds for the choice $\eta = (m/M)\sqrt{(8\ln N)/n}$. Here we give a simple new proof of this result, mostly because the main idea is at the basis of other arguments that follow. Recall that the worst-case logarithmic wealth ratio is

$$\max_{\mathbf{x}_1^n} \max_{\mathbf{B}\in\mathcal{X}} \ln \frac{\prod_{t=1}^{n}\mathbf{B}\cdot\mathbf{x}_t}{\prod_{t=1}^{n}\mathbf{P}_t\cdot\mathbf{x}_t}$$

where in this case the first maximum is taken over market sequences satisfying the boundedness assumption. By using the elementary inequality $\ln(1+u) \leq u$, we obtain

$$\ln \frac{\prod_{t=1}^{n}\mathbf{B}\cdot\mathbf{x}_t}{\prod_{t=1}^{n}\mathbf{P}_t\cdot\mathbf{x}_t} = \sum_{t=1}^{n}\ln\left(1 + \frac{(\mathbf{B}-\mathbf{P}_t)\cdot\mathbf{x}_t}{\mathbf{P}_t\cdot\mathbf{x}_t}\right)$$

$$\leq \sum_{t=1}^{n}\sum_{i=1}^{N}\frac{(B_i - P_{i,t})x_{i,t}}{\mathbf{P}_t\cdot\mathbf{x}_t}$$

$$= \sum_{t=1}^{n}\left(\sum_{j=1}^{N}\sum_{i=1}^{N}P_{i,t}\frac{B_j x_{j,t}}{\mathbf{P}_t\cdot\mathbf{x}_t} - \sum_{i=1}^{N}\sum_{j=1}^{N}B_j\frac{P_{i,t}x_{i,t}}{\mathbf{P}_t\cdot\mathbf{x}_t}\right)$$

$$= \sum_{j=1}^{N}B_j\left(\sum_{t=1}^{n}\sum_{i=1}^{N}P_{i,t}\left(\frac{x_{j,t}}{\mathbf{P}_t\cdot\mathbf{x}_t} - \frac{x_{i,t}}{\mathbf{P}_t\cdot\mathbf{x}_t}\right)\right) . \tag{3.2}$$

Under the boundedness assumption $0 < m \leqslant x_{i,t} \leqslant M$, the quantities $\ell_{i,t} = M/m - x_{i,t}/(\mathbf{P}_t \cdot \mathbf{x}_t)$ are within $[0, M/m]$ and can therefore be interpreted as bounded loss functions. Thus, the minimizing the above upper bound on the worst-case logarithmic wealth ratio may be cast as a sequential prediction problem as described in Section 2. Observing that the EG investment algorithm is just the exponentially weighted average predictor for this prediction problem, and using the performance bound (2.1) we obtain the cited inequality of [14].

*Remark 1. (Suboptimality of the* EG *investment strategy.)* Using the approach of bounding the worst-case logarithmic wealth ratio linearly as above is inevitably suboptimal. Indeed, the linear upper bound

$$\sum_{j=1}^{N} B_j \left( \sum_{t=1}^{n} \left( \sum_{i=1}^{N} P_{i,t} \ell_{i,t} \right) - \ell_{j,t} \right) = \sum_{j=1}^{N} B_j \sum_{i=1}^{N} \left( \sum_{t=1}^{n} P_{i,t} \left( \ell_{i,t} - \ell_{j,t} \right) \right) .$$

is minimized for a constantly rebalanced portfolio $\mathbf{B}$ lying in a corner of the simplex $\mathcal{X}$, whereas the worst-case logarithmic wealth ratio is concave in $\mathbf{B}$ and therefore is minimized in the interior of the simplex. Thus, no algorithm trying to minimize the linear upper bound on the external regret can be minimax optimal. However, as it is shown in [14], on real data good performance may be achieved. This good behavior may be explained by observing that the linear upper bound (3.2) is almost tight whenever the wealth ratios are close to each other, which is typically the case on real data. On the other hand, the exponentially weighted average predictor is optimal in a certain sense for minimizing the linear upper bound. Note also that the bound obtained for the worst-case logarithmic wealth ratio of the EG strategy grows as $\sqrt{n}$ whereas that of Cover's universal portfolio has only a logarithmic growth. In [14] it is asked whether the suboptimal bound for the EG strategy is an artifact of the analysis or it is inherent in the algorithm. The next simple example shows that no bound of a smaller order than $\sqrt{n}$ holds. Consider a market with two assets and market vectors $\mathbf{x}_t = (1, 1 - \epsilon)$, for all $t$. Then every wealth allocation $\mathbf{P}_t$ satisfies $1 - \epsilon \leqslant \mathbf{P}_t \cdot \mathbf{x}_t \leqslant 1$. Now, the best constantly rebalanced portfolio is clearly $(1, 0)$, and the worst-case logarithmic wealth ratio is simply

$$\sum_{t=1}^{n} \ln \frac{1}{1 - P_{2,t}\epsilon} \geqslant \sum_{t=1}^{n} P_{2,t}\epsilon .$$

In the case of the EG strategy, $P_{2,t}$ equals

$$\frac{\exp\left(\eta \sum_{t=1}^{n} \frac{(1-\epsilon)}{\mathbf{P}_t \cdot \mathbf{x}_t}\right)}{\exp\left(\eta \sum_{t=1}^{n} \frac{1}{\mathbf{P}_t \cdot \mathbf{x}_t}\right) + \exp\left(\eta \sum_{t=1}^{n} \frac{(1-\epsilon)}{\mathbf{P}_t \cdot \mathbf{x}_t}\right)} = \frac{\exp\left(-\eta\epsilon \sum_{t=1}^{n} \frac{1}{\mathbf{P}_t \cdot \mathbf{x}_t}\right)}{1 + \exp\left(-\eta\epsilon \sum_{t=1}^{n} \frac{1}{\mathbf{P}_t \cdot \mathbf{x}_t}\right)}$$

$$\geqslant \frac{\exp\left(-\eta \left(\epsilon/(1 - \epsilon)\right) t\right)}{2} .$$

Thus, the logarithmic wealth ratio of the EG algorithm is lower bounded by

$$\sum_{t=1}^{n} \epsilon \frac{\exp\left(-\eta\left(\epsilon/(1-\epsilon)\right)t\right)}{2} = \frac{\epsilon}{2} \frac{1-\exp\left(-\eta\left(\epsilon/(1-\epsilon)\right)(n+1)\right)}{1-\exp\left(-\eta\left(\epsilon/(1-\epsilon)\right)\right)}$$

$$= \frac{1}{2}\sqrt{\frac{n}{8\ln N}} + o(\sqrt{n}) .$$

## 4   Internal Regret of Investment Strategies

The aim of this section is to introduce the notion of internal regret to the sequential investment problem. Recall that in the framework of sequential prediction described in Section 2, the cumulative internal regret $R_{(i,j),n}$ for the pair of experts $(i,j)$ may be interpreted as how much the predictor would have gained had he replaced all values $P_{i,t}$ $(t \le n)$ by zero and all values $P_{j,t}$ by $P_{i,t} + P_{j,t}$. Analogously, given an investment strategy $P = (\mathbf{P}_1, \mathbf{P}_2, \ldots)$, we may define the *internal regret of $P$ with respect to the pair of assets $(i,j)$* (where $1 \le i, j \le N$) by

$$\overline{r}_{(i,j),t} = \ln \frac{\mathbf{P}_t^{i \to j} \cdot \mathbf{x}_t}{\mathbf{P}_t \cdot \mathbf{x}_t}$$

where the probability vector $\mathbf{P}_t^{i \to j}$ is defined such that its $i$-th component equals zero, its $j$-th component equals $P_{j,t} + P_{i,t}$, and all other components are equal to those of $\mathbf{P}_t$. $\overline{r}_{(i,j),t}$ expresses the regret the investor using strategy $P$ suffers after trading day $t$ by not having invested all his capital he invested in stock $i$ in stock $j$ instead, where the regret is expressed as the logarithmic ratio of the wealth factor the investor would have achieved by moving all his capital from stock $i$ to stock $j$ and the wealth factor he achieves actually. The *cumulative internal regret of $P$ with respect to the pair $(i,j)$* after $n$ trading periods is simply

$$\overline{R}_{(i,j),n} = \sum_{t=1}^{n} \overline{r}_{(i,j),n} .$$

It is a desirable property of an investment strategy that its cumulative internal regret grows sublinearly for all possible pairs of assets, independently of the market outcomes. Indeed, otherwise the investor could exhibit a simple modification of his betting strategy which would have led to exponentially larger wealth. In this sense, the notion of internal regret is a measure of the efficiency of the strategy. Based on this, we define the *internal regret* of the investment strategy $P$ by

$$\overline{R}_n = \max_{1 \le i,j \le N} \overline{R}_{(i,j),n}$$

and ask wether it is possible to guarantee that $\overline{R}_n = o(n)$ for all possible market sequences. Thus, an investor using a strategy with a small internal regret is guatanteed that for any pair of stocks the total regret of not investing in one stock instead of the other becomes negligible.

The next two examples show that it is not trivial to achieve a small internal regret. Indeed, the buy-and-hold and EG investment strategies have linearly increasing internal regret for some bounded market sequences.

*Example 2. (Buy-and-hold strategies may have large internal regret.)* As a first example we point out that buy-and-hold stategies are not guaranteed to have a small internal regret. To this end, consider a market with $N = 3$ assets which evolves according to the following repeated scheme:

$$(1 - \epsilon, \epsilon, \epsilon), \ (\epsilon, 1 - \epsilon, 1 - \epsilon), \ (1 - \epsilon, \epsilon, \epsilon), \ (\epsilon, 1 - \epsilon, 1 - \epsilon), \ \ldots$$

where $\epsilon < 1$ is a fixed positive number. Straightforward calculation shows that for an even $n$, the cumulative internal regret $\overline{R}_{(2,1),n}$ of the buy-and-hold strategy which distributes its initial wealth uniformly among the assets equals

$$\frac{n}{2} \left( \ln \frac{(2 - \epsilon)^2}{3(1 - \epsilon)(1 + \epsilon)} \right) \ ,$$

showing that even for bounded markets, the naive buy-and-hold strategy may incur a large internal regret. Later we will see a generalization of buy-and-hold with small internal regret.

*Example 3. (The EG strategy may have large internal regret.)* The next example, showing that for some market sequence the EG algorithm of [14] has a linearly growing internal regret, is inspired by Example 1 above. Consider a market of three stocks $A$, $B$, and $C$. Divide the $n$ trading periods into three different regimes of lengths $L_1$, $L_2$, and $L_3$. The wealth ratios (which are constant in each regime) are summarized in the table below.

| Regimes | $x_{A,t}$ | $x_{B,t}$ | $x_{C,t}$ |
|---|---|---|---|
| $1 \leqslant t \leqslant T_1 = L_1$ | 2 | 1 | 0.5 |
| $T_1 + 1 \leqslant t \leqslant T_2 = L_1 + L_2$ | 1 | 2 | 0.5 |
| $T_2 + 1 \leqslant t \leqslant T_3 = n$ | 1 | 2 | 2.05 |

In the first period, the weight of $B$ quickly becomes negligible and remains small in most of the second period, except at the end of it, when it recovers. In the last period, it is always more than a constant and a large internal regret is suffered. It is possible to show that $L_1, L_2$, and $L_3$ may be set in such a way that the cumulative internal regret $R_{(B,C),n}$ is lower bounded by a positive constant times $n$ for $n$ sufficiently large. The details of the proof are omitted.

## 5   Investment Strategies with Small Internal Regret

The purpose of this section is to introduce some investment strategies with guaranteed small internal regret. The first may be considered a generalization of the buy-and-hold strategy.

## 5.1   Generalized Buy-and-Hold Strategy

The intuition behind the first algorithm is that we try to construct an algorithm which satisfies the Blackwell condition (2.2) with the instantaneous internal regret

$$\overline{r}_{(i,j),t} = \ln\left(\mathbf{P}_t^{i\to j} \cdot \mathbf{x}_t\right) - \ln\left(\mathbf{P}_t \cdot \mathbf{x}_t\right) \ .$$

(Note that satisfying the Blackwell condition is not sufficient in this case, since the $\overline{r}_{(i,j),t}$ are not necessarily bounded, but in spite of the unbounded regrets, this intuition turns out to lead to a strategy with a small internal regret.) Now using the exponential potential function, the Blackwell condition may be rewritten as

$$\frac{1}{W_t} \sum_{i\neq j} W_{t-1}^{i\to j} \ln\left(\frac{\mathbf{P}_t^{i\to j} \cdot \mathbf{x}_t}{\mathbf{P}_t \cdot \mathbf{x}_t}\right) \leqslant 0 \ ,$$

where $W_t = \prod_{s=1}^{t} \mathbf{P}_s \cdot \mathbf{x}_s$ is the wealth achieved by strategy $P$ and $W_t^{i\to j} = \prod_{s=1}^{t} \mathbf{P}_s^{i\to j} \cdot \mathbf{x}_s$ is the fictitious wealth obtained by the $i \to j$ modified version of it. To construct a method satisfying this inequality, we note that $W_{t-1}^{i\to j} \geqslant 0$, so that, using $\ln(1 + u) \leqslant u$, it suffices to find a strategy $P$ satisfying

$$\sum_{i\neq j} W_{t-1}^{i\to j} P_{i,t} \left(\frac{x_{j,t}}{\mathbf{P}_t \cdot \mathbf{x}_t} - \frac{x_{i,t}}{\mathbf{P}_t \cdot \mathbf{x}_t}\right) = 0 \ . \tag{5.1}$$

Thus, we define the *generalized buy-and-hold* (GBH) investment strategy as one satisfying the above equality. The validity of this definition follows by a similar argument to that in Section 2. Indeed, the GBH strategy $\mathbf{P}_t$ may be calculated, at time $t$, as a fixed probability vector of the positive matrix

$$\left[\frac{W_{t-1}^{j\to i}}{\sum_{1\leqslant k\leqslant N} W_{t-1}^{i\to k}}\right]_{(i,j)} \ .$$

The proof of the theorem below shows that the GBH strategy performs buy-and-hold on the $N(N - 1)$ fictitious modified strategies and, in the particular case of $N = 2$ assets, it reduces to the simple buy-and-hold strategy–hence its name. The main property of this investment strategy is that its internal regret is bounded by a constant, as stated by the theorem below.

**Theorem 1.** *The* GBH *investment strategy incurs a cumulative internal regret* $\overline{R}_n \leq \ln N(N - 1)$ *for all* $n$.

*Proof.* Denote by $\nu_t^{i\to j}$ the quantity

$$\nu_t^{i\to j} = \frac{\mathbf{P}_t^{i\to j} \cdot \mathbf{x}_t}{\mathbf{P}_t \cdot \mathbf{x}_t} - 1 = P_{i,t}\left(\frac{x_{j,t}}{\mathbf{P}_t \cdot \mathbf{x}_t} - \frac{x_{i,t}}{\mathbf{P}_t \cdot \mathbf{x}_t}\right) \ .$$

Then the condition (5.1) may be written equivalently as

$$\sum_{i\neq j} \left(\prod_{s=1}^{t-1} \left(1 + \nu_s^{i\to j}\right)\right) \nu_t^{i\to j} = 0 \ .$$

Using this property, we have

$$
\frac{\sum_{i \neq j} W_t^{i \to j}}{W_t} = \sum_{i \neq j} \left( \prod_{s=1}^{t} \left( 1 + \nu_s^{i \to j} \right) \right) = \sum_{i \neq j} \left( \prod_{s=1}^{t-1} \left( 1 + \nu_s^{i \to j} \right) \right) \left( 1 + \nu_t^{i \to j} \right)
$$

$$
= \sum_{i \neq j} \left( \prod_{s=1}^{t-1} \left( 1 + \nu_s^{i \to j} \right) \right) = \ldots = N(N-1) \, .
$$

Thus,

$$
\overline{R}_{(i,j),n} = \ln \frac{W_t^{i \to j}}{W_t} \leqslant \ln N(N-1) \, .
$$

The advantage of this algorithm is that its performance bounds do not depend on the market. However, unlike in the sequential prediction problem described in Section 2, in the problem of sequential portfolio selection, a small internal regret does not necessarily imply a small worst-case logarithmic wealth ratio with respect to the class of all buy-and-hold strategies. (This may be seen by considering the example of GBH.) However, there is a simple modification of the GBH strategy leading to internal regret less than $2 \ln N$ and external regret with respect to buy-and-hold strategies less than $2 \ln N$.

The investment algorithm introduced in the next section has the surprising property that, apart from a guaranteed sublinear internal regret, it also achieves a sublinear worst-case logarithmic wealth ratio not only with respect to the class of buy-and-hold strategies, but also with respect to the class of all constantly rebalanced portfolios.

## 5.2   A Strategy with Small Internal and External Regrets

The investment strategy introduced in this section–which we call B1EXP–is based on the same kind of linear upper bound on the internal regret as the one that was used in our proof of the performance of the EG strategy in Section 3. The same argument may be used to upper bound the cumulative internal regret as

$$
\overline{R}_{(i,j),n} = \sum_{t=1}^{n} \ln \left( \mathbf{P}_t^{i \to j} \cdot \mathbf{x}_t \right) - \ln \left( \mathbf{P}_t \cdot \mathbf{x}_t \right) \leq \sum_{t=1}^{n} P_{i,t} \left( \frac{x_{j,t}}{\mathbf{P}_t \cdot \mathbf{x}_t} - \frac{x_{i,t}}{\mathbf{P}_t \cdot \mathbf{x}_t} \right) \, .
$$

Introducing

$$
r_{(i,j),t} = P_{i,t} \left( \frac{x_{j,t}}{\mathbf{P}_t \cdot \mathbf{x}_t} - \frac{x_{i,t}}{\mathbf{P}_t \cdot \mathbf{x}_t} \right)
$$

we may use the internal-regret minimizing prediction algorithm of Section 2 to compute $\mathbf{P}_t$ as a fixed point of the nonnegative matrix $S = A/\alpha + I_N$ as defined at the end of Section 2. For simplicity, we use the exponential potential function. This definition, of course, requires the boundedness of the values of $r_{(i,j),t}$. This may be guaranteed by the same assumption as in the analysis of the EG investment strategy, that is, by assuming that the returns $x_{i,t}$ all fall in the interval $[m, M]$ where $m < M$ are positive constants. Then the internal regret of the algorithm B1EXP may be bounded by the result of Cesa-Bianchi and Lugosi mentioned in Section 2. An important additional property of the algorithm is that its worst-case logarithmic wealth ratio, with respect to the the class of all constantly rebalanced portfolios, may be bounded similarly as that of the the EG algorithm. These main properties are summarized in the following theorem.

**Theorem 2.** *Assume that* $m \le x_{i,t} \le M$ *for all* $1 \le i \le N$ *and* $1 \le t \le n$. *Then the cumulative internal regret of the* B1EXP *strategy* $P$ *is bounded by*

$$\overline{R}_n \le \frac{\ln N(N-1)}{\eta} + \frac{n\eta}{2} \frac{M^2}{m^2} = 2\frac{M}{m}\sqrt{n \ln N} \ ,$$

*where we set* $\eta = 2(m/M)\sqrt{(\ln N)/n}$. *In addition, if* $\mathcal{Q}$ *denotes the class of all constantly rebalanced portfolios, then the worst-case logarithmic wealth ratio of* $P$ *is bounded by*

$$W_n(P, \mathcal{Q}) \le 2N\frac{M}{m}\sqrt{n \ln N} \ .$$

*Proof.* The bound for the internal regret $\overline{R}_n$ follows from the linear upper bound described above and Corollary 8 of Cesa-Bianchi and Lugosi [5].

To bound the worst-case logarithmic wealth ratio $W_n(P, \mathcal{Q})$, recall that by inequality (3.2), for any constantly rebalanced portfolio **B**,

$$W_n(P, \mathcal{Q}) \le \sum_{j=1}^{N} B_j \sum_{i=1}^{N} \left( \sum_{t=1}^{n} P_{i,t} (\ell_{i,t} - \ell_{j,t}) \right)$$

$$\le N \max_{1 \le i,j \le N} \sum_{t=1}^{n} P_{i,t} \left( \frac{x_{j,t}}{\mathbf{P}_t \cdot \mathbf{x}_t} - \frac{x_{i,t}}{\mathbf{P}_t \cdot \mathbf{x}_t} \right)$$

which is not larger than $N$ times the upper bound obtained on the cumulative internal regret $\overline{R}_n$ which completes the proof.

*Remark 2.* The computation of the investment strategy requires the inversion of an $N \times N$ matrix at each trading period. This is quite feasible even for large markets in which $N$ may be as large as about 100.

*Remark 3.* The B1EXP strategy may be seen as another instance of the exponentially weighted average predictor, which uses the fictitious strategies as experts. Thus, instead of considering the single stocks, as EG, B1EXP and GBH consider stocks pairs and their relative behaviors. This may explain the greater stability observed on real data.

*Remark 4.* Just like in the case of the sequential prediction problem, the exponential potential function may be replaced by others such as polynomial potentials. In that case the cumulative internal regret is bounded by $\frac{M}{m}\sqrt{n(p-1)}N^{2/p}$ which is approximately optimized by the choice $p = 4\ln N$. We call this investment strategy B1POL. Even though this strategy has comparable theoretical guarantees to those of B1EXP, our experiments show a clear superiority of the use of the exponential potential. This and other practical issues will be discussed elsewhere.

*Remark 5.* Just like EG, the strategy B1EXP requires the knowledge of two parameters: the time horizon $n$ and the ratio $M/m$ of the bounds assumed on the market. This disadvantage may be fixed by either using the well-known doubling trick or recalling remark 3 and considering a time-varying value of $\eta$ similarly to the algorithms suggested by Auer, Cesa-Bianchi, and Gentile [1]. The details are omitted from this summary and will be given elsewhere.

## 6    A Generalized Universal Portfolio

The definition of internal regret $\overline{R}_n$ considers the regret suffered by not moving one's capital from one stock to another. Still considering only simple modifications of the investor's allocation strategy, a significantly more general definition may be given as follows: let $\mathcal{F}$ be the class of all functions $f : \{1, \ldots, N\} \to \{1, \ldots, N\}$ and let $\mathbf{B} = (B_1, \ldots, B_N) \in [0, 1]^N$. The function $f$ indicates the capital transfers considered in the regret and the vector $\mathbf{B}$ is the vector of proportions of capital moved from stocks to others. More precisely, at each time instant $t$, the modified strategy $\mathbf{P}_t^{f,\mathbf{B}}$ corresponding to the pair $(f, \mathbf{B})$ is defined by

$$P_{i,t}^{f,\mathbf{B}} = (1 - B_i)\, P_{i,t} + \sum_{j \in f^{-1}\{i\}} B_j P_{j,t} \ .$$

Note that by taking $f$ to be the function which maps every index to itself except for index $i$ which is mapped to $j$, and $\mathbf{B} = (1, \ldots, 1)$ then $P_{i,t}^{f,\mathbf{B}}$ becomes $P_t^{i \to j}$ considered in our original definition of the internal regret.

Now the generalized internal regret is defined as

$$\max_{f \in \mathcal{F}} \max_{\mathbf{B} \in [0,1]^N} \ln \frac{W_n^{f,\mathbf{B}}}{W_n}$$

where $W_n^{f,\mathbf{B}} = \prod_{t=1}^n \sum_{i=1}^N P_{i,t}^{f,\mathbf{B}} x_{i,t}$.

It is quite surprising that even this very general notion of internal regret may be made small. Note that the GBH strategy suffers a large generalized internal regret, for it may have a large external regret with respect to buy-and-hold strategies, as noted in the remark following Theorem 1, while this new notion of internal regret encapsulates external regret with respect to buy-and-hold strategies (take $\mathbf{B} = (1, \ldots, 1)$ and a constant $f$ to see it).

But a linear upper bounding shows that B1EXP and B1POL have a low generalized internal regret, with exactly the same bound on it as proved in Section 5.2. This may be another explanation of the good performance of B1EXP on real data. Indeed, it turns out that generalized internal regret can be made much smaller, as the next theorem shows. The proof is directly inspired by Theorem 1 and uses Blum and Kalai's point of view of Cover's universal portfolio, [2].

**Theorem 3.** *There exists an investment strategy $P$ such that*

$$\max_{f \in \mathcal{F}} \max_{\mathbf{B} \in [0,1]^N} \ln \frac{W_n^{f,\mathbf{B}}}{W_n} \leqslant N \ln(n+1) + N \ln N + 1 \ .$$

*Remark 6.* The algorithm given in the proof has a computational complexity exponential in the number of stocks (at least in its straightforward implementation). However, it provides a theoretical bound which is likely to be of the best achievable order.

## Acknowledgements

We thank Yoram Singer for sending us the NYSE data set used in the experiments. We also thank Dean Foster for his suggestions that lead us to the example showing that the exponential weighted average predictor has a large internal regret.

## References

1. P. Auer, N. Cesa-Bianchi, and C. Gentile. Adaptive and self-confident on-line learning algorithms. *Journal of Computer and System Sciences*, 64:48–75, 2002.
2. A. Blum and A. Kalai. Universal portfolios with and without transaction costs. *Machine Learning*, 35:193–205, 1999.
3. N. Cesa-Bianchi, Y. Freund, D.P. Helmbold, D. Haussler, R. Schapire, and M.K. Warmuth. How to use expert advice. *Journal of the ACM*, 44(3):427–485, 1997.
4. N. Cesa-Bianchi and G. Lugosi. Minimax values and entropy bounds for portfolio selection problems. In *Proceedings of the First World Congress of the Game Theory Society*, 2000.
5. N. Cesa-Bianchi and G. Lugosi. Potential-based algorithms in on-line prediction and game theory. *Machine Learning*, 51, 2003.
6. T.M. Cover. Universal portfolios. *Mathematical Finance*, 1:1–29, 1991.
7. T.M. Cover and E. Ordentlich. Universal portfolios with side information. *IEEE Transactions on Information Theory*, 42:348–363, 1996.
8. D. Foster and R. Vohra. Asymptotic calibration. *Biometrica*, 85:379–390, 1998.
9. D. Foster and R. Vohra. Regret in the on-line decision problem. *Games and Economic Behavior*, 29:7–36, 1999.
10. D. Fudenberg and D. Levine. Universal consistency and cautious fictitious play. *Journal of Economic Dynamics and Control*, 19:1065–1089, 1995.
11. D. Fudenberg and D. Levine. Universal conditional consistency. *Games and Economic Behavior*, 29:104–130, 1999.
12. S. Hart and A. Mas-Colell. A simple adaptive procedure leading to correlated equilibrium. *Econometrica*, 68:1127–1150, 2000.
13. S. Hart and A. Mas-Colell. A general class of adaptive strategies. *Journal of Economic Theory*, 98:26–54, 2001.
14. D. P. Helmbold, R. E. Schapire, Y. Singer, and M. K. Warmuth. On-line portfolio selection using multiplicative updates. *Mathematical Finance*, 8:325–344, 1998.
15. E. Ordentlich and T.M. Cover. The cost of achieving the best portfolio in hindsight. *Mathematics of Operations Research*, 23:960–982, 1998.

# Lower Bounds on the Sample Complexity of Exploration in the Multi-armed Bandit Problem

Shie Mannor and John N. Tsitsiklis

Laboratory for Information and Decision Systems
Massachusetts Institute of Technology, Cambridge, MA 02139
{shie,jnt}@mit.edu

**Abstract.** We consider the Multi-armed bandit problem under the PAC ("probably approximately correct") model. It was shown by Even-Dar et al. [5] that given $n$ arms, it suffices to play the arms a total of $O\big((n/\varepsilon^2)\log(1/\delta)\big)$ times to find an $\varepsilon$-optimal arm with probability of at least $1 - \delta$. Our contribution is a matching lower bound that holds for any sampling policy. We also generalize the lower bound to a Bayesian setting, and to the case where the statistics of the arms are known but the identities of the arms are not.

## 1   Introduction

The multi-armed bandit problem is a classical problem in decision theory. There is a number of alternative arms, each with a stochastic reward with initially unknown statistics. We play these arms in some order, which may depend on the sequence of rewards that have been observed so far. The objective is to find a policy for playing the arms, under which the sum of the expected rewards comes as close as possible to the ideal reward, i.e., the expected reward that would be obtained if we were to play the "best" arm at all times. One of the attractive features of the multi-armed bandit problem is that despite its simplicity, it encompasses many important decision theoretic issues, such as the tradeoff between exploration and exploitation.

The multi-armed bandit problem has been widely studied in a variety of setups. The problem was first considered in the 50's, in the seminal work of Robbins [10], which derives strategies that asymptotically attain an average reward that converges in the limit to the reward of the best arm. The multi-armed bandit problem was later studied in discounted, Bayesian, Markovian, expected reward, and adversarial setups. (See [4] for a review of the classical results on the multi-armed bandit problem.)

Lower bounds for different variants of the multi-armed bandit have been studied by several authors. For the expected regret model, where the regret is defined as the difference between the ideal reward (if the best arm were known) and the reward of an online policy, the seminal work of Lai and Robbins [9] provides tight bounds in terms of the Kullback-Leibler divergence between the distributions of the rewards of the different arms. These bounds grow logarithmically with the number of steps. The adversarial multi-armed bandit problem (i.e., without any

B. Schölkopf and M.K. Warmuth (Eds.): COLT/Kernel 2003, LNAI 2777, pp. 418–432, 2003.

probabilistic assumptions) was considered in [2, 3], where it was shown that the expected regret grows proportionally to the square root of the number of steps. Of related interest is the work of Kulkarni and Lugosi [8]. It was shown there that for any specific time $t$, one can choose probability distributions so that the expected regret is linear in $t$.

The focus of this paper is the classical multi-armed bandit problem, but rather than looking at the expected regret, we are concerned with PAC-type bounds on the number of steps needed to identify a near-optimal arm. In particular, we are interested in the expected number of steps that are required in order to identify with high probability (at least $1 - \delta$) an arm whose expected reward is within $\varepsilon$ from the expected reward of the best arm. This naturally abstracts the case where one must eventually commit to one specific arm, and quantifies the amount of exploration necessary. This is in contrast to most of the results for the multi-armed bandit problem, where the main aim is to maximize the expected cumulative reward while both exploring and exploiting.

In [5] an algorithm, called the Median Elimination algorithm, was shown to require $O\big((n/\varepsilon^2) \log(1/\delta)\big)$ arm plays to find, with probability of at least $1-\delta$, an $\varepsilon$-optimal arm. A matching lower bound was also derived [5], but it only applied to the case where $\delta > 1/n$, and therefore did not capture the case where high confidence (small $\delta$) is desired. In this paper, we derive a matching lower bound which applies for every $\delta > 0$. Let us note here that some results with a similar flavor have been provided in [7]. However, they refer to the case of Gaussian rewards and only consider the case of asymptotically vanishing $\delta$.

Our main result can be viewed as a generalization of a $O(1/\varepsilon^2 \log(1/\delta))$ lower bound provided in [1] for the case of two bandits. The proof in [1] is based on a simple interchange argument, and relies on the fact there are only two underlying hypotheses. The technique we use is based on a likelihood ratio argument and a tight martingale bound. Let us note that the inequalities used in [3] to derive lower bounds for the expected regret in an adversarial setup can also be used to derive a lower bound for our problem, but do not appear to be tight enough to capture the $\log(1/\delta)$ dependence on $\delta$.

Our work also provides fundamental lower bounds in the context of sequential analysis (see, e.g., [12]). In the language of [12], we provide a lower bound on the expected length of a sequential sampling algorithm under any adaptive allocation scheme. For the case of two arms, it was shown in [12] (p. 148) that if one restricts to sampling strategies that only take into account the empirical average rewards from the different arms, then the problems of inference and arm selection can be treated separately. As a consequence, and under this restriction, [12] shows that an optimal allocation cannot be much better than a uniform one. Our results are different in a number of ways. First, we consider multiple hypotheses (multiple arms). Second, we allow the allocation rule to be completely general and to depend on the whole history. Third, unlike most of the sequential analysis literature (see, e.g., [7]), we do not restrict ourselves to the limiting case where the probability of error converges to zero. Finally, we consider finite time bounds, rather than asymptotic ones.

The paper is organized as follows. In Section 2, we set up our framework, and since we are interested in lower bounds, we restrict to the special case where each arm is a "coin," i.e., the rewards are Bernoulli random variables, but with unknown parameters ("biases"). In Section 3, we provide a lower bound on the sample complexity. In fact, we show that the lower bound holds true even in the special case where the set of coin biases is known, but the identity of the coins is not. In Section 4, we derive similar lower bounds within a Bayesian setting, where there is a prior distribution on the set of biases of the different coins. In Section 5, we provide a lower bound that depends on the specific (though unknown) biases of the coins. Finally, Section 6 contains some brief concluding remarks.

## 2    Problem Definition

The exploration problem for multi-armed bandits is defined as follows. We are given $n$ arms. Each arm $i$ is associated with a sequence of identically distributed Bernoulli (i.e., taking values in $\{0,1\}$) random variables $X_k^i$, $k = 1, 2, \ldots$, with mean $p_i$. Here, $X_k^i$ corresponds to the reward obtained the $k$th time that arm $i$ is played. We assume that the random variables $X_k^i$, for $i = 1, \ldots, n$, $k = 1, 2, \ldots$, are independent, and we define $p = (p_1, \ldots, p_n)$. Given that we restrict to the Bernoulli case, we will use in the sequel the term "coin" instead of "arm."

A *policy* is a mapping that given a history, chooses a particular coin to be tried next, or selects a particular coin and stops. We allow a policy to use randomization when choosing a coin to sample or when making a final selection. However, we only consider policies that are guaranteed to stop with probability 1, for every possible vector $p$. (Otherwise, the expected number of steps would be infinite.) Given a particular policy, we let $\mathbf{P}_p$ be the corresponding probability measure (on the natural probability space for this model). This probability space captures both the randomness in the coins (according to the vector $p$), as well as any additional randomization carried out by the policy. We introduce the following random variables, which are well defined, except possibly on the set of measure zero where the policy does not stop. We let $T_i$ be the total number of times that coin $i$ is tried, and let $T = T_1 + \cdots + T_n$ be the total number of trials. We also let $I$ be the coin which is selected when the policy decides to stop.

We say that a policy is $(\varepsilon,\delta)$-*correct* if

$$\mathbf{P}_p\Big(p_I > \max_i p_i - \varepsilon\Big) \geq 1 - \delta,$$

for *every* $p \in [0,1]^n$. It was shown in [5] that there exist constants $c_1$ and $c_2$ such that for every $n$, $\varepsilon > 0$, and $\delta > 0$, there exists an $(\varepsilon,\delta)$-correct policy under which

$$\mathbf{E}_p[T] \leq c_1 \frac{n}{\varepsilon^2} \log \frac{c_2}{\delta}, \qquad \forall\, p \in [0,1]^n.$$

A matching lower bound was also established in [5], but only for "large" values of $\delta$, namely, for $\delta > 1/n$. In contrast, we aim at deriving bounds that capture the dependence of the sample-complexity on $\delta$, as $\delta$ becomes small.

## 3    A Lower Bound on the Sample Complexity

In this section, we present our main results. Theorem 1 below matches the upper bounds in [5]. Throughout, log stands for the natural logarithm.

**Theorem 1.** *There exist positive constants $c_1$, $c_2$, $\varepsilon_0$, and $\delta_0$, such that for every $n \geq 2$, $\varepsilon \in (0, \varepsilon_0)$, and $\delta \in (0, \delta_0)$, and for every ($\varepsilon,\delta$)-correct policy, there exists some $p \in [0, 1]^n$ such that*

$$\mathbf{E}_p[T] \geq c_1 \frac{n}{\varepsilon^2} \log \frac{c_2}{\delta}.$$

*In particular, $\varepsilon_0$ and $\delta_0$ can be taken equal to $1/4$ and $e^{-4}/4$, respectively.*

Instead of proving Theorem 1, we will establish a stronger result, which refers to the case where the values of the biases $p_i$ are known up to a permutation. More specifically, we are given a vector $q \in [0, 1]^n$, and we are told that the true vector $p$ of coin biases is of the form $p = q \circ \sigma$, where $\sigma$ is an unknown permutation of the set $\{1, \ldots, n\}$, and where $q \circ \sigma$ stands for permuting the components of the vector $q$ according to $\sigma$, i.e., $(q \circ \sigma)_i = q_{\sigma(i)}$. We say that a policy is ($q, \varepsilon, \delta$)-correct if

$$\mathbf{P}_{q \circ \sigma}\left(p_I > \max_i q_i - \varepsilon\right) \geq 1 - \delta,$$

for every permutation $\sigma$ of the set $\{1, \ldots, n\}$.

Theorem 2 below establishes a lower bound of the same form as the one in Theorem 1, for the special case discussed here. In essence it provides a lower bound on the number of trials needed in order to identify, with high probability, a coin with bias $(1/2)+\varepsilon$, out of a population consisting of this coin and $n-1$ fair coins. Theorem 1 is a straightforward corollary of Theorem 2. This is because any ($\varepsilon,\delta$)-correct policy must also be ($q, \varepsilon, \delta$)-correct for every given $q$.

**Theorem 2.** *There exist positive constants $c_1$, $c_2$, $\varepsilon_0$, and $\delta_0$, such that for every $n \geq 2$, $\varepsilon \in (0, \varepsilon_0)$, and $\delta \in (0, \delta_0)$, there exists $q \in [0, 1]^n$ such that every ($q, \varepsilon, \delta$)-correct policy satisfies*

$$\mathbf{E}_{\sigma \circ q}[T] \geq c_1 \frac{n}{\varepsilon^2} \log \frac{c_2}{\delta},$$

*for every permutation $\sigma$. In particular, $\varepsilon_0$ and $\delta_0$ can be taken equal to $1/4$ and $e^{-4}/4$, respectively.*

*Proof.* Let us fix $n$, $\varepsilon_0 = 1/4$, $\delta_0 = e^{-4}/4$, and some $\varepsilon \in (0, \varepsilon_0)$, and $\delta \in (0, \delta_0)$. Let

$$q = \left(\frac{1}{2} + \varepsilon, \frac{1}{2}, \ldots, \frac{1}{2}\right).$$

Suppose that we have a policy which is ($q, \varepsilon, \delta$)-correct. We need to show that under such a policy the lower bound in the theorem statement holds.

We introduce a collection of hypotheses $H_1, \ldots, H_n$, defined by

$$H_\ell : \qquad p_\ell = \frac{1}{2} + \varepsilon, \qquad p_i = \frac{1}{2}, \qquad \text{for } i \neq \ell.$$

Since the policy is $(q, \varepsilon, \delta)$-correct, the following must be true for every hypothesis $H_\ell$: if $H_\ell$ is true, the policy must have probability at least $1 - \delta$ of eventually stopping and selecting coin $\ell$. We denote by $\mathbf{E}_\ell$ and $\mathbf{P}_\ell$ the expectation and probability, respectively, under the policy being considered and under hypothesis $H_\ell$.

As in Section 2, we denote by $T_i$ the number of times coin $i$ is tried. We also define $K_t^i = X_1^i + \cdots + X_t^i$, which is the number of unit rewards ("heads") if the coin $i$ is tried $t$ times (not necessarily consecutively.) Let $t^* = \frac{1}{c\varepsilon^2} \log \frac{1}{4\delta}$, where $c$ is an absolute constant whose value will be specified later. We also introduce the following events:

(i) $A_i = \{T_i \leq 4t^*\}$. (Coin $i$ was not tried too many times.)
(ii) $B_i = \{I = i\}$. (Coin $i$ was selected upon termination.)
(iii) $C_i = \left\{ \max_{1 \leq t \leq 4t^*} \left| K_t^i - \frac{1}{2}t \right| < \sqrt{t^* \log(1/4\delta)} \right\}$. (Coin $i$ appears fair throughout the process.)

We now establish two lemmas that will be used in the sequel.

**Lemma 1.** *If $\ell \neq i$, then $\mathbf{P}_\ell(C_i) > 3/4$.*

*Proof.* First, note that $K_t^i - p_i t$ is a $\mathbf{P}_\ell$-martingale, where $p_i = 1/2$ is the bias of coin $i$ under hypothesis $H_\ell$. (We are developing the proof for a general $p_i$, because this will be useful later.) Using Kolmogorov's inequality (Corollary 7.66, in p. 244 of [11]), the probability of the complement of $C_i$ can be bounded as follows:

$$\mathbf{P}_\ell \left( \max_{1 \leq t \leq 4t^*} \left| K_t^i - p_i t \right| \geq \sqrt{t^* \log(1/4\delta)} \right) \leq \frac{\mathbf{E}_\ell \left[ (K_{4t^*}^i - 4p_i t^*)^2 \right]}{t^* \log(1/4\delta)}.$$

Since $\mathbf{E}_\ell \left[ (K_{4t^*}^i - 4p_i t^*)^2 \right] = 4p_i(1 - p_i)t^*$, we obtain

$$\mathbf{P}_\ell(C_i) \geq 1 - \frac{4p_i(1 - p_i)}{\log(1/4\delta)} > \frac{3}{4},$$

where the last inequality follows because $4\delta < e^{-4}$ and $4p_i(1 - p_i) \leq 1$. $\square$

**Lemma 2.** *If $0 \leq x \leq 3/4$ and $y \geq 0$, then*

$$(1 - x)^y \geq e^{-dxy},$$

*where $d = 2$.*

*Proof.* A straightforward calculation shows that $\log(1 - x) + dx \geq 0$ for $0 \leq x \leq 3/4$. Therefore, $y(\log(1 - x) + dx) \geq 0$ for every $y \geq 0$. Rearranging and exponentiating leads to $(1 - x)^y \geq e^{-dxy}$. $\square$

The next key lemma is the central part of the proof. It uses a likelihood ratio argument to show that if a coin $i$ is not tried enough times under hypothesis $H_\ell$, the probabilities of selecting coin $\ell$ under hypothesis $H_i$ is substantial.

**Lemma 3.** *Suppose that $\ell \neq i$ and $\mathbf{E}_\ell[T_i] \leq t^*$. If the constant $c$ in the definition of $t^*$ is larger than 128, then $\mathbf{P}_i(B_\ell) > \delta$.*

*Proof.* We first observe that

$$t^* \geq \mathbf{E}_\ell[T_i] > 4t^* \mathbf{P}_\ell(T_i > 4t^*) = 4t^* \big(1 - \mathbf{P}_\ell(T_i \leq 4t^*)\big),$$

from which it follows that $\mathbf{P}_\ell(A_i) > 3/4$. We now define the event

$$S_i^\ell = A_i \cap B_\ell \cap C_i.$$

Since $\delta < \delta_0 < 1/4$, and the policy is $(q, \varepsilon, \delta)$-correct, we must have $\mathbf{P}_\ell(B_\ell) > 3/4$. Furthermore, $\mathbf{P}_\ell(C_i) > 3/4$ (by Lemma 1). It follows that $\mathbf{P}_\ell(S_i^\ell) > \frac{1}{4}$.

We let $W$ be the history of the process until the policy terminates. Thus, $W$ consists of the sequence of observed rewards, and if the policy uses randomization, the sequence of coin choices as well. We define the likelihood function $L_i$ by letting

$$L_i(w) = \mathbf{P}_i(W = w),$$

for every possible history $w$, and an associated random variable $L_i(W)$. We also let $K_i$ be a shorthand notation for $K_{T_i}^i$, the total number of unit rewards ("heads") obtained from coin $i$. Because the underlying hypothesis only affects the coin biases but not the statistics of the policy's randomizations, we have

$$\frac{L_i(W)}{L_\ell(W)} = \frac{(\frac{1}{2} + \varepsilon)^{K_i}(\frac{1}{2} - \varepsilon)^{T_i - K_i} \frac{1}{2}^{T_\ell}}{\frac{1}{2}^{T_i}(\frac{1}{2} + \varepsilon)^{K_\ell}(\frac{1}{2} - \varepsilon)^{T_\ell - K_\ell}} = \frac{(1 + 2\varepsilon)^{K_i}(1 - 2\varepsilon)^{T_i - K_i}}{(1 + 2\varepsilon)^{K_\ell}(1 - 2\varepsilon)^{T_\ell - K_\ell}}$$

$$= \frac{(1 - 4\varepsilon^2)^{K_i}(1 - 2\varepsilon)^{T_i - 2K_i}}{(1 - 4\varepsilon^2)^{K_\ell}(1 - 2\varepsilon)^{T_\ell - 2K_\ell}}.$$

Since $\varepsilon < \varepsilon_0 = 1/4$, the denominator is smaller than 1, so that

$$\frac{L_i(W)}{L_\ell(W)} \geq (1 - 4\varepsilon^2)^{K_i}(1 - 2\varepsilon)^{T_i - 2K_i}. \tag{1}$$

We will now proceed to lower bound the terms in the right-hand side of Eq. (1) when event $S_i^\ell$ occurs. If event $S_i^\ell$ occurs, then $A_i$ occurs, so that $K_i \leq T_i \leq 4t^*$. We therefore have

$$(1 - 4\varepsilon^2)^{K_i} \geq (1 - 4\varepsilon^2)^{4t^*} = (1 - 4\varepsilon^2)^{(4/(c\varepsilon^2))\log(1/4\delta)}$$
$$\geq e^{-(16d/c)\log(1/4\delta)} = (4\delta)^{16d/c}.$$

(In the inequalities above, we made use of the assumption that $\varepsilon < \varepsilon_0 = 1/4$ and Lemma 2.) Similarly, if the event $A_i \cap C_i$ occurs, then $T_i - 2K_i \leq 2\sqrt{t^* \log(1/4\delta)}$, so that

$$(1 - 2\varepsilon)^{T_i - 2K_i} \geq (1 - 2\varepsilon)^{2\sqrt{t^* \log(1/4\delta)}} \geq e^{-(4d/\sqrt{c})\log(1/4\delta)} = (4\delta)^{4d/\sqrt{c}}.$$

Using the above inequalities, and by picking $c$ large enough ($c > 128$ will suffice), we obtain that $L_1(W)/L_0(W)$ is at least $4\delta$, whenever the event $S_i^\ell$ occurs. More precisely, we have $\frac{L_i(W)}{L_\ell(W)} 1_{S_i^\ell} \geq 4\delta 1_{S_i^\ell}$, where $1_D$ is the indicator function of an event $D$. We then have

$$\mathbf{P}_i(B_\ell) \geq \mathbf{P}_i(S_i^\ell) = \mathbf{E}_i[1_{S_i^\ell}] = \mathbf{E}_\ell\left[\frac{L_i(W)}{L_\ell(W)} 1_{S_i^\ell}\right] \geq \mathbf{E}_\ell[4\delta 1_{S_i^\ell}] = 4\delta \mathbf{P}_\ell(S_i^\ell) > \delta,$$

where the last inequality made use of the already established fact $\mathbf{P}_\ell(S_i^\ell) > 1/4$.

□

Since the policy is $(q, \varepsilon, \delta)$-correct, we must have $\mathbf{P}_i(B_\ell) \leq \delta$ for every $i \neq \ell$. Lemma 3 then implies that for all $i \neq \ell$ we have that $\mathbf{E}_\ell[T_i] > t^* = \frac{1}{c\varepsilon^2} \log \frac{1}{4\delta}$. By summing over all $i \neq \ell$, we obtain $\mathbf{E}_\ell[T] \geq \frac{n-1}{c\varepsilon^2} \log \frac{1}{4\delta}$, which is of the required form, with $c_1 \geq (n-1)/nc \geq 1/2c$ and $c_2 = 1/4$.

□

## 4    The Bayesian Setup

In this section, we study another variant of the problem, which is based on a Bayesian formulation. In this variant, the parameters $p_i$ associated with each arm are not unknown constants, but random variables described by a given prior. In this case, there is a single underlying probability measure which we denote by $\mathbf{P}$, and which is a mixture of the measures $\mathbf{P}_p$. We also use $\mathbf{E}$ to denote expectation with respect to $\mathbf{P}$. We then define a policy to be $(\varepsilon, \delta)$-correct, under a particular prior and associated measure $\mathbf{P}$, if

$$\mathbf{P}\left(p_I > \max_i p_i - \varepsilon\right) \geq 1 - \delta.$$

We then have the following result.

**Theorem 3.** *There exist positive constants $c_1$, $c_2$, $\varepsilon_0$, and $\delta_0$, such that for every $n \geq 2$, $\varepsilon \in (0, \varepsilon_0)$, and $\delta \in (0, \delta_0)$, there exists a prior such that every $(\varepsilon, \delta)$-correct policy under this prior satisfies*

$$\mathbf{E}[T] \geq c_1 \frac{n}{\varepsilon^2} \log \frac{c_2}{\delta}.$$

*In particular, $\varepsilon_0$ and $\delta_0$ can be taken equal to $1/4$ and $e^{-4}/12$, respectively.*

*Proof.* Let us fix some $\varepsilon \in (0, \varepsilon_0)$, $\delta \in (0, \delta_0)$, and some $(\varepsilon, \delta)$-correct policy. Consider the hypotheses $H_1, \ldots, H_n$, introduced in the proof of Theorem 2. For $i = 1, \ldots, n$, let the prior probability of $H_i$ be equal to $1/n$. It follows that

$$\mathbf{E}[T] = \frac{1}{n} \sum_{\ell=1}^n \sum_{i=1}^n \mathbf{E}_\ell[T_i].$$

Using the same definition for events as in Theorem 2, we have

$$\frac{1}{n} \sum_{\ell=1}^n \mathbf{P}_\ell(B_\ell) = \mathbf{P}\left(p_I > \max_i p_i - \varepsilon\right) \geq 1 - \delta. \tag{2}$$

Let $G$ be the set of coins $\ell$ for which $\mathbf{P}_\ell(B_\ell) > 1 - 3\delta$. From Eq. (2), we obtain that the cardinality of $G$ satisfies $|G| \geq \lfloor 2n/3 \rfloor$.

We now proceed as in the proof of Theorem 2, except that we replace throughout $\delta$ by $3\delta$. The condition $\delta < e^{-4}/4$ becomes $\delta < e^{-4}/12 = \delta_0$. The analogs of Lemmas 1 and 3 go through. In particular, Lemma 3 implies that if $\ell \neq i$ and $\mathbf{E}_\ell[T_i] \leq (1/c\varepsilon^2)\log(1/12\delta)$, then $\mathbf{P}_i(B_\ell) \geq 3\delta$. However, this can never happen for $\ell \in G$. Hence,

$$\mathbf{E}_\ell[T_i] \geq \frac{1}{c\varepsilon^2}\log\frac{1}{12\delta}, \qquad \forall\, \ell \in G,\ \forall\, i \neq \ell.$$

We conclude that

$$\mathbf{E}[T] \geq \frac{1}{n}\sum_{\ell \in G}^{n}\sum_{i \neq \ell}\mathbf{E}_\ell[T_i] \geq \frac{|G|(n-1)}{n} \cdot \frac{1}{c\varepsilon^2}\log\frac{1}{12\delta} \geq c_1\frac{n}{\varepsilon^2}\log\frac{1}{12\delta},$$

where the selection of $c_1$ is such that the last inequality holds for all $n > 1$.   $\square$

## 5    A Lower Bound on the Sample Complexity – General Probabilities

In Theorem 1, we developed a lower bound on the amount of exploration required for any $(\varepsilon, \delta)$-correct policy, by exhibiting an unfavorable vector $p$ of coin biases, under which a lot of exploration is necessary. But this leaves open the possibility that for other, more favorable choices of $p$, less exploration might suffice.

In this section, we refine Theorem 1 by developing a lower bound that explicitly depends on the actual (though unknown) vector $p$. Of course, for any given vector $p$, there is an "optimal" policy, which selects the best coin without any exploration: e.g., if $p_* \geq p_i$ for all $i$, the policy that immediately selects coin 1 is "optimal." However, such a policy will not be $(\varepsilon, \delta)$-correct for all possible vectors $p$.

We start with a lower bound that applies when all coin biases $p_i$ lie in the range $[0, 1/2]$. We will later use a reduction technique to extend the result to a generic range of biases. In the rest of the paper, we use the notational convention $(x)^+ = \max\{0, x\}$.

**Theorem 4.** *Fix some $\underline{p} \in (0, 1/2)$. There exists a constant $c_1$ that depends only on $\underline{p}$ such that for every $\varepsilon \in (0, 1/2)$, every $\delta \in (0, e^{-4}/4)$, every $p \in [0, 1/2]^n$, and every $(\varepsilon, \delta)$-correct policy, we have*

$$\mathbf{E}_p[T] \geq c_1\left\{\frac{(|M(p,\varepsilon)| - 3)^+}{\varepsilon^2} + \sum_{\ell \in N(p,\varepsilon)}\frac{1}{(p_* - p_\ell)^2}\right\}\log\frac{1}{4\delta},$$

*where $p_* = \max_i p_i$,*

$$M(p,\varepsilon) = \left\{\ell :\ p_\ell \geq p_* - \varepsilon,\ \text{and } p_\ell > \underline{p},\ \text{and } p_\ell \geq \frac{\varepsilon + p_*}{1 + \sqrt{1/2}}\right\}, \qquad (3)$$

*and*

$$N(p, \varepsilon) = \left\{ \ell : p_\ell < p_* - \varepsilon, \text{ and } p_\ell > \underline{p}, \text{ and } p_\ell \geq \frac{\varepsilon + p_*}{1 + \sqrt{1/2}} \right\}. \quad (4)$$

**Remarks:**

(a) The lower bound involves two sets of coins whose biases are not too far from the best bias $p_*$. The first set $M(p, \varepsilon)$ contains coins that are within $\varepsilon$ from the best and would therefore be legitimate selections. In the presence of multiple such coins, a certain amount of exploration is needed to obtain the required confidence that none of these coins is significantly better than the others. The second set $N(p, \varepsilon)$ contains coins whose bias is more than $\varepsilon$ away from $p_*$; they come into the lower bound because some exploration is needed in order to avoid selecting one of these coins.

(b) The expression $(\varepsilon + p_*)/(1 + \sqrt{1/2})$ in Eqs. (3) and (4) can be replaced by $(\varepsilon + p_*)/(2 - \alpha)$ for any positive constant $\alpha$, by changing some of the constants in the proof.

(c) This result actually provides a family of lower bounds, one for every possible choice of $\underline{p}$. A tighter bound can be obtained by optimizing the choice of $\underline{p}$, while also taking into account the dependence of the constant $c_1$ on $\underline{p}$. This is not hard (the dependence of $c_1$ on $\underline{p}$ can be extracted from the details of the proof), but is not pursued any further.

*Proof.* Let us fix some $\underline{p} \in (0, 1/2)$, $\varepsilon \in (0, 1/2)$, $\delta \in (0, e^{-4}/4)$, an $(\varepsilon, \delta)$-correct policy, and some $p \in [0, 1/2]^n$. Without loss of generality, we assume that $p_* = p_1$. Let us denote the true (unknown) bias of each coin by $q_i$. We consider the following hypotheses:

$$H_0 : q_i = p_i, \text{ for } i = 1, \dots, n,$$

and for $\ell = 1, \dots, n$,

$$H_\ell : q_\ell = p_1 + \varepsilon, \qquad q_i = p_i, \text{ for } i \neq \ell.$$

If hypothesis $H_0$ is true, when the policy terminates, it must select some coin $i$ in the set $M(p, \varepsilon)$, in order to have an $\varepsilon$-optimal coin. If hypothesis $H_\ell$ is true, it must select coin $\ell$.

We will bound from below the expected number of times the coins in the sets $N(p, \varepsilon)$ and $M(p, \varepsilon)$ must be tried, when hypothesis $H_0$ is true. As in Section 3, we use $\mathbf{E}_\ell$ and $\mathbf{P}_\ell$ to denote the expectation and probability, respectively, under the policy being considered and under hypothesis $H_\ell$.

Let

$$t_\ell^* = \begin{cases} \dfrac{1}{c\varepsilon^2} \log \dfrac{1}{4\delta}, & \text{if } \ell \in M(p, \varepsilon), \\[2mm] \dfrac{1}{c(p_1 - p_\ell)^2} \log \dfrac{1}{4\delta}, & \text{if } \ell \in N(p, \varepsilon), \end{cases}$$

where $c$ is a constant that only depends on $\underline{p}$, and whose value will be chosen later. Recall that $T_i$ stands for the total number of times that coin $i$ is tried. We define the event

$$A_\ell = \{T_\ell \leq 4t_\ell^*\}.$$

As in the proof of Theorem 2, if $\mathbf{E}_0[T_\ell] < t_\ell^*$, then $\mathbf{P}_0(A_\ell) > 3/4$.

We define $K_t^\ell = X_1^\ell + \cdots + X_t^\ell$, which is the number of unit rewards ("heads") if the $\ell$-th coin is tried $t$ times (not necessarily consecutively.) We let $C_\ell$ be the event defined by

$$C_\ell = \left\{ \max_{1 \leq t \leq 4t_\ell^*} \left| K_t^\ell - p_\ell t \right| < \sqrt{t_\ell^* \log\left(1/4\delta\right)} \right\}.$$

We have, similar to Lemma 1, $\mathbf{P}_0(C_\ell) > 3/4$. In that lemma, we had $p_\ell = 1/2$, but the proof is also valid for general $p_\ell$.

Let $B_\ell$ be the event $\{I = \ell\}$, i.e., that the policy eventually selects coin $\ell$, and let $B_\ell^c$ be its complement. Since the policy is $(\varepsilon, \delta)$-correct with $\delta < 1/4$, we must have

$$\mathbf{P}_0(B_\ell^c) > 3/4, \qquad \forall\, \ell \in N(p, \varepsilon).$$

We also have $\sum_{\ell \in M(p,\varepsilon)} \mathbf{P}_0(B_\ell) \leq 1$, so that the inequality $\mathbf{P}_0(B_\ell) > 1/4$ can hold for at most three elements of $M(p, \varepsilon)$. Equivalently, the inequality $\mathbf{P}_0(B_\ell^c) < 3/4$ can hold for at most three elements of $M(p, \varepsilon)$. Let

$$M_0(p, \varepsilon) = \left\{ \ell \in M(p, \varepsilon) \text{ and } \mathbf{P}_0(B_\ell^c) \geq \frac{3}{4} \right\}.$$

It follows that $|M_0(p, \varepsilon)| \geq \left( |M(p, \varepsilon)| - 3 \right)^+$.

The following lemma is an analog of Lemma 3.

**Lemma 4.** *Suppose that $\mathbf{E}_0[T_\ell] < t_\ell^*$ and that the constant $c$ in the definition of $t^*$ is chosen large enough (possibly depending on $p$). Then $\mathbf{P}_\ell(B_\ell^c) > \delta$, for every $\ell \in M_0(p, \varepsilon) \cup N(p, \varepsilon)$.*

*Proof.* Fix some $\ell \in M_0(p, \varepsilon) \cup N(p, \varepsilon)$. We define the event $S_\ell$ by

$$S_\ell = A_\ell \cap B_\ell^c \cap C_\ell.$$

Since $\mathbf{P}_0(A_\ell)$, $\mathbf{P}_0(B_\ell^c)$, $\mathbf{P}_0(C_\ell)$ are all larger than $3/4$, we have $\mathbf{P}_0(S_\ell) > \frac{1}{4}$ for all $\ell \in M_0(p, \varepsilon) \cup N(p, \varepsilon)$.

As in the proof of Lemma 3, we define the likelihood function $L_\ell$ by letting $L_\ell(w) = \mathbf{P}_\ell(W = w)$, for every possible history $w$, and use again $L_\ell(W)$ to define the corresponding random variable. Let $K$ be a shorthand notation for $K_{T_\ell}^\ell$, the total number of unit rewards ("heads") obtained from coin $\ell$. We have

$$\frac{L_\ell(W)}{L_0(W)} = \frac{(p_1 + \varepsilon)^K (1 - p_1 - \varepsilon)^{T_\ell - K}}{p_\ell^K (1 - p_\ell)^{T_\ell - K}} = \left( \frac{p_1}{p_\ell} + \frac{\varepsilon}{p_\ell} \right)^K \left( \frac{1 - p_1}{1 - p_\ell} - \frac{\varepsilon}{1 - p_\ell} \right)^{T_\ell - K}$$

$$= \left( 1 + \frac{\varepsilon + \Delta_\ell}{p_\ell} \right)^K \left( 1 - \frac{\varepsilon + \Delta_\ell}{1 - p_\ell} \right)^{T_\ell - K},$$

where $\Delta_\ell = p_1 - p_\ell$. It follows that

$$
\frac{L_\ell(W)}{L_0(W)}
$$

$$
= \left(1 + \frac{\varepsilon + \Delta_\ell}{p_\ell}\right)^K \left(1 - \frac{\varepsilon + \Delta_\ell}{p_\ell}\right)^K \left(1 - \frac{\varepsilon + \Delta_\ell}{p_\ell}\right)^{-K} \left(1 - \frac{\varepsilon + \Delta_\ell}{1 - p_\ell}\right)^{T_\ell - K}
$$

$$
= \left(1 - \left(\frac{\varepsilon + \Delta_\ell}{p_\ell}\right)^2\right)^K \left(1 - \frac{\varepsilon + \Delta_\ell}{p_\ell}\right)^{-K} \left(1 - \frac{\varepsilon + \Delta_\ell}{1 - p_\ell}\right)^{T_\ell - K}. \tag{5}
$$

Note that the fact that $(p_1 + \varepsilon)/2 < p_\ell$ (cf. Eqs. (3) and (4)) implies that $0 \le (\varepsilon + \Delta_\ell)/p_\ell \le 1$.

We will now proceed to lower bound the right-hand side of Eq. (5) for histories under which event $S_\ell$ occurs.

If event $S_\ell$ has occurred, then $A_\ell$ has occurred, and we have $K \le T_\ell \le 4t^*$, so that for every $\ell \in N(\varepsilon, p)$, we have

$$
\left(1 - \left(\frac{\varepsilon + \Delta_\ell}{p_\ell}\right)^2\right)^K \ge \left(1 - \left(\frac{\varepsilon + \Delta_\ell}{p_\ell}\right)^2\right)^{4t_\ell^*} = \left(1 - \left(\frac{\varepsilon + \Delta_\ell}{p_\ell}\right)^2\right)^{\frac{4}{c\Delta_\ell^2}\log(1/4\delta)}
$$

$$
\overset{a}{\ge} \exp\left\{-d\frac{4}{c}\left(\frac{(\varepsilon/\Delta_\ell) + 1}{p_\ell}\right)^2 \log(1/4\delta)\right\}
$$

$$
\overset{b}{\ge} \exp\left\{-d\frac{16}{cp_\ell^2}\log(1/4\delta)\right\} = (4\delta)^{16d/p_\ell^2 c}.
$$

In step (a), we have used Lemma 2 and the fact $(\varepsilon + p_1)/(1 + (1/\sqrt{2})) < p_\ell$; in step (b), we used the fact $\varepsilon/\Delta_\ell \le 1$. (Both facts hold because $\ell \in N(\varepsilon, p)$.)

Similarly, for $\ell \in M(\varepsilon, p)$, we have

$$
\left(1 - \left(\frac{\varepsilon + \Delta_\ell}{p_\ell}\right)^2\right)^K \ge \left(1 - \left(\frac{\varepsilon + \Delta_\ell}{p_\ell}\right)^2\right)^{4t_\ell^*} = \left(1 - \left(\frac{\varepsilon + \Delta_\ell}{p_\ell}\right)^2\right)^{\frac{4}{c\varepsilon^2}\log(1/4\delta)}
$$

$$
\overset{a}{\ge} \exp\left\{-d\left(\frac{1 + (\Delta_\ell/\varepsilon)}{p_\ell}\right)^2 \frac{4}{c}\log(1/4\delta)\right\}
$$

$$
\overset{b}{\ge} \exp\left\{-d\frac{16}{cp_\ell^2}\log(1/4\delta)\right\} = (4\delta)^{16d/p_\ell^2 c}.
$$

In step (a), we have used Lemma 2 and the fact $(\varepsilon + p_1)/(1 + (1/\sqrt{2})) < p_\ell$; in step (b), we used the fact $\Delta_\ell/\varepsilon \le 1$. (Both facts hold because $\ell \in M(\varepsilon, p)$.)

We now bound the product of the second and third terms in Eq. (5). Note that if $p_\ell \le 1/2$, then $1/p_\ell > 1/(1 - p_\ell)$. It follows that

$$
\left(1 - \frac{\varepsilon + \Delta_\ell}{p_\ell}\right)^{-K} \ge \left(1 - \frac{\varepsilon + \Delta_\ell}{1 - p_\ell}\right)^{-K}. \tag{6}
$$

We start with the case where $\ell \in N(p, \varepsilon)$. Using Eq. (6) we obtain

$$\left(1 - \frac{\Delta_\ell + \varepsilon}{p_\ell}\right)^{-K} \left(1 - \frac{\varepsilon + \Delta_\ell}{1 - p_\ell}\right)^{T_\ell - K} \geq \left(1 - \frac{\varepsilon + \Delta_\ell}{1 - p_\ell}\right)^{T_\ell - 2K}$$

$$\overset{a}{\geq} \left(1 - \frac{\varepsilon + \Delta_\ell}{1 - p_\ell}\right)^{T_\ell - 4p_\ell K}$$

$$\overset{b}{\geq} \left(1 - \frac{\varepsilon + \Delta_\ell}{1 - p_\ell}\right)^{2\sqrt{t_\ell^* \log(1/4\delta)}}$$

$$\overset{c}{\geq} \exp\left\{\frac{-2d(\varepsilon + \Delta_\ell)}{\sqrt{c}\Delta_\ell(1 - p_\ell)}\sqrt{\log(1/4\delta)}\right\} \tag{7}$$

$$\overset{d}{\geq} \exp\left\{\frac{-4d}{(1 - p_\ell)\sqrt{c}}\sqrt{\log(1/4\delta)}\right\} \tag{8}$$

$$\overset{e}{\geq} \exp\left\{-4d\frac{1}{1 - p_\ell}\frac{1}{\sqrt{c}}\log(1/4\delta)\right\}$$

$$\overset{f}{\geq} \exp\left\{-8d\frac{1}{\sqrt{c}}\log(1/4\delta)\right\} = (4\delta)^{8d/\sqrt{c}}.$$

Here, (a) holds because $p_\ell \leq 1/2$; (b) holds because we are assuming that the event $A_\ell \cap C_\ell$ has occurred; (c) follows by Lemma 2 and by noticing that if $(\varepsilon + p_1)/(1 + \sqrt{1/2}) \leq p_\ell$ and $p_\ell \leq 1/2$, then $(\varepsilon + \Delta_\ell)/(1 - p_\ell) \leq 1/\sqrt{2}$; (d) follows from the fact that $\Delta_\ell > \varepsilon$; (e) follows because the assumption $\delta < e^{-4}/4$ implies that $\sqrt{\log(1/4\delta)} < \log(1/4\delta)$; and (f) holds because $0 \leq p_\ell \leq 1/2$, which implies that $1/(1 - p_\ell) \leq 2$.

Consider now the case where $\ell \in M(p, \varepsilon)$. Developing a bound for the product of the second and third terms in Eq. (5) is similar to the case where $\ell \in N(p, \varepsilon)$. The only difference is that in step (b), $t_\ell^*$ should be replaced with $1/c\varepsilon^2 \log(1/4\delta)$ (we assume here too that $(\varepsilon + p_1)/(1 + \sqrt{1/2}) \leq p_\ell$). Then, the right-hand side in Eq. (7) becomes $\exp\left\{-d\frac{\varepsilon + \Delta_\ell}{1 - p_\ell} \cdot \frac{2}{\sqrt{c\varepsilon}}\sqrt{\log(1/4\delta)}\right\}$. For $\ell \in M(p, \varepsilon)$, we have $\Delta_\ell \leq \varepsilon$, which implies that $(\varepsilon + \Delta_\ell)/\varepsilon \leq 2$, which then leads to the same expression as in Eq. (8). The rest of the derivation is identical.

Summarizing the above, we have shown that if $\ell \in M(p, \varepsilon) \cup N(p, \varepsilon)$, and event $S_\ell$ has occurred, then $\frac{L_\ell(W)}{L_0(W)} \geq (4\delta)^{\frac{8d}{\sqrt{c}}}(4\delta)^{\frac{16d}{p_\ell^2 c}}$. For $\ell \in M(p, \varepsilon) \cup N(p, \varepsilon)$, we have $p < p_\ell$. We can choose $c$ large enough so that $L_\ell(W)/L_0(W) \geq 4\delta$; the value of $c$ depends only on the constant $p$.

Similar to the proof of Theorem 2, we have $\frac{L_\ell(W)}{L_0(W)}1_{S_\ell} \geq 4\delta 1_{S_\ell}$, where $1_{S_\ell}$ is the indicator function of the event $S_\ell$. It follows that

$$\mathbf{P}_\ell(B_\ell^c) \geq \mathbf{P}_\ell(S_\ell) = \mathbf{E}_\ell[1_{S_\ell}] = \mathbf{E}_0\left[\frac{L_\ell(W)}{L_0(W)}1_{S_\ell}\right] \geq \mathbf{E}_0[4\delta 1_{S_\ell}] = 4\delta \mathbf{P}_0(S_\ell) > \delta,$$

where the last inequality relies on the already established fact $\mathbf{P}_\ell(S_\ell) > 1/4$.

$\square$

Since the policy is $(\varepsilon,\delta)$-correct, we must have $\mathbf{P}_\ell(B_\ell^c) \leq \delta$, for every $\ell$. Lemma 4 then implies that $\mathbf{E}_0[T_\ell] \geq t_\ell^*$ for every $\ell \in M_0(p,\varepsilon) \cup N(p,\varepsilon)$. We sum over all $\ell \in M_0(p,\varepsilon) \cup N(p,\varepsilon)$, use the definition of $t_\ell^*$, together with the fact $|M_0(p,\varepsilon)| \geq (|M(p,\varepsilon)| - 3)^+$, to conclude the proof of the theorem. $\qquad\square$

**Remark:** A close examination of the proof reveals that the dependence of $c_1$ on $p$ is captured by a requirement of the form $c_1 \leq \min\{c_2, c_3 p^2\}$, for some absolute constants $c_2$ and $c_3$. This suggests that there is a tradeoff in the choice of $p$. By choosing a large $p$, the constant $c_1$ is made large, but the sets $M$ and $N$ become smaller, and vice versa.

The preceding result may give the impression that the sample complexity is high only when the $p_i$ are bounded by $1/2$. The next result shows that similar lower bounds hold (with a different constant) whenever the $p_i$ can be assumed to be bounded away from 1. However, the lower bound becomes weaker (i.e., the constant $c_1$ is smaller) when the upper bound on the $p_i$ approaches 1. This is because no $O(1/\varepsilon^2)$ lower bound on $\mathbf{E}_p[T]$ is possible when $\max_i p_i = 1$. In fact, there exists an $(\varepsilon,\delta)$-correct algorithm such that $\mathbf{E}_p[T]$ is proportional to $1/\varepsilon$ for every $p$ with $\max_i p_i = 1$.

**Theorem 5.** *Fix an integer $s \geq 2$, and some $p \in (0,1/2)$. There exists a constant $c_1$ that depends only on $p$ such that for every $\varepsilon \in (0,2^{-(s+1)})$, every $\delta \in (0,e^{-4}/4)$, every $p \in [0,1-2^{-s}]^n$, and every $(\varepsilon,\delta)$-correct policy, we have*

$$\mathbf{E}_p[T] \geq \frac{c_1}{s\eta^2}\left\{\frac{(|M(\tilde{p},\varepsilon\eta)| - 3)^+}{\varepsilon^2} + \sum_{\ell \in N(\tilde{p},\eta\varepsilon)}\frac{1}{(p_* - p_\ell)^2}\right\}\log\frac{1}{4\delta},$$

*where $p_* = \max_i p_i$, $\eta = 2^s/s$, $\tilde{p}$ is the vector with components $\tilde{p}_i = 1-(1-p_i)^{1/s}$, and $M$ and $N$ are as defined in Theorem 4.*

*Proof.* Let us fix $s \geq 2$, $p \in (0,1/2)$, $\varepsilon \in (0,2^{-(s+1)})$, and $\delta \in (0,e^{-4}/4)$. Suppose that we have an $(\varepsilon,\delta)$-correct policy $\pi$ whose expected time to termination is $\mathbf{E}_p[T]$, whenever the vector of coin biases happens to be $p$. We will use the policy $\pi$ to construct a new policy $\tilde{\pi}$ such that

$$\mathbf{P}\left(p_I > \max_i p_i - \eta\varepsilon\right) \geq 1 - \delta, \qquad \forall\, p \in [0,(1/2) + \eta\varepsilon]^n;$$

(we will then say that $\tilde{\pi}$ is $(\eta\varepsilon,\delta)$-correct on $[0,(1/2) + \eta\varepsilon]^n$). Finally, we will use the lower bounds from Theorem 4, applied to $\tilde{\pi}$, to obtain a lower bound on the sample complexity of $\pi$.

The new policy $\tilde{\pi}$ is described as follows. Run the original policy $\pi$. Whenever $\pi$ chooses to try a certain coin $i$ once, policy $\tilde{\pi}$ tries coin $i$ for $s$ consecutive times. Policy $\tilde{\pi}$ then "feeds" $\pi$ with 0 if all $s$ trials resulted in 0, and feeds $\pi$ with 1 otherwise. If $\tilde{p}$ is the true vector of coin biases faced by policy $\tilde{\pi}$, and if policy $\pi$ chooses to sample coin $i$, then policy $\pi$ "sees" an outcome which equals 1 with probability $p_i = 1 - (1 - \tilde{p}_i)^s$. Let us define two mappings $f, g : [0, 1] \mapsto [0, 1]$, which are inverses of each other by

$$f(p_i) = 1 - (1 - p_i)^{1/s}, \qquad g(\tilde{p}_i) = 1 - (1 - \tilde{p}_i)^s,$$

and with a slight abuse of notation, let $f(p) = (f(p_1), \ldots, f(p_n))$, and similarly for $g(\tilde{p})$. With our construction, when policy $\tilde{\pi}$ is faced with a bias vector, it evolves in an identical manner as the policy $\pi$ faced with a bias vector $p = g(\tilde{p})$. But under policy $\tilde{\pi}$, there are $s$ trials associated with every trial under policy $\pi$, which implies that $\tilde{T} = sT$ ($\tilde{T}$ is the number of trials under policy $\tilde{\pi}$) and therefore

$$\mathbf{E}_{\tilde{p}}[\tilde{T}] = s\mathbf{E}_{g(\tilde{p})}[T], \qquad \mathbf{E}_{f(p)}[\tilde{T}] = s\mathbf{E}_p[T]. \tag{9}$$

We will now determine the "correctness" guarantees of policy $\tilde{\pi}$. We first need some algebraic preliminaries.

Let us fix some $\tilde{p} \in [0, (1/2) + \eta\varepsilon]^n$ and a corresponding vector $p$, related by $\tilde{p} = f(p)$ and $p = g(\tilde{p})$. Let also $p_* = \max_i p_i$ and $\tilde{p}_* = \max_i \tilde{p}_i$. Using the definition $\eta = 2^s/s$ and the assumption $\varepsilon < 2^{-(s+1)}$, we have $\tilde{p}_* \leq (1/2) + (1/2s)$, from which it follows that

$$p_* \leq 1 - \left(\frac{1}{2} - \frac{1}{2s}\right)^s = 1 - \frac{1}{2^s}\left(1 - \frac{1}{s}\right) \leq 1 - \frac{1}{2^s} \cdot \frac{1}{2} = 1 - 2^{-(s+1)}.$$

The derivative $f'$ of $f$ is monotonically increasing on $[0, 1)$. Therefore,

$$f'(p_*) \leq f'(1 - 2^{-(s+1)}) = \frac{1}{s}\left(2^{-(s+1)}\right)^{(1/s)-1} = \frac{1}{s}2^{-(s+1)(1-s)/s}$$
$$= \frac{1}{s}2^{s-(1/s)} \leq \frac{1}{s}2^s = \eta.$$

Thus, the monotonically decreasing derivative $g'$ of the inverse mapping is at least $1/\eta$ in the set $[0, (1/2) + \eta\varepsilon]$. Hence, $g'(\tilde{p}_*) \geq \frac{1}{\eta}$, which implies that $g(\tilde{p}_* - \eta\varepsilon) \leq g(\tilde{p}_*) - g'(\tilde{p}_*)\varepsilon\eta \leq g(\tilde{p}_*) - \varepsilon$.

Let $I$ be the coin index finally selected by policy $\tilde{\pi}$ when faced with $\tilde{p}$, which is the same as the index chosen by $\pi$ when faced with $p$. We have

$$\mathbf{P}(\tilde{p}_I \leq \tilde{p}_* - \eta\varepsilon) = \mathbf{P}\big(g(\tilde{p}_I) \leq g(\tilde{p}_* - \eta\varepsilon)\big) \leq \mathbf{P}\big(g(\tilde{p}_I) \leq g(\tilde{p}_*) - \varepsilon\big)$$
$$= \mathbf{P}(p_I \leq p_* - \varepsilon) \leq 1 - \delta,$$

where the last inequality follows because policy $\pi$ was assumed to be $(\varepsilon, \delta)$-correct. We have therefore established that $\tilde{\pi}$ is $(\eta\varepsilon, \delta)$-correct on $[0, (1/2) + \eta\varepsilon]^n$. We now apply Theorem 4, with $\eta\varepsilon$ instead of $\varepsilon$. Even though that theorem is stated for a policy which is $(\varepsilon, \delta)$-correct for all possible $p$, the proof shows that it also applies to $(\varepsilon, \delta)$-correct policies on $[0, (1/2) + \varepsilon]^n$. This gives a lower bound on $\mathbf{E}_{\tilde{p}}[\tilde{T}]$ which, using Eq. (9), translates to the claimed lower bound on $\mathbf{E}_p[T]$. This lower bound applies whenever $p = g(\tilde{p})$, for some $\tilde{p} \in [0, 1/2]^n$, and therefore whenever $p \in [0, 1 - 2^{-s}]^n$.                             $\square$

# 6    Concluding Remarks

We have addressed the problem of deriving lower bounds on the number of steps required to identify a near optimal arm, with high probability, in a multi-armed bandit setting. For the problem formulations studied in Section 3 and 4, the lower bounds match the existing upper bounds of $\Theta\big((n/\varepsilon^2)\log(1/\delta)\big)$.

Our results have been derived under the assumption of Bernoulli rewards. Clearly, the lower bounds also apply to more general problem formulations, as long as they include the special case of Bernoulli rewards. It would be of some interest to derive similar lower bounds for other special cases of reward distributions. It is reasonable to expect that essentially the same results will carry over, as long as the divergence between the reward distribution associated with different arms is finite (as in [9]).

**Acknowledgments.** This research was partially supported by a Fulbright post-doctoral fellowship, by the MIT-Merrill Lynch partnership, and by the ARO under grant DAAD10-00-1-0466.

# References

1. M. Anthony and P.L. Bartlett. *Neural Network Learning; Theoretical Foundations.* Cambridge University Press, 1999.
2. P. Auer, N. Cesa-Bianchi, Y. Freund, and R. E. Schapire. Gambling in a rigged casino: The adversarial multi-armed bandit problem. In *Proc. 36th Annual Symposium on Foundations of Computer Science*, pages 322–331. IEEE Computer Society Press, 1995.
3. P. Auer, N. Cesa-Bianchi, Y. Freund, and R. E. Schapire. The non-stochastic multi-armed bandit problem. To appear in SIAM journal of Computation, 2002.
4. D.A. Berry and B. Fristedt. *Bandit Problems.* Chapman and Hall, 1985.
5. E. Even-Dar, S. Mannor, and Y. Mansour. PAC Bounds for Multi-Armed Bandit and Markov Decision Processes In *Fifteenth Annual Conference on Computation Learning Theory*, pages 255–270, 2002.
6. J. Gittins and D. Jones. A dynamic allocation index for the sequential design of experiments. In J. Gani, K. Sarkadi, and I. Vincze, editors, *Progress in Statistics*, pages 241–266. North-Holland, Amsterdam, 1974.
7. C. Jennison, I. M. Johnstone and B.W. Turnbull. Asymptotically optimal procedures for sequential adaptive selection of the best of several normal means. In S. S. Gupta and J. Berger, editors, *Statistical decision theory and related topics III, Vol 2*, pages 55–86. Academic Press, 1982.
8. S. R. Kulkarni and G. Lugosi. Finite-time lower bounds for the two-armed bandit problem *IEEE Trans. Aut. Control*, 45(4):711-714, 2000.
9. T.L. Lai and H. Robbins. Asymptotically efficient adaptive allocation rules. *Advances in Applied Mathematics*, 6:4–22, 1985.
10. H. Robbins. Some aspects of sequential design of experiments. *Bull. Amer. Math. Soc.*, 55:527–535, 1952.
11. S. M. Ross. *Stochastic processes.* Wiley, 1983.
12. D. Siegmund. *Sequential analysis–tests and confidence intervals.* Springer Verlag, 1985.

# Smooth ε-Insensitive Regression by Loss Symmetrization

Ofer Dekel, Shai Shalev-Shwartz, and Yoram Singer

School of Computer Science, Hebrew University, Jerusalem, Israel
{oferd,shais,singer}@cs.huji.ac.il

**Abstract.** We describe a framework for solving regression problems by reduction to classification. Our reduction is based on symmetrization of margin-based loss functions commonly used in boosting algorithms, namely, the logistic loss and the exponential loss. Our construction yields a smooth version of the ε-insensitive hinge loss that is used in support vector regression. A byproduct of this construction is a new simple form of regularization for boosting-based classification and regression algorithms. We present two parametric families of batch learning algorithms for minimizing these losses. The first family employs a log-additive update and is based on recent boosting algorithms while the second family uses a new form of additive update. We also describe and analyze online gradient descent (GD) and exponentiated gradient (EG) algorithms for the ε-insensitive logistic loss. Our regression framework also has implications on classification algorithms, namely, a new additive batch algorithm for the log-loss and exp-loss used in boosting.

## 1 Introduction

The focus of the paper is supervised learning of real-valued regression functions. In the settings we discuss in this paper, we observe a sequence $S = \{(\mathbf{x}_1, y_1), \ldots, (\mathbf{x}_m, y_m)\}$ of instance-target pairs. For concreteness, we assume that the instances are vectors in $\mathbb{R}^n$ and that the targets are real-valued scalars, $y_i \in \mathbb{R}$. We denote the $j$'th component of an instance $\mathbf{x}_i$ by $x_{i,j}$. Our goal is to learn a function $f : \mathbb{R}^n \to \mathbb{R}$ which provides a good approximation of target values from their corresponding instance vectors. Such a function is often referred to as a regression function or a regressor for short. In this paper we focus on learning linear regressors, that is, $f$ is of the form $f(\mathbf{x}) = \boldsymbol{\lambda} \cdot \mathbf{x}$. This setting is also suitable for learning a linear combination of base regressors of the form $f(\mathbf{x}) = \sum_{j=1}^{l} \lambda_j h_j(\mathbf{x}) = \boldsymbol{\lambda} \cdot \mathbf{h}(\mathbf{x})$ where $h_j : X \to \mathbb{R}$, $X$ is an instance domain, and $\mathbf{h}(\mathbf{x}) = (h_1(\mathbf{x}), \ldots, h_l(\mathbf{x}))$. The latter form enables us to employ kernels by setting $h_j(\mathbf{x}) = K(\mathbf{x}_j, \mathbf{x})$. Since the class of regressors we consider is rather restricted and due to the existence of noise, a perfect mapping such that for all $(\mathbf{x}_i, y_i) \in S$, $f(\mathbf{x}_i) = y_i$ might not exist. Hence, we employ a loss function $L : \mathbb{R} \times \mathbb{R} \to \mathbb{R}_+$ which measures the discrepancy between the *predicted* target, $f(\mathbf{x})$, and the *true* (observed) target $y$. As we discuss shortly, the loss functions we consider in this paper depend only on the discrepancy $\delta = f(\mathbf{x}) - y$ hence

B. Schölkopf and M.K. Warmuth (Eds.): COLT/Kernel 2003, LNAI 2777, pp. 433–447, 2003.

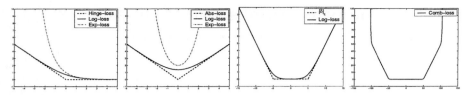

**Fig. 1.** Constructing regression losses (second-left) by symmetrization of margin losses (left). The smooth $\varepsilon$-insensitive log-loss (second-right) and the combined loss (right).

$L$ can be viewed as a function from $\mathbb{R}$ into $\mathbb{R}_+$ and is denoted by $L(\delta)$. Given a loss function $L$, the goal of a regression algorithm is to find a regressor $f$ which attains a small *cumulative* loss on the training set $S$,

$$\text{Loss}(\boldsymbol{\lambda}, S) = \sum_{i=1}^{m} L(f(\mathbf{x}_i) - y_i) = \sum_{i=1}^{m} L(\boldsymbol{\lambda} \cdot \mathbf{x}_i - y_i) .$$

Regression problems have long been the focus of many research papers in statistics and learning theory. See for instance the book by Hastie, Tibshirani, and Friedman [6] and the references therein. Denote the discrepancy $\boldsymbol{\lambda} \cdot \mathbf{x}_i - y_i$ by $\delta_i$. Two common approaches for regression minimize either the sum of the absolute discrepancies over the sample ($\sum_i |\delta_i|$) or the square of the discrepancies ($\sum_i \delta_i^2$). It has been argued that the squared loss is sensitive to outliers, hence robust regression algorithms often employ the absolute loss [7].

Furthermore, it is often the case that the *exact* discrepancy between $\boldsymbol{\lambda} \cdot \mathbf{x}$ and $y$ is unimportant so long as this discrepancy falls below an insensitivity parameter $\varepsilon$. Formally, the $\varepsilon$-insensitive hinge loss, denoted $|\delta|_\varepsilon$, is zero if $|\delta| \leq \varepsilon$ and is $|\delta| - \varepsilon$ for $|\delta| > \varepsilon$ (see also Fig. 1). Whether $\varepsilon = 0$ or not, the $\varepsilon$-insensitive hinge loss is not smooth as its derivative is discontinuous at $\delta = \pm\varepsilon$. While the non-smooth nature of the $\varepsilon$-insensitive hinge loss led to the design and analysis of efficient batch learning algorithms (cf. [14, 13]), it also poses algorithmic difficulties. In this paper we discuss and analyze a smooth approximation of the $\varepsilon$-insensitive hinge loss. Formally, we define the following loss,

$$L_{\log}(\delta; \varepsilon) = \log\left(1 + e^{\delta - \varepsilon}\right) + \log\left(1 + e^{-\delta - \varepsilon}\right) + \kappa . \tag{1}$$

Whenever it is clear from context we simply denote the loss as $L_{\log}(\delta)$. We term this loss the *symmetric $\varepsilon$-insensitive logistic loss* and for brevity, we refer to it simply as the log-loss. The constant $\kappa$ equals $2\log(1 + e^{-\varepsilon})$ and is set so that $L_{\log}(0) = 0$. Since additive constants do not change the form of the optimal regressor we henceforth omit this constant. In Fig. 1 we depict the above loss along with the $\varepsilon$-insensitive hinge loss for $\varepsilon = 5$. Note that the $\varepsilon$-insensitive log-loss provides a smooth upper bound on the $\varepsilon$-insensitive hinge loss, and that with this particular choice of $\varepsilon$ we get that for $|\delta| < 2$ and $|\delta| > 8$ the smooth and non-smooth $\varepsilon$-insensitive losses are graphically indistinguishable.

To motivate our construction, let us make a short detour and discuss a recent view of classification algorithms. In the binary classification setting discussed in [5, 2, 10], we are provided with *instance-label* pairs, $(\mathbf{x}, y)$, where, in contrast to regression, each label takes one of two values, namely $y \in \{-1, +1\}$. A real-valued classifier is a function $f$ into the reals such that $\text{sign}(f(\mathbf{x}))$ is the predicted label and the magnitude, $|f(\mathbf{x})|$, is the confidence of $f$ in its prediction. The product $yf(\mathbf{x})$ is called the (signed) margin of the instance-label pair $(\mathbf{x}, y)$. The goal of a margin-based classifier is to attain large margin values on as many instances as possible. Learning algorithms for margin-based classifiers typically employ a margin-based loss function $L_c(yf(\mathbf{x}))$ and attempt to minimize the cumulative loss over a given sample. One of the margin losses discussed is the logistic loss, that takes the form

$$L_c(yf(\mathbf{x})) = \log\left(1 + e^{-yf(\mathbf{x})}\right) . \tag{2}$$

We use the loss in Eq. (2) as a building block in the construction of the regression loss (Eq. (1)). Denote by $[\mathbf{u}\,;\,v]$ the concatenation of an additional element $v$ to the end of a vector $\mathbf{u}$. We replace every instance-*target* pair $(\mathbf{x}, y)$ from the regression problem with *two* classification instance-*label* pairs,

$$(\mathbf{x}, y) \;\mapsto\; \begin{cases} ([\mathbf{x}\,;\,-y+\varepsilon]\,,\,+1) \\ ([\mathbf{x}\,;\,-y-\varepsilon]\,,\,-1) \end{cases} .$$

In words, we duplicate each regression instance and create two classification instances. We then increase the dimension by one and concatenate $-y + \varepsilon$ to the first newly created instance and set its label to $+1$. Symmetrically, we concatenate $-y - \varepsilon$ to the second duplicate and set its label to $-1$. We define the linear *classifier* to be the vector $[\boldsymbol{\lambda}\,;\,1] \in \mathbb{R}^{n+1}$. It is simple to verify that,

$$L_{\log}(\boldsymbol{\lambda} \cdot \mathbf{x} - y\,;\,\varepsilon) = L_c([\boldsymbol{\lambda}\,;\,1] \cdot [\mathbf{x}\,;\,-y+\varepsilon]) + L_c(-[\boldsymbol{\lambda}\,;\,1] \cdot [\mathbf{x}\,;\,-y-\varepsilon]) .$$

In Fig. 1 we give an illustration of the above construction. We have thus reduced a regression problem of $m$ instances in $\mathbb{R}^n$ and targets in $\mathbb{R}$ to a classification problem with $2m$ instances in $\mathbb{R}^{n+1}$ and binary labels.

The work in [2] gave a unified view of two margin losses: the logistic loss defined by Eq. (2) and an exponential loss. An immediate benefit of our construction is a similar unified account of the two respective regression losses. Formally, we define the *symmetric exponential loss* for regression as follows,

$$L_{\exp}(\delta) \;=\; e^{\delta} + e^{-\delta} .$$

As for the log-loss, we simply refer to this loss as the exp-loss. The exp-loss was first presented and analyzed by Duffy and Helmbold [3] in their pioneering work on leveraging regressors. Their view though is somewhat different as it builds upon the notion of weak-learnability, yielding a different (sequential) algorithm for regression. The exp-loss is by far less forgiving than the log-loss, i.e. small discrepancies are amplified exponentially. While this property might be undesirable in regression problems with numerous outliers, it can also serve as a barrier that prevents the existence of any large discrepancy on the training set.

A nice property of this loss is that it provides a bound on the maximal absolute discrepancy in the sample. To see this, note that the minimizer of $\sum_i L_{\exp}(\delta_i)$ is also the minimizer of $\log(\sum_i L_{\exp}(\delta_i))$ which is a smooth approximation to $\max_i |\delta_i|$. We can also combine the log-loss and the exp-loss with two different insensitivity parameters and benefit both from a discrepancy insensitivity region and from enforcing a smooth barrier on the maximal discrepancy. Formally, let $\varepsilon_1 > 0$ and $\varepsilon_2 > \varepsilon_1$ be two insensitivity parameters. We define the *combined loss*, abbreviated as *comb-loss*, by $L_{\text{comb}}(\delta; \varepsilon_1, \varepsilon_2) = L_{\log}(\delta; \varepsilon_1) + L_{\exp}(\delta; \varepsilon_2)$ , where $L_{\exp}(\delta; \varepsilon_2) = e^{-\varepsilon_2} L_{\exp}(\delta)$. An illustration of the combined loss with $\varepsilon_1 = 50$ and $\varepsilon_2 = 100$ is given in Fig. 1.

The paper is organized as follows. In Sec. 2 we describe a simple use of the symmetric losses defined above as a means of regularizing $\boldsymbol{\lambda}$. In Sec. 3 we describe and analyze a family of log-additive update algorithms for batch learning settings. The algorithms are derived using the reduction outlined above and by adapting proof techniques from [2] to our setting. In Sec. 4 we describe a new family of additive update regression algorithms based on modified gradient descent. For both the log-additive and the additive updates, we provide a boosting-style analysis of the decrease in loss. In Sec. 5 we shift our attention to *online* learning algorithms for the $\varepsilon$-insensitive log-loss. Our algorithms and regularization technique have implications on *classification* algorithms with both the log-loss and the exp-loss. We briefly discuss these implications, illustrate the merits of the two losses and conclude in Sec. 6.

## 2    Regularization

Regularization is a means of controlling the complexity of the regressor being learned. In particular for linear regressors, regularization serves as a soft limit on the magnitude of the elements of $\boldsymbol{\lambda}$ (cf. [11]). The losses we discussed in the previous section can provide a new form of regularization. For the log-loss, the regularization applied to the $j$'th coordinate of $\boldsymbol{\lambda}$ is, $\log\left(1 + e^{\lambda_j}\right) + \log\left(1 + e^{-\lambda_j}\right)$. The minimum of the above equation is obtained at $\lambda_j = 0$. It is straightforward to show that the regularization term above is bounded below by $|\lambda_j|$ and above by $|\lambda_j| + 2$. Therefore, summing over all possible indices $j$, the regularization term on $\boldsymbol{\lambda}$ lies between $\|\boldsymbol{\lambda}\|_1$ and $\|\boldsymbol{\lambda}\|_1 + 2n$. Thus, this form of regularization can be viewed as a smooth approximation to the $\ell_1$ norm. A similar regularization can be imposed using the exp-loss, namely, $e^{\lambda_j} + e^{-\lambda_j}$. For both losses, the $j$'th regularization term equals $L(\lambda_j ; 0)$. An equivalent way to impose this form of regularization is to introduce a set of pseudo examples $S_{\text{reg}} = \{\mathbf{x}_k, 0\}_{k=1}^n$ where $\mathbf{x}_k = \mathbf{1}_k$ (a vector with 1 at its $k$'th position and zeros elsewhere).

Let $\nu > 0$ denote a regularization parameter that governs the relative importance of the regularization term with respect to the empirical loss. The sample loss with regularization becomes, $\text{Loss}(\boldsymbol{\lambda}, \nu, S) = \text{Loss}(\boldsymbol{\lambda}, S) + \nu \text{Loss}(\boldsymbol{\lambda}, S_{\text{reg}})$. The batch algorithms we describe in the sequel easily accommodate a weighted sample. Therefore, by introducing a set of $n$ pseudo-examples weighted by $\nu$, we can incorporate regularization into our batch algorithms without any modifica-

INPUT:   Training set $S = \{(\mathbf{x}_i, y_i) \mid \mathbf{x}_i \in \mathbb{R}^n,\ y_i \in \mathbb{R}\}_{i=1}^m$  ;  Insensitivity $\varepsilon \in \mathbb{R}_+$

Update templates $\mathcal{A} \subseteq \mathbb{R}_+^n$ s.t. $\forall \mathbf{a} \in \mathcal{A}$  $\max_i \left( \sum_{j=1}^n a_j |x_{i,j}| \right) \leq 1$

INITIALIZE: $\boldsymbol{\lambda}_1 = (0, 0, \ldots, 0)$

ITERATE: **For** $t = 1, 2, \ldots$

$$\delta_{t,i} = \boldsymbol{\lambda}_t \cdot \mathbf{x}_i - y_i \qquad q_{t,i}^- = \frac{1}{1 + e^{-\delta_{t,i}+\varepsilon}} \qquad q_{t,i}^+ = \frac{1}{1 + e^{\delta_{t,i}+\varepsilon}} \qquad (1 \leq i \leq m)$$

$$W_{t,j}^- = \sum_{i:x_{i,j}\geq 0} q_{t,i}^-\, x_{i,j} - \sum_{i:x_{i,j}<0} q_{t,i}^+\, x_{i,j} \qquad\qquad (1 \leq j \leq n)$$

$$W_{t,j}^+ = \sum_{i:x_{i,j}\geq 0} q_{t,i}^+\, x_{i,j} - \sum_{i:x_{i,j}<0} q_{t,i}^-\, x_{i,j} \qquad\qquad (1 \leq j \leq n)$$

$$\mathbf{a}_t = \operatorname*{argmax}_{\mathbf{a}\in\mathcal{A}} \sum_{j=1}^n a_j \left( \sqrt{W_{t,j}^-} - \sqrt{W_{t,j}^+} \right)^2$$

$$\Lambda_{t,j} = \frac{a_{t,j}}{2} \log \left( \frac{W_{t,j}^+}{W_{t,j}^-} \right) \qquad\qquad (1 \leq j \leq n)$$

$$\boldsymbol{\lambda}_{t+1} = \boldsymbol{\lambda}_t + \Lambda_t$$

**Fig. 2.** A log-additive update algorithm for minimizing the log-loss.

tion to the core of the algorithms. It is simple to verify that the above regularization forces the optimal solution $\boldsymbol{\lambda}^\star$ to be unique and with finite elements. We use this property in the convergence analysis of the batch algorithms.

## 3   Log-Additive Update for Batch Regression

In the previous section we discussed a general reduction from regression problems to margin-based classification problems. As a first application of this reduction, we devise a family of batch regression learning algorithms based on boosting techniques. We term these algorithms *log-additive update* algorithms as they iteratively add to $\boldsymbol{\lambda}$ a logarithmic function of the gradient of the loss.

Our implicit goal is to obtain the (global) minimizer of the empirical loss function $\sum_{i=1}^m L(\boldsymbol{\lambda} \cdot \mathbf{x}_i - y_i)$ where $L$ is either the log-loss, the exp-loss or the comb-loss. For the sake of clarity, we present algorithms and proofs only for the log-loss. We then complete our presentation with a brief discussion on how everything carries over to settings that employ the exp-loss or the comb-loss.

Following the general paradigm of boosting, we make the assumption that we have access to a set of predefined base regressors. These base regressors are analogous to the weak hypotheses commonly discussed in boosting. The goal of the learning algorithm is to select a subset of base regressors and combine them linearly to obtain a highly accurate strong regressor. We assume that the set of base regressors is of finite cardinality though our algorithms can be generalized to a countably infinite number of base regressors. In the finite case we can simply map each input instance to the vector of images with respect to each of the base-regressors, $\mathbf{x} \mapsto (h_1(\mathbf{x}), \ldots, h_n(\mathbf{x}))$ where $n$ is the number or base-regressors. Using this transformation, each input instance is a vector $\mathbf{x}_i \in \mathbb{R}^n$ and the strong regressor's prediction is $\boldsymbol{\lambda} \cdot \mathbf{x}$.

Boosting was initially described and analyzed as a *sequential* algorithm that iteratively selects a base-hypothesis or a feature and changes its weight. All of the elements of $\boldsymbol{\lambda}$ are initialized to be zero, so after performing $T$ sequential update iterations, at most $T$ elements of $\boldsymbol{\lambda}$ are non-zero. Thus, the sequential update can be used for feature selection as well as loss optimization. An alternative approach is to simultaneously update all of the elements of $\boldsymbol{\lambda}$ on every iteration. This approach is the more common among regression algorithms. Collins et al. [2] described a unified framework of boosting algorithms for *classification*. In that framework, the sequential and parallel update schemes are actually two extremes of a general approach for applying iterative updates to $\boldsymbol{\lambda}$. Following Collins et al. we describe and analyze an algorithm that employs *update templates* to determine specifically which subsets of the coordinates of $\boldsymbol{\lambda}$ may be updated in parallel. This algorithm includes both sequential update and parallel update paradigms as special cases by setting the templates accordingly, and allows us to discuss and prove correctness of both algorithms in a unified manner.

In this unified approach, we are required to pre-specify to the algorithm which subsets of the coordinates of $\boldsymbol{\lambda}$ may be updated simultaneously. Formally, the algorithm is given a set of update templates $\mathcal{A}$, where every template $\mathbf{a} \in \mathcal{A}$ is a vector in $\mathbb{R}_+^n$. On every iteration, the algorithm selects a template $\mathbf{a} \in \mathcal{A}$ and updates only those elements $\lambda_j$ for which $a_j$ is non-zero. We require that every $\mathbf{a} \in \mathcal{A}$ conform with the constraint $\sum_j a_j |x_{i,j}| \leq 1$ for every instance $\mathbf{x}_i$ in the training set. The purpose of this requirement will become apparent in the proof of Thm. 1. The parallel update is obtained by setting $\mathcal{A}$ to contain the single vector $(\rho, \ldots, \rho)$ where $\rho = (\max_i \|\mathbf{x}_i\|_1)^{-1}$. The sequential update is obtained by setting $\mathcal{A}$ to be the set of vectors $\mathbf{a}_1, \ldots, \mathbf{a}_n$ defined by

$$a_{k,j} = \begin{cases} (\max_i |x_{i,j}|)^{-1} & \text{if } j = k \\ 0 & \text{if } j \neq k \end{cases}.$$

The algorithm that we discuss is outlined in Fig. 2 and operates as follows. During the process of building $\boldsymbol{\lambda}$, we may encounter two different types of discrepancies: underestimation and overestimation. If the predicted target $\boldsymbol{\lambda} \cdot \mathbf{x}_i$ is less than the correct target $y_i$, we say that $\boldsymbol{\lambda}$ underestimates $y_i$, if it is greater we say that $\boldsymbol{\lambda}$ overestimates $y_i$. For every instance-target pair in the training set, we use a pair of weights $q_{t,i}^-$ and $q_{t,i}^+$ to represent its discrepancies: $q_{t,i}^-$ represents the degree to which $y_i$ is overestimated by $\boldsymbol{\lambda}_t$ and analogously $q_{t,i}^+$ represents the degree to which $y_i$ is underestimated by $\boldsymbol{\lambda}_t$. We then proceed to calculate two weighted sums over each coordinate of the instances: $W_{t,j}^-$ can be thought of as the degree to which $\lambda_{t,j}$ should be decreased in order to compensate for overestimation discrepancies. Symmetrically, $W_{t,j}^+$ represents the degree to which $\lambda_{t,j}$ should be increased. At this point, the algorithm selects the update template $\mathbf{a}_t \in \mathcal{A}$ with respect to which it will apply the update to $\boldsymbol{\lambda}$. $\mathbf{a}_t$ is selected so as to maximize the decrease in loss, according to a criterion that follows directly from Thm. 1.

Finally, the update applied to each coordinate of $\boldsymbol{\lambda}_t$ is half the log ratio between the respective elements of $W_t^+$ and $W_t^-$, times the scaling factor $a_{t,j}$.

In the following theorem we prove a lower bound on the decrease in loss on every iteration of the algorithm. We later use this bound to show that the algorithm converges to the unique globally optimal regressor $\boldsymbol{\lambda}^\star$.

**Theorem 1.** *Let $\{(\mathbf{x}_i, y_i)\}_{i=1}^m$ be a training set of instance-target pairs where for all $i$ in $1, \ldots, m$, $\mathbf{x}_i \in \mathbb{R}^n$ and $y_i \in \mathbb{R}$. Then using the notation defined in the algorithm outlined in Fig. 2, on every iteration $t$ the decrease in the log-loss satisfies,*

$$\text{Loss}(\boldsymbol{\lambda}_t, S) - \text{Loss}(\boldsymbol{\lambda}_{t+1}, S) \geq \sum_{j=1}^n a_{t,j} \left( \sqrt{W_{t,j}^-} - \sqrt{W_{t,j}^+} \right)^2 .$$

**Proof** Define $\Delta_t(i)$ to be the difference between the loss attained by $\boldsymbol{\lambda}_t$ and that attained by $\boldsymbol{\lambda}_{t+1}$ on an instance-target pair $(\mathbf{x}_i, y_i)$ in the training set, namely $\Delta_t(i) = L_{\log}(\delta_{t,i}) - L_{\log}(\delta_{t+1,i})$. Since $\boldsymbol{\lambda}_{t+1} = \boldsymbol{\lambda}_t + \boldsymbol{\Lambda}_t$ then $\delta_{t+1,i} = \delta_{t,i} + \boldsymbol{\Lambda}_t \cdot \mathbf{x}_i$. Using this equality, and the identity $1/(1 + e^\alpha) = 1 - 1/(1 + e^{-\alpha})$, $\Delta_t(i)$ can be rewritten as follows,

$$\Delta_t(i) = -\log\left(\frac{1 + e^{\delta_{t+1,i} - \varepsilon}}{1 + e^{\delta_{t,i} - \varepsilon}}\right) - \log\left(\frac{1 + e^{-\delta_{t+1,i} - \varepsilon}}{1 + e^{-\delta_{t,i} - \varepsilon}}\right)$$

$$= -\log\left(1 - \frac{1}{1 + e^{-(\delta_{t,i} - \varepsilon)}} + \frac{e^{\boldsymbol{\Lambda}_t \cdot \mathbf{x}_i}}{1 + e^{-(\delta_{t,i} - \varepsilon)}}\right)$$

$$- \log\left(1 - \frac{1}{1 + e^{-(-\delta_{t,i} - \varepsilon)}} + \frac{e^{-\boldsymbol{\Lambda}_t \cdot \mathbf{x}_i}}{1 + e^{-(-\delta_{t,i} - \varepsilon)}}\right) .$$

We can now plug the definitions of $q_{t,i}^+$ and $q_{t,i}^-$ into this expression to get

$$\Delta_t(i) = -\log\left(1 - q_{t,i}^-\left(1 - e^{\boldsymbol{\Lambda}_t \cdot \mathbf{x}_i}\right)\right) - \log\left(1 - q_{t,i}^+\left(1 - e^{-\boldsymbol{\Lambda}_t \cdot \mathbf{x}_i}\right)\right) .$$

Next we apply the inequality $-\log(1 - \alpha) \geq \alpha$ (which holds wherever $\log(1 - \alpha)$ is defined):

$$\Delta_t(i) \geq q_{t,i}^-\left(1 - e^{\boldsymbol{\Lambda}_t \cdot \mathbf{x}_i}\right) + q_{t,i}^+\left(1 - e^{-\boldsymbol{\Lambda}_t \cdot \mathbf{x}_i}\right) . \tag{3}$$

We rewrite the scalar product $\boldsymbol{\Lambda}_t \cdot \mathbf{x}_i$ in a more convenient form,

$$\boldsymbol{\Lambda}_t \cdot \mathbf{x}_i = \sum_{j=1}^n \frac{a_{t,j}}{2} \log\left(W_{t,j}^+ / W_{t,j}^-\right) x_{i,j}$$

$$= \sum_{j=1}^n (a_{t,j} |x_{i,j}|) \, \text{sign}(x_{i,j}) \log\left(\sqrt{W_{t,j}^+ / W_{t,j}^-}\right) . \tag{4}$$

We recall the assumptions made on the vectors in $\mathcal{A}$, namely that $\mathbf{a}_t$ and $\mathbf{x}_i$ comply with $\sum_{j=1}^n a_{t,j} |x_{i,j}| \leq 1$ and that $a_{t,j} |x_{i,j}|$ is non-negative. We now use the fact that $(1 - e^\alpha)$ is a concave function and is equal to zero at $\alpha = 0$. Replacing $\mathbf{\Lambda}_t \cdot \mathbf{x}_i$ in Eq. (3) with the form given by Eq. (4) we get,

$$
\begin{aligned}
\Delta_t(i) &\geq q_{t,i}^- \left(1 - e^{\mathbf{\Lambda}_t \cdot \mathbf{x}_i}\right) + q_{t,i}^+ \left(1 - e^{-\mathbf{\Lambda}_t \cdot \mathbf{x}_i}\right) \\
&\geq \sum_{j=1}^n a_{t,j} q_{t,i}^- |x_{i,j}| \left(1 - e^{\operatorname{sign}(x_{i,j}) \log\left(\sqrt{W_{t,j}^+/W_{t,j}^-}\right)}\right) \\
&\quad + \sum_{j=1}^n a_{t,j} q_{t,i}^+ |x_{i,j}| \left(1 - e^{-\operatorname{sign}(x_{i,j}) \log\left(\sqrt{W_{t,j}^+/W_{t,j}^-}\right)}\right) .
\end{aligned}
$$

We now rewrite,

$$
\begin{aligned}
\Delta_t(i) &\geq \sum_{j:x_{i,j}>0} a_{t,j} q_{t,i}^- |x_{i,j}| \left(1 - \sqrt{\frac{W_{t,j}^+}{W_{t,j}^-}}\right) + \sum_{j:x_{i,j}<0} a_{t,j} q_{t,i}^- |x_{i,j}| \left(1 - \sqrt{\frac{W_{t,j}^-}{W_{t,j}^+}}\right) \\
&\quad + \sum_{j:x_{i,j}>0} a_{t,j} q_{t,i}^+ |x_{i,j}| \left(1 - \sqrt{\frac{W_{t,j}^-}{W_{t,j}^+}}\right) + \sum_{j:x_{i,j}<0} a_{t,j} q_{t,i}^+ |x_{i,j}| \left(1 - \sqrt{\frac{W_{t,j}^+}{W_{t,j}^-}}\right) .
\end{aligned}
$$

Summing $\Delta_t(i)$ over $i$ and using the definition of the $q$'s and $W$'s we finally get that,

$$
\begin{aligned}
\sum_{i=1}^m \Delta_t(i) &\geq \sum_{j=1}^n a_{t,j} \left(W_{t,j}^- \left(1 - \sqrt{W_{t,j}^+/W_{t,j}^-}\right) + W_{t,j}^+ \left(1 - \sqrt{W_{t,j}^-/W_{t,j}^+}\right)\right) \\
&= \sum_{j=1}^n a_{t,j} \left(\sqrt{W_{t,j}^-} - \sqrt{W_{t,j}^+}\right)^2 .
\end{aligned}
$$

This concludes the proof.                                                          □

For the remainder of this section, we assume that the set of update templates $\mathcal{A}$ is not degenerate, in the sense that every coordinate of $\mathbf{\lambda}$ is accessible. We now show that the incorporation of a regularization term (Sec. 2) into the loss function implies that the algorithm converges to the unique global minimizer of the loss. First, it is easily verified that the regularization term guarantees that the loss function is strictly convex and attains its unique minimum at the point denoted $\mathbf{\lambda}^\star$. Second, the regularization term guarantees that all admissible values for $\mathbf{\lambda}_t$ lie within a compact set $C$. To see this, note that the initial loss with regularization is

$$
\operatorname{Loss}(\mathbf{0}, \nu, S) = \operatorname{Loss}(\mathbf{0}, S) + \nu \operatorname{Loss}(\mathbf{0}, S_{\text{reg}}) .
$$

Denote the initial loss above by $\mathcal{L}_0$. Since the loss attained by the algorithm on every iteration is non-increasing, the contribution of the regularization term to the total loss cannot exceed $\mathcal{L}_0/\nu$. Also, the regularization term for both the exp-loss and the log-loss bounds the $\ell_\infty$ norm of $\mathbf{\lambda}_t$ by

$$
\|\mathbf{\lambda}_t\|_\infty \leq \operatorname{Loss}(\mathbf{\lambda}_t, S_{\text{reg}}) \leq \operatorname{Loss}(\mathbf{\lambda}_t, \nu, S)/\nu \leq \mathcal{L}_0/\nu .
$$

Therefore, the compact set $C$ of admissible values for $\boldsymbol{\lambda}_t$ is $\{\boldsymbol{\lambda} : \|\boldsymbol{\lambda}\|_\infty \leq \mathcal{L}_0/\nu\}$. The lower bound on the decrease in loss given in Thm. 1 can be thought of as a function of the current regressor $\boldsymbol{\lambda}_t$ and is equal to zero only when the gradient of the loss function equals zero, that is, at $\boldsymbol{\lambda}^\star$.

Assume by contradiction that the sequence of regressors $\boldsymbol{\lambda}_1, \boldsymbol{\lambda}_2, \ldots$ does *not* converge to $\boldsymbol{\lambda}^\star$. An immediate consequence of this assumption is that there exists $\gamma > 0$ such that an infinite subsequence of regressors $\boldsymbol{\lambda}_{s_1}, \boldsymbol{\lambda}_{s_2}, \ldots$ remains outside of $B(\boldsymbol{\lambda}^\star, \gamma)$, the open ball of radius $\gamma$ centered at $\boldsymbol{\lambda}^\star$. The set $C \setminus B(\boldsymbol{\lambda}^\star, \gamma)$ is also compact. Therefore, the lower bound from Thm. 1 attains a minimum value over $C \setminus B(\boldsymbol{\lambda}^\star, \gamma)$ at $\tilde{\boldsymbol{\lambda}} \neq \boldsymbol{\lambda}^\star$. Denoting this minimum by $\mu$, we conclude that $\mu$ is a positive lower bound on the decrease in loss on each of the iterations $s_1, s_2, \ldots$. If the loss decreases by at least $\mu$ an unbounded number of times then it must eventually become negative. We therefore get a contradiction since the loss is a non-negative function. We thus conclude that the sequence $\boldsymbol{\lambda}_t$ converges to $\boldsymbol{\lambda}^\star$.

So far, we have focused on the log-loss function. The algorithm described in Fig. 2 can easily be adapted to minimize the exp-loss or the comb-loss by simply redefining the overestimation and underestimation weights $q^-$ and $q^+$. For exp-loss regression problems, we define $q_{t,i}^- = e^{\delta_{t,i}}$ and $q_{t,i}^+ = e^{-\delta_{t,i}}$.

Similarly, we can redefine $q^-$ and $q^+$ to minimize the comb-loss. Recall that the comb-loss function is defined by a pair of insensitivity parameters, $\varepsilon_1$ and $\varepsilon_2$. To minimize the comb-loss, we define

$$q_{t,i}^- = \frac{e^{\delta_{t,i}-\varepsilon_1}}{1 + e^{\delta_{t,i}-\varepsilon_1}} + e^{\delta_{t,i}-\varepsilon_2} \qquad q_{t,i}^+ = \frac{e^{-\delta_{t,i}-\varepsilon_1}}{1 + e^{-\delta_{t,i}-\varepsilon_1}} + e^{-\delta_{t,i}-\varepsilon_2} .$$

All of the formal discussion given in this section carries over to the exp-loss and the comb-loss cases with only minor technical adaptations necessary.

## 4   Additive Update for Batch Regression

In this section we describe a family of additive batch learning algorithms that advance on each iteration in a direction which is a linear transformation of the gradient of the loss. We term these algorithm *additive update* algorithms. These algorithms bear a resemblance to the log-additive algorithms described in the previous section, as do their proofs of progress. As in the previous section, we first restrict the discussion to the log-loss and then outline the adaptation to the exp-loss at the end of the section.

We again devise a template-based family of updates. This family includes a parallel update which modifies all the elements of $\boldsymbol{\lambda}$ simultaneously and a sequential update which updates a single element of $\boldsymbol{\lambda}$ on each iteration. We denote the set of update templates by $\mathcal{A}$ and assume that every $\mathbf{a} \in \mathcal{A}$ is a vector in $\mathbb{R}_+^n$. For each $\mathbf{a} \in \mathcal{A}$ we require that $\sum_{i=1}^m \sum_{j=1}^n a_j x_{i,j}^2 \leq 2$.

The pseudo-code of the additive update algorithm is given in Fig. 3. Intuitively, on each iteration $t$, the algorithm computes the negative of the gradient with respect to $\boldsymbol{\lambda}_t$, denoted $(W_{t,1}, \ldots, W_{t,n})$. It then selects the update template $\mathbf{a}_t \in \mathcal{A}$ which, as we shortly show in Thm. 2, guarantees a maximal drop in the loss.

INPUT:  Training set $S = \{(\mathbf{x}_i, y_i) \,|\, \mathbf{x}_i \in \mathbb{R}^n, \ y_i \in \mathbb{R}\}_{i=1}^m$  ;  Insensitivity $\varepsilon \in \mathbb{R}_+$
  Update templates $\mathcal{A} \subseteq \mathbb{R}_+^n$  s.t.  $\forall \mathbf{a} \in \mathcal{A} \ \ \sum_{i=1}^m \sum_{j=1}^n a_j x_{i,j}^2 \leq 2$

INITIALIZE: $\boldsymbol{\lambda}_1 = (0, 0, \ldots, 0)$

ITERATE: **For**  $t = 1, 2, \ldots$

$$\delta_{t,i} = \boldsymbol{\lambda}_t \cdot \mathbf{x}_i - y_i \qquad q_{t,i}^- = \frac{1}{1 + e^{-\delta_{t,i}+\varepsilon}} \qquad q_{t,i}^+ = \frac{1}{1 + e^{\delta_{t,i}+\varepsilon}} \qquad (1 \leq i \leq m)$$

$$W_{t,j} = \sum_{i=1}^n (q_{t,i}^+ - q_{t,i}^-) \, x_{i,j} \qquad\qquad (1 \leq j \leq n)$$

$$\mathbf{a}_t = \underset{\mathbf{a} \in \mathcal{A}}{\text{argmax}} \sum_{j=1}^n a_j W_{t,j}^2$$

$$\Lambda_{t,j} = a_{t,j} W_{t,j} \qquad\qquad (1 \leq j \leq n)$$

$$\boldsymbol{\lambda}_{t+1} = \boldsymbol{\lambda}_t + \boldsymbol{\Lambda}_t$$

**Fig. 3.** An additive update algorithm for minimizing the log-loss.

**Theorem 2.** *Let $\{(\mathbf{x}_i, y_i)\}_{i=1}^m$ be a training set of instance-target pairs where for all $i$ in $1, \ldots, m$, $\mathbf{x}_i \in \mathbb{R}^n$ and $y_i \in \mathbb{R}$. Then using the notation defined in the algorithm outlined in Fig. 3, on every iteration $t$ the decrease in the log-loss, denoted $\Delta_t$, satisfies*

$$\Delta_t = \text{Loss}(\boldsymbol{\lambda}_t, S) - \text{Loss}(\boldsymbol{\lambda}_{t+1}, S) \geq \frac{1}{2} \sum_{j=1}^n a_{t,j} W_{t,j}^2 \ .$$

**Proof**  To prove the theorem we construct a parametric quadratic function $Q : \mathbb{R} \to \mathbb{R}$ which bounds the log-loss along the direction $\boldsymbol{\Lambda}$ from $\boldsymbol{\lambda}$. Concretely, the function $Q$ is defined as

$$Q_{\boldsymbol{\lambda}, \boldsymbol{\Lambda}}(\alpha) = \text{Loss}(\boldsymbol{\lambda}, S) + (\nabla \text{Loss}(\boldsymbol{\lambda}, S) \cdot \boldsymbol{\Lambda})(\alpha - \alpha^2/2) \ . \qquad (5)$$

Next, we show that for all $\alpha$, $Q_{\boldsymbol{\lambda}_t, \boldsymbol{\Lambda}_t}(\alpha) \geq \text{Loss}(\boldsymbol{\lambda}_t + \alpha \boldsymbol{\Lambda}_t, S)$ where $\boldsymbol{\Lambda}_t$ is defined as in Fig. 3. For convenience, we define $\Gamma(\alpha) = Q_{\boldsymbol{\lambda}_t, \boldsymbol{\Lambda}_t}(\alpha) - \text{Loss}(\boldsymbol{\lambda}_t + \alpha \boldsymbol{\Lambda}_t, S)$ and prove that $\Gamma$ is a non-negative function.

By construction, we get that $\Gamma(0) = 0$. Since the derivative of $Q_{\boldsymbol{\lambda}_t, \boldsymbol{\Lambda}_t}$ at zero is equal to $\nabla \text{Loss}(\boldsymbol{\lambda}_t, S) \cdot \boldsymbol{\Lambda}_t$, we get that the derivative of $\Gamma$ at zero is also zero. To prove that $\Gamma$ is non-negative it remains to show that $\Gamma$ is convex and thus $\alpha = 0$ attains its global minimum. To prove convexity it is sufficient to show that the second derivative of $\Gamma$ (denoted $\Gamma''$) is non-negative. Routine calculations yield that,

$$\Gamma''(\alpha) = -\boldsymbol{\Lambda} \cdot \nabla \text{Loss}(\boldsymbol{\lambda}, S) - \boldsymbol{\Lambda}^{\mathrm{T}} H \boldsymbol{\Lambda} \ , \qquad (6)$$

where $H = \sum_{i=1}^m L''_{\log}(\boldsymbol{\lambda} + \alpha \boldsymbol{\Lambda}) \mathbf{x}_i \mathbf{x}_i^{\mathrm{T}}$ and $L''_{\log}$ is the second derivative of the log-loss. It is simple to show that this derivative is in $[0, 1/2]$. Plugging the value of $H$ into Eq. (6) we get that,

$$\Gamma''(\alpha) \geq -\boldsymbol{\Lambda} \cdot \nabla \mathrm{Loss}(\boldsymbol{\lambda}, S) - \frac{1}{2} \sum_{i=1}^{m} (\boldsymbol{\Lambda} \cdot \mathbf{x}_i)^2 \ . \tag{7}$$

Note that on the $t$'th iteration, the $j$'th element of $\boldsymbol{\Lambda}_t$ equals $a_{t,j} W_{t,j}$ where $W_{t,j} = -\nabla_j \mathrm{Loss}(\boldsymbol{\lambda}_t, S)$. Therefore, we rewrite Eq. (7) as,

$$
\begin{aligned}
\Gamma''(\alpha) \ &\geq \ \sum_{j=1}^{n} a_{t,j} W_{t,j}^2 - \frac{1}{2} \sum_{i=1}^{m} \left( \sum_{j=1}^{n} a_{t,j} W_{t,j} x_{i,j} \right)^2 \\
&= \ \sum_{j=1}^{n} a_{t,j} W_{t,j}^2 - \frac{1}{2} \sum_{i=1}^{m} \left( \sum_{j=1}^{n} \sqrt{a_{t,j}} \, W_{t,j} \sqrt{a_{t,j}} \, x_{i,j} \right)^2 \ . 
\end{aligned} \tag{8}
$$

Using Cauchy-Schwartz inequality ($\mathbf{u} \cdot \mathbf{v} \leq \|\mathbf{u}\| \|\mathbf{v}\|$) we further bound $\Gamma''$ as,

$$
\begin{aligned}
\Gamma''(\alpha) \ &\geq \ \sum_{j=1}^{n} a_{t,j} W_{t,j}^2 - \frac{1}{2} \sum_{i=1}^{m} \left( \sum_{j=1}^{n} a_{t,j} W_{t,j}^2 \right) \left( \sum_{k=1}^{n} a_{t,k} x_{i,k}^2 \right) \\
&= \ \sum_{j=1}^{n} a_{t,j} W_{t,j}^2 \left( 1 - \frac{1}{2} \sum_{i=1}^{m} \sum_{k=1}^{n} a_{t,k} x_{i,k}^2 \right) \ . 
\end{aligned} \tag{9}
$$

Finally, we use the constraint $\sum_i \sum_{k=1}^{n} a_{t,k} x_{i,k}^2 \leq 2$ which immediately implies that $\Gamma''(\alpha) \geq 0$.

Summing up, we have shown that $\mathrm{Loss}(\boldsymbol{\lambda}_t + \alpha \boldsymbol{\Lambda}_t, S)$ is upper bounded by $Q_{\boldsymbol{\lambda}_t, \boldsymbol{\Lambda}_t}(\alpha)$. Therefore, $\mathrm{Loss}(\boldsymbol{\lambda}_{t+1}, S) = \mathrm{Loss}(\boldsymbol{\lambda}_t + \boldsymbol{\Lambda}_t, S) \leq Q_{\boldsymbol{\lambda}_t, \boldsymbol{\Lambda}_t}(1)$, hence,

$$\Delta_t \ \geq \ \mathrm{Loss}(\boldsymbol{\lambda}_t, S) \ - \ Q_{\boldsymbol{\lambda}_t, \boldsymbol{\Lambda}_t}(1) \ = \ \frac{1}{2} \sum_{j=1}^{n} a_{t,j} W_{t,j}^2 \ .$$

This concludes the proof.                                                           $\square$

The proof of convergence for the additive update algorithm follows identical lines as the proof of convergence for the log-additive update algorithm. If the loss function includes a regularization term then the lower bound discussed in Thm. 2 attains a value of zero only at $\boldsymbol{\lambda}^\star$, the unique global optimum of $\mathrm{Loss}(\boldsymbol{\lambda}, \nu, S)$. This fact implies convergence of $\boldsymbol{\lambda}$ to $\boldsymbol{\lambda}^\star$.

To conclude this section, we briefly outline the adaptation of the additive update algorithm to the exp-loss. Since the gradient of the exp-loss is itself exponential, we cannot hope to minimize the exp-loss by straightforward gradient descent. However, we can apply a gradient descent approach to the *logarithm* of the exp-loss on the entire sample, as both the empirical exp-loss and its logarithm share the same global optimum. For this modified loss, we can also apply the proof technique of Thm. 2.

## 5   Online Regression Algorithms

In this section we describe online regression algorithms for the log-loss. We follow the notation and techniques used in [9, 8, 1]. In online learning settings, we

| Online EG | Online GD |
|---|---|
| INPUT: upper bound $X$<br>$\quad$ insensitivity parameter $\varepsilon$<br>INITIALIZE: $\boldsymbol{\lambda}_1 = (\frac{1}{n}, \ldots, \frac{1}{n})$ | INPUT: upper bound $R$<br>$\quad$ insensitivity parameter $\varepsilon$<br>INITIALIZE: $\boldsymbol{\lambda}_1 = (0, 0, \ldots, 0)$ |
| **For** $t = 1, 2, \ldots$<br>$\quad$ Receive an example $\mathbf{x}_t$<br>$\quad$ Predict $\boldsymbol{\lambda}_t \cdot \mathbf{x}_t$<br>$\quad$ Receive target $y_t$ and update:<br>$\quad\quad \delta_t = \boldsymbol{\lambda}_t \cdot \mathbf{x}_t - y_t$<br>$\quad\quad L'_{\log}(\delta_t) = \frac{1}{1+e^{-\delta_t+\varepsilon}} - \frac{1}{1+e^{\delta_t+\varepsilon}}$<br>$\quad\quad \beta_t = L'_{\log}(\delta_t)/X^2$<br>$\quad$ For $1 \le j \le n$ :<br>$\quad\quad \lambda_{t+1,j} = \frac{\lambda_{t,j}e^{-\beta_t\,x_{t,j}}}{\sum_{k=1}^{n}\lambda_{t,k}e^{-\beta_t\,x_{t,k}}}$ | **For** $t = 1, 2, \ldots$<br>$\quad$ Receive an example $\mathbf{x}_t$<br>$\quad$ Predict $\boldsymbol{\lambda}_t \cdot \mathbf{x}_t$<br>$\quad$ Receive target $y_t$ and update:<br>$\quad\quad \delta_t = \boldsymbol{\lambda}_t \cdot \mathbf{x}_t - y_t$<br>$\quad\quad L'_{\log}(\delta_t) = \frac{1}{1+e^{-\delta_t+\varepsilon}} - \frac{1}{1+e^{\delta_t+\varepsilon}}$<br>$\quad\quad \beta_t = L'_{\log}(\delta_t)/(2R^2)$<br>$\quad\quad \boldsymbol{\lambda}_{t+1} = \boldsymbol{\lambda}_t - \beta_t \mathbf{x}_t$ |

**Fig. 4.** The EG and GD algorithms for online regression with the log-loss.

observe a sequence of instance-target pairs, in rounds, one by one. On round $t$ we first receive an instance $\mathbf{x}_t$. Based on the current regressor, $\boldsymbol{\lambda}_t$, we extend a prediction $\boldsymbol{\lambda}_t \cdot \mathbf{x}_t$. We then receive the true target $y_t$ and suffer an instantaneous loss which is in our case, $L_{\log}(\boldsymbol{\lambda}_t \cdot \mathbf{x}_t - y_t)$. Our goal is to suffer a small cumulative loss. The learning algorithm employs an *update rule* which modifies its current regressor after each round. We describe and analyze two online regression algorithms that differ in the update rules that they employ. The first is additive in the gradient of the loss and is thus called *Gradient Descent* (GD) while the second is exponential in the gradient of the loss and is analogously called *Exponentiated Gradient* (EG).

**The GD algorithm:** The pseudo-code of the algorithm is given on the right hand side of Fig. 4. Note that the GD algorithm updates its current regressor, $\boldsymbol{\lambda}_t$, by subtracting the gradient of the loss function from it. The GD algorithm assumes an upper bound $R$ on the norm of the instances, that is, $\|\mathbf{x}_t\|_2 \le R$. In the following analysis we give a bound on the cumulative loss for any number of rounds. However, rather than bounding the loss per se we bound the cumulative loss *relative* to the cumulative loss suffered by a *fixed* regressor $\boldsymbol{\mu}$. The bound holds for any linear regressor $\boldsymbol{\mu}$ and any number of rounds, hence we get that the GD algorithm is competitive with the optimal (fixed) linear regressor for any number of rounds. Formally, the following theorem states that the cumulative loss attained by the GD algorithm is at most twice the cumulative loss of any fixed linear regressor plus an additive constant.

**Theorem 3.** *Let $S = \{(\mathbf{x}_1, y_1), \ldots, (\mathbf{x}_T, y_T)\}$ be a sequence of instance-target pairs such that $\forall t : \|x_t\|_2 \le R$ and let $\boldsymbol{\lambda}_1, \ldots, \boldsymbol{\lambda}_T$ be the regressors generated* *by the GD online algorithm (Fig. 4) on the sequence. Then for any fixed linear regressor* $\boldsymbol{\mu} \in \mathbb{R}^n$ *we have*

$$\sum_{t=1}^{T} L_{log}(\boldsymbol{\lambda}_t \cdot \mathbf{x}_t - y_t) \leq 2 \sum_{t=1}^{T} L_{log}(\boldsymbol{\mu} \cdot \mathbf{x}_t - y_t) + 2R^2 \|\boldsymbol{\mu}\|_2^2 \quad . \tag{10}$$

The proof of the theorem is based on the following lemma that underscores an invariant property of the update rule.

**Lemma 1.** *Consider the setting of Thm. 3, then for each round $t$ we have*

$$L_{log}(\boldsymbol{\lambda}_t \cdot \mathbf{x}_t - y_t) - 2L_{log}(\boldsymbol{\mu} \cdot \mathbf{x}_t - y_t) \leq 2R^2 \left( \|\boldsymbol{\lambda}_t - \boldsymbol{\mu}\|_2^2 - \|\boldsymbol{\lambda}_{t+1} - \boldsymbol{\mu}\|_2^2 \right) \quad . \tag{11}$$

The proof of the lemma is omitted due to the lack of space. Intuitively, the lemma states that if the loss of GD on round $t$ is greater than the loss of a fixed regressor $\boldsymbol{\mu}$, then the algorithm updates its regressor so that $\boldsymbol{\lambda}_{t+1}$ gets closer to $\boldsymbol{\mu}$ than $\boldsymbol{\lambda}_t$. In contrast, if the loss of $\boldsymbol{\mu}$ is greater than the loss of GD, the algorithm may move its regressor away from $\boldsymbol{\mu}$. With Lemma 1 handy it is almost immediate to prove Thm. 3.

**Proof of Theorem 3:**     Summing Eq. (11) for $t = 1, ..., T$ we get

$$\sum_{t=1}^{T} L_{log}(\boldsymbol{\lambda}_t \cdot \mathbf{x}_t - y_t) - 2 \sum_{t=1}^{T} L_{log}(\boldsymbol{\mu} \cdot \mathbf{x}_t - y_t) \leq 2R^2 \left( \|\boldsymbol{\lambda}_1 - \boldsymbol{\mu}\|_2^2 - \|\boldsymbol{\lambda}_{T+1} - \boldsymbol{\mu}\|_2^2 \right)$$
$$\leq 2R^2 \|\boldsymbol{\lambda}_1 - \boldsymbol{\mu}\|_2^2$$
$$= 2R^2 \|\boldsymbol{\mu}\|_2^2 \quad ,$$

where in the last equality we use the fact that the initial regressor, $\boldsymbol{\lambda}_1$, is the zero vector. $\qquad\square$

**The EG algorithm:** The algorithm is described on the left hand side of Fig. 4. The algorithm assumes that the regressor is in the probability simplex, $\boldsymbol{\lambda} \in \mathbb{P}^n$ where $\mathbb{P}^n = \{\boldsymbol{\mu} : \boldsymbol{\mu} \in \mathbb{R}^n_+, \sum_{j=1}^n \mu_j = 1\}$. We would like to note in passing that following an analogous construction to the one employed in [9, 8], it is possible to derive a generalized version of EG in which the elements of $\boldsymbol{\lambda}$ can be either negative or positive, so long as the sum of their absolute values is less than 1. The EG algorithm assumes an upper bound, denoted $X$, on the difference between the maximal value and minimal value of any two elements in all of the instances it receives, $X \geq (\max_j x_{t,j} - \min_j x_{t,j})$. Since EG maintains a regressor from the probability simplex, we measure the cumulative loss of the EG algorithm *relative* to the cumulative loss achieved by any fixed regressor from the probability simplex. The following theorem gives a bound on the loss of the EG algorithm relative to the loss of any fixed regressor from $\mathbb{P}^n$.

**Theorem 4.** *Let* $S = \{(\mathbf{x}_1, y_1), ..., (\mathbf{x}_T, y_T)\}$ *be a sequence of instance-target pairs, and let* $\boldsymbol{\lambda}_1, ..., \boldsymbol{\lambda}_T$ *be the regressors generated by the EG online algorithm (Fig. 4) on the sequence. Then, for any fixed regressor* $\boldsymbol{\mu} \in \mathbb{P}^n$ *we have*

$$\sum_{t=1}^{T} L_{log}(\boldsymbol{\lambda}_t \cdot \mathbf{x}_t - y_t) \leq \frac{4}{3}\sum_{t=1}^{T} L_{log}(\boldsymbol{\mu} \cdot \mathbf{x}_t - y_t) + \frac{4}{3}X^2 D_{RE}(\boldsymbol{\mu}, \boldsymbol{\lambda}_1) \quad , \qquad (12)$$

*where* $D_{RE}(p, q) = \sum_j p_j \log(p_j/q_j)$ *is the relative entropy.*

The proof of the theorem is analogous to the proof of Thm. 3 and employs a relative entropy based progress lemma.

## 6   Discussion

We described a framework for solving regression problems by a symmetrization of margin loss functions. Our approach naturally lent itself to a shifted and symmetric loss function which is approximately zero in a pre-specified interval and can thus be used as a smooth alternative to the $\varepsilon$-insensitive hinge loss. We presented both batch and online algorithms for solving the resulting regression problems. The updates of the batch algorithms we presented have a log-additive and an additive form. Our framework also results in a new and very simple to implement regularization scheme. As a byproduct, we tacitly derived a new additive algorithm for boosting-based classification, which can be used in conjunction with the newly introduced regularization scheme. There are numerous extensions of this work. One of them is the application of Thms. 1 and 2 as splitting criteria for learning regression trees. Another interesting direction is the marriage of the loss symmetrization

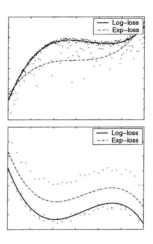

**Fig. 5.** A comparison of log-loss and exp-loss.

technique with other boosting related techniques such as drifting games [12, 4].

We conclude the paper with a synthetic example that underscores the different merits of the log-loss and the exp-loss. In Fig. 5 we show results obtained for both losses on two synthetic datasets. Each dataset was generated by uniformly sampling from a univariate third degree polynomial. One-sided noise, generated by taking minus the absolute value of a normal random variable, was added to the first dataset (top plot in Fig. 5). Regressors were learned using both the log-loss and the exp-loss, using a degree 3 polynomial kernel. The regressor obtained by minimizing the log-loss is very close to the function used to generate the data, demonstrating the robustness of the log-loss to noise. The regressor attained by minimizing the exp-loss, however, attempts to minimize the maximal discrepancy over the entire data set and therefore lies significantly below. The other facet of this behavior is illustrated on the bottom plot of Fig. 5. For this dataset, a third of the targets were shifted by a positive constant. The regressor obtained by minimizing the exp-loss lies between the two groups of points and as such approximately minimizes the $\ell_\infty$ regression loss on the sample. The regressor found by minimizing the log-loss practically ignores the shifted third of the sample. The log-loss shares the same asymptotic behavior as the absolute loss and as such its solution resembles the median. The different merits of the two losses can be exploited in more complex decision tasks such as ranking problems. We leave this and the extensions mentioned above for future research.

## Acknowledgements

We are in debt to Rob Schapire for making the connection to regularization and for numerous comments. Part of this research was funded by the Bi-national Science Foundation grant no. 1999-038.

## References

1. Nicolò Cesa-Bianchi. Analysis of two gradient-based algorithms for on-line regression. *Journal of Computer and System Sciences*, 59(3):392–411, 1999.
2. M. Collins, R.E. Schapire, and Y. Singer. Logistic regression, AdaBoost and Bregman distances. *Machine Learning*, 47(2/3):253–285, 2002.
3. N. Duffy and D. Helmbold. Leveraging for regression. In *Proceedings of the Thirteenth Annual Conference on Computational Learning Theory*. ACM, 2000.
4. Y. Freund and M. Opper. Drifting games and Brownian motion. *Journal of Computer and System Sciences*, 64:113–132, 2002.
5. Jerome Friedman, Trevor Hastie, and Robert Tibshirani. Additive logistic regression: a statistical view of boosting. *Annals of Statistics*, 28(2):337–374, April 2000.
6. Trevor Hastie, Robert Tibshirani, and Jerome Friedman. *The Elements of Statistical Learning*. Springer, 2001.
7. P.J. Huber. *Robust Statistics*. John Wiley and Sons, New York, 1981.
8. J. Kivinen, D.P Helmbold, and M. Warmuth. Relative loss bounds for single neurons. *IEEE Transactions on Neural Networks*, 10(6):1291–1304, 1999.
9. J. Kivinen and M. K. Warmuth. Exponentiated gradient versus gradient descent for linear predictors. *Information and Computation*, 132(1):1–64, January 1997.
10. G. Lebanon and J. Lafferty. Boosting and maximum likelihood for exponential models. In *Advances in Neural Information Processing Systems 14*, 2001.
11. T. Poggio and F. Girosi. Networks for approximation and learning. *Proceedings of the IEEE*, 78(9), 1990.
12. Robert E. Schapire. Drifting games. In *Proceedings of the Twelfth Annual Conference on Computational Learning Theory*, 1999.
13. A. Smola and B. Schölkopf. A tutorial on support vector regression. Technical Report NC2-TR-1998-030, NeuroCOLT2, 1998.
14. Vladimir N. Vapnik. *The Nature of Statistical Learning Theory*. Springer, 1995.

# On Finding Large Conjunctive Clusters

Nina Mishra[1], Dana Ron[2], and Ram Swaminathan[3]

[1] HP Labs and Stanford University[†]
nmishra@theory.stanford.edu
[2] Tel-Aviv University[‡]
danar@eng.tau.ac.il.
[3] HP Labs.
swaram@hpl.hp.com.

**Abstract.** We propose a new formulation of the clustering problem that differs from previous work in several aspects. First, the goal is to explicitly output a collection of simple and meaningful *conjunctive descriptions* of the clusters. Second, the clusters might overlap, i.e., a point can belong to multiple clusters. Third, the clusters might not cover all points, i.e., not every point is clustered. Finally, we allow a point to be assigned to a conjunctive cluster description even if it does not completely satisfy all of the attributes, but rather only satisfies most.

A convenient way to view our clustering problem is that of finding a collection of large bicliques in a bipartite graph. Identifying one largest conjunctive cluster is equivalent to finding a maximum edge biclique. Since this problem is NP-hard [28] and there is evidence that it is difficult to approximate [12], we solve a relaxed version where the objective is to find a large subgraph that is close to being a biclique. We give a randomized algorithm that finds a relaxed biclique with almost as many edges as the maximum biclique. We then extend this algorithm to identify a good collection of large relaxed bicliques. A key property of these algorithms is that their running time is *independent* of the number of data points and linear in the number of attributes.

**Keywords:** Conceptual Clustering, Max Edge Biclique, Unsupervised Learning

## 1 Introduction

It has become evident that clustering is not a single problem, but rather a collection of application-specific optimization problems. Conductance-based clustering [22] is appealing when the objective is to maximize edge connectivity within a cluster and minimize the weight of inter-cluster edges. Correlation clustering [6] is practical when each pair of data points can be given a label according to whether they should or should not belong to the same cluster and when the objective is to minimize the number of disagreements/maximize the number of

[†] Research partially supported by NSF grant EIA-0137761.
[‡] Part of this reserach was done while visiting HP Labs. The Research is supported by the Israel Science Foundation (grant number 32/00-1).

B. Schölkopf and M.K. Warmuth (Eds.): COLT/Kernel 2003, LNAI 2777, pp. 448–462, 2003.

agreements with the given labels. As clustering becomes more clearly defined for other applications, many new and important formulations will follow.

In this paper we are motivated by applications where the goal is to identify tight descriptions of large groups of points. One example is customer segmentation where one may be interested in describing common customers via a simple conjunctive description like people who care about "Price AND Quality" when making product purchase decisions. Such cluster descriptions can then be used as a basis for target marketing.

We introduce a new kind of clustering that we call *Conjunctive Clustering* *(CC)* where the objective is to identify long conjunctive cluster descriptions that cover a dense region of the space. More formally, a conjunctive cluster is a conjunction of attributes $c$ together with the points $Y$ in the data set that satisfy the conjunction $c$. In general we are interested in longer, more specific conjunctions since then the points that satisfy the conjunction have more in common. We are also interested in having a large number of points satisfy that conjunction. A natural way to combine these objectives is to maximize $|c| \cdot |Y|$ so that we cover as many points as possible that have much in common.

A convenient way to think about a conjunctive cluster is as a biclique in a bipartite graph. For a bipartite graph $G = (U, W, E)$, let $U$ be the points to be clustered, $W$ the attributes that describe the data, and let there be an edge between $(u, w)$ if the point $u$ has attribute $w$. (In the more general categorical case, there is a vertex in $W$ for each attribute/value combination.) A biclique is a subgraph $(U^*, W^*)$ with $|U^*| \cdot |W^*|$ edges, in other words there is an edge between each vertex in $U^*$ and each vertex in $W^*$. A biclique naturally corresponds to a conjunctive cluster since each point $u$ in $U^*$ satisfies the conjunction of attributes in $W^*$. A maximum edge biclique corresponds to the best conjunctive cluster, since $|W^*|$ is precisely the length of the conjunction and $|U^*|$ is the number of points that satisfy the conjunction. We define the $k$ best conjunctive clusters as the $k$ largest clusters that don't overlap too much (a formal definition can be found in Section 2).

## 1.1   Advantages of the Conjunctive Clustering Formulation

Our interpretation of clustering as the problem of identifying large bicliques is appealing for many reasons:

**Cluster Descriptions:** For the applications we have in mind, it is not sufficient for a clustering algorithm to output subsets of points that each belong to the same cluster. Rather, the identification of a cluster description is crucial.

In practice, the problem of identifying cluster descriptions is overcome by using a machine learning algorithm. Points in the same cluster are assigned the same class label, and a machine learning algorithm is used to learn a function that distinguishes the classes from each other. The problem with this approach is that typically the clustering algorithm optimizes a cost function unrelated to the type of cluster description sought. Thus a common byproduct of the machine learning step is a collection of descriptions that are not necessarily conjunctive, and usually hard to understand. If on the other hand the learning algorithm is forced to output conjunctions as hypotheses, then they may serve as poor descriptions of clusters (since the clusters found may be inherently more complex). Thus by performing clustering and learning separately, one may be sacrificing the descriptive quality of the final clusters – either because they are too complicated to understand, or they are too simple to describe the clusters.

**Clusters Overlap / Some Points Not Clustered:** The objective of many existing clustering algorithms is to identify a strict partition of the points [21, 8, 11, 18, 22]. In practice such a condition is far too stringent: Each point need not be clustered and further some points can be assigned to multiple clusters. By viewing a clustering as a collection of bicliques, we allow clusters to overlap, both in that each point can belong to multiple clusters and that an attribute can be used to describe multiple clusters.

We also allow our algorithm to ignore some points if they don't fall into one of the $k$ desired clusters. In contrast to outlier detection methods, which typically are viewed as a preprocessing step employed prior to clustering, we directly allow the clustering algorithm to ignore some points. Furthermore, while clustering algorithms like EM [10] allow points to be assigned to multiple clusters, such approaches do not typically produce cluster descriptions.

**Move Away from Metric Space:** Much of the existing research on clustering assumes that the data to be clustered falls in some metric space, e.g., $k$–Median [21, 8, 5, 27] and $k$–Center [20, 11, 18]. Such a measure is useful in situations where the goal is to ensure that pairs of points in the same cluster are "close" according to the metric space. In the CC formulation, if the points to be clustered are in $\{0, 1\}^d$, for example, then it is possible that two points in the same cluster are "far" according to the metric space, but placed in the same cluster since they share some common subset of variables. In other words, some dimensions are completely ignored when placing points in the same conjunctive cluster.

Furthermore, there may be applications where data does not inherently fall in a metric space, e.g., text and images. In such situations, it may be difficult to both quantify the distance between two objects as well as ensure that the distance measure satisfies the triangle inequality. The CC view of the clustering problem moves away from quantifying the distance between points. Instead it attempts to find large subsets of points that have many attributes in common.

## 1.2   Our Results

**Maximum Conjunctive Cluster/Maximum Edge Biclique.** We start by considering the problem of finding a maximum conjunctive cluster, that is a cluster/biclique $(U^*, W^*)$ with the most edges. Since this problem is NP hard [28] and there is evidence that it is difficult to approximate [12], we consider a relaxation of the maximum edge biclique problem where the algorithm is allowed to output a pair $(\hat{U}, \hat{W})$, where $\hat{U} \subseteq U$ and $\hat{W} \subseteq W$, that is $\epsilon$-close to being a conjunctive cluster/biclique. That is, every point in $\hat{U}$ has at least $(1 - \epsilon)$ of the attributes in $\hat{W}$. More precisely, the algorithm only outputs $\hat{W}$ (which corresponds to the cluster description), and $\hat{U}$ is implicitly determined by $\hat{W}$ (that is, it contains all vertices in $U$ that neighbor at least $(1 - \epsilon)$ of the vertices in $\hat{W}$). We refer to such an approximate biclique (cluster) as an $\epsilon$-biclique ($\epsilon$-cluster). We give an algorithm that outputs a subset $\hat{W}$ such that $(\hat{U}, \hat{W})$ has almost as many edges as the optimum biclique $(U^*, W^*)$.

Our algorithm runs efficiently provided that $\epsilon$ is constant and the fraction of points in both $U^*$ and $W^*$ is sufficiently large. In other words, that the length of the conjunction and the number of points that satisfy the conjunction is large. Indeed, if $|U^*| \geq \rho_{\mathrm{U}} \cdot |U|$ and $|W^*| \geq \rho_{\mathrm{w}} \cdot |W|$, for certain size parameters $0 < \rho_{\mathrm{U}}, \rho_{\mathrm{w}} \leq 1$, then our algorithm draws a sample of size polynomial in all input parameters, and runs in time linear in $|W|$, *independent* of $|U|$, quasi-polynomial in $1/\rho_{\mathrm{U}}$ and $1/\rho_{\mathrm{w}}$, and exponential in $\log(1/\epsilon)/\epsilon^2$.

While it would be more desirable to have an algorithm with running time polynomial in all problem parameters, we cannot expect to have polynomial dependence in $1/\epsilon$ since in such a case we could use the algorithm to solve the original NP-hard problem in polynomial time by setting $\epsilon < \frac{1}{|U||W|}$. We leave open the question of whether it is possible to obtain an algorithm with polynomial dependence on $1/\rho_{\mathrm{U}}, 1/\rho_{\mathrm{w}}$. This paper addresses the situation when both $1/\rho_{\mathrm{U}}$ and $1/\rho_{\mathrm{w}}$ are small (for example, constant); such a situation has practical motivation. For instance, target marketing schemes are often designed to affect large portions (e.g., 20-30%) of the customer population.

**Collection of Large Conjunctive Clusters.** We next discuss the more general problem of identifying a collection of large conjunctive clusters. We define the $k$ best conjunctive clusters as the largest conjunctive clusters that don't overlap too much. Given size parameters $0 < \rho_{\mathrm{U}}, \rho_{\mathrm{w}} \leq 1$, and given $k$ the number of clusters, we give an algorithm that outputs $k$ subsets $\hat{W} \subseteq W$ for which the following holds: $|\hat{W}| \geq \rho_{\mathrm{w}} \cdot |W|$; $|\hat{U}| \geq \rho_{\mathrm{U}} \cdot |U|$ (where $\hat{U}$ is as defined above given $\hat{W}$); the different $\epsilon$-bicliques $(\hat{U}, \hat{W})$ don't overlap too much in terms of edges. Further, for every true conjunctive cluster $(U', W')$ such that $|U'| \geq \rho_{\mathrm{U}} \cdot |U|$ and $|W'| \geq \rho_{\mathrm{w}} \cdot |W|$, either there is an $\epsilon$-cluster in our collection that approximately covers $(U', W')$ or $(U', W')$ is smaller (not much bigger) than every $\epsilon$-cluster in the collection. The running time of our algorithm is quasi-polynomial in $k$, $1/\rho_{\mathrm{U}}$ and $1/\rho_{\mathrm{w}}$, exponential in $\log(1/\epsilon)/\epsilon^2$, linear in $|W|$, and independent of $|U|$.

**Finding Approximations to $\epsilon$-Bicliques.** The above algorithms can also be adapted to finding approximations to large $\epsilon$-bicliques. This may be useful when there is no large "perfect" conjunctive cluster, but there are large $\epsilon$-clusters. The modified algorithm will output an $O(\epsilon^{1/3})$-biclique that is almost as large as the largest $\epsilon$-biclique and can be further extended to output a collection of such large approximate bicliques.

## 1.3   Related Work

As mentioned previously, the maximum-edge biclique problem is NP-hard [28]. Recently, Feige [12] has shown that under the assumption that refuting 3SAT is hard on average, the maximum-edge biclique problem is hard to approximate to within a certain constant. Furthermore, for certain constants $\alpha < \beta$, it is hard to distinguish between the case in which the maximum biclique has size at least $\beta \cdot |U| \cdot |W|$ (where $G = (U, W, E)$ is the given bipartite graph) and the case in which the maximum biclique has size less than $\alpha \cdot |U| \cdot |W|$.

Related to the problem of finding almost bicliques is finding dense subgraphs (i.e., with maximum average degree). Finding a densest subgraph of a particular size is NP-hard (since CLIQUE is NP-hard). The algorithm in [30] gives an approximation factor of $O(n^{1/3})$ and the algorithm of [4] gives a PTAS for dense graphs. Finding the densest subgraph (without size constraints) can be performed in polynomial time (cf. [16, 7]).

Our algorithms are related to Property Testing algorithms on dense graphs [17] (and in particular are inspired by the CLIQUE-testing algorithm in [17]). Such algorithms are designed to decide whether a given (dense) graph has a certain property or whether many edge modifications should be performed so that it obtains the property. Many testing algorithms can be modified so as to obtain approximate solutions to the corresponding search problems, similarly to the approximate solutions studied in this paper. However, none of the known property testing algorithms (and their extensions to approximation algorithms) directly applies to our problem. In particular, the most general family of graph properties studied in [17] does not capture our definition of clustering which allows for overlapping subsets of vertices. Other related work on approximation algorithms and testing algorithm on dense graphs includes [4, 14, 3].

The general notion of finding cluster descriptions is known as conceptual clustering [24]. Pitt and Reinke [29] show that the Hierarchical Agglomerative Clustering (HAC) algorithm finds an optimum clustering under particular conditions on intra and inter cluster distance. A separate conjunctive clustering problem, considered in [25], was that of finding $k \geq 2$ disjoint conjunctive descriptions $c_1 \ldots, c_k$ such that $\sum_{i=1}^{k} |c_i||Y_i|$ is maximized, and no point satisfies both $c_i$ and $c_j$. These two results are not applicable to our problem since in particular we do not require that each point be assigned to a cluster, that the clusters be disjoint, or that a point exactly satisfy a conjunction in order to be assigned to it. Another paper on identifying descriptions of clusters, by Agrawal et al [1], gives algorithms for identifying DNF descriptions for each cluster. In this work the objective function is different in that a cluster is a union of connected, high density regions, where a region has high density if it has more density than the area around it.

Research on discovering web communities [23, 15, 13] is also related to CC. A web community is a set of web pages that are all relevant to each other. One way to view the community discovery problem is as a bipartite graph $G = (U, W, E)$ where $U = W$ are the pages on the web and $E$ consists of edges $(u, w)$ if there is a hyperlink from $u$ to $w$ or if $u = w$. A biclique $(U', W')$ forms a community since each page in $U'$ is linked to each page in $W'$. Our results can be used to identify a good cover of the *large* communities on the web. In contrast, our algorithms are not designed to find small communities, also known as "cores" as studied by [23], where the goal is to for example find all $K_{3,2}$'s.

The frequent itemset problem [2, 19] is also closely related to CC. Given a collection of points $P$ in $\{0,1\}^d$, the frequent itemset problem is that of identifying all subsets of variables that have high support, i.e., all subsets of variables that satisfy a sufficiently large fraction of $P$. A large conjunctive cluster is in some sense a maximally frequent itemset. The key difference between the two is that whereas in the frequent set formulation the identification of a border separating the frequent from the infrequent sets is critical, our objective is to find a collection of $k$ conjunctions that don't overlap too much and that "dominate" all the big conjunctions.

## 2    Preliminaries and Problem Definitions

As noted in the introduction, it will be convenient to define our problems using a graph-theoretic formulation. Given a bipartite graph $G = (U, W, E)$ and two subsets $U' \subseteq U$ and $W' \subseteq W$, we denote by $E(U', W')$ the subset of all edges between vertices in $U'$ and vertices in $W'$. That is, $E(U', W') \stackrel{\text{def}}{=} \{(u, w) \in E : u \in U', w \in W'\}$. We refer to such a pair $(U', W')$ as a *bisubgraph*. For a vertex $v$ we denote the neighbor set of $v$ by $\Gamma(v)$. For a subset $S$ of vertices, we let $\Gamma(S) \stackrel{\text{def}}{=} \cap_{v \in S} \Gamma(v)$ denote the set of vertices that neighbor *every* vertex in $S$. For a subset $S$ and a parameter $\epsilon < 1$, we let $\Gamma_\epsilon(S) \stackrel{\text{def}}{=} \{w : |\Gamma(w) \cap S| \geq (1 - \epsilon)|S|\}$ denote the set of vertices that neighbor all but an $\epsilon$-fraction of $S$.

**Definition 1.** *Given a bipartite graph $G = (U, W, E)$, a bisubgraph $(U', W')$ is a **biclique** if $E(U', W') = U' \times W'$. That is, $W' \subseteq \Gamma(U')$. The (edge-)**size** of a biclique $(U', W')$ is $|E(U', W')| = |U'| \cdot |W'|$, and a **maximum biclique** is a biclique $(U', W')$ for which $|U'| \cdot |W'|$ is maximized over all bicliques.*

Note that if we have one side of the biclique $W^*$ then we can obtain the other side of the biclique $U^*$ since $U^* = \Gamma(W^*)$ (and vice versa). This implies that outputting the conjunctive description $W^*$ suffices for identifying the cluster.

As noted previously, the maximum biclique problem is NP-hard. Here we suggest a relaxation of the maximum biclique problem which allows the output to be close to a biclique.

**Definition 2.** *We say that $(U', W')$ is $\epsilon$-**close** to being a biclique, for $0 \leq \epsilon \leq 1$, if every vertex in $U'$ neighbors at least $(1 - \epsilon)$ of the vertices in $W'$. For the sake of succinctness, we say that $(U', W')$ is an $\epsilon$-**biclique**. The size of an $\epsilon$-biclique is $|E(U', W')|$ (which is $\geq |U'| \cdot |W'| \cdot (1 - \epsilon)$).*

In the context of conjunctive clusters, an $\epsilon$-biclique corresponds to a pair $(Y, c)$ such that every point in $Y$ satisfies most (at least $(1-\epsilon)$) of the attributes in $c$. Note that the asymmetry between $U'$ and $W'$ in the definition of an $\epsilon$-biclique corresponds to our needs in the context of clustering where the two sides of the $\epsilon$-biclique in fact have a different role. Similarly to the biclique case, if we discover $W'$ then $U'$ is completely determined, i.e., $(U', W') = (\Gamma_\epsilon(W'), W')$. This is especially useful in the context of clustering since $W' = c$ is the description of the cluster, and so we do not need to output explicitly all points $Y$ in the cluster.

Our first problem formulation follows.

*Problem 1.* Given a bipartite graph $G = (U, W, E)$, find a subset $W' \subseteq W$ such that the $\epsilon$-biclique $(\Gamma_\epsilon(W'), W')$ is at least $(1 - b\epsilon)$ times as large as the maximum biclique for a small constant $b$.

For our sublinear result, $b = 2$. If we are allowed time linear in $|U|$, then we can show that $b = 0$.

**Collections of Large Bicliques.** The above relaxation addresses the issue of finding a *single* approximate maximum biclique. We now turn to defining a good *collection* of at most $k$ bicliques where $k$ is a given parameter.

As in the case of a single biclique, we would like the bicliques in the collection to be large. On the other hand, the number of bicliques in the collection should be bounded. Therefore, if there are several large bicliques that are very similar, we may prefer including only one of them in the collection as a "representative", so as to allow ourselves to include other bicliques that are possibly smaller but less similar. We next introduce the notion of coverage.

**Definition 3.** *Let $G = (U, W, E)$ be a bipartite graph and let $U', U'' \subseteq U$ and $W', W'' \subseteq W$. We say that $(U', W')$ is a $\boldsymbol{\delta}$-cover of $(U'', W'')$ if*

$$\frac{|E(U'', W'') \setminus E(U', W')|}{|E(U'', W'') \cup E(U', W')|} \leq \delta \ .$$

We next define *domination* which essentially states that a subgraph $(U', W')$ is dominated by a collection of subgraphs $C$ if there is a subgraph in $C$ that covers $(U', W')$ or if every pair in $C$ is either larger or only slightly smaller than $(U', W')$.

**Definition 4.** *Let $G = (U, W, E)$ be a bipartite graph and let $C = \{(U_i, W_i)\}_{i=1}^k$ be a collection of pairs of vertex subsets where $U_i \subseteq U$, and $W_i \subseteq W$. We say that $C$ $(\boldsymbol{\delta}, \boldsymbol{\epsilon})$-dominates a pair $(U', W')$ if either there exists a pair $(U_i, W_i) \in C$ that $\delta$-covers $(U', W')$, or $|E(U', W')| \leq (1 + \epsilon) \cdot \min_j \{|E(U'_j, W'_j)|\}$.*

We will also sometimes say that a collection $C_1$ of subgraphs dominates another collection of subgraphs $C_2$ if $C_1$ dominates each subgraph $(U_2, W_2) \in C_2$.

The following definition ensures that the collection of subgraphs output by the algorithm don't overlap with each other too much.

**Definition 5.** *Let $G = (U, W, E)$ be a bipartite graph and let $C = \{(U_i, W_i)\}_{i=1}^k$ be a collection of pairs of vertex subsets where $U_i \subseteq U$, and $W_i \subseteq W$. We say that $C$ is $\boldsymbol{\delta}$-diverse if for every two different pairs $(U_i, W_i)$ and $(U_j, W_j)$ in $C$, neither is a $\delta$-cover of the other.*

Since this paper is focused on identifying large conjunctive clusters, we introduce two lower-bound parameters, $\rho_U$ and $\rho_W$, which the algorithm is provided with, and consider only bicliques $(U', W')$ such that $|U'| \geq \rho_U \cdot |U|$ and $|W'| \geq \rho_W \cdot |W|$. These parameters prevent the algorithm from outputting clusters with few points ($\rho_U$) or with little in common ($\rho_W$). Let $\mathcal{B}(\rho_U, \rho_W)$ denote the set of all bicliques $(U', W')$ in $G$ such that $|U'| \geq \rho_U \cdot |U|$ and $|W'| \geq \rho_W \cdot |W|$.

Given the above definitions, a natural problem is to find a collection of at most $k$ bicliques in $\mathcal{B}(\rho_\mathrm{U}, \rho_\mathrm{w})$, that is both $\delta$-diverse and $(\delta, \epsilon)$-dominates every $(U', W') \in \mathcal{B}(\rho_\mathrm{U}, \rho_\mathrm{w})$. Here we define a relaxation:

*Problem 2.* Let $G = (U, W, E)$ be a given bipartite graph, $0 < \rho_\mathrm{U}, \rho_\mathrm{w} \le 1$ two size parameters, $k$ an integer, $0 \le \delta \le 1$ a diversity/covering parameter, and $0 \le \epsilon \le 1$ an approximation parameter. Find a collection $\tilde{\mathcal{C}}$ of at most $k$ $\epsilon$-bicliques in $\mathcal{B}_\epsilon(\rho_\mathrm{U}, \rho_\mathrm{w})$ such that $\tilde{\mathcal{C}}$ is $\delta$-diverse and for every $(U', W') \in \mathcal{B}(\rho_\mathrm{U}, \rho_\mathrm{w})$, $(U', W')$ is $(b \cdot (\delta + \epsilon), b' \cdot \epsilon)$-dominated by $\tilde{\mathcal{C}}$ for some small constants $b$ and $b'$.

For our sublinear result, $b = 4$ and $b' = 2$. If we are given time linear in $|U|$ then we can show that $b = 3$ and $b' = 0$.

Note that Problem 2 allows clusters to overlap in the sense that a given point may belong to multiple clusters. Note also that the problem definition doesn't require that all points be clustered. These two facts are an interesting contrast to clustering problem formulations that require a strict partition of the points [21, 8, 11, 18, 22, 6].

## 3   A Good Seed

In this section we discuss a central building block of our algorithms. Consider a fixed biclique $(U^*, W^*)$ and assume it is maximal. As noted in the preliminaries section, if we knew $U^*$ we could obtain $W^*$ exactly by simply considering $\Gamma(U^*)$. We can then get $U^*$ back by considering $\Gamma(\Gamma(U^*))$. Clearly we do not have $U^*$, or else we would be done. Suppose instead, as a mental experiment, that we were able to obtain a (small) *random sample* $S$ from $U^*$. Then for every sample $S \subset U$, $W^*$ is contained in $\Gamma(S)$. However, $\Gamma(S)$ may contain many additional vertices outside of $W^*$. As a consequence, if we now take $\Gamma(\Gamma(S))$ we may get a very small subset (or even an empty set). However, as we show below, if we instead take $\Gamma_\epsilon(\Gamma(S))$, then with high probability over the choice of a sufficiently large sample $S$, the $\epsilon$-biclique $(\Gamma_\epsilon(\Gamma(S)), \Gamma(S))$ is at least as large as the biclique $(U^*, W^*)$.

We think of the sample $S$ as being a "good seed" for the biclique $(U^*, W^*)$. In the next section we shall get rid of the imaginary assumption that we can directly sample from $U^*$ in order to obtain the good seed. Let $\rho_\mathrm{w}$ be a lower bound on $|W^*|/|W|$, and let $\hat{m} = \frac{16}{\epsilon^2} \log \frac{40}{\rho_\mathrm{w}\epsilon}$.

**Good Seed Algorithm**
1. $S \leftarrow$ sample from $U^*$ of size $\hat{m}$
2. $\hat{W} \leftarrow \Gamma(S)$
3. Output $\hat{W}$

**Lemma 1.** *Let $\hat{W}$ be as constructed in the Good Seed Algorithm on a sample $S$ of size $\hat{m}$ drawn uniformly from $U^*$. With probability at least $\frac{9}{10}$ over the choice of $S \subset U^*$, $|E(\Gamma_\epsilon(\hat{W}), \hat{W})| \ge |U^*| \cdot |W^*|$.*

In order to prove the lemma, it will be helpful to partition the vertices in $\hat{W}$, i.e., the intersection of the neighbors of $S$, into those that are in the optimum biclique, $W^*$, those that neighbor a significant fraction of $U^*$ ($H$, for high degree) and those that don't ($L$, for low degree). Note again that since $S$ is a subset of $U^*$, $\hat{W}$ must contain all of $W^*$. We'll show that with high probability there are very few $L$ vertices. Thus, since most of the vertices in $\hat{W}$ are either in the optimum biclique or have high degree with $U^*$, we'll argue that the bisubgraph $(\Gamma_\epsilon(\hat{W}), \hat{W})$ has at least as many edges as the optimum. We now precisely define the terms High and Low.

**Definition 6.** *We say that a vertex $w \in W$ has **high degree with respect to** $U^*$ if*

$$\frac{|\Gamma(w) \cap U^*|}{|U^*|} \geq 1 - (\epsilon/4)^2 .$$

*Otherwise it has **low degree with respect to** $U^*$.*

Note that in particular, every $w \in W^*$ has high degree with respect to $U^*$ (since for every $w \in W^*$, $\frac{|\Gamma(w) \cap U^*|}{|U^*|} = 1$). We will be interested in samples of $U^*$ that are "good seeds": we would like a sample $S$ so that $\Gamma(S)$ contains $W^*$ plus mostly vertices that have high degree with respect to $U^*$.

**Definition 7.** *We say that a subset $S \subseteq U^*$ is **a good seed** of $U^*$ if the number of vertices in $\Gamma(S) \subseteq W$ that have low degree with respect to $U^*$ is at most $(\epsilon/4)|W^*|$.*

We now claim that our sample $S$ is sufficiently large to ensure that $\Gamma(S)$ has few low degree vertices with respect to $U^*$, i.e., that $S$ is a good seed of $U^*$. The lemma (proof in [26]) can be proved via probabilistic techniques.

**Lemma 2.** *With probability at least $\frac{9}{10}$ the sample $S$ drawn in step 1 of the Good Seed Algorithm is a good seed of $U^*$.*

We next show that if $S$ is a good seed of $U^*$ then the $\epsilon$-biclique $(\Gamma_\epsilon(\hat{W}), \hat{W}) = (\Gamma_\epsilon(\Gamma(S)), \Gamma(S))$ has as many edges as $(U^*, W^*)$.

**Lemma 3.** *Let $\hat{W}$ be as constructed in the Good Seed Algorithm on a sample $S$ of size $\hat{m}$ drawn from $U^*$. If $S$ is a good seed of $U^*$ then $(\Gamma_\epsilon(\hat{W}), \hat{W})$ is an $\epsilon/4$-cover of $(U^*, W^*)$ and $|E(\Gamma_\epsilon(\hat{W}), \hat{W})| \geq |U^*| \cdot |W^*|$.*

*Proof.* The subset $\hat{W}$ consists of three parts: (1) the vertices of $W^*$; (2) a subset of vertices, denoted $H$, that have high degree with respect to $U^*$; (3) a subset of vertices, denoted $L$, having low degree with respect to $U^*$. We will show that most of $U^*$ neighbors $\hat{W}$ by considering two cases based on whether $|H|$ is small or large. In what follows, let $\hat{U} \stackrel{\text{def}}{=} \Gamma_\epsilon(\hat{W})$.

$|H| \leq \frac{\epsilon}{2}|W^*|$: If $W^*$ accounts for at least $(1 - \epsilon)$ of $\hat{W}$ then by Step 3 of the algorithm, $U^*$ will be part of $\hat{U}$. Indeed this is true:

$$\frac{|W^*|}{|\hat{W}|} = \frac{|W^*|}{|H| + |L| + |W^*|} > \frac{|W^*|}{\frac{\epsilon}{2}|W^*| + \frac{\epsilon}{4}|W^*| + |W^*|} = \frac{1}{1 + \frac{\epsilon}{2} + \frac{\epsilon}{4}} \geq (1-\epsilon) \quad (1)$$

(recall that $|L| < \frac{\epsilon}{4}|W^*|$ since $S$ is a good seed). Since $U^* \subseteq \hat{U}$ and $W^* \subseteq \hat{W}$ we have that $(\hat{U}, \hat{W})$ completely covers $(U^*, W^*)$ and so $|E(\hat{U}, \hat{W})| \geq |U^*||W^*|$ as desired.

$|H| > \frac{\epsilon}{2}|W^*|$: We first show that all but at most an $\epsilon/4$-fraction of the vertices in $U^*$ have at least $(1 - \epsilon/4)|H|$ neighbors in $H$. Let the subset of vertices in $U^*$ having at least $(1 - \epsilon/4)|H|$ neighbors in $H$ be denoted $Q^*$. Thus we would like to show that $|Q^*| \geq (1 - \epsilon/4)|U^*|$.

Let $\alpha$ be such that $|Q^*| = (1 - \alpha)|U^*|$. Assume contrary to the claim, that $\alpha > \epsilon/4$. Then the total number of edges between $U^*$ and $H$ would be less than:

$$|Q^*| \cdot |H| + |U^* \setminus Q^*| \cdot (1 - \epsilon/4)|H|$$
$$= (1 - \alpha)|U^*| \cdot |H| + \alpha|U^*| \cdot (1 - \epsilon/4)|H|$$
$$= (1 - \alpha + \alpha - \alpha \cdot (\epsilon/4))|U^*| \cdot |H| < (1 - (\epsilon/4)^2)|U^*| \cdot |H| . \tag{2}$$

But by definition of $H$, $|E(U^*, H)| \geq |H| \cdot (1 - (\epsilon/4)^2)|U^*|$, and we have reached a contradiction.

Since $|L| \leq (\epsilon/4)|W^*|$, every vertex in $Q^*$ has at least $(1 - \epsilon)|\hat{W}|$ neighbors in $\hat{W}$, and hence $Q^* \subseteq \hat{U}$. Since we have shown that $|Q^*| \geq (1 - \epsilon/4)|U^*|$ (where $Q^* \subseteq U^*$), we have that $E(\hat{U}, \hat{W})$ contains all edges in $E(U^*, W^*)$ but at most $(\epsilon/4) \cdot |U^*| \cdot |W^*|$ And so $(\hat{U}, \hat{W})$ certainly $(\epsilon/4)$-covers $(U^*, W^*)$. Finally, by definition of $Q^*$ and what we have shown concerning its size,

$$|E(Q^*, \hat{W})| \geq |Q^*| \cdot (|W^*| + (1 - \epsilon/4)|H|)$$
$$\geq (1 - \epsilon/4)|U^*| \cdot (|W^*| + |H|(1 - \epsilon/4))$$
$$> |U^*| \cdot |W^*| \cdot (1 - \epsilon/4) \cdot (1 + \epsilon/2(1 - \epsilon/4)) > |U^*| \cdot |W^*| \tag{3}$$

Since $|E(\hat{U}, \hat{W})| \geq |E(Q^*, \hat{W})|$, we are done. $\qquad\square$

The proof of Lemma 1 directly follows from Lemmas 2 and 3.

## 4    Conjunctive Clustering Algorithm

We now turn to the problem of identifying conjunctive clusters. We begin by considering the problem of finding one large approximate conjunctive cluster. Then we consider finding a good collection of them.

### 4.1    Approximate Maximum Biclique

Given $\rho_U$ and $\rho_W$ (for which $\mathcal{B}(\rho_U, \rho_W)$ is non-empty) we shall show how to find an $\epsilon$-biclique in which the number of edges is almost as large as in a maximum biclique in $\mathcal{B}(\rho_U, \rho_W)$.[1] Solving this problem is interesting in its own right and the solution is also later used to identify $k$ conjunctive clusters.

---

[1] If the algorithm is not provided with lower bounds $\rho_U$ and $\rho_W$ then it can search for them using a standard doubling process.

Since we cannot actually sample from the left-hand-side $U^*$, we instead use what is sometimes referred to as *exhaustive sampling* (see e.g. [9, 4, 17, 14]). Namely, we sample from $U$, and consider all subsets of the sample whose size is lower bounded by a certain threshold. It can then be verified that if the sample is sufficiently large, then with high probability one of these subsets is a good seed. However, now we have to address a new problem: How do we decide which subset is the good seed? We could of course check the resulting $\epsilon$-biclique for each subset, but this would take time linear in $U$, and we are interested in an algorithm having time *independent* of $|U|$. As one may guess at this point, we solve this by sampling again from $U$.

Let $\hat{m}$ be as defined in the Good Seed Algorithm. Also, let $m = m(\epsilon, \rho_\mathsf{U}, \rho_\mathsf{W}) = \frac{2}{\rho_\mathsf{U}} \cdot \hat{m}$, and let $t = t(\epsilon, \rho_\mathsf{U}) = \frac{96}{\rho_\mathsf{U} \cdot \epsilon^2} \cdot m$.

## Algorithm Approximate Maximum Biclique

1. Draw a sample $X$ of $m$ vertices uniformly and independently from $U$.
2. Draw another sample $T$ of $t$ vertices uniformly and independently from $U$.
3. For each subset $S$ of $X$ that has size $\hat{m}$ do:
   (a) $\hat{W}(S) \leftarrow \Gamma(S)$
   (b) $\hat{T}(S) \leftarrow$ vertices in $T$ that neighbor most of $\hat{W}$, i.e., $T \cap \Gamma_\epsilon(\hat{W}(S))$.
4. Among all subsets $S$ considered by the algorithm for which $\hat{T}(S) \geq (3\rho_\mathsf{U}/4)t$, let $Z$ be the one for which $|\hat{T}(Z)| \cdot |\hat{W}(Z)|$ is maximized. Output $\hat{W}(Z)$.

Let $(U^*, W^*)$ be a maximum biclique. For any subset $S$, let $\hat{W}(S) = \Gamma(S)$ and let $\hat{U}(S) = \Gamma_\epsilon(\hat{W}(S))$. Let $\hat{G}(S) = (\hat{U}(S), \hat{W}(S))$ be the bisubgraph determined by $S$. We define the *true relative size* of $\hat{G}(S)$ to be $(|\hat{U}(S)| \cdot |\hat{W}(S)|)/(|U| \cdot |W|)$ and the *estimated relative size* of $\hat{G}(S)$ to be $(|\hat{T}(S)| \cdot |\hat{W}(S)|)/(t \cdot |W|)$. (Recall that $|T| = t$.) We also define a *good subset* $S_g$ to be one for which $|\hat{U}(S_g)|/|U| \geq \rho_\mathsf{U}/2$ and a *bad subset* $S_b$ to be one for which $|\hat{U}(S_b)|/|U| < \rho_\mathsf{U}/2$.

The algorithm works via the following reasoning. We show that one of the subsets $S$ considered in step 3 of the algorithm is a good seed of $U^*$ with high probability. We denote this subset by $S^*$. By Lemma 3, we will then know that the bisubgraph $(\Gamma_\epsilon(\hat{W}(S^*)), \hat{W}(S^*))$ has at least as many edges as the optimum. We then show that, with high probability, the algorithm won't consider any bad subset $S_b$ (since for bad subsets, $\hat{T}(S_b)$ will be too small). On the other hand, the estimated relative size of $\hat{G}(S_g)$ for any good subset $S_g$ is close to its true relative size. Thus in particular, the estimated relative size of $\hat{G}(S^*)$ for the seed $S^*$ (which is a good subset), is close to its true relative size. It will then follow that for $\hat{W}(Z)$ output by the algorithm, the bisubgraph $(\hat{U}(Z), \hat{W}(Z))$ must have about as many (not much fewer) edges as the optimum true maximum biclique $(U^*, W^*)$.

**Theorem 1.** *With probability at least 2/3, Algorithm Approximate Maximum Biclique outputs a subset $\hat{W} = \hat{W}(Z)$ so that $|E(\Gamma_\epsilon(\hat{W}), \hat{W}))| \geq (1 - 2\epsilon) \cdot |U^*| \cdot |W^*|$. The running time of the algorithm is exponential in $\frac{\log(1/\epsilon)}{\epsilon^2}$, quasi-polynomial in $\frac{1}{\rho_\mathsf{U}}$ and $\frac{1}{\rho_\mathsf{W}}$, linear in $|W|$ and independent of $|U|$.*

*Proof.* It can be shown via multiplicative Chernoff bounds, that the following holds with probability at least 9/10: (1) One of the subsets considered in step 3 of Algorithm Approximate Maximum Biclique is a good seed. (2) In step 4 of Algorithm Approximate Maximum Biclique, no bad subset $X$ of size $\hat{m}$ will be considered. (3) In step 4 of Algorithm Approximate Maximum Biclique, for any good subset $S_g$ of $X$ of size $\hat{m}$,

$$(1 - \epsilon/4)\frac{|\hat{U}(S_g)|}{|U|} \leq \frac{|\hat{T}(S_g)|}{t} \leq (1 + \epsilon/4)\frac{|\hat{U}(S_g)|}{|U|}$$

For the rest of the proof, assume that these events in fact happen.

Now we show that the specific subset $S^*$ will not (with high probability) be excluded by Step 4 of the algorithm. First observe that the subset $S^*$ is good since $|\hat{U}(S^*)| \geq (1 - \epsilon/4)|U^*| > (\rho_U/2)|U|$. Further, it can be shown that $\hat{T}(S^*)/t \geq 3\rho_U/4$ since $\epsilon < 1/2$:

$$|\hat{T}(S^*)|/t \geq (1 - \epsilon/4)|\hat{U}(S^*)|/|U| \geq (1 - \epsilon/4)(1 - \epsilon/4)\rho_U \geq (1 - \epsilon/2)\rho_U \geq 3\rho_U/4$$

and thus $S^*$ will be considered by the algorithm. By the proof of Lemma 3, we have that

$$\frac{|\hat{T}(S^*)| \cdot |\hat{W}(S^*)|}{t \cdot |W|} \geq (1 - \epsilon/4) \cdot \frac{|\hat{U}(S^*)| \cdot |\hat{W}(S^*)|}{|U| \cdot |W|} . \tag{4}$$

Next we show that the number of edges in the bisubgraph output by the algorithm $(\hat{U}(Z), \hat{W}(Z))$ is not much smaller than the number of edges in the maximum biclique $(U^*, W^*)$.

$$|E(\hat{U}(Z), \hat{W}(Z))| \geq (1 - \epsilon)|\hat{U}(Z)| \cdot |\hat{W}(Z)| \tag{5}$$

$$\geq \frac{1 - \epsilon}{1 + \epsilon/4} \cdot \frac{|U|}{t} \cdot |\hat{T}(Z)| \cdot |\hat{W}(Z)| \tag{6}$$

$$\geq \frac{1 - \epsilon}{1 + \epsilon/4} \cdot \frac{|U|}{t} \cdot |\hat{T}(S^*)| \cdot |\hat{W}(S^*)| \tag{7}$$

$$\geq \frac{(1 - \epsilon)(1 - \epsilon/4)}{1 + \epsilon/4} \cdot |\hat{U}(S^*)| \cdot |\hat{W}(S^*)| \tag{8}$$

$$\geq (1 - 2\epsilon)|U^*| \cdot |W^*| \tag{9}$$

The bound on the running time follows from the fact that we enumerate over all subsets of size $\hat{m}$ of the $m$ vertices drawn in Step 1. The total number of such subsets is $\binom{m}{\hat{m}}$. For each subset $S$ we compute $\Gamma(S)$ and $T \cap \Gamma_\epsilon(\Gamma(S))$. Thus for each subset $S$, the algorithm spends time $O(t \cdot |W|)$. Hence the total running time is $O(m^{\hat{m}}|W|t) = O((\frac{1}{\rho_U \epsilon^2} \log \frac{1}{\rho_W \epsilon})^{O(\frac{1}{\epsilon^2} \log \frac{1}{\rho_W \epsilon})}|W|(\frac{1}{(\rho_U \epsilon^2)^2} \log \frac{1}{\rho_W \epsilon}))$. □

## 4.2   Conjunctive Clustering

Recall that given $\rho_U, \rho_W, k, \epsilon$ and $\delta$, our goal is to output a collection $\tilde{C}$ of $k$ $\epsilon$-bicliques that is $\delta$-diverse and that $(b(\delta + \epsilon), b'\epsilon)$-dominates every biclique in $\mathcal{B}(\rho_U, \rho_W)$ for small constants $b$ and $b'$.

We reset $\hat{m}, m$ and $t$ as follows: $\hat{m} = \hat{m}(k, \epsilon, \rho_U, \rho_w) = \Theta\left(\frac{1}{\epsilon^2} \log \frac{k}{\rho_w \cdot \epsilon}\right)$, $m = m(k, \epsilon, \rho_U, \rho_w) = \frac{2 \log k}{\rho_U} \cdot \hat{m}$, and $t = t(k, \epsilon, \rho_U, \rho_w) = \Theta\left(\frac{\log(1/\epsilon)}{\rho_U \cdot \rho_w \cdot \epsilon^3}\right) \cdot m$.

### Conjunctive Clustering Algorithm

1. Draw a sample $X$ of $m$ vertices uniformly and independently from $U$.
2. Draw another sample $T$ of $t$ vertices uniformly and independently from $U$. Let $\hat{W} \leftarrow \emptyset$.
3. For each subset $S$ of $X$ that has size $\hat{m}$ do
   (a) $\hat{W}(S) \leftarrow \Gamma(S)$.
   (b) $\hat{T}(S) \leftarrow T \cap \Gamma_\epsilon(\hat{W}(S))$.
   (c) If $|\hat{W}(S)| \geq \rho_w \cdot |W|$ and $|\hat{T}(S)| \geq (\rho_U/2) \cdot t$ then add $\hat{W}(S)$ to $\hat{\mathcal{W}}$.
4. Order the subsets $\hat{W}(S)$ in $\hat{\mathcal{W}}$ according to the magnitude of $|\hat{T}(S)| \cdot |\hat{W}(S)|$. Perform the following at most $k$ times: Add to $\hat{\mathcal{W}}$ the next subset $\hat{W}(S)$ (according to the above order) such that $(\hat{T}(S), \hat{W}(S))$ is not yet $(\delta + 2\epsilon)$-covered by any $(\hat{T}(S'), \hat{W}(S'))$ where $\hat{W}(S') \in \hat{\mathcal{W}}$.

The next theorem establishes that our algorithm works as desired. Due to space constraints its proof appears in the full version of this paper [26].

**Theorem 2.** *With probability at least 4/5 Algorithm Conjunctive Clustering outputs a collection $\tilde{\mathcal{W}}$ of at most $k$ $\epsilon$-bicliques such that $\tilde{\mathcal{C}} = \left\{\left(\Gamma_\epsilon(\hat{W}), \hat{W}\right) : \hat{W} \in \tilde{\mathcal{W}}\right\}$ is $\delta$-diverse, and $\tilde{\mathcal{C}}$ $((2\delta + 4\epsilon), 2\epsilon)$-dominates every biclique in $\mathcal{B}(\rho_U, \rho_w)$. The running time of the algorithm is exponential in $\frac{\log 1/\epsilon}{\epsilon^2}$, quasi-polynomial in $k$, $1/\rho_U$, and $1/\rho_w$ linear in $|W|$ and independent of $|U|$.*

An algorithm that runs in time independent of both $|U|$ and $|W|$ can be found in the full version of this paper [26].

## 5    Finding Approximate $\epsilon$-Bicliques

In Section 4.1 we showed that if the graph contains a large biclique $(U^*, W^*)$, then we can find a subset $\hat{W}$ such that $|E(\Gamma_\epsilon(\hat{W}), \hat{W})| \geq (1 - 2\epsilon)|U^*| \cdot |W^*|$. Let us define a *strong* $\epsilon$-biclique to be a pair $(U', W')$ such that every vertex in $U'$ neighbors at least $(1 - \epsilon)$ of the vertices in $W'$ and every vertex in $W'$ neighbors at least $1 - \epsilon$ of the vertices in $U'$. Thus this is a strengthening of the definition of an $\epsilon$-biclique. Suppose we know that there exists a strong $\epsilon$-biclique $(\tilde{U}, \tilde{W})$ such that $|\tilde{U}| \geq \rho_U \cdot |U|$ and $|\tilde{W}| \geq \rho_w \cdot |U|$ (but there isn't necessarily such a large biclique). We next show how the Approximate Maximum Biclique algorithm can be modified so as to obtain an $O(\epsilon^{1/2})$-biclique $(\hat{U}, \hat{W})$ such that $|E(\hat{U}, \hat{W})| \geq (1 - O(\epsilon^{1/2}))|E(\tilde{U}, \tilde{W})|$. By small modifications it is possible to deal with the case in which $(\tilde{U}, \tilde{W})$ is an $\epsilon$-biclique (i.e., not a strong one). The extension of finding a collection of large $O(\epsilon^{1/2})$-bicliques is done analogously to what is described in Section 4.2.

Let $\hat{m}$ and $m$ be as in the Approximate Maximum Biclique algorithm, where we assume that $\rho_U \cdot |U|$ and $\rho_w \cdot |W|$ are lower bounds on the sizes of $\tilde{U}$ and $\tilde{W}$, respectively. We also assume that $\epsilon$ is sufficiently small ($\epsilon < 1/12$), or else we can replace each occurrence of $\epsilon$ with $\min\{\epsilon, 1/12\}$.

**Algorithm Approximate Maximum $\epsilon$-Biclique**

1. Draw a sample $X$ of $m$ vertices uniformly and independently from $U$.
2. Draw another sample $T$ of $t$ vertices uniformly and independently from $U$.
3. For each subset $S$ of $X$ that has size $\hat{m}$ do:
   (a) $\hat{W}(S) \leftarrow \Gamma_{2\epsilon}(S)$
   (b) $\hat{T}(S) \leftarrow T \cap \Gamma_{2\sqrt{\epsilon}}(\hat{W}(S))$.
4. Among all subsets $S$ considered by the algorithm for which $\hat{T}(S) \geq (3\rho_U/4)t$, let $Z$ be such that $|\hat{T}(Z)| \cdot |\hat{W}(Z)|$ is maximized. Output $\hat{W}(Z)$.

The proof of the following theorem can be found in the full version [26].

**Theorem 3.** *With probability at least 2/3, Algorithm Approximate Maximum $\epsilon$-biclique outputs a subset $\hat{W} = \hat{W}(S)$ such that $|E(\Gamma_{2\sqrt{\epsilon}}(\hat{W}), \hat{W})| \geq (1 - 3\sqrt{\epsilon}) \cdot \bar{\rho}|U||W|$, where $\bar{\rho}|U||W|$ is the size of a maximum strong $\epsilon$-biclique.*

## 6    Future Work

Some interesting problems left open by our research include: (1) Algorithms with polynomial dependence on $\frac{1}{\rho_U}$ and $\frac{1}{\rho_W}$; (2) Variations where the vertices or edges are weighted; (3) Alternate definitions of $k$ best conjunctive clusters; and (4) Extensions to descriptions that are not conjunctive in nature, e.g., disjunctions.

## References

1. R. Agrawal, J.E. Gehrke, D. Gunopulos, and P. Raghavan. Automatic subspace clustering of high dimensional data for data mining applications. In *Proceedings of SIGMOD*, pages 94–105, 1998.
2. R. Agrawal, T. Imielinski, and A. Swami. Mining association rules between sets of items in large databases. In *Proceedings of SIGMOD*, pages 207–216, 1993.
3. N. Alon, E. Fischer, M. Krivelevich, and M. Szegedy. Efficient testing of large graphs. *Combinatorica*, 20:451–476, 2000.
4. S. Arora, D. Karger, and M Karpinski. Polynomial time approximation schemes for dense instances of NP-hard problems. *Journal of Computer and System Sciences*, 58:193–210, 1999.
5. Arya, Garg, Khandekar, Munagala, and Pandit. Local search heuristic for k-median and facility location problems. In *Proceedings of STOC*, 2001.
6. N. Bansal, A. Blum, and S. Chawla. Correlation clustering. In *Proceedings of FOCS*, pages 938–247, 2002.
7. M. Charikar. Greedy approximation algorithms for finding dense components in a graph. *Proceedings of the 3rd International Workshop on Approximation Algorithms for Combinatorial Optimization Problems*, pages 84–95, 2000.
8. M. Charikar and S. Guha. Improved combinatorial algorithms for the facility location and k-median problems. In *Proceedings of FOCS*, pages 378–388, 1999.
9. W. Fernandez de la Vega. MAX-CUT has a randomized approximation scheme in dense graphs. *Random Structures and Algorithms*, 8:187–198, 1996.

10. A. P. Dempster, N. M. Laird, and D. B. Rubin. Maximum likelihood from incomplete data via the EM algorithm (with discussion). *Journal of the Royal Statistical Society series B*, 39:1–38, 1977.
11. T. Feder and D. Greene. Optimal algorithms for approximate clustering. In *Proceedings of STOC*, pages 434–444, 1988.
12. U. Feige. Average case complexity and approximation complexity. In *Proceedings of STOC*, 2002.
13. G. Flake, S. Lawrence, and C. Lee Giles. Efficient identification of web communities. In *Proceedings of KDD*, pages 150–160, 2000.
14. A. Frieze and R. Kannan. Quick approximation to matrices and applications. *Combinatorica*, 19(2):175–220, 1999.
15. D. Gibson, J. Kleinberg, and P. Raghavan. Inferring web communities from link topology. In *Proceedings of the 9th ACM Conference on Hypertext*, Structural Queries, pages 225–234, 1998.
16. A. V. Goldberg. Finding a maximum density subgraph. *UC Berkeley Tech Report, CSD-84-171*, 1984.
17. O. Goldreich, S. Goldwasser, and D. Ron. Property testing and its connection to learning and approximation. *Journal of the ACM*, 45(4):653–750, 1998.
18. T. F. Gonzalez. Clustering to minimize the maximum intercluster distance. *Theoretical Computer Science*, 38(2-3):293–306, June 1985.
19. D. Gunopulos, H. Mannila, R. Khardon, and H. Toivonen. Data mining, hypergraph transversals, and machine learning (extended abstract). In *Proceedings of PODS*, pages 209–216, 1997.
20. D. Hochbaum and D. Shmoys. A unified approach to approximate algorithms for bottleneck problems. *Journal of the ACM*, 33(3):533–550, July 1986.
21. N. Jain and V.V. Vazirani. Primal-dual approximation algorithms for metric facility location and k-median problems. In *Proceedings of FOCS*, pages 2–13, 1999.
22. R. Kannan, S. Vempala, and A. Vetta. On clusterings — good, bad and spectral. In IEEE, editor, *Proceedings of the 41st Annual Symposium on Foundations of Computer Science*, pages 367–377, 2000.
23. R. Kumar, P. Raghavan, S. Rajagopalan, and A. Tomkins. Trawling the Web for emerging cyber-communities. *Computer Networks (Amsterdam, Netherlands: 1999)*, 31(11–16):1481–1493, May 1999.
24. R. S. Michalski. Knowledge acquisition through conceptual clustering: A theoretical framework and an algorithm for partitioning data into conjunctive concepts. Technical Report 1026, Department of Computer Science, University of Illinois at Urbana-Champaign, Urbana, Illinois, 1980.
25. N. Mishra, D. Oblinger, and L. Pitt. Sublinear time approximate clustering. In *Proceedings of SODA*, pages 439–447, 2001.
26. N. Mishra, D. Ron, and R. Swaminathan. Large conjunctive clusters and bicliques. Available from the authors, 2002.
27. R. Ostrovsky and Y. Rabani. Polynomial time approximation schemes for geometric k-clustering. In IEEE, editor, *41st Annual Symposium on Foundations of Computer Science*, pages 349–358, 2000.
28. R. Peeters. The maximum edge biclique problem is NP-complete. Unpublished manuscript, 2000.
29. L. Pitt and R.E. Reinke. Criteria for polynomial-time (conceptual) clustering. *Machine Learning*, 2:371, 1987.
30. D. Peleg U. Feige, G. Kortsarz. The dense-k-subgraph problem. *Algorithmica*, 29(3):410–421, 2001.

# Learning Arithmetic Circuits
# via Partial Derivatives

Adam R. Klivans[1] and Amir Shpilka[2]

[1] Division of Engineering and Applied Sciences, Harvard
Cambridge, MA 02139, USA
`klivans@eecs.harvard.edu`
[2] DEAS, Harvard
LCS, MIT
Cambridge, MA, USA
`amirs@deas.harvard.edu`

**Abstract.** We present a polynomial time algorithm for learning several models of algebraic computation. We show that any arithmetic circuit whose partial derivatives induce a "low"-dimensional vector space is exactly learnable from membership and equivalence queries. As a consequence we obtain the first polynomial time algorithm for learning depth three multilinear arithmetic circuits. In addition, we give the first polynomial time algorithms for learning restricted algebraic branching programs and noncommutative arithmetic formulae. Previously only restricted versions of depth-2 arithmetic circuits were known to be learnable in polynomial time. Our learning algorithms can be viewed as solving a generalization of the well known *polynomial interpolation problem* where the unknown polynomial has a succinct representation. We can learn representations of polynomials encoding *exponentially* many monomials. Our techniques combine a careful algebraic analysis of arithmetic circuits' partial derivatives with the "multiplicity automata" techniques due to Beimel et al [BBB+00].

**Keywords:** PAC learning, learning with queries.

## 1 Introduction

Let $p$ be an unknown multivariate polynomial over a fixed field. Given random input/output pairs chosen from some distribution $D$, can a computationally bounded learner output a hypothesis which will correctly approximate $p$ with respect to future random examples chosen from $D$? This problem, known as the multivariate polynomial learning problem, continues to be a fundamental area of research in computational learning theory. If the learner is allowed to query the unknown polynomial at points of his choosing (instead of receiving random examples) and is required to output the exact polynomial $p$, then this problem is precisely the well-known polynomial interpolation problem. Both the learning and the interpolation problem have received a great deal of attention from the theoretical computer science community. In a learning context, multivariate polynomials are expressive structures for encoding information (sometimes

B. Schölkopf and M.K. Warmuth (Eds.): COLT/Kernel 2003, LNAI 2777, pp. 463–476, 2003.

referred to as the "algebraic" analogue of DNF formulae) while polynomial interpolation has been studied in numerous contexts and has important applications in complexity theory, among other fields [ALM+98,STV01].

Previous research on this problem has focused on giving algorithms whose running time is polynomial in the number of terms or monomials of the unknown polynomial. This is a natural way to measure the complexity of learning and interpolating polynomials when the unknown polynomial is viewed in the usual "sum of monomials" representation. That is to say, given that the polynomial $p = \sum_{i=1}^{t} m_i$ is the sum of $t$ monomials, we may wish to output a list of these monomials (and their respective coefficients), hence using at least $t$ time steps simply to write down the list of coefficients. Several researchers have developed powerful interpolation and learning algorithms for a variety of contexts which achieve time bounds polynomial in all the relevant parameters, including $t$ (see for example [BBB+00,BM02,GKS94,HR99,KS01,SS96]).

## 1.1   Arithmetic Circuits

In this paper we are concerned with learning succinct representations of polynomials via alternate algebraic models of computation, most notably *arithmetic circuits*. An arithmetic circuit syntactically represents a multivariate polynomial in the obvious way: a multiplication (addition) gate outputs the product (sum) of the polynomials on its inputs. The input wires to the circuit correspond to the input variables of the polynomial and thus the output of the circuit computes some polynomial of the input variables. We measure the size of an arithmetic circuit as the number of gates. For example, the standard "sum of monomials" representation of a polynomial $p = \sum_{i=1}^{t} \alpha_i x_{i_1} \cdots x_{i_n}$ ($\alpha_i$ is an arbitrary field element) corresponds precisely to a depth-2 arithmetic circuit with a single sum gate at the root and $t$ product gates feeding into the sum gate (each product gate multiplies some subset of the input variables). To rephrase previous results on learning and interpolating polynomials in terms of arithmetic circuits, we could say that depth-2 arithmetic circuits with a sum gate at the root are learnable in time polynomial in the size of the circuit.

Moving beyond the standard "sum of products" representation, we consider the complexity of learning higher depth arithmetic circuits. It is easy to see that there exist polynomial size depth-3 (or even depth-2 with a product gate at the root) arithmetic circuits capable of computing polynomials with *exponentially* many monomials. For example, let $\{L_{i,j}\}, 1 \leqslant i, j \leqslant n$ be a family of $n^2$ distinct linear forms over $n$ variables. Then $\sum_{i=1}^{n} \prod_{i=1}^{n} L_{i,j}$ is a polynomial size depth-3 arithmetic circuit but cannot be written as a sum of polynomially many monomials. Although arithmetic circuits have received a great deal of attention in complexity theory and, more recently, derandomization, the best known result for learning arithmetic circuits in a representation other than the depth-2 sum of products representation is due to Beimel et al. [BBB+00] who show that depth-2 arithmetic circuits with a product gate of fan in $O(\log n)$ at the root and addition gates of unbounded fan-in in the bottom level are learnable in polynomial time.

## 1.2   Our Results

We learn various models of algebraic computation capable of encoding exponentially many monomials in their input size. Our algorithms work with respect to any distribution and require membership query access to the concept being learned. More specifically we show that any class of polynomial size arithmetic circuits whose partial derivatives induce a vector space of dimension polynomial in the circuit size are learnable in polynomial time. This characterization generalizes the work of Beimel et al. [BBB+00] and yields the following results:

- The first polynomial time algorithm for learning the class of depth-3 multilinear circuits: polynomials $p = \sum_{i=1}^{n} \prod_{j=1}^{m} L_{i,j}(X_j)$ where each $L_{i,j}$ is a linear form and the $X_j$'s are a partition of the input variables.
- An algorithm for learning general depth-3 arithmetic circuits with $s$ product gates each of fan in at most $d$ in time polynomial in $s$, $2^d$, and $n$, the number of variables.
- The first polynomial time algorithm for learning polynomial size noncommutative formulae computing polynomials over a fixed partition of the variables (note there are no depth restrictions on the size of the formula).
- The first polynomial time algorithm for learning polynomial size read once, oblivious algebraic branching programs.

The last two results appear in the full version of this paper (see the authors' web pages). Finally we show that, with respect to known techniques, it is hard to learn polynomial size depth-3 homogeneous arithmetic circuits in polynomial time. This indicates that our algebraic techniques give a fairly tight characterization of the learnability of arithmetic circuits with respect to current algorithms.

## 1.3   Our Techniques

We use as a starting point the work on multiplicity automata due to Beimel et al. [BBB+00]. A multiplicity automaton is a nondeterministic finite automaton where each transition edge has an integer weight (for a precise definition see Section 2). On input $x$, $f(x)$ is equal to to the sum over all accepting paths of the automaton on input $x$ of the product of the edge weights on that accepting path. In [BBB+00], the authors, building on work due to [OSK94], show that multiplicity automata can be learned in polynomial time and that these multiplicity automata can compute polynomials in their standard sum of products representation[1]. Their analysis centers on the Hankel matrix of a multiplicity automata (see section 2 for a definition).

We generalize their results and show that any polynomial whose partial derivatives induce a low dimensional vector space has a low rank Hankel matrix. We conclude that any arithmetic circuit or branching program whose partial

---

[1] More generally they can learn any polynomial $p$ of the form $p = \sum_{i=1}^{n} \prod_{j=1}^{m} p_{ij}(x_j)$ where $p_{ij}(x_j)$ is a univariate polynomial of low degree.

derivatives form a low dimensional vector space can be computed by polynomial size multiplicity automata and are amenable to the learning algorithms developed by Beimel et al. As such, we output a multiplicity automaton as our learner's hypothesis.

Our next task is to show which circuit classes have partial derivatives that induce low dimensional vector spaces. At this point we build on work due to Nisan [Nis91] and Nisan and Wigderson [NW97] (see also [SW01]) who analyzed the partial derivatives of certain arithmetic circuit classes in the context of proving lower bounds and show that a large class of algebraic models have "well-behaved" partial derivatives. For example we show that the dimension of the vector space of partial derivatives induced by a multilinear depth-3 arithmetic circuit is polynomial in the size of the circuit.

We feel that partial derivatives are the "correct" algebraic quantity to analyze for learning irreducible polynomials[2]. By considering partial derivatives, we can show that there are depth-3 polynomial size homogeneous arithmetic circuits which are not computed by polynomial size multiplicity automata and are thus not learnable by these techniques. As depth-3 homogeneous circuits would be the natural next step in this line of research, we feel that we have captured precisely which circuits are learnable with respect to known techniques. Finally, we feel that that a function's partial derivatives are more easily understood than its Hankel matrix and hence may lead to more improvements in learning polynomials.

## 1.4   The Relationship to Lower Bounds

In the case of learning Boolean functions, the ability to prove lower bounds against a class of Boolean circuits usually coincides with the ability to give strong learning algorithms for those circuits. For example the well known lower bounds of Håstad [Has86] against constant depth Boolean circuits are used heavily in the learning algorithm due to Linial, Mansour, and Nisan [LMN93]. Jackson et al. [JKS02] have shown that constant depth circuits with a majority gate, one of the strongest circuit classes for which we can prove lower bounds (see [ABFR91]), also admit nontrivial learning algorithms. Furthermore Jackson et al. [JKS02] show that we will not be able to learn more complicated Boolean circuits unless certain cryptographic assumptions are false.

We believe our work furthers this relationship in the algebraic setting. The models of algebraic computation we can learn correspond to a large subset of the models of algebraic computation for which lower bounds are known. For example Nisan [Nis91] gives lower bounds for noncommutative formulae. Nisan and Wigderson [NW97] prove lower bounds against depth-3 multilinear circuits. Moreover, in both papers the authors prove lower bounds by considering the partial derivatives spanned by the circuit and the function computed by it, a method similar to ours. No exponential lower bounds are known for general depth-3 arithmetic circuits (see [GR98,SW01]). As in the Boolean case, we exploit many of the

---

[2] Reducible polynomials can first be factored.

insights from the lower bound literature to prove the correctness of our learning algorithms.

## 2  Preliminaries

### 2.1  The Learning Model

We will work in the model of exact learning from membership and equivalence queries. See Angluin [Ang87] for details.

### 2.2  Multiplicity Automata

A multiplicity automaton is a nondeterministic automaton where each transition is assigned a weight, and the output of the automaton for any input $x$ is the sum over all accepting paths of $x$ of the products of the weights on each path.

**Definition 1.** *Fix $\Sigma$ an alphabet with $s = |\Sigma|$ elements. A multiplicity automaton $A$ of size $r$ over alphabet $\Sigma$ is a vector of integers $\bar{\gamma} = \{\gamma_1, \ldots, \gamma_r\}$ and a set of $s$ matrices $\mu_\sigma$, one for each $\sigma \in \Sigma$, where each $\mu_\sigma$ is an $r \times r$ matrix of integers. The output of $A$ on input $x = (x_1, \ldots, x_n)$ is defined to be the inner product of $(\prod_{i=1}^n \mu_{x_i})_1$ and $\bar{\gamma}$ where $(\prod_{i=1}^n \mu_{x_i})_1$ equals the first row of $\prod_{i=1}^n \mu_{x_i}$. In other words the output is the first coordinate of the vector $(\prod_{i=1}^n \mu_{x_i}) \cdot \bar{\gamma}$.*

Intuitively each matrix $\mu_\sigma$ corresponds to the transition matrix of the automaton for symbol $\sigma \in \Sigma$. Iterative matrix multiplication keeps track of the weighted sum of paths from state $i$ to state $j$ for all $i, j \leqslant r$. The first row of the iterated product corresponds to transition values starting from the initial state and $\bar{\gamma}$ determines the acceptance criteria.

Next we define the Hankel matix of a function:

**Definition 2.** *Let $\Sigma$ be an alphabet and $f : |\Sigma|^n \to \mathbb{F}$. Consider an ordering of all strings in $\Sigma^{\leqslant n}$ and let $x \in \Sigma^d$ and $y \in \Sigma^{n-d}$ for some $d \leqslant n$. Construct a matrix $H$ where the $(x, y)$ entry of $H$ is equal to $f(x \cdot y)$. For any other pair of strings $(a, b)$ such that $|a| + |b| \neq n$ let $H_{a,b} = 0$. $H$ is called the Hankel matrix of $f$ for strings of length $n$. We define $H_k$ to be the $k$th "block" of $H$, i.e. $H_k$ is the submatrix defined by all rows of $H$ indexed by strings of length exactly $k$ and all columns of $H$ indexed by strings of length exactly $n - k$.*

The following key fact relates the rank of the Hankel matrix of a function for strings of length $n$ with the size of multiplicity automaton computing $f$ on inputs of length $n$:

**Theorem 1.** *[CP71,Fli74,BBB⁺00] Let $f : \Sigma^n \to \mathbb{F}$ for some fixed field $\mathbb{F}$. Then the rank of the Hankel matrix of $f$ (over $\mathbb{F}$) is equal to the size of the smallest multiplicity automaton computing $f$ on inputs of length $n$.*

Previous learning results have computed the rank of the Hankel matrices of particular polynomials yielding a bound on the size of their multiplicity automata. In fact, Beimel et al. [BBB+00], improving on [OSK94], learn functions computed by multiplicity automata by iteratively learning their corresponding Hankel matrices:

**Theorem 2.** *[BBB+00] Let $f : \Sigma^n \to \mathbb{F}$ for some fixed field $\mathbb{F}$. Let $r$ be the rank of the Hankel matrix of $f$ for strings of length $n$. Then there exists an exact learning algorithm for $f$ running in time polynomial in $n, r$, and $|\Sigma|$. Furthermore the final hypothesis output by the learning algorithm is a multiplicity automaton of size $r$ over alphabet $\Sigma$.*

Our main technical contribution is to show that the rank of a function's Hankel matrix is bounded by (and in most cases equal to) the dimension of the vector space of a function's partial derivatives. Thus we reduce the problem of learning a polynomial to bounding the dimension of the vector space of its partial derivatives.

## 2.3   Structured Polynomials

In this paper we will work primarily with polynomials that respect a fixed partition of the input variables:

**Definition 3.** *Let $X = \dot{\cup}_{i=1}^d X_i$ be a partition of the variables into $d$ sets each of size $n$. A polynomial over the variables $X$ is called* structured *and has degree $d$ if every monomial $m$ is of the form $y_1 \cdot y_2 \cdots y_d$ where each $y_i$ is some variable from $X_i$. Thus any structured $f$ is also homogeneous and multilinear.*

For example, the class of depth-3 multilinear circuits, as defined by Nisan and Wigderson [NW97] (see Definition 11), computes only structured polynomials. To see this note that any polynomial computed by a depth-3 multilinear circuits is of the form $p = \sum_{i=1}^n \prod_{j=1}^m L_{i,j}(X_j)$ where each $L_{i,j}$ is a linear form and the $X_j$'s are a partition of the input variables. In later sections we will show that certain algebraic branching programs also compute structured polynomials and will therefore be amenable to our learning techniques.

Another notation that we use is the following:

**Definition 4.** *Let $X = \dot{\cup}_{i=1}^d X_i$. For any $1 \leqslant k \leqslant d$ define*

$$\mathbb{M}[X_1, ..., X_k] = \{ \, M \mid M = \prod_{i=1}^k x_i \, , x_i \in X_i \, \}.$$

Thus $\mathbb{M}[X_1, ..., X_k]$ is the set of all structured monomials of degree $k$.

## 2.4    Partial Derivatives

In this subsection we introduce some notation for computing partial derivatives.

**Definition 5.** *Let $d = \sum_{i=1}^{k} d_i$. For a function $f(x_1, ..., x_n)$ and a a monomial $M = \prod_{i=1}^{k} x_i^{d_i}$ we define*

$$\frac{\partial f}{\partial M} = \frac{1}{M!} \cdot \frac{\partial^d f}{\prod_{i=1}^{k} \partial x_i^{d_i}}$$

*Where $M! = \prod_{i=1}^{k} (d_i!)$.*

**Example 3** *Let $f(x, y, z) = x^2 y + z$, $M(x, y, x,) = xy$. We have that*

$$\frac{\partial f}{\partial M} = 2x, \ M! = 1$$

**Definition 6.** *For a function $f(x_1, ..., ..., x_n)$ and $k \leqslant n$ define*

$$\partial_k(f) = \{ \ \frac{\partial f}{\partial M} \mid \text{monomials } M \in \mathbb{F}[x_1, ..., x_k] \ \}$$

*We define*

$$\text{rank}_k(f) = \dim\left(\text{span}\left(\partial_k(f)\right)\right)$$

In the case that $f$ is a sturctured multilinear polynomial we define $\partial_k(f)$ in a slightly different way.

**Definition 7.** *Let $f$ be a structured polynomial of degree $d$ over $X = \dot\cup_{i=1}^{d} X_i$. We define*

$$\partial_k(f) = \{ \ \frac{\partial f}{\partial M} \mid M \in \mathbb{M}[X_1, ..., X_k] \ \}$$

*As before we define*

$$\text{rank}_k(f) = \dim\left(\text{span}\left(\partial_k(f)\right)\right)$$

Notice that for every $M \in \mathbb{M}[X_1, ..., X_k]$ we have that $\frac{\partial f}{\partial M}$ is a stuctured polynomial in $X_{k+1}, ..., X_d$.

We now show how to compute $\text{rank}_k(f)$ by considering the rank of the partial derivative *evaluation* matrix and *coefficient* matrix:

**Definition 8.** *(Evaluation Matrix) Let $f$ be a structured polynomial over $X = \dot\cup_{i=1}^{d} X_i$. Fix a field $\mathbb{F}$ and lexicographically order all elements of $\mathbb{F}^{d-k}$. Construct a matrix $E_k$ where the rows are indexed by elements of $\mathbb{M}[X_1, ..., X_k]$ and the columns are indexed by elements of $\mathbb{F}^{d-k}$. Then the $M, \rho$ entry of $E_k$ is equal to*

$$\frac{\partial f}{\partial M}(\rho)$$

*That is the value of the partial derivative of $f$ with respect to $M$ at the point $\rho$.*

**Definition 9.** *(Coefficient Matrix) Let $f$ be a structured polynomial over $X = \dot{\bigcup}_{i=1}^{d} X_i$. Lexicographically order the sets $\mathbb{M}[X_1, \ldots, X_k]$ and $\mathbb{M}[X_{k+1}, \ldots, X_d]$. Construct a matrix $N_k$ where the rows are indexed by elements of $\mathbb{M}[X_1, \ldots, X_k]$ and the columns are indexed by elements of $\mathbb{M}[X_{k+1}, \ldots, X_d]$. Then the $M_1, M_2$ entry of $N_k$ is equal to the coefficient of monomial $M_2$ in $\frac{\partial f}{\partial M_1}$.*

The following is a standard fact from linear algebra:

**Fact 4** *Let $f$ be a structured polynomial over $X = \dot{\bigcup}_{i=1}^{d} X_i$. Then $\mathrm{rank}_k(f)$ is equal to both the rank of $E_k$ and the rank of $N_k$ where $E_k$ and $N_k$ are defined as above.*

Although we use $\mathrm{rank}_k(f)$ both for structured and unstructured polynomials it will be clear from the context which is the case.

## 3     Characterizing Learnability via Partial Derivatives

In this section we present our main criterion for determining whether an arithmetic circuit or algebraic branching program is learnable. We prove that any structured polynomial whose partial derivatives form a low degree vector space induce low rank Hankel matrices. To relate the rank of the Hankel matrix of $C$ to its partial derivatives we will need the following multivariate version of Taylor's theorem:

**Fact 5** *Let $X = \dot{\bigcup}_{i=1}^{d} X_i$ and let $f(X_1, \ldots, X_d)$ be a polynomial in nd variables respecting the partition. Let $\rho = (\rho_1, \ldots, \rho_d)$ be an assignment to the variables. For a monomial $M$ define $M(\rho)$ be value of $M$ on assignment $\rho$. Then*

$$f(\rho_1, \ldots, \rho_d) = \sum_{M \in \mathbb{M}[X_1, \ldots, X_k]} M(\rho) \frac{\partial f}{\partial M}(\rho)$$

Now we can state the main technical theorem of the paper:

**Theorem 6.** *Let $X = \dot{\bigcup}_{i=1}^{d} X_i$ be a partition of at most nd variables and let $f(X_1, \ldots, X_d)$ be a polynomial respecting this partition. Then for every $k \leqslant d$,*

$$\dim(H_k(f)) = \mathrm{rank}_k(f)$$

**Proof of Theorem 6:**

We will define two matrices $V$ and $D$ such that the rank of $D$ will equal $\mathrm{rank}_k(f)$ and that $H_k = V \cdot D$. Then we will show that the rank of $H_k = \mathrm{rank}(D) = \mathrm{rank}_k(f)$.

– **Construction of $V$:**
Fix a lexicographic ordering of all monomials in $\mathbb{M}[X_1, \ldots, X_k]$ and all assignments $\rho$ to the variables $X_1, \ldots, X_k$ (note that there might be infinitely many such assignments). Create a generalized Vandermonde matrix $V$ where the rows are indexed by all assignments $\rho$ and the columns are indexed by all elements of $\mathbb{M}[X_1, \ldots, X_k]$. For an assignment $\rho$ and a monomial $M \in \mathbb{M}[X_1, \ldots, X_k]$ the $(\rho, M)$ entry of $V$ is defined to be $M(\rho)$.

– **Construction of $D$:**
Again fix a lexicographic ordering of all monomials in $\mathbb{M}[X_1, \ldots, X_k]$ and all assignments $\sigma$ to the variables $X_{k+1}, \ldots, X_d$. Create a matrix $D$ where the rows are indexed by all elements in $\mathbb{M}[X_1, \ldots, X_k]$ and the columns are indexed by all assignments $\sigma$. For a monomial $M$ and an assignment $\sigma$ the $(M, \sigma)$ entry of $D$ is defined to be $\frac{\partial f}{\partial M}(\sigma)$.

*Claim.* $\mathrm{rank}(D) = \mathrm{rank}_k(f)$

*Proof.* Row $M$ of $D$ is the evaluation of $\frac{\partial f}{\partial M}$ on all inputs. Hence each vector corresponds to the "truth table" of a particular partial derivative of $f$. By Fact 4, the rank of this matrix equals the dimension of the span of the partial derivatives of $f$ with respect to all $M \in \mathbb{M}[X_1, \ldots, X_k]$.

*Claim.* $V \cdot D = H_k(f)$

*Proof.* Consider $V \cdot D$. Notice that for $\rho = \rho_1, \ldots, \rho_k$ and $\sigma = \sigma_{k+1}, \ldots, \sigma_d$, the $(\rho, \sigma)$ entry of $V \cdot D$ is equal to

$$(V \cdot D)_{\rho, \sigma} = \sum_{M \in \mathbb{M}[X_1, \ldots, X_k]} M(\rho) \frac{\partial f}{\partial M}(\sigma)$$

which by Fact 5 equals $f(\rho_1, \ldots, \rho_k, \sigma_{k+1}, \ldots, \sigma_d)$.

Thus $H_k$ is exactly equal to $V \cdot D$. Furthermore it is easy to check that $V$ is a generalized Vandermonde matrix and has full rank. Therefore we can conclude

$$\mathrm{rank}(H_k) = \mathrm{rank}(D) = \mathrm{rank}_k(f).$$

$\square$

By summing over all values of $k$ we obtain

**Corollary 1.** *Let $f$ be a polynomial respecting a partition $X = \dot{\cup}_{i=1}^d X_i$. Then*

$$\dim(H(f)) = \sum_{i=1}^d \mathrm{rank}_k(f).$$

Using a similar argument we can prove an analogous theorem for polynomials that are not necessarily structured:

**Theorem 7.** *Let $f : \mathbb{F}^n \to \mathbb{F}$ be a polynomial in $n$ variables where each variable has degree less than $d$. Then $\dim(H(f)) \leqslant \sum_{i=1}^n \mathrm{rank}_k(f)$. If $|\mathbb{F}|$ is larger than $d$ then the previous equation is an equality.*

# 4    Learning Multilinear Depth-3 Arithmetic Circuits

In this section we learn a form of depth-3 arithmetic circuits first studied by Nisan and Wigderson [NW97] called multilinear depth-3 arithmetic circuits. Although strong lower bounds have been proved for this circuit class (see [NW97]), previously no learning algorithms were known. We begin by defining general depth-3 arithmetic circuits:

**Definition 10.** *A depth 3 arithmetic circuit is a layered graph with 3 levels and unbounded fan-in. At the top we have either a sum gate or a product gate. A depth 3 arithmetic circuit C with a sum (product) gate at the top is called a ΣΠΣ (ΠΣΠ) circuit and has the following structure:*

$$C = \sum_{i=1}^{s} \prod_{j=1}^{d} L_{i,j}(X)$$

*where each $L_{i,j}$ is a linear function in the input variables $X = x_1, \ldots, x_n$. The size of the circuit is the number of gates, in this case $O(sd)$.*

A ΣΠΣ circuit is a homogeneous circuit if all the linear forms are homogeneous linear forms and all the product gates have the same fan in (or degree). In other words every gate of the circuit computes a homogeneous polynomial. To define a multilinear depth-3 circuit we need to impose a partition on the variables:

**Definition 11.** *A ΣΠΣ circuit is called multilinear with respect to $X = \dot{\cup}_{i=1}^{d} X_i$ if every linear function computed at the bottom is a homogeneous linear form in one of the sets $X_i$, and each multiplication gate multiplies d homogeneous linear forms $L_1, \ldots, L_d$ where every $L_i$ is over a distinct set of variables $X_i$. That is to say a depth-3 multilinear circuit C has the following structure:*

$$C = \sum_{i=1}^{s} \prod_{j=1}^{d} L_{i,j}(X_j)$$

*where $L_{i,j}$ is an homogeneous linear form.*

The following lemma characterizes the dimension of a multilinear circuit's partial derivatives:

**Lemma 1.** *If a polynomial f is computed by a multilinear depth 3 circuit with s product gates then for every $1 \leqslant k \leqslant d$,*

$$\mathrm{rank}_k(f) \leqslant s.$$

*Proof.* First notice that for every product gate

$$P = \prod_{i=1}^{d} L_i(X_i)$$

we have $\text{rank}_k(P) \leqslant 1$. Indeed for any monomial $M \in \mathbb{M}[X_1, ..., X_k]$ we have that

$$\frac{\partial P}{\partial M} = \alpha_M \cdot \prod_{i=k+1}^{d} L_i(X_i)$$

for some constant $\alpha_M$ depending on $M$ and $P$. The proof of the lemma now follows from the linearity of the partial derivative operator.

Applying Lemma 1, Theorem 6, and Theorem 2 we obtain the following learning result:

**Theorem 8.** *Let $C$ be a multilinear depth-3 circuit with $s$ product gates over $n$ variables with coefficients from a field $\mathbb{F}$. Then $C$ is learnable in time polynomial in $s$,$n$, and $|\mathbb{F}|$.*

## 4.1   Learning General Depth 3 Circuits

In this subsection we give a learning algorithm for general depth-3 arithmetic circuits. Unlike the algorithm in the multilinear case, our algorithm runs in time exponential in the degree of the circuit (and polynomial in the other parameters). Thus we can learn in subexponential time any depth-3 circuit of sublinear degree. Our algorithm follows from the following lemma:

**Lemma 2.** *If a polynomial $f : \mathbb{F}^n \to \mathbb{F}$ be a polynomial over a variable set $X$ of size $n$ computed by a depth-3 circuit with $s$ product gates each of degree at most $d$ then for every $1 \leqslant k \leqslant d$,*

$$\text{rank}_k(f) \leqslant \binom{d}{k} \cdot s$$

*Proof.* The proof is similar to the case of multilinear depth-3 circuits. Notice that for every product gate

$$P = \prod_{i=1}^{d} L_i(X)$$

we have $\text{rank}_k(P) \leqslant \binom{d}{k}$. For any monomial $M$ of degree $k$ we have that

$$\frac{\partial P}{\partial M} \in \text{span} \left\{ \prod_{i \in T} L_i(X) \mid T \subset [d], \; |T| = d - k \right\}$$

Since there are at most $s$ product gates we obtain the claimed bound.

Applying the above lemma with Theorem 7 and Theorem 2 we obtain the following learning result:

**Theorem 9.** *Let $f : \mathbb{F}^n \to \mathbb{F}$ be computed by a depth-3 arithmetic circuit with $s$ product gates each of fan in at most $d$. Then $f$ is learnable in time polynomial in $n, 2^d$, and $s$.*

## 4.2   Discussion

The fact that the rank of $f$ was bounded by the number of product gates is unique to multilinear depth-3 circuits. For example consider the following depth-2 $\Pi\Sigma$ circuit:

$$f(z, x_1, ..., x_n) = \prod_{i=1}^{n}(z + x_i).$$

For every ordering of the variables the dimension of the span of the partial derivatives of $f$, and hence the rank of the Hankel matrix of $f$, is exponential in $n$; this follows from the observation that the coefficient of $z^d$ is the $n - d$ symmetric polynomial whose partial derivatives have dimension $2^{\Omega(n-d)}$ (see [SW01]). Thus it is no surprise that Beimel et al. [BBB+00] only considered depth-2 $\Pi\Sigma$ circuits where the product gate at the root has fan in at most $O(\log n)$; fan in larger than $O(\log n)$ would correspond to Hankel matrices of superpolynomial dimension and thus would not be learnable by multiplicity automata techniques.

On the other hand, in the full version of this paper we show how to learn $\Pi\Sigma$ circuits where the product gate has large fan in (our learning results hold only over large enough finite fields) using black box factorization techniques. To show the limits of current learning techniques we point out that the following homogeneous depth-3 arithmetic circuit

$$C' = \prod_{i=1}^{n}(z + x_i) + \prod_{i=1}^{n}(v + u_i)$$

is both irreducible and has exponentially many independent partial derivatives. As its degree is $n$ we can only learn it in time exponential in $n$. We leave open the problem of learning homogeneous depth-3 arithmetic circuits (as well as the more difficult problem of learning general depth-3 arithmetic circuits) of super logarithmic degree.

## 5   Further Results

We can also give new learning algorithms for polynomial size noncommutative formulae and read once, oblivious, algebraic branching programs using the previous techniques. In addition, we can use black box factoring techniques to learn certain depth 4 arithmetic circuits with a product gate at the root. Due to space considerations we defer these results to the full version (which can be found on the authors' web pages).

## Acknowledgments

We thank Ran Raz for many helpful discussions in all stages of this work. We also thank Eli Ben-Sasson for important conversations at an early stage of this research.

# References

[ABFR91]  J. Aspnes, R. Beigel, M. Furst, and S. Rudich. The expressive power of voting polynomials. In Baruch Awerbuch, editor, *Proceedings of the 23rd Annual ACM Symposium on the Theory of Computing*, pages 402–409, New Orleans, LS, May 1991. ACM Press.

[ALM+98]  Sanjeev Arora, Carsten Lund, Rajeev Motwani, Madhu Sudan, and Mario Szegedy. Proof verification and the hardness of approximation problems. *Journal of the ACM*, 45(3):501–555, May 1998.

[Ang87]  Dana Angluin. Queries and concept learning. *Machine Learning*, 2:319, 1987.

[BB98]  Daoud Bshouty and Nader H. Bshouty. On interpolating arithmetic read-once formulas with exponentiation. *Journal of Computer and System Sciences*, 56(1):112–124, February 1998.

[BBB+00]  Amos Beimel, Francesco Bergadano, Nader H. Bshouty, Eyal Kushilevitz, and Stefano Varricchio. Learning functions represented as multiplicity automata. *J. ACM*, 47(3):506–530, 2000.

[BBTV97]  F. Bergadano, N. H. Bshouty, C. Tamon, and S. Varricchio. On learning branching programs and small depth circuits. In Shai Ben-David, editor, *Proceedings of the 3rd European Conference on Computational Learning Theory*, volume 1208 of *LNAI*, pages 150–161, Berlin, March 17–19 1997. Springer.

[BM02]  N. Bshouty and Y. Mansour. Simple learning algorithms for decision trees and multivariate polynomials. *SICOMP: SIAM Journal on Computing*, 31, 2002.

[BTW96]  Nader H. Bshouty, Christino Tamon, and David K. Wilson. On learning width two branching programs. In *Proc. 9th Annu. Conf. on Comput. Learning Theory*, pages 224–227. ACM Press, New York, NY, 1996.

[CP71]  J. W. Carlyle and A. Paz. Realizations by stochastic finite automata. *Journal of Computer and System Sciences*, 5(1):26–40, February 1971.

[Fli74]  Michel Fliess. Matrices de Hankel. *J. Math. Pures et Appl.*, 53:197–224, 1974.

[GKS94]  Dima Grigoriev, Marek Karpinski, and Michael F. Singer. Computational complexity of sparse rational interpolation. *SIAM Journal on Computing*, 23(1):1–11, February 1994.

[GR98]  D. Grigoriev and A. A. Razborov. Exponential complexity lower bounds for depth 3 arithmetic circuits in algebras of functions over finite fields. In IEEE, editor, *39th Annual Symposium on Foundations of Computer Science: proceedings: November 8–11, 1998, Palo Alto, California*, pages 269–278, 1109 Spring Street, Suite 300, Silver Spring, MD 20910, USA, 1998. IEEE Computer Society Press.

[Has86]  Johan Hastad. Almost optimal lower bounds for small depth circuits. In *Proceedings of the Eighteenth Annual ACM Symposium on Theory of Computing*, pages 6–20, Berkeley, California, 28–30 May 1986.

[HR99]  M. Huang and T. Rao. Interpolation of sparse multivariate polynomials over large finite fields with applications. *ALGORITHMS: Journal of Algorithms*, 33, 1999.

[JKS02]  Jeffrey C. Jackson, Adam R. Klivans, and Rocco A. Servedio. Learnability beyond AC⁰. In *Proceedings of the 34th Annual ACM Symposium on Theory of Computing (STOC-02)*, pages 776–784, New York, May 19–21 2002. ACM Press.

[KS01]      Adam R. Klivans and Daniel Spielman. Randomness efficient identity test-
            ing of multivariate polynomials. In ACM, editor, *Proceedings of the 33rd
            Annual ACM Symposium on Theory of Computing: Hersonissos, Crete,
            Greece, July 6–8, 2001*, pages 216–223, New York, NY, USA, 2001. ACM
            Press.

[KT90]      Erich Kaltofen and Barry M. Trager. Computing with polynomials given
            by black boxes for their evaluations: Greatest common divisors, factor-
            ization, separation of numerators and denominators. *Journal of Symbolic
            Computation*, 9(3):300–320 (or 301–320??), March 1990.

[LMN93]     Nathan Linial, Yishay Mansour, and Noam Nisan. Constant depth circuits,
            Fourier transform and learnability. *Journal of the ACM*, 40(3):607–620,
            July 1993.

[Nis91]     Noam Nisan. Lower bounds for non-commutative computation (extended
            abstract). In *Proceedings of the Twenty Third Annual ACM Symposium on
            Theory of Computing*, pages 410–418, New Orleans, Louisiana, 6–8 May
            1991.

[NW97]      N. Nisan and A. Wigderson. Lower bounds on arithmetic circuits via
            partial derivatives. *CMPCMPL: Computational Complexity*, 6, 1997.

[OSK94]     H. Ohnishi, H. Seki, and T. Kasami. A polynomial time learning algo-
            rithm for recognizable series. *TIEICE: IEICE Transactions on Communi-
            cations/Electronics/Information and Systems*, 1994.

[SS96]      Robert E. Schapire and Linda M. Sellie. Learning sparse multivariate
            polynomials over a field with queries and counterexamples. *Journal of
            Computer and System Sciences*, 52(2):201–213, April 1996.

[Sch80]     J. T. Schwartz. Fast probabilistic algorithms for verification of polynomial
            identities. *Journal of the ACM*, 27(4):701–717, October 1980.

[STV01]     M. Sudan, L. Trevisan, and S. Vadhan. Pseudorandom generators without
            the XOR lemma. *JCSS: Journal of Computer and System Sciences*, 62,
            2001.

[SW01]      A. Shpilka and A. Wigderson. Depth-3 arithmetic circuits over fields of
            characteristic zero. *CMPCMPL: Computational Complexity*, 10, 2001.

[Zip79]     R. Zippel. Probabilistic algorithms for sparse polynomials. In *ISSAC '79:
            Proc. Int'l. Symp. on Symbolic and Algebraic Computation*, Lecture Notes
            in Computer Science, Vol. 72. Springer-Verlag, 1979.

# Using a Linear Fit
# to Determine Monotonicity Directions

Malik Magdon-Ismail[1] and Joseph Sill[2]

[1] Dept. of Computer Science, RPI, Rm 207 Lally
110 8th Street, Troy, NY 12180, USA
magdon@cs.rpi.edu
[2] Plumtree Software
500 Sansome Street, San Francisco, CA 94111, USA
joe_sill@yahoo.com

**Abstract.** Let $f$ be a function on $\mathbb{R}^d$ that is monotonic in every variable. There are $2^d$ possible assignments to the directions of monotonicity (two per variable). We provide sufficient conditions under which the optimal linear model obtained from a least squares regression on $f$ will identify the monotonicity directions correctly. We show that when the input dimensions are independent, the linear fit correctly identifies the monotonicity directions. We provide an example to illustrate that in the general case, when the input dimensions are not independent, the linear fit may not identify the directions correctly. However, when the inputs are jointly Gaussian, as is often assumed in practice, the linear fit will correctly identify the monotonicity directions, even if the input dimensions are dependent. Gaussian densities are a special case of a more general class of densities (Mahalanobis densities) for which the result holds. Our results hold when $f$ is a classification or regression function.
If a finite data set is sampled from the function, we show that if the exact linear regression would have yielded the correct monotonicity directions, then the sample regression will also do so asymptotically (in a probabilistic sense). This result holds even if the data are noisy.

## 1 Introduction and Results

A function $f : \mathbb{R}^d \mapsto \mathbb{R}$ is said to be monotonic with positive direction in dimension $i$ if

$$f(x_1, \ldots, x_{i-1}, x_i + \Delta, x_{i+1}, \ldots, x_d) \geq f(x_1, \ldots, x_{i-1}, x_i, x_{i+1}, \ldots, x_d), \quad (1)$$

for all $\Delta > 0$ and all $\mathbf{x} \in \mathbb{R}^d$. When the context is clear, we will use the notation $f_i(x_i)$ to denote the function $f$ of $x_i$ with all other variables held constant. We assume throughout that we are in $\mathbb{R}^d$. The direction of monotonicity is negative if the condition $\Delta > 0$ is replaced by $\Delta < 0$. A function is *monotonic* if it is monotonic in every dimension. If $f$ is only defined on some subset of $\mathbb{R}^d$, then the monotonicity conditions need hold only in this subset. We can represent the monotonicity directions of such a function by a $d$ dimensional

B. Schölkopf and M.K. Warmuth (Eds.): COLT/Kernel 2003, LNAI 2777, pp. 477–491, 2003.

vector $\mathbf{m}$ of $\pm 1$'s. There are $2^d$ possible choices for $\mathbf{m}$. A classification function, $f : \mathbb{R}^d \mapsto \{+1, -1\}$ is monotonic if it can be represented as $f(\mathbf{x}) = \text{sign}(g(\mathbf{x}))$, where $g$ is a monotonic function. Condition (1) can now be more compactly written as $f_i(x_i + m_i \Delta) \geq f_i(x_i)$, for all $\Delta \geq 0$.

Monotonicity is a property that might be true of a function that one might like to determine on the basis of some data. For example, the creditworthiness of an individual would be a monotonic function of variables such as income, [1]. The severity of a heart condition should be a monotonic function of cholesterol level. One might wish to learn such a function from a finite data set, for predictive purposes. In such cases, incorporating the monotonicity constraint can significantly enhance the performance of the resulting predictor, because the capacity[1] of monotonic functions can be considerably less than the capacity of an unrestricted class, which has consequences on the generalization ability of the learned function, [1–3].

Some tests for the monotonocity of a regression function have been considered in the literature, see for example [4, 5]. Algorithms for enforcing monotonicity have also been considered, for example [1, 6–12]. Most of these (especially the nonparametric regression approaches) focus on the single variable case, and it is always assumed that the monotonicity direction is known (usually positive). For the credit and heart problems above, it is reasonable to guess that the direction of the monotonicity is positive. However, it can often be the case that while monotonicity is known to hold, the direction is not known, and needs to be determined. An example is when the identity of the variables is kept secret for privacy or propriety reasons. Exactly such a problem was encountered in [1]. It can also be argued that the general multilevel classification problem admits a monotonicity constraint, even though the directions are not known *apriori* [7]. In such cases, it is not practical to enforce monotonicity in one of the $2^d$ possible directions, especially when $d$ is large. Rather, one would like to determine a specific direction in which to enforce the monotonicity.

A linear function $l$ is defined by $l(\mathbf{x}; \mathbf{w}, w_0) = \mathbf{w}^T \mathbf{x} + w_0$. Since a linear model is monotonic, one approach would be to fit a linear model to the data, and use the monotonicity direction implied by the optimal linear model as an estimate of the monotonicity direction of $f$. Such an approach was used in [1]. The purpose here is to show that such an approach is valid. Assume that the inputs are distributed according to $p_\mathbf{x}(\mathbf{x})$. The expected mean square error $\mathcal{E}$ of the linear function $l(\mathbf{x}; \mathbf{w}, w_0)$ is given by

$$\mathcal{E}(\mathbf{w}, w_0) = \int d\mathbf{x}\, p_\mathbf{x}(\mathbf{x})\, (\mathbf{w}^T \mathbf{x} + w_0 - f(\mathbf{x}))^2. \tag{2}$$

The optimal linear fit (which we will refer to more simply as the linear fit) is given by the choice of $\mathbf{w}$ and $w_0$ that minimize $\mathcal{E}(\mathbf{w}, w_0)$. We will assume throughout that the linear fit exists. Without loss of generality, we can also assume that

---

[1] The capacity of a set of functions is related to the expected number of dichotomies that the set of functions can implement on a set of points. For formal definitions of the capacity, VC dimension, etc., can be found in [3].

$E[\mathbf{x}] = \mathbf{0}$ (Lemmas 4, 5). In general we will postpone proofs to Section 2. First we state how to obtain the linear fit.

**Lemma 1 (Linear fit.).** *Let $\boldsymbol{\Sigma} = \int d\mathbf{x}\, p_{\mathbf{x}}(\mathbf{x})\, \mathbf{x}\mathbf{x}^T$ be invertible. The linear fit is then given by*

$$\mathbf{w}^l = \boldsymbol{\Sigma}^{-1} \int d\mathbf{x}\, p_{\mathbf{x}}(\mathbf{x})\, f(\mathbf{x})\mathbf{x}, \qquad w_0^l = \int d\mathbf{x}\, p_{\mathbf{x}}(\mathbf{x})\, f(\mathbf{x}) \tag{3}$$

PROOF: See any standard book on statistics for a proof, for example [13].     ∎

The main content of this paper is to determine conditions under which the linear fit in (3) will produce the correct monotonicity directions for the function $f(\mathbf{x})$. First we give the result for independent input densities.

**Theorem 1 (Independent densities).** *Let $f(\mathbf{x})$ be monotonic with monotonicity direction $\mathbf{m}$, and let the input probability density be any independent density[2]. Let $\mathbf{w}^l, w_0^l$ be given by the linear fit. Then $m_i = \mathrm{sign}(w_i^l)$ for all $i$ such that $w_i^l \neq 0$. Further, if $f_i(x_i)$ is non-constant for all $\mathbf{x}$ in a compact set of positive probability, then $w_i^l \neq 0$.*

Thus, when the inputs are independent, the linear fit deduces the correct monotonicity directions for $f$, even though $f$ may not resemble a linear function in any way. Further, note that the theorem does not differentiate between classification or regression functions, and thus the optimal linear fit for a classification problem will also yield the correct directions of monotonicity. An immediate corollary of this theorem is that when the input dimension is $d = 1$, the linear fit will always yield the correct monotonicity direction. An important special case is when the function is defined on a hyper–rectangle, and the measure is uniform on the rectangle.

Independence in the input dimensions is quite a strong restriction, and much of the benefit of the monotonicity constraint is due to the fact that the input dimensions are *not independent*. This is evident from the fact that the VC-dimencion of the class of monotonic classification functions is $\infty$, but the capacity of this class is heavily dependent on the input distribution. When the input dimensions are independent, the capacity of the class of monotonic functions grows exponentially in $N$, but when the input dimensions are dependent, the capacity can be a much more slowly growing function. Such issues are discussed in greater detail in [2]. Unfortunately, if we remove the independence requirement, then we cannot guarantee that the optimal linear fit will induce the correct monotonicity directions. The following proposition establishes this fact, and an explicit example is constructed in the proof in Section 2.

**Proposition 1.** *There exist monotonic functions $f$ and input densities $p_{\mathbf{x}}(\mathbf{x})$ for which the optimal linear fit induces the incorrect monotonicity directions.*

The essential idea is to choose a function like $f(\mathbf{x}) = x_1^3 - x_2$. By suitably choosing the correlation between $x_1$ and $x_2$, the linear regression can be "tricked" into

---

[2] i.e., $p_{\mathbf{x}}(\mathbf{x}) = p_1(x_1)p_2(x_2)\cdots p_d(x_d)$.

believing that the function is increasing in the $x_2$ dimension, because the $x_1$ behavior of the function dominates. The details are given in the proof.

We cannot remove the independence restriction in general, however, for certain special cases we can. In particular, a common assumption is that the inputs are jointly Gaussian. In this case, the linear fit will correctly induce the monotonicity directions. This result is a special case of a more general one dealing with a class of input densities which we call *Mahalanobis densities*.

**Definition 1.** *A density $p_{\mathbf{x}}(\mathbf{x})$ is a Mahalanobis density if it can be written as*

$$p_{\mathbf{x}}(\mathbf{x}) = g\left((\mathbf{x} - \boldsymbol{\mu})^T \boldsymbol{\Sigma}^{-1}(\mathbf{x} - \boldsymbol{\mu})\right).$$

*The mean vector and covariance matrix are given by $\boldsymbol{\mu}$ and $\boldsymbol{\Sigma}$ respectively. $g(x)$ is a function defined on $\mathbb{R}_+$ that is the derivative of a non-decreasing function $G(x) < 0$, i.e., $g(x) = G'(x)$. By definition, $\boldsymbol{\Sigma} = \int d\mathbf{x} \, g(\mathbf{x}^T \boldsymbol{\Sigma}^{-1}\mathbf{x})\mathbf{x}\mathbf{x}^T$. Further, we require the following constraints on $G(x)$: $\lim_{|x| \to \infty} G(x^2)x = 0$; $\int d\mathbf{x} \, G'(\mathbf{x}^T \boldsymbol{\Sigma}^{-1}\mathbf{x}^T) = 1$; $\int d\mathbf{x} \, G(\mathbf{x}^T \boldsymbol{\Sigma}^{-1}\mathbf{x}^T) = -2$. $G(x)$ is called the associated Mahalanobis distribution function.*

The first constraint on $G$ is merely technical, stating that $G$ decays "quickly" to zero[3]. The second ensures the $p_{\mathbf{x}}$ is a legitimate density, integrating to 1. The third merely enforces the consistency constraint that $\boldsymbol{\Sigma} = \int d\mathbf{x} \, g(\mathbf{x}^T \boldsymbol{\Sigma}^{-1}\mathbf{x})\mathbf{x}\mathbf{x}^T$. The Gaussian density function is defined by

$$N(\mathbf{x}; \boldsymbol{\Sigma}) = \frac{1}{(2\pi)^{d/2}|\boldsymbol{\Sigma}|^{1/2}} e^{-\frac{1}{2}\mathbf{x}^T \boldsymbol{\Sigma}^{-1}\mathbf{x}}$$

where $\boldsymbol{\Sigma}$ is the covariance matrix for $\mathbf{x}$ and the mean is zero. A Gaussian distribution with mean $\boldsymbol{\mu}$ has a density function given by $N(\mathbf{x} - \boldsymbol{\mu}; \boldsymbol{\Sigma})$. It is easily verified that every Gaussian density is a Mahalanobis density with Mahalanobis distribution function $G(x) = -2e^{-\frac{1}{2}x}/(2\pi)^{d/2}|\boldsymbol{\Sigma}|^{1/2}$. The next theorem shows that the linear fit is faithful to the monotonicity directions of $f(\mathbf{x})$ whenever the input density is a Mahalanobis density.

**Theorem 2 (Mahalanobis densities).** *Let $f(\mathbf{x})$ be monotonic with monotonicity direction $\mathbf{m}$, and let the input probability density be a Mahalanobis density. In the regression case, assume that $f$ is differentiable and does not grow too quickly, i.e.,*

$$\lim_{|x_i| \to \infty} G(\mathbf{x}^T \boldsymbol{\Sigma}^{-1}\mathbf{x}^T)f(\mathbf{x}) = 0 \qquad \forall i = 1, \dots, d. \tag{4}$$

*Let $\mathbf{w}^l$ be given by the linear fit. Then $m_i = \text{sign}(w_i^l)$ for all $i$ such that $w_i^l \neq 0$. Further, if $f_i(x_i)$ is non-constant for all $\mathbf{x}$ in some compact set of positive measure, then $w_i^l \neq 0$.*

---

[3] This is not a serious constraint if moments of $p_{\mathbf{x}}(\mathbf{x})$ are to exist. In fact, since $p_{\mathbf{x}}(\mathbf{x})$ integrates to 1, this constraint becomes vacuous when $d \geq 3$.

Since the Gaussian density is a Mahalanobis density, the theorem applies, and an immediate corollary is that the linear fit will induce the correct monotonocity directions, provided a certain technical condition regarding the growth of $f$ is met. The technical condition essentially amounts to the fact that $\log |f(\mathbf{x})| = o(\mathbf{x}^T\mathbf{x})$, which is a reasonable assumption if the moments of $f$ are to exist. Other Mahalanobis densities are given in Appendix A.

Practically, from the learning perspective, one does not have access to the target function $f(\mathbf{x})$, which is assumed to be monotonic, nor does one have access to the input distribution $p_{\mathbf{x}}(\mathbf{x})$. Rather, one has a data set, $\mathcal{D}_N = \{\mathbf{x}_i, y_i\}_{i=1}^N$. The particular way in which the data set was sampled defines the regression model. The model we will assume is the standard homoskedastic regression model. $\mathbf{x}_i$ are sampled independently from $p_{\mathbf{x}}(\mathbf{x})$ and $y_i = f(\mathbf{x}_i) + \epsilon_i$, where $\epsilon_i$ is noise. In the regression case, we assume that the $\epsilon_i$ are independent zero mean noise, with bounded fourth moments.

$$E[\epsilon_i|\mathbf{x}_i] = 0, \quad E[\epsilon_i\epsilon_j|\mathbf{x}_i, \mathbf{x}_j] = \sigma^2\delta_{ij}, \tag{5}$$

where $\delta_{ij}$ is the Kronecker delta function. Often, one assumes the noise to be Gaussian, but this is not a necessary requirement. For technical reasons, we will generally assume that all fourth moments that include powers of the noise variable, powers of $\mathbf{x}$ and powers of $f$ are bounded. For example, $E[f^2(\mathbf{x})\mathbf{x}\mathbf{x}^T] < \infty$, etc. Some of these restrictions can be dropped, however for simplicity, we maintain them. For the classification case, we assume that the noise $\epsilon_i$ is independent flip noise, i.e., independent flips of the output values from $y_i$ to $-y_i$ with some probability $p < \frac{1}{2}$.

$$\epsilon_i = \begin{cases} 0 & \text{w.p. } 1 - p, \\ -2f(\mathbf{x}_i) & \text{w.p. } p. \end{cases} \tag{6}$$

Define the augmented input vector by

$$\hat{\mathbf{x}}_i = \begin{bmatrix} 1 \\ \mathbf{x}_i \end{bmatrix},$$

and define $\mathbf{X}_N$ by

$$\mathbf{X}_N = \frac{1}{N}\sum_{i=1}^N \hat{\mathbf{x}}_i\hat{\mathbf{x}}_i^T = \frac{1}{N}\sum_{i=1}^N \begin{bmatrix} 1 & \mathbf{x}_i^T \\ \mathbf{x}_i & \mathbf{x}_i\mathbf{x}_i^T \end{bmatrix}.$$

An approximation to the linear fit is given by the Ordinary Least Squares (OLS) estimator, which minimizes the sample average of the squared error. The OLS estimator is given in the following lemma,

**Lemma 2.** *The OLS estimates* $w_0^*, \mathbf{w}^*$, *of* $w_0^l, \mathbf{w}^l$ *are given by*

$$\boldsymbol{\beta}^* = \begin{bmatrix} w_0^* \\ \mathbf{w}^* \end{bmatrix} = \frac{\mathbf{X}_N^{-1}}{N}\sum_{i=1}^N y_i\hat{\mathbf{x}}_i.$$

PROOF: See any standard book on statistics, for example [13].    ∎

Under reasonable conditions, when $N \to \infty$, we expect sample averages to converge to expectations, i.e.,

$$\frac{1}{N}\sum_i \mathbf{x}_i \to E[\mathbf{x}] = \mathbf{0}, \qquad \mathbf{X}_N^{-1} \to \begin{bmatrix} 1 & \mathbf{0}^T \\ \mathbf{0} & \Sigma^{-1} \end{bmatrix}, \qquad \sum_{i=1}^N y_i \hat{\mathbf{x}}_i \to \begin{bmatrix} E[f(\mathbf{x})] \\ E[f(\mathbf{x})\mathbf{x}] \end{bmatrix}.$$

Thus, the OLS estimates should converge to the true linear fit. The following lemma is therefore not surprising.

**Lemma 3.** *Let $w_0^l, \mathbf{w}^l$ be the linear fit to $f(\mathbf{x})$ with respect to input density $p_{\mathbf{x}}(\mathbf{x})$. Assume that all fourth order moments of $p_{\mathbf{x}}$ with respect to $\mathbf{x}$, $f(\mathbf{x})$ and $\epsilon_i$ are bounded, and that $E[\mathbf{x}] = \mathbf{0}$. Suppose that $N$ points $\{\mathbf{x}_i\}_{i=1}^N$ are sampled i.i.d. from $p_{\mathbf{x}}$ with $y_i = f(\mathbf{x}_i) + \epsilon_i$ where $\epsilon_i$ is independent noise. For regression, the noise satisfies (5), and for classification, the noise is independent flip noise (6). Let $\mathbf{w}^*$ be the OLS estimator of $\mathbf{w}^l$. Then,*

$$\mathbf{w}^* \xrightarrow{P} \begin{cases} \mathbf{w}^l & regression, \\ (1-2p)\mathbf{w}^l & classification. \end{cases}$$

We use the standard notation $\xrightarrow{P}$ to denote convergence in probability. Notice that while $\mathbf{w}^*$ converges in probability to $\mathbf{w}^l$ for regression, it *does not* for classification, unless $p = 0$. However, since $p < \frac{1}{2}$, the sign of $\mathbf{w}^*$ converges in probability to the sign of $\mathbf{w}^l$ for both cases. Thus, if the linear fit $\mathbf{w}^l$ induces the correct monotonicity directions, then so will $\mathbf{w}^*$, asymptotically as $N \to \infty$. The following theorem is therefore evident.

**Theorem 3 (OLS).** *Let $f(\mathbf{x})$ be monotonic with direction $\mathbf{m}$, and suppose that $N$ points $\{\mathbf{x}_i\}_{i=1}^N$ are sampled i.i.d. from $p_{\mathbf{x}}(\mathbf{x})$ with $y_i = f(\mathbf{x}_i) + \epsilon_i$ where $\epsilon_i$ is independent noise. For classification, $\epsilon_i$ is flip noise with probability $p < \frac{1}{2}$ (6), otherwise it is a zero mean random variable with variance $\sigma^2$ (5). Assume all fourth order moments are finite. Let $\mathbf{w}^l$ be given by the exact linear fit, and let $\mathbf{w}^*$ be the OLS estimators for $\mathbf{w}^l$. Suppose further that the linear fit induces the correct monotonicity directions, i.e., $sign(\mathbf{w}^l) = \mathbf{m}$. Then,*

$$\lim_{N\to\infty} P[sign(\mathbf{w}^*) = \mathbf{m}] = 1.$$

This theorem states that if the linear fit extracts the correct monotonicity directions, then with high probability (for large $N$), the OLS estimator will do so as well, even in the presence of noise. The theorem thus applies to independent input densities and Mahalanobis densities. This convergence is illustrated in Figure 1 where we show the dependence of $P[sign(\mathbf{w}) = \mathbf{m}]$ as a function of $N$ for different noise levels, for both classification and regression. The data were sampled uniformly from $[0,1]^2$ and $f(x,y) = e^{y-x} - \frac{1}{2}$ for regression and the sign of this function for classification.

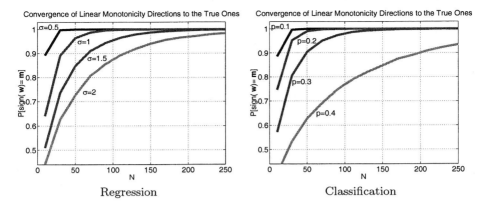

**Fig. 1.** Probability of obtaining the correct monotonocity directions vs. sample size.

## Discussion

Before a monotonicity constraint can be enforced, most algorithms will require knowledge of the direction of the monotonicity. We have shown that under quite general assumptions, the correct monotonicity directions are induced by fitting a linear model to the data, in particular, when the inputs have a Gaussian distribution. Athrough we have assumed that the function $f$ is monotonic in every dimension, this need not be so. It is possible that a function be monotonic in some dimensions and non-monotonic in others. The proofs do not require monotonicity in every dimension, thus, it is straightforward to extend the proofs to this situation. In this case, the linear model will extract the correct monotonicity directions for those dimensions in which monotonicity is known to hold. Once the direction of monotonicity has been determined, it can be incorporated into more complicated learning models such as neural networks, a task that would have been considerably tougher had the monotonicity directions not been known.

The linear model has a number of appealing features: it is easy to implement; once it has been implemented, the monotonicity directions are easy to determine; the linear model developed on a finite data set converges rapidly to the true linear fit, though we did not address this issue rigorously here – the asymptotic distribution of the OLS estimator is given in Lemma 11 which is Gaussian with a variance that is $O(\frac{1}{N})$; these convergence rates could be used to determine how much data is needed to make an accurate determiniation of the monotonicity directions. The main drawback of the linear model is that it is useful for certain classes of input densities, in particular independent densities and Gaussian densities. Enlarging this class of densities would be useful progress.

Other approaches to determining the monotonicity of a function that are as simple and efficient as fitting a linear model would also be useful. There is potential that some non-parametric techniques could prove successful in this respect, for example regression approaches that are consistent, in that they approach the true function $f$ in a distribution-independent manner. The main drawbacks of such a general approach are that the convergence will be much slower than for linear models, and the monotonicity directions of the resulting function may not be easy to determine – this function may not even be monotonic. Our motivation is that a simple, effective algorithm be used to obtain the monotonicity directions which can then be used to *constrain* more powerful models so that the more powerful model will attain a better generalization performance.

How bad can the linear model be? The example constructed in Proposition 1 required one dimension to dominate the other. In such a situation, one might suspect that this second dimension is not important in the implementation of the true monotonic fit. To be more specific, if the linear model gave monotonicity direction $\mathbf{m}' \neq \mathbf{m}$, and one obtains the best monotonic fit subject to the incorrect monotonicity constraints $\mathbf{m}'$, then how bad can the expected fit error be?

We assumed monotonicity in the variables. Perhaps $f$ is monotonic in features that are not the individual variables. Are their efficient algorithms to determine the monotonic features? We leave such questions as food for future thought.

## 2    Proofs

The following lemmas will be useful in the proof of Theorem 1. The first two state that the monotonicity directions of $f$ and the monotonicity directions that would be induced by a linear fit are unchanged under scaling and translation of the input space. The third states a useful property of monotonic functions.

**Lemma 4 (Monotonicity direction is scale and translation invariant).** *Let $f(\mathbf{x})$ be monotonic with direction $\mathbf{m}$. Let $\mathbf{A}$ be any invertible diagonal matrix and $\mathbf{b}$ be any vector. Then, $g(\mathbf{x}) = f(\mathbf{A}\mathbf{x} + \mathbf{b})$ is monotonic. Further, the monotonicity direction of $g$ is $\text{sign}(\mathbf{A})\mathbf{m}$.*

PROOF: Suppose $m_i = +1$ and let $\Delta > 0$. $\hat{g}(x_i + \Delta) = f_i(A_{ii}x_i + b_i + A_{ii}\Delta)$. If $A_{ii} > 0$, then $f_i(A_{ii}x_i + b_i + A_{ii}\Delta) \geq f_i(A_{ii}x_i + b_i) = \hat{g}(x_i)$. Similarly if $A_{ii} < 0$, then $f_i(A_{ii}x_i + b_i + A_{ii}\Delta) \leq f_i(A_{ii}x_i + b_i) = \hat{g}(x_i)$. An analogous argument with $m_i = -1$ and $\Delta < 0$ completes the proof.    ∎

**Lemma 5.** *Let $\mathbf{w}, w_0$ be the linear fit for $f(\mathbf{x})$ with respect to input density $p_{\mathbf{x}}(\mathbf{x})$. Let $\mathbf{A}$ be any invertible diagonal matrix and $\mathbf{b}$ be any vector. Let $\mathbf{x}' = \mathbf{A}\mathbf{x} + \mathbf{b}$ be a scaled and translated coordinate system, with respect to $\mathbf{x}$. In the $\mathbf{x}'$ coordinate system, let $\mathbf{v}, v_0$ be the linear fit. Then $\mathbf{w} = \mathbf{A}\mathbf{v}$.*

PROOF: $\mathbf{w}, w_0$ are minimizers of $\int d\mathbf{x}\, p_{\mathbf{x}}(\mathbf{x})\, (\mathbf{w}^T\mathbf{x} + w_0 - f(\mathbf{x}))^2$, and $\mathbf{v}, v_0$ are minimizers of $\int d\mathbf{x}'\, p_{\mathbf{x}'}(\mathbf{x}')(\mathbf{v}^T\mathbf{x}' + v_0 - f(\mathbf{A}^{-1}(\mathbf{x}' - \mathbf{b})))^2$ where $p_{\mathbf{x}'}(\mathbf{x}') = p_{\mathbf{x}}(\mathbf{A}^{-1}(\mathbf{x}' - \mathbf{b}))/|\mathbf{A}|$. Making a change of variables to $\mathbf{x} = \mathbf{A}^{-1}(\mathbf{x}' - \mathbf{b})$ we have that $\mathbf{v}, v_0$ are minimizers of $\int d\mathbf{x}\, p_{\mathbf{x}}(\mathbf{x})\, (\mathbf{v}^T\mathbf{A}\mathbf{x} + \mathbf{v}^T\mathbf{b} + v_0 - f(\mathbf{x}))^2$. Consequently, we identify $\mathbf{w}^T = \mathbf{v}^T\mathbf{A}$, and since $\mathbf{A}$ is diagonal, the lemma follows.    ∎

**Lemma 6.** *Let $f(\mathbf{x})$ be monotonic with direction $\mathbf{m}$. Then,*

$$m_i x_i f_i(x_i) \geq m_i x_i f_i(0).$$

*Further, if $f_i(x_i)$ is non-constant, then $\exists x_i^- < 0$ such that the inequality is strict $\forall x_i \leq x_i^-$, or $\exists x_i^+ \geq 0$ such that the inequality is strict $\forall x_i \geq x_i^+$.*

PROOF: Let $m_i = +1$. If $x_i \geq 0$, then $f_i(x_i) \geq f_i(0)$ therefore $x_i f_i(x_i) \geq x_i f_i(0)$. If $x_i < 0$, then $f_i(x_i) \leq f_i(0)$ therefore $x_i f_i(x_i) \geq x_i f_i(0)$. An exactly analogous argument holds with inequalities reversed when $m_i = -1$. Further, suppose that $f_i(x_i)$ is non-constant, and that $m_i = 1$. Then one of the following two cases must hold.

(i) $\exists x_i^+ > x \geq 0$ such that $f_i(x_i^+) > f_i(x) \geq f_i(0)$.
(ii) $\exists x_i^- < x \leq 0$ such that $f_i(x_i^+) < f_i(x) \leq f_i(0)$.

In both cases, it is easy to see that the inequality becomes strict in the respective ranges for $x_i$ as claimed. An analogous argument with $m_i = -1$ and the inequality signs reversed completes the proof of the lemma. ∎

*Proof of Theorem 1.* By Lemmas 4 and 5, after suitable scaling and translation, we can assume, without loss of generality, that $E[\mathbf{x}] = \mathbf{0}$ and that $E[\mathbf{x}\mathbf{x}^T] = \mathbf{I}$. Then, using Lemma 1, we have that

$$\mathbf{w} = \int_{-\infty}^{\infty} d\mathbf{x}\, p_{\mathbf{x}}(\mathbf{x})\mathbf{x}f(\mathbf{x}) \qquad\qquad w_0 = \int_{-\infty}^{\infty} d\mathbf{x}\, p_{\mathbf{x}}(\mathbf{x})\, f(\mathbf{x}). \qquad (7)$$

It remains to show that $m_i w_i \geq 0$, as follows.

$$m_i w_i \overset{(a)}{=} \int d\mathbf{x}' \int_{-\infty}^{\infty} dx_i\, p_{\mathbf{x}}(\mathbf{x})\, m_i x_i f_i(x_i),$$

$$\overset{(b)}{\geq} \int d\mathbf{x}'\, p_{\mathbf{x}'}(\mathbf{x}') \int_{-\infty}^{\infty} dx_i\, p_{x_i}(x_i) m_i x_i f_i(0),$$

$$= \int d\mathbf{x}'\, p_{\mathbf{x}'}(\mathbf{x}') m_i f_i(0) \int_{-\infty}^{\infty} dx_i\, p_{x_i}(x_i) x_i,$$

$$\overset{(c)}{=} 0,$$

where $\mathbf{x}' = (x_1, \ldots, x_{i-1}, x_{i+1}, \ldots, x_d)$. (a) follows since the measure is independent, (b) by Lemma 6 and (c) because $E[\mathbf{x}] = \mathbf{0}$, concluding the proof. Note that if $w_i = 0$, the result is ambiguous and could be an artifact of the measure. However, from Lemma 6 we see that if $f_i$ is non-constant for all $\mathbf{x}$ in a compact set of positive probability, then the $x_i^{\pm}$ can be chosen so as to specify sets of positive probability with the inequality being strict, and hence the result is that $m_i w_i > 0$, concluding the proof of the theorem. ∎

*Proof of Proposition 1.* It suffices to construct an example where the optimal linear fit gives the wrong monotonicity directions. We use a two dimensional example $f(\mathbf{x}) = x_1^3 - x_2$, and for the input density, we use a mixture of Gaussians,

$$p_{\mathbf{x}}(x_1, x_2) = \frac{1}{2}N(x_1 - a_1)N(x_2 - 1) + \frac{1}{2}N(x_1 + a_1)N(x_2 + 1).$$

where $N(x)$ is the standard Gaussian density function, $N(x) = e^{-\frac{1}{2}x^2}/\sqrt{2\pi}$. Notice that $E[\mathbf{x}] = \mathbf{0}$. Denote the covariance matrix of this distribution by $\Sigma$.

Using the moments of the Gaussian distribution, see for example [13], we find that

$$\boldsymbol{\Sigma} = \begin{bmatrix} 1+a_1^2 & a_1 \\ a_1 & 2 \end{bmatrix}, \qquad E[x_1^4] = a_1^4 + 6a_1^2 + 3, \qquad E[x_1^3 x_2] = a_1^3 + 3a_1.$$

The optimal linear fit is given by

$$\mathbf{w} = \boldsymbol{\Sigma}^{-1} E[f(\mathbf{x})\mathbf{x}] = \boldsymbol{\Sigma}^{-1} \begin{bmatrix} E[x_1^4] - E[x_1 x_2] \\ E[x_1^3 x_2] - E[x_2^2] \end{bmatrix},$$

$$= \frac{1}{2+a_1^2} \begin{bmatrix} a_1^4 + 9a_1^2 + 6 \\ -2a_1^3 - a_1^2 - 2 \end{bmatrix}.$$

The monotonicity direction of $f$ is $\mathbf{m} = [1, -1]$. The first component is always positive, which is consistent with $\mathbf{m}$, however for sufficently negative $a_1$, for example $a_1 < -2$, the second component becomes positive which is inconsistent with $\mathbf{m}$, thus concluding the proof. ∎

Let $p_{\mathbf{x}}(\mathbf{x})$ be a density that depends on $\mathbf{x}$ only through $\mathbf{x}^T \boldsymbol{\Sigma}^{-1} \mathbf{x}$, where $\boldsymbol{\Sigma}$ is the covariance matrix for $\mathbf{x}$ under density $p_{\mathbf{x}}$. Thus, $p_{\mathbf{x}}(\mathbf{x}) = g(\mathbf{x}^T \boldsymbol{\Sigma}^{-1} \mathbf{x})$ for some function $g$ defined on $\mathbb{R}_+$. By construction, $E[\mathbf{x}] = \mathbf{0}$, since $p_{\mathbf{x}}$ is a symmetric function. Let $G$ be the indefinite integral of $g$, so $G'(x) = g(x)$. Assume that $G(x) \leq 0, \forall x \geq 0$, and that $G$ is a sufficiently decreasing function such that

$$\lim_{|x| \to \infty} G(x^2)x = 0 \tag{8}$$

Note that $g$ must satisfy some constraints. It must normalize to 1, and the covariance must be $\boldsymbol{\Sigma}$. Thus,

$$\boldsymbol{\Sigma} = \int d\mathbf{x}\, g(\mathbf{x}^T \boldsymbol{\Sigma}^{-1} \mathbf{x})\mathbf{x}\mathbf{x}^T$$

$$= \boldsymbol{\Sigma} \int d\mathbf{x}\, g(\mathbf{x}^T \boldsymbol{\Sigma}^{-1} \mathbf{x})\boldsymbol{\Sigma}^{-1}\mathbf{x}\mathbf{x}^T$$

$$= \frac{1}{2}\boldsymbol{\Sigma} \int d\mathbf{x}\, \left[\nabla_{\mathbf{x}} G(\mathbf{x}^T \boldsymbol{\Sigma}^{-1} \mathbf{x})\right]\mathbf{x}^T$$

$$= \frac{1}{2}\boldsymbol{\Sigma} \int d\mathbf{x}\, \nabla_{\mathbf{x}}\left(G(\mathbf{x}^T \boldsymbol{\Sigma}^{-1} \mathbf{x})\mathbf{x}^T\right) - G(\mathbf{x}^T \boldsymbol{\Sigma}^{-1} \mathbf{x})\nabla_{\mathbf{x}}\mathbf{x}^T$$

$$= -\frac{1}{2}\boldsymbol{\Sigma} \int d\mathbf{x}\, G(\mathbf{x}^T \boldsymbol{\Sigma}^{-1} \mathbf{x})$$

where the last line follows because, using the fundamental theorem of calculus and (8), the first term is zero, and, $\nabla_{\mathbf{x}}\mathbf{x}^T = \mathbf{I}$. Thus we have the two constraints,

$$\int d\mathbf{x}\, G'(\mathbf{x}^T \boldsymbol{\Sigma}^{-1} \mathbf{x}) = 1 \qquad \int d\mathbf{x}\, G(\mathbf{x}^T \boldsymbol{\Sigma}^{-1} \mathbf{x}) = -2. \tag{9}$$

The first constraint can always be effected by multiplying $G$ by some positive scalar. The second then leads to a constraint on $G$. Using some standard multidimensional integration techniques, these two constraints can be reduced to

$$\int_0^\infty ds\, s^{d-1} G'(s^2) = \frac{\Gamma(d/2)}{2|\boldsymbol{\Sigma}|^{1/2}\pi^{d/2}} \qquad \int_0^\infty ds\, s^{d-1} G(s^2) = -\frac{\Gamma(d/2)}{|\boldsymbol{\Sigma}|^{1/2}\pi^{d/2}}, \tag{10}$$

where the Gamma function is defined by $\Gamma(x) = \int_0^\infty ds\, s^{x-1}e^{-s}$. In terms of $g(x)$, these constraints become

$$\int_0^\infty ds\, s^{d-1}g(s^2) = \frac{\Gamma(d/2)}{2|\boldsymbol{\Sigma}|^{1/2}\pi^{d/2}} \qquad \int_0^\infty ds\, s^{d+1}g(s^2) = \frac{\Gamma(d/2+1)}{|\boldsymbol{\Sigma}|^{1/2}\pi^{d/2}}. \qquad (11)$$

The classification boundary with respect to dimension $x_i$ is a function $f_i^c(\mathbf{x}')$ : $\mathbb{R}^{d-1} \mapsto \{\mathbb{R}, \infty, -\infty\}$, that determines the point at which $f_i(x_i)$ changes sign. Here $\mathbf{x}' = (x_1, \ldots, x_{i-1}, x_{i+1}, \ldots, x_d)$. Thus,

$$f_i(x_i) = \begin{cases} m_i & x_i \geq f_i^c(\mathbf{x}') \\ -m_i & x_i < f_i^c(\mathbf{x}') \end{cases}$$

An interesting fact about the classification boundary is that it is a monotonic function. In fact, its monotonicity directions $\mathbf{m}^c$ can be obtained from the original monotonicity directions by $\mathbf{m}^c = -m_i\mathbf{m}'$.

*Proof of Theorem 2.* Let $p_{\mathbf{x}}(\mathbf{x}) = g(\mathbf{x}^T\boldsymbol{\Sigma}^{-1}\mathbf{x}^T)$ satisfy the properties described above. Let $f$ be a monotonic function with monotonicity direction $\mathbf{m}$ satisfying[4]

$$\lim_{|x_i|\to\infty} G(\mathbf{x}^T\boldsymbol{\Sigma}^{-1}\mathbf{x}^T)f(\mathbf{x}) = 0 \qquad \forall i = 1, \ldots, d. \qquad (12)$$

Let's first consider the regression case, then $\mathbf{w}$ from the linear fit is given by

$$\mathbf{w} = \int d\mathbf{x}\, g(\mathbf{x}^T\boldsymbol{\Sigma}^{-1}\mathbf{x})\boldsymbol{\Sigma}^{-1}\mathbf{x}f(\mathbf{x}),$$

$$\overset{(a)}{=} \frac{1}{2}\int d\mathbf{x}\, \left[\nabla_{\mathbf{x}}G(\mathbf{x}^T\boldsymbol{\Sigma}^{-1}\mathbf{x})\right]f(\mathbf{x}),$$

$$= \frac{1}{2}\int d\mathbf{x}\, \nabla_{\mathbf{x}}\big(G(\mathbf{x}^T\boldsymbol{\Sigma}^{-1}\mathbf{x})f(\mathbf{x})\big) - G(\mathbf{x}^T\boldsymbol{\Sigma}^{-1}\mathbf{x})\nabla_{\mathbf{x}}f(\mathbf{x}),$$

$$\overset{(b)}{=} -\frac{1}{2}\int d\mathbf{x}\, G(\mathbf{x}^T\boldsymbol{\Sigma}^{-1}\mathbf{x})\nabla_{\mathbf{x}}f(\mathbf{x}),$$

$$\overset{(c)}{=} -\frac{1}{2}\left(\int d\mathbf{x}\, G(\mathbf{x}^T\boldsymbol{\Sigma}^{-1}\mathbf{x})\boldsymbol{\Lambda}(\mathbf{x})\right)\mathbf{m},$$

$$\overset{(d)}{=} \boldsymbol{\Lambda}\mathbf{m},$$

where $\boldsymbol{\Lambda}(\mathbf{x})$ and $\boldsymbol{\Lambda}$ are a non-negative diagonal matrices. (a) follows by the definition of $G$; (b) follows by using the fundamental theorem of calculus and (12); (c) follows because $f$ is monotonic with direction $\mathbf{m}$, therefore $\nabla_{\mathbf{x}}f(\mathbf{x})$ must have the same sign as $\mathbf{m}$ and hence can be written as $\boldsymbol{\Lambda}(\mathbf{x})\mathbf{m}$; (d) follows because $-G$ is non-negative. Thus all the non-zero components of $\mathbf{w}$ have the same sign as $\mathbf{m}$ and the theorem follows. Note that if for each $i$ and some $\epsilon > 0$, $|G(\mathbf{x}^T\boldsymbol{\Sigma}^{-1}\mathbf{x})\Lambda_{ii}(\mathbf{x})| \geq \epsilon$ holds in some set of measure greater than zero, then

---

[4] Note that for the classification case this restriction is vacuous as $|f(\mathbf{x})| = 1$.

every component of $\mathbf{w}$ will be non-zero. Certainly this will be the case if $f_i(x_i)$ is non-constant for all $\mathbf{x}$ in a compact set of positive probability.

For the classification case, (13) gives

$$
w_i \overset{(a)}{=} -\frac{m_i}{2} \int d\mathbf{x}' \left[ \int_{-\infty}^{f_i^c(\mathbf{x}')} \frac{\partial}{\partial x_i} G(\mathbf{x}^T \boldsymbol{\Sigma}^{-1} \mathbf{x}) - \int_{f_i^c(\mathbf{x}')}^{\infty} \frac{\partial}{\partial x_i} G(\mathbf{x}^T \boldsymbol{\Sigma}^{-1} \mathbf{x}) \right],
$$

$$
\overset{(b)}{=} -m_i \int d\mathbf{x}' \, G(\mathbf{x}^T \boldsymbol{\Sigma}^{-1} \mathbf{x})|_{x_i = f_i^c(\mathbf{x}')}
$$

$$
\overset{(c)}{=} \lambda_i m_i
$$

where $\lambda_i \geq 0$. (a) follows by definition of $f_i^c(\mathbf{x}')$; (b) follows by the fundamental theorem of calculus; and (c) follows because $G(x) < 0$. If $f_i^c(\mathbf{x}')$ is bounded on a compact positive probability set, which will happen if $f_i(x_i)$ is non-constant for all $\mathbf{x}$ in a compact set of positive probability, then $\lambda_i > 0$, and the theorem follows.  ∎

The following lemmas will prove useful in the proof of Theorem 3. Let the data be $\{\mathbf{x}_i, y_i\}_{i=1}^N$ and let $\mathbf{X}_N = \frac{1}{N} \sum_{i=1}^N \hat{\mathbf{x}}_i \hat{\mathbf{x}}_i^T$, and $y_i = f(\mathbf{x}_i) + \epsilon_i$. The noise $\epsilon_i$ satisfies (5) for regression, and (6) for classification.

**Lemma 7 (Expectation of the OLS estimator).** *Let $\mathbf{w}^*$ be the OLS estimator and $\mathbf{w}'$ be the OLS estimator had the data been noiseless. Then*

$$
E_\epsilon[\mathbf{w}^*] = \begin{cases} \mathbf{w}'(1 - 2p) & \text{classification,} \\ \mathbf{w}' & \text{regression,} \end{cases}
$$

*where the expectation is with respect to the noise.*

PROOF: By Lemma 2,

$$
\mathbf{w}^* = \mathbf{w}' + \frac{\mathbf{X}_N^{-1}}{N} \sum_{i=1}^N \epsilon_i \hat{\mathbf{x}}_i,
$$

because $\mathbf{w}' = \frac{1}{N} \mathbf{X}_N^{-1} \sum_{i=1}^N f(\mathbf{x}_i) \hat{\mathbf{x}}_i$. Taking expectations, for regression noise we have $E[\epsilon_i] = 0$, and for the flip noise we have $E[\epsilon_i] = -2pf(\mathbf{x}_i)$, from which the lemma follows.  ∎

**Lemma 8 (Covariance of the OLS estimator).** *Let $\mathbf{w}^*$ be the OLS estimator, then*

$$
Cov(\mathbf{w}^*) = \begin{cases} \dfrac{\sigma^2 \mathbf{X}_N^{-1}}{N} & \text{regression,} \\[2mm] \dfrac{4p(1 - p) \mathbf{X}_N^{-1}}{N} & \text{classification.} \end{cases}
$$

PROOF: $Cov(\mathbf{w}^*) = E[(\mathbf{w}^* - \mathbf{E}[\mathbf{w}^*])(\mathbf{w}^* - \mathbf{E}[\mathbf{w}^*])^T]$. For regression,

$$
Cov(\mathbf{w}^*) = \frac{\mathbf{X}_N^{-1}}{N} \left( \sum_{i=1}^N \sum_{j=1}^N \hat{\mathbf{x}}_i \hat{\mathbf{x}}_j^T \mathbf{E}[\epsilon_i \epsilon_j] \right) \frac{\mathbf{X}_N^{-1}}{N},
$$

$$
\overset{(a)}{=} \frac{\sigma^2 \mathbf{X}_N^{-1}}{N},
$$

where (a) follows because $\mathbf{E}\left[\epsilon_i \epsilon_j\right] = \sigma^2 \delta_{ij}$. For classification,

$$Cov(\mathbf{w}^*) = \frac{\mathbf{X}_N^{-1}}{N}\left(\sum_{i=1}^{N}\sum_{j=1}^{N}\hat{\mathbf{x}}_i\hat{\mathbf{x}}_j^T \mathbf{E}\left[(2pf(\mathbf{x}_i) + \epsilon_i)(2pf(\mathbf{x}_j) + \epsilon_j)\right]\right)\frac{\mathbf{X}_N^{-1}}{N},$$

$$\overset{(b)}{=} \frac{4p(1-p)\mathbf{X}_N^{-1}}{N},$$

where (b) follows because $f(\mathbf{x}_i)^2 = 1$ and so using (6) and the independence of the $\epsilon_i$, we get that $\mathbf{E}\left[(2pf(\mathbf{x}_i) + \epsilon_i)(2pf(\mathbf{x}_j) + \epsilon_j)\right] = 4p(1-p)\delta_{ij}$, from which the lemma follows. ∎

**Lemma 9.** *Let $Y_N$, $Z_N$ be random variables such that $Y_N \overset{P}{\longrightarrow} Z_N$, and let $g$ be a continuous function. Then $g(Y_N) \overset{P}{\longrightarrow} g(Z_n)$. Further, if $Z_N$ is the constant $z$, then $g$ need only be continuous at $z$.*

PROOF: See for example [14]. ∎

**Lemma 10.**

$$\mathbf{X}_N \overset{P}{\longrightarrow} \begin{bmatrix} 1 & \mathbf{0}^T \\ \mathbf{0} & \Sigma \end{bmatrix} \qquad \mathbf{X}_N^{-1} \overset{P}{\longrightarrow} \begin{bmatrix} 1 & \mathbf{0}^T \\ \mathbf{0} & \Sigma^{-1} \end{bmatrix}$$

PROOF: The first result follows by the weak law of large numbers because the fourth order moments are bounded. Since $\Sigma$ is invertible, the function $\mathbf{X}_N^{-1}$ is continuous at $\mathbf{X}_N = \Sigma$. Therefore, by Lemma 9, the second result also holds. ∎
    The following is a well known lemma about the distribution of the OLS estimator, essentially stating that it has an asymptotically Gaussian distribution.

**Lemma 11.** *The OLS estimator has a distribution that is asymptotically Gaussian, given by*

$$\beta^* \overset{P}{\longrightarrow} N(\bar{\beta}; Q)$$

*where $\bar{\beta}$ is the mean of the estimator, given in Lemma 7 and the covariance matrix $Q$ is given by Lemma 8. Therefore, $\beta^* \overset{P}{\longrightarrow} \bar{\beta}$. 10.*

PROOF: The fact that $\beta^* \overset{P}{\longrightarrow} N(\bar{\beta}, Q)$ is a standard result, see for example [13]. by Lemmas 8, 10, we have that $Q \overset{P}{\longrightarrow} 0$, and so $\beta^* \overset{P}{\longrightarrow} N(\bar{\beta}, 0)$, implying that $\beta^* \overset{P}{\longrightarrow} \bar{\beta}$. ∎

*Proof of Lemma 3.* Let $\hat{\Sigma} = E[\hat{\mathbf{x}}\hat{\mathbf{x}}^T]$. By Lemma 10, $X_N^{-1} \overset{P}{\longrightarrow} \hat{\Sigma}^{-1}$. By the weak law of large numbers, $\frac{1}{N}\sum_i f(x_i)\hat{\mathbf{x}}_i \overset{P}{\longrightarrow} E[f(\mathbf{x})\hat{\mathbf{x}}]$, so $\mathbf{w}' \overset{P}{\longrightarrow} \Sigma^{-1}E[f(\mathbf{x})\hat{\mathbf{x}}] = \mathbf{w}^l$. By Lemma 11, $\mathbf{w}^* \overset{P}{\longrightarrow} \mathbf{w}'$ for regression, and $\mathbf{w}^* \overset{P}{\longrightarrow} (1-2p)\mathbf{w}'$ for classification. Since $\mathbf{w}' \overset{P}{\longrightarrow} \mathbf{w}^l$, we therefore conclude that $\mathbf{w}^* \overset{P}{\longrightarrow} \mathbf{w}^l$ for regression and $\mathbf{w}^* \overset{P}{\longrightarrow} (1-2p)\mathbf{w}^l$ for classification. ∎

# A    Some Mahalanobis Densities

We list some Mahalanobis densities, and their associated Mahalanobis distribution functions.

| Name | $G(x)/g(x)$ | $p(\mathbf{x})$ |
|---|---|---|
| Gamma Density | $g(x) = Ax^k e^{-\alpha x^\rho}$ | $A(\mathbf{x}^T \mathbf{\Sigma}^{-1}\mathbf{x})^k e^{-\alpha(\mathbf{x}^T \mathbf{\Sigma}^{-1}\mathbf{x})^\rho}$ <br><br> $k > -\dfrac{d}{2},\ \rho > 0,\ \alpha = \left[\dfrac{\Gamma(\frac{d+2(k+1)}{2\rho})}{d\,\Gamma(\frac{d+2k}{2\rho})}\right]^\rho$ <br><br> $A = \dfrac{\Gamma(\frac{d}{2})\rho\alpha^{(d+2k)/2\rho}}{\Gamma(\frac{d+2k}{2\rho})|\mathbf{\Sigma}|^{1/2}\pi^{d/2}}$ |
| Gaussian | $G(x) = -\dfrac{2e^{-\frac{1}{2}x}}{(2\pi)^{d/2}|\mathbf{\Sigma}|^{1/2}}$ | $N(\mathbf{x};\mathbf{\Sigma}) = \dfrac{1}{(2\pi)^{d/2}|\mathbf{\Sigma}|^{1/2}}e^{-\frac{1}{2}\mathbf{x}^T \mathbf{\Sigma}^{-1}\mathbf{x}}$ |
| Exponential square root | $G(x) = -Ae^{-\sqrt{(d-1)x}}$ | $A\sqrt{d-1}\,\dfrac{e^{-\sqrt{(d-1)\mathbf{x}^T \mathbf{\Sigma}^{-1}\mathbf{x}}}}{2\sqrt{\mathbf{x}^T \mathbf{\Sigma}^{-1}\mathbf{x}}}$ <br> $d > 1$ <br> $A = \dfrac{(d-1)^{d/2}\Gamma(\frac{d}{2})}{\Gamma(d)|\mathbf{\Sigma}|^{1/2}\pi^{d/2}}$ |
| Polynomial ratio | $g(x) = \dfrac{Ax^p}{(1+ax)^{q+1}}$ <br> For integer $p \geq 0$: <br> $G(x) = -\dfrac{A}{a^{p+1}}\displaystyle\sum_{i=0}^{p}G_i(x),$ <br> $G_i(x) = \dfrac{p!(q-i-1)!(ax)^{p-i}}{(p-i)!q!(1+ax)^{q-i}}$ | $\dfrac{A(\mathbf{x}^T \mathbf{\Sigma}^{-1}\mathbf{x})^p}{(1+a\mathbf{x}^T \mathbf{\Sigma}^{-1}\mathbf{x})^{q+1}}$ <br> $\dfrac{d}{2}+p > 0,\ q > \dfrac{d}{2}+p$ <br> $a = \dfrac{1}{d}\left(\dfrac{\frac{d}{2}+p}{q-\frac{d}{2}-p}\right)$ <br> $A = \dfrac{a^{d/2+p}\Gamma(q+1)\Gamma(\frac{d}{2})}{|\mathbf{\Sigma}|^{1/2}\pi^{d/2}\Gamma(\frac{d}{2}+p)\Gamma(q+1-\frac{d}{2}-p)}$ |
| Linear combination | $G(x) = \displaystyle\sum_i A_i\alpha_i^{d/2}G_i(\alpha_i x)$ <br> $G_i(x)$ are Mahalanobis | $\displaystyle\sum_i A_i\alpha_i^{d/2+1}g_i(\alpha_i\mathbf{x}^T \mathbf{\Sigma}^{-1}\mathbf{x})$ <br> $\displaystyle\sum_i A_i = 1,\ \ \sum_i A_i\alpha_i = 1,\ \alpha_i > 0,\ A_i > 0$ <br> $g_i(x)$ are Mahalanobis |

# References

1. Sill, J., Abu-Mostafa, Y.S.: Monotonicity hints. In Mozer, M.C., Jordan, M.I., Petsche, T., eds.: Advances in Neural Information Processing Systems (NIPS). Volume 9., Morgan Kaufmann (1997) 634–640
2. Sill, J.: The capacity of monotonic functions. Discrete Applied Mathematics **Special Issue on VC Dimension** (1998)

3. Vapnik, V.N.: Statistical Learning Theory. Adaptive and Learning Systems for Signal Processing, Communications and Control. John Wiley & Sons, Inc., New york (1998)
4. Bowman, A.W., Jones, M.C., Gubels, I.: Testing monotonicity of regression. Journal of Computational and Graphical Statistics **7** (1998) 489–500
5. Schlee, W.: Non-parametric tests of the monotony and convexity of regression. in Non–Parametric Statistical Inference **2** (1982) 823–836
6. Ben-David, A.: Monotonicity maintenance in information theoretic machine learning algorithms. Machine Learning **19** (1995) 29–43
7. Magdon-Ismail, M., Chen, J.H.C., Abu-Mostafa, Y.S.: The multilevel classification problem and a monotonicity hint. Intelligent Data Engineering and Learning (IDEAL 02), Third International Conference (2002)
8. Mammen, E.: Estimating a smooth monotone regression function. Annals of Statistics **19** (1991) 724–740
9. Mukerjee, H.: Monotone nonparametric regression. Annals of Statistics **16** (1988) 741–750
10. Mukerjee, H., Stern, S.: Feasible nonparametric estimation of multiargument monotone functions. Journal of the American Statistical Association **89** (1994) 77–80
11. Potharst, R., Feelders, A.J.: Classification trees for problems with monotonicity constraints. SIGKDD Explorations **4** (2002) 1–10
12. Sill, J.: Monotonic networks. In: Advances in Neural Information Processing Systems (NIPS). Volume 10. (1998)
13. DeGroot, M.H.: Probability and Statistics. Addison–Wesley, Reading, Massachusetts (1989)
14. Billingsley, P.: Probability and Measure. Wiley Series in Probability and Mathematical Statistics. Wiley (1986)

# Generalization Bounds for Voting Classifiers Based on Sparsity and Clustering

Vladimir Koltchinskii[*], Dmitry Panchenko, and Savina Andonova

**Abstract.** We prove new margin type bounds on the generalization error of voting classifiers that take into account the sparsity of weights and certain measures of clustering of weak classifiers in the convex combination. We also present experimental results to illustrate the behavior of the parameters of interest for several data sets.

## 1 Introduction

We introduce in this paper several measures of complexity of functions from the convex hull of a given base class. These complexity measures take into account the "sparsity" of the weights as well as the "clustering" properties of the base functions and we use them to prove some new margin type bounds on generalization performance of voting classification algorithms. This continues the line of research started in [12] and further pursued in [6–9, 11].

Let $\mathcal{X}$ be a measurable space (space of instances) and $\mathcal{Y} = \{-1, +1\}$ be the set of labels. Let $\mathbb{P}$ be a probability measure on $\mathcal{X} \times \mathcal{Y}$, that describes the underlying distribution of instances and their labels. We do not assume that the label $y$ is a deterministic function of $x$, in general it can also be random, which means that the probability $\mathbb{P}(y = 1|x)$ may be different from 0 or 1. Let $\mathcal{H}$ be a class of measurable functions $h : \mathcal{X} \to [-1, 1]$. Denote by $\mathcal{P}(\mathcal{H})$ the set of all discrete distributions on $\mathcal{H}$ and let $\mathcal{F}$ be the convex hull of $\mathcal{H}$,

$$\mathcal{F} \text{conv}(\mathcal{H}) := \left\{ \int h(\cdot)\lambda(dh) : \lambda \in \mathcal{P}(\mathcal{H}) \right\}.$$

For $f \in \mathcal{F}$, we assume that $\text{sign}(f(x))$ is used to classify $x \in \mathcal{X}$ ($\text{sign}(f(x)) = 0$ meaning that no decision is made). The generalization error of $f$ is defined as

$$\mathbb{P}(\text{sign}(f(x)) \neq y)\mathbb{P}(yf(x) \leq 0). \tag{1.1}$$

Most often, the distribution $\mathbb{P}$ is unknown and the training data $(X_1, Y_1), \ldots, (X_n, Y_n)$ consisting of $n$ independent training examples with common distribution $\mathbb{P}$ allows us to estimate $\mathbb{P}$ by the empirical measure $\mathbb{P}_n$ :

$$\mathbb{P}_n(A) := n^{-1} \sum_{i=1}^{n} I_A(X_i, Y_i), \ A \subset \mathcal{X} \times \mathcal{Y}.$$

[*] Partially supported by NSA Grant MDA904-02-1-0075

B. Schölkopf and M.K. Warmuth (Eds.): COLT/Kernel 2003, LNAI 2777, pp. 492–505, 2003.

Let us describe now the typical complexity assumptions on the class of weak classifiers $\mathcal{H}$. Given a probability distribution $Q$ on $\mathcal{X}$, a class $\mathcal{H}$ of measurable functions on $\mathcal{X}$ and $f, g \in \mathcal{H}$ we denote

$$d_{Q,2}(f,g) = (Q(f-g)^2)^{1/2}$$

the $L_2$−distance on $\mathcal{H}$ with respect to $Q$. Given $u > 0$ we say that a subset $\mathcal{H}' \subset \mathcal{H}$ is $u$−separated if for any $f \neq g \in \mathcal{H}'$ we have $d_{Q,2}(f,g) > u$. Let the packing number $D(\mathcal{H}, u, d_{Q,2})$ be the maximal cardinality of a $u$−separated set.

We will assume that the family of weak classifiers $\mathcal{H}$ satisfies the following condition

$$D(\mathcal{H}; u) := \sup_{Q} D(\mathcal{H}, u, L_2(Q)) \leq K(V) u^{-V}, \ u > 0, \tag{1.2}$$

for some $V > 0$ and $K > 0$ depending only on $V$, and where the supremum is taken over all discrete probability measures. For example, if $\mathcal{H}$ is a VC-subgraph class with VC dimension $d$, then the result of Haussler [5] implies that (1.2) holds with $V = 2d$, namely,

$$D(\mathcal{H}, u) \leq e(V+1) \left( \frac{2e}{u^2} \right)^d. \tag{1.3}$$

In a well known paper [12], it was proved that if $\mathcal{H} := \{2I_C - 1 : C \in \mathcal{C}\}$, where $\mathcal{C}$ is a VC class with VC−dimension $V$ (the condition (1.2) is satisfied in this case), then for all $t > 0$ with probability at least $1 - e^{-t}$ $\forall f \in \mathrm{conv}(\mathcal{H})$ :

$$\mathbb{P}(yf(x) \leq 0) \leq \inf_{\delta \in (0,1]} \left( \mathbb{P}_n(yf(x) \leq \delta) + K\left( \left( \frac{V \log^2(n/V)}{n\delta^2} \right)^{1/2} + \left( \frac{t}{n} \right)^{1/2} \right) \right), \tag{1.4}$$

where $K$ is a numerical constant. In [7–9], the dependence of this type of bounds on the margin parameter $\delta$ and on the sample size $n$ was explored further. In particular, it was proved that if for some $\alpha \in (0,2)$

$$\log D(\mathcal{G}, u, L_2(P_n)) \leq K u^{-\alpha}, \ u > 0,$$

where $P_n$ is the empirical distribution based on the sample $(X_1, \ldots, X_n)$, then for all $t > 0$ with probability at least $1 - e^{-t}$ $\forall f \in \mathcal{G}$ :

$$\mathbb{P}(yf(x) \leq 0) \leq \inf_{\delta \in (0,1]} \left( \mathbb{P}_n(yf(x) \leq \delta) + K\left( \frac{1}{n^{2/(2+\alpha)} \delta^{2\alpha/(2+\alpha)}} + \frac{t}{n} \right) \right). \tag{1.5}$$

This result applies, in particular, to $\mathcal{G} := \mathrm{conv}(\mathcal{H})$ with $\mathcal{H}$ satisfying the condition (1.2) and with $\alpha = \frac{2V}{2+V}$. It also shows that if a classifier $f$ has been picked from a class $\mathcal{G}$ that is smaller than the whole convex hull $\mathrm{conv}(\mathcal{H})$, then the margin type bound on the generalization error of such a classifier can be drastically better than (1.4). However, to take advantage of this improvement one has to know the class $\mathcal{G}$ (to which the classifier belongs and which is smaller than the whole convex hull) *prior* to the run of the algorithm that produces the classifier.

For most of the voting algorithms used in classification, this information is not available and this leads to the question whether reasonable margin type bounds on generalization error can be expressed in terms of *individual* complexities of classifiers $f$ from the convex hull rather than in terms of global complexity measures (such as metric entropy, Rademacher complexities, etc.) of the whole class or even localized versions of these complexities (where localization means restriction of the complexity to small enough balls with respect to the empirical distances). One individual complexity measure (based on the notion of approximate $\Delta$–dimension of $f \in \text{conv}(\mathcal{H})$) was suggested and explored in [9] and some further measures in [11]. Our goal in this paper is to develop this technique further by looking not only at the measures based on "sparsity" of the weights involved in the convex combination but also at the "clustering" properties of the base classifiers.

## 2    Main Results

We will describe our first bound on the generalization error of voting classifiers where we take into account the sparsity of weights in the convex combination. Given $\lambda \in \mathcal{P}(\mathcal{H})$ and $f(x) = \int h(x)\lambda(dh)$, we can also represent $f$ as $f = \sum_{k=1}^{T} \lambda_k h_k$ with $T \leq \infty$ (since $\lambda$ is a discrete probability measure). Without loss of generality let us assume that $\lambda_1 \geq \lambda_2 \geq \ldots \geq 0$. We define $\gamma_d(f) = \sum_{k=d+1}^{T} \lambda_k$ and for $\delta > 0$ we define the *effective dimension* function by

$$e_n(f, \delta) = \min_{0 \leq d \leq T} \left( d + \frac{2\gamma_d^2(f)}{\delta^2} \log n \right). \tag{2.1}$$

This name is motivated by the fact that (as will become clear from the proof of Theorem 1 below) it can be interpreted as a dimension of a subset of the convex hull $\text{conv}(\mathcal{H})$ that contains a "good" approximation of $f$.

We state our first result.

**Theorem 1.** *(Sparsity bound) If (1.2) holds then there exists an absolute constant $K > 0$ such that for all $t > 0$ with probability at least $1 - e^{-t}$ for all $\lambda \in \mathcal{P}(\mathcal{H})$ and $f(x) = \int h(x)\lambda(dh)$,*

$$\mathbb{P}(yf(x) \leq 0) \leq \inf_{\delta \in (0,1]} \left( U^{1/2} + (\mathbb{P}_n(yf(x) \leq \delta) + U)^{1/2} \right)^2,$$

*where*

$$U = K\left( \frac{V e_n(f, \delta)}{n} \log \frac{n}{\delta} + \frac{t}{n} \right).$$

It follows from the bound of the theorem that for all $\varepsilon > 0$

$$\mathbb{P}(yf(x) \leq 0) \leq \inf_{\delta \in (0,1]} \left( (1+\varepsilon)\mathbb{P}_n(yf(x) \leq \delta) + \left(2 + \frac{1}{\varepsilon}\right) U \right), \tag{2.2}$$

which is a more explicit version of the result. Some results of similar nature were also proved in [9], but the method here is different and, in some sense, simpler.

The major drawback of this type of bounds is that they take into account only the size of the coefficients of the convex combination, but not the "closeness" of the base functions involved in it. Such a "closeness" (reflected, for instance, in the fact that the base functions classify most of the examples the same way or, more generally, can be divided into several groups with the functions within each group classifying similarly) could possibly lead to further complexity reduction. We give below two bounds on the generalization error of voting classifiers that take into account the clustering of weak classifiers in a convex combination. Given $\lambda \in \mathcal{P}(\mathcal{H})$, consider

$$f(x) = \int h(x)\lambda(dh) = \sum_{k=1}^{T} \lambda_k h_k(x).$$

We ask the following question - what if the functions $h_1, \ldots, h_T$ are, in some sense, close to each other? For example, $n^{-1}\sum_{k=1}^{n}(h_i(X_k) - h_j(X_k))^2$ is small for all couples $i \neq j$. In that case, the convex combination can be approximated "well" by one function from $\mathcal{H}$. Or, more generally, one can imagine the situation when there are several clusters of functions among $h_1, \ldots, h_T$ such that within each cluster all functions are close to each other. This information should be reflected in the generalization error of classifier $f$, since it can be approximated by a classifier from a small subset of $\mathcal{F}$. Below we prove two results in this direction. We will start by describing the result where we consider $h_1, \ldots, h_T$ as one (hopefully "small") cluster, and then we will naturally generalize it to any number of clusters.

We define a pointwise variance of $h$ with respect to the distribution $\lambda$ by

$$\sigma_\lambda^2(x) \int \left( h(x) - \int h(x)\lambda(dh) \right)^2 \lambda(dh). \tag{2.3}$$

Clearly, $\sigma_\lambda^2(x) = 0$ if and only if $h_1(x) = h_2(x)$ for all $h_1, h_2 \in \mathcal{H}$.
The following theorem holds.

**Theorem 2.** *If (1.2) holds then there exists an absolute constant $K > 0$ such that for all $t > 0$ with probability at least $1 - e^{-t}$ for all $\lambda \in \mathcal{P}(\mathcal{H})$ and $f(x) = \int h(x)\lambda(dh)$,*

$$\mathbb{P}(yf(x) \leq 0) \leq K \inf_{0 < \delta \leq \gamma \leq 1} \left( \mathbb{P}_n(yf(x) \leq \delta) + \mathbb{P}_n(\sigma_\lambda^2(x) \geq \gamma) + \frac{V\gamma}{n\delta^2} \log^2 \frac{n}{\delta} + \frac{t}{n} \right).$$

**Remark.** The constant $K$ in the bound of this Theorem can, in principle, be redistributed among terms similarly to (2.2), by writing a factor $1 + 1/\varepsilon$ in front of $\mathbb{P}_n(yf(x) \leq \delta) + \mathbb{P}_n(\sigma_\lambda^2(x) \geq \gamma)$ and a factor proportional to $1/\varepsilon$ in front of other terms. Similar comment applies to Theorem 3 below.

This result is, probably, of limited interest since there is no reason to expect that the "global variances" of convex combinations output by popular learning algorithms are necessarily small [however, it might be of interest to design classification algorithms of boosting type that involve a complexity penalization suggested by the above bound; for instance, the algorithm might be designed to optimize the expression $\mathbb{P}_n\ell(yf(x)) + \mathbb{P}_n\phi(\sigma_\lambda(x))$ for properly chosen smooth cost functions $\ell, \phi$]. It is much more likely that it would be possible to split a convex combination into several clusters, each having a small variance. This is reflected in the following definition.

Given $m \geq 1$ and $\lambda \in \mathcal{P}(\mathcal{H})$, define a set

$$\mathcal{C}^m(\lambda) = \{(\alpha_1, \ldots, \alpha_m, \lambda^1, \ldots, \lambda^m) \ : \ \lambda^k \in \mathcal{P}(\mathcal{H}), \ \alpha_k \geq 0, \ \sum_{k=1}^m \alpha_k \lambda^k = \lambda\}.$$

For an element $c \in \mathcal{C}^m(\lambda)$, we define a weighted variance over clusters by

$$\sigma^2(c; x) = \sum_{k=1}^m \alpha_k^2 \sigma_{\lambda^k}^2(x), \qquad (2.4)$$

where $\sigma_{\lambda^k}^2(x)$ are defined in (2.3). If indeed there are $m$ small clusters among functions $h_1, \ldots, h_T$, then one should be able to choose element $c \in \mathcal{C}^m(\lambda)$ so that $\sigma^2(c; x)$ will be small on the majority of data points $X_1, \ldots, X_n$.

The following theorem holds.

**Theorem 3.** *If (1.2) holds then there exists an absolute constant $K > 0$ such that for all $t > 0$ with probability at least $1 - e^{-t}$ for all $\lambda \in \mathcal{P}(\mathcal{H})$ and $f(x) = \int h(x)\lambda(dh)$,*

$$\mathbb{P}(yf(x) \leq 0)$$

$$\leq K \inf_{m \geq 1} \inf_{c \in \mathcal{C}^m(\lambda)} \inf_{0 < \delta \leq \gamma \leq 1} \left(\mathbb{P}_n(yf(x) \leq \delta) + \mathbb{P}_n(\sigma^2(c; x) \geq \gamma) + \frac{Vm\gamma}{n\delta^2} \log^2 \frac{n}{\delta} + \frac{t}{n}\right).$$

If we define the number of $(\gamma, \delta)$-clusters of $\lambda$ as the smallest $m$ for which there exists $c \in \mathcal{C}_\lambda$ such that

$$\mathbb{P}_n(\sigma^2(c; x) \geq \gamma) \leq \frac{Vm\gamma}{n\delta^2} \log^2 \frac{n}{\delta}$$

and denote this number by $\hat{m}_\lambda(n, \gamma, \delta)$, then the bound implies that for all $\lambda \in \mathcal{P}(\mathcal{H})$

$$\mathbb{P}(yf(x) \leq 0) \leq K \inf_{0 < \delta \leq \gamma} \left(\mathbb{P}_n(yf(x) \leq \delta) + \frac{V\hat{m}_\lambda(n, \gamma, \delta)\gamma}{n\delta^2} \log^2 \frac{n}{\delta} + \frac{t}{n}\right).$$

The choice of $\gamma = \delta$ gives an upper bound with the error term (added to the empirical margin distribution) of the order

$$\frac{\hat{m}_\lambda(n, \delta, \delta)}{n\delta} \log^2 \frac{n}{\delta},$$

which significantly improves earlier bounds provided that we are lucky to have a small number of clusters $\hat{m}_\lambda(n, \delta, \delta)$ in the convex combination.

## 3  Proofs

We give a detailed proof of Theorem 1, and only sketches of the proofs of Theorems 2 and 3. Let us introduce the notations

$$\mathbb{P}g = \int g(x, y) d\mathbb{P}(x, y), \quad \mathbb{P}_n g = n^{-1} \sum_{i=1}^{n} g(X_i, Y_i).$$

Given integer $d \geq 1$, denote

$$\mathcal{F}_d = \mathrm{conv}_d(\mathcal{H}) \Big\{ \sum_{i=1}^{d} \lambda_i h_i : \sum_{i=1}^{d} \lambda_i \leq 1, \lambda_i \geq 0, h_i \in \mathcal{H} \Big\}.$$

Let $\Phi = \{ \varphi_\delta : \mathbb{R} \to [0, 1] : \delta \in \Delta \subset \mathbb{R}_+ \}$ be a countable family of Lipschitz functions such that Lipschitz norm of $\varphi_\delta$ is equal to $\delta^{-1}$ and $\sum_{\delta \in \Delta} \delta < \infty$. One can use a specific choice of $\Delta = \{ 2^{-k} : k \geq 1 \}$. Denote

$$\phi(a, b) = \frac{(a - b)^2}{a} I(a \geq b).$$

The following theorem holds.

**Theorem 4.** *If (1.2) holds then there exists $K > 0$ such that for all $t > 0$ with probability at least $1 - e^{-t}$ we have for all $d \geq 1, f \in \mathcal{F}_d$ and $\delta \in \Delta$,*

$$\phi \Big( \mathbb{P}\varphi_\delta(yf(x)), \mathbb{P}_n\varphi_\delta(yf(x)) \Big) \leq K \Big( \frac{dV}{n} \log \frac{n}{\delta} + \frac{t}{n} \Big). \tag{3.1}$$

**Proof.** See [11].  □

We make a specific choice of functions $\varphi_\delta$. For each $\delta \in \Delta$ we set $\varphi_\delta$ to be $\varphi_\delta(s) = 1$ for $s \leq \delta$, $\varphi_\delta(s) = 0$ for $s \geq 2\delta$ and linear on $[\delta, 2\delta]$.

**Proof of Theorem 1.** Let us fix $f = \sum_{k=1}^{T} \lambda_k h_k \in \mathcal{F}_T$. For a fixed $0 \leq d \leq T$, let us represent $f$ as

$$f = \sum_{k=1}^{d} \lambda_k h_k + \gamma_d(f) \sum_{k=d+1}^{T} \lambda_k' h_k,$$

where $\gamma_d(f) = \sum_{k=d+1}^{T} \lambda_k$, and $\lambda_k' = \lambda_k / \gamma_d(f)$.

Given $N \geq 1$ we generate an i.i.d. sequence of functions $\xi_1, \ldots, \xi_N$ according to the distribution $\mathbb{P}_\xi(\xi_i = h_k) = \lambda_k'$ for $k = d + 1, \ldots, T$ and independent of $\{(X_k, Y_k)\}$. Clearly, $\mathbb{E}_\xi \xi_i(x) = \sum_{k=d+1}^{T} \lambda_k' h_k(x)$. Consider a function

$$g(x) = \sum_{k=1}^{d} \lambda_k h_k(x) + \gamma_d(f) \frac{1}{N} \sum_{k=1}^{N} \xi_k(x),$$

which plays the role of a random approximation of $f$ in the following sense. We can write,

$$\mathbb{P}(yf(x) \le 0) = \mathbb{E}_\xi \mathbb{P}(yf(x) \le 0, yg(x) < \delta) + \mathbb{E}_\xi \mathbb{P}(yf(x) \le 0, yg(x) \ge \delta)$$
$$\le \mathbb{E}_\xi \mathbb{P}\varphi_\delta(yg(x)) + \mathbb{E}\mathbb{P}_\xi(yg(x) \ge \delta, \mathbb{E}_\xi yg(x) \le 0). \tag{3.2}$$

In the last term for a fixed $(x, y) \in \mathcal{X} \times \mathcal{Y}$, we have

$$\mathbb{P}_\xi(yg(x) \ge \delta, \mathbb{E}_\xi yg(x) \le 0) \le \mathbb{P}_\xi(yg(x) - \mathbb{E}_\xi yg(x) \ge \delta)$$
$$\mathbb{P}_\xi\Big(\sum_{i=1}^{N}(y\xi_i(x) - y\mathbb{E}_\xi\xi_i(x)) \ge N\delta/\gamma_d(f)\Big) \le \exp\big(-N\delta^2/2\gamma_d^2(f)\big).$$

where in the last step we used Hoeffding's inequality. Hence,

$$\mathbb{P}(yf(x) \le 0) - e^{-N\delta^2/2\gamma_d^2(f)} \le \mathbb{E}_\xi \mathbb{P}\varphi_\delta(yg(x)). \tag{3.3}$$

Similarly, one can write

$$\mathbb{E}_\xi \mathbb{P}_n \varphi_\delta(yg(x)) \le \mathbb{E}_\xi \mathbb{P}_n(yg(x) \le 2\delta) \le \mathbb{P}_n(yf(x) \le 3\delta)$$
$$+\mathbb{E}_\xi \mathbb{P}_n(yg(x) \le 2\delta, yf(x) \ge 3\delta) \le \mathbb{P}_n(yf(x) \le 3\delta) + e^{-N\delta^2/2\gamma_d^2(f)}. \tag{3.4}$$

Clearly, for any random realization of the sequence $\xi_1, \ldots, \xi_N$, a random function $g$ belongs to a class $\mathcal{F}_{d+N}$. Convexity of the function $\phi(a, b)$ and Theorem 4 imply that for any $t > 0$ with probability at least $1 - e^{-t}$ for all $\delta \in \Delta$ and all $f \in \mathcal{F}$

$$\phi\Big(\mathbb{E}_\xi \mathbb{P}\varphi_\delta(yg(x)), \mathbb{E}_\xi \mathbb{P}_n\varphi_\delta(yg(x))\Big) \le \mathbb{E}_\xi \phi\Big(\mathbb{P}\varphi_\delta(yg(x)), \mathbb{P}_n\varphi_\delta(yg(x))\Big)$$
$$\le K\Big(\frac{V(d+N)}{n}\log\frac{n}{\delta} + \frac{t}{n}\Big).$$

The fact that $\phi(a, b)$ is decreasing in $b$ and increasing in $a$ combined with (3.3) and (3.4) implies that

$$\phi\Big(\mathbb{P}(yf(x) \le 0) - e^{-N\delta^2/2\gamma_d^2(f)}, \mathbb{P}_n(yf(x) \le 3\delta) + e^{-N\delta^2/2\gamma_d^2(f)}\Big)$$
$$\le K\Big(\frac{V(d+N)}{n}\log\frac{n}{\delta} + \frac{t}{n}\Big).$$

Setting $N = 2(\gamma_d^2(f)/\delta^2)\log n$, we get

$$\phi\Big(\mathbb{P}(yf(x) \le 0) - 1/n, \mathbb{P}_n(yf(x) \le 3\delta) + 1/n\Big) \le K\Big(\frac{Ve_n(f, \delta, d)}{n}\log\frac{n}{\delta} + \frac{t}{n}\Big),$$

where $e_n(f, \delta, d) = d + 2(\gamma_d^2(f)/\delta^2)\log n$. Solving the last inequality for $\mathbb{P}(yf(x) \le 0)$ and changing variable $3\delta \to \delta$ gives the bound (that holds with probability at least $1 - e^{-t}$)

$$\mathbb{P}(yf(x) \le 0) \le \Big(W^{1/2} + (\mathbb{P}_n(yf(x) \le \delta) + W)^{1/2}\Big)^2, \tag{3.5}$$

where

$$W = W(f, n, d, \delta, t) := K\left(\frac{Ve_n(f, \delta, d)}{n}\log\frac{n}{\delta} + \frac{t}{n}\right).$$

It remains to make the bound uniform over $d$ and $\delta$, which is done using standard union bound techniques. More specifically, replace $t$ in the above bound by $t'(d, \delta) = t + 2\log(1/\delta) + 2\log d + c$, where $\delta \in \{2^{-k} : k \geq 1\}$ and

$$c := 2\log\left(\sum_{k=1}^{\infty} k^{-2}\right).$$

Then the union bound can be used to show that (3.5) (with $t$ replaced by $t'(d, \delta)$) holds for all $d$ and all $\delta \in \{2^{-k} : k \geq 1\}$ simultaneously with probability at least $1 - p$, where

$$p \leq e^{-t-c}\sum_{k=1,d=1}^{\infty} e^{-2\log k - 2\log d}e^{-t-c}\left(\sum_{k=1}^{\infty} k^{-2}\right)^2 = e^{-t}.$$

and, hence, we also have with probability at least $1 - e^{-t}$

$$\mathbb{P}(yf(x) \leq 0) \leq \inf_{\delta \in \{2^{-k}:k\geq 1\}} \inf_d \left(W^{1/2}(f, n, d, \delta, t'(d, \delta))\right.$$

$$\left. + (\mathbb{P}_n(yf(x) \leq \delta) + W(f, n, d, \delta, t'(d, \delta)))^{1/2}\right)^2.$$

Taking into account the monotonicity of the function $e_n(f, \delta, d)$ with respect to $\delta$ (and increasing the value of the constant $K$) it is now easy to extend the infimum over $\delta$ to all $\delta \in (0, 1]$. Increasing the value of $K$ further allows one to rewrite the bound as

$$\mathbb{P}(yf(x) \leq 0) \leq \inf_{\delta \in (0,1]} \left(U^{1/2} + (\mathbb{P}_n(yf(x) \leq \delta) + U)^{1/2}\right)^2$$

with $U$ defined in the formulation of the theorem, which completes the proof. $\square$

**Sketch of the Proof of Theorem 2.** First of all, given $f(x) = \sum_{k=1}^{T} \lambda_k h_k(x)$, and given $N \geq 1$, we generate an i.i.d. sequence of functions $\xi_1, \ldots, \xi_N$ independently of $\{(X_i, Y_i)\}$ and according to the distribution $\mathbb{P}_\xi(\xi_i = h_k) = \lambda_k$, for $k = 1, \ldots, T$, and consider a function

$$g = \frac{1}{N}\sum_{i=1}^{N} \xi_i,$$

which plays the role of random approximation of $f$.

The main difference from the proof of Theorem 1 is that in equation (3.2) we also introduce the condition on the variance $\sigma_\lambda^2(x)$. Namely, one can write

$$\mathbb{P}(yf(x) \leq 0) \leq \mathbb{E}_\xi\mathbb{P}(yg(x) \leq \delta) + \mathbb{P}(\sigma_\lambda^2(x) \geq \gamma)$$
$$+ \mathbb{E}\mathbb{P}_\xi(yg(x) \geq \delta, yf(x) \leq 0, \sigma_\lambda^2(x) \leq \gamma). \tag{3.6}$$

To bound the last term we note that we explicitly introduced the condition on the variance of $\xi_i$'s, since for a fixed $x \in \mathcal{X}$,

$$\text{Var}_\xi(\xi_i(x)) = \sigma_\lambda^2(x).$$

Therefore, instead of using Hoeffding's inequality it is advantageous to use Bernstein's inequality, since it takes into account the information about the variance, namely,

$$\mathbb{P}_\xi(yg(x) \geq \delta, yf(x) \leq 0, \sigma^2(f(x)) \leq \gamma)$$

$$\leq \mathbb{P}_\xi(\sum_{i=1}^{T}(y\xi_i(x) - y\mathbb{E}_\xi\xi_i(x)) \geq N\delta | \text{Var}_\xi(\xi_1(x)) \leq \gamma)$$

$$\leq 2\exp\left(-\frac{1}{4}\min\left(\frac{N\delta^2}{\gamma}, N\delta\right)\right)2\exp\left(-\frac{1}{4}\frac{N\delta^2}{\gamma}\right),$$

since we assume that $\gamma \geq \delta$. We make this term negligible by taking $N = K(\gamma/\delta^2)\log n$, which (almost) explains the appearance of this factor in the statement of Theorem 2. The rest of the proof is quite similar to Theorem 1. The main technical difficulty left is to relate the term $\mathbb{P}(\sigma_\lambda^2(x) \geq \gamma)$ to the term $\mathbb{P}_n(\sigma_\lambda^2(x) \geq \gamma/2)$ that will appear in the analog of (3.4). This is done by another random approximation and a more subtle application of Bernstein's inequality. We leave the details for the extended version of the paper. □

**Sketch of the Proof of Theorem 3.** The idea of the proof of Theorem 3 is similar to that of Theorem 2.

Consider $\lambda \in \mathcal{P}(\mathcal{H})$ and $f(x) = \int h(x)\lambda(dh)$. Consider an element $c \in \mathcal{C}^m(\lambda)$, i.e. $c = (\alpha_1, \ldots, \alpha_m, \lambda^1, \ldots, \lambda^m)$, such that $\lambda = \sum_{i=1}^{m}\alpha^j\lambda^j$, and $\lambda^j \in \mathcal{P}(\mathcal{H})$. We interpreted $c$ as a decomposition of $\lambda$ into $m$ clusters, or in other words - the decomposition of the set $\{h_i\}$ into $m$ clusters. This time we will generate functions from each cluster independently from each other (and, as before, independently of the data) and take their weighted sum to approximate $f(x)$. Given $N \geq 1$, let us generate $\xi_k^j(x), k \leq N, j \leq m$, where for each $j \leq m$, $\xi_k^j$'s have the distribution $\mathbb{P}_\xi(\xi_k^j = h_i) = \lambda_i^j, i \leq T$. Consider a function

$$g(x) = \frac{1}{N}\sum_{j=1}^{m}\alpha_j\sum_{k=1}^{N}\xi_k^j(x).$$

For a fixed $x \in \mathcal{X}$, the variance of $g$ with respect to the distribution $\mathbb{P}_\xi$ is

$$\text{Var}_\xi(g(x)) = N^{-1}\sum_{j=1}^{m}\alpha_j^2\text{Var}_\xi(\xi_1^j(x)) = N^{-1}\sum_{j=1}^{m}\alpha_j^2\sigma_{\lambda^j}^2(x) = N^{-1}\sigma^2(c; x).$$

Instead of (3.6), we can write,

$$\mathbb{P}(yf(x) \leq 0) \leq \mathbb{E}_\xi\mathbb{P}(yg(x) \leq \delta) + \mathbb{P}(\sigma^2(c; x) \geq \gamma)$$
$$+ \mathbb{E}\mathbb{P}_\xi(yg(x) \geq \delta, yf(x) \leq 0, \sigma^2(c; x) \leq \gamma). \tag{3.7}$$

Similarly, taking $N = 4(\gamma/\delta^2)\log n$ will make the last term negligible. With this choice of $N$ the function $g(x)$ has at most $mN = 4m(\gamma/\delta^2)\log n$ terms in the convex combination and, thus, belongs to $\mathrm{conv}_{mN}(\mathcal{H})$. Via application of Theorem 4 this explains the appearance of this factor in the bound of Theorem 3. As in the case of Theorem 2, we omit the details of the proof.    □

## 4    Experiments with Learning Algorithms

We applied two voting algorithms, AdaBoost ([12]) and Arc-Gv ([2]), to four data sets and compared the behavior of several parameters of interest, such as effective dimension function, distribution of margin and distribution of weighted variance for different number of clusters. We also examined the behavior of the bound of Theorem 3 in order to see whether it could be used as a selection criterion for the predictor with better generalization. In the experiments we ignore the constants in the bounds of our main theorems and explore the following bound:

$$\inf_{m\geq 1}\inf_{c\in\mathcal{C}^m(\lambda)}\inf_{0<\delta\leq\gamma\leq 1}\left(\mathbb{P}_n(yf(x)\leq\delta)+\mathbb{P}_n(\sigma^2(c;x)\geq\gamma)+\frac{m\gamma}{n\delta^2}\right).$$

First, we consider the so called interval problem, which is a one-dimensional classification problem with the space of instances $\mathcal{X} = [0,1]$ endowed with uniform distribution. Given a finite union of disjoint intervals $\mathcal{C}_0 \subset \mathcal{X}$, the label $y$ is assigned to a point $x \in \mathcal{X}$ according to the rule $y = 1$ if $x \in \mathcal{C}_0$, and $y = -1$ if $x \in \mathcal{X} \setminus \mathcal{C}_0$. In our experiments, we divided the interval $[0,1]$ in 20 equal subintervals and formed the set $\mathcal{C}_0$ by taking alternating subintervals. We generated a training data set and test data set, both of size 1000, according to the uniform distribution on $[0,1]$, and then ran AdaBoost and Arc-Gv and recorded all parameters of interest. We repeated this procedure ten times and averaged each parameter over 10 repetitions.

Next, we considered threenorm, heart, and ionosphere data sets, which were considered in [2]. In the case of threenorm data set, we used a random subset of size 300 for training and subset of size 5000 for test data. For heart and ionosphere data sets, we randomly selected 90% of the data for training and used the remaining 10% to compute the test error. Again, we repeated each procedure 10 times and averaged the results.

In each problem, we used decision stumps as weak classifiers, i.e.

$$\mathcal{H}\{2I(x \in \mathbb{R}^d : x_i \leq c) - 1, c \in \mathbb{R}, i \leq d\}$$
$$\cup\{2I(x \in \mathbb{R}^d : x_i \geq c) - 1, c \in \mathbb{R}, i \leq d\}.$$

The results are given in Figures 1 and 2. In rows (1) through (6) the parameters of AdaBoost are plotted with solid line, and the parameters of Arc-Gv - with dashed line:

(1) Cumulative distribution function of the margin $\mathbb{P}_n(yf(x \leq \delta))$.
(2) Effective dimension function $e_n(f, \delta)$ defined in (2.1), on the last boosting round.

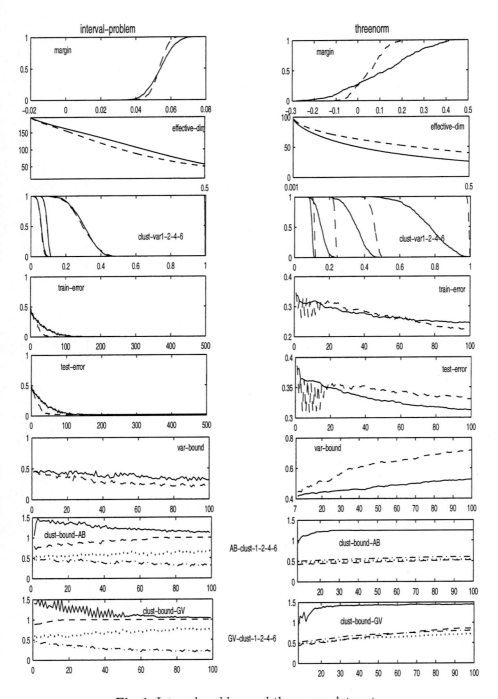

**Fig. 1.** Interval problem and threenorm data set.

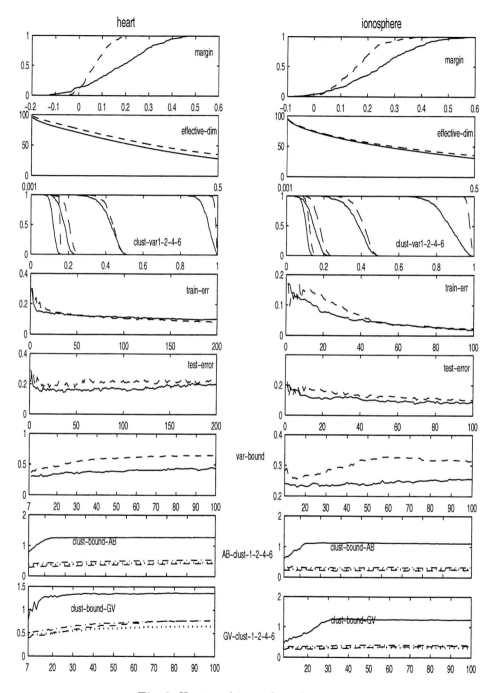

**Fig. 2.** Heart and ionosphere data sets.

(3) The tail distribution of the weighted variance $\mathbb{P}_n(\sigma^2(c; x) \geq \gamma)$, where $\sigma^2(c; x)$ is defined in (2.4), and where $c \in \mathcal{C}^m(\lambda)$ was determined by the best among the following algorithms (i.e. the one that gives the smallest value for $\mathbb{P}_n(\sigma^2(c; x) \geq \gamma)$,): (a) $k$-means; (b) clustering based on splitting the sample in the direction with maximum variance; (c) clustering based on grouping the classifiers in such a way that the weights $\alpha_1, \ldots, \alpha_m$ are as close to uniform as possible; (d) clustering (a) and (b) applied to points chosen with respect the distribution $\lambda$ and the rest of the points are clustered with respect to the received clusters. (The last two methods were usually the most successful in decreasing $\sigma^2(c; x)$.) The graphs for $m = 1, 2, 4$ and 6 are shifting right to left, showing the significant improvement of the distribution of weighted variance with increasing the number of clusters.
(4) Training error over boosting rounds.
(5) Test error over boosting rounds.
(6) The bound above over boosting rounds. Here, for a fixed $\gamma$, to approximate the infimum over $m$ and $c \in \mathcal{C}^m$, we used four clustering algorithms mentioned above and then picked the one that gives the smallest value of $\mathbb{P}(\sigma^2(c; x) \geq \gamma)$. The bounds usually predicted correctly which one of two algorithms produces a classifier with smaller test error. Moreover, all the parameters in the bound (rows 1 through 3) were usually consistent with the test error.
(7) For AdaBoost, and
(8) for Arc-Gv: Graphs of the bounds

$$\inf_{c \in \mathcal{C}^m(\lambda)} \inf_{0 < \delta \leq \gamma \leq 1} \left( \mathbb{P}_n(yf(x) \leq \delta) + \mathbb{P}_n(\sigma^2(c; x) \geq \gamma) + \frac{m\gamma}{n\delta^2} \right).$$

over boosting rounds for a fixed number of clusters $m = 1$ (solid line), $m = 2$ (dashed line), $m = 4$ (dot line) and $m = 6$ (dot-dash line). We see that using 2 or more clusters improves the bounds.

## 5    Conclusion

The results obtained so far show that the generalization bounds based on individual complexities of convex combinations and on margin parameters can be useful in better understanding and predicting the performance of the existing large margin classification algorithms. There might be a variety of ways to define useful quantities of this type, especially, the quantities describing the cluster structure of the set of base classifiers (for example, instead of the definitions based on the notion of variance used in the current paper one can use $L_2(P_n)$- or other covering numbers of the set of base classifiers). Both theoretical and experimental work will be needed to understand these bounds better.

## References

1. Breiman, L. (1996) Bagging predictors. *Machine Learning*, 24, 2, 123–140.
2. Breiman, L. (1999) Prediction games and arcing algorithms. *Neural Computation*, 11, 7, 1493 - 1517.

3. Dudley, R.M. (1999) Uniform Central Limit Theorems. Cambridge University Press.
4. Friedman, J., Hastie, T. and Tibshirani, R. (2000) Additive logistic regression: a statistical view of boosting. *Ann. Statist.*, 28, 337-374.
5. Haussler, D., (1995) Sphere packing numbers for subsets of the boolean $n$−cube with bounded Vapnik-Chervonenkis dimension, *J. Combin. Theory Ser. A*, **69**, 217 - 232.
6. Antos, A., Kégl, B., Linder, T. and Lugosi, G., (2002), Data-dependent margin-based generalization bounds for classification, Journal of Machine Learning Research.
7. Koltchinskii, V. (2002) Bounds on margin distributions in learning problems, *Annales de l'Institut Henri Poincaré,* to appear.
8. Koltchinskii, V. and Panchenko, D. (2002) Empirical margin distributions and bounding the generalization error of combined classifiers. *Ann. Statist.*, 30, 1.
9. Koltchinskii, V., Panchenko, D. and Lozano, F. (2003) Bounding the generalization error of convex combinations of classifiers: balancing the dimensionality and the margins, *Ann. Appl. Probab.*, 13, 1.
10. Panchenko, D. (2002) Some extensions of an inequality of Vapnik and Chervonenkis, *Elect. Comm. in Probab.* 7, 55-65.
11. Panchenko, D. (2002) On the generalization ability of voting classifiers, submitted.
12. Schapire, R., Freund, Y., Bartlett, P. and Lee, W. S. (1998) Boosting the margin: A new explanation of effectiveness of voting methods. *Ann. Statist.*, 26, 1651-1687.
13. van der Vaart, A.W. and Wellner, J.A. (1996) Weak convergence and Empirical Processes. With Applications to Statistics. Springer-Verlag, New York.
14. Vapnik, V.N. (1968) Chervonenkis, A.Ya., On the uniform convergence of relative frequencies of event to their probabilities, *Soviet Math. Dokl.,***9**, 915 - 918.
15. Vapnik, V. (1998) Statistical Learning Theory. John Wiley & Sons, New York.

# Sequence Prediction
# Based on Monotone Complexity

Marcus Hutter

IDSIA, Galleria 2, CH-6928 Manno-Lugano, Switzerland[*]
marcus@idsia.ch
http://www.idsia.ch/~marcus

**Abstract.** This paper studies sequence prediction based on the monotone Kolmogorov complexity $Km = -\log m$, i.e. based on universal deterministic/one-part MDL. $m$ is extremely close to Solomonoff's prior $M$, the latter being an excellent predictor in deterministic as well as probabilistic environments, where performance is measured in terms of convergence of posteriors or losses. Despite this closeness to $M$, it is difficult to assess the prediction quality of $m$, since little is known about the closeness of their posteriors, which are the important quantities for prediction. We show that for deterministic computable environments, the "posterior" and losses of $m$ converge, but rapid convergence could only be shown on-sequence; the off-sequence behavior is unclear. In probabilistic environments, neither the posterior nor the losses converge, in general.

## 1 Introduction

**Complexity Based Sequence Prediction.** In this work we study the performance of Occam's razor based sequence predictors. Given a data sequence $x_1$, $x_2$, ..., $x_{n-1}$ we want to predict (certain characteristics) of the next data item $x_n$. Every $x_t$ is an element of some domain $\mathcal{X}$, for instance weather data or stock-market data at time $t$, or the $t^{th}$ digit of $\pi$. Occam's razor [LV97], appropriately interpreted, tells us to search for the simplest explanation (model) of our data $x_1,...,x_{n-1}$ and to use this model for predicting $x_n$. Simplicity, or more precisely, effective complexity can be measured by the length of the shortest program computing sequence $x := x_1...x_{n-1}$. This length is called the algorithmic information content of $x$, which we denote by $\tilde{K}(x)$. $\tilde{K}$ stands for one of the many variants of "Kolmogorov" complexity (plain, prefix, monotone, ...) or for $-\log \tilde{k}(x)$ of universal distributions/measures $\tilde{k}(x)$. For simplicity we only consider binary alphabet $\mathcal{X} = \{0,1\}$ in this work.

The most well-studied complexity regarding its predictive properties is $KM(x) = -\log M(x)$, where $M(x)$ is Solomonoff's universal prior [Sol64,Sol78]. Solomonoff has shown that the posterior $M(x_t|x_1...x_{t-1})$ rapidly converges to the true data generating distribution. In [Hut01b,Hut02] it has been shown that

---

[*] This work was supported by SNF grant 2000-61847.00 to Jürgen Schmidhuber.

B. Schölkopf and M.K. Warmuth (Eds.): COLT/Kernel 2003, LNAI 2777, pp. 506–521, 2003.
© Springer-Verlag Berlin Heidelberg 2003

$M$ is also an excellent predictor from a decision-theoretic point of view, where the goal is to minimize loss. In any case, for prediction, the posterior $M(x_t|x_1...x_{t-1})$, rather than the prior $M(x_{1:t})$, is the more important quantity.

Most complexities $\tilde{K}$ coincide within an additive logarithmic term, which implies that their "priors" $\tilde{k} = 2^{-\tilde{K}}$ are close within polynomial accuracy. Some of them are extremely close to each other. Many papers deal with the proximity of various complexity measures [Lev73,Gác83, ...]. Closeness of two complexity measures is regarded as indication that the quality of their prediction is similarly good [LV97, p.334]. On the other hand, besides $M$, little is really known about the closeness of "posteriors", relevant for prediction.

**Aim and Conclusion.** The main aim of this work is to study the predictive properties of complexity measures, other than $KM$. The monotone complexity $Km$ is, in a sense, closest to Solomonoff's complexity $KM$. While $KM$ is defined via a mixture of infinitely many programs, the conceptually simpler $Km$ approximates $KM$ by the contribution of the single shortest program. This is also closer to the spirit of Occam's razor. $Km$ is a universal deterministic/one-part version of the popular Minimal Description Length (MDL) principle. We mainly concentrate on $Km$ because it has a direct interpretation as a universal deterministic/one-part MDL predictor, and it is closest to the excellent performing $KM$, so we expect predictions based on other $\tilde{K}$ not to be better.

The main conclusion we will draw is that closeness of priors does neither necessarily imply closeness of posteriors, nor good performance from a decision-theoretic perspective. It is far from obvious, whether $Km$ is a good predictor in general, and indeed we show that $Km$ can fail (with probability strictly greater than zero) in the presence of noise, as opposed to $KM$. We do not suggest that $Km$ fails for sequences occurring in practice. It is not implausible that (from a practical point of view) minor extra (apart from complexity) assumptions on the environment or loss function are sufficient to prove good performance of $Km$. Some complexity measures like $K$, fail completely for prediction.

**Contents.** *Section 2* introduces notation and describes how prediction performance is measured in terms of convergence of posteriors or losses. *Section 3* summarizes known predictive properties of Solomonoff's prior $M$. *Section 4* introduces the monotone complexity $Km$ and the prefix complexity $K$ and describes how they and other complexity measures can be used for prediction. In *Section 4* we enumerate and relate eight important properties, which general predictive functions may posses or not: proximity to $M$, universality, monotonicity, being a semimeasure, the chain rule, enumerability, convergence, and self-optimizingness. Some later needed normalization issues are also discussed. *Section 6* contains our main results. Monotone complexity $Km$ is analyzed quantitatively w.r.t. the eight predictive properties. Qualitatively, for deterministic, computable environments, the posterior converges and is self-optimizing, but rapid convergence could only be shown on-sequence; the (for prediction equally important) off-sequence behavior is unclear. In probabilistic environments, $m$ neither converges, nor is it self-optimizing, in general. The proofs are presented in *Section 7*. *Section 8* contains an outlook and a list of open questions.

## 2   Notation and Setup

**Strings and Natural Numbers.** We write $\mathcal{X}^*$ for the set of finite strings over binary alphabet $\mathcal{X} = \{0,1\}$, and $\mathcal{X}^\infty$ for the set of infinity sequences. We use letters $i,t,n$ for natural numbers, $x,y,z$ for finite strings, $\epsilon$ for the empty string, $l(x)$ for the length of string $x$, and $\omega = x_{1:\infty}$ for infinite sequences. We write $xy$ for the concatenation of string $x$ with $y$. For a string of length $n$ we write $x_1 x_2 ... x_n$ with $x_t \in \mathcal{X}$ and further abbreviate $x_{1:n} := x_1 x_2 ... x_{n-1} x_n$ and $x_{<n} := x_1 ... x_{n-1}$. For a given sequence $x_{1:\infty}$ we say that $x_t$ is on-sequence and $\bar{x}_t \neq x_t$ is off-sequence. $x_t'$ may be on- or off-sequence.

**Prefix Sets/Codes.** String $x$ is called a (proper) prefix of $y$ if there is a $z(\neq \epsilon)$ such that $xz = y$. We write $x* = y$ in this case, where $*$ is a wildcard for a string, and similarly for infinite sequences. A set of strings is called prefix-free if no element is a proper prefix of another. A prefix-free set $\mathcal{P}$ is also called a prefix-code. Prefix-codes have the important property of satisfying Kraft's inequality $\sum_{x \in \mathcal{P}} 2^{-l(x)} \leq 1$.

**Asymptotic Notation.** We abbreviate $\lim_{t\to\infty}[f(t) - g(t)] = 0$ by $f(t) \overset{t\to\infty}{\longrightarrow} g(t)$ and say $f$ converges to $g$, without implying that $\lim_{t\to\infty} g(t)$ itself exists. We write $f(x) \overset{\times}{\leq} g(x)$ for $f(x) = O(g(x))$ and $f(x) \overset{+}{\leq} g(x)$ for $f(x) \leq g(x) + O(1)$. Corresponding equalities can be defined similarly. They hold if the corresponding inequalities hold in both directions. $\sum_{t=1}^\infty a_t^2 < \infty$ implies $a_t \overset{t\to\infty}{\longrightarrow} 0$. We say that $a_t$ converges fast or rapidly to zero if $\sum_{t=1}^\infty a_t^2 \leq c$, where $c$ is a constant of reasonable size; $c = 100$ is reasonable, maybe even $c = 2^{30}$, but $c = 2^{500}$ is not[1]. The number of times for which $a_t$ deviates from 0 by more than $\varepsilon$ is finite and bounded by $c/\varepsilon^2$; no statement is possible for *which* $t$ these deviations occur. The cardinality of a set $\mathcal{S}$ is denoted by $|\mathcal{S}|$ or $\#\mathcal{S}$.

**(Semi)measures.** We call $\rho : \mathcal{X}^* \to [0,1]$ a (semi)measure iff $\sum_{x_n \in \mathcal{X}} \rho(x_{1:n}) \overset{(\leq)}{=} \rho(x_{<n})$ and $\rho(\epsilon) \overset{(\leq)}{=} 1$. $\rho(x)$ is interpreted as the $\rho$-probability of sampling a sequence which starts with $x$. The conditional probability (posterior)

$$\rho(x_t | x_{<t}) := \frac{\rho(x_{1:t})}{\rho(x_{<t})} \tag{1}$$

is the $\rho$-probability that a string $x_1 ... x_{t-1}$ is followed by (continued with) $x_t$. We call $\rho$ deterministic if $\exists \omega : \rho(\omega_{1:n}) = 1 \; \forall n$. In this case we identify $\rho$ with $\omega$.

**Convergent Predictors.** We assume that $\mu$ is "true"[2] sequence generating measure, also called environment. If we know the generating process $\mu$, and given past data $x_{<t}$ we can predict the probability $\mu(x_t | x_{<t})$ of the next data item $x_t$. Usually we do not know $\mu$, but estimate it from $x_{<t}$. Let $\rho(x_t | x_{<t})$ be

---

[1] Environments of interest have reasonable complexity $K$, but $2^K$ is not of reasonable size.

[2] Also called *objective* or *aleatory* probability or *chance*.

an estimated probability[3] of $x_t$, given $x_{<t}$. Closeness of $\rho(x_t|x_{<t})$ to $\mu(x_t|x_{<t})$ is expected to lead to "good" predictions:

Consider, for instance, a weather data sequence $x_{1:n}$ with $x_t = 1$ meaning rain and $x_t = 0$ meaning sun at day $t$. Given $x_{<t}$ the probability of rain tomorrow is $\mu(1|x_{<t})$. A weather forecaster may announce the probability of rain to be $y_t := \rho(1|x_{<t})$, which should be close to the true probability $\mu(1|x_{<t})$. To aim for

$$\rho(x_t'|x_{<t}) \stackrel{(fast)}{\longrightarrow} \mu(x_t'|x_{<t}) \quad \text{for} \quad t \to \infty \tag{2}$$

seems reasonable. A sequence of random variables $z_t = z_t(\omega)$ (like $z_t = \rho(x_t|x_{<t}) - \mu(x_t|x_{<t})$) is said to converge to zero with $\mu$-probability 1 (w.p.1) if the set $\{\omega : z_t(\omega) \stackrel{t\to\infty}{\longrightarrow} 0\}$ has $\mu$-measure 1. $z_t$ is said to converge to zero in mean sum (i.m.s) if $\sum_{t=1}^{\infty} \mathbf{E}[z_t^2] \leq c < \infty$, where $\mathbf{E}$ denotes $\mu$-expectation. Convergence i.m.s. implies convergence w.p.1 (rapid if $c$ is of reasonable size).

Depending on the interpretation, a $\rho$ satisfying (2) could be called consistent or self-tuning [KV86]. One problem with using (2) as performance measure is that closeness cannot be computed, since $\mu$ is unknown. Another disadvantage is that (2) does not take into account the value of correct predictions or the severity of wrong predictions.

**Self-optimizing Predictors.** More practical and flexible is a decision-theoretic approach, where performance is measured w.r.t. the true outcome sequence $x_{1:n}$ by means of a loss function, for instance $\ell_{x_t y_t} := (x_t - y_t)^2$, which does not involve $\mu$. More generally, let $\ell_{x_t y_t} \in [0,1] \subset \mathbb{R}$ be the received loss when performing some prediction/decision/action $y_t \in \mathcal{Y}$ and $x_t \in \mathcal{X}$ is the $t^{th}$ symbol of the sequence. Let $y_t^\Lambda \in \mathcal{Y}$ be the prediction of a (causal) prediction scheme $\Lambda$. The true probability of the next symbol being $x_t$, given $x_{<t}$, is $\mu(x_t|x_{<t})$. The $\mu$-expected loss (given $x_{<t}$) when $\Lambda$ predicts the $t^{th}$ symbol is

$$l_t^\Lambda(x_{<t}) := \sum_{x_t} \mu(x_t|x_{<t}) \ell_{x_t y_t^\Lambda}.$$

The goal is to minimize the $\mu$-expected loss. More generally, we define the $\Lambda_\rho$ sequence prediction scheme

$$y_t^{\Lambda_\rho} := \arg\min_{y_t \in \mathcal{Y}} \sum_{x_t} \rho(x_t|x_{<t}) \ell_{x_t y_t}, \tag{3}$$

which minimizes the $\rho$-expected loss. If $\mu$ is known, $\Lambda_\mu$ is obviously the best prediction scheme in the sense of achieving minimal expected loss ($l_t^{\Lambda_\mu} \leq l_t^\Lambda$ for all $\Lambda$). An important special case is the error-loss $\ell_{xy} = 1 - \delta_{xy}$ with $\mathcal{Y} = \mathcal{X}$. In this case $\Lambda_\rho$ predicts the $y_t$ which maximizes $\rho(y_t|x_{<t})$, and $\sum_t \mathbf{E}[l_t^{\Lambda_\rho}]$ is the expected number of prediction errors (where $y_t^{\Lambda_\rho} \neq x_t$). The natural decision-theoretic counterpart of (2) is to aim for

$$l_t^{\Lambda_\rho}(x_{<t}) \stackrel{(fast)}{\longrightarrow} l_t^{\Lambda_\mu}(x_{<t}) \quad \text{for} \quad t \to \infty \tag{4}$$

what is called (without the fast supplement) self-optimizingness in control-theory [KV86].

---

[3] Also called *subjective* or *belief* or *epistemic* probability.

# 3    Predictive Properties of $M = 2^{-KM}$

We define a prefix Turing machine $T$ as a Turing machine with binary unidirectional input and output tapes, and some bidirectional work tapes. We say $T$ halts on input $p$ with output $x$ and write "$T(p) = x$ halts" if $p$ is to the left of the input head and $x$ is to the left of the output head after $T$ halts. The set of $p$ on which $T$ halts forms a prefix-code. We call such codes $p$ *self-delimiting* programs. We write $T(p) = x*$ if $T$ outputs a string starting with $x$; $T$ need not to halt in this case. $p$ is called *minimal* if $T(q) \neq x*$ for all proper prefixes of $p$. The set of all prefix Turing-machines $\{T_1, T_2, ...\}$ can be effectively enumerated. There exists a universal prefix Turing machine $U$ which can simulate every $T_i$. A function is called computable if there is a Turing machine, which computes it. A function is called enumerable if it can be approximated from below. Let $\mathcal{M}_{comp}^{msr}$ be the set of all computable measures, $\mathcal{M}_{enum}^{semi}$ the set of all enumerable semimeasures, and $\mathcal{M}_{det}$ be the set of all deterministic measures ($\hat{=} \mathcal{X}^\infty$) [4].

Levin [ZL70,LV97] has shown the existence of an enumerable universal semimeasure $M$ ($M \overset{\times}{\geq} \nu \; \forall \nu \in \mathcal{M}_{enum}^{semi}$). An explicit expression due to Solomonoff [Sol78] is

$$M(x) := \sum_{p:U(p)=x*} 2^{-l(p)}, \qquad KM(x) := -\log M(x). \tag{5}$$

The sum is over all (possibly non-halting) minimal programs $p$ which output a string starting with $x$. This definition is equivalent to the probability that $U$ outputs a string starting with $x$ if provided with fair coin flips on the input tape. $M$ can be used to characterize randomness of individual sequences: A sequence $x_{1:\infty}$ is (Martin-Löf) $\mu$-random, *iff* $\exists c : M(x_{1:n}) \leq c \cdot \mu(x_{1:n}) \forall n$. For later comparison, we summarize the (excellent) predictive properties of $M$ [Sol78,Hut01a,Hut02] (the numbering will become clearer later):

**Theorem 1 (Properties of $M = 2^{-KM}$).** *Solomonoff's prior $M$ defined in (5) is a (i) universal, (v) enumerable, (ii) monotone, (iii) semimeasure, which (vi) converges to $\mu$ i.m.s., and (vii) is self-optimizing i.m.s. More quantitatively:*

(vi) $\sum_{t=1}^{\infty} \mathbf{E}[\sum_{x_t'} (M(x_t'|x_{<t}) - \mu(x_t'|x_{<t}))^2] \overset{+}{\leq} \ln 2 \cdot K(\mu)$, *which implies*
$M(x_t'|x_{<t}) \overset{t \to \infty}{\longrightarrow} \mu(x_t'|x_{<t})$ *i.m.s. for* $\mu \in \mathcal{M}_{comp}^{msr}$.

(vii) $\sum_{t=1}^{\infty} \mathbf{E}[(l_t^{\Lambda_M} - l_t^{\Lambda_\mu})^2] \overset{+}{\leq} 2\ln 2 \cdot K(\mu)$, *which implies*
$l_t^{\Lambda_M} \overset{t \to \infty}{\longrightarrow} l_t^{\Lambda_\mu}$ *i.m.s. for* $\mu \in \mathcal{M}_{comp}^{msr}$,

*where $K(\mu)$ is the length of the shortest program computing function $\mu$.*

# 4    Alternatives to Solomonoff's Prior $M$

The goal of this work is to investigate whether some other quantities which are closely related to $M$ also lead to good predictors. The prefix Kolmogorov

---

[4] $\mathcal{M}_{enum}^{semi}$ is enumerable, but $\mathcal{M}_{comp}^{msr}$ is not, and $\mathcal{M}_{det}$ is uncountable.

complexity $K$ is closely related to $KM$ ($K(x) = KM(x) + O(\log l(x))$). $K(x)$ is defined as the length of the shortest halting program on $U$ with output $x$:

$$K(x) := \min\{l(p) : U(p) = x \text{ halts}\}, \qquad k(x) := 2^{-K(x)}. \tag{6}$$

In Section 8 we briefly discuss that $K$ completely fails for predictive purposes. More promising is to approximate $M(x) = \sum_{p:U(p)=x*} 2^{-l(p)}$ by the dominant contribution in the sum, which is given by

$$m(x) := 2^{-Km(x)} \quad \text{with} \quad Km(x) := \min_p\{l(p) : U(p) = x*\}. \tag{7}$$

$Km$ is called *monotone complexity* and has been shown to be *very* close to $KM$ [Lev73,Gác83] (see also Theorem 5(*o*)). It is natural to call a sequence $x_{1:\infty}$ *computable* if $Km(x_{1:\infty}) < \infty$. $KM$, $Km$, and $K$ are ordered in the following way:

$$0 \leq K(x|l(x)) \overset{+}{\leq} KM(x) \leq Km(x) \leq K(x) \overset{+}{\leq} l(x) + 2\log l(x). \tag{8}$$

There are many complexity measures (prefix, Solomonoff, monotone, plain, process, extension, ...) which we generically denote by $\tilde{K} \in \{K, KM, Km, ...\}$ and their associated "predictive functions" $\tilde{k}(x) := 2^{-\tilde{K}(x)} \in \{k, M, m, ...\}$. This work is mainly devoted to the study of $m$.

Note that $\tilde{k}$ is generally not a semimeasure, so we have to clarify what it means to predict using $\tilde{k}$. One popular approach which is at the heart of the (one-part) MDL principle is to predict the $y$ which minimizes $\tilde{K}(xy)$ (maximizes $\tilde{k}(xy)$), where $x$ are past given data: $y_t^{MDL} := \operatorname{argmin}_{y_t} \tilde{K}(x_{<t}y_t)$.

For complexity measures $\tilde{K}$, the conditional version $\tilde{K}_|(x|y)$ is often defined[5] as $\tilde{K}(x)$, but where the underlying Turing machine $U$ has additionally access to $y$. The definition $\tilde{k}_|(x|y) := 2^{-\tilde{K}_|(x|y)}$ for the conditional predictive function $\tilde{k}$ seems natural, but has the disadvantage that the crucial the chain rule (1) is violated. For $\tilde{K} = K$ and $\tilde{K} = Km$ and most other versions of $\tilde{K}$, the chain rule is still satisfied approximately (to logarithmic accuracy), but this is not sufficient to prove convergence (2) or self-optimizingness (4). Therefore, we define $\tilde{k}(x_t|x_{<t}) := \tilde{k}(x_{1:t})/\tilde{k}(x_{<t})$ in the following, analogously to semimeasures $\rho$ (like $M$). A potential disadvantage of this definition is that $\tilde{k}(x_t|x_{<t})$ is not enumerable, whereas $\tilde{k}_|(x_t|x_{<t})$ and $\tilde{k}(x_{1:t})$ are.

We can now embed MDL predictions minimizing $\tilde{K}$ into our general framework: MDL coincides with the $\Lambda_{\tilde{k}}$ predictor for the error-loss:

$$y_t^{\Lambda_{\tilde{k}}} = \arg\max_{y_t} \tilde{k}(y_t|x_{<t}) = \arg\max_{y_t} \tilde{k}(x_{<t}y_t) = \arg\min_{y_t} \tilde{K}(x_{<t}y_t) = y_t^{MDL} \tag{9}$$

In the first equality we inserted $\ell_{xy} = 1 - \delta_{xy}$ into (3). In the second equality we used the chain rule (1). In both steps we dropped some in argmax ineffective additive/multiplicative terms independent of $y_t$. In the third equality we used $\tilde{k} = 2^{-\tilde{K}}$. The last equality formalizes the one-part MDL principle: given $x_{<t}$ predict the $y_t \in \mathcal{X}$ which leads to the shortest code $p$. Hence, validity of (4) tells us something about the validity of the MDL principle. (2) and (4) address what (good) prediction *means*.

---

[5] Usually written without index $|$.

# 5    General Predictive Functions

We have seen that there are predictors (actually the major one studied in this work) $\Lambda_\rho$, but where $\rho(x_t|x_{<t})$ is not (immediately) a semimeasure. Nothing prevents us from replacing $\rho$ in (3) by an arbitrary function $b_| : \mathcal{X}^* \to [0,\infty)$, written as $b_|(x_t|x_{<t})$. We also define general functions $b : \mathcal{X}^* \to [0,\infty)$, written as $b(x_{1:n})$ and $b(x_t|x_{<t}):=\frac{b(x_{1:t})}{b(x_{<t})}$, which may not coincide with $b_|(x_t|x_{<t})$. Most terminology for semimeasure $\rho$ can and will be carried over to the case of general predictive functions $b$ and $b_|$, but one has to be careful which properties and interpretations still hold:

**Definition 2 (Properties of Predictive Functions).** *We call functions $b,b_| :$ $\mathcal{X}^* \to [0,\infty)$ (conditional) predictive functions. They may possess some of the following properties:*

*o)* Proximity: $b(x)$ *is "close" to the universal prior* $M(x)$

*i)* Universality: $b \overset{\times}{\geq} M$, *i.e.* $\forall \nu \in \mathcal{M} \exists c > 0 : b(x) \geq c \cdot \nu(x) \forall x$.

*ii)* Monotonicity: $b(x_{1:t}) \leq b(x_{<t})$ $\forall t, x_{1:t}$

*iii)* Semimeasure: $\sum_{x_t} b(x_{1:t}) \leq b(x_{<t})$ *and* $b(\epsilon) \leq 1$

*iv)* Chain rule: $b(x_{1:t}) = b.(x_t|x_{<t}) b(x_{<t})$

*v)* Enumerability: $b$ *is lower semi-computable*

*vi)* Convergence: $b.(x'_t|x_{<t}) \overset{t\to\infty}{\longrightarrow} \mu(x'_t|x_{<t})$ $\forall \mu \in \mathcal{M}, x'_t \in \mathcal{X}$ *i.m.s. or w.p.1*

*vii)* Self-optimizingness: $l_t^{\Lambda_b.} \overset{t\to\infty}{\longrightarrow} l_t^{\Lambda_\mu}$ *i.m.s. or w.p.1*

*where $b.$ refers to $b$ or $b_|$*

The importance of the properties $(i)-(iv)$ stems from the fact that they together imply convergence $(vi)$ and self-optimizingness $(vii)$. Regarding proximity $(o)$ we left open what we mean by "close". We also did not specify $\mathcal{M}$ but have in mind all computable measures $\mathcal{M}_{comp}^{msr}$ or enumerable semimeasures $\mathcal{M}_{enum}^{semi}$, possibly restricted to deterministic environments $\mathcal{M}_{det}$.

**Theorem 3 (Predictive Relations).**

*a)* $(iii) \Rightarrow (ii)$: *A semimeasure is monotone.*

*b)* $(i),(iii),(iv) \Rightarrow (vi)$: *The posterior $b.$ as defined by the chain rule $(iv)$ of a universal semimeasure $b$ converges to $\mu$ i.m.s. for all $\mu \in \mathcal{M}$.*

*c)* $(i),(iii),(v) \Rightarrow (o)$: *Every w.r.t. $\mathcal{M}_{enum}^{semi}$ universal enumerable semimeasure coincides with $M$ within a multiplicative constant.*

*d)* $(vi) \Rightarrow (vii)$: *Posterior convergence i.m.s./w.p.1 implies self-optimizingness i.m.s./w.p.1.*

**Proof Sketch.** $(a)$ follows trivially from dropping the sum in $(ii)$, $(b)$ and $(c)$ are Solomonoff's major results [Sol78,LV97,Hut01a], $(d)$ follows from $0 \leq l_t^{\Lambda_b.} - l_t^{\Lambda_\mu} \leq \sum_{x'_t} |b.(x'_t|x_{<t}) - \mu(x'_t|x_{<t})|$, since $\ell \in [0,1]$ [Hut02, Th.4$(ii)$]. $\qquad\square$

We will see that $(i),(iii),(iv)$ are crucial for proving $(vi),(vii)$.

**Normalization.** Let us consider a scaled $b$ version $b_{norm}(x_t|x_{<t}) := c(x_{<t}) b(x_t|x_{<t})$, where $c > 0$ is independent of $x_t$. Such a scaling does not affect the prediction scheme $\Lambda_b$ (3), i.e. $y_t^{\Lambda_b} = y_t^{\Lambda_{b_{norm}}}$, which implies $l_t^{\Lambda_{b_{norm}}} = l_t^{\Lambda_b}$.

Convergence $b(x'_t|x_{<t}) \to \mu(x'_t|x_{<t})$ implies $\sum_{x'_t} b(x'_t|x_{<t}) \to 1$ if $\mu$ is a measure, hence also $b_{norm}(x'_t|x_{<t}) \to \mu(x'_t|x_{<t})$ for[6] $c(x_{<t}) := [\sum_{x'_t} b(x'_t|x_{<t})]^{-1}$. Speed of convergence may be affected by normalization, either positively or negatively. Assuming the chain rule (1) for $b_{norm}$ we get

$$b_{norm}(x_{1:n}) = \prod_{t=1}^{n} \frac{b(x_{1:t})}{\sum_{x_t} b(x_{1:t})} = d(x_{<n})b(x_{1:n}), \qquad d(x_{<n}) := \frac{1}{b(\epsilon)} \prod_{t=1}^{n} \frac{b(x_{<t})}{\sum_{x_t} b(x_{1:t})}$$

Whatever $b$ we start with, $b_{norm}$ is a measure, i.e. $(iii)$ is satisfied with equality. Convergence and self-optimizingness proofs are now eligible for $b_{norm}$, provided universality $(i)$ can be proven for $b_{norm}$. If $b$ is a semimeasure, then $d \geq 1$, hence $M_{norm} \geq M \overset{\times}{\geq} \mathcal{M}_{enum}^{semi}$ is universal and converges $(vi)$ with same bound (Theorem 1$(vi)$) as for $M$. On the other hand $d(x_{<n})$ may be unbounded for $b=k$ and $b=m$, so normalization does not help us in these cases for proving $(vi)$. Normalization transforms a universal non-semimeasure into a measure, which may no longer be universal.

# 6    Predictive Properties of $m = 2^{-Km}$

We can now state which predictive properties of $m$ hold, and which not. In order not to overload the reader, we first summarize the qualitative predictive properties of $m$ in Corollary 4, and subsequently present detailed quantitative results in Theorem 5, followed by an item-by-item explanation and discussion. The proofs are deferred to the next section.

**Corollary 4 (Properties of $m = 2^{-Km}$).** *For $b = m = 2^{-Km}$, where $Km$ is the monotone Kolmogorov complexity (7), the following properties of Definition 2 are satisfied/violated: (o) For every $\mu \in \mathcal{M}_{comp}^{msr}$ and every $\mu$-random sequence $x_{1:\infty}$, $m(x_{1:n})$ equals $M(x_{1:n})$ within a multiplicative constant. m is (i) universal (w.r.t. $\mathcal{M} = \mathcal{M}_{comp}^{msr}$), (ii) monotone, and (v) enumerable, but is $\neg(iii)$ not a semimeasure. m satisfies (iv) the chain rule by definition for $m. = m$, but for $m. = m_|$ the chain rule is only satisfied to logarithmic order. For $m. = m$, m (vi) converges and (vii) is self-optimizing for deterministic $\mu \in \mathcal{M}_{comp}^{msr} \cap \mathcal{M}_{det}$, but in general not for probabilistic $\mu \in \mathcal{M}_{comp}^{msr} \setminus \mathcal{M}_{det}$.*

The lesson to learn is that although $m$ is very close to $M$ in the sense of $(o)$ and $m$ dominates all computable measures $\mu$, predictions based on $m$ may nevertheless fail (cf. Theorem 1).

**Theorem 5 (Detailed Properties of $m = 2^{-Km}$).** *For $b = m = 2^{-Km}$, where $\mathring{K}m(x) := \min_p\{l(p) : U(p) = x*\}$ is the monotone Kolmogorov complexity, the following properties of Definition 2 are satisfied / violated:*

> $(o)$ $\forall \mu \in \mathcal{M}_{comp}^{msr}$ $\forall \mu$-random $\omega$ $\exists c_\omega : Km(\omega_{1:n}) \leq KM(\omega_{1:n}) + c_\omega$ $\forall n$,    *[Lev73]*
> $KM(x) \leq Km(x) \leq KM(x) + 2\log Km(x) + O(1)$ $\forall x$.    *[ZL70, Th.3.4]*
> $\neg(o)$ $\forall c : Km(x) - KM(x) \geq c$ for infinitely many $x$.    *[Gác83]*

---

[6] Arbitrarily we define $b_{norm}(x_t|x_{<t}) = \frac{1}{|\mathcal{X}|}$ if $\sum_{x'_t} b(x'_t|x_{<t}) = 0$.

(i)  $Km(x) \overset{+}{\leq} -\log \mu(x) + K(\mu)$ if $\mu \in \mathcal{M}^{msr}_{comp}$,                    [LV97, Th.4.5.4]

  $m \overset{\times}{\geq} \mathcal{M}^{msr}_{comp}$, but $m \overset{\times}{\ngeq} \mathcal{M}^{semi}_{enum}$ (unlike $M \overset{\times}{\geq} \mathcal{M}^{semi}_{enum}$).

(ii)  $Km(xy) \geq Km(x) \in \mathbb{N}_0$,    $0 < m(xy) \leq m(x) \in 2^{-\mathbb{N}_0} \leq 1$.

¬(iii)  If $x_{1:\infty}$ is computable, then $\sum_{x_t} m(x_{1:t}) \nleq m(x_{<t})$ for almost all $t$,

  If $Km(x_{1:t}) = o(t)$,   then $\sum_{x_t} m(x_{1:t}) \nleq m(x_{<t})$ for most $t$.

(iv)  $0 < m(x|y) := \frac{m(yx)}{m(y)} \leq 1$.

¬(iv)  if $m_|(x|y) := 2^{-\min_p\{l(p):U(p,y)=x*\}}$, then $\exists x,y : m(yx) \neq m_|(x|y) \cdot m(y)$,

  $Km(yx) = Km_|(x|y) + Km(y) \pm O(\log l(xy))$.

(v)  $m$ is enumerable, i.e. lower semi-computable.

(vi)  $\sum_{t=1}^n |1 - m(x_t|x_{<t})| \leq \frac{1}{2} Km(x_{1:n})$,   $m(x_t|x_{<t}) \overset{fast}{\longrightarrow} 1$ for comp. $x_{1:\infty}$,

  Indeed, $m(x_t|x_{<t}) \neq 1$ at most $Km(x_{1:\infty})$ times,

  $\sum_{t=1}^n m(\bar{x}_t|x_{<t}) \leq 2^{Km(x_{1:n})}$,   $m(\bar{x}_t|x_{<t}) \overset{slow?}{\longrightarrow} 0$ for computable $x_{1:\infty}$.

¬(vi)  $\exists \mu \in \mathcal{M}^{msr}_{comp} \setminus \mathcal{M}_{det} : m_{(norm)}(x_t|x_{<t}) \nrightarrow \mu(x_t|x_{<t}) \; \forall x_{1:\infty}$

(vii)  $l_t^{\Lambda m}(x_{<t}) \overset{slow?}{\longrightarrow} l_t^{\Lambda \omega} := \operatorname{argmin}_{y_t} \ell_{x_t y_t}$ if $\omega \equiv x_{1:\infty}$ is computable.

  $\Lambda_m = \Lambda_{m_{norm}}$, i.e. $y_t^{\Lambda m} = y_t^{\Lambda m_{norm}}$ and $l_t^{\Lambda m} = l_t^{\Lambda m_{norm}}$.

¬(vii)  $\forall |\mathcal{Y}| > 2 \; \exists \ell, \mu : l_t^{\Lambda m}/l_t^{\Lambda \mu} = c > 1 \, \forall t$   ($c = \frac{6}{5} - \varepsilon$ possible).

  $\forall$ non-degenerate $\ell \; \exists U, \mu : l_t^{\Lambda m}/l_t^{\Lambda \mu} \overset{t \to \infty}{\nrightarrow} 1$ with high probability.

**Explanation and Discussion.** (*o*) The first line shows that $m$ is close to $M$ within a multiplicative constant for nearly all strings in a very strong sense. $\sup_n \frac{M(\omega_{1:n})}{m(\omega_{1:n})} \leq 2^{c_\omega}$ is finite for every $\omega$ which is random (in the sense of Martin-Löf) w.r.t. *any* computable $\mu$, but note that the constant $c_\omega$ depends on $\omega$. Levin falsely conjectured the result to be true for *all* $\omega$, but could only prove it to hold within logarithmic accuracy (second line).

¬(*o*) A later result by Gács, indeed, implies that $Km - KM$ is unbounded (for infinite alphabet it can even increase logarithmically).

(*i*) The first line can be interpreted as a "continuous" coding theorem for $Km$ and recursive $\mu$. It implies (by exponentiation) that $m$ dominates all computable measures (second line). Unlike $M$ it does *not* dominate all enumerable semimeasures. Dominance is a key feature for good predictors. From a practical point of view the assumption that the true generating distribution $\mu$ is a proper measure and computable seems not to be restrictive. The problem will be that $m$ is not a semimeasure.

(*ii*) The monotonicity property is obvious from the definition of $Km$ and is the origin of calling $Km$ monotone complexity.

¬(*iii*) shows and quantifies how the crucial semimeasure property is violated for $m$ in an essential way, where *almost all $n$* means "all but finitely many," and *most $n$* means "all but an asymptotically vanishing fraction.".

(*iv*) the chain rule can be satisfied by definition. With such a definition, $m(x|y)$ is strictly positive like $M(x|y)$, but not necessarily strictly less than 1, unlike $M(x|y)$. Nevertheless it is bounded by 1 due to monotonicity of $m$, unlike for $k$.

¬$(iv)$ If a conditional monotone complexity $Km_| = -\log m_|$ is defined similarly to the conditional Kolmogorov complexity $K_|$, then the chain rule is only valid within logarithmic accuracy.

$(v)$ $m$ shares the obvious enumerability property with $M$.

$(vi)$ (first line) shows that the on-sequence predictive properties of $m$ for deterministic computable environments are excellent. The predicted $m$-probability[7] of $x_t$ given $x_{<t}$ converges rapidly to 1 for reasonably simple/complex $x_{1:\infty}$. A similar result holds for $M$. The stronger result (second line), that $m(x_t|x_{<t})$ deviates from 1 at most $Km(x_{1:\infty})$ times, does not hold for $M$. Note that perfect on-sequence prediction could trivially be achieved by always predicting 1 ($b_. \equiv 1$). Since we do not know the true outcome $x_t$ in advance, we need to predict $m(x'_t|x_{<t})$ well for all $x'_t \in \mathcal{X}$. $m(|)$ also converges off-sequence for $\bar{x}_t \neq x_t$ (to zero as it should be), but the bound (third line) is much weaker than the on-sequence bound (first line), so rapid convergence cannot be concluded, unlike for $M$, where $M(x_t|x_{<t}) \xrightarrow{fast} 1$ implies $M(\bar{x}_t|x_{<t}) \xrightarrow{fast} 0$, since $\sum_{x'_t} M(x'_t|x_{<t}) \leq 1$. Consider an environment $x_{1:\infty}$ describable in 500 bits, then bound $(vi)$ line 2 does not exclude $m(\bar{x}_t|x_{<t})$ from being 1 (maximally wrong) for all $t = 1..2^{500}$; with asymptotic convergence being of pure academic interest.

¬$(vi)$ The situation is provably worse in the probabilistic case. There are computable measures $\mu$ for which neither $m(x_t|x_{<t})$ nor $m_{norm}(x_t|x_{<t})$ converge to $\mu(x_t|x_{<t})$ for any $x_{1:\infty}$.

$(vii)$ Since $(vi)$ implies $(vii)$ by continuity, we have convergence of the instantaneous losses for computable environments $x_{1:\infty}$, but since we do not know the speed of convergence off-sequence, we do not know how fast the losses converge to optimum.

¬$(vii)$ Non-convergence ¬$(vi)$ does not necessarily imply that $\Lambda_m$ is not self-optimizing, since different predictive functions can lead to the same predictor $\Lambda$. But it turns out that $\Lambda_m$ is not self-optimizing even in Bernoulli environments $\mu$ for particular losses $\ell$ (first line). A similar result holds for *any non-degenerate loss function* (especially for the error-loss, cf. (9)), for specific choices of the universal Turing-machine $U$ (second line). Loss $\ell$ is defined to be non-degenerate iff $\bigcap_{x \in \mathcal{X}} \{\tilde{y} : \ell_{x\tilde{y}} = \min_y \ell_{xy}\} = \{\}$. Assume the contrary that a *single* action $\tilde{y}$ is optimal for *every* outcome $x$, i.e. that ($\arg\min_y$ can be chosen such that) $\arg\min_y \ell_{xy} = \tilde{y} \forall x$. This implies $y_t^{\Lambda_\rho} = \tilde{y} \forall \rho$, which implies $l_t^{\Lambda_m}/l_t^{\Lambda_\mu} \equiv 1$. So the non-degeneracy assumption is necessary (and sufficient).

# 7    Proof of Theorem 5

$(o)$ The first two properties are due to Levin and are proven in [Lev73] and [ZL70, Th.3.4], respectively. The third property is an easy corollary from Gács result [Gác83], which says that if $g$ is some monotone co-enumerable function

---

[7] We say "probability" just for convenience, not forgetting that $m(\cdot|x_{<t})$ is not a proper (semi)probability distribution.

for which $Km(x) - KM(x) \leq g(l(x))$ holds for all $x$, then $g(n)$ must be $\overset{+}{\geq} K(n)$. Assume $Km(x) - KM(x) \geq \log l(x)$ only for finitely many $x$ only. Then there exists a $c$ such that $Km(x) - KM(x) \leq \log l(x) + c$ for all $x$. Gács' theorem now implies $\log n + c \overset{+}{\geq} K(n) \, \forall n$, which is wrong due to Kraft's inequality $\sum_n 2^{-K(n)} \leq 1$.

**(i)** The first line is proven in [LV97, Th.4.5.4]. Exponentiating this result gives $m(x) \geq c_\mu \mu(x) \, \forall x, \mu \in \mathcal{M}_{comp}^{msr}$, i.e. $m \overset{\times}{\geq} \mathcal{M}_{comp}^{msr}$. Exponentiation of $\neg(o)$ gives $m(x) \leq M(x)/l(x)$, which implies $m(x) \overset{\times}{\not\geq} M(x) \in \mathcal{M}_{enum}^{semi}$, i.e. $m \overset{\times}{\not\geq} \mathcal{M}_{enum}^{semi}$.

**(ii)** is obvious from the definition of $Km$ and $m$.

**¬(iii)** Simple violation of the semimeasure property can be inferred indirectly from $(i),(iv),\neg(vi)$ and Theorem $3b$. To prove $\neg(iii)$ we first note that $Km(x) < \infty$ for all finite strings $x \in \mathcal{X}^*$, which implies $m(x_{1:n}) > 0$. Hence, whenever $Km(x_{1:n}) = Km(x_{<n})$, we have $\sum_{x_n} m(x_{1:n}) > m(x_{1:n}) = m(x_{<n})$, a violation of the semimeasure property. $\neg(iii)$ now follows from $\#\{t \leq n : \sum_{x_t} m(x_{1:t}) \leq m(x_{<t})\} \leq \#\{t \leq n : Km(x_{1:t}) \neq Km(x_{<t})\} \leq \sum_{t=1}^n Km(x_{1:t}) - Km(x_{<t}) = Km(x_{1:n})$, where we exploited $(ii)$ in the last inequality.

**(iv)** immediate from $(ii)$.

**¬(iv)** (first line) follows from the fact that equality does not even hold within an additive constant, i.e. $Km(yx) \overset{+}{\neq} Km(x|y) + Km(y)$. The proof of the latter is similar to the one for $K$ (see [LV97]). $\neg(iv)$ (second line) follows within log from $Km = K + O(\log)$ and $K(yx) = K(x|y) + K(y) + O(\log)$ [LV97].

**(v)** immediate from definition.

**(vi)** $\#\{t \leq n : m(x_t|x_{<t}) \neq 1\} \leq \sum_{t=1}^n 2|1 - m(x_t|x_{<t})| \leq -\sum_{t=1}^n \log m(x_t|x_{<t}) = -\log m(x_{1:n}) = Km(x_{1:n}) < \infty$. In the first inequality we used $m := m(x_t|x_{<t}) \in 2^{-\mathbb{N}_0}$, hence $1 \leq 2|1-m|$ for $m \neq 1$. In the second inequality we used $1 - m \leq -\frac{1}{2}\log m$, valid for $m \in [0,\frac{1}{2}] \cup \{1\}$. In the first equality we used (the log of) the chain rule $n$ times. For computable $x_{1:\infty}$ we have $\sum_{t=1}^\infty |1 - m(x_t|x_{<t})| \leq \frac{1}{2} Km(x_{1:\infty}) < \infty$, which implies $m(x_t|x_{<t}) \to 0$ (fast if $Km(x_{1:\infty})$ is of reasonable size). This shows the first two lines of $(vi)$. The last line is shown as follows: Fix a sequence $x_{1:\infty}$ and define $\mathcal{Q} := \{x_{<t}\bar{x}_t : t \in \mathbb{N}, \bar{x}_t \neq x_t\}$. $\mathcal{Q}$ is a prefix-free set of finite strings. For any such $\mathcal{Q}$ and any semimeasure $\mu$, one can show that $\sum_{x \in \mathcal{Q}} \mu(x) \leq 1$ [8]. Since $M$ is a semimeasure lower bounded by $m$ we get

$$\sum_{t=1}^n m(x_{<t}\bar{x}_t) \leq \sum_{t=1}^\infty m(x_{<t}\bar{x}_t) = \sum_{x \in \mathcal{Q}} m(x) \leq \sum_{x \in \mathcal{Q}} M(x) \leq 1.$$

With this, and using monotonicity of $m$ we get

$$\sum_{t=1}^n m(\bar{x}_t|x_{<t}) = \sum_{t=1}^n \frac{m(x_{<t}\bar{x}_t)}{m(x_{<t})} \leq \sum_{t=1}^n \frac{m(x_{<t}\bar{x}_t)}{m(x_{1:n})} \leq \frac{1}{m(x_{1:n})} = 2^{Km(x_{1:n})}$$

---

[8] This follows from $1 \geq \mu(A \cup B) \geq \mu(A) + \mu(B)$ if $A \cap B = \{\}$, $\Gamma_x \cap \Gamma_y = \{\}$ if $x$ not prefix of $y$ and $y$ not prefix of $x$, where $\Gamma_x := \{\omega : \omega_{1:l(x)} = x\}$, hence $\sum_{x \in \mathcal{Q}} \mu(\Gamma_x) \leq \mu(\bigcup_{x \in \mathcal{Q}} \Gamma_x) \leq 1$, and noting that $\mu(x)$ is actually an abbreviation for $\mu(\Gamma_x)$.

Finally, for an infinite sum to be finite, its elements must converge to zero.

¬**(vi)** follows from the non-denseness of the range of $m_{(norm)}$: We choose $\mu(1|x_{<t}) = \frac{3}{8}$, hence $\mu(0|x_{<t}) = \frac{5}{8}$. Since $m(x_t|x_{<t}) \in 2^{-\mathbb{N}_0} = \{1, \frac{1}{2}, \frac{1}{4}, \frac{1}{8}, ...\}$, we have $|m(x_t|x_{<t}) - \mu(x_t|x_{<t})| \geq \frac{1}{8}$ $\forall t, \forall x_{1:\infty}$. Similarly for

$$m_{norm}(x_t|x_{<t}) = \frac{m(x_t|x_{<t})}{m(0|x_{<t}) + m(1|x_{<t})} \in \{\frac{2^{-n}}{2^{-n} + 2^{-m}} : n, m \in \mathbb{N}_0\} =$$

$$= \{\frac{1}{1+2^z} : z \in \mathbb{Z}\} = \frac{1}{1+2^{\mathbb{Z}}} = \{..., \frac{1}{9}, \frac{1}{5}, \frac{1}{3}, \frac{1}{2}, \frac{2}{3}, \frac{4}{5}, \frac{8}{9}, ...\}$$

we choose $\mu(1|x_{<t}) = 1 - \mu(0|x_{<t}) = \frac{5}{12}$, which implies $|m_{norm}(x_t|x_{<t}) - \mu(x_t|x_{<t})| \geq \frac{1}{12}$ $\forall t, \forall x_{1:\infty}$.

**(vii)** The first line follows from $(vi)$ and Theorem 3d. That normalization does not affect the predictor, follows from the definition of $y_t^{\Lambda_\rho}$ (3) and the fact that argmin() is not affected by scaling its argument.

¬**(vii)** Non-convergence of $m$ does not necessarily imply non-convergence of the losses. For instance, for $\mathcal{Y} = \{0,1\}$, and $\omega_t' := 1/0$ for $\mu(1|x_{<t}) \underset{<}{\overset{>}{\gtrless}} \gamma := \frac{\ell_{01} - \ell_{00}}{\ell_{01} - \ell_{00} + \ell_{10} - \ell_{11}}$, one can show that $y_t^{\Lambda_\mu} = y_t^{\Lambda_{\omega'}}$, hence convergence of $m(x_t|x_{<t})$ to 0/1 and not to $\mu(x_t|x_{<t})$ could nevertheless lead to correct predictions.

Consider now $y \in \mathcal{Y} = \{0,1,2\}$. To prove the first line of ¬(vii) we define a loss function such that $y_t^{\Lambda_\mu} \neq y_t^{\Lambda_\rho}$ for any $\rho$ with same range as $m_{norm}$ and for some $\mu$. The loss function $\ell_{x0} = x$, $\ell_{x1} = \frac{3}{8}$, $\ell_{x2} = \frac{2}{3}(1-x)$, and $\mu := \mu(1|x_{<t}) = \frac{2}{5}$ will do. The $\rho$-expected loss under action $y$ is $l_\rho^y :=$ $\sum_{x_t=0}^{1} \rho(x_t|x_{<t})\ell_{x_t y}$; $l_\rho^0 = \rho$, $l_\rho^1 = \frac{3}{8}$, $l_\rho^2 = \frac{2}{3}(1-\rho)$ with $\rho := \rho(1|x_{<t})$ (see Figure).

Since $l_\mu^0 = l_\mu^2 = \frac{2}{5} > \frac{3}{8} = l_\mu^1$, we have $y_t^{\Lambda_\mu} = 1$ and $l_t^{\Lambda_\mu} = l_\mu^1 = \frac{3}{8}$. For $\rho \leq \frac{1}{3}$, we have $l_\rho^0 < l_\rho^1 < l_\rho^2$, hence $y_t^{\Lambda_\rho} = 0$ and $l_t^{\Lambda_\rho} = l_\mu^0 = \frac{2}{5}$. For $\rho \geq \frac{1}{2}$, we have $l_\rho^2 < l_\rho^1 < l_\rho^0$, hence $y_t^{\Lambda_\rho} = 2$ and $l_t^{\Lambda_\rho} = l_\mu^2 = \frac{2}{5}$. Since $m_{norm} \notin (\frac{1}{3}, \frac{1}{2})$, $\Lambda_{m_{norm}}$ predicts 0 or 2, hence $l_t^{\Lambda_m} = l_\mu^{0/2} = \frac{2}{5}$. Since $\Lambda_{m_{norm}} = \Lambda_m$, this shows that $l_t^{\Lambda_m}/l_t^{\Lambda_\mu} = \frac{16}{15} > 1$. The constant $\frac{16}{15}$ can be enlarged to $\frac{6}{5} - \varepsilon$ by setting $\ell_{x1} = \frac{1}{3} + \varepsilon$ instead of $\frac{3}{8}$.

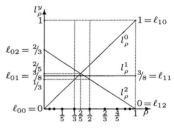

For $\mathcal{Y} = \{0,...,|\mathcal{Y}|-1\}$, $|\mathcal{Y}| > 3$, we extend the loss function by defining $\ell_{xy} = 1$ $\forall y \geq 3$, ensuring that actions $y \geq 2$ are never favored. With this extension, the analysis of the $|\mathcal{Y}| = 3$ case applies, which finally shows ¬$(vii)$. In general, a non-dense range of $\rho(x_t|x_{<t})$ implies $l_t^{\Lambda_\rho} \not\to l_t^{\Lambda_\mu}$, provided $|\mathcal{Y}| \geq 3$.

We now construct a monotone universal Turing machine $U$ satisfying ¬$(vii)$ (second line). In case where ambiguities in the choice of $y$ in $\text{argmin}_y \ell_{xy}$ matter we consider the set of solutions $\{\text{argmin}_y \ell_{xy}\} := \{\tilde{y} : \ell_{x\tilde{y}} = \min_y \ell_{xy}\} \neq \{\}$. We define a one-to-one (onto $A$) decoding function $d : \{0,1\}^s \to A$ with $A = \{0^{s+1}\} \cup 1\{0,1\}^s \setminus 1\{0^s\} \subset \mathcal{X}^{s+1}$ as $d(0_{1:s}) = 0_{1:s+1}$ and $d(x_{1:s}) = 1x_{1:s}$ for $x_{1:s} \neq 0_{1:s}$ with a large $s \in \mathbb{N}$ to be determined later. We extend $d$ to $d : (\{0,1\}^s)^* \to A^*$ by defining $d(z_1...z_k) = d(z_1)...d(z_k)$ for $z_i \in \{0,1\}^s$ and define the inverse coding function $c : A \to \{0,1\}^s$ and its extension $c : A^* \to (\{0,1\}^s)^*$ by $c = d^{-1}$. Roughly,

$U$ is defined as $U(1p_{1:sn}0_{1:s}) = d(p_{1:sn})0_{1:s+1}$. More precisely, if the first bit of the binary input tape of $U$ contains 1, $U$ decodes the successive blocks of size $s$, but always withholds the output until a block $0_{1:s}$ appears. $U$ is obviously monotone. Universality will be guaranteed by defining $U(0p)$ appropriately, but for the moment we set $U(0p) = \epsilon$. It is easy to see that for $x \in A^*$ we have

$$Km(x0) = Km(x0_{1:s+1}) = l(c(x)) + s + 1 \quad \text{and} \tag{10}$$
$$Km(x1) = Km(x1z0_{1:s+1}) = l(c(x)) + 2s + 1,$$

where $z$ is any string of length $s$. Hence, $m_{norm}(0|x) = [1 + 2^{-s}]^{-1} \overset{s\to\infty}{\longrightarrow} 1$ and $m_{norm}(1|x) = [1 + 2^s]^{-1} \overset{s\to\infty}{\longrightarrow} 0$. For $t - 1 \in (s+1)\mathbb{N}$ we get $l_m^{y_t} := \sum_{x_t} m_{norm}(x_t|x_{<t})\ell_{x_t y_t} \overset{s\to\infty}{\longrightarrow} \ell_{0y_t}$. This implies

$$y_t^{\Lambda_m} \in \{\arg\min_{y_t} l_m^{y_t}\} \subseteq \{\arg\min_y \ell_{0y}\} \quad \text{for sufficiently large finite } s. \tag{11}$$

We now define $\mu(z) = |A|^{-1} = 2^{-s}$ for $z \in A$ and $\mu(z) = 0$ for $z \in \mathcal{X}^{s+1} \setminus A$, extend it to $\mu(z_1...z_k) := \mu(z_1) \cdot ... \cdot \mu(z_k)$ for $z_i \in \mathcal{X}^{s+1}$, and finally extend it uniquely to a measure on $\mathcal{X}^*$ by $\mu(x_{<t}) := \sum_{x_{t:n}} \mu(x_{1:n})$ for $\mathbb{N} \ni t \leq n \in (s+1)\mathbb{N}$. For $x \in A^*$ we have $\mu(0|x) = \mu(0) = \mu(0_{1:s+1}) = 2^{-s} \overset{s\to\infty}{\longrightarrow} 0$ and $\mu(1|x) = \mu(1) = \sum_{y\in\mathcal{X}^s}\mu(1y) = \sum_{z\in A\setminus\{0^{s+1}\}}\mu(z) = (2^s - 1)\cdot 2^{-s} = 1 - 2^{-s} \overset{s\to\infty}{\longrightarrow} 1$. For $t - 1 \in (s+1)\mathbb{N}$ we get $l_\mu^{y_t} := \sum_{x_t}\mu(x_t|x_{<t})\ell_{x_t y_t} \overset{s\to\infty}{\longrightarrow} \ell_{1y_t}$. This implies

$$y_t^{\Lambda_\mu} \in \{\arg\min_{y_t} l_\mu^{y_t}\} \subseteq \{\arg\min_y \ell_{1y}\} \quad \text{for sufficiently large finite } s. \tag{12}$$

By definition, $\ell$ is non-degenerate iff $\{\arg\min_y \ell_{0y}\} \cap \{\arg\min_y \ell_{1y}\} = \{\}$. This, together with (11) and (12) implies $y_t^{\Lambda_m} \neq y_t^{\Lambda_\mu}$, which implies $l_t^{\Lambda_m} \neq l_t^{\Lambda_\mu}$ (otherwise the choice $y_t^{\Lambda_m} = y_t^{\Lambda_\mu}$ would have been possible), which implies $l_t^{\Lambda_m}/l_t^{\Lambda_\mu} = c > 1$ for $t - 1 \in (s+1)\mathbb{N}$, i.e. for infinitely many $t$.

What remains to do is to extend $U$ to a universal Turing machine. We extend $U$ by defining $U(0zp) = U'(p)$ for any $z \in \{0,1\}^{3s}$, where $U'$ is some universal Turing machine. Clearly, $U$ is now universal. We have to show that this extension does not spoil the preceding consideration, i.e. that the shortest code of $x$ has sufficiently often the form $1p$ and sufficiently seldom the form $0p$. Above, $\mu$ has been chosen in such a way that $c(x)$ is a Shannon-Fano code for $\mu$-distributed strings, i.e. $c(x)$ is with high $\mu$-probability a shortest code of $x$. More precisely, $l(c(x)) \leq Km_T(x) + s$ with $\mu$-probability at least $1 - 2^{-s}$, where $Km_T$ is the monotone complexity w.r.t. any decoder $T$, especially $T = U'$. This implies $\min_p\{l(0p) : U(0p) = x*\} = 3s + 1 + Km_{U'}(x) \geq 3s + 1 + l(c(x)) - s > l(c(x)) + s + 1 \geq \min_p\{l(1p) : U(1p) = x*\}$, where the first $\geq$ holds with high probability $(1 - 2^{-s})$. This shows that the expressions (10) for $Km$ are with high probability not affected by the extension of $U$. Altogether this shows $l_t^{\Lambda_m}/l_t^{\Lambda_\mu} \overset{t\to\infty}{\not\longrightarrow} 1$ with high probability. $\qquad\square$

## 8  Outlook and Open Problems

**Speed of Off-Sequence Convergence of $m$ for Computable Environments.** The probably most interesting open question is how fast $m(\bar{x}_t|x_{<t})$ converges to zero in the deterministic case.

**Non-self-optimizingness for General $U$ and $\ell$.** Another open problem is whether for every non-degenerate loss-function, self-optimizingness of $\Lambda_m$ can be violated. We have shown that this is the case for particular choices of the universal Turing machine $U$. If $\Lambda_m$ were self-optimizing for some $U$ and general loss, this would be an unusual situation in Algorithmic Information Theory, where properties typically hold for all or no $U$. So we expect $\Lambda_m$ not to be self-optimizing for general loss and $U$ (particular $\mu$ of course). A first step may be to try to prove that for all $U$ there exists a computable sequence $x_{1:\infty}$ such that $K_U(x_{<t}\bar{x}_t) < K_U(x_{<t}x_t)$ for infinitely many $t$ (which shows $\neg(vii)$ for $K$ and error-loss), and then try to generalize to probabilistic $\mu$, $Km$, and general loss functions.

**Other Complexity Measures.** This work analyzed the predictive properties of the monotone complexity $Km$. This choice was motivated by the fact that $m$ is the MDL approximation of the sum $M$, and $Km$ is *very* close to $KM$. We expect all other (reasonable) alternative complexity measure to perform worse than $Km$. But we should be careful with precipitative conclusions, since closeness of unconditional predictive functions not necessarily implies good prediction performance, so distantness may not necessarily imply poor performance. What is easy to see is that $K(x)$ (and $K(x|l(x))$) are completely unsuitable for prediction, since $K(x0) \overset{+}{=} K(x1)$ (and $K(x0|l(x0)) \overset{+}{=} K(x1|l(x1))$), which implies that the predictive functions do not even converge for deterministic computable environments. Note that the larger a semimeasures, the more distributions it dominates, the better its predictive properties. This simple rule does not hold for non-semimeasures. Although $M$ predicts better than $m$ predicts better than $k$ in accordance with (8), $2^{-K(x|l(x))} \overset{\times}{\geq} M(x)$ is a bad predictor disaccording with (8). Besides the discussed prefix Kolmogorov complexity $K$, monotone complexity $Km$, and Solomonoff's universal prior $M = 2^{-KM}$, one may investigate the predictive properties of the historically first plain Kolmogorov complexity $C$, Schnorr's process complexity, Chaitin's complexity $Kc$, Cover's extension semimeasure $Mc$, Loveland's uniform complexity, Schmidhuber's cumulative $K^E$ and general $K^G$ complexity and corresponding measures, Vovk's predictive complexity $KP$, Schmidhuber's speed prior $S$, Levin complexity $Kt$, and several others [LV97,VW98,Sch00]. Many properties and relations are known for the unconditional versions, but little relevant for prediction of the conditional versions is known.

**Two-Part MDL.** We have approximated $M(x) := \sum_{p:U(p)=x*} 2^{-l(p)}$ by its dominant contribution $m(x) = 2^{-Km(x)}$, which we have interpreted as deterministic or one-part universal MDL. There is another representation of $M$ due to Levin [ZL70] as a mixture over semi-measures: $M(x) = \sum_{\nu \in \mathcal{M}_{enum}^{semi}} 2^{-K(\nu)}\nu(x)$ with dominant contribution $m_2(x) = 2^{-Km_2(x)}$ and universal two-part MDL $Km_2(x) := \min_{\nu \in \mathcal{M}_{enum}^{semi}} \{-\log \nu(x) + K(\nu)\}$. MDL "lives" from the validity of this approximation. $K(\nu)$ is the complexity of the probabilistic model $\nu$, and $-\log \nu(x)$ is the (Shannon-Fano) description length of data $x$ in model $\nu$. MDL usually refers to two-part MDL, and not to one-part MDL. A natural question is to ask about the predictive properties of $m_2$, similarly to $m$. $m_2$ is even closer to $M$ than $m$ is ($m_2 \stackrel{\times}{=} M$), but is also not a semi-measure. Drawing the analogy to $m$ further, we conjecture slow posterior convergence $m_2 \to \mu$ w.p.1 for computable probabilistic environments $\mu$. In [BC91], MDL has been shown to converge for computable i.i.d. environments.

**More abstract proofs** showing that violation of some of the criteria $(i) - (iv)$ necessarily lead to violation of $(vi)$ or $(vii)$ may deal with a number of complexity measures simultaneously. For instance, we have seen that any non-dense posterior set $\{\tilde{k}(x_t|x_{<t})\}$ implies non-convergence and non-self-optimizingness; the particular structure of $m$ did not matter.

**Extra Conditions.** Non-convergence or non-self-optimizingness of $m$ do not necessarily mean that $m$ fails in practice. Often one knows more than that the environment is (probabilistically) computable, or the environment possess certain additional properties, even if unknown. So one should find sufficient and/or necessary extra conditions on $\mu$ under which $m$ converges / $\Lambda_m$ self-optimizes rapidly. The results of this work have shown that for $m$-based prediction one *has* to make extra assumptions (as compared to $M$). It would be interesting to characterize the class of environments for which universal MDL alias $m$ is a good predictive approximation to $M$. Deterministic computable environments were such a class, but a rather small one, and convergence is possibly slow.

# References

[BC91]    A. R. Barron and T. M. Cover. Minimum complexity density estimation. *IEEE Transactions on Information Theory*, 37:1034–1054, 1991.

[Gác83]   P. Gács. On the relation between descriptional complexity and algorithmic probability. *Theoretical Computer Science*, 22:71–93, 1983.

[Hut01a]  M. Hutter. Convergence and error bounds of universal prediction for general alphabet. *Proceedings of the 12th Eurpean Conference on Machine Learning (ECML-2001)*, pages 239–250, 2001.

[Hut01b]  M. Hutter. New error bounds for Solomonoff prediction. *Journal of Computer and System Sciences*, 62(4):653–667, 2001.

[Hut02]   M. Hutter. Convergence and loss bounds for Bayesian sequence prediction. Technical Report IDSIA-09-01, IDSIA, Manno(Lugano), CH, 2002. http://arxiv.org/abs/cs.LG/0301014.

[KV86]    P. R. Kumar and P. P. Varaiya. *Stochastic Systems: Estimation, Identification, and Adaptive Control.* Prentice Hall, Englewood Cliffs, NJ, 1986.

[Lev73]   L. A. Levin. On the notion of a random sequence. *Soviet Math. Dokl.*, 14(5):1413–1416, 1973.

[LV97]    M. Li and P. M. B. Vitányi. *An introduction to Kolmogorov complexity and its applications.* Springer, 2nd edition, 1997.

[Sch00]   J. Schmidhuber. Algorithmic theories of everything. Report IDSIA-20-00, quant-ph/0011122, IDSIA, Manno (Lugano), Switzerland, 2000.

[Sol64]   R. J. Solomonoff. A formal theory of inductive inference: Part 1 and 2. *Inform. Control*, 7:1–22, 224–254, 1964.

[Sol78]   R. J. Solomonoff. Complexity-based induction systems: comparisons and convergence theorems. *IEEE Trans. Inform. Theory*, IT-24:422–432, 1978.

[VW98]    V. G. Vovk and C. Watkins. Universal portfolio selection. In *Proceedings of the 11th Annual Conference on Computational Learning Theory (COLT-98)*, pages 12–23, New York, 1998. ACM Press.

[ZL70]    A. K. Zvonkin and L. A. Levin. The complexity of finite objects and the development of the concepts of information and randomness by means of the theory of algorithms. *Russian Mathematical Surveys*, 25(6):83–124, 1970.

# How Many Strings Are Easy to Predict?

Yuri Kalnishkan, Vladimir Vovk, and Michael V. Vyugin

Department of Computer Science
Royal Holloway, University of London
Egham, Surrey, TW20 0EX, United Kingdom
{yura,vovk,misha}@cs.rhul.ac.uk

**Abstract.** It is well known in the theory of Kolmogorov complexity that most strings cannot be compressed; more precisely, only exponentially few ($\Theta(2^{n-m})$) strings of length $n$ can be compressed by $m$ bits. This paper extends the 'incompressibility' property of Kolmogorov complexity to the 'unpredictability' property of predictive complexity. The 'unpredictability' property states that predictive complexity (defined as the loss suffered by a universal prediction algorithm working infinitely long) of most strings is close to a trivial upper bound (the loss suffered by a trivial minimax constant prediction strategy). We show that only exponentially few strings can be successfully predicted and find the base of the exponent.

## 1   Introduction

We consider the following on-line prediction problem: given observed outcomes $x_1, x_2, \ldots, x_{n-1}$, the prediction algorithm is required to output a prediction $\gamma_n$ for the new outcome $x_n$. Let all outcomes be either 0 or 1 and predictions be real numbers from the interval $[0, 1]$. A loss function $\lambda(\omega, \gamma)$ is used to measure the discrepancy between predictions and actual outcomes. The performance of the algorithm is measured by the cumulative loss $\sum_{i=1}^{n} \lambda(x_i, \gamma_i)$. This problem has been extensively studied; see, e.g., [CBFH+97,HKW98,LW94]. The existing literature is mainly concerned with construction of specific prediction algorithms and studying their properties. This paper deals with a more abstract question: how many strings can be successfully predicted?

The difficulty of predicting a sequence $x_1, x_2, \ldots, x_n$ is formalized by the notion of predictive complexity (introduced in [VW98]). The loss suffered by any prediction algorithm on a sequence is at least the predictive complexity of the sequence and predictive complexity can be approached in the limit if a universal prediction algorithm is allowed to work infinitely long.

This paper shows that most strings have predictive complexity close to the loss of a trivial minimax constant strategy. In other words, we prove that on most strings even the idealized optimal algorithm performs little better than the trivial strategy. Of course, this result is hardly surprising: one would not expect a random string to be predictable. The interesting part is the number of predictable sequences: even though the fraction of such sequences is tiny,

B. Schölkopf and M.K. Warmuth (Eds.): COLT/Kernel 2003, LNAI 2777, pp. 522–536, 2003.

we happen to be especially interested in them. Our main result (Theorem 1) says that the idealized optimal algorithm beats the trivial strategy by $m$ on the fraction $\Theta(\beta_0^m)$ of strings of length $n$, where $\beta_0 \in (0, 1)$ is a constant determined by the loss function.

The situation is similar to that with Kolmogorov complexity, which formalizes our intuition concerning the shortest description of an object. Results of the theory of predictive complexity are expressed in the same asymptotical fashion as the results about Kolmogorov complexity. In fact, Kolmogorov complexity coincides with predictive complexity for a particular loss function called the logarithmic loss function.

One of the important properties of Kolmogorov complexity is the so called incompressibility property (see [LV97], Sect. 2.2). It states that for most strings Kolmogorov complexity is close to their length (see Appendix A for the exact statements). The intuitive interpretation is that for a random string there is no substantially shorter way to describe it than to list its elements in the most straightforward way. The unpredictability property generalizes the incompressibility property and states that most strings have predictive complexity close to a trivial upper bound. The fraction of strings of length $n$ that have Kolmogorov complexity less than $n - m$ is $\Theta(2^{-m})$; therefore, $\beta_0 = 1/2$ for the logarithmic loss. In general, $\beta_0$ is determined by both the local behaviour of the loss function in the neighbourhood of the minimax and its global behaviour.

Sect. 2 defines predictive complexity. Sect. 3 contains the statement of the main theorem followed by a discussion. The main result is proven in Sect. 4; some technical parts of the proof have been moved to appendices.

## 2 Preliminaries

We consider finite strings of elements from the binary alphabet $\mathbb{B} = \{0, 1\}$ and denote these strings by bold letters. The set of all finite binary strings is denoted by $\mathbb{B}^*$. The length of a string $x \in \mathbb{B}^*$ is denoted by $|x|$. We use similar notation $|A|$ for the number of elements of a set $A$. The notation $x^{(k)}$ refers to the prefix of $x$ of length $k$. The notation $\mathbb{N}$ refers to the set of non-negative integers $\{0, 1, 2, \ldots\}$.

We will now define predictive complexity and discuss some of its properties.

### 2.1 The Definition of Predictive Complexity

An *on-line prediction game* (or simply *game*) $\mathfrak{G}$ is a triple $(\mathbb{B}, [0, 1], \lambda)$, where $\mathbb{B} = \{0, 1\}$ is the *outcome space*, $[0, 1]$ is the *prediction space*, and $\lambda : \mathbb{B} \times [0, 1] \to [0, +\infty]$ is a *loss function*. We suppose that $\lambda$ is computable and continuous.

The following are examples of games: the *square-loss* game with the loss function $\lambda(\omega, \gamma) = (\omega - \gamma)^2$ and the *logarithmic* game with

$$\lambda(\omega, \gamma) = \begin{cases} -\log_2(1 - \gamma) & \text{if } \omega = 0 \\ -\log_2 \gamma & \text{if } \omega = 1 \end{cases} .$$

Consider a computable *prediction strategy* $\mathfrak{A} : \mathbb{B}^* \to [0,1]$; it maps a sequence of outcomes into a prediction. We say that on a finite sequence $x_1 x_2 \ldots x_n \in \mathbb{B}^n$, where $n \in \mathbb{N}$, the strategy $\mathfrak{A}$ suffers loss

$$\mathrm{Loss}_{\mathfrak{A}}^{\mathfrak{G}}(x_1 x_2 \ldots x_n) = \sum_{i=1}^{n} \lambda(x_i, \mathfrak{A}(x_1 x_2 \ldots x_{i-1})) \ .$$

A function $L : \mathbb{B}^* \to [0, +\infty]$ is a *loss process* if it coincides with the loss of a computable prediction strategy.

An equivalent definition of a loss process can be given as follows. A computable function $L : \mathbb{B}^* \to [0, +\infty]$ is a loss process if $L(\Lambda) = 0$, where $\Lambda$ is the empty string, and for every $\boldsymbol{x} \in \mathbb{B}^*$ there is $\gamma \in [0,1]$ such that

$$\begin{cases} L(\boldsymbol{x}0) - L(\boldsymbol{x}) = \lambda(0, \gamma) \ , \\ L(\boldsymbol{x}1) - L(\boldsymbol{x}) = \lambda(1, \gamma) \ . \end{cases} \tag{1}$$

Unfortunately, for the majority of nontrivial games the class of loss processes does not have a universal element. It can be easily shown using a simple diagonalization argument that every strategy is greatly outperformed by some other strategy on some sequences. To overcome this problem we extend the class of loss processes to the class of superloss processes. The original idea (for what is in our terms the logarithmic game) goes back to Kolmogorov and Levin. A *superloss process* is a function $L : \mathbb{B}^* \to [0, +\infty]$ such that

− $L$ is semi-computable from above,
− $L(\Lambda) = 0$, and
− for every $\boldsymbol{x} \in \mathbb{B}^*$ there is $\gamma \in [0,1]$ such that

$$\begin{cases} L(\boldsymbol{x}0) - L(\boldsymbol{x}) \geq \lambda(0, \gamma) \ , \\ L(\boldsymbol{x}1) - L(\boldsymbol{x}) \geq \lambda(1, \gamma) \ , \end{cases} \tag{2}$$

We say that a superloss process $\mathcal{K}$ is *universal* if for every superloss process $L$ there is a constant $C$ such that $\mathcal{K}(\boldsymbol{x}) \leq L(\boldsymbol{x}) + C$ for all strings $\boldsymbol{x}$. As we will see below, many games, including the logarithmic and the square-loss, have universal superloss processes. A universal process for some game is called *predictive complexity* for that game.

We will need a more general definition of conditional complexity. Let $\Xi$ be an ensemble of constructive objects containing the representations of all finite sequences $\mathbb{B}^*$ and natural numbers $\mathbb{N}$. A function $L : \mathbb{B}^* \times \Xi \to (-\infty, +\infty]$ (we will separate arguments of $L$ by the vertical line | rather than by the comma) is a *conditional superloss process* if

− $L(\Lambda \mid \boldsymbol{y}) = 0$ for all $\boldsymbol{y} \in \mathbb{B}^*$,
− $L$ is semi-computable from above, and
− for every $\boldsymbol{x}, \boldsymbol{y} \in \mathbb{B}^*$ there is $\gamma \in [0,1]$ such that

$$\begin{cases} L(\boldsymbol{x}0 \mid \boldsymbol{y}) - L(\boldsymbol{x} \mid \boldsymbol{y}) \geq \lambda(0, \gamma) \ , \\ L(\boldsymbol{x}1 \mid \boldsymbol{y}) - L(\boldsymbol{x} \mid \boldsymbol{y}) \geq \lambda(1, \gamma) \ . \end{cases} \tag{3}$$

In other terms, $L(x \mid y)$ is uniformly semicomputable from above and for each fixed $y$ it is a superloss process. The intuition behind this concept is that the learner may have access to certain additional information.

A conditional superloss process $\mathcal{K}$ is *universal* if for every conditional superloss process $L$ there is a constant $C$ such that the inequality $\mathcal{K}(x \mid y) \leq L(x \mid y) + C$ holds for all $x, y \in \mathbb{B}^*$. A universal conditional superloss process is called *conditional predictive complexity*. It is easy to see that the existence of conditional predictive complexity $\mathcal{K}(x \mid y)$ implies the existence of $\mathcal{K}(x)$, and $\mathcal{K}(x \mid \Lambda)$ coincides with $\mathcal{K}(x)$ up to an additive constant.

## 2.2   Superpredictions and the Existence of Predictive Complexity

We call a point $(x_0, x_1) \in [0, +\infty]^2$ a *superprediction* w.r.t. $\mathfrak{G}$ if there is a prediction $\gamma \in [0, 1]$ such that $x_0 \geq \lambda(0, \gamma)$ and $x_1 \geq \lambda(1, \gamma)$; let $S$ be the set of superpredictions. Geometrically, $S$ is the set of points lying to the north-east of the curve $\{(\lambda(0, \gamma), \lambda(1, \gamma) \mid \gamma \in [0, 1]\}$.

We need to define some classes of games in terms of $S$. We say that $\mathfrak{G}$ is *symmetrical* if $S$ is symmetrical w.r.t. the straight line $x = y$. For example, if $\lambda$ is such that $\lambda(0, t) = \lambda(1, 1 - t)$, then the game is symmetrical.

Mixability is a less trivial property introduced in [VW98]. Take a parameter $\beta \in (0, 1)$ and consider the homeomorphism $\mathfrak{B}_\beta : (-\infty, +\infty]^2 \to [0, +\infty)^2$ specified by

$$\mathfrak{B}_\beta(x, y) = (\beta^x, \beta^y) \ . \tag{4}$$

A game $\mathfrak{G}$ with the set of superpredictions $S$ is called *$\beta$-mixable* if the set $\mathfrak{B}_\beta(S)$ is convex. A game $\mathfrak{G}$ is *mixable* if it is $\beta$-mixable for some $\beta \in (0, 1)$.

**Proposition 1 ([VW98]).** *If a game $\mathfrak{G}$ with the set of superpredictions $S$ is mixable then there is conditional predictive complexity w.r.t. $\mathfrak{G}$.*

It is easy to see that there is a positive constant $C$ such that for all strings $x$ and $y$ the inequality $\mathcal{K}(x \mid y) \leq \mathcal{K}(x) + C$ holds. On the other hand, by applying the Aggregating Algorithm (see [VW98]) it may be shown that, if the game is mixable, then there is a positive constant $c$ such that $\mathcal{K}(x) \leq \mathcal{K}(x \mid y) + c\mathrm{KP}(y)$ for all strings $x$ and $y$, where KP stands for prefix complexity.

The square-loss and the logarithmic games are both mixable and thus they specify conditional and unconditional complexities. We denote them by $\mathcal{K}^{\mathrm{sq}}$ and $\mathcal{K}^{\mathrm{log}}$, respectively. It follows straight from the definition that the (unconditional) complexity w.r.t. the logarithmic game coincides with KM, the negative logarithm of Levin's a priori semimeasure. It differs from plain Kolmogorov complexity K by a term of logarithmic order in the length of the string, i.e. there is $c > 0$ such that for all strings $x \neq \Lambda$ we have $|\mathrm{K}(x) - \mathrm{KM}(x)| \leq c \ln |x|$. A proof may be found in [LV97]. The definition of plain Kolmogorov complexity K is given in Appendix A.

# 3   Main Results and Discussion

**Theorem 1 (Unpredictability Property).** *Let $\mathfrak{G}$ be a mixable symmetrical game specifying conditional predictive complexity $\mathcal{K}$. Suppose that the set $S$ of superpredictions for $\mathfrak{G}$ is such that the boundary $\partial S$ is a twice differentiable curve in a vicinity of the point $(B, B)$, where $B = \inf\{t \in \mathbb{R} \mid (t, t) \in S\}$. Then the inequalities*

$$\sup_{n,m \in \mathbb{N}} \frac{|\{x \in \mathbb{B}^n \mid \mathcal{K}(x \mid m) \leq Bn - m\}|}{2^n \beta_0^m} \leq 1 \tag{5}$$

*and*

$$\inf_{m \in \mathbb{N}} \lim_{n \to \infty} \frac{|\{x \in \mathbb{B}^n \mid \mathcal{K}(x \mid m) \leq Bn - m\}|}{2^n \beta_0^m} > 0 \tag{6}$$

*hold, where $\beta_0 \in (0, 1)$ is the infimum of all $\beta \in (0, 1)$ such that the set $\mathfrak{B}_\beta(S)$ lies below the straight line $x + y = 2\beta^B$.*

This theorem assumes not only that the loss function is computable but also that $\beta_0$ is computable and that the set

$$S \cap \{(x, y) \mid x \neq y \ \& \ x + y = 2\beta_0^B\}$$

contains a computable point (if non-empty). For specific loss functions studied in the literature this is always the case.

Let us discuss the theorem informally. Inequality (5) means that for all positive integers $n$ and $m$ the inequality

$$\frac{|\{x \in \mathbb{B}^n \mid \mathcal{K}(x \mid m) \leq Bn - m\}|}{2^n} \leq \beta_0^m$$

holds. This can be interpreted as a statement about the probability provided we assign equal probabilities to all strings of length $n$. Lemma 1 proves this inequality for any $\beta \in (0, 1)$ such that $\mathfrak{B}_\beta(S)$ lies below the straight line $x/2 + y/2 = \beta^B$. The value $\beta_0$ just provides the best bound.

Note that values of $\beta$ such that $\mathfrak{B}_\beta(S)$ lies below the straight line $x/2 + y/2 = \beta^B$ exist. Indeed, since $\mathfrak{G}$ is mixable, the set $\mathfrak{B}_\beta(S)$ is convex for some $\beta \in (0, 1)$. Since the set $\mathfrak{B}_\beta(S)$ is symmetrical in the bisector $x = y$, the line $x + y = 2\beta^B$ is a support line for $\mathfrak{B}_\beta(S)$ and convex sets are not cut by their support lines (see, e.g., [Egg58]).

However, in the general case, $\mathfrak{G}$ is not necessarily $\beta_0$-mixable. It is possible that for some values of $\beta$ the game is not $\beta$-mixable, i.e., the set $\mathfrak{B}_\beta(S)$ is not convex, but $\mathfrak{B}_\beta(S)$ still lies below the straight line in question.

Inequality (6) shows that the value $\beta_0$ cannot be decreased further. The inequality can be reformulated as follows. There is a constant $\theta > 0$ such that for every positive integer $m$ there is a number $n_0(m)$ such that for all integers $n > n_0(m)$ the inequality

$$\frac{|\{x \in \mathbb{B}^n \mid \mathcal{K}(x \mid m) \leq Bn - m\}|}{2^n} \geq \theta \beta_0^m \tag{7}$$

holds. If we portray a pair $(n, m)$ by a corresponding point in the positive quadrant, (7) holds inside a certain 'wedge'. Lemmas 3 and 4 give insight into the shape of this wedge. Depending on the set $S$, there are two cases, which are addressed by the lemmas. In one of the cases we show that $n_0(m)$ can be taken to be equal $cm$, where $c$ is a constant independent of $m$ and in the other case we take $n_0(m) = cm^3$ (given certain regularity conditions, it is possible to reduce the degree and to take $n_0(m) = cm^2$). The exact shape of the 'wedge' is an open problem.

It is easy to see that for the logarithmic game $\beta_0 = 1/2$ and thus our theorem states that $|\{x \in \mathbb{B}^n \mid \mathrm{KM}(x \mid m) \leq Bn - m\}| \leq 2^{n-m}$ for all $n, m$, while $\varliminf_{n \to \infty} |\{x \in \mathbb{B}^n \mid \mathrm{KM}(x \mid m) \leq Bn - m\}| \geq \theta 2^{n-m}$ for some positive $\theta$.

Appendix A reviews the definition of the plain Kolmogorov complexity K and the incompressibility property. It is remarkable that similar estimates exist for the plain Kolmogorov complexity while their short proof is based on completely different ideas.

## 4   Proof of the Main Theorem

This section contains the proof of the main theorem. The proof splits into a number of lemmas, two of which are proved in appendices.

*Proof (of Theorem 1).* First the existence of values of $\beta \in (0, 1)$ such that $\mathfrak{B}_\beta(S)$ lies below the line $x + y = 2\beta^B$ is proved in the discussion in Section 3.

Secondly the infimum of such values of $\beta$ is less than 1. This is implied by the formula for the second derivative of the function $g(x)$ whose graph represents $\partial \mathfrak{B}_\beta(S)$ in a vicinity of $(\beta^B, \beta^B)$. Indeed, let $x(t)$ and $y(t)$ be smooth functions parameterizing the boundary $\partial S$ in a vicinity of $(B, B)$. For definiteness sake, assume that $x(t)$ strictly increases and $y(t)$ strictly decreases. Then $g_\beta(\beta^x) = \beta^y$ and

$$\frac{d^2 \beta^{y(t)}}{d \left(\beta^{x(t)}\right)^2} =$$
$$\frac{\beta^{y(t) - 2x(t)}}{\ln \beta \cdot (x'(t))^2} \left( (y'(t) - x'(t))y'(t) \ln \beta + \frac{y''(t)x'(t) - y'(t)x''(t)}{x'(t)} \right) .$$

The inequality $g''_\beta(\beta^x) \leq 0$ is equivalent to

$$(y'(t) - x'(t))y'(t) \ln \beta \geq -\frac{y''(t)x'(t) - y'(t)x''(t)}{x'(t)} . \tag{8}$$

For every fixed value of $t$, the left-hand side is a negative value which tends to $-\infty$ as $\beta \to 0$, while the right-hand side is a fixed number. Thus the inequality gets violated for small values of $\beta$.

Inequality (5) follows from Lemma 1 below.

In order to prove (6), we need to consider two cases. Either there is $\Delta \in (0, \beta_0^B]$ such that the inverse image $\mathfrak{B}_{\beta_0}^{-1}(\beta_0^B - \Delta, \beta_0^B + \Delta)$ is a superprediction,

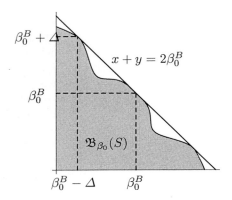
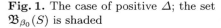

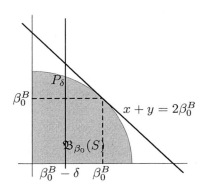

**Fig. 1.** The case of positive $\Delta$; the set $\mathfrak{B}_{\beta_0}(S)$ is shaded

**Fig. 2.** The case of the touch of the second order; the set $\mathfrak{B}_{\beta_0}(S)$ is shaded

or the line $x + y = 2\beta_0^B$ and the curve $\partial \mathfrak{B}_{\beta_0}(S)$ have a touch of the second order at $(\beta_0^B, \beta_0^B)$ (see Figs. 1 and 2).

Indeed, suppose that $g_{\beta_0}$ has a strictly negative second derivative at the point $\beta_0^B$. By continuity, for some small $\beta > \beta_0$ the second derivative of $g_\beta$ at $\beta^B$ will remain negative and thus there are $\varepsilon, \delta > 0$ such that for every $\beta \in [\beta_0 - \varepsilon, \beta_0]$ the part of $\mathfrak{B}_\beta(S)$ in the stripe $[\beta^B - \delta, \beta^B + \delta] \times \mathbb{R}$ lies below the line $x + y = 2\beta^B$. Since $\beta_0$ is the infimum, there exists $\Delta$ in question.

The cases are considered in Lemmas 3 and 4.    $\square$

### 4.1   The Upper Bound on Probability

In this subsection we derive the upper bound on the number of strings of low complexity.

**Lemma 1.** *Let $\mathfrak{G}$ be a symmetrical game with the set of superpredictions $S$; let $B = \inf\{t \in \mathbb{R} \mid (t, t) \in S\}$ and let $L$ be a conditional superloss process w.r.t. $\mathfrak{G}$. Let $\beta \in (0, 1)$ be such that $\mathfrak{B}_\beta(S)$ lies below the straight line $x + y = 2\beta^B$. Then for all positive integers $n$ and $m$ we have*

$$\frac{|\{\boldsymbol{x} \in \mathbb{B}^n \mid \exists k \in \{1, 2, \ldots, n\} : L(\boldsymbol{x}^{(k)} \mid m) \leq Bk - m\}|}{2^n} \leq \beta^m . \tag{9}$$

*Proof.* Consider the function $\beta^{L(\boldsymbol{x}|m) - B|\boldsymbol{x}|}$. If we show that for every fixed $m$ it is a supermartingale and apply a variant of Doob's inequality, the bound will follow. The definitions of a martingale and a supermartingale and the required inequality may be found in Appendix B.

**Lemma 2.** *Under the conditions of Lemma 1, for every $\boldsymbol{x} \in \mathbb{B}^*$, the inequality*

$$\frac{1}{2}\beta^{L(\boldsymbol{x}1|m) - B(|\boldsymbol{x}1|)} + \frac{1}{2}\beta^{L(\boldsymbol{x}0|m) - B(|\boldsymbol{x}0|)} \leq \beta^{L(\boldsymbol{x}|m) - B|\boldsymbol{x}|}$$

*holds for every positive integer $m$.*

*Proof.* By definition of predictive complexity, the pair $(L(\boldsymbol{x}1 \mid m) - L(\boldsymbol{x} \mid m), L(\boldsymbol{x}0 \mid m) - L(\boldsymbol{x} \mid m))$ is a superprediction, i.e., belongs to $S$. The conditions of Lemma 1 imply that for every $(x, y) \in \mathfrak{B}_\beta(S)$, the inequality $x/2 + y/2 \leq \beta^B$ holds. The lemma follows. $\qquad\square$

It follows from this lemma that $\beta^{L(\boldsymbol{x}\mid m) - B\mid\boldsymbol{x}\mid}$ is a supermartingale. $\qquad\square$

## 4.2 Tightness of the Bound

In this subsection we show that the bound from the previous subsection is tight.

**Lemma 3.** *Let $\mathfrak{G}$ be a symmetrical game with the set of superpredictions $S$; let $B = \inf\{t \in \mathbb{R} \mid (t, t) \in S\}$ and let $\mathfrak{G}$ specify conditional complexity $\mathcal{K}$. Let $\beta_0 \in (0, 1)$ and $\Delta \in (0, \beta_0^B]$ be such that the point $\mathfrak{B}_{\beta_0}^{-1}((\beta_0^B - \Delta, \beta_0^B + \Delta))$ is a superprediction. Then there are positive constants $c$ and $\theta$ such that for every positive integer $m$ and positive integer $n \geq cm$ the inequality*

$$\theta\beta_0^m \leq \frac{|\{\boldsymbol{x} \in \mathbb{B}^n \mid \mathcal{K}(\boldsymbol{x} \mid m) \leq Bn - m\}|}{2^n}$$

*holds.*

The conditions of the lemma are pictured in Fig. 1.

**Lemma 4.** *Let $\mathfrak{G}$ be a symmetrical game with the set of superpredictions $S$, let $B = \inf\{t \in \mathbb{R} \mid (t, t) \in S\}$, and let the boundary $\partial S$ be represented by a twice differentiable curve in a vicinity of the point $(B, B)$; let $\mathfrak{G}$ specify conditional predictive complexity $\mathcal{K}$. Let $\beta_0 \in (0, 1)$ be such that the curves $x/2 + y/2 = \beta_0^B$ and $\mathfrak{B}(\partial S)$ have a touch of the second order at the point $(\beta_0^B, \beta_0^B)$. Then there are positive constants $c$ and $\theta$ such that for every positive integer $m$ and positive integer $n \geq cm^3$ the inequality*

$$\theta\beta_0^m \leq \frac{|\{\boldsymbol{x} \in \mathbb{B}^n \mid \mathcal{K}(\boldsymbol{x} \mid m) \leq Bn - m\}|}{2^n} \tag{10}$$

*holds.*

The statement of the lemma and some details of the proof are pictured in Fig. 2.

The proofs are given in Appendices C and D.

*Remark 1.* If the boundary $\partial S$ can be represented by a thrice differentiable curve in a vicinity of the point $(B, B)$, the construction from the proof of Lemma 4 can be strengthened to show that (10) holds for all $n > cm^2$ for some $c$. See Appendix E for details.

# References

[CBFH+97] N. Cesa-Bianchi, Y. Freund, D. Haussler, D. P. Helmbold, R. E. Schapire, and M. K. Warmuth. How to use expert advice. *Journal of the ACM*, 44(3):427–485, 1997.

[Egg58]     H. G. Eggleston. *Convexity*. Cambridge University Press, 1958.

[Gal68]     R. G. Gallager. *Information Theory and Reliable Communication*. John Wiley and Sons, INC, 1968.

[HKW98]     D. Haussler, J. Kivinen, and M. K. Warmuth. Sequential prediction of individual sequences under general loss functions. *IEEE Transactions on Information Theory*, 44(5):1906–1925, 1998.

[KT75]     S. Karlin and H. M. Taylor. *A First Course in Stochastic Processes*. Academic Press, Inc, 1975.

[LV97]     M. Li and P. Vitányi. *An Introduction to Kolmogorov Complexity and Its Applications*. Springer, New York, 2nd edition, 1997.

[LW94]     N. Littlestone and M. K. Warmuth. The weighted majority algorithm. *Information and Computation*, 108:212–261, 1994.

[VW98]     V. Vovk and C. J. H. C. Watkins. Universal portfolio selection. In *Proceedings of the 11th Annual Conference on Computational Learning Theory*, pages 12–23, 1998.

[V'y94]     V. V. V'yugin. Algorithmic entropy (complexity) of finite objects and its applications to defining randomness and amount of information. *Selecta Mathematica formerly Sovietica*, 13:357–389, 1994.

[Wil91]     D. Williams. *Probability with Martingales*. Cambridge University Press, 1991.

[ZL70]     A. K. Zvonkin and L. A. Levin. The complexity of finite objects and the development of the concepts of information and randomness by means of the theory of algorithms. *Russian Math. Surveys*, 25:83–124, 1970.

# Appendix A: Kolmogorov Complexity

In this appendix we briefly survey the definition of Kolmogorov complexity and the incompressibility property.

A *programming language* $P$ is a partial computable function from $\mathbb{B}^*$ to $\mathbb{B}^*$. Informally, an argument $p$ of $P$ is a program and the value $P(p)$ is the result of executing this program; this result may be undefined since binary strings are not all syntactically correct programs which can be executed and print a result within a finite lapse of time. Given a programming language $P$, one may define complexity w.r.t. $P$ by the equation

$$\mathrm{K}_P(\boldsymbol{x}) = \min\{n \mid \exists \boldsymbol{y} \in \mathbb{B}^n : P(\boldsymbol{y}) = \boldsymbol{x}\} \ , \qquad (11)$$

where $\min(\varnothing) = +\infty$ by definition.

A fundamental Kolmogorov's theorem (see any of [ZL70,V'y94,LV97]) states that there is a universal programming language $U$, i.e. a language such that for every $P$ there is a constant $C > 0$ such that for every $\boldsymbol{x} \in \mathbb{B}^*$ we have $\mathrm{K}_U(\boldsymbol{x}) \leq \mathrm{K}_P(\boldsymbol{x}) + C$. Clearly, the difference between the two complexities specified by universal functions is bounded by a constant. We may pick one universal function $U$ and define *plain Kolmogorov complexity* $\mathrm{K} = \mathrm{K}_U$.

**Proposition 2 (Incompressibility Property).**

*(i) There is a constant $C$ such that for every $x \in \mathbb{B}^*$ the inequality*

$$K(x) \leq |x| + C \tag{12}$$

*holds.*

*(ii) For every positive integer $n$ and every $m < n$ we have*

$$|\{x \mid |x| = n \text{ and } K(x) \leq n - m\}| \leq 2^{n-m+1} . \tag{13}$$

This statement can be found in any of the sources [ZL70,V'y94,LV97]. For completeness, we give a short proof.

*Proof.* The proof of (i) is by considering the programming language which performs the identity mapping. The statement (ii) follows from the observation that there can be no more then $2^s$ strings of complexity $s$ since each of them is generated by its own program of length $s$.  □

The bound in (ii) is tight since the following holds:

**Proposition 3.** *There is a positive constant $\theta$ such that for all positive integers $n$ and $m < n$ we have*

$$|\{x \mid |x| = n \text{ and } K(x) \leq n - m\}| \geq \theta 2^{n-m+1} . \tag{14}$$

*Proof.* The proposition is implied by the bound (12).  □

# Appendix B: Martingales

Here we briefly review a general definition of a *(super)martingale*, adapt it to our special case, and formulate an inequality necessary for the derivation of the incompressibility property.

We are going to use (more or less) the terminology and notation from [Wil91]. Throughout this appendix $\Omega$ refers to a *sample space*; its elements $\omega \in \Omega$ are *sample points*. A *filtered space* is a quadruple $(\Omega, \mathcal{F}, \{\mathcal{F}\}_n, \text{Pr})$ where $\mathcal{F}$ is a $\sigma$-algebra on $\Omega$, the sets $\mathcal{F}_n$, $n = 0, 1, 2, \ldots$, are sub-$\sigma$-algebras of $\mathcal{F}$ such that

$$\mathcal{F}_0 \subseteq \mathcal{F}_1 \subseteq \ldots \subseteq \mathcal{F} ,$$

and Pr is a probability measure on $(\Omega, \mathcal{F})$. A sequence of random variables $X_0, X_1, X_2, \ldots$ on $\Omega$ is a *martingale* w.r.t. $(\Omega, \mathcal{F}, \{\mathcal{F}\}_n, \text{Pr})$ if for every $n = 0, 1, 2, \ldots$ the variable $X_n$ is measurable w.r.t. $\mathcal{F}_n$, and for every $n \geq 1$ we have

  − $\mathbf{E}_{\text{Pr}}(|X_n|) < +\infty$, and
  − $\mathbf{E}_{\text{Pr}}(X_n \mid \mathcal{F}_{n-1}) = X_{n-1}$.

In the definition of a supermartingale the last condition should be replaced by $\mathbf{E}_{\text{Pr}}(X_n \mid \mathcal{F}_{n-1}) \leq X_{n-1}$. In the above expressions $\mathbf{E}_{\text{Pr}}$ stands for the expectations taken w.r.t. the probability Pr.

Non-negative martingales satisfy Doob's inequality (see, e.g., [Wil91]); we need a version of this inequality for supermartingales. The following statement may be found, e.g., in [KT75] (Lemma 5.2):

**Proposition 4.** *If non-negative random variables* $Z_0, Z_1, Z_2, \ldots$ *form a super-martingale w.r.t.* $(\Omega, \mathcal{F}, \{\mathcal{F}\}_n, \Pr)$, *then for every* $c > 0$ *and positive integer* $n$ *we have*

$$\Pr\left\{\max_{k=0,1,2,\ldots} Z_k \geq c\right\} \leq \frac{\mathbf{E}Z_0}{c}.$$

Consider the case of the Bernoulli distribution with the probability of 1 equal to $p$. The sample space is the set of all infinite binary strings $\mathbb{B}^\infty$. The $\sigma$-algebra $\mathcal{F}$ is generated by all cylinders $\Gamma_{\boldsymbol{x}}$, $\boldsymbol{x} \in \mathbb{B}^*$, where

$$\Gamma_{\boldsymbol{x}} = \{\boldsymbol{x}\tau \mid \tau \in \mathbb{B}^\infty\}.$$

For every $n = 0, 1, 2, \ldots$, the $\sigma$-algebra $\mathcal{F}_n$ is generated by the cylinders $\Gamma_{\boldsymbol{x}}$ such that $|\boldsymbol{x}| = n$. A function measurable w.r.t. $\mathcal{F}_n$ may be identified with a function defined on $\mathbb{B}^n$. Thus a sequence of random variables $X_0, X_1, X_2, \ldots$ such that $X_n$ is measurable w.r.t. $\mathcal{F}_n$, $n = 0, 1, 2, \ldots$, may be identified with a function $L : \mathbb{B}^* \to \mathbb{R}$. In order to be a martingale, it should satisfy the condition $pL(\boldsymbol{x}1) + (1-p)L(\boldsymbol{x}0) = L(\boldsymbol{x})$ for every $\boldsymbol{x} \in \mathbb{B}^*$. If for every $\boldsymbol{x} \in \mathbb{B}^*$ we have $pL(\boldsymbol{x}1) + (1-p)L(\boldsymbol{x}0) \leq L(\boldsymbol{x})$, it is a supermartingale.

## Appendix C: Proof of Lemma 3

Let $(\log_{\beta_0}(\beta_0^B - \Delta), \log_{\beta_0}(\beta_0^B + \Delta))$ be a superprediction. For every positive integer $m$ we will construct a superloss process $L_m$ that achieves

$$p(n, m) = \frac{|\{\boldsymbol{x} \in \mathbb{B}^n \mid L_m(\boldsymbol{x}) \leq Bn - m\}|}{2^n} \geq \frac{1}{4}\beta_0^m \tag{15}$$

for every $n \geq c_1 m + c_2$, where $c_1$ and $c_2$ are some constant independent of $m$ or $n$.

In order to construct these superloss processes, we need the metaphor of a 'superstrategy'. Within this proof the word 'superstrategy' is taken to mean a prediction algorithm that on every trial outputs a superprediction and suffers corresponding loss. The total loss of a superstrategy is a superloss process.

Let $\mathfrak{A}$ be the superstrategy that always outputs the same superprediction $(\log_{\beta_0}(\beta_0^B - \Delta), \log_{\beta_0}(\beta_0^B + \Delta))$ and let $L(\boldsymbol{x})$ be the loss of this superstrategy. The superstrategy $\mathfrak{A}_m$ works as follows. It imitates $\mathfrak{A}$ as long as the inequality $L(\boldsymbol{x}) > B|\boldsymbol{x}| - m$ holds. After the inequality gets violated, the superstrategy switches to the superprediction $(B, B)$. Let $L_m(\boldsymbol{x})$ be the loss of $\mathfrak{A}_m$. Put $A = B - \log_{\beta_0}(\beta_0^B + \Delta) > 0$ so that $(B|\boldsymbol{x}| - m) - L_m(\boldsymbol{x})$ does not exceed $A$.

Let $M(\boldsymbol{x}) = \beta_0^{L(\boldsymbol{x})-B|\boldsymbol{x}|}$ and $M_m(\boldsymbol{x}) = \beta_0^{L_m(\boldsymbol{x})-B|\boldsymbol{x}|}$. These processes are martingales w.r.t. the Bernoulli distribution with the probability of success being equal to $1/2$. We have

$$\mathbf{E}M(\xi_1^{(1/2)}, \xi_2^{(1/2)}, \ldots, \xi_n^{(1/2)}) = \mathbf{E}M_m(\xi_1^{(1/2)}, \xi_2^{(1/2)}, \ldots, \xi_n^{(1/2)}) = 1$$

for every positive integer $m$, where $\xi_1^{(1/2)}, \xi_2^{(1/2)}, \ldots, \xi_n^{(1/2)}$ are results of $n$ independent Bernoulli trials with the probability of success being equal to $1/2$. Note that $M_m(\boldsymbol{x}) \leq \beta_0^{-m-A} \leq 2\beta_0^{-m}$ for every $\boldsymbol{x} \in \mathbb{B}^m$.

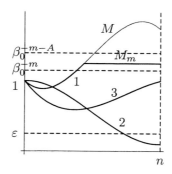

**Fig. 3.** Three options for trajectories from the proof of Lemma 3

Fix a positive integer $m$ as in the statement of the theorem. Pick $x$ of length $n$ and consider the 'trajectories'

$$\langle 1, M(x^{(1)}), M(x^{(2)}), \ldots, M(x^{(n)}) \rangle$$

and

$$\langle 1, M_m(x^{(1)}), M_m(x^{(2)}), \ldots, M_m(x^{(n)}) \rangle \ .$$

Consider $\varepsilon > 0$ such that $\varepsilon < 1 \leq \beta_0^{-m}$. There are three mutually exclusive options:

1. $M(x^{(k)}) \geq \beta_0^{-m}$ for some $k \leq n$ and thus $\beta_0^{-m} \leq M_m(x) \leq 2\beta_0^{-m}$.
2. $M(x^{(k)}) < \beta_0^{-m}$ for all $k \leq n$ and $M_m(x) = M(x) \leq \varepsilon$.
3. $M(x^{(k)}) < \beta_0^{-m}$ for all $k \leq n$ and $\beta_0^{-m} > M_m(x) = M(x) > \varepsilon$.

These three options are shown in Fig. 3, where the values of $M(x^{(k)})$ and $M_m(x^{(k)})$ are plotted against values of $k$.

The expectation of $M_n(x)$ over all $x$ of length $n$ splits into the sum of three terms corresponding to the three classes of trajectories

$$1 = \mathbf{E}M_m(\xi_1^{(1/2)}, \xi_2^{(1/2)}, \ldots, \xi_n^{(1/2)}) = \Sigma_1 + \Sigma_2 + \Sigma_3 \ , \tag{16}$$

where $\xi_1^{(1/2)}, \xi_2^{(1/2)}, \ldots, \xi_n^{(1/2)}$ are as above. The following bounds hold:

$$\Sigma_1 \leq 2\beta_0^{-m} \Pr\{M_m(\xi_1^{(1/2)}, \xi_2^{(1/2)}, \ldots, \xi_n^{(1/2)}) \geq \beta_0^{-m})\},$$
$$\Sigma_2 \leq \varepsilon,$$
$$\Sigma_3 \leq \beta_0^{-m} \Pr\{\varepsilon < M_m(\xi_1^{(1/2)}, \xi_2^{(1/2)}, \ldots, \xi_n^{(1/2)}) < \beta_0^{-m}\}$$
$$\leq \beta_0^{-m} \Pr\{M(\xi_1^{(1/2)}, \xi_2^{(1/2)}, \ldots, \xi_n^{(1/2)}) > \varepsilon\} \ .$$

The event $\{M_m(x) \geq \beta_0^{-m})\}$ coincides with the event $\{L_m(x) \leq Bn - m\}$ and thus $\Pr\{M_m(\xi_1^{(1/2)}, \xi_2^{(1/2)}, \ldots, \xi_n^{(1/2)}) \geq \beta_0^{-m})\} = p(n, m)$. If we denote the value

$$\Pr\{M(\xi_1^{(1/2)}, \xi_2^{(1/2)}, \ldots, \xi_n^{(1/2)}) > \varepsilon\} =$$
$$\Pr\{L(\xi_1^{(1/2)}, \xi_2^{(1/2)}, \ldots, \xi_n^{(1/2)}) - Bn < \log_{\beta_0} \varepsilon\}$$

by $\alpha_\varepsilon(n)$, we obtain the inequality

$$1 \leq 2\beta_0^{-m} p(n, m) + \varepsilon + \beta_0^{-m} \alpha_\varepsilon(n) \tag{17}$$

and thus

$$p(n, m) \geq \frac{\beta_0^m}{2} - \varepsilon\beta_0^m - \alpha_\varepsilon(n) \ . \tag{18}$$

We will construct an upper bound on $\alpha_\varepsilon(n)$ by means of the Chernoff bound. A derivation of the Chernoff bound may be found in [Gal68]; we need the following simple form of the bound. If $X_1, X_2, \ldots, X_n$ are independent Bernoulli trials with the probability of success equal to $p \in (0, 1)$, $S = X_1 + X_2 + \cdots + X_n$, and $\gamma \in [0, 1]$, then

$$\Pr\{S < (1 - \gamma)pn\} \leq e^{-np\gamma^2/2} \ . \tag{19}$$

The function $L(x) - B|x|$ may be treated as a biased random walk. We will straighten it in order to apply the Chernoff bound. The value

$$d = \frac{(L(x0) - B|x0|) + (L(x1) - B|x1|)}{2} - (L(x) - B|x|)$$

$$= \frac{1}{2}(\log_{\beta_0}(\beta_0^B + \Delta) + \log_{\beta_0}(\beta_0^B - \Delta) - 2B)$$

$$= \frac{\ln\left(1 - \left(\frac{\Delta}{\beta_0^B}\right)^2\right)}{2\ln\beta_0}$$

$$> 0$$

is independent of $x \in \mathbb{B}^*$ so that $\mathbf{E}(L(\xi_1^{(1/2)}, \xi_2^{(1/2)}, \ldots, \xi_n^{(1/2)}) - Bn) = nd$; let $r = (\log_{\beta_0}(\beta_0^B - \Delta) - B) - d = d - (\log_{\beta_0}(\beta_0^B + \Delta) - B) > 0$. The function

$$S(x) = \frac{L(x) - B|x| - d|x|}{2r} + \frac{|x|}{2}$$

can be treated as the sum of outcomes of independent Bernoulli trials and thus satisfies (19). The Chernoff bound implies that for every $\gamma \in [0, 1]$ and $p \in (0, 1)$ we have $\Pr(S(\xi_1^{(p)}, \xi_2^{(p)}, \ldots, \xi_n^{(p)}) < (1 - \gamma)pn) \leq e^{-np\gamma^2/2}$, where $\xi_1^{(p)}, \xi_2^{(p)}, \ldots, \xi_n^{(p)}$ are results of $n$ independent Bernoulli trials with probability of success equal to $p$. If we take $p = 1/2$, we get

$$\Pr\{L(\xi_1^{(1/2)}, \xi_2^{(1/2)}, \ldots, \xi_n^{(1/2)}) - Bn \leq -\gamma rn + dn\} \leq e^{-n\gamma^2/4} \ .$$

Therefore if $n$ and $\varepsilon$ are such that the value $\gamma(\varepsilon) = \frac{d}{r} - \frac{1}{rn}\log_{\beta_0}\varepsilon$ falls within the segment $[0, 1]$, then $\alpha_\varepsilon(n) \leq e^{-n\gamma^2(\varepsilon)/4}$. It is easy to check that $d/r < 1$. Indeed,

$$d - r = \log_{\beta_0}(\beta_0^B + \Delta) - B$$

$$= \log_{\beta_0}\left(1 + \frac{\Delta}{\beta_0^B}\right)$$

$$< 0 \ .$$

Hence for every $\varepsilon \in (0,1)$ and $n \geq \frac{2}{d} \log_{\beta_0} \varepsilon$ the inequalities $0 < d/(2r) < \gamma(\varepsilon) < d/r < 1$ and thus $\alpha_\varepsilon(n) \leq e^{-\frac{n}{16}\left(\frac{d}{r}\right)^2}$ hold.

Fix $\varepsilon = 1/8$. For every $n > \max(\frac{2}{d} \log_{\beta_0} \varepsilon, 16\left(\frac{r}{d}\right)^2 (m \ln(1/\beta_0) + \ln 8))$ we get $\alpha_{1/8}(n) \leq \beta_0^m/8$. The substitution to (18) yields $p(n,m) \geq \beta_0^m/4$. We can take $c_1 = 16\left(\frac{r}{d}\right)^2 \ln(1/\beta_0)$ and $c_2 = \max\left(-\frac{2}{d}\log_{\beta_0} 8, 16\left(\frac{r}{d}\right)^2 \ln 8\right)$.

## Appendix D: Proof of Lemma 4

The proof is based upon the proof of Lemma 3.

For every small $\delta > 0$, consider the point $(\beta_0^B - \delta, \beta_0^B + \delta)$. It is not the image of a superprediction, but we still can define the function $L_m^{(\delta)}$ treating the point $(\log_{\beta_0}(\beta_0^B - \delta), \log_{\beta_0}(\beta_0^B + \delta))$ in the same fashion as we treated $(\log_{\beta_0}(\beta_0^B - \Delta), \log_{\beta_0}(\beta_0^B + \Delta))$ in the definition of $L_m$ above. The processes $\tilde{L}_m^{(\delta)}$ are no longer superloss processes w.r.t. $\mathfrak{G}$, but for every fixed $\delta$ they still satisfy (15). We will use the notation $d(\delta)$, $r(\delta)$, $c_1(\delta)$, and $c_2(\delta)$ for numbers defined in the same fashion as $d$, $r$, $c_1$, and $c_2$ in the construction above.

We will use these processes to construct $\tilde{L}_m$ and a constant $C > 0$ such that

$$p(n,m) = \frac{\left|\{x \in \mathbb{B}^n \mid \tilde{L}_m(x) \leq Bn - m + C\}\right|}{2^n} \geq \frac{1}{4}\beta_0^m \qquad (20)$$

for every $n \geq \tilde{c}_1 m^3 + \tilde{c}_2$, where $\tilde{c}_1$ and $\tilde{c}_2$ are some constants independent of $m, n$.

Now take points on $\partial\mathfrak{B}_{\beta_0}(S)$ approximating $(\beta_0^B - \delta, \beta_0^B + \delta)$. For definiteness sake, for every small $\delta > 0$ let $P_\delta$ be the intersection of $x = \beta_0^B - \delta$ and the boundary $\partial\mathfrak{B}_{\beta_0}(S)$. The distance between $P_\delta$ and $(\beta_0^B - \delta, \beta_0^B + \delta)$ is $O(\delta^3)$ as $\delta$ approaches 0. Let $\tilde{L}_m^{(\delta)}$ be the superloss process which uses the components of the superprediction $\mathfrak{B}_{\beta_0}^{-1}(P_\delta)$ exactly where $\tilde{L}_m^{(\delta)}$ uses numbers $\log_{\beta_0}(\beta_0^B - \delta)$ and $\log_{\beta_0}(\beta_0^B + \delta)$. Since

$$\log_{\beta_0}(\beta_0^B \pm \delta + O(\delta^3)) - \log_{\beta_0}(\beta_0^B \pm \delta) = \log_{\beta_0}\left(1 + \frac{O(\delta^3)}{\beta_0^B \pm \delta}\right)$$
$$= O(\delta^3)$$

as $\delta \to 0$, there is $t > 0$ such that $|\tilde{L}_m^{(\delta)}(x) - L_m^{(\delta)}(x)| \leq t|x|\delta^3$ for every small positive $\delta$ and every string $x$.

The superloss processes $\tilde{L}_m$ are constructed as follows. For every $m$ we will choose $\delta(m)$ and $n_0(m)$. The process $\tilde{L}_m$ imitates $\tilde{L}_m^{(\delta(m))}$ as long as the length of the string is less then or equal to $n_0(m)$. The remaining 'tail' is provided by the trivial strategy predicting $(B, B)$. The problem is to choose $\delta(m)$ and $n_0(m)$ such that $\tilde{L}_m$ will still be close enough to $L_m^{(\delta(m))}(x)$ for strings of length up to $n_0(m)$ and the inequality (20) will be achieved.

It is easy to check that

$$d(\delta) = \frac{\ln\left(1 - \left(\frac{\delta}{\beta_0^B}\right)^2\right)}{2\ln\beta_0} \qquad \sim \bar{d}\delta^2$$

and

$$r(\delta) = (\log_{\beta_0}(\beta_0^B - \delta) - B) - d(\delta) \sim \bar{r}\delta$$

as $\delta \to 0$, where $\bar{d}$ and $\bar{r}$ are some positive numbers. Thus we obtain the inequalities $c_1(\delta) \leq \bar{c}_1/\delta^2$ and $c_2(\delta) \leq \bar{c}_2/\delta^2$ for small $\delta$ and some constants $\bar{c}_1$ and $\bar{c}_2$.

Consider a pair of inequalities

$$n_0(m) \geq m\frac{\bar{c}}{\delta^2(m)} \tag{21}$$

$$1 \geq tn_0(m)\delta^3(m) , \tag{22}$$

where $\bar{c} = \bar{c}_1 + \bar{c}_2$. The former implies that $n_0(m) \geq c_1(\delta(m))m + c_2(\delta(m))$ while the latter ensures that the difference $\tilde{L}_m^{(\delta(m))}(x) - L_m^{(\delta(m))}(x)$ is bounded by a constant in the absolute value. They are satisfied if we let $\delta(m) = \frac{1}{mt\bar{c}}$ and $n_0(m) = m^3\bar{c}^3t^2$.

The lemma follows.

## Appendix E: An Improvement for Smoother Functions

Remark 1 states that if $\partial S$ is thrice differentiable in a vicinity of $(B, B)$, then the condition $n > cm^3$ in the statement of Lemma 4 can be relaxed to $n > cm^2$.

Indeed, since the set $\mathfrak{B}_{\beta_0}(S)$ is symmetrical in the straight line $x = y$, the touch between the boundary and the line $x + y = 2\beta^B$ at $(\beta^B, \beta^B)$ has the third order. This observation implies that $|\tilde{L}_m^{(\delta(m))}(x) - L_m^{(\delta(m))}(x)| \leq t|x|\delta^4(m)$. Inequality (22) may thus be replaced by $1 \geq tn_0(m)\delta^4(m)$.

# Polynomial Certificates
# for Propositional Classes[*]

Marta Arias[1], Roni Khardon[1], and Rocco A. Servedio[2]

[1] Department of Computer Science, Tufts University
Medford, MA 02155, USA
{marias,roni}@cs.tufts.edu
[2] Department of Computer Science, Columbia University
New York, NY 10027, USA
rocco@cs.columbia.edu

**Abstract.** This paper studies the query complexity of learning classes of expressions in propositional logic from equivalence and membership queries. We give new constructions of polynomial size certificates of non-membership for monotone, unate and Horn CNF functions. Our constructions yield quantitatively different bounds from previous constructions of certificates for these classes. We prove lower bounds on certificate size which show that for some parameter settings the certificates we construct for these classes are exactly optimal. Finally, we also prove that a natural generalization of these classes, the class of renamable Horn CNF functions, does *not* have polynomial size certificates of non-membership, thus answering an open question of Feigelson.

## 1 Introduction

This paper is concerned with the model of exact learning from equivalence and membership queries [1]. Since its introduction [1] this model has been extensively studied and many classes have been shown to be efficiently learnable. Of particular relevance for the current paper are learning algorithms for monotone DNF expressions [26, 1], unate DNF expressions [7], and Horn CNF expressions [2, 11]. Some results in this model have also been obtained for sub-classes of Horn expressions in first order logic but the picture there is less clear. Except for a "monotone-like case" [24] the query complexity is either exponential in one of the crucial parameters (e.g. universally quantified variables) [17, 4] or the algorithms use additional syntax based oracles [5, 25]. It is thus interesting to investigate whether this gap is necessary. The current paper takes a first step in this direction by studying the query complexity in the propositional case.

Query complexity can be characterized using the combinatorial notion of *polynomial certificates* [14, 12] (see also [6, 3]). In particular, [14, 12] show that

---

[*] This work has been partly supported by NSF Grant IIS-0099446 (M.A. and R.K.) and by an NSF Mathematical Sciences Postdoctoral Research Fellowship (R.S). Work done while R.S. was at the Division of Engineering and Applied Sciences, Harvard University.

B. Schölkopf and M.K. Warmuth (Eds.): COLT/Kernel 2003, LNAI 2777, pp. 537–551, 2003.
© Springer-Verlag Berlin Heidelberg 2003

a class $\mathcal{C}$ is learnable from a polynomial number of proper equivalence queries (using hypotheses in $\mathcal{C}$) and membership queries if and only if the class $\mathcal{C}$ has polynomial certificates. This characterization is information theoretic and ignores run time. Certificates have already proved to be a useful tool for studying learnability. For example, conjunctions of unate formulas are learnable with a polynomial number of queries but not learnable in polynomial time unless P=NP [10]. A recent result [15] shows that DNF expressions require a super-polynomial number of queries even when the hypotheses are larger than the target function by some (relatively small) factor.

Our own results establish lower and upper bounds on certificates for several classes. We give constructions of polynomial certificates for (1) monotone CNF where no variables are negated, (2) unate CNF where by renaming some variables as their negations we get a monotone formula, and (3) Horn CNF where each clause has at most one positive literal. We give certificates in the standard learning model as well as the model of learning from entailment [11] which is studied extensively in Inductive Logic Programming (see e.g. [8]). The construction of certificates for the Horn case is based on an analysis of *saturation* forming a "standardized representation" for Horn expressions that has useful properties.

The learnability results that follow from these certificate results are weaker than the results in [26, 1, 7, 2] since we obtain query complexity results and the results cited are for time complexity. However, the certificate constructions which we give are different from those implied by these earlier algorithms, so our results may be useful in suggesting new learning algorithms. We also give new lower bounds on certificate size for each of these concept classes. For some parameter settings, our lower bounds imply that our new certificate constructions are exactly optimal.

Finally, we also consider the class of renamable Horn CNF expressions. Note that unate CNF and Horn CNF generalize monotone expressions in two different ways. Renamable Horn expressions combine the two allowing to get a Horn formula after renaming variables. Renamable Horn formulas can be identified in polynomial time and have efficient satisfiability algorithms and are therefore interesting as a knowledge representation. While unate CNF and Horn CNF each have polynomial certificates, we give an exponential lower bound on certificate size for renamable Horn CNF. This answers an open question of Feigelson [9] and proves that renamable Horn CNF is not learnable in polynomial time from membership and equivalence queries.

## 2   Preliminaries

We assume that the reader is familiar with basic propositional logic. For completeness we give some of the definitions we use repeatedly in the paper.

We consider families of expressions built from $n \geq 1$ propositional variables. We assume some fixed ordering so that an element of $\{0, 1\}^n$ specifies an assignment of a truth value to these variables. A *literal* is a variable or its negation. A *term* is a conjunction of literals. A *clause* is a disjunction of literals. A *Horn clause* is a clause in which there is at most one positive literal. A *DNF* expression is a disjunction of terms. A *CNF* expression is a conjunction of clauses; it is Horn if all its clauses are Horn.

Let $x, y \in \{0,1\}^n$ be two assignments. Their intersection $x \cap y$ is the assignment that sets to 1 only those variables that are 1 in both $x$ and $y$.

The *DNF size* of a boolean function $f \subseteq \{0,1\}^n$, denoted $|f|_{DNF}$, is the minimum number of terms in a DNF representation of $f$. The *CNF size* of $f$, $|f|_{CNF}$, is defined analogously. In general, let $\mathcal{R}$ be a representation class for boolean formulas. Then $|f|_{\mathcal{R}}$ is the size of a minimal representation for $f$ in $\mathcal{R}$. If $f \notin \mathcal{R}$, we assign $|f|_{\mathcal{R}} = \infty$.

Let $\mathcal{C}$ be a boolean class, i.e. $\mathcal{C} \subseteq 2^{\{0,1\}^n}$. Then $\mathcal{C}_m$ denotes the subclass of $\mathcal{C}$ whose concepts have size at most $m$.

**Definition 1 (Polynomial Certificates, from [14]).** *Let $\mathcal{R}$ be a class of representations defining a boolean concept class $\mathcal{C}$. The class $\mathcal{R}$ has* polynomial certificates *if there exist two-variable polynomials $p(\cdot, \cdot)$ and $q(\cdot, \cdot)$ such that for every $n, m > 0$ and for every boolean function $f \subseteq \{0,1\}^n$ s.t. $|f|_{\mathcal{R}} > p(m, n)$, there is a set $Q \subseteq \{0,1\}^n$ satisfying the following: (1) $|Q| \leq q(m, n)$ and (2) for every $g \in \mathcal{C}_m$ there is some $x \in Q$ s.t. $g(x) \neq f(x)$. In other words, (2) states that no function in $\mathcal{C}_m$ is consistent with $f$ over $Q$.*

We also need the notion of redundant expressions:

**Definition 2.** *A* clause *$C$ in a Horn expression $f$ is* redundant *if $f \setminus \{C\} \equiv f$. An expression $f$ is* redundant *if it contains a redundant clause.*

## 3   Certificates for Monotone and Unate CNFs

In this section we construct polynomial certificates for anti-monotone CNFs (generalizable to unate CNF/DNF). This is to facilitate the presentation of certificates for Horn CNF. A certificate for unate DNF was given in [9]:

**Theorem 1 (Lemma 5 from [9], page 26).** *The classes of monotone and unate functions under DNF have polynomial size certificates with $p(m, n) = m$ and $q(m, n) = O(mn)$.*

Feigelson's construction is based on the fact that to show that a unate DNF function has more than $m$ terms, it is sufficient to prove that it has $m + 1$ minterms, which can be done by including in the certificate $m + 1$ positive assignments corresponding to the minterms and $O(mn)$ negative assignments corresponding to the assignments one level below the positive ones.

We next show a construction that achieves a certificate of size $O(m^2)$ which improves Feigelson's construction when $m < n$.

An anti-monotone CNF expression is a CNF where all variables appear negated. In this case we have that anti-monotone CNFs satisfy:

$$\forall x, y \in \{0,1\}^n : (x < y \implies f(x) \geq f(y)),$$

where $<$ between assignments denotes the standard bit-wise relational operator.

Notice that an anti-monotone CNF expression can be seen as a Horn CNF whose clauses have empty consequents. As an example, the anti-monotone CNF $(\bar{a} \vee \bar{b}) \wedge (\bar{b} \vee \bar{c})$ is equivalent to the Horn CNF $(ab \rightarrow \texttt{false}) \wedge (bc \rightarrow \texttt{false})$.

**Theorem 2.** *The class of anti-monotone CNF has polynomial size certificates with $p(m, n) = m$ and $q(m, n) = \binom{m+1}{2} + m + 1$.*

*Proof.* Fix $m, n > 0$. Fix any $f \subseteq \{0, 1\}^n$ s.t. $|f|_{anti-monCNF} > p(m, n) = m$. We proceed by cases.

*Case 1.* $f$ is not anti-monotone. In this case, there must exist two assignments $x, y \in \{0, 1\}^n$ s.t. $x < y$ but $f(x) < f(y)$ (otherwise $f$ would be anti-monotone). Let $Q = \{x, y\}$. Notice that by definition no anti-monotone CNF can be consistent with $Q$. Moreover, $|Q| \leq q(m, n)$.

*Case 2.* $f$ is anti-monotone. Let $c_1 \wedge c_2 \wedge \ldots \wedge c_m \wedge \ldots \wedge c_k$ be a minimal representation for $f$. Notice that $k \geq m+1$ since $|f|_{anti-monCNF} > p(m, n) = m$. Define assignment $x^{[c_i]}$ as the assignment that sets to 1 exactly those variables that appear in $c_i$'s antecedent. For example, if $n = 5$ and $c_i = v_3 v_5 \rightarrow \texttt{false}$ then $x^{[c_i]} = 00101$.

*Remark 1.* Notice that every $x^{[c_i]}$ falsifies $c_i$ (antecedent is satisfied but consequent is $\texttt{false}$) but satisfies every other clause in $f$. If this were not so, then we would have that some other clause $c_j$ in $f$ is falsified by $x^{[c_i]}$, that is, the antecedent of $c_j$ is true and therefore all variables in $c_j$ appear in $c_i$ as well (i.e. $c_j \subseteq c_i$). This is a contradiction since $c_i$ would be redundant and we are looking at a minimal representation of $f$.

Now, define the set $Q = Q^+ \cup Q^-$ where

$$Q^- = \left\{ x^{[c_i]} \mid 1 \leq i \leq m+1 \right\} \text{ and } Q^+ = \left\{ x^{[c_i]} \cap x^{[c_j]} \mid 1 \leq i < j \leq m+1 \right\}.$$

Notice that $|Q| \leq \binom{m+1}{2} + m + 1 = q(m, n)$. The assignments in $Q^-$ are negative for $f$, since $x^{[c_i]}$ clearly falsifies clause $c_i$ (and hence it falsifies $f$). The assignments in $Q^+$ are positive for $f$. To see this, suppose some $x^{[c_i]} \cap x^{[c_j]} \in Q^+$ is negative. This implies that there is some clause $c$ in $f$ that is falsified by $x^{[c_i]} \cap x^{[c_j]} \in Q^+$. That is, all variables in $c$ are set to 1 by $x^{[c_i]} \cap x^{[c_j]} \in Q^+$. Therefore, all variables in $c$ are set to 1 by $x^{[c_i]}$ and $x^{[c_j]}$. Hence, they falsify the same clause which is a contradiction by the remark above. Hence, all assignments in $Q^+$ are positive for $f$.

It is left to show that no anti-monotone CNF $g$ s.t. $|g|_{anti-monCNF} \leq m$ is consistent with $f$ over $Q$. Fix any $g = c'_1 \wedge \ldots \wedge c'_l$ with $l \leq m$. If $g$ is consistent with $Q^-$, then there is a $c' \in g$ falsified by two different $x^{[c_i]}, x^{[c_j]} \in Q^-$ (because we have $m+1$ assignments in $Q^-$ but less than $m+1$ clauses in $g$). Since they falsify $c'$, all variables in $c'$ are set to 1 in both $x^{[c_i]}$ and $x^{[c_j]}$. Therefore, all variables in $c'$ are set to 1 in their intersection $x^{[c_i]} \cap x^{[c_j]}$. Hence, clause $c'$ (and therefore $g$) is falsified by $x^{[c_i]} \cap x^{[c_j]}$. Thus, $x^{[c_i]} \cap x^{[c_j]} \in Q^+$ is negative for $g$ and $g$ is not consistent with $f$ over $Q$. $\square$

By duality of the boolean operators and DNF/CNF representations we get that Monotone CNF, monotone DNF and anti-monotone DNF have polynomial certificates of size $O(min(mn, m^2))$.

## 3.1 Unate CNF

**Definition 3.** *Let $a, x, y \in \{0, 1\}^n$ be three assignments. The inequality between assignments $x \leq_a y$ is defined as $x \oplus a \leq y \oplus a$, where $\leq$ is the bit-wise standard relational operator and $\oplus$ is the bit-wise exclusive OR.*

**Definition 4.** *A boolean CNF function $f$ (of arity $n$) is* unate *if there exists some assignment $a$ such that:*

$$\forall x, y \in \{0, 1\}^n : (x <_a y \implies f(x) \leq f(y))$$

*Equivalently, a variable cannot appear both negated and unnegated in any minimal CNF representation of $f$. Variables are either monotone or anti-monotone.*

The construction above can be used to give certificates for unate CNF. Case 2 in the proof follows along the same lines but reversing $\cap$ with $\cup$ for variables on which the function is anti-monotone. Case 1 can be dealt with using 4 assignments showing that $f$ is neither monotone nor anti-monotone in one of the variables ([13]). We therefore get:

**Theorem 3.** *Unate CNFs have polynomial certificates of size $O(min(mn, m^2))$.*

## 4 Saturated Horn CNFs

This section develops a "standardized" representation for Horn expression which can be obtained by an operation we call saturation. We establish properties on saturated expressions that makes it possible to construct a set of certificates in a similar way to the case of anti-monotone CNF.

**Definition 5.** *Let $f$ be a Horn expression. We define Saturation($f$) as the Horn expression returned by the following function:*

- *$Sat := f$*
- ***repeat*** *until no changes are made to Sat*
    - ***if*** *there are two clauses $s_i \to b_i$ and $s_j \to b_j$ in Sat s.t.*
      *(i) $b_i \neq b_j$, (ii) $s_j \subseteq s_i$ and (iii) $b_j \notin s_i$* ***then***
        * *$s'_i := s_i \cup \{b_j\}$*
        * *replace $s_i \to b_i$ with $s'_i \to b_i$ in Sat.*
- ***return*** *Sat*

*Example 1.* Notice that an expression can have many possible saturations. As an example, take $f = \{a \to b, a \to c\}$; this expression has two possible saturations: $Sat_1 = \{ac \to b, a \to c\}$ and $Sat_2 = \{a \to b, ab \to c\}$. Clearly, the result depends on the order in which we saturate clauses.

The proofs of the next two lemmas are omitted due to space limit; both can be done by induction on the number of modifications in the saturation process.

**Lemma 1.** *Every Horn expression is logically equivalent to its saturation.*

Notice that we use the notion of a "sequential" saturation in the sense that we use the updated expression to continue the process of saturation. There is a notion of "simultaneous" saturation that uses the original expression to saturate all the clauses. Lemma 1 does not hold for simultaneous saturation. An easy example illustrates this. Let $f = \{a \to b, a \to c\}$. Clearly, $SimSat(f) = \{ac \to b, ab \to c\}$ is not logically equivalent to $f$ (notice $f \models a \to b$ but $SimSat(f) \not\models a \to b$).

**Definition 6.** *An expression $f$ is saturated iff $f = Saturation(f)$.*

**Lemma 2.** *If a Horn expression $f$ is non-redundant, then all of its saturations are non-redundant, too.*

The converse of the previous lemma does not hold. That is, there are redundant expressions $f$ with non-redundant saturations. As an example: $f = \{ab \to c, c \to d, ab \to d\}$ is clearly redundant since the third clause $ab \to d$ can be deduced from the first two. If we saturate the first clause with the third, we obtain: $Saturation(f) = \{abd \to c, c \to d, ab \to d\}$ which is not redundant! However, if we saturate the third clause with the first, we obtain a redundant saturation $Saturation'(f) = \{ab \to c, c \to d, \underline{abc \to d}\}$

**Lemma 3.** *Let $f$ be a non-redundant Horn expression. Let $s_i \to b$ and $s_j \to b$ be any two distinct clauses in $f$ with the same consequent. Then, $s_i \not\subseteq s_j$.*

*Proof.* If $s_i \subseteq s_j$, then $s_i \to b$ subsumes $s_j \to b$ and $f$ is redundant.     □

**Lemma 4.** *Let $f$ be a non-redundant, saturated Horn expression. Let $c$ be any clause in $f$. Let $x^{[c]}$ be the assignment that sets to one exactly those variables in the antecedent of $c$. Then, $x^{[c]}$ falsifies $c$ but satisfies every other clause $c'$ in $f$.*

*Proof.* Let $c = s \to b$. Clearly, $x^{[c]}$ falsifies $c$: its antecedent is satisfied but its consequent is not. It also satisfies every other clause $c' = s' \to b'$ in $f$. To see this, we look at the following two cases: if $s' \not\subseteq s$, there is a variable in $s'$ not in $s$. Hence $x^{[c]} \not\models s'$ and $x^{[c]} \models c'$. Else, $s' \subseteq s$ and Lemma 3 guarantees that $b \neq b'$ (otherwise there would be a redundant clause in $f$). Furthermore, $b' \in s$ (otherwise $f$ would not be saturated). Thus, $x^{[c]} \models b'$ and $x^{[c]} \models c'$.     □

## 5    Certificates for Horn CNF

We proceed with the construction of the certificates for Horn CNFs. The following characterization is due to [22], although it was stated in a different context and in more general terms. It was further explored by [16]. Finally, a proof adapted to our setting can be found e.g. in [19]. Horn CNF expressions are characterized by

$$\forall x, y \in \{0,1\}^n : (x \models f) \land (y \models f) \implies (x \cap y \models f) \qquad (1)$$

**Theorem 4.** *Horn CNFs have polynomial size certificates with* $p(m,n) = m(n+1)$ *and* $q(m,n) = \binom{m+1}{2} + m + 1$.

*Proof.* Fix $m, n > 0$. Fix any $f \subseteq \{0,1\}^n$ s.t. $|f|_{hornCNF} > p(m,n) = m(n+1)$. Again, we proceed by cases.

*Case 1.* $f$ is not Horn. In this case, there must exist two assignments $x, y \in \{0,1\}^n$ s.t. $x \models f$ and $y \models f$ but $x \cap y \not\models f$ (otherwise $f$ would be Horn). Let $Q = \{x, y, x \cap y\}$. Notice that by (1) no Horn CNF can be consistent with $Q$. Moreover, $|Q| \leq q(m,n)$.

*Case 2.* $f$ is Horn. Let $c_1 \wedge c_2 \wedge \ldots \wedge c_{k'}$ be a minimal, saturated representation of $f$. Notice that $k' \geq m(n+1) + 1$ since $|f|_{hornCNF} > p(m,n) = m(n+1)$ and saturation does not produce redundant clauses when starting from a non-redundant representation (see Lemma 2). Since there are more than $m(n+1)$ clauses, there must be at least $m+1$ clauses sharing a single consequent in $f$ (there are at most $n+1$ different consequents among the clauses in $f$ – we must count the constant `false`, too). Let these clauses be $c_1 = s_1 \rightarrow b, \ldots, c_k = s_k \rightarrow b$, with $k \geq m+1$. Define assignment $x^{[c_i]}$ as the assignment that sets to 1 exactly those variables that appear in $c_i$'s antecedent. For example, if $n = 5$ and $c_i = v_3 v_5 \rightarrow v_2$ then $x^{[c_i]} = 00101$. Define the set $Q = Q^+ \cup Q^-$ where

$$Q^- = \left\{ x^{[c_i]} \mid 1 \leq i \leq m+1 \right\} \text{ and } Q^+ = \left\{ x^{[c_i]} \cap x^{[c_j]} \mid 1 \leq i < j \leq m+1 \right\}.$$

Notice that $|Q| = |Q^+| + |Q^-| \leq \binom{m+1}{2} + m + 1 = q(m,n)$. The assignments in $Q^-$ are negative for $f$, since $x^{[c_i]}$ clearly falsifies clause $c_i$ (and hence it falsifies $f$). The assignments in $Q^+$ are positive for $f$. To see this, we show that every assignment in $Q^+$ satisfies every clause in $f$. Take any assignment $x^{[c_i]} \cap x^{[c_j]} \in Q^+$. For clauses $c$ with a different consequent than $c_i$ (thus $c \neq c_i, c \neq c_j$), Lemma 4 shows that $x^{[c_i]} \models c$ and $x^{[c_j]} \models c$. Since $c$ is a Horn clause, we obtain that $x^{[c_i]} \cap x^{[c_j]} \models c$. For clauses with the same consequent as $c_i$ (and $c_j$), we have two cases. Either (1) $c \neq c_i$ or (2) $c \neq c_j$. If (1) holds, then Lemma 3 guarantees that $s \not\subseteq s_i$, where $s$ is $c$'s antecedent. Therefore some variable in $s$ is set to 0 by $x^{[c_i]}$ and hence by $x^{[c_i]} \cap x^{[c_j]}$, too. Thus, $x^{[c_i]} \cap x^{[c_j]} \models c$. Case (2) is analogous. Hence, all assignments in $Q^+$ are positive for $f$.

It is left to show that no Horn CNF $g$ s.t. $|g|_{hornCNF} \leq m$ is consistent with $f$ over $Q$. Fix any $g = c_1' \wedge \ldots \wedge c_l'$ with $l \leq m$. If $g$ is consistent with $Q^-$, then there is a $c' \in g$ falsified by two different $x^{[c_i]}, x^{[c_j]} \in Q^-$ (because we have $m+1$ assignments in $Q^-$ but less than $m+1$ clauses in $g$). Since they falsify $c'$, all variables in the antecedent of $c'$ are set to 1 in both $x^{[c_i]}$ and $x^{[c_j]}$. Also, in both assignments the consequent of $c'$ is set to 0. Therefore, the assignment $x^{[c_i]} \cap x^{[c_j]}$ sets all variables in the antecedent of $c'$ to 1 and the consequent to 0, too. Hence, clause $c'$ (and therefore $g$) is falsified by $x^{[c_i]} \cap x^{[c_j]}$. Thus, $x^{[c_i]} \cap x^{[c_j]} \in Q^+$ is negative for $g$ and $g$ is not consistent with $f$ over $Q$.  $\square$

## 6  Learning from Entailment

The learning model we have been using, where an example is an assignment to propositional variables is natural in the propositional setting. Models for learnability of first order logic have generalize this in two ways [8]. *Learning from interpretations* is a direct lifting of the above. In *learning from entailment*, formalized in [11] examples are *clauses*. An example is positive iff it is implied by the target expression. This model has been widely used in inductive logic programming both in theoretical studies and in practice. We can adapt the query model to treat such examples in a natural manner. Membership queries accept clauses and give their classification and equivalence queries return clauses as counterexamples.

We present a general transformation that allows us to obtain an entailment certificate from an interpretation certificate for propositional logic. Similar observations have been made before in different context (e.g. [18, 8]) where one transforms efficient algorithms not just certificates. Note however, that for efficiency we must be able to solve the implication problem for the language of hypotheses used by the algorithm.

**Definition 7.** *Let $x$ be an interpretation. Then $ones(x)$ is the set of variables that are set in $x$.*

**Lemma 5.** *Let $f$ be a boolean expression and $x$ an interpretation. Then,*

$$x \models f \iff f \not\models ones(x) \to \bigvee_{b \notin ones(x)} b.$$

*Proof.* Suppose $x \models f$. By construction, $x \not\models ones(x) \to \bigvee_{b \notin ones(x)} b$. Suppose by way of contradiction that $f \models ones(x) \to \bigvee_{b \notin ones(x)} b$. But since $x \not\models ones(x) \to \bigvee_{b \notin ones(x)} b$ we conclude that $x \not\models f$, which contradicts our initial assumption. Now, suppose $x \not\models f$. Hence, there is a clause $s \to \bigvee_i b_i$ in $f$ falsified by $x$. This can happen only if $s \subseteq ones(x)$ and $b_i \notin ones(x)$ for all $i$. Clearly, $s \to \bigvee_i b_i \models ones(x) \to \bigvee_{b \notin ones(x)} b$. Therefore $f \models ones(x) \to \bigvee_{b \notin ones(x)} b$ and the result follows. $\qquad\square$

**Theorem 5.** *Let $S$ be an interpretation certificate for a boolean expression $f$ w.r.t. a class $\mathcal{C}$ of boolean expressions. Then, the set of clauses $\{ones(x) \to \bigvee_{b \notin ones(x)} b \mid x \in S\}$ is an entailment certificate for $f$ w.r.t. $\mathcal{C}$.*

*Proof.* If $S$ is an interpretation certificate for $f$ w.r.t. some class $\mathcal{C}$ of propositional expressions, then for all $g \in \mathcal{C}$ there is some assignment $x \in S$ such that $x \models f$ and $x \not\models g$ or vice versa. Therefore, by Lemma 5, it follows that $f \not\models ones(x) \to \bigvee_{b \notin ones(x)} b$ and $g \models ones(x) \to \bigvee_{b \notin ones(x)} b$ or vice versa. Given the arbitrary nature of $g$ the theorem follows. Moreover, both sets have the same cardinality. $\qquad\square$

## 7    Certificate Size Lower Bounds

The certificate results above imply that Monotone and Horn CNF are learnable with queries but as mentioned in the introduction this was already known. It is therefore useful to review the relationship between the certificate size of a class and its query complexity. From [12, 14] we know that if $CS(\mathcal{C})$ is the certificate size of a certain class $\mathcal{C}$, then its query complexity (denoted $QC(\mathcal{C})$) satisfies:

$$CS(\mathcal{C}) \leq QC(\mathcal{C}) \leq CS(\mathcal{C}) \log(|\mathcal{C}|)$$

For the class of monotone DNF there is an algorithm that achieves query complexity $O(mn)$ [26, 1]. Since $\log(|MonotoneDNF_m|) = \Theta(mn)$, a certificate result is not likely to improve the known learning complexity. In the case of Horn CNF, there is an algorithm that achieves query complexity $O(m^2 n)$ [2]. Since again $\log(|HornCNF_m|) = \Theta(mn)$ improving on known complexity would require a certificate for Horn of size $o(m)$. The results in this section show that this is not possible and in fact that our certificate constructions are optimal.

In particular, for every $m, n$ with $m < n$ we construct an $n$-variable monotone DNF $f$ of size greater than $m$ and show that any certificate that $f$ has more than $m$ terms must have cardinality at least $q(m, n) = m + 1 + \binom{m+1}{2}$. We also show that if $m > n$ then there is a monotone DNF of size greater than $m$ that requires a certificate of size $\Omega(mn)$. These results also apply to both unate and Horn CNF/DNF as described below. We first give the result for $m < n$:

**Theorem 6.** *Any certificate construction for monotone DNF for $m < n$ with $p(m, n) = m$ has size $q(m, n) \geq m + 1 + \binom{m+1}{2}$.*

*Proof.* Let $X_n = \{x_1, .., x_n\}$ be the set of $n$ variables and let $m < n$. Let $f = t_1 \vee \cdots \vee t_{m+1}$ where $t_i$ is the term containing all variables (unnegated) except $x_i$. Such a representation is minimal and hence $f$ has size exactly $m + 1$. We show that any set with less than $m + 1 + \binom{m+1}{2}$ assignments cannot certify that $f$ has more than $m$ terms. That is, for any set $Q$ of size less than $m + 1 + \binom{m+1}{2}$ assignments we will show that there is a monotone DNF with at most $m$ terms consistent with $f$ over $Q$.

If $Q$ contains at most $m$ positive assignments of weight $n - 1$ then it easy to see that the function with minterms corresponding to these positive assignments is consistent with $f$ over $Q$. Hence we may assume that $Q$ contains at least $m + 1$ positive assignments of weight $n - 1$. Since $f$ only has $m + 2$ positive assignments, one of which is $1^n$, $Q$ must include all $m + 1$ positive assignments corresponding to the minterms of $f$. Thus if $|Q| < m + 1 + \binom{m+1}{2}$ then $Q$ must contain strictly less than $\binom{m+1}{2}$ negative assignments. Notice that all the intersections between pairs of positive assignments of weight $n - 1$ are different and there are $\binom{m+1}{2}$ such intersections. It follows that $Q$ must be missing some intersection between some pair of positive assignments in $Q$. But then there is an $m$-term monotone DNF consistent with $Q$ which uses one term for the missing intersection and $m - 1$ terms for the other $m - 1$ positive assignments.     $\square$

We can strengthen the previous theorem so that for every $n$ a fixed function $f$ serves for all $m < n$. The motivation behind this is that the lower bound in Theorem 6 implies a lower bound on the query complexity of any strongly proper learning algorithm [15, 23]. Such algorithms are only allowed to output hypotheses that are of size at most that of the target expression; this is in contrast with the usual scenario in which learning algorithms are allowed to present hypotheses of size polynomial in the size of the target. In the following certificate lower bound we use a function $f$ of DNF size $n$, so the resulting lower bound for learning algorithms applies to algorithms which may use hypotheses of size at most $n - 1$ (even if the target function is much smaller).

**Theorem 7.** *Any certificate construction for monotone DNF for $m < n$ with $p(m,n) < n$ has size $q(m,n) \geq m + 1 + \binom{m+1}{2}$.*

*Proof.* Let $q(m,n) = m + 1 + \binom{m+1}{2}$ and let $f$ be defined as $f = \bigvee_{i \in \{1,..,n\}} t_i$ where $t_i$ is the term containing all variables (unnegated) except $x_i$. Clearly, all $t_i$ are minterms, $f$ has size exactly $n$ and $f$ is monotone. We will show that for any $m < n$ and any set of assignments $Q$ of cardinality strictly less than $q(m,n)$, there is a monotone function $g$ of at most $m$ terms consistent with $f$ over $Q$.

We first claim that w.l.o.g. we can assume that all the assignments in the potential certificate $Q$ have exactly one bit set to zero (positive assignments) or two bits set to zero (negative assignments). We prove that if $Q$ contains the positive assignment $1^n$, or a negative assignment with more than 2 bits set to zero, then we can replace these by appropriate assignments with exactly 1 or 2 zeros so that any monotone function $g$ consistent with the latter set of assignments (call it $Q'$) is also consistent with $Q$. Suppose first that we have a function $g$ consistent with $f$ over $Q'$ where the positive assignment $b \in Q$ with all its bits set to 1 has been changed to $b'$ with just one bit set to 0 (choose it arbitrarily). Since $g$ is monotone, $g$ is consistent with $f$ over $Q'$, $b' \leq b$, and $g(b') = 1$, it follows that $g(b) = 1$ and hence $g$ is also consistent with $f$ over the initial $Q$. Now suppose that we have a function $g$ consistent with the set $Q$ where one negative assignment $a$ with more than two bits set to zero has been (arbitrarily) changed so that some of the extra zero bits are set to one (call the new assignment $a'$). Since $g$ is consistent with $Q'$, $g(a') = 0$, and since $g$ is also monotone and $a \leq a'$ it follows that $g(a) = 0$, too. Hence, $g$ is consistent with $Q$ in this second case. By induction, our assumption results in no loss of generality.

We may assume, then, that $Q$ is a set of fewer than $q(m,n)$ assignments each of which has either 1 or 2 zeros. We model the problem of finding a suitable monotone function as a graph coloring problem. We map $Q$ into a graph $G_Q = (V, E)$ where $V = \{p \in Q \mid f(p) = 1\}$ and $E = \{(p_1, p_2) \mid \{p_1, p_2, p_1 \cap p_2\} \subseteq Q\}$. Let $|V| = v$ and $|E| = e$.

First we show that if $G_Q$ is $m$-colorable then there is a monotone function $g$ of DNF size at most $m$ that is consistent with $f$ over $Q$. It is sufficient that for each color we find a single term $t_c$ that (1) is satisfied by the positive assignments in $Q$ that have been assigned some color $c$, with the additional condition that (2) $t_c$ is not satisfied by any of the negative assignments in $Q$. We define $t_c$ as the minterm corresponding to the intersection of all the assignments colored $c$ by the $m$-coloring. Property (1) is clearly satisfied, since no variable set to zero in any of the assignments is present in $t_c$. To see that (2) holds it suffices to notice that the assignments colored $c$ form an independent set in $G_Q$ and therefore none of their pair-wise intersections is in $Q$. By the assumption no negative point below the intersections is in $Q$ either. The resulting consistent function $g$ contains all minterms $t_c$. Since the graph is $m$-colorable, $g$ has at most $m$ terms.

It remains to show that $G_Q$ is $m$-colorable. Note that the condition $|Q| < q(m, n)$ translates into $v + e < q(m, n)$ in $G_Q$. If $v \leq m$ then there is a trivial $m$-coloring. For $v \geq m + 1$, it suffices to prove the following: any $v$-node graph with $v \geq m + 1$ with at most $\binom{m+1}{2} + m - v$ edges is $m$ colorable. We prove this by induction on $v$.

The base case is $v = m + 1$; in this case since the graph has at most $\binom{m+1}{2} - 1$ edges it can be colored with only $m$ colors (reuse one color for the missing edge). For the inductive step, note that any $v$-node graph which has at most $\binom{m+1}{2} + m - v$ edges must have some node with fewer than $m$ neighbors (otherwise there would be at least $vm/2$ nodes in the graph, and this is more than $\binom{m+1}{2} + m - v$ since $v$ is at least $m + 2$ in the inductive step). By the induction hypothesis there is an $m$-coloring of the $(v - 1)$-node graph obtained by removing this node of minimum degree and its incident edges. But since the degree of this node was less than $m$ in $G_Q$, we can color $G_Q$ using at most $m$ colors.    □

Finally, we give an $\Omega(mn)$ lower bound on certificate size for monotone DNF for the case $m > n$. Like Theorem 6 this result gives a lower bound on query complexity for any strongly proper learning algorithm.

**Theorem 8.** *Any certificate construction for monotone DNF for $m > n$ with $p(m, n) = m$ has size $q(m, n) = \Omega(mn)$.*

*Proof.* Fix any constant $k$. We show that for all $n$ and for all $m = \binom{n}{k} - 1$, there is a function $f$ of monotone DNF size $m + 1$ such that any certificate showing that $f$ has more than $m$ terms must contain $\Omega(nm)$ assignments.

Fix $n$, fix $k$. We define $f$ as the function whose satisfying assignments have at least $n - k$ bits set to 1. Notice that the size of $f$ is exactly $\binom{n}{k} = m + 1$. Let $P$ be the set of assignments corresponding to the minterms of $f$, i.e. $P$ consists of all assignments that have exactly $n - k$ bits set to 1. Let $N$ be the set of assignments that have exactly $n - (k + 1)$ bits set to 1. Notice that $f$ is positive for the assignments in $P$ but negative for those in $N$. Clearly, assignments in $P$ are minimal weight positive assignments and assignments in $N$ are maximal weight negative assignments. As in the previous proof, we may assume w.l.o.g. that any certificate $Q$ contains assignments in $P \cup N$ only. Notice, too, that $|P| = \binom{n}{k}$ and $|N| = \frac{(m+1)(n-k)}{k+1} = \binom{n}{k+1} = \Omega(mn)$ for constant $k$. Moreover, any assignment in $N$ is the intersection of two assignments in $P$.

Let $Q \subseteq P \cup N$. If $Q$ has at most $m$ positive assignments then it is easy to construct a function consistent with $Q$ regardless of how negative examples are placed. Otherwise, $Q$ contains all the $m + 1$ positive assignments in $P$ and the rest are assignments in $N$. If $Q$ misses any assignment in $N$ then we build a consistent function as follows: use the minterm corresponding to the missing intersection to "cover" two of the positive assignments with just one term. The remaining $m - 1$ positive assignments in $P$ are covered by one minterm each. Hence, any certificate $Q$ must contain $P \cup N$ and thus is of size $\Omega(nm)$.    □

We note that all of the lower bounds above apply to unate or Horn CNF/DNF as well. This follows from the fact that monotone CNF/DNF is a special case of unate or Horn CNF/DNF and that the function $f$ is outside the class (has size more than $m$ in all cases).

It is known [20] that the VC-dimension of $m$-term monotone DNF is $\Omega(mn)$, so a result in [21] implies a $\Omega(mn)$ lower bound on the number of queries to learn this class. Our result gives an alternative proof of this fact. For the Horn case we have a gap between the $\Omega(mn)$ and $O(m^2)$ bounds on certificate size, and the $O(m^2n)$ query complexity of the algorithm from [2]. Closing this gap is an interesting problem for future work.

## 8    An Exponential Lower Bound for Renamable Horn

In this section we show that Renamable Horn CNF expressions do not have polynomial certificates. This answers an open question posed in [9] and implies that the class of Renamable Horn CNF is not exactly learnable using a polynomial number of membership and equivalence queries [14, 12].

**Definition 8.** *A boolean CNF function $f$ (of arity $n$) is* renamable Horn *if there exists some assignment $c$ such that $f_c$ is Horn, where $f_c(x) = f(x \oplus c)$ for all $x \in \{0,1\}^n$. In other words, the function obtained by renaming the variables according to $c$ is Horn. We call such an assignment $c$ an* orientation *for $f$.*

To show non-existence of certificates, we need to prove the negation of the property in Definition 1, namely: for all two-variable polynomials $p(\cdot, \cdot)$ and $q(\cdot, \cdot)$ there exist $n, m > 0$ and a boolean function $\hat{f} \subseteq \{0,1\}^n$ s.t. $\left|\hat{f}\right|_{ren\mathcal{H}} > p(m, n)$ such that for every $Q \subseteq \{0,1\}^n$ it holds (1) $|Q| > q(m, n)$ or (2) some $g \in \mathcal{C}_m$ is consistent with $f$ over $Q$.

In particular, we define an $\hat{f}$ that is not renamable Horn, so that $\left|\hat{f}\right|_{ren\mathcal{H}} = \infty > p(m, n)$ holds for any function $p(m, n)$.

Hence, we need to show: there exist $n, m > 0$ and a non-renamable Horn $\hat{f} \subseteq \{0,1\}^n$ s.t. if no $g \in \mathcal{C}_m$ is consistent with $\hat{f}$ over some set of assignments $Q$, then $|Q| > q(m, n)$ for every polynomial $q(m, n)$. We say that a set $Q$ such that no $g \in \mathcal{C}_m$ is consistent with $\hat{f}$ over $Q$ is a *certificate that $\hat{f}$ is not small renamable Horn.*

What we actually show is: for each $n$ which is a multiple of 3, there exists a non-renamable Horn $\hat{f} \subseteq \{0,1\}^n$ s.t. if no $g \in \mathcal{C}_{n^6}$ is consistent with $\hat{f}$ over some set of assignments $Q$, then $|Q| \geq \frac{1}{3}2^{2n/3}$. Equivalently, for every such $n$ every certificate $Q$ that $\hat{f}$ is not a renamable Horn CNF function of size $n^6$ has to be of super-polynomial (in fact exponential) size. This is clearly sufficient to prove the non-existence of polynomial certificates for renamable Horn boolean functions. The following lemma due to Feigelson will be useful:

**Lemma 6 (Lemma 44 from [9], page 86).** *Let $f$ be a renamable Horn function. Then there is an orientation $c$ for $f$ such that $c \models f$.*

**Definition 9.** *The function $\hat{f}$ which we use is as follows: Let $n = 3k$ for some $k \geq 1$. We define $\hat{f} : \{0,1\}^n \to \{0,1\}$ to be the function whose only satisfying assignments are $0^k 1^k 1^k$, $1^k 0^k 1^k$, and $1^k 1^k 0^k$.*

**Lemma 7.** *The function $\hat{f}$ defined above is not renamable Horn.*

*Proof.* To see that a function $f$ is not renamable Horn with orientation $c$ it suffices to find a triple $(p_1, p_2, q)$ such that $p_1 \models f$, $p_2 \models f$ but $q \not\models f$ where $q = p_1 \cap_c p_2$. By Lemma 6 it is sufficient to check that the three positive assignments are not valid orientations for $f$:
The triple $(1^k 1^k 0^k, 1^k 0^k 1^k, 1^k 1^k 1^k)$ rejects $c = 0^k 1^k 1^k$.
The triple $(0^k 1^k 1^k, 1^k 1^k 0^k, 1^k 1^k 1^k)$ rejects $c = 1^k 0^k 1^k$.
The triple $(0^k 1^k 1^k, 1^k 0^k 1^k, 1^k 1^k 1^k)$ rejects $c = 1^k 1^k 0^k$. □

The following lemma is an extension of Lemma 57 from [9]. We say that a triple $(p_1, p_2, q)$ such that $p_1 \models f$, $p_2 \models f$ but $q \not\models f$ is *suitable* for $c$ if $q \leq_c p_1 \cap_c p_2$.

**Lemma 8.** *If $Q$ is a certificate that $\hat{f}$ is not small renamable Horn with orientation $c$, then $Q$ includes a suitable triple $(p_1, p_2, q)$ for $c$.*

*Proof.* Following the same strategy as in [9], suppose that a certificate $Q$ that $\hat{f}$ is not small renamable Horn with orientation $c$ does not include a suitable triple $(p_1, p_2, q)$ for $c$. That is, $p_1 \models \hat{f}$, $p_2 \models \hat{f}$ but $q \not\models \hat{f}$ where $q \leq_c p_1 \cap_c p_2$. Feigelson [9] defines a function $g$ that is consistent with $\hat{f}$ on $Q$ as follows:

$$g(x) = \begin{cases} 1 \text{ if } x \in Q \text{ and } x \models \hat{f} \\ 1 \text{ if } x \leq_c (s_1 \cap_c s_2) \text{ for any } s_1, s_2 \in Q \text{ s.t. } s_1 \models \hat{f} \text{ and } s_2 \models \hat{f} \\ 0 \text{ otherwise.} \end{cases}$$

The function $g$ is consistent with $Q$ since by assumption no negative example is covered by the second condition. Feigelson [9] shows that $g$ is renamable Horn with orientation $c$; here, we show that it is also *small*. We use the fact that our particular $\hat{f}$ is designed to have very few positive assignments. First notice that $g$ only depends on the positive assignments in $Q$. Moreover, these must be positive assignments for $\hat{f}$. Suppose that $Q$ contains any $l \leq 3$ of these positive assignments. Let these be $x_1, .., x_l$. A DNF representation for $g$ is:

$$g = \bigvee_{1 \leq i \leq l} t_i \vee \bigvee_{1 \leq i < j \leq l} t_{i,j}$$

where $t_i$ is the term that is true for the assignment $x_i$ only and $t_{i,j}$ is the term that is true for the assignment $x_i \cap_c x_j$ and all assignments below it (w.r.t. $c$). Notice that we can represent this with just one term by removing literals that correspond to maximal values (w.r.t. $c$).

Since $l \leq 3$, $g$ has at most $3 + \binom{3}{2} = 6$ terms. Hence, $g$ has CNF size at most $n^6$ (multiply out all terms to get the clauses). Now we use the fact that if there is a CNF formula representing $g$ of size at most $n^6$, then there must be a (syntactically) renamable Horn representation $\tilde{g}$ for $g$ which is also of size at most $n^6$. (It is well known that if a function $h$ is Horn and $g$ is a non-Horn CNF representation for $h$, then every clause in $g$ can be replaced with a Horn clause which uses a subset of its literals; see e.g. [22] or Claim 6.3 in [19].) We arrive at a contradiction: $Q$ is not a certificate that $\hat{f}$ is not small renamable Horn with orientation $c$ since $\tilde{g}$ is not rejected. □

**Theorem 9.** *For all $n = 3k$, there is a function $\hat{f} : \{0,1\}^n \to \{0,1\}$ which is not renamable Horn such that any certificate $Q$ showing that the renamable Horn size of $\hat{f}$ is more than $n^6$ must have $|Q| \geq \frac{1}{3}2^{2n/3}$.*

*Proof.* The Hamming distance between any two positive assignments for $\hat{f}$ is $2n/3$. Since, as observed in [9, 10], the intersection of two different bits equals the minimum of the two bits, any triple can be suitable for at most $2^{n/3}$ orientations. A negative example in $Q$ can appear in at most 3 triples (only 3 choices for $p_1, p_2$). Hence any negative example in $Q$ contributes to at most $3 \cdot 2^{n/3}$ orientations. The theorem follows since we must reject all orientations. □

**Corollary 1.** *Renamable Horn CNFs do not have polynomial size certificates.*

## Acknowledgments

We thank José Luis Balcázar for comments on earlier drafts, and Lisa Hellerstein for raising the question of certificate lower bound for strong learnability.

## References

1. D. Angluin. Queries and concept learning. *Machine Learning*, 2(4):319–342, April 1988.
2. D. Angluin, M. Frazier, and L. Pitt. Learning conjunctions of Horn clauses. *Machine Learning*, 9:147–164, 1992.
3. Dana Angluin. Queries revisited. In *Proceedings of the 12th International Conference on ALT*, volume 2225 of *Lecture Notes in Computer Science*, pages 12–31, Washington, DC, USA, November 25-28 2001. Springer.
4. Marta Arias and Roni Khardon. Learning closed horn expressions. *Information and Computation*, pages 214–240, 2002.
5. Hiroki Arimura. Learning acyclic first-order Horn sentences from entailment. In *Proceedings of the International Conference on ALT*, Sendai, Japan, 1997. Springer-Verlag. LNAI 1316.
6. José L. Balcázar, Jorge Castro, and David Guijarro. The consistency dimension and distribution-dependent learning from queries. In *Proceedings of the 10th International Conference on ALT*, Tokyo, Japan, December 6-8 1999. Springer. LNAI 1702.
7. Nader H. Bshouty. Simple learning algorithms using divide and conquer. In *Proceedings of the Conference on COLT*, 1995.
8. L. De Raedt. Logical settings for concept learning. *Artificial Intelligence*, 95(1):187–201, 1997. See also relevant Errata (forthcoming).

9. Aaron Feigelson. On boolean functions and their orientations: Learning, monotone dimension and certificates. Ph.D. Thesis, Northwestern University, Department of Electrical and Computer Engineering. 1998.

10. Aaron Feigelson and Lisa Hellerstein. Conjunctions of unate DNF formulas: Learning and structure. *Information and Computation*, 140(2):203–228, 1988.

11. M. Frazier and L. Pitt. Learning from entailment: An application to propositional Horn sentences. In *Proceedings of the International Conference on Machine Learning*, pages 120–127, Amherst, MA, 1993. Morgan Kaufmann.

12. T. Hegedus. On generalized teaching dimensions and the query complexity of learning. In *Proceedings of the 8th Annual Conference on Computational Learning Theory (COLT'95)*, pages 108–117, New York, NY, USA, July 1995. ACM Press.

13. Lisa Hellerstein. On generalized constraints and certificates. *Discrete Mathematics*, 226:211–232, 2001.

14. Lisa Hellerstein, Krishnan Pillaipakkamnatt, Vijay Raghavan, and Dawn Wilkins. How many queries are needed to learn? *Journal of the ACM*, 43(5):840–862, September 1996.

15. Lisa Hellerstein and Vijay Raghavan. Exact learning of DNF formulas using DNF hypotheses. In *Proceedings of the 34th Annual ACM Symposium on Theory of Computing (STOC-02)*, pages 465–473, New York, May 19–21 2002. ACM Press.

16. A. Horn. On sentences which are true of direct unions of algebras. *Journal of Symbolic Logic*, 16:14–21, 1956.

17. R. Khardon. Learning function free Horn expressions. *Machine Learning*, 37:241–275, 1999.

18. R. Khardon and D. Roth. Learning to reason with a restricted view. *Machine Learning*, 35(2):95–117, 1999.

19. Roni Khardon and Dan Roth. Reasoning with models. *Artificial Intelligence*, 87(1–2):187–213, 1996.

20. N. Littlestone. Learning quickly when irrelevant attributes abound: A new linear-threshold algorithm. *Machine Learning*, 2:285–318, 1988.

21. Wolfgang Maass and György Turán. Lower bound methods and separation results for on-line learning models. *Machine Learning*, 9:107–145, 1992.

22. J. C. C. McKinsey. The decision problem for some classes of sentences without quantifiers. *J. Symbolic Logic*, 8:61–76, 1943.

23. Krishnan Pillaipakkamnatt and Vijay Raghavan. On the limits of proper learnability of subclasses of DNF formulas. *Machine Learning*, 25:237, 1996.

24. C. Reddy and P. Tadepalli. Learning Horn definitions with equivalence and membership queries. In *International Workshop on Inductive Logic Programming*, pages 243–255, Prague, Czech Republic, 1997. Springer. LNAI 1297.

25. C. Reddy and P. Tadepalli. Learning first order acyclic Horn programs from entailment. In *International Conference on Inductive Logic Programming*, pages 23–37, Madison, WI, 1998. Springer. LNAI 1446.

26. Leslie G. Valiant. A theory of the learnable. *Communications of the ACM*, 27(11):1134–1142, November 1984.

# On-Line Learning with Imperfect Monitoring

Shie Mannor[1] and Nahum Shimkin[2]

[1] Laboratory for Information and Decision Systems
Massachusetts Institute of Technology, Cambridge, MA 02139
shie@mit.edu
[2] Department of Electrical Engineering
Technion, Haifa 32000, Israel
shimkin@ee.technion.ac.il

**Abstract.** We study on-line play of repeated matrix games in which the observations of past actions of the other player and the obtained reward are partial and stochastic. We define the Partial Observation Bayes Envelope (POBE) as the best reward against the worst-case stationary strategy of the opponent that agrees with past observations. Our goal is to have the (unobserved) average reward above the POBE. For the case where the observations (but not necessarily the rewards) depend on the opponent play alone, an algorithm for attaining the POBE is derived. This algorithm is based on an application of approachability theory combined with a worst-case view over the unobserved rewards. We also suggest a simplified solution concept for general signaling structure. This concept may fall short of the POBE.

## 1 Introduction

Repeated games provide the opportunity for each player to adjust her play according to the observed past, in particular the observed actions of the other players, or the rewards obtained for different choices of actions. The regret minimization framework allows to exploit this idea in a non-strategic framework, without imposing any restrictions or rationality assumptions on the strategies employed by the other players. The idea in regret minimization is to set a desired goal for the average payoff, depending on the observed moves in the game, and show that this goal may be obtained asymptotically. The most common goal is the Bayes envelope – the maximal average payoff that a player could secure for herself had she known in advance the relative empirical frequencies of the other players' actions. Obviously, with such prior knowledge, this payoff could be secured simply by playing the stationary strategy which repeats at every stage the best response (in the single-shot game) to the given relative empirical frequencies. The difference between the actual average payoff and the current Bayes envelope is termed the average regret. A strategy which asymptotically secures non-positive average regret for all possible strategies of the other player has been termed *regret minimizing*, and more recently *universally consistent* ([1]).

To motivate the following discussion let us consider a doctor that attends many patients. Suppose that each patient may either have disease A or disease

B. Schölkopf and M.K. Warmuth (Eds.): COLT/Kernel 2003, LNAI 2777, pp. 552–566, 2003.

B. The doctor may treat each patient using one of two treatments - 1 or 2. Treatment 1 is effective only against disease A while treatment 2 is effective only against disease B. Suppose that the doctor does not know if treatment 1 is successful or not, however she does know if treatment 2 is successful or not. As many patients arrive, the doctor's overall goal is to have the best success rate as if she knew in advance the patients' disease distribution. This situation can be captured in the following table. Each entry $(r, s)$ in the table represents the doctor's reward, $r$, and by the observation, $s$, she receives.

|  | Disease A | Disease B |
|---|---|---|
| Treatment 1 | $(1, a)$ | $(0, a)$ |
| Treatment 2 | $(0, b)$ | $(1, c)$ |

If the doctor was informed the results of each treatment the game reduces to a matching pennies game, and the doctor can obtain the best rate possible. Since this is not the case, a refined machinery is needed. Suppose that by time $t$ the doctor observed signals $a, b$, and $c$ for $\pi_a, \pi_b$, and $\pi_c$ fraction of the time (respectively). If it was known in advance that the patients' disease is a stationary process, then (assuming $\pi_b + \pi_c \neq 0$) the best response is $r^*(\pi_a, \pi_b, \pi_c) = \frac{\max(\pi_b, \pi_c)}{\pi_b + \pi_c}$. If $\pi_a = 1$ then no information is gathered and the worst case disease distribution is $1/2 - 1/2$, in which case the doctor cannot hope to gain more than $1/2$. The function $r^*$ is shown in Figure 1(a). We will show that while $r^*$ may not be attainable in general its lower convex hull, $r^c$, is attainable. $r^c$ is presented in Figure 1(b). The difference between $r^*$ and $r^c$ is plotted in Figure 1(c). We note that by attaining $r^c$ a higher reward than the pessimistic $\frac{1}{2}$ is obtained for most observation frequency vectors.

The case of perfect monitoring is well studied. Regret minimizing strategies were originally provided in [2] and later in [3] (see also [1] for a more modern approach). Recently, the feasibility of regret minimization has been established even when a perfect monitoring of the opponents actions is not available. The adversarial bandit formulation of [4] considers the case where only the reward at each stage is observed (in addition to the player's own action). It was shown

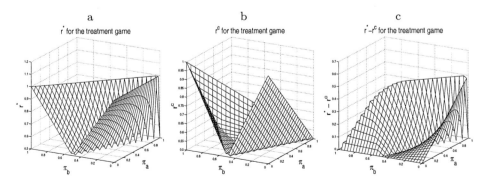

**Fig. 1.** $r^*$ (a), $r^c$ (b), and the difference $r^* - r^c$ (c) for the treatment game.

that regret minimizing strategies exist in this case as well. In [5] the regret minimization framework was extended to a general signalling structure, where the
observed signals are random functions of the two players' actions at each stage.
The Bayes envelope in this case must be weakened to take into account the imperfect monitoring. This modified Bayes envelope is still defined in the space of
the (now unobserved) empirical actions frequency of the other player, but now
the worst-case payoff over all stationary strategies of the other player, which
induce the same signal frequencies as the empirically observed signal frequencies, is considered. This envelope is termed Partial Observation Bayes Envelope
(POBE). The existence of regret minimizing strategies with respect to the POBE
was established in [5]. The proofs there rely on the approachability theory, lifted
to the space of measures over mixed actions. Concrete algorithms that attain
the POBE were not supplied in [5]. A simplified model was suggested in [6]. In
the model analyzed there the average reward can be consistently estimated from
the available signal data. Since the model of [6] essentially allows observing the
reward, the POBE of that model coincides with the perfect monitoring Bayes
envelope and efficient algorithms which are based on multiplicative weights were
derived.

   In this paper we consider the general signalling model where the reward is
not assumed observed. We provide an explicit algorithm for attaining the POBE
when P2 alone affects the observation. We also suggest a simplified concept for
arbitrary signaling structure. This concept can be easily attained, possess some
non-trivial performance guarantees, but may fall short of the POBE. We note
in passing that an essential part of our imperfect monitoring model is that the
game and signalling are *known* to the player. This is required in order to allow
meaningful inference from the observed signals. A note about the terminology is
due. We use the words "game" and "opponent" in this paper, however the model
does *not* assume that the other participating agents are rational. Consequently,
the model may be considered as a game against Nature (as in the treatment
game above), where Nature's play is not assumed stationary nor adversarial.

## 2   The Model

In order to model imperfect monitoring we consider a finite action two-person
game that is repeated in time. We refer to the players as P1 (the regret-minimi-
zing player) and P2. The stage game is assumed here to be a finite game in
strategic form, namely a matrix game. Let $a \in \mathcal{A}$ and $b \in \mathcal{B}$ denote the (finite)
set of actions of P1 and P2 in this game, respectively. The strategies of P1 and
P2 in the repeated game will be denoted by $\sigma$ and $\rho$, respectively. A strategy is
a map from the set of all possible histories to the set of mixed actions of each
respective player in the stage game.

   When P1 plays an action $a$ and P2 plays an action $b$, P1 obtains a stochastic
reward with expected value $r(a, b)$. This reward is assumed to be a positive
bounded random variable. The average reward until time $t$ is $\hat{r}_t \triangleq \frac{1}{t} \sum_{\tau=1}^{t} r_\tau$
($r_\tau$ is the reward at time $\tau$). When P1 plays a mixed strategy $p \in \Delta(\mathcal{A})$ ($\Delta(\mathcal{A})$ is

the set of probability vectors on $\mathcal{A}$) and P2 plays a mixed strategy $q \in \Delta(\mathcal{B})$ the obtained reward has the expected value of $r(p, q) \overset{\triangle}{=} \sum_{a \in \mathcal{A}} \sum_{b \in \mathcal{B}} p(a)q(b)r(a, b)$. The value of the associated one shot zero-sum game is denoted by v. Note that since P2's reward is unknown and possibly not relevant, v is not the value of any concrete game.

We assume that there are "signals" that are received by P1 after each stage of the game. These signals carry some information regarding P2's last action. Let $\mathcal{S} = \{1, \ldots, S\}$ denote the (finite) set of possible signals. Given that actions $a$ and $b$ were played at a given stage $t$, the observed signal $s_t$ is a random variable with a given distribution $P(s|a, b)$. We further denote by $s(p, q)$ the expected signal frequency vector in $\Delta(\mathcal{S})$ which is generated when P1 plays $p$ and P2 plays $q$. That is, if $\pi = s(p, q)$ then $\pi(s) = \sum_{a,b} P(s|a, b)p(a)q(b)$ for every $s \in \mathcal{S}$.

Let P2's empirical strategy by time $t$ be denoted by $q_t$. That is, $q_t(b) = \frac{1}{t} \sum_{\tau=1}^{t} 1_{\{b_\tau = b\}}$. The Bayes envelope with respect to $q_t(b)$ is defined as $r_{BE}^*(q_t) \overset{\triangle}{=} \max_{p \in \Delta(A)} r(p, q_t)$. If P1 knew $q_t$ in advance, then P1 could have played the maximizing (one-shot game) action against $q_t$ repeatedly, and attain an average reward as high as $r_{BE}^*(q_t)$. Since $q_t$ is not known in advance, an adaptive framework is needed. Even if we suppose that $q_t$ is estimated as the repeated game is played, one must limit the performance comparison to $q_t$ which are distinguishable. For that purpose we define the follows congruence class of $q$:

$$Q(q) = \{q' \in \Delta(\mathcal{B}) \; : \text{for every } p \in \Delta(\mathcal{A}) \quad s(p, q') = s(p, q)\}. \tag{1}$$

It can be shown that it suffices to examine the set of pure actions for P2 in (1). Essentially, P1 cannot distinguish between different $q$ in $Q(q)$, therefore any scheme cannot strive to achieve more than:

$$r^*(q) \overset{\triangle}{=} \max_{p \in \Delta(A)} \min_{q \in Q(q)} r(p, q). \tag{2}$$

We call (2) the Partial Observation Bayes Envelope (POBE) and consider it as the target to be achieved. Note that $r^*(q)$ depends on the *actual* unobserved strategy of P2. Formally, our goal is to attain envelopes in the sense of the following definition:

**Definition 1.** *A function* $r : \Delta(\mathcal{B}) \to \mathbb{R}$ *is attainable by P1 if there exists a strategy* $\sigma$ *of P1 such that for every strategy* $\rho$ *of P2:*

$$\liminf_{t \to \infty}(\hat{r}_t - r(q_t)) \geq 0 \quad P_{\sigma,\rho} \text{ a.s.}$$

*where* $P_{\sigma,\rho}$ *is the probability measure induced by* $\sigma$ *and* $\rho$.

## 3   P2 Determines the Signals

This section discusses the case where P2 alone determines the signal probability that is $P(s|a, b) = P(s|b)$. As a result one can write $s(q)$ for the expected signal frequency when $q$ is played (rather than $s(p, q)$). We will show that for the sake of consistency it suffices to consider the empirical signal frequency vector $\pi_t \in \Delta(\mathcal{S})$ which is defined as $\pi_t(s) \triangleq \frac{1}{t}\sum_{\tau=1}^{t} 1_{\{s_\tau=s\}}$. With some abuse of notation, let $Q(\pi) = \{q \in \Delta(\mathcal{B}) : \pi = s(q)\}$ denote the set of all possible stationary strategies (or, equivalently, mixed single stage strategies) that can possibly result in the observation $\pi$. Furthermore, we define the set of "possible" observations as $\Pi \triangleq \{\pi \in \Delta(\mathcal{S}) : Q(\pi) \neq \emptyset\}$. Observe that $\Pi$ is a convex set. Since every $q$ induces a single $\pi$ it stands to reason to define a Bayes-like envelope as a function of the signal frequency $\pi$:

$$r^*(\pi) \triangleq \min_{q \in Q(J(\pi))} r^*(q) = \max_{p \in \Delta(\mathcal{A})} \min_{q \in Q(J(\pi))} r(p,q), \tag{3}$$

where we define $J(\pi) : \Delta(\mathcal{S}) \to \Pi$ to be the Euclidean projection to of $\Delta(\mathcal{S})$ to $\Pi$. The following proposition provides the basic property of the POBE in the special case considered in this section.

**Proposition 1.** *If P1 does not affect the signals then $r^*(\pi)$ is a convex function of $\pi$ on $\Pi$.*

*Proof.* Let $\pi_1,\ldots,\pi_k$ be probability vectors in $\Pi$. We have to show that for a convex combination $\alpha_1,\ldots,\alpha_k$ we have that $r^*(\sum_{i=1}^{k}\alpha_i\pi_i) \leq \sum_{i=1}^{k}\alpha_i r^*(\pi_i)$. Since P1 does not affect the signal probability we can write $Q(\pi) = \{q : Hq = \pi\}$ for the signalling matrix $H$ ($H_{bs} = P(s|b)$). Let $q_i$ denote a minimax mixed action in the stage game that agrees with $\pi_i$, that is $r^*(\pi_i) = \max_p r(p,q_i)$ (such a mixed action exists by the minimax theorem since $Q(\pi)$ is convex for every $\pi$.) Let $q_\alpha \triangleq \sum_{i=1}^{k}\alpha_i q_i$, we have that $Hq_\alpha = \sum_{i=1}^{k}\alpha_i Hq_i = \sum_{i=1}^{k}\alpha_i\pi_i$. Recalling the definition:

$$r^*\left(\sum_{i=1}^{k}\alpha_i\pi_i\right) = \min_{q \in Q(\sum_{i=1}^{k}\alpha_i\pi_i)} \max_{p \in \Delta(\mathcal{A})} r(p,q) = \max_{p \in \Delta(\mathcal{A})} \min_{q \in Q(\sum_{i=1}^{k}\alpha_i\pi_i)} r(p,q)$$

$$\leq \max_{p \in \Delta(\mathcal{A})} r(p,q_\alpha) = \max_{p \in \Delta(\mathcal{A})} \sum_{i=1}^{k}\alpha_i r(p,q_i)$$

$$\leq \sum_{i=1}^{k}\max_{p \in \Delta(\mathcal{A})} \alpha_i r(p,q_i) = \sum_{i=1}^{k}\alpha_i r^*(\pi_i).$$

The second equality follows from the minimax theorem and the convexity of $Q(\pi)$. The first inequality holds since we fixed a specific $q$ that agrees with the signals $\alpha_i\pi_i$. The third equality is a result of the linearity of the reward $r$ in $q$. The second inequality is justified by the convexity of the max operator. $\square$

Since P2 alone affects the signals probability, and by the continuity of $r^*(\pi)$ and $r^*(q)$ we next claim that $r^*(q_t) \to r^*(\pi_t)$ almost surely.

**Proposition 2.** *Suppose P1 does not affect the signals. Then for every pair of strategies $\sigma, \rho$*

$$\lim_{t\to\infty} r^*(q_t) - r^*(\pi_t) = 0 \quad \mathbf{P}_{\sigma,\rho}\text{-a.s.}$$

*Proof.* Since $Q(q)$ is convex and $r$ is bilinear it follows that there exists $\tilde{q}_t \in \Delta(\mathcal{B})$ such that $r^*(q_t) = \max_p r(p, \tilde{q}_t)$. Let $\tilde{\pi}_t = s(\tilde{q}_t)$. It follows by our definitions so far that $r^*(\tilde{\pi}_t) = r^*(q_t)$. If the signals were deterministic then $\tilde{\pi}_t = \pi_t$ and the result follows. Generally, the signals are random so we need a more complicated argument. By Proposition 1, $r^*(\pi)$ is convex and therefore Lipschitz continuous over $\Pi$. It is therefore enough to show that $\|\pi_t - \tilde{\pi}_t\| \to 0$ almost surely. Note that the strategy $\rho$ which governs the distribution of $q_t$ and $\pi_t$ is *not* assumed stationary so standard large deviation bounds cannot be immediately applied. Let $n_t(b)$ be the number of times action $b$ was played by time $t$ (i.e. $tq_t(b)$), and similarly let $n_t(b, s) = \sum_{\tau=1}^{t} 1_{\{b_\tau = b \& s_\tau = s\}}$ count how many times action $b$ was used by P2 and signal $s$ observed. Define the event $E_t(b, s) = \{|n_t(b, s) - n_t(b)P(s|b)| \geq \delta t\}$. By the union bound we have that:

$$\mathbf{P}(\|\pi_t - \tilde{\pi}_t\| \geq \epsilon) \leq \sum_{b,s} \mathbf{P}(E_t(b, s)),$$

with $\delta = \epsilon/SB$. To bound the probability of $E_t(b, s)$ define the events $F_\ell(b, s) = \{|f_\ell(b, s) - \ell P(s|b)| \geq \delta t\}$ where $f_\ell$ is the sum of $\ell$ independently distributed Bernoulli random variables with bias $P(s|b)$. Let $F(b, s) = \bigcup_{1 < \ell \leq t} F_\ell(b, s)$. We will now reason in terms of a single probability space on which the controlled process can be defined, under any strategy. Formally speaking, we need to define a joint probability space, but as this is standard we omit it for the sake of brevity. It follows that

$$\mathbf{P}(E_t(b, s)) \leq \mathbf{P}(F(b, s)) \leq \sum_{\ell=1}^{t} \mathbf{P}(F_\ell(b, s)) \leq \sum_{\ell=1}^{t} 2e^{-(\frac{\delta t}{\ell})^2 \ell c(b,s)} \leq 2te^{-\delta^2 t c'(b,s)},$$

where the third inequality is due to Hoeffding's inequality, and $c(b, s), c'(b, s)$ are some constants. Applying the union bound again gives $\mathbf{P}(\|\pi_t - \tilde{\pi}_t\| \geq \epsilon) \leq cte^{-t\epsilon^2 c'}$ for some constants $c, c'$. By the Borel-Cantelli Lemma it follows that $\mathbf{P}(\|\pi_t - \tilde{\pi}_t\| \geq \epsilon \text{ i.o}) = 0$. □

We can therefore term $r^*(\pi)$ the POBE as well. We start with discussing the case where the reward is observed in Section 3.1. We then discuss the case where the reward is not observed and a refined scheme is required. An example for a game where P2 determines the signals is presented in Section 3.3.

## 3.1   Reward is Observed

When the reward is observed, the Bayes envelope itself is attainable, as in, e.g., [4]. We now provide some insight to the case where the reward is not observed, using the proof technique of [3] for the perfect monitoring case. Let us recall the following definition. The setup is a repeated game with vector-valued reward vector $m_t$ which average by time $t$ is denoted by $\hat{m}_t = \frac{1}{t} \sum_{\tau=1}^{t} m_\tau$; see [7].

**Definition 2.** *A set $B \subseteq \mathbb{R}^k$ is* approachable *by P1 if there exists a* $B$-*approaching* strategy $\sigma^*$ *of P1 such that*

$$d(\hat{m}_t, B) \to 0 \quad P_{\sigma^*, \rho}\text{-a.s., for every } \rho$$

*where $d$ is the Euclidean point to set distance.*

If the reward itself is observed then a straightforward application of approachability theory would result in attaining $r^*(q_t)$.

**Theorem 1.** *If the reward is observed then the set*

$$\mathbf{B} = \{(\hat{r}, \pi) :\ \pi \in \Pi\ ;\ \hat{r} \geq r^*(\pi)\} \subseteq \mathbb{R} \times \Pi\,. \tag{4}$$

*is approachable. Consequently, every $\mathbf{B}$-approaching strategy attains the POBE.*

*Proof.* We apply approachability theory for repeated matrix games (e.g., [7]). $r^*(\pi)$ is convex on $\Pi$ and therefore continuous (e.g., [8]). In order to apply approachability arguments, we construct the following game with vector-valued payoffs. Define the $1 + S$ dimensional reward vector $m = (\hat{r}, \pi) \in \mathbb{R} \times \Delta(\mathcal{S})$, indexed by $k \in \{0\} \cup \mathcal{S}$. When the observed signal was $s$ and the observed reward was $r$,

$$m(k) \triangleq \begin{cases} r \text{ if } k = 0 \\ 0 \text{ if } k \in \mathcal{S},\ k \neq s \\ 1 \text{ if } k \in \mathcal{S},\ k = s \end{cases} \tag{5}$$

Thus, the first coordinate of the vector-valued average payoff vector is the average reward, the other coordinates are the relative frequencies of the signals. We note that $m$ is generally a random vector, and is observed by P1 according to our assumptions. For a pair of mixed strategies $p \in \Delta(\mathcal{A})$ and $q \in \Delta(\mathcal{B})$, let

$$m(p, q) \triangleq \sum_{a \in \mathcal{A}} p(a) \sum_{b \in \mathcal{B}} q(b) m(a, b)\,, \tag{6}$$

where $m(a, b)$ is the entry of the vector-valued game defined in Eq. (5). Since $\mathbf{B}$ is convex it suffices to prove that $\forall q \in \Delta(\mathcal{B})$ the set $M(\mathcal{A}, q) \triangleq \text{co}(\{m(a, q)\}_{a \in \mathcal{A}})$ (co is the convex hull operator) intersects $\mathbf{B}$ ($m(a, q)$ denotes the expected reward vector in the one shot game when P1 plays the action $a$ and P2 plays the strategy $q$). Fix $q$, in the original game P1 has an optimal deterministic action $a^* \in \mathcal{A}$ against $q$. Consider the signal $\pi$ that satisfies $\pi(s) = \sum_{b \in \mathcal{B}} P(s|a^*, b) q(b)$ for every $s \in \mathcal{S}$. By definition $q \in Q(\pi)$. $r^*$ satisfies $r^*(\pi) = \max_{p \in \Delta(\mathcal{A})} \min_{q \in Q(\pi)} r(p, q)$ but since the pure strategy $a^*$ is optimal against $q$, we have that $\forall p \in \Delta(\mathcal{A})$, $r(p, q) \leq r(a^*, q)$ so at $\pi$ we have that $r^*(\pi) \leq r(a^*, q)$. We conclude that $\mathbf{B}$ is approachable since $(r(a^*, q), s(q)) \in \mathbf{B}$ holds for every $q \in \Delta(\mathcal{B})$. Since $\mathbf{B}$ is approachable and since $r^*$ is continuous it follows that by our definitions that by approaching $\mathbf{B}$ the first coordinates difference decreases to 0 so the result follows. $\qquad \square$

It follows by [7] that the approaching strategy is to play at time $t$ a minimax mixed action in the one shot matrix game defined by the projection of the vector reward, defined in Eq. (5), on the direction from $(\hat{r}_t, \pi_t)$ to a closest point in $\mathbf{B}$ (defined in Eq. (4)).

## 3.2   Unobserved Reward

In this section we discuss the case where the reward is not observed. Surprisingly, we are still able to attain the POBE when P1 does not affect the signaling structure.

The following strategy attains the POBE in the case where the reward is not observed by approaching the set **B**. The strategy advances is stages. In each stage, the same mixed action is used repeatedly. A note about the notations is due. We use superscripts for stage indices and subscript for time indices.

**Algorithm 1: An Attaining Strategy when the Reward is Unobserved**

---

1. Start: $t = 0$, $i = 1$, $t^0 = 0$.
2. Choose an arbitrary $p^1$, Goto 6.
3. If $\tilde{r}_t \geq r^*(\pi_t)$ let $p^i$ be arbitrary, Goto 6.
4. If $\tilde{r}_t < r^*(\pi_t)$ find the direction $u^i$ from the point $(\tilde{r}_t, \pi_t)$ to the closest point in the set **B** defined in Eq. (4).
5. Let $p^i$ be a maximizer of $\max_{p \in \Delta(\mathcal{A})} \min_{q \in \Delta(\mathcal{B})} m(p, q) \cdot u^i$, where $m(p, q)$ is given in (6), and $\cdot$ is the standard dot product.
6. Repeat $T^i$ times:
   $t = t + 1$.
   Pick a random action $a_t$ according to $p^i$, play $a_t$ and observe $s_t$.
7. $t^i = t$. Set: $\pi^i(s) = \frac{1}{T^i} \sum_{\tau = t^{i-1}+1}^{t^i} 1_{\{s_\tau = s\}}$; $\tilde{r}^i = \min_{q \in Q(J(\pi^i))} r(p^i, q)$;
   $\tilde{r}_{t^i} = \frac{1}{t^i} \sum_{j=1}^{i} T^j \tilde{r}^j$.
8. $i = i + 1$. Goto 3.

---

**Theorem 2.** *By playing Algorithm 1 with $T^i = i^2$ the POBE is attained.*

*Proof.* The proof is deferred to the Appendix.

The basic idea behind Algorithm 1 is that the fictitious reward $\tilde{r}$ replaces the true (unobserved) reward. For large $t$ the average reward and the observed signals frequency change slowly, so that by choosing $T^i$ small enough the same strategy is almost optimal during the $i$-th interval. By choosing $T^i$ large enough we guarantee that the average reward is asymptotically not lower than the fictitious reward. We also note that any polynomial $T^i$ would lead to a similar convergence result.

## 3.3   An Example

We now provide an example to the case where the signals depend only on P2's actions. This example is related to the field of Internet Protocols and is motivated by source routing and the ability of modern routers to supply information to the sending machine. In TCP communication protocol a node (e.g., a computer) sends a packet and receives an acknowledgement signal from the destination node. It may happen that a packet gets lost in the way and should be resent. The packet is resent if there is an indication that the packet is lost (i.e., after enough time). Suppose a node sends packets with not only destination address but also route of the packet (this is called source routing). The router sends the packet in the route required by the node, however since the router has a better picture of the network it may know if the packet has a good chance to get

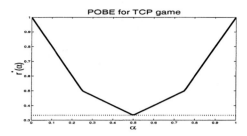

**Fig. 2.** $r^*(\alpha)$ is the convex line above the value $v = 1/3$ (dotted).

lost. The router may be able to return a small message containing some limited information (this is not an acknowledge - just an indication). See [9] for an example of a scheme where a single bit is used to provide information regarding congestion. The following example demonstrates such a situation. Suppose that there are three links, out of which only one is operative. The node does not know which link is operative. The router may use only a single bit to hint the node which of the three links was working. The performance measure is to get as many packets across. Let P1 be the node that sends packets (the row player) and P2 is the network (the column player), P1's reward-signal matrix is (each entry is denoted by $(r, s)$):

|  | Link 1 up | Link 2 up | Link 3 up |
|---|---|---|---|
| Send via link 1 | $(1, a)$ | $(0, a\vert b)$ | $(0, b)$ |
| Send via link 2 | $(0, a)$ | $(1, a\vert b)$ | $(0, b)$ |
| Send via link 3 | $(0, a)$ | $(0, a\vert b)$ | $(1, b)$ |

The available signals are $\{a, b\}$. The signals generating probability $P(s\vert b)$ satisfies $P(a\vert 1) = P(b\vert 3) = 1$ and $P(a\vert 2) = P(b\vert 2) = 1/2$. This means that when P2 plays action 1 or 3 P1 observes signals $a, b$ deterministically (respectively), and when action 2 is played a random signal is observed with equal probabilities. Observe that this example cannot be cast into the model of [6], and that the Bayes envelope (rather than the POBE) cannot be attained. To see that consider two strategies of P2, the first is to always play action 2, and the second to always play actions 1 and 3 with equal probability. P1 cannot distinguish between the two strategies. The POBE of either strategies is $1/3$, however the best response reward against the first is 1 and against the second is $1/2$. It follows that if P2 throws a coin before the game begins and with probability $1/3$ plays the first strategy and with probability $2/3$ plays the second, then no matter what strategy P1 employs a reward of no more than $1/3$ can be guaranteed. Let $\alpha$ be the frequency of signal $a$. We identify the signal frequency with $0 \le \alpha \le 1$. Obviously, $r^*(\alpha)$ is symmetric around $1/2$. The possible stage game strategies that agree with $\alpha$ satisfy $Q(\alpha) = \mathrm{co}\{(\alpha, 0, 1 - \alpha), (0, 2\alpha, 1 - 2\alpha)\}$, which leads to the conclusion that $r^*(\alpha) = 1 - 2\alpha$ for $\alpha \le 1/4$. For $1/4 \le \alpha \le 1/2$ a straight forward calculation shows that $r^*(\alpha) = \min_{0 \le \beta \le 1} \max\{\alpha\beta, 2\alpha - 2\alpha\beta, 1 + \alpha\beta - 2\alpha\} = \frac{2}{3} - \frac{2\alpha}{3}$. The graph of $r^*(\alpha)$ is given in Figure 2. The value of the game is v = 1/3 which is the result of the unique single stage game minimax strategy $q^* = (1/3, 1/3, 1/3)$. Note that $r^*(\pi) > v$ for every $\pi$ for which $q^* \notin Q(\pi)$. This behavior is typical, as explained in Remark 1.

## 4   The General Case

In this section we study the general model (i.e., both players affect the signals). We suggest a simplified target which is fairly easy to attain, though it does not promise a reward as high as $r^*(q_t)$.

The idea is to define a function of the signal frequency, which is attainable. Redefine

$$Q(\pi) \triangleq \{q \in \Delta(\mathcal{B}) : \text{ there exists } p \in \Delta(\mathcal{A}) \text{ such that } \pi = s(p, q)\}.$$

$Q(\pi)$ is the set of all possible stationary strategies (or, equivalently, mixed actions) that can possibly result in the observation $\pi$. As before, let $\Pi = \{\pi : Q(\pi) \neq \emptyset\}$. Note that in this case $\Pi$ may be not convex. We can now formulate the empirical Bayes envelope in the reward signal space, $r_E^*(\pi) : \Delta(\mathcal{S}) \to \mathbb{R}$, as

$$r_E^*(\pi) \triangleq \max_{p \in \Delta(\mathcal{A})} \min_{q \in Q(J(\pi))} r(p, q),$$

with $J(\pi)$ being the projection onto $\Pi$ (with ambiguities resolved in arbitrary manner). This definition coincides with Eq. (3) for games where P1 does not affect the signalling structure. It turns out that in general $r_E^*$ is *not* attainable ([10]). This may be the case even if $r_E^*$ is well defined for all $\pi$ and $Q(\pi) \neq \emptyset$ for all $\pi$. An attainable solution concept we suggest is the *convex Bayes envelope* that is defined as the lower convex hull of $r_E^*(\pi)$ on $\Pi$ and is denoted by $r^c$ (where $r^c(\pi) = r^c(J^c(\pi))$ for $\pi \notin \text{co}(\Pi)$, and $J^c(\pi)$ is the projection of $\Delta(\mathcal{S})$ onto $\text{co}(\Pi)$.) Let $\mathbf{C}$ as the set $\{(r, \pi) : r \geq r^c(\pi)\}$.

**Theorem 3.** *Suppose that Algorithm 1 is used with $\mathbf{C}$ replacing $\mathbf{B}$. Then for every strategy of P2:*

$$\liminf_{t \to \infty} \hat{r}_t - r^c(\pi_t) \geq 0 \quad a.s.$$

*Proof.* (Outline) The set $\mathbf{C}$ is convex by definition. Showing that $\mathbf{C}$ is approachable in a game were both signals and reward are observed follows exactly as in Theorem 1. When the reward is not observed, an analogue algorithm to Algorithm 1 may be suggested with replacing $\mathbf{B}$ with $\mathbf{C}$ and the analysis of Theorem 2 still holds.                                                                                    □

*Remark 1.* By attaining $r^c(\pi_t)$ instead of $r^*(q_t)$ the performance guarantees deteriorate. Obviously $r^c(\pi) \geq v$ where v is the value of the one shot zero-sum game. It can be shown ([10]) that if P2 has a unique minimax strategy $q^*$ then $r^c(\pi) > v$ for every $\pi$ for which $q^* \notin Q(\pi)$.

Recall the treatment game from the introduction. In this game both players affect the signals. As shown in Figure 1, $r^*$ is not convex. Moreover, it is not even continuous near the point $(\pi_a, \pi_b) = (1, 0)$. The difference between the attainable envelope, $r^c$ and the $r^*$ is plotted in Figure 1c. In this game $r^c(\pi) > $ v for every $\pi$ that does not agree with the unique minimax strategy $(1/2, 1/2)$ of Nature.

The main question which remains open is how to attain the POBE (from Definition 1) in the general case where both players affect the signalling probabilities. We believe that combining the idea of fictitious reward with a prediction with expert advice framework may be used for attaining the POBE.

## Acknowledgements

This research was supported by the fund for the promotion of research at the Technion.

## References

1. D. Fudenberg and D. Levine. Universal consistency and cautious fictitious play. *Journal of Economic Dynamic and Control*, 19:1065–1190, 1995.
2. J. Hannan. Approximation to Bayes risk in repeated play. In M. Dresher, A. W. Tucker, and P. Wolde, editors, *Contribution to The Theory of Games, III*, pages 97–139. Princeton University Press, 1957.
3. D. Blackwell. Controlled random walks. In *Proc. International Congress of Mathematicians, 1954*, volume III, pages 336–338. North-Holland, 1956.
4. P. Auer, N. Cesa-Bianchi, Y. Freund, and R. E. Schapire. The non-stochastic multi-armed bandit problem. To appear in SIAM journal of Computation, 2002.
5. A. Rustichini. Minimizing regret: the general case. *Games and Economic Behavior*, 29:224–243, November 1999.
6. A. Piccolboni and C. Schindelhauer. Discrete prediction games with arbitrary feedback and loss. In D. Helmbold and B. Williamson, editors, *Fourteenth Annual Conference on Computation Learning Theory*, pages 208–223. Springer, 2001.
7. D. Blackwell. An analog of the minimax theorem for vector payoffs. *Pacific J. Math.*, 6(1):1–8, 1956.
8. R.T. Rockafellar. *Convex Analysis*. Princeton University Press, 1970.
9. K. Ramakrishnan, S. Floyd, and D. Black. The addition of explicit congestion notification (ECN) to IP. IETF, Tech. Rep., 2001.
10. S. Mannor and N. Shimkin. Regret minimization in signal space for repeated matrix games with partial observations. Technical report EE- 1242, Faculty of Electrical Engineering, Technion, Israel, March 2000. Available from http://web.mit.edu/~shie/www/pubs.htm.
11. N. Shimkin. Extremal large deviations in controlled I.I.D. processes with applications to hypothesis testing. *Adv. Appl. Prob.*, 25:875–894, 1993.
12. D.P. Bertsekas and J.N. Tsitsiklis. *Neuro-Dynamic Programming*. Athena Scientific, 1996.

## A    Proof of Theorem 2

Let $r^i = \frac{1}{T^i} \sum_{\tau=t^{i-1}+1}^{t^i} r_\tau$ be the actual (unobserved) reward in the $i$-th interval. The actual (unobserved) average reward can be written as

$$\hat{r}_{t^i} = \frac{1}{t^i} \sum_{j=1}^{i} T^j r^j. \tag{7}$$

First, let us bound the probability that the worst case estimate is too optimistic:

**Lemma 1.** *There exist constants $C$ and $D$ such that for every $i$:*

$$\mathbf{P}(\tilde{r}^i \geq r^i + \epsilon) \leq CT^i e^{-D\epsilon^2 T^i}.$$

*Proof.* Let $q^i$ denote P2's true unobserved empirical frequency by the $i$th interval. That is, $q^i(b) = \frac{1}{T^i}\sum_{\tau=t^{i-1}+1}^{t^i} 1_{\{b_\tau=b\}}$. We have that:

$$\mathbf{P}(\tilde{r}^i \geq r^i + \epsilon) \leq \mathbf{P}(r(p^i, q^i) - r^i \geq \epsilon/2) + \mathbf{P}(\tilde{r}^i - r(p^i, q^i) \geq \epsilon/2). \quad (8)$$

Recall that $r(p^i, q^i)$ is the expected reward in the one shot game when P1 plays $p^i$ and P2 plays $q^i$. We now bound each of the terms in Eq. (8). As in the proof of Proposition 2 we cannot assume stationarity of the strategy of P2, so we will use a similar technique. One can use the results of [11], however, this is at the expense of finite time bounds. Let us reset the time of the beginning of the $i$th interval to 1. Consider the event

$$E(a,b) = \{|\sum_{\tau=1}^{T^i} 1_{\{a_\tau=a, b_\tau=b\}} r_\tau - n_{T^i}(a,b)r(a,b)| > \delta T^i\},$$

where $r(a,b)$ is the expected reward when P1 plays $a$ and P2 plays $b$, and $n_{T^i}(a,b) = \sum_{\tau=1}^{T^i} 1_{\{a_\tau=a, b_\tau=b\}}$ counts the number of time P1 played $a$ and P2 played $b$. It follows by the union bound that

$$\mathbf{P}(r(p^i, q^i) - r^i \geq \epsilon/2) \leq \sum_{a,b} E(a,b),$$

with $\delta = \frac{\epsilon}{2AB}$. Consider the event $F_\ell(a,b) = \{|\sum_{k=1}^{\ell} f_k(a,b) - \ell r(a,b)| > \delta T^i\}$ where $f_k(a,b)$ is an I.I.D. random variable with the same distribution as $r$ when $a$ and $b$ are played by P1 and P2, respectively. Reasoning in terms of a single probability space we get that:

$$\mathbf{P}(E(a,b)) \leq \sum_{\ell=1}^{T^i} \mathbf{P}(F_\ell(a,b)) \leq \sum_{\ell=1}^{T^i} 2e^{-c(a,b)(\frac{\delta T^i}{\ell})^2 \ell} \leq 2T^i e^{-c'(a,b)\epsilon^2 T^i},$$

where the second inequality follows by Hoeffding's inequality, and $c(a,b), c'(a,b)$ are some constants. Summing over $a, b$ and using the union bound we get that $\mathbf{P}(r(p^i, q^i) - r^i \geq \epsilon/2) \leq C_1 T^i e^{-D_1 T^i \epsilon^2}$ for every $p^i$ and $q^i$. Note that the inequality holds with the same constants for all $p^i$ and $q^i$ since $r$ is bounded for every $a$ and $b$ and therefore for all $a$ and $b$ ($\mathcal{A}$ and $\mathcal{B}$ are finite.)

To bound the second term of Eq. (8) let $\tilde{\pi}^i = s(q^i)$. In Proposition 2 we proved that there are constants $c$ and $c'$ such that: $\mathbf{P}(\|\pi^i - \tilde{\pi}^i\| > \epsilon) \leq cT^i e^{-c'T^i \epsilon^2}$. Consider the function $r_{p^i}(\pi) = \inf_{q \in Q(J(\pi))} r(p^i, q)$. It follows that $r_{p^i}(\pi) : \Delta(\mathcal{S}) \to \mathbb{R}$ is a continuous function. Moreover, it is easily verified that $\{r_{p^i}\}_{p^i \in \Delta(\mathcal{A})}$ are Lipschitz continuous, and that the Lipschitz constant of all $\{r_{p^i}\}_{p^i \in \Delta(\mathcal{A})}$ is bounded by some $K$. By our definitions, we have that $r_{p^i}(\tilde{\pi}^i) \leq r(p^i, q^i)$. Using the uniform continuity it follows that with probability of at least $1 - cT^i e^{-\frac{c'}{4K^2}T^i\epsilon^2}$ we have that $\|\tilde{\pi} - \pi^i\| \leq \frac{\epsilon}{2K}$ so that $|r_{p^i}(\tilde{\pi}^i) - r_{p^i}(\pi^i)| \leq \epsilon/2$. Recalling that $\tilde{r}^i = r_{p^i}(\pi^i)$, it follows that the probability of the event $\{\tilde{r}^i - r(p^i, q^i) \geq \epsilon/2\}$ is at most $cT^i e^{-\frac{c'}{4K^2}T^i\epsilon^2}$. The lemma follows by combining the bounds for the two terms. $\qquad\square$

The asymptotical relation between $\tilde{r}$ and $\hat{r}$ is given in the following lemma.

**Lemma 2.** *For every strategy of P2* $\liminf_{i\to\infty} \hat{r}_{t^i} - \tilde{r}_{t^i} \geq 0$ *almost surely.*

*Proof.* By our choice of $T^i = i^2$ we can apply the Borel-Cantelli Lemma to deduce that for every $\epsilon > 0$ we have that $\mathbf{P}(\tilde{r}^i \geq r^i + \epsilon \text{ i.o}) = 0$. Recalling our definitions we have that $\hat{r}_{t^i} - \tilde{r}_{t^i} = \frac{1}{t^i}\sum_{j=1}^{i} T^j(r^j - \tilde{r}^j)$. Since after some random index $k$ we have that $r^j - \tilde{r}^j > -\epsilon/2$ for every $j > k$, and since the reward is bounded until $t^k$ we have that for some random $\ell$ for all $j > \ell$ we have that $\hat{r}_{t^j} - \tilde{r}_{t^j} \geq -\epsilon$. The lemma follows since this is true for every $\epsilon > 0$. $\qquad\square$

We can now imitate the proof of Blackwell's theorem. In order to provide a Blackwell like theorem we need to provide a geometric condition regarding the behavior of the fictitious reward in every interval. Let $C^i$ be the closest point in $\mathbf{B}$ to the point $(\tilde{r}_{t^{i-1}}, \pi_{t^{i-1}})$ in the $S+1$ dimensional space (using Euclidean norm). That is $C^i = \operatorname{argmin}_{c\in\mathbf{B}} d(c, (\tilde{r}_{t^{i-1}}, \pi_{t^{i-1}}))$. Note that $C^i$ is well defined by the convexity of $\mathbf{B}$. When $\tilde{r}_{t^{i-1}} < r^*(\pi_{t^{i-1}})$ (step 4 of the algorithm) the direction $u^i$ is set as $u^i = \frac{C^i - (\tilde{r}_{t^{i-1}}, \pi_{t^{i-1}})}{\|C^i - (\tilde{r}_{t^{i-1}}, \pi_{t^{i-1}})\|}$. Though not critical to the following when $\tilde{r}_{t^{i-1}} \geq r^*(\pi_{t^{i-1}})$ we define $u^i = 0$. Finally, we set $\tilde{m}^i = (\tilde{r}^i, \pi^i) \in \mathbb{R} \times \Delta(\mathcal{S})$ the $S+1$ dimensional vector whose first coordinate is the added fictitious reward, and whose remaining $S$ coordinates are added to the observation frequency vector (normalized by the length of the $i$th stage.)

**Lemma 3.** *When Algorithm 1 is used then for every strategy $\rho$ of P2 we have that*

$$\liminf_{i\to\infty} u^i \cdot (\tilde{m}^i - C^i) \geq 0 \quad a.s.$$

*Proof.* Fix $\epsilon > 0$, we will show that $\liminf_{i\to\infty} u^i \cdot (\tilde{m}^i - C^i) \geq -\epsilon$ almost surely. If $\tilde{r}_{t^{i-1}} \geq r^*(\pi_{t^{i-1}})$ then $u^i = 0$ and equality holds. Assume $\tilde{r}_{t^{i-1}} < r^*(\pi_{t^{i-1}})$. By Proposition 1 the set $\mathbf{B}$ is approachable in the original game when the reward is observed. It follows from Blackwell's theorem that in the original game by choosing $p^i$ we have that for every $q \in \Delta(\mathcal{B})$

$$u^i \cdot (m(p^i, q) - C^i) \geq 0, \tag{9}$$

where $m(p, q)$ is given in Eq. (6). Suppose first that $\pi^i \in \Pi$. Recalling our definitions, there exists $q' \in \Delta(\mathcal{B})$ such that $\tilde{r}^i = r(p^i, q')$ and $\pi^i = s(q')$. Now, Eq. (9) holds for $q'$, so that $u^i \cdot (m(p^i, q') - C^i) \geq 0$, and therefore $u^i \cdot (\tilde{m}^i - C^i) \geq 0$. As in the proof of Lemma 1, we can show that $\mathbf{P}(\|\pi^i - \tilde{\pi}^i\| \geq \epsilon) \leq cT^i e^{-c'T^i\epsilon^2}$, so that by our choice of $T^i$ and using the Borel-Cantelli lemma $\mathbf{P}(\|\pi^i - \tilde{\pi}^i\| \geq \epsilon \text{ i.o}) = 0$. Let $\tilde{q}^i$ be the minimizer of $\min_{q\in J(\pi^i)} r(p^i, q)$. We have that:

$$u^i \cdot (\tilde{m}^i - C^i) = u^i \cdot ((\tilde{r}^i, J(\pi^i)) - C^i) + u^i \cdot ((\tilde{r}^i, \pi^i) - (\tilde{r}^i, J(\pi^i)))$$
$$\geq -\|\pi^i - J(\pi^i)\|,$$

where we used Eq. (9) for the first term and the Cauchy-Schwartz inequality for the second. The result follows from some random time on since from some time on $\|\pi^i - \tilde{\pi}^i\| \leq \epsilon$.  $\square$

We can now use Lemma 3 to show that $(\tilde{r}_{t^i}, \pi_{t^i})$ converge to $\mathbf{B}$.

**Lemma 4.** *Suppose that Algorithm 1 is used. Then for every strategy of P2:*

$$\lim_{i \to \infty} d\left((\tilde{r}_{t^i}, \pi_{t^i}), \mathbf{B}\right) = 0 \quad a.s.$$

*Proof.* Let $\mathbf{B}^\eta$ be the $\eta$-expansion of $\mathbf{B}$ (i.e. the union of all the points whose distance from $\mathbf{B}$ is $\eta$ or less). Let $\tilde{m}_{t^i} \stackrel{\triangle}{=} (\tilde{r}_{t^i}, \pi_{t^i})$ be the $S+1$ vector whose first coordinate is the fictitious reward and whose remaining $S$ coordinates are the empirical signal frequency. We will show that $d\left(\tilde{m}_{t^i}, \mathbf{B}^\eta\right) \to 0$.

Fix $\eta > 0$. By our choices of $T^i$ we have that $t^i = \frac{i(i+1)(2i+1)}{6}$. By Lemma 3 we have that after some finite random time either $\tilde{m}_{t^{i-1}} \in \mathbf{B}^\eta$ or that there is an advancement in direction $u^i$, i.e.:

$$\tilde{m}^i \cdot u^i \geq u^i \cdot C^i - \eta \,,$$

where $C^i$ is the closest point to $\tilde{m}_{t^{i-1}}$ in $\mathbf{B}$. Let $y_{t^i}$ be the closest point to $\tilde{m}_{t^i}$ in $\mathbf{B}^\eta$. It follows that if $\tilde{m}_{t^i} \notin \mathbf{B}^\eta$ then $y_{t^i} = C^{i+1} - \eta u^{i+1}$. We therefore have that after some finite (a.s.) random time

$$\tilde{m}^{i+1} \cdot u^{i+1} \geq u^{i+1} \cdot C^i - \eta u^{i+1} \cdot u^{i+1} = u^{i+1} \cdot y_{t^i}. \qquad (10)$$

Let $d_i$ denote the distance from $\tilde{m}_{t^i}$ to $\mathbf{B}^\eta$, i.e., $d_i = d((\tilde{r}_{t^i}, \pi_{t^i}), \mathbf{B}^\eta)$. Consider the square of the distance, $d_i^2$. It follows that:

$$d_{i+1}^2 = \|\tilde{m}_{t^{i+1}} - y_{t^{i+1}}\|_2^2 \leq \|\tilde{m}_{t^{i+1}} - y_{t^i}\|_2^2 = \|\tilde{m}_{t^{i+1}} - \tilde{m}_{t^i} + \tilde{m}_{t^i} - y_{t^i}\|$$
$$= \|\tilde{m}_{t^i} - y_{t^i}\|_2^2 + \|\tilde{m}_{t^{i+1}} - \tilde{m}_{t^i}\|_2^2 + 2(\tilde{m}_{t^i} - y_{t^i}) \cdot (\tilde{m}_{t^{i+1}} - \tilde{m}_{t^i}).$$

The first element is simply $d_i^2$. Since $t_i = O(i^3)$ and the reward is bounded, the second element can be bounded by $\frac{D}{i^2}$. The third element is more tricky. Since

$$\tilde{m}_{t^{i+1}} - \tilde{m}_{t^i} = \left(\frac{1}{t^{i+1}} - \frac{1}{t^i}\right) t^i \tilde{m}_{t^i} + \frac{T^{i+1}}{t^{i+1}} \tilde{m}^{i+1} = \frac{t^i - t^{i+1}}{t^{i+1}} \tilde{m}_{t^i} + \frac{T^i}{t^{i+1}} \tilde{m}^{i+1}$$

we have that:

$$(\tilde{m}_{t^i} - y_{t^i}) \cdot (\tilde{m}_{t^{i+1}} - \tilde{m}_{t^i}) = (\tilde{m}_{t^i} - y_{t^i}) \cdot \left(\tilde{m}_{t^{i+1}} - \frac{t^i - t^{i+1}}{t^{i+1}} y_{t^i} + \frac{t^i - t^{i+1}}{t^{i+1}} y_{t^i} - \tilde{m}_{t^i}\right)$$

$$= \frac{t^i - t^{i+1}}{t^{i+1}} (\tilde{m}_{t^i} - y_{t^i}) \cdot (\tilde{m}_{t^i} - y_{t^i}) \qquad (11)$$

$$+ \frac{t^i - t^{i+1}}{t^{i+1}} (\tilde{m}_{t^i} - y_{t^i}) \cdot (\tilde{m}^{i+1} - y_{t^i}) \,.$$

Since $i^3 c \geq t^i$ (for some $c$) and recalling that $T^i = i^2$, we can bound the fraction $\frac{t^{i+1} - t^i}{t^{i+1}} \geq C/i$. The first term (Eq. (11)) is therefore bounded by $-d_i^2 \frac{C_1}{i}$. We get the following inequality:

$$d_{i+1}^2 \leq (1 - \frac{C_1}{i})d_i^2 + \frac{C_2}{i^2} + 2C_3 \frac{(\tilde{m}_{t^i} - y_{t^i}) \cdot (\tilde{m}^{i+1} - y_i)}{i+1}, \qquad (12)$$

where $C_1, C_2$, and $C_3$ are positive constants. Now according to Eq. (10) the last term in (12) is negative after some random time. We therefore have that $d_{i+1}^2 \leq (1 - \frac{C_1}{i})d_i^2 + \frac{C_2}{i^2}$ from some point on. It now follows that $d_{i+1}^2 \to 0$ almost surely using, e.g., [12, Page 117].                                                          □

Using Lemma 4 we have that $d((\tilde{r}_{t^i}, \pi_{t^i}), \mathbf{B}) \to 0$ almost surely. By Lemma 2 we have that $\liminf_{i \to \infty} \hat{r}_{t^i} - \tilde{r}_{t^i} \geq 0$. Since $\mathbf{B}$ is the epigraph of $r^*$ we therefore have that also $d(\hat{m}_{t^i}, \mathbf{B}) \to 0$ almost surely, where $\hat{m}_t = (\hat{r}_{t^i}, \pi_{t^i})$. To conclude the proof we need to show that the above bound holds for all $t$ and not just for $t^i$. Let $i(t)$ denote the maximal $t^i$ smaller than $t$ (i.e. $i(t) = \max\{i : t^i \leq t\}$). By the triangle inequality

$$d(\hat{m}_t, \mathbf{B}) \leq d(\hat{m}_{t^{i(t)}}, \mathbf{B}) + \|\hat{m}_{t^{i(t)}} - \hat{m}_t\|_2.$$

The first term converges to 0 by the above. To bound the second term we let $m_\tau = (r_\tau, \pi_\tau)$.

$$\|\hat{m}_{t^{i(t)}} - \hat{m}_t\|_2 = \left\| \frac{1}{t} \sum_{\tau=1}^{t} m_\tau - \frac{1}{t^{i(t)}} \sum_{\tau=1}^{t^{i(t)}} m_\tau \right\|_2$$

$$= \left\| \frac{1}{t} \sum_{\tau=t^{i(t)}+1}^{t} m_\tau + \frac{t^{i(t)} - t}{t t^{i(t)}} \sum_{\tau=1}^{t^{i(t)}} m_\tau \right\|_2$$

$$\leq \frac{1}{t} \left\| \sum_{\tau=t^{i(t)}+1}^{t} m_\tau \right\|_2 + \frac{t - t^{i(t)}}{t t^{i(t)}} \left\| \sum_{\tau=1}^{t^{i(t)}} m_\tau \right\|_2$$

$$= \frac{t - t^{i(t)}}{t} \left( \frac{1}{t - t^{i(t)}} \left\| \sum_{\tau=t^{i(t)}+1}^{t} m_\tau \right\|_2 + \frac{1}{t^{i(t)}} \left\| \sum_{\tau=1}^{t^{i(t)}} m_\tau \right\|_2 \right), \qquad (13)$$

where the inequality is due to the triangle inequality. By our construction of $t^i$ it follows that $\lim_{t \to \infty} \frac{t - t^{i(t)}}{t} = 0$. By the boundedness of $m_t$ it follows that both terms inside the parenthesis of Eq. (13) are contained in some ball of finite radius. Consequently, Eq. (13) converges to 0 almost surely.

Since $d(\hat{m}_t, \mathbf{B})$ converges to 0 almost surely it follows using the same continuity argument in Theorem 1 that $\liminf_{t \to \infty} \hat{r}_t - r^*(\pi_t) \geq 0$ almost surely. Finally, using Proposition 2 we have that $\lim_{t \to \infty} r^*(\pi_t) - r^*(q_t) = 0$ almost surely. The result follows by combining the two limits.                                                          □

# Exploiting Task Relatedness
# for Multiple Task Learning

Shai Ben-David[1,3] and Reba Schuller[2]

[1] Cornell University, School of Electrical and Computer Engineering
Ithaca, NY 14853 USA
`shai@ece.cornell.edu`
[2] Cornell University, Department of Mathematics
Ithaca, NY 14853 USA
`ras51@cornell.edu`
[3] Technion, Department of Computer Science
Haifa 32000, Israel

**Abstract.** The approach of learning of multiple "related" tasks simultaneously has proven quite successful in practice; however, theoretical justification for this success has remained elusive. The starting point for previous work on multiple task learning has been that the tasks to be learned jointly are somehow "algorithmically related", in the sense that the *results* of applying a specific learning algorithm to these tasks are assumed to be similar. We offer an alternative approach, defining relatedness of tasks on the basis of similarity between the example generating distributions that underline these task.

We provide a formal framework for this notion of task relatedness, which captures a sub-domain of the wide scope of issues in which one may apply a multiple task learning approach. Our notion of task similarity is relevant to a variety of real life multitask learning scenarios and allows the formal derivation of generalization bounds that are strictly stronger than the previously known bounds for both the learning-to-learn and the multitask learning scenarios. We give precise conditions under which our bounds guarantee generalization on the basis of smaller sample sizes than the standard single-task approach.

## 1 Introduction

Most of the work in machine learning focuses on learning tasks that are encountered separately, one task at a time. While great success has been achieved in this type of framework, it is clear that it neglects certain fundamental aspects of human and animal learning. Human beings face each new learning task equipped with knowledge gained from previous similar learning tasks. Furthermore, human learning frequently involves approaching several learning tasks simultaneously; in particular, humans take advantage of the opportunity to compare and contrast similar categories in learning to classify entities into those categories.

It is natural to attempt to apply these observations to machine learning–what kind of advantage is there in setting a learner to work on several tasks

B. Schölkopf and M.K. Warmuth (Eds.): COLT/Kernel 2003, LNAI 2777, pp. 567–580, 2003.

sequentially or simultaneously? Intuitively, there should certainly be some advantage, especially if the tasks are closely related in some way. And, indeed, much experimental work [Bax95,IE96,Thr96,Hes98,Car97] has validated this intuition. However, thus far, there has been relatively little progress on theoretical justification for these results.

Relatedness of tasks is key to the multitask learning (MTL) approach. Obviously, one cannot expect that information gathered through the learning of a set of tasks will be relevant to the learning of another task that has nothing in common with the already learned tasks.

Previous work on MTL (or Learning to Learn) treated the notion of relatedness using a 'functional' approach. Consider for example Baxter's Learning To Learn work, e.g., [Bax00] (which is, to our knowledge, the most systematic theoretical analysis of the simultaneous learning approach). In Baxter's work the similarity between jointly learned tasks is manifested solely through a model selection criterion, namely, the advantage of learning tasks together relies on the assumption that the tasks share a common optimal (or near-optimal) hypothesis class (i.e., inductive bias).

We try to determine under what circumstances one can expect a sequence of tasks to be related in a 'learning useful' way. We focus on the sample generating distributions underlying the learning tasks, and define task relatedness as an explicit relationship between these distributions. Our notion seems to capture a sub-domain of the realm of applications to which multitask learning may be relevant.

Not surprisingly, by limiting the discussion to problems that can be modeled by our data generating mechanism we leave many potential MTL scenarios outside the scope of our discussion. However, there are several interesting problems that can be treated within our framework. For these problems we can reap the benefits of having a mathematical notion of relatedness and prove sample size upper bounds for MTL learning that are better than any previous proven bounds.

The rest of the paper is organized as follows: Section 2 formally introduces multiple task learning and describes our notion of task relatedness. We state and prove our generalization error bound for this framework in section 3. In section 4, we analyze the generalized VC-dimension parameter on which this bound depends, and we compare this bound for multiple task learning to the known bounds for the single task approach. That is, we examine when can the error bounds for learning a given task improve by allowing the learner to access samples generated by different but related tasks.

## 1.1   Previous Work

The only theoretical analysis of multitask learning that we are aware of is the work of Baxter [Bax00], and the recent work of Ben-David et. al. [BDGS02].

The main question that we are interested in is when does multitask learning provide an advantage over the single task approach. In order to achieve this, we introduce a concrete notion of what it means for tasks to be "related," and evaluate multi- versus single-task learning for tasks related in this manner. Our notion of relatedness between tasks is inspired by [BDGS02] which deals with the problem of integrating disparate databases. We extend the main generalization error result from [BDGS02] to the multitask learning setting, strengthen it, and analyze the extent to which it offers an improvement over single task learning.

The main technical tool that we use is the generalized VC-dimension of Baxter and his results bounding the average error over a class of tasks in terms of this dimension. However, since we view multitask learning as having one 'focus of interest' task that one wishes to learn and extra related tasks that are mainly used as an aid towards learning the main task, bounds on the average error over all tasks are not good enough. We show that when one is dealing with tasks that are related in the sense that we define, the Baxter generalization bound can be strengthened to hold for every single error, on every one of the tasks at hand.

We should point out the distinction between the problem considered herein and the co-training approach of [BM98]. Co-training makes use of extra "tasks" to compensate for having only a small amount of labeled data. However, in co-training, the extra tasks are assumed to be different "views" of the same sample, whereas our extra tasks are independent samples from different distributions. Thus, in spite of its relevance to multitask learning, previous work on co-training cannot be directly applied to the problem at hand.

## 2   A Data Generation Model for Related Tasks

Formally, the typical (single-task) classification learning problem is modeled as follows: Given a domain $\mathcal{X}$ and a random sample $S$ drawn from some unknown distribution $P$ on $\mathcal{X} \times \{0, 1\}$, find a hypothesis $h : \mathcal{X} \to \{0, 1\}$ such that for randomly drawn $(x, b)$, with high probability $h(x) = b$. This problem is some times referred to as "statistical regression".

The multiple task learning problem is the analogous problem for multiple distributions. That is, given domain $\mathcal{X}$ and sequence of random samples $S_1, \ldots, S_n$ drawn from some unknown distributions $P_1, \ldots P_n$, respectively, on $\mathcal{X} \times \{0, 1\}$, find hypotheses $h_1, \ldots, h_n : \mathcal{X} \to \{0, 1\}$ such that for each $i$, for $(x, b)$ drawn randomly from $P_i$, $h_i(x) = b$ with high probability.

Note that this is an extension of the *agnostic* learning framework.

As we have mentioned previously, it is intuitive that the advantage of the multiple task approach depends on the "relatedness" between the different tasks. While there has been empirical success with sets of tasks related in various ways, thus far, no formal definition of "relatedness" has provided any theoretical results to this effect.

### 2.1   Our Notion of Relatedness between Learning Tasks

We define a data generation mechanism which serves to determine our notion of related tasks.

The basic ingredient in our definition is a set $\mathcal{F}$ of transformations $f : \mathcal{X} \to \mathcal{X}$. We say that tasks are $\mathcal{F}$- related if, for some fixed probability distribution over

$\mathcal{X} \times \{0, 1\}$, the data in each of these tasks is generated by applying some $f \in \mathcal{F}$ to this distribution.

**Definition 1.** *Let $\mathcal{F}$ be a set of transformations $f : \mathcal{X} \to \mathcal{X}$, and let $P_1$, $P_2$ be probability distributions over $\mathcal{X} \times \{0, 1\}$. We say that $P_1$, $P_2$ are $\mathcal{F}$-related if there exists some $f \in \mathcal{F}$ such that for any $T \subseteq \mathcal{X} \times \{0, 1\}$, $T$ is $P_1$-measurable iff $f[T] = \{(f(x), b) \mid (x, b) \in T)\}$ is $P_2$ - measurable and $P_1(T) = P_2(f[T])$. We say that two samples are $\mathcal{F}$-related if they are samples from $\mathcal{F}$-related distributions.*

In our learning scenario for such $\mathcal{F}$-related tasks, we assume that the learner knows the family of functions $\mathcal{F}$ but does not know which specific function $f$ relates any given pair of distributions. Consequently, the advantage that a learner can derive for a specific task from access to a sample drawn from some other $\mathcal{F}$-related task depends of the richness of the family of transformations $\mathcal{F}$. The larger this set gets, the looser the notion of $\mathcal{F}$- relatedness is.

Clearly there are many examples of potential applications of simultaneous learning that do not fit into this model of relatedness. However, there are various interesting examples where this notion seems to provide a satisfactory mathematical model of the similarity between the tasks in a set of related learning problems.

Typically our notion of $\mathcal{F}$-relatedness arises in situations where many different sensors collect data for the same classification problem. For example, consider a set of cameras located in the lobbies of several high security buildings. Assume that they are all used to automatically detect unauthorized visitors, based on the images they record. Clearly, each of these cameras has its own bias, due to a different height, light conditions, angle, etc. While it may be difficult to determine the exact bias of each camera, it may be feasible to define mathematically a set of image transformations $\mathcal{F}$ such that the data distributions of images collected by of all these recorders are $\mathcal{F}$-related.

Another area in which such a notion of similarity is applicable is that of database integration. Suppose there are several databases available, each of which obtains its information from the same data pool, yet represents its information with a different database schema. For the purpose of classification prediction, our results in the next section eliminate the need for the difficult undertaking of database integration, treating each database as one task in a multiple task learning problem.

## 3 Learning $\mathcal{F}$-Related Tasks

In this section, we analyze multiple task learning for $\mathcal{F}$-related tasks. We provide a technique for incorporating examples coming from extra related tasks in order to reduce the hypothesis space in such a way that the reduced hypothesis space contains a near-optimal hypothesis for each of the tasks. In particular, given a set of data transformations and a hypothesis space, we partition the latter into subspaces and use the samples from the extra tasks to choose a subspace that minimizes the average empirical error over the different tasks. To solve the original learning problem, we then focus the hypothesis search on this chosen subspace of the hypothesis space. We give a sample complexity bound that justifies this algorithmic approach.

Formally, the problem at hand is as follows: given domain $\mathcal{X}$, hypothesis space $\mathbb{H}$ on $\mathcal{X}$, set of transformations $\mathcal{F}$ on $\mathcal{X}$, and sequence $S_1, \ldots, S_n$ of samples from some sequence of $\mathcal{F}$-similar distributions, $P_1, \ldots, P_n$ on $\mathcal{X} \times \{0,1\}$, select hypotheses $h_1, \ldots, h_n \in \mathbb{H}$ such that for each $i$, for $(x, b)$ drawn randomly from $P_i$, $h_i(x) = b$ with high probability.

We proceed by addressing this problem in two phases. The first phase makes use of all of the samples to reduce the size of our hypothesis space by selecting a subspace of $\mathbb{H}$. The second phase then uses standard learning techniques to select a hypothesis from this subspace for each task separately. The advantage of multitask learning is obtained through the reduction in complexity of the hypothesis space achieved in the first phase.

In general, our approach to the first phase is as follows: Define a partition of $\mathbb{H}$ into a family of subspaces. Then choose a subspace, $H$, to minimize the average empirical error over the different tasks.

One of our main results is a bound on the generalization error for this approach.

We now describe explicitly our method for partitioning $\mathbb{H}$. From the given hypothesis space, $\mathbb{H}$, we create a family, $\mathbf{H}$, of hypothesis spaces consisting of sets of hypothesis in $\mathbb{H}$ which are equivalent up to transformations in $\mathcal{F}$. We assume that $\mathcal{F}$ forms a group under function composition and that $\mathbb{H}$ is closed under the action of $\mathcal{F}$ (i.e., for each $f \in \mathcal{F}$ and each $h \in \mathbb{H}$, we have $h \circ f \in \mathbb{H}$). As is standard, we will write $[h]_{\sim_{\mathcal{F}}}$, or simply $[h]$, to denote the equivalence class of $h$ under $\sim_{\mathcal{F}}$.

**Definition 2.** *Given hypothesis space $\mathbb{H}$ and transformation family $\mathcal{F}$ on domain $\mathcal{X}$, define equivalence relation $\sim_{\mathcal{F}}$ on $\mathbb{H}$ by:*

$$h_1 \sim_{\mathcal{F}} h_2 \text{ iff there exists } f \in \mathcal{F} \text{ such that } h_2 = h_1 \circ f.$$

Now, we let our family of hypothesis spaces, $\mathbf{H}$, be the family of all equivalence classes of $\mathbb{H}$ under $\sim_{\mathcal{F}}$, i.e., $\mathbf{H} = \mathbb{H}/\sim_{\mathcal{F}}$.

As is standard, we denote the *true error*, and *empirical error*, respectively, of a hypothesis as follows. For distribution $P$,

$$Er^P(h) = P(\{(x, b) \in \mathcal{X} \times \{0,1\} : h(x) \neq b\}).$$

And for a sample, $S$, of points in $\mathcal{X} \times \{0,1\}$,

$$\hat{Er}^S(h) = \frac{|\{(x, b) \in S : h(x) \neq b\}|}{|S|}.$$

Observe that, for any hypothesis, $h$, if $P_1, P_2$ are $\mathcal{F}$-related distributions, then

$$\exists f \in \mathcal{F} \text{ such that } Er^{P_1}(h \circ f) = Er^{P_2}(h). \tag{1}$$

This is an immediate consequence of the the definition of $\mathcal{F}$-related distributions and our assumption that $\mathcal{F}$ forms a group under function composition.

Using this fact, we can deduce that the equivalence classes of $\mathbb{H}$ perform equally well on the different tasks in the following sense.

**Definition 3.** *For any hypothesis space, $H$, define*

$$Er^P(H) = \inf_{h \in H} Er^P(h).$$

Thus, we judge the performance of a hypothesis space on a given task by the performance of the best hypothesis in the space on that task.

**Lemma 1.** *Let $P_1$, $P_2$ be $\mathcal{F}$-related distributions and $\mathcal{F}$ be a group under function composition. If $H$ is closed under the action of $\mathcal{F}$ then $Er^{P_1}(H) = Er^{P_2}(H)$.*

*Proof.* We need to show that

$$\inf_{h \in H} Er^{P_1}(h) = \inf_{h \in H} Er^{P_2}(h).$$

It suffices to show that for every $h \in H$ there exist $h', h'' \in H$ such that $Er^{P_2}(h') \leq Er^{P_1}(h)$ and $Er^{P_1}(h'') \leq Er^{P_2}(h)$.

By equation 1, there exist $f, f'$ such that if $h' = h \circ f$, and $h'' = h' \circ f'$, then $Er^{P_2}(h') = Er^{P_1}(h)$ and $Er^{P_1}(h'') = Er^{P_2}(h)$, so we are done. $\qquad\square$

Before we continue, we require some background.

## 3.1   Background from Baxter [Bax00]

Baxter [Bax00] discusses the following problem. Given a set of tasks and a set of hypothesis spaces, choose the hypothesis space which performs best on the set of the tasks. He provides a bound for the generalization error for this problem in terms of a generalized VC-dimension parameter. In particular, he bounds the rate of convergence of the *average* (over all the tasks) of the empirical errors to the true error.

Baxter's generalization error bound depends on the following notion of generalized VC-dimension for families of hypothesis spaces.

*Notation:* For function $g : Y \to Z$ and $\bar{y} = (y_1, \ldots, y_n) \in Y^n$, $\bar{g}(\bar{y})$ will denote $(g(y_1), \ldots, g(y_n)) \in Z^n$.

**Definition 4.** *For family $\mathbf{H}$ of hypothesis spaces, and $n, m \in \mathbb{Z}^+$,*

$$\Pi_{\mathbf{H}}(n, m) = \max_{\bar{x}_1, \ldots, \bar{x}_n \in X^m} \left| \left\{ \begin{bmatrix} \overline{h_1(\bar{x}_1)} \\ \vdots \\ \overline{h_n(\bar{x}_n)} \end{bmatrix} : \exists H \in \mathbf{H} \text{ with } h_1, \ldots, h_n \in H \right\} \right|.$$

**Definition 5.** $d_{\mathbf{H}}(n) = \max\{m : \Pi_{\mathbf{H}}(n, m) = 2^{nm}\}$.

We can now state the necessary result from [Bax00] on multitask learning, which appears as corollary 13 in [Bax00][1].

**Theorem 1.** *Let* **H** *be any permissible boolean hypothesis space family[2], and let* $S_1, \ldots, S_n$ *be a sequence of random samples from distributions* $P_1, \ldots, P_n$ *on* $\mathcal{X} \times \{0, 1\}$. *If the number of examples,* $m$, *in each sample* $S_i$ *satisfies*

$$m \geq \frac{88}{\epsilon^2} \left[ 2d_{\mathbf{H}}(n) \log \frac{22}{\epsilon} + \frac{1}{n} \log \frac{4}{\delta} \right],$$

*then with probability at least* $1 - \delta$ *(over the choice of* $S_1, \ldots, S_n$), *for any* $H \in \mathbf{H}$, *and* $h_1, \ldots, h_n \in H$,

$$\left| \frac{1}{n} \sum_{i=1}^{n} Er^{P_i}(h_i) - \frac{1}{n} \sum_{i=1}^{n} \hat{Er}^{S_i}(h_i) \right| \leq \epsilon.$$

Note that this theorem only bounds the *average* generalization error over the different tasks.

## 3.2   Bounding the Generalization Error for *Each* Task

We are now ready to state and prove one of our main results, which gives an upper bound on the sample complexity of finding a $\sim_{\mathcal{F}}$-equivalence class which is near-optimal for *each* of the tasks. This is significant, since the goal of multitask learning is to use extra tasks to improve performance on one particular task.

**Theorem 2.** *For any* $0 \leq \epsilon, \delta \leq 1$ *and* $h \in \mathbb{H}$, *if* $S_1, \ldots, S_n$ *is an* $\mathcal{F}$-similar *sequence of samples corresponding to* $P_1, \ldots, P_n$, *with* $|S_i| \geq m$ *for all* $i$, *where*

$$m \geq \frac{88}{\epsilon^2} \left[ 2d_{\mathbf{H}}(n) \log \frac{22}{\epsilon} + \frac{1}{n} \log \frac{4}{\delta} \right], \tag{2}$$

*then with probability at least* $1 - \delta$, *for any* $1 \leq j \leq n$,

$$\left| Er^{P_j}([h]_{\sim_{\mathcal{F}}}) - \inf_{h_1, \ldots, h_n \in [h]_{\sim_{\mathcal{F}}}} \frac{1}{n} \sum_{i=1}^{n} \hat{Er}^{S_i}(h_i) \right| \leq \epsilon.$$

*Proof.* We first observe that it follows from lemma 1 that for any $h \in \mathbb{H}$ and any $1 \leq j \leq n$,

$$Er^{P_j}([h]_{\sim_{\mathcal{F}}}) = \inf_{h_1, \ldots, h_n \in [h]_{\sim_{\mathcal{F}}}} \frac{1}{n} \sum_{i=1}^{n} Er^{P_i}(h_i).$$

The result now follows from theorem 1. $\qquad\square$

---

[1] Note that although [Bax00] only states that $\frac{1}{n} \sum_{i=1}^{n} Er^{P_i}(h_i) \leq \frac{1}{n} \sum_{i=1}^{n} \hat{Er}^{S_i}(h_i) + \epsilon$, it is clear from the proofs in [Bax00] that this stronger form holds.

[2] Permissibility, discussed in [BEHW89] is a "weak measure-theoretic condition satisfied by almost all 'real-world' hypothesis space families" ([Bax00], Appendix D). Throughout this paper we shall assume that all our classes are permissible.

Note that combining the standard generalization error result for single task learning with theorem 2 gives an information complexity bound for these two phases together. We state this bound explicitly in the next section. First, though, we examine what this theorem says for a particular learning scenario.

## 3.3    Analysis of Axis-Aligned Rectangles under Euclidean Shifts

Let $\mathcal{X} = \mathbb{R}^d$, and $\mathbb{H}$ be the set of characteristic functions of axis-aligned rectangles, i.e., functions that map to 1 all points within some fixed rectangle $[a_1, a_1+b_1] \times \ldots \times [a_d, a_d+b_d]$ and map to 0 to all other points. Let $\mathcal{F}$ be the set of Euclidean shifts, i.e., functions of the form $f(x_1, \ldots, x_d) = (x_1+v_1, \ldots, x_d+v_d)$, where $v_1, \ldots v_d \in \mathbb{R}$. As above, we let $\mathbf{H}$ denote $\mathbb{H}/\sim_{\mathcal{F}}$.

*Claim.* For $d > 1$ and $n > d$, $d_{\mathbf{H}}(n) \leq d + \frac{d}{2}$.

*Proof.* We will see in theorem 4 that for $H$ as above and $n > d$,

$$d_{\mathbf{H}}(n) = max_{[h] \in \mathbf{H}} \text{VC-dim}([h]).$$

So, it suffices to show that for any $[h] \in \mathbf{H}$, VC-dim$([h]) \leq d + \frac{d}{2}$. We prove this as the following lemma.

**Lemma 2.** *Let* $\mathbf{r}$ *be an axis-aligned rectangle in* $\mathbb{R}^d$, *and let* $F(\mathbf{r})$ *be the class of all Euclidean shifts of* $\mathbf{r}$. *Then* $VC\text{-}dim(F(\mathbf{r})) \leq d + \frac{d}{2}$.

*Proof.* Suppose $[h]$ shatters set $U$. (I.e., for any $V \subseteq U$, there exists $h' \in [h]$ such that for all $x \in U$, $h'(x) = 1 \iff x \in V$. We say that such an $h'$ *obtains* subset $V$ of $U$.)

Then, in order to obtain the complements of each of the singleton subsets of $U$, each point $x \in U$ must have some coordinate $k_x$ in which its value is either the greatest or the least among the $k_x$th coordinate of all points in $U$.

For a given point, $p \in \mathbb{R}^m$, let $p(k)$ denote its $k$th coordinate.

Assume $|U| > d + \frac{d}{2}$. Then, there must exist at least $d + 1$ points $p \in U$ for which $k_p$ is unique, i.e., for every other coordinate $k$, there exist points $y, z \in U$ such that $y(k) > p(k)$ and $z(k) < p(k)$. And since we are in $\mathbb{R}^d$, there exist two such points, $p$ and $q$ such that $k_p = k_q$ and both $k_p$ and $k_q$ are unique. Call this coordinate $k$.

Now, what we have is points $p, q \in U$ such that $p(k) > x(k)$, and $q(k) > x(k)$ for all $x \in U - \{p, q\}$, and for every $k' \neq k$ there exist points $y, z \in S$ such that $y(k) > p(k), q(k)$ and $z(k) < p(k), q(k)$.

We proceed to show that no $h' \in [h]$ obtains the subset $U - \{p, q\}$.

Since $[h]$ must obtain the subset of $S$ consisting of $U$ itself, the length of the side in coordinate $j$ for any $h' \in [h]$ must be at least $max_{x,y \in U}|x(j) - y(j)|$. Without loss of generality, let us say that $h$ obtains $U$. Then, any subset of $U$ obtained by any $h' \in [h]$ consists of those points in $U$ that remain after removing axis-parallel slices of $h$ on up to $d$ of its faces, with no two opposing faces sliced.

However, the only slices that can remove $p$ and $q$ without removing any other points from $S$ are the two opposing slices in coordinate $k$, so, indeed, the subset $U - \{p, q\}$ cannot be obtained by any $h' \in [h]$ .                                      $\square$

Note that the VC-dimension of the class of axis-aligned rectangles in $\mathbb{R}^d$ is $2d$. Comparing equation 2 to the corresponding standard VC-dimension generalization error bound [VC71] (shown in equation 3), we have the following.

*Claim.* For the purpose of learning the rectangle side lengths, VC-dimension considerations provide better accuracy guarantees for $n$ shifted samples each of size $m$ than for a single sample of size $n(\frac{8}{11}m - c)$, where $c$ is a constant depending on the desired accuracy and the Euclidean dimension. Furthermore, c is small enough so that each sample may be smaller than that needed to obtain the same guarantees for a single data set of size m.

Previously, [BDGS02] showed that, for this example in the PAC setting, $n$ shifted samples each of size $m$ provide better accuracy guarantees under the standard ad hoc considerations [KV97] than a single sample of size $n(m - c')$, where $c'$ is also a constant depending on the desired accuracy and the Euclidean dimension. We are pleased to see that our analysis provides nearly as strong a result for the agnostic setting.

## 4   Multiple Task Learning versus the Single Task Approach

We have provided upper bounds on the information complexity of multiple task learning where the tasks are related via some set of transformations, $\mathcal{F}$. We now address the question of how this compares to the information complexity of single task learning.

In the following, let $D =$ VC-dim$(\mathbb{H})$, and

$$d_{max} = \max_{h \in \mathbb{H}} \text{VC-dim}([h]_{\sim_{\mathcal{F}}}).$$

The standard single task learning result [VC71] guarantees that for a single sample $S_0$ sampled from distribution $P_0$,

$$|S_0| \geq (64/\epsilon^2)[\log(4/\delta) + 2D\log(12/\epsilon)] \tag{3}$$

is sufficient to ensure that with probability at least $1 - \delta$,

$$\left| Er^{P_0}(h) - \hat{Er}^{S_0}(h) \right| \leq \epsilon.$$

Analogously, the results in this paper guarantee that for $n$ $\mathcal{F}$-similar tasks, the total number of examples needed is at most

$$n \times \max\left( \frac{352}{\epsilon^2}\left[2d_{\mathbf{H}}(n)\log\frac{44}{\epsilon} + \frac{1}{n}\log\frac{8}{\delta}\right], \left(\frac{256}{\epsilon^2}\right)\left[2d_{max}\log\frac{24}{\epsilon} + \log\frac{8}{\delta}\right] \right) \tag{4}$$

It is clear that if n is relatively large, then this bound for the total number examples required for the multitask approach is not an improvement over the single task approach. This is not surprising. However, the number of examples needed *per task* is at most $\frac{1}{n}th$ of this quantity. Thus, if

$$d_{\mathbf{H}}(n) < \frac{4D\log\frac{12}{\epsilon} + 2\log\frac{4}{\delta} - \frac{11}{n}\log\frac{8}{\delta}}{22\log\frac{44}{\epsilon}},$$

and

$$d_{max} < \frac{2D\log\frac{12}{\epsilon} + 2\log\frac{4}{\delta} - 4\log\frac{8}{\delta}}{8\log\frac{24}{\epsilon}},$$

then the information complexity *per task* is less for learning $n$ tasks than for learning a single data task. This means that if the $\sim_{\mathcal{F}}$-equivalence classes of $\mathbb{H}$ are sufficiently less rich than $\mathbb{H}$ itself, then one can compensate for insufficient training data for a task by using additional tasks.

Now, in order to evaluate the per-task information complexity advantage of multiple task learning, we must analyze the parameter $d_{\mathbf{H}}(n)$ and its relationship to VC-dim($\mathbb{H}$).

### 4.1 Analysis of $d_{\mathbf{H}}(n)$

It is clear that $d_{\mathbf{H}}(n+1) \leq d_{\mathbf{H}}(n)$ for any $n$. Thus, we see from eq. 2 that once we have committed ourselves to the multitask approach, extra tasks can only be beneficial.

It is also easy to see that $d_{max} \leq d_{\mathbf{H}}(n) \leq D$. Thus, the best we can hope for is $d_{\mathbf{H}}(n) = d_{max}$. We conjecture that for any $\mathbb{H}$ of finite VC-dimension and any $\mathcal{F}$, this lower bound is attained for all sufficiently large $n$. The following two theorems support this conjecture.

*Notation:* Let $|h|$ denote the cardinality of the support of $h$, i.e., $|h|$ denotes $|\{x \in \mathcal{X} : h(x) = 1\}|$.

**Theorem 3.** *If there exists $M$ such that $|h| \leq M$ for all $h \in \mathbb{H}$, then there exists $n_0$ such that for all $n \geq n_0$,*

$$d_{\mathbf{H}}(n) = \max_{h \in \mathbb{H}} VC\text{-}dim([h]_{\sim_{\mathcal{F}}}).$$

*(Recall that $\mathbf{H}$ denotes $\mathbb{H}/\sim_{\mathcal{F}}$. )*

*Proof.* Assume $d_{\mathbf{H}}(n) \geq m$, and let $\overline{x_1}, \ldots, \overline{x_n}$ be such that

$$\left| \left\{ \begin{bmatrix} \overline{h \circ f_1(\overline{x_1})} \\ \vdots \\ \overline{h \circ f_n(\overline{x_n})} \end{bmatrix} : f_1 \ldots f_n \in \mathcal{F}, h \in \mathbb{H} \right\} \right| = 2^{nm}$$

Consider $h_0 \in \mathbb{H}$ and $f_1, \ldots, f_n$ such that

$$\begin{bmatrix} \overline{h_0 \circ f_1(\overline{x_1})} \\ \vdots \\ \overline{h_0 \circ f_n(\overline{x_n})} \end{bmatrix} = \begin{bmatrix} 1 \ldots 1 \\ \vdots \ddots \vdots \\ 1 \ldots 1 \end{bmatrix}$$

Note that for each $i$, there exists $S_i \subseteq h_0$ such that $\overline{x_i}$ is some permutation of $\{f_i^{-1}(z) : z \in S_i\}$.

Say $|h_0| = K$. Then if $n > \left(\binom{K}{m} - 1\right) 2^m$, then there exists $S \subseteq h_0$ and $i_1, \ldots i_{2^m}$ such that $S_{i_j} = S$ for $1 \leq j \leq 2^m$. Let $\sigma_1, \ldots \sigma_{2^m}$ be the corresponding permutations.

Finally, letting $v_1, \ldots, v_{2^m}$ be an enumeration of all vectors of length $m$ over $\{0, 1\}$, letting $N$ be any $m \times n$ matrix over $\{0, 1\}$ whose $i_j^{th}$ row is $\sigma_j(v_{i_j})$, and letting $h_*$ and $f_1', \ldots, f_n'$ be such that

$$\begin{bmatrix} \overline{h_* \circ f_1'(\overline{x_1})} \\ \vdots \\ \overline{h_* \circ f_n'(\overline{x_n})} \end{bmatrix} = N,$$

we see that $[h_*]_{\sim_{\mathcal{F}}}$ shatters $S$, so $m \leq$ VC-dim$([h_*]_{\sim_{\mathcal{F}}})$.

To eliminate the dependence on $|h_0| = K$, we set $n_0 = \left(\binom{M}{M/2} - 1\right) 2^M$, noting that $n_0 \geq \left(\binom{K}{m} - 1\right) 2^m$ for all $K, m \leq M$.   $\square$

So, we see that for any class of hypotheses bounded in size (i.e., the size of their support), for sufficiently large $n$, $d_{\mathbf{H}}(n)$ obtains it's minimum possible value of $d_{max}$. However, many natural hypothesis spaces consist of hypotheses that are not only unbounded, but infinite in size. In the following theorem, we show that this conjecture also holds for a natural hypothesis space consisting of infinite hypotheses.

**Theorem 4.** *Let $\mathcal{X}, \mathbb{H}$, and $\mathcal{F}$ be the rectangles with shifts as in section 3.3, and let $\mathbf{H}$ denote $\mathbb{H}/\sim_{\mathcal{F}}$ as usual. For $n > d$,*

$$d_{\mathbf{H}}(n) = \max_{h \in \mathbb{H}} \text{VC-dim}([h]_{\sim_{\mathcal{F}}}).$$

*Proof.* let $\overline{x_1}, \ldots, \overline{x_n} \in \left(\mathbb{R}^d\right)^m$ be such that

$$\left| \left\{ \begin{bmatrix} \overline{h \circ f_1(\overline{x_1})} \\ \vdots \\ \overline{h \circ f_n(\overline{x_n})} \end{bmatrix} : f_1 \ldots f_n \in \mathcal{F}, h \in \mathbb{H} \right\} \right| = 2^{nm}.$$

For $y \in \mathbb{R}^d$, and $1 \leq k \leq d$, we will denote by $y(k)$ the $k$th coordinate of $y$.

For $k = 1, \ldots, d$, let $w_k = \max\{|y(k) - z(k)| : y, z \in \overline{x_i} \text{ for some } 1 \leq i \leq n\}$. $w_1, \ldots, w_d$ is the sequence of minimal possible side lengths for any rectangle $h$ such that

$$\begin{bmatrix} \overline{h \circ f_1(\overline{x_1})} \\ \vdots \\ \overline{h \circ f_n(\overline{x_n})} \end{bmatrix} = \begin{bmatrix} 1 \ldots 1 \\ \vdots \ \vdots \\ 1 \ldots 1 \end{bmatrix}.$$

Without loss of generality, let us assume that $\overline{x_1} \ldots, \overline{x_n}$ are ordered such that these maxima are attained within $\overline{x_1} \ldots, \overline{x_d}$.

Now, for any binary sequence $b = (b_1, \ldots b_m)$, there exists some $h_b \in \mathbb{H}$ such that

$$\begin{bmatrix} \overline{h_b \circ f_1(\overline{x_1})} \\ \vdots \\ \overline{h_b \circ f_n(\overline{x_n})} \end{bmatrix} = \begin{bmatrix} 1 & \cdots & 1 \\ \vdots & & \vdots \\ 1 & \cdots & 1 \\ b_1 & \cdots & b_m \end{bmatrix}$$

Clearly, no such $h_b$ can have its $k$th side length less than $w_k$. Furthermore, there is no advantage in having any $k$th side length greater than $w_k$. Thus, we see that if $h = [0, w_1] \times \ldots \times [0, w_k]$, then $[h]_{\sim_{\mathcal{F}}}$ shatters $\overline{x_n}$, so VC-dim$([h]_{\sim_{\mathcal{F}}}) \geq m$. □

So, we see that it is not uncommon for $d_{\mathbf{H}}(n)$ to attain its minimum possible value, $d_{max}$. As this value can be significantly less than $D$, this gives great hope for equation 4 to be significantly less than equation 3. Thus our bounds can guarantee generalization on the basis of smaller size than the standard VC-dimension considerations for the single-task approach.

Ben-David, et. al. [BDGS02] provide the following further results on $d_{\mathbf{H}}(n)$.

**Theorem 5.** *If $\mathcal{F}$ is finite and $\frac{n}{\log(n)} \geq$ VC-dim$(\mathbb{H})$, then*

$$d_{\mathbf{H}}(n) \leq 2\log(|\mathcal{F}|).$$

Note that this result leads us to scenarios under which $d_{\mathbf{H}}(n)$ is arbitrarily smaller than VC-dim$(\mathbb{H})$. Indeed, as long as $\mathcal{F}$ is finite, no matter how complex $\mathbb{H}$ is, $d_{\mathbf{H}}(n)$ remains bounded by $2\log(|\mathcal{F}|)$. Furthermore, in practice, the requirement that $\mathcal{F}$ be finite is not an unreasonable one, since real world problems come with bounded domains and real world computations have limited numerical accuracy.

Furthermore, [BDGS02] provides the following generalization of this result.

**Theorem 6.** *If $\sim_{\mathcal{F}}$ is of finite index[3], $k$, and $n \geq \frac{\log k}{4b\log b}$, then*

$$d_{\mathbf{H}}(n) \leq \frac{\log k}{n} + 4b\log b,$$

*where*

$$b = \max\left(\max_{H \in \mathbb{H}/\sim_{\mathcal{F}}} VC\text{-}dim(H), 3\right).$$

This shows that even if $\mathcal{F}$ is infinite, $d_{\mathbf{H}}(n)$ cannot grow arbitrarily with increasing complexity of $\mathbf{H}$.

---

[3] The *index* of an equivalence relation is the number of equivalence classes into which it partitions its domain.

# 5    Conclusions and Future Work

We have presented a useful notion of relatedness between tasks for multiple task learning. This notion of relatedness provides a natural model for a variety of real world learning scenarios. We have derived generalization error bounds for learning of multiple tasks related in this manner. These bounds depend on a generalized VC-dimension parameter, which can be significantly less than the ordinary VC-dimension, thus improving on the usual bounds for the single task approach. We have provided analysis of this parameter and its relationship to the usual VC-dimension, and we have given precise conditions under which our multitask approach provides generalization guarantees based on smaller sample size than the single task approach.

This work is a significant step towards the goal of a full theory of multiple task learning. With the restriction to a special type of relatedness of tasks, we have been able to obtain sample size bounds which are significantly better than previously proven bounds for the learning to learn scenario.

Hopefully, this work will stimulate future work in several directions. There is room for a more thorough understanding of the conditions under which multi-task learning is advantageous over the single task approach in our scenario; in particular, a greater understanding of the generalized VC-dimension parameter would provide such insight. It would also be fruitful to relax the requirements on the set of transformations through which the tasks are related, allowing these transformations to be arbitrary rather than bijections, and perhaps even allowing the actual transformations between the tasks to be merely approximated by the set of known transformations. Finally, the quest for further applicable notions of relatedness between tasks remains the key to a thorough understanding of multiple task learning.

We believe that this work provides convincing evidence that a theoretical understanding of multiple task learning and its advantage over the single task approach is a promising research endeavor worth pursuing.

# References

[Bax95]     Jonathan Baxter. Learning Internal Representations. In *COLT: Proceedings of the Workshop on Computational Learning Theory, Morgan Kaufmann Publishers*, 1995.

[Bax00]     Jonathan Baxter. A Model of Inductive Bias Learning. *Journal of Artificial Intelligence Research*, 12:149–198, 2000.

[BDGS02]   Shai Ben-David, Johannes Gehrke, and Reba Schuller.  A Theoretical Framework for Learning from a Pool of Disparate Data Sources. In *Proceedings of the The Eighth ACM SIGKDD International Conference on Knowledge Discovery and Data Mining*, 2002.

[BEHW89]   Anselm Blumer, Andrzej Ehrenfeucht, David Haussler, and Manfred K. Warmuth. Learnability and the Vapnik-Chervonenkis Dimension. *Journal of the Association for Computing Machinery*, 36(4):929–965, 1989.

[BM98]     Avrim Blum and Tom Mitchell. Combining labeled and unlabeled data with co-training. In *COLT: Proceedings of the Workshop on Computational Learning Theory, Morgan Kaufmann Publishers*, 1998.

[Car97]    Rich Caruana. Multitask Learning. *Machine Learning*, 28(1):41–75, 1997.

[Hes98]    Tom Heskes. Solving a Huge Number of Similar Tasks: A Combination of Multi-Task Learning and a Hierarchical Bayesian Approach. In *International Conference on Machine Learning*, pages 233–241, 1998.

[IE96]     N. Intrator and S. Edelman. How to Make a Low-Dimensional Representation Suitable for Diverse Tasks. *Connection Science*, 8, 1996.

[KV97]     Michael J. Kearns and Umesh V. Vazirani. *An Introduction to Computational Learning Theory*. MIT Press, Cambridge, Massachusetts, 1997.

[Thr96]    S. Thrun. Is learning the n-th thing any easier than learning the first? In D. Touretzky and M Mozer, editors, *Advances in Neural Information Processing Systems (NIPS)*, pages 640–646, 1996.

[VC71]     V. Vapnik and A. Chervonenkis. On the Uniform Convergence of Relative Frequencies of Events to Their Probabilities. *Theoret. Probl. And Its Appl*, 16(2):264–280, 1971.

# Approximate Equivalence
# of Markov Decision Processes

Eyal Even-Dar and Yishay Mansour

School of Computer Science
Tel Aviv University, Tel-Aviv 69978, Israel
{evend,mansour}@cs.tau.ac.il

**Abstract.** We consider the problem of finding the minimal $\epsilon$-equivalent MDP for an MDP given in its tabular form. We show that the problem is NP-Hard and then give a bicriteria approximation algorithm to the problem. We suggest that the right measure for finding minimal $\epsilon$-equivalent model is $L_1$ rather than $L_\infty$ by giving both an example, which demonstrates the drawback of using $L_\infty$, and performance guarantees for using $L_1$. In addition, we give a polynomial algorithm that decides whether two MDPs are equivalent.

## 1 Introduction

In Reinforcement Learning, an agent wanders in an unknown environment and tries to maximize its long term return by performing actions and receiving rewards. The challenge is to understand how a current action will affect future rewards. A good way to model this task is the Markov Decision Process (MDP), which has become the dominating approach in Reinforcement Learning [2, 10].

An MDP includes states, which abstract the environment, actions, which are available to the agent, and for each state and action a distribution of next states, the state reached after performing the action in the given state. In addition there is a reward function that assigns a stochastic reward for each state and action; we combine a sequence of rewards into a single value, the return. A policy assigns a distribution over actions for each state.

We focus on the following problem: given an MDP compute an MDP, which is similar to the original MDP and has smaller state space. Our major requirement is that a good policy in the reduced MDP should translate back to a good policy in the original MDP. This will allow us to consider policies in the reduced MDP, and be guaranteed a similar performance in the original MDP. This problem is clearly interesting from the theoretical perspective. Other benefits of a reduced MDP might be, like any other reduced model, better understandability by humans and better generalization ability.

A related line of research is using compact models such as factored MDPs to represent MDPs. Factored MDPs [3] provide a compact representation of MDPs by using state variables instead of enumerating the entire state space. This compact representation has the potential of significantly reducing the number

B. Schölkopf and M.K. Warmuth (Eds.): COLT/Kernel 2003, LNAI 2777, pp. 581–594, 2003.

of states. However, this compact representation does not yield neither an efficient method to compute optimal policies [8] nor an efficient way to represent the optimal policy [1]. Givan *et al.* [5] derive an algorithm, which computes an equivalent minimal model for an MDP, when the MDP is given in its tabular form. For a factored MDP they show that the minimization problem is NP-Hard [5] and supply a heuristic that calculates a reduced model, but does not have any performance guarantee. In [4] they supply a method, which computes some $\epsilon$-equivalent model in factored MDPs, but they do not show any performance guarantees or approximation ratio on the resulting MDP.

In this paper we study the problem of finding an $\epsilon$-equivalent model for an MDP in its tabular form. We show that the right measure of computing an $\epsilon$-equivalent model is $L_1$, rather than $L_\infty$ that was used in [4, 5]. We show that an optimal policy in an $\epsilon$-equivalent model, with respect to $L_\infty$, might be arbitrarily far from the optimal policy in the original MDP, independent of $\epsilon$. On the other hand we show that if a policy is optimal in an $\epsilon$-equivalent model with respect to $L_1$, then its induced policy in the original model is close to the optimal policy.

We also show that computing the minimal $\epsilon$-equivalent MDP for an MDP, given in its tabular form, is NP-Hard. This holds for both $L_1$ and $L_\infty$ norm, and is done by a reduction from metric $k$ cluster. Given that the problem is NP-Hard, one would like to derive an approximate solution. Usually in approximation algorithms we are given one objective function, which we try to minimize. In bicriteria approximations we are given two objective functions that we try to minimize. Thus, a bicriteria is an approximate solution in two parameters of the problem. Our criteria are both the MDP size and the $\epsilon$ of the $\epsilon$-equivalence. We give an approximation algorithm for finding the $\epsilon$-equivalent MDP and prove that this is an $(2\sqrt{|S|}, \sqrt{|S|})$-approximation. We actually prove that the resulting MDP is either 0-equivalent and with size no more than $2\sqrt{|S|}$ times the size of the minimal $\epsilon$-equivalent MDP, or $\sqrt{|S|}\epsilon$-equivalent and with size no larger than the minimal $\epsilon$-equivalent MDP.

Finally, we also present a simple polynomial algorithm which checks whether two MDPs are equivalent based on the algorithm which computes the minimal MDP [5].

## 2    Model

We define a Markov Decision process (MDP) as follows

**Definition 1.** *A Markov Decision process (MDP) M is a 4-tuple $(S, A, P, R)$, where S is a set of the states, A is a set of actions ($A(i)$ is the set of actions available at state i), $P_M(i, j, a)$ is the transition probability from state i to state j when performing action $a \in A(i)$ in state i, and $R_M(s, a)$ is the reward received when performing action a in state s.*

Whenever it is clear from the context we use $V^\pi$ instead of $V_M^\pi$. Next we give a definition of MDP equivalence and of an $\epsilon$-homogenous partition.

**Definition 2.** *An MDP $M_1 = (S_1, A, R_1, P_1)$ and MDP $M_2 = (S_2, A, R_2, P_2)$ are $\epsilon$-equivalent with respect to $L_k$ norm if there exist mappings $\phi_1 : S_1 \to S$ and $\phi_2 : S_2 \to S$ to MDP $M = (S, A, R, P)$, such that $\phi_1$ and $\phi_2$ are surjective and for every $s_1 \in S_1, s_2 \in S_2$ such that $\phi_1(s_1) = \phi_2(s_2) = s$ the following holds:*

1. $\forall a \in A \quad \left( \sum_{s' \in S} \left( \sum_{\hat{s}; \phi_i(\hat{s}) = s'} P_i(s_i, \hat{s}, a) - P(s, s', a) \right)^k \right)^{1/k} \leq \epsilon \quad i = 1, 2$

2. $\forall a \in A \quad |R_i(s_i, a) - R(s, a)| \leq \epsilon \qquad\qquad\qquad i = 1, 2$

**Definition 3.** *An MDP $M_1 = (S_1, A, R_1, P_1)$ is an $\epsilon$-homogenous partition of MDP $M = (S, A, R, P)$ with respect to $L_k$ norm if there exists mapping $\phi : S \to S_1$, such that $\phi$ is surjective and for every $s$ the following holds:*

1. $\forall a \in A \quad \left( \sum_{s' \in S} \left( \sum_{\hat{s}; \phi(\hat{s}) = s'} P(s, \hat{s}, a) - P_1(\phi(s), s', a) \right)^k \right)^{1/k} \leq \epsilon$

2. $\forall a \in A \quad \max_{\tilde{s}; \phi(\tilde{s}) = s} |R(\tilde{s}, a) - R_1(s, a)| \leq \epsilon$

We note that if an MDP $M_\epsilon$ is an $\epsilon$-homogenous partition of MDP $M$ then they are $\epsilon$-equivalent. We also note that the minimal equivalent MDP to an MDP $M$ must be an $\epsilon$-homogenous partition of $M$ with $\epsilon = 0$, and that this MDP is unique.

A stochastic stationary policy for an MDP assigns, for each state $s$ a probability for performing action $a \in A(s)$. While following a policy $\pi$ we perform at time $t$ action $a_t$ at state $s_t$ and observe a reward $r_t$ (distributed according to $R_M(s, a)$), and the next state $s_{t+1}$ (distributed according to $P_M(s_t, s_{t+1}, a_t)$). We combine the sequence of rewards to a single value called the return, and our goal is to maximize the return. The discounted return of policy $\pi$ is $V_M^\pi = \sum_{t=0}^\infty \gamma^t r_t$, where $r_t$ is the reward observed at time $t$. Since all the rewards are bounded by $R_{max}$ the discounted return is bounded by $V_{max} = \frac{R_{max}}{1-\gamma}$.

We define a value function for each state $s$, under policy $\pi$, as $V_M^\pi(s) = E[\sum_{i=0}^\infty r_i \gamma^i]$, where the expectation is over a run of policy $\pi$ starting at state $s$. We define a state-action value function $Q^\pi(s, a) = R(s, a) + \gamma \sum_{\tilde{s}} P(s, \tilde{s}, a) V^\pi(\tilde{s})$, whose value is the return of initially performing action $a$ at state $s$ and then following policy $\pi$.

Let $\pi^*$ be an optimal policy, which maximizes the return from any start state. (It is well known that there exists an optimal strategy, which is a deterministic policy, see [9].) This implies that for any policy $\pi$ and any state $s$ we have $V^{\pi^*}(s) \geq V^\pi(s)$, and $\pi^*(s) = argmax_a(R(s, a) + \gamma(\sum_{s'} P(s, s', a) \max_b Q(s', b)))$. We say that a policy $\pi$ is an $\epsilon$-optimal if $\|V^* - V^\pi\|_\infty \leq \epsilon$.

## 3   Markov Decision Process Minimization

Since we build on some of Givan *et al.* [5] techniques, we describe briefly their minimization process. We first introduce a few notations and definitions. An equivalence relation is defined as a transitive binary relation, $E$. The equivalence relation groups similar states in the original MDP and in the reduced MDP and each equivalence class translates into one state. We often denote by a block a group of states in a specific equivalence class. Given an MDP, $M$ and an equivalence relation $E \subseteq S \times S$, an operator $I$ is defined as

$$I(E) = \{(i, j)|R(i) = R(j) \wedge E(i, j) \wedge P(i, i'|E, a) = P(j, i'|E, a)\},$$

where $P(i, j'|E, a) = \sum_{j:E(j,j')=1} P(i, j, a)$. The minimal model is the fixed point of the process $E_{n+1} = I(E_n)$, where $I(E) \subseteq E$.

We define the reward partition as the equivalence relation, $E(i, j) = \{i, j|$ $\|R(i, \cdot) - R(j, \cdot)\|_\infty = 0\}$. We say that a block $B \subseteq S$ is stable with respect to block $C$ if every state in $B$ has the same transition probability with respect to $C$, i.e., for every $i, i' \in B$ we have $P(i, C, a) = P(i', C, a)$, where $P(i', C, a) = \sum_{j \in C} P(i', j, a)$. Let $B = (B_1, \dots, B_m)$, where if $i \in B_k$ then $j \in B_k \iff E(i, j) = 1$. We define the procedure $SPLIT(B_i, B_j, P)$ that replaces the block $B_i$ by the uniquely determined sub-blocks of $B_i$, $B_{i1}, \dots, B_{ik}$ such that each sub-block is the maximal stable sub-block with respect to $B_j$. In other words, all the states $s \in B_{il}$ have the same probability $P(s, B_j, a)$ for every action $a$ and no two sub-blocks $B_{il}$ and $B_{ik}$ have the same set of probabilities.

The algorithm of Givan et al. [5] works as follows. It begins by making $E_0$ the reward partition. It then iterates and checks for every pair of blocks if they are stable; if not, it performs the procedure $SPLIT$. The algorithm terminates when all blocks are stable with respect to every other block. The algorithm clearly terminates, since each SPLIT increases the number of blocks and the number of blocks is bounded by $|S|$.

**Theorem 1.** [5] *The minimization problem for MDP, given in its tabular form, is in P.*

## 4    Hardness of Epsilon Equivalence

In [5] it was shown that finding the minimal model is in $P$. On the other hand they have shown that finding the minimal (or minimal $\epsilon$-equivalent) model is NP-Hard for factored MDPs. We show that finding the minimal $\epsilon$-equivalent model is NP-Hard even for MDPs that are represented in a tabular form. We use here a variant of the $k$-center problem known as **metric k cluster**.

**Lemma 1.** [6] *Let $G = (V, E)$ be a complete undirected graph with edge costs satisfying the triangle inequality, and let $k$ be a positive integer. Find a partition of $V$ into sets $V_1, \dots, V_k$ such that the maximum cost of an edge between two vertices in the same set is minimized.*

We will use different notations and a more restricted problem to simplify the reduction.

**Corollary 1.** *The following $\epsilon$-cover problem is NP-Complete. Given $n$ points, $X = (x_1, \dots, x_n)$, where $x_i$ is in $\Re^m$, a positive number $K$ and a norm distance, $L_q$. Partition the points into $K$ sets, $X_1, \dots X_K$ such that $\max_{1 \le i \le K} {}_{p,p' \in X_i} \|p - p'\|_q \le \epsilon$.*

We obtain our theorem by a reduction from the $\epsilon$-cover problem.

**Theorem 2.** *Given an MDP, M, and a positive number K the problem of determining whether there exists an $\epsilon$-homogenous partition, in $L_q$, of size no more than K is NP-Complete.*

*Proof.* The problem is clearly in NP. Next we show a reduction from metric $k$ cluster to this problem. We reduce the $n$ points, $x_1, ..., x_n$ to MDP $M = (s_1, ..., s_n)$ and keep $K$ and $\epsilon$ identical in both problems. In $M$ each state has $m$ actions, the reward function is $R(s_i, a_j) = x_i^j$, where $x_i^j$ is the $j$th coordinate of $x_i$, and the next state distribution is uniform, i.e. $\forall i, j, k$  $P(s_i, s_j, a_k) = \frac{1}{n}$. We show that there exists an $\epsilon$ - homogenous partition of size no more than $K$ if and only if there exists a partition of $X$ into sets $X_1, ..., X_K$ such that $\max_{1 \leq i \leq K, p, p' \in X_i} \|p - p'\|_q \leq \epsilon$. We first prove that if there exists an $\epsilon$ - homogenous partition of size $K$ then there exists a $K$ cluster. Since the next state distribution is uniform for every state-action pair, then an $\epsilon$ - homogenous partition of the MDP has to be according to the reward. Let $B_1, ..., B_K$ be the partition for the MDP, then we have that $\max_{1 \leq i \leq K, s, s' \in B_i} \|R(s, \cdot) - R(s', \cdot)\|_q \leq \epsilon$ and let $X_1, ..., X_K$ be the matching partition in $X$. Now we show that the partition that $X_i$ induces on $X$ is an $\epsilon$ cover. We observe that

$$\max_{1 \leq i \leq K, u, v \in X_i} \|u - v\|_q = \max_{1 \leq i \leq K, u, v \in X_i} (\sum_{j=1}^m |u_j - v_j|^q)^{1/q}$$

$$= \max_{1 \leq i \leq K, s, s' \in B_i} (\sum_{j=1}^m |R(s, a_j) - R(s', a_j)|^q)^{1/q} \leq \epsilon.$$

Using the fact that every block is stable with respect to every block, the proof of the other direction is identical.                                                          $\square$

## 5   $L_1$ versus $L_\infty$

In this section we present an example, which demonstrates the drawback of using $L_\infty$ as measure for an $\epsilon$-homogenous partition of the MDP. On the other hand we derive performance guarantees for the $L_1$ measure.

**Lemma 2.** *For every $\epsilon > 0$, there exists an MDP M with an $\epsilon$-homogenous partition, $M_\epsilon$, with respect to $L_\infty$, such that an optimal policy in $M_\epsilon$ induces a policy in M that is arbitrarily far from from the optimal policy.*

*Proof.* Consider the MDPs in Figure 1, where $M$ and $M_\epsilon$ are $\epsilon$-equivalent for $\epsilon = 1/n$. There are only two policies in $M$, $\pi_a$, which performs action $a$ in state 1 and $\pi_u$, which performs action $u$ in state 1. Note that in $M_\epsilon$ both policies are optimal. We consider in $M_\epsilon$ the policy, $\pi_a$, which performs action $a$ in state 1. The induced policy, $\pi_a$ in $M$, satisfies $V_M^{\pi_a}(1) \leq 6$ for any $\gamma$. The optimal policy, $\pi_u$, satisfies $V_M^*(1) \geq \frac{R_{max}\gamma^3}{1-\gamma} = \gamma^3 V_{max}$. For constant $\gamma$ the difference can be arbitrarily large, independent of $\epsilon$.                                                          $\square$

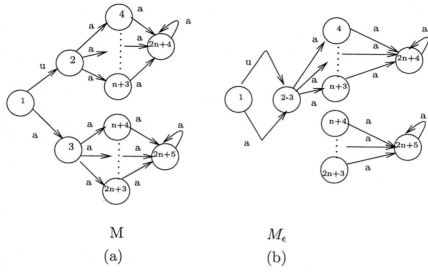

M $\qquad$ $M_\epsilon$

(a) $\qquad$ (b)

**Fig. 1.** An example in which two MDPs are $\epsilon$-equivalent in $L_\infty$ norm but an optimal policy in $M_\epsilon$ is far from optimal in M. Let $n = \lceil 1/\epsilon \rceil$. The rewards are $R(1, u) = R(1, a) = 0, R(2, a) = R(3, a) = 1, R(2n + 4, a) = R_{max}, R(2n + 5, a) = 0 \; \forall k \in \{4, 2n + 3\} \; R(k, a) = 2\epsilon k$. In states 2, 3 the next state distribution is uniform. We note that there are only two policies in $M$, one performs $a$ at state 1 and other performs $u$ at state 1. In $M_\epsilon$ the two policies coincide.

In the next lemma we show that for every policy, $\pi^\epsilon$ in an $\epsilon$-homogenous partition of an MDP, with respect to $L_1$ norm, its induced policy, $\pi$ is at most $\epsilon \frac{V_{max}}{1-\gamma}$ from the value of $\pi^\epsilon$ in $M_\epsilon$ for every state. The proof is done by relying on the following fact:

**Fact 3** *For any phase in Value Iteration algorithm we have that if $\|V_{t+1} - V_t\|_\infty \le \epsilon$ then $\|V_t - V^*\|_\infty \le \frac{\epsilon}{1-\gamma}$*

**Lemma 3.** *Let $M_\epsilon$ be an $\epsilon$-homogenous partition of MDP $M$, with respect to $L_1$ norm, and $\pi$ any policy in $M_\epsilon$, then the induced policy $\pi^M$ on $M$, that is $\pi^M(s) = \pi(\phi(s))$, satisfies*

$$\forall s \in S \quad |V_M^{\pi^M}(s) - V_{M_\epsilon}^\pi(\phi(s))| \le \frac{\epsilon V_{max}}{1-\gamma}$$

*Proof.* The proof is done by estimating the value of $\pi^M$ using Value Iteration with initial value $V_0^{\pi^M}(s) = V_{M_\epsilon}^\pi(\phi(s))$. Since we use $L_1$ norm, each state can deviate only in $\epsilon$ from its representative state in $M_\epsilon$ and the difference $\|V_0^{\pi^M} - V_1^{\pi^M}\|_\infty$ is bounded by $\epsilon V_{max}$. Using the fact that $\|V_0^{\pi^M} - V_1^{\pi^M}\|_\infty \le \epsilon V_{max}$ and Fact 3 we can conclude that

$$\max_{s \in S} |V_M^{\pi^M}(s) - V_{M_\epsilon}^\pi(\phi(s))| = \|V_0^{\pi^M} - V_M^{\pi^M}\|_\infty = \|V_0^{\pi^M} - V_\infty^{\pi^M}\|_\infty \le \frac{\epsilon V_{max}}{1-\gamma},$$

where $V_\infty^{\pi^M} = V_M^{\pi^M}$ is the value of $\pi^M$ in $M$. $\qquad\square$

The next lemma shows that the optimal policy in $M_\epsilon$ induces a nearly optimal policy in $M$.

**Lemma 4.** *Let $M_\epsilon$ be an $\epsilon$-homogenous partition of MDP $M$, with respect to $L_1$ norm, then the optimal policy in $M_\epsilon$ induces an $\frac{2\epsilon V_{max}}{1-\gamma}$-optimal policy in $M$.*

*Proof.* Let $\sigma$ be the optimal policy in $M_\epsilon$ and $\sigma^M$ be the induced policy in $M$. By Lemma 3 we have that $\max_s |V_M^{\sigma^M}(s) - V_{M_\epsilon}^\sigma(\phi(s))| \leq \frac{\epsilon V_{max}}{1-\gamma}$. Next we show that if we use a Value Iteration on $M$ with initial value $V_0^M(s) = V_{M_\epsilon}^\sigma(\phi(s))$ then we have that

$$\|V_0^M - V_\infty^M\|_\infty = \|V_0^M - V_M^*\|_\infty \leq \frac{\epsilon V_{max}}{1-\gamma}.$$

Since we use $L_1$ norm, once again we have that $\|V_0^M - V_1^M\|_\infty$ is bounded by $\epsilon V_{max}$. Combining the two parts, we obtain that $\sigma^M$ is an $\frac{2\epsilon V_{max}}{1-\gamma}$-optimal policy in $M$. □

## 6   Approximation Scheme

Since finding the minimal $\epsilon$-equivalent MDP is NP-Hard, we would like to find an approximate solution to the problem. The natural approximation is to give an MDP, which is $\epsilon$-equivalent and is $K$ times larger than the minimal $\epsilon$-equivalent MDP. Unfortunately, we do not present such approximation. We present a bi-criteria approximation algorithm for finding an $\epsilon$-equivalent model for an MDP. Usually in approximation algorithms we are given one objective function, which we try to minimize. In bicriteria approximations two objective functions that we try to minimize are given. Thus, a bicriteria is an approximate solution in two parameters of the problem. Our criteria are both the MDP size and the parameter $\epsilon$ in the $\epsilon$-equivalence. We prove that our algorithm is $(2\sqrt{|S|}, \sqrt{|S|})$ approximation with respect to (size, $\epsilon$), that is our MDP might be $\sqrt{|S|}\epsilon$-equivalent and $2\sqrt{|S|}$ times larger than the minimal $\epsilon$-equivalent MDP. In fact, for our algorithm either (1) produces an equivalent MDP, which is $2\sqrt{|S|}$ larger than the minimal size $\epsilon$-equivalent MDP, or (2) produces an MDP which is $\sqrt{|S|}\epsilon$-equivalent, whose size is at most the size of the minimal $\epsilon$-equivalent MDP.

We first give a high level description of our approximation algorithm. We initially build a graph $G = (S, E)$, where the vertices are the MDP states and there is an edge between states if their rewards are $\epsilon$-close. After the initialization, we run in phases. In each phase we check for each edge if it is consistent with some legal partition. A partition is legal with respect to $G$ if every vertex in it is connected to every other vertex. If we observe that the edge is not consistent with any legal partition, then we delete that edge. To check whether an edge $(s, t)$ is consistent, we compute the connected components of $G$ and see if $s$ and $t$ have similar next state transition with respect to them. (The detailed procedure *CheckConsistent* is formally described in Alg. 6.) We terminate when we cannot delete any edges. Clearly the algorithm terminates after at most $|S|^2$ phases. (The Algorithm is formally described in Alg. 1).

**Algorithm 1:** An algorithm which calculates an $\epsilon$-equivalent MDP

---

**Input**  : MDP $M$, $\epsilon > 0$ precision
**Output** : A partition of M to Equivalence Relations
Build a graph $G = (S, E)$, where $(s, t) \in E$ if $\forall a \in A$ $|R(s, a) - R(t, a)| \leq \epsilon$;
**repeat**
    $Deleted = FALSE$;
    **foreach** $(s, t) \in E$ **do**
        **foreach** $a \in A$ **do**
            **if** $CheckConsistent(s,t,a,E,S,P) = FALSE$ **then**
                $Deleted = TRUE$ ;
                $E = E - (s, t)$ ;
        **end**
    **end**
**until** $Deleted = FALSE$;
Compute $C_1, \ldots, C_l$ the connected components of G= (S,E);
**if** $\max_i Diameter(C_i) \geq \sqrt{S}$ **then**
    Return $S$
**else**
    Return $C = \cup_i C_i$
**end**

---

Since our algorithm returns an MDP partition, we show how to construct an MDP from an MDP partition. We note that for an MDP $M$ a partition of $S$ by itself does not define a unique MDP, but a family of MDPs. This family can be viewed also as a bounded MDP [7]; we take a different approach and choose arbitrarily representative MDP for each partition.

**Definition 4.** *Let $M = (S, A, P, R)$ and $\phi$ be a mapping from $S$ to $S_1$. Then the MDP, $M_1 = (S_1, A, P_1, R_1)$ induced by $(M, \phi)$ is defined as follows. For each $s \in S_1$ we choose arbitrarily $s'$ such that $\phi(s') = s$. The reward in $s \in S_1$ is $R_1(s, a) = R(s', a)$ and the next state distribution is $P_1(s, t, a) = \sum_{\phi(t')=t} P(s', t', a)$.*

In the following lemmas we provide correctness proof of Algorithm 1. We first prove that if $s$ and $t$ are in the same equivalence class in some $\epsilon$-homogenous partition, then the edge $(s, t)$ is never removed from the graph during Algorithm 1.

**Lemma 5.** *Let $s$ and $t$ be two states such that there exists an $\epsilon$-homogenous partition MDP in which $s$ and $t$ are in the same equivalence class, then the edge $(s, t)$ is never removed from the graph in Algorithm 1.*

*Proof.* Let $C_1^k, \ldots, C_l^k$ be the connected components of $G$ at the $k$th stage and $EC_1, \ldots, EC_m$ be the equivalence classes of an $\epsilon$-homogenous partition MDP in which $s$ and $t$ are in the same equivalence class. We prove by induction on the algorithm steps (number of calls to $CheckConsistent$) that (1) the edge $(s, t)$ is never removed (2) $C_i^k = \cup_{EC_j \subseteq C_i^k} EC_j$ for every $i$, i.e., each connected component is a union of equivalence classes from an $\epsilon$-homogenous partition

**Algorithm 2:** CheckConsistent(s,t,E,S,P) Procedure

---

**Input**   : state s , state t, action a, Edges between states E, MDP states S,
              Next state distribution P
**Output** : Boolean answer whether $s$ and $t$ are consistent
Compute the connected components of $G = (S, E)$, $C_1, \ldots, C_l$;
**if** $\sum_{i=1}^{l} |P(s, C_i, a) - P(t, C_i, a)| \leq \epsilon$ **then**
    Return TRUE;
**else**
    Return FALSE;
**end**

---

MDP. The basis is due to the fact that the first stage is the reward partition. We assume that the induction hypothesis holds for the first $k$ stages and prove for the $k + 1$ stage. WLOG, we assume that the edge $(s, t)$ is checked at this stage. By the induction assumption we have that $C_i^k = \cup_{j:EC_j \subseteq C_i^k} EC_j$ for every $i$. Therefore, for every action $a$ we obtain the following

$$\sum_{i=1}^{l} |P(s, C_i^k, a) - P(t, C_i^k, a)| = \sum_{i=1}^{l} \left| \sum_{j:EC_j \subseteq C_i^k} P(s, EC_j, a) - P(t, EC_j, a) \right|$$

$$\leq \sum_{i=1}^{l} \sum_{j:EC_j \subseteq C_i^k} |P(s, EC_j, a) - P(t, EC_j, a)|$$

$$= \sum_{j=1}^{m} |P(s, EC_j, a) - P(t, EC_j, a)| \leq \epsilon.$$

We conclude that $(s, t)$ is never removed from the graph if $(s, t)$ are in the same equivalence class in some $\epsilon$-homogenous partition MDP. Therefore, all states in an equivalence class form a clique at every stage and each equivalence class is contained in a single connected component.                                □

Next we prove that at the end of the algorithm we have a $(2\sqrt{S}, \sqrt{S})$-approximation. We first show that the size of the resulting MDP is no larger than $2\sqrt{S}$ the minimal $\epsilon$-equivalent MDP.

**Lemma 6.** *If* $\max_i Diameter(C_i) \geq \sqrt{|S|}$ *then there are at least* $\frac{\sqrt{|S|}}{2}$ *states in the minimal $\epsilon$-equivalent MDP.*

*Proof.* Consider the diameter's path, $s_1, ..., s_{\sqrt{|S|}}$, of a connected component $C$. By Lemma 5 we have that no three states in the path can be in the same equivalence class. (Otherwise the diameter would have been smaller.) Thus there are at least $\left\lfloor \sqrt{|S|}/2 \right\rfloor$ states in the minimal $\epsilon$-equivalent MDP.                □

Next we claim that if we take each connected component as an equivalence class, then they are $\epsilon D$-stable, where $D = \max_i Diameter(C_i)$.

**Lemma 7.** *Consider an MDP, $M_1$, which is induced by $(M, \phi)$, such that if $s, s' \in C_i$ in Algorithm 1 then $\phi(s) = \phi(s')$. Then we have that $M_1$ is $\epsilon D$-equivalent to $M$, where $D = \max_i Diameter(C_i)$.*

*Proof.* Since $\phi$ maps all the states in a connected component $C_i$ to a single state in M, we let the states of $M_1$ be the connected components. This implies that if $s \in C_i$ then $\phi(s) = C_i$. First we show that for every connected component

$$\forall a \forall s, t \in C_i \quad |R(s, a) - R(t, a)| \leq \epsilon D$$

We prove it by induction on the length of the path between the states in $C_i$. For the basis we have that if the path length between $s$ and $t$ is one, then there is an edge between them. This implies that $max_a |R(s, a) - R(t, a)| \leq \epsilon$. Assume the induction assumption holds for $k - 1$ and prove for $k$ and let $s = s_1, \ldots, s_k = t$ be the path between $s$ and $t$. From the induction assumption we have that $max_a |R(s_1, a) - R(s_{k-1}, a)| \leq (k-1)\epsilon$ and since there is an edge between $s_{k-1}$ to $s_k$ we have that $max_a |R(s_{k-1}, a) - R(s_k, a)| \leq \epsilon$. Using the triangle inequality we complete the induction. Next we prove that for any $s, t$ in a connected component the following holds:

$$\max_{a \in A} \sum_{C_i} \left| \sum_{\hat{s}; \phi(\hat{s}) = C_i} P_M(s, \hat{s}, a) - \sum_{\hat{s}; \phi(\hat{s}) = C_i} P_M(t, \hat{s}, a) \right| \leq \epsilon D$$

Fix an action $a$. We prove by induction on the path length that $\sum_{i=1}^m |P(s_1, C_i, a) - P(s_j, C_i, a)| \leq j\epsilon$, where $m$ is the number of connected component. The basis of the induction is due to the fact that when the algorithm terminates, it cannot delete more edges, and therefore for every edge we have that $\sum_{i=1}^m |P(s_j, C_i, a) - P(s_{j+1}, C_i, a)| \leq \epsilon$. We assume that the induction assumption holds for $k-1$ and prove for $k$. For a path $s = s_1, \ldots, s_k = t$ in $G$, we show that $\sum_{i=1}^m |P(s_1, C_i, a) - P(s_k, C_i, a)| \leq k\epsilon$. Since $\sum_{i=1}^m |P(s_{k-1}, C_i, a) - P(s_k, C_i, a)| \leq \epsilon$ and by the induction assumption we have that $\sum_{i=1}^m |P(s_1, C_i, a) - P(s_{k-1}, C_i, a)| \leq (k-1)\epsilon$, we can conclude that $\sum_{i=1}^m |P(s_1, C_i, a) - P(s_k, C_i, a)| \leq k\epsilon$. □

Combining Lemma 6 and Lemma 7 we obtain our main theorem.

**Theorem 4.** *Given an MDP $M$, Algorithm 1 terminates in polynomial time and returns an MDP partition, $\phi$ with induced MDP, $M_\epsilon = (M, \phi)$, that is at most $\sqrt{|S|}\epsilon$-equivalent and with size no larger than $2\sqrt{|S|}$ time the size of the minimal $\epsilon$-equivalent MDP.*

## 6.1 A Heuristic Finer Partition

In this section, we suggest a "better" *CheckConsistent* procedure. This procedure always performs at least as good as the original *CheckConsistent* procedure. However, this procedure is more complicated and we could not provide a better performance grantees using it. The procedure *CheckConsistent*1 checks

**Algorithm 3:** CheckConsistent1(s,t,E,S,P) Procedure

---

**Input**    : state s , state t, action a, Edges between states E, MDP states S,
            Next state distribution P
**Output** : Answer whether $s$ and $t$ are consistent
Build a graph with four layres;
The first layer contains $s$ ;
The second layer contains $S$ ;
The third layer contains $S$ ;
The fourth layer contains $t$;
Connect $s$ to every vertex $s'$ in the second layer with capacity $c(s, s') = P(s, s', a)$;
If $(s', s'') \in E$ then connect $s'$ in the second layer to a vertex $s''$ in the third layer with capacity $c(s', s'') = 1$ ;
Connect every vertex in the third layer to $t$ with capacity $c(s', t) = P(t, s', a)$;
Calculate the max flow from $s$ to $t$;
**if** *max flow* $< 1 - \epsilon/2$ **then**
    Return FALSE;
**else**
    Return TRUE;
**end**

---

whether an edge $(s, t)$ is consistent by building the graph (in Fig. 2) for each action and check if the max flow is close to 1, more precisely if it is at least $1 - \epsilon/2$. (The detailed procedure *CheckConsistent1* is formally described in Alg. 3.) We also note that the difference between the procedures is that in *CheckConsistent* procedure we connect states between the second and the third layer if they are in the same connected component, while in *CheckConsistent1* procedure we connect them only if they have an edge in $G$.

## 7 Markov Decision Process Equivalence

We present a polynomial method to check whether two MDPs are equivalent. Our algorithm is very simple and uses any procedure to compute the minimal MDP, which we call minimal equivalent MDP. For instance such a procedure is given in [5].

Assuming the algorithm for finding the minimal equivalent model is polynomial in the MDP size as in [5], then our algorithm is polynomial as well.

**Lemma 8.** *Algorithm 4 runs in polynomial time in the MDP size.*

Next we show the correctness of the algorithm. We first show that any two states from the same minimal MDP $D_1$ or $D_2$ have to be in the same equivalence relation of $M$.

**Lemma 9.** *No equivalence relation in the minimal partition of $M$ contains two states from either $D_1$ or $D_2$.*

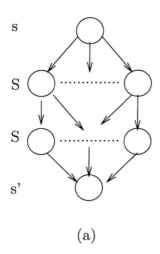

s

S

S

s'

(a)

**Fig. 2.** The graph built by *CheckConsistent* procedure

*Proof.* We let $D_1 = (s_1^1, ..., s_1^m)$ and let $D_2 = (s_2^1, ..., s_2^m)$. The proof is done by contradiction. Assume there are two states from $D_1$, $s_1^i$ and $s_1^j$, in the same equivalence class in $M$, then we can construct to $M_1$ an equivalent model, which consists of at most $size(D_1) - 1$ states. Since $s_1^i$ and $s_1^j$ are stable with respect to any other block in $D$, then they are stable with respect to the projection of $D$ to $D_1$ and can be in the same equivalence class. This contradicts the minimality of $D_1$. □

**Lemma 10.** *MDPs $M_1$ and $M_2$ are equivalent if and only if all the equivalence relations of $D$ consists only pairs $(s_i, s_j)$ for which $s_i \in D_1$ and $s_j \in D_2$, i.e. $size(D) = size(D_1) = size(D_2)$.*

*Proof.* (a) $\Leftarrow$
Trivial and we have a mapping from $M_1$ and $M_2$ to $D$.
(b)$\Rightarrow$
We assume that $M_1$ and $M_2$ are equivalent; thus their minimal models, $D_1 = (s_1^1, ..., s_1^m)$ and $D_2 = (s_2^1, ..., s_2^m)$, satisfy $\forall i \; s_1^i \equiv s_2^i$. (we do not assume that we know which state in $D_1$ corresponds to which state in $D_2$).

Now we follow the construction of the minimal model as appears in [5]. We prove by induction on the construction steps that for each block $B$ the following holds

$$\forall i \; : \; s_1^i \in B \iff s_2^i \in B$$

For the induction basis. Since for any $i$ states $s_1^i$ and $s_2^i$ must have the same reward, then they must be in the same block in the initial reward partition. Next we assume that the claim holds for any $j < k$ and prove for $k$. We assume that in the $k$th step we check the stability of block $B$ which consists $s_1^i$ and $s_2^i$ with respect to block $C$. By the induction assumption for every action $a$ we

**Algorithm 4:** An algorithm which finds whether two MDPs are equivalent

---

**Input**   : MDPs $M_1, M_2$
**Output** : Answer whether the MDPs are equivalent
Calculate $D_1$, the minimal Equivalent MDP of $M_1$;
Calculate $D_2$, the minimal Equivalent MDP of $M_2$;
**if** *(size($D_1$) $\neq$ size($D_2$))* **then**
    Return FALSE;
**end**
Calculate $D$, the minimal Equivalent MDP of $M = D_1 \cup D_2 = (S_1 \cup S_2, R_1 \cup R_2, P_1 \cup P_2, A)$;
**if** *(size($D$) = size($D_1$))* **then**
    Return TRUE;
**else**
    Return FALSE;
**end**

---

have $P(s_1^i, C, a) = P(s_2^i, C, a)$ and since $SPLIT(B, C, P)$ replaces the block $B$ by the uniquely determined sub-blocks $B_i$, we have that $s_1^i$ and $s_2^i$ will be in the same sub block after the $k$th step. Together with Lemma 9 we conclude the lemma.                                                                    □

By Lemma 10 we have that Algorithm 4 checks whether two MDPs are equivalent and by Lemma 8 we have that it is polynomial. Therefore, we derive the following theorem.

**Theorem 5.** *The equivalence problem for MDPs, given in their tabular form, is in P.*

## Acknowledgements

This research was supported in part by a grant from the Israel Science Foundation. Eyal Even-dar was partially supported by the Deutsch Institute.

## References

1. E. Allender, S. Arora, M. Kearns, C. Moore, and A. Russell. Note on the representational incompatabilty of function approximation and factored dynamics. In *Advances in Neural Information Processing Systems 15*, 2002.
2. Dimitri P. Bertsekas and John N. Tsitsiklis. *Neuro-Dynamic Programming*. Athena Scientific, Belmont, MA, 1996.
3. T. Dean and K. Kanazawa. A model for reasoning about persistence and causation. *Computational Intelligence*, 5(3):142–150, 1989.
4. Thomas Dean, Robert Givan, and Sonia Leach. Model reduction techniques for computing approximately optimal solutions for Markov decision processes. In *UAI*, pages 124–131, 1997.
5. Robert Givan, Thomas Dean, and Matthew Greig. Equivalence notions and model minimization in markov decision processes. *Artificial Intelligence*, 2003. To appear.

6. T.F. Gonzalez. Clustering to minimize the maximum inter-cluster distance. *Theoretical Computer Science*, 38: 293-306, 1985.

7. Robert Givan, Sonia Leach and Thomas Dean. Bounded parameter markov decision processes. *Artificial Intelligence*, 122:71–109, 2000.

8. C. Lusena, J. Goldsmith, and M. Mundhenk. Nonapproximability results for partially observable markov decision processes. *Journal of Artificial Intelligence Research*, 14:83–103, 2001.

9. M. Puterman. *Markov Decision Processes : Discrete Stochastic Dynamic Programming*. John Wiley & Sons, 1994.

10. R. Sutton and A. Barto. *Reinforcement Learning*. MIT Press, Cambridge, MA, 1998.

# An Information Theoretic Tradeoff between Complexity and Accuracy

Ran Gilad-Bachrach, Amir Navot, and Naftali Tishby

School of Computer Science and Engineering and
Interdisciplinary Center for Neural Computation
The Hebrew University, Jerusalem, Israel
{ranb,anavot,tishby}@cs.huji.ac.il

**Abstract.** A fundamental question in learning theory is the quantification of the basic tradeoff between the complexity of a model and its predictive accuracy. One valid way of quantifying this tradeoff, known as the *"Information Bottleneck"*, is to measure both the complexity of the model and its prediction accuracy by using Shannon's mutual information. In this paper we show that the Information Bottleneck framework answers a well defined and known coding problem and at same time it provides a general relationship between complexity and prediction accuarcy, measured by mutual information. We study the nature of this complexity-accuracy tradeoff and discuss some of its theoretical properties. Furthermore, we present relations to classical information theoretic problems, such as *rate-distortion theory, cost-capacity tradeoff* and *source coding with side information*.

## 1    Introduction

Learning, in human and machine, is known to be related to the ability to find compact representations of data. In supervised learning this is done by choosing an hypothesis which somehow summarizes the training data, where as in unsupervised learning - clusters or low dimensional features play the same role. In both cases we are interested in a concise description that preserves the *relevant* essence of the data. Therefore any learning process has to deal with the basic tradeoff between the complexity (conciseness) of the data representation available and the best accuracy (goodness of fit) that this complexity enables. The measures of complexity and accuracy may change from one task to another. In learning theory complexity is commonly measured by the VC-dimension, covering numebrs, metric entropies of the class, or by the description (coding) length of the representation. Accuracy can be measured by generalization error, mistake bound, clusters purity, feature efficiency, and various other ways.

In this paper we choose study the nature of the tradeoff between complexity and accuracy using information theoretic concepts. The main advantage of this choice is in its model independece and its powerful asymthotic properties. We therefore measure the representation complexity by the minimal number of bits needed to describe the data per sample - known as rate. We choose to measure

B. Schölkopf and M.K. Warmuth (Eds.): COLT/Kernel 2003, LNAI 2777, pp. 595–609, 2003.

the accuracy by the amount of information our data representation preserves on the target variable. While the precise nature of the target variable depends on the task, labels in supervised learning, it can be categories, noisy data, or other weakly dependent random variable. Statistical dependence with the data seems to be the only general property of the target - thus universally quantified by mutual information. The fact that both complexity and accuarcy can be quantifed by mutual information - as proposed in the *Information Bottleneck* (IB) framework - enables us to quantify their traedoff in a general yet very precise way, as shown in this study.

The Information-Bottleneck (IB) method was first introduced by Tishby, Pereira and Bialek [12] about 5 years ago. The *relevant information* in a one variable (signal) - with respect to another one - is defined as the (mutual) information that this variable provides about the other. One can think about it as the minimal number of binary questions, on average, that should be asked about the values of one variable, in order to reduce as much as possible the uncertainty in the value of the other. Examples include the relationship between document category and its words statistics, face features and person's identity, speech sounds and spoken words, gene expression levels and tissue samples, etc. In all such cases, the problem is how to map one of the variables, considered as the source signal, $X$ into a more concise reproduction signal $\hat{X}$ while preserving the information about the relevant (predicted) signal $Y$.

The Information-Bottleneck was found useful in various learning applications. Slonim et. al. [9, 10] used it for clustering data. Note that since IB uses information theoretic point of view it does not suffer from basic flaws of geometric based algorithms as presented by Kleinberg [5]. In [8] the IB was used for feature selection. Poupart et. al. [6] used it while studying POMDPs, and Baram et. al. [2] used it for evaluating the expected performance of active learning algorithms. For a comprehensive study of the IB see [11].

The IB is related to several classic problems in information theory such as *rate-distortion* and *cost-capacity* [7]. In rate-distortion problem the goal is to encode a source in a way that minimizes the code length under a constraint on the average distortion. In cost-capacity problem a cost is assigned to each symbol of the channel alphabet. The task is to minimize the ambiguity at the receiver under a constraint on the average cost. The IB can be presented in "rate-distortion like" formulation, but with non-fixed distortion measure and at the same time it can take the form of "cost capacity like" problem with non-fixed cost function. Moreover it combines these two problems in a way that is free of the arbitrary nature of both the distortion measure and channel cost. Another formally related problem is *source coding with side information*[14, 1]. The setting of this problem is very different but the solution happen to be similar. See section 3 for a detailed discussion of this relationship.

## 1.1 Summary of Results

- We define the IB coding problem and the IB optimization problem in section 2.

- We discuss the relationship between the IB and the problem of source coding with side information in section 3.
- We show that the IB optimization problem provides a tight lower bound for the IB coding problem in section 4.
- We define the IB-tradeoff (information-curve) which assigns to any restriction on $I(\hat{X}; Y)$ the minimal possible value of $I(X; \hat{X})$, where the free variables are the conditional distributions $p(\hat{x}|x)$. In section 5 we study this functional optimization and utilize its formal relation to source coding with side information to prove that the IB-curve is a smooth, monotone and convex function. Furthermore we show that $|\hat{\mathcal{X}}| = |\mathcal{X}| + 2$ is sufficient to achieve the best encoding.
- In section 6, we show that the Information Bottleneck optimization is locally equivalent to a Rate-Distortion problem with an adequate distortion measure, and thus can be considered as a rate-distortion problem with a variable distortion measure. We also show that the information curve is the envelope of all such "locally equivalent" rate-distortion functions.
- In section 7, a dual representation of the IB problem is presented. In the dual representation the IB takes the form of a cost-capacity problem with non fixed cost function. However the optimum of the primal (rate-distortion like) and the dual (cost-capacity like) is equivalent.

## 1.2   Preliminaries and Notation

We use the following notation: $X, Y, \hat{X}$ are random variables over a finite alphabets $\mathcal{X}, \mathcal{Y}$ and $\hat{\mathcal{X}}$ respectively. $x, y, \hat{x}$ are instances of these variables. $H(X)$ denote the Entropy of the random variable $X$, the Mutual Information between $X$ and $Y$ is denoted by $I(X; Y)$ and $D_{KL}[p(x)||q(x)]$ is the Kullback and Liebler (KL)-Divergence between the two distributions $p(x)$ and $q(x)$. We also assume that $|\hat{\mathcal{X}}| \geq |\mathcal{X}| + 2$ in this paper unless specified otherwise[1]. All logarithms are base 2.

## 2   Problem Setting

Assume that we have two random variables $X$ and $Y$, and their joint distribution $p(x, y)$, $x \in \mathcal{X}$, $y \in \mathcal{Y}$. We would like to encode $X$ using reproduction alphabet $\hat{\mathcal{X}}$ in a way that keeps the maximum information on $Y$ for a given rate or alternatively, use the minimal rate for a given value $I_Y$ of information on $Y$).

As usually done in Information Theory we use block encoding and thus discuss average rate and *average information*. We will show that the tradeoff between these two values can be discovered using the optimization problem presented in definition 3. Before going any further we introduce the definitions of encoding and how do we measure its average information. Note that the definition is similar to the one of rate-distortion code [4]. The only difference is that the average distortion is replaced by the $Y$-information.

---

[1] This last assumption is used for proving the convexity of the information curve (lemma 5), which by itself is used in some other proofs.

**Definition 1 (Rate Information Code).** *A $(2^{nR}, n)$ rate information code consists of:*

$$\text{an encoding function:} \qquad f_n : \mathcal{X}^n \longrightarrow \{1, 2, \cdots, 2^{nR}\}$$
$$\text{a decoding function:} \qquad g_n : \{1, 2, \cdots, 2^{nR}\} \longrightarrow \hat{\mathcal{X}}^n$$

*The $Y$-information associated with the $(2^{nR}, n)$ is defined as*

$$Y_{info}(f_n, g_n) = \frac{1}{n} \sum_{i=1}^{n} I\Big( (g_n \circ f_n(X^n))_i \; ; \; (Y^n)_i \Big)$$

*where the information of the $i$'s element is calculated with respect to the distribution defined by the code for this coordinate as follows:*

$$\bar{p}_i(x, \hat{x}) = \sum_{x^n \; : \; (x^n)_i = x \; \wedge \; (g_n \circ f_n(x^n))_i = \hat{x}} p(x^n) \tag{1}$$

A rate information pair $(R, I_Y)$ is said to be *achievable* if there exists a sequence of rate information codes $(f_n, g_n)$ with asymptotic rate $R$ and asymptotic $Y$-information larger than or equal to $I_Y$, i.e. with $\lim_{n \to \infty} Y_{info}(f_n, g_n) \geq I_Y$

The *rate information region* is the closure of the set of achievable rate information pairs $(R, I_Y)$.

**Definition 2 (Rate Information Function).** *The* rate information function *$R(I_Y) : [0, I(X, Y)] \to [0, h(X)]$ is the infimum of rates $R$ such that $(R, I_Y)$ is in the rate information region for a given constraint on the information on $Y$, $I_Y$.*

**Definition 3 (IB-Function).** *The* IB-function *$R^{(I)}(I_Y)$ for two random variables $X$ and $Y$ is defined as*

$$R^{(I)}(I_Y) = \min_{p(\hat{x}|x) : I(\hat{X}; Y) \geq I_Y} I(X; \hat{X})$$

*Where the minimization is over all the normalized distributions $p(\hat{x}|x)$.*

Note that the constraint depends on $p(y|\hat{x})$ which does not appear explicitly in the minimization problem, but is given by $p(y|\hat{x}) = \sum_x p(y|x)p(x|\hat{x})$, which follows from the Markov chain $\hat{X} \to X \to Y$. The minimum exists as $I(\hat{X}, X)$ is a continuous function of $p(\hat{x}|x)$ and the minimization is over a compact set.

It is also possible to define the dual function

$$I_Y^{(I)}(R) = \max_{p(\hat{x}|x) \; : \; I(\hat{X}; X) \leq R} I(\hat{X}; Y) \tag{2}$$

later on we will show that the two functions are indeed equivalent, i.e. that they defines the same curve. Theorem 2 shows that the curve of $R(I_Y)$ is also the same. We will refer to this curve later on as the *IB-curve*. See figure 1 for an illustration of this curve.

Tishby et al. [12] used Lagrange multipliers to analyze the IB optimization problem. They proved that the conditional distribution $p(\hat{x}|x)$ which achieves the minimum has an exponential form, as stated in theorem 1.

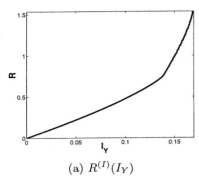

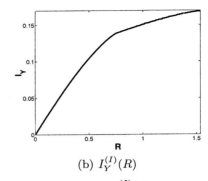

(a) $R^{(I)}(I_Y)$                                   (b) $I_Y^{(I)}(R)$

**Fig. 1.** A typical IB-curve. The graphs of $R^{(I)}(I_Y)$ (left) and of $I_Y^{(I)}(R)$ (right). The curve was computed empirically for a joint distribution of size $3 \times 3$.

**Theorem 1 (Tishby et al. 1999).** *The optimal assignment, that minimizes the IB minimization problem given in definition 3, satisfies the equation*

$$p(\hat{x}|x) = \frac{p(\hat{x})}{Z(x,\beta)} e^{-\beta D_{KL}[p(y|x)||p(y|\hat{x})]} \tag{3}$$

*where $\beta$ is the Lagrange multiplier corresponds to the constraint $I(\hat{X};Y) \geq I_Y$ and $Z(x,\beta) = \sum_{\hat{x}} p(\hat{x})e^{-\beta D_{KL}[p(y|x)||p(y|\hat{x})]}$ is a normalization function. and the distribution $p(y|\hat{x})$ in the exponent is given via Bayes' rule and the Markov chain condition $\hat{X} \leftarrow X \leftarrow Y$, as,*

$$p(y|\hat{x}) = \frac{1}{p(\hat{x})} \sum_{x} p(y|x)p(\hat{x}|x)p(x) \tag{4}$$

Note that this solution is a *formal* solution since $p(y|\hat{x})$ in the exponent is defined implicitly in the terms of the assignment mapping $p(\hat{x}|x)$.

## 3   Relation to Source Coding with Side Information

The problem of source coding with side information at the decoder is being studied in the Information Theory community since the mid seventies [14, 1]. It is also known as the Wyner-Ahlswede-Koroner (WAK) problem. Lately it was discovered [3] that it is closely related to the Information Bottleneck. In order to explore the relations between the two frameworks we first give here a short description of the WAK problem.

The WAK framework study the situation where one would like to encode information about one variable in a way that allow to reconstruct it in the presence of some information about another variable. More formally, let $X$ and $Y$ be two (non independent) random variables. Each of them is encoded separately with rates $R_0$ and $R_1$ accordingly. Both codes are available at the decoder. A pair of rates $R_0, R_1$ is *achievable* if it allows exact reconstruction of $Y$ in the usual Shannon sense. $X$ is referred as *side information*. See figure 2 for an illustration.

[14, 1] found independently, at the same time, that the minimal achievable rate $R_1$ for a given constraint $R_0 \leq r_0$ is given by

$$F(r_0) = \min_{p(\hat{x}|x):I(\hat{X};X) \leq r_0} H(Y|\hat{X})$$

By adding the constant $H(Y)$, we get

$$F(r_0) = H(Y) - I_Y^{(I)}(r_0) \tag{5}$$

where $I_Y^{(I)}(\cdot)$ is as defined in (2).

Although surprising, this equivalence (5) can be explained as follows: The value $F(r_0)$ measures the rate one should add on top of the side information in order to fully reconstruct $Y$. The compliment of this quantity is the amount of information known about $Y$ from the side information $\hat{X}$. The last measures the quality of the quantization (accuracy) in the IB framework.

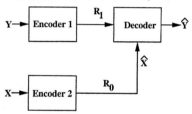

**Fig. 2.** The network correspond to the WAK problem.

Using the similarity between the two problems it is possible to share the knowledge about the optimization problem. For an example, any algorithms that was developed for the IB is also valid for WAK. Anyway, despite the technical similarity, the motivation and the applications are very different and therefore the kind of questions arises are different. For an example, the coding theorems for IB and for WAK are related but different.

## 4    The Coding Theorem

In this section we state and prove our main results, that the IB-function is the solution of the coding problem presented in definition 2.

**Theorem 2.** *The rate information function for i.i.d sampling of $(X, Y)$ is equal to the associated IB-function. Thus*

$$R(I_Y) = R^{(I)}(I_Y) \triangleq \min_{p(\hat{x}|x):I(\hat{X};Y) \geq I_Y} I(X; \hat{X}) \tag{6}$$

### 4.1    The IB-Function Lower Bounds R($I_Y$)

First we show that any code which achieves $Y$-information larger than $I_Y$ has rate of $R^{(I)}(I_Y)$ at least. The proof is very similar to the converse proof of the *rate-distortion theorem* (see [4]) and is given here for the sake of completeness. The proof uses some properties of $R^{(I)}(I_Y)$, that will be presented later on in section 5. We complete the proof of the theorem in section 4.2.

*Proof (Lower bound in theorem 2).* Consider any $(2^{nR}, R)$ code defined by functions $f_n$ and $g_n$. Let $\hat{X}^n = \hat{X}^n(X^n) = g_n \circ f_n(X^n)$ be the reproducing sequence corresponding to $X^n$. The joint distribution induced by the code is:

$$\bar{p}(x^n, \hat{x}^n) = \begin{cases} p(x^n) & \text{if } \hat{x} = g_n \circ f_n(x^n) \\ 0 & \text{otherwise} \end{cases}$$

Since at most $2^{nR}$ elements of $\hat{\mathcal{X}}^n$ are in use, the elements of $X^n$ are independent and the fact that conditioning reduces entropy, we have that

$$nR \geq H(\hat{X}^n) = H(\hat{X}^n) - H(\hat{X}^n|X^n) = I(\hat{X}^n; X^n)$$

$$= H(X^n) - H(X^n|\hat{X}^n) = \sum_{i=1}^{n} H(X_i) - \sum_{i=1}^{n} H(X_i|\hat{X}^n, X_{1\dots i-1})$$

$$\geq \sum_{i=1}^{n} H(X_i) - \sum_{i=1}^{n} H(X_i|\hat{X}_i) = \sum_{i=1}^{n} I(X_i; \hat{X}_i) \tag{7}$$

using the definition and convexity of $R^{(I)}(\cdot)$ we have that

$$\sum_{i=1}^{n} I(X_i; \hat{X}_i) \geq \sum_{i=1}^{n} R^{(I)}(I(\hat{X}_i; Y_i)) = n \sum_{i=1}^{n} \frac{1}{n} R^{(I)}(I(\hat{X}_i; Y_i))$$

$$\geq nR^{(I)}\left(\sum_{i=1}^{n} \frac{1}{n} I(\hat{X}_i; Y_i)\right) \tag{8}$$

and since the marginals of $\bar{p}$ are exactly the $\bar{p}_i$'s defined in (1), and the fact that $R^{(I)}(\cdot)$ is non-decreasing,

$$nR^{(I)}\left(\sum_{i=1}^{n} \frac{1}{n} I(\hat{X}_i; Y_i)\right) = nR^{(I)}\left(Y_{info}(f_n, g_n)\right) \geq nR^{(I)}(I_Y) \tag{9}$$

Combining (7), (8) and (9) we get the stated result.  □

## 4.2  Achievability of the IB-Function

We now prove the achievability of the IB-function $R^{(I)}(I_Y)$, or in other words that this function is a tight bound. Given any $p(\hat{x}|x)$, a series of codes with $R_n \to I(\hat{X}; X)$ and $Y_{info_n} \to I(\hat{X}; Y)$ is constructed. We enhance the standard construction of the rate-distortion in two ways: first we encode with respect to multiple distortion measures at the same time. Moreover, we require that the distortion for each coordinate of the block will be close to the distortion induced by $p(\hat{x}|x)$, while in rate-distortion only the average distortion counts. By selecting the appropriate distortion measures we complete the proof. First we introduce a few definitions and lemmas.

**Definition 4 (Multi Distortion Jointly Typical).** *Let $p(x, \hat{x})$ be a joint probability distribution on $\mathcal{X} \times \hat{\mathcal{X}}$. Let $d_1, \ldots, d_k$ be a set of distortion measures on $\mathcal{X} \times \hat{\mathcal{X}}$. For any $\epsilon > 0$, a pair of sequences $(x^n, \hat{x}^n)$ is said to be* multi distortion jointly $\epsilon$-typical *if*

$$\left| -\frac{1}{n} \log p(x^n) - H(X) \right| < \epsilon$$

$$\left| -\frac{1}{n} \log p(\hat{x}^n) - H(\hat{X}) \right| < \epsilon$$

$$\left| -\frac{1}{n} \log p(x^n, \hat{x}^n) - H(X, \hat{X}) \right| < \epsilon$$

$$\left| d_j(x^n, \hat{x}^n) - E d_j(X, \hat{X}) \right| < \epsilon \qquad \forall j, \; 1 \leq j \leq k$$

*where $d_j(x^n, \hat{x}^n)$ is defined as $\frac{1}{n} \sum_{i=1}^{n} d_j((x^n)_i, (\hat{x}^n)_i)$.*
*This set is denoted $A_\epsilon^{(n)}$*

**Lemma 1.** *Let $(X_i, \hat{X}_i)$ be drawn i.i.d $\sim p(x, \hat{x})$. Then $Pr(A_\epsilon^{(n)}) \to 1$ as $n \to \infty$*

This result follows from the *central limit theorem*.

**Lemma 2.** *Given $p(x, \hat{x}) = p(\hat{x}|x)p(x)$ and a finite set of bounded distortion measures $d_1 \ldots d_k$ there exists a series of codes $(f_n, g_n)$ with asymptotic rate $I(\hat{X}; X)$, and such that for any $d_j$ the average distortion of the code converges uniformly to $E_{p(\hat{x}, x)} d_j(X, \hat{X})$. i.e. for any $\epsilon > 0$ there exist $N$ such that for any $d_j$ and any $n > N$ we have that*

$$\left| E_{x^n} d_j(X^n, g_n \circ f_n(X^n)) - E_{p(\hat{x}, x)} d_j(X, \hat{X}) \right| < \epsilon$$

*Proof.* We use random codebook and mapping by multi distortion joint typicality as follows:

**Generation of codebook.** Randomly generate a codebook $\mathcal{C}$ consisting of $2^{nI(X; \hat{X})}$ sequences $\hat{x}^n$ drawn i.i.d from $p(\hat{x})$. Index these codewords by $w \in \{1, 2, \ldots, 2^{nI(X; \hat{X})}\}$.

**Encoding.** Encode $x^n$ by $w$ if there exist a $w$ s.t. $(x^n, \hat{x}^n(w)) \in A_\epsilon^{(n)}$. If there is more than one such $w$ send the least. If There is no such $w$ let $w = 1$.

The rest of the proof, i.e. showing that with probability greater than zero this construction achieves the required distortion, is the same as the one used in the rate-distortion theorem that can be found for example in [4] (pp.350).    □

**Definition 5 (The Distortion of a Coordinate).** *Given source $p(x)$, a distortion measure $d$ and a code $(f_n, g_n)$. The distortion of a coordinate $i$ is*

$$E_{p^n(x^n)} d((X^n)_i, (g_n \circ f_n(X^n))_i)$$

*Note that the total distortion of the code $(f_n, g_n)$ is the average of its coordinate distortions.*

**Lemma 3.** *In the setting of lemma 2, It is possible to add the requirement that for each distortion measure $d_j$, the distortion of all the coordinates is the same.*

*Proof.* We will achieve the additional demand by making the code symmetric. Start with the code that satisfies the requirements of lemma 2. For each $\hat{x}^n$ in the code add all its cyclic permutations to the codebook. This will enlarge the codebook by factor $n$ at most, and thus does not change the asymptotic rate. Let $\sigma$ be any cyclic permutation, note that $(x^n, \hat{x}^n) \in A_\epsilon^{(n)}$ implies $(\sigma(x^n), \sigma(\hat{x}^n)) \in A_\epsilon^{(n)}$. Hence it is possible to change the encoding such that the following hold:

$$\sigma(g_n \circ f_n(x^n)) = g_n \circ f_n(\sigma(x^n)) \tag{10}$$

without sacrificing the average distortion. Fix a distortion measure $d_j$ and let $i$ be one of the coordinates of the code. For any cyclic permutation $\sigma$ the following holds:

$$E_{p^n(x^n)} d((X^n)_i, (g_n \circ f_n(X^n))_i) = \sum_{x^n} p(x^n) d((X^n)_i, (g_n \circ f_n(X^n))_i)$$

$$= \sum_{x^n} p(\sigma(x^n)) d((\sigma(X^n))_i, (g_n \circ f_n(\sigma(X^n)))_i)$$

$$= \sum_{x^n} p(x^n) d((X^n)_{\sigma(i)}, (g_n \circ f_n(X^n))_{\sigma(i)})$$

$$= E_{p^n(x^n)} d((X^n)_{\sigma(i)}, (g_n \circ f_n(X^n))_{\sigma(i)})$$

These equalities follows from equation (10) and since $p(x^n) = p(\sigma(x^n))$.  □

We are now ready to complete the proof of theorem 2.

*Proof (Achievability in theorem 2).* It suffices to show that for any joint distribution $p(\hat{x}, x) = p(\hat{x}|x)p(x)$ it is possible to construct a series of codes $(f_n, g_n)$ with asymptotic rate $I(X; \hat{X})$ and asymptotic $Y$-information $I(Y; \hat{X})$.

Let define for any pair $(x_0, \hat{x}_0)$ a distortion measure as follows:

$$d = d_{x_0, \hat{x}_0}(x, \hat{x}) = \begin{cases} 1 \text{ if } (x_0, \hat{x}_0) = (x, \hat{x}) \\ 0 \text{ otherwise} \end{cases}$$

Then we have:

$$E_{p(x, \hat{x})} d_{x_0, \hat{x}_0}(X, \hat{X}) = p(x_0, \hat{x}_0) \tag{11}$$

and

$$E_{p(x^n)} d_{x_0, \hat{x}_0}(X^n, g_n \circ f_n(X^n)) = \frac{1}{n} \sum_{i=1}^n \bar{p}_i(x_0, \hat{x}_0) \tag{12}$$

where $\bar{p}_i$ are as defined in (1).

Using these distortion measures, the construction in lemma 3 and equations (11) and (12) we build a series of codes $(f_n, g_n)$ with asymptotic rate $I(X; \hat{X})$ such that for large enough $n$, any $(x_0, \hat{x}_0)$ and any $i$

$$|\bar{p}_i(x_0, \hat{x}_0) - p(x_0, \hat{x}_0)| < \epsilon$$

Since the $Y$-information of the code is continuous function with respect to the $\bar{p}_i$ it follows that the $Y$-information convergence to $I(Y; \hat{X})$.  □

## 5    Properties of the IB-Curve

In this section we study the IB-function $R^{(I)}(I_Y)$ and present some properties it poses. We use the similarity to the WAK problem (see section 3) to adopt results from [13].

First note that $R^{(I)}(I_Y)$ is the minimum of $I(X; \hat{X})$ over decreasingly smaller sets as $I_Y$ increases. Thus $R^{(I)}(I_Y)$ is non-decreasing function of $I_Y$.

Second, note that in contrary to the rate-distortion scenario, where the elements of $\hat{\mathcal{X}}$ get meaning from the distortion measure, in our scenario only the size of $\hat{\mathcal{X}}$ matter. It is clear that if $|\hat{\mathcal{X}}| < |\mathcal{X}|$ the solution may not be optimal. However the following lemma shows that $|\hat{\mathcal{X}}|$ does not have to be much bigger.

**Lemma 4.** $\hat{\mathcal{X}}$ of cardinality $|\mathcal{X}| + 2$ is sufficient to achieve the optimal $I(X; \hat{X})$ for any constraint $I_Y$ on $I(\hat{X}; Y)$

And for this case we also have convexity:

**Lemma 5.** For $|\hat{\mathcal{X}}| \geq |\mathcal{X}| + 2$, the IB-function $R^{(I)}(I_Y)$ is a convex function of $I_Y$ and $I_Y^{(I)}(R)$ is concave function of $R$.

The above two lemmas were proved in [13]. Note that [13] prove it for a slightly different setting, but the modifications are straightforward.

The curve is continuous in the interior since it is monotonic and convex. Moreover it is smooth under mild conditions as stated in the following lemma.

**Lemma 6.** For a $p(x, y) > 0$ the slope of $R^{(I)}(I_Y)$ is continuous and approaches $\infty$ as $I_Y$ approaches $I(X; Y)$

*Proof.* Let $(I_Y^*, R^*)$ be a point on the curve and let $p^*(\hat{x}|x)$ be a distribution that achieves this point. From convexity we know that there is a straight line that pass through $(I_Y^*, R^*)$ such that all the curve lies in the upper half space defined by this line. Denote by $\beta$ the slope of this line. Then

$$R - \beta I_Y \geq R^* - \beta I_Y^* \qquad \forall \, (I_Y, R) \tag{13}$$

Thus $p^*$ is optimal and has the following exponential form:

$$p^*(\hat{x}|x) = \frac{p^*(\hat{x})}{Z(x, \beta)} e^{-\beta D_{KL}[p(y|x)||p^*(y|\hat{x})]} \tag{14}$$

Assume that there is a line with slope $\beta' \neq \beta$ with the same properties (i.e. that the curve is not smooth at this point). Then it is also true that:

$$p^*(\hat{x}|x) = \frac{p^*(\hat{x})}{Z(x, \beta')} e^{-\beta' D_{KL}[p(y|x)||p^*(y|\hat{x})]} \tag{15}$$

From (14) and (15) and the fact that $D_{KL}$ is finite for $p(x, y) > 0$ we have that for every $\hat{x}$ with $p(\hat{x}) > 0$:

$$\frac{Z(x, \beta)}{Z(x, \beta')} = e^{(\beta - \beta') D_{KL}[p(y|x)||p^*(y|\hat{x})]}$$

The left-hand side is independent of $\hat{x}$ and thus the right-hand side must as well. It follow then that $p(\hat{x}|x) = p(\hat{x})$ and therefore $I(X;\hat{X}) = 0$.                    □

It is easy to see that the assumption that there are no zeros in $p(x,y)$ in the above lemma is necessary, for example the curve correspond to the following block matrix has a constant finite slope.

$$p(x,y) = \frac{1}{8} \begin{pmatrix} 1\,1\,0\,0 \\ 1\,1\,0\,0 \\ 0\,0\,1\,1 \\ 0\,0\,1\,1 \end{pmatrix}$$

**Corollary 1.** *From equation (13) it follows that any optimal solution is a global minimum[2] of the Lagrangian $I(X;\hat{X}) - \beta I(\hat{X};Y)$ and $\beta$ is the slope of $R^{(I)}(I_Y)$ in that point.*

**Lemma 7.** *The IB function $R^{(I)}(I_Y)$ is continuous as a function of $p(x,y)$.*

The proof follows from the continuity of both mutual information and $R^{(I)}(I_Y)$ (as a function of $I_Y$).

## 6    Information Bottleneck and Rate Distortion

In this section we show that the Information Bottleneck is locally equivalent to a rate-distortion problem (RDT) [7] with adequate distortion measure and can be considered as a RDT with a non fixed distortion measure. We also show that the information curve is the envelope of all these "locally equivalent" RDT curves.

**Definition 6.** *For given $p(y|x)$ and $p(y|\hat{x})$ we define the following distortion measure on $\mathcal{X} \times \hat{\mathcal{X}}$:*

$$d_{IB}(x,\hat{x}) = D_{KL}[p(y|x)||p(y|\hat{x})]$$

**Lemma 8.** *For fixed $p(\hat{x}|x)$ and $p(y|\hat{x}) = \sum_x p(y|x)p(x|\hat{x})$*

$$\langle d_{IB} \rangle_{x,\hat{x}} = I(X;Y) - I(\hat{X};Y)$$

The proof of lemma 8 follows from the Markov chain $\hat{X} \to X \to Y$ and simple algebric manipulation.
Now define the "rate-distortion like" minimization problem

$$R_{DT}(D) = \min_{p(\hat{x}|x)\,:\,\langle d_{IB}\rangle \leq D} I(\hat{X};X) \qquad (16)$$

and from the lemma we have that $R_{DT}(D) = R^{(I)}(I(X;Y) - D)$. Note that $R_{DT}(D)$ is not a rate-distortion problem as the "distortion measure" $d_{IB}$ is not

---

[2] note that generally when using Lagrange multipliers, the optimum can be any point where the gradient of the Lagrangian vanishes.

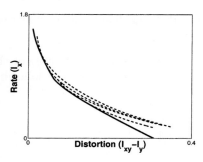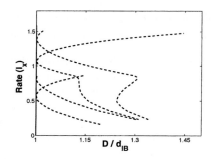

**Fig. 3.** IB-curve as an envelope of rate-distortion curves for a random 4x4 matrix. The bold line is the IB curve with switched x-axis. The dashed lines are the rate distortion curves for the same source, with different distortion measures induced from substituting different $p(y|\hat{x})$ in the $D_{KL}$. The right figure shows the normalized graph, i.e. each curve was divided by the IB curve.

fixed. Where "not fixed" means that it depends on the minimization parameter $p(\hat{x}|x)$. The dependency is as follows:

$$d_{IB}(x,\hat{x}) = D_{KL}[p(y|x)||p(y|\hat{x})] \tag{17}$$

$$= D_{KL}\left[p(y|x)||\frac{1}{p(\hat{x})}\sum_{x'}p(y|x')p(\hat{x}|x')p(x')\right] \tag{18}$$

**Lemma 9.** *Let $D \geq 0$. For a conditional distribution $q(y|\hat{x})$ define the rate-distortion problem:*

$$R(q,D) = \min_{p(\hat{x}|x)\ :\ \sum_{x,\hat{x}}p(\hat{x}|x)p(x)D_{KL}[p(y|x)||q(y|\hat{x})]\leq D} I(X;\hat{X}) \tag{19}$$

*Then*

$$R^{(I)}(I(X;Y) - D) = \min_{q(y|\hat{x})} R(q,D)$$

The proof of lemma 9 is omitted due to space limitation.

**Corollary 2.** *For any $p(x|\hat{x})$, let $p(y|\hat{x}) = \sum_{x'}p(y|x')p(x'|\hat{x})$ and consider the rate-distortion problems given by the source $X$ and the distortion measure $d(x,\hat{x}) = D_{KL}[p(y|x)|p(y|\hat{x})]$. Then the following hold:*

- *The IB-curve (with switched x-axis) is below the rate-distortion curve.*
- *If the $p(x|\hat{x})$ is correspond to a point on the IB-curve, the rate-distortion curve is tangent to the IB-curve at this point.*
- *The IB-curve is a tight lower bound ("envelope") for all the rate-distortion curves of the above form.*

A demonstration of corollary 2 is given in figure 3.

## 7   Information Bottleneck and Cost Capacity

In the previous section we have shown that the information bottleneck can be considered as a rate-distortion problem with a non-fixed distortion measure. In this section we consider a dual representation. This representation takes the form of a cost-capacity problem with a non-fixed cost function. We show that these two dual problems are indeed equivalent.

**Definition 7.** *Given a noisy channel $p(b|a)$ and a cost function $c : A \to \mathbb{R}^+$, let $e(p) = \sum_a c(a)p(a)$ then the* cost-capacity *function is defined as*

$$C(E) = \max_{p(a)\ :\ e(p) \leq E} I(A; B)$$

Consider $p(y|\hat{x})$ as defining a noisy channel and define a cost function

$$c(\hat{x}) = \sum_x p(x|\hat{x}) \log \frac{p(x|\hat{x})}{p(x)}$$

then    $$e(p) = \sum_{\hat{x}} c(\hat{x})p(\hat{x}) = \sum_{x,\hat{x}} p(x|\hat{x})p(\hat{x}) \log \frac{p(x|\hat{x})}{p(x)} = I_p(X; \hat{X})$$

and    $$C(R) = \max_{p(\hat{x}|x)\ :\ e(p) \leq R} I(\hat{X}; Y) = \max_{p(\hat{x}|x)\ :\ I(\hat{X};X) \leq R} I(\hat{X}; Y) = I_Y^{(I)}(R)$$

Note that $p(\hat{x}|x)$ defines $p(\hat{x})$ as $p(x)$ is fixed and thus it is sound to maximize over $p(\hat{x}|x)$ instead of over $p(\hat{x})$.

Next we show that this maximization problem is really dual to our original minimization problem, i.e. that the two optimization problems defines the same curve.

**Lemma 10.** *The two optimization problems $R^{(I)}(I_Y)$ and $I_Y^{(I)}(R)$ defines the same curve with switched axes for $0 \leq I_Y \leq I(X; Y)$ and $0 \leq R \leq R^{(I)}(I(X; Y))$*

*Proof.* We have to prove that for any $I_Y$, $R^{(I)}(I_Y) = I_Y^{(I)}(R)$ for some $R$ and vice-versa, i.e. for any $R$ there exists $I_Y$ such that $I_Y^{(I)}(R) = R^{(I)}(I_Y)$. For this purpose it suffices to show that the following two properties hold:

- for any relevant $I_Y$, it is not possible to achieve $I(\hat{X}; Y)$ larger than $I_Y$ with $I(X; \hat{X})$ equal to or smaller than $R^{(I)}(I_Y)$
- for any relevant $R$, it is not possible to achieve $I(\hat{X}; X)$ smaller than $R$ with $I(\hat{X}; Y)$ equal to or larger than $I_Y^{(I)}(R)$

The first property is clear from the convexity of $R^{(I)}(I_Y)$ and the obvious fact that it is impossible to achieve $I(\hat{X}; Y) > 0$ with $I(X; \hat{X}) = 0$.

The second property follows from the concavity of $I_Y^{(I)}(R)$ as follows: if it is possible to move down from any $(I_Y^{(I)}(R), R)$ point (i.e. to achieve a smaller $I(X, \hat{X})$ with $I(\hat{X}; Y) = I_Y^{(I)}(R)$) then concavity is possible only if $I_Y^{(I)}(R)$ is the maximal possible value of $I(\hat{X}; Y)$, and this possible only for $R \geq R^{(I)}(I(X; Y))$. $\qquad\square$

# 8   Conclusions and Further Research

In this paper we provided a rigorous formulation of the Information Bottleneck method as a fumdamental information theoretic question: what is the lower bound on the rate of a code that preserves mutual information on another variable. This method was successfully applied for finding efficient representations for numerous learning problems for which co-occurance distribution of two variables can be estimated, so-far without proper information theoretic justification. We showed that the IB method indeed solves a natural information theoretic problem, formally related to source coding with side information. In a well defined sense this problem unifies aspects of Rate-Distortion Theory and Cost-Capacity tradeoff, but in both cases the effective distortion and the channel cost function are simultaneously determined from the joint statistics of the data, given a single tradeoff parameter. We proved that given the joint distribution, there is a tight achievable convex and smooth bound on the representation length of one variable, for a given mutual information that this representation maintains on the other variable. Since the problem is continuous as a function of the joint distribution (lemma 7), we expect that calculating the bound using a sampled version of the joint distribution can give a good approximation. We also showed that the representation cardinality should not exceed - by more than 2 - the cardinality of the original variable.

Finding a compact representation is a crucial known component in learning (Occam razor, MDL, etc.). In this work we used information theoretic tools in order to quantify the quality of representations, when the accuracy is measured by mutual information as well. A natural extention to these ideas should connect our bounds to generalization error bounds, more common in learning theory.

Many related interesting issues are left outside of this paper, such as analytic properties of the IB-curve for specific joint distributions, or simpler conditions that ensure its convexity and smoothness. We know that for some interesting classes of joint distributions there are analytic expressions for this curve, but for general distributions finding this curve can be computationally very difficult. Some most intriguing remaining questions are: (i) What is the optimal compexity-accuarcy tradeoff for bounded computational complexity? (ii) What is the nature of the deviations from the optimal when given only a finite sample from the joint distribution $p(x, y)$ (the sample complexity - over-fitting - probelm)? (iii) Is there a similar coding theoretic formulation for the multivariate IB, which is in fact a network information theoretic tradeoff?

# Acknowledgment

We would like to thank Eyal Krupka and Noam Slonim for many invaluable discussions and ideas. RB is supported by the Clore foundation. AN is supported by the Horowitz foundation. This work is partly supported by a grant from the Israel Science Foundation.

# References

1. R. F. Ahlswede and J. Korner. Source coding with side information and a converse for degraded broadcast channels. *IEEE transaction on information theory*, 21(6):629–637, November 1975.
2. Y. Baram, R. El-Yaniv, and K. Luz. Online choice of active learning algorithms. Submitted for publication.
3. J. Cardinal. Compression of side information. In *IEEE International Conference on Multimedia and Expo*, 2003.
4. T. M. Cover and J. A. Thomas. *Elements Of Information Thory*. Wiley Interscience, 1991.
5. J. Kleinberg. An impossibility theorem for clustering. In *Proc. of the 16th conference on Neural Information Processing Systems*, 2002.
6. P. Poupart and C. Boutilier. Value-directed compression of pomdps. In *Proc. of the 16th conference on Neural Information Processing Systems*, 2002.
7. C. E. Shannon. A mathematical theory of communication. *Bell System Technical Journal*, 27, July and October 1948.
8. N. Slonim and Tishby N. The power of word clustering for text classification. In *Proc. of the 23rd European Colloquium on Information Retrieval Research*, 2001.
9. N. Slonim, R. Somerville, N. Tishby, and O. Lahav. Objective classification of galaxy spectra using the information bottleneck method. *Monthly Notes of the Royal Astronomical Society*, 323:270–284, 2001.
10. N. Slonim and N. Tishby. Document clustering using word clusters via the information bottleneck method. In *Proc. of the 23rd Annual International ACM-SIGIR Conference on Research and Development in Information Retrieval*, 2000.
11. N. Slonim. *The Information Bottleneck: Theory and Applications*. PhD thesis, The Hebrew University, 2002.
12. N. Tishby, F.C. Pereira, and W. Bialek. The information bottleneck method. In *Proc. of the 37-th Annual Allerton Conference on Comunnication, Control and Computing*, pages 368–377, 1999.
13. H. S. Witsenhausen and A. D. Wyner. A conditional entropy bound for a pair of discrete random variables. *IEEE transaction on information theory*, 21(5):493–501, September 1975.
14. A. D. Wyner. On source coding with side information at the decoder. *IEEE transaction on information theory*, 21(3):294–300, May 1975.

# Learning Random Log-Depth Decision Trees under the Uniform Distribution

Jeffrey C. Jackson[1,*] and Rocco A. Servedio[2]

[1] Department of Mathematics and Computer Science
Duquesne University, Pittsburgh, PA 15282
jackson@mathcs.duq.edu
[2] Department of Computer Science
Columbia University, New York, NY 10027, USA
rocco@cs.columbia.edu

**Abstract.** We consider three natural models of random log-depth decision trees. We give an efficient algorithm that for each of these models learns—as a decision tree—all but an inverse polynomial fraction of such trees using only uniformly distributed random examples.

## 1 Introduction

Decision trees are widely used to represent various forms of knowledge. The apparent ease with which humans can understand and work with decision trees has also made them a popular form of representation for knowledge obtained through heuristic machine learning algorithms (see, e.g., [3,8]). While heuristic algorithms have proved reasonably successful for many applications, there is some reason to believe that arbitrary decision trees are not efficiently learnable from random examples alone, as the class of decision trees is provably not efficiently learnable in the Statistical Query model, even when the examples are uniformly distributed [2].

Given the apparent difficulty of learning decision trees in polynomial time, many researchers have considered alternate learning scenarios. One line of work which has been pursued is to consider algorithms that run in superpolynomial time. Ehrenfeucht and Haussler [5] have shown that the class of size-$s$ decision trees over $\{0,1\}^n$ can be PAC learned in $n^{\log s}$ time steps. This result was later simplified by Blum [1]. Another approach which has been pursued is to study decision tree learnability in alternate learning models in which the learner has more power. Kushilevitz and Mansour [7] gave a polynomial time algorithm which uses membership queries and can learn decision trees under the uniform distribution. The hypothesis produced by this algorithm is a weighted threshold of parity functions. Using different techniques, Bshouty [4] gave a polynomial time algorithm which learns decision trees in the model of exact learning from membership and (non-proper) equivalence queries; this implies that decision trees can be PAC learned in polynomial time under any distribution if membership queries are allowed. The hypothesis in this case is a depth-three Boolean circuit.

---

* This material is based upon work supported by the National Science Foundation under Grant No. CCR-0209064.

B. Schölkopf and M.K. Warmuth (Eds.): COLT/Kernel 2003, LNAI 2777, pp. 610–624, 2003.

In this work we propose a third approach to coping with the difficulty of learning decision trees: looking at the average case. Specifically, since we have been unable to design algorithms which can learn *all* decision trees, we focus instead on algorithms which can efficiently learn "average" decision trees. Another difference between our approach and some of the earlier theoretical work is that the hypothesis produced by our algorithm is a decision tree. A limitation of our algorithm is that we assume that examples are uniformly distributed.

In Section 2 we give the necessary background on uniform distribution learning and decision trees, and describe the three models of random decision trees which we consider. Section 3 gives useful Fourier properties of decision trees. In Section 4 we present the learning algorithm, and Sections 5 through 7 contain the proofs of correctness for the learning algorithm. We conclude in Section 8.

## 2    Preliminaries

A *Boolean decision tree* $T$ is a rooted binary tree in which each internal node has two children and is labeled with a variable, and each leaf is labeled with a bit $b \in \{-1, +1\}$. Children are ordered, i.e., each internal node has a definite left child and right child. We refer to an internal node whose two children are both leaves as a *pre-leaf node*. Because we will deal exclusively with Boolean decision trees in this paper, for convenience we will refer to them simply as decision trees.

A decision tree $T$ computes a Boolean function $f : \{-1, 1\}^n \to \{-1, 1\}$ in the obvious way: on input $x$, if variable $x_i$ is at the root of $T$ we go to either the left or right subtree depending on whether $x_i$ is $-1$ or $1$. We continue in this fashion until reaching a bit leaf; the value of this bit is $f(x)$.

We define the *depth of a node* in a decision tree as follows. First, every decision tree must have at least one node; we do not admit the empty (0-node) decision tree. In a tree consisting of a single leaf node (labeled with some bit), the depth of this node is $-1$; we call such a tree *trivial*. The depth of the root in a non-trivial tree is $0$, and the depth of any non-root node is one greater than the depth of its parent. The *depth of a decision tree* $T$ is $-1$ if $T$ is trivial and the maximum depth over all pre-leaf nodes of $T$ otherwise.

A decision tree is *non-redundant* if no variable occurs more than once on any root-to-leaf path. We consider only non-redundant decision trees in this paper.

We let $\mathcal{U}$ be the uniform distribution on $\{-1, 1\}^n$. We write $EX(f, \mathcal{U})$ to denote a uniform random example oracle for $f : \{-1, 1\}^n \to \{-1, 1\}$ which, when invoked, outputs a labeled example $\langle x, f(x) \rangle$ where $x$ is drawn from $\mathcal{U}$.

We consider three models of random decision trees. Our primary model is the uniform distribution over the set of all non-redundant decision tree representations of depth at most $d$ on the variable set $\{x_1, \ldots, x_n\}$. We call this the *uniform* model and will represent this distribution by $\mathcal{T}_{d,n}^U$. Note that not every Boolean function that can be represented by a depth-$d$ tree has the same probability mass under $\mathcal{T}_{d,n}^U$; some functions may have more $\mathcal{T}_{d,n}^U$-good trees which represent them than others. That is, $\mathcal{T}_{d,n}^U$ is a distribution over syntactic representations of decision tree functions, and not over the functions themselves.

In each of our other two models, the internal nodes form a complete tree of depth $d$ and are labeled uniformly at random using the variables $\{x_1, \ldots, x_n\}$, with the restriction that the tree must be non-redundant. These models, denoted by $\mathcal{T}_{d,n}^C$ and $\mathcal{T}_{d,n}^B$, differ in that the leaves in $\mathcal{T}_{d,n}^C$ are selected independently and uniformly from $\{-1, 1\}$ while in $\mathcal{T}_{d,n}^B$ each sibling pair must have opposite signs, although the sign of the left node is independently and uniformly chosen from $\{-1, 1\}$. We call these the *complete* and *balanced* models, respectively.

Due to the space restrictions in these proceedings, here we prove our main learning result (Theorem 2) only for the complete model $\mathcal{T}_{d,n}^C$. We have proved exact analogues of this result for for the uniform and balanced models $\mathcal{T}_{d,n}^U$ and $\mathcal{T}_{d,n}^B$ as well; the proofs for these models will be contained in the full version of the paper.

We assume throughout that $d$ is $O(\log n)$, and that the learning algorithm knows the exact value of $d$. This latter assumption is w.l.o.g. since the algorithm can try all values $d = 1, 2, \ldots$ until it succeeds.

## 3    Fourier Properties of Decision Trees

We will be interested in carefully measuring the correlation between a decision tree $f$ and each of $f$'s variables. Define $e_i$ to be the $n$-bit vector that has a 1 in position $i$ and 0's elsewhere and define $\hat{f}(e_i)$ to be $E_{a \sim \mathcal{U}}[a_i f(a)]$. Since $f(a)$ and $a_i$ take values in $\{-1, 1\}$ we have $\hat{f}(e_i) = \Pr_{a \sim \mathcal{U}}[f(a) = a_i] - \Pr_{a \sim \mathcal{U}}[f(a) \neq a_i]$. Each $\hat{f}(e_i)$ is a *first-order Fourier coefficient* of $f$.

Kushilevitz and Mansour [7] showed that decision trees have some particularly useful Fourier properties[1]. Define $L(i)$ to be the set of all leaves in a decision tree $f$ that are descendants of some node labeled by variable $x_i$, and let $d(\ell)$ represent the depth of a leaf $\ell$ in $f$. The analysis of [7] directly implies:

**Corollary 1 (Kushilevitz Mansour).** *For every decision tree $f$ and every $1 \leq i \leq n$, there is a function $\sigma : L(i) \to \{-1, 1\}$ such that*

$$\hat{f}(e_i) = \sum_{\ell \in L(i)} 2^{-d(\ell)} \sigma(\ell).$$

(Note that this corollary implies that any tree of depth $d$ has each $\hat{f}(e_i)$ of the form $i/2^d$ for some integer $i$. This is because any leaf at depth $d + 1$ must have a sibling leaf, so the total number of $\pm 1/2^{d+1}$ contributions to $\hat{f}(e_i)$ is even.)

From this we easily obtain:

**Corollary 2.** *For every decision tree $f$ of depth $d$ and every $1 \leq i \leq n$, there is an integer $k$ such that $\hat{f}(e_i) = \frac{2k+1}{2^d}$ if and only if the total number of nodes/pairs of leaves satisfying the following conditions is odd for $x_i$:*

1. *A node at depth $d$ is labeled with $x_i$ and the children of this node (both leaves) have opposite signs;*

---

[1] [7] considered decision trees in which internal nodes can contain arbitrary parity functions; however as noted earlier we only allow single variables at internal nodes.

2. *A leaf at depth $d$ has an ancestor labeled with $x_i$;*
3. *A pair of sibling leaves at depth $d+1$ have the same sign, $x_i$ labels an ancestor of this pair of leaves, and $x_i$ is not the label of the parent of the pair.*

We say that any first-order Fourier coefficient of the form $\frac{2k+1}{2^d}$ is an *odd coefficient*, and all other first-order coefficients are *even coefficients*. Conditions 2 and 3 may seem redundant, since a tree with two sibling leaves having the same sign is equivalent to a tree that has a single leaf in place of the parent of the siblings. We include both conditions because these are syntactically different structures both of which may arise in the various trees we consider.

A key observation, which follows easily from the above corollaries, is:

**Lemma 1.** *Fix any Boolean decision tree structure of depth $d$ and assign variables $x_1$ through $x_n$ arbitrarily to the internal nodes of the tree, with the constraint that the resulting tree is non-redundant. Assign each leaf bit by independently and uniformly selecting from $\{-1, 1\}$. Then for every $1 \leq i \leq n$ such that $x_i$ is an ancestor of at least one leaf at depth $d + 1$, we have $\Pr[\hat{f}(e_i)$ is an odd coefficient $] = \frac{1}{2}$.*

*Moreover, let $S$ be any subset of variables $x_1, \ldots, x_n$ with the following property: there is a collection $C$ of $|S|$ pre-leaves in $T$, each of which is at depth $d$ and is labeled with a different element of $S$, such that no variable in $S$ occurs on any of the paths from the root to any of these pre-leaves. Then we have that $\Pr[\forall x_i \in S \ \hat{f}(e_i)$ is an even coefficient $] = \frac{1}{2^{|S|}}$.*

*Proof.* We can view certain leaves of the tree as defining the "parity" of the internal nodes in a way that corresponds to the conditions of Corollary 2. More precisely, all internal nodes begin with even parity, and then their parities are computed by applying the following rules to each leaf and each pair of leaves (each leaf or leaf pair will meet the conditions of at most one rule):

1. If a pair of sibling leaves are at depth $d + 1$ and have opposite signs, then the parity of their depth-$d$ parent node is toggled.
2. If a leaf is at depth $d$ then the parity of each ancestor node is toggled.
3. If a pair of sibling leaves are at depth $d + 1$ and have identical signs, then the parity of each ancestor node except their parent node is toggled.

We can then define the parity of a variable $x_i$ as the parity of the parity of all nodes that are labeled by $x_i$. It is clear that for each $i$, the first-order Fourier coefficient $\hat{f}(e_i)$ is odd if and only if $x_i$ has odd parity according to this definition.

Next, notice that since sibling leaves are labeled uniformly at random, any pair of sibling leaves at depth $d + 1$ is equally likely to satisfy rule 1 or rule 3 above. So the probability that any given ancestor node of a pair of such sibling leaves has its parity toggled by a random assignment to these leaf bits is exactly $1/2$. The same is true of the parity of the variable labeling the node. Since all leaves at depth $d+1$ have sibling leaves (because the tree depth is $d$), all possible assignments to leaves at depth $d+1$ are covered by the conditions of rules 1 and 3. Thus, any variable $x_i$ that is an ancestor of at least one leaf at depth $d+1$ will have odd parity with probability exactly $1/2$, and the first equation is proved.

To see that the second equation also holds, observe that the $|S|$ pre-leaves in $C$ will each toggle the parity of the corresponding variable with probability $1/2$. Since no variable in $S$ occurs on any path to a node in $C$, the final parities of these variables are all independent of each other, and the lemma follows.   □

Kushilevitz and Mansour also observed that it follows from Corollary 1 and Chernoff bounds that for any decision tree $f$ and any $\delta > 0$, a uniformly distributed sample $A$ of $m$ labeled pairs $\langle a, f(a) \rangle$ is—with probability at least $1 - \delta$ over the choice of $A$—sufficient to compute all of the first-order Fourier coefficients of $f$ exactly, for $m$ exponential in the depth $d$ of $f$ and polynomial in $\log(n/\delta)$. In particular, with probability at least $1 - \delta$ over the random draw of $A$, $\hat{f}(e_i) = R\left((\sum_{a \in A} a_i f(a))/m\right)$ where $R(\cdot)$ represents "rounding" the argument to the nearest rational number having denominator $2^d$. Therefore, we also have

**Corollary 3 (Kushilevitz Mansour).** *There is an algorithm* **FCExact** *such that, given* $\delta > 0$ *and access to* $EX(f, \mathcal{U})$ *for any decision tree* $f$ *of depth* $O(\log n)$, *with probability at least* $1 - \delta$ **FCExact**$(n, \delta, EX(f, \mathcal{U}))$ *computes all of the first-order Fourier coefficients of* $f$ *exactly in time* $poly(n, \log(1/\delta))$.

For our algorithm we will need uniform random examples which are labeled not only according to the original tree $f$, but also according to certain subtrees obtained by restricting a subset of the variables of $f$. Each such subset will lie along a root-to-leaf path in $f$ and—since we consider only trees of depth $O(\log n)$—will therefore have cardinality $O(\log n)$. We can simulate exactly an example oracle for such a restricted $f'$ given an oracle $EX(f, \mathcal{U})$ by simply drawing examples from $EX(f, \mathcal{U})$ until we obtain one that satisfies the restriction on the $O(\log n)$ variables. Since each example from $EX(f, \mathcal{U})$ will satisfy such a restriction with probability $1/poly(n)$, the probability of failing to obtain such an example after $poly(n)$ many draws from $EX(f, \mathcal{U})$ can be made exponentially small. Thus the simulation of these subtree oracles is both exact and efficient. We will use $EX(f', \mathcal{U})$ to represent the simulated oracle for a restriction $f'$.

## 4    The Algorithm for Learning Random Decision Trees

Our algorithm for learning random decision trees (Figure 1) operates in two phases. In the first phase (lines 4-11) the algorithm uses the Fourier properties outlined above to find a root-like variable for the original tree. (Informally, a root-like variable has the property that it can be taken as the root of the tree without increasing the depth of the tree; we give precise definitions later.) Once this is done, it recursively finds a good root for each of the two subtrees induced by this root, and so on. The process stops at depth $d - \frac{1}{2} \log n$, so when it stops there are at most $2^d/\sqrt{n}$ subtrees remaining, each of depth at most $\frac{1}{2} \log n$. (Recall that w.l.o.g. we may assume the algorithm knows the exact value of $d$.) In the second phase (lines 1-3) we employ an algorithm **UnikDTLearn**$(n, \epsilon, \delta, EX(T, \mathcal{U}))$ due to Hancock [6] to learn these remaining "shallow" decision trees.

**LearnTree**$(n, d, \delta, \epsilon, EX(T, \mathcal{U}))$

1.    **if** $d \leq (\frac{1}{2} \log n)$
2.        **return UnikDTLearn**$(n, \epsilon, \delta, EX(T, \mathcal{U}))$
3.    **endif**
4.    **for** $i = 1 \ldots n$
5.        **for** $b = -1, 1$
6.            Call **FCExact**$(n - 1, \delta/(4n^2), EX(T_{x_i \leftarrow b}, \mathcal{U}))$ to compute
                $\widehat{T_{x_i \leftarrow b}}(e_j)$ for all $j \neq i$
7.        **endfor**
8.        **if** none of the coefficients $\widehat{T_{x_i \leftarrow b}}(e_j)$ is odd
9.            **return** tree consisting of root $x_i$ and children defined by
                **LearnTree**$(n - 1, d - 1, \delta/4, \epsilon, EX(T_{x_i \leftarrow b}), \mathcal{U})$ for $b \in \{-1, 1\}$.
10.      **endif**
11.    **endfor**
12.    **return** "fail"

**Fig. 1.** Algorithm for learning random decision trees.

The intuition underlying the algorithm is that at each step in the first phase, each of the two subtrees of the root $x_i$ of a decision tree $T$ will obviously have depth at least one less than that of the original tree. These subtrees will therefore contain no odd first-order Fourier coefficients by Corollary 2, and thus the root $x_i$ will pass the test at line 8. On the other hand, we will show that in our random decision tree models, if we consider a variable $x_j$ which is not the root (or, more accurately, is not root-like in a sense defined below) then projecting on $x_j$ will result in at least one projection containing odd first-order coefficients. (This will follow from our earlier Fourier analysis of decision trees plus some combinatorial arguments showing that if $x_j$ is not root-like, then with very high probability the trees resulting from restricting on $x_j$ will have an $\omega(\log n)$ size collection $C$ of pre-leaves as in Lemma 1.) Furthermore, we will argue in section 6 that Hancock's **UnikDTLearn** efficiently learns random trees of depth at most $\frac{1}{2} \log n$, so **LearnTree** clearly runs in time poly$(n)$ for any value $d = O(\log n)$. The rest of this paper shows that the algorithm with high probability outputs an accurate decision tree for the complete random tree model $\mathcal{T}_{d,n}^C$.

## 5  Bottlenecks and Recursing the Algorithm

The first phase of our algorithm attempts to recursively select the root of the original tree $T$ and its subtrees. One obvious difficulty is that there may be a tree $T'$ that computes the same function as $T$ and that has the same depth but that has a different root variable; consider any tree representing $x_1 \oplus x_2$, for example. We will therefore be content with finding any of a set of "root-like" variables of $T$, which we call *bottlenecks*:

**Definition 1.** *A variable* $x_i$ *is a* bottleneck *for a decision tree* $T$ *if* $T$ *is non-trivial and* $x_i$ *occurs on every root-to-leaf path in* $T$.

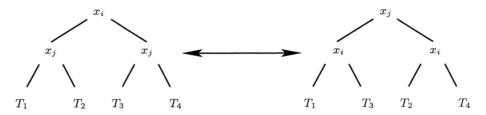

**Fig. 2.** Replacing the left structure by the right structure, or vice versa, is a swap.

Clearly the variable labeling the root is a bottleneck for any tree. We note that if $x_i$ is the root of a tree $T$, then a variable $x_j \neq x_i$ is a bottleneck in $T$ if and only if $x_j$ is a bottleneck in both the left and right subtrees of $T$. Notice also that if a bottleneck variable is chosen as the root at each stage of the recursion and **FCExact** returns accurate values for all first-order Fourier coefficients then at every stage any bottleneck variable will pass the test at line 8 of **LearnTree**.

In later sections we will show that for a random tree $T$ drawn from $\mathcal{T}_{d,n}^C$, any non-bottleneck variable will with very high probability not pass the test of line 8. Thus each recursive call of **LearnTree** is performed by restricting on some bottleneck variable; however, the bottleneck may or may not be the root. If the root is the bottleneck chosen, then it is easy to see that each of the two subtrees will be drawn from $\mathcal{T}_{d-1,n-1}^C$ (over a suitable set of $n-1$ variables) as desired, and the inductive assumption of **LearnTree** (that the tree it is given is drawn from $\mathcal{T}_{d,n}^C$) will be valid. If a non-root bottleneck is chosen, however, it is not *a priori* clear that the two resulting subfunctions for the recursive call correspond to draws from $\mathcal{T}_{d-1,n-1}^C$.

We now show that as long as any bottleneck is chosen, the two resulting subfunctions do indeed correspond to draws from $\mathcal{T}_{d-1,n-1}^C$. While the two draws are not independent of each other, this does not negatively impact the algorithm.

We say that two decision trees $T$ and $T'$ are *structurally equivalent* if $T'$ can be obtained from $T$ by performing a sequence of "swaps" of subtrees, where a swap is a replacement of one subtree by another subtree as shown in Figure 2. Note that if two trees are structurally equivalent then they compute the same function and have the same depth. The following lemma, which can be proved inductively (omitted due to space limitations), shows that any bottleneck variable can be swapped to the root of a tree in a way that preserves structural equivalence.

**Lemma 2.** *Let $T$ be any decision tree. If variable $x_i$ is a bottleneck for $T$, then there is a tree $T'$ having $x_i$ at its root that is structurally equivalent to $T$.*

Let $\mathcal{T}_{d,n}^i$ be the induced distribution over trees obtained by restricting $\mathcal{T}_{d,n}^C$ to trees for which $x_i$ is a bottleneck, and let $\mathcal{T}_{d,n}^{\tilde{i}}$ be the distribution over trees obtained by first selecting a tree $T$ according to $\mathcal{T}_{d,n}^i$ and then performing a minimal sequence of swap operations (implicit in the proof Lemma 2) to produce a structurally equivalent $\tilde{T}$ having $x_i$ as its root. Finally, let $\mathcal{T}_{d-1,n-1}^{-1}$ (resp. $\mathcal{T}_{d-1,n-1}^1$) represent the distribution over trees corresponding to a random variable that selects a tree $\tilde{T}$ according to $\mathcal{T}^{\tilde{i}}_{d,n}$ and then returns the left (resp. right) subtree as the value of the random variable. Then for the complete model, it suffices to prove the following lemma:

**Lemma 3.** *Let* $\mathcal{T}^i_{d,n}$, $\mathcal{T}^{-1}_{d-1,n-1}$ *and* $\mathcal{T}^1_{d-1,n-1}$ *be as defined above. Then for all* $1 \leq i, d \leq n$, $\mathcal{T}^{-1}_{d-1,n-1}$ *and* $\mathcal{T}^1_{d-1,n-1}$ *are both identical to* $\mathcal{T}^C_{d-1,n-1}$.

*Proof.* The proof is by induction on $d$. For the base case $d = 1$, any tree $T$ drawn from $\mathcal{T}^i_{1,n}$ either has $x_i$ at the root or some other variable $x_j$ at the root and $x_i$ as the root of both children of $x_j$. In either case, the corresponding tree $\tilde{T}$ of the process defining $\mathcal{T}^{\tilde{i}}_{1,n}$ will have $x_i$ at the root with two depth 0 children. It is easy to see that, over random draws from $\mathcal{T}^{\tilde{i}}_{1,n}$, the root variables of these children of $x_i$ are each uniformly distributed over the $n-1$ variables excluding $x_i$ (although the distributions of these root variables are not necessarily independent). The values of the leaves are also uniformly and independently distributed. Therefore, the base case has been shown.

For the inductive case, consider a tree $T$ drawn from $\mathcal{T}^i_{d,n}$, for fixed $d > 1$. Since $x_i$ must be a bottleneck in $T$, it is either the root of $T$ or is a bottleneck in both children of the root of $T$. If $x_i$ is the root of $T$, the lemma obviously holds. So we are left with the case in which some variable $x_j$—uniformly chosen from the $n-1$ variables excluding $x_i$—labels the root of $T$ and $x_i$ is a bottleneck in both children of $x_j$. Let $T_{-1}$ ($T_1$) represent the left (right) subtree of $T$, and let $\tilde{T}_{-1}$ ($\tilde{T}_1$) represent the tree obtained by swapping $x_i$ to the root of $T_{-1}$ ($T_1$). Since $x_i$ is a bottleneck in $T_{-1}$ ($T_1$), the children of $x_i$ in $\tilde{T}_{-1}$ ($\tilde{T}_1$) are drawn from $\mathcal{T}^C_{d-2,n-2}$, by the inductive hypothesis[2]. Notice also that, although the distribution over each child of $x_i$ in $\tilde{T}_{-1}$ may be dependent on its sibling's distribution, each is independent of both of the distributions over children of $x_i$ in $\tilde{T}_1$. Therefore, after performing a final swap of the $x_i$'s at the roots of $\tilde{T}_{-1}$ and $\tilde{T}_1$ with the root $x_j$ of $T$, we obtain a tree $\tilde{T}$ in which each child of the root $x_i$ is a tree rooted at uniformly (over $n-1$ variables) chosen $x_j$ and in which the children of $x_j$ are independently distributed according to $\mathcal{T}^C_{d-2,n-2}$. That is, each child of $x_i$ in $\tilde{T}$ is distributed according to $\mathcal{T}^C_{d-1,n-1}$. Since $\tilde{T}$ is by construction distributed according to $\mathcal{T}^{\tilde{i}}_{d,n}$, the lemma follows.                                              $\square$

It remains to show that **LearnTree** will with high probability choose a bottleneck at each stage of the recursion in the first phase, and that Hancock's algorithm can be used to efficiently learn $\mathcal{T}^C_{d,n}$-random trees of depth $\frac{1}{2} \log n$ with high probability. We address the second point first in the next section.

---

[2] Strictly speaking, the children of $x_i$ are fixed for any given $T$. What we are actually claiming here is that over draws of $T$ from $\mathcal{T}^i_{d,n}$, for fixed $d > 1$, the children of $x_i$ in $\tilde{T}_{-1}$ are distributed according to $\mathcal{T}^C_{d-2,n-2}$. But for ease of exposition, here and below we often blur the distinction between a single tree produced by one application of a random process defining a distribution over trees and the distribution itself.

# 6   Learning Random ($\frac{1}{2} \log n$)-Depth Trees

We stop the recursion in **LearnTree** at depth $\frac{1}{2} \log n$ because our analysis depends on trees being somewhat deep. So we use another method for learning random trees of depth less than $\frac{1}{2} \log n$, which is based on the following lemma plus the **UnikDTLearn** algorithm due to Hancock [6].

Recall that a decision tree $T$ is *read-k* if each variable labels at most $k$ nodes in $T$. The following lemma is easily proved (proof omitted due to space):

**Lemma 4.** *Let $r = ((1 - \epsilon) \log n) - 2$ for some constant $\epsilon > 0$. Let $C$ be any constant. Then we have $\Pr_{T \in \mathcal{T}_{r,n}^C}[T$ is not read-$k] \leq 1/n^C$ for $k = (C+2)/\epsilon$.*

Thus, if $r = (\frac{1}{2} \log n)$, then for any constant $C$ we may take $k = 8C + 16$, and with probability at least $1 - \frac{4}{(n-2)^C}$ a tree $T$ drawn from $\mathcal{T}_{d,n}^C$ is read-$k$ (since each of the four subtrees of depth $r - 2$ is not read-$(2C + 4)$ with probability at most $1/(n - 2)^C$).

Hancock [6] has given an algorithm **UnikDTLearn** and shown that it (or more precisely, a version which takes $k$ as an input along with the parameters given earlier) efficiently learns read-$k$ trees with respect to the uniform distribution, producing a decision tree (not necessarily read-$k$) as its hypothesis. Given any constant $k$, his algorithm terminates in time polynomial in $n$, $1/\epsilon$, and $1/\delta$, regardless of whether or not the target function $f$ is actually a read-$k$ decision tree. So our version of **UnikDTLearn**$(n, \epsilon, \delta, EX(T, \mathcal{U}))$ will begin by finding the smallest integer $C$ such that $1/n^C \leq \delta/2$. If the $\delta$ originally provided to **LearnTree** is inverse polynomial in $n$, then this value $C$ will be a constant independent of $n$. Taking $k = 8C + 16$, this means that the target function provided to **UnikDTLearn** is a read-$k$ decision tree with probability at least $1 - \delta/2$. Then running Hancock's original **UnikDTLearn** with this value of $k$ and with $\delta/2$ as the confidence parameter will succeed at learning an $\epsilon$-approximating tree with probability at least $1 - \delta/2$, for an overall success probability at the bottom of the recursion of $1 - \delta$. In short, we have the following:

**Lemma 5.** *If the oracle $EX(T, \mathcal{U})$ in the call to **UnikDTLearn** in **LearnTree** represents a tree $T$ distributed according to $\mathcal{T}_{d,n}^C$, then **UnikDTLearn** returns a decision tree that $\epsilon$-approximates $T$ with probability (over the random choice of $T$ and the randomness in $EX(T, \mathcal{U})$) at least $1 - \delta$.*

It remains to show that the first stage of the algorithm successfully finds a bottleneck variable with high probability given a decision tree drawn at random according to one of our tree models and with depth at least $\frac{1}{2} \log n$. Throughout the rest of the paper we thus have $d = \Theta(\log n), d \geq \frac{1}{2} \log n$.

# 7   Identifying Bottlenecks in the Complete Model $\mathcal{T}_{d,n}^C$

Since we have already shown that any bottleneck makes an equally good root in the hypothesis, and since it is easily seen that all bottlenecks (including the root of $T$) will pass the test at line 8 of **LearnTree**, it remains to show the following: for each $i = 1, \ldots, n$, if $x_i$ is *not* a bottleneck in a random tree $T$ then the probability that $x_i$ passes the test in line 8 is negligibly small.

Our general plan of attack is as follows: we will prove that if $x_1$ is *not* a bottleneck, then with $1 - \frac{1}{n^{\omega(1)}}$ probability there are many root-to-leaf paths in $T$ that do not include $x_1$. We then argue that, conditioned on there being many such paths, among these pre-leaves there is a collection $C$ satisfying the condition of Lemma 1 which has $|C| = \omega(\log n)$. Combining this with the Fourier properties of random decision trees derived earlier gives us our result.

More precisely, the argument is as follows. Let $S$ be a random variable which denotes the number of $x_1$-free paths from the root to a pre-leaf in $T \in \mathcal{T}_{d,n}^C$. (Note that each such path ends at a depth-$d$ pre-leaf since we are in the complete model. Note also that $S > 0$ iff $x_1$ is not a bottleneck). We will prove the following lemmas in Appendix A.

**Lemma 6.** *For* $0 \leq d \leq n - 1$, $\Pr_{T \in \mathcal{T}_{d,n}^C}[S = 0] \leq \frac{1}{n-d}$.

**Lemma 7.** *For any value* $1 \leq k \leq (\log n)^{3/2}$ *we have* $\Pr[S = k] = 1/n^{\omega(1)}$.

**Lemma 8.** *Let* $T$ *be drawn from* $\mathcal{T}_{d,n}^C$ *conditioned on its having some set of* $(\log n)^{3/2}$ *pre-leaves at depth* $d$, *each of which has no* $x_1$-*labeled node as an ancestor. Then with probability* $1 - 1/n^{\omega(1)}$ *there is a set* $C$ *of* $(\log n)^{5/4}$ *pre-leaves at depth* $d$, *each labeled with a distinct variable, each of which has no ancestor labeled with* $x_1$ *or with a variable that labels any element of* $C$.

From these lemmas it is easy to prove that each non-bottleneck will pass the test at line 8 with negligible probability:

**Theorem 1.** *Let* $T \in \mathcal{T}_{d,n}^C$ *where* $d = \Theta(\log n), d \geq \frac{1}{2}\log n$. *If* $x_1$ *is not a bottleneck then the probability that* $x_1$ *passes the test in line 8 is* $1/n^{\omega(1)}$.

*Proof.* Since $S = 0$ iff $x_1$ is a bottleneck, we have

$$\Pr_{T \in \mathcal{T}_{d,n}^C}[S < (\log n)^{3/2} \mid x_1 \text{ is not a bottleneck}] = \frac{\Pr[S < (\log n)^{3/2} \ \& \ S > 0]}{\Pr[S > 0]}$$

$$= \frac{\Pr[1 \leq S < (\log n)^{3/2}]}{\Pr[S > 0]}$$

$$= 1/n^{\omega(1)}$$

where the last equality follows from Lemmas 6 and 7. Thus we may assume that $S \geq (\log n)^{3/2}$. Lemma 8 now implies that there is a set $C$ of $(\log n)^{5/4}$ pre-leaves with the stated properties. Now we observe that if a pre-leaf belongs to $C$, then under any restriction $x_1 \leftarrow b$, the pre-leaf will still occur at depth $d$ with the desired property (that no variable labeling any node of $C$ occurs as an ancestor of any node of $C$) in the tree resulting from the restriction. Thus by Lemma 1, the probability that all variables labeling nodes in $C$ have even coefficients in the restricted tree is at most $1/2^{(\log n)^{5/4}} = 1/n^{\omega(1)}$. Hence $x_1$ passes the test at line 8 with negligible probability and the theorem is proved.     $\square$

Combined with our earlier remarks, this establishes

**Theorem 2.** *For any $d = O(\log n)$, any polynomial $p(\cdot)$, any $\delta > 1/p(n)$, and any $\epsilon > 0$, algorithm* **LearnTree** *will with probability at least $1 - \delta$ (over a random choice of tree $T$ from $\mathcal{T}_{d,n}^C$ and the randomness of the example oracle) produce a hypothesis decision tree $T'$ that $\epsilon$-approximates the target with respect to the uniform distribution.* **LearnTree** *runs in time polynomial in $n$ and $1/\epsilon$.*

*Proof.* By Lemma 5, the base case of the algorithm will succeed with probability at least $1-\delta$ as long as it is run on a tree drawn from $\mathcal{T}_{c,n}^C$ for some $c \leq \frac{1}{2} \log n$. In the recursive phase, all first-order Fourier coefficients will be computed exactly with probability at least $1 - \delta/4$. Furthermore, assuming that the coefficients are correctly computed, every bottleneck variable will pass the test at line 8 of **LearnTree**, and by the preceding theorem the probability is negligible that any non-bottleneck variable will pass this test. Thus, in the recursive phase of the algorithm, with probability at least $1-\delta/4$ a bottleneck variable will be chosen by the test. By the arguments of Section 5, if the initial tree is distributed according to $\mathcal{T}_{d-k,n-k}^C$ then the two functions obtained by restricting on either value of this bottleneck variable will both be distributed according to $\mathcal{T}_{d-k-1,n-k-1}^C$. Therefore, the two recursive calls to **LearnTree** will succeed with probability at least $1 - \delta/2$, so that overall the recursive phase succeeds with probability at least $1 - \delta$. Furthermore, it is easy to see that the tree returned by the recursive phase will be an $\epsilon$-approximator to the target if each of the subtrees returned by the recursive call is an $\epsilon$-approximator. Finally, for $d = O(\log n)$, the number of recursive calls is clearly polynomially bounded, and thus the algorithm runs in the time claimed given the previously mentioned bounds on **UnikDTLearn** and **FCExact**. $\qquad\square$

## 8  Conclusions and Future Work

We have given positive results for learning several natural models of random log-depth decision trees under uniform. Many interesting questions remain about related models of average case learning:

- Can similar results be established for natural models of random decision trees of polynomial size (as opposed to logarithmic depth)?
- Can similar results be established for random monotone DNF?
- Can our results be extended to learning under broader classes of distributions, either over examples or over trees?

It seems possible that progress in these directions could eventually lead to useful practical algorithms.

## References

1. A. Blum. Rank-$r$ decision trees are a subclass of $r$-decision lists. *Information Processing Letters*, 42(4):183–185, 1992.

2. A. Blum, M. Furst, J. Jackson, M. Kearns, Y. Mansour, and S. Rudich. Weakly learning DNF and characterizing statistical query learning using Fourier analysis. In *Proceedings of the 26th Annual ACM Symposium on Theory of Computing*, pages 253–262, 1994.
3. L. Breiman, J. Friedman, R. Olshen, and C. Stone. *Classification of Regression Trees*. Wadsworth, 1984.
4. N. Bshouty. Exact learning boolean functions via the monotone theory. *Information and Computation*, 123(1):146–153, 1995.
5. A. Ehrenfeucht and D. Haussler. Learning decision trees from random examples. *Information and Computation*, 82(3):231–246, 1989.
6. T. Hancock. Learning $k\mu$ decision trees on the uniform distribution. In *Proceedings of the Sixth Annual Conference on Computational Learning Theory*, pages 352–360, 1993.
7. E. Kushilevitz and Y. Mansour. Learning decision trees using the Fourier spectrum. *SIAM J. on Computing*, 22(6):1331–1348, 1993.
8. J. Quinlan. *C4.5: Programs for Machine Learning*. Morgan Kaufmann, 1993.

# A    Proofs of Lemmas 6, 7, and 8

We first prove Lemma 6. Let us write $p_{d,n}$ to denote the probability that $S = 0$ for a random $T$ drawn from $\mathcal{T}_{d,n}^C$, i.e. $p_{d,n} = \Pr_{T \in \mathcal{T}_{d,n}^C}[x_1 \text{ is a bottleneck in } T]$. Lemma 6 follows directly from the following:

**Proposition 1.** *For $0 \leq d \leq n-1$ we have $p_{d,n} \leq \frac{1}{n-d}$.*

*Proof.* Clearly $p_{0,n} = \frac{1}{n}$. For $d \geq 1, n \geq 1$ we have $p_{d,n} = \frac{1}{n} + \frac{n-1}{n}(p_{d-1,n-1})^2$. This is because with probability $1/n$ the root is $x_1$. With probability $\frac{n-1}{n}$ the root is some $x_j \neq x_1$ in which case each of the subtrees of the root is drawn from $\mathcal{T}_{d-1,n-1}^C$, and $x_1$ is a bottleneck iff it is a bottleneck in each of these two subtrees.

Fix any $m > 0$. We prove that for all $d \geq 0$ we have $p_{d,d+m} \leq \frac{1}{m}$; the proof is by induction on $d$. The base case holds since $p_{0,m} = \frac{1}{m}$. For the induction step, we have

$$p_{d+1,d+m+1} = \frac{1}{d+m+1} + \frac{d+m}{d+m+1}(p_{d,d+m})^2$$

$$\leq \frac{1}{d+m+1} + \frac{d+m}{d+m+1}\left(\frac{1}{m}\right)^2 = \frac{m^2+m+d}{m^2(m+d+1)}.$$

This is at most $1/m$ iff $m^3 + dm + m^2 \leq m^3 + dm^2 + m^2$ which is true since $m \geq 1$, so the proposition is proved. $\square$

We will prove Lemma 7 in a moment using using Lemma 9 below. First, a definition and some introductory analysis.

Let $p_{k,d,n}$ denote $\Pr_{T \in \mathcal{T}_{d,n}^C}[S = k]$. For $k \geq 1$ and $d \geq 1$ we have

$$p_{k,d,n} = \frac{n-1}{n}\sum_{i=0}^{k} p_{i,d-1,n-1}p_{k-i,d-1,n-1}. \tag{1}$$

To see this, note that there are exactly $k$ $x_1$-free root-to-preleaf paths in $T$ iff (1) the root is some variable other than $x_1$, and (2) the left and right subtrees (each of which is drawn from $\mathcal{T}^C_{d-1,n-1}$) have $i$ and $k-i$ $x_1$-free root-to-preleaf paths, respectively, for some $0 \le i \le k$. For the base cases, we have $p_{c,0,n} = 0$ for $c \ge 2$ since it is impossible to have two paths to pre-leaves in a tree of depth 0. $p_{1,0,n} = \frac{n-1}{n}$ since there is exactly one $x_1$-free path as long as the root is not $x_1$. $p_{0,0,n} = \frac{1}{n}$ by the same reasoning. Finally, $p_{0,d,n} \le \frac{1}{n-d}$ by Lemma 6.

The following lemma is proved in section A.1:

**Lemma 9.** *Let $c = \Theta(\log n)$, $c \ge \frac{3}{8} \log n$ and $\ell \le poly(n)$. Then*

$$p_{\ell,c,n} \le t(n) + \sum_{j=1}^{(\log n)^{1/3}} \sum_{i=(1/4)\log n+1}^{\ell-(1/4)\log n-1} p_{i,c-j,n-j} \qquad (2)$$

*where $t(n) = 1/n^{\omega(1)}$.*

*Proof of Lemma 7.* Recall that $k \le (\log n)^{3/2}$, $d = \Theta(\log n)$ and $d \ge \frac{1}{2} \log n$. By Lemma 9 we have

$$p_{k,d,n} \le t(n) + \sum_{j=1}^{(\log n)^{1/3}} \sum_{i=(1/4)\log n+1}^{k-(1/4)\log n-1} p_{i,d-j,n-j} \qquad (3)$$

We now repeatedly apply Lemma 9 to the right-hand side of inequality (3). The key observation is that each time we apply Lemma 9 to bound some $p_{\ell,c,n'}$ by the right side of (2), the first subscript ($\ell$) decreases by at least $\frac{1}{4} \log n$ in every new occurrence of $p_{.,.,.}$. Hence the "depth" of this repeated replacement will be at most $4(\log n)^{1/2}$ (since $k \le (\log n)^{3/2}$), at which point the summation over $i$ in the right hand side of (2) will be empty.

We now observe that each application of Lemma 9 replaces one $p_{.,.,.}$ with at most $(\log n)^{1/3} \cdot (\log n)^{3/2} < (\log n)^2$ new $p_{.,.,.}$'s. Since the replacement depth is at most $4(\log n)^{1/2}$ and $t(n) = 1/n^{\omega(1)}$, it follows that

$$p_{k,d,n} \le \frac{1}{n^{\omega(1)}} \cdot \left((\log n)^2\right)^{4(\log n)^{1/2}} = \frac{1}{n^{\omega(1)}} \cdot 2^{8(\log n)^{1/2} \log\log n} = \frac{1}{n^{\omega(1)}}$$

and Lemma 7 is proved. $\qquad \square$

Now we prove Lemma 8.

*Proof of Lemma 8.* Fix any set $R$ of $(\log n)^{3/2}$ pre-leaf nodes in a complete binary tree structure of depth $d$. Fix any non-redundant labeling of all of the ancestors of all of these pre-leaves which does not use $x_1$ anywhere. Now each labeling of the nodes in $R$ which does not use $x_1$ and maintains non-redundancy is equally likely under the conditioning of the lemma. Note that for each node in $R$ there are $n - d - 1$ legal labelings (since the label must not use $x_1$ or any of the $d$ ancestors of the node).

Consider a random legal labeling of the nodes in $R$. Partition the nodes of $R$ into $(\log n)^{5/4}$ disjoint subsets $R_1, \ldots, R_{(\log n)^{5/4}}$ each of size $(\log n)^{1/4}$. Let

$F$ denote a set of "forbidden" labels; initially $F$ is the set of all variables which label ancestors of nodes in $R$ (plus $x_1$). Let $F_0$ denote the size of this initial set, so initially we have $|F| = F_0 \leq 1 + d(\log n)^{3/2} = O((\log n)^{5/2})$. We consider the subsets $R_1, \ldots$ in turn. The probability that every node in $R_1$ is assigned a forbidden label is at most $\left(\frac{F_0}{n-d-1}\right)^{(\log n)^{1/4}} = 1/n^{\omega(1)}$. Thus we may suppose that there is some pre-leaf $v_1 \in R_1$ which receives a non-forbidden label; we add this label to $F$. Now the probability that every node in $R_2$ receives a forbidden label is at most $\left(\frac{F_0+1}{n-d-1}\right)^{(\log n)^{1/4}} = 1/n^{\omega(1)}$, so we may suppose that there is some pre-leaf $v_2 \in R_2$ which receives a non-forbidden label; we add this label to $F$. Continuing in this fashion for $(\log n)^{5/4}$ steps, and noting that $|F|$ never exceeds $O((\log n)^{5/2})$, we have that with probability $1 - 1/n^{\omega(1)}$ there is a set $v_1, \ldots, v_{(\log n)^{5/4}}$ of nodes each of which receives a non-forbidden label. This set is easily seen to satisfy the desired conditions for $C$. $\qquad\square$

## A.1    Proof of Lemma 9

Our proof of Lemma 9 will use the following intermediate lemma. Note that we allow a slightly weaker bound on $d$ than usual in this lemma; we will need this slightly weaker bound later.

**Lemma 10.** *For any value $1 \leq k \leq \frac{1}{4}\log n$ and any value $d \geq \frac{1}{3}\log n$ we have* $p_{k,d,n} = \Pr_{T \in \mathcal{T}_{d,n}^C}[S = k] = 1/n^{\omega(1)}.$

*Proof.* We first consider the case $k = 1$. There are exactly $2^d$ possible locations (pre-leaves) where an $x_1$-free path from the root to a pre-leaf could end. Consider any such location. In order for this to be the only $x_1$-free path to a pre-leaf in $T$, it must be the case that every node on this path (except the root) has the property that the subtree rooted at its sibling has $x_1$ as a bottleneck. These $d$ subtrees are clearly disjoint; the one at depth $\ell$ is drawn from $\mathcal{T}_{d-\ell,n-\ell}^C$ (over a suitable set of $n - \ell$ variables which includes $x_1$ since the path is $x_1$-free) and hence by Lemma 6 each subtree has $x_1$ as a bottleneck with probability at most $\frac{2}{n}$. Thus $\Pr[S = 1]$ is at most $2^d \cdot \left(\frac{2}{n}\right)^d = \left(\frac{4}{n}\right)^d$ which is $1/n^{\omega(1)}$ since $d \geq \frac{1}{3}\log n$.

The general case for any $1 \leq k \leq \frac{1}{4}\log n$ is similar. We use the following fact which we prove later:

**Fact 3** *Fix any set of $k$ root-to-preleaf paths in $T$. Let $N$ be the number of subtrees of $T$ which are rooted at an internal node and (1) are not rooted on any of these $k$ paths, but (2) have their parent on one of these $k$ paths. Then $N \geq d - \log k$.*

There are $\binom{2^d}{k}$ possible sets of $k$ pre-leaves where the $x_1$-free paths might end. As in the case $k = 1$, each subtree as in Fact 3 must have $x_1$ as a bottleneck, but as in the $k = 1$ case each such subtree has $x_1$ as a bottleneck with probability at most $2/n$. Thus the probability that $S = k$ is at most (by Fact 3)

$$\binom{2^d}{k} \cdot \left(\frac{2}{n}\right)^{d-\log k} \leq 2^{dk} \left(\frac{2}{n}\right)^{d-\log k} \leq n^{d/4} \cdot \left(\frac{2}{n}\right)^d \cdot n^{\log k} = n^{\log k} \left(\frac{2}{n^{3/4}}\right)^d,$$

where the second inequality uses $k \le \frac{1}{4}\log n$. This is $1/n^{\omega(1)}$ since $d \ge \frac{1}{3}\log n$ and $k \le \frac{1}{4}\log n$. $\qquad\square$

*Proof of Fact 3.* It is clear that there are exactly $2^d - k$ pre-leaves contained in the desired subtrees of $T$. Each subtree contains $2^i$ of these pre-leaves for some $i$, and clearly different subtrees have disjoint sets of pre-leaves. Since the binary representation of $2^d - k$ starts with $d - \log k$ ones, there must be at least $d - \log k$ such subtrees (it is impossible to add up $t$ powers of 2 and get a binary number with more than $t$ ones). $\qquad\square$

Now we prove Lemma 9. From the recursive equation (1) we have

$$p_{\ell,c,n} \le 2p_{0,c-1,n-1}p_{\ell,c-1,n-1} + \sum_{i=1}^{\ell-1} p_{i,c-1,n-1}p_{\ell-i,c-1,n-1}$$

$$\le \frac{4}{n}p_{\ell,c-1,n-1} + \sum_{i=1}^{\ell-1} p_{i,c-1,n-1}p_{\ell-i,c-1,n-1} \qquad (4)$$

where the last inequality holds (with room to spare) by Lemma 6 since $c = \Theta(\log n) < n/2$. Repeatedly applying (4) we have

$$p_{\ell,c,n} \le \left(\frac{4}{n}\right)^2 p_{\ell,c-2,n-2} + \frac{4}{n}\sum_{i=1}^{\ell-1} p_{i,c-2,n-2}p_{\ell-i,c-2,n-2}$$

$$+ \sum_{i=1}^{\ell-1} p_{i,c-1,n-1}p_{\ell-i,c-1,n-1}$$

$$\le \left(\frac{4}{n}\right)^c p_{\ell,0,n-c} + \sum_{j=1}^{c}\left(\frac{4}{n}\right)^{j-1}\sum_{i=1}^{\ell-1} p_{i,c-j,n-j}p_{\ell-i,c-j,n-j}.$$

Since each value $p_{\cdot,\cdot,\cdot}$ is a probability it is easy to see that for any value of $j$ the inner sum over $i$ is at most $\ell = \mathrm{poly}(n)$. Recalling that $c \ge \frac{3}{8}\log n$, we may truncate the sum over $j$ at (say) $(\log n)^{1/3}$ and thus have

$$p_{\ell,c,n} \le \frac{1}{n^{\omega(1)}} + \sum_{j=1}^{(\log n)^{1/3}}\sum_{i=1}^{\ell-1} p_{i,c-j,n-j}p_{\ell-i,c-j,n-j}$$

$$\le \frac{1}{n^{\omega(1)}} + \sum_{j=1}^{(\log n)^{1/3}}\left[2\sum_{i=1}^{(1/4)\log n} p_{i,c-j,n-j} + \sum_{i=(1/4)\log n+1}^{\ell-(1/4)\log n-1} p_{i,c-j,n-j}\right].$$

Since $c - (\log n)^{1/3}$ is at least $(1/3)\log n$, Lemma 10 implies that the first sum over $i$ inside the brackets is $1/n^{\omega(1)}$ for all $j = 1, \ldots, (\log n)^{1/3}$. We thus have

$$p_{\ell,c,n} \le \frac{1}{n^{\omega(1)}} + \sum_{j=1}^{(\log n)^{1/3}}\sum_{i=(1/4)\log n+1}^{\ell-(1/4)\log n-1} p_{i,c-j,n-j}$$

as desired, and Lemma 9 is proved.

# Projective DNF Formulae and Their Revision

Robert H. Sloan[1,*], Balázs Szörényi[2], and György Turán[3,*]

[1] U. of Illinois at Chicago
sloan@uic.edu
[2] U. of Szeged, Hungary
szorenyi@inf.u-szeged.hu
[3] U. of Illinois at Chicago and RGAI Hungarian Academy of Sciences
gyt@uic.edu

## 1 Introduction

Valiant argued that biology imposes various constraints on learnability, and, motivated by these constraints, introduced his model of *projection learning* [14]. Projection learning aims to learn a target concept over some large domain, in this paper $\{0, 1\}^n$, by learning some of its projections to a class of smaller domains, and combining these projections. Valiant proved a general mistake bound for the resulting algorithm under certain conditions. The basic assumption underlying projection learning is that there is a family of simple projections that cover all positive instances of the target, where simple means belonging to some efficiently learnable class. The projections describing the target in this way can also be thought of as a set of experts, each specialized to classify a subset of the instances, such that whenever two experts overlap they always agree in their classification.

Perhaps the most natural special case of this framework, also discussed by Valiant, is when the projection domains are subcubes of a fixed dimension, and the restrictions of the target to these domains are conjunctions. In this case, the algorithm learns a class of disjunctive normal forms (DNF) called *projective* DNF, which appears to be a new class of DNF expressions. As the learnability of DNF is a major open problem, it is of interest to identify new learnable subclasses and to understand their scope.

We give some basic properties of projective DNF by comparing them to standard classes such as DNF with terms of bounded size or with a bounded number of terms, and we present lower and upper bounds for the *exclusion dimension* of projective DNF. The exclusion dimension, or certificate size [1, 6, 7], of a concept class is a combinatorial parameter that is closely related to its learning complexity in the model of proper learning with equivalence and membership queries. Thus we obtain bounds for the complexity of learning projective DNF in this model. For the subclass of 1-projective DNF we prove a characterization theorem that gives an explicit description of all such expressions.

One of the main goals of Valiant's work is to find *attribute-efficient* learning algorithms. The notion of an attribute-efficient learning algorithm goes back to the seminal work of Littlestone [10]. His Winnow algorithm learns a (monotone)

---

* Partially supported by NSF grant CCR-0100336.

B. Schölkopf and M.K. Warmuth (Eds.): COLT/Kernel 2003, LNAI 2777, pp. 625–639, 2003.

disjunction of $k$ variables out of a total of $n$ variables with $O(k \log n)$ mistakes. Thus Winnow is very efficient for learning problems where there are many attributes but most of them are irrelevant. It is argued that learning in the brain, and also many real-life applications have exactly that property [14, 15]. In general, a learning algorithm is called attribute efficient if it has a mistake bound that is polynomial in the number of relevant variables, and only polylogarithmic in the total number of variables. One of the most attractive features of Valiant's projection learning algorithm is its attribute efficiency.

The apparently unrelated area of *theory revision* in machine learning is concerned with the revision, or correction, of an initial theory that is assumed to be a good approximation of a correct theory. A typical application of theory revision is the refinement of an initial version of a theory provided by a domain expert. In that context it is argued that a large and complex theory cannot be learned from scratch, but it is necessary to start with a reasonably close initial theory. The usual assumption of theory revision is that the correct theory can be obtained from the initial one by a small number of syntactic modifications, such as the deletion or the addition of a literal. An efficient revision algorithm is required to be polynomial in the number of literals that need to be modified and polylogarithmic in the total number of literals. Wrobel surveys the complete theory revision literature [16, 17]; efficient revision in the framework of learning with queries is discussed in detail in [4, 5].

Thus, the situation in theory revision is similar to the case of attribute-efficient learning, but instead of assuming that only a few literal occurrences are relevant, one assumes that only a few literal occurrences need to be modified. Roughly speaking, attribute efficient learning requires efficient revision of an empty initial formula. The argument for the biological relevance of attribute-efficient learning can be extended to apply to revision, for example, in the case of information hard-wired at birth.

In view of this relationship, it is an interesting general question whether attribute-efficient learnability results can be extended to results on efficient revision. Previously we gave a positive answer in the case of parity function, where the relationship between the two tasks is straightforward [4]. As a next step, we show here that Winnow is in fact an efficient algorithm for revising disjunctions as well. This in turn raises the question whether Valiant's more general results on the attribute-efficient learnability of projective DNF can also be extended to efficient revision. We show that projective DNF can be revised efficiently by using, just as Valiant does, the original Winnow algorithm on two levels. In our setting, the initial weights are adapted to the task of revision. The correctness proof uses a potential function argument.

We note that the problem of revising is somewhat related to the problem of tracking changing target concepts, which is discussed in several previous papers (see, e.g., [2, 12]). Compared to the model of tracking a changing target concept, our model is less general, as it assumes only a single change from an initial concept to the target. On the other hand, the tracking model starts from scratch, and thus, in order to simulate our setting, the initial formula (which may be large) has to be built up by adding all its relevant variables, and all these additions may enter into the mistake bound of the algorithm. Thus it appears that there is no direct implication between our results and those of Auer and Warmuth on tracking disjunctions [2].

After some preliminaries given in Section 2, Section 3 contains the definition of projective DNF and a discussion of some of their properties, and Section 4 contains the bounds for the exclusion dimension. The characterization of 1-PDNF is presented in Section 5. Section 6 contains the revision algorithms.

## 2    Preliminaries

The weight of $\mathbf{x} \in \{0,1\}^n$ is the number of its ones, denoted $|\mathbf{x}|$. The vector $\mathbf{e}_I^n$ is the characteristic vector of $I \subseteq [n]$, and the vector $\mathbf{g}_I^n$ is its componentwise complement ($[n] = \{1, \ldots, n\}$). The all 1's vector, $\mathbf{e}_{[n]}^n$, is written $\mathbf{1}$; the all 0's vector is written $\mathbf{0}$. For a Boolean function $f : \{0,1\}^n \to \{0,1\}$, we write $T(f) = \{\mathbf{x} \in \{0,1\}^n : f(\mathbf{x}) = 1\}$. For $\mathbf{x} = (x_1, \ldots, x_n), \mathbf{y} = (y_1, \ldots, y_n) \in \{0,1\}^n$ we write $\mathbf{x} \leq \mathbf{y}$ if $x_i \leq y_i$ for $1 \leq i \leq n$, and we write $\mathbf{x} \wedge \mathbf{y}$ (resp. $\mathbf{x} \vee \mathbf{y}$) for $(x_1 \wedge y_1, \ldots, x_n \wedge y_n)$ (resp. $(x_1 \vee y_1, \ldots, x_n \vee y_n)$).

A Boolean function $f$ is monotone if $\mathbf{x} \leq \mathbf{y}$ implies $f(\mathbf{x}) \leq f(\mathbf{y})$, it is a-unate if it holds that $g(\mathbf{x}) = f(\mathbf{x} \oplus \mathbf{a})$ is monotone, where $\mathbf{a} \in \{0,1\}^n$ and $\oplus$ is componentwise exclusive-or, and it is unate if it is a-unate for some $\mathbf{a} \in \{0,1\}^n$.

We use the standard model of *mistake bounded* learning [10], which proceeds in a sequence of *rounds* (or trials). In each round the learner receives an instance $\mathbf{x}$, and produces a prediction $\hat{y}$. Then the correct classification $y$ is revealed. If $\hat{y} \neq y$ then the learner made a *mistake*. The mistake bound of the learning algorithm is the maximal number of mistakes, taken over all possible runs, i.e., sequences of instances.

In addition to the standard mistake-bounded model, as a technical tool for the learning result, we also consider the more general model of learning monotone disjunctions with *attribute errors* (Auer and Warmuth [2], also used by Valiant [14] with a different name). In this model $y$ may *not* be the correct classification of $\mathbf{x}$. It is assumed that the error comes from some components of $\mathbf{x}$ being incorrect, and the number of attribute errors committed in a round is the minimal number of components that need to be changed in order to get the correct classification. More precisely, if in round $r$ the $y_r$ is not the correct classification of $\mathbf{x}_r$, and $y_r = 1$ then $AttrErr(r) = 1$, and if $y_r = 0$ then $AttrErr(r)$ is the number of variables, which are included in the target disjunction and which are set to 1 in $\mathbf{x}_r$. The total number of attribute errors for a given run, denoted $\#AttributeErrors$, is the sum of the attribute errors of the rounds.

For a conjunction (or term) $t$, we write $Lit(t)$ for the set of literals in $t$. A term is monotone if it consists of unnegated variables. Given $\mathbf{a} \in \{0,1\}^n$, a term is **a**-unate if every literal in it is unnegated iff the corresponding component of $\mathbf{a}$ is 0. A *subcube* (or simply *cube*) is any set of vectors that is of the form $T(t)$ for some conjunction (i.e., term) $t$. For terms $t_1, t_2$ it holds that $t_1 \to t_2$ iff $T(t_1) \subseteq T(t_2)$ iff $Lit(t_1) \supseteq Lit(t_2)$.

**Proposition 1** *A set $A \subseteq \{0,1\}^n$ is a cube iff for every $\mathbf{x}, \mathbf{y} \in A$ and every $\mathbf{z} \in \{0,1\}^n$ such that $\mathbf{x} \wedge \mathbf{y} \le \mathbf{z} \le \mathbf{x} \vee \mathbf{y}$, it also holds that $\mathbf{z} \in A$.*

It follows, in particular, that if a cube contains two vectors with weights $w_1 < w_2$, then it also contains vectors of weight $w$ for every $w_1 < w < w_2$.

## 3   Projective DNF

In this section we introduce projective disjunctive normal forms and we briefly discuss some of their properties.

**Definition 2** *A DNF formula $\varphi$ is a $k$-projective DNF, or $k$-PDNF if it is of the form*

$$\varphi = \rho_1 c_1 \vee \cdots \vee \rho_\ell c_\ell,$$

*where every $\rho_i$, referred to as a $k$-conjunction, is a conjunction of exactly $k$ literals, $c_i$ is a conjunction and for every $i$ it holds that*

$$\rho_i \varphi \equiv \rho_i c_i. \tag{1}$$

Note that in order to specify a $k$-PDNF, it is *not* sufficient to specify its terms, but for each term one has to specify its $\rho$-part and its $c$-part; that is, the projection and the corresponding conjunction have to be distinguished. If necessary, we indicate this distinction by placing a dot between the two parts. For example,

$$(x \cdot y) \vee (z \cdot y) \quad \text{and} \quad (x \cdot y) \vee (\bar{x} \cdot yz) \tag{2}$$

are two different 1-PDNF for the same function. The dots are omitted whenever this does not lead to confusion. The conjunctions $\rho_i$ and $c_i$ may have common literals in general. The requirement (1) is equivalent to requiring that $\rho_j \rho_i c_i \equiv \rho_i \rho_j c_j$ for every $i$ and $j$. This makes it easy to verify that a given expression, such as those in (2), is indeed a $k$-PDNF. It also shows that the disjunction of any set of terms of a $k$-PDNF is again a $k$-PDNF.

A function $f : \{0,1\}^n \to \{0,1\}$ is $k$-*projective* if it can be written as a $k$-PDNF formula. If a function is $k$-projective, then it is $k'$-projective for every $k'$ with $k \le k' \le n$. The class of $n$-variable $k$-projective functions is denoted by $k$-$\mathrm{PDNF}_n$.

We briefly discuss the relationship between projective DNF and some other standard classes. Let $k$-$\mathrm{DNF}_n$, resp. $K$-term-$\mathrm{DNF}_n$, denote the class of $n$-variable Boolean functions expressible as a DNF with all terms having size at most $k$, resp. with at most $K$ terms. Let $k$-$\mathrm{DL}_n$ denote the class of $k$-decision lists on $n$ variables [13].

**Proposition 3** *Assume $k < n$, and let $K = 2^k \binom{n}{k}$. Then*

$$k\text{-}DNF_n \subset k\text{-}PDNF_n \subset K\text{-}term\text{-}DNF_n.$$

**Proposition 4** *$k$-$PDNF_n \subset (k+1)$-$DL_n$.*

We also give some bounds for the number of $n$-variable $k$-projective functions. In view of Proposition 3, an upper bound is provided by the straightforward upper bound for the number of $K$-term DNF's. The exponent of the lower bound matches the exponent of the upper bound for every fixed $k$.

**Proposition 5**

$$3^{\lfloor \frac{n}{k+1} \rfloor (\lceil \frac{k}{k+1} n \rceil)} \leq |k\text{-}PDNF_n| \leq 3^{n\,2^k \binom{n}{k}}.$$

## 4   Exclusion Dimension

We present the definitions of specifying sets and the exclusion dimension for the case of $k$-projective functions, following the terminology of Angluin [1] ([6,7] use unique specification dimension and certificate size for the same notion).

Let $f$ be an $n$-variable Boolean function. A set $A \subseteq \{0,1\}^n$ is a *specifying set* of $f$ (with respect to the class of $k$-projective functions) if there is at most one $k$-projective function that agrees with $f$ on $A$. (So clearly $\{0,1\}^n$ is always a specifying set.) The *specifying set size* of $f$ is

$$spec(f) = \min\{|A| : A \text{ is a specifying set for } f\},$$

and the *exclusion dimension* of the class of $n$-variable $k$-projective functions is

$$XD(k\text{-}PDNF_n) = \max\{spec(f) : f \text{ is an } n\text{-variable non-}k\text{-projective function}\}.$$

A function $f$ is *minimally* non-$k$-projective if it is not $k$-projective, but any $f'$ with $T(f') \subset T(f)$ is $k$-projective.

**Proposition 6** *If $f$ is minimally non-$k$-projective, then $spec(f) \geq |T(f)| - 1$.*

We now present a lower and an upper bound for the exclusion dimension of $k\text{-}PDNF_n$, which show that for fixed $k$ the exclusion dimension is $\Theta(n^k)$. We begin with a lemma that characterizes $k$-PDNF, give some examples, and then continue to the main theorem of this section that gives the bound.

**Lemma 7** a) *A function $f$ is $k$-projective iff for every $\mathbf{x} \in T(f)$ there is a $k$-conjunction $\rho$ such that $\mathbf{x} \in T(\rho)$ and $T(f) \cap T(\rho)$ is a cube.*

   b) *If for every $\mathbf{x} \in T(f)$ there is a $k$-conjunction $\rho$ such that $T(f) \cap T(\rho) = \{\mathbf{x}\}$, then $f$ is $k$-projective.*

(Proof of lemma omitted due to space constraints.)

We illustrate Lemma 7 with the following example. We claim that the function $f(x_1, x_2, x_3, x_4) = x_1 x_2 \vee x_3 x_4$ is not 1-projective. Call a vector that violates condition (a) of the lemma *deviant*. It suffices to show that $\mathbf{1}$ is deviant. For symmetry reasons, we only need to show that $T(f) \cap T(x_1)$ is not a cube. Indeed, it contains 1100 and 1011, but it does not contain $1100 \wedge 1011 = 1001$.

**Proposition 8** *For every $k$ and $n \geq k+2$ there is a non-$k$-projective function with $|T(f)| = k+3$.*

**Theorem 9 a)** $XD(k\text{-}PDNF_n) \leq 3\binom{n}{k} + 1$.
**b)** *If $n \geq 4k(k+1)$, then $XD(k\text{-}PDNF_n) \geq \binom{\lfloor n/4 \rfloor}{k} - 1$.*

*Proof.* The upper bound follows directly from Lemma 7 and Proposition 1.

For the lower bound, in view of Proposition 6, it is sufficient to construct a minimally non-$k$-projective $n$-variable function $f_{n,k}$ that takes the value 1 at many points. First we describe the construction in the case when $n$ is even and $k = 1$. Let $n = 2s$, and let $T(f_{n,k}) = \{\mathbf{a}_i = (\mathbf{g}_i^s, \mathbf{e}_i^s) : i = 1, \ldots, s\} \cup \{\mathbf{0}\}$. We claim that $f_{n,k}$ is minimally non-1-projective. The non-1-projectivity of $f_{n,k}$ follows from the fact that $\mathbf{0}$ is deviant: any 1-projection $\rho$ containing $\mathbf{0}$ is of the form $\bar{x}_j$, and thus it contains some vector(s) $\mathbf{a}_i$, but it does not contain any vector of positive weight less than $s$. Thus, by the remark following Proposition 1, $T(f_{n,k}) \cap T(\rho)$ is not a cube. On the other hand, the $\mathbf{a}_i$'s are *not* deviant for $f_{n,k}$. This holds as they satisfy the condition of part *b)* of Lemma 7: the 1-conjunction $x_{s+i}$ contains only $\mathbf{a}_i$ from $T(f_{n,k})$. Now we show that every $f'$ with $T(f') \subset T(f_{n,k})$ is 1-projective. Indeed, if $f'(\mathbf{0}) = 0$ then this follows from part *b)* of Lemma 7 directly. Otherwise the only thing to note is that if $f'(\mathbf{a}_i) = 0$, then the 1-conjunction $\bar{x}_i$ contains only $\mathbf{0}$ from $T(f')$.

For the construction in the general case we use the following lemma. In the lemma we consider $\{0,1\}^p$ to be the $p$-dimensional vector space over $GF(2)$.

**Lemma 10** *Let $A$ be a $p \times p$ 0-1 matrix such that both $A$ and $A \oplus I$ are non-singular. Assume that $k(k+1) < 2^p$ and define the mapping*

$$h(b_1, \ldots, b_k) = (b_1 \oplus Ab, \ldots, b_k \oplus Ab),$$

*where $b_1, \ldots, b_k \in \{0,1\}^p$ and $b = b_1 \oplus \ldots \oplus b_k$. Then it holds that*
   a) *$h$ is a bijection,*
   b) *for every $b_1, \ldots, b_{k-1}$ and $c_1, \ldots, c_k$ there is a $b_k$ different from $b_1, \ldots, b_{k-1}$, such that the components of $h(b_1, \ldots, b_k)$ are all different from the $c_i$'s.*

(Proof of lemma omitted due to space constraints.)

It is easily verified that, for example, the matrix $A$ with all 0's except $a_{1,1} = a_{1,p} = a_{i,i+1} = 1$ (where $i = 2, \ldots, p-1$) satisfies the conditions of the lemma. It is clear from the definition of $h$ that if the $b_i$'s are all different, then the components of $h(b_1, \ldots, b_s)$ are also all different, and if we permute the $b_i$'s then the components of the image are permuted in the same way. Thus if $I = \{b_1, \ldots, b_k\} \subseteq \{0,1\}^p$, then with an abuse of notation we can write $h(I)$ for the $k$-element subset of $\{0,1\}^p$ formed by the components of $h(b_1, \ldots, b_k)$.

Now let $p = \lfloor \log \frac{n}{2} \rfloor$, and put $s = 2^p$. If $I$ is a $k$-element subset of $[s]$, define $\mathbf{a}_I = (\mathbf{g}_I^s, \mathbf{e}_{h(I)}^s, \mathbf{0}^{n-2s})$, and let $T(f_{n,k}) = \{\mathbf{a}_I : I \subseteq [s], |I| = k\} \cup \{\mathbf{0}\}$.

We claim that $f_{n,k}$ is minimally non-$k$-projective. This follows very similarly to the special case above.  $\square$

Using the results on the relation between the exclusion dimension and the complexity of learning with membership and proper equivalence queries $[1, 6, 7]$ we get the following.

**Proposition 11** *The class $k - PDNF_n$ can be learned with $O\left(n\, 2^k \binom{n}{k}^2\right)$ membership and proper equivalence queries.*

The number of queries is polynomial in $n$ for every fixed $k$. On the other hand, the running time of the learning algorithm is not necessarily polynomial.

Blum [3], using ideas from Littlestone and Helmbold et al. [8, 11], shows that 1-DL is efficiently learnable in the mistake-bounded model. It follows from a straightforward generalization of this result and Proposition 4 that for every fixed $k$, the class $k$-PDNF is learnable with polynomially many *improper* equivalence queries and with polynomial running time.

## 5   A Characterization of 1-PDNF

In this section we give a description of 1-projective functions. First let us note that if $\varphi$ is a 1-PDNF with two complementary projections, i.e., of the form $x t_1 \vee \bar{x} t_2 \vee \cdots$ for some variable $x$, then by deleting everything else besides these two terms, we get an equivalent formula. Indeed, as every $\mathbf{x}$ satisfying $\varphi$ satisfies either $x$ or $\bar{x}$, it follows from the definition of projective $DNF$ that $\mathbf{x}$ also satisfies the corresponding term.

We formulate a notion of irredundancy for 1-PDNF, which we call $p$-irredundancy to distinguish it from the usual notion of irredundancy for DNF. Unlike the standard notion, $p$-irredundancy of a 1-PDNF is easy to decide.

**Definition 12** *A 1-PDNF formula $\varphi = \rho_1 t_1 \vee \cdots \vee \rho_\ell t_\ell$ is $p$-irredundant if the following conditions hold:*

  *a) $Lit(\rho_i t_i) \nsubseteq Lit(\rho_j t_j)$ for every $1 \le i, j \le \ell$,*
  *b) $\rho_i \notin Lit(t_i)$ for every $1 \le i \le \ell$,*
  *c) if $\ell \ge 3$ then $\rho_i \ne \bar{\rho}_j$ for every $1 \le i, j \le \ell$.*

The first condition says that no term implies another, the second that in each term the projection and conjunction parts are disjoint, and the third that if there are at least three terms, then no two projections are complementary.

**Proposition 13** *There is a polynomial algorithm which, given a 1-projective DNF, transforms it into an equivalent $p$-irredundant 1-projective DNF.*

First we give a description of those $p$-irredundant 1-projective DNF that represent either a monotone or an **a**-unate function, and then we give the general description. We assume throughout this section that the 1-PDNF formulas in question are nonempty; thus they represent a function that is not identically 0.

**Theorem 14** *A formula $\varphi$ is a p-irredundant 1-PDNF formula representing a monotone (resp. $\mathbf{a}$-unate) function if and only if it is either of the form*

$$\varphi = \rho_1 t \vee \cdots \vee \rho_\ell t,$$

*where $\rho_1, \ldots, \rho_\ell$ are different unnegated variables (resp. literals whose signs agree with $\mathbf{a}$) not contained in $t$, and $t$ is a monotone (resp. $\mathbf{a}$-unate) term, or $t$ is of the form*

$$\varphi = \rho t \vee \bar{\rho} t t',$$

*where $\rho$ is an unnegated variable (resp. agrees with $\mathbf{a}$) and $t, t'$ are monotone (resp. $\mathbf{a}$-unate) terms not containing $\rho$ or $\bar{\rho}$.*

*Proof.* We prove only the monotone case, as the $\mathbf{a}$-unate case follows by considering the monotone function obtained by replacing $\mathbf{x}$ with $\mathbf{x} \oplus \mathbf{a}$. One direction of the theorem follows immediately from the definition of $p$-irredundancy.

Separating the negated and unnegated projections, let us write $\varphi$ as

$$\varphi = \bigvee_{i \in I} x_i t_i \vee \bigvee_{j \in J} \bar{x}_j t'_j.$$

As $\varphi(\mathbf{1}) = 1$, it must be the case that $I$ is nonempty. Also, as $\mathbf{1}$ is contained in every unnegated projection, projectivity implies that it satisfies every term $x_i t_i$ with $i \in I$, thus it must be the case that every $t_i$ is monotone. We claim that

$$T(\varphi) \subseteq T(t_i) \tag{3}$$

for every $i \in I$. Indeed, if $\varphi(\mathbf{x}) = 1$, then by monotonicity $\varphi(\mathbf{x}^{x_i=1}) = 1$, by projectivity $t_i(\mathbf{x}^{x_i=1}) = 1$, and by $b)$ of $p$-irredundancy $t_i(\mathbf{x}) = 1$. (Here $\mathbf{x}^{x_i=1}$ is $\mathbf{x}$ with its first component fixed to 1.)

Now consider any two terms $x_i t_i$ and $x_j t_j$ from $\varphi$. From (3) we get $T(x_i t_i) \subseteq T(\varphi) \subseteq T(t_j)$ and $T(x_j t_j) \subseteq T(\varphi) \subseteq T(t_i)$. Thus

$$Lit(t_j) \subseteq Lit(x_i t_i) \quad \text{and} \quad Lit(t_i) \subseteq Lit(x_j t_j). \tag{4}$$

However, $x_j \notin Lit(x_i t_i)$ and $x_i \notin Lit(x_j t_j)$, as otherwise using (4) it follows that $\varphi$ is $p$-redundant. But then $Lit(t_j) = Lit(t_i)$. Thus so far we know that $\varphi$ is of the form

$$\varphi = \bigvee_{i \in I} x_i t \vee \bigvee_{j \in J} \bar{x}_j t'_j,$$

where $I \neq \emptyset$. If $J = \emptyset$, we are done. Otherwise let us consider a term $\bar{x}_j t'_j$ with $j \in J$. By projectivity, $T(\bar{x}_j t'_j) = T(\bar{x}_j \varphi)$, and monotonicity implies that $t'_j$ is monotone. It follows from (3) that $T(\bar{x}_j t'_j) \subseteq T(\varphi) \subseteq T(t)$, thus $Lit(t) \subseteq Lit(\bar{x}_j t'_j)$, and so $Lit(t) \subseteq Lit(t'_j)$. Thus $\varphi$ can further be written as

$$\varphi = \bigvee_{i \in I} x_i t \vee \bigvee_{j \in J} \bar{x}_j t t''_j,$$

where now $I, J \neq \emptyset$ and $t, t_j''$ are monotone terms. If $|J| = 1$ and $I = J = \{i\}$ for some $i$, then we are done. Otherwise, there are terms $x_i t$ and $\bar{x}_j t t_j''$ in $\varphi$ such that $i \neq j$. Now $T(\bar{x}_j x_i t) = T(x_i \bar{x}_j t t_j'') \neq \emptyset$, and so either $t_j'' = x_i$ or $t_j''$ is the empty term. But $t_j'' = x_i$ would imply that $\varphi$ is $p$-redundant, thus $t_j''$ is the empty term. Hence $T(\bar{x}_j t) \subseteq T(\varphi)$, and by monotonicity $T(t) \subseteq T(\varphi)$. With (3) this implies $T(t) = T(\varphi)$. But then for every other term $\bar{x}_k t t_k''$ of $\varphi$ it holds that $T(\bar{x}_k t t_k'') = T(\bar{x}_k \varphi) = T(\bar{x}_k t)$, and so $t_k''$ is the empty term. Therefore

$$t \equiv \varphi = \bigvee_{i \in I} x_i t \vee \bigvee_{j \in J} \bar{x}_j t \equiv \left( \bigvee_{i \in I} x_i \vee \bigvee_{j \in J} \bar{x}_j \right) t.$$

This can only hold if some variable occurs both in $I$ and $J$, contradicting condition $c)$ of the $p$-irredundancy of $\varphi$.    $\square$

The example of (2) shows that the representation as a $p$-irredundant 1-PDNF is not always unique. Also, it is an interesting consequence of the theorem that there are 1-projective monotone functions, which cannot be expressed with monotone 1-projective DNF. Consider, for example the 1-PDNF

$$(x \cdot 1) \vee (\bar{x} \cdot yz),$$

representing the monotone function $x \vee yz$. If there is an equivalent monotone 1-PDNF, then it can be transformed into a monotone $p$-irredundant 1-PDNF, which must look like the first case in the theorem. But then the minimal true vectors must have Hamming distance at most 2, which is not the case for this function.

**Theorem 15** *A formula $\varphi$ is a p-irredundant 1-PDNF formula if and only if it is either of the form*

$$\varphi = \bigvee_{i=1}^{s} (\rho_1^i t_i \vee \cdots \vee \rho_{\ell_i}^i t_i),$$

*where $\rho_u^i \notin Lit(t_i)$ and $\bar{\rho}_u^j \in Lit(t_i)$ for every $i \neq j$ and $1 \leq u \leq \ell_j$, or it is of the form*

$$\varphi = xt \vee \bar{x}t' \ ,$$

*where $x \notin Lit(t_i)$ and $\bar{x} \notin Lit(t')$.*

*Proof.* Again one direction of the theorem is immediate from the definition of $p$-irredundant. For the other direction, if there are two complementary projections in $\varphi$, then by condition $c)$ of $p$-irredundancy, it must be of the form $xt \vee \bar{x}t'$. Otherwise, let us assume that $\varphi$ is of the form $\varphi = \rho_1 t_1 \vee \cdots \vee \rho_\ell t_\ell$. Consider any two terms $\rho_i t_i$ and $\rho_j t_j$. If $T(\rho_i t_i) \cap T(\rho_j t_j) \neq \emptyset$, then $\rho_i t_i \vee \rho_j t_j$ is unate, and by Theorem 14 it must be the case that $t_i = t_j$. On the other hand, if $T(\rho_i t_i) \cap T(\rho_j t_j) = \emptyset$, then by projectivity, it holds that $T(\rho_i \rho_j t_j) = \emptyset$, thus $\bar{\rho}_i \in Lit(t_j)$. Thus for every term $\rho_i t_i$, those terms $\rho_j t_j$ for which $T(\rho_i t_i) \cap T(\rho_j t_j) \neq \emptyset$ have the same conjunction part, and all the other terms contain $\bar{\rho}_i$ in their conjunction part.    $\square$

# 6    Revising Disjunctions and $k$-PDNF

In this section we consider two different revision algorithms. First we define the *revision distance* between two $k$-PDNF's, which is used in our complexity measure.

The distance of two terms $t$ and $t^*$ is $|t \oplus t^*|$, the number of literals occurring in exactly one of the two terms. The revision distance between an *initial* formula

$$\varphi_0 = \rho_1 t_1 \vee \cdots \vee \rho_\ell t_\ell \vee \rho_{\ell+1} t_{\ell+1} \vee \cdots \vee \rho_{\ell+d} t_{\ell+d}$$

and a *target* formula $\varphi = \rho_1 t_1^* \vee \cdots \vee \rho_\ell t_\ell^* \vee \rho_1' t_1' \vee \cdots \vee \rho_a' t_a'$ is

$$dist(\varphi_0, \varphi) = d + \sum_{i=1}^{\ell} |t_i \oplus t_i^*| + \sum_{i=1}^{a} \max(|t_i'|, 1).$$

The distance is *not* symmetric, and this reflects the fact that we are interested in the number of edit operations required to transform $\varphi_0$ to $\varphi$. These edit operations are the deletion of a literal or a term, and the addition of a literal. For example, the $d$ term in the definition of $dist$ corresponds to the deletion of the $d$ terms $\rho_{\ell+1} t_{\ell+1}, \cdots, \rho_{\ell+d} t_{\ell+d}$.

Given an initial formula $\varphi_0$ and a target formula $\varphi$, we want our mistake bound to be polynomial in the revision distance $e = dist(\varphi_0, \varphi)$, and logarithmic (or polylogarithmic) in all other parameters. In this case, that means logarithmic in $n$ and, for $k$-PDNF, in the total number of projections of size $k$.

We begin by demonstrating that the original Winnow, with appropriately modified initial weights, is an efficient revision algorithm—even in the presence of attribute errors, if we are willing to tolerate mistakes polynomial in the number of attribute errors as well as the usual parameters. (Previous work on theory revision has not given much consideration to noise.) We will use this result to show how to use an algorithm similar to Valiant's PDNF learning algorithm to revise PDNF. There, two levels of Winnow are run, and even with noise-free data, mistakes made by the lower-level Winnows will represent attribute errors in the input to the top-level Winnow.

Throughout this section, we will sometimes need to discuss both the components of vectors and which round of a mistake-bounded algorithm a vector is used in. When we need to discuss both, we will write $\mathbf{v}_{r,i}$ to denote component $i$ of the value that vector $\mathbf{v}$ takes on in round $r$.

## 6.1    Revising Disjunctions

Consider a version of Winnow, which we call RevWinn, presented as Algorithm 1. Note that this is Littlestone's Winnow2 [10] using different initial weights, with his parameters set to $\alpha = 2$, and $\theta = n/2$ (except that we have divided all the weights by $n$, because we feel it makes the analysis below a little easier to follow).

Note that throughout, all of the weights are always strictly between 0 and 1.

---

**Algorithm 1** Algorithm RevWinn($\varphi_0$)

---

Initialization: For $i = 1, \ldots, n$ initialize the weights to

$$w_{0,i} = \begin{cases} 1 & \text{if variable } x_i \text{ appears in } \varphi_0 \\ \frac{1}{2n} & \text{otherwise} \end{cases}$$

The hypothesis function in round $r$ is

$$h_r(\mathbf{x}) = \begin{cases} 0 & \text{if } \mathbf{w}_{r-1} \cdot \mathbf{x} < 1/2 \\ 1 & \text{otherwise} \end{cases}$$

In round $r$ predict $\hat{y}_r = h_r(\mathbf{x}_r)$

If $\hat{y}_r \neq y_r$, then update the weights for $i = 1, \ldots, n$ to

$$w_{r,i} = w_{r-1,i} \cdot 2^{\mathbf{x}_r(y_r - \hat{y}_r)}$$

---

**Theorem 16** *The number of mistakes made by Algorithm RevWinn with initial (monotone) disjunction $\varphi_0$ and target (monotone) disjunction $\varphi$ is*

$$O(\#AttributeErrors + e \log n) ,$$

*where $e = dist(\phi_0, \phi)$.*

*Proof.* Consider any run of the algorithm of length $R$. Let $I$ be the set of indices $i$ of variables that appear in both the initial and target disjunctions, such that for at least one round $r$ variable $\mathbf{x}_{r,i} = 1$ but $y_r = 0$. Let $J$ be the set of indices of variables that appear in the target disjunction but not in the initial disjunction. Let us also introduce the notation $\overline{I \cup J} = \{1, \ldots, n\} \setminus (I \cup J)$. When no confusion arises, we will sometimes refer to a variable $x_i$ belonging to one of these sets when we really should say that the variable's index belongs to the set.

We will use later the fact that any variable in both $\varphi_0$ and $\varphi$ that is *not* in $I$ never has its weight changed from 1.

For the proof we use a potential function $\Phi(\mathbf{w})$ that is somewhat different from those used in some other cases for analyzing Winnow (e.g., in [2, 9]). Put $\Phi(\mathbf{w}) = \sum_{i=1}^{n} \Phi_i(\mathbf{w})$, where

$$\Phi_i(\mathbf{w}) = \begin{cases} w_i - 1 + \ln \frac{1}{w_i} & \text{if } i \in I \cup J \\ w_i & \text{otherwise.} \end{cases}$$

It can be verified that $\Phi_i(\mathbf{w}) \geq 0$ for any $\mathbf{w} \in (0, 1]^n$.

Let $\Delta_r = \Phi(\mathbf{w}_{r-1}) - \Phi(\mathbf{w}_r)$ denote the change of the potential function during round $r$. We will derive both upper and lower bounds on $\sum_{r=1}^{R} \Delta_r$ that will allow us to relate the number of mistakes made by RevWinn to $e$, $n$, and $\#AttributeErrors$.

First we derive an upper bound:

$$\sum_{r=1}^{R} \Delta_r = \Phi(\mathbf{w}_0) - \Phi(\mathbf{w}_R) \leq \Phi(\mathbf{w}_0) - \sum_{i \in \overline{I \cup J}} w_{R,i}$$

$$= \sum_{i \in I} \Phi_i(\mathbf{w}_0) + \sum_{j \in J} \Phi_j(\mathbf{w}_0) + \sum_{i \in \overline{I \cup J}} (w_{0,i} - w_{R,i}) \ . \tag{5}$$

For $i \in I$ we initialized $\mathbf{w}_{0,i} = 1$ so $\Phi_i(\mathbf{w}_{0,i}) = 0$. Also, $|J| \le e$, and $\Phi_j(\mathbf{w}_{0,j}) = \ln(2n) - (2n-1)/2n < \ln(2n)$ for $j \in J$, so the sum of the first two terms is at most $e \ln(2n)$. Now we need to bound the third term. The variables that appear neither in $\varphi$ nor in $\varphi_0$ have initial weights $1/2n$, and so altogether can contribute at most $1/2$ to the sum. There are at most $e$ variables in $\varphi_0 \setminus \varphi$, so those variables can contribute at most $e$ to the sum. Finally, as noted earlier, the weights never change for those variables in both $\varphi_0$ and $\varphi$ but not in $I$. Thus we get

$$\sum_{r=1}^{R} \Delta_r \le e \ln 2n + e + 1/2 \ . \tag{6}$$

To get a lower bound on the sum, we begin by deriving a lower bound on the change in potential in one round. Now

$$\Delta_r = \sum_{i \in I \cup J} \left( w_{r-1,i} - w_{r,i} + \ln \frac{w_{r,i}}{w_{r-1,i}} \right) + \sum_{i \in \overline{I \cup J}} (w_{r-1,i} - w_{r,i})$$

$$= \sum_{i=1}^{n} (w_{r-1,i} - w_{r,i}) + \sum_{i \in I \cup J} \ln \frac{w_{r,i}}{w_{r-1,i}} \ . \tag{7}$$

There are three cases for a round $r$: no change in weights, a demotion, and a promotion. Obviously, when no update is done in round $r$ (i.e., $\hat{y}_r = y_r$), then $\Delta_r = 0$.

In a demotion step, $\hat{y}_r = 1$ and $y_r = 0$. By the definition of $I$ and $J$, in this case $AttrErr(r) = |(I \cup J) \cap \mathbf{x}_r|$ [1]. Also, the total weight of components being on in $\mathbf{x}_r$ is at least $1/2$, and the weight of each of those components is halved. So, using (7),

$$\Delta_r \ge 1/4 + |(I \cup J) \cap \mathbf{x}_r| \ln \left( \frac{1}{2} \right) = 1/4 - \ln 2 \, AttrErr(r) \ . \tag{8}$$

In a promotion step, $\hat{y}_r = 0$ and $y_r = 1$. We know that the components of $\mathbf{x}_r$ that are on have total weight at most $1/2$, and that each of these components is multiplied by 2. So the first term in (7) is at least $-1/2$. Thus $\Delta_r \ge -1/2 + |(I \cup J) \cap \mathbf{x}_r| \ln 2$. Now if $y_r = \varphi(\mathbf{x}_r)$, then $|(I \cup J) \cap \mathbf{x}_r| \ge 1$, because we know that $\hat{y}_r = 0$ and we know that all the weights of variables in $\varphi$ but not in $I$ are 1. If $y_r \neq \varphi(\mathbf{x}_r)$, then $AttrErr(r) = 1$. Thus, in a promotion step, it always holds that

$$\Delta_r \ge -1/2 + \ln 2(1 - AttrErr(r)) \ . \tag{9}$$

---

[1] With mild abuse of notation, we write $S \cap \mathbf{x}_r$ to denote the set of indices that are both in the set $S$ and set to 1 in the vector $\mathbf{x}_r$.

Finally, let $M^-$ denote the total number of demotions and $M^+$ the total number of promotions. Then (8) and (9) give us

$$\sum_{r=1}^{R} \Delta_r \geq \sum_{\hat{y}_r=1, y_r=0} (1/4 - \ln 2 \, AttrErr(r))$$

$$+ \sum_{\hat{y}_r=0, y_r=1} (\ln 2 - 1/2) - \ln 2 \, AttrErr(r)$$

$$= M^-/4 + (\ln 2 - 1/2)M^+ - \ln 2 \# AttributeErrors \ .$$

Combining this with (6) gives the desired mistake bound.     □

Note that the potential function used depends on the particular run of the algorithm, and that it does not appear to be any obvious measure of distance between the actual weight vector $\mathbf{w}_r$ and a weight vector for the target.

**Remark 17** *Using the De Morgan rules one can easily modify the code of Algorithm RevWinn to make it revise conjunctions instead of disjunctions, and have the same mistake bound. Call the resulting algorithm RevWinnC.*

## 6.2  Revising $k$-PDNF

Now we give a revision algorithm for PDNFs. We use Valiant's two-level algorithm [14] for learning PDNFs, except that we use the different initial weights in the individual copies of Winnow that were discussed in the previous subsection. We present this as Algorithm Rev-$k$-PDNF (see Algorithm 2). Rev-$k$-PDNF consists of a top-level RevWinn algorithm that handles the selection of the appropriate projections. On the lower level, instances of RevWinnC are run, one for each projection, to find the appropriate term for that particular projection. Each instance of RevWinnC maintains its own separate hypothesis $h^\rho$ for one of the $2^k \binom{n}{k}$ projections $\rho$. We will write this as $h_r^\rho$ when we need to indicate the current hypothesis in a particular round $r$.

For each projection $\rho$, introduce a new Boolean variable $v_\rho$. We denote by $\mathbf{v}$ the vector formed by all these variables. The top level RevWinn learns a disjunction over these variables; its hypothesis in round $r$ is denoted by $h_r$. In round $r$, we define variable

$$v_{r,\rho} = \rho(\mathbf{x}_r) h_r^\rho(\mathbf{x}_r) \ .$$

Algorithm Rev-$k$-PDNF predicts $h_r(\mathbf{v}_r)$ in round $r$.

**Theorem 18** *Suppose that the initial and target formulas are, respectively, the $k$-PDNF$_n$ formulas*

$$\varphi_0 = \rho_1 t_1 \vee \cdots \vee \rho_\ell t_\ell \vee \rho_{\ell+1} t_{\ell+1} \vee \cdots \vee \rho_{\ell+d} t_{\ell+d} \ ,$$
$$\varphi = \rho_1 t_1^* \vee \cdots \vee \rho_\ell t_\ell^* \vee \rho_1' t_1' \vee \cdots \vee \rho_a' t_a' \ ,$$

*and $e = dist(\varphi_0, \varphi)$. Then algorithm Rev-$k$-PDNF makes $O(ek \log n)$ mistakes.*

---

**Algorithm 2** The procedure Rev-$k$-PDNF($\varphi_0$)

---

1: {$\varphi_0 = \rho_1 t_1 \vee \cdots \vee \rho_{\ell+d} t_{\ell+d}$ is the $k$-PDNF to be revised to another $k$-PDNF}
2: Initialize a RevWinn instance for the top level algorithm with initial disjunction $v_{\rho_1} \vee \cdots \vee v_{\rho_{\ell+d}}$.
3: Initialize a RevWinnC instance for each $k$-projection $\rho_i$ with parameter $t_i$ for $\rho_1, \ldots, \rho_{\ell+d}$ respectively and with parameter the empty conjunction for the rest.
4: **for** each round $r$ with instance $\mathbf{x}_r$ **do**
5:     Set each $v_{r,\rho} = \rho(\mathbf{x}_r) h_r^\rho(\mathbf{x}_r)$
6:     Predict $\hat{y}_r = h_r(\mathbf{v}_r)$
7:     **if** $\hat{y}_r \neq y_r$ **then**
8:         Update top-level RevWinn for a $\hat{y}_r \neq y_r$ mistake on $\mathbf{v}_r$.
9:         **for** each $\rho$ with $\rho(\mathbf{x}_r) = 1$ and $v_{r,\rho} \neq y_r$ **do**
10:            Update the low-level RevWinnC instance $\rho$ for a $v_{r,\rho} \neq y_r$ mistake on $\mathbf{x}_r$.

---

*Proof.* The top-level RevWinn is revising a disjunction over the $v_\rho$'s. There will be two sources of mistakes. First, the initial disjunction is not correct; it needs revising. Second, the values of the $v_\rho$'s will sometimes be erroneous, because the low-level RevWinnC's are imperfect. (The actual $\mathbf{x}$ input and $y$ classification are assumed to be noiseless.)

Theorem 16 tells us how to calculate the overall number of mistakes of the top-level RevWinn as a function of three quantities: the revision distance, which is $d + a$, the total number of variables, both relevant and irrelevant for the disjunction, which is $2^k \binom{n}{k}$, and the total number of attribute errors, which we will now calculate.

In fact, we will *not* count all the attribute errors. We will count (actually provide an upper bound on) only those attribute errors that occur when RevWinn is charged with a mistake.

For $i = 1, \ldots, \ell$, the RevWinnC instance corresponding to projection $\rho_i$ predicts $v_{\rho_i}$ according to $h^{\rho_i}$. That RevWinnC instance updates for a mistake only when the overall algorithm makes a mistake (i.e., $\hat{y}_r \neq y_r$), its prediction was different from $y_r$, and $\rho_i(\mathbf{x}_r) = 1$. Now $y_r = \varphi(\mathbf{x}_r) = t_i^*(\mathbf{x}_r)$ (the last equation holds because of projectivity and because $\rho_i(\mathbf{x}_r) = 1$). This means that the mistake bound for this RevWinnC tells us how many times this RevWinnC can make errors on rounds when the overall algorithm makes an error; after that number of mistakes, this RevWinnC will then always predict correctly. By Remark 17 the mistake bound on this RevWinnC is $O(|t_i \oplus t_i^*| \ln n)$.

For $j = 1, \ldots, a$ a similar argument shows that there are at most $O(|t_j'| \ln n)$ rounds $r$ where $v_{r,\rho_j'} \neq \rho_j'(\mathbf{x}_r) t_j'(\mathbf{x}_r)$ and the top-level RevWinn makes a mistake. Put $F = (\sum_{i=1}^\ell |t_i \oplus t_i^*| + \sum_{j=1}^a |t_j'|) \ln n$.

How many times can Rev-$k$-PDNF err when predicting? We just argued that the total number of attribute errors that occur when the top-level RevWinn makes a mistake is $O(F)$. The total number of variables that the top-level RevWinn is working with is $2^k \binom{n}{k}$. Thus, the overall mistake bound is, by Theorem 16, $O(F + (d + a) \log (2^k \binom{n}{k})) = O(ek \log n)$, since $F = O(e \log n)$. $\square$

*Remark:* For learning an $m$-term $k$-PDNF$_n$ from scratch, that is, for revising the empty $k$-PDNF$_n$ to a target $k$-PDNF$_n$, this algorithm has the same asymptotic mistake bound as Valiant's learning algorithm [14]: $O(kms \log n)$, where $s$ is the maximum number of variables in any term in the target.

# References

1. Dana Angluin. Queries revisited. In *Algorithmic Learning Theory, 12th International Conference, ALT 2001, Washington, DC, USA, November 25–28, 2001, Proceedings*, volume 2225 of *Lecture Notes in Artificial Intelligence*, pages 12–31. Springer, 2001.
2. Peter Auer and Manfred K. Warmuth. Tracking the best disjunction. *Machine Learning*, 32(2):127–150, 1998. Earlier version in 36th FOCS, 1995.
3. Avrim Blum. On-line algorithms in machine learning. Available from http:// www-2.cs.cmu.edu/~avrim/Papers/pubs.html, 1996.
4. Judy Goldsmith, Robert H. Sloan, B. Szörényi, and György Turán. Theory revision with queries: Horn, read-once, and parity formulas. Technical Report TR03-039, Electronic Colloquium on Computational Complexity (ECCC), 2003. Available at http://www.eccc.uni-trier.de/eccc/. Also submitted for journal publication.
5. Judy Goldsmith, Robert H. Sloan, and György Turán. Theory revision with queries: DNF formulas. *Machine Learning*, 47(2/3):257–295, 2002.
6. Tibor Hegedüs. Generalized teaching dimensions and the query complexity of learning. In *Proc. 8th Annu. Conf. on Comput. Learning Theory*, pages 108–117. ACM Press, New York, NY, 1995.
7. Lisa Hellerstein, Krishnan Pillaipakkamnatt, Vijay Raghavan, and Dawn Wilkins. How many queries are needed to learn? *J. ACM*, 43(5):840–862, 1996.
8. David Helmbold, Robert Sloan, and Manfred K. Warmuth. Learning nested differences of intersection closed concept classes. *Machine Learning*, 5(2):165–196, 1990. Special Issue on Computational Learning Theory; first appeared in 2nd COLT conference (1989).
9. Jyrki Kivinen and Manfred K. Warmuth. Additive versus exponentiated gradient updates for linear prediction. In *Proc. 27th Annual ACM Symposium on Theory of Computing*, pages 209–218. ACM Press, New York, NY, 1995.
10. N. Littlestone. Learning quickly when irrelevant attributes abound: A new linear-threshold algorithm. *Machine Learning*, 2(4):285–318, 1988.
11. N. Littlestone. A mistake-bound version of Rivest's decision-list algorithm. Personal communication to Avrim Blum, 1989.
12. Chris Mesterharm. Tracking linear-threshold concepts with Winnow. In *15th Annual Conference on Computational Learning Theory, COLT 2002, Sydney, Australia, July 2002, Proceedings*, volume 2375 of *Lecture Notes in Artificial Intelligence*, pages 138–152. Springer, 2002.
13. Ronald L. Rivest. Learning decision lists. *Machine Learning*, 2:229–246, 1987.
14. Leslie G. Valiant. Projection learning. *Machine Learning*, 37(2):115–130, 1999.
15. Leslie G. Valiant. A neuroidal architecture for cognitive computation. *Journal of the ACM*, 47(5):854–882, 2000.
16. S. Wrobel. *Concept Formation and Knowledge Revision*. Kluwer, 1994.
17. S. Wrobel. First order theory refinement. In L. De Raedt, editor, *Advances in ILP*, pages 14–33. IOS Press, Amsterdam, 1995.

# Learning with Equivalence Constraints and the Relation to Multiclass Learning

Aharon Bar-Hillel and Daphna Weinshall

School of Computer Sci. and Eng. & Center for Neural Computation
Hebrew University, Jerusalem 91904, Israel
{aharonbh,daphna}@cs.huji.ac.il
http://www.ca.huji.ac.il/~daphna

**Abstract.** We study the problem of learning partitions using equivalence constraints as input. This is a binary classification problem in the product space of pairs of datapoints. The training data includes pairs of datapoints which are labeled as coming from the same class or not. This kind of data appears naturally in applications where explicit labeling of datapoints is hard to get, but relations between datapoints can be more easily obtained, using, for example, Markovian dependency (as in video clips).

Our problem is an unlabeled partition problem, and is therefore tightly related to multiclass classification. We show that the solutions of the two problems are related, in the sense that a good solution to the binary classification problem entails the existence of a good solution to the multiclass problem, and vice versa. We also show that bounds on the sample complexity of the two problems are similar, by showing that their relevant 'dimensions' (VC dimension for the binary problem, Natarajan dimension for the multiclass problem) bound each other. Finally, we show the feasibility of solving multiclass learning efficiently by using a solution of the equivalent binary classification problem. In this way advanced techniques developed for binary classification, such as SVM and boosting, can be used directly to enhance multiclass learning.

## 1 Introduction

Multiclass learning is about learning a concept over some input space, which takes a discrete set of values $\{0, 1, \ldots, M-1\}$. A tightly related problem is data partitioning, which is about learning a partitioning of data to $M$ discrete sets. The latter problem is equivalent to unlabelled multiclass learning, namely, all the multiclass concepts which produce the same partitioning but with a different permutation of labels are considered the same concept.

Most of the work on multiclass partitioning of data has focused on the first variant, namely, the learning of an explicit mapping from datapoints to $M$ discrete labels. It is assumed that the training data is obtained in the same form, namely, it is a set of datapoints with attached labels taken from the set $\{0, 1, \ldots, M-1\}$. On the other hand, unlabeled data partitioning requires as training data only equivalence relations between pairs of datapoints; namely, for

B. Schölkopf and M.K. Warmuth (Eds.): COLT/Kernel 2003, LNAI 2777, pp. 640–654, 2003.

each pair of datapoints a label is assigned to indicate whether the pair originates from the same class or not. While it is straightforward to generate such binary labels on pairs of points from multiclass labels on individual points, the other direction is not as simple.

It is therefore interesting to note that equivalence constraints between pairs of datapoints may be easier to obtain in many real-life applications. More specifically, in data with natural Markovian dependency between successive datapoints (e.g., a video clip), there are automatic means to determine whether two successive datapoints (e.g., frames) come from the same class or not. In other applications, such as distributed learning where labels are obtained from many uncoordinated teachers, the subjective labels are meaningless, and the major information lies in the equivalence constraints which the subjective labels impose on the data. More details are given in [12].

Multiclass classification appears like a straightforward generalization of the binary classification problem, where the concept takes only two values $\{0, 1\}$. But while there is a lot of work on binary classification, both theoretical and algorithmic, the problem of multiclass learning is less understood. The VC dimension, for example, can only be used to characterize the learnability and sample complexity of binary functions. Generalizing this notion to multiclass classification has not been straightforward; see [4] for the details regarding a number of such generalizations and the relations between them.

On a more practical level, most of the algorithms available are best suitable (or only work for) the learning of binary functions. Support vector machines (SVM) [14] and boosting techniques [13] are two important examples. A possible solution is to reduce the problem to the learning of a number of binary classifiers ($O(\mathbf{M})$ or $O(\mathbf{M}^2)$), and then combine the classifiers using for example a winner-takes-all strategy [7]. The use of error correcting code to combine the binary classifiers was first suggested in [5]. Such codes were used in several successful generalizations to existing techniques, such as multiclass SVM and multiclass boosting [6, 1]. These solutions are hard to analyze, however, and only recently have we started to understand the properties of these algorithms, such as their sample complexity [7]. Another possible solution is to assume that the data distribution is known and construct a generative model, e.g., a Gaussian mixture model. The main drawback of this approach is the strong dependence on the assuption that the distribution is known.

In this paper we propose a different approach to multiclass learning. For each multiclass learning problem, define an equivalent binary classification problem. Specifically, if the original problem is to learn a multiclass classifier over data space $X$, define a binary classification problem over the product space $X \times X$, which includes all pairs of datapoints. In the binary classification problem, each pair is assigned the value 1 if the two datapoints come from the same class, and 0 otherwise. Hence the problem is reduced to the learning of a *single* binary classifier, and any existing tool can be used. Note that we have eliminated the problem of combining $\mathbf{M}$ binary classifiers. We need to address, however, the problems of how to generate the training sample for the equivalent binary problem, and how to obtain a partition of $X$ from the learned concept in the product space.

A related idea was explored algorithmically in [11], where multiclass learning was translated to a binary classification problem over the *same* space $X$, using the difference between datapoints as input. This embedding in rather problematic, however, since the binary classification problem is ill-defined; it is quite likely that the same value would correspond to the difference between two vectors from the same class, and the difference between two other vectors from two different classes.

In the rest of this paper we study the properties of the binary classification problem in the product space, and their relation to the properties of the equivalent multiclass problem. Specifically, in Section 2.1 we define, given a multiclass problem, the equivalent binary classification problem, and state its sample complexity using the usual PAC framework. In Section 2.2 we show that for any solution of the product space problem with error $e_{pr}$, there is a solution of the multiclass problem with error $e_o$, such that

$$\frac{e_{pr}}{2} < e_o < \sqrt{2\mathbf{M}e_{pr}}$$

However, under mild assumptions, a stronger version for the right inequality exists, showing that the errors in the original and the product space are lineary related:

$$e_o < (\frac{e_{pr}}{K})$$

where $K$ is the frequency of the smallest class. Finally, in Section 2.3 we show that the sample complexity of the two problems is similar in the following sense: for $S_N$ the Natarajan dimension of the the multiclass problem, $S_{VC}$ the VC-dimension of the equivalent binary problem, and $\mathbf{M}$ the number of classes, the following relation holds

$$\frac{S_N}{f_1(\mathbf{M})} - 1 \le S_{VC} \le f_2(\mathbf{M})S_N$$

where $f_1(\mathbf{M})$ is $O(\mathbf{M}^2)$ and $f_2(\mathbf{M})$ is $O(log\mathbf{M})$.

In order to solve a multiclass learning problem by solving the equivalent binary classification problem in the product space, we need to address two problems. First, a sample of independent points in $X$ does not generate an independent sample in the product space. We note, however, that every $n$ independent points in $X$ trivially give $\frac{n}{2}$ independent pairs in the product space, and therefore the bounds above still apply up to a factor of $\frac{1}{2}$. We believe that the bounds are actually better, since a sample of $n$ independent labels gives an order of $\mathbf{M}n$ non-trivial labels on pairs. By non-trivial we mean that given less than $\mathbf{M}n$ labels on pairs of points from $\mathbf{M}$ classes of the same size, we cannot deterministically derive the labels of the remaining pairs. This problem is more acute in the other direction, namely, it is actually not possible to generate a set of labels on individual points from a set of equivalence constraints on pairs of points.

Second, and more importantly, the approximation we learn in the product space may not represent any partition. A binary product space function $f$ represents a partition only if it is an indicator of an equivalence relation, i.e. the relation $f(x1, x2) = 1$ is reflexive, symetric and transitive. It can be readily shown that $f$ represents a partition, i.e., $\exists g, s.t. f = U(g))$ iff the function $1 - f$ is a binary metric. While this condition holds for our target concept, it doesn't hold for its approximation in the general case, and so an approximation will not induce any obvious partition on the original space.

To address this problem, we show in section 3 how an $\varepsilon$-good hypothesis $f$ in the product space can be used to build an original space classifier with error linear in $\varepsilon$. First we show how $f$ enables us, under certain conditions, to partition data in the original space with error linear in $\varepsilon$. Given the partitioning, we claim that a classifier can be built by using $f$ to compare new presented data points to the partitioned sample. A similar problem was studied in [2], using the same kind of approximation. However, different criteria are optimized in the two papers: in [2] $e_{pr}(\bar{g}, f)$ is minimized (i.e., the product space error), while in our work a partition $g$ is sought which minimizes $e_o(g, c)$ (i.e., the error in the original space of $g$ w.r.t. the original concept).

## 2   From M-Partitions to Binary Classifiers

In this section we show that multiclass classification can be translated to binary classification, and that the two problems are equivalent in many ways. First, in section 2.1 we formulate the binary classification problem whose solution is equivalent to a given multiclass problem. In section 2.2 we show that the solutions of the two problems are closely related: a good hypothesis for the multiclass problem provides a good hypothesis for the equivalent binary problem, and vice versa. Finally, in section 2.3 we show that the sample complexity of the two problems is similar.

### 2.1   PAC Framework in the Product Space

Let us introduce the following notations:

- $X$: the input space.
- **M**: the number of classes.
- $D$: the sampling distribution (measure) over $X$.
- $c$: a target concept over $X$; it is a labeled partition of $X$, $c : X \rightarrow \{0, \ldots, \mathbf{M}-1\}$. For each such concept, $c^{-1}(j) \in X$ denotes the cluster of points labeled $j$ by $c$.
- $\mathcal{H}$: a family of hypotheses; each hypothesis is a function $h : X \rightarrow \{0, \ldots, \mathbf{M}-1\}$.
- $e(h, c)$: the error in $X$ of a hypothesis $h \in \mathcal{H}$ with respect to $c$, defined as

$$e(h, c) = D(c(x) \neq h(x))$$

Given an unknown target concept $c$, the learning task is to find a hypothesis $h \in \mathcal{H}$ with low error $e(h, c)$. Usually it is assumed that a set of labeled datapoints is given during training. In this paper we do not assume to have access to such training data, but instead have access to a set of labeled equivalence constraints on pairs of datapoints. The label tells us whether the two points come from the same (unknown) class, or not. Therefore the learning problem is transformed as follows:

For any hypothesis $h$ (or $c$), define a functor $U$ which takes the hypothesis as an argument and outputs a function $\bar{h}, \bar{h} : X \times X \rightarrow \{0, 1\}$. Specifically:

$$\bar{h}(x, y) = 1_{h(x)=h(y)}$$

Thus $\bar{h}$ expresses the implicit equivalence relations induced by the concept $h$ on pairs of datapoints.

The functor $U$ is not injective: two different hypotheses $h_1$ and $h_2$ may result in the same $\bar{h}$. This, however, happens only when $h_1$ and $h_2$ differ only by a permutation of their corresponding labels, while representing the same partition; $\bar{h}$ therefore represents an unlabeled partition.

We can now define a second notion of error between unlabeled partitions over the product space $X \times X$:

$$e(\bar{h}, \bar{c}) = D \times D(\bar{h}(x, y) \neq \bar{c}(x, y))$$

where $\bar{c}$ is obtained from $c$ by the functor $U$. This error measures the probability of disagreement between $\bar{h}$ and $\bar{c}$ with regard to equivalence queries. It is a rather intuitive measure for the comparison of unlabeled partitions. The problem of learning a partition can now be cast as a regular PAC learning problem, since $\bar{h}$ and $\bar{c}$ are binary hypotheses. Specifically:

Let $X \times X$ denote the input space, $D \times D$ denote the sampling probability over the input space, and $\bar{c}$ denote the target concept. Let the hypotheses family be the family $\bar{\mathcal{H}} = \{\bar{h} : h \in \mathcal{H}\}$ [1].

Now we can use the VC dimension and PAC-learning theory on sample complexity, in order to characterize the sample complexity of learning the binary hypothesis $\bar{h}$. More interestingly, we can then compare our results with results on sample complexity obtained directly for the multiclass problem.

## 2.2     The Connection between Solution Quality of the Two Problems

In this section we show that a good (binary) hypothesis in the product space can be used to find a good hypothesis (partition) in the original space, and vice versa. Note that the functor $U$, which connects hypotheses in the original space to hypotheses in the product space, is not injective, and therefore it has no inverse. Therefore, in order to asses the difference between two hypotheses $\bar{h}$ and

---

[1] Note that $\bar{\mathcal{H}}$ is of the same size as $\mathcal{H}$ only when $\mathcal{H}$ does not contain hypotheses which are identical with respect to the partition of $X$.

$\bar{c}$, we must choose $h$ and $c$ such that $\bar{h} = U(h)$ and $\bar{c} = U(c)$, and subsequently compute $e(h, c)$.

We proceed by showing three results: Thm. 1 shows that in general, if we have a hypothesis in product space with some error $\varepsilon$, there is a hypothesis in the original space with error $O(\sqrt{M\varepsilon})$. However, if $\varepsilon$ is small with respect to the smallest class probability $K$, Thm. 2 shows that the bound is linear, namely, there is a hypothesis in the original space with error $O(\frac{\varepsilon}{K})$. In most cases, this is the range of interest. Finally, Thm. 3 shows the other direction: if we have a hypothesis in the original space with some error $\varepsilon$, its product space hypothesis $U(h) = \bar{h}$ has an error smaller than $2\varepsilon$.

Before proceeding we need to introduce some more notations: Let $c$ and $h$ denote two partitions of $X$ into $\mathbf{M}$ classes. Define the joint distribution matrix $P = \{p_{ij}\}_{i,j=0}^{\mathbf{M}-1}$ as follows:

$$p_{ij} \overset{\Delta}{=} D(c(x) = i, h(x) = j)$$

Using this matrix we can express the probability of error in the original space and the product space.

1. The error in $X$ is

$$e(h, c) = D(c(x) \neq h(x)) = \sum_{i=0}^{\mathbf{M}-1} \sum_{j \neq i} p_{ij}$$

2. The error in the product space is

$$e(\bar{h}, \bar{c}) = D \times D([\bar{c}(x, y) = 1 \wedge \bar{h}(x, y) = 0] \vee [\bar{c}(x, y) = 0 \wedge \bar{h}(x, y) = 1])$$

$$= \sum_{i=0}^{\mathbf{M}-1} \sum_{j=0}^{\mathbf{M}-1} D(c(x) = i, h(x) = j) \cdot (D(\{y | c(y) = i, h(y) \neq j\})$$

$$+ D(\{y | c(y) \neq i, h(y) = j\}))$$

$$= \sum_{i=0}^{\mathbf{M}-1} \sum_{j=0}^{\mathbf{M}-1} p_{ij} \left( \sum_{k \neq i} p_{kj} + \sum_{k \neq j} p_{ik} \right)$$

**Theorem 1.** *For any two product space hypotheses $\bar{h}, \bar{c}$, there are $h, c$ such that $\bar{h} = U(h), \bar{c} = U(c)$ and*

$$e(h, c) \leq \sqrt{2\mathbf{M}e(\bar{h}, \bar{c})}$$

*where $\mathbf{M}$ is the number of equivalence classes of $\bar{h}, \bar{c}$.*

The proof appears in the technical report [3], appendix A. We note that the bound is tight as a function of $\varepsilon$ since there are indeed cases where $e(c, h) = O(\sqrt{(e(\bar{h}, \bar{c}))})$. A simple example of such 3-class problem occurs when the matrix of joint distribution is the following:

$$P = \begin{pmatrix} 1 - 3q & 0 & 0 \\ 0 & q & q \\ 0 & 0 & q \end{pmatrix}$$

Here $e(c, h) = q$ and $e(\bar{c}, \bar{h}) = 4q^2$. The next theorem shows, however, that this situation cannot occur if $e(\bar{c}, \bar{h})$ is small compared to the smallest class frequency.

**Theorem 2.** *Let $c$ denote a target partition and $h$ a hypothesis, and let $\bar{c}, \bar{h}$ denote the corresponding hypotheses in the product space. Denote the size of the minimal class of $c$ by $K = \min\limits_{i \in \{0,...,M-1\}} D(c^{-1}(i))$, and the product space error $\varepsilon = e(\bar{c}, \bar{h})$.*

$$\varepsilon < \frac{K^2}{2} \quad \implies \quad e(f \circ h, c) < \frac{\varepsilon}{K} \tag{1}$$

*where $f : \{0, \dots, M-1\} \to \{0, \dots, M-1\}$ is a bijection matching the labels of $h$ and $c$.*

*Proof.* We start by showing that if the theorem's condition holds, then there is a natural correspondence between the classes of $c$ and $h$:

**Lemma 1.** *If the condition in (1) holds, then there exists a bijection $J : \{0, \dots, M-1\} \to \{0, \dots, M-1\}$ such that*

- $p_{i,J(i)} > \sqrt{\frac{\varepsilon}{2}}$
- $p_{i,l} < \sqrt{\frac{\varepsilon}{2}}$ for all $l \neq J(i)$
- $p_{l,J(i)} < \sqrt{\frac{\varepsilon}{2}}$ for all $l \neq i$

*Proof.* Denote the class probabilities as $p_i^c = D(c^{-1}(i))$; clearly

$$p_i^c = \sum_{j=0}^{M-1} p_{ij}$$

We further define for each class $i$ of $c$ its internal error $\varepsilon_i = \sum_{j=0}^{M-1} p_{ij}(p_i^c - p_{ij})$. The rationale for this definition follows from the following inequality:

$$\varepsilon = \sum_{i=0}^{M-1}\sum_{j=0}^{M-1} p_{ij}\Big(\sum_{\substack{k=0\\k\neq i}}^{M-1} p_{kj} + \sum_{\substack{k=0\\k\neq j}}^{M-1} p_{ik}\Big) \geq \sum_{i=0}^{M-1}\sum_{j=0}^{M-1} p_{ij}(p_i^c - p_{ij}) = \sum_{i=0}^{M-1} \varepsilon_i$$

We first observe that each row in matrix $P$ contains at least one element bigger than $\sqrt{\frac{\varepsilon}{2}}$. Assume to the contrary that no such element exists in class $i$; then

$$\varepsilon \geq \varepsilon_i = \sum_{j=0}^{M-1} p_{ij}(p_i^c - p_{ij}) > \sum_{j=0}^{M-1} p_{ij}\Big(\sqrt{2\varepsilon} - \sqrt{\frac{\varepsilon}{2}}\Big) = \sqrt{\frac{\varepsilon}{2}}\sum_{j=0}^{M-1} p_{ij}$$

$$\geq \sqrt{\frac{\varepsilon}{2}} \cdot \sqrt{2\varepsilon} = \varepsilon$$

in contradiction.

Second, we observe that the row element bigger than $\sqrt{\frac{\varepsilon}{2}}$ is unique. This follows from the following argument: for any two elements $p_{ij_1}, p_{ij_2}$ in the same row:

$$\varepsilon \geq \sum_{j=0}^{M-1} p_{ij}\Big(\sum_{\substack{k=0\\k\neq i}}^{M-1} p_{kj} + \sum_{\substack{k=0\\k\neq j}}^{M-1} p_{ik}\Big) \geq \sum_{j=0}^{M-1} p_{ij} \sum_{\substack{k=0\\k\neq j}}^{M-1} p_{ik} \geq 2p_{ij_1}p_{ij_2}$$

Hence it is not possible that both the elements $p_{ij_1}$ and $p_{ij_2}$ are bigger than $\sqrt{\frac{\varepsilon}{2}}$. The uniqueness of an element bigger than $\sqrt{\frac{\varepsilon}{2}}$ in a column follows from an analogous argument with regard to the columns, which completes the proof of the lemma. $\qquad\square$

Denote $f = J^{-1}$, and let us show that $\sum_{i=0}^{M-1} p_{i,f(i)} > 1 - \frac{\varepsilon}{K}$. We start by showing that $p_{i,f(i)}$ cannot be 'too small':

$$\varepsilon_i = \sum_{j=0}^{M-1} p_{ij}(p_i^c - p_{ij}) = p_{i,f(i)}(p_i^c - p_{i,f(i)}) + \sum_{\substack{j=0\\j\neq f(i)}}^{M-1} p_{ij}(p_i^c - p_{ij})$$

$$\geq p_{i,f(i)}(p_i^c - p_{i,f(i)}) + \sum_{\substack{j=0\\j\neq f(i)}}^{M-1} p_{ij}p_{i,f(i)} = 2p_{i,f(i)}(p_i^c - p_{i,f(i)})$$

This gives a quadratic inequality

$$p_{i,f(i)}^2 - p_i^c p_{i,f(i)} + \frac{\varepsilon_i}{2} \geq 0$$

which holds for $p_{i,f(i)} \geq \frac{p_i^c + \sqrt{(p_i^c)^2 - 2\varepsilon_i}}{2}$ or for $p_{i,f(i)} \leq \frac{p_i^c - \sqrt{(p_i^c)^2 - 2\varepsilon_i}}{2}$. Since

$$\sqrt{(p_i^c)^2 - 2\varepsilon_i} = \sqrt{(p_i^c)^2\Big(1 - \frac{2\varepsilon_i}{(p_i^c)^2}\Big)} = p_i^c\sqrt{1 - \frac{2\varepsilon_i}{(p_i^c)^2}} > p_i^c\Big(1 - \frac{2\varepsilon_i}{(p_i^c)^2}\Big) = p_i^c - \frac{2\varepsilon_i}{p_i^c}$$

it must hold that either $p_{i,f(i)} > p_i^c - \frac{\varepsilon_i}{p_i^c}$ or $p_{i,f(i)} < \frac{\varepsilon_i}{p_i^c}$. But the second possiblity that $p_{i,f(i)} < \frac{\varepsilon_i}{p_i^c}$ leads to contradiction with condition (1) since

$$\sqrt{\frac{\varepsilon}{2}} < p_{i,f(i)} < \frac{\varepsilon_i}{p_i^c} \leq \frac{\varepsilon}{K} \implies K < \sqrt{2\varepsilon}$$

Therefore $p_{i,f(i)} > p_i^c - \frac{\varepsilon_i}{p_i^c}$. Summing the inequalities over $i$, we get

$$\sum_{i=0}^{M-1} p_{i,f(i)} > \sum_{i=0}^{M-1} p_i^c - \frac{\varepsilon_i}{p_i^c} \geq 1 - \sum_{i=0}^{M-1} \frac{\varepsilon_i}{K} \geq 1 - \frac{\varepsilon}{K}$$

This completes the proof of the theorem since

$$e(J \circ h, c) = p(J \circ h(x) \neq c(x)) = 1 - p(J \circ h(x) = c(x))$$

$$= 1 - \sum_{i=0}^{M-1} p(\{c(x) = i, h(x) = J^{-1}(i)\}) = 1 - \sum_{i=0}^{M-1} p_{i,f(i)} < \frac{\varepsilon}{K}$$

$$= \frac{e(\bar{c}, \bar{h})}{K}$$

$\square$

**Corollary 1.** *If the classes are equiprobable, namely $\frac{1}{K} = M$, we get a bound of $M\varepsilon$ on the error in the original space.*

**Corollary 2.** *As $K \to \sqrt{2\varepsilon}$, the lowest allowed value according to the theorem condition, we get an error bound approaching $\frac{\varepsilon}{\sqrt{2\varepsilon}} = \sqrt{\frac{\varepsilon}{2}}$. Hence the linear behavior of the bound on the original space error is lost near this limit, in accordance with Thm. 1.*

A bound in the other direction is much simpler to achieve:

**Theorem 3.** *For every two labeled partitions $h, c$: if $e(h, c) < \varepsilon$ then $e(\bar{h}, \bar{c}) < 2\varepsilon$.*

*Proof.*

$$e(\bar{h}, \bar{c}) = \sum_{i=0}^{M-1} \sum_{j=0}^{M-1} p_{ij} \left[ \sum_{k \neq i} p_{kj} + \sum_{k \neq j} p_{ik} \right]$$

$$= \sum_{i=0}^{M-1} p_{ii} [\sum_{k \neq i} p_{ki} + \sum_{k \neq i} p_{ik}] + \sum_{i=0}^{M-1} \sum_{j \neq i} p_{ij} [\sum_{k \neq i} p_{kj} + \sum_{k \neq j} p_{ik}]$$

$$\leq \sum_{i=0}^{M-1} p_{ii} \cdot \varepsilon + \sum_{i=0}^{M-1} \sum_{j \neq i} p_{ij} \leq \varepsilon + \varepsilon = 2\varepsilon$$

$\square$

## 2.3   The Connection between Sample Size Complexity

Several dimension-like measures of the sample complexity exist for multiclass probelms. However, these measures can be shown to be closely related [4]. We use here the Natarajan dimension, denoted as $S_N(\mathcal{H})$, to characterize the sample size complexity of the hypotheses family $\mathcal{H}$ [10, 4]. Since $\bar{\mathcal{H}}$ is binary, its sample size is characterized by its VC dimension $S_{VC}(\bar{\mathcal{H}})$ [14]. We will now show that each of these dimensions bounds the other up to a scaling factor which depends on $M$. Specifically, we will prove the following double inequality:

$$\frac{S_N(\mathcal{H})}{f_1(M)} - 1 \leq S_{VC}(\bar{\mathcal{H}}) \leq f_2(M) S_N(\mathcal{H}) \tag{2}$$

where $f_1(M) = O(M^2)$ and $f_2(M) = O(log M)$.

**Theorem 4.** *Let $S_N^U(\mathcal{H})$ denote the uniform Natarajan dimension of $\mathcal{H}$ as defined by Ben-David et al. [4]; then*

$$S_N^U(\mathcal{H}) - 1 \leq S_{VC}(\bar{\mathcal{H}})$$

*Proof.* Let $d$ denote the uniform Natarajan dimension, $d = S_N^U(\mathcal{H})$. It follows that there are $k, l \in \{0, \ldots, \mathbf{M} - 1\}$ and $\{x_i\}_{i=1}^d$ points in $X$ such that

$$\{0,1\}^d \subseteq \{(\psi_{k,l} \circ h(x_1), \ldots, \psi_{k,l} \circ h(x_d))|h \in \mathcal{H}\}$$

where $\psi_{k,l} : \{0, \ldots, \mathbf{M} - 1\} \to \{0, 1, *\}$, $\psi_{k,l}(k) = 1$, $\psi_{k,l}(l) = 0$, and $\psi_{k,l}(u) = *$ for every $u \neq k, l$.

Next we show that the set of product space points $\{\bar{x}_i = (x_i, x_{i+1})\}_{i=1}^{d-1}$ is VC-shattered by $\bar{\mathcal{H}}$. Assume an arbitrary $\bar{b} \in \{0,1\}^{d-1}$. Since by definition $\{x_i\}_{i=1}^d$ is $\psi_{k,l}$-shattered by $\mathcal{H}$, we can find $h \in \mathcal{H}$ which assigns $h(x_1) = l$ and gives the following assignments over the points $\{x_i\}_{i=2}^d$:

$$h(x_i) = \begin{pmatrix} k \ if \ h(x_{i-1}) = l \ and \ \bar{b}(i-1) = 0 \\ l \ if \ h(x_{i-1}) = l \ and \ \bar{b}(i-1) = 1 \\ l \ if \ h(x_{i-1}) = k \ and \ \bar{b}(i-1) = 0 \\ k \ if \ h(x_{i-1}) = k \ and \ \bar{b}(i-1) = 1 \end{pmatrix}$$

By construction $(\bar{h}(\bar{x}_1), \ldots, \bar{h}(\bar{x}_{d-1})) = \bar{b}$. Since $\bar{b}$ is arbitrary, $\{\bar{x}_i\}_{i=1}^{d-1}$ is shattered by $\bar{\mathcal{H}}$, and hence $S_{vc}(\bar{\mathcal{H}}) \geq d - 1$. $\qquad \square$

The relation between the uniform Natarajan dimension and the Natarajan dimension is given by theorem 7 in [4]. In our case it is

$$S_N(H) \leq \frac{M(M-1)}{2} S_N^U(H)$$

Hence the proof of theorem 4 gives us the left bound of inequality 2.

**Theorem 5.** *Let $d_{pr} = S_N(\mathcal{H})$ denote the Natarajan dimension of $\mathcal{H}$, and $d_o = S_{VC}(\bar{\mathcal{H}})$ denote the VC dimension of $\bar{\mathcal{H}}$. Then*

$$S_{VC}(\bar{\mathcal{H}}) \leq 4.87 S_N(\mathcal{H}) \log(\mathbf{M} + 1)$$

*Proof.* Let $X_{pr} = \{\bar{x}_i = (x_i^1, x_i^2)\}_{i=1}^{d_{pr}}$ denote a set of points in the product space which are shattered by $\bar{\mathcal{H}}$. Let $X_o = \{x_1^1, x_1^2, x_2^1, \ldots, x_{d_{pr}}^1, x_{d_{pr}}^2\}$ denote the corresponding set of points in the original space.

There is a set $Y_{pr} = \{\bar{h}_j\}_{j=1}^{2^{d_{pr}}}$ of $2^{d_{pr}}$ hypotheses in $\bar{\mathcal{H}}$, which are different from each other on $X_{pr}$. For each hypothesis $\bar{h}_j \in Y_{pr}$ there is a hypothesis $h \in \mathcal{H}$ such that $\bar{h} = U(h)$. If $\bar{h}_1 \neq \bar{h}_2 \in Y_{pr}$ then the corresponding $h_1, h_2$ are different on $X_o$. To see this, note that $\bar{h}_1 \neq \bar{h}_2$ implies the existence of $\bar{x}_i = (x_i^1, x_i^2) \in X_{pr}$ on which $\bar{h}_1(\bar{x}_i) \neq \bar{h}_2(\bar{x}_i)$. It is not possible in this case that both $h_1(x_i^1) = h_2(x_i^1)$ and $h_1(x_i^2) = h_2(x_i^2)$. Hence there are $2^{d_{pr}}$ hypotheses in $\mathcal{H}$ which are different on $X_o$, from which it follows that

$$|\{(h(x_1^1), h(x_1^2), \ldots, h(x_{d_{pr}}^1), h(x_{d_{pr}}^2))|h \in \mathcal{H}\}| \geq 2^{d_{pr}} \qquad (3)$$

The existence of an exponential number of assignments of $\mathcal{H}$ on the set $X_o$ is not possible if $|X_o|$ is much larger than the Natarajan dimension of $\mathcal{H}$. We use Thm. 9 in [4] (proved in [8]) to argue that if the Natarajan dimension of $\mathcal{H}$ is $d_o$, then

$$|\{(h(x_1^1), h(x_1^2), \ldots, h(x_{d_{pr}}^1), h(x_{d_{pr}}^2)) | h \in \mathcal{H}\}| \leq (\frac{2d_{pr}e(\mathbf{M}+1)^2}{2d_o})^{d_o} \qquad (4)$$

where $\mathbf{M}$ is the number of classes. Combining (3) and (4) we get

$$2^{d_{pr}} \leq (\frac{2d_{pr}e(\mathbf{M}+1)^2}{2d_o})^{d_o}$$

Here the term on left side is exponential in $d_{pr}$, and the term on the right side is polynomial. Hence the inequality cannot be true asymptotically and $d_{pr}$ is bounded.

We can find a convenient bound by following the proof of Thm. 10 in [4]. The algebraic details completing the proof are left for the technical report [3], appendix B. □

**Corollary 3.** $\bar{\mathcal{H}}$ *is learnable iff* $\mathcal{H}$ *is learnable.*

# 3   From Product Space Approximations to Original Space Classifiers

In section 3.1 we present an algorithm to partition a data set $Y$ using a product space function which is $\varepsilon$-good over $Y \times Y$. $f$ should only satisfy $e(f, \bar{c}) < \varepsilon$, but it doesn't have to be an equivalence relation indicator, and so in general there is no $h$ such that $f = U(h)$. The partition generated is shown to have an error linear in $\varepsilon$. Then in section 3.2 we briefly discuss (without proof) how an $\varepsilon$-good product space hypothesis can be used to build a classifier with error $O(\varepsilon)$.

## 3.1   Partitioning Using a Product Space Hypothesis

Assume we are given a data set $Y = \{x_i\}_{i=1}^N$ of points drawn independently from the distribution over $X$. Let $f$ denote a learned hypothesis from $\bar{\mathcal{H}}$, and denote the error of $f$ over the product space $Y \times Y$ by

$$\varepsilon = e(\bar{c}, f) = \frac{1}{N^2} \sum_{i=1}^N \sum_{j=1}^N 1_{\bar{c}(x_i, y_j) \neq f(x_i, y_j)}$$

Denote by $K$ the frequency $\frac{classsize}{N}$ of the smallest class in $Y$.

Note that since no explicit labels are given, we can only hope to find an approximation to $c$ over $Y$ up to a permutation of the labels. The following theorem shows that if $\varepsilon$ is small enough compared to $K$ and given $f$, there is a simple algorithm which is guaranteed to achieve an approximation to the partition represented by concept $c$ with error linear in $\varepsilon$.

**Theorem 6.** *Using the notation defined above, if the following condition hold*

$$\varepsilon < \frac{K^2}{6},$$ (5)

*then we can find a partition $g$ of $Y$ with a simple procedure, such that $e(c, J \circ g) < \frac{6\varepsilon}{K}$. $J$ here denotes a permutation $J : \{0, \ldots, M-1\} \to \{0, \ldots, M-1\}$ matching the labels of $c$ and $g$.*

In order to present the algorithm and prove the error bound as stated above, we first define several simple concepts.

Define the 'fiber' of a point $x \in Y$ under a function $h : X \times X \to \{0,1\}$ as the following restriction of $h$:

$$fiber^h(x) : Y \to \{0, 1\}, \quad [fiber^h(x)](y) = h(x, y)$$

$fiber^h(x)$ is an indicator function of the points in $Y$ which are in the same class with $x$ according to $h$.

Let us now define the distance between two fibers. For two indicator functions $I_1, I_2 : Y \to \{0, 1\}$ let us measure the distance between them using the $L1$ metric over $Y$:

$$d(I_1, I_2) = Prob(I_1(x) \neq I_2(x)) = \frac{1}{N} \sum_{i=1}^{N} 1_{I_1(x_i) \neq I_2(x_i)} = \frac{1}{N} \sum_{i=1}^{N} |I_1(x_i) - I_2(x_i)|$$

Given two fibers $fiber^h(x)$, $fiber^h(z)$ of a product space hypothesis, the $L_1$ distance between them has the form of

$$d(fiber^h(x), fiber^h(z)) = \frac{\#(Nei^h(x) \Delta Nei^h(z))}{N}$$

where $Nei^h(x) = \{y | h(x, y) = 1\}$. This gives us an intuitive meaning to the inter-fiber distance, namely, it is the frequency of sample points which are neighbors of $x$ and not of $z$ or vice versa.

The operator taking a point $x \in Y$ to $fiber^h(x)$ is therefore an embedding of $Y$ in the metric space $L_1(Y)$. In the next lemma we see that if the conditions of Thm. 6 hold, most of the data set is well separated under this embedding, in the sense that points from the same class are near while points from different classes are far. This allows us to define a simple algorithm which uses this separability to find a good partitioning of $Y$, and prove that its error is bounded as required.

**Lemma 2.** *There is a set of 'good' points $\mathcal{G} \in Y$ such that $|Y \backslash \mathcal{G}| \leq \frac{3\varepsilon}{K} N$ (i.e., the set is large), and for every two points $x, y \in \mathcal{G}$:*

$$c(x) = c(y) \implies d(fiber^f(x), fiber^f(y)) < \frac{2K}{3}$$

$$c(x) \neq c(y) \implies d(fiber^f(x), fiber^f(y)) \geq \frac{4K}{3}$$

*Proof.* Define the 'good' set $\mathcal{G}$ as

$$\mathcal{G} = \{x | d(fiber^f(x), fiber^c(x)) < \frac{K}{3}\}$$

We start by noting that the complement of $\mathcal{G}$, the set of 'bad' points $\mathcal{B} = \{x | d(fiber^f_x, fiber^c_x) \geq \frac{K}{3}\}$, is small as the lemma requires. The argument is the following

$$\varepsilon = e(\bar{c}, f) = \frac{1}{N^2} \sum_{i=1}^{N} \sum_{j=1}^{N} 1_{\bar{c}(x_i, y_j) = f(x_i, y_y)} = \frac{1}{N^2} [ \sum_{x_i \in \mathcal{B}} \sum_{j=1}^{N} 1_{\bar{c}(x_i, y_j) = f(x_i, y_y)}$$

$$+ \sum_{x_i \in \mathcal{G}} \sum_{j=1}^{N} 1_{\bar{c}(x_i, y_j) = f(x_i, y_y)}] \geq \frac{1}{N^2} \sum_{x_i \in \mathcal{B}} \frac{K}{3} N = \frac{K}{3N} |\mathcal{B}|$$

Next, assume that $c(x) = c(y)$ holds for two points $x, y \in \mathcal{G}$. Since $fiber^c(x) = fiber^c(y)$ we get

$$d(fiber^f(x), fiber^f(y)) \leq d(fiber^f(x), fiber^c(x)) + d(fiber^c(x), fiber^c(y))$$
$$+ d(fiber^c(y), fiber^f(y)) < \frac{K}{3} + 0 + \frac{K}{3} = \frac{2K}{3}$$

Finally, if $c(x) \neq c(y)$ then $fiber^c(x)$ and $fiber^c(y)$ are indicators of disjoint sets, each bigger or equal to $K$. Hence $d(fiber^c(x), fiber^c(y)) \geq 2K$ and we get

$$\begin{aligned} 2K &\leq d(fiber^c(x), fiber^c(y)) \\ &\leq d(fiber^c(x), fiber^f(x)) + d(fiber^f(x), fiber^f(y)) \\ &\quad + d(fiber^f(y), fiber^c(y)) \\ &\leq \frac{K}{3} + d(fiber^f(x), fiber^f(y)) + \frac{K}{3} \\ &\implies d(fiber^f(x), fiber^f(y)) \geq \frac{4K}{3} \end{aligned}$$

$\square$

It follows from the lemma that over the 'good' set $\mathcal{G}$, which contains more than $(1 - \frac{3\varepsilon}{K})N$ points, the classes are very well separated. Each class is concentrated in a $\frac{K}{3}$-ball and the different balls are $\frac{4K}{3}$ distant from each other. Intuitively, under such conditions almost any reasonable clustering algorithm can find the correct partitioning over this set; since the size of the remaining set of 'bad' points $\mathcal{B}$ is linear in $\varepsilon$, the total error is expected to be linear in $\varepsilon$ too.

However, in order to prove a worst case bound we still face a certain problem. Since we do not know how to tell $\mathcal{G}$ from $\mathcal{B}$, the 'bad' points might obscure the partition. We therefore suggest the following greedy procedure to define a partition g over $Y$:

- Compute the fibers $fiber^f(x)$ for all $x \in Y$.
- Let $i = 0$, $S_0 = Y$; while $|S_i| > \frac{KN}{2}$ do:

- for each point $x \in S_i$, compute the set of all points lying inside a sphere of radius $\frac{2K}{3}$ around $x$:

$$B_{\frac{2k}{3}}(x) = \{y \in S_i : d(fiber^f(x), fiber^f(y)) < \frac{2K}{3}\}$$

- find $z = \underset{x \in S_i}{\arg\max} |B_{\frac{2K}{3}}(x)|$ and define $g(y) = i$ for every $y \in B_{\frac{2k}{3}}(z)$;
- remove the points of $B_{\frac{2k}{3}}(z)$ from $S_i$: let $S_{i+1} = S_i \backslash B_{\frac{2k}{3}}(z)$, and $i = i+1$.
- Let $\mathbf{M}_g$ denote the number of rounds completed. Denote the domain on which $g$ has been defined so far as $G_0$. Define $g$ for the remaining points in $Y \backslash G_0$ as follows:

$$g(x) = \underset{i \in \{0, \ldots, \mathbf{M}_g - 1\}}{\arg\min} d(fiber^f(x), I_{\{g^{-1}(i)\}})$$

where $I_{\{g^{-1}(i)\}}$ is the indicator function of cluster $i$ of $g$. Note, however, that the way $g$ is defined over this set is not really important since, as we shall see, the set is small.

The proof for the error bound of $g$ starts with two lemmas:

1. The first lemma uses lemma 2 to show that each cluster defined by $g$ intersects only a single set of the form $c^{-1}(i) \cap \mathcal{G}$.
2. The second lemma shows that due to the greedy nature of the algorithm, the sets $g^{-1}(i)$ chosen at each step are big enough so that each intersects at least one of the sets $\{c^{-1}(j) \cap \mathcal{G}\}_{j=1}^{\mathbf{M}-1}$.
   It immediately follows that each set $g^{-1}(i)$ intersects a single set $\{c^{-1}(j) \cap \mathcal{G}\}$, and a match between the clusters of $g$ and the classes of $c$ can be established, while $Y \backslash G_0$ can be shown to be $O(\varepsilon)$ small.
3. Finally, the error of $g$ is bounded by showing that if $x \in G_0 \cap \mathcal{G}$ then $x$ is classified correctly by $g$.

Details of the lemmas and proofs are given in the technical report [3], appendix C, which completes the proof of Thm. 6.

## 3.2   Classifing Using a Product Space Hypothesis

Given an $\varepsilon$ good product space hypothesis $f$, we can build a multiclass classifier as follows: Sample $N$ unlabeled data points $Y = \{x_i\}_{i=1}^N$ from $X$ and partition them using the algorithm presented in the previous subsection. A new point $Z$ is classified as a member of the class $l$ where

$$l = \underset{i \in \{0, \ldots, M-1\}}{\arg\min} d(fiber^f(z), I_{g^{-1}(i)})$$

The following theorem bounds the error of such a classifier

**Theorem 7.** *Assume the error probability of $f$ over $X \times X$ is $e(f, \bar{c}) = \varepsilon < \frac{K^2}{8}$. For each $\delta > 0$, $l > 4$: if $N > \frac{3l}{K(\frac{l}{4}-1)^2} \log(\frac{1}{\delta})$, then the error of the classifier proposed is lower than $\frac{l\varepsilon}{K} + \delta$*

The proof is omitted.

# 4    Concluding Remarks

We showed in this paper that learning in the product space produces good multi-class classifiers of the original space, and that the sample complexity of learning in the product space is comparable to the complexity of learning in the original space. We see the significance of these results in two aspects: First, since learning in the product space always involves only binary functions, we can use the full power of binary classification theory and its many efficient algorithms to solve multiclass classification problems. In contrast, the learning toolbox for multi-class problems in the original space is relatively limited. Second, the automatic acquisition of product space labels is plausible in many domains in which the data is produced by some Markovian process. In such domains the learning of interesting concepts without any human supervision may be possible.

# References

1. E. Allwein, R. Schapire, and Y. Singer. Reducing Multiclass to Binary: A Unifying Approach for Margin Classifiers. *Journal of Machine Learning Research*, 1:113-141, 2000.
2. N. Bansal, A. Blum, and S. Chawla. Correlation Clustering. In Proc. FOCS 2002, pages 238-247.
3. A. Bar-Hillel, and D. Weinshall. Learning with Equivalence Constraints. HU Technical Report 2003-38, in http://www.cs.huji.ac.il/~daphna.
4. S. Ben-David, N. Cesa-Bianchi, D. Haussler, and P. H. Long. Characterizations of learnability for classes of 0, . . . , n-valued functions.
5. T. G. Dietterich, and G. Bakiri. Solving multiclass learning problems via error-correcting output codes. *Journal of Artifical Intelligence Research*, 2:263-286, 1995.
6. V. Guruswami and Amit Sahai. Multiclass learning, Boosting, and Error-Correcting codes. In Proc. COLT, 1999.
7. S. Har-Peled, D. Roth, D. Zimak. Constraints classification:A new approach to multiclass classification and ranking. In Proc. NIPS, 2002.
8. D. Haussler and P.M. Long. A generalization of Sauer's lemma. Technical Report UCSU-CRL-90-15. UC Santa Cruz, 1990.
9. M. J. Kearns and U. V. Vazirani. An Introduction to Computational Learning Theory. MIT Press, 1994.
10. B. K. Natarajan. On learning sets and functions. *Machine Learning*, 4:67-97, 1989.
11. P. J. Phillips. Support vector machines applied to face recognition. In M. C. Mozer, M. I. Jordan, and T. Petsche, editors, *Advances in Neural Information Processing Systems 11*, page 803. MIT Press, 1998.
12. T. Hertz, N. Shental, A. Bar-Hillel, and D. Weinshall. Enhancing Image and Video Retrieval: Learning via Equivalence Constraints. In Proc. of IEEE Conference on Computer Vision and Pattern Recognition, 2003.
13. R. E. Schapire. A brief introduction to boosting. In Proc. of the Sixteenth International Joint Conference on Artificial Intelligence, 1999.
14. V. N. Vapnik. The Nature of Statistical Learning. Springer, 1995.

# Tutorial: Machine Learning Methods in Natural Language Processing

Michael Collins

MIT AI Lab

Statistical or machine learning approaches have become quite prominent in the Natural Language Processing literature. Common techniques include generative models such as Hidden Markov Models or Probabilistic Context-Free Grammars, and more general noisy-channel models such as the statistical approach to machine translation pioneered by researchers at IBM in the early 90s. Recent work has considered discriminative methods such as (conditional) markov random fields, or large-margin methods. This tutorial will describe several of these techniques. The methods will be motivated through a number of natural language problems: from part-of-speech tagging and parsing, to machine translation, dialogue systems and information extraction problems. I will also concentrate on links to the COLT and kernel methods literature: for example covering kernels over the discrete structures found in NLP, online algorithms for NLP problems, and the issues in extending generalization bounds from classification problems to NLP problems such as parsing.

B. Schölkopf and M.K. Warmuth (Eds.): COLT/Kernel 2003, LNAI 2777, p. 655, 2003.
© Springer-Verlag Berlin Heidelberg 2003

# Learning from Uncertain Data

Mehryar Mohri

AT&T Labs – Research
180 Park Avenue, Florham Park, NJ 07932, USA
mohri@research.att.com

**Abstract.** The application of statistical methods to natural language processing has been remarkably successful over the past two decades. But, to deal with recent problems arising in this field, machine learning techniques must be generalized to deal with *uncertain data*, or datasets whose elements are distributions over sequences, such as weighted automata. This paper reviews a number of recent results related to this question. We discuss how to compute efficiently basic statistics from a weighted automaton such as the expected count of an arbitrary sequence and higher moments of that distribution, by using weighted transducers. Both the corresponding transducers and related algorithms are described. We show how general classification techniques such as Support Vector Machines can be extended to deal with distributions by using general kernels between weighted automata. We describe several examples of positive definite kernels between weighted automata such as kernels based on counts of common *n*-gram sequences, counts of common factors or suffixes, or other more complex kernels, and describe a general algorithm for computing them efficiently. We also demonstrate how machine learning techniques such as clustering based on the edit-distance can be extended to deal with unweighted and weighted automata representing distributions.

## 1 Introduction

The application of statistical methods to natural language processing has been remarkably successful over the past two decades. Many of the components of speech recognition systems, language models, pronunciation models, context-dependency models, Hidden-Markov Models (HMMs), are statistical models [10, 25, 22]. Sophisticated statistical learning techniques have also been used in all other areas of natural language processing from the design of high-accuracy statistical parsers [3, 4, 26] and morphological analyzers to that of accurate text classification systems [27, 11].

As for all machine learning techniques, these methods heavily rely on data and the availability of text and speech corpora in several areas has played a critical role in their success. But, new machine learning techniques in natural language processing must deal with *uncertain data*. To illustrate this, consider the case of large-vocabulary speech recognition systems designed to transcribe broadcast programs. A virtually unlimited amount of unlabeled audio data can

B. Schölkopf and M.K. Warmuth (Eds.): COLT/Kernel 2003, LNAI 2777, pp. 656–670, 2003.

be collected from a television feed. An existing speech recognizer can be applied to this data to produce, for each speech utterance, a set of uncertain alternative transcriptions, typically represented by a weighted automaton [13]. Such an automaton can then be used as a *label* for the corresponding speech utterance and constitute the input data for training acoustic or grammar models.

A similar situation can be found in the case of a complex information extraction system or a complex search engine. These systems are typically not fully certain about the correct response. This may be because of the ambiguities affecting the input query, which are quite common in natural language, or because the complex information sources used by the system just cannot uniquely determine the response. Thus, they generate a range of alternative hypotheses with some associated weights or probabilities used to rank these hypotheses. When the accuracy of a system is relatively low, it is not safe to rely only on the best hypothesis output by the system. It is then preferable to use instead the full range of hypotheses and their weights since that set most often contains the correct response.

These observations apply similarly to many other areas of natural language processing and in fact to other domains such as computational biology. The input data for many machine learning techniques in such contexts is *uncertain* and can be viewed as a set of *distributions*. More specifically, in natural language processing, these are distributions over sequences, such as sequences of words or phonemes. Thus, statistical learning techniques must be generalized to deal with distributions of strings, or sequences.

The data uncertainty and the distributions we are referring to here should not be confused with the sampling distribution inherent to any learning problem – that distribution is typically assumed to be *i.i.d.* and the corresponding assumptions hold similarly in our case. Here, each object of the input data is a distribution. To further clarify the problem we are describing, consider the toy classification problem of predicting gender based on height and weight. The input data for this problem is typically a set of pairs (height, weight) for a large sample of the population. The problem we are facing here is similar to having instead for each member of that population not the exact height or weight but a height or weight distribution.

It is possible to reformulate this problem as a classical machine learning problem if we resort to an approximation. Indeed, we can extract random samples from each distribution and use the samples to augment the feature set. The sample sizes must be sufficiently large to be representative of each distribution. But, this may dramatically affect the efficiency of the learning algorithm by significantly increasing the size of the feature set, while still solving only an approximate problem. In what follows, we are interested in exact solutions and efficient algorithms exploiting the input distributions directly.

In most cases, such as those just discussed, the distributions can be represented by weighted automata, in fact acyclic, since their support is a large but finite number of sequences. Dealing with objects represented by weighted automata arises many new algorithmic questions. This paper discusses and reviews a number of recent results related to these questions [7, 6, 21].

A general question for any statistical learning technique dealing with weighted automata is that of collecting statistics. How can we count efficiently sequences appearing in weighted automata? How do we take into account the weight or probability associated to each path? We present simple algorithms for computing efficiently the expected count and even higher moments of the count of an arbitrary sequence in a weighted automaton.

The application of discriminant classification algorithms to weighted automata arises other issues. We briefly describe a general kernel framework, *rational kernels*, that extends kernel methods to the analysis of weighted automata. These kernels can be computed efficiently and include many of the kernels introduced in text classification and computational biology [9, 30, 16, 14]. They have been used successfully in applications such as spoken-dialog classification. We give several examples of positive definite rational kernels and illustrate their generality.

We also show how machine learning techniques such as clustering based on the edit-distance can be generalized to deal with unweighted and weighted automata representing distributions. We extend the definition of the edit-distance to automata and describe efficient algorithms for the computation of the edit-distance and the longest common subsequence of two automata. We start with some basic definitions and notation related to weighted automata and transducers.

## 2   Preliminaries

**Definition 1 ([12]).** *A system* $(\mathbb{K}, \oplus, \otimes, \overline{0}, \overline{1})$ *is a* semiring *if* $(\mathbb{K}, \oplus, \overline{0})$ *is a commutative monoid with identity element* $\overline{0}$, $(\mathbb{K}, \otimes, \overline{1})$ *is a monoid with identity element* $\overline{1}$, $\otimes$ *distributes over* $\oplus$, *and* $\overline{0}$ *is an annihilator for* $\otimes$: *for all* $a \in \mathbb{K}, a \otimes \overline{0} = \overline{0} \otimes a = \overline{0}$.

Thus, a semiring is a ring that may lack negation. Some familiar examples are the Boolean semiring $\mathcal{B} = (\{0, 1\}, \vee, \wedge, 0, 1)$, or the probability semiring $\mathcal{R} = (\mathbb{R}_+, +, \times, 0, 1)$ used to combine probabilities. Two semirings often used in natural language processing are: the *log semiring* $\mathcal{L} = (\mathbb{R} \cup \{\infty\}, \oplus_{\log}, +, \infty, 0)$ [20] which is isomorphic to $\mathcal{R}$ via a log morphism with: $\forall a, b \in \mathbb{R} \cup \{\infty\}, a \oplus_{\log} b = -\log(\exp(-a) + \exp(-b))$ (by convention: $\exp(-\infty) = 0$ and $-\log(0) = \infty$), and the *tropical semiring* $\mathcal{T} = (\mathbb{R}_+ \cup \{\infty\}, \min, +, \infty, 0)$ which is derived from the log semiring using the Viterbi approximation.

**Definition 2.** *A* weighted finite-state transducer $T$ *over a semiring* $\mathbb{K}$ *is an 8-tuple* $T = (\Sigma, \Delta, Q, I, F, E, \lambda, \rho)$ *where* $\Sigma$ *is the finite input alphabet of the transducer,* $\Delta$ *is the finite output alphabet,* $Q$ *is a finite set of states,* $I \subseteq Q$ *the set of initial states,* $F \subseteq Q$ *the set of final states,* $E \subseteq Q \times (\Sigma \cup \{\epsilon\}) \times (\Delta \cup \{\epsilon\}) \times \mathbb{K} \times Q$ *a finite set of transitions,* $\lambda : I \rightarrow \mathbb{K}$ *the initial weight function, and* $\rho : F \rightarrow \mathbb{K}$ *the final weight function mapping* $F$ *to* $\mathbb{K}$.

A *Weighted automaton* $A = (\Sigma, Q, I, F, E, \lambda, \rho)$ is defined in a similar way by simply omitting the input or output labels. We denote by $L(A) \subseteq \Sigma^*$ the set of strings accepted by an automaton $A$ and similarly by $L(X)$ the strings described by a regular expression $X$.

Given a transition $e \in E$, we denote by $i[e]$ its input label, $p[e]$ its origin or previous state and $n[e]$ its destination state or next state, $w[e]$ its weight, $o[e]$ its output label (transducer case). Given a state $q \in Q$, we denote by $E[q]$ the set of transitions leaving $q$.

A *path* $\pi = e_1 \cdots e_k$ is an element of $E^*$ with consecutive transitions: $n[e_{i-1}] = p[e_i]$, $i = 2, \ldots, k$. We extend $n$ and $p$ to paths by setting: $n[\pi] = n[e_k]$ and $p[\pi] = p[e_1]$. A *successful path* in a weighted automaton or transducer is a path from an initial state to a final state. We denote by $P(q, q')$ the set of paths from $q$ to $q'$ and by $P(q, x, q')$ and $P(q, x, y, q')$ the set of paths from $q$ to $q'$ with input label $x \in \Sigma^*$ and output label $y$ (transducer case). These definitions can be extended to subsets $R, R' \subseteq Q$, by: $P(R, x, R') = \cup_{q \in R, \, q' \in R'} P(q, x, q')$. The labeling functions $i$ (and similarly $o$) and the weight function $w$ can also be extended to paths by defining the label of a path as the concatenation of the labels of its constituent transitions, and the weight of a path as the $\otimes$-product of the weights of its constituent transitions: $i[\pi] = i[e_1] \cdots i[e_k]$, $w[\pi] = w[e_1] \otimes \cdots \otimes w[e_k]$. We also extend $w$ to any finite set of paths $\Pi$ by setting: $w[\Pi] = \bigoplus_{\pi \in \Pi} w[\pi]$, and even to an automaton or transducer $M$ by $w[M] = \bigoplus_{\pi \in \Pi_M} w[\pi]$, where $\Pi_M$ is the set of successful paths of $M$. An automaton $A$ is *regulated* if the output weight associated by $A$ to each input string $x \in \Sigma^*$:

$$[\![A]\!](x) = \bigoplus_{\pi \in P(I, x, F)} \lambda(p[\pi]) \otimes w[\pi] \otimes \rho(n[\pi]) \qquad (1)$$

is well-defined and in $\mathbb{K}$. This condition is always satisfied when $A$ contains no $\epsilon$-cycle since the sum then runs over a finite number of paths. It is also always satisfied with *k-closed* semirings such as the tropical semiring [20]. $[\![A]\!](x)$ is defined to be $\bar{0}$ when $P(I, x, F) = \emptyset$.

Similarly, a transducer $T$ is *regulated* if the output weight associated by $T$ to any pair of input-output string $(x, y)$ by:

$$[\![T]\!](x, y) = \bigoplus_{\pi \in P(I, x, y, F)} \lambda(p[\pi]) \otimes w[\pi] \otimes \rho(n[\pi]) \qquad (2)$$

is well-defined and in $\mathbb{K}$. $[\![T]\!](x, y) = \bar{0}$ when $P(I, x, y, F) = \emptyset$. In the following, we will assume that all the automata and transducers considered are regulated. We denote by $|M|$ the sum of the number of states and transitions of an automaton or transducer $M$.

For any transducer $T$, we denote by $\Pi_2(T)$ the automaton obtained by projecting $T$ on its output, that is by omitting its input labels.

## 3    Collecting Statistics

Statistical methods used in natural language processing are typically based on very large amounts of data, e.g., statistical language models are derived from text corpora of several million words. The first step for the creation of these models is the computation of the counts of some sequences. For language models used in speech recognition, these sequences are often $n$-gram sequences, but other applications may require the computation of the counts of non-contiguous units or even that of sequences given by a regular expression.

In new applications such as task adaptation, one needs to construct these models from distributions of sequences. For example, one may need to construct a language model based on the output of a speech recognition system, which is an acyclic weighted automaton called a *word* or a *phone lattice*. In traditional language modeling tasks, the count of the relevant sequences is computed from the input text. To deal with distributions of sequences instead of just text, we need to compute efficiently the *expected count* of a sequence or a set of sequences.[1]

A weighted automaton contains typically a very large set of alternative sequences with corresponding weights or probabilities. Collecting such statistics cannot be done by counting the number of occurrences of the sequence considered in each path since the number of paths of even a small automaton may be more than a billion. We present a simple and efficient algorithm for computing efficiently the expected count and higher moments of the count of an arbitrary sequence appearing in a weighted automaton.

### 3.1    Definition

Let $A = (Q, I, F, \Sigma, \delta, \sigma, \lambda, \rho)$ be an arbitrary weighted automaton over the probability semiring and let $X$ be a regular expression defined over the alphabet $\Sigma$. We are interested in *counting* the occurrences of the sequences $x \in L(X)$ in $A$ while taking into account the weight of the paths where they appear.

When $A$ is *stochastic*, i.e. when it is deterministic and the sum of the weights of the transitions leaving any state is 1, it can be viewed as a probability distribution $P$ over all strings $\Sigma^*$.[2] The weight $[\![A]\!](u)$ associated by $A$ to a string $u \in \Sigma^*$ is then $P(u)$. Thus, we define the *expected count* of the sequence $x$ in $A$, $c(x)$, as:

$$c(x) = \sum_{u \in \Sigma^*} |u|_x \, P(u) = \sum_{u \in \Sigma^*} |u|_x \, [\![A]\!](u) \tag{3}$$

where $|u|_x$ denotes the number of occurrences of $x$ in the string $u$. We will define the count of $x$ as above regardless of whether $A$ is stochastic or not. More

---

[1]  Many modeling algorithms can be naturally generalized to deal with input distributions by replacing the quantity $X$ originally derived from text by its expectation $E[X]$ based on the probability distribution considered.

[2]  There exist a general weighted determinization and a weight pushing algorithm that can be used to create a deterministic and stochastic automaton equivalent to an input weighted automaton [17].

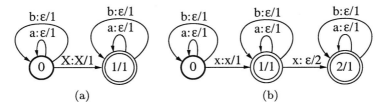

**Fig. 1.** Weighted transducers over the probability semiring used for counting with the alphabet $\Sigma = \{a, b\}$. (a) Transducer $T_1$ used to compute the expected counts of the sequences $x \in L(X)$. The transition weights and the final weight at state 1 are all equal to 1. (b) Weighted transducer $T_2$ used to compute $c_2(x)$, the second moment of the counts of a sequence $x \in L(X)$.

generally, for $m \geq 1$, the *m-th moment of the count* of the sequence $x$ is defined by:

$$c_m(x) = \sum_{u \in \Sigma^*} |u|_x^m \, [\![A]\!](u) \tag{4}$$

In many applications, the weighted automaton $A$ is acyclic, e.g., it is the output of a speech recognition system. But our algorithm is general and does not assume $A$ to be acyclic.

## 3.2   Algorithm

We describe an algorithm for computing the expected counts of the sequences $x \in L(X)$. Let $A_1$ be a weighted automaton over the probability semiring representing the weighted regular expression (or *formal power series* [12]) $\Sigma^* x \Sigma^*$. Figure 1(a) shows a weighted transducer whose input automaton is $A_1$ if $X = x$ and $\Sigma = \{a, b\}$.

**Lemma 1.** *For all $u \in \Sigma^*$, $[\![A_1]\!](u) = |u|_x$.*

*Proof.* Let $u \in \Sigma^*$. For any occurrence of $x$ in $u$, $u$ can be decomposed into $u = u_1 x u_2$, with $u_1, u_2 \in \Sigma^*$. Thus, for any occurrence of $x$ in $u$, $A_1$ contains one distinct path labeled with $u$ and with weight 1. Since $[\![A_1]\!](u)$ is the sum of the weights of all these paths, this proves the lemma. □

Since $X$ is regular, the weighted transduction defined by $(\Sigma \times \{\epsilon\})^*(X \times X)(\Sigma \times \{\epsilon\})^*$ is rational. Thus, by the theorem of Schützenberger [28], there exists a weighted transducer $T_1$ defined over the alphabet $\Sigma$ and the probability semiring realizing that transduction. Figure 1(a) shows the transducer $T_1$ in the particular case of $\Sigma = \{a, b\}$.

**Proposition 1.** *Let $A$ be a weighted automaton over the probability semiring, then:*

$$[\![\Pi_2(A \circ T_1)]\!](x) = c(x)$$

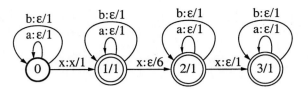

**Fig. 2.** Weighted transducer $T_3$ used to compute $c_3(x)$, the third moment of the counts of a sequence $x \in L(X)$.

*Proof.* By definition of $T_1$, for any $u \in \Sigma^*$, $[\![T_1]\!](u, x) = [\![A_1]\!](x)$, and by Lemma 1, $[\![A_1]\!](x) = |u|_x$. Thus, by definition of composition:

$$[\![\Pi_2(A \circ T_1)]\!](x) = \sum_{\pi \in P(I,F),\, u=i[\pi]} [\![A]\!](u) \times |u|_x = \sum_{u \in \Sigma^*} |u|_x\, [\![A]\!](u) = c(x)$$

This ends the proof of the proposition. □

The weighted automaton $B = \Pi_2(A \circ T_1)$ contains $\epsilon$-transitions. A general $\epsilon$-removal algorithm can be used to compute an equivalent weighted automaton with no $\epsilon$-transition [19]. The computation of $[\![B]\!](x)$ for a given $x$ is done by composing $B$ with an automaton representing $x$ and by using a simple shortest-distance algorithm [20] to compute the sum of the weights of all the paths of the result.

The proposition gives a simple algorithm for computing the expected counts of $X$ in a weighted automaton $A$ based on several general and well-studied algorithms: composition algorithm for weighted transducers [23], projection of weighted transducers, $\epsilon$-removal of weighted transducers, forward-backward algorithm or shortest-distance algorithm.

The algorithm is also based on the transducer $T_1$ which is quite easy to construct. The size of $T_1$ is in $O(|\Sigma| + |A_X|)$, where $A_X$ is a finite automaton accepting $X$. With a lazy implementation of $T_1$, only one transition can be used instead of $|\Sigma|$, thereby reducing the size of the representation of $T_1$ to $O(|A_X|)$. The worst case complexity of composition is quadratic and that of projection is linear, thus the time complexity of the construction of the automaton $B$ giving the expected counts of sequences $x \in L(X)$ is $O(|A||A_X|)$.

One can compute other moments of the count of a sequence $x$ in a similar way. Indeed, let $A_m$, $m \geq 1$, be the automaton obtained by composing or intersecting $A_1$ with itself $m - 1$ times, and let $T_m$ be a weighted transducer corresponding to $A_m \times \{x\}$, then $T_m$ can be used to compute the $m\text{-}th$ moment of the count of $x$.

**Corollary 1.** *Let $A$ be a weighted automaton over the probability semiring, then:*

$$[\![\Pi_2(A \circ T_m)]\!](x) = c_m(x)$$

*Proof.* In view of lemma 1, $[\![A]\!](u) = |u|_x$. Thus, by definition of composition:

$$\forall u \in \Sigma^*, [\![A_m]\!](u) = |u|_x^m \tag{5}$$

The result follows.                                                           □

In the worst case, the size of the composition of an automaton with itself may be quadratic in the size of the original automaton. But, it can be shown that there exists a compact representation of $A_m$ whose size is in $O(m(|x| + \Sigma))$, thus the size of a lazy representation of $T_m$ is in $O(m|x|)$. Figure 1(a) shows the transducer $T_2$ and Figure 2 the transducer $T_3$, when the alphabet is reduced to $\Sigma = \{a, b\}$.

These transducers can be used to compute efficiently the moments of the counts of sequences appearing in weighted automata, which are needed for the design of statistical models derived from distributions of sequences given by weighted automata.

# 4    Classification

Classification is a key task in many natural language processing applications. In document or text classification, it may consist of assigning a specific topic to each document, or to a set of sentences. Typically, features such as some specific sequences are extracted from these sentences and used by a machine learning algorithm. In spoken-dialog systems, the task consists of assigning to each speech utterance a category, out of a finite set, based on the output of a speech recognizer for that utterance. Due to the word error rate of conversational speech recognizers, it is preferable to use to full output of the recognizer which is a weighted automaton containing a large set of alternative transcriptions with their corresponding weights.

Recently, we introduced a general kernel framework based on weighted transducers, *rational kernels*, to extend kernel methods to deal with weighted automata [7, 6]. These kernels can be used in combination with a statistical learning technique such as Support Vector Machines (SVMs) [2, 8, 29] for efficient classification of weighted automata. This section briefly introduces rational kernels and describes several examples of positive definite rational kernels that can be used in a variety of applications.

## 4.1    Definition

Let $\Omega$ denote the set of weighted automata over the alphabet $\Sigma$.

**Definition 3.** $K : \Omega \times \Omega \to \mathbb{R}$ *is a* rational kernel *if there exists a weighted transducer* $T$ *and a function* $\psi : \mathbb{R} \to \mathbb{R}$ *such that for all* $X, Y \in \Omega$:

$$K(X, Y) = \psi(w[X \circ T \circ Y]) \tag{6}$$

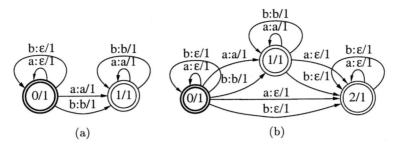

**Fig. 3.** (a) Weighted transducer $T_s$ mapping any sequence $x$ to the set of suffixes of $x$. (b) Weighted transducer $T_f$ mapping any sequence $x$ to the set of factors of $x$.

No special assumption is made about the function $\psi$ in this definition. In most cases of interest, however, $\psi$ is simply the identity function. Since the worst cost complexity of composition is quadratic, assuming that $\psi$ can be computed in constant time, the cost of the computation of $K(X, Y)$ is in $O(|T||X||Y|)$. This complexity can be improved to be linear in $|X|$ and $|Y|$ in the case of automata representing strings by using failure functions.

Rational kernels define a general set of kernels based on weighted transducers that can be computed efficiently using composition. But not all rational kernels are *positive definite symmetric* (PDS), or equivalently verify Mercer's condition [1], a condition that guarantees the convergence to a global optimum of discriminant classification algorithms such as Support Vector Machines (SVMs). A kernel $K$ is a PDS kernel iff the matrix $K(x_i, x_j)_{i,j \leq n}$ for all $n \geq 1$ and all $\{x_1, \ldots, x_n\} \subseteq X$ is symmetric and all its eigenvalues are non-negative. There exists however a systematic method for constructing a PDS kernel. Assume that the function $\psi$ in the definition of rational kernels is a continuous morphism. Then, the following result [6] shows that one can in fact construct a PDS rational kernel from an arbitrary weighted transducer $T$. The construction is based on the composition of $T$ with its inverse $T^{-1}$, that is the transducer obtained from $T$ by swapping input and output labels of each transition.

**Proposition 2 ([6]).** *Let $T$ be a weighted finite-state transducer and assume that the weighted transducer $T \circ T^{-1}$ is well-defined, then $T \circ T^{-1}$ defines a PDS rational kernel over $\Sigma^* \times \Sigma^*$.*

### 4.2   Examples of Rational Kernels

A kernel can be viewed as a measure of similarity between two elements. A common method used for the definition of kernels is based on the idea that two sequences are similar if they share many common subsequences of some kind. This idea can be generalized to weighted automata by considering the expected counts of the subsequences of the paths of an automaton instead of the

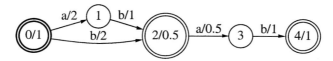

**Fig. 4.** Result of the application of the transducer $T_s$ to an acceptor for the sequence *abab*. This weighted automaton contains all the suffixes of the string *abab* with their multiplicities.

counts. We present several examples of construction of PDS rational kernels for automata.

*Suffix kernel.* The transduction from $\Sigma^*$ to $\Sigma^*$ which associates to each string the set of its suffixes is rational. Figure 3(a) shows a weighted transducer, $T_s$, realizing that transduction. By Proposition 2, we can use $T_s$ to define a PDS rational kernel $K_s$ measuring the similarity of two weighted automata $X$ and $Y$ based on the expected counts of the common suffixes of the sequences of $X$ and $Y$ by

$$K_s(X,Y) = w[X \circ (T_s \circ T_s^{-1}) \circ Y] \tag{7}$$

We can define similarly a PDS rational kernel based on prefixes. Figure 4 shows the result of the application of the transducer $T_s$ to the input sequence *abab* after $\epsilon$-removal and determinization.

*Factor kernel.* Similarly, the transduction from $\Sigma^*$ to $\Sigma^*$ which associates to each string the set of its factors is rational.[3] Figure 3(b) shows a weighted transducer, $T_f$, realizing that transduction. By Proposition 2, we can use $T_f$ to define a PDS rational kernel $K_f$ measuring the similarity of two weighted automata $X$ and $Y$ based on the expected counts of the common factors of the sequences of $X$ and $Y$.

*Gappy n-gram kernels.* Measures of similarity are often based on common $n$-gram sequences. Since the set of $n$-gram sequences over a finite alphabet is a regular language, by Proposition 1, there exists a simple weighted transducer that can be used to compute the expected counts of $n$-gram sequences of a weighted automaton $A$. That transducer can be slightly modified to compute the expected counts of non-contiguous or gappy $n$-grams using a decay factor $\lambda$, $0 \le \lambda < 1$, penalizing long gaps. Figure 5 shows a weighted transducer over the alphabet $\Sigma = \{a, b\}$, $T_\lambda$, that computes the expected counts of gappy trigrams with a decay factor $\lambda$ as defined by [16]. By Proposition 2, the composed transducer $T_\lambda \circ T_\lambda^{-1}$ defines a PDS kernel measuring the similarity of two weighted automata based on the expected counts of their common gappy $n$-grams.

---

[3] A *factor* $f$ of a string $x$ is a subsequence of $x$ with contiguous symbols. Thus, if $f$ is a factor of $x$, $x$ can be written as $x = x_1 f x_2$ for some $x_1, x_2 \in \Sigma^*$.

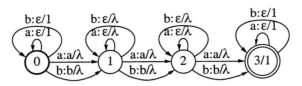

**Fig. 5.** Weighted transducer $T_\lambda$ over the probability semiring computing the expected counts of gappy trigrams with a decay factor $0 \leq \lambda < 1$.

*More powerful n-gram kernels.* The results of Section 3 can be used to design more complex PDS rational kernels. The previous examples were all based on the expected counts of some subsequences. By Corollary 1, one can use a weighted transducer to compute other moments of the counts of $n$-gram sequences. That transducer can be composed with its inverse to construct a PDS rational kernel. Thus, we can define more general rational kernels based on both the expectation and the variance of common $n$-gram sequences between two automata. These kernels are likely to lead to a more refined classification.

We have reported elsewhere the results of experiments using SVMs with $n$-gram kernels in a spoken-dialog classification task [7]. The results show the benefits of the use of kernels applied to weighted automata over the use of just the best paths of these machines.

## 5   Clustering

The significant increase in size of text and speech datasets, in some cases data generated by continuous streams, has created an even stronger need for clustering, in particular because of its use for data summarization. Clustering consists of grouping objects of a large dataset into classes based on a metric, or a similarity measure. Many of the kernels presented in the previous section can be used as a similarity measure for clustering algorithms. Another metric relevant to clustering often used in natural language processing applications is that of the *edit-distance*, that is the minimal cost of a series of edit operations (symbol insertions, deletions, or substitutions) transforming one sequence into the other [15], e.g., the accuracy of a speech recognition system for an input speech utterance is often measured by the edit-distance between the output of the recognizer and the correct transcription.

To use the notion of edit-distance and apply clustering algorithms to uncertain data where each element is represented by a set of alternatives, we need to extend the edit-distance to that of a distance between two languages, the sets of sequences accepted by two automata and provide an efficient algorithm for its computation. Let $d(x, y)$ denote the edit-distance between two strings $x$ and $y$ over the alphabet $\Sigma$. A natural extension of the definition of the edit-distance which coincides with the usual definition of the distance between two subsets of a metric space is given by the following.

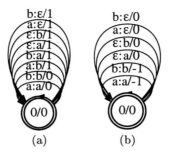

Fig. 6. (a) Weighted transducer $T_e$ over the tropical semiring computing the edit-distance of two strings or automata. (b) Weighted transducer $T_s$ over the tropical semiring computing the longest common subsequence of two strings of two automata.

**Definition 4 ([21]).** *The edit-distance of two languages $X \subseteq \Sigma^*$ and $Y \subseteq \Sigma^*$ is denoted by $d(X, Y)$ and defined by:*

$$d(X, Y) = \inf \{ d(x, y) : x \in X, \, y \in Y \} \tag{8}$$

This definition can be naturally generalized to (unweighted) automata: the edit-distance of two automata $A_1$ and $A_2$ is that of the languages accepted by these automata $d(L(A_1), L(A_2))$. The general problem of the computation of the edit-distance between two languages is not trivial. In fact, it can be proven that this problem is *undecidable* for arbitrary context-free languages [21]. But the edit-distance of two automata can be computed efficiently using a weighted transducer over the tropical semiring [24, 21].

Let $U$ be the weighted transducer over the tropical semiring defined by:

$$\forall a, b \in \Sigma \cup \{\epsilon\}, \quad [\![U]\!](a, b) = \begin{cases} 1 & \text{if } (a \neq b) \\ 0 & \text{otherwise} \end{cases} \tag{9}$$

and define $T_e$ by $T_e = U^*$. Figure 6(a) shows that transducer for $\Sigma = \{a, b\}$.

**Proposition 3 ([24, 21]).** *Let $A_1$ and $A_2$ be two (unweighted) finite automata over the alphabet $\Sigma$. Then,*

$$d(A_1, A_2) = w[A_1 \circ T_e \circ A_2] \tag{10}$$

*Proof.* By definition of $U$, $A_1 \circ T_e \circ A_2$ contains a successful path corresponding to each alignment of a sequence accepted by $A_1$ and a sequence accepted by $A_2$ and the weight of that path is exactly the cost of that alignment, i.e. the number of mismatches in that alignment. Since $A_1 \circ T_e \circ A_2$ is defined over the tropical semiring, $w[A_1 \circ T_e \circ A_2]$ is the minimum alignment cost, which is the edit-distance. □

Note that the best path of $A_1 \circ T_e \circ A_2$ provides also the best alignment of the two automata $A_1$ and $A_2$. The proposition leads to an efficient algorithm for computing the edit-distance of two automata based on the composition algorithm and a classical single-source shortest-paths algorithm. This computation can be done on-the-fly since composition admits a natural on-the-fly implementation. Since the worst case complexity of composition is quadratic, and since the transducer $T_e$ can be constructed on-demand (not all symbols of $\Sigma$ might be needed for a specific choice of $A_1$ and $A_2$), the time and space complexity of the construction of $A_1 \circ T_e \circ A_2$ is $O(|A_1||A_2|)$. When $A_1$ and $A_2$ are acyclic, the result of composition is also an acyclic transducer and the shortest path can be found using the classical linear-time single-source shortest paths algorithm [5]. Thus, the total time complexity of the algorithm is $O(|A_1||A_2|)$.

The notion of edit-distance can be similarly extended to measure the similarity between two distributions of sequences given by weighted automata. It can be defined as the expected edit-distance of the strings accepted by $A_1$ and $A_2$.

**Definition 5** **([21]).** *Let $A_1$ and $A_2$ be two acyclic weighted automata over the probability semiring. Then the edit-distance of $A_1$ and $A_2$ is denoted by $d(A_1, A_2)$ and defined by:*

$$d(A_1, A_2) = \sum_{x,y} d(x,y) [\![A_1]\!](x) [\![A_2]\!](y) \tag{11}$$

It can be shown that this generalized definition of the edit-distance can also be computed *exactly* using standard weighted automata algorithms such as weighted determinization, synchronization, and $\epsilon$-removal [21].

A notion closely related to the edit-distance of two strings is that of the *longest common subsequence*, that is the longest subsequence of symbols (not necessarily contiguous) common to two strings. Let $lcs(x,y)$ denote the longest common subsequence of $x$ and $y$. This definition can be naturally extended to two languages or two finite automata.

**Definition 6.** *The* longest common subsequence of two languages $X \subseteq \Sigma^*$ and $Y \subseteq \Sigma^*$ *is denoted by $lcs(X,Y)$ and defined by:*

$$lcs(X,Y) = \sup \{lcs(x,y) : x \in X, y \in Y\} \tag{12}$$

*The longest common subsequence of two finite automata $A_1$ and $A_2$ over the alphabet $\Sigma$ is denoted by $lcs(A_1, A_2)$ and defined by $lcs(A_1, A_2) = lcs(L(A_1), L(A_2))$.*

Let $U'$ be the weighted transducer over the tropical semiring defined by:

$$\forall a \in \Sigma, \ [\![U']\!](a, \epsilon) = [\![U']\!](\epsilon, a) = 0 \tag{13}$$

$$[\![U']\!](a, a) = -1 \tag{14}$$

and define $T_s$ by $T_s = U'^*$. Figure 6(b) shows that transducer for $\Sigma = \{a, b\}$.

**Proposition 4.** *Let $A_1$ and $A_2$ be two (unweighted) finite automata over the alphabet $\Sigma$. Then,*

$$lcs(A_1, A_2) = -w[A_1 \circ T_s \circ A_2] \tag{15}$$

*Proof.* The proof is similar to that of Proposition 4. $A_1 \circ T_s \circ A_2$ contains a path corresponding to each subsequence common to a string accepted by $A_1$ and a string accepted by $A_2$, and the weight of that path is the negative length of that subsequence. Since $A_1 \circ T_s \circ A_2$ is defined over the tropical semiring, $-w[A_1 \circ T_s \circ A_2]$ is the maximum length of a common subsequence, which is $lcs(A_1, A_2)$. □

As in the case of the edit-distance, the longest common subsequence of two acyclic automata $A_1$ and $A_2$ can be computed in $O(|A_1||A_2|)$ using the composition algorithm and a linear-time single-source shortest path algorithm.

# 6    Conclusion

We discussed several algorithms related to the use of statistical learning techniques in natural language processing when the input data is given as a set of distributions over strings, each compactly represented by a weighted automaton. We described efficient algorithms for computing the expected count of an arbitrary sequence and other moments of that distribution from a weighted automaton. We also demonstrated how several general similarity measures between weighted automata can be efficiently computed using algorithms based on weighted transducers.[4] This extends machine learning techniques such as SVMs and clustering to deal with distributions.

# References

1. Christian Berg, Jens Peter Reus Christensen, and Paul Ressel. *Harmonic Analysis on Semigroups*. Springer-Verlag: Berlin-New York, 1984.
2. B. E. Boser, I. Guyon, and V. N. Vapnik. A training algorithm for optimal margin classifiers. In *Proceedings of the Fifth Annual Workshop of Computational Learning Theory*, volume 5, pages 144–152, Pittsburg, 1992. ACM.
3. Eugene Charniak. Statistical parsing with a context-free grammar and word statistics. In *AAAI/IAAI*, pages 598–603, 1997.
4. Michael Collins. Three Generative, Lexicalised Models for Statistical Parsing. In *35th Meeting of the Association for Computational Linguistics (ACL '96), Proceedings of the Conference, Santa Cruz, California*, 1997.
5. T. Cormen, C. Leiserson, and R. Rivest. *Introduction to Algorithms*. The MIT Press: Cambridge, MA, 1992.
6. Corinna Cortes, Patrick Haffner, and Mehryar Mohri. Positive Definite Rational Kernels. In *Proceedings of The Sixteenth Annual Conference on Computational Learning Theory (COLT 2003)*, Washington D.C., August 2003.
7. Corinna Cortes, Patrick Haffner, and Mehryar Mohri. Rational Kernels. In *Advances in Neural Information Processing Systems (NIPS 2002)*, volume 15, Vancouver, Canada, March 2003. MIT Press.
8. Corinna Cortes and Vladimir N. Vapnik. Support-Vector Networks. *Machine Learning*, 20(3):273–297, 1995.
9. David Haussler. Convolution Kernels on Discrete Structures. Technical Report UCSC-CRL-99-10, University of California at Santa Cruz, 1999.
10. Frederick Jelinek. *Statistical Methods for Speech Recognition*. The MIT Press, Cambridge, Massachusetts, 1998.

---

[4] Efficient implementations of many of the general algorithms that we used are incorporated in two software libraries, the AT&T FSM library [24] and the GRM Library [18], whose binary executables are available for download for non-commercial use.

11. Thorsten Joachims. Text categorization with support vector machines: learning with many relevant features. In Claire Nédellec and Céline Rouveirol, editors, *Proceedings of ECML-98, 10th European Conference on Machine Learning*, pages 137–142, Chemnitz, DE, 1998. Springer Verlag, Heidelberg, DE.

12. Werner Kuich and Arto Salomaa. *Semirings, Automata, Languages*. Number 5 in EATCS Monographs on Theoretical Computer Science. Springer-Verlag, Berlin, Germany, 1986.

13. Fabrice Lefevre, Jean-Luc Gauvain, and Lori Lamel. Towards task-independent speech recognition. In *Proceedings of the International Conference on Acoustics, Speech, and Signal Processing (ICASSP 2001)*, 2001.

14. Christina Leslie, Eleazar Eskin, Jason Weston, and William Stafford Noble. Mismatch String Kernels for SVM Protein Classification. In *Advances in Neural Information Processing Systems 15 (NIPS 2002)*. MIT Press, March 2003.

15. Vladimir I. Levenshtein. Binary codes capable of correcting deletions, insertions, and reversals. *Soviet Physics - Doklady*, 10:707–710, 1966.

16. Huma Lodhi, John Shawe-Taylor, Nello Cristianini, and Chris Watkins. Text classification using string kernels. In Todd K. Leen, Thomas G. Dietterich, and Volker Tresp, editors, *Advances in Neural Information Processing Systems 13 (NIPS 2000)*, pages 563–569. MIT Press, 2001.

17. Mehryar Mohri. Finite-state transducers in language and speech processing. *Computational Linguistics*, 23:2, 1997.

18. Mehryar Mohri. Weighted Grammar Tools: the GRM Library. In Jean claude Junqua and Gertjan van Noord, editors, *Robustness in Language and Speech Technology*, pages 165–186. Kluwer Academic Publishers, The Netherlands, 2001. http://www.research.att.com/sw/tools/grm.

19. Mehryar Mohri. Generic Epsilon-Removal and Input Epsilon-Normalization Algorithms for Weighted Transducers. *International Journal of Foundations of Computer Science*, 13(1):129–143, 2002.

20. Mehryar Mohri. Semiring Frameworks and Algorithms for Shortest-Distance Problems. *Journal of Automata, Languages and Combinatorics*, 7(3):321–350, 2002.

21. Mehryar Mohri. Edit-Distance of Weighted Automata: General Definitions and Algorithms. *International Journal of Foundations of Computer Science*, 2003.

22. Mehryar Mohri, Fernando Pereira, and Michael Riley. Weighted Finite-State Transducers in Speech Recognition. *Computer Speech and Language*, 16(1):69–88, 2002.

23. Mehryar Mohri, Fernando C. N. Pereira, and Michael Riley. Weighted automata in text and speech processing. In *ECAI-96 Workshop, Budapest, Hungary*, 1996.

24. Mehryar Mohri, Fernando C. N. Pereira, and Michael Riley. The Design Principles of a Weighted Finite-State Transducer Library. *Theoretical Computer Science*, 231:17–32, January 2000. http://www.research.att.com/sw/tools/fsm.

25. Lawrence Rabiner and Biing-Hwang Juang. *Fundamentals of Speech Recognition*. Prentice-Hall, Englewood Cliffs, NJ, 1993.

26. Brian Roark. Probabilistic top-down parsing and language modeling. *Computational Linguistics*, 27(2):249–276, 2001.

27. Robert E. Schapire and Yoram Singer. BoosTexter: A boosting-based system for text categorization. *Machine Learning*, 39(2/3):135–168, 2000.

28. Marcel Paul Schützenberger. On the definition of a family of automata. *Information and Control*, 4, 1961.

29. Vladimir N. Vapnik. *Statistical Learning Theory*. John Wiley & Sons, NY, 1998.

30. Chris Watkins. Dynamic alignment kernels. Technical Report CSD-TR-98-11, Royal Holloway, University of London, 1999.

# Learning and Parsing Stochastic Unification-Based Grammars

Mark Johnson

Cognitive and Linguistic Sciences and Computer Science
Brown University, Providence RI 02912, USA
Mark_Johnson@Brown.edu

**Abstract.** Stochastic Unification-Based Grammars combine knowledge-rich and data-rich approaches to natural language processing. This provides a rich structure to the learning and parsing (decoding) tasks that can be described with undirected graphical models. While most work to date has treated parsing as a straight-forward multi-class classification problem, we are beginning to see how this structure can be exploited in learning and parsing. Exploiting this structure is likely to become more important as the research focus moves from parsing to more realistic tasks such as machine translation and summarization.

## 1 Introduction

This paper summarizes recent research into Stochastic Unification-Based Grammars (SUBGs), which attempt to combine linguistic insights expressed by grammars with modern machine-learning techniques. So far most work has focused on parsing, i.e., identifying the syntactic and semantic structure of sentences, and this paper focuses on this application. But the community is beginning to investigate applications of these techniques such as automatic summarization [1] and machine translation, which are more challenging and present interesting opportunities for machine learning.

A *parse* consists of a string of words, called its *yield*, together with its syntactic structure and/or semantics. A syntactic structure describes how words are organized into phrases and clauses, while the semantics is the meaning of a sentence. While trees are most commonly used to represent syntactic structure, the linguistic theories discussed in this paper use both trees and attribute-value structures to represent the syntactic and semantic properties of a sentence. Even though modern linguistics has been investigating syntax and semantics since the mid-1950s and before, there are still large gaps in our knowledge of English and other languages, and considerable dispute over exactly what the structure of particular sentences actually is.

The parsing problem is to identify the parse of a sentence intended by its speaker or author. Undoubtedly this depends on a wide variety of factors, including the discourse context and world knowledge, but most work on statistical parsing ignore these. Not surprisingly, ambiguity is a pervasive problem in parsing: many different parses have the same yield (e.g., consider sentences such as

B. Schölkopf and M.K. Warmuth (Eds.): COLT/Kernel 2003, LNAI 2777, pp. 671–683, 2003.

"I saw the man with the T.V."). Currently statistical and machine-learning approaches provide the most systematic way to identify the most likely intended parse.

The basic assumption behind the work described here is that linguists have identified reasonably well the general principles that determine the possible structures of a language, but they have not identified a satisfactory method for disambiguating sentences, so this must be inferred from training data. By contrast, most work on statistical parsing seems to assume that linguists can only accurately determine the structures of particular sentences (specifically, those in the treebank training data), and only incorporates much weaker linguistic assumptions [2, 3].

SUBGs define probability distributions over the parses defined by Unification-Based Grammars (UBGs). These grammars can incorporate virtually all kinds of linguistically important constraints. There are several different kinds of UBGs, including Head-Driven Phrase-Structure Grammar (HPSG) [4, 5] and Lexical-Functional Grammar (LFG) [6, 7]. This paper uses LFG, but the approach is general and can be used with virtually any UBG. Section 2 describes LFG representations in some more detail, and section 4 explains how probability distributions are defined over these structures.

We chose LFG because two decades of work have produced in broad-coverage grammars [8] and well-developed non-statistical parsing technology [9, 10]. In particular, there are parsing algorithms that produce "packed" representations of a set of parses which can often find an exponential number of different parses for a sentence in polynomial time and represent them in polynomial space. Section 5 outlines dynamic programming algorithms for estimating statistical models and identifying the most probable parse from the set of parses encoded by a packed representation.

The notation used in this paper is as follows. Variables are written in upper case italic, e.g., $X, Y$, etc., the sets they range over are written in script, e.g., $\mathcal{X}, \mathcal{Y}$, etc., while specific values are written in lower case italic, e.g., $x, y$, etc. In the case of vector-valued entities, subscripts indicate particular components.

## 2     Lexical-Functional Grammar

An LFG parse describes the different aspects of a sentence's syntactic structure and semantics using several different structures; for simplicity we only discuss two of these here. The constituent or c-structure of a parse is a tree that describes how words and phrases combine to form larger syntactic units. The functional or f-structure is a particular kind of directed graph known as an attribute-value structure that identifies the function-argument dependencies of the parse.

Figure 1 depicts the c-structure and f-structure for the sentence "Alex promised Sasha to leave". The fact that the single phrase "Alex" fills two functional roles in this sentence (it is the subject of "promise" as well as the subject of "leave") is not represented in the c-structure tree, but it is represented by the re-entrancy in the f-structure (which is depicted by co-indexation in the figure). LFG parses use similar f-structure re-entrancies to encode long-distance depen-

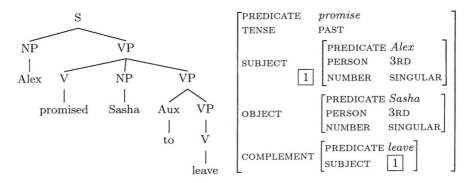

**Fig. 1.** The c-structure and f-structure for "Alex promised Sasha to leave".

dencies in phrases such as "Sam bought the program that Alex wants to use", where "the program" is both the object of "bought" and of "use".

The precise way in which grammars specify how strings are associated with parses differs in different kinds of UBGs, and is not important for what follows. Let $\Omega$ be the set of parses for the sentences of a language, and for each parse $\omega \in \Omega$ let $Y(\omega)$ be its yield. If $y$ is a string then $\Omega(y) = \{\omega \in \Omega | Y(\omega) = y\}$ is the set of parses with yield $y$. We require that $\Omega(y)$ be a finite for all $y$; this is almost always true of (bug-free) UBGs. For our LFGs $|\Omega(y)|$ ranges from one to the hundreds of thousands.

It important for the dynamic programming algorithms described below that each parse $\omega$ consist of a finite set of parse *fragments*[1]. Precisely what a fragment is is unimportant, but typically fragments are units directly or indirectly defined by the grammar (e.g., chart edges, local trees, attribute-value pairs, etc.) out of which parses are constructed. For example, in Figure 1 one fragment might consists of all of the information associated with the word "Alex", i.e., the NP c-structure node and the f-structure node with the index "1". This fragment would also appear in other parses containing the word "Alex". This sharing of fragments is key to the dynamic programming algorithms described below. If $y$ is a string let $\mathcal{F}(y) = \bigcup_{\omega \in \Omega(y)} \{f \in \omega\}$ be the set of fragments appearing in any parse of $y$. $\mathcal{F}(y)$ is finite since $\Omega(y)$ and each $\omega \in \Omega(y)$ are finite.

## 3   Maxwell-Kaplan Packed Parse Representations

As mentioned earlier, ambiguity is a pervasive problem in parsing, and much of the work on parsing over the past several decades has focused on methods for efficiently finding and compactly representing the parses of a sentence. Maxwell and Kaplan [9, 10] developed a dynamic programming framework for UBG parsing that seems to be more general than other approaches. The dynamic programming algorithms described below take the packed representations produced by their

---

[1] Fragments were called "features" in [11], but we use the word "fragment" here to avoid confusion with the machine learning use of the word "feature".

parsing algorithm as input, so we describe them here. The intuition motivating the Maxwell-Kaplan packed representations is that for most strings $y$, many of the fragments in $\mathcal{F}(y)$ occur in many of the parses $\Omega(y)$. This is often the case in natural language, since the same substructure can appear as a component of many different parses.

Maxwell-Kaplan packed representations are defined in terms of conditions on the values assigned to a vector of auxiliary variables $X$. These variables have no direct linguistic interpretation; rather, each different assignment of values to these variables identifies a set of fragments which constitutes one of the parses represented by the packed representation. A *condition* on $X$ is a function from $\mathcal{X}$ (the range of $X$) to $\{0, 1\}$. While for uniformity we write conditions as functions on the entire vector $X$, in practice the Maxwell-Kaplan parsing algorithm usually produces conditions whose value depends only on a few of the variables in $X$, and the efficiency of the algorithms described here depends on this.

A *packed representation* of a finite set of parses is a quadruple $R = (\mathcal{F}', X, N, \alpha)$, where:

- $\mathcal{F}' \supseteq \mathcal{F}(y)$ is a finite set of fragments,
- $X$ is a finite vector of *variables*, where each variable $X_\ell$ ranges over the finite set $\mathcal{X}_\ell$,
- $N$ is a finite set of conditions on $X$ called the *no-goods*[2], and
- $\alpha$ is a function that maps each fragment $f \in \mathcal{F}'$ to a condition $\alpha_f$ on $X$.

A vector of values $x$ *satisfies the no-goods* $N$ iff $N(x) = 1$, where $N(x) = \prod_{\eta \in N} \eta(x)$. Each $x$ that satisfies the no-goods *identifies* a parse $\omega(x) = \{f \in \mathcal{F}' | \alpha_f(x) = 1\}$, i.e., $\omega$ is the set of features whose conditions are satisfied by $x$. We require that each parse be identified by a *unique* value satisfying the no-goods. That is, we require that:

$$\forall x, x' \in \mathcal{X} \text{ if } N(x) = N(x') = 1 \text{ and } \omega(x) = \omega(x') \text{ then } x = x' \qquad (1)$$

A packed representation $R$ *represents* the set of parses $\Omega(R)$ that are identified by values that satisfy the no-goods, i.e., $\Omega(R) = \{\omega(x) | x \in \mathcal{X}, N(x) = 1\}$.

Maxwell and Kaplan describe a parsing algorithm for unification-based grammars that takes as input a string $y$ and returns a packed representation $R$ such that $\Omega(R) = \Omega(y)$, i.e., $R$ represents the set of parses of the string $y$. The SUBG parsing and estimation algorithms described here use the Maxwell-Kaplan parsing algorithm as a subroutine.

*Example.* Figure 2 depicts in extremely schematic form a packed parse representation for the sentence "Sam saw a man with a T.V. driving a car". This admittedly rather contrived sentence contains two interacting ambiguities[3]. First, "with a T.V." can either modify "saw" or "a man" (i.e., either Sam used the

---

[2] The name "no-good" comes from the TMS literature, and was used by Maxwell and Kaplan. However, here the no-goods actually identify the *good* variable assignments.

[3] Interestingly, most of the ambiguities that cause so much trouble in parsing are extremely difficult for humans to detect.

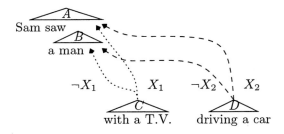

**Fig. 2.** A depiction of a packed parse forest encoding possible parses of "Sam saw a man with a T.V. driving a car".

T.V., or the man had the T.V.). The boolean variable $X_1$ encodes which phrase "with a T.V." modifies.

Second, "driving a car" can also either modify "saw" or "a man" (either the seeing was done while driving, or else the man was driving a car; the semantically implausible reading where the T.V. was driving a car is not represented). The boolean variable $X_2$ encodes which phrase "driving a car" modifies.

Many linguists would claim that not all combinations of these ambiguities are possible. Specifically, if "with a T.V." modifies "saw" then "driving a car" cannot modify "a man", since that would result in a crossing dependency of a kind not found in English. This constraint is encoded by the no-good $\neg X_1 \vee X_2$.

Suppose that $\xi_A$ is the parse fragment for the phrase "Sam saw", $\xi_B$ is the fragment for "a man", $\xi_C$ for "with a T.V." and $\xi_D$ for "driving a car". Let $\xi_{CA}$ be the parse fragment representing the attachment of $\xi_C$ to $\xi_A$ (i.e., the c-structure and f-structure elements representing the attachment of "with a T.V." to "Sam saw"), and let $\xi_{CB}, \xi_{DA}, \xi_{DB}$ be the other corresponding attachment fragments. Then the following schematic packed representation encodes the possible parses:

$$\mathcal{F}' = \{\xi_A, \xi_B, \xi_C, \xi_D, \xi_{CA}, \xi_{CB}, \xi_{DA}, \xi_{DB}\}$$
$$X = (X_1, X_2)$$
$$N = \{\neg X_1 \vee X_2\}$$
$$\alpha(\xi_{CA}) = X_1, \alpha(\xi_{CB}) = \neg X_1, \alpha(\xi_{DA}) = X_2, \alpha(\xi_{DB}) = \neg X_2,$$
$$\alpha(\xi_A) = \alpha(\xi_B) = \alpha(\xi_C) = \alpha(\xi_D) = 1.$$

In LFGs and similiar grammars the fragments containing lexical items (i.e., words) are usually very large, since these grammars typically contain a lot of lexical information. Notice that the fragments $\xi_A, \ldots, \xi_D$ corresponding to the phrases in the sentence occur only once in the packed representation, rather than appearing three times, as they would if the parses were enumerated. In the packed representation these fragments are associated with the constant condition 1, which indicates that they all appear in every parse. Only the fragments required to connect up these phrasal fragments have non-constant conditions, indicating that they are the only fragments that vary across the parses of this sentence. Such structure sharing, especially of lexical information, is a goal of the Maxwell-Kaplan approach.

# 4    Stochastic Unification-Based Grammars

SUBGs use exponential models (also known as log-linear or MaxEnt models or Markov Random Fields) extend UBGs by defining probability distributions over the parses of a UBG. Abney [12] proposed the use of exponential models for defining probability distributions over the parses of a UBG. Johnson et al. [13] noted that calculating the partition function and the various expectations required for estimation (see below) is computationally very expensive because they require integrating over all parses of all sentences. However, Johnson et al. pointed out that parsing and related tasks only require the conditional distribution of parses given their yields, and that these conditional distributions are much less computationally demanding to estimate.

A SUBG is a triple $(U, g, \theta)$, where $U$ is a unification grammar that defines a set $\Omega$ of parses as described above, $g = (g_1, \ldots, g_m)$ is a vector of features, and $\theta = (\theta_1, \ldots, \theta_m)$ is a vector of non-negative real-valued parameters called *feature weights*. A *feature* is a real-valued function of parses $\Omega$ [4].

If we are prepared to enumerate all of the parses of the sentences in our training and test data then features can be any real-valued function of parses whatsoever. However, the dynamic programming algorithms described below require the information encoded in features to be local with respect to the fragments $\mathcal{F}$ of packed parse representations. Specifically, they require that features be linear in terms of the fragments of parses, i.e., each fragment $f \in \mathcal{F}$ is associated with a finite vector of real values $(g_1(f), \ldots, g_m(f))$ which define the feature functions for parses as follows:

$$g_k(\omega) = \sum_{f \in \omega} g_k(f), \text{ for } k = 1 \ldots m. \tag{2}$$

This requires features be very local with respect to fragments, which gives up the ability to define features arbitrarily. Note that we can encode essentially arbitrary non-local information in the attributes of the underlying unification grammar and then define features locally in terms of those attributes.

We now describe how SUBGs define conditional probability distributions over parses given yields. The conditional probability $P_\theta(\omega|y)$ of a parse $\omega \in \Omega(y)$ given a yield $y$ is:

$$P_\theta(\omega|y) = \frac{W_\theta(\omega)}{Z_\theta(y)}, \text{ where } W_\theta(\omega) = \prod_{j=1}^{m} \theta_j^{g_j(\omega)}, \text{ and } Z_\theta(y) = \sum_{\omega' \in \Omega(y)} W_\theta(\omega').$$

Intuitively, if $g_j(\omega)$ is the number of times that feature $j$ occurs in $\omega$ then $\theta_j$ is the weight or cost of each occurrence of feature $j$, and $Z_\theta(y)$ is a normalising constant that ensures that the probability of all parses of $y$ sum to 1.

---

[4] Features were called "properties" in [11, 13] in order to avoid confusion with the linguistic use of the word "feature".

Such a distribution can be used for a variety of tasks. The most straight-forward application is parsing: the most likely parse of a string of words $y$ is:

$$\hat{\omega}(y) = \operatorname*{argmax}_{\omega \in \Omega(y)} P(\omega|y) = \operatorname*{argmax}_{\omega \in \Omega(y)} W_\theta(\omega).$$

$\hat{\omega}(y)$ can be found by exhaustively enumerating $\Omega(y)$. But even though $\Omega(y)$ is finite, with large grammars and long sentences finding the most likely parse by direct enumeration can be extremely time-consuming. The dynamic programming algorithm described below exploits the structure of packed representations to avoid this exhaustive search.

Now we turn to estimation. Suppose we have a training corpus $D$ of sentences $y_i$ and their correct parses $\omega_i$, i.e., $D = ((y_1, \omega_1), \ldots, (y_n, \omega_n))$, from which we wish to estimate the feature weights $\theta$ [5]. The $\hat{\theta}$ that maximizes the *conditional likelihood* $L_D(\theta)$ is a consistent estimator of the conditional distribution[6].

$$\hat{\theta} = \operatorname*{argmax}_\theta L_D(\theta) = \prod_{i=1}^n P_\theta(\omega_i|y_i)$$

Practial methods for optimizing $L_D$, such as the Conjugate Gradient and L-BFGS algorithms as well as the various iterative scaling algorithms, require the partial derivatives of $L_D$ as well as $L_D$ itself.

$$\frac{\partial L_D}{\partial \theta_k} = \frac{L_D(\theta)}{\theta_k} \sum_{i=1}^n (g_k(\omega_i) - E_\theta[g_k|y_i]) \text{, where:}$$

$$E_\theta[g|y] = \sum_{\omega \in \Omega(y)} g(\omega)P_\theta(\omega|y) = \sum_{\omega \in \Omega(y)} \frac{g(\omega)W_\theta(\omega)}{Z_\theta(y)}$$

Here $E_\theta[g|y]$ is the *conditional expectation* of $g$ with respect to distribution $P_\theta$ over parses $\Omega(y)$ of the sentence $y$. As with parsing, computing this conditional expectation by explicit summation over $\Omega(y)$ can be computationally expensive.

## 5    Packed Representations and Graphical Models

The previous section treated parses in SUBGs as atomic (i.e., the features are functions of the entire parse), whereas they actually have a rich internal structure. As explained earlier the Maxwell-Kaplan parsing algorithm exploits the sharing of fragments in parses to produce a "packed representation" of a set of parses. This section describes explains how dynamic programming algorithms for graphical models can be used to compute the most likely parse and the expected value of features directly from these packed representations [11].

---

[5] We call $D$ *fully labelled* because it identifies the correct parse $\omega_i$ for each sentence $y_i = Y(\omega_i)$ in $D$; see [14] for conditional estimation from partially labelled data.

[6] In fact [13] and later work estimate $\theta$ by maximizing a regularized conditional likelihood obtained by multiplying $L_D$ by a zero-mean diagonal-variance Gaussian.

These methods are analogues of the well-known dynamic programming algorithms for Probabilistic Context-Free Grammars (PCFGs); specifically the Viterbi algorithm for finding the most probable parse of a string and the Inside-Outside algorithm for estimating a PCFG from unparsed training data (which we use to calculate the expected number of times each feature occurs). In fact, because the Maxwell-Kaplan packed representations are just Truth Maintenance System (TMS) representations [15], the statistical techniques described here should extend to non-linguistic applications of TMSs as well.

Dynamic programming techniques have been applied to log-linear models in other setting. Lafferty et al. show how dynamic programming can be used to compute the statistics required for conditional estimation of log-linear models of labeled sequences where the properties can include arbitrary functions of the input string [16]. The closest work we know of to the approach described here is that of Miyao, Tsujii and colleagues [17, 18]. They also describe a technique for calculating the statistics required to estimate a log-linear model from packed parse forests.

The previous section introduced several important quantities for parsing and maximum likelihood estimation of SUBGs. In each case we show that the quantity can be expressed as the value that maximises a product of functions or else as the sum of a product of functions, each of which depends on a small subset of the variables $X$ of a packed parse representation. These are the kinds of quantities for which dynamic programming algorithms for graphical models have been developed.

As explained in section 4, the most probable parse is $\hat{\omega}(y) = \text{argmax}_{\omega \in \Omega(y)} W_\theta(\omega)$. Given a packed representation $(\mathcal{F}', X, N, \alpha)$ for the parses $\Omega(y)$, let $\hat{x}(y)$ be the $x$ that identifies $\hat{\omega}(y)$, i.e., $\hat{\omega}(y) = \{f \in \mathcal{F}' | \alpha_f(\hat{x}(y)) = 1\}$. Since $W_\theta(\hat{\omega}(y)) > 0$, it can be shown that:

$$\hat{x}(y) = \underset{x \in \mathcal{X}}{\text{argmax}} \, N(x) \prod_{j=1}^{m} \theta_j^{g_j(\omega(x))}$$

$$= \underset{x \in \mathcal{X}}{\text{argmax}} \, N(x) \prod_{j=1}^{m} \theta_j^{\sum_{f \in \omega(x)} g_j(f)}$$

$$= \underset{x \in \mathcal{X}}{\text{argmax}} \, N(x) \prod_{j=1}^{m} \theta_j^{\sum_{f \in \mathcal{F}'} \alpha_f(x) g_j(f)}$$

$$= \underset{x \in \mathcal{X}}{\text{argmax}} \, N(x) \prod_{j=1}^{m} \prod_{f \in \mathcal{F}'} \theta_j^{\alpha_f(x) g_j(f)}$$

$$= \underset{x \in \mathcal{X}}{\text{argmax}} \, N(x) \prod_{f \in \mathcal{F}'} \left( \prod_{j=1}^{m} \theta_j^{g_j(f)} \right)^{\alpha_f(x)}$$

$$= \underset{x \in \mathcal{X}}{\text{argmax}} \prod_{\eta \in N} \eta(x) \prod_{f \in \mathcal{F}'} h_{\theta, f}(x) \tag{3}$$

where $h_{\theta,f}(x) = \prod_{j=1}^{m} \theta_j^{g_j(f)}$ if $\alpha_f(x) = 1$ and $h_{\theta,f}(x) = 1$ if $\alpha_f(x) = 0$. That is, $h_{\theta,f}(x)$ is the weight of the fragment $f$ in the parse $\omega(x)$. Note that $h_{\theta,f}(x)$ depends on exactly the same subset of variables in $X$ as $\alpha_f$ does. As (3) makes clear, finding $\hat{x}(y)$ involves maximising a product of functions where each function depends on a subset of the variables $X$. As explained below, this is exactly the kind of maximisation that can be solved using graphical model techniques.

We now turn to the partition function. As mentioned earlier, calculating the partition function $Z_\theta(y) = \sum_{\omega \in \Omega(y)} W_\theta(\omega)$ by explicitly summing over all parses $\Omega(y)$ can be computationally expensive. However, there is an alternative method for calculating $Z_\theta(y_i)$ that does not involve this enumeration. As noted above, for each yield $y_i, i = 1, \ldots, n$, the Maxwell-Kaplan algorithm returns a packed parse $R_i$ that represents the parses of $y_i$, i.e., $\Omega(y_i) = \Omega(R_i)$. A derivation parallel to the one for (3) shows that for $R = (\mathcal{F}', X, N, \alpha)$:

$$Z_\theta(\Omega(R)) = \sum_{x \in \mathcal{X}} \prod_{\eta \in N} \eta(x) \prod_{f \in \mathcal{F}'} h_{\theta,f}(x) \tag{4}$$

This derivation relies on the isomorphism between parses and variable assignments in (1). It turns out that sums of products of this kind can also be calculated using graphical model techniques.

Similar remarks apply to the computation of the conditional expectations $E_\theta[g_k|y_i]$. Again, let $R = (\mathcal{F}, X, N, \alpha)$ be a packed representation such that $\Omega(R) = \Omega(y_i)$. First, note that (2) implies that:

$$E_\theta[g_k|y_i] = \sum_{f \in \mathcal{F}'} g_k(f) \, \mathrm{P}(\{\omega : f \in \omega\}|y_i).$$

Note that $\mathrm{P}(\{\omega : f \in \omega\}|y_i)$ involves the sum of weights over all $x \in \mathcal{X}$ subject to the conditions that $N(x) = 1$ and $\alpha_f(x) = 1$. Thus $\mathrm{P}(\{\omega : f \in \omega\}|y_i)$ can also be expressed in a form that is easy to evaluate using graphical techniques.

$$Z_\theta(\Omega(R))\mathrm{P}_\theta(\{\omega : f \in \omega\}|y_i) = \sum_{x \in \mathcal{X}} \alpha_f(x) \prod_{\eta \in N} \eta(x) \prod_{f' \in \mathcal{F}'} h_{\theta,f'}(x) \tag{5}$$

## 5.1   Graphical Model Calculations

In this subsection we briefly review graphical model algorithms for maximizing and summing products of functions of the kind presented above. The quantities (3), (4) and (5) involve maximisation or summation over a product of functions, each of which depends only on the values of a subset of the variables $X$. There are dynamic programming algorithms for calculating all of these quantities, but for reasons of space we only describe an algorithm that finds the most probable parse $\hat{\omega}(y)$ of a string $y$. As explained above, this is equivalent to finding $x \in \mathcal{X}$ that maximizes (3).

It turns out that the algorithm for maximisation is a generalisation of the Viterbi algorithm for HMMs, and the algorithm for computing the summation in (5) is a generalisation of the forward-backward algorithm for HMMs [19]. Viewed abstractly, these algorithms simplify these expressions by moving common factors over the max or sum operators respectively. These techniques are now relatively standard; the most well-known approach involves junction trees [20, 21]. We adopt the approach approach described by [22], which is a straightforward generalization of HMM dynamic programming with minimal assumptions and programming overhead.

To explain the algorithm we use the following notation. If $x$ and $x'$ are both vectors of length $m$ then $x =_j x'$ iff $x$ and $x'$ disagree on at most their $j$th components, i.e., $x_k = x'_k$ for $k = 1, \ldots, j-1, j+1, \ldots m$. If $f$ is a function whose domain is $\mathcal{X}$, we say that $f$ *depends on* the set of variables $d(f) = \{X_j | \exists x, x' \in \mathcal{X}, x =_j x', f(x) \neq f(x')\}$. That is, $X_j \in d(f)$ iff changing the value of $X_j$ can change the value of $f$.

The algorithm relies on the fact that the variables in $X = (X_1, \ldots, X_n)$ are ordered (e.g., $X_1$ precedes $X_2$, etc.), and while the algorithm is correct for any variable ordering, its efficiency may vary dramatically depending on which ordering is chosen. Let $\mathcal{H}$ be any set of functions whose domains are $X$. We partition $\mathcal{H}$ into disjoint subsets $\mathcal{H}_1, \ldots, \mathcal{H}_{n+1}$, where $\mathcal{H}_j$ is the subset of $\mathcal{H}$ that depend on $X_j$ but do not depend on any variables ordered before $X_j$, and $\mathcal{H}_{n+1}$ is the subset of $\mathcal{H}$ that do not depend on any variables at all (i.e., they are constants)[7]. That is, $\mathcal{H}_j = \{H \in \mathcal{H} | X_j \in d(H), \forall i < j \, X_i \notin d(H)\}$ and $\mathcal{H}_{n+1} = \{H \in \mathcal{H} | d(H) = \emptyset\}$.

In order to find the most probable parse we must find the $x$ that maximizes the product of functions (3). Here we describe a general algorithm for finding $M_{\max}$ and $\hat{x}$ that satisfy (6-7).

$$M_{\max} = \max_{x \in \mathcal{X}} \prod_{A \in \mathcal{A}} A(x) \tag{6}$$

$$\hat{x} = \operatorname*{argmax}_{x \in \mathcal{X}} \prod_{A \in \mathcal{A}} A(x). \tag{7}$$

The procedure depends on two sequences of functions $M_i, i = 1, \ldots, n+1$ and $V_i, i = 1, \ldots, n$. Informally, $M_i$ is the maximum value attained by the subset of the functions $\mathcal{A}$ that depend on one of the variables $X_1, \ldots, X_i$, and $V_i$ identifies the $x$ at which this maximum is attained.

To simplify notation we write these functions as functions of the entire set of variables $X$, but the efficiency of the algorithm requires that they depend on a much smaller set of variables. The $M_i$ are real valued, while each $V_i$ ranges over $\mathcal{X}_i$. Let $\mathcal{M} = \{M_1, \ldots, M_n\}$. $\mathcal{A}$ and $\mathcal{M}$ are both partitioned into disjoint subsets $\mathcal{A}_1, \ldots, \mathcal{A}_{n+1}$ and $\mathcal{M}_1, \ldots, \mathcal{M}_{n+1}$ respectively as described above on the basis of the variables each $A_i$ and $M_i$ depend on.

$$M_i(x) = \max_{\substack{x' \in \mathcal{X} \\ \text{s.t. } x' =_i x}} \prod_{A \in \mathcal{A}_i} A(x') \prod_{M \in \mathcal{M}_i} M(x') \tag{8}$$

---

[7] Strictly speaking this does not necessarily define a partition, as some of the subsets $\mathcal{H}_j$ may be empty.

$$V_i(x) = \underset{\substack{x' \in \mathcal{X} \\ \text{s.t. } x' =_i x}}{\operatorname{argmax}} \prod_{A \in \mathcal{A}_i} A(x') \prod_{M \in \mathcal{M}_i} M(x')$$

$M_{n+1}$ receives a special definition, since there is no variable $X_{n+1}$.

$$M_{n+1} = \left( \prod_{A \in \mathcal{A}_{n+1}} A \right) \left( \prod_{M \in \mathcal{M}_{n+1}} M \right) \tag{9}$$

The $M_i(x)$ and $V_i(x)$ correspond to the intermediate quantities computed in the well-known Viterbi algorithm for HMMs. $M_i(x)$ is the maximum value of the product of terms $A \in \mathcal{A}$ that depend directly or indirectly (through some $M$) on the variable $X_i$, and the $i$th component of $V_i(x)$ gives the value of $x_i$ at this maximum. That is, each $M_i$ can be recursively expanded into the maximum of a product of functions $A \in \mathcal{A}$. If any of these functions also depend on variables ordered after $X_i$, $M_i$ and $V_i$ must also.

The definition of $M_i$ in (8) may look circular (since $M$ appears in the right-hand side), but in fact it is not. First, note that $M_i$ depends only on variables ordered after $X_i$, so if $M_j \in \mathcal{M}_i$ then $j < i$. More specifically,

$$d(M_i) = \left( \bigcup_{A \in \mathcal{A}_i} d(A) \cup \bigcup_{M \in \mathcal{M}_i} d(M) \right) \setminus \{X_i\}.$$

Thus we can compute the $M_i$ in the order $M_1, \ldots, M_{n+1}$, inserting $M_i$ into the appropriate set $\mathcal{M}_k$, where $k > i$ is the next variable $M_i$ depends on, when $M_i$ is computed. By recursively expanding each $M_i$, a simple induction shows that $M_{\max} = M_{n+1}$ and that $V_i(\hat{x}) = \hat{x}_i$ (the value $\hat{x}$ assigns to $X_i$). Because $V_i$ only depends on variables ordered after $x_i$, we can evaluate the $V_i$ in the order $V_n, \ldots, V_1$ to find the maximising assignment $\hat{x}$.

We now briefly consider the computational complexity of this process. Clearly, the number of steps required to compute each $M_i$ is a polynomial of order $|d(M_i)| + 1$, since we need to enumerate all possible values for the argument variables $d(M_i)$ and for each of these, maximise over the set $\mathcal{X}_i$.

Since computational effort is bounded above by a polynomial of order $|d(M_i)| + 1$, we seek a variable ordering that bounds the maximum value of $|d(M_i)|$. Unfortunately, finding the ordering that minimises the maximum value of $|d(M_i)|$ is an NP-complete problem. However, there are several efficient heuristics that are reputed in graphical models community to produce good visitation schedules. It may be that they will perform well in the SUBG parsing applications as well.

# 6   Conclusion

This paper described recent research in SUBGs, concentrating on dynamic programming algorithms for estimating and parsing using exponential models that do not require explicit enumeration of all parses. These algorithms are likely to play an increasingly important role as SUBGs are applied to complex natural language processing tasks such as machine translation.

The key observation is that the set of parses of a sentence possesses a non-trivial structure that can be represented using an undirected graphical model. The Maxwell-Kaplan parsing algorithm takes advantage of this structure to produce a packed representation of a set of parses, and the dynamic programming algorithms described above exploit the same structure to compute the statistics needed for parsing and estimation without enumerating all possible parses.

While almost all of the work on SUBGs has been based on exponential models, the astute reader will have noticed identifying the correct parse of a sentence is essentially just a discriminative learning task, and virtually any discriminative learning algorithm could be used. It would be interesting to see if standard discriminative learning algorithms, such as Support Vector Machines, yield better parsing performance. It would also be interesting to see if these algorithms can be trained from partially labelled data [14] and possess dynamic programming parsing and estimation algorithms.

# References

1. Stefan Riezler, Tracy H. King, R.C., Zaenen, A.: Statistical sentence condensation using ambiguity packing and stochastic disambiguation methods for lexical-functional grammar. In: Proceedings of the Human Language Technology Conference of the North American Chapter of the Association for Computational Linguistics, The Association for Computational Linguistics (2003) 197–204
2. Charniak, E.: A maximum-entropy-inspired parser. In: The Proceedings of the North American Chapter of the Association for Computational Linguistics. (2000) 132–139
3. Collins, M.: Three generative, lexicalised models for statistical parsing. In: The Proceedings of the 35th Annual Meeting of the Association for Computational Linguistics, San Francisco, Morgan Kaufmann (1997)
4. Pollard, C., Sag, I.A.: Information-based Syntax and Semantics. Number 13 in CSLI Lecture Notes Series. Chicago University Press, Chicago (1987)
5. Pollard, C., Sag, I.: Head-driven Phrase Structure Grammar. The University of Chicago Press, Chicago (1994)
6. Bresnan, J.: Control and complementation. In Bresnan, J., ed.: The Mental Representation of Grammatical Relations. The MIT Press, Cambridge, Massachusetts (1982) 282–390
7. Bresnan, J.: Lexical-Functional Syntax. Blackwell, Malden, MA (2001)
8. Butt, M., King, T.H., no, M.E.N., Segon, F.: A Grammar Writer's Cookbook. CSLI Publications, Stanford, CA (1999)
9. Maxwell III, J.T., Kaplan, R.M.: The interface between phrasal and functional constraints. In Dalrymple, M., Kaplan, R.M., Maxwell III, J.T., Zaenen, A., eds.: Formal Issues in Lexical-Functional Grammar. Number 47 in CSLI Lecture Notes Series. CSLI Publications (1995) 403–430
10. Maxwell III, J.T., Kaplan, R.M.: A method for disjunctive constraint satisfaction. In Dalrymple, M., Kaplan, R.M., Maxwell III, J.T., Zaenen, A., eds.: Formal Issues in Lexical-Functional Grammar. Number 47 in CSLI Lecture Notes Series. CSLI Publications (1995) 381–401

11. Geman, S., Johnson, M.: Dynamic programming for parsing and estimation of stochastic unification-based grammars. In: Proceedings of the 40th Annual Meeting of the Association for Computational Linguistics, Morgan Kaufmann (2002) 279–286

12. Abney, S.: Stochastic Attribute-Value Grammars. Computational Linguistics **23** (1997) 597–617

13. Johnson, M., Geman, S., Canon, S., Chi, Z., Riezler, S.: Estimators for stochastic "unification-based" grammars. In: The Proceedings of the 37th Annual Conference of the Association for Computational Linguistics, San Francisco, Morgan Kaufmann (1999) 535–541

14. Riezler, S., King, T.H., Kaplan, R.M., Crouch, R., Maxwell, J.T.I., Johnson, M.: Parsing the wall street journal using a lexical-functional grammar and discriminative estimation techniques. In: Proceedings of the 40th Annual Meeting of the Association for Computational Linguistics, Morgan Kaufmann (2002) 271–278

15. Forbus, K.D., de Kleer, J.: Building problem solvers. The MIT Press, Cambridge, Massachusetts (1993)

16. Lafferty, J., McCallum, A., Pereira, F.: Conditional Random Fields: Probabilistic models for segmenting and labeling sequence data. In: Machine Learning: Proceedings of the Eighteenth International Conference (ICML 2001), Stanford, California (2001)

17. Miyao, Y., Tsujii, J.: Maximum entropy estimation for feature forests. In: Proceedings of Human Language Technology Conference 2002. (2002)

18. Miyao, Y., Tsujii, J.: A model of syntactic disambiguation based on lexicalized grammars. In: Proceedings of the Seventh Conference on Natural Language Learning. (2003) 1–8

19. Smyth, P., Heckerman, D., Jordan, M.: Probabilistic Independence Networks for Hidden Markov Models. Neural Computation **9** (1997) 227–269

20. Pearl, J.: Probabalistic Reasoning in Intelligent Systems: Networks of Plausible Inference. Morgan Kaufmann, San Mateo, California (1988)

21. Cowell, R.: Introduction to inference for Bayesian networks. In Jordan, M., ed.: Learning in Graphical Models. The MIT Press, Cambridge, Massachusetts (1999) 9–26

22. Geman, S., Kochanek, K.: Dynamic programming and the representation of soft-decodable codes. Technical report, Division of Applied Mathematics, Brown University (2000)

# Generality's Price
## Inescapable Deficiencies in Machine-Learned Programs

John Case[1], Keh-Jiann Chen[2], Sanjay Jain[3],
Wolfgang Merkle[4], and James S. Royer[5]

[1] Dept. of Computer and Information Sciences, University of Delaware
Newark, DE 19716-2586 USA
`case@cis.udel.edu`
[2] Institute of Information Science, Academia Sinica
Nankang 115, Taipei, Taiwan, ROC
`kchen@iis.sinica.edu.tw`
[3] School of Computing, National University of Singapore
3 Science Drive 2, Singapore 117543, Republic of Singapore
`sanjay@comp.nus.edu.sg`
[4] Universität Heidelberg, Mathematisches Institut
Im Neuenheimer Feld 294, D-69120 Heidelberg, Germany
`merkle@math.uni-heidelberg.de`
[5] Dept. of Elec. Eng. and Computer Science, Syracuse University
Syracuse, NY 13244 USA
`royer@ecs.syr.edu`

**Abstract.** This paper investigates some delicate tradeoffs between the *generality* of an algorithmic learning device and the *quality* of the programs it learns successfully. There are results to the effect that, thanks to small increases in generality of a learning device, the computational complexity of some successfully learned programs is provably unalterably *sub*optimal. There are also results in which the complexity of successfully learned programs *is* asymptotically optimal and the learning device is general, but, still thanks to the generality, some of those optimal, learned programs are provably unalterably *information deficient* — in some cases, deficient as to safe, algorithmic extractability/provability of the fact that they are even approximately optimal. The paper is on the borderline between learning theory, complexity theory and logic.

## 1 Introduction

We abbreviate *class of characteristic functions of languages* by CCFL. Suppose $\mathcal{C}_0 \subseteq \mathcal{C}_1$ is a pair of complexity CCFLs which *do* (perhaps barely) separate. For example, let $\alpha$ be a *very slow growing*, linear time computable inverse of Ackermann's function as from [CLRS01, §21.4]; let $\mathcal{C}_1$ be $\text{DTIME}(n \cdot (\log n) \cdot \alpha(n))$; and let $\mathcal{C}_0$ be $\text{DTIME}(n)$ [1]. These classes have long been known to separate

---

[1] $\text{DTIME}(t(n))$ denotes the set of languages decidable by a deterministic, multi-tape Turing machine within $O(t(n))$ time, where $n$ is the length of the machine's input. $\text{DTimeF}(t(n))$ denotes the set of *functions* over strings computable by this same class of machines within $O(t(n))$ time.

B. Schölkopf and M.K. Warmuth (Eds.): COLT/Kernel 2003, LNAI 2777, pp. 684–698, 2003.

[HS65,HU79]. Furthermore, it is straightforward that *some* learning device (synonymously, inductive inference machine or IIM) $\mathbf{M}_0$, fed the values of any element $f$ of this $\mathcal{C}_0$, outputs nothing but linear-time programs and eventually converges to a fixed linear-time program which correctly computes $f$. This kind of syntactically converging learning in the limit is called EX-*learning* (or EX-*identification*) [Gol67,BB75,CS83,JORS99]. Let $\mathcal{Z}^*$ be the CCFL for (all and only) the *finite* languages. Clearly, $\mathcal{Z}^*$ is an especially simple, proper subclass of our example $\mathcal{C}_0$. Two of our main theorems (Theorems 19 and 20 in §6 below) each implies that, nonetheless, if $\mathbf{M}_1$ is *any* learning device which is slightly more general than $\mathbf{M}_0$ in that it EX-learns every function in our example $\mathcal{C}_1$, then, for some especially "easy" function $f$, more particularly for an $f \in \mathcal{Z}^*$, $\mathbf{M}_1$ on $f$ syntactically converges to a correct program $p$ for $f$, *but* this $p$ runs in worse than any linear-time bound *on all but finitely many inputs*. This *inherent* run-time deficiency of $p$ is the *inescapable* price for employing a more general learning device to learn $\mathcal{C}_1$ instead of learning only $\mathcal{C}_0$. Theorems 19 and 20 on which this example is based are proved by delayed diagonalization (or slowed simulation) [Lad75,RC94] with cancellation [Blu67] (or zero injury), complexity-bounded self-reference [RC94], and careful subrecursive programming [RC94].

Fix $k \geq 1$. Let $\mathcal{C}_1 = \mathrm{DTIME}(n^k \cdot (\log n) \cdot \alpha(n))$ and $\mathcal{C}_0 = \mathrm{DTIME}(n^k)$. These classes separate [HS65,HU79], and it is straightforward that some learning device EX-learns this $\mathcal{C}_0$ outputting only conjectures that run in $k$-degree polytime. However, again from Theorems 19 and 20, for any slightly more general learning device $\mathbf{M}$ which EX-learns this $\mathcal{C}_1$, there will be an easy $f$, an $f \in \mathcal{Z}^*$, so that, on $f$, $\mathbf{M}$'s final program $p$ will run worse than any $k$-degree polytime bound on all but finitely many inputs.

One way to circumvent the complexity-deficiency-in-learned-programs price of generality in the above examples is to consider a most general learning criterion called BC$^*$-*learning* [CS83,CCJ01]. In this type of learning, in contrast to EX-learning, one foregoes syntactic convergence in favor of semantic convergence and one foregoes requiring the final programs to be perfectly correct at computing the input function: convergence is to an infinite sequence of programs all but finitely many of which are each correct on all but finitely many inputs. Harrington [CS83] showed that there is a learning device that BC$^*$-learns *every* computable function. (On the other hand, fairly simple classes of computable functions cannot be EX-learned [CS83].) One of our main positive results (Theorem 23 in §8 below) says that there is a learning device $\mathbf{M}_*$ that BC$^*$-learns the CCFL for the polytime decidable languages in such a way that: (i) all of $\mathbf{M}_*$'s output conjectures run in polytime, (ii) for each $k \geq 1$, on each $f \in \mathrm{DTIME}(n^k)$, all but finitely many of $\mathbf{M}_*$'s outputs run in $k$-degree polytime; *and* (iii) $\mathbf{M}_*$ EX-learns all the linear-time computable functions.

There is, though, another kind of deficiency-in-learned-programs price for generality of learning, and this affects BC$^*$-learning, EX-learning, and the learning criteria of strength in between them and which are discussed beginning in §2 below. Let $\mathcal{PF}^k = \mathrm{DTimeF}(n^k)$, and let $\mathcal{QF}_\alpha^k = \mathrm{DTimeF}(n^k \cdot (\log n) \cdot \alpha(n))$. Let $\varphi_q$ be the (partial) function computed by multi-tape Turing machine $q$. Suppose

**M** is any device BC*-learning $\mathcal{QF}_\alpha^k$ [2]. Corollary 6 in §4 below says, then, that there is an easy $f$, an $f \in \mathcal{Z}^*$, so that, if **M** is fed the values of $f$ (which it at least BC*-learns), then for all but finitely many of **M**'s corresponding output conjectures $p$, Peano Arithmetic [Men97] (PA) *fails* to prove that some finite variant of $\varphi_p$ is $k$-degree polytime computable. Of course, for such $p$'s, some finite variant of $\varphi_p$, e.g., $f$, *is* trivially *linear-time* computable. Hence, these $p$'s are *information-deficient*. If, for example, $\mathbf{M}_*$, the learning device of Theorem 23 (discussed in the previous paragraph), is used for **M**, then, on the corresponding $f$, this **M** outputs a *perfectly correct* final program $p$ which runs in linear-time, but Peano Arithmetic can*not* prove the weaker result about this $p$ that some finite variant of $\varphi_p$ is $k$-degree polytime computable. Hence, for the device of Theorem 23, its final output on $f$ is information-deficient, but *not* complexity-deficient. Corollary 6 discussed in this paragraph (as well as Corollaries 7 and 8 in the same section and other corollaries that will be included in an expanded version of this paper) is a consequence of one of our main sufficient condition results, Theorem 5 (also in the same section).

Here is another example. Let $(\mathcal{C}_0, \mathcal{C}_1) = (\mathcal{REG}, \mathcal{CF})$, where $\mathcal{REG}$ and $\mathcal{CF}$ are the CCFLs of regular and context free languages, respectively. Of course, for this example, the separation is not particularly tight. However, importantly, for this example, direct, aggressive diagonalization methods such those as mentioned above are not available. Let $\mathcal{U}^*$ be the CCFL for the *co-finite* languages, i.e., the languages whose complements are finite. Clearly, $\mathcal{U}^*$ is an especially simple, proper subclass of $\mathcal{REG}$. First note that some learning device outputs only deterministic finite automata and EX-learns $\mathcal{REG}$ [Gol67], where deterministic finite automata should be thought of as a degenerate case of Turing machines which use *no* tape squares for workspace [HU79]. EX*-learning is the variant of EX-learning in which the final program need be correct only on all but finitely many inputs. By contrast, still in §4 below, as a corollary of our other main sufficient condition result, Theorem 9, we have Corollary 12 as follows. Suppose **M** EX*-learns $\mathcal{CF}$ and $k, n \geq 1$ [3]. Then there is an easy $f$, an $f \in \mathcal{U}^*$, such that, if $p$ is **M**'s final program on $f$, for *some distinct* $x_0, \ldots, x_{n-1}$, program $p$ uses more than $k$ workspace squares on each of the inputs $x_0, \ldots, x_{n-1}$. This is a complexity-deficiency result for $(\mathcal{REG}, \mathcal{CF})$. Theorem 9 has other complexity-deficiency corollaries, e.g., Corollary 13, an interesting one for (P, NP) — *assuming* they separate. Corollaries 7 and 8 of Theorem 5 provide information-deficiency results for $(\mathcal{REG}, \mathcal{CF})$ and (P, NP), respectively.

Those corollaries, discussed in the previous paragraph, of our sufficient condition results, Theorems 5 and 9, involve classes $(\mathcal{C}_0, \mathcal{C}_1)$ for which direct, aggressive diagonalization is (apparently) not available. These sufficient condition results are proved herein with the aid of some refined *inseparability* results from [RC94]. §3 below provides the details. In [RC94] the inseparabilities were used to characterize relative program succinctness between (possibly barely) sepa-

---

[2] One of many *special cases of this hypothesis* is that **M** actually EX-learns $\mathcal{QF}_\alpha^k$.

[3] One of many special cases of the hypothesis that **M** EX*-learns $\mathcal{CF}$ is that **M** actually EX-learns $\mathcal{CF}$.

rated subrecursive programming systems. Herein they are used to obtain higher-type inseparabilities providing our sufficient conditions (not characterizations) for deficiencies in machine-learned programs. We also use Theorem 5 to obtain all our *information-deficiency* results, including the one for $(\mathcal{PF}^k, \mathcal{QF}_\alpha^k)$ described above. Actually, Theorem 9 can be used to prove a weak special case of our strong complexity-deficiency result (Theorem 20) for $(\mathcal{PF}^k, \mathcal{QF}_\alpha^k)$. This is Corollary 11. In this corollary the quantifier *order* between the $f \in \mathcal{Z}^*$ and the $k$-degree polynomial time bounds is weakened and the for-all-but-finitely-many-inputs-$x$ quantifier is weakened to exists-$n$-distinct-inputs.

*Some* of our results herein whose proofs employ tricks from [RC94] can likely be proved employing instead related methods from [Sch85,Sch82,Reg88]. We may pursue this in an expanded version of the present paper. We also hope to provide, in a future expansion, results in the style of the present paper for P versus various quantum polynomial time classes — assuming separation.

The order of presentation in this introduction differs from that of the remaining sections. The latter order was dictated, to some extent, by the need to introduce required technology in a particular order. Due to space limitations, the proofs of many results have been omitted in this version of the paper.

## 2    Conventions and Notation

*Strings and numbers.* Each $x \in \mathbb{N}$, the set of non-negative integers, is identified with its dyadic representation over $\{0, 1\}$. Thus, $0 \equiv \epsilon$, $1 \equiv \mathbf{0}$, $2 \equiv \mathbf{1}$, $3 \equiv \mathbf{00}$, etc.[4]. For each $x \in \mathbb{N}$, $|x|$ denotes the length of its dyadic representation. By convention, for $\boldsymbol{x} \in \mathbb{N}^n$, $|\boldsymbol{x}|$ denotes $|x_0| + \cdots + |x_{n-1}|$. (By convention, $\boldsymbol{x}, \boldsymbol{y}, \ldots$ range over finite sequences of numbers, the length of which will always be clear from context.) We will freely pun between $x \in \mathbb{N}$ as a number and a $\mathbf{0\text{-}1}$-string.

Let $\langle \cdot, \cdot \rangle$ be a standard, poly-time computable pairing function, e.g., the one from Rogers [Rog67]. By convention, for each $n \geq 2$ and each $x_1, \ldots, x_{n+1} \in \mathbb{N}$, we recursively define $\langle x_1, \ldots, x_{n+1} \rangle =_{\text{def}} \langle x_1, \langle x_2, \ldots, x_{n+1} \rangle \rangle$.

*Encoding lists.*    For each $x, y \in \mathbb{N}$, let $x \diamond y$ denote the concatenation of (the dyadic representations of) $x$ and $y$. For each $x \in \mathbb{N}$, let $E(x) = \mathbf{1}^{|x|}\mathbf{0} \diamond x$. (Note that the image of $E$ in $\{\mathbf{0, 1}\}^*$ is a collection of prefix codes [LV97, §1.4].) We use $E$ to provide a low complexity encoding of lists of numbers as follows. Let $[\,] = 0$, and for each $x_0, \ldots, x_k \in \mathbb{N}$, let $[x_0, \ldots, x_k] = E(x_0) \diamond \cdots \diamond E(x_k)$. By convention, any element of $\mathbb{N}$ that is not of the form $[x_0, \ldots, x_j]$ is considered as coding the empty list. It is clear from our definition of $[\cdot]$ that concatenations, projections, and so on, involving coded lists are all linear-time computable.

*Functions.*    $A \to B$ denotes the set of all total functions from $A$ to $B$ and $A \rightharpoonup B$ denotes the set of (possibly) partial functions from $A$ to $B$. Let $\mathcal{F} = (\mathbb{N} \to \mathbb{N})$. For each $\mathcal{C} \subseteq \mathcal{F}$, let $\mathcal{C}_{0\text{-}1}$ denote the 0–1 valued elements of $\mathcal{C}$. $\mathcal{PR}$ denotes the set of partial recursive functions and $\mathcal{R}$ denotes the total recursive functions.

---

[4] We employ dyadic representation instead of the more standard binary number representation to avoid problems with the degeneracy of lead zeros in the latter [RC94].

For each $f\colon \mathbb{N} \to \mathbb{N}$, we define $O(f) = \{\, g\colon \mathbb{N} \to \mathbb{N} \mid (\exists a)(\forall x)[\, g(x) \leq a \cdot (f(x)+1)\,]\,\}$. By convention $O(f(n))$ is short for $O(\lambda x \boldsymbol{.} f(|x|))$.

Suppose $f, g\colon \mathbb{N} \to \mathbb{N}$. We say that $f$ and $g$ are *finite variants* if and only if $\{\, x \mid f(x) \neq g(x)\,\}$ is finite. Let $\mathcal{FV}(f) = $ the set of finite variants of $f$. For $\mathcal{S} \subseteq (\mathbb{N} \to \mathbb{N})$, let $\mathcal{FV}(\mathcal{S}) = \bigcup_{f \in \mathcal{S}} \mathcal{FV}(f)$. For each $n \in \mathbb{N}$, $f =^{n} g$ means that $\{\, x \mid f(x) \neq g(x)\,\}$ is of size $n$ or less; and $f =^{*} g$ means $g \in \mathcal{FV}(f)$.

*Programming systems.* We say that a partial recursive $\psi\colon \mathbb{N}^2 \to \mathbb{N}$ is a *programming system* for a class of functions $\mathcal{S} \subseteq \mathcal{PR}$ if and only if $\mathcal{S} = \{\, \lambda x \boldsymbol{.} \psi(i, x) : i \in \mathbb{N}\,\}$. We typically write $\psi_i(x)$ for $\psi(i, x)$. We say that $\psi$ is an *acceptable programming system* of $\mathcal{S}$ [Rog67,RC94] if and only if it is the case that for any other programming system for $\mathcal{S}$, say $\theta$, there is a recursive function $t$ such that, for all $i$, $\psi_{t(i)} = \theta_i$, that is, there is an effective way of translating (or reducing) $\theta$-programs into equivalent $\psi$-programs. Let $\varphi$ be an acceptable programming system of $\mathcal{PR}$ based on deterministic multi-tape Turing machines [HU79,Jon97]. By convention, for each $i$ and $x_0, \ldots, x_k$, $\varphi_i(x_0, \ldots, x_k) = \varphi_i(\langle x_0, \ldots, x_k\rangle)$. Also, for each $i$ and $x$, let $\Phi_i(x)$ denote the run time of the computation of the TM encoded by $i$ on input $x$ and let $\Phi_i^{\mathrm{WS}}(x) = $ the work space used by the TM encoded by $i$ on input $x$, provided $\varphi_i(x)\!\downarrow$; $\infty$, otherwise.

*Arithmetic sets.* The $\Sigma_0$- and $\Pi_0$-predicates over $\mathbb{N}^k$ are just the recursive predicates over $\mathbb{N}^k$. $P$ is a $\Sigma_{n+1}$ predicate over $\mathbb{N}^k$ if and only if for some $m$, there is a $\Pi_n$ predicate $Q$ over $\mathbb{N}^{k+m}$ such that $P(\boldsymbol{x}) \equiv (\exists y_1)\ldots(\exists y_m)Q(\boldsymbol{x}, \boldsymbol{y})$ for each $x \in \mathbb{N}^k$. $P$ is a $\Pi_{n+1}$ predicate over $\mathbb{N}^k$ if and only if for some $m$, there is a $\Sigma_n$ predicate $Q$ over $\mathbb{N}^{k+m}$ such that $P(\boldsymbol{x}) \equiv (\forall y_1)\ldots(\forall y_m)Q(\boldsymbol{x}, \boldsymbol{y})$ for each $\boldsymbol{x}$. $A$ is a $\Sigma_n$ (respectively, $\Pi_n$) set if and only if for some $\Sigma_n$ (respectively, $\Pi_n$) predicate $P$ we have $A = \{\, x \mid P(x)\,\}$. Let $\langle W_i^n\rangle_{i \in \mathbb{N}}$ be an acceptable indexing of the $\Sigma_n$ sets [Rog67].

*Subrecursive classes of functions.* For each recursive $t\colon \mathbb{N} \to \mathbb{N}$, let $\mathrm{DTimeF}(t) = \{\, \varphi_i \mid (\exists a)(\forall x)[\,\Phi_i(x) \leq a \cdot (t(x)+1)\,]\,\}$ and $\mathrm{DTIME}(t) = (\mathrm{DTimeF}(f))_{0\text{-}1}$. For each $k > 0$, we define $\mathcal{PF}^k = \mathrm{DTimeF}(\lambda x \boldsymbol{.} |x|^k) = $ the class of functions computable in $O(n^k)$ time on a deterministic multi-tape TM, and $\mathcal{PF} = \cup_{k>0}\mathcal{PF}^k = $ the class of poly-time computable functions. Let $\mathcal{LS}low = \{\, f \in \mathcal{PF}^1 \mid f \text{ is non-decreasing and unbounded}\,\}$. By standard results [CM81,LLR81], for each recursive, increasing, unbounded $f$, there is an $s \in \mathcal{LS}low$ that grows slower than the inverse of $f$ in the sense that, for all $x$, $s(f(x)) \leq x$. $\mathcal{QF}_s^k = \mathrm{DTimeF}(\lambda x \boldsymbol{.} |x|^k \cdot (\log|x|)\cdot s(|x|))$, for $k > 0$ and $s \in \mathcal{LS}low$. By standard results from [HS65,HU79], for all $k > 0$ and $s \in \mathcal{LS}low$, $(\mathcal{QF}_s^k - \mathcal{PF}^k)_{0\text{-}1} \neq \emptyset$.

Let $\mathcal{NP}$, $\mathcal{P}$, $\mathcal{CF}$, and $\mathcal{REG}$ respectively denote the classes of characteristic functions of NP, poly-time decidable, context free, and regular languages over $\{\,\boldsymbol{0}, \boldsymbol{1}\,\}^*$. (Recall that we are punning between $\mathbb{N}$ as the natural numbers and $\boldsymbol{0}$-$\boldsymbol{1}$-strings.) $\mathcal{Z}^*$ (respectively, $\mathcal{U}^*$) denotes the class of 0–1 valued functions that are 0 (respectively, 1) almost everywhere.

$\mathcal{S} \subseteq \mathcal{R}$ is an *r.e. subrecursive class* when there is a programming system for $\mathcal{S}$. By standard results, $\mathcal{P}$, $\mathcal{P}^k$, $\mathcal{QF}_s^k$, $\mathcal{NP}$, ... are each r.e. subrecursive classes.

*Finite initial segments.* For $f \in \mathcal{F}$ and $n \in \mathbb{N}$, $f|_n$ denotes the sequence $f(0), f(1), \ldots, f(n-1)$, the finite initial segment of $f$ of length $n$. Clearly, $f|_0$ denotes the empty segment. Let SEG denote the set of all such finite initial segments; $\sigma$, with or without decorations, will range over SEG. If $\sigma = a_0, a_1, \ldots, a_{n-1}$ and $m \leq n$, then $\sigma|_m = a_0, a_1, \ldots, a_{m-1}$.

*Inductive inference machines.* An *inductive inference machine* [Gol67] is an algorithmic device that computes a possibly partial function from SEG to $\mathbb{N}$. $\mathbf{M}$, with or without decorations, ranges over such machines. Since SEG can be coded into $\mathbb{N}$, we can view an $\mathbf{M}$ as computing a partial function over $\mathbb{N}$. We say that $\mathbf{M}(f)$ *converges* to $i$ (written: $\mathbf{M}(f){\downarrow} = i$) if and only if, for all but finitely many $n$, $\mathbf{M}(f|_n) = i$; $\mathbf{M}(f)$ is undefined if no such $i$ exists. The *point of convergence* of $\mathbf{M}$ on $f$ is, if it exists, the smallest $m \in \mathbb{N}$ such that $\mathbf{M}(f|_m)$ is defined and, for all $n \geq m$, $\mathbf{M}(f|_n) = \mathbf{M}(f|_m)$.

*The EX and EX\* identification criteria.* Suppose $f \in \mathcal{R}$ and $\mathcal{S} \subseteq \mathcal{R}$. We say that $\mathbf{M}$ EX-identifies $f$ if and only if, for some $i$, $\mathbf{M}(f){\downarrow} = i$ and $i$ is a program for $f$ (i.e., $\varphi_i = f$). We say that $\mathbf{M}$ EX-identifies $\mathcal{S}$ if and only if $\mathcal{S} \subseteq \mathrm{EX}(\mathbf{M}) =_{\mathrm{def}} \{ f \in \mathcal{R} \mid \mathbf{M} \text{ EX-identifies } f \}$. EX denotes $\{ \mathcal{S} \mid \text{ some } \mathbf{M} \text{ EX-identifies } \mathcal{S} \}$. The notion of EX-identification originated with Gold [Gol67]. Gold [Gol67] showed that every r.e. subrecursive class is in EX. We say that $\mathbf{M}$ EX\*-identifies $f$ if and only if, for some $i$, $\mathbf{M}(f){\downarrow} = i$ and $\varphi_i =^* f$. We define EX\*$(\mathbf{M})$ and EX\* analogously to our definitions of EX$(\mathbf{M})$ and EX. EX\*-identification is due to Blum and Blum [BB75] who showed that EX $\subsetneq$ EX\*.

*The BC, BC$^n$, and BC\* identification criteria.* Suppose $f \in \mathcal{R}$ and $\mathcal{S} \subseteq \mathcal{R}$. For each $k \in \mathbb{N} \cup \{ * \}$, we say that $\mathbf{M}$ BC$^k$-identifies $f$ if and only if, for all but finitely many $n$, $\varphi_{\mathbf{M}(f|_n)} =^k f$. We say that $\mathbf{M}$ BC$^k$-identifies $\mathcal{S}$ if and only if $\mathcal{S} \subseteq$ BC$^k(\mathbf{M}) =_{\mathrm{def}} \{ f \in \mathcal{R} \mid \mathbf{M} \text{ BC}^k\text{-identifies } f \}$. BC$^k$ denotes $\{ \mathcal{S} \mid \text{ some } \mathbf{M} \text{ BC}^k\text{-identifies } \mathcal{S} \}$. We usually write BC$^0$ as simply BC. BC-identification was first formalized by Bārzdiņš [Bar74]. Independently, Case and Smith [CS83] defined BC$^m$- and BC\*-identification. Steel [CS83] showed EX\* $\subseteq$ BC, Harrington and Case showed this inclusion to be proper [CS83], and Case and Smith [CS83] showed BC$^0 \subsetneq$ BC$^1 \subsetneq$ BC$^2 \subsetneq \cdots \subsetneq$ BC\*. Moreover, as noted in §1, Harrington [CS83] showed that $\mathcal{R} \in$ BC\*.

## 3   Inseparability Notions

Suppose $A$, $B$, and $S$ are sets. We say that $S$ *separates* $B$ from $A$ if and only if $B \subseteq S \subseteq \overline{A}$. (See Figure 1.)

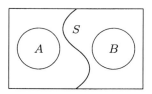

**Definition 1.** Suppose $A$ and $B \subseteq \mathbb{N}$.

(a) $B$ is *$\Sigma_n$-inseparable* from $A$ if and only if $A$ and $B$ are nonempty and disjoint, but no $\Sigma_n$ set separates $B$ from $A$.

**Fig. 1.** $S$ separates $B$ from $A$.

(b) $B$ is *effectively $\Sigma_n$-inseparable* from $A$ if and only if $A$ and $B$ are nonempty and disjoint and there is a recursive $f$ such that, for each $i$, $f(i) \in (W_i^n \cap A) \cup (\overline{W_i^n} \cap B)$, i.e., $f(i)$ witnesses that $B \subseteq W_i^n \subseteq \overline{A}$ fails.  $\diamond$

**Definition 2.** Suppose $R \subseteq \mathcal{F}^k \times \mathbb{N}^\ell$.

(a) $R$ is *recursive* if and only if the characteristic function of $R$ is a total recursive functional of type $\mathcal{F}^k \times \mathbb{N}^\ell \to \{0, 1\}$.

(b) $R$ is *arithmetical* if and only if either $R$ is recursive or

$$R = \{ (\boldsymbol{f}, \boldsymbol{x}) : (Q_1 \, y_1) \ldots (Q_m \, y_m)[\, S(\boldsymbol{f}, \boldsymbol{x}, \boldsymbol{y})\,]\} \tag{1}$$

where each $Q_i$ is either $\exists$ or $\forall$ and where $S \subseteq \mathcal{F}^k \times \mathbb{N}^{\ell+m}$ is recursive. (**N.B.** All the quantifiers in (1) are numeric.)

(c) $R$ is in $\Sigma_n^{(\mathrm{fn})}$ if and only if $R$ is recursive or $R$ is expressible as in (1) with the quantifiers in $\Sigma_n$ form.

(d) $R$ is in $\Pi_n^{(\mathrm{fn})}$ if and only if $R$'s complement is in $\Sigma_n^{(\mathrm{fn})}$.     ◇

*Indexings.* For each $k$, $\ell$, and $n$, let $\langle W_i^{(\mathrm{fn}),k,\ell,n} \rangle_{i \in \mathbb{N}}$ be an acceptable indexing of the class of all $R \subseteq \mathcal{F}^k \times \mathbb{N}^\ell$ in $\Sigma_n^{(\mathrm{fn})}$. For each $i$, let $\mathcal{W}_i^n = W_i^{(\mathrm{fn}),1,0,n}$.

Next we introduce the higher-type inseparabilities needed for our results.

**Definition 3.** Suppose $\mathcal{A}$ and $\mathcal{B} \subseteq \mathcal{F}$.

(a) $\mathcal{B}$ is $\Sigma_n^{(\mathrm{fn})}$-*inseparable* from $\mathcal{A}$ if and only if $\mathcal{A}$ and $\mathcal{B}$ are nonempty and disjoint, but no $\Sigma_n^{(\mathrm{fn})}$ set separates $\mathcal{B}$ from $\mathcal{A}$.

(b) $\mathcal{B}$ is *effectively* $\Sigma_n^{(\mathrm{fn})}$-*inseparable* from $\mathcal{A}$ if and only if $\mathcal{A}$ and $\mathcal{B}$ are nonempty and disjoint and there is a recursive $f$ such that for each $i$, $\varphi_{f(i)} \in (\mathcal{W}_i^n \cap \mathcal{A}) \cup (\overline{\mathcal{W}_i^n} \cap \mathcal{B})$.     ◇

In the journal version of this paper we establish several sufficient conditions for $\Sigma_2^{(\mathrm{fn})}$-inseparability. From these sufficient conditions we can deduce:

**Corollary 4.**

(a) Suppose that $k > 0$ and $s \in \mathcal{LS}low$. Then $(\mathcal{QF}_s^k - \mathcal{PF}^k)_{0\text{-}1}$ is effectively $\Sigma_2^{(\mathrm{fn})}$-inseparable from $\mathcal{Z}^*$.

(b) $(\mathcal{CF} - \mathcal{REG})$ is effectively $\Sigma_2^{(\mathrm{fn})}$-inseparable from $\mathcal{U}^*$.

(c) If $\mathrm{P} \neq \mathrm{NP}$, then $(\mathcal{NP} - \mathcal{P})$ is effectively $\Sigma_2^{(\mathrm{fn})}$-inseparable from $\mathcal{Z}^*$.

## 4     Sufficient Conditions Theorems

In the following, think of $\mathcal{A}$ as some set of very modest functions (e.g., $\mathcal{Z}^*$ above), $\mathcal{B}$ as some set of immodest functions, and $G$ as some set of "good" programs such that no finite variant of a member of $\mathcal{B}$ has a program in $G$ [5].

Theorem 5, our first sufficient condition theorem, provides us with our information deficiency corollaries (Corollaries 6 through 8).

**Theorem 5.** Suppose that: (i) $\mathcal{B}$ is $\Sigma_2^{(\mathrm{fn})}$-inseparable from $\mathcal{A}$. (ii) $G$ is a $\Sigma_1$-set such that $\mathcal{FV}(\mathcal{B}) \cap \{\varphi_i : i \in G\} = \emptyset$. (iii) $\mathbf{M}$ is an IIM such that $\mathcal{B} \subseteq \mathrm{BC}^*(\mathbf{M})$. Then there is an $f \in \mathcal{A}$ such that for all but finitely many $n$, $\mathbf{M}(f|_n) \notin G$.

---

[5] For example, the members of $G$ may run efficiently and/or be easy to prove things about.

*Proof.* Since $G$ is a $\Sigma_1$ set, we know that there is a recursive $R_G$ such that $G = \{\, x \mid (\exists m) R_G(x, m)\,\}$. Consider $\mathcal{S} = \{\, f \in \mathcal{F} \mid (\overset{\infty}{\forall} n)[\mathbf{M}(f|_n) \notin G]\,\} = \{\, f \in \mathcal{F} \mid (\exists n_0)(\forall n > n_0)(\forall m)[\neg R_G(\mathbf{M}(f|_n), m)]\,\}$. Thus, $\mathcal{S} \in \Sigma_2^{(\mathrm{fn})}$. Also, by (ii) and (iii) it follows that $\mathcal{B} \subseteq \mathcal{S}$. Now suppose by way of contradiction that, for all $f \in \mathcal{A}$, we have: $(\overset{\infty}{\exists} n)[\mathbf{M}(f|_n) \in G]$. Clearly, $\mathcal{A} \cap \mathcal{S} = \emptyset$. Therefore, $\mathcal{S}$ is a $\Sigma_2^{(\mathrm{fn})}$-set that separates $\mathcal{B}$ from $\mathcal{A}$, contradiction.    $\square$

The next three corollaries involve provability and PA, Peano Arithmetic [Men97]. We write $\vdash$ for the provability relation and $\nvdash$ for 'does *not* prove.' The following predicates are expressible in Peano Arithmetic (and herein we do not distinguish between expressions in Peano Arithmetic and expressions in the metalanguage).

$$P_k(i) \equiv_{\mathrm{def}} (\exists c)(\forall x)[\Phi_i(x) \le c \cdot (|x| + 1)^k].\quad S_k(i) \equiv_{\mathrm{def}} (\forall x)[\Phi_i^{\mathrm{WS}}(x) \le k].$$
$$P_k^*(i) \equiv_{\mathrm{def}} (\exists j \mid \varphi_j =^* \varphi_i)[P_k(j)].\quad P^*(i) \equiv_{\mathrm{def}} (\exists j \mid \varphi_j =^* \varphi_i)(\exists k)[P_k(j)].$$
$$REG^*(i) \equiv_{\mathrm{def}} (\exists k)(\exists j \mid \varphi_j =^* \varphi_i)[S_k(j)].$$

**N.B.** Each of Corollaries 6, 7, and 8 remains true if PA is replaced by any true and computably axiomatized theory [Men97] extending the language of PA. Such theories, including PA itself, should be thought of as safe, algorithmic extractors of information: the safety is they prove only true sentences; and, since they are computably axiomatized, there is an associated automatic theorem prover, i.e., the set of theorems is r.e. [Men97].

**Corollary 6.** *Suppose that* $k > 0$, $s \in \mathcal{LS}low$, *and* $BC^*(\mathbf{M}) \supseteq \mathcal{QF}_s^k$. *Then there is an* $f \in \mathcal{Z}^*$ *such that, for all but finitely many* $n$, *PA* $\nvdash P_k^*(\mathbf{M}(f|_n))$.

*Proof.* Let $\mathcal{A} = \mathcal{Z}^*$, $\mathcal{B} = (\mathcal{QF}_s^k - \mathcal{PF}^k)$, and $G = \{\, i \mid \text{PA} \vdash P_k^*(i)\,\}$. Now, applying Corollary 4(a) and Theorem 5, we are done.    $\square$

*Interpretation.* Let $\mathbf{M}$ and $f$ be as in Corollary 6[6]. Then it must be the case that, for all but finitely many $n$, the program $\mathbf{M}(f|_n)$ computes a (finite variant of a) function $f$ that is almost everywhere zero. Of course *some* program computes $f$ in *linear time*. Yet, even so, for sufficiently large $n$, the programs $\mathbf{M}(f|_n)$ are so information deficient that PA fails to prove of them that they compute a finite variant of something (like $f$) that has *some* program running in $k$-degree polynomial time. Analogous interpretive remarks apply to the next two corollaries (which, by the way, have proofs similar to that just above for Corollary 6).

**Corollary 7.** *Suppose* $BC^*(\mathbf{M}) \supseteq \mathcal{CF}$. *Then there is an* $f \in \mathcal{U}^*$ *such that, for all but finitely many* $n$, *PA* $\nvdash REG^*(\mathbf{M}(f|_n))$.

**Corollary 8.** *Suppose* $BC^*(\mathbf{M}) \supseteq \mathcal{NP}$ *and that* $P \ne NP$. *Then there is an* $f \in \mathcal{Z}^*$ *such that, for all but finitely many* $n$, *PA* $\nvdash P^*(\mathbf{M}(f|_n))$.

---

[6] As noted in §1, an allowed special case is that $\mathbf{M}$ actually EX-learns $\mathcal{QF}_\alpha^k$.

Theorem 9, our second sufficient condition theorem, provides us with complexity deficiency corollaries (Corollaries 11 through 13).

**Theorem 9.** *Suppose that: (i) $\mathcal{B}$ is $\Sigma_2^{(\text{fn})}$-inseparable from $\mathcal{A}$. (ii) $G$ is a $\Pi_2$-set such that $\mathcal{FV}(\mathcal{B}) \cap \{\varphi_i \mid i \in G\} = \emptyset$. (iii) $\mathbf{M}$ is an IIM such that (a) $\mathcal{A} \subseteq \text{EX}^*(\mathbf{M})$ and (b) $\mathcal{B} \subseteq \text{EX}^*(\mathbf{M})$. Then there is an $f \in \mathcal{A}$ such that $\mathbf{M}(f) \notin G$.*

**Scholium 10.** The fact that $G \in \Pi_2$ in Theorem 9 does not provide as much generality as one might hope. Here is why. It is a well-worn observation that if $\mathcal{C}$ is closed under finite variants and $P$ is a $\Sigma_2$ set such that $\mathcal{C} \subseteq \{\varphi_i \mid i \in P\} \subseteq \mathcal{F}$, then there is an r.e. set $P'$ such that $\mathcal{C} \subseteq \{\varphi_i \mid i \in P\} \subseteq \{\varphi_i \mid i \in P'\} \subseteq \mathcal{F}$. It is a minor variation on this observation that if hypotheses (ii) and (iii) of Theorem 9 hold, then there is a $\Pi_1$-set $G'$ such that $\mathcal{A} \subseteq \{\varphi_i \mid i \in G\} \subseteq \{\varphi_i \mid i \in G'\} \subseteq (\mathcal{PR} - \mathcal{B})$. Hence, $G$ in Theorem 9 might as well be $\Pi_1$—which is what it is in our applications of this theorem.    $\diamond$

As was mentioned in §1, the following corollary of Theorem 9 provides a weak special case of our strong complexity-deficiency result (Theorem 20) for $(\mathcal{PF}^k, \mathcal{QF}_\alpha^k)$: the quantifier *order* between the $f \in \mathcal{Z}^*$ and the $k$-degree polynomial time bounds is weakened and the for-all-but-finitely-many-inputs-$x$ quantifier is weakened to exists-$n$-distinct-inputs.

**Corollary 11.** *Suppose $a, k, n > 0$, $s \in \mathcal{LS}low$, and $\text{EX}^*(\mathbf{M}) \supseteq \mathcal{QF}_s^k$. Then there is an $f \in \mathcal{Z}^*$ such that, for some $i$, $\mathbf{M}(f)\downarrow = i$, but there are distinct $x_0, \ldots, x_{n-1}$ such that for each $j < n$, $\Phi_i(x_i) > a \cdot (|x_j| + 1)^k$.*

*Proof.* Let $\mathcal{A} = \mathcal{Z}^*$, $\mathcal{B} = (\mathcal{QF}_s^k - \mathcal{PF}^k)$, and $G = \{i \mid (\forall x_0)(\forall x_1 > x_0) \ldots (\forall x_{n-1} > x_{n-2})(\exists j < n)[\Phi_i(x_j) \leq a \cdot (|x_j| + 1)^k]\}$. Now, applying Corollary 4(a) and Theorem 9, we are done.    $\square$

As mentioned in §1, the next two corollaries seem difficult to establish by aggressive diagonalization techniques. It is open for each as to whether the quantifier on the inputs to the programs $i$ can be strengthened.

**Corollary 12.** *Suppose $\text{EX}^*(\mathbf{M}) \supseteq \mathcal{CF}$ and $k, n > 0$. Then there is an $f \in \mathcal{U}^*$ such that, for some $i$, $\mathbf{M}(f)\downarrow = i$, but, there are distinct $x_0, \ldots, x_{n-1}$ such that for each $j < n$, $\Phi_i^{\text{WS}}(x_j) > k$.*

*Proof.* Let $\mathcal{A} = \mathcal{U}^*$, $\mathcal{B} = (\mathcal{CF} - \mathcal{REG})$, and $G = \{i \mid (\forall x_0)(\forall x_1 > x_0) \ldots (\forall x_{n-1} > x_{n-2})(\exists j < n)[\Phi_i^{\text{WS}}(x_j) \leq k]\}$. Now, applying Corollary 4(b) and Theorem 9, we are done.    $\square$

*Interpretation.* Suppose $\mathbf{M}$ $\text{EX}^*$-identifies $\mathcal{CF}$ [7]. Then Corollary 12 implies that there are members of $\mathcal{U}^*$ for which $\mathbf{M}$ infers programs that use arbitrarily large (but finite) amounts of workspace on arbitrarily large (but finite) sets of inputs. Thus $\mathbf{M}$ is quite far from inferring space efficient programs for easy

---

[7] As noted in §1, an allowed special case is that $\mathbf{M}$ actually EX-learns $\mathcal{CF}$.

members of $\mathcal{REG}$, and members of $\mathcal{REG}$ have programs that use no workspace at all.

The next corollary has a similar proof to that for Corollary 12.

Let $\varphi^{\mathrm{ND}}$ be based on a natural programming system of non-deterministic, multi-tape Turing machines for accepting sets.

**Corollary 13.** *Suppose* P $\neq$ NP. *Suppose* **M** EX*-*identifies* $\mathcal{NP}$ *using poly-nomial-time (deterministic and nondeterministic)* $\varphi^{\mathrm{ND}}$*-programs*[8], *q is a poly-nomial, and* $n > 0$. *Then there is an* $f \in \mathcal{Z}^*$ *such that, for some* $i$, $\mathbf{M}(f)\!\downarrow = i$, *but, there are distinct* $x_0, \ldots, x_{n-1}$ *such that for each* $j < n$, $\varphi^{\mathrm{ND}}$*-program* $i$ *on input* $x_j$ *runs* non-*deterministically and, in fact, has a computation tree of more than* $q(|x_j|)$ *paths.*

*Interpretation.* Suppose **M** EX*-identifies $\mathcal{NP}$ using polynomial-time (deter-ministic and nondeterministic) $\varphi^{\mathrm{ND}}$-programs. Then the above corollary implies that there are members of $\mathcal{Z}^*$ for which **M** infers programs that employ arbi-trarily polynomially much unpleasant non-determinism on arbitrarily large (but finite) sets of inputs. Thus **M** is far from inferring efficient programs for easy members of P.

## 5   A Few More Diagonalization and Structural Tools

Here we state a few more tools for the proofs of the results in the next three sections. These depend on a few special features of our programming system $\varphi$ and its associated complexity measure $\Phi$. The details of these features are mostly straightforward and are omitted here, but can be found in Chapter 3 of [RC94].

**Proposition 14 (The Cost of Simulations, [RC94] Theorem 3.6).** *Sup-pose* $S, T \colon \mathbb{N}^3 \to \mathbb{N}$ *are given by:*

$$S(i, x, t) = \begin{cases} \varphi_i(x), & \text{if } \Phi_i(x) \leq |t|; \\ 0, & \text{otherwise.} \end{cases} \quad T(i, x, t) = \begin{cases} 1, & \text{if } \Phi_i(x) \leq |t|; \\ 0, & \text{otherwise.} \end{cases}$$

*Then* $S$ *and* $T$ *are computable in time* $O(|x| + (|i| + 1) \cdot (|t| \cdot \log |t| + 1))$.

**Proposition 15.** *Suppose that* $m, n \geq 1$. *In the following* $i$, $j$, *and* $k$ *range over* $\mathbb{N}$, *and* $x$ *and* $y$ *over* $\mathbb{N}^m$ *and* $\mathbb{N}^n$, *respectively.*

*(a)* COMPLEXITY-BOUNDED CONDITIONALS, [RC94] LEMMA 3.14. *There is a poly-time computable* $\mathrm{if}_m$ *and an* $a_m \in \mathbb{N}$ *such that, for all* $i, j, k$, *and* $x$:

$$\varphi_{\mathrm{if}_m(i,j,k)}(x) = \begin{cases} \varphi_j(x), & \text{if } \varphi_i(x) > 0; \\ \varphi_k(x), & \text{if } \varphi_i(x) = 0; \\ \uparrow, & \text{if } \varphi_i(x)\!\uparrow. \end{cases}$$

$$\Phi_{\mathrm{if}_m(i,j,k)}(x) \leq \begin{cases} \Phi_i(x) + \Phi_j(x) + a_m \cdot (|x| + 1), & \text{if } \varphi_i(x) > 0; \\ \Phi_i(x) + \Phi_k(x) + a_m \cdot (|x| + 1), & \text{if } \varphi_i(x) = 0; \\ \infty, & \text{if } \varphi_i(x)\!\uparrow. \end{cases}$$

---

[8] *Note:* NP is trivially in EX as witnessed by some **M**′ also outputting $\varphi^{\mathrm{ND}}$-programs.

*(b)* COMPLEXITY-BOUNDED SELF-REFERENCE, [RC94] THEOREM 4.6. *There is a poly-time computable* $r_{m,n}$ *and an* $a_{m,n} \in \mathbb{N}$ *such that, for all* $i$, $\boldsymbol{x}$, *and* $\boldsymbol{y}$:

$$\varphi^n_{r_{m,n}(i,\boldsymbol{x})}(\boldsymbol{y}) = \varphi^{m+n+1}_i(r_{m,n}(i,\boldsymbol{x}),\boldsymbol{x},\boldsymbol{y}).$$

$$\Phi^n_{r_{m,n}(i,\boldsymbol{x})}(\boldsymbol{y}) \leq \Phi^{m+n+1}_i(r_{m,n}(i,\boldsymbol{x}),\boldsymbol{x},\boldsymbol{y}) + a_{m,n} \cdot (|\boldsymbol{x}| + |\boldsymbol{y}| + 1).$$

**Proposition 16 (Low Complexity Delayed Enumeration, [RC94] Theorem 7.1).** *For each* $m > 0$ *and* $s \in \mathcal{LS}low$, *there is a linear time computable function* $\mathrm{rng}_{m,s}$ *such that, for all* $i$ *with* $\varphi_i$ *total and all* $\boldsymbol{w} \in \mathbb{N}^m$, *there is a strictly increasing sequence of numbers* $y_0, y_1, y_2, \ldots$ *such that*
  *(a) for each* $y \in \{0, \ldots, y_0 - 1\}$, $\mathrm{rng}_{m,s}(i,\boldsymbol{w},y) = 0$, *and*
  *(b) for each* $x$ *and each* $y \in \{y_x \ldots, y_{x+1}-1\}$, $\mathrm{rng}_{m,s}(i,\boldsymbol{w},y) = 1+\varphi_i(\boldsymbol{w},x)$,
*and moreover,* $|\varphi_i(\boldsymbol{w},x)| \leq s(|\max(i,\boldsymbol{w},y)|)$.

*Convention:* For each $m$, let $\mathrm{rng}_m$ denote $\mathrm{rng}_{m,s}$ where $s = \lambda n.\log^{(2)}(n)$.

# 6   Negative, Almost Everywhere Results for EX$^*$ and BC$^0$

For simplicity of proof exposition we begin with two theorems essentially announced in [Che81] and based on a suggestion of Sipser for the EX case. In [Che81] it was merely asserted without proof that the constructions could be done in polytime. At that time, the machinery to supply really convincing proofs of these results was not yet available (at least to us). For the present paper we have the needed machinery for this and for proving the main theorems of this section (Theorems 19 and 20) which follow. These main theorems provide considerably tighter complexity bounds *and* stronger quantifier order.

Although EX$^* \subsetneq$ BC$^0$, Theorems 17 through 20 handle separately the cases of EX$^*$ and BC$^0$. This is because, if **M** witnesses that a class is in EX$^*$, the same **M** need not witness the class is in BC$^0$: the latter can require a different machine **M**$'$.

**Theorem 17.** *Suppose that* BC$^0$(**M**) $\supseteq \mathcal{PF}$. *Then for each polynomial* $q$, *there is an* $f \in \mathcal{Z}^*$ *such that* $(\overset{\infty}{\forall}n)(\overset{\infty}{\forall}x)[\Phi_{\mathbf{M}(f|_n)}(x) > q(|x|)]$.

**Theorem 18.** *Suppose that* EX$^*$(**M**) $\supseteq \mathcal{PF}$. *Then, for each polynomial* $q$, *there is an* $f \in \mathcal{Z}^*$ *such that* $(\overset{\infty}{\forall}x)[\Phi_{\mathbf{M}(f)}(x) > q(|x|)]$.

*Proof (of Theorem 17).* Fix a polynomial $q$. *Terminology:* We say that $p$ is *available* at $w$ if and only if $\Phi_p(w) \leq q(|w|)$. For each $\sigma$, define the set

$$\mathrm{Candidates}(\sigma) = \left\{ p \; \middle| \; \begin{array}{l} \text{for some } n \leq |\sigma|+1, \ p = \mathbf{M}(\sigma|_n) \text{ and, for each } w \in \\ \mathrm{dom}(\sigma), \text{ if } p \text{ is available at } w, \text{ then } \varphi_p(w) = \sigma(w) \end{array} \right\}.$$

Let $d$ be a $\varphi$-program such that, for all $e$ and $x$,

$$\varphi_d(e,x) = \begin{cases} \uparrow, & \text{if, for some } w < x, \ \varphi_e(w)\uparrow; \\ [p_1,\ldots,p_k] & \text{otherwise, where } \{p_1 < \cdots < p_k\} = \\ & \quad \mathrm{Candidates}(\varphi_e|_x). \end{cases}$$

Intuitively, when $\varphi_d(e,x){\downarrow} = [p_1,\ldots,p_k]$, then $p_1,\ldots,p_k$ is a list of conjectures that $\mathbf{M}$ makes on $\varphi_e$ that are candidates for diagonalization. Now let $u$ be a $\varphi$-program such that, for all $e$ and $y$, $\varphi_u(e,y) =$

$$\begin{cases} 0, & \text{if (i) } \mathrm{rng}_1(d,e,y) = 0 \text{ or } \mathrm{rng}_1(d,e,y) = 1 + [p_1, \\ & \ldots,p_k], \text{ but none of the } p_i\text{'s is available at } y; \\ 1 \dot{-} S(p,y,\mathbf{0}^{q(|y|)}), & \text{(ii) otherwise, where } p \text{ is the least } p_i \text{ available at } y. \end{cases}$$

*Terminology:* If (ii) holds above for a particular input $e$ and $y$, we then say that the $p$ is *canceled* for $e$ at $y$. Since $S$, $\mathrm{rng}_1$, and the availability predicate are all poly-time computable, it is straightforward that $\varphi_u$ is poly-time computable. So, without loss of generality, we assume that $\Phi_u$ is polynomially bounded. Thus by Proposition 15(b), there is a $\varphi$-program $e_0$ and a polynomial $q_0$ such that, for all $y$, $\varphi_{e_0}(y) = \varphi_u(e_0,y)$ and $\Phi_{e_0}(y) \leq q_0(|y|)$. Hence, $\varphi_{e_0} \in \mathcal{PF}$. Thus, $\lambda x.\varphi_d(e_0,x)$ is total.

*Claim 1:* No $p$ is canceled for $e_0$ infinitely many times. *Proof:* Suppose $p$ is canceled for $e_0$ on some number. Then it follows by the definition of $\varphi_d$ that, for all but finitely many $x$, $p$ is not on the list output by $\varphi_d(e_0,x)$. Hence, by the definition of $\mathrm{rng}_1$, for all but finitely many $y$, $p \notin \{p_1^y,\ldots,p_{k_y}^y\}$ where $1 + [p_1^y,\ldots,p_{k_y}^y] = \mathrm{rng}_1(d,e_0,y)$. Thus, by the definition of $u$, Claim 1 follows.

*Claim 2:* Suppose $\varphi_{\mathbf{M}(\varphi_{e_0}|_n)} = \varphi_{e_0}$. Then $\mathbf{M}(\varphi_{e_0}|_n)$ is never canceled for $e_0$ on any $y$. *Proof:* If $p$ is canceled for $e_0$ on some $y$, then $\varphi_p \neq \varphi_{e_0}$. Hence the claim follows.

*Claim 3:* Suppose $\varphi_{\mathbf{M}(\varphi_{e_0}|_n)} = \varphi_{e_0}$. Then it is the case that, for all but finitely many $y$, $\Phi_{\mathbf{M}(\varphi_{e_0}|_n)}(y) > q(|y|)$. *Proof:* Suppose by way of contradiction that $\mathbf{M}(\varphi_{e_0}|_n)$ is available for $e_0$ on infinitely many $y$. Then it follows by standard arguments that $\mathbf{M}(\varphi_{e_0}|_n)$ is eventually canceled for $e_0$ on some $y$, contradicting Claim 2. Hence, the present claim follows.

Since $\mathbf{M}$ BC-identifies $\varphi_{e_0}$, it follows from Claim 3 that, for all but finitely many $n$ and all but finitely many $y$, $\Phi_{\mathbf{M}(\varphi_{e_0}|_n)}(y) > q(|y|)$.

It follows from Claims 1 and 2 and the BC-identification of $\varphi_{e_0}$ by $\mathbf{M}$ that there are only finitely many $y$ on which any $p$ is canceled for $e_0$. Thus, by the definition of $u$, $\varphi_{e_0} \in \mathcal{Z}^*$. Therefore, the theorem follows. $\qquad\square$

By a more delicate choice of complexity functions and a correspondingly more careful complexity analysis of the proofs of the previous two theorems, we can obtain the following two improvements which are our main theorems of the present section.

**Theorem 19.** *Suppose* $\mathbf{M}$ $BC^0$*-identifies* $\mathcal{QF}_s^k$, *where* $k \geq 1$ *and* $s \in \mathcal{LS}low$. *Then there is an* $f \in \mathcal{Z}^*$ *such that* $(\forall a)(\overset{\infty}{\forall} n)(\overset{\infty}{\forall} x)[\Phi_{\mathbf{M}(f|_n)}(x) > a \cdot (|x|+1)^k]$.

**Theorem 20.** *Suppose* $\mathbf{M}$ $EX^*$*-identifies* $\mathcal{QF}_s^k$, *where* $k \geq 1$ *and* $s \in \mathcal{LS}low$. *Then there is an* $f \in \mathcal{Z}^*$ *such that* $(\forall a)(\overset{\infty}{\forall} x)[\Phi_{\mathbf{M}(f)}(x) > a \cdot (|x|+1)^k]$.

*Interpretation.* Let $\mathbf{M}$, $k$, $s$ and $f$ be as in Theorem 19[9]. Then for all most all $n$, the program $\mathbf{M}(f|_n)$ must compute $f$, an almost everywhere zero function, yet the run time of this program is almost everywhere worse than any degree-$k$ polynomial in the size of the input. This is a profound failure of $\mathbf{M}$ to infer anything like asymptotically optimal programs for even easy members of $\mathcal{PF}^k$. Similar remarks apply to Theorem 20.

*Proof (of Theorem 19).* Let $s' \in \mathcal{LS}low$ be such that $\lim_{n \to \infty}(s'(n))^2/s(n) = 0$. The construction is identical to the one given in the proof of Theorem 17 with $q$ replaced by $\lambda n.s'(n) \cdot (n+1)^k$ and $\mathrm{rng}_1$ replaced by $\mathrm{rng}_{1,s'}$. Without loss of generality we assume that, for all $x$, $s(x)$ and $s'(x) > 0$.

Let us consider the cost of computing the function computed by $\varphi_u$. Recall that $p$ is available at $y$ if and only if $\Phi_p(y) \le s'(|y|) \cdot (|y| + 1)^k$ if and only if $T(p, y, \mathbf{0}^{s'(|y|) \cdot (|y|+1)^k}) = 1$. By standard time-constructibility results [HU79], given $y$ (in dyadic representation), constructing a string of $\mathbf{0}$'s of length $s'(|y|) \cdot (|y| + 1)^k$ can be done in time $O(s'(|y|) \cdot (|y| + 1)^k)$. Hence by Proposition 14, testing, for a given $p$ and $y$, whether $p$ is available at $y$ can be done in $O((|p| + 1) \cdot (|y| + 1)^k \cdot (1 + \log |y|) \cdot s'(|y|))$ time.

Recall from Proposition 16 that $\mathrm{rng}_{1,s'}$ is linear time computable *and*, for all $d$, $e$, and $y$, $|\mathrm{rng}_1(d, e, y)| \le s'(\max(|d|, |e|, |y|))$. Consequently it follows that when $\mathrm{rng}_1(d, e, y) = 1 + [p_1, \ldots, p_m]$, we have that each of $m$, $|p_1|, \ldots, |p_m|$ is less that $s'(\max(|d|, |e|, |m|))$. Hence it follows that searching for the least $i$ such that $p_i$ is available at $y$ can be done in $O((s'(\max(|d|, |e|, |y|)))^2 \cdot (|y|+1)^k \cdot (1 + \log |y|))$ time. Since, by Proposition 14, computing $S(p, y, \mathbf{0}^{s'(|y|) \cdot (|y|+1)^k})$ has the same complexity as testing whether $p$ is available at $y$, it follows from Proposition 15(a) that $\varphi_u$ on input $(e, y)$ is computable in $O((s'(\max(|e|, |y|)))^2 \cdot (|y| + 1)^k \cdot (1 + \log |y|))$ time. (Since $d$ is a constant, we can absorb its contribution into the constant hidden by the $O$.) Without loss of generality, we can assume that $\Phi_u$ has such an upper bound. Therefore, by Proposition 15(b), there is an $e_0$ such that, for all $y$, $\varphi_{e_0} = \varphi_u(e_0, y)$ and $\Phi_{e_0}(y)$ has an upper bound which is in $O((s'(\max(|e_0|, |y|)))^2 \cdot (|y| + 1)^k \cdot (1 + \log |y|) + (|y| + 1))$ which by some algebra is contained in $O(|y|^k (\log |y|) \cdot s(|y|))$. It thus follows that $\mathbf{M}$ $\mathrm{BC}^0$ identifies $\varphi_{e_0}$. Now the rest of the proof follows the argument given for Theorem 17.   □

# 7   Infinitely Often Results for $\mathrm{BC}^m$

In this section we deal with the criteria $\mathrm{BC}^m$, especially for $m \ge 1$. The stronger version of the $m = 0$ case was handled in Theorem 19. It is technically surprising that the $m \ge 1$ cases provably do not permit as strong a quantifier on the inputs $x$ as does the $m = 0$ case.

**Theorem 21.** *Suppose $\mathbf{M}$ $\mathrm{BC}^m$-identifies $\mathcal{QF}^k_s$, where $k \ge 1$ and $s \in \mathcal{LS}low$. Then there is an $f \in \mathcal{Z}^*$ such that $(\forall a)(\overset{\infty}{\forall} n)(\overset{\infty}{\exists} x)[\Phi_{\mathbf{M}(f|_n)}(x) > a \cdot (|x| + 1)^k]$.*

---

[9] As noted in §1, an allowed special case is that $\mathbf{M}$ actually EX-learns $\mathcal{QF}^k_s$.

The proof is a straightforward modification of the proof of Theorem 19; however, to prove Theorem 21 we need to diagonalize over $m+1$ points at once. It is *not* possible to replace the $(\overset{\infty}{\exists} x)$ in Theorem 21 with an $(\overset{\infty}{\forall} x)$ as shown by:

**Theorem 22.** *There is an* **M** *that both: (i)* $\mathrm{BC}^1$*-identifies* $\mathcal{PF}$ *using programs having polynomial-bounded run times, and (ii)* EX*-identifies* $\mathcal{PF}^1$ *and moreover, for each* $f \in \mathcal{PF}^1$, *there is a constant* $c_f$ *such that* $(\overset{\infty}{\exists} x)[\,\Phi_{\mathbf{M}(f)}(x) \leq c_f \cdot |x|\,]$.

# 8    Positive, Almost Everywhere Results for $\mathrm{BC}^*$

This section contains our strongest positive results. After the theorem, we state informally a generalization.

**Theorem 23.** *There is an IIM* $\mathbf{M}_*$ *that* $\mathrm{BC}^*$*-identifies* $\mathcal{PF}$ *with all outputs running in polynomial time and such that:*

(a) *For each* $k \geq 1$ *and each* $f \in \mathcal{PF}^k$, $(\overset{\infty}{\forall} n)[\,\Phi_{\mathbf{M}_*(f|_n)} \in O(\lambda x.\,|x|^k)\,]$.

(b) *Moreover,* $\mathbf{M}_*$ EX*-identifies* $\mathcal{PF}^1$.

*Interpretation.* In contrast to Theorems 17 through 21, the above result is quite a surprise. Not only does the $\mathbf{M}_*$ of the theorem $\mathrm{BC}^*$-infer programs that have $O(n^k)$ run-time bounds for each member of $\mathcal{PF}^k$ for every $k$, but for each $f \in \mathcal{PF}^1$, $\mathbf{M}_*$ also *syntactically* converges to a program for this $f$ that has an $O(n)$ run-time bound. However, as noted in §1, Corollary 6 applies to $\mathbf{M}_*$ of the above theorem. Hence, for each $\ell \geq 1$, there is an $f \in \mathcal{Z}^*$ such that $\mathbf{M}_*$ EX-identifies $f$ and the perfectly correct $\varphi$-program $\mathbf{M}_*(f)$ has a *linear run-time bound* (by Theorem 23); *however*, by Corollary 6, $\mathbf{M}_*(f)$ is so *information deficient* that PA fails to prove even that it computes a finite variant of something having *some* program running in $\ell$-degree polynomial time. Thus part of the price $\mathbf{M}_*$ pays for the asymptotically optimal run times of its output programs is that these programs, even on some easy functions, must necessarily be highly information deficient.

A generalization of Theorem 23 also holds by a similar proof. In the generalization one introduces an arbitrary $j \geq 1$ but requires $k \geq j$; then part (b) becomes $\mathbf{M}_*$ EX-identifies $\mathcal{PF}^j$ with all but finitely many of $\mathbf{M}_*$'s conjectures running in time $O(n^j)$.

# Acknowledgments

Special thanks go to Prof. Dr. Klaus Ambos-Spies for some very helpful suggestions and observations. Grant support was received by J. Case from NSF grant CCR-0208616, by S. Jain from NUS grant R252-000-127-112, and by J. Royer from NSF grant CCR-0098198.

# References

[Bar74]    J. A. Barzdin, *Two theorems on the limiting synthesis of functions*, In Theory of Algorithms and Programs, Latvian State University, Riga, U.S.S.R **210** (1974), 82–88.

[BB75]    L. Blum and M. Blum, *Toward a mathematical theory of inductive inference*, Information and Control **28** (1975), 125–155.

[Blu67]    M. Blum, *A machine independent theory of the complexity of recursive functions*, Journal of the ACM **14** (1967), 322–336.

[CCJ01]    J. Case, K. Chen, and S. Jain, *Costs of general purpose learning*, Theoretical Computer Science **259** (2001), 455–473.

[Che81]    K. Chen, *Tradeoffs in machine inductive inference*, Ph.D. thesis, SUNY at Buffalo, 1981.

[CLRS01]    T. Cormen, C. Leiserson, R. Rivest, and C. Stein, *Introduction to algorithms*, 2 ed., MIT Press, 2001.

[CM81]    P. Chew and M. Machtey, *A note on structure and looking back applied to the relative complexity of computable functions*, Journal of Computer and System Sciences **22** (1981), 53–59.

[CS83]    J. Case and C. Smith, *Comparison of identification criteria for machine inductive inference*, Theoretical Computer Science **25** (1983), 193–220.

[Gol67]    E. M. Gold, *Language identification in the limit*, Information and Control **10** (1967), 447–474.

[HS65]    J. Hartmanis and R. Stearns, *On the computational complexity of algorithms*, Transactions of the American Mathematical Society **117** (1965), 285–306.

[HU79]    J. Hopcroft and J. Ullman, *Introduction to automata theory languages and computation*, Addison-Wesley Publishing Company, 1979.

[Jon97]    N. Jones, *Computability and complexity from a programming perspective*, MIT Press, 1997.

[JORS99]    S. Jain, D. Osherson, J. Royer, and A. Sharma, *Systems that learn: An introduction to learning theory*, second ed., MIT Press, Cambridge, Mass., 1999.

[Lad75]    R. Ladner, *On the structure of polynomial time reducibility*, Journal of the ACM **22** (1975), 155–171.

[LLR81]    L. Landweber, R. Lipton, and E. Robertson, *On the structure of sets in NP and other complexity classes*, Theoretical Computer Science **15** (1981), 181–200.

[LV97]    M. Li and P. Vitányi, *An introduction to Kolmogorov complexity and its applications, second edition*, Springer-Verlag, 1997.

[Men97]    E. Mendelson, *Introduction to mathematical logic*, fourth ed., Chapman & Hall, London, 1997.

[RC94]    J. Royer and J. Case, *Subrecursive programming systems: Complexity & succinctness*, Birkhäuser, 1994.

[Reg88]    K. Regan, *The topology of provability in complexity theory*, Journal of Computer and System Sciences **36** (1988), 384–432.

[Rog67]    H. Rogers, *Theory of recursive functions and effective computability*, McGraw Hill, New York, 1967, Reprinted. MIT Press. 1987.

[Sch82]    U. Schöning, *A uniform approach to obtain diagonal sets in complexity classes*, Theoretical Computer Science **18** (1982), 95–103.

[Sch85]    D. Schmidt, *The recursion-theoretic structure of complexity classes*, Theoretical Computer Science **38** (1985), 143–156.

# On Learning to Coordinate

## Random Bits Help, Insightful Normal Forms, and Competency Isomorphisms

John Case[1], Sanjay Jain[2], Franco Montagna[3], Giulia Simi[3], and Andrea Sorbi[3]

[1] Department of Computer and Information Sciences
University of Delaware, Newark, DE 19716-2586 (USA)
case@cis.udel.edu
[2] School of Computing
National University of Singapore, Singapore 117543, Republic of Singapore
sanjay@comp.nus.edu.sg
[3] Dipartimento di Scienze Matematiche ed Informatiche "R. Magari"
University of Siena, 53100 Siena, Italy
{montagna,simi,sorbi}@unisi.it

**Abstract.** A mere bounded number of random bits judiciously employed by a probabilistically correct algorithmic coordinator is shown to increase the power of learning to coordinate compared to deterministic algorithmic coordinators. Furthermore, these probabilistic algorithmic coordinators are provably *not* characterized in power by *teams* of deterministic ones.

An insightful, enumeration technique based, normal form characterization of the classes that are learnable by total computable coordinators is given. These normal forms are for insight only since it is shown that the complexity of the normal form of a total computable coordinator can be infeasible compared to the original coordinator.

Montagna and Osherson showed that the competence class of a total coordinator cannot be strictly improved by another total coordinator. It is shown in the present paper that the competencies of any two total coordinators are the same modulo isomorphism. Furthermore, a completely effective, index set version of this competency isomorphism result is given, where all the coordinators are total computable.

## 1 Introduction

The learning theory paradigms descending from Gold's [7], as summarized say in [8], do not generally take into account the delicacies of learning with timing, feedback, and interaction as one would see with agents learning to *coordinate* their activities in real time. In practice such agents could range from the environment together with individual muscle and brain cells of animals to furniture movers verbally negotiating in real time how to get a large, irregularly shaped object through a doorway. On the other hand, also descending from the Gold paradigm, are [3,9] which study learning to win reactive process-control games

B. Schölkopf and M.K. Warmuth (Eds.): COLT/Kernel 2003, LNAI 2777, pp. 699–713, 2003.

and [1] which studies learning to predict concepts which are changing with time. These studies, in a sense, capture *some* aspects of learning to coordinate. A new paradigm (under Gold's) very specifically aimed at learning to coordinate was introduced in [11]. In this paradigm one studies, say, two, agents, called *players* (or *coordinators*) which simultaneously play bits (i.e., elements of $\{0,1\}$), *each taking into account the prior bits played by the other*[1]. Their goal, successful coordination, is to have their bit streams perfectly match past some point. [11] gives an example of two people who show up in a park each day at one of noon (bit 0) or 6pm (bit 1); each *silently* watches the others past behavior; and each *tries*, based on the past behavior of the other, to show up eventually exactly when the other shows up. If they manage it, they have learned to coordinate.

Mathematically, we model players as (partial) functions from (finite) bit strings to bits (or bit strings). A player can be, for example, total, partial computable, computable, or probabilistic (the latter with some probability of success).

In the present paper we extend [11] in three interesting directions which we will discuss briefly in turn. Each direction is considered in a separate section below and, in the present section, for each direction, we informally discuss only our main results in that direction.

We are interested in single coordinators which do or do not (learn to) coordinate with a whole class $\mathcal{C}$ of coordinators.

The main results of Section 3 concern probabilistic algorithmic coordinators $PM$ surprisingly beating deterministic ones (Theorems 2, 3, 4, and 5) or beating probabilistic ones (Corollary 1) — each at coordinating with some class $\mathcal{C}$ of algorithmic deterministic players. One nice property, of these main results of Section 3, is that each features a $PM$ which tosses a bounded number of coins, i.e., the $PM$'s do not require coin tosses on infinitely many inputs. The $PM$'s and other (deterministic) machines which are shown to exist also do not have to remember very much about their past inputs — in memory limited senses identical to or similar to the senses studied in [13, Page 66] and [2, 5, 6, 11].

Theorems 2 and 3 essentially show that there are classes $\mathcal{C}$ of deterministic algorithmic coordinators such that *no* deterministic algorithmic coordinator can (learn to) coordinate with each element of $\mathcal{C}$, but *some* probabilistic algorithmic coordinator can.

For $1 \leq i \leq m$, $\mathbf{Team}_m^i\mathbf{Coord}$ denotes the collection of classes $\mathcal{C}$ of algorithmic *deterministic* players such that we have $m$ deterministic algorithmic coordinators $M_1, \ldots, M_m$ so that for each element $F$ of $\mathcal{C}$, at least $i$ of $M_1, \ldots, M_m$ coordinate with $F$.

In the setting of learning programs for total computable functions, team learning by deterministic machines is completely characterized by single machines learning probabilistically and vice versa [14–16]. Furthermore, the analog of $\mathbf{Team}_m^i$ in *that* context has exactly the inferring power of single machines which succeed with probability at least $\frac{i}{m}$. One might suspect that such a char-

---

[1] More agents than two can easily be accommodated in the model as can allowing outputs besides bits.

acterization holds for learning to coordinate, and that Theorems 2 and 3 mentioned above are readily explainable as deterministic team learning in disguise. Theorems 4 and 5 show this is not the case, and that no such characterization holds in the case of learning to coordinate! A few random bits make a big difference in learning to coordinate. One wonders, then, in conceiving the brain and its environment as a collection of coordinators working together (somewhat as in [10]) for tasks such as muscle movement and speech, if random bits may need to be employed to achieve learning to coordinate.

Corollary 1 shows that, for probabilities $p < q$, there are classes $\mathcal{C}$ of deterministic algorithmic coordinators, such that some probabilistic algorithmic coordinator $PM$ learns to coordinate with each player in $\mathcal{C}$ with probability $p$, but none can do it with probability $q$.

The $PM$'s of Theorems 2 and 4 and Corollary 1 are additionally *blind*, i.e., they depend functionally only on the length of the bit strings they see. Theorems 3 and 5 are uniformizations of Theorems 2 and 4, respectively. More particularly, Theorems 3 and 5 feature the strong quantifier order $(\exists \mathcal{C})(\forall$ probabilities $p < 1)[\cdots]$; whereas, Theorems 2 and 4 essentially feature the weaker order $(\forall$ probabilities $p < 1)(\exists \mathcal{C})[\cdots]$. There are, however, some apparent costs for the stronger quantifier order of Theorems 3 and 5: the $PM$'s in the proofs of Theorems 3 and 5 are not blind, and, as we shall see, they are not as memory limited as the $PM$'s in the proofs of Theorems 2 and 4[2].

[11, (6), Page 367] shows that any indexed class of total computable players is learnable (by a total computable player), and the learning strategy employed is an enumeration strategy [8]. In Section 4 we show (Theorem 8) that *any* total computable player $P$ is (extensionally) equivalent to a player $E_P$ based on enumeration strategy for a suitable indexed class of blind players. The enumeration strategy based $E_P$ can and should be thought of as a *canonical normal form of* $P$. The canonical computable coordinator $E_P$ corresponding to a pre-given total computable coordinator $P$ may, though, take exponentially more time than $P$ (Theorem 10 also in Section 4), but, of course, the point of the existence of $E_P$ (and the "converse" result [11, (6), Page 367]) is the interesting insight that total coordinators can be *extensionally* conceptualized as exploiting an enumeration technique. From Theorem 10, though, *intensionally* a total coordinator $P$ can be quite different, e.g., in run time, from its (enumeration technique based) canonical form $E_P$.

TSCOPE($P$) denotes the class of total coordinators learnable by a total coordinator $P$ and represents the *competence* of $P$. In [11] it is shown that the competence, [11, Page 369], of a total player cannot be strictly improved by another total player. In Section 5 we prove that the competencies of any two total players are the same modulo isomorphism. More specifically, Theorem 11 of Section 5 says that, for every pair $P$ and $Q$ of total players, the sets TSCOPE($P$) and TSCOPE($Q$) are homeomorphic in Cantor space [12] (computably homeomorphic, if $P$ and $Q$ are computable). Then we provide a completely *effective version* of this competency isomorphism theorem. Let IND($P$) denote the in-

---

[2] It is open whether these costs are necessary.

dex set of the restriction of TSCOPE($P$) to total computable players for a computable coordinator $P$. Theorem 12 of Section 5 says that IND($P$) and IND($Q$) are computably isomorphic for every pair $P, Q$ of total computable coordinators.

## 2    Mathematical Preliminaries

We denote by $\{0,1\}^*$ the set of all (finite) binary strings. If $\sigma \in \{0,1\}^*$ then $|\sigma|$ denotes the length of $\sigma$; $\sigma(i)$, with $i < |\sigma|$, is the $i$-th bit of $\sigma$; $\sigma\lceil n$ denotes the initial segment of $\sigma$ of length equal to $n$; (clearly $\sigma\lceil 0$ is the empty string, denoted by $\emptyset$); if $|\sigma| > 0$ then $\sigma^- = \sigma\lceil(|\sigma|-1)$. The concatenation of two strings $\sigma$ and $\tau$ is denoted by $\sigma \cdot \tau$.

We let $\mathbb{N}$ denote the set of natural numbers. Suppose $p_m(x_1, \ldots, x_m)$ is a computable bijection from $\mathbb{N}^m$ to $\mathbb{N}$. Then $\pi_1^m, \ldots, \pi_m^m$ denote the corresponding computable inverse of $p_m$, i.e., $\pi_j^m(p_m(x_1, \ldots, x_m)) = x_j$.

A *player* (synonym: a *coordinator*) is a partial function from $\{0,1\}^*$ into $\{0,1\}$. Given two players $F$ and $G$, define two sequences $R_{F,G}$ and $R_{G,F}$ by induction as follows. For every $n$, let

$$R_{F,G}(n) = F(R_{G,F}\lceil n) \qquad R_{G,F}(n) = G(R_{F,G}\lceil n),$$

where $R_{F,G}(n)$ is defined if and only if, for every $i < n$ $R_{G,F}(i)$ is defined, and $F(R_{G,F}\lceil n)$ is defined; similarly for $R_{G,F}(n)$. We say that $F$ and $G$ *coordinate* or that $F$ *learns* $G$, or else that $G$ *learns* $F$ if and only if both $R_{F,G}$ and $R_{G,F}$ are infinite strings and for almost all $i$, $R_{F,G}(i) = R_{G,F}(i)$. A *total player* is simply a player which is total. Deterministic players will usually be denoted by upper case Latin letters. A *probabilistic player* is a player, with the ability to toss coins. Probability of player coordinating with another deterministic player, is the probability (over all possible coin tosses) that the two players coordinate (we will not need to consider coordination among two probabilistic players in this paper). Probabilistic players will usually be denoted by $PM$ (with or without subscripts).

A class $\mathcal{C}$ of players is said to be *learnable by a player* $F$ if and only if $F$ learns all elements of $\mathcal{C}$: in this case, we say that $F$ *learns* $\mathcal{C}$ or $F$ *coordinates* $\mathcal{C}$.

We observe that alternatively a player can also be viewed as a function from $\{0,1\}^*$ into $\{0,1\}^*$. Indeed, any player $F$ originates a function from $\{0,1\}^*$ into $\{0,1\}^*$ as follows: $F$ maps a string $\sigma$ into a string $F[\sigma]$ with $|F[\sigma]| = |\sigma| + 1$, and for every $i < |\sigma| + 1$, $F[\sigma](i) = F(\sigma\lceil i)$ if $F[\sigma](j)$ converges for all $j < i$ and $F(\sigma\lceil i)$ converges; divergent otherwise. $F[\sigma]$ denotes the sequence $\tau$ (of length $|\sigma| + 1$) that $F$ outputs while coordinating with some player which starts with $\sigma$ when coordinating with $F$.

Conversely, every monotonic partial function $h : \{0,1\}^* \longrightarrow \{0,1\}^*$ such that $|h[\sigma]| = |\sigma| + 1$ (again denoting by $h[\sigma]$ the image of $\sigma$ under $h$) can be viewed as a player, by letting $h(\sigma) = h[\sigma](|\sigma|)$.

Throughout the paper we will refer to some effective listing $\{M_i\}_{i \in \mathbb{N}}$ of all (partial) computable deterministic players, and to some effective listing $\{PM_i\}_{i \in \mathbb{N}}$ of all (partial) computable probabilistic players.

## 3    Probabilistic vs. Deterministic Coordinators

N.B. Throughout *this* section all of our players are *algorithmic*; also all our random bits are *uniformly distributed*, e.g., from fair coin tosses.

The first result in this section is just a lift of a result from [11].

**Theorem 1.** *For all $n > 1$, there exist classes $\mathcal{C}_1, \ldots, \mathcal{C}_n$ of coordinators such that:*

1. *For each $i$, $1 \leq i \leq n$, all members of $\mathcal{C}_i$ coordinate with each other; and*
2. *If any coordinator $M$ (even outside above classes) coordinates with all of $\mathcal{C}_i$, then $M$ cannot coordinate with any member of $\bigcup_{1 \leq j \leq n, j \neq i} \mathcal{C}_j$.*

*Proof.* This can be handled by straightforwardly generalizing the proof for the $n = 2$ case in [11]. ∎

In a sense, then, $\mathcal{C}_1, \ldots, \mathcal{C}_n$ from Theorem 1 are *incompatible* "camps" of computable coordinators.

**Definition 1.** [11] *A player $Q$ is* blind *if $Q(\sigma) = Q(\tau)$ for all $\sigma, \tau \in \{0, 1\}^*$ such that $|\sigma| = |\tau|$.*

The remaining results of this section concern the power of probabilistic coordinators, deterministic coordinators, or teams thereof.

We say a coordinator is *$k$-memory limited* iff it depends functionally only on the (up to) $k$ last bits of its input.

The next four results are among the main results of this section mentioned in Section 1 above.

**Theorem 2.** *Suppose $0 \leq p < 1$. There exists a class of deterministic players $\mathcal{C}$ such that:*

1. *No deterministic coordinator can coordinate with all of $\mathcal{C}$; and*
2. *For $k$ chosen large enough that $1 - 2^{-k} \geq p$, there exists a* blind *probabilistic coordinator $PM$, such that, for each member $M$ of $\mathcal{C}$, $PM$ can coordinate with $M$ with probability $1 - 2^{-k} \geq p$.*

*Interpretation. PM* of Theorem 2 just above succeeds in coordinating with the class $\mathcal{C}$ of deterministic players with probability (at least) $p$, but *no* deterministic coordinator can coordinate with every player in $\mathcal{C}$. Hence, probabilistic coordinators beat deterministic ones! Furthermore, *PM* is blind, i.e., it depends functionally only on the length of the bit strings it sees.

*Proof.* As above, let $k$ be chosen large enough that $1 - 2^{-k} \geq p$. Let $M_n$ be the $n$-th deterministic player. Define player $F_n$ as follows. Let $\tau$ be any sequence (over 0, 1). $F_n[\tau]$ is defined as follows.

$$
F_n[\tau](r) = \begin{cases}
1, & \text{if } r < n; \\
0, & \text{if } r = n; \\
1, & \text{if } n < r \leq n + k + 1; \\
1, & \text{if } r \geq n + k + 2, \text{ and } (M_n[1^n 01^k] \\
& \text{does not halt within } r \text{ steps, or} \\
& \tau \text{ does not start with } M_n[1^n 01^k]); \\
1 - M_n[F_n[\tau \lceil (r-1)]]](r), & \text{otherwise.}
\end{cases}
$$

Note that $F_n$ does not coordinate with $M_n$. Thus no deterministic machine can coordinate with $\mathcal{C} = \{F_i \mid i \in \mathbb{N}\}$.

Now define $PM$ as follows. $PM[\tau] = [k \text{ random bits}]1^{|\tau|-k+1}$.

Note that if the random $k$ bits chosen by $PM$ are such that $PM[1^n 01^k] \neq M_n[1^n 01^k]$, then $PM$ coordinates with $F_n$. Thus, $PM$ coordinates with each $F_n$ with probability at least $1 - 2^{-k}$. ∎

*Furthermore,* we can see from the proof just above of Theorem 2 that $PM$ employs only $k$ random bits and is $k$-memory limited, i.e., it depends functionally only on the (up to) $k$ last bits of its input. This is only so it can keep track if it is to output one of its first $k$ bits, its only random bits.

As mentioned in Section 1, the next theorem provides a variant of Theorem 2 with significantly stronger quantifier order: $(\exists \mathcal{C})(\forall \text{ probabilities } p < 1)[\cdots]$ instead of $(\forall \text{ probabilities } p < 1)(\exists \mathcal{C})[\cdots]$. Our witnessing $PM$ is no longer blind.

**Theorem 3.** *There exists a class of deterministic players $\mathcal{C}$ such that:*

1. *No deterministic coordinator can coordinate with all of $\mathcal{C}$; and*
2. *For all $p$ such that $0 \leq p < 1$, for $k$ chosen large enough that $1 - 2^{-k} \geq p$, there exists a probabilistic coordinator $PM$ such that, for each member $M$ of $\mathcal{C}$, $PM$ can coordinate with $M$ with probability $1 - 2^{-k} \geq p$.*

*Furthermore,* from the omitted proof of Theorem 3, it can be seen that this theorem's $PM$ employs only $k$ random bits and is *not* $k$-memory limited before the first 0 it sees since it needs to remember how many 1's it saw before the first 0. However, right after the first 0 it sees, it outputs either a deterministic bit or $k$ random bits and no more random bits. Hence, after the first 0 it sees, it becomes $k$-memory limited from there onward.

**Theorem 4.** *Suppose $0 \leq p < 1$, and $m \in \mathbb{N}^+$. Let $k$ be chosen large enough that $\frac{2^k - m}{2^k} \geq p$. Then there exists a class of deterministic players $\mathcal{C}$ such that:*

1. $\mathcal{C} \notin \mathbf{Team}_m^1 \mathbf{Coord}$;
2. *There are $m + 1$ blind deterministic machines such that, these machines witness that $\mathcal{C} \in \mathbf{Team}_{m+1}^1 \mathbf{Coord}$.*
3. *There exists a probabilistic coordinator $PM$, such that, for each member $M$ of $\mathcal{C}$, $PM$ can coordinate with $M$ with probability $\frac{2^k - m}{2^k} \geq p$.*

*Interpretation.* $PM$ of Theorem 4 just above succeeds in coordinating with the class $\mathcal{C}$ of deterministic players with probability (at least) $p$. However, $\mathcal{C} \in (\mathbf{Team}_{m+1}^1 \mathbf{Coord} - \mathbf{Team}_m^1 \mathbf{Coord})$. Therefore, probablistic coordination is *not* characterized by deterministic team coordination. That $\mathcal{C} \in \mathbf{Team}_{m+1}^1 \mathbf{Coord}$ is witnessed by $m + 1$ blind deterministic coordinators.

*Furthermore,* from the omitted proof of Theorem 4 just above, it can be seen that this theorem's $PM$ employs only $k$ random bits and *is* $k$-memory limited. Also, each of the $m + 1$ blind deterministic coordinators witnessing $\mathcal{C} \in \mathbf{Team}_{m+1}^1 \mathbf{Coord}$ is $\lceil \log_2(m + 1) \rceil$-memory limited.

As mentioned in Section 1, the next theorem provides a variant of Theorem 4 with significantly stronger quantifier order. Our witnessing $PM$ is no longer blind.

**Theorem 5.** *Suppose $m \in \mathbb{N}^+$. Then there exists a class of deterministic players $\mathcal{C}$ such that:*

1. $\mathcal{C} \notin \textbf{Team}_m^1\textbf{Coord}$;
2. *There are $m + 1$ blind deterministic machines such that, these machines witness that $\mathcal{C} \in \textbf{Team}_{m+1}^1\textbf{Coord}$; and*
3. *For all $p$ such that $0 \leq p < 1$, for $k$ chosen large enough that $\frac{2^k - m}{2^k} \geq p$, there exists a probabilistic coordinator PM such that, for each member $M$ of $\mathcal{C}$, PM can coordinate with $M$ with probability $\frac{2^k - m}{2^k} \geq p$.*

*Furthermore,* from the omitted proof of Theorem 5 just above, it can be seen that this theorem's *PM* employs only $k$ random bits and is *not* $k$-memory limited. However, after the first 0 it sees, it becomes $k$-memory limited from there onward. Also, each of the $m+1$ blind deterministic coordinators witnessing $\mathcal{C} \in \textbf{Team}_{m+1}^1\textbf{Coord}$ is $\lceil \log_2(m + 1) \rceil$-memory limited.

For probabilities $p$, $\textbf{Prob}_p\textbf{Coord}$ denotes the collection of classes $\mathcal{C}$ of *deterministic* players such that some probabilistic coordinator coordinates with each element of $\mathcal{C}$ with probability $\geq p$.

**Theorem 6.** *Suppose $\ell, m \in \mathbb{N}^+$ and $0 \leq p \leq 1$ are given such that $\frac{\ell}{m} < p$. Then, there is a class of deterministic players $\in$ ($\textbf{Team}_m^\ell\textbf{Coord} - \textbf{Prob}_p\textbf{Coord}$).*

*Moreover, for $k$ such that $2^k \geq m$, the positive half of this theorem is witnessed by a team of blind, deterministic coordinators which are $k$-memory limited.*

The next corollary is one of the main results of this section mentioned in Section 1 above. It shows that the power of probabilistic coordination of deterministic classes of players is strict in the associated probability.

**Corollary 1.** *Suppose $0 \leq p < q \leq 1$. Then, there is a class of deterministic players $\in$ ($\textbf{Prob}_p\textbf{Coord} - \textbf{Prob}_q\textbf{Coord}$). Moreover, for $\ell, m$ such that $p \leq \frac{\ell}{m} < q$ and $k$ such that $k = \lceil \log_2(m) \rceil$, the positive half of this corollary is witnessed by a blind probabilistic coordinator which employs only $k$ random bits and is $k$-memory limited.*

The next two results together completely characterize the relative power of the coordination classes of the form $\textbf{Team}_m^i\textbf{Coord}$.

**Theorem 7.** *Suppose $\ell, m, v, w \in \mathbb{N}^+$ such that $\ell \leq m$, $v \leq w$, and there is no way to distribute $w$ balls among $m$ boxes such that any combination of $\ell$ boxes receives at least $v$ balls. Then, $\textbf{Team}_m^\ell\textbf{Coord} - \textbf{Team}_w^v\textbf{Coord} \neq \emptyset$.*

*Proof.* Let $k$ be such that $2^k \geq m$. Let $M_i$ be the $i$-th deterministic player. Define player $F_n$ as follows. Let $\tau$ be any sequence (over 0, 1). $F_n[\tau]$ is defined as follows.

Let $X$ be the first $m$ elements of $\{0,1\}^k$. Let $S_n^t$ be the lexicographically least subset $Y$ of $X$ of cardinality $\ell$, such that card($\{j \mid 1 \leq j \leq w$ and $M_{\pi_j^w(n)}[1^n 01^k]$ halts within $t$ steps, and starts with $\sigma \in Y\}$) $< v$.

Define $F_n[\tau]$ as follows:

– if $r < n + k$ then let

$$F_n[\tau](r) = \begin{cases} 1, & \text{if } r < n; \\ 0, & \text{if } r = n; \\ 1, & \text{if } n < r < n + k. \end{cases}$$

– if $r \geq n + k$ then search for the first $t \geq r - 1$ such that either
  (i) $\tau$ starts with an element of $S_n^t$; or
  (ii) otherwise and within $t - r - 1$ steps, one can find an $x$ such that $M_{\pi_j^w(n)}[F_n[\tau\lceil(r-1)]]\!\downarrow \supseteq \tau\lceil r \cdot x$ for some $j$.
If such a $t$ is found then let

$$F_n[\tau](r) = \begin{cases} 1, & \text{if (i) holds;} \\ 1 - x & \text{if (ii) holds for some first such } x, j. \end{cases}$$

Let $F_n[\tau](r)$ be undefined otherwise.

Let $S_n = \lim_{t \to \infty} S_n^t$. Note that $S_n$ is well defined, as the limit of $S_n^t$ exists. Let $\mathcal{C} = \{F_n \mid n \in \mathbb{N}\}$.

Now, (a) Let $r > n + 1 + k$ be large enough so that $S_n^t = S_n$, for any $t \geq r$. Now consider any $\sigma \in \{0,1\}^r$ such that $\sigma$ does not start with any element of $S_n$. Then by the diagonalization clause in the construction of $F_n$, we have that none of the machines in $M_{\pi_1^w(n)}, \ldots, M_{\pi_w^w(n)}$, which starts with $\sigma$ while interacting with $F_n$, can coordinate with $F_n$.

On the other hand, the number of machines in $M_{\pi_1^w(n)}, \ldots, M_{\pi_w^w(n)}$, which start with $\sigma \in S_n$ while interacting with $F_n$ is $< v$. Thus, $\{M_{\pi_j^w(n)} \mid 1 \leq j \leq w\}$, do not **Team$_w^v$Coord** identify $F_n$ and thus do not **Team$_w^v$Coord** identify $\mathcal{C}$.

(b) $F_n$ coordinates with any string $\tau$ which starts with an element of $S_n$ and converges to 1. Define $m$ machines $M^1, \ldots, M^m$, such that $M^i[\tau] = \tau_i 1^{|\tau| - |\tau_i| + 1}$, for any text $\tau$, where $\tau_i$ is the $i$-th string in $X$. It follows that, for any $n$, at least $\text{card}(S_n) = \ell$ of the machines $M^1, \ldots, M^m$, coordinate with $F_n$.

Theorem follows.    ∎

**Proposition 1.** *Suppose $\ell, m, v, w \in \mathbb{N}^+$ such that $\ell \leq m$, $v \leq w$, and there exists a way to distribute $w$ balls among $m$ boxes such that any combination of $l$ boxes receives at least $v$ balls. Then,* **Team$_m^\ell$Coord** $\subseteq$ **Team$_w^v$Coord**.

*Proof.* Assume the boxes and balls in above to be numbered (from 1 to $m$ and 1 to $w$ respectively). Now suppose $M^1, \ldots, M^m$ are given. Define $M^{',1}, \ldots, M^{',w}$ such that $M^{',i}$ follows $M^j$, if the $i$-ball in the above distribution falls in $j$-th box. Now it is easy to verify that the players which can be **Team$_m^\ell$Coord** identified by $M^1, \ldots, M^m$ are also **Team$_w^v$Coord** identified by $M^{',1}, \ldots, M^{',w}$.    ∎

## 4    Normal Form Characterization of Learnable Classes of Total Computable Players

N.B. Throughout *this* section players are always *total computable*.

**Definition 2.** An *indexed class* of total computable binary functions (*indexed class* for short) is a class $\mathcal{C}$ of total computable binary functions such that there is a total computable function $C(i, x)$ from $\mathbb{N}^2$ into $\{0, 1\}$ such that

$$\mathcal{C} = \{\lambda x.\, C(i, x) \mid i \in \mathbb{N}\}.$$

In this case, $C(i, x)$ is said to be an *enumerating function* for $\mathcal{C}$.

**Definition 3.** Let $\mathcal{C}$ be an indexed, and dense class ("dense" means that for every $\sigma \in \{0,1\}^*$ there is some $f \in \mathcal{C}$ such that $\sigma \subset f$), and let $C(i, x)$ be an enumerating function for $\mathcal{C}$. We define a total computable function $\mathrm{LE}(C)$ from $\{0,1\}^*$ into $\{0,1\}$ as follows. Given $\sigma \in \{0,1\}^*$, let

$$\mathrm{LE}(C)(\sigma) = C(i(\sigma), |\sigma|)$$

where

$$i(\sigma) = \min(\{i \in \mathbb{N} : (\forall j < |\sigma|)[\sigma(j) = C(i, j)]\})$$

(such an $i$ exists because $\mathcal{C}$ is dense).

Note that $\mathrm{LE}(C)$ is an algorithm which $NV$-identifies [8] $\mathcal{C}$ by enumeration: given $\sigma$, $\mathrm{LE}(C)$ first finds the first $i$ such that $\lambda x.C(i, x)$ is consistent with $\sigma$, and then outputs the next value $C(i, |\sigma|)$ of $\lambda x.C(i, x)$. Of course, $\mathrm{LE}(C)$ is also a total computable player. Note also that $\mathrm{LE}(C)$ depends on the enumeration function $C(i, x)$ and not only on $\mathcal{C}$.

**Definition 4.** Let $\sigma \in \{0,1\}^*$, and let $P$ be a total computable player. We define a total computable function $P_\sigma$ from $\mathbb{N}$ into $\{0,1\}$ as follows:

$$P_\sigma(n) = \begin{cases} \sigma(n) & \text{if } n < |\sigma|; \\ P(P_\sigma \lceil n) & \text{otherwise.} \end{cases}$$

**Definition 5.** Let $\mathcal{C}$ and $C(i, x)$ be as in Definition 3. Define

$$\mathcal{P}(C) = \{P \mid (\exists \sigma \in \{0,1\}^*)[R_{P, \mathrm{LE}(C)} = \mathrm{LE}(C)_\sigma]\}$$

(where we identify $\mathrm{LE}(C)_\sigma$ with the infinite string of its values).

Roughly speaking, $\mathcal{P}(C)$ consists of all players which, as far as the opponent behaves like $\mathrm{LE}(C)$, behave as $\mathrm{LE}(C)_\sigma$ for a suitable $\sigma \in \{0,1\}^*$. A moment's reflection shows that $\mathcal{P}(C)$ is precisely the class of all total computable players which are learned by $\mathrm{LE}(C)$.

Theorem 8 next is a main result of this section mentioned above in Section 1. The player $\mathrm{LE}(C_P)$ of Theorem 8 can and should be thought of as an enumeration strategy based *canonical normal form* of $P$.

**Theorem 8.** *(a) For every total computable player $P$ there are a dense indexed class $\mathcal{C}_P$ and an enumerating function $C_P(i, x)$ for $\mathcal{C}_P$ such that $P = \mathrm{LE}(C_P)$.*

*(b) Hence a class $\mathcal{D}$ of total computable players is learnable by a total computable player if and only if there are a dense indexed class $\mathcal{C}$ and an enumerating function $C(i, x)$ for $\mathcal{C}$ such that $\mathcal{D} \subseteq \mathcal{P}(C)$.*

*Proof.* (a) Let $P$ be a total computable player. Let $\{\sigma_i\}_{i \in \mathbb{N}}$ be a 1-1 computable numbering of all finite binary strings, such that $|\sigma_i| < |\sigma_j|$ implies $i < j$. Let $C_P(i, n) = P_{\sigma_i}(n)$. Clearly, $C_P(i, n)$ is a total computable function from $\mathbb{N}^2$ into $\{0, 1\}$. Let $f_i = \lambda n.C_P(i, n)$, and let $\mathcal{C}_P = \{f_i : i \in \mathbb{N}\}$. We prove (a) by means of the following claims.

(i) $\mathcal{C}_P$ is a dense indexed class.
(ii) If $\sigma \subseteq \tau \subseteq P_\sigma$, then $P_\tau = P_\sigma$.
(iii) $\sigma_{i(\sigma)} \subseteq \sigma$, where $i(\sigma) = \min(\{i \in \mathbb{N} : (\forall j < |\sigma|)[C_P(i, j) = \sigma(j)]\})$.
(iv) $P_\sigma = P_{\sigma_{i(\sigma)}}$.
(v) $\mathrm{LE}(\mathcal{C}_P) = P$.

We omit the proof of above claims. These claims imply part (a).

As regards part (b), let $\mathcal{D}$ be a learnable class of total computable players, and let $P$ be a total computable player that learns $\mathcal{D}$. By claim (a), there are an indexed class $\mathcal{C}_P$ and an enumerating function $C_P(i, x)$ for $\mathcal{C}_P$ such that $P = \mathrm{LE}(\mathcal{C}_P)$. Moreover, we observed before that $\mathcal{P}(\mathcal{C}_P)$ is the class of all total computable players learned by $\mathrm{LE}(\mathcal{C}_P) = P$. Thus $\mathcal{D} \subseteq \mathcal{P}(\mathcal{C}_P)$, as desired. ∎

**Definition 6.** Given a player $P$, we define:

$$\mathrm{BLINDSCOPE}(P) = \{Q : Q \text{ total computable blind player and } P \text{ learns } Q\}.$$

**Definition 7.** An *indexed class of players* is a class $\mathcal{C}$ such that there is a total computable function $C(i, \sigma)$ from $\mathbb{N} \times \{0, 1\}^*$ into $\{0, 1\}$ (called an *enumerating function for $\mathcal{C}$*) such that, for all $P \in \mathcal{C}$, there is an $i \in \mathbb{N}$ such that, for all $\sigma \in \{0, 1\}^*$, $P(\sigma) = C(i, \sigma)$.

**Theorem 9.** *A class of total computable blind players is learnable by a total computable player if and only if it is contained in an indexed class of players.*

*Proof.* To any total computable function $f$ from $\mathbb{N}$ into $\{0, 1\}$ we associate a blind player $Q_f$ defined by $Q_f(\sigma) = f(|\sigma|)$. It is easy to see that for every total computable player $P$, $\mathrm{BLINDSCOPE}(P) = B(P)$ where $B(P) = \{Q_{P_\sigma} : \sigma \in \{0, 1\}^*\}$. Hence a class of total computable blind players is learnable by a total computable player if and only if it is contained in $B(P)$ for some total computable player $P$, and $B(P)$ is an indexed class of players, being enumerated by $C_P(i, \tau) = P_{\sigma_i}(|\tau|)$. ∎

The last result in this section provides a complexity upper bound for canonical normal forms for total coordinators — in terms of the complexity of the coordinators being put into normal form.

Let $P$ be a given total coordinator. Let $C_P$ denote the enumerating function of the indexed family $\mathcal{C}_P$ generated for this $P$, and let $E_P = \mathrm{LE}(\mathcal{C}_P)$ be the canonical coordinator provided by Theorem 8 exploiting learning by enumeration for $\mathcal{C}_P$. Clearly,

$$Time(C_P(i, n)) \leq O\left(\begin{cases} |\sigma_i|, & \text{if } n < |\sigma_i|; \\ \Sigma_{|\sigma_i| \leq j \leq n} Time(P(\lambda x.C_P(i, x)\lceil j)) & \text{if } n \geq |\sigma_i|. \end{cases}\right)$$

Furthermore, note that in above time, one can calculate not only $C_P(i, n)$, but all of $C_P(i, 0), C_P(i, 1), \ldots, C_P(i, n)$. Note also that for all $\sigma$, there is $i \leq 2^{|\sigma|+1}$, such that $\sigma_i = \sigma$ and $\sigma_{i(\sigma)} \subseteq \sigma$ by (iii) in the proof of Theorem 8 (a). Thus, $E_P(\sigma)$ can be computed in time

$$O(2^{|\sigma|+1} * \max(\{Time(C_P(i, |\sigma|) \mid i \leq 2^{|\sigma|+1}\}))   \qquad (1)$$

We get, then, our last main result of this section (mentioned above in Section 1) showing that, while the canonical forms featured above in this section are insightful, running them in place of the originals can be inefficient.

**Theorem 10.** *Assume the time $Time_P(\cdot)$ used by $P$ is monotonically increasing on length of input and yields the complexity lengthwise (i.e., as the maximum over a particular length of inputs).*
*Then, the time to compute $E_P(\sigma)$ is $\leq$*

$$O(2^{|\sigma|} * |\sigma| * Time_P(|\sigma|)).$$

*Proof.* Clearly (1) above is upperbounded by $O(2^{|\sigma|} * |\sigma| * Time_P(|\sigma|))$. ∎


# 5    Topological and Computability Theoretic Aspects of Learnable Classes of Total Players

A total player can be regarded as an element of the topological space $\{0, 1\}^{\{0,1\}^*}$ (with respect to the product topology, where $\{0, 1\}$ is equipped with the discrete topology. This space is usually called *Cantor space*). Given $P$, a mapping $\Gamma : \{0, 1\}^{\{0,1\}^*} \longrightarrow \{0, 1\}^{\{0,1\}^*}$ is called *$P$-computable* (or simply *computable* if $P$ is computable) if $\Gamma(F) = \lambda\sigma. \varphi_z^{F,P}(\sigma)$, for some index $z$ (where $\varphi_z^{F,P}$ is the function computed by the Turing machine with index $z$ and an oracle for $F, P$). It turns out that $\Gamma$ is *continuous* if and only if it is $P$-computable for some $P$.

Next, as mentioned in Section 1 above, we show a main result of this section, that the competencies, [11, Page 369], of any two total players are the same modulo isomorphism, that is,

**Theorem 11.** *If $P$ and $Q$ are arbitrary total players, then TSCOPE($P$) and TSCOPE($Q$) are $P, Q$-computably homeomorphic. In particular if $P, Q$ are computable then TSCOPE($P$) and TSCOPE($Q$) are computably homeomorphic.*

*Proof.* We define, for any ordered pair $(P, Q)$ of total players, a map $\lambda S. S^{PQ}$ on $\{0, 1\}^{\{0,1\}^*}$, and we show that the map $\lambda S. S^{QP}$ associated to the pair $(Q, P)$ is the inverse of $\lambda S. S^{PQ}$. Moreover, we prove that for every total player $S$, one has: $S \in$ TSCOPE($P$) if and only if $S^{PQ} \in$ TSCOPE($Q$). Finally, $\lambda S. S^{PQ}$ is $P, Q$-computable. Thus $\lambda S. S^{PQ}$ is a $P, Q$-computable homeomorphism of $\{0, 1\}^{\{0,1\}^*}$ onto itself. This is clearly sufficient to prove Theorem 11.

First of all some notation: for every quadruple of (not necessarily total) players $A, B, C, D$ defined on all strings $\tau$ with $|\tau| < n$ and for every nonempty string $\sigma \in \{0,1\}^*$ with $|\sigma| = n$ we define $\sigma^{ABCD} \in \{0,1\}^*$, with $|\sigma^{ABCD}| = |\sigma|$ as follows: For $i < |\sigma|$, let

$$\sigma^{ABCD}(i) = \begin{cases} R_{C,D}(i) & \text{if } \sigma(i) = R_{A,B}(i); \\ 1 - R_{C,D}(i) & \text{otherwise.} \end{cases}$$

Let $S$ be any total player. We define a player $S^{PQ}$ (computable in $S, P, Q$) by induction as follows:

First of all, we define:

$$S^{PQ}(\emptyset) = \begin{cases} Q(\emptyset) & \text{if } P(\emptyset) = S(\emptyset); \\ 1 - Q(\emptyset) & \text{otherwise.} \end{cases}$$

Now let $\sigma \in \{0,1\}^*$ with $|\sigma| = n > 0$, and assume that we have defined $S^{PQ}(\tau)$ for all $\tau \in \{0,1\}^*$ with $|\tau| < n$. Note that under this assumption we can compute (with an oracle for $P, Q, S$) $R_{Q,S^{PQ}}(i)$ and $R_{S^{PQ},Q}(i)$ for all $i < n$. Then we define $S^{PQ}(\sigma)$ by cases:

Case (a) For all $i < n$, $\sigma(i) = R_{Q,S^{PQ}}(i)$. Then:

(a1) If $S(\sigma^{QS^{PQ}PS}) = P(S[(\sigma^{QS^{PQ}PS})^-])$ then $S^{PQ}(\sigma) = Q(S^{PQ}[\sigma^-])$.
(a2) Otherwise, $S^{PQ}(\sigma) = 1 - Q(S^{PQ}[\sigma^-])$.

Case (b) There is $i < n$ such that $\sigma(i) \neq R_{Q,S^{PQ}}(i)$. Then let $S^{PQ}(\sigma) = S(\sigma^{QS^{PQ}PS})$.

This concludes the definition of $S^{PQ}$. Note that $S^{PQ}$ is computable in $S, P$ and $Q$, thus if $P$ and $Q$ are computable players, then $S^{PQ}$ is computable in $S$, and the map $\lambda S. S^{PQ}$ is computable.

Moreover our procedure allows us to define $\lambda S. S^{PQ}$ for all pairs $(P, Q)$ of total players, thus it makes sense to consider e.g. $(S^{AB})^{CD}$, (the result of applying to $S$ the composition of the operators $^{AB}$ and $^{CD}$) where $S, A, B, C, D$ are arbitrary total players.

The rest of the proof relies on the following:

**Claim.** For all total players $P, Q$ and $S$, and for all $\rho \in \{0,1\}^*$, $S(\rho) = (S^{PQ})^{QP}(\rho)$.

In order to prove the claim one can use the following fact: If $\delta \in \{0,1\}^*$ has length $|\delta| > 0$ and $\gamma = \delta^{P(S^{PQ})^{QP}QS^{PQ}}$ then for every $i < |\delta|$, we have

$$\delta(i) = R_{P,(S^{PQ})^{QP}}(i) \Leftrightarrow \gamma(i) = R_{Q,S^{PQ}}(i) \Leftrightarrow \gamma^{Q(S^{PQ})PS}(i) = R_{P,S}(i).$$

We omit the proof of the claim. By Claim, for all total players $P$ and $Q$, the map $\lambda S. S^{PQ}$ is a bijection, and is also $P, Q$-computable, because for all $\tau \in \{0,1\}^*$, and for every total player $S$, $S^{PQ}(\tau)$ only depends on the values of $S$ on a finite subset of $\{0,1\}^*$. Finally, it is straightforward to show that $S \in \mathrm{TSCOPE}(P)$ if and only if $S^{PQ} \in \mathrm{TSCOPE}(Q)$. $\blacksquare$

In the rest of this section we give a completely *effective version* of the competency isomorphism result above (Theorem 11). Specifically, we show that, if

$P, Q$ are total computable players then the classes of total computable players learned by $P$ and $Q$, respectively, have computably isomorphic index sets.

Given a player $P$ define $\mathrm{IND}(P)$ to be the index set of the class of total computable players learned by $P$, i.e.,

$$\mathrm{IND}(P) = \{n : \varphi_n \text{ total and } \varphi_n \text{ is learned by } P\}.$$

Let $\mathrm{Tot} = \{n : \varphi_n \text{ total}\}$. It is well known (see e.g. [18, Page 66]) that Tot is a $\Pi_2^0$ set, in fact $\Pi_2^0$ complete. Now,

$$n \in \mathrm{IND}(P) \Leftrightarrow n \in \mathrm{Tot} \text{ and } (\exists k_0)(\forall k \geq k_0)[R_{P,\varphi_n}(k) = R_{\varphi_n, P}(k)].$$

Thus if $P$ is computable then an easy calculation shows that $\mathrm{IND}(P)$ is $\Delta_3^0$. We can be more precise about the arithmetical complexity of $\mathrm{IND}(P)$. Let us say that a subset $X \subseteq \mathbb{N}$ is 2-$\Sigma_2^0$ if $X = Y - Z$, where $Y, Z \in \Sigma_2^0$. (The 2-$\Sigma_2^0$ sets constitute one of the levels of the Ershov difference hierarchy of the $\Sigma_2^0$ sets. For more on the Ershov hierarchy, see e.g. [4]).

What we have seen above clearly amounts to the following:

**Lemma 1.** *If $P$ is total computable then $\mathrm{IND}(P)$ is 2-$\Sigma_2^0$.*

Next is the completely effective competency isomorphism result mentioned in Section 1 as one of the main results of the present section.

**Theorem 12.** *If $P$ and $Q$ are total computable players then $\mathrm{IND}(P)$ and $\mathrm{IND}(Q)$ are computably isomorphic.*

*Proof.* By the previous lemma and by the Myhill Isomorphism Theorem (see e.g. [17, Page 85]) we need only show that for every total computable player $P$, the set $\mathrm{IND}(P)$ is 2-$\Sigma_2^0$-complete, i.e. for every 2-$\Sigma_2^0$ set $X$ one has $X \leq_1 \mathrm{IND}(P)$, as this would imply that $\mathrm{IND}(P) \leq_1 \mathrm{IND}(Q)$ and $\mathrm{IND}(Q) \leq_1 \mathrm{IND}(P)$ for every pair of total computable players $P$ and $Q$. To this end, let $X = Y \cap Z$ where $X \in \Sigma_2^0$ and $Z \in \Pi_2^0$, and let $R_Y(x, t, s), R_Z(x, t, s)$ be computable relations such that

$$Y = \{i : (\exists t)(\forall s) R_Y(i, t, s)\} \qquad Z = \{i : (\forall t)(\exists s) R_Z(i, t, s)\}.$$

Moreover let $P$ be any total computable player.

By the $s_n^m$-Theorem let $g$ be a $1 - 1$ computable function such that:

– $\varphi_{g(i)}(\emptyset) = 0$; let also $m_0 = 0$;
– if $|\sigma| = k + 1$ and we have inductively defined $m_k$ and $\varphi_{g(i)}(\tau)$ for all $\tau$ such that $|\tau| \leq k$, then let $\varphi_{g(i)}(\sigma) =\uparrow$ if $\varphi_{g(i)}(\tau) =\uparrow$ for some $\tau$ with $|\tau| \leq k$. Otherwise let:

$$\varphi_{g(i)}(\sigma) = \begin{cases} \uparrow & \text{if } (\forall s)[\neg R_Z(i, k, s)]; \\ P(\varphi_{g(i)}[\sigma^-]) & \text{if } (\exists s)[R_Z(i, k, s)] \text{ and} \\ & (\forall s \leq k)[R_Y(i, m_k, s)]; \\ 1 - P(\varphi_{g(i)}[\sigma^-]) & \text{otherwise.} \end{cases}$$

Moreover, let

$$m_{k+1} = \begin{cases} m_k & \text{if } (\forall s \le k)[R_Y(i, m_k, s)]; \\ m_k + 1 & \text{otherwise.} \end{cases}$$

To verify that for all $i$

$$i \in X \Leftrightarrow g(i) \in \text{IND}(P)$$

first note that if $i \notin Z$, then there exists some $k$ such that, for no $s$ do we have $R_Z(i, k, s)$; hence $g(i) \notin \text{IND}(P)$ as $\varphi_{g(i)}$ is not total. Next suppose that $i \in Z$. In this case $\varphi_{g(i)}$ is total. If $i \in Y$ then $m = \lim_k m_k$ exists, and $m$ is the least number such that $R_Y(i, m, s)$ for all $s$. If $k_0$ is such that $m_k = m$ for all $k \ge k_0$, then for all strings $\sigma$ with $|\sigma| \ge k_0$ we have that $\varphi_{g(i)}(\sigma) = P(\varphi_{g(i)}[\sigma^-])$; hence $\varphi_{g(i)}(\sigma)$ is learned by $P$. If $i \notin Y$ then there are infinitely many $k$ such that $m_{k+1} \ne m_k$, and for all strings $\sigma$ with $|\sigma| = k + 1$ we have that $\varphi_{g(i)}(\sigma) \ne P(\varphi_{g(i)}[\sigma^-])$; hence $\varphi_{g(i)}$ and $P$ do not coordinate. ∎

# Acknowledgments

Grant support was received by J. Case from NSF grant CCR-0208616 and by S. Jain from NUS grant R252-000-127-112.

# References

1. J. Case, S. Jain, S. Kaufmann, A. Sharma, and F. Stephan. Predictive learning models for concept drift. *Theoretical Computer Science*, 268:323–349, 2001. Special Issue for *ALT'98*.
2. J. Case, S. Jain, S. Lange, and T. Zeugmann. Incremental concept learning for bounded data mining. *Information and Computation*, 152:74–110, 1999.
3. J. Case, M. Ott, A. Sharma, and F. Stephan. Learning to win process-control games watching game-masters. *Information and Computation*, 174(1):1–19, 2002.
4. Yu. L. Ershov. A hierarchy of sets, I. *Algebra i Logika*, 7(1):47–74, January–February 1968. English Translation, Consultants Bureau, NY, pp. 25–43.
5. R. Freivalds, E. Kinber, and C. Smith. On the impact of forgetting on learning machines. *Journal of the ACM*, 42:1146–1168, 1995.
6. M. Fulk, S. Jain, and D. Osherson. Open problems in Systems That Learn. *Journal of Computer and System Sciences*, 49(3):589–604, December 1994.
7. E.M. Gold. Language identification in the limit. *Information and Control*, 10:447–474, 1967.
8. S. Jain, D. Osherson, J. Royer, and A. Sharma. *Systems that Learn: An Introduction to Learning Theory*. MIT Press, Cambridge, Mass., second edition, 1999.
9. M. Kummer and M. Ott. Learning branches and closed recursive games. In *Proceedings of the Ninth Annual Conference on Computational Learning Theory*, Desenzano del Garda, Italy. ACM Press, July 1996.
10. M. Minsky. *The Society of Mind*. Simon and Schuster, NY, 1986.
11. F. Montagna and D. Osherson. Learning to coordinate: A recursion theoretic perspective. *Synthese*, 118:363–382, 1999.

12. Y. N. Moschovakis. *Descriptive Set Theory*. North–Holland Publishing Co., Amsterdam, New York, Oxford, 1980.

13. D. Osherson, M. Stob, and S. Weinstein. *Systems that Learn: An Introduction to Learning Theory for Cognitive and Computer Scientists*. MIT Press, Cambridge, Mass., 1986.

14. L. Pitt. *A Characterization of Probabilistic Inference*. PhD thesis, Yale University, 1984.

15. L. Pitt. Probabilistic inductive inference. *Journal of the ACM*, 36:383–433, 1989.

16. L. Pitt and C. Smith. Probability and plurality for aggregations of learning machines. *Information and Computation*, 77:77–92, 1988.

17. H. Rogers, Jr. *Theory of Recursive Functions and Effective Computability*. McGraw-Hill, New York, 1967.

18. R. I. Soare. *Recursively Enumerable Sets and Degrees*. Perspectives in Mathematical Logic, Omega Series. Springer–Verlag, Heidelberg, 1987.

# Learning All Subfunctions of a Function

Sanjay Jain[1],[*], Efim Kinber[2], and Rolf Wiehagen[3]

[1] School of Computing, National University of Singapore
3 Science Drive 2, Singapore 117543
sanjay@comp.nus.edu.sg
[2] Department of Computer Science, Sacred Heart University
Fairfield, CT 06432-1000, USA
kinbere@sacredheart.edu
[3] Department of Computer Science, University of Kaiserslautern
D-67653 Kaiserslautern, Germany
wiehagen@informatik.uni-kl.de

**Abstract.** *Sublearning*, a model for learning of subconcepts of a concept, is presented. Sublearning a class of total recursive functions informally means to learn all functions from that class together with all of their *subfunctions*. While in *language* learning it is known to be impossible to learn any infinite language together with all of its sublanguages, the situation changes for sublearning of *functions*.

Several types of sublearning are defined and compared to each other as well as to other learning types. For example, in some cases, sublearning coincides with *robust* learning. Furthermore, whereas in usual function learning there are classes that cannot be learned *consistently*, all sublearnable classes of some natural types *can* be learned consistently.

Moreover, the power of sublearning is characterized in several terms, thereby establishing a close connection to *measurable* classes and variants of this notion. As a consequence, there are rich classes which do not need any self-referential coding for sublearning them.

**Keywords:** inductive inference, learning in the limit, learning of functions.

## 1 Introduction

In Gold's model of learning in the limit, see [Gol67], the machine learner gets all examples of a total recursive function $f$, without loss of generality in natural order $(0, f(0)), (1, f(1)), (2, f(2)), \ldots$. Based on this information, the learner creates a sequence of hypotheses which eventually converges to a hypothesis exactly describing this function $f$. One might argue that getting *all* examples may be somewhat unrealistic, at least in some situations. On the other hand, what one can learn depends, intuitively, on the information one gets. Thus, also intuitively, the less information the learner gets the less it can learn. If it receives only information describing some *subconcept* of a certain "master" concept, then it seems

---

[*] Supported in part by NUS grant number R252-000-127-112.

B. Schölkopf and M.K. Warmuth (Eds.): COLT/Kernel 2003, LNAI 2777, pp. 714–728, 2003.

reasonable that it can learn only this subconcept. From another, positive, point of view, the less data the learner is provided with, the wider is the spectrum of hypotheses which are consistent with these data and hence can serve as correct descriptions of the corresponding (sub-)concept to be learned. Situations like these of learning subconcepts of concepts we want to model and to study in the present paper. Possible scenarios of such "hierarchies" of concepts and corresponding subconcepts might include:

— learning a "theory of the universe", or learning only "subconcepts of nature" such as gravitation, quantum theory, or relativity,
— diagnosing the complete health status of a patient, or detecting only some of his/her deficiencies, or only one illness,
— forecasting the weather for a whole country or for some smaller region, or for a town only.

We do not intend, of course, to solve these problems within a model from abstract computation theory. What we want is to present a, in our opinion, technically easy model for learning of concepts and subconcepts and to study the corresponding learning capabilities.

In our model, we represent concepts by total recursive functions, i.e. computable functions mapping the natural numbers into the natural numbers and being everywhere defined (total). Subconcepts are then, consequently, represented by subfunctions of total recursive functions. Informally, we will call a class $C$ of total recursive functions *sublearnable* iff all the functions from that class $C$ *together with all of their subfunctions*, finite and infinite ones, are learnable. This goal might seem too ambitious, since, for example, in learning of *languages* from positive data it is known to be impossible to learn any infinite language together with all of its finite sublanguages, see [Gol67]. However, in learning of *functions*, the situation changes provided we consider a hypothesis as correct if this hypothesis is consistent with all the data presented to the learner. In other words, we allow the learner to converge to a hypothesis describing a *superfunction* of the (finite, infinite or total) function to be learned. This approach was introduced in the paper of the Blums [BB75]. Within this approach, if the learner is provided with all examples of any *total* function, then it is supposed to learn that function exactly. But if the learner is provided with exactly all examples of any finite or infinite *subfunction* of some total function, then it suffices to create a final hypothesis which, on the one hand, is consistent with this subfunction, but which, on the other hand, describes a function that, on arguments never shown, can be arbitrarily defined or even undefined. Thus, indeed, when learning a *proper* subfunction of a total function by being presented only all the examples of that subfunction, the learner has "more freedom" to generate a correct final hypothesis.

We will also modify this approach, namely by strengthening and by weakening it, respectively. *Strengthening* means that we always require the final hypothesis to be *total* even when the learner was presented only a *partial* function. However, we do not require that this total final hypothesis has to describe a (total) function *from the learnable class* $C$. The reason for not considering this additional strengthening is that then already simple classes (namely subclasses of recursively enumerable classes) would be no longer sublearnable. Nevertheless, it may be worth to study this additional strengthening as well in more detail in future work. *Weakening* the approach above means to require to learn only all the *infinite* subfunctions of the functions from $\mathcal{C}$, that is missing the finite subfunctions. As it turns out, this weakening indeed increases the learning possibilities. Finally, we will also combine this strengthening and this weakening, that is learning only infinite subfunctions but requiring total hypotheses as the final result of the learning process.

As for some historical background, note that in the seminal paper [Gol67], Gold showed that in his model every *recursively enumerable* class of total recursive functions is learnable by the so-called identification-by-enumeration principle. Informally, this kind of learning strategy always outputs the minimal hypothesis (with respect to a given total recursive enumeration of the class to be learned) which is consistent with all the data seen so far. It is then easy to see that this strategy converges to the minimal correct hypothesis within the given enumeration. The naturalness of this strategy led Gold to conjecture that *every* learnable class can be learned using identification-by-enumeration. In other words, Gold's conjecture was that every learnable class is contained in a recursively enumerable class. However, as Bārzdiņš [Bār71] proved, this conjecture is false. He exhibited the following "self-describing" class SD of total recursive functions, SD $= \{f \mid f(0)$ is a program for $f\}$. Each function $f$ in SD can be trivially learned by just outputting the program $f(0)$. On the other hand, no recursively enumerable class contains SD.

It seems worth to be noted that the class SD above can also be learned *without* making explicit use of its self-coding, namely by some "generalized" identification-by-enumeration. The same is true for other classes learnable in Gold's model. This in turn led to the thesis that for *each* type of Gold-style learning, there is an *adequate* enumeration technique, i.e. an enumeration technique which can be used to learn exactly the concept classes of that type. This thesis is stated and technically motivated in [KSW01]. In the present paper, we verify this thesis for several types of sublearning, see Theorems 11 and 12.

Also in the 1970's, Bārzdiņš suggested a more sophisticated version of Gold's conjecture above designed to transcend such self-referential counterexamples as the class SD. He reasoned that if a class is learnable by way of such a self-referential property, then there would be an "effective transformation" that would transform the class into another one that is no longer learnable. The idea is that if a learner is able to find the embedded self-referential information in the functions of the class, so can an effective transformation, which then can weed out this information. A reasonable way to make the notion of an effective transformation precise consists in using the concept of general recursive operators, i.e. effective and total mappings from total functions to total functions. In order to illustrate Bārzdiņš' intuition in the context of the class SD above, consider the operator $\Theta$ weeding out the self-referential information $f(0)$ as follows: $\Theta(f) = g$, where $g(x) = f(x + 1)$ for all arguments $x$. Then one can show that

$\Theta(\text{SD}) = \{\Theta(f) \mid f \in \text{SD}\} = \mathcal{R}$, the class of *all* the total recursive functions. Since $\mathcal{R}$ is not learnable, see [Gol67], $\Theta(\text{SD})$ is not learnable as well. Informally, Bārzdiņš' conjecture can then be stated as follows: If all the projections of a class of total recursive functions under all general recursive operators *are* learnable (or, in other words, if the class is learnable *robustly*), then the class is contained in a recursively enumerable class of total recursive functions, and, consequently, it is learnable by use of identification-by-enumeration. This was how the notion of robust learning appeared historically. This notion was then studied in several papers, see [Zeu86,Ful90,OS99,CJO+00,JSW01,CJSW01].

Clearly, the notion of sublearning in the present paper can intuitively be viewed as some special case of learning robustly. Indeed, while general robust learning requires that *all* projections of a given class of total recursive functions under all general recursive operators be learnable, in sublearning only a *special* kind of projections is required so, namely the given class of total recursive functions together with all of their subfunctions (or all of their infinite subfunctions, respectively). Thus, the question of comparing the capabilities of these two learning paradigms, sublearning and robust learning, naturally arises. As we will show, in general, these capabilities turn out to be set-theoretically incomparable, see Theorems 13 and 14. Consequently, each of these notions has its "right of existence", since no one of them majorizes the other one by its learning power. On the other hand, in some natural cases, sublearning and robust learning *coincide*! This is true if the function classes to be learned are closed under finite variations, i.e. if some total function $f$ belongs to such a class then any total function which differs from $f$ at most on finitely many arguments also belongs to that class. Thus, intuitively, changing a function a "little bit" will keep the resulting function still within the class. In this case, we can show that sublearning and robust learning are of the same power, and, moreover, any such class is even contained in a recursively enumerable class, see Theorem 15.

Further note that Gold's classical identification-by-enumeration was later shown to be successfully applicable to learning of more than merely the recursively enumerable classes of functions. Actually, this technique can directly be applied also to learning of so-called *measurable* classes, see Definition 12. Informally, a function class is measurable iff it can be embedded into a computable numbering $\eta$ such that the predicate $\eta_i(x) = y$ is decidable uniformly in $i, x$ and $y$. For example, the running times of the total recursive functions form a measurable class. Somewhat more generally, any complexity measure in the sense of [Blu67] also constitutes a measurable class. Clearly, measurability here just ensures the *computability* of the identification-by-enumeration strategy, i.e. the *effectiveness* of finding the corresponding minimal hypothesis which is consistent with the data received so far. As to our concept of sublearning, we will see that some of the corresponding types of sublearning contain *all* the measurable classes, as it follows from Theorem 9. This result has yet another interesting consequence, namely that there are sublearnable classes beyond the world of recursive enumerability which turn out to be not at all self-referential!

There are further results showing that the connection between sublearnable classes and measurable classes is really close. Actually, if we confine ourselves again to classes being closed under finite variations, then sublearnability and measurability *coincide*, see Theorem 10. Moreover, if we drop the property of closedness under finite variations, then sublearnability coincides with *weak* measurability, see Definition 13 and Theorem 11. Furthermore, the close connection between sublearnability and measurability can be considered as the substantial reason for another unexpected phenomenon. It is known that in Gold's model there are learnable classes which cannot be learned consistently; i.e. every learner of such a class must be allowed to produce intermediate hypotheses that are not consistent with the data seen so far, see [Bär74a,Wie76,WZ95]. Thus, paradoxically, the learners of such classes are forced to output intermediate hypotheses which *contradict known* data. Conversely, as it will be shown in Theorem 4, sublearnable classes *can* always be learned consistently!

The paper is organized as follows. In Section 2, the needed definitions and results from existing function learning theory are presented. In Section 3, the types of sublearning are formally introduced. In Section 4, we compare these types with respect to their corresponding learning power. In Section 5, we prove some characterizations for several sublearning types. In Section 6, we compare sublearning with robust learning.

## 2   Notation and Preliminaries

Recursion-theoretic concepts not explained below are treated in [Rog67]. $N$ denotes the set of natural numbers. The empty set is denoted by $\emptyset$. For sets $A$ and $B$, we write $A \triangle B$ iff $A$ and $B$ are incomparable, that is neither $A \subseteq B$ nor $B \subseteq A$ holds.

$\langle \cdot, \cdot \rangle$ denotes a 1-1 computable mapping from pairs of natural numbers onto natural numbers. $\pi_1, \pi_2$ are the corresponding projection functions. $\eta$, with or without subscripts, ranges over partial functions. $f$ ranges over total functions. $\mathcal{R}$ denotes the class of all total recursive functions, i.e. total computable functions with arguments and values from $N$. $\mathcal{C}$ ranges over subsets of $\mathcal{R}$. $\varphi$ denotes a *fixed* acceptable numbering of all partial recursive functions. $\varphi_i$ denotes the partial recursive function computed by the $\varphi$-program $i$. Below we will interpret the hypotheses of our learning machines just as programs in this numbering $\varphi$. Let $\Phi$ be an arbitrary Blum complexity measure [Blu67] associated with $\varphi$. $\varphi_{i,s}$ is defined as follows:

$$\varphi_{i,s}(x) = \begin{cases} \varphi_i(x), & \text{if } x < s \text{ and } \Phi_i(x) < s; \\ \uparrow, & \text{otherwise.} \end{cases}$$

A class $\mathcal{C} \subseteq \mathcal{R}$ is said to be *recursively enumerable* iff there exists an r.e. set $X$ such that $\mathcal{C} = \{\varphi_i \mid i \in X\}$. For any non-empty recursively enumerable class $\mathcal{C}$, there exists a total recursive function $f$ such that $\mathcal{C} = \{\varphi_{f(i)} \mid i \in N\}$.

A class $\mathcal{C} \subseteq \mathcal{R}$ is said to be *closed under finite variations* iff for all $f, g \in \mathcal{R}$ such that $\{x \mid f(x) \neq g(x)\}$ is finite, $f \in \mathcal{C}$ iff $g \in \mathcal{C}$.

## 2.1   Function Identification

For learning of (partial) functions, the learner receives the graph of the function to be learned which is presented as an infinite sequence (called *text*) consisting of pairs from that graph or a special pause symbol #.

Formally, a text is a mapping from $N$ to $(N \times N) \cup \{\#\}$, such that if $(x, y)$ and $(x, z)$ are in the range of the text, then $y = z$. $\mathbf{T}$ denotes the set of all texts. A segment is an initial sequence of a text. That is, a segment is a mapping from $\{x \in N \mid x < n\}$ to $(N \times N) \cup \{\#\}$, for some natural number $n$. For a segment $\sigma$, content($\sigma$) denotes the set of pairs in the range of $\sigma$: content($\sigma$) = range($\sigma$) $- \{\#\}$. Similarly, for a text $T$, content($T$) = range($T$) $- \{\#\}$. $T[n]$ denotes the initial segment of $T$ of length $n$. A text $T$ is for a (partial) function $\eta$, iff content($T$) = $\eta$. SEG denotes the set of all segments. $\sigma$ and $\tau$ range over SEG. Let $\sigma \cdot \tau$ denote the concatenation of $\sigma$ and $\tau$, and let $\sigma \cdot (x, w)$ denote the concatenation of $\sigma$ with the segment of length one consisting of $(x, w)$. $\Lambda$ denotes the empty segment.

An *inductive inference machine* (IIM) $\mathbf{M}$ [Gol67] is an algorithmic device that computes a (possibly partial) mapping from SEG into $N$. We say that $\mathbf{M}(T){\downarrow} = i$ iff the sequence $\mathbf{M}(T[n])$ converges to $i$. $\mathbf{M}(T)$ is undefined if no such $i$ exists.

**Definition 1.** [Gol67] Let $f \in \mathcal{R}$ and $\mathcal{C} \subseteq \mathcal{R}$.
  (a) $\mathbf{M}$ **Ex**-*identifies* $f$ (written: $f \in \mathbf{Ex}(\mathbf{M})$) just in case, for all texts $T$ for $f$, there exists a $\varphi$-program $i$ for $f$ such that $\mathbf{M}(T){\downarrow} = i$.
  (b) $\mathbf{M}$ **Ex**-*identifies* $\mathcal{C}$ iff $\mathbf{M}$ **Ex**-identifies each $f \in \mathcal{C}$.
  (c) $\mathbf{Ex} = \{\mathcal{C} \subseteq \mathcal{R} \mid (\exists \mathbf{M})[\mathcal{C} \subseteq \mathbf{Ex}(\mathbf{M})]\}$.

By the definition of convergence, only finitely many data points from a function $f$ have been observed by an IIM $\mathbf{M}$ at the (unknown) point of convergence. Hence, some form of learning must take place in order for $\mathbf{M}$ to identify $f$. For this reason, hereafter the terms *identify*, *learn* and *infer* are used interchangeably.

Note that in the literature, often canonical ordering of data for the input function is considered: the input consists of $(0, f(0)), (1, f(1)), \ldots$. For **Ex**-learning of functions, the ordering is not important. However, for the criteria considered in this paper, ordering is often important. Thus, it is more suitable for us to use *arbitrary* ordering in the input.

**Definition 2.** [Bār74b,CS83] Let $f \in \mathcal{R}$ and $\mathcal{C} \subseteq \mathcal{R}$.
  (a) $\mathbf{M}$ **Bc**-*identifies* $f$ (written: $f \in \mathbf{Bc}(\mathbf{M})$) iff, for all texts $T$ for $f$, for all but finitely many $n \in N$, $\mathbf{M}(T[n])$ is a $\varphi$-program for $f$.
  (b) $\mathbf{M}$ **Bc**-*identifies* $\mathcal{C} \subseteq \mathcal{R}$ iff $\mathbf{M}$ **Bc**-identifies each $f \in \mathcal{C}$.
  (c) $\mathbf{Bc} = \{\mathcal{C} \subseteq \mathcal{R} \mid (\exists \mathbf{M})[\mathcal{C} \subseteq \mathbf{Bc}(\mathbf{M})]\}$.

**Definition 3.** [Bār74a] $\mathbf{M}$ is said to be *consistent* on $f$ iff, for all texts $T$ for $f$, for all $n$, $\mathbf{M}(T[n]){\downarrow}$ and content($T[n]$) $\subseteq \varphi_{\mathbf{M}(T[n])}$.

**Definition 4.** (a) [Bār74a] $\mathbf{M}$ **Cons**-*identifies* $f \in \mathcal{R}$ iff $\mathbf{M}$ is consistent on $f$, and $\mathbf{M}$ **Ex**-identifies $f$.

(b) [Bār74a] **M Cons**-*identifies* $\mathcal{C} \subseteq \mathcal{R}$ iff **M Cons**-identifies each $f \in \mathcal{C}$.
(c) **Cons** $= \{\mathcal{C} \subseteq \mathcal{R} \mid (\exists \mathbf{M})[\mathbf{M} \ \mathbf{Cons}\text{-identifies } \mathcal{C}]\}$.

Note that for **M** to **Cons**-identify a function $f$, it must be defined on each initial segment of each text for $f$.

**Definition 5.** **NUM** $= \{\mathcal{C} \mid (\exists \mathcal{C}' \mid \mathcal{C} \subseteq \mathcal{C}' \subseteq \mathcal{R})[\mathcal{C}' \text{ is recursively enumerable}]\}$.

The following theorem relates the criteria of inference discussed above.

**Theorem 1.** [Bār74a,Bār74b,BB75,Wie76,CS83] **NUM** $\subset$ **Cons** $\subset$ **Ex** $\subset$ **Bc**.

Finally, we define *robust* learning.

**Definition 6.** [Ful90,JSW01]
**RobustEx** $= \{\mathcal{C} \subseteq \mathcal{R} \mid (\forall \text{ general recursive operators } \Theta)[\Theta(\mathcal{C}) \in \mathbf{Ex}]\}$.

**Proposition 1.** [Zeu86,JSW01] **NUM** $\subseteq$ **RobustEx**.


## 3   Definitions for Sublearning

In this section, we formally define our types of sublearning. Then we show that all the *recursively enumerable* classes are sublearnable with respect to *every* of our sublearning criteria, see Proposition 2.

In our first definition, the learner is required to stabilize on a program for a *total* function extending the concept to be learned.

**Definition 7.** (a) We say that **M AllTotSubEx**-*identifies* $f \in \mathcal{R}$ (written: $f \in \mathbf{AllTotSubEx}(\mathbf{M})$), iff, for all subfunctions $\eta \subseteq f$, for all texts $T$ for $\eta$, $\mathbf{M}(T)\!\downarrow$, $\varphi_{\mathbf{M}(T)} \supseteq \eta$, and $\varphi_{\mathbf{M}(T)} \in \mathcal{R}$.
(b) **M AllTotSubEx**-identifies $\mathcal{C} \subseteq \mathcal{R}$, iff **M AllTotSubEx**-identifies each $f \in \mathcal{C}$.
(c) **AllTotSubEx** $= \{\mathcal{C} \subseteq \mathcal{R} \mid (\exists \mathbf{M})[\mathcal{C} \subseteq \mathbf{AllTotSubEx}(\mathbf{M})\}$.

In the next definition, the final conjecture is *not* required to be total.

**Definition 8.** (a) We say that **M AllPartSubEx**-*identifies* $f \in \mathcal{R}$ (written: $f \in \mathbf{AllPartSubEx}(\mathbf{M})$), iff, for all subfunctions $\eta \subseteq f$, for all texts $T$ for $\eta$, $\mathbf{M}(T)\!\downarrow$, and $\varphi_{\mathbf{M}(T)} \supseteq \eta$.
(b) **M AllPartSubEx**-identifies $\mathcal{C} \subseteq \mathcal{R}$, iff **M AllPartSubEx**-identifies each $f \in \mathcal{C}$.
(c) **AllPartSubEx** $= \{\mathcal{C} \subseteq \mathcal{R} \mid (\exists \mathbf{M})[\mathcal{C} \subseteq \mathbf{AllPartSubEx}(\mathbf{M})\}$.

In the next definition, the final conjecture must be total, but only all *infinite* subconcepts are required to be learned.

**Definition 9.** (a) We say that **M InfTotSubEx**-*identifies* $f \in \mathcal{R}$ (written: $f \in \mathbf{InfTotSubEx}(\mathbf{M})$), iff, for all subfunctions $\eta \subseteq f$ with infinite domain, for all texts $T$ for $\eta$, $\mathbf{M}(T)\!\downarrow$, $\varphi_{\mathbf{M}(T)} \supseteq \eta$, and $\varphi_{\mathbf{M}(T)} \in \mathcal{R}$.
(b) **M InfTotSubEx**-identifies $\mathcal{C} \subseteq \mathcal{R}$, iff **M InfTotSubEx**-identifies each $f \in \mathcal{C}$.
(c) **InfTotSubEx** $= \{\mathcal{C} \subseteq \mathcal{R} \mid (\exists \mathbf{M})[\mathcal{C} \subseteq \mathbf{InfTotSubEx}(\mathbf{M})\}$.

The next definition requires only infinite subconcepts to be learned, but does not require the final conjecture to be total.

**Definition 10.** (a) We say that **M InfPartSubEx**-*identifies* $f \in \mathcal{R}$ (written: $f \in$ **InfPartSubEx(M)**), iff, for all subfunctions $\eta \subseteq f$ with infinite domain, for all texts $T$ for $\eta$, $\mathbf{M}(T)\downarrow$, and $\varphi_{\mathbf{M}(T)} \supseteq \eta$.

(b) **M InfPartSubEx**-identifies $\mathcal{C} \subseteq \mathcal{R}$, iff **M InfPartSubEx**-identifies each $f \in \mathcal{C}$.

(c) **InfPartSubEx** $= \{\mathcal{C} \subseteq \mathcal{R} \mid (\exists \mathbf{M})[\mathcal{C} \subseteq$ **InfPartSubEx(M)**$\}$.

One can extend the above definitions to use other criteria of inference such as **Bc** or require consistency by machine. Such criteria are named, **AllTotSubBc** and **InfPartSubCons**, etc. We define **AllTotSubBc** as an example.

**Definition 11.** (a) We say that **M AllTotSubBc**-*identifies* $f \in \mathcal{R}$ (written: $f \in$ **AllTotSubBc(M)**), iff, for all subfunctions $\eta \subseteq f$, for all texts $T$ for $\eta$, for all but finitely many $n$, $\varphi_{\mathbf{M}(T[n])} \supseteq \eta$ and $\varphi_{\mathbf{M}(T[n])} \in \mathcal{R}$.

(b) **M AllTotSubBc**-identifies $\mathcal{C} \subseteq \mathcal{R}$, iff **M AllTotSubBc**-identifies each $f \in \mathcal{C}$.

(c) **AllTotSubBc** $= \{\mathcal{C} \subseteq \mathcal{R} \mid (\exists \mathbf{M})[\mathcal{C} \subseteq$ **AllTotSubBc(M)**$\}$.

Using identification-by-enumeration one can easily show that already the strongest among the sublearning types, **AllTotSubEx**, contains all the recursively enumerable classes. Notice that, by Proposition 1 and Theorem 14 below, the inclusion of Proposition 2 is even *proper*.

**Proposition 2. NUM $\subseteq$ AllTotSubEx.**

# 4    Comparisons between Sublearning Criteria

In this section, we first compare various criteria of sublearning to each other. Then we exhibit that the classes from **AllPartSubEx** and from **AllTotSubEx** can even be learned *consistently*. Finally, we present some surprising results for **Bc**-sublearning.

## 4.1    Comparing the Basic Types of Sublearning to Each Other

As it turns out, the trivial inclusions immediately implied by the definitions are all *proper*, while **AllPartSubEx** and **InfTotSubEx** are incomparable, see Corollaries 1 and 2, which follow from Theorems 2 and 3.

**Theorem 2. AllPartSubEx $-$ InfTotSubBc $\neq \emptyset$.**

**Theorem 3. InfTotSubEx $-$ AllPartSubEx $\neq \emptyset$.**

*Proof.* Let $\mathcal{C} = \{f \in \mathcal{R} \mid (\exists e)(\forall^\infty x)[\pi_1(f(x)) = e \text{ and } \varphi_e = f]\}$.

Clearly, $\mathcal{C} \in$ **InfTotSubEx**.

Now suppose by way of contradiction that **M** witnesses that $\mathcal{C} \in$ **AllPartSubEx**.

We will first construct a function $\varphi_e$. If $\varphi_e$ is total, then $\varphi_e$ will be in $\mathcal{C}$ and $\varphi_e$ will be a diagonalizing function.

If $\varphi_e$ is not total, then we will construct another diagonalizing function $\varphi_{e'}$ based on $\varphi_e$.

By Kleene recursion theorem [Rog67], there exists an $e$ such that $\varphi_e$ may be described as follows. Let $x_s$ denote the least $x$ such that $\varphi_e(x)$ has not been defined before stage $s$. Initially, $x_0 = 0$. Let $\sigma_0 = \Lambda$. Go to stage 0.

**Stage $s$**

Dovetail steps 1 and 2, until one of them succeeds. If step 1 succeeds before step 2, then go to step 3. If step 2 succeeds before step 1, then go to step 4.

1.  Search for a $\tau$ extending $\sigma_s$ such that:
    (a) content$(\tau) \subseteq \{(x, \langle e, z \rangle) \mid x, z \in N\}$,
    (b) $\mathbf{M}(\tau) \neq \mathbf{M}(\sigma_s)$.
2.  Search for a $w$ such that
    (a) for all $y$, $(w, y) \notin$ content$(\sigma_s)$,
    (b) $\varphi_{\mathbf{M}(\sigma_s)}(w)\!\downarrow$.
3.  Let $\varphi_e(x) = \langle e, z \rangle$, for all $(x, \langle e, z \rangle)$ in content$(\tau)$.
    Let $x'$ be the maximum $x$ such that, for some $z$, $(x, \langle e, z \rangle) \in$ content$(\tau)$.
    Let $\varphi_e(x) = \langle e, 0 \rangle$ for $x \leq x'$ such that $\varphi_e(x)$ has not been defined up to now.
    Let $\sigma_{s+1}$ be an extension of $\tau$ such that content$(\sigma_{s+1})$ is the graph of $\varphi_e$ defined up to now.
    Go to stage $s + 1$.
4.  Let $\varphi_e(w) = \langle e, 0 \rangle$, if $\varphi_{\mathbf{M}(\sigma_s)}(w)\!\downarrow = \langle e, 1 \rangle$; $\varphi_e(w) = \langle e, 1 \rangle$, otherwise.
    Let $\varphi_e(x) = \langle e, 0 \rangle$ for $x_s \leq x < w$.
    Let $\sigma_{s+1}$ be an extension of $\tau$ such that content$(\sigma_{s+1})$ is the graph of $\varphi_e$ defined up to now.
    Go to stage $s + 1$.

**End stage $s$**

If all stages in the above construction complete, then clearly, $\varphi_e$ is total, is a member of $\mathcal{C}$ and $\mathbf{M}$ either makes infinitely many mind changes on $\bigcup_s \sigma_s$ (due to success of step 1 infinitely often), or the final program output by $\mathbf{M}$ on $\bigcup_s \sigma_s$ makes infinitely many convergent errors on $\varphi_e$ (due to success of step 2 infinitely often, and diagonalization in step 4). Thus, $\mathbf{M}$ cannot **AllPartSubEx**-identify $\mathcal{C}$.

We now consider the case that some stage $s$ does not complete. This means that step 1 in stage $s$ does not succeed. In particular, it means that for some finite function $\eta$ extending $\sigma_s$, $\mathbf{M}$ does not partially extend $\eta$ on some input text for $\eta$. Fix one such $\eta$. Now again using Kleene recursion theorem [Rog67] there exists an $e'$ such that

$$\varphi_{e'} = \begin{cases} \eta(x), & \text{if } x \in \text{domain}(\eta); \\ \langle e', 0 \rangle, & \text{otherwise.} \end{cases}$$

Clearly, $\varphi_{e'}$ is in $\mathcal{C}$. However, $\mathbf{M}$ does not partially extend the subfunction $\eta$ of $\varphi_{e'}$, on some text for $\eta$. Thus, $\mathbf{M}$ does not **AllPartSubEx**-identify $\mathcal{C}$. $\blacksquare$

**Corollary 1. AllPartSubEx $\triangle$ InfTotSubEx.**

**Corollary 2. AllTotSubEx $\subset$ AllPartSubEx.**
**InfTotSubEx $\subset$ InfPartSubEx.**
**AllPartSubEx $\subset$ InfPartSubEx.**
**AllTotSubEx $\subset$ InfTotSubEx.**

## 4.2   Consistent Sublearning

While in Gold's model there are learnable classes which *cannot* be learned consistently, see [Bār74a,Wie76,WZ95], all the classes from **AllPartSubEx** as well as from **AllTotSubEx** *can* be learned consistently. The proof of the following theorem uses a technique from [CJSW01].

**Theorem 4. AllPartSubEx = AllPartSubCons.**
**AllTotSubEx = AllTotSubCons.**

*Proof.* Suppose $\mathbf{M}$ **AllPartSubEx**-identifies (**AllTotSubEx**-identifies) $\mathcal{C}$. We define a (monotonic) mapping $F$ from SEG to SEG $\cup$ **T**, such that either (a) or (b) holds.

(a) $F(\sigma)$ is infinite, content$(F(\sigma)) \subseteq$ content$(\sigma)$, and either $\mathbf{M}(F(\sigma))$ is not defined or $\varphi_{\mathbf{M}(F(\sigma))}$ is not an extension of content$(F(\sigma))$. (Thus content$(\sigma)$ is not extended by any function in $\mathcal{C}$).

(b) $F(\sigma)$ is of finite length, content$(F(\sigma))$ = content$(\sigma)$, and $\varphi_{\mathbf{M}(F(\sigma))}$ extends content$(\sigma)$.

This can be done by defining $F(\Lambda) = \Lambda$,

$$F(\sigma \cdot (x,w)) = \begin{cases} F(\sigma), & \text{if } F(\sigma) \text{ is of infinite length;} \\ F(\sigma) \cdot (x,w) \cdot \#^{\infty}, & \text{if } F(\sigma) \text{ is of finite length, and} \\ & \text{there does not exist a } j \text{ such that} \\ & \varphi_{\mathbf{M}(F(\sigma) \cdot (x,w) \cdot \#^j),j} \supseteq \text{content}(\sigma \cdot (x,w)); \\ F(\sigma) \cdot (x,w) \cdot \#^j, & \text{if } F(\sigma) \text{ is of finite length, and } j \text{ is the} \\ & \text{least number such that} \\ & \varphi_{\mathbf{M}(F(\sigma) \cdot (x,w) \cdot \#^j),j} \supseteq \text{content}(\sigma \cdot (x,w)). \end{cases}$$

$F$ is clearly computable and satisfies the properties (a) and (b) above. Furthermore, for all $\eta$ with an extension in $\mathcal{C}$, for all texts $T$ for $\eta$, it is easy to verify that $\bigcup_n F(T[n])$ is also a text for $\eta$.

Define $\mathbf{M}'$ as follows. $\mathbf{M}'(\sigma) = \mathbf{M}(F(\sigma))$, if $F(\sigma)$ is finite in length. $\mathbf{M}'(\sigma)$ is undefined otherwise.

Now, as $\mathbf{M}$ **AllPartSubEx**-identifies (**AllTotSubEx**-identifies) $\mathcal{C}$, it follows using property (b) of $F$ above, that $\mathbf{M}'$ **AllPartSubCons**-identifies (**AllTotSubCons**-identifies) $\mathcal{C}$. $\blacksquare$

### 4.3    Behaviourally Correct Sublearning

While **AllPartSubEx** is a *proper* subset of **InfPartSubEx**, see Corollary 2, this is no longer true for **Bc**-sublearning.

**Theorem 5. AllPartSubBc = InfPartSubBc.**

Another difference comes with the **AllTot**-type of sublearning. While in traditional learning **Ex** $\subset$ **Bc** holds, see [Bär74b,CS83], this is not valid for **AllTot**-sublearning.

**Theorem 6. AllTotSubBc = AllTotSubEx.**

*Proof.* Suppose **M AllTotSubBc**-identifies a class $\mathcal{C}$. Note that, without loss of generality, we may assume that **M** is consistent on all inputs, i.e., for all $\sigma \in$ SEG, content$(\sigma) \subseteq \varphi_{\mathbf{M}(\sigma)}$.

For an r.e. set $S$ of programs, we let $Union(S)$ denote a program for the partial recursive function defined as follows: $\varphi_{Union(S)}(x) = \varphi_p(x)$, for the first $p \in S$ found such that $\varphi_p(x)$ is defined, using some standard dovetailing mechanism for computing $\varphi_p$'s. If $\varphi_p(x)$ is undefined for all $p \in S$, then $\varphi_{Union(S)}(x)$ is undefined. Note that one can get a program for $Union(S)$ effectively from an index for the r.e. set $S$.

For each segment $\sigma$, define $F(\sigma)$ as follows:
Let $Cand_\sigma = \{\mathbf{M}(\sigma') \mid \sigma \subseteq \sigma' \wedge \text{content}(\sigma) = \text{content}(\sigma')\}$.
Then, $F(\sigma) = Union(Cand_\sigma)$.
$F$ satisfies the following properties.

(a) For all $\sigma \in$ SEG such that content$(\sigma)$ has an extension in $\mathcal{C}$, $F(\sigma)$ is a program for a total function extending content$(\sigma)$ (by definition of **AllTotSubBc** and consistency assumption on **M**).

(b) For all partial functions $\eta$ with an extension in $\mathcal{C}$, there exists a $\sigma \in$ SEG such that content$(\sigma) \subseteq \eta \subseteq \varphi_{F(\sigma)}$ (since there exists a locking sequence, see [BB75], for **M** on $\eta$, for **AllTotSubBc**-identification).

Now define $\mathbf{M}'$ as follows. $\mathbf{M}'$ on input $\sigma$ outputs $F(\tau)$, for the least segment $\tau$ (in some ordering of elements of SEG) such that content$(\tau) \subseteq$ content$(\sigma)$ and $\varphi_{F(\tau)}$ extends content$(\sigma)$.

Now consider any subfunction $\eta$ of $f \in \mathcal{C}$ and any text $T$ for $\eta$. It follows using property (b) that $\mathbf{M}'(T)$ converges to $F(\tau)$ such that $\tau$ is the least element of SEG satisfying content$(\tau) \subseteq \eta \subseteq \varphi_{F(\tau)}$ (such $\tau$ exists due to property (b)). Furthermore, $\varphi_{F(\tau)}$ in the previous statement is total (by property (a)). Theorem follows.    ∎

The following result completes the picture.

**Theorem 7. InfTotSubBc $\triangle$ InfPartSubEx.**

## 5    Characterizations for Sublearning

In this section, we derive some characterizations for several types of sublearning. The first of these characterizations, for **AllTotSubEx**, turns out to be useful for proving other results.

**Theorem 8.** $C \in$ **AllTotSubEx** *iff there exists a total recursive function $F$ mapping finite functions to programs such that:*

*(a) For all finite functions $\alpha$ with an extension in $C$, $F(\alpha)$ is a program for a total function extending $\alpha$.*

*(b) For all infinite partial functions $\eta$ with an extension in $C$, there exists a finite subfunction $\alpha$ of $\eta$ such that $F(\alpha)$ is a program for an extension of $\eta$.*

**Corollary 3.** *Let $C$ be closed under finite variations. Then $C \in$ **AllTotSubEx** iff $C \in$ **NUM**.*

*Proof.* Let $C$ be as given in the hypothesis. Without loss of generality assume $C$ is non-empty.

Suppose $C \in$ **AllTotSubEx**. Since $C$ is non-empty and closed under finite variations, every finite function has an extension in $C$. Hence, Theorem 8 above implies that range of $F$ (as defined in Theorem 8) contains programs for only total functions. As range of $F$ contains programs for all functions in $C$, we immediately have that $C \in$ **NUM**. Corollary now follows from Proposition 2. ∎

Note that Corollary 3 does not hold for **InfTotSubEx** as the class: $\{f \in \mathcal{R} \mid (\exists e \mid \varphi_e = f)(\forall^\infty x)[\pi_1(f(x)) = e]\}$ shows. This class and its closure under finite variations are in **InfTotSubEx**. However, the class is not contained in **NUM**.

Our next results show that there is a close connection between **AllPartSubEx**-learnability and measurability.

**Definition 12.** A class $C \subseteq \mathcal{R}$ is said to be *measurable* iff there exists a numbering $\eta$ such that (a) $C \subseteq \{\eta_i \mid i \in N\}$, and (b) there exists a total recursive function $F$ such that, for all $i, x, y$,

$$F(i, x, y) = \begin{cases} 1, & \text{if } \eta_i(x) = y; \\ 0, & \text{otherwise.} \end{cases}$$

**Theorem 9.** *If $C$ is measurable, then $C \in$ **AllPartSubEx**.*

*Proof.* Suppose $C$ is measurable, as witnessed by numbering $\eta$. Let $h$ be a total recursive function reducing $\eta$-programs to equivalent $\varphi$-programs. Then one can define **M** as follows: $\mathbf{M}(\sigma) = h(\min(\{i \mid \text{content}(\sigma) \subseteq \eta_i\}))$. By measurability, it immediately follows that **M** **AllPartSubEx**-identifies $C$. ∎

The converse of Theorem 9 is also valid provided the corresponding classes are closed under finite variations.

**Theorem 10.** *Let $C$ be closed under finite variations. Then $C \in$ **AllPartSubEx** iff $C$ is measurable.*

*Proof.* The sufficiency follows from Theorem 9. For the necessity, note that **AllPartSubEx** $\subseteq$ **AllPartSubCons**, by Theorem 4. Thus, if $C$ is closed under finite variations, then $C$ must be sublearnable by a machine **M** which is consistent on *arbitrary* input.

For any $\sigma \in$ SEG, define a (possibly partial) function $\eta_\sigma$ as follows.

$$\eta_\sigma(x) = \begin{cases} y, & \text{if } (x, y) \in \text{content}(\sigma); \\ y, & \text{if } (x, z) \notin \text{content}(\sigma) \text{ for all } z, \text{ and } \varphi_{\mathbf{M}(\sigma)}(x) = y \text{ and} \\ & \mathbf{M}(\sigma) = \mathbf{M}(\sigma \cdot (x, y)). \\ \uparrow, & \text{otherwise.} \end{cases}$$

Note that one can test whether $\eta_\sigma(x) = y$ as follows. If $\sigma$ contains $(x, y)$, then clearly, $\eta_\sigma(x) = y$. Otherwise, $\eta_\sigma(x) = y$, iff $\mathbf{M}(\sigma \cdot (x, y)) = \mathbf{M}(\sigma)$. To see this, suppose $\mathbf{M}(\sigma \cdot (x, y)) = \mathbf{M}(\sigma)$. Then, by consistency of $\mathbf{M}$ on all inputs, we have $\varphi_{\mathbf{M}(\sigma)}(x) = y$, and thus $\eta_\sigma(x) = y$. On the other hand, if $\mathbf{M}(\sigma \cdot (x, y)) \neq \mathbf{M}(\sigma)$, then, by definition of $\eta_\sigma$, we have that $\eta_\sigma(x)$ cannot be $y$. Thus, in all cases, we can determine if $\eta_\sigma(x) = y$.

Moreover, for every function $f \in \mathcal{C}$, there is $\sigma \in \text{SEG}$ with $\eta_\sigma = f$ due to the locking sequence property (see [BB75]) for $\mathbf{M}$ on functions from $\mathcal{C}$. Finally, define a numbering $\psi$ by $\psi_i = \eta_{\sigma_i}$, where $\sigma_0, \sigma_1, \ldots$ is an effective enumeration of SEG. Then, obviously, $\mathcal{C}$ is measurable as witnessed by the numbering $\psi$. ∎

In general, a class is **AllPartSubEx**-learnable iff it is *weakly measurable*, as we will see now. Intuitively, for a weakly measurable class $\mathcal{C}$, the measurability property is required only for those functions within the corresponding numbering which have a "good chance" to belong to $\mathcal{C}$.

**Definition 13.** A class $\mathcal{C} \subseteq \mathcal{R}$ is said to be *weakly measurable* iff there exist a computable numbering $\eta$ and a recursive sequence $\alpha_0, \alpha_1, \ldots$ of finite functions (here recursive sequence $\alpha_0, \alpha_1, \ldots$ means that there exists a program which, on input $i$, enumerates all of $\alpha_i$ and then stops) such that

(1) for each $i$, $\alpha_i \subseteq \eta_i$,

(2) for each partial function $\psi$ which has an extension in $\mathcal{C}$, there exists an $i$ such that $\alpha_i \subseteq \psi \subseteq \eta_i$,

(3) there exists a partial recursive function $F$ such that, for all $i, x, y$ such that $\alpha_i \cup \{(x, y)\}$ has an extension in $\mathcal{C}$,

$$F(i, x, y) = \begin{cases} 1, & \text{if } \eta_i(x) = y; \\ 0, & \text{otherwise.} \end{cases}$$

**Theorem 11.** $\mathcal{C} \in$ **AllPartSubEx** *iff* $\mathcal{C}$ *is weakly measurable.*

Finally, we characterize the classes from **AllTotSubEx** to be exactly the *weakly enumerable* classes. In a certain analogy to the notion of weak measurability, intuitively, a class $\mathcal{C}$ is weakly enumerable if any function within the corresponding numbering is *total* in case this function has a "good chance" to belong to $\mathcal{C}$.

**Definition 14.** A class $\mathcal{C} \subseteq \mathcal{R}$ is said to be *weakly enumerable* iff there exist a computable numbering $\eta$ and a recursive sequence $\alpha_0, \alpha_1, \ldots$ of finite functions such that

(1) for each $i$, $\alpha_i \subseteq \eta_i$,

(2) for each partial function $\psi$ which has an extension in $\mathcal{C}$, there exists an $i$ such that $\alpha_i \subseteq \psi \subseteq \eta_i$,

(3) for all $i$, such that $\alpha_i$ has an extension in $\mathcal{C}$, $\eta_i$ is total.

**Theorem 12.** $\mathcal{C} \in$ **AllTotSubEx** *iff* $\mathcal{C}$ *is weakly enumerable.*

# 6   Sublearning versus Robust Learning

In this section, we compare the capabilities of sublearning and robust learning. In general, these capabilities turn out to be *incomparable*. Indeed, on the one hand, **RobustEx** contains classes which do not belong to the largest type of **Ex**-sublearning, **InfPartSubEx**, see Theorem 13. On the other hand, we derive that already the smallest sublearning type, **AllTotSubEx**, contains classes which are out of **RobustEx**, see Theorem 14. Finally, we exhibit that, under certain circumstances, the power of sublearning and robust learning *coincides*, see Theorem 15.

**Theorem 13.** RobustEx − InfPartSubEx $\neq \emptyset$.

**Theorem 14.** AllTotSubEx − RobustEx $\neq \emptyset$.

*Proof.* Let $\mathcal{C} = \{f \in \mathcal{R} \mid (\forall x)[\varphi_{\pi_1(f(x))} = f]\}$. $\mathcal{C}$ is clearly in **AllTotSubEx**, as any data point gives away a program for $f$.

On the other hand, $\mathcal{C} \notin$ **RobustEx**. To see this, consider $\Theta(f)(x) = \pi_2(f(x))$. Now $\Theta(\mathcal{C})$ contains every recursive function, as for any recursive function $g$, there exists an $e$ such that $\varphi_e(x) = \langle e, g(x) \rangle$. As $\mathcal{R} \notin$ **Ex** (see [Gol67]), we immediately have that $\mathcal{C} \notin$ **RobustEx**.     ∎

**Theorem 15.** *Let $\mathcal{C}$ be closed under finite variations. Then $\mathcal{C} \in$ **AllTotSubEx** iff $\mathcal{C} \in$ **RobustEx** iff $\mathcal{C} \in$ **NUM**.*

*Proof.* Let $\mathcal{C} \subseteq \mathcal{R}$ be closed under finite variations. Then, by Corollary 3, $\mathcal{C} \in$ **AllTotSubEx** iff $\mathcal{C} \in$ **NUM**. On the other hand, $\mathcal{C} \in$ **RobustEx** iff $\mathcal{C} \in$ **NUM** was shown in [OS99].     ∎

## Acknowledgements

We would like to thank the anonymous referees for valuable comments and suggestions.

## References

[Bär71]   J. Bārzdiņš. Prognostication of automata and functions. *Information Processing*, 1:81–84, 1971.

[Bär74a]  J. Bārzdiņš. Inductive inference of automata, functions and programs. In *Int. Math. Congress, Vancouver*, pages 771–776, 1974.

[Bär74b]  J. Bārzdiņš. Two theorems on the limiting synthesis of functions. In *Theory of Algorithms and Programs, vol. 1*, pages 82–88. Latvian State University, 1974. In Russian.

[BB75]    L. Blum and M. Blum. Toward a mathematical theory of inductive inference. *Information and Control*, 28:125–155, 1975.

[Blu67]   M. Blum. A machine-independent theory of the complexity of recursive functions. *Journal of the ACM*, 14:322–336, 1967.

[CJO+00]  J. Case, S. Jain, M. Ott, A. Sharma, and F. Stephan. Robust learning aided by context. *Journal of Computer and System Sciences (Special Issue for COLT'98)*, 60:234–257, 2000.

[CJSW01]  J. Case, S. Jain, F. Stephan, and R. Wiehagen. Robust learning – rich and poor. In David Helmbold and Bob Williamson, editors, *Computational Learning Theory, 14th Annual Conference on Computational Learning Theory, COLT 2001, and 5th European Conference on Computational Learning Theory, EuroCOLT 2001*, volume 2111 of *Lecture Notes in Artificial Intelligence*, pages 143–159. Springer-Verlag, 2001.

[CS83]  J. Case and C. Smith. Comparison of identification criteria for machine inductive inference. *Theoretical Computer Science*, 25:193–220, 1983.

[Ful90]  M. Fulk. Robust separations in inductive inference. In *31st Annual IEEE Symposium on Foundations of Computer Science*, pages 405–410. IEEE Computer Society Press, 1990.

[Gol67]  E. M. Gold. Language identification in the limit. *Information and Control*, 10:447–474, 1967.

[JSW01]  S. Jain, C. Smith, and R. Wiehagen. Robust learning is rich. *Journal of Computer and System Sciences*, 62(1):178–212, 2001.

[KSW01]  S. Kurtz, C. Smith, and R. Wiehagen. On the role of search for learning from examples. *Journal of Experimental and Theoretical Artificial Intelligence*, 13:24–43, 2001.

[OS99]  M. Ott and F. Stephan. Avoiding coding tricks by hyperrobust learning. In P. Vitányi, editor, *Fourth European Conference on Computational Learning Theory*, volume 1572 of *Lecture Notes in Artificial Intelligence*, pages 183–197. Springer-Verlag, 1999.

[Rog67]  H. Rogers. *Theory of Recursive Functions and Effective Computability*. McGraw-Hill, 1967. Reprinted by MIT Press in 1987.

[Wie76]  R. Wiehagen. Limes-Erkennung rekursiver Funktionen durch spezielle Strategien. *Journal of Information Processing and Cybernetics (EIK)*, 12:93–99, 1976.

[WZ95]  R. Wiehagen and T. Zeugmann. Learning and consistency. In K. P. Jantke and S. Lange, editors, *Algorithmic Learning for Knowledge-Based Systems*, volume 961 of *Lecture Notes in Artificial Intelligence*, pages 1–24. Springer-Verlag, 1995.

[Zeu86]  T. Zeugmann. On Bārzdiņš' conjecture. In K. P. Jantke, editor, *Analogical and Inductive Inference, Proceedings of the International Workshop*, volume 265 of *Lecture Notes in Computer Science*, pages 220–227. Springer-Verlag, 1986.

# When Is Small Beautiful?

Amiran Ambroladze[1] and John Shawe-Taylor[2]

[1] Lunds University, Lund
[2] Department of Computer Science, Royal Holloway, England

The basic bound on the generalisation error of a PAC learner makes the assumption that a consistent hypothesis exists. This makes it appropriate to apply the method only in the case where we have a guarantee that a consistent hypothesis can be found, something that is rarely possible in real applications. The same problem arises if we decide not to use a hypothesis unless its error is below a prespecified number.

In this open problem we examine the implications of this fact for learning bounds.

Let $S = ((\mathbf{x}_1, y_1), \cdots, (\mathbf{x}_l, y_l))$ be a training set, where the elements $(\mathbf{x}_i, y_i)$ of $S$ are generated independently and identically (i.i.d.) according to an unknown but fixed distribution over input/output pairings $(\mathbf{x}, y) \in X \times \{-1, 1\}$. Here $y_i$ is called the label of the example $\mathbf{x}_i$. Let $H$ be a hypothesis space, that is a collection of functions $h \in H$ mapping the input space $X$ to the output space $\{-1, 1\}$. Denote: $\mathrm{err}(h) := \mathrm{Prob}\{(\mathbf{x}, y) : h(\mathbf{x}) \neq y\}$.

Fix $\epsilon > 0$. For the brevity we use the following terminology: A hypothesis $h$ is *bad* if $\mathrm{err}(h) > \epsilon$; otherwise $h$ is *good*. We say that $h$ is a *separator* for $S$ if $h$ is consistent with $S$: $h(\mathbf{x}_i) = y_i, i = 1, \cdots, l$.

Denote $\delta(l) := \mathrm{Prob}\{S : \exists \text{ a bad separator for } S\}$. It is easy to check that $\delta(l)$ is a monotonically decreasing function of $l$. This means that choosing big training sets is a winning strategy (at least theoretically) for getting better bounds for the classification error. In addition, if $d := \mathrm{VCdim}(H) < \infty$ then we have (see [1]), that

$$\delta(l) < C(\epsilon, d) \cdot l^{2d} \cdot e^{-\epsilon l}, \tag{1}$$

where $C(\epsilon, d)$ depends only on $\epsilon$ and $d$. In particular, $\delta(l) \to 0$, as $l \to \infty$.

The smallness of $\delta(l)$ is partly guaranteed on the account of those training sets $S$ for which there are no hypotheses $h \in H$ separating $S$. Some algorithms use an inference rule that selects a hypothesis $h \in H$ separating $S$, under the a-priori assumption that such a hypothesis exists for the given training set $S$. This makes relevant the following question about the conditional probability: How big is the probability of existence of a bad separator if we know that a separator (bad or good) exists? So, we are interested in the following quantity: $\delta(l)/\Delta(l) := \mathrm{Prob}\{\exists \text{ a bad separator}\}/\mathrm{Prob}\{\exists \text{ a separator}\}$.

Some natural questions about this quotient are:
1) Is $\delta(l)/\Delta(l)$ still a monotonically decreasing function of $l$?
2) Do we still have convergence to zero: $\delta(l)/\Delta(l) \to 0$ as $l \to \infty$?

B. Schölkopf and M.K. Warmuth (Eds.): COLT/Kernel 2003, LNAI 2777, pp. 729–730, 2003.
© Springer-Verlag Berlin Heidelberg 2003

In Example 1 below we have $\delta(l)/\Delta(l) \to 1$ and at the same time $\delta(l)/\Delta(l) < 1$. This implies that $\delta(l)/\Delta(l)$ does not decrease monotonically: there exists $l_0$ such that:

$$\delta(l_0)/\Delta(l_0) > \delta(l_0 - 1)/\Delta(l_0 - 1). \tag{2}$$

In this example VCdim$(H) = \infty$. In Example 2 we modify Example 1 so that VCdim$(H)$ becomes finite. We still have inequality (2), but it turns out that in this modified case we get

$$\delta(l)/\Delta(l) \to 0 \text{ as } l \to \infty. \tag{3}$$

Here a natural question arises: Does the condition VCdim$(H) < \infty$ always guarantee the limit relation (3)? A very trivial Example 3 below shows that this is not so. But Example 3 is 'too' trivial in the sense that there is no good hypothesis at all in that case; so trivially there is $\delta(l) = \Delta(l)$ for all $l$. Now we formulate our

**Conjecture:** If VCdim$(H) < \infty$. Then a necessary and sufficient condition for (3) to be true is that $H$ contains at least one good hypothesis.

**Theorem 1.** *If VCdim$(H) < \infty$ and if in addition $H$ contains at least one hypothesis $h$, err$(h) < 1 - e^{-\epsilon}$, then we have (3).*

Note here that $1 - e^{-\epsilon} \approx \epsilon$ and by the definition the condition err$(h) < \epsilon$ means that $h$ is good. This shows that the result of this theorem is very close to the statement in the conjecture. The proof of the theorem is essentially based on [1].

Theorem 1 shows that in most cases $\delta(l)/\Delta(l)$ decreases to zero, but we have no guarantee of monotonicity. This means that choosing big training sets for classification purposes may not always be a winning strategy.

**Problem:** Which conditions on the hypothesis space $H$ guarantee that the conditional probability $\delta(l)/\Delta(l)$ is a monotonically decreasing function of $l$?

*Example 1.* $X = (-1, 1)$, Prob$\{y = 1\}$ = Prob$\{y = -1\}$ = $1/2$. The density functions for the positive and negative classes are $(x + 1)/2$ and $(1 - x)/2$, respectively. $\epsilon = 1/3$. For an arbitrary finite set $S = \{(\mathbf{x}_i, y_i)\}$ define $h_S(\mathbf{x}) = y_i$ if $\mathbf{x} = \mathbf{x}_i, \mathbf{x} \notin (-0.1, 0.1)$ and $h_S(\mathbf{x}) = 1$ otherwise. Let $H$ consists of all such $h_S$ (bad hypotheses) and plus the function $h_0 = \text{sgn}(x)$ (a good hypothesis).

*Example 2.* Here we define $H$ in the same way as in Example 1, but take only those $S$ which contain no more then $l_0$ elements. $l_0$ defined from (2).

*Example 3.* $X = \{1\}$, Prob$\{y = 1\}$ = Prob$\{y = -1\}$ = $1/2$, $H = \{\text{sgn}(\mathbf{x})\}$.

# References

[1] Shave-Taylor J., Anthony M., Biggs N.L.: Bounding Sample Size with the Vapnik-Chervonenkis Dimension. Discrete Applied Maths **42** (1993) 65-73.

# Learning a Function of $r$ Relevant Variables

Avrim Blum[*]

Carnegie Mellon University

This problem has been around for a while but is one of my favorites. I will state it here in three forms, discuss a number of known results (some easy and some more intricate), and finally end with small financial incentives for various kinds of partial progress. This problem appears in various guises in [2, 3, 10]. To begin we need the following standard definition: a boolean function $f$ over $\{0,1\}^n$ has (at most) $r$ relevant variables if there exist $r$ indices $i_1, \ldots, i_r$ such that $f(x) = g(x_{i_1}, \ldots, x_{i_r})$ for some boolean function $g$ over $\{0,1\}^r$. In other words, the value of $f$ is determined by only a subset of $r$ of its $n$ input variables. For instance, the function $f(x) = x_1 \bar{x}_2 \vee x_2 \bar{x}_5 \vee x_5 \bar{x}_1$ has three relevant variables. The "class of boolean functions with $r$ relevant variables" is the set of all such functions, over all possible $g$ and sets $\{i_1, \ldots, i_r\}$. The problems are:

(a) Does there exist a polynomial time algorithm for learning the class of boolean functions that have $\lg(n)$ relevant variables, over the uniform distribution on $\{0,1\}^n$?

(b) Does there exist a polynomial time algorithm for learning the class of boolean functions that have $\lg\lg(n)$ relevant variables, over the uniform distribution on $\{0,1\}^n$? Notice that since there are only $2^{2^{\lg \lg n}}$ possible $g$'s, we can assume the function $g$ is known, and the only difficulty is determining which are the relevant variables.

(c) Does there exist an algorithm for learning the class of boolean functions that have $r$ relevant variables, over the uniform distribution on $\{0,1\}^n$, in time "substantially" better than $n^r$?

**Motivation:** These problems are all a special case of the question of whether DNF or Decision Trees can be learned in polynomial time. In particular, any function of $r$ relevant variables can be written as a decision tree of depth $r$ (branching on a different variable at each level) or as a DNF formula with at most $2^r$ terms (one for each positive entry in the truth-table for $g$). These both have polynomial size for $r = O(\log n)$, and so progress on the relevant-variable problem is necessary for any positive answers to those questions. Furthermore, the relevant-variable problem is arguably more basic than the DNF or Decision-Tree questions, since the target class is defined semantically rather than syntactically. Lastly, these problems suggest specific "challenge" distributions on target functions that could be used to test heuristics (see below).

**Current Status:** A recent and very nice result of Mossel, O'Donnell, and Servedio [10], building on ideas of Kalai and Mansour [9], achieves roughly $O(n^{0.7r})$ for problem (c). In the other direction, there exists a *specific* function $g$ for which (if the set of relevant variables is chosen at random), all current techniques appear

[*] Supported in part by NSF grants CCR-0105488 and NSF-ITR CCR-0122581.

B. Schölkopf and M.K. Warmuth (Eds.): COLT/Kernel 2003, LNAI 2777, pp. 731–733, 2003.
© Springer-Verlag Berlin Heidelberg 2003

to break down at $O(n^{r/3})$ [2]. In addition to the question of whether [10] can be improved, a natural question is whether this specific case can be learned more efficiently, and whether one can construct "harder" functions $g$ for which, say, beating $n^{r/2}$ appears hard. See below for rewards related to these statements.

## Some Observations:

1. If membership queries are allowed, then learning is easy. (This makes a good homework question). Given a positive and negative example, one can "walk" them together to identify one relevant bit, put that at the top of a decision tree, and then recursively learn each subtree. Or, one can apply the more general algorithms of Bshouty [4] or Jackson [7].

2. If the target function is unbiased, then weak learning, strong learning, and exact identification are equivalent. (This also makes a good homework problem.) In particular, if $A$ is a weak-learning algorithm, then one can identify a relevant variable by running $A$ on data in which the first $i$ bits of every example are replaced by new, truly random bits. If we do this for $i = 0, 1, \ldots, n$, then at some point $A$ must fail to perform better than random guessing, and this will occur at one of the relevant variables. If $f$ is a *biased* function, then for this to work we need to change the definition of "weak learning" to mean an algorithm that performs noticeably better than the underlying bias of the target function.

3. We can assume without loss of generality that the relevant variables are chosen at random (since the algorithm can always randomly permute the indices if it so chooses).

4. Here is a specific function $g$ proposed in [2] as a candidate hard case. Split the relevant variables into two sets $A$ and $B$. On input $x$, compute the Parity function over $A$, and the Majority function over $B$, and then XOR the two results together.[1] This class can be easily learned in time $O(n^{|A|})$ (by guessing the set $A$ and reducing to majority) or in time $O(n^{|B|/2})$ (by guessing half of $B$ and examining only the examples in which those bits are all 0, reducing to parity). The worst case is when $|A| = r/3, |B| = 2r/3$, yielding an algorithm that runs in time $O(n^{r/3})$, but no better algorithm is known.

   Notice that this specific function $g$ gives a samplable distribution on target functions $f$ (pick a random subset of $r$ variables, split into $A$ and $B$, and feed it into $g$). Thus one can test proposed heuristics.

5. Problems (a) and (b) are not solvable by SQ algorithms [8, 1]. This holds even for the specific $g$ above. However, learning is easy for "most" functions $g$ (e.g., if the truth table is picked at random). The difficult cases seem to be the functions $g$ that are "similar to parity functions, but not exactly."

6. The theory of fixed-parameter tractability [5, 6] has been used to analyze the complexity of problems as a function of the size of the solution. For example,

---

[1] For instance, if $A = \{1, 2, 3\}$ and $B = \{4, 5, 6\}$ then the classification of the example 011101001010 would be positive, since the first three bits have an even number of ones (making their parity 0), and the next three bits have more ones than zeros (so the majority function is 1), and the XOR of those two quantities is 1.

suppose we want to determine if an instance of the set-cover problem has a cover of size $r$. If there are $n$ sets total, then it is easy to do this in time $O(n^r)$, but the results of [5] suggest that achieving running time of $f(r)poly(n)$ for any function $f$ (e.g., $f(r) = 2^{2^r}$) may be hard. This has immediate consequences for the "proper learning" problem, if we allow examples to be arbitrary. For instance, it implies that determining if the data is consistent with a conjunction of size $r$ is likely to be hard even if $r = O(\log n)$. However it is unclear whether this theory can be used to show (or suggest) hardness for the prediction problem.

## Monetary Rewards:

**$100:** Improve the results of [10] to $O(n^{0.666r})$.

**$200:** Improve the results of [10] to $O(n^{0.499r})$.

**$100:** Find an algorithm to learn the class described in Observation (4) in time $O(n^{r/4})$.

**$500:** Find an algorithm to learn the class described in (4) in polynomial time, for $r = O(\log n)$.

**$50:** Find a function $g$ as in (4) but for which achieving $O(n^{r/2})$ appears hard.

**$1000:** Give a positive solution to open problem (a) or (b).

**$50+:** Give a convincing argument why nobody will ever be able to solve the above $1000 problem. (Prize depends on how convincing.)

## References

1. A. Blum, M. Furst, J. Jackson, M. Kearns, Y. Mansour, and S. Rudich. Weakly learning DNF and characterizing statistical query learning using fourier analysis. In *Proceedings of the 26th Annual ACM Symposium on Theory of Computing*, pages 253–262, May 1994.

2. A. Blum, M. Furst, M. Kearns, and D. Lipton. Cryptographic primitives based on hard learning problems. In D. Stinson, editor, *13th Annual International Cryptology Conference (CRYPTO)*. Springer, 1993. Lecture Notes in Computer Science No. 773.

3. Avrim Blum. Relevant examples and relevant features: Thoughts from computational learning theory. In *AAAI-94 Fall Symposium, Workshop on Relevance*, 1994.

4. N. H. Bshouty. Exact learning via the monotone theory. In *Proceedings of the IEEE Symposium on Foundation of Computer Science*, pages 302–311, Palo Alto, CA., 1993.

5. Rodney G. Downey and Michael R. Fellows. Fixed-parameter tractability and completeness i: Basic results. *SIAM Journal on Computing*, 24(4):873–921, 1995.

6. Rodney G. Downey and Michael R. Fellows. *Parameterized Complexity*. Monographs in Computer Science of Springer-Verlag, 1999.

7. J. Jackson. An efficient membership-query algorithm for learning DNF with respect to the uniform distribution. In *Proceedings of the IEEE Symposium on Foundation of Computer Science*, 1994.

8. M. Kearns. Efficient noise-tolerant learning from statistical queries. *Journal of the ACM*, 45(6):983–1006, 1998.

9. Adam Kalai and Yishay Mansour. Perosnal communication. 2001.

10. Elchanan Mossel, Ryan O'Donnell, and Rocco Servedio. Learning juntas. In *Proceedings of the 35th Annual ACM Symposium on Theory of Computing*, 2003.

# Subspace Detection:
# A Robust Statistics Formulation

Sanjoy Dasgupta

UC San Diego

If data in $\mathbb{R}^d$ actually lie in a linear subspace, then principal component analysis (PCA) will find this subspace. If the data are corrupted by benign (eg. independent Gaussian) noise, then approximation bounds can quite easily be shown for the solution returned by PCA. What if the noise is malicious?

$\varepsilon$-NOISY HYPERPLANE
*Input:* Points $x_1, \ldots, x_n \in R^d$
*Output:* A vector $w \in \mathbb{R}^d$ such that $w \cdot x_i = 0$ for at least $(1 - \varepsilon)$ fraction of the points

This is the typical sort of problem studied in the field of *robust statistics* ([2]). They typically consider data which has been corrupted by two types of noise: benign perturbation, as well as a small amount of malicious noise. The perturbation is generally easy to handle, and the main question is, how much malicious noise can be tolerated? The statistics literature offers two standard tricks.

1. Randomly sample $d$ points, and hope they contain no outliers. Try this repeatedly, obtaining a candidate hyperplane each time; and return the best answer you get. The number of trials needed is something like $(1 - \varepsilon)^{-d}$, which is polynomial in $d$ only for error rates $\varepsilon \leq O(\log d/d)$. Notice that this particular scheme assumes that the points are in general position (ie. any $d$ good points specify the hyperplane).
2. Run PCA on the data to get a candidate hyperplane $w$; throw away the point $x$ with largest $|w \cdot x|$, and repeat. The behavior of this scheme has not been fully characterized, although Dunagan and Vempala ([1]) have analyzed something very similar.

There is a popular class of robust statistical estimators called M-estimators. It is known ([2]) that these can tolerate no more than a fraction $\varepsilon = \frac{1}{d+1}$ of outliers. Is it possible to do much better?

On the computational complexity side of things, the problem as stated above is NP-hard for any $\varepsilon = 1/\text{poly}(d)$; it is equivalent to being given a set of linear equalities and trying to satisfy as many of them as possible. However the reductions naively produce instances in which the points are not in general position.

# References

1. J. Dunagan and S. Vempala. Optimal outlier removal in high-dimensional spaces. *Proceedings of the 32nd ACM Symposium on the Theory of Computing*, 2000.
2. P.J. Huber. *Robust statistics.* Wiley, 1984.

B. Schölkopf and M.K. Warmuth (Eds.): COLT/Kernel 2003, LNAI 2777, p. 734, 2003.
© Springer-Verlag Berlin Heidelberg 2003

# How Fast Is $k$-Means?

Sanjoy Dasgupta

UC San Diego

The $k$-means algorithm is probably the most widely used clustering heuristic, and has the reputation of being fast. How fast is it exactly? Almost no non-trivial time bounds are known for it.

Let's say $k$-means is used to cluster $n$ data points in $\mathbb{R}^d$. At any given time, it maintains a set of $k$ "centers" $\mu_1, \ldots, \mu_k$. These are often initialized by choosing randomly from the data set. The update rule is as follows:

1. Assign each data point to its closest center. This gives a Voronoi partitioning $C_1, \ldots, C_k$ of the data.
2. Reset each center $\mu_j$ to be the mean of (the data points in) its cluster $C_j$.

There is a particular cost function which strictly decreases on each step (if it doesn't, the algorithm halts):

$$\sum_{j=1}^{k} \sum_{x \in C_j} \|x - \mu_j\|^2,$$

where the inner summation is over the data points in cluster $C_j$.

The monotonic decrease of this cost function means that any particular configuration (a Voronoi $k$-partitioning) is never revisited, and therefore the number of iterations is at most the number of such partitionings (a simple upper bound is $n^{(d+1)\binom{k}{2}}$). This is the only general bound known!

For the *one-dimensional* case I have checked the following.

1. For $k = 2$, there are instances which force $\Omega(n)$ iterations.
2. For $k < 5$, the number of iterations is at most $O(n)$.
3. If the ratio between the largest interpoint distance and the smallest interpoint distance is bounded by $\sigma$, then the number of iterations is $O(1/\sigma^2)$.

This appears to be the state of present knowledge.

Note that the quality of the final clustering is not the issue here: it is easy to show that it can be arbitrarily bad. The question is, how many iterations are needed until convergence?

B. Schölkopf and M.K. Warmuth (Eds.): COLT/Kernel 2003, LNAI 2777, p. 735, 2003.
© Springer-Verlag Berlin Heidelberg 2003

# Universal Coding of Zipf Distributions

Yoav Freund[1], Alon Orlitsky[2], Prasad Santhanam[2], and Junan Zhang[2]

[1] Mitsubishi Electric Research Labs. Cambridge, MA
[2] ECE Department, UC San Diego, La Jolla, CA 92093
alon@ucsd.edu

**Background.** One of the best known results in information theory says that a data sequence $x_1, x_2, \ldots, x_n$ produced by independent random draws from a fixed distribution $P$ over a discrete domain can be compressed into a binary sequence, or *code* whose expected length is at most $nH(P) + 1$ bits, where $H(P) = - \sum_i P_i \log P_i$ is the *entropy* of $P$. It is also known that this compression is near optimal as $nH(P)$ is the smallest achievable expected number of code bits.

In many data-compression applications the distribution $P$ is not known except that it belongs to a given collection $\mathcal{P}$ of distributions. In such situations the expected code length is longer and the difference between the expected code length and $nH(P)$ is the code's *redundancy*. Coding schemes whose redundancy increases slower than $n$ are called *universal*.

For collections of distributions over finite alphabets, many results are known. For example, for the collection $\mathcal{P}_k$ of iid distributions over an alphabet of size $k$ it has been shown [1] that the optimal redundancy is $\frac{k-1}{2} \log n + o(\log n)$, hence iid distributions over finite alphabets can be universally compressed.

Considering these results from an online learning point of view, the set of distributions $\mathcal{P}$ corresponds to a set of fixed experts (i.e. each experts makes a fixed prediction, independent of the past.) The universal coding scheme can be seen as an algorithm for combining expert advice, the code length is equal to the cumulative log loss (up to rounding error) and the redundancy is the difference between the loss of the combining algorithm and the loss of the best expert. See Freund [7] for an example of this type of analysis.

**Large Alphabets.** When compressing natural-language text, it is reasonable to code the text a word at a time, thereby relying on the distribution of the words. In that case, the alphabet size $k$ is the number of words in the language, which may be very large. Hence the $\frac{k-1}{2} \log n$ redundancy bound is not very meaningful.

One approach to reducing the redundancy in that case would be to restrict the collection of possible distributions over the words. The most popular way for characterizing such distributions is to sort the words in decreasing order of probability and characterize the probability of a word as a function of its place in the sorted list, also called its "rank". Specifically, Zipf [2] observed that in many textual corpora, the distribution of words follows a power law whereby the probability of the $i$th ranked word is $P_i \approx \frac{C}{i^\alpha}$ where $\alpha$ is a constant close to

B. Schölkopf and M.K. Warmuth (Eds.): COLT/Kernel 2003, LNAI 2777, pp. 736–737, 2003.

1 and $C$ is a normalization factor[1]. This observation underlies many applications of statistical natural language processing, see, e.g., [3].

**Unknown Alphabets.** Another approach for compressing large, possibly infinite or even unknown, alphabets, is to decompose the description of a string into two parts: a description of the symbols, and of the order, or *pattern*, in which they appear. This is done for example, in the facsimile transmission of a document where the images corresponding to each character in the document are conveyed, then the order of the characters is transmitted.

This approach was taken in [4], and, in a slightly different context in [5]. Formally, the *index* $I(x)$ of a symbol $x$ in a string $\bar{x}$ is one more than the number of distinct symbols preceding $x$ in $\bar{x}$, and the pattern of $\bar{x}$ is the string $I(x_1), \ldots, I(x_n)$ of indices. For example, in the string "abracadabra", $I(a) = 1$, $I(b) = 2$, $I(r) = 3$, $I(c) = 4$, and $I(d) = 5$, hence the pattern of "abracadabra" is 12314151231.

It was shown in [6] that patterns of sequences generated by iid distributions can be universally compressed, regardless of the alphabet size. Specifically, that the redundancy of compressing the patterns of length-$n$ sequences is $O(\sqrt{n})$.

Note however that this redundancy bound applies to patterns of strings generated by any iid distribution. As with standard compression, we would like to know whether there are lower-redundancy coding schemes for patterns of sequences generated by a distribution from a restricted class.

One such class is that of Zipf distributions with parameter $\alpha$. It would be interesting to know whether one can achieve a redundancy bound of $O(n^\beta)$ where $\beta < 1/2$ and what is smallest achievable $\beta$ as a function of $\alpha$.

# References

1. R.E. Krichevsky and V.K. Trofimov. The preformance of universal coding. *IEEE Transactions on Information Theory*, 27:199–207, 1981.
2. G. Zipf. Selective studies and the principle of relative frequency in language. Technical report, Harvard university press, 1932.
3. W. Li. http://linkage.rockefeller.edu/wli/zipf/. *North Shore LIJ Research Institute*.
4. N. Jevtic, A. Orlitsky, and N.P. Santhanam. Universal compression of unknown alphabets. In *IEEE Symposium on Information Theory*, 2002.
5. J. Aberg, Y.M. Shtarkov, and B.J.M. Smeets. Multialphabet coding with separate alphabet description. In *Proceedings of compression and complexity of sequences*, 1997.
6. A. Orlitsky, N.P. Santhanam, and J. Zhang. Bounds on compression of unknown alphabets. In *IEEE Symposium on Information Theory*, 2003.
7. Y. Freund. Predicting a binary sequence almost as well as the optimal biased coin. *Information and Computation* 182 (2003) 73-94.

---

[1] For those that would like a more precise definition, a reasonable one might be to restrict $P_i$ to be in the range $\left[\frac{C_1}{i^\alpha}, \frac{C_2}{i^\alpha}\right]$ where $C_2 > C_1 > 0$ are two constants.

# An Open Problem Regarding the Convergence of Universal A Priori Probability

Marcus Hutter[*]

IDSIA, Galleria 2, CH-6928 Manno-Lugano, Switzerland
marcus@idsia.ch
http://www.idsia.ch/~marcus

**Abstract.** Is the textbook result that Solomonoff's universal posterior converges to the true posterior for all Martin-Löf random sequences true?

**Universal Induction.** Induction problems can be phrased as sequence prediction tasks. This is, for instance, obvious for time series prediction, but also includes classification tasks. Having observed data $x_t$ at times $t < n$, the task is to predict the $t$-th symbol $x_t$ from sequence $x = x_1...x_{t-1}$. The key concept to attack general induction problems is Occam's razor and to a less extent Epicurus' principle of multiple explanations. The former/latter may be interpreted as to keep the simplest/all theories consistent with the observations $x_1...x_{t-1}$ and to use these theories to predict $x_t$. Solomonoff [4, 5] formalized and combined both principles in his universal prior $M(x)$ which assigns high/low probability to simple/complex environments, hence implementing Occam and Epicurus. $M(x)$ is defined as the probability that a universal Turing machine $U$ outputs a string starting with $x$, when provided with fair coin flips on the input.

**Posterior Convergence.** Solomonoff's [5] central result is that if the probability $\mu(x_t|x_1...x_{t-1})$ of observing $x_t$ at time $t$, given past observations $x_1...x_{t-1}$ is a computable function, then the universal posterior $M_t := M(x_t|x_1...x_{t-1})$ converges (rapidly!) *with $\mu$-probability 1* (w.p.1) for $t \to \infty$ to the true posterior $\mu_t := \mu(x_t|x_1...x_{t-1})$, hence $M$ represents a universal predictor in case of unknown $\mu$. Convergence of $M_t$ to $\mu_t$ w.p.1 tells us that $M_t$ is close to $\mu_t$ for sufficiently large $t$ for "almost all" sequences $x_{1:\infty}$ (we abbreviate $x_{1:n} := x_1...x_n$). It says nothing about whether convergence is true for any *particular* sequence (of measure 0).

**Martin-Löf Randomness** is the standard notion to capture convergence for individual sequences and is closely related to Solomonoff's universal prior. Levin gave a characterization equivalent to Martin-Löf's (M.L.) original definition [2]:

*A sequence $x_{1:\infty}$ is $\mu$-random (in the sense of M.L.) iff there is a constant $c$ such that $M(x_{1:n}) \leq c \cdot \mu(x_{1:n})$ for all $n$.*

---

[*] A prize of 128 Euro for a solution of this problem is offered.

B. Schölkopf and M.K. Warmuth (Eds.): COLT/Kernel 2003, LNAI 2777, pp. 738–740, 2003.

One can show that a $\mu$-random sequence $x_{1:\infty}$ passes *all* thinkable effective randomness tests, e.g. the law of large numbers, the law of the iterated logarithm, etc. In particular, the set of all $\mu$-random sequences has $\mu$-measure 1.

**Open Problem.** An interesting open question is whether $M_t$ converges to $\mu_t$ (in difference or ratio) individually for all Martin-Löf random sequences. Clearly, Solomonoff's result shows that convergence may at most fail for a set of sequences with $\mu$-measure zero. A convergence result for $\mu$-random sequences is particularly interesting and natural in this context, since $\mu$-randomness can be defined in terms of $M$ itself (see above).

**Proof Attempts.** Attempts to convert the convergence results w.p.1 to effective $\mu$-randomness tests fail, since $M_t$ is not lower semi-computable. In [3, Th.5.2.2] and [6, Th.10] the following Theorem is stated:

"*Let $\mu$ be a positive recursive measure. If the length of $y$ is fixed and the length of $x$ grows to infinity, then $M(y|x)/\mu(y|x) \to 1$ with $\mu$-probability one. The infinite sequences $\omega$ with prefixes $x$ satisfying the displayed asymptotics are precisely ['$\Rightarrow$' and '$\Leftarrow$'] the $\mu$-random sequences.*"

While convergence w.p.1 is correct if appropriately interpreted[1], the proof that convergence holds for $\mu$-random sequences is incomplete: "$M(x_{1:n}) \leq c \cdot \mu(x_{1:n}) \forall n \Rightarrow \lim_{n\to\infty} M(x_{1:n})/\mu(x_{1:n})$ *exists*" has been used, but not proven, and may indeed be wrong. Vovk [7] shows that for two finitely computable semi-measures $\mu$ and $\rho$, and $x_{1:\infty}$ being $\mu$- *and* $\rho$-random that $\rho_t/\mu_t \to 1$. If $M$ were recursive, then this would imply $M_t/\mu_t \to 1$ for every $\mu$-random sequence $x_{1:\infty}$, since *every* sequence is $M$-random. Since $M$ is *not* recursive Vovk's theorem cannot be applied and it is not obvious how to generalize it. So the question of individual convergence remains open.

**Conclusions.** Contrary to what was believed before, the question of posterior convergence $M_t/\mu_t \to 1$ (also $M_t \to \mu_t$) for all $\mu$-random sequences is still open. In [1] we introduce a new flexible notion of randomness which contains Martin-Löf randomness as a special case. This notion is used to show that standard proof attempts of $M_t/\mu_t \xrightarrow{M.L.} 1$ based on so called dominance only must fail, indicating that this problem may be a hard one.

# References

1. M. Hutter. On the existence and convergence of computable universal priors. Technical Report IDSIA-05-03, 2003. http://arxiv.org/abs/cs.LG/0305052.
2. L. A. Levin. On the notion of a random sequence. *Soviet Math. Dokl.*, 14(5):1413–1416, 1973.

---

[1] The formulation of the Theorem is quite misleading in general: First, for off-sequence $y$ convergence w.p.1 does not hold ($xy$ must be demanded to be a prefix of $x_{1:\infty}$). Second, the proof of '$\Leftarrow$' has loopholes (see main text). Last, '$\Rightarrow$' is given without proof and is probably wrong. Also the assertion in [3, Th.5.2.1] that $S_t$ converges to zero faster than $1/t$ cannot be made, since $S_t$ may not decrease monotonically.

3. M. Li and P. M. B. Vitányi. *An introduction to Kolmogorov complexity and its applications.* Springer, 2nd edition, 1997.
4. R. J. Solomonoff. A formal theory of inductive inference: Part 1 and 2. *Inform. Control,* 7:1–22, 224–254, 1964.
5. R. J. Solomonoff. Complexity-based induction systems: comparisons and convergence theorems. *IEEE Trans. Inform. Theory,* IT-24:422–432, 1978.
6. P. M. B. Vitányi and M. Li. Minimum description length induction, Bayesianism, and Kolmogorov complexity. *IEEE Transactions on Information Theory,* 46(2):446–464, 2000.
7. V. G. Vovk. On a randomness criterion. *Soviet Mathematics Doklady,* 35(3):656–660, 1987.

# Entropy Bounds for Restricted Convex Hulls

Vladimir Koltchinskii

Department of Mathematics and Statistics, University of New Mexico, Albuquerque, NM, 87131-1141, USA

**Abstract.** An unsolved problem of bounding the entropy of a "restricted" convex hull of a set in a Hilbert space is discussed. The problem is related to bounding the generalization error of convex combinations of base classifiers.

Let $H$ be a separable Hilbert space and $K \subset H$. Without loss of generality, one can assume that $H$ is the space $\ell_2$ of all square summable sequences equipped with the canonical inner product. Let $\text{conv}(K)$ denote the convex hull of $K$ :

$$\text{conv}(K) := \Big\{ \sum_j \lambda_j x_j : x_j \in K, \lambda_j \geq 0, \sum_j \lambda_j = 1 \Big\}.$$

For a set $T \subset H$, $N(T; \varepsilon)$ denotes the minimal number of balls of radius $\varepsilon > 0$ covering $T$ and let $H(T; \varepsilon) := \log N(T; \varepsilon)$ be the $\varepsilon$-entropy of $T$. We assume in what follows that for some $V > 0$ $N(K; \varepsilon) = O(\varepsilon^{-V})$ as $\varepsilon \to 0$.
Then, it is well known (see, e.g., [1], Theorem 2.6.9) that

$$H(\text{conv}(K); \varepsilon) = O\Big( \varepsilon^{-2V/(2+V)} \Big) \text{ as } \varepsilon \to 0.$$

Convex hulls are of importance in learning theory since boosting type algorithms output combined classifiers from the convex hull of a given base class of functions. The analysis of such algorithms and, especially, the development of subtle probabilistic bounds on their generalization error often require the knowledge of not only the entropy of the whole convex hull, but also the entropy of its subsets defined in terms of various restrictions on the coefficients of convex combinations as well as on the vectors involved in them. We describe below an important version of this problem.
Given $x \in \text{conv}(K)$, define

$$\mathcal{N}(x, \varepsilon) := \inf\Big\{ N(K'; \varepsilon), \ K' \subset K, \ x \in \text{conv}(K') \Big\}.$$

Clearly, if $x = \sum_{j=1}^m \lambda_j x_j$, then

$$\mathcal{N}(x, \varepsilon) \leq N(\{x_1, \dots, x_m\}; \varepsilon).$$

So, if $x$ is a convex combination of a base classifiers $x_j$, $\mathcal{N}(x; \varepsilon)$ can be bounded by the $\varepsilon$-covering number of the set $\{x_j\}$ of base classifiers.

B. Schölkopf and M.K. Warmuth (Eds.): COLT/Kernel 2003, LNAI 2777, pp. 741–742, 2003.

If now $N$ is a nonincreasing nonnegative function on $(0, +\infty)$, let us define

$$\mathrm{conv}_N(K) := \Big\{ x \in \mathrm{conv}(K) : \forall \varepsilon > 0 : \ \mathcal{N}(x, \varepsilon) \le N(\varepsilon) \Big\}.$$

**Problem:** Find a sharp upper bound on the $\varepsilon$-entropy of the set $\mathrm{conv}_N(K)$. It is easy to prove that

$$H\Big( \mathrm{conv}_N(K); \varepsilon \Big) = O(N(\varepsilon) \log(1/\varepsilon)) \text{ as } \varepsilon \to 0,$$

which is sharp if $N(\varepsilon) \equiv d$, $d$ is a constant. However, if $N(\varepsilon) = C\varepsilon^{-V} \ge N(K; \varepsilon)$, then $\mathrm{conv}_N(K) = \mathrm{conv}(K)$, and the above bound becomes much worse than $O\Big(\varepsilon^{-2V/(2+V)}\Big)$, which also holds in this case. So, the problem is to find a subtle interpolation between these two cases.

# References

1. van der Vaart, A.W. and Wellner, J. Weak Convergence and Empirical Processes. Springer, New York (1996)

# Compressing to VC Dimension Many Points

Manfred K. Warmuth

UC Santa Cruz

Any set of labeled examples consistent with some hidden orthogonal rectangle can be "compressed" to at most four examples: An upmost, a leftmost, a rightmost and a bottommost positive example. These four examples represent an orthogonal rectangle (the smallest such rectangle that contains them) that is consistent with all examples.

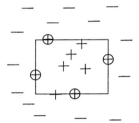

Note that the VC dimension of orthogonal rectangles is four and this is exactly the number of examples needed to represent the consistent orthogonal rectangle.

A compression scheme of size $k$ for a concept class $C$ picks from any set of examples consistent with some concept in $C$ a subset of up to $k$ examples and this subset represents (via a mapping that that is specific to the class $C$) a hypothesis consistent with the whole original set of examples.

**Conjecture**: Any concept class of VC dimension d has a compression scheme of size $d$.

What evidence do we have that this conjecture might be true?

Call a concept class of VC dimension $d$ maximum if for every subset of $m$ instances, the concept class induces exactly $\sum_{i=1}^{d} \binom{m}{i}$ concepts on the subset. That is, for every subset of $m$ instances, we have exactly the maximum number of induced concepts so that Sauer's lemma is tight.

In [1] it was shown that every maximum concept class of VC dimension $d$ has a compression scheme that compresses example sets of size larger than $d$ to a subset of exactly $d$ examples.

Compression schemes were introduced in [2]. In that note a PAC bound is given (See also appendix of [1]). The size of the compression scheme takes the role of the VC dimension in the PAC bound and the constants are small. The proof is very short and interesting in its own right.

Various variants of the above definition of compression scheme are discussed in [2] and [1], Section 9.

B. Schölkopf and M.K. Warmuth (Eds.): COLT/Kernel 2003, LNAI 2777, pp. 743–744, 2003.

**Monetary rewards:** $600 for resolving the conjecture by either proving that for any concept class of VC dimension $d$ there always is a compression scheme of size $O(d)$, or by providing a counter example that shows that such compressions schemes are not always possible.

# References

1. S. Floyd and M. K. Warmuth. Sample compression, learnability, and the Vapnik-Chervonenkis dimension. *Machine Learning*, 21(3):269–304, 1995.
2. N. Littlestone and M. K. Warmuth. Relating data compression and learnability. Unpublished manuscript, obtainable at http://www.cse.ucsc.edu/m̃anfred, June 10 1986.

# Author Index